Y0-BEI-994

Twentieth-Century Literary Criticism

Guide to Gale Literary Criticism Series

For criticism on	Consult these Gale series
Authors now living or who died after December 31, 1959	***CONTEMPORARY LITERARY CRITICISM* (CLC)**
Authors who died between 1900 and 1959	***TWENTIETH-CENTURY LITERARY CRITICISM* (TCLC)**
Authors who died between 1800 and 1899	***NINETEENTH-CENTURY LITERATURE CRITICISM* (NCLC)**
Authors who died between 1400 and 1799	***LITERATURE CRITICISM FROM 1400 TO 1800* (LC)** ***SHAKESPEAREAN CRITICISM* (SC)**
Authors who died before 1400	***CLASSICAL AND MEDIEVAL LITERATURE CRITICISM* (CMLC)**
Authors of books for children and young adults	***CHILDREN'S LITERATURE REVIEW* (CLR)**
Dramatists	***DRAMA CRITICISM* (DC)**
Poets	***POETRY CRITICISM* (PC)**
Short story writers	***SHORT STORY CRITICISM* (SSC)**
Black writers of the past two hundred years	***BLACK LITERATURE CRITICISM* (BLC)**
Hispanic writers of the late nineteenth and twentieth centuries	***HISPANIC LITERATURE CRITICISM* (HLC)**
Native North American writers and orators of the eighteenth, nineteenth, and twentieth centuries	***NATIVE NORTH AMERICAN LITERATURE* (NNAL)**
Major authors from the Renaissance to the present	***WORLD LITERATURE CRITICISM, 1500 TO THE PRESENT* (WLC)**

ISSN 0276-8178

Volume 76

Twentieth-Century Literary Criticism

Excerpts from Criticism of the Works of Novelists, Poets, Playwrights, Short Story Writers, and Other Creative Writers Who Lived between 1900 and 1960, from the First Published Critical Appraisals to Current Evaluations

Jennifer Gariepy
Editor

Thomas Ligotti
Associate Editor

DETROIT • NEW YORK • LONDON

REF
PN
771
T85
V. 76

STAFF

Jennifer Gariepy, *Editor*

Thomas Ligotti, *Associate Editor*

Susan Trosky, *Permissions Manager*
Kimberly F. Smilay, *Permissions Specialist*
Sarah R. Chesney, Steve Cusack, Kelly A. Quin, *Permissions Associate*

Victoria B. Cariappa, *Research Manager*
Michele P. LaMeau, Andrew Guy Malonis, Barbara McNeil, Gary J. Oudersluys, Maureen Richards, *Research Specialists*
Julia C. Daniel, Tamara C. Nott, Tracie A. Richardson, Norma Sawaya, Cheryl L. Warnock, *Research Associates*

Mary Beth Trimper, *Production Director*
Deborah L. Milliken, *Production Assistant*

Ninette Saad, *Desktop Publisher Assistant*
Randy Bassett, *Image Database Supervisor*
Robert Duncan, Michael Logusz, *Imaging Specialists*
Pamela Reed, *Photography Coordinator*

Since this page cannot legibly accommodate all copyright notices, the acknowledgments constitute an extension of the copyright notice.

While every effort has been made to ensure the reliability of the information presented in this publication, Gale Research neither guarantees the accuracy of the data contained herein nor assumes any responsibility for errors, omissions or discrepancies. Gale accepts no payment for listing, and inclusion in the publication of any organization, agency, institution, publication, service, or individual does not imply endorsement of the editors or publisher. Errors brought to the attention of the publisher and verified to the satisfaction of the publisher will be corrected in future editions.

The paper used in this publication meets the minimum requirements of American National Standard for Information Sciences—Permanence Paper for Printed Library Materials, ANSI Z39.48-1984. ∞™

This publication is a creative work fully protected by all applicable copyright laws, as well as by misappropriation, trade secret, unfair competition, and other applicable laws. The authors and editors of this work have added value to the underlying factual material herein through one or more of the following: unique and original selection, coordination, expression, arrangement, and classification of the information.

All rights to this publication will be vigorously defended.

Copyright © 1998
Gale Research
835 Penobscot Building
Detroit, MI 48226-4094

All rights reserved including the right of reproduction in whole or in part in any form.

Library of Congress Catalog Card Number 76-46132
ISBN 0-7876-2022-X
ISSN 0276-8178

Printed in the United States of America
10 9 8 7 6 5 4 3 2 1

Contents

Preface

Since its inception more than fifteen years ago, *Twentieth-Century Literary Criticism* has been purchased and used by nearly 10,000 school, public, and college or university libraries. *TCLC* has covered more than 500 authors, representing 58 nationalities, and over 25,000 titles. No other reference source has surveyed the critical response to twentieth-century authors and literature as thoroughly as *TCLC*. In the words of one reviewer, "there is nothing comparable available." *TCLC* "is a gold mine of information—dates, pseudonyms, biographical information, and criticism from books and periodicals—which many libraries would have difficulty assembling on their own."

Scope of the Series

TCLC is designed to serve as an introduction to authors who died between 1900 and 1960 and to the most significant interpretations of these author's works. The great poets, novelists, short story writers, playwrights, and philosophers of this period are frequently studied in high school and college literature courses. In organizing and excerpting the vast amount of critical material written on these authors, *TCLC* helps students develop valuable insight into literary history, promotes a better understanding of the texts, and sparks ideas for papers and assignments. Each entry in *TCLC* presents a comprehensive survey of an author's career or an individual work of literature and provides the user with a multiplicity of interpretations and assessments. Such variety allows students to pursue their own interests; furthermore, it fosters an awareness that literature is dynamic and responsive to many different opinions.

Every fourth volume of *TCLC* is devoted to literary topics. These topic entries widen the focus of the series from individual authors to such broader subjects as literary movements, prominent themes in twentieth-century literature, literary reaction to political and historical events, significant eras in literary history, prominent literary anniversaries, and the literatures of cultures that are often overlooked by English-speaking readers.

TCLC is designed as a companion series to Gale's *Contemporary Literary Criticism,* which reprints commentary on authors now living or who have died since 1960. Because of the different periods under consideration, there is no duplication of material between *CLC* and *TCLC*. For additional information about *CLC* and Gale's other criticism titles, users should consult the Guide to Gale Literary Criticism Series preceding the title page in this volume.

Coverage

Each volume of *TCLC* is carefully compiled to present:

- criticism of authors, or literary topics, representing a variety of genres and nationalities
- both major and lesser-known writers and literary works of the period
- 6-12 authors or 3-6 topics per volume
- individual entries that survey critical response to each author's work or each topic in literary history, including early criticism to reflect initial reactions; later criticism to represent any rise or decline in reputation; and current retrospective analyses.

Organization of This Book

An author entry consists of the following elements: author heading, biographical and critical introduction, list of principal works, excerpts of criticism (each preceded by an annotation and a bibliographic citation), and a bibliography of further reading.

- The **Author Heading** consists of the name under which the author most commonly wrote, followed by birth and death dates. If an author wrote consistently under a pseudonym, the pseudonym will be listed in the author heading and the real name given in parentheses on the first line of the biographical and critical introduction. Also located at the beginning of the introduction to the author entry are any name variations under which an author wrote, including transliterated forms for authors whose languages use nonroman alphabets.

- The **Biographical and Critical Introduction** outlines the author's life and career, as well as the critical issues surrounding his or her work. References to past volumes of *TCLC* are provided at the beginning of the introduction. Additional sources of information in other biographical and critical reference series published by Gale, including *Short Story Criticism, Children's Literature Review, Contemporary Authors, Dictionary of Literary Biography,* and *Something about the Author,* are listed in a box at the end of the entry.

- Some *TCLC* entries include **Portraits** of the author. Entries also may contain reproductions of materials pertinent to an author's career, including manuscript pages, title pages, dust jackets, letters, and drawings, as well as photographs of important people, places, and events in an author's life.

- The **List of Principal Works** is chronological by date of first book publication and identifies the genre of each work. In the case of foreign authors with both foreign-language publications and English translations, the title and date of the first English-language edition are given in brackets. Unless otherwise indicated, dramas are dated by first performance, not first publication.

- Critical excerpts are prefaced by **Annotations** providing the reader with information about both the critic and the criticism that follows. Included are the critic's reputation, individual approach to literary criticism, and particular expertise in an author's works. Also noted are the relative importance of a work of criticism, the scope of the excerpt, and the growth of critical controversy or changes in critical trends regarding an author. In some cases, these annotations cross-reference excerpts by critics who discuss each other's commentary.

- A complete **Bibliographic Citation** designed to facilitate location of the original essay or book precedes each piece of criticism.

- Criticism is arranged chronologically in each author entry to provide a perspective on changes in critical evaluation over the years. All titles of works by the author featured in the entry are printed in boldface type to enable the user to easily locate discussion of particular works. Also for purposes of easier identification, the critic's name and the publication date of the essay are given at the beginning of each piece of criticism. Unsigned criticism is preceded by the title of the journal in which it appeared. Some of the excerpts in *TCLC* also contain translated material. Unless otherwise noted, translations in brackets are by the editors; translations in parentheses or continuous with the text are by the critic. Publication information (such as footnotes or page and line references to specific editions of works) have been deleted at the editor's discretion to provide smoother reading of the text.

- An annotated list of **Further Reading** appearing at the end of each author entry suggests secondary sources on the author. In some cases it includes essays for which the editors could not obtain reprint rights.

Cumulative Indexes

- Each volume of *TCLC* contains a cumulative **Author Index** listing all authors who have appeared in Gale's Literary Criticism Series, along with cross references to such biographical series as *Contemporary Authors* and *Dictionary of Literary Biography.* For readers' convenience, a complete list of Gale titles included appears on the first page of the author index. Useful for locating authors within the various series, this index is particularly valuable for those authors who are identified by a certain period but who, because of their death dates, are placed in another, or for those authors whose careers span two periods. For example, F. Scott Fitzgerald is found in *TCLC,* yet a writer often associated with him, Ernest Hemingway, is found in *CLC.*

- Each *TCLC* volume includes a cumulative **Nationality Index** which lists all authors who have appeared in *TCLC* volumes, arranged alphabetically under their respective nationalities, as well as Topics volume entries devoted to particular national literatures.

- Each new volume in Gale's Literary Criticism Series includes a cumulative **Topic Index,** which lists all literary topics treated in *NCLC, TCLC, LC 1400-1800,* and the *CLC* yearbook.

- Each new volume of *TCLC,* with the exception of the Topics volumes, includes a **Title Index** listing the titles of all literary works discussed in the volume. In response to numerous suggestions from librarians, Gale has also produced a **Special Paperbound Edition** of the *TCLC* title index. This annual cumulation lists all titles discussed in the series since its inception and is issued with the first volume of *TCLC* published each year. Additional copies of the index are available on request. Librarians and patrons will welcome this separate index; it saves shelf space, is easy to use, and is recyclable upon receipt of the following year's cumulation. Titles discussed in the Topics volume entries are not included *TCLC* cumulative index.

Citing Twentieth-Century Literary Criticism

When writing papers, students who quote directly from any volume in Gale's literary Criticism Series may use the following general forms to footnote reprinted criticism. The first example pertains to materials drawn from periodicals, the second to material reprinted from books.

[1]William H. Slavick, "Going to School to DuBose Heyward," *The Harlem Renaissance Reexamined,* (AMS Press, 1987); excerpted and reprinted in *Twentieth-Century Literary Criticism,* Vol. 59, ed. Jennifer Gariepy (Detroit: Gale Research, 1995), pp. 94-105.

[2]George Orwell, "Reflections on Gandhi," *Partisan Review,* 6 (Winter 1949), pp. 85-92; excerpted and reprinted in *Twentieth-Century Literary Criticism,* Vol. 59, ed. Jennifer Gariepy (Detroit: Gale Research, 1995), pp. 40-3.

Suggestions Are Welcome

In response to suggestions, several features have been added to *TCLC* since the series began, including annotations to excerpted criticism, a cumulative index to authors in all Gale literary criticism series, entries devoted to criticism on a single work by a major author, more extensive illustrations, and a title index listing all literary works discussed in the series since its inception.

Readers who wish to suggest authors or topics to appear in future volumes, or who have other suggestions, are cordially invited to write the editors.

Acknowledgments

The editors wish to thank the copyright holders of the excerpted criticism included in this volume and the permissions managers of many book and magazine publishing companies for assisting us in securing reproduction rights. We are also grateful to the staffs of the Detroit Public Library, the Library of Congress, the University of Detroit Mercy Library, Wayne State University Purdy/Kresge Library Complex, and the University of Michigan Libraries for making their resources available to us. Following is a list of the copyright holders who have granted us permission to reproduce material in this volume of *TCLC*. Every effort has been made to trace copyright, but if omissions have been made, please let us know.

COPYRIGHTED EXCERPTS IN *TCLC*, VOLUME 76, WERE REPRODUCED FROM THE FOLLOWING PERIODICALS:

The Academy of Management Review, v. 1, July, 1976; v. 7, January, 1982. Both reproduced by permission of the publisher.—***American Quarterly,*** v. 43, March, 1991. © The American Studies Association. Reproduced by permission of The Johns Hopkins University Press.—***Black American Literature Forum,*** v. 25, Summer, 1991 for "Micheaux: Celebrating Blackness" by Bell Hooks. Copyright © 1991 by the author. Reprinted by permission of Bell Hooks and the Watkins/Loomis Agency.—***The Centennial Review,*** v. 23, 1979 for "Walden on Halsted Street: Jane Addams' Twenty Years at Hull-House" by James Hurt. © 1979 by The Centennial Review. Reproduced by permission of the publisher and the author.—***Cinefantastique,*** v. 12, May-June, 1982 for "Val Lewton's Cat People" by George Turner. Copyright © 1982 by Frederick S. Clarke.—***Film Comment,*** October, 1985 for "'B'. . . for Black" by Donald Bogle. Copyright © 1985 by Film Comment Publishing Corporation. Reproduced by permission of the author.—***History of Education Quarterly,*** v. 14, Spring, 1974 for "The Education of Jane Addams" by J. O. C. Phillips.—***Journal of Film and Video,*** v. 40, Winter, 1988. Copyright © 1988 by the University Film and Video Association. All rights reserved. Reproduced by permission.—***Journal of Popular Film and Television,*** v. 10, Fall, 1982. Copyright © 1982 Helen Dwight Reid Educational Foundation. Reproduced with permission of the Helen Dwight Reid Educational Foundation, published by Heldref Publications, 1319 18th Street, NW, Washington, DC 20036-1802.—***Journal of the History of Ideas,*** v. XXII; v. 54, April, 1993. Copyright © 1993 by Journal of the History of Ideas, Inc. Both reproduced by permission of Johns Hopkins University Press.—***Journal of Women's History,*** v. 7, Summer, 1995. Reproduced by permission of Indiana University Press.—***Journalism Quarterly,*** v. 67, Autumn, 1990. Reproduced by permission.—***Literature/Film Quarterly,*** v. 10, 1982. © copyright 1982 Salisbury State College. Reproduced by permission.—***Monthly Film Bulletin,*** v. 48, August, 1981. Copyright © The British Film Institute, 1981. Reproduced by permission.—***The New York Times Book Review,*** June 15, 1997. Copyright © 1997 by The New York Times Company. Reproduced by permission.—***Nineteenth-Century Literature,*** v. 48, March 1994. © 1994 by The Regents of the University of California. Reprinted by permission of the publisher and the author.—***The Old Northwest: A Journal of Regional Life and Letters,*** v. 2, September, 1976. Copyright © Miami University 1976. Reproduced by permission.—***Romanian Review,*** v. 26, 1972; v. 41, 1987. Both reproduced by permission.—***South Dakota Review,*** v. 11, Winter, 1973-74. © 1973, University of South Dakota. Reproduced by permission.—***Theatre Journal,*** v. 34, May, 1982. © 1982 Johns Hopkins University Press. Reproduced by permission of The Johns Hopkins University Press.—***The Village Voice,*** v. 34, December 5, 1989 for "A Man For All Seasons: Miyazawa Kenji Cultivates His Garden" by Geoffrey O'Brien. Copyright © V. V. Publishing Corporation. Reproduced by permission of the author.

COPYRIGHTED EXCERPTS IN *TCLC*, VOLUME 76, WERE REPRODUCED FROM THE FOLLOWING BOOKS:

Abbott, Philip. From ***States of Perfect Freedom.*** The University of Massachusetts Press, 1987. Copyright © 1987 by The University of Massachusetts Press. All rights reserved. Reproduced by permission.—Bester, John. From the foreword to ***Once and Forever: The Tales of Kenji Miyazawa.*** Translated by John Bester. Kodansha International Ltd., 1993. Copyright © 1993, by Kodansha International Ltd. All rights reserved. Reproduced by permission.—Bowser, Pearl and Louise Spence. From "Identity and Betrayal: The Symbol of the Unconquered and Oscar Micheaux's 'Biographical Legend'" in ***The Birth of Whiteness: Race and the Emergence of U. S. Cinema.*** Edited by Daniel Bernardi. Rutgers University Press, 1996. Copyright © 1996 by Rutgers, The State University. All rights reserved. Reproduced by permission.—Davis, Allen F. From ***The Spirit of Youth and the City Streets by Jane Addams.*** University of Illinois Press, 1972. © 1972 by The Board of Trustees of the University of Illinois. Reproduced by permission of the publisher and the author.—DeKoven, Marianne. From ***Rereading Modernism: New Directions in Feminist Criticism.*** Edited with an introduction by Lisa Rado. Garland Publishing, 1994. Copyright © 1994 Lisa Rado. Reproduced by permission.—Drucker, Peter F. From ***Toward the Next Economics and Other Essays.*** Harper & Row, Publishers. Copyright © 1981 by Peter F. Drucker. All rights reserved. Reproduced by permission of the author.—Elshtain, Jean Bethke. From ***Power Trips and Other Journeys: Essays in Feminism as Civic Discourse.*** The University of

Wisconsin Press, 1990. Copyright © 1990 The Board of Regents of the University of Wisconsin System. All rights reserved. Reproduced by permission.—Everson, William K. From ***Classics of the Horror Film.*** The Citadel Press, 1974. Copyright © 1974 by William K. Everson. All rights reserved. Reproduced by permission.—Fontenot, Chester J., Jr. From "Oscar Micheaux, Black Novelist and Film Maker" in ***Vision and Refuge: Essays on the Literature of the Great Plains.*** Edited by Virginia Faulkner. University of Nebraska Press, 1982. Copyright © 1982 by the University of Nebraska Press. All rights reserved. Reproduced by permission.—Gloster, Hugh M. From ***Negro Voices in American Fiction.*** The University of North Carolina Press, 1948. Copyright © 1948 by The University of North Carolina, renewed 1975 by Hugh M. Gloster. Used by permission of the publisher and the author.—Haber, Samuel. From ***Efficiency and Uplift: Scientific Management in the Progressive Era 1890-1920.*** The University of Chicago Press, 1964. © 1964 by The University of Chicago. All rights reserved. Reproduced by permission.—Herman, Sondra R. From ***Eleven Against War: Studies in American Internationalist Thought, 1898-1921.*** Stanford University, 1969. Copyright © 1969 by the Board of Trustees of the Leland Stanford Junior University. Reproduced with the permission of the publishers, Hoover Institution Press.—Knight, Louise W. From ***The Responsibilities of Wealth.*** Edited by Dwight F. Burlingame. Indiana University Press, 1992. © 1992 by Indiana University Press. All rights reserved. Reproduced by permission.—Lagemann, Ellen Condliffe. From ***Jane Addams on Education.*** Edited by Ellen Condliffe Lagemann. Teachers College Press, 1985. Copyright © 1985 by Teachers College, Columbia University. All rights reserved. Reproduced by permission.—Lehmkuhl, Ursula. From ***Reconstructing American Literary and Historical Studies.*** St. Martin's Press, 1990. Copyright © 1990 in Frankfurt am Main by Campus Verlag. All rights reserved. Reproduced by permission of Campus Verlag. In North America by St. Martin's Press.—Nadworny, Milton J. From ***Scientific Management and the Unions 1900-1932: A Historical Analysis.*** Harvard University Press, 1955. © Copyright, 1955, by The President and Fellows of Harvard College. Renewed, 1983, by Milton Joseph Nadworny. Reproduced by permission.—Rimer, J. Thomas. From ***A Reader's Guide to Japanese Literature.*** Kodansha International, 1988. Copyright © 1988 by Kodansha International Ltd. All rights reserved. Reproduced by permission.—Sampson, Henry T. From ***Blacks in Black and White: A Source Book on Black Films.*** The Scarecrow Press, Inc., 1977. Copyright © 1977 by Henry T. Sampson. Reproduced by permission.—Sato, Hiroaki. From an introduction to ***A Future of Ice: Poems and Stories of a Japanese Buddhist, Miyazawa Kenji.*** Translated by Hiroaki Sato. North Point Press, 1989. Reproduced by permission of the author.—Schachter, Hindy Lauer. From ***Frederick Taylor and the Public Administration Community: A Reevaluation.*** State University of New York Press, 1989. © 1989 SUNY Press. All rights reserved. Reproduced by permission.—Siegel, Joel E. From ***Val Lewton: The Reality of Terror.*** The Viking Press, 1973. Copyright 1973 by Joel E. Siegel. All rights reserved. Reproduced by permission of The British Film Institute.—Stroup, Herbert. From ***Social Work Pioneers.*** Nelson-Hall, 1986. Copyright © 1986 Nelson-Hall. Reproduced by permission. Telotte, J. P. From ***Dreams of Darkness: Fantasy and the Films of Val Lewton.*** University of Illinois Press, 1985. © 1985 b the Board of Trustees of the University of Illinois. Reproduced by permission of the publisher and the author.—Telotte, J. P. From "Val Lewton and the Perspective of Horror" in ***Forms of the Fantastic: Selected Essays from the Third International Conference on the Fantastic in Literature and Film.*** Edited by Jan Hokenson and Howard Pearce. Greenwood Press, 1986. Copyright © 1986 by The Thomas Burnett Swann Fund. All rights reserved. Reproduced by permission of Greenwood Publishing Group, Inc., Westport, CT.—Ueda, Makoto. From ***Modern Japanese Poets and the Nature of Literature.*** Stanford University Press, 1983. © 1983 by the Board of Trustees of the Leland Stanford Junior University. Reproduced with the permission of the publishers, Stanford University Press.—Watson, Burton. From the introduction to ***Spring & Asura: Poems of Kenji Miyazawa.*** Translated by Hiroaki Sato. Chicago Review Press, 1973. Copyright © 1973 by Chicago Review Press. Reproduced by permission of the author.

PHOTOGRAPHS AND ILLUSTRATIONS APPEARING IN *TCLC,* VOLUME 76, WERE RECEIVED FROM THE FOLLOWING SOURCES:

Addams, Jane, photograph. The Library of Congress.—Lewton, Val, photograph. Archive Photos, Inc. Reproduced by permission.—Pulitzer, Joseph, photograph. Archive Photos, Inc. Reproduced by permission.—Taylor, Frederick Winslow, photograph of sketch. The Library of Congrcss.

Jane Addams

1860-1935

American social worker, essayist and autobiographer.

INTRODUCTION

Jane Addams is known primarily as a social reformer, a reputation built during the many years she devoted to serving the poor through Hull House in Chicago. But that was only one level of her achievements. She created the foundations for the profession of social work, contributed significantly to the discipline of sociology, developed the idea of parks and playgrounds as places vital for reducing urban tension, and established a model of progressive-minded activism which helped form the basis of the welfare state that emerged under the administration of President Franklin D. Roosevelt in the 1930s. In the process she became one of America's best-known and best-loved women, and her fame spread with the publication of her books—including the autobiographical *Twenty Years at Hull-House* (1910)—and hundreds of articles. Addams challenged her compatriots' understanding of urban life, wealth and poverty, democracy, and peace, and was instrumental in founding numerous organizations such as the American Civil Liberties Union (ACLU) and the National Association for the Advancement of Colored People (NAACP). A popularizer rather than an innovator in the realm of ideas, she transformed the pragmatism of William James and John Dewey, along with the mystic agrarian socialism of Leo Tolstoy, into a workable program of social action that transformed the American landscape.

Biographical Information

Addams was born in Cedarville, Illinois, on the eve of the Civil War. Her father, John Addams, who would become her most significant role model, was an entrepreneur and politician who had served in the Illinois legislature with another of Addams's later heroes, Abraham Lincoln. Addams seldom spoke of her mother, who died when she was three, or of her stepmother, who her father married soon afterward. She was a sickly child, and like many young women of her day, was discouraged from pursuing too high a degree of education. Giving up a dream to attend Smith College, she went instead to Rockford Seminary, and soon after her graduation, a series of unhappy events threw her young life into turmoil. Her beloved father died, and after six months at a medical college in Philadelphia, she withdrew in 1882 for reasons of illness, and never went back. A year of convalescence followed, and then two tours of Europe, but her travels did not make her happy. Later she would write of being caught in "the snare of preparation" which she said impeded young women from wealthy backgrounds, keeping them locked in a state of continual preparation for life rather than permitting them to commence an actual career. Partly as a result of experiences in Europe, however, she discovered her life's mission, and with her friend and lifelong companion Ellen Gates Starr founded Hull House in a run-down Chicago mansion on September 18, 1889. At Hull House (which Addams referred to in her writing as "Hull-House"), she established numerous innovative programs to provide not just food and shelter, but a sense of purpose and belonging, both to the people served by the house and to the upper-class women and men who ran it. During the next two decades, Addams's work on behalf of the poor and immigrants of the nearby slums made her a figure of national and ultimately international prominence, and she published numerous articles and books. She was also instrumental in the founding and development of dozens of organizations, and through Hull House, helped create a model for a vital community center which could transform a troubled urban environment. In the years leading up to World War I, her outspoken pacifism began to strike a raw nerve in a nation mobilizing for the defeat of Germany, and she became almost as much a figure of scorn as she had been of admiration. But her reputation ultimately rose to its former level, a resurrection which culminated in her receiving the Nobel Peace Prize in 1931. During her career, Addams spent time with a number of notable writers and philosophers, including James, Dewey, Tolstoy, W. E. B. Du Bois, and many others. In politics she campaigned for Theodore Roosevelt in his unsuccessful bid to regain the White House under the Progressive Party banner in 1912; and later she put her support behind a man with whom she had worked in the area of famine relief following the First World War, President Herbert Hoover. Addams never married, and had few interests outside her social concerns. She was an astute manager and promoter who devoted all her efforts—and the proceeds from her publications and prizes—to Hull House and its activities.

Major Works

As with many writers, it is virtually impossible to separate Addams' published work from the conditions that surrounded their creation. This is not only because Addams's life was defined by action rather than thought, but also because most of her writings were in response to specific situations that she encountered first as the director of Hull House, and later as a campaigner for world peace. Furthermore, with a few notable exceptions, most of her books were actually composed of essays, speeches, and articles she had presented earlier, again in response to specific conditions. Such was certainly the case with her first book, *Democracy and Social Ethics* (1902), in which she identified a spirit of alienation pervading modern life, and as an antidote offered active involvement in the project of establishing a more humane public order. Likewise *The Spirit of Youth and City Streets* (1909) came from a series of essays, and it, like *A New Conscience and an Ancient Evil* (1912) explored the problems of the slums and the unhealthy lifestyles they bred. Her examination of prostitution in the latter work scandalized readers, but it was the pacifism expressed in volumes such as *Newer Ideals of Peace* (1909) and *Peace and Bread in Time of War* (1922) which would earn her the disapprobation of conservative leaders and institutions from the Daughters of the American Revolution to the Ku Klux Klan. The condemnation of Addams for her vocal opposition to the First World War perhaps marked the low point of her career; *Twenty Years at Hull-House* (1910), on the other hand, came at the high point. Ostensibly an autobiography, it was in fact the story of how Addams came to find her mission as a crusader for social justice, and then pursued that mission without wavering. Critically acclaimed at the time and thereafter, it is usually considered the best of her works, whereas the sequel, *The Second Twenty Years at Hull-House* (1930)—which sums up activity in the two decades that followed the writing of its predecessor—is often viewed as one of her least well-written. Her later works included a collection of essays called *The Excellent Becomes the Permanent* (1932), which helped to sum up an extraordinarily distinguished career.

PRINCIPAL WORKS

Democracy and Social Ethics (essays) 1902
Newer Ideals of Peace (essays) 1907
The Spirit of Youth and the City Streets (essays) 1909
Twenty Years at Hull-House (autobiography) 1910
A New Conscience and an Ancient Evil (nonfiction) 1912
Peace and Bread in Time of War (nonfiction) 1922
The Second Twenty Years at Hull-House; September 1909 to September 1929, with a Record of a Growing World Conscience (autobiography) 1930
The Excellent Becomes the Permanent (essays) 1932

CRITICISM

C. C. Arbuthnot (essay date 1903)

SOURCE: *The Journal of Political Economy,* Vol. XI, December, 1902-September, 1903, pp. 169-171.

[*In the following essay, Arbuthnot reviews* Democracy and Social Ethics *with a focus on its economic and political insights.*]

Among the matters of particularly economic interest in Miss Addams's [***Democracy and Social Ethics***] is the discussion of the domestic service problem, in the chapter on **"Household Adjustment."** The family has given up to the factory most of the manufacture which contributes to the welfare of its members, but it retains the preparation of food and ministration to personal comfort, as essential to family life. This domestic industry is out of line with economic development, and is "ill-adjusted and belated." As a result the household employee is more or less isolated in the social world with whose growing democratic ideas the factory system is in harmony. She is discriminated against by the young men of her acquaintance, and has to work long hours and every day, with proportionate remuneration a little doubtful, when the prospect of promotion in the factory is taken into account. The manufacture of more household necessities in factories, and the elimination of personal service for healthy adults, would open a way to an adjustment which promises relief.

"Political Reform" is the caption of the last chapter, and the question turns largely on the ethical ideas of the people in the district around Hull House. The alderman who represents the ward is noisomely corrupt, as the reform element count corruptness, but his constituents "admire him as a great man and a hero because his individual acts are, on the whole, kindly and generous." The very poor, whose kindnesses to each other, in the nature of the case, take the form of supplying immediate wants, estimate a man by his willingness to furnish the necessities of life. Considerations of abstract justice or social policy are secondary and are treated as such. They do not much concern people who have to struggle in order to provide for actual needs. The ethical precept to fit such conditions seems to be: do the substantial thing and do it immediately. The alderman is a good man because in his relations with the people of the ward he closely acts in obedience to this injunction. He bails his constituents when they are arrested; "fixes up" matters with the justice or the state's attorney; pays the rent when one is hard pressed; sees that a respectable funeral is provided in case of need; and gets jobs for those who are out of work. He is a good friend and neighbor. There is no doubt about it, and he is voted for because he is such a man. If he pays for votes that is another of his good acts.

When the vote commands a price it becomes a part of the assets of the owner. A citizen in the ward complained "that his vote had sold for only two dollars this year," in much the same way that a farmer might regret that the price of wheat had fallen. Efforts are made to get the best prices for this intangible property. The ranks of reform clubs are swelled by voters who join in order to bull the market and sell out to the opposition at an advance. This is merely making the most of a commercial opportunity.

These people have a strong sense of moral obligation and a wrongdoer is liable to punishment as direct and palpable as their kindness. "A certain lodginghouse keeper sold the votes of his entire house to a political party and 'was well paid for it too.'" He then turned around and sold them to the rival party. This was outrageous. The scoundrel was held under a street hydrant in November, and died of pneumonia contracted in consequence. The alderman, under these circumstances, is the model of aspiring politicians. His methods of getting on are imitated, and politics becomes "a matter of favors and positions," to be had by necessary manipulation, which is of the same moral quality as the operations of ordinary business.

If the voter can be persuaded "that his individual needs are common needs, that is, public needs, and that they can only be legitimately supplied for him when they are supplied for all," Miss Addams thinks, the structure of civic virtue can be built up. The provision by the city of kindergartens for the children; playgrounds and readingrooms for the youth; gymnasiums and swimming-tanks for men; and the enactment and enforcement of a civil service law that would relieve the city employee from dependence on the alderman for the tenure of his job; such methods are suggested as means for promoting civic consciousness. When people's minds are constantly occupied with the difficulties of satisfying substantial wants, they cannot be reached by appeals for political righteousness and pure politics. They do not think in these terms.

The Nation (essay date 1910)

SOURCE: A review of *Twenty Years at Hull-House,* in *The Nation,* Vol. 91, No. 2374, December 29, 1910, pp. 634-35.

[*In the following review, the critic considers* Twenty Years at Hull-House *primarily from the standpoint of the biographical information it offers on Addams.*]

"Which is better," asks Professor Cooley in his *Social Organization,* "fellowship or distinction? There is much to be said on both sides, but the finer spirits of our day lean toward the former, and find it more human and exhilarating to spread abroad the good things the world already has than to prosecute a lonesome search for new ones. I notice among the choicest people I know—those who seem to me most representative of the inner trend of democracy—a certain generous contempt for distinction and a passion to cast their lives heartily on the general current." This penetrating observation is suggested by Miss Jane Addams's new book on her life at Hull-House. About a third of the material has previously appeared in the magazines; but unlike the author's previous books setting forth conclusions based on her experience, this traces the experiences themselves with the invaluable sidelight emanating from her own early history.

Miss Addams was born in the village of Cedarville, Illinois, in 1860, the daughter of a Hicksite Quaker who, from 1854 to 1870, was a member of the State Senate, and sufficiently conversant with politics to enjoy the intimate confidence of Lincoln. Her mother died when the future founder of Hull-House was a baby. Despite her physical infirmity—a curvature of the spine—her childhood was a joyous one. The family was well-to-do, if not prosperous; there was an ample air of public interest and public spirit stirring in the household circle; and more than the ordinary heritage of culture. She records that even as a child, her "mind was busy, however, with the old question eternally suggested by the inequalities of the human lot". Like her older sisters before her, Miss Addams went to the seminary, now college, at Rockford, Illinois, one of the earliest schools in the West for the higher education of women, and dubbed, because of affinity of spirit, "The Mount Holyoke of the West." All the fine enthusiasms of those early days of collegiate education for women found in Miss Addams hospitable lodgment, though she records with a bit of waggishness how once upon occasion, in an intercollegiate oratorical contest, she was pitted against no less a competitor than William Jennings Bryan. Her father's death occurred soon after she left college. Diverted from the professional study of medicine by a long illness, she spent some years in study, and in travel and residence abroad, until Hull-House in Chicago was opened in 1889. She speaks with an amusing impatience of "the snare of preparation," and with true feminine relief at the thought that "I had at last finished with the everlasting preparation for life," however ill-prepared I might be".

The social settlement has become so familiar an institution that an estimate of its nature and functions is less necessary than an insight into the convictions and character of the best known of its early founders in this country—and this, for the reason that Miss Addams's work has had so strong a formative influence upon settlements everywhere in the United States. The fundamental motive which seems to have actuated her proceeded from her conviction of the utter futility of a detached attainment of moral excellence. This root idea she expresses at times negatively in terms of revolt, or at least of reaction, against a premature overdose or individualistic cultivation, "a moral revulsion against this feverish search after culture". Positively, the same dominant impulse she describes almost passionately as a belief in the supreme moral worth of democracy in social relationships. During the eight years that fell wasted in "the snare of preparation" she "was absolutely at sea so far as any moral purpose was concerned, clinging only to the desire to live in a really living world and refusing to be content with a shadowy intellectual or aesthetic reflection of it". At times, a note almost bitter against the intellectual surfeiting of college training is sounded—"lumbering our minds with literature that only served to cloud the really vital situation spread before our eyes". Or again, when she avers that the "first generation of college women had taken their learning too quickly, had departed too suddenly from the active emotional life led by their grandmothers" . . . "had lost that simple almost automatic response to the human appeal".

Her positive attachment to democracy, in the sense of "universal fellowship" in the life-adventure of the race, will appear most clearly if treated conjointly with Miss Addams's second ruling trait, a curious detachment coupled with skepticism about any system, religion, or panacea which falls short of her dominating idea of "universal fellowship." She herself ascribes her rejection of the evangelical assault upon her at college as due to her father's insistence upon "moral integrity" in the forum of conscience as the supreme law of the soul. But some years after, when all outside pressure was withdrawn, she voluntarily was baptized and became a communicant. The recital of the episode is exquisite—as "mere literature" finer than St. Augustine's conversion, in our opinion—but, while explicit as to the absence of disturbance of soul or strong compunction, she adds this revelatory comment:

> There was also growing within me an almost passionate devotion to the ideals of democracy, and when in all history had these ideals been so thrillingly expressed as when the faith of the fisherman and slave had been boldly opposed to the accepted moral belief that the well-being of a privileged few might justly be built upon the ignorance and sacrifice of the many?

After this one does not wonder that the single-taxer who sought to convert her to his cult by sudden prayer for her in her presence went away sorrowful; or that she failed to convert herself to Socialism, though she conscientiously made the effort.

It is interesting to notice how this underlying conviction and motive determine her attitude—and incidentally the attitude of settlement workers so largely—upon public issues. Of factory legislation in behalf of the weak, children and women, they approve. With trades-unionism so far as "it is a general social movement concerning all members of society and not merely a class struggle", they are in sympathy. For a discriminating State regimentation they stand, for "if certain industrial conditions are forcing workers below the standard of decency, it becomes possible to deduce the right of State regulation" on the ground that "the very existence of the State depends upon the character of its citizens".

There is a fortunate sanity of temper and attitude flowing from the ground idea of "universal fellowship" in social relations which, while misrepresented and at times maligned, has kept the settlements close on the track of their quest of social betterment. Even when outbreaks of individual anarchists have driven the proud logicians into panic and grotesque absurdity, the settlement workers, and Miss Addams in particular, have emerged with signal credit. Even their hero-worship has been in a way transfigured by their guiding motive. Miss Addams confesses that, instead of Carlyle's "Heroes and Hero-Worship" which she had once purposed to give to young boys of promise, she actually presented Schurz's "Abraham Lincoln." Moreover, in retrospect as to "the actual attainment of these early hopes," she remarks, "so far as they have been realized at all, [they] seem to have come from men of affairs rather than from those given to speculation".

The various experiments of Hull House, its failures and triumphs, its inner life as well as its outer activities, are all set forth engagingly in this volume, with a surprising modesty as regards general scientific conclusions such as the professional sociologist would expect. Miss Addams has generally a direct way of putting things, and an enjoyment of humorous by-products. Occasionally, however, there is a note of wistful pathos—"the sense of universality thus imparted to that mysterious injustice, the burden of which we are all forced to bear and with which I have become only too familiar".

Miss Addams's narration of her visit to Tolstoy, and her appraisal of Tolstoyism, will be of particular interest at this juncture. The prophet in his peasant's garb glanced disapprovingly at her large sleeves which were then in vogue, and, "pulling out one sleeve to an interminable breadth, said quite simply that 'there was enough stuff on one arm to make a frock for a little girl'." He would have said something similar about an historic alabaster box of ointment. Miss Addams is fortunate in her illustrator. There are an arresting power and a suggestive charm about some of the plates that entitle the artist to distinction.

Thomas C. Hall (essay date 1911)

SOURCE: A review of *Twenty Years at Hull-House,* in *Political Science Quarterly,* Vol. 26, 1911, pp. 317-19.

[*In the following review of* Twenty Years at Hull-House, *Hall concentrates on the role models who instilled in Addams a spirit of selflessness.*]

[***Twenty Years at Hull-House***] is invaluable as a human document. It is a beautiful memorial to a father and a wonderful revelation of a life given to a great purpose. In its style it is transparent and simple, but it is filled with subtle suggestion. It is not a book that should be lightly skimmed. Throughout there is a constant searching for the fuller meaning of human life; and underneath all the tentative inquiry and sometimes apparent groping there is a strong faith and a definite and clear conviction that have given unity to the whole life so vividly described.

The first chapter shows us an almost super-sensitive child, brought up under simple conditions, which yet were most advantageous for intellectual and spiritual development. The picture of the father, who evidently dominated the girl's early life, is attractive in the extreme; and subsequent chapters reveal many of his traits as those of the subject of the biography. Upon the spiritual development of both father and daughter the influence of Lincoln seems to have been in some respects controlling; so that when boarding-school was reached the social sympathies born of the home life and the political sympathies developed during the great national struggle asserted themselves, only with a clearer intelligence and with a more defined program for the lifework. For although Hull House was established only after a good deal of wandering in Europe and some intellectual hesitation on the part of its founder, it is easy to see that with Miss Addams the plan of a home shared with a larger humanity was always the underlying thought.

The subsequent chapters, dealing with the first days of Hull House and some of its early undertakings, are a most effective apologetic for the whole social settlement movement. If the movement has not broken down the wall of partition between class and class, it at least has opened windows, and sometimes doors, through which one class may have access to the hopes and ambitions of the other.

Miss Addams frankly acknowledges both her lack of a political program and her realization of the comfort and sustaining strength which a cut-and-dried and dogmatic political program may afford to the social worker. But it is easy to see that in mind and temperament alike Miss Addams is incapable of dogmatism, either broad or narrow. In action she is decided and prompt, and willing courageously to face the issue and take a prophet's risk of being wrong. But when it is a matter of far-reaching answers to perplexing problems, she is intellectually too sincere to be satisfied with clear-cut but untested formulas. Her sympathy with Tolstoi in no way prevented her from realizing the weak points in his position. Her admiration for particular socialists and her willingness to coöperate largely with them has in no wise determined her judgment of socialism; and her analysis of its fundamental philosophy has left her unsatisfied and unable to include herself in the party. Even her intense activity in the social settlement movement does not prevent her seeing clearly its tentative character; and she looks forward to a possible future society so organized that the ideals of the social settlement can be more largely realized.

Nothing is more striking than the insistent modesty with which these memoirs are written. The reader might almost imagine that some one else was responsible for all the good things accomplished by Hull House and that Miss Addams had made all the mistakes; whereas anyone who has had personal contact with the activities of that settlement knows that in a hundred exigencies Miss Addams's sanity, gentleness and indwelling grace have been its salvation.

The book is one that should be read both by partisans and by non-partisans in the present movement for social betterment; and happily it is so written that it will be widely read. And in years to come it will be studied page by page by those who may be puzzled to comprehend the manifold confusions of our American life at this turning-point of the road. For the reviewer feels assured that, when the orgy of individualism that followed the occupation of free land and the exploitations of the natural resources of the continent by a restless immigrant population under the unorganized conditions of competitive struggle shall be over, and when we shall have entered upon a more ordered social state, men will eagerly seek just such a human document as this to explain a social situation which may well seem inexplicably unintelligent and needlessly tragic. We must surely all be grateful to Miss Addams that she has given to us, while the memories are still vivid and the situation not yet too idealized, this most illuminating account of the activities of Hull House, in which one sees reflected so much of the restless longing of our generation for a new world of social sympathy and human understanding.

The Sociological Review **(essay date 1911)**

SOURCE: A review of *Twenty Years at Hull-House,* in *The Sociological Review,* Vol. IV, 1911, pp. 153-54.

[*The following essay appraises* Twenty Years at Hull-House *as not just a personal account of one life, but of a time and place.*]

[***Twenty Years at Hull-House*** is] a book which is assured of a place among the noblest life records of the time. . . . It is not formally autobiographic in method, but Miss Addams has the rare faculty of stating or implying the essential personal facts, in the fewest possible words, during the process of describing the experiences which led her to follow a certain course of public action, or showing the relation in which Hull House has stood to the political and economic forces of the past two decades. It is a wonderful and deeply moving record, the power and inspiration of which no reviewer can hope to reproduce.

We get, in the opening pages, an exquisite reminiscence of the Addams home at Cedarville, Illinois; a glimpse of the American worship of Lincoln; an account of the boarding-school ideals and the varied European influences which led, by ways not difficult to follow, to the founding of the settlement among the slums of Chicago. Halstead Street, in which Hull House stands, has a length of thirty-two miles.

> Polk Street crosses it midway between the stockyards to the south and the shipbuilding yards on the north bank of the Chicago River. For six miles between these two industries the street is lined with shops and saloons. Polk Street running west becomes more prosperous; running a mile east to State Street it grows steadily worse, and crosses a network of vice on the corners of Clark Street and Fifth Avenue. . . . Between Halstead Street and the river live about 10,000 Italians, Neapolitans, Sicilians, and Calabrians, with an occasional Lombard or Venetian. To the south on Twelfth Street are many Germans, and side-streets are given over almost entirely to Polish and Russian Jews. Still further south, these Jewish colonies merge into a huge Bohemian colony, so vast that Chicago ranks as the third Bohemian city in the world.

Settlement life, still in its infancy in England, was in 1889 unknown in the United States and Miss Addams and her colleagues began work in an atmosphere of critical bewilderment, so far as observers were concerned, and with, on their own part, theories of happily sufficient fluidity to reinforce their abundant enthusiasms. The story of the first days is brilliantly told, and it is followed by a rapid and vivid description of the years of discussion and experiment—the invention and adjustment of social machinery, the gradual conquest of the neighbourhood, the many experiments undertaken, not merely in providing means of culture and recreation, but in co-operative enterprise, and later in general civic reconstruction. The narrative of schemes begun and developed, or attempted and abandoned, is interwoven with passages of personal reminiscence and confession, with stories of tragedy and heroism, drawn from a marvellously full store. At intervals, too, we learn of visits to Europe and contact with kindred workers on this side.

Miss Addams has some interesting comments to make on the changes in the intellectual and emotional aspects of England, at intervals of a few years before and during the South African War; and she tells of a visit to Tolstoy, which had a disconcerting effect upon her spiritual outlook. Beaten by the old prophet's questions as to her mode of life in the city, and caught by the idea of "bread labour," she resolved to pay toll, on her return to Chicago, by spending two hours every morning in the little bakery of Hull House—with this result:—

> It may be that I had thus to pacify my aroused conscience before I could settle down to hear Wagner's "Ring" at Bayreuth; it may be that I had fallen a victim to the phrase "bread labour"; but at any rate I held fast to the belief that I should do this, throughout the entire journey homeward, on land and sea, until I actually arrived in Chicago, when suddenly the whole scheme seemed to me as utterly preposterous, as it undoubtedly was. The half-dozen people invariably waiting to see me after breakfast, the piles of letters to be opened and answered, the demand of actual and pressing human wants,—were these all to be pushed aside and asked to wait while I saved my soul by two hours' work at baking bread?

It would need many pages of quotation to give any adequate impression of a book which breathes on every page the spirit of the dedicated life. No one who would know the best of the religion of service, which is the highest ethical product of our age, can afford to miss the reading.

John Dewey (essay date 1945)

SOURCE: An introduction to *Peace and Bread in Time of War,* by Jane Addams, King's Crown Press, 1945, pp. i-xx.

[*In the following essay, Dewey comments on the timely reissue of* Peace and Bread *at the end of World War II.*]

The present republication of ***Peace and Bread*** is peculiarly timely. Some of the external reasons for this timeliness are evident without need of prolonged analysis. The book is a record, searching and vivid, of human aspects of the First World War. It gives a picture of the development of American sentiment from 1914 to 1922, the year of its publication. It is a forceful reminder of things that would be unforgettable, did we not live on the surface of the current of the day's events. The book takes us through the period when the war seemed remote and unreal, and the American public reacted with incredulity and exasperation; through the phase of gradual hardening into sullen acceptance of war as a fact; to the time when, after a delay of two and a half years, we responded to the declaration of war with enthusiastic participation in which the earlier all but universal pacifism was treated as cowardly retreat or as actively treasonable; and then through the post-war years of disillusionment and reaction.

These facts the older ones among us have largely forgotten and the younger ones never knew. The picture the book gives would be of great present value if it merely gave the instruction and communicated the warning provided by the traits common to the First World War and to the present war which now afflicts the world on an even greater scale. But the instruction and the warning are increased rather than diminished, when we include in the reckoning certain matters which make the American attitude and response during the present war very different from that of thirty years ago, and that of the eight or ten years immediately following. A brief statement of some of these differences will, I think, disclose the nature of the increased timeliness.

Conditions at home as well as abroad produced a reaction to the outbreak of the European war in 1939 very different from that which greeted the events of 1914. Even only eight years after that date Miss Addams could write, "It is impossible now to reproduce that basic sense of desolation, of suicide, of anachronism, which the first news of war brought to thousands of men and women who had come to consider war as a throwback in the scientific sense." And she could also write, "It is very difficult after five years of war to recall the attitude of most normal people during those first years"—years when the reaction against war "was almost instantaneous throughout the country." What was difficult then is practically impossible now. Instead, we have an accentuation of that later development when, as Miss Addams wrote, "We have perforce become accustomed to a world of widespread war with its inevitable consequences of divisions and animosities."

It is characteristic of the change that, while some thirty years ago the idea of a war to end wars could be taken seriously, we now indulge only in the modest hope of being able to establish a peace that will last a generation or two. Even more significant is the change in the attitude of those who opposed our taking part in the two wars. In the case of the first war, it was the sense of the stupidity and immorality of war *as war* that animated the opposition. In the case of the present war, vocal opposition came most conspicuously from the nationalistic isolationism that wanted to keep *us* out of the devastation of war, while those who favored participation were those who, for the most part, took the ground of moral obligation.

There is, I believe, nothing paradoxical in saying that such differences as these, great as they are, increase, instead of lessen, the instruction and the warning, the timeliness, of the book written almost a quarter of a century ago. The warning is against adoption and use of methods which are so traditional that we are only too likely to adopt them:—methods which are called "terms of peace," but which in fact are but terms of a precarious interim between wars. The instruction concerns the need for adoption of methods which break with political tradition and which courageously adventure in lines that are new in diplomacy and in the political relations of governments, and which are consonant with the vast social changes going on everywhere else.

The term "pacifist" has unfortunately assumed a more restricted meaning during recent years. It used to apply to all persons who hoped and worked for a world free from the curse of war. It has now come to stand almost exclusively for those who are opposed to war under any and all conditions. On the other hand, the significance of the phrase "Peace Movement" has deepened. It used to stand for something which upon the whole was negative, for an attitude that made it easy to identify pacifism with passivism. A large measure of credit for producing this latter change must go to Jane Addams. In her book ***The Newer Ideals of Peace,*** published some years before the outbreak of World War One, she set forth aims and methods that are so intimately connected with ***Peace and Bread*** that the two books form a whole. The aims and methods set forth in both are of a kind that more than justify her in referring to them as "vital and dynamic."

Their nature may be gathered from the vigor with which she repudiated accusations that were freely and ungenerously brought against her and her fellow-workers. Speaking of the state of affairs before the war, she writes, "The world was bent on change, for it knew that the real denial and surrender of life is not physical death but acquiescence in hampered conditions and unsolved problems. . . . We pacifists, so far from passively wishing nothing to be done, contended on the contrary that this world crisis should be utilized for the creation of an international government able to make the necessary political and economic changes which were due; . . . it was unspeakably stupid that the nations should fail to create an international government through which each one, without danger to itself, might recognize and even encourage the impulses toward growth in other nations." And again she writes, "We were constantly accused of wishing to isolate the United States and to keep our country out of world politics. We were of course urging a policy exactly the reverse, that this country should lead the nations of the world into a wider life of coördinated political activity."

Miss Addams repeatedly calls attention to the fact that all social movements *outside* of traditional diplomacy and "international law" were drawing the peoples of different countries together in ever closer bonds, while war, under present conditions, was affecting civilian populations as it had never done before. Both of these factors have immensely increased since she wrote. The futility of dependence upon old methods, which is referred to in the passage just quoted, has correspondingly increased. Many persons, among whom the present writer enrolls himself, who are not pacifists in the absolute sense in which Miss Addams was one, believe that she has clearly indicated the directions which all peace efforts must take if they are not to be doomed in advance to futility.

Miss Addams remarks in the present book that "Social advance depends as much upon the process through which it is secured as upon the result itself." When one considers the intimately human quality of her writings it sounds pedantic to say that this sentence conveys a philosophy, one which underlies what she has to say about war and the conditions of enduring peace. But the human quality of her position and proposals in this case *is* a philosophy that gives the key to understanding her. Her dynamic and vital contribution to the Peace Movement is her insistence upon the necessity of international organization. Today the idea is a commonplace. The Wilsonian League of Nations at least accomplished that much. We are assured from all quarters that the War is being fought in order to achieve an organization of nations that will maintain peace. But when we ask about the *process* that is depended upon, we find the word "organization" covers very different things.

The process that looms largest in current discussions is "political" action, by which we usually mean governmental and legal action, together with coercive economic measures. Miss Addams does employ the *word* "political." But the context invariably shows that she uses it in a wide human sense. And while this usage of hers confers upon the word a moral, and in so far an idealistic, significance, her attitude is in fact much more *realistic* than is the attitude that puts its trust in "organization" of the traditional political type. For one can say, with as much justice as is consonant with brevity, that to trust to traditional political "organization" to create peaceful relations between nations involves reliance upon just that exaggerated nationalistic and power politics that has brought the world to its present pass.

In contrast, the process of organization upon which Miss Addams would have us depend is one which cuts *across* nationalistic lines. Moreover, instead of setting up a super-state, it also cuts *under* those lines. Its nature is indicated in a passage which follows the one already quoted, in which Miss Addams expressed the desire that the United States take the lead in guiding the world "into a wider life of coördinated political activity." What fits the United States, she holds, for assuming this leadership is precisely the fact that democratic development in this country has in fact increasingly cut under and cut across barriers of race and class. In nothing is Miss Addams' book more timely than in its sense of the positive values contributed by our immigrant populations. The pattern of American life, composed of multiple and diversified peoples, hostile in the countries from which they came but living in reasonable amity here, can and should be used to provide the pattern of international organization. One of the ironies of the present situation is that a war caused in large measure by deliberate Nazi provocation of racial and class animosity has had the effect in this country of stimulating the growth of racial fear and dislike, instead of leading to intelligent repudiation of Nazi doctrines of hate. The heart of the democratic movement, as Miss Addams saw and felt it, is "to replace coercion by the full consent of the governed, to educate and strengthen the free will of the people through the use of democratic institutions" in which "the cosmopolitan inhabitants of this great nation might at last become united in a vast common endeavor for social ends." Since the United States had demonstrated on a fairly large scale the practicability of this method, Miss Addams put her faith in extension of the democratic process to the still wider world of peoples. Its exact opposite she found in the use of "opposition to a common enemy, which is an old method of welding peoples together," a method "better fitted to military than to social use, adapted to a government resulting from coercion rather than one founded by free men."

There are today, as I have said, many persons not pacifists in the present technical sense who believe that Miss Addams' book is timely because it points directly to the source of the failure of the hopes so ardently entertained a generation ago. Men then thought they could attain peace through an international organization of the traditional political kind, which relies more upon coercive force than upon constructive meeting of human needs. When I try to formulate what Miss Addams said informally yet clearly, I come out with a sense of the difference between two methods and attitudes. On the one hand, we can trust to an international political organization of an over-all type to create the organs it requires. On the other, we can rely upon organs that have been formed to take care of human needs (including the need for change) to develop in the course of their own use an organization which can be depended upon, because it has become ingrained in practice. If history has proved anything, it is, I believe, that only the latter kind of organization is so "vital and dynamic" as to endure, while the former kind is likely to yield a mechanical structure of forces so uncertainly "balanced" as to be sure to collapse when old stresses and strains recur in new shapes. It has become customary to give the name "realistic" to the kind of organization that is based upon opposition to an enemy and that relies upon armed force to maintain itself. In contrast, the road indicated by Miss Addams is, I submit, infinitely more "realistic."

There are chapters in ***Peace and Bread,*** notably the fourth and the tenth, which supply material that makes concrete and definite the difference between processes or organizations of the traditional political-legal type, with their emphasis upon force—already war *in posse*—and the human and socially humane processes to which Miss Addams appealed for help. The formation of the UNRRA, even while war is still going on, is, as far as it goes, a recognition of the "Food Challenge" for world organization. The energy with which we use and extend this kind of process as the working model for other endeavors at international organization will decide the success or failure of efforts to achieve lasting peace. This is no mere prediction, but is based on the solid experience of the past.

The importance attached by Miss Addams to need for food points to a trait which animates almost every page of ***Peace and Bread,*** for the association of the two words in the title is fundamental. The need for bread is a symbol of the importance attached by Miss Addams to natural impulse and primitive affection. Her faith in them was the source of her interest in "social settlements"; it was nourished by the experiences that centered in Hull House. All who knew Miss Addams also know of her insistence that sharing in the activities which issued from it was not a matter of doing good to others as beneficiaries; those who took part had more to receive than to give. Miss

Addams had a deep feeling that the simple, the "humble" peoples of the earth are those in whom primitive impulses of friendly affection are the least spoiled, the most spontaneous. Her faith in democracy was indissolubly associated with this belief. It permeates what she wrote because it was a part of the life she lived from day to day. Her own life was an active anticipation of what a recent writer has put into words: "Society will develop by living it, not by policing it." Miss Addams did not put her trust in the "Carlyle contention that the peoples must be led into the ways of righteousness by the experience, acumen, and virtues of the great man." Her faith was at the opposite pole. Leaders, whether political or intellectual, were to her trustees for the interests of the common people. Theirs was the duty and the task of giving articulate and effective form to the common impulses she summed up in the word "Fellowship." Were Jane Addams with us today her voice and pen would tell us how the events of the years which have intervened between two World Wars have intensified the evils which will surely follow if leaders betray the trust committed to them—events which have deepened the need for those humane processes and organs which alone can bring hope of enduring peace to a tragically torn and bleeding world.

Merle Curti (essay date 1960)

SOURCE: "Jane Addams on Human Nature," in *Ideas in Cultural Perspective,* edited by Philip P. Wiener and Aaron Noland, Rutgers University Press, 1962, pp. 468-81.

[*In the following essay, which was originally presented as the first William I. Hull Lecture at Swarthmore College on 16 October 1960, Curti discusses Addams's views on the self and the place of the individual in society.*]

It is somewhat curious that in tributes to Jane Addams (1860-1935) occasioned by her centennial year, no serious consideration has been given to her place in American intellectual history. One finds merited praise of her personality and of her contributions to the woman's movement, to social welfare, and to international peace. Her understanding and appreciation of the immigrants in our midst and what she did to help them become Americans without losing a feeling for their Old World heritage have been rightly recalled. But the ideas she held, their relation to her time and her life, have not apparently seemed worthy of analysis and evaluation.

Three main considerations go a long way toward explaining this. Jane Addams did not in any of her writings systematically set forth her social ideas in a way to please the scholars nowadays who set great store on what is called intellectual sophistication. Her ideas, in her books and essays, are subordinated to the larger social and human purposes and activities to which her life was dedicated. The pages abound with straightforward, unpretentious but often moving and penetrating reports of interviews with well known public figures and of participation in meetings of social workers and advocates of peace. Her writings are chiefly concerned with her everyday experiences over forty odd years at Hull House.

A second reason for the neglect of Jane Addams' thought may be that in her own day a public image was developed in some quarters which did her scant justice. She was widely appreciated, but certain critics, influenced by the stereotype of the sentimental do-gooder which was common among intellectuals, were close to condescension in their judgments of her. Agnes Repplier, for example, wrote of her "ruthless sentimentality." Theodore Roosevelt once dubbed her "poor bleeding Jane" and "a progressive mouse." Such judgments no doubt have lingered and confirmed many in accepting a stereotype—a Jane Addams whose easy optimism blinded her to the depth of the "tragic view of life" so popular now in many intellectual circles.

The neglect of her ideas may also be related to a present discouragement over the uses women have made of the vote, to which she attached so much importance, and, even more likely, to the contemporary strength of nationalism and of the forces in the world that make the abolition of war seem at best remote.

It is not my purpose to try to elevate Jane Addams into a major figure in our intellectual life. But on re-reading her ten books[1] it seems clear that if justice has been done her heart and her social vision, it has not been done her mind. Her ideas illuminate in sensitive and often keen ways major movements of thought in her time. Nor can the significance of her life be understood unless thoughtful attention is given to the rôle that ideas played in that life. Further, at its best, the writing in which her ideas are expressed rises to a level of literary distinction.

The thought of Jane Addams might be considered in any of a number of ways. I have chosen to use a central theme as a key to her ideas and feelings—her conception of human nature. The term itself occurs frequently in her writings. It was not common in her time to give the term an explicit, formal definition, and she herself did not do so. But it is clear that she did not limit it to the native equipment of men. For her, human nature encompassed the experiences and potentialities of the growing organism, in infancy, childhood, adolescence, and old age. She appreciated the dynamic factors in motivation and saw in the universal desire of individuals to be recognized and appreciated as unique persons, and the consequence of society's failure to make such recognition, the key to much behavior. She recognized the nature and rôle of sex in the life of the individual, but she also saw its relation to civilization. In her view of human nature, play and recreation are basic needs which brook denial only at heavy cost. Fighting is of course a part of human nature, but so is cooperation. Above all, her image of man emphasized the idea that the differences separating social classes and distinguishing immigrants and Negroes from old stock Americans, are far less important than the capacities, impulses, and motives they share in common.

In ***Twenty Years at Hull House*** the author noted that in 1889, when she went to live on Halstead Street, she was without any preconceived social theories and economic views. These, she added, were developed out of her experiences in Chicago. True, but the foundations for these theories and views rested on already formulated conceptions of human nature which, as she herself recognized, began to take shape in early childhood. Such recognition was natural enough, for by 1910, when the book was published, social workers as well as parents and educators were familiar with the great importance G. Stanley Hall had long been attaching to childhood experiences. And so it was natural for Miss Addams to begin her autobiography by referring to the theory that "our genuine impulses may be connected with our childish experiences, that one's bent may be traced back to that 'No man's land' where character is formless but nevertheless settling into definite lines of future development."

These reminiscences reveal some of the basic conceptions of human nature later to be more or less explicitly formulated in writing and richly implemented in living. One finds repeated reference, for example, to the presumably innate tendency of children to seek in ceremonial expression a sense of identification with man's primitive life and kinship with the past, perhaps a compensation for the child's slowness to understand the real world about him, and certainly an instrument toward that end. This conviction, made intellectually respectable by early XIXth-century German philosophers and in Jane Addams' young womanhood by G. Stanley Hall (the recapitulation theory), was to figure in the importance she attached to the esthetic impulse and to children's play. The theory that in play children satisfy an innate need to live over the experience of the race seemed to her both reasonable and realistic. Adolescent behavior, which some thought stemmed from original sin, she looked upon as a natural expression of an instinct too old and too powerful to be easily recognized and wisely controlled. She noted also that children love to carry on, either actually or in play, activities proper to older people. This trait she thought of as also grounded in the need to repeat racial experience, and as expressing itself regardless of precept or inculcation. "The old man," as she put it, "clogs our earliest years."

Another early formed foundation stone for her image of man was the conviction that the basis of childhood's timidity, never altogether outworn, stems from "a sense of being unsheltered in a wide world of relentless and elemental forces." It is at least in part because of this fear and loneliness, she thought, that the child, and the adult which he becomes, needs affection and companionship. Jane Addams realized, of course, long before she wrote the autobiography, that in her own case this feeling of being unsheltered was accentuated by the fact that she had been deprived of her mother by death in her third year and by the further fact that a physical deformity both isolated her and gave her a sense of inadequacy and inferiority. But she was sure that all children share in greater or less degree this sense of fear and loneliness and that its major antidote is understanding and love. Also in her case the sense of timidity and loneliness was compensated for by the close and affectionate father-daughter relationship. The father's way of assuring her of his acceptance of her cemented the bond more tightly. It is hard, she reflected, to account fully for a child's adoring affection for a parent, "so emotional, so irrational, so tangled with the affairs of the imagination."

It came to be clear to Jane Addams, as it is so patently clear to us, that her father greatly influenced her ideas about the nature of mankind. A substantial miller imbued with the democracy of the Illinois frontier and of his hero Mazzini, John Addams' views of human nature reflected his abolitionism, his great admiration of Lincoln, and his commitment to Hicksite Quakerism. His complete lack of racial prejudice and his firm conviction that the similarities of men far outweigh the differences, were an indelible influence in the forming of the daughter's view of human nature. So too was his belief in the essential equality of men and women. These beliefs were reinforced by his Quaker heritage and the essentially classless society of this Illinois farm community. When his young daughter was troubled about the doctrine of foreordination, and asked her father to explain it to her, he replied that probably neither she nor he had the kind of minds capable of understanding the doctrine. In other words, as Jane Addams later recalled the conversation, some minds are capable and fond of dealing with abstractions while others are at home with concrete facts and immediate problems: this simple typology explained much that she later observed at Hull House in heated discussions over socialism and anarchism. Her father continued by adding that it made little difference whether one was the sort to understand such doctrines as predestination as long as he did not pretend to understand what he didn't. "You must always be honest with yourself inside, no matter what happens." This idea, so basic in Quaker tradition, stuck with the girl. The discussion ended with the suggestion that there may be areas of unfathomed complexity, incapable at least at the present stage of man's rational development, of being fully comprehended. In Jane Addams' view of human nature there was a large place for the contemplation of life's mysteries.

The instruction and associations of Rockford Seminary did not greatly alter these foundations for a conception of human nature. Jane Addams, like her fellow-students, read textbooks on mental philosophy, but the static and sterile approach in most treatises of this kind at best stimulated discussions outside class on such questions as the freedom of the will. The reading of Emerson strengthened her sense that human nature includes both rational and intuitive capacities. But as she was introduced to new ranges of feminism, she felt dissatisfied with the old belief in the ascendancy of intuition in the feminine mind. Under the influence of the positivism which she discovered, she concluded that women ought to study intensively at least one branch of natural science to make the faculties clear and more acute. Following graduation from Rockford, she tried studying medicine in Philadelphia but found she had little taste or aptitude for the sciences and dropped the course.

During the Rockford years and the brief Philadelphia experiment, Miss Addams' awareness of death and sorrow took on, especially through her study of Plato, a universal dimension: human existence had always been an unceasing flow and ebb of justice and oppression, of life and death. She heard about Darwinism and accepted it. The acceptance and interpretations she gave to evolution became a frcsh and vastly important component in her image of man.

Like so many young women college graduates of the time, Jane Addams went to Europe in search of further culture. The four years she spent abroad were shadowed by long and painful illnesses and a depressing sense of failure. Thus her years of further education were not altogether roseate. But she continued to learn. Experiences in the great art galleries and study of man's early artistic expressions in the pyramids and in the catacombs sharpened her vague feeling that the esthetic component is basic in man's nature. But this was not all, for she interested herself further in the positivism which she had discovered in her reading at Rockford.

When she saw that for all their enthusiasm about human brotherhood, the positivists did little or nothing to implement the idea, she sought light elsewhere. This she found in her growing awareness of the human wretchedness in the great urban slums and in the programs of the British social settlement pioneers. Increasingly she felt that many college women in their zest for learning and in their search for individual culture departed too suddenly from the active, emotional life led by their grandmothers and great grandmothers. The rewards of the search for individual knowledge and culture paled as she became more deeply convinced of the far greater importance of learning from life itself. Education and artistic effort, she decided, were futile when considered apart from the ultimate test of the conduct it inspired, when there was no relationship between these and the human need of the poor and the suffering. Thus without benefit of William James and John Dewey, who only later reenforced her views of human nature, she became, as her friend Dr. Alice Hamilton said, something of a pragmatist, determined to test ideas and values about life in the actual laboratory of life. But the pragmatism that later provided support for an enlarged view of human nature did not lead to a rejection of presuppositions more or less unconsciously acquired and interwoven with Christian humanism and Christian mystery.

Closely related to pragmatism and more important in her own intellectual growth had been the doctrine of evolution. No one of the other late XIXth- and early XXth-century movements of thought—the so-called new psychology of the experimental laboratory, or Freudianism, or Marxism—to all of which she responded, exerted so far-reaching an influence on Jane Addams' view of the nature of man as did the teachings of Darwin and his disciple Kropotkin, who spent some time at Hull House in 1901.

For Jane Addams, the evolutionary view of human nature postulated certain primordial types of behavior and potential types of behavior. On many occasions she referred to these, in the fashion of those days, as instincts. Man shared some of these with other animals. But in the process of evolution, of survival through adaptation, he came to have impulses that set him apart from other animals in somewhat the way that the human hand enabled him to claw his way to a civilization denied his less well equipped fellow creatures.

Her view of the inherited basic equipment of man emphasized the special importance of the extremely early appearance in man's long struggle upwards, of the tribal feeding of the young. This human instinct sprang out of or was at least closely related to man's innate gregariousness and to the ability first of mothers and then of males to see in the hunger of any young symbolical relationship to the hunger of their own offspring. Our very organism, Jane Addams wrote, holds memories and glimpses of "that long life of our ancestors which still goes on among so many of our contemporaries. Nothing," she continued, "so deadens the sympathies and shrivels the power of enjoyment, as the persistent keeping away from the great opportunities for helpfulness, as a continual ignoring of the starvation struggle which makes up the life of at least half the race. To shut oneself away from the race life is to shut one's self away from the most vital part of it; it is to live out but half the humanity to which we have been born and to use but half our faculties." This desire for action to fulfil social obligation was so deep-seated a heritage that to deny its expression, she thought, was more fatal to well-being than anything save disease, indigence, and a sense of guilt.

Here we have the corner stone of all that Jane Addams did in sharing her life with less fortunate neighbors, in encouraging measures designed to prevent the young and the old from being exploited, and in mobilizing in wartime food for helpless hungry mouths wherever they might be. For marvelous though human nature was in its adaptability, it had never "quite fitted its back to the moral strain involved in the knowledge that fellow creatures are starving."

The reading of Kropotkin and others led to the belief that this human instinct or trait appeared perhaps a million years or more before man developed a proclivity to kill masses of his own kind. This method of settling differences, many anthropologists held, had become common among human beings a mere twenty thousand years ago. It was used by only one other species, ants, which like human beings, were property holders. Thus Jane Addams might respectably hold, and she did, that the earlier instinct, with its implications of human solidarity, could under proper conditions exert an even stronger pull over behavior than competing forces, less deeply seated. In other words, man's primordial concern for group feeding of the young and the sense of responsibility for helping those in need which was related to it, might check and control the more recently acquired habit of mass killing of one's own kind. In the growth of international institutions and the evidences that love of man was crossing provincial and national boundaries, she saw hope for an emerging pacifism that in time would make war as obsolete as slavery had become. In sum, her reading convinced her that war, like slavery, was a relatively recent man-made institution. The argument that pacifism could never triumph because of man's inborn and unchangeable pugnacity, was no more valid, she thought, than the pre-Civil War argument of Southerners that slavery could never be abolished because it is ingrained in human nature itself.

In an address at the Boston Peace Congress of 1904, Miss Addams began to spell out the implications of this position, a position more positive in character than the non-resistance ideas of her hero, Tolstoy. In that address she anticipated William James' "Moral Equivalents of War" in suggesting that the subhuman and dark forces which so easily destroy the life of mankind might be diverted into organized attacks on social maladjustments, on poverty, disease, and misfortune, on one hand, and into the closely related "nurture of human life" on the other. It might in particular be diverted from destructive outburst into war by taking heed from the successful example of the immigrants of diverse and even hostile traditions who had learned to live as friends in America's cities. This view was developed in her book ***Newer Ideals of Peace,*** published in 1907. In the poorer quarters of our cosmopolitan cities she found multitudes of immigrants surrendering habits of hate and of aggression cherished for centuries, and customs that could be traced to habits of primitive man. She not only saw that they surrendered these habits, she also witnessed innumerable and sustained examples of the pity and kindness based on an equally ancient, or even more ancient, instinct: the instinct of pity and kindness toward those in the group whose need was even greater than that of the others. "In seeking companionship in the new world the immigrants are reduced to the fundamental equalities and universal necessities of life itself. They develop power of association which comes from daily contact with those who are unlike each other in all save the universal characteristics of man." To put it in other words, the pressures of a cosmopolitan neighborhood seemed to be the simple and inevitable foundations for an international order in somewhat the same way that the foundations of tribal and national morality had already been laid.

This hope suffered a blow during the first world war when an emotional crisis showed that many immigrants had not in living together actually shed the heritage of Old World hatreds. But the outbreak of the war brought to the fore another belief also rooted in her conception of human nature. Jane Addams found a great many soldiers in hospitals in the several belligerent countries who expressed the wish that women everywhere would use their influence to end the struggle. She knew, of course, that women as well as men in all the fighting countries were supporting the war. Yet she reflected that, just as an artist in an artillery corps commanded to fire on a beautiful cathedral would be "deterred by a compunction unknown to the man who had never given himself to creating beauty and did not know the intimate cost of it, so women, who have brought men into the world and nurtured them until they reach the age of fighting, must experience a peculiar revulsion when they see them destroyed, irrespective of the country in which these may have been born."

Such intimations received confirmation at the meeting of women from several countries at The Hague in 1915. Here it was said again and again that appeals against war and for a peaceful organization of the world had been made too largely a matter of reason and a sense of justice. If reason is only part of the human endowment, then emotion and the deepest racial impulses must be recognized, modified, utilized. These deep racial impulses admittedly include the hatred of the man who differs from the crowd: but this would be softened by understanding and education. Also involved are those primitive human urgings to foster life and to protect the helpless of which women were the earliest custodians. Involved too are the gregarious instincts shared with the animals themselves—instincts which women as noncombatants might now best keep alive. Such were some of the supports in her concept of human nature on which Jane Addams now leaned.

When her own country entered the war in 1917 she kept faith with the instrumentalist conviction that the processes or methods by which goals are approached or achieved, are more important than acceptance of so-called practical means that are in fact incompatible with the ends. She had always felt that temperament and habit—also important ingredients in human nature—kept her in the middle of the road. Now circumstances drove her to the extreme left of what had been the peace movement. She faced the opprobrium of society and the loneliness of standing out against mass judgment, wondering at times if such deviation as hers might not be only arrogance. But she fell back on the lesson her Quaker father had taught her: that what was most important was always to be honest with oneself inside, no matter what happened, that the ability to hold out against friends and society in a time of crisis depends "upon the categorical belief that a man's primary allegiance is to his own vision of the truth and that he is under an obligation to affirm it."

She also found comfort in reminding herself of the universality of sorrow and death and in pondering—she knew it was at the risk of rationalization—on what seemed to be one of the lessons of the evolutionary view of human nature. If the deviant pacifist invited the deeply rooted biological hatred meted out to one who by non-conforming threatened the security of the group, there was after all another side of the evolutionary coin. All forms of growth begin with a variation from the mass. Might not the individual or group that differed from the mass be initiating moral changes and growth in human behavior and affairs? Might not he who was damned as a crank or pitied as a freak in times of stern crisis actually be leading in the growth of a new moral sense for his society? In view of the complexity and mystery of life's purposes, who could say? And finally, the difficulties of being a pacifist in war time were made a bit more bearable by keeping in mind what seemed another lesson from evolution: that the virtues of patriotism and the martial traits remained only as vestiges after they had actually become a deterrent to future social progress.

In other ways, too, the evolutionary view deeply influenced without moulding Jane Addams' ideas about human nature. This view also influenced, in an unknown measure, her own conduct. During the first years on Halstead Street nothing was more pitifully clear to her than "the fact that pliable human nature is relentlessly pressed upon by its physical environment." The Socialists, more than any other group, seemed to realize this, and seemed also to be making an earnest effort to relieve that heavy pressure. She would have been glad to have the comradeship of that "gallant company" had the Socialists not so firmly insisted that fellowship depended on identity of creed. In making this comment she was for the moment probably overlooking a Socialist emphasis on class conflict: for though she recognized the existence of such a conflict, she was not convinced that it was inevitable.

And so, unable to find comfort in a definite ideology which "explained" social chaos and pointed to logical bettering of physical conditions, Jane Addams went at the matter differently. Without bitterness or self-righteousness she tried to help labor and management learn the lesson of cooperation. She tried to educate public opinion and legislators to an appreciation of the fact that there is a definite relation between physical conditions and human behavior: that long and exhausting hours of labor at deadening tasks are likely to be followed by a quest for lurid and exciting pleasures. Moreover, the power to overcome such temptation reaches its limit almost automatically with that of physical resistance. "The struggle for existence," she wrote in ***Democracy and Social Ethics*** (1902), "which is so much harsher among people near the edge of pauperism, sometimes leaves ugly marks on character." Society had begun to apply this evolutionary principle to the bringing up of children. It had finally come to expect certain traits and behavior under certain conditions, to adapt methods and matter to the child's growing and changing needs. But society was slow to apply this principle to human affairs in general. In our attitudes toward the poor, the alcoholic, the prostitute, the outcast, she wrote, we think much more of what a man or woman ought to be than of what he is or what he might become under different and better conditions.

Here is an important factor in Jane Addams' approach to social work. She sensed the limitations in what the scientific charity groups and case workers had come to look on as the only true kind of helpfulness but what all too often seemed to those to be aided, ruthless imposition of conventions and standards that were incomprehensible. Pity might seem capricious and harmful to the new type of social case worker, but she should not forget that a theory of social conduct is a poor substitute for tenderness of heart which need not be blind to the complexity of the situation.

The deeply human interest in and appreciation of all sorts of people, including those in trouble, led Jane Addams to an early appreciation of the rôle of sex in deviant behavior and tragedy. It is noteworthy that a girl reared in the Victorian period was able to speak as frankly as she did and to recognize sex as "the most basic and primordial instinct of human beings." It is remarkable that she so early saw in the sex instinct a source of creativity in the arts and that she recognized its close association with play, which she also thought to be an inherent need in humankind. Basic and all important as the sex instinct was, it had always, from the beginnings of the race itself, been in some way controlled in the expression it took. But, in her view, our modern industrial city as it was in the 1890's not only failed to provide sensible, humane, and necessary forms of regulation of the instinct but invited its commercial degradation and exploitation and encouraged its expression in delinquent behavior and in enduring human tragedy.

More specifically, the American city with its anonymity, its uprooted families, its ill-adjusted immigrants, its commercial exploitation of the labor of girls and boys and young men and women in grim shops and factories in an almost never-ending workday, provided no opportunities for the development of comradeship and recreation save in gaudy and sensation-evoking saloons, dance halls and similar money-making establishments. Loneliness was the fate of innumerable girls who struggled against poverty and who had no decent opportunities for making friendships. "It is strange," wrote Miss Addams in 1911, "that we are so slow to learn that no one can safely live without companionship and affection, that the individual who tries the hazardous experiment of going without at least one of them is prone to be swamped by a black mood from within. It is as if we had to build little islands of affection in the vast sea of impersonal forces lest we be overwhelmed by them." Boys, to be sure, found companionship in gangs. But deprived of opportunities for natural expression of adolescent revolt in healthy recreation, the gang was at best an antisocial institution leading naturally to delinquency and a life of defeat, alcoholism, violence, and crime.

One might suppose in view of the innumerable examples of the rôle of sex in leading to ruthless exploitation one the one hand and to grim tragedy on the other, that Jane Addams would have accepted the Calvinist theory, with which she was familiar, of the innate depravity of mankind. On the contrary, with her faith in the pliability of human nature she held that just as our society brings out unfortunate behavior, so it is also capable of evoking wholesome relationships, social idealism, and artistic creativity if society assumes responsibility in a great area of human drive and experience, sex, which it had ignored, or condemned, or permitted to be degraded. She quoted General Bingham, Police Commissioner of New York, to the effect that there is "not enough depravity in human nature" to keep alive the very large business of commercial prostitution. "The immorality of women and the brutishness of men have to be persuaded, coaxed, and constantly stimulated in order to keep the social evil in its present state of business prosperity."

Jane Addams, like other Americans imbued with the teachings of pragmatism, did not draw any separating line between theory and practice. If, as she insisted, the regulation of this great primitive instinct had a long history and if that regulation had evolved with civilization, indeed, with the race itself, it was important to recognize the fact that its regulation now needed to be better adapted to the conditions of urban and industrial life.

Understanding the nature of sex was the first step in developing a better regulation of it. The cooperation of parents and schools might do much to bring about a more healthy understanding of and attitude toward sex. Sane education could be furthered not only through classes in biology and hygiene. It could also be encouraged through the study of literature and history which provide rich examples of the ill-effects of mere suppression or mere indulgence, and which also give abundant illustration of the ennobling expression of sex in altruism. Also important in her view was the expression of the creative aspects of the sex instinct in music and art—which the ancient Greeks had so well understood. "In failing to diffuse and utilize this fundamental instinct of sex through the imagination," she wrote, "we not only inadvertently foster vice and enervation, but we throw away one of the most precious implements for ministering to life's highest need." It is, to be sure, no easy thing to substitute the love of beauty for mere desire, to place the mind above the senses. But "the whole history of civilization," as she kept reminding her generation, "has been one long effort to substitute psychic impulsion for the driving force of blind appetite." Jane Addams took pains again and again to make clear that this was quite different from the mere parental and social imposition of repression.

Understanding the nature and potential relationships between sex, altruism, and esthetic creativity was, however, not enough. What was also needed was community provision for the expression of the sex impulse in wholesome companionship, in social idealism put into practice, and in the provision by society of adequate means for the expression and development of the play instinct. For this too was so basic and inherent a constituent of human nature that it could neither be safely repressed nor, in modern urban life, left to chance. The thwarting of all these basic instincts, the failure of contemporary society to provide proper channels for their expression, explained, Jane Addams insisted, much of the tragedy that stemmed from leaving the sex instinct isolated from intelligent direction and manifestation. It is worth noting in passing that she came to these views without benefit of Freud, at least as far as we know. When, in the 1920's, she first spoke of him in her writings, it was less to find support for her thesis than to regret the popular interpretation which focused attention on the driving need for direct and overt sex expression.

But understanding and sublimation of the sex instinct are not in her view enough. Society, she insisted, must put an end to certain conditions that tempted boys and girls into degrading expressions of the sex impulse. It can not do this merely by sanctioning benevolent welfare capitalism, such as that exemplified in the paternalism at Pullman. For like a modern King Lear, George Pullman could not understand that his regimentation of the workers presumably in their own interest led to "a revolt of human nature" against the denial of their own participation in what affected every detail of their lives. State intervention against long hours, poor pay, and the grueling monotony of tending machines in factory and sweatshop was a more positive need. The trade unions were working in this direction and early found in Jane Addams a strong supporter. But the community, she said, must also provide an environment in which, after an exhausting workday, youth and older workers might find the right sort of companionship and release from nervous tensions. Only by this means and through adequate pay would the toilers be freed from the temptation and necessity of finding pleasure in saloons and dubious dance halls.

Society can, in short, Miss Addams believed, reestablish under modern conditions the ancient tie between the sex impulse and artistic creativity and wholesome relaxation from the nervous tension of modern industrial labor. And it can also provide the means by which the social idealism of adolescence can find constructive outlet in helping others. Hull House pioneered in all this; but Jane Addams was sufficiently realistic to appreciate the need of a broader institutionally and socially supported program, and to work toward that end. In brief, people need not be allowed to fall into esthetic and social insensibility and into an indulgence of basic instincts that is unsatisfying, wasteful, and often tragic.

How much of the analysis of human nature which Jane Addams so unpretentiously made seems valid in the light of experience and present-day knowledge? One must report that some of her concepts are no longer entertained by competent psychologists. The theory that children in their growth recapitulate racial experiences, for example, now has few adherents. Nor would psychologists describe as instincts some of the motives and behavior she regarded as inborn and unlearned. But in her day psychologists did accept the instinct theory, and in following them she was *au courant.* She was on more solid ground in early emphasizing the importance of childhood experiences and of sex well before even psychologists had generally recognized it. It is true that she was too optimistic in thinking that degrading forms of expression of the sex impulse would disappear if bitter poverty were eliminated and adequate recreation made available. Our society has gone far toward achieving these ends, yet the degrading forms of expression seem to be as much of a problem as ever. But it is hard to measure the effects of changing conditions, and a great deal can of course be said for her conviction that the sex impulse can be modified and channeled into varied and often elevating expressions.

Miss Addams was also a pioneer in America in appreciating and using constructively the now well established fact that the great modes of adjustment in life, whether considered individually or socially, develop through influences of which each participant is often unconscious as he struggles to adapt himself to continuing and changing conditions. And though motivation research, unknown in her day, has made substantial progress, her discussion of motivation was unusually perceptive and is still largely acceptable. Her explanation of the deviant behavior of youth as a blundering effort to find adventure and self-expression in a society which provides few opportunities for either, is still central in the most informed approaches to the problems of delinquency. A case can also be made for her thesis that the talents and experiences of women in bearing children, in nurturing life, and in housekeeping and homemaking have been important factors in what they have done with the vote and through organization in helping to raise standards of community welfare.

It is perhaps in Miss Addams' discussion of the relation of war to human nature that the limitations of her analysis and her program are most apparent. One need not minimize the contributions of women in the continuing struggle against war. But her ideas about the potential rôle of women in this struggle, which she associated with a strongly ingrained compassion and reverence for life, would probably seem to her, were she alive today, to have been overstressed. The fact that immigrants in the United States seem quickly to forget ancient hatreds and learn to live together in peace, has been cited by various writers here and abroad. But Miss Addams' expectation that this demonstration would have an effect on international cooperation does not appear to have been realized. It also seems clear that she overstressed as a factor for peace what she regarded as the primordial appearance in the race of group responsibility for feeding infants and children regardless of parentage. The fact that loyalty to the nation and mass killing appeared historically late has not thus far rendered these patterns of behavior subordinate to the compassionate traits in human nature which she thought to be much older and therefore stronger in pull.

On the other hand, social scientists generally endorse Miss Addams's early arrived at insistence that the things that make men alike are more important than the things that differentiate them. If this is the case, then it may be that in our trials and errors and in our efforts to adjust our behavior to the world community we now recognize as a fact, we have not yet found adequate means for institutionalizing the implications of the fact that men share common characteristics regardless of culture. Also relevant to the discussion is the general agreement of psychologists and other social scientists that man's action or behavior is largely explained in terms of his social relationships.

Perhaps we have not yet sufficiently tested Jane Addams' conviction that there will be no peace until the world community is no longer divided into the repressed, dimly conscious that they have no adequate outlet for normal life, and the repressing, the self-righteous and the cautious who hold fast to their own. Perhaps we have not yet tested sufficiently her overarching conviction that if life is often mean, unprofitable and tragic, if it is at other times feeble and broken, it is because we have not yet learned the lesson, and acted on it, that these evidences of what some call the tragic flaw in human nature, result not from man's essential and unchangeable limitations, but rather follow from our failure to understand ourselves and others.

NOTES

[1] All of Jane Addams' books were published by the Macmillan Company: *Democracy and Social Ethics* (1902), *Newer Ideals of Peace* (1907), *The Spirit of Youth and the City Streets* (1909), *Twenty Years at Hull House* (1910), *A New Conscience and an Ancient Evil* (1912), *The Long Road of Woman's Memory* (1916), *Peace and Bread in Time of War* (1922), *The Second Twenty Years at Hull House* (1930), *The Excellent Becomes the Permanent* (1932), and *My Friend Julia Lathrop* (1935); *Jane Addams, A Centennial Reader,* edited by Emily Cooper Johnson, 1960. The Jane Addams papers are in the Swarthmore College Peace Collection.

Sondra R. Herman (essay date 1969)

SOURCE: "Jane Addams: The Community as a Neighborhood," in *Eleven Against War: Studies in American Internationalist Thought, 1898-1921,* Stanford University, 1969, pp. 114-49.

[*In the following excerpt, Herman explores the path by which Addams moved from philanthropic works to pacifism.*]

> Cease to be the shadow of man and of his passion of pride and destruction. Have a clear vision of the duty of pity! Be a living peace in the midst of war—the eternal Antigone refusing to give herself up to hatred and knowing no distinction between her suffering brothers who make war on each other.
>
> —Romain Rolland, quoted by Jane Addams, ***The Long Road of Woman's Memory,*** 1916

The pragmatism that Royce regarded as only a partial account of truth because it ignored the community of truth-seekers, had its own communal ethic. Grounded in evolutionary science, rather than in metaphysical logic, this pragmatism produced plans for social reconstruction and experiments in community living. John Dewey's attempt to make the school a miniature community—peaceful as well as active—was one such expression of this philosophy. Like Royce, Dewey was indebted to Hegel for the distinction between community and civil society. He too retained a certain nostalgia for small rural communities in the midst of his urban living. But while Royce's method was to elucidate the logical structure of the community of interpretation, and then to seek a practical application of it, Dewey encouraged intelligent scientific planning to further social welfare. Jane Addams and other settlement-house pioneers owed more to the insights of John Dewey[1] than to the idealism of Josiah Royce. Dewey himself learned much from the settlement-house communities.

Absolute idealism was not then a necessary component of international communalism. It was not even essential for a religious view of the international community. Positivists, for example, rejected supernaturalism and made of humanity itself an object of worship. The ministers of the social gospel made human solidarity, cooperation, and brotherhood conditions for individual salvation. One could save one's soul only by redeeming the society. Even revolutionary nationalism could infuse political movements with mystical hopes for an international brotherhood. Mazzinian nationalism, paradoxically, was internationalist in just this way. In general, however, it was difficult to combine religious fervor with a pragmatic temperament. As Royce suspected, the two did not go well together. William James's appreciation of the "varieties of religious experience" was pragmatic, indeed, but not in itself religious. Still, this peculiar combination of an almost mystical reverence for humanity and a very pragmatic approach to social problems, leading to radical criticism of the *status quo,* was possible.

Jane Addams made this combination her own. As a pacifist she criticized the passive "dove-like" ideal of the peace movement. As a pragmatist she relied upon experience more heavily than upon theory. And then she would theorize. She had an almost mystical faith in the people, but never hesitated to point to their corrupt and often selfish behavior. She was an ardent feminist with Victorian standards of femininity, sentimental in the extreme, and yet an effective executive. Her contemporaries and more recent historians, as Christopher Lasch has pointed out, have been prone to sanctify her. "Praising her goodness, her saintliness, was a way to avoid answering her questions."[2]

The questions, however, had a disturbing way of reemerging: Was industrial materialism crushing the spontaneous joy of youth? Could any group loyalty, even loyalty to the workers of the world, foster human unity? Could a war that intensified nationalistic hatreds "make the world safe for democracy"? Her questions turned most of all to her own beliefs, for she was never certain she was right. Thus when her friends deserted her in 1917, she asked whether her pacifism had degenerated into a dogma. It was not the loneliness, nor even her own mistakes, she feared, but the tendency toward self-righteousness in anyone who held himself apart from a mass emotion. Too much was at stake, however, for her to give up pacifism even for the sake of "mixing on the thronged and common road."[3] She would have had to sacrifice her faith that individual loyalty to one's "vision of the truth" was the beginning of social change; she would have had to deny her perception that a pervasive desire for peace and unity underlay even the hatreds of war. Above all, she was convinced that one could only teach by the deed.

For Jane Addams, loyalty to one's own vision was an overly individualistic, doctrinaire belief. Her pacifism did not stem primarily from doctrine. It was, in fact, fused with a belief in international community, and this came as much from experience as from theory. She identified herself with the interests and hopes of the immigrant community. This was truly a radical identification for so middle-class a lady although not really unusual among American intellectuals of the time.[4] Her experience on Chicago's West Side revealed that the crippling environment that drove apart immigrant and old American, young idealist and parent, rich and poor, also forced cooperation among the poor themselves. She appreciated that the immigrants were, in Oscar Handlin's words, "the uprooted," divorced from the familiar rural-village environment and longing for community. While Handlin has shown that the immigrant associations were community-creating instruments for the Germans, the Russians, and the Italians, separately, Jane Addams saw the birth of an international community in the tendency of the Polish neighbor to help the Austrian one, the Italian worker to join a union with the Jewish worker. The immigrant community was international not because many nationalities lived side by side, but because they were helping each other and "fusing."[5] Undoubtedly, observers with a lesser faith in natural gregariousness would have been more keenly aware of intergroup tensions; nor did Jane Addams completely ignore them. Like Prince Kropotkin, however, she argued that man would have to rely for his very existence upon mutual aid rather than upon competition. Like Tolstoy she saw salvation in the masses and the humble.

Tolstoyan Christianity and the settlement-house experience worked together in the creation of her pacifism, with the settlement and practical needs always taking the upper hand. She had very early been attracted to Tolstoyan beliefs, not particularly because they were pacifist, but because the great teacher of nonresistance embodied ethics in action. In 1896 she had gone to Yasnaya Polyana to visit the master, and had returned more a critic than a disciple, but with uneasy feelings of guilt. Tolstoy had examined the luxuriant sleeves on her dress and had commented upon the uses the peasant women would have applied to so much material. Learning that she derived part of her income from a farm in Illinois, he noted that she was an absentee landlord. Jane Addams was to observe many years later that she was disappointed in Tolstoy's position on nonresistance. "It seemed to me that he made too great a distinction between the use of physical force and that of moral energy which can override another's differences and scruples with equal ruthlessness."[6] But she did not mean to imply that Tolstoy had been wrong about her privileges in contrast with those around her. Upon returning from Yasnaya Polyana she determined to work in the Hull House bakery every day for two hours. Her father, a miller, had taught her to bake bread; and, as we shall see, the bread itself had as great a significance for her as for the advocates of "bread labor." But as always, realism prevailed over doctrine.

> I held fast to the belief that I should do this, through the entire journey homeward . . . until I actually arrived in Chicago when suddenly the whole scheme seemed to me as utterly preposterous as it doubtless was. The half dozen people invariably waiting to see me after breakfast, the piles of letters to be opened and answered, the demand of actual and pressing human wants—were these all to be pushed aside and asked to wait while I saved my soul by two hours' work at baking bread?[7]

Here was a very early instance, but a crucial one, in her attempts to test theory by practice. Her experience with Tolstoy put an end once and for all to the irrelevant preaching of perfectionist dogmas. Yet she gained more than she lost through this experience, for she soon would apply to social problems what John Dewey called the "creative imagination," dealing with the materials at hand for the sake of what could be. William James caught the spirit of her work in a review of her ***The Spirit of Youth and the City Streets*** (1909). "She simply inhabits reality and everything she says necessarily expresses its nature."[8]

COMMUNITIES IN CEDARVILLE AND CHICAGO

Neither Jane Addams' pacifism nor her awareness of poverty stemmed from childhood experiences. She had grown up in the prosperous farming community of Cedarville, Illinois, under the guidance of her well-to-do father, a miller and grain merchant. Following her sisters to Rockford Seminary for girls, she had become a genteel, cultured young lady. Her determination to live among the poor in some great cosmopolitan city had come only in her late twenties, when she was seeking a fulfillment of the new woman's role in public affairs. If she had not struggled so painfully to discover herself, it is unlikely that she would have discovered "the depressed tenth." Her motives, as she herself implied, were subjective rather than charitable.[9]

Undoubtedly her father, whom she worshipped with a "doglike affection," was the strongest influence in her early years. Her mother had died in 1863 when Jane was only two, and the little girl turned to her father for love and for an interpretation of the life around her. John Addams, Cedarville's most respected citizen, a friend of Lincoln and a State Senator, had little use for religious doctrine. When his bewildered daughter had asked him what he was, he had replied without further elucidation that he was a Hicksite Quaker. Her questions about foreordination finally led to his revelation that such disputes meant nothing to him. He believed simply that "you must always be honest with yourself inside whatever happened." Throughout her childhood and her college years, Jane Addams searched for a secure religious haven. She entered settlement work partly out of religious motives. Eventually, however, Chicago taught her the limitations of traditional individual rectitude. She became a contented and a more democratic-minded agnostic.[10]

Her father's heroes, Lincoln and Mazzini, became her own. The Lincoln ideal taught her that democracy grew out of the fund of common experience between leader and people. The experiment in self-government could succeed only if the people themselves cooperated to foster it. The frontier community symbolized this ideal, and her father's experience in building a railroad with the financial aid of his Pennsylvania Dutch neighbors stood as a living example of it.[11]

The rural setting, the free and prosperous farmers who cooperated to bring the wheat of northern Illinois to Freeport and Chicago by rail, always spelled community to Jane Addams. The whole life of Cedarville seemed a natural setting for youth and age. It was perhaps here that Jane Addams' vision of an organic, classless society began.

Between her father's internationalism and her own there existed a tenuous connection, even though Jane Addams appreciated it only after she had discovered the meaning of her past. One day in 1872 the little girl found her father in mourning for the Italian patriot Joseph Mazzini. Why should he care about some foreigner he had never met? John Addams explained that just as he himself had formed the "Addams guard" to fight with the Union Army for freedom in America, Mazzini had fought for Italian liberty and for the freedom of all Europe's peoples. "I obtained a sense," she recalled in 1910, "of the genuine relationship which may exist between men who shared large hopes, and like desires, even though they may differ in nationality, language and creed."[12]

Rockford Seminary (later Rockford College) was one of the first institutions for higher learning for women in the Midwest. The environment of serious study and dedication, the girls' sense of unique opportunity, awakened Jane Addams' feminism. But Rockford was also a training ground for foreign missionaries, and the evangelism of the headmistress, Miss Sill, repelled the young doubter whose ideas of the divine were still in flux. Nevertheless, Jane Addams acquired a sense of Christian mission all her own and strong ideas of woman's role in society, which were just enough to make her restive with the life her vivacious, cultured stepmother had planned for her.

Women's education, she told her fellow students in her junior class oration, neither confined them to the "arts of pleasing," nor sought to make them like men. Women claimed the right to "independent thought and action" while retaining the old ideal of the Saxon lady as "bread giver." Jane then planned a career combining scientific study with feminine service. She would become a doctor.[13]

The matter was not so quickly settled, however. In August 1881 John Addams died. His daughter lost all sense of purpose and plunged into an emotional and spiritual crisis from which she did not recover completely for eight years. She went on to the Woman's Medical College in Philadelphia only to decide, after six months, that she had mistaken her aptitude for science. A spinal disease temporarily immobilized her physically as well as emotionally. A trip to Europe with her stepmother failed to revive her spirits. When her stepmother moved the family to Baltimore, where Jane studied French and attended lectures at Johns Hopkins, she "reached the nadir of . . . [her] nervous depression and sense of maladjustment." She wrote her friend, Ellen Gates Starr, that she was "filled with shame that with all my apparent leisure I do nothing at all. . . . I have found my faculties, memory receptive faculties and all, perfectly inaccessible locked up away from me."[14] A second trip to Europe in 1887-88 turned the key, not because she had discovered "the other half" but because she decided to act at last upon a plan she had considered even before she embarked.

One evening in Madrid after she and her friends had enjoyed the bloody spectacle of a bullfight and she had stayed all day at the arena, the shock of her love for a beauty that was also cruel impelled her to stop cloaking her idleness in a "dreamer's scheme." She would tell Ellen of her plan and bring the dream to reality. She wanted to rent a large house in the cosmopolitan industrial district of a great city "where many primitive and actual needs are found," to give herself and others like her, too swamped with privileges and too steeped in intellectual pursuits alone, the "solace of activity."[15] The next day Jane Addams and her friend set out for Paris and London. They visited Toynbee Hall, the first settlement house, to learn how such an enterprise worked.

In 1889 as she and Ellen opened up Hull House in Chicago's immigrant district, Jane Addams saw that two needs were meeting and answering each other—the objective needs of a torn, divided, and impoverished area and the subjective needs of her own generation to create some harmony between their Christian ideals and their lives.[16] The settlement movement was a very class-conscious one. In England it was inspired by a sense of *nobless oblige*. John Ruskin, whose writings first impelled Canon Barnett and the young men of Oxford and Cambridge to set up Toynbee Hall in the Whitechapel district, was concerned chiefly with the intellectual's obligation to relieve the sins of his society.[17] In spite of all Jane Addams' efforts to understand rather than sympathize with the poor, she never quite lost this feeling of condescension. Hull House was to bring high culture to the slums, if only to prove that the poor were not a lower order of men. The settlement workers learned neighborliness from their clients, but largely because these clients retained the "primitive" virtues of pity and mutual aid. Canon Barnett of Toynbee Hall had taught that whatever draws men together was deeper and more real than the environment that drove them apart. Jane Addams accepted this as her guiding philosophy. Yet the subjective and objective needs were, after all, different needs, and behind her goal of the classless society lay the haunting sense that such differences might not so quickly disappear.[18]

The salvation of privileged youth lay in answering the cries of the slums. For if they held aloof from the poor and from the "starvation struggle which makes up the life of at least half the race," not only would their sympathies deaden, but their guilt would bring a loss of vitality, which could only make them "pitifully miserable." Jane Addams regarded this longing for helpfulness and action as a "race memory" of the "starvation struggle" of ancestors. But when she spoke of girls trained to altruism and then bound by the "family claim," just as they would go out into the world to fulfill their obligations, it was clear that her own experience rather than any evolutionism molded her interpretation.[19]

In 1887, on her second trip to London, Miss Addams had heard the positivist Frederick Harrison speak of loyalty to humanity. Without yet understanding the practical implications of the idea, she was attracted to it. Her notebook recorded a visit to Ulm cathedral, where in the choir stalls were carved figures of Hebrew prophets, Greek philosophers, and Christian saints, symbols of the rich diversity of this "humanity" and of the "fellowship of common purpose" which transcended it.[20] Her vision of Hull House became this vision of human solidarity, and she quickly saw its fulfillment in her own activity. She plunged into work, minding the children of working mothers, preparing the dead for burial, acting as midwife for an unmarried pregnant girl whom all the good Irish matrons of the neighborhood had deserted. The Nineteenth Ward of Chicago, where Hull House stood, was the center of the tenement sweat-shop garment industry. Evening after evening, the Russian and Bohemian and Italian women staggered home under the weight of huge piles of garments to be finished in their crowded rooms. There the children waited for supper, and the ill lay on bedrolls on the floor. There the stink of the slaughterhouses and the noise of the streetcars and crowds drifted through the narrow windows. Typhoid, tuberculosis, smallpox, and diphtheria ran rampant through these tenements. And often the most pitiful savings went for funeral trappings much more magnificent than the clothing or shelter of the living.[21]

Jane Addams and Ellen Starr were learning what the "love of humanity" meant. It did not mean charity nor the handing out of a pittance of help.

> Our very first Christmas at Hull House, when we

> as yet knew nothing of child labor, a number of little girls refused the candy which was offered them as part of the Christmas good cheer saying simply that they "worked in a candy factory and could not bear the sight of it." We discovered that for six weeks they had worked from seven in the morning until nine at night, and that they were exhausted as well as satiated. The sharp consciousness of stern economic conditions was thus thrust upon us in the midst of the season of good will.[22]

The clash between the dream of Christian fulfillment and the harsh reality of the slums brought the genteel Miss Addams and her friends up sharply. They were soon transformed from missionary philanthropists into radical critics of the ugly commercialism of the cities. Not only did they see youth and love and work degraded, but they learned at close hand that it was no simple matter to bridge the chasm of values between the rich and the poor. The traditional puritan virtues of hard work, abstinence, and thrift which the middle-class charity worker usually preached to her clients were meaningless to families who could find no work, or who could not possibly save when they needed every penny merely to live. The poor understood their naturally helpful and kindly neighbors. They understood the selfish rich who stayed uptown. What they could not understand was middle-class charity doled out as a reward for impossible "virtues."[23] Thus in the very first years of Hull House, the settlement workers discovered that the "overdifferentiation" of the lives of rich and poor could not be ended by even the most generous giving. Community had to start with mutuality. The women of Hull House, wanting to open the lines of communication between the classes, had to transform charity into equality and comradeship. Only if they joined the real struggles—for labor legislation, for union rights, for accident insurance, for adequate medical care, for tenement legislation—would the community grow. Even the most immediate problems provided opportunities.

> We quickly discovered that nothing brought us so absolutely into comradeship with our neighbors as *mutual and sustained efforts* such as the paving of a street, the closing of a gambling house, or the restoration of a veteran policeman.[24]

Thus the settlement workers became fighters. They campaigned against the ward boss (while quite appreciating why he held the neighbors' loyalty). They organized the Juvenile Protective Association, the Consumers' League, and women's trade unions. During these struggles Jane Addams began to appreciate two cardinal points that would later mold her pacifism. First of all, the struggle for social justice held forth as great a challenge and as much adventure as any war. Secondly, the very process of fostering the growth of human solidarity required the use of all the resources of government. A government so transformed by the demands of its own society might be compelled to adapt even its foreign policy to those demands.

All the while the settlement house was becoming a community—a community whose goal was to make city life more organic. And this meant, at the very least, hospitality to all visitors and to every viewpoint. The problems of industrial society were too complex to permit the social workers to apply any limited insight to the solutions. The neighbors must be heard, for it was their city. Evangelists and housewives, respectable reformers and eccentrics, conservatives, atheists, socialists—all used the Hull House platform. Chicagoans often misunderstood this hospitality and assumed that the residents agreed with those who spoke. Following the assassination of President McKinley, night after night the great house was surrounded by the Chicago police as they combed the district hunting for anarchists. After one particularly noisy meeting, a policeman turned to Dr. Alice Hamilton with a few pointed words: "Lady, you oughtn't to let bums like these come here. If I had my way, they'd all be lined up against a wall at sunrise and shot."[25] But the ladies found it all very stimulating. They understood that the real purpose of free speech was mutual enlightenment. One could not be "dogmatic concerning the final truth."[26]

The settlement house was more than a community of diverse viewpoints; it was a community of nationalities and individuals as well. In the Nineteenth Ward, Russians and Poles, Jews and Hungarians, Italians and Irish, Czechs and Germans lived and worked together. And the Hull House little theater performed the Shakespearean histories and Greek tragedies for them all, while the immigrants themselves wrote and performed plays, gave dances, parties, and staged grand parades. "When men and women, boys and girls, work all day in sweatshops," Jane Addams observed realistically, "they want to have fun." Yet neither the residents nor the neighbors lost their identities in the mass. They were too strikingly individual to do so. Clarence Darrow often visited at Hull House and welcomed Governor John Peter Altgeld and Beatrice and Sydney Webb there. John Dewey served on the Board of Trustees and lectured at the Plato Club, both learning from and teaching the residents of Hull House. Julia Lathrop, a friend of Jane Addams from Rockford, combined law and social work and eventually directed the US Children's Bureau while furthering plans for psychiatric treatment of juvenile criminals. Dr. Alice Hamilton's studies of the "dangerous trades" helped to open the whole new field of industrial medicine. Florence Kelley, the most vociferous battler of them all, joined the movement for an eight-hour day and became chief factory-inspector in Illinois. Grace Abbott was superintendent of the League for the Protection of Immigrants, while her sister Edith joined Julia Lathrop and Sophonisba Breckinridge in founding the department of social research at the University of Chicago's School of Civics and Philanthropy.[27]

In brief, the residents of Hull House started out as amateur philanthropists; but within a decade they became scientific reformers, using the best available professional tools for the creation of an urban community. One of

Jane Addams' first principles was her insistence upon expert knowledge and precise information as instruments of social progress. The settlement was not just a laboratory. Fellow feeling was more important to early social work than were analytical motives. Nevertheless, the acquisition of thorough information about urban society signalized the residents' break with the condescending and genteel charity work of the past. One of the most famous early collections of studies of urban population patterns, labor movements, and housing problems was *Hull House Maps and Papers, a presentation of nationalities and wages in a congested district in Chicago . . .* (1895). Not only did their investigations of urban problems greatly strengthen the settlement workers' arguments before city and state governing bodies, but they helped significantly to launch university studies in urban sociology.[28]

Thus the devoted expert played as crucial a role in Addams' Chicago programs as did the interpreter in Royce's insurance plans. And in many ways the social worker and expert served as interpreters between parties in conflict, even as in Royce's triadic scheme. It is not surprising, therefore, that during the international disintegration of 1914 Jane Addams, like Royce, would be mindful of the potentially helpful role of the neutral expert. She came to believe that the fundamental problems that gave rise to war could be understood better by scientists and doctors than by statesmen.

Within the settlement house itself many activities became bridges between groups isolated by class distinction, by generational experience, or by national background. Like Tolstoy, Jane Addams valued the arts for their inherent unifying qualities and for the emotional involvement they produced in the residents. She was delighted to discover that her neighbors cherished their native cultures and that they remembered the arts and crafts of their homelands.[29] Like Tolstoy, too, Miss Addams put to good use both in her writing and in her social reform work her own sensitivity to family misunderstandings. In a sense, perhaps because her own struggle for independence against the "family claim" had been so painful and so crucial to her development, she discovered the now familiar clash between immigrants and their Americanized children. Characteristically she discovered an activity reflecting the genuine cultural heritage of the European parents, to heal the alienation between them and their children. The women who used to spin and weave garments in the old country displayed their skills in the Hull House Labor Museum, teaching their children the origins of the garment industry in which those children worked. With a new pride in their parents, some of the children gained a sympathetic insight into all their parents had left behind in the peasant villages—acceptable social roles, useful work, respect.[30]

Class isolation presented more difficult problems. In Chicago, memories of strikes, police hunts, and the Haymarket bomb were bitter and enduring. The socialists did not entirely trust the Hull House ladies. Jane Addams, in fact, had indicated that although she fully sympathized with their goals and appreciated that they realized the true situation of the workers better than any, she found their interpretation of human nature too dogmatic and too rigid.[31] But these same middle-class ladies were useful interpreters to "respectable" Chicago of the immigrants' feelings and conditions. Both unionists and socialists recognized this fact. Often the residents arbitrated labor disputes when no one else could. They were profoundly sympathetic with the worker's drives for concrete gains and for the theme of solidarity, but they regarded the violence of the strikes as tragic. Still, Miss Addams rather idolized the labor movement. She criticized it only after its first struggling days, when it showed signs of adopting the business ethic which was so thoroughly corrupt in Chicago.[32]

Thus, long before Jane Addams knew she was a pacifist, her pacifism was growing, primarily out of her practice of reconciling conflicting interests without weak compromises. She would probe beneath appearances and look for some motive in her opponents that might be transformed into an instrument for reconciliation. This ceaseless activity of discovering bonds of unity in mutual needs formed the core of Addams' community.

THE PEACEFUL IMPULSES

In 1893 Chicago held a world's fair, the Columbian Exposition. A great white city, elaborate and overdecorated, arose in the midst of the filth and the smoke. A group of boys at Hull House joined the "Columbian Guards" and drilled in the gymnasium. One day Jane Addams visited them and told them that since the purpose of the Guards was to clean up the city, it would be more appropriate to parade with sewer spades than with rifles. The moment her back was turned they dropped the spades and took up the rifles once more. It was Miss Addams' first "Quixotic experiment" in pacifism,[33] inspired more by the needs of the city than by her readings in Tolstoy. She was reaching the conclusion that war and soldiering were futile, ineffective instruments for social change.

As she observed her neighbors in the Nineteenth Ward, especially during the Spanish-American War and the Philippines campaign that followed, she began to consider the sources of man's warlike tendencies. There was the basic human need to identify oneself with a group—a family, a class, or a nation. This primitive core of patriotism derived from the ancient tribe's need for self-protection against outsiders, and was infused with distrust and hatred. She felt that a civilized people could outgrow such aggressive patriotism, just as adolescents emerged from their gang loyalties into a fuller and more meaningful adult life.[34]

Men also showed a spirit of adventure, particularly when they were young. The same longing for excitement stirred the primitive hunter and warrior and the young men who revolted against factory labor by committing petty crimes and experimenting with drink and drugs.[35] The blandness of traditional peace dogma, not peace itself, repelled such adventurous spirits. Thus Jane Addams connected the activism of the 1890s with man's primitive needs. She concluded, however, that the martial spirit was not the only outlet for this desire for action and vitality.

In 1904, in two addresses to the thirteenth Universal Peace Congress in Boston, Miss Addams began to suggest two moral substitutes for war—the labor movement, with its ideal of human solidarity, and social reform, an experiment in trusting the people.[36] William James, at the same time, was developing his "moral equivalent of war." He commended Addams' suggestions, and called for the actual recruitment of youth in the tasks of building the industrial city. The heroism of physical labor, of socially useful work, might assume the same martial trappings as a soldier's life. James was convinced that warlike tendencies were deeply imbedded in human nature.[37] Addams believed that only the longing for adventure and group approval was. But the plans of both coalesced.

The concern for human nature, Jane Addams observed in 1907, had lately evinced an aggressive character; and yet it was international and might inspire an international loyalty. The campaign of German, British, French and American doctors against tuberculosis, for example, had

> . . . its international congresses, its discoverers and veterans, also its decorations and rewards for bravery. Its discipline is severe; it requires self-control, endurance, self-sacrifice and constant watchfulness.[38]

This cause of service to the most primitive needs of humanity became Addams' equivalent of "loyalty to loyalty." It was universal, without restricting individual choice; peaceful, but far from passive. The choice also demonstrated why the Addams pacifism never assumed the isolationist character of Bryan's nor of some other anti-war progressives. She had conceived of social reform as international from the very beginning, and had found her own efforts for labor legislation supplemented by the efforts of reformers in other lands. For example, the Hull House residents quickly joined the International League for Labor Legislation because their own knowledge of the immigrants' past convinced them that the need was world-wide. Even campaigns in Illinois identified them with similar campaigns in Europe.[39]

The second substitute for war was a vital internationalism growing up among the immigrants themselves in the slums. In contrast to Butler's international mind with its cool rationality and patrician connotations, Addams' new internationalism was sentimental, empirical, and above all democratic. Both Root and Butler argued that the irrational masses drove the leaders to war. But Addams proclaimed the very opposite.

> It is possible that we shall be saved from warfare by the "fighting rabble" itself . . . turned into kindly citizens of the world through the pressure of the cosmopolitan neighborhood. It is not that they are shouting for peace—on the contrary, if they shout at all, they will continue to shout for war—but they are really attaining cosmopolitan relations through daily experience.[40]

While there was nothing unusual in the belief in a natural progress toward internationalism—it was part of the motif of the turn-of-the century peace movement—the contention that the lowliest shall save was too thoroughly Tolstoyan for most of the peace society leadership. The labor movement that did form a part of the American peace movement was an aristocracy among workers. But Jane Addams was speaking out for the unskilled, unassimilated masses whom neither the peace societies nor the American Federation of Labor embraced. What was it that caused her to adopt this course? Actually it was more than her own identification with the immigrants that impelled her in this direction. She had drawn for herself a blueprint of human nature that conformed in no way to the pattern of "fighting rabble."

Man, she believed, was a complex organism, changing psychologically throughout his life, molding his environment because he was a creature of dynamic instincts. Yet he was so "extraordinarily pliable" that the settlement workers could see no bounds to his moral capabilities "under ideal civic and educational conditions."[41] The old concept of sinful human nature was refuted both by newer instinct theory and by the environmentalism which Jane Addams paradoxically combined.

It was not that she argued for the perfectibility of man. On the contrary, she often spoke of "our imperfect human nature" as being more real than eighteenth-century humanitarians thought. But in emphasizing man's pliability and vitality she was denying all rigid categorizations—the economic man of the classical economists, the political man of political scientists, even the proletariat and capitalist categories of socialist thought. Human beings were too complex and whole for these descriptions to be meaningful. To the Spencerians, she replied that man's economic success was no test of his fitness. There were virtues more important than the commercial ones. And if one individual or one family could barely endure the industrial environment, "larger social groupings," neighborhood organizations and unions, would find a greater fitness to cope with crushing burdens.[42] For man, above all, was an instinctively cooperative, gregarious, and creative creature. The few potent impulses (the "handful of incentives" Jane Addams called them) that really directed human conduct were life-giving and peaceful.

While recognizing the prevalent practice of immigrant families to send their children to work at an early age (as if the factories were no different from their old-country fields or the home workshop) and even importing young relatives to help support them, she insisted that such evidence of the corruption of poverty did not make child labor reforms, or any other reforms, in the phrase of William Graham Sumner "absurd efforts to make the world over."[43] On the contrary, conditions such as child labor only proved the need to free much deeper motives—the motives that inspired other poor people to sacrifice everything for family unity and the children's education, the motive that led old mothers to protect their criminal sons from further degradation. It was "family devotion," or as she frequently would term it, the "maternal anxieties," that kept the world sane and whole when every social force drove the family apart.[44] This instinct for nurturing the young, and the love of men and women which was so closely tied to it, became Miss Addams' basic explanation for the "revolt against war" in 1915.

Love and the nurturing instinct were not confined to the family. A sense of primitive pity served peasant peoples as much as a "thirst for righteousness" served young revolutionaries and as an impulse to justice served more sophisticated reformers.

In the depression winter of 1893, Jane Addams observed neighbors lending each other clothing and shoes, giving bread, advancing rent to families close to the breaking-point. The charity workers' concerns could hardly rival the kindnesses of the poor to one another.[45] True, other observers would have seen more terrible psychological effects of poverty. Jane Addams was hardly implying that poverty brought out the best in man. The fact remains that she observed that these primitive kindly instincts survived even in the worst environment, and faltered only when the young were overprotected, isolated from the "starvation struggle."

One reason for her insistence upon the basic nature of man's gregariousness was her observation that youth and primitive peoples exhibited more of it than the sophisticated. This Rousseauian romanticism she confirmed in describing the play instinct as the source of man's aesthetic and social drives. Children entered a world of imagination with their peers and could hardly be kept apart unless literally locked up. In adolescence the longing to assert individuality and vitality took the form of trying to prove oneself to others. The sexual instinct was, when not perverted by the glare of the dance halls, tender and romantic.[46]

All these longings for other beings and for love were fundamentally creative. Addams wrote of each of them not merely to prove man's sociability but also to attack the sordid ugliness of industrial life that thwarted man's normal nature. It was not the city she deplored (although she implied that rural life was more natural to man), but the crass materialism that corrupted the city and made it a place for profits instead of for civilization. For example, one of the social and creative instincts, man's "free labor quality" (similar to Veblen's "instinct of workmanship"), deteriorated in the tedium of mechanical and repetitious tasks in the factory. This quality found renewed expression in the immigrants' handicraft hobbies and artistic efforts. Having read John Ruskin and William Morris, Addams was aware of the attack upon the factory system in the name of the artistic sense. She realized at the same time that the handicraft system would never come into its own again. But she called for a new socialized education that would put this instinct to use, bringing the workman a consciousness of the social usefulness of the product he shared in making. Like Veblen, she associated workmanship with peace, believing that even in the midst of war men longed to return to creative tasks.[47] Thus the "free labor quality" discussions were in reality a reformer's pleas. The same purpose pervaded her descriptions of the peasants who longed to cultivate the earth, a task which war thwarted. The instinct for labor was to become one of the bases of her association of peace and bread.

THE STATE—MILITARISTIC OR NURTURING

Jane Addams perceived the necessity of a radical transformation of the state into a community. She did not, however, call the change "community." Instead she spoke of ***Democracy and Social Ethics*** (1902), but what she had in mind was clearly a community transformation. Government would answer the primitive needs of the people. The population in turn would feel the government an extension of itself. In ***Newer Ideals of Peace*** (1907) Jane Addams insisted that peace itself was dependent upon such a transformation. Her 1902 collection of essays did not yet make the connection to international relations, but it did prepare the ground.

Democracy and Social Ethics was a rejection of the individualistic and commercial morality of the Gilded Age. Like the ministers of the social gospel, Jane Addams viewed the success ethic as a perversion of Christianity and a pervasive disorder throughout American society, infecting the relationship of parents to children, of teacher to students, of philanthropist to the recipient of aid. Her revolt against the gospel of wealth and economic individualism was not unique, but a part of the welfare-progressivism of the turn of the century. But it established certain themes for her later internationalism that were unique. First, there was the emphasis upon the importance of means for achieving any desirable goal. Failure in any reform effort, Miss Addams stressed, could come "quite as easily from ignoring the adequacy of one's method as from social or ignoble aims."[48] This emphasis upon processes really defined her democratic faith. She could never look upon violent means as necessary for the achievement of any worth while goal, and rejected both the war to "make the world safe for democracy" and collective security on this ground. It was not the illogic of waging war for peace that troubled her, so much as a realistic appreciation that processes were always caught up in the results.

Second, her early ideas of leadership and individuality were to make themselves keenly felt during the war in her response to Wilson. She insisted, in 1902, that good could never be done to people, or even for them, but only with them. Certainly the Hull House experience confirmed this, but in ***Democracy and Social Ethics*** Jane Addams raised participatory democracy to a moral law. She recognized the importance and the effectiveness of organization, but questioned closely any organization that drew sharp lines between leaders and followers.

> We have learned to say that the good must be extended to all of society before it can be held secure by one person or any one class; but we have not yet learned to add the statement that unless all men and classes contribute to the good, we cannot even be sure it is worth having.[49]

Thus, what Jane Addams perceived in the great strikes of her time was not simply class conflict, but a contest between an outdated individualistic ethic, which included even philanthropy, and a social ethic that was the essence of democracy. Her perceptive analysis of George Pullman as a well-meaning self-righteous Lear who would not let the labor movement, with its impulse toward brotherhood, grow up,[50] was the sharpest case in point. Her refutation of Spencer's contention that capitalistic individualism was peaceful began here—in her conception of capitalism's domineering character.

In ***Newer Ideals of Peace*** she developed the theme further, arguing that both the ideal and the reality of *laissez faire* were militaristic. The ideology of limited government, which so captured the American mind, had been a weapon against British royalism. *Laissez faire* still reflected martial origins. It was supported by static eighteenth-century ideas of human nature that had no relationship to real, imperfect human beings. The eighteenth-century idealists, Addams contended, had an aristocratic distaste for the masses. The distinction they drew between government and freedom was but an extension of the English common-law distinction between ruler and ruled. No one who truly trusted the people to find their own solutions through government would have clung to the government-freedom dichotomy.[51]

Moreover, the eighteenth-century theories proved militaristic in their nineteenth-century applications. A government that took no account of the instincts for fellowship and mutual aid among the people naturally confined itself to military functions. Keeping order was, after all, a policeman's or a soldier's task. More than that, it encouraged a colonial relationship between employers and workers. The symbol of authority in the city was the privately-owned factory, just as the symbol of authority in medieval times was the fortified castle. From the factory, the employer looked down upon the workers as if they were a lower order of being. The workers responded with their group morality. Insofar as this morality bespoke the solidarity of all, it was an example of the social ethic. But it could become an exclusive and intolerant class-consciousness. The result of both attitudes was warfare. Terror was a proper instrument against class enemies, and violence characterized labor relations on both sides.[52] The negligent state became military, largely because it tolerated militaristic social relations.

Having thus denied Spencer's distinction between the peaceful capitalist order and the older militarism (Veblen was to do the same thing with very different methods), Jane Addams applied this interpretation to foreign affairs. Her life on Chicago's West Side had given her a unique insight into the connection between militarism at home and imperialism abroad. The ideal of enforcing order in the cities resembled the Anglo-Saxon idea of the rule of law over backward, colored peoples. Disparagement of the immigrant's culture enforced the racism of the expansionist mind.

> Unrestricted commercialism is an excellent preparation for governmental aggression. The nation which is accustomed to condone the questionable business methods of a rich man because of his success will find no difficulty in obscuring the moral issues involved in any undertaking that is successful. It becomes easy to deny the moral basis of self-government and to substitute militarism.[53]

Perhaps the barest explanation of imperialism that one could find among any of the American internationalists, this statement neglected Addams' own interpretation of primitive patriotism with its hatreds and fears. However, her tempering of economic interpretation with a socio-psychological one enabled her to make a unique analysis of the expansionist mind as one that equated morality with power, and thus denied the potential creativity both of the poor and of the inhabitants of the backward areas.

The real difficulty came when Miss Addams sought to prove that the welfare-state would be less inclined to imperialism and more toward peace. The evidence of Progressives who supported both welfare reforms and expansionism contradicted her contention. The Tory democracy of Disraeli was also the climax of Victorian imperialism; the Germany of Kaiser Wilhelm, with its elaborate provisions for social insurance had not abandoned militarism. Nevertheless, Jane Addams argued that a subtle psychological change was taking place in Germany and Britain that might eventually turn them away from the course of empire. In Britain the workers discovered that the cheap products of colonial labor debased their own standard of living. In Germany, the police who enforced health, insurance, and safety regulations were assuming the attitude of "helpers and protectors."[54] Orthodox Spencerians might doubt that either of these changes was taking place or that they would affect foreign policy. Addams' point was more pedagogical than logical. She was trying to make Americans feel guilty that more class-conscious, militaristic societies should have advanced social legislation while America with its egalitarian ideals had none.

She sought to indicate the connections between participatory democracy, welfare legislation, and peace. The welfare state, like the unions, would teach the immigrants the real rudiments of self-government in the only way these could be taught, by an appeal to the peoples' reliance on basic necessities.[55] The immigrants in turn would create a new patriotism, full of compassion for others, whether they were blood brothers or not. Therefore, if the government were to infuse this vital concern for human welfare into its activities, it would utilize this compassion. There was a kind of mystical "back to the people" fervor in all this, and perhaps Addams realized it; for she defended her conception of immigrant life. "We are often told that men under this pressure of life [poverty and the experience of being uprooted] become calloused and cynical, whereas anyone who lives with them knows that they are sentimental and compassionate."[56] It was a difficult argument for those without settlement experience to counter; those with the experience tended to agree.

Even more determinative in the welfare state's peacefulness would be the women, who would connect their "maternal anxieties" with the new state's nurturing activities. Jane Addams did not claim that women were inherently more pacifist than men, but she did associate the maternal instinct with peacefulness. She was developing, along with Charlotte Gilmore Perkins and others, a new argument for female suffrage that had very little to do with the dogma of equal rights. The argument ran as follows: Woman's traditional functions had been the nurturing of the family, the protection of their health, the education of children. In an industrial city these tasks were literally stolen from her, for she no longer controlled the environment for raising children. The family health was undermined by industrial disease. She worked in a factory where she couldn't regulate her own hours as she could at home. She was being dehumanized. On the other hand, the government, as it began to concern itself with urban problems, was almost acting the mother role for its citizens. Clearly, the need of women for the vote, to regain their old functions, and the need of government for women, to gain their experience and motivation, were reciprocal.[57] In brief, women should have the vote not because they were like men, but because they were different.

By identifying women and the nurturing state in this manner, Jane Addams also connected exclusive male suffrage with an extinct militarism. Man's ability to bear arms was surely an irrelevant criterion for citizenship in an industrial democracy. She asserted finally that the military state and the nurturing state confronted each other as opposites in psychology, function, qualifications for citizenship, and the use of natural resources. The people could not have both butter and guns. They would have to choose. Thus she concluded her defense of the maternal state by interpreting Isaiah's prophecy of peace.

> He contended that peace could be secured only as men abstained from the gains of oppression and responded to the cause of the poor; that swords would finally be beaten into plowshares and pruning hooks, not because men resolved to be peaceful, but because the metal of the earth would be turned to its proper use when the poor and their children should be abundantly fed. It was as if the ancient prophet foresaw that under an enlightened industrialism peace would no longer be an absence of war, but the unfolding of world-wide processes making for the nurture of human life.[58]

It was not many years later that Jane Addams put the identification of peace and nurture to the test of action. The National Conference of Charities and Corrections (a national social workers' organization) elected her president in 1909, and in the same year began to draw up programs for "industrial minimums" that required immediate government action. In spite of their achievements in state welfare legislation, the social workers felt increasingly frustrated by serious discrepancies in state standards and by the attacks of the courts upon this legislation. They had reached the conclusion that some national party must take up their cause, but neither of the major parties was receptive. In the contest between the Taft Republicans and the insurgents, in the emerging Progressive Party the social workers saw a unique opportunity. Jane Addams, who had never held any public office higher than that of garbage inspector for the Nineteenth Ward, took the step of committing herself to Roosevelt's cause, because Roosevelt and his cohorts adopted the "minimums" into the platform.

She now began to realize the full difficulty and complexity of ethics in action even more than she had in the old campaign against ward boss Jimmy Powers. First, there was the lily-white complexion of the Progressives, which Jane Addams, a founder of the National Association for the Advancement of Colored People, found so repugnant that she almost bolted. Then she had to decide upon the platform that recommended the fortification of the Panama Canal and the building of two battleships a year.[59] Roosevelt and his fellow Progressives so identified the new nationalism with balance of power politics and expansionism that it was impossible to win a compromise on these points.

Addams defended the logic of her new pacifism. How could a government willing to expend hundreds of thousands of dollars to protect the Canal workers against malaria and yellow fever and the industrial workers against long hours, accidents, and the dangerous trades, threaten with destruction "the same sort of human stuff which it had so painstakingly" kept alive? A rift was evident between two streams within the Progressive Party—social welfare progressivism, which in part tended toward pacifism, and the new nationalism, which valued the state as a powerful arbitrator between inevitably conflicting interests at home and abroad.

Jane Addams was never particularly inspired by Herbert Croly's thought, although she advocated a strong state as a popular instrument. The realism of Roosevelt with its emphasis upon the continual international struggle for power was not her variety of realism with its focus upon the human results of such struggles and the waste of human resources in military preparations. Nevertheless, after considerable soul-searching Addams decided that the chance to enact significant welfare legislation should not be ignored. Supporting the Progressives and campaigning in their behalf, she reasoned that any group so committed to saving lives in industry (where more were lost than on the battlefields) was "surely on the road to peace."[60] Many years later she granted that perhaps this was a rationalization and she experienced a vague sense of guilt, even though she was still passionately committed to the reforms the Progressives had advocated. What she would not observe, perhaps because it was too self-complimentary, was that this stand above all indicated the realistic nature of her pacifism. The cause she cared about was the cause of the poor. Only in 1914 did this cause and the changing reality propel her into an extreme course.

"THE REVOLT AGAINST WAR"

All through the prewar years Jane Addams clung to her faith in the progress of peace through the progress of the nurturing state. The 1912 defeat was not the end of progressivism, although after 1914 she parted company with the Progressive Party. That summer, when the confrontation between nurture and militarism emerged into the open, she experienced a sense of desolation that was almost as suicidal as the great war itself. The whole world was changing, and her position would change with it, not because she became less the pacifist, but because she began to feel the full impact of an idea that formed the bedrock of her revolt against war: namely, that the real evil of war was not the destruction of property or life but the destruction of the human community. The nobility and sacrifice of war-time patriotism were purchased at a frightful cost, the creation of a dogmatic nationalism which consumed truth, fellowship, and the hope for the future of the coming generation. No other communalist, not even Royce, saw the conflict between war and community in such stark terms. Veblen and Dewey, and most Wilsonian progressives, hoped to use the opportunity of the war to achieve long-sought goals of social control. But Jane Addams testified that the social reformer would have to combat the effects of the world war for years before the psychological foundation for social progress was re-established.

Most of her friends were to disagree with her and desert her in 1917, but in 1914 there was a glimmering of a social workers' revolt against war. In September, Lillian Wald of the Henry Street Settlement, Paul Kellogg, editor of the social worker's magazine, *Survey,* and veteran of the National Conference of Charities and Corrections, joined Miss Addams in calling upon other social workers to form a Union Against Militarism. Their anti-war protest reflected professional interests very directly. War eroded the generous impulses upon which the willingness to do justice depended. It shattered the immigrant community, turning neighbor against neighbor. It reduced the state to its primitive defensive functions, forcing an abandonment of those normal activities which governments had lately begun. War reversed democracy by unifying a population on the basis of coercion, instead of winning "inner consent." It "curbed the intelligence" by brutalizing men and demanding conformity.[61]

The social workers' revolt was a small and relatively weak one, but Jane Addams and Lillian Wald soon expanded it by making it a women's revolt. Never was American feminism more militant than in its pacifist crusade. The fighting spirit of the British suffragettes infused the American movement with an aggressive tone. Mrs. Emmeline Pethick-Lawrence, a veteran of the most violent phase of the British women's campaigns, came to Chicago. She was now, in 1914, an ardent pacifist. She pleaded with the women to follow their instincts and to demand an end to the war through American mediation. She brought with her the emerging program of the British Liberal-Labour organization, the Union of Democratic Control. In the fall of 1914 Mme. Rosika Schwimmer of Hungary, a journalist and founder of the International Suffrage Alliance, entered the fray. Both women were old comrades of Jane Addams, and their presence reminded her that she had considered suffrage an internationalist movement. Feminism was "spontaneous and universal," uniting the secluded Oriental women with the Western activists, the hard-working factory laborer and the privileged lady.[62]

As the women of Chicago and New York gathered to receive Mme. Schwimmer and Mrs. Pethick-Lawrence, Jane Addams conceived of a plan to unite the peace societies and the suffragettes. She asked Lillian Wald to contact New York pacifists and feminists to ask them to lend their support to an Emergency Peace Committee that would call for immediate American mediation. "It does seem a pity," she observed, "not to utilize all this enthusiasm."[63] The Chicago Emergency Peace Committee soon pondered the idea of a nation-wide organization. Carrie Chapman Catt, President of the International Suffrage Alliance, agreed to invite women's groups all over the country to attend a national peace meeting. The leading pacifists, such as Anna Garland Spencer and Lucia Ames Mead, quickly accepted and began to organize the conference. Every type of organization, from women's trade unions to associations of teachers to the Daughters of the American Revolution accepted the invitation, although some patriotic associations dropped out as soon as the platform emerged. This emergency meeting organized the Woman's Peace Party. Jane Addams became its president. During the war the party affiliated with British, German, Dutch, Belgian, Hungarian, and French peace groups, emerging in 1919 as the Woman's International League for Peace and Freedom. Their cause became Jane Addams' own as completely as Hull House had been in the early days.[64]

The ideas of feminine pacifism fused with the ideals of the nurturing state and of the internationalism of immigrants to form the whole *Weltanschauung* of Jane Addams' community. The association of maternal instinct with Tolstoyan "bread labor" gave Jane Addams' internationalism both its mystical and its empirical dimensions.

The Woman's Peace Party was a minority of a minority from the very beginning. In spite of their rejection of the Victorian sheltered life,[65] most American women related feminism to the rather barren ideals of career-women and to the sacrifice of family security. But the pacifists were even a minority of the feminist minority, and Jane Addams recognized this in declaring that most women allowed their political views to be molded by men.[66] Hers was a skillful and pointed argument, therefore, quite in keeping with her arguments for women's votes. It pictured the pacifist as not only a freer woman than her traditionally patriotic sister, but also as a more feminine one. Femininity did not mean frills and passivity and dependency, but a love-giving, life-giving assertion. In short, it was the maternal instinct that defined a woman, and this instinct created a unique obligation, for " . . . quite as an artist in an artillery corps commanded to fire on the *duomo* at Florence would be deterred by a compunction unknown to the man who had never given himself to creating beauty and did not know the intimate cost of it, so women, who have brought men into the world and nurtured them until they reach the age for fighting, must experience a peculiar revulsion when they see them destroyed, irrespective of the country in which these men may have been born."[67]

Jane Addams and the others traveled throughout the country asking the women to heed this instinct for life and utilize it. Instinct, she believed, could be a force for change. It was not religious conversion but true femininity in revolt that had, after thousands of years, brought to an end the ancient practice of human sacrifice to the gods, although the high priests were still declaring sacrifice essential to the survival of the tribe.[68] The ironic association of war patriotism and ancient superstition remained in the minds of her listeners, and Jane Addams, especially after 1917, spent an increasing proportion of her speeches in proving that the pacifists were not unpatriotic, but rather strongly insistent that patriotism retain its civilized meaning of nurturing all citizens and responding to economic changes through "rational and peaceful means."[69]

Nevertheless, it was quite clear from the beginning that the cause would mean considerable sacrifice for the women in belligerent countries who would be torn between their pacifism and the desire to be at one with their countrymen.[70] The feminine revolt was useful, however, in two respects. It could expose other "revolts against war," and it might encourage practical changes in national policy. Jane Addams was sure there were other, more silent, rebellions against the war. In the summer of 1915, while she presented the Woman's Peace Party program for neutral mediation to the officials of belligerent and neutral nations, she discovered these revolts and used them as anti-war arguments.

During the war there were two currents in European thought flowing in opposite directions. The surface current was wartime nationalism, heroic, loyal, and full of passionate hatreds. Each additional day of war intensified this current, which was cutting disastrous channels into the foundations of democratic fellowship. Jane Addams, recalling her father's admiration of Mazzini, asserted that nationalism had once provided a unifying ideal. After the turn of the century, however, and especially after 1914, it became divisive and dogmatic. Like the religious fervor of the Spanish Inquisitors, the nationalism of modern Europe lived on its intolerance and persecutions. In 1919 she would interpret the red scare as but another manifestation of this religious nationalism, which feared heresy above all else.[71]

But beneath the obvious national hatreds flowed a deeper current seeking the channels of fellowship and a hopeful future. Civil leaders on both sides confided to Jane Adams their fears that the psychology of war would fix militarism and authoritarianism upon Europe for years to come. So prevalent was this apprehension that Miss Addams puzzled over the fact that neither the Allies nor the Central Powers understood the actual thinking of their supposed enemies. The waters of mutual interest were still and deep while violence frothed on the surface. She attributed this situation largely to a press which deliberately ignored such stirrings while adding color and emphasis to atrocities.[72]

The soldiers also revolted against war, although they fought well. Jane Addams learned that some refused to shoot, that many could be led into the brutal bayonet charges only after their scruples had been dulled by absinthe or brandy. It was not cowardice that gave rise to these scruples, she insisted, after Richard Harding Davis accused her of demeaning brave men—not cowardice but fellowship. The young soldiers had been outgrowing the rigid Victorian nationalism of their fathers when the old men's war thrust them back into it. (It is significant in view of her own experience that she interpreted the war itself as a conflict of generations more than as a conflict of nationalities.) The German lieutenant who told her that he realized there were good men on all sides, the French and British soldiers who confided they found it impossible to kill men who may have been fellow-students or business associates before the war, confirmed Jane Addams' idea that the new internationalism was as much a possession of youth as of the urban immigrants. The war was constricting it, just as the city constricted the family instincts. The wounded soldiers in the ambulances and field hospitals characteristically turned to women for support: "Cannot the women do something about this war? Are you kind to us only when we are wounded?"[73]

It was a sentimental view of women and war—the vision of Florence Nightingale and the mothers who did not raise their boys to be soldiers—but the pacifists drew enough inspiration from it to draw up a very concrete program. The January 1915 meeting of the Woman's Peace Party and the International Congress of Women at The Hague in April 1915 drew very heavily upon the British Union of Democratic Control platform. They advocated parliamentary control over the formulation of foreign policy, including, of course, feminine participation in parliaments and in executive positions. Self-determination meant the recognition of the rights of small nations and of primitive peoples at the peace conference, not great-power domination. They advocated an international organization with a legislature, a judiciary, and an international police force, viewing the latter as a replacement for national armies rather than as an instrument for enforcing peace.

The entire program, which emerged at the same time as the League to Enforce Peace, offered a sharp contrast to that organization. Where the League leaders troubled over questions of structure and sovereignty, the Woman's Peace Party neglected these issues entirely. The League to Enforce Peace was concerned with the nature of sanctions; the pacifists barely mentioned moral and economic sanctions to encourage arbitration. The women opposed the use of military force, and failed to examine the arbitral process. There was no fine distinction between juridical and non-juridical disputes in the Woman's Peace Party platform. The women did not consider the machinery of peaceful settlement as important as the prevention of the economic conflicts that led to war. Most of their program was substantive rather than methodological. The Hague Congress called for an end to all governmental protection of investors conducting business in foreign lands, for the opening of the Panama Canal and the Suez Canal and other international waterways to all traffic in peace and war, for nationalization of the arms industries preceding universal disarmament, and above all for neutral mediation.[74]

The idea of a continuous conference of neutrals mediating between the belligerents even before an armistice was the keystone of the Peace Party platform. Julia Grace Wales, a young English teacher at the University of Wisconsin, had formulated the plan. The Wisconsin legislature and Senator Robert M. La Follette endorsed it. The Wisconsin plan assumed that an open challenge to the belligerents, offered by men without diplomatic status or functions, would awaken latent peace sentiment in Europe. It would provide a means for mediation when the belligerents decided they wanted it. The continuous conference would draw up a peace settlement without consulting the two sides, would receive their replies and suggestions, would revise the proposals, and would continue this process until a settlement had been reached.[75]

Jane Addams, however, interpreted the Wisconsin plan somewhat differently. Emphasizing the apolitical character of the mediators, she declared that if the conference were composed of scientific experts, labor representatives, artists, and humanitarians all of whom shared an "international viewpoint" it would not attempt to split the difference between the belligerents, but instead would probe beneath nationalistic division to discover the real causes of conflict. It would reveal the frustrations of economic and moral needs, the resistance to change, the static and impractical character of international relations that had characterized the prewar period. The mediators might do something about these. For example, they might consider

> . . . the necessity of feeding those people in the southeast portion of Europe who are pitifully underfed when there is a shortage of crops, in relation to the possession of warm-water harbors which would enable Russia to send them her great stores of wheat. Such harbors would be considered . . . not from a point of view of the claims of Russia nor the counter claims of some other nation, but from the point of view of the needs of Europe.[76]

The mediators would act for the international community just as Royce's insurance board and Veblen's technical administrators were to act. There was no evidence, however, that the belligerents would accept such an interpretation of the mediator's role, or, for that matter, the idea of mediation at all. In April 1915, at the joint invitation of the British, German, and Dutch suffragettes, women representing over fifteen countries met at the Hague. After electing Jane Addams chairman of the Congress, they adopted the platform and instructed Jane Addams, Alice Hamilton, Dutch leader Aletta Jacobs, and others to present the Wisconsin plan to neutral and belligerent leaders. These representatives soon discovered the two sides of public opinion in the belligerent countries, calling them the "democratic" and "imperialist" forces. Historian Arno Mayer has called them the "parties of movement" and the "parties of order."[77] They learned that the neutrals at least would support the plan on condition that President Wilson endorsed it.

In 1915 Wilson did not yet appreciate, as he would two years later, the significance (one might say the revolutionary significance) of the "parties of movement." Colonel Edward House had quietly explored with the British, French, and German governments the possibilities for American mediation, and had concluded that Addams naively misinterpreted the views of Lord Grey and others.[78] Moreover, he had been at work during the winter of 1915, while Addams' tour took place the following spring and summer, right after the sinking of the *Lusitania.* The positions of both sides had hardened. With Secretary of State Lansing opposing neutral mediation, and House ridiculing the innocent lady pacifists, Wilson declined to risk his future usefulness by supporting an official neutral conference.[79] The International Woman's Committee turned to support of an unofficial neutral conference.

Just at this juncture the irrepressible Madame Schwimmer decided that the whole plan needed funds, color, and publicity. She appealed to Henry Ford for help. Ford lost no time in stepping front and center, and promptly informed the press that he not only would finance a neutral conference at Stockholm, but that he would attend himself and would hire a ship to bring the delegates to the meeting. He would have the "boys out of the trenches by Christmas." Jane Addams realized that Ford's showmanship was discouraging the most serious participants, but she decided to go to the conference without committing either the Woman's Peace Party or the International Committee. But just before the *Oscar II* sailed forth on a wave of press ridicule, she experienced a serious recurrence of an old kidney and bladder disturbance that sent her to the hospital. Emily Green Balch took her place.[80]

PEACE AND BREAD

American entry into the war killed the last prospects for neutral mediation. Henry Ford had left the neutral conference expedition in Norway. Madame Schwimmer also had resigned. But the Stockholm conference had assembled. It addressed appeals to neutral and belligerent governments alike, appeals embodying much of the Woman's Peace Party program. In February 1917, after the United States broke diplomatic relations with Germany, Ford withdrew his financial support and the conference ended a short time later.[81]

More than the conference died in 1917. The Woman's Peace Party had placed great faith in Woodrow Wilson. Disagreeing with his Caribbean diplomacy, they nevertheless were convinced that he was a rational, peace-loving man. Now Addams and the others felt a sense of betrayal. Was it too much for one man to formulate ideals and then live them, Addams asked. Had Wilson overvalued his own leadership in the future peace conference, as he once had at Princeton? The first note of real bitterness now crept into Addams' writings, measuring the depth of her disillusionment. It was as if Wilson's actions had awakened memories of George Pullman. "What was this curious break between speech and deed," she asked, "how could he expect to know the doctrine [of democracy] if he refused to do the will?"[82] But Wilson had no obligation to the pacifists, while many leaders of social reform did. Most of them abandoned the cause in 1917. The loss of friends, the public ridicule and misunderstanding, and the terrible treatment of conscientious objectors almost drove Jane Addams to complete despair. She never wrote more personally or perceptively than of the psychological effects of war upon the pacifists.

> I experienced a bald sense of social opprobrium and wide-spread misunderstanding which brought me very near to self pity, perhaps the lowest pit into which human nature can sink. Indeed the pacifist in war time, with his precious cause in the keeping of those who control the sources of publicity and consider it a patriotic duty to make all types of peace propaganda obnoxious, constantly faces two dangers. Strangely enough he finds it possible to travel from the mire of self-pity straight to the barren hills of self-righteousness and to hate himself equally in both places.[83]

Fairly soon, Jane Addams found that her loyalty to her "vision of the truth" was not enough. If she hoped to make her stand practical, she would have to act. It is significant that the two most critical decisions in her life, the establishment of Hull House and her adherence to the cause of pacifism during the war, both stemmed from and answered "subjective" as well as "objective" needs. Both had religious overtones. Jane Addams returned to the religious symbol of bread for comfort, and found her new task in working for the Food Administration. She pleaded with American women to conserve food so that others might live. Although she recognized that Hoover's Food Administration was a wartime agency, she considered the implications of inter-Allied control of a common food supply enormous. For the first time an international agency had regulated commercial competition, not in response to an economic theory, but in response to primitive actual needs. If the League of Nations took up this work after the war, it would have all the positive incentive it needed to begin to create an international ethic and an international community.[84]

All her life Jane Addams had searched for union of the practical and the religious, for salvation and the new woman's role, for the humanitarian spirit and the action that should make the difference in the way men actually lived. This was the double meaning that "peace and bread" had for her. The wheat loaf symbolized man's primitive affections and mutual aid, the maternal impulse to nurture the young, the Russian peasant's longing to work the land in peace so that he and his family would not face starvation.[85] Bread now came to mean as well the small, practical beginnings of an international organization, not the grand creation as loudly heralded as Ford's peace ship, but quiet, effective work—the ending of the blockade as a beginning.

In 1919 the Second International Congress of Women, held in Zurich, telegraphed this appeal to the Versailles Conference, asking President Wilson to use his influence to keep the Inter-Allied Commissions in operation as relief agencies.[86] Then the League might extend credits for postwar reconstruction to all needy nations, whether former enemies or not. The international agencies should control strategic waterways, protecting the food trade against nationalistic interference. There should be a specific agency to guard the welfare of migratory laborers who had lost the protection both of their native land and of the nations where they worked. Finally, the mandates commission should act as a probate court protecting the interests of the mandated territories and not of the guardians.[87]

This peculiar linking of the mystical and the practical had begun when Jane Addams explored the anthropological interpretations of the primitive adoration of such figures as the "corn mother." She believed that savage peoples had conceived of nurture and war as opposing forces. Their earliest training was not in fighting but in feeding the young. "Anthropologists insist that war has not been in the world for more than 20,000 years. It is in fact so recent that existing remnants of primitive people do not understand it." Whether or not the anthropology of her day actually confirmed such a generalization is questionable, but the uses that Jane Addams made of it are clear. "Could not the earlier instinct and training in connection with food be aroused and would it not quench the later tendency to war?"[88]

This, indeed, was a key question. Could such functionalism as Jane Addams advocated ever neutralize the conflicting interests of national states and dampen their ardor for plunging into war? In the 1940s most realists thought not. Jane Addams' latter-day critics have pointed out that her stress upon human solidarity neglected the ethnocentric character of human groupings. Critics of functionalism and communalism have maintained that getting the nations to work on programs such as health, food distribution, the fight against illiteracy, where they are likely to agree, does nothing to mitigate their actual struggles for power.[89] John Dewey, on the other hand, contrasted Jane Addams' realism with the mechanistic and force-ridden ideas of collective security and legal-political structures. He maintained that it was eminently more practical to seek to undercut nationalistic motives by appealing to actual needs than to rely upon force, whether national or international.[90] Paradoxically, some of the realists who criticized the world federalists in the 1940s used arguments for the slow growth of internationalism through small practical efforts[91] which resembled the basic tenet of Jane Addams' radicalism.

In the last analysis, Jane Addams' thought was indeed radical. So completely did she identify with all peoples that she refused to ally with any movement that was exclusively of one class or of one nationality. Her ideal remained the peaceful, classless community. And yet her radicalism, as active as it was, never became revolutionary. She neither planned nor advocated the violent destruction of one system of government in order to achieve something more humane. The processes of change were ever as important to her as the results. She unswervingly refused to sacrifice for a cause the precious lives of those for whom she fought. Her romantic discovery of the immigrants of Chicago sustained her and remained her raison d'etre throughout her life. A deep interest in human motives and the faith in human resiliency overcame even the disillusion of war. For in the closing years of her career she still hoped that people would work to create the international community because they would understand their mutual needs. For this most cosmopolitan of women the only eternal truths were those that might be called household truths.

NOTES

[1] Jane Addams, "John Dewey and Social Welfare," *John Dewey, the Man and His Philosophy: Addresses Delivered in New York in Celebration of His Seventieth Birthday* (Cambridge, Harvard Univ. Press, 1930), pp. 141-43; Morton White, *Social Thought in America: The Revolt Against Formalism,* 2nd ed. (Boston, Beacon Press, 1959), p. 96; Morton and Lucia White, *The Intellectual versus the City: From Thomas Jefferson to Frank Lloyd Wright* (New York, Mentor Books, 1964), p. 160.

[2] "Introduction," *The Social Thought of Jane Addams* (Indianapolis, Bobbs-Merrill, 1965), p. xiv.

[3] *Democracy and Social Ethics,* ed. Anne Firor Scott (Cambridge, Harvard Univ. Press, 1964), p. 6.

[4] Christopher Lasch, *The New Radicalism in America, 1889-1963: The Intellectual as a Social Type* (New York, Knopf, 1965), p. 147.

[5] Jane Addams, "Class Conflict in America," *American Sociological Society: Papers and Proceedings,* XI (Dec. 28-31, 1907), 153; "Toward Internationalism," *Woman's Auxiliary Conference of the Second Pan-American Scientific Congress* (Washington, D.C., Dec. 28, 1915-Jan. 7, 1916), p. 59; Oscar Handlin, *The Uprooted: The Epic Story of the Great Migrations That Made the American People* (New York, University Library, n.d.), pp. 173, 185-89.

[6] *Twenty Years at Hull House, with Autobiographical Notes* (New York, Macmillan, 1910), pp. 268, 273.

[7] *Ibid.,* pp. 276-77.

[8] James quoted by Anne Firor Scott, "Introduction," *Democracy and Social Ethics,* p. lxii. For Dewey's definition of creative intelligence, see White, *Social Thought in America,* p. 145.

[9] "The Subjective Necessity for Social Settlements," *Philanthropy and Social Progress: Seven Essays . . . Delivered Before the School of Applied Ethics at Plymouth, Mass., During the Session of 1892* (New York, Crowell, 1893), pp. 12-16; *Twenty Years at Hull House,* pp. 72-73, 77, 88.

[10] *Twenty Years at Hull House,* pp. 15-16; Margaret Tims, *Jane Addams of Hull House* (New York, Macmillan, 1961), pp. 17-19; John C. Farrell, *Beloved Lady: A History of Jane Addams' Ideas on Reform and Peace* (Baltimore, Johns Hopkins Press, 1967), pp. 61-63.

[11] *Twenty Years at Hull House,* pp. 35-36; James Weber Linn, *Jane Addams: A Biography* (New York, Appelton, 1935), pp. 11-13, 16-17, indicates that John Addams business ventures played a central role in the development of Cedarville.

[12] *Twenty Years at Hull House,* p. 21.

[13] "Bread Givers," Address at Rockford Seminary, April 21, 1880, Jane Addams MSS, Swarthmore College Peace Collection; Linn, *Addams Biography,* pp. 42-44, 54, 61; Lasch, *New Radicalism,* pp. 8-10, 16, 21-22.

[14] Jane Addams to Ellen Gates Starr, Feb. 7, 1886, quoted in Lasch, *Social Thought of Addams,* p. 5; cf. *Twenty Years at Hull House,* p. 77.

[15] *Twenty Years at Hull House,* pp. 85-86.

[16] In *Philanthropy and Social Progress,* see "Subjective Necessity for Social Settlements" pp. 1-2, 6, 17, 19; and "The Objective Value of a Social Settlement," pp. 29, 31.

[17] Arthur Mann, "British Social Thought and American Reformers of the Progressive Era," *Mississippi Valley Historical Review,* XLII (March 1956), 683-84.

[18] Daniel Levine, *Varieties of Reform Thought* (Madison, State Historical Society of Wisconsin, 1964), p. 21; Addams, "Subjective Necessity for Social Settlements," p. 26.

[19] "Subjective Necessity for Social Settlements," pp. 10, 12-16.

[20] *Twenty Years at Hull House,* pp. 82-83.

[21] *Ibid.,* pp. 109-10; "Objective Value of Social Settlements," pp. 29-31; Ray Ginger, *Altgeld's America: The Lincoln Ideal versus Changing Realities* (Chicago, Quadrangle Paperbacks, 1965), pp. 27-29.

[22] *Twenty Years at Hull House,* p. 198.

[23] *Democracy and Social Ethics,* pp. 29-31, 34-40, 51.

[24] *Twenty Years at Hull House,* p. 315 (italics added).

[25] Ginger, *Altgeld's America,* pp. 129, 138.

[26] *Twenty Years at Hull House,* pp. 447-48.

[27] "Objective Value of Social Settlements," p. 28; Nicholas Kelley, "Early Days at Hull House," *Social Service Review,* XXVIII (Dec. 1954), 424-29; Ginger, *Altgeld's America,* pp. 129, 132-33, 135-36; Scott, "Introduction," *Democracy and Social Ethics,* pp. xxviii-xxx.

[28] *Hull House Maps and Papers, a presentation of nationalities and wages in a congested district in Chicago. . . .* (New York, Crowell, 1895); Addams, "A Function of the Social Settlement," 1899, *Jane Addams: A Centennial Reader,* ed. Emily Cooper Johnson (New York, Macmillan, 1960), pp. 24-25; A. Elson, "First Principles of Jane Addams," *Social Service Review,* XXVIII (March 1954), 5-6.

[29] Addams, "Tolstoy's Theory of Life," *Chautauqua Assembly Herald,* XXVII (July 14, 1902), 2; Farrell, *Beloved Lady,* p. 65.

[30] *Twenty Years at Hull House,* pp. 235-37.

[31] *Ibid.,* pp. 186-87.

[32] "The Significance of Organized Labor," *Machinists Monthly Journal,* X (Sept. 1898), 551-52; "The Present Crisis in Trade Union Morals," *North American Review,* CLXXIX (Aug. 1904), 179-93; "Trade Unions and Public Duty," *American Journal of Sociology,* IV (Jan. 1899), 448-62, offered her most extended discussion of the labor movement's faults and virtues. Most of the faults stemmed from the efforts of a "partial" movement to correct abuses that could only be cured by the whole public, represented by the government.

[33] *Twenty Years at Hull House,* pp. 444-45.

[34] *Newer Ideals of Peace* (New York, Macmillan, 1907), pp. 12, 91, 210-11.

[35] *Ibid.,* p. 10; *The Spirit of Youth and the City Streets* (New York, Macmillan, 1912), pp. 51-52, 55, 59, 63, 70-71.

[36] In *Universal Peace Congress: Official Report of the Thirteenth Congress* (Boston, Oct. 3-8, 1904), see: "The Responsibilities and Duties of Women toward the Peace Movement," p. 121; and "The Interests of Labor in International Peace," pp. 145-46.

[37] William James, "The Moral Equivalent of War," 1910, *Essays on Faith and Morals,* ed. Ralph Barton Perry (Cleveland, Meridian Books, 1962), pp. 314, 323-26.

[38] *Newer Ideals of Peace,* p. 25.

[39] *Twenty Years at Hull House,* p. 230.

[40] *Newer Ideals of Peace,* p. 18.

[41] *Twenty Years at Hull House,* p. 452; Merle Curti, "Jane Addams on Human Nature," *Journal of the History of Ideas,* XXII (Oct. 1961), 252-53. Curti emphasizes Addams' extraordinary appreciation of unconscious motivations, as well as her knowledge of human growth.

[42] "In Memoriam, Henry Demarest Lloyd," Address, Chicago, Nov. 29, 1903, Jane Addams MSS typescript, p. 2; "Larger Social Groupings," *Charities,* XII (1904), 675; Donald Fleming, "Social Darwinism," *Paths of American Thought,* eds. Arthur M. Schlesinger, Jr. and Morton White (Boston, Houghton Mifflin, 1963), p. 140.

[43] Tims, *Jane Addams,* p. 11; Addams, "The Operation of the Illinois Child Labor Law," *Annals of the American Academy of Political and Social Science,* XXVII (March 1906), 328; Sumner, "The Absurd Effort to Make the World Over," 1894, in *The Conquest of the United States by Spain and Other Essays,* ed. Murray Polner (Chicago, Regnery, 1965), p. 55.

[44] *Twenty Years at Hull House,* p. 133; *Spirit of Youth,* pp. 31-33.

[45] *Twenty Years at Hull House,* p. 162; *Spirit of Youth,* pp. 142-43; *The Long Road of Woman's Memory* (New York, Macmillan, 1916), pp. 64-65; *Democracy and Social Ethics,* pp. 19-22.

[46] *Spirit of Youth,* pp. 15-16, 25-27, 29-30; "Work and Play as Factors in Education," *Chautauguan,* XLII (Nov. 1905), 253; *Newer Ideals of Peace,* pp. 171-72.

[47] "Child Labor Legislation—A Requisite for Industrial Efficiency," *Annals of the American Academy of Political and Social Science,* XXV (May 1905), 543-44; "Arts and Crafts and the Settlement," *Chautauqua Assembly Herald,* XXVII (July 9, 1902), 2-3; *Democracy and So-*

cial Ethics, pp. 209-10, 219-20; "Labor as a Factor in the Newer Conception of International Relationships," Address, National Conference on Foreign Relations of the United States, Academy of Political Science at Long Beach, New York, May 31, 1917, Jane Addams MSS, pamphlet, p. 7.

[48] *Democracy and Social Ethics,* p. 6.

[49] *Ibid.,* p. 220.

[50] *Ibid.,* pp. 141-48; "A Modern Lear: Strike at Pullman," *Survey,* XXIX (Nov. 2, 1912), 131-37. In *Democracy and Social Ethics* Jane Addams did not mention Pullman directly, but her reference was clear. Instead she used the Lear image to portray generational conflict (see pp. 94-99). In "A Modern Lear," she gave not only a fuller account but her most sensitive portrayal of the ethical issues involved between Pullman and Debs's union. For another definition of democratic leadership, see "Exercises in Commemoration of the Birthday of Washington," Address, Chicago, Feb. 23, 1903, Union League Club of Chicago: *Memorial Bulletin* (1903), p. 6.

[51] *Newer Ideals of Peace,* pp. 33-36; see also p. 37: [We] "obstensibly threw off traditional governmental oppression only to encase ourselves in a theory of virtuous revolt against oppressive government, which in many instances has proved more binding than the actual oppression itself."

[52] *Ibid.,* pp. 149-50.

[53] *Ibid.,* p. 223. For a later interpretation of imperialism, emphasizing its relationships to dominant economic interests in the United States, see "Impressions of Mexico," *Women's International League for Peace and Freedom: U.S. Section,* pamphlet (April 1925), pp. 1-2, Society Publications, Hoover Institution.

[54] *Newer Ideals of Peace,* pp. 89, 166.

[55] "Recent Immigration, A Field Neglected by the Scholar," Address, University of Chicago, Dec. 20, 1904, *University Record,* IX (Jan. 1905), 282.

[56] *Newer Ideals of Peace,* p. 18; "Recent Immigration," pp. 277-78, has specific suggestions for immigrant participation in the welfare government of the cities.

[57] *Newer Ideals of Peace,* pp. 184-88, 206-208; "Larger Aspects of the Woman's Movement," *Annals of the American Academy of Political and Social Science,* LVI (Nov. 1914), 4-6; "Votes for Women and Other Votes," *Survey Graphic,* XXVIII (June 1, 1912), 367-68. In 1912 Addams compared the need for women's votes by the welfare state to the need for middle-class votes by the commercial *laissez-faire* states of the early nineteenth century.

[58] *Newer Ideals of Peace,* pp. 237-38.

[59] *The Second Twenty Years at Hull House, September, 1909 to September, 1929, With a Record of Growing World Consciousness* (New York, Macmillan, 1930), pp. 20, 25-27, 31, 34-35, 37; "Charity and Social Justice," Address, National Conference of Charities and Corrections, St. Louis, May 19, 1910, *Survey,* XXIV (June 11, 1910), 441-43, indicates the change in the concept of philanthropy from aid to prevention, a change that required governmental action. Allen F. Davis, "The Social Workers and the Progressive Party, 1912-1916," *American Historical Review,* LXIX (April 1964), 673-74, 676-77, describes the development of the social workers' planks, and their difficulty with all-white Southern delegations.

[60] *Second Twenty Years,* p. 37; William E. Leuchtenberg, "Progressivism and Imperialism: The Progressive Movement and American Foreign Policy, 1898-1916," *Mississippi Valley Historical Review,* XXIX (Dec. 1952), 483-86, 492, 497-98, 500, shows how compatible the ideas of the new nationalism were with imperialism. His description of the majority of Progressives contrasts with Davis' description of the social worker Progressives.

[61] Jane Addams, *Peace and Bread in Time of War,* reprinted with a 1945 introduction by John Dewey (Boston, G. K. Hall, 1960), pp. 3-4, 6; Jane Addams, Paul U. Kellogg, Lillian Wald, "Towards a Peace that Shall Last," *Towards An Enduring Peace: A Symposium of Peace Proposals and Programs 1914-1916* (New York, American Association for International Conciliation, 1916), pp. 233-37; Jane Addams, "Women and Internationalism," *Women at the Hague: The International Congress of Women and Its Results* (New York, Macmillan, 1915), p. 137.

[62] Marie Louise Degen, *History of the Woman's Peace Party* (Baltimore, Johns Hopkins Press, 1939), pp. 28-29, 31-33; Jane Addams, "Larger Aspects of the Woman's Movement," *Annals of the American Academy of Political and Social Science,* LVI (Nov. 1914), 8. The Union of Democratic Control was formed in the fall of 1914 by C. P. Trevelyan, Ramsay McDonald, Norman Angell, and other leaders of the Liberal and Labour Parties. Its platform made parliamentary control of foreign policy, renunciation of secret alliances, nationalization of the arms industries preceding disarmament prerequisites for a democratic league of nations. See Henry R. Winkler, *The League of Nations Movement in Great Britain, 1914-1919* (New Brunswick, Rutgers Univ. Press, 1952), pp. 23-26.

[63] Jane Addams to Lillian Wald, Dec. 8, 1914, Papers of Lillian Wald, New York Public Library.

[64] The self-chosen epitaph on Jane Addams' tombstone reads, "Jane Addams of Hull House and the Woman's International League for Peace and Freedom"; Tims, *Jane Addams,* p. 15; Degan, *Woman's Peace Party,* pp. 35-38; Jane Addams and Carrie Chapman Catt's invitation to the women's organizations, Dec. 28, 1914, is in

Jane Addams' Correspondence, Swarthmore College Peace Collection.

[65] John Higham, "The Reorientation of American Culture in the 1890's," *Origins of Modern Consciousness,* ed. John Weiss (Detroit, Wayne State Univ. Press, 1965), p. 31.

[66] *Second Twenty Years,* pp. 109-10.

[67] "Women and Internationalism," p. 128.

[68] *Second Twenty Years,* p. 120.

[69] "Patriotism and Pacifism in Wartime," Address, Chicago, May 15, 1917, Evanston, Ill., June 10, 1917, Jane Addams MSS, separate pamphlet, p. 2; Linn, *Jane Addams,* 327-33, 349-56, 436, documents Jane Addams' isolation from former friends, and her defenses of her position.

[70] Addams, *Long Road of Woman's Memory,* 116 ff.; "Women and Internationalism," pp. 124-25.

[71] "Americanization," *American Sociological Society: Papers and Proceedings,* XIV (Dec. 29-31, 1919), 206-209, 211-12; *Second Twenty Years,* pp. 153-55.

[72] In *Women at the Hague,* see: "The Revolt Against War," pp. 75-77; and "Factors in Continuing the War," pp. 88-89; in the *Independent,* see: "Peace and the Press," LXXXIV (Oct. 11, 1915), 55-56; and "The Food of War," LXXXIV (Dec. 13, 1915), 430-31.

[73] "Revolt Against War," pp. 59-69, 73-75. Jane Addams' address at Carnegie Hall, New York, July 9, 1915, on the "revolt" raised a storm of protest centering on her charge that stimulants were used before bayonet charges. See New York *Times,* July 13, 1915, p. 10; July 15, 1915, p. 3; July 16, 1915, p. 8; July 24, 1915, p. 4. She observed: "It brought me an enormous number of letters, most of them abusive, but a minimum number from soldiers who had actually been through bayonet charges, and these letters, I am happy to say, were always sympathetic and corroborative" (see *Second Twenty Years,* pp. 131-33; quotation from p. 133).

[74] "Program for a Constructive Peace of the Woman's Peace Party," Jan. 10, 1915, in *The Overthrow of the War System,* ed. Lucia Ames Mead (Boston, Forum Publications, 1915), pp. 125-28; "Resolutions of the International Congress of Women at the Hague," May 1, 1915, *Women at the Hague,* pp. 150-59. Jane Addams later acknowledged the debt of the Woman's Peace Party to the Union of Democratic Control, and called attention to resemblances between the Hague program and the Fourteen Points, without, however, claiming any influence over Wilson. See "Public Address," May 12, 1919, *Bericht des Internationalen Frauenkongress* (Zurich, May 12-17, 1919), p. 196.

[75] Julia Grace Wales, "Continuous Mediation Without Armistice," Pamphlet (Chicago, 1915), pp. 1-13, Woman's Peace Party Pamphlet, Society Publications, Hoover Institution; Degen, *Woman's Peace Party,* pp. 46-47.

[76] "Women and Internationalism," pp. 132-33. Jane Addams repeatedly expressed her faith in the internationalism of scientists, labor unionists, women, and social workers, believing that a basic concern for the advancement of knowledge or of human welfare was the essence of this kind internationalism. See *Long Road of Woman's Memory,* p. 121; *Newer Ideals of Peace,* pp. 113-15; "Public Address," *Bericht des Frauenkongress,* p. 197; "Women's Special Training for Peacemaking," *Proceedings of the Second National Peace Congress* (Chicago, May 2-5, 1909), pp. 252-54; "International Cooperation for Social Welfare," *National Conference of Social Work: Proceedings* (1924), pp. 107-13.

[77] *Wilson vs. Lenin: Political Origins of the New Diplomacy, 1917-1918* (Cleveland, Meridian Books, 1964), pp. vii, 4-8; Emily G. Balch, "The Time for Making Peace," *Women at the Hague,* pp. 113-14.

[78] Charles Seymour, *The Intimate Papers of Colonel House,* 4 vols. (Boston, Houghton Mifflin, 1926-28), II, 22.

[79] Degen, *Woman's Peace Party,* pp. 115-25; Ray Stannard Baker, *Woodrow Wilson: Life and Letters,* 8 vols. (Garden City, N.Y., Doubleday, 1927-39), VI, 122-24.

[80] Degen, *Woman's Peace Party,* pp. 128-48; Louise Bowen to Lillian Wald, Dec. 1, 1915, Wald Papers; Chicago Woman's Peace Party to Aletta Jacobs, Dec. 13, 24, 1915, Woman's Peace Party Correspondence, Addams' folder, Swarthmore College Peace Collection; Addams to David Starr Jordan, Dec. 28, 1915, David Starr Jordan Peace Collection, Hoover Institution.

[81] *Peace and Bread,* pp. 41-46; Neutral Conference for Continuous Mediation: "Appeal to the Governments, Parliaments and Peoples of the Warring Nations," Easter 1916, *Towards an Enduring Peace,* pp. 243-46. The Stockholm program resembled that of the International Congress of Women at the Hague with a much greater emphasis, however, upon the particulars of self-determination. It called for the restoration of Belgium and Alsace-Lorraine; for boundary adjustments between Austria and Italy; and for autonomy for Armenia and other Turkish possessions.

[82] *Peace and Bread,* p. 65. See also pp. 56-60 and 62 for Addams' mixed reactions to Wilson's foreign policies. Lillian Wald to Wilson, Jan. 24, 1917, Wald Papers, describes the pacifists' enthusiastic reaction to Wilson's "peace without victory" speech. The American Union Against Militarism was particularly active during the armed neutrality period, having several specific sugges-

tions to prevent America from going to war. See Wald to Wilson, February 8, 1917, March 16, 1917, *Wald Papers.*

[83] *Peace and Bread,* p. 139.

[84] "The World's Food and World Politics," *National Conference of Social Work* Pamphlet, no. 128 (1918), 2-5; "Statement of the Executive Board of the National Woman's Peace Party," Oct. 27, 1917, Pamphlet, p. 3, Woman's Peace Party, Society Publications, Hoover Institution. The Woman's Peace Party hoped that inter-Allied commissions, working on non-military problems, would become the "nucleus of a permanent international parliament." The contrast with J. B. Clark's idea of an Entente nucleus, united by the threat from outside, could not have been stronger.

[85] *Peace and Bread,* pp. 82, 93-94; "Tolstoy and the Russian Soldiers," *New Republic,* XII (Sept. 29, 1917), 240-42.

[86] This resolution of Mrs. Pethick-Lawrence was adopted unanimously. See *Bericht des Frauenkongress,* p. 195; *Peace and Bread,* pp. 160-61.

[87] *Peace and Bread,* pp. 95-96; "Labor as a Factor in International Relations," p. 5; "Women, War and Suffrage," *Survey,* XXXV (Nov. 6, 1915), 148-49; "The Potential Advantages of the Mandate System," *Annals of the American Academy of Political and Social Sciences,* XCVI (July 1921), 71-73; "Feed the World and Save the League," *New Republic,* XXIV (Nov. 24, 1920), 326. Addams and Alice Hamilton considered the food shortage so critical that they could not wait for governmental or League action, but personally distributed Quaker relief supplies in Germany, Austria, and Poland. Their report on the living conditions in postwar Europe and on the psychological aftermath of war stimulated other relief movements. See "Official Report of Jane Addams and Dr. Alice Hamilton to the American Society of Friends Service Committee, Philadelphia," *Nebraska Branch American Relief Fund for Central Europe* (1919), Pamphlet, 14 pp., Woman's Peace Party, Society Publications. Addams appealed to Congress for a thirty-three million dollar loan to supplement the work of the League and Hoover's American Relief Committee to ease the "hunger oedema" (see U.S. Congress, Senate, Committee on Banking and Currency, *Rehabilitation and Provisions for European Countries: The Need of Assistance in Exporting Our Goods and Rendering Financial Aid Generally in Rehabilitating European Countries: Addams' Statement,* Jan. 21, 1921, 66th Cong., third sess. (Washington, 1921), pp. 3-8.

[88] *Peace and Bread,* pp. 75-76, 78-80. For her ideas of the comparative lateness of war Addams was evidently relying upon Fraser's *The Golden Bough* and possibly upon Kropotkin's *Mutual Aid.* The "peacefulness" of primitive man was one of the communalists' unproven assumptions. Cf. Franz Boas, *Anthropology and Modern Life* (New York, Norton, 1928), pp. 67-68, 93-95, 97-98, for contrary anthropological conclusions.

[89] T. V. Smith, *et al.,* "Discussion of the Theory of International Relations based upon the Introduction by John Dewey to a Re-Issue of Jane Addams' *Peace and Bread in Time of War,*" *Journal of Philosophy,* XLIII (Aug. 30, 1945), 478-79, 481; Frederick L. Schuman, *The Commonwealth of Man: An Inquiry into Power Politics and World Government* (New York, Knopf, 1952), pp. 335-43.

[90] John Dewey, "Democratic vs. Coercive International Organization," 1945, Introduction, *Peace and Bread,* p. xviii.

[91] Carl Becker, *How New Will the Better World Be* (New York, Knopf, 1944), pp. 241-43; Edward Hallett Carr, *Nationalism and After* (London, Macmillan, 1945), pp. 64-70.

Allen F. Davis (essay date 1972)

SOURCE: An introduction to *The Spirit of Youth and the City Streets,* by Jane Addams, University of Illinois Press, 1972, pp. vii-xxx.

[*In the following essay, Davis introduces a new edition of* The Spirit of Youth and the City Streets *with a brief recap of Addams's biography, as well as details of the book's history.*]

Jane Addams always claimed that ***The Spirit of Youth and the City Streets*** was her favorite book. Published in 1909, it received praise from sociologists, psychologists, and other critics. William James wrote in the *American Journal of Sociology*

> Certain pages of Miss Addams' book seem to me to contain immortal statements of the fact that the essential and perennial function of the Youth-period is to reaffirm authentically the value and the charm of Life. All the details of the little book flow from this central insight or persuasion. Of how they flow I can give no account, for the wholeness of Miss Addams' embrace of life is her own secret. She simply inhabits reality, and everything she says necessarily expresses its nature. She *can't help writing truth.*[1]

This was extravagant praise, but it was in no way unique, for in 1909 Jane Addams was probably the most famous woman in America. In that year she became the first woman to receive an honorary degree from Yale University and the first woman to be elected president of the National Conference on Charities and Corrections. Yet she was more than a celebrity; she was treated as a kind of spiritual leader, even a saint. One reviewer called her "The Lady Abbess of Chicago"; another said simply, "Miss Addams is a prophet. She brings us messages from God." But the review continued, "They are always messages for the time."[2] The last sentence was crucial, for Jane Addams was considered by many to be a special American kind of saint—practical, realistic, and useful, with special feminine insight into the problems of urban America. At a time when women were just beginning to take an active role in public life, she became the symbol of what woman could do. "Alert, a deep thinker, progressive, strong and tender-hearted, Jane Addams is a true type of useful American womanhood," *Leslie's Weekly* announced. Mrs. Ethelbert Stewart, wife of the labor leader and journalist, wrote, "I thank God for the intuitive motherhood that has made you see the needs so plainly, and the education and opportunity that has enabled you to express what you see, as we mothers of large families cannot."[3]

The legend of Jane Addams, which depicted her as a heroine and saint, influenced all those in her day who read what she wrote and continues to affect her reputation today. The legend is important in itself, but it obscures what she actually did. A careful reading of ***The Spirit of Youth*** may help separate the myth from the reality, but there are other reasons for a new edition at this time. ***The Spirit of Youth*** is certainly one of Jane Addams's best books. It establishes beyond doubt that she was a literary craftsman as well as a reformer. The book has been overshadowed by her autobiography, ***Twenty Years at Hull House,*** which appeared the next year, and her writing on peace, especially ***The Newer Ideals of Peace*** (1907) and ***Peace and Bread in Time of War*** (1922). Yet ***Spirit of Youth*** has much to tell us today; it offers perspective on youth culture, juvenile delinquency, drug addiction, the generation gap, the search for community in the city, and many other problems that still beset urban America. It is also an important book for understanding the emergence of concern for adolescence in the early twentieth century.

The concept of adolescence, of a time between childhood and adulthood, is such a commonly held assumption about the process of human development that it is accepted without thinking by most people today. Yet, as a number of scholars have recently pointed out, the idea of adolescence has had a relatively short history. The concept of a special time between childhood and adulthood developed gradually during the nineteenth century, but it was not until the first decade of the twentieth century that the idea became firmly planted in the national consciousness.[4]

In pre-industrial, rural societies there was usually no conception of children as a special group. They were seen as miniature adults. The boys were potential farmers or craftsmen, the girls potential mothers and homemakers. In Puritan Massachusetts a child seems to have been considered depraved and treated like an adult, dressed like an adult, and given adult tasks sometime between the ages of six and eight. The eighteenth and nineteenth centuries witnessed a developing concern for childhood as a special time of innocence and development, and gradually the concept of an intermediate period of storm and stress and preparation emerged. This change was tied closely to industrial and urban developments and to the movement of population into the cities. A farm family had a great deal of unity; adults and children shared the same work, entertainment, and friends. But a move to the city often caused the breakdown of the family as an economic unit. Children and adults were separated during the day, and adolescents had much more contact with others of their age group. At the same time new employment opportunities, and eventually state laws, required longer periods of schooling and the extension of childhood. There were class and ethnic distinctions and differences, of course, but industrial and urban changes affected all families to some extent and contributed to the discovery of childhood and adolescence.

After 1825 in the United States there was a great increase in the number of child-rearing books published; examples are Lydia M. Child's *The Mother's Book* (Boston, 1835) and H. W. Bulkeley's *A Word to Parents* (Philadelphia, 1858). These books decried the breakdown of parental authority and the increasing separation of young and old. Also published in greater numbers were books offering advice to adolescents (though the term generally used was "youth"). Such books as Henry Ward Beecher's *Lectures to Young Men* (Boston, 1844), Theodore Munger's *On the Threshold* (Boston, 1881), and Henrietta Keddie's *Papers for Thoughtful Girls* (Boston, 1860) had a wide sale. These books depicted youth as a critical transition period of life, a time when "passions" increased, when temptations had to be faced and overcome. Many writers associated these temptations and dangers with the corrupting influence of the city. Urban life as a corrupter of youth was also a favorite theme in the McGuffey Readers and in much of the popular fiction of the nineteenth century. In the 1890s books began to appear which dealt specifically with the problem of the slum child. Franklin H. Briggs in *Boys as They Are Made and How to Remake Them* (New York, 1894) blamed heredity for most delinquency. But Jacob Riis in *The Children of the Poor* (New York, 1892) argued that crowded tenements and filthy streets had something to do with juvenile crime in the city.

The point is that there was a considerable popular literature relating to youth and the city in the nineteenth century before there was any systematic attempt to study "youth" or adolescence. There was also, beginning in mid-century, a greater concern for "child study," stimulated by Darwin and especially by Friedrich Froebel and the kindergarten movement in Germany. The movement sought to develop the whole personality of the child, not through harsh discipline but, rather, through creative play and an introduction to art and music. In America the leader in the systematic child-study movement was G. Stanley Hall, a psychologist who after 1881 was president of Clark University. Hall's most influential work in this area, published in 1904, was *Adolescence: Its Psychology, and Its Relations to Physiology, Anthropology, Sociology, Sex, Crime and Education.* This encyclopedic work contained an immense amount of information and had a large impact on thinking about adolescence in many fields; indeed, it introduced the term "adolescence" into common usage. Perhaps his most important theory was his idea of "recapitulation," that a child in his growth and development "recapitulated" the history of the race, that babies in their need to grasp and small children in the urge to climb were showing their kinship with the apes. Adolescence in this theory took on a crucial importance, for it represented the most recent of man's great leaps, and the adolescent had the possibility of advancing beyond the present stage of civilization. But Hall also saw this transitional stage as a troubled time of contradiction and emotional stress. Not everyone accepted Hall's ideas, and his theory of "recapitulation" was repudiated within two decades, but his work did serve to focus attention on the child and especially the adolescent.[5]

Jane Addams was familiar with Hall's work, and she used his theories in arguing for more parks and playgrounds for the children who needed an outlet for their animal energies. The romantic belief in the civilizing possibilities of youth that permeates ***The Spirit of Youth*** also owes something to Hall, as do constant references to primitive instincts. Yet she never once used the term "adolescence" in the book, preferring the older and more general word "youth." Her first thought was to call the book "Juvenile Delinquency and Public Morality" or "Juvenile Crime and Public Morals." She rejected these titles because they seemed too sociological, implying facts and figures and footnotes, and she had something more literary in mind, something that would appeal to a wide audience.[6]

Obviously Jane Addams was influenced by the writing of G. Stanley Hall and by the work of sociologists and other experts on adolescence and juvenile crime. But of greater importance were her observations in Chicago and the memories of her own childhood and youth. Part of her genius and success as a writer was her ability to adapt the theories of others and to make universal her own experience. Everything she wrote was in a real sense autobiographical.

Jane Addams grew up in Cedarville, Illinois, a small town near the Wisconsin border. She went to a one-room school, attended church and Sunday school, and roamed the hills and fields with her step-brother and the village children. They played chess, "King and Queen," and "crusades," or occasionally the girls watched the boys organize a sham battle or a parade. In winter they could slide down the gentle hills or skate on the mill pond. On special days, such as the Fourth of July, there were celebrations, and now and then a lecture, a revival meeting, or a wedding became a social occasion for young and old alike. Of course there were daily chores to do: cooking, cleaning, sewing, and needlework for the girls, feeding the cows and horses, splitting wood, and hoeing the garden for the boys. It was assumed by all in the village that girls were more domestic and more submissive than boys. There was little sense of social class in Cedarville. Jane Addams, whose father owned the mill and several farms, as well as the largest house in town, played with the sons and daughters of the hired hands with little idea that she was superior. There was domestic help, of course, yet she learned how to sew and knit and bake bread. There was a sense of community in the small Illinois town, a close association between work and play, between young and old, between men and women of all backgrounds. Distinctions were made, but there was a feeling of belonging.

Cedarville was an important influence on Jane Addams. Like a great many others of her generation, she left the small town. She went away to college, she traveled twice for extended periods in Europe, and eventually she moved permanently to Chicago, but she always found time to visit Cedarville, even in her busiest years. The memories of her childhood became a reference point for evaluating and understanding the massive changes taking place in America during her own lifetime, and they enabled her to become an interpreter of those changes.

In January 1889 Jane Addams and Ellen Starr, a college classmate, moved to Chicago and began to talk about their "scheme." They had a difficult time explaining that their object was not to uplift the masses but to restore communications between the various parts of society, and that they were going to live in the slums as much to help themselves as to aid the poor. Some laughed at their idea, others ignored them, but a surprisingly large number of men and women rallied to their cause and offered assistance. They quickly learned that they were not the first people in America to have the idea of a settlement. Stanton Coit, also influenced by Toynbee Hall, had established a settlement in New York in 1886. In 1887 a group of Smith College graduates organized College Settlement Association, which founded a settlement in New York barely a week before Miss Addams and Miss Starr moved into the dilapidated mansion that would become Hull House. It was obvious even before they began that they were a part of a national, indeed an international, movement, and still they had only the vaguest notion of what they would do once they had moved in. They knew they wanted to be neighbors to the poor, but beyond that they were not sure.

They furnished the house, put the pictures they had collected in Europe on the walls, and began doing what they knew best—teaching, lecturing, and explaining their art objects. Ellen Starr started a reading group to discuss George Eliot's *Romola,* and they organized art exhibits. One of their tasks, they firmly believed, was to bring an appreciation of beauty and art to those forced to live in the drab environment of the slums. But they soon discovered that the neighbors had more immediate concerns than art and literature. They needed better food, clothing, and housing. The cultural activities of Hull House remained important, but very quickly the settlement became involved in attempts to improve conditions in the neighborhood, the city, and the nation.[7]

From the beginning it was the plight of the children and the young people that depressed the settlement workers most. They opened a kindergarten, began clubs and classes for the older children, and established the first public playground in Chicago in 1893. They also became aware of the horrors of child labor. The sallow-cheeked youngster forced to work twelve hours a day in a factory, the stunted and deformed and crippled children in the neighborhood were constant reminders of the problem. But the campaign against child labor really began when Florence Kelley moved to Hull House at the end of 1891. A large and powerful woman, educated at Cornell and the University of Zurich, she was an expert social investigator and a socialist. More radical than Jane Addams and the other residents, she forced them to confront the working and living conditions in the city. As chief factory inspector for Illinois, a job she held for four years, she made careful studies documenting the extent of child labor in the area and then mobilized a campaign to pass a state law against the abuse.

Florence Kelley was only one of a remarkable group of talented women who made Hull House the vital institution it became. There was also Julia Lathrop, a graduate of Vassar, an executive with a sense of humor and a passion for research. Alzina Stevens, a former labor leader, and Mary Kenny, a vivacious Irish girl from the neighborhood who became a labor organizer for the American Federation of Labor, both participated. Later there were Alice Hamilton, a doctor who became an expert on industrial disease, Grace and Edith Abbott, two sisters from Nebraska who pioneered in working with immigrants and became leaders in a variety of reform movements, and many more. A number of wealthy and socially prominent Chicago women never became residents, but they gave their time and money to the settlement. Most important of these talented and dedicated women were Mary Rozet Smith, Jane Addams's long-time friend and constant companion, and Mrs. Louise deKoven Bowen, a strong-minded woman who donated several buildings at Hull House as well as the summer camp and who served as treasurer and trustee of the settlement.

There were men too: residents like Edward Burchard and George Hooker, as well as others who came for a few months or a few years, such as the historian Charles Beard, William Lyon Mackenzie King, the future prime minister of Canada, and Gerard Swope, who would one day be president of General Electric. Many others, some famous, others unknown, visited the settlement or dropped in for a meal or a lecture. Over it all presided Jane Addams, called "Miss Addams" by all but her closest friends and treated with awe and almost reverence by many of the residents. She was occasionally resented, even hated, but she had the ability to solve differences, calm disagreements, and engineer compromises. She was given credit in the press for all that was accomplished at Hull House when often it was someone else who was responsible for an innovation. But Jane Addams was the acknowledged leader, the publicist, the one who wrote the articles and the books, made the speeches, and related the activities in and around Hull House to broader conceptions and movements.

Jane Addams and the others at Hull House were constantly studying their neighborhood, discovering problems which led them to initiate reforms at the city, state, or national level. Their concern for playgrounds and the need for parks and recreation led them to promote recreation centers in the city and to participate in the national play movement. When the National Playground Association of America was formed in 1906, Jane Addams was on the executive committee. The Hull House residents' experiments with kindergartens and adult education made them pioneers in progressive education. They tried to make the classroom relate to the reality of the world, and they believed that the school should be the center of the community. Their thinking paralleled that of John Dewey, and for good reason. Dewey was a good friend of the Hull House group, a frequent visitor to the settlement, and a member of the board of trustees. He learned from Hull House as the settlement workers learned from him.

Interest in young people in the neighborhood led the settlement residents to begin many other programs. Jane Addams was concerned with the widening split she observed between the immigrants and their children. As the children became Americanized, they tended to rebel against the language, customs, religion, and even the clothes of their mothers and fathers. In order to illustrate that the ways of the old country were not useless, she encouraged festivals and the preservation of native handicrafts, and in 1900 she organized the Hull House Labor Museum. By employing some of the older artisans as teachers, the Hull House reformers hoped to restore some of the immigrants' pride in the heritage of the Old World while at the same time giving the younger generation an appreciation of that heritage. They also believed that by showing the history of the textile industry or the process by which wheat was made into bread, or by teaching the ancient art of pottery making or wood carving, that they could demonstrate the relationship between raw material and finished product, a relationship that had disappeared in the modern factory. They also hoped to restore a pride in workmanship and a respect for useful things of beauty. Unfortunately, it was often a forlorn hope and a romantic dream.

The Labor Museum, the clubs and classes, and other activities did not keep the young people who lived in the Hull House neighborhood from getting into trouble with the law. The settlement workers were disturbed that many juvenile offenders were picked up for minor offenses and then were thrown together with hardened criminals. The spirit of adventure, the impulsive action, that would be of little consequence for the rural youth often resulted in a prison term and a life of crime for the city youngster. Concerned about this situation, the Hull House group agitated for the new law that, in 1899, provided for the first juvenile court in the nation. The juvenile court was not a criminal court, and it was supposed to keep the rights and interests of the offender chiefly in mind. The judge could put the delinquent on probation, make him a ward of the state, or assign him to an institution. While the main idea was to help rather than to penalize the child, it did not always work out that way, for the judge had great power while the offender had none of the rights of due process. Not until 1967 did a U.S. Supreme Court decision recognize that even juvenile offenders were entitled to procedural rights. Still, at the time, the juvenile court represented a major breakthrough in the treatment of boys and girls in trouble. Alzina Stevens of Hull House was the first probation officer of the court, and Julia Lathrop and then Mrs. Bowen were successively chairwomen of the Juvenile Court Committee. Through the cases that came before the court the Hull House residents had a chance to study systematically the problem of the juvenile delinquent and to try to understand why he got into trouble with the law. Jane Addams used material collected by the juvenile court to illustrate ***Spirit of Youth,*** and she dedicated the book to Mrs. Bowen, the chairman of the court committee.

The tragedy and pathos of the young offenders who came before the juvenile court not only inspired Jane Addams's book but also stimulated further attempts to solve the problem of juvenile crime. In 1909, the same year that ***The Spirit of Youth*** was published, the Hull House reformers organized the Juvenile Protective Association, an outgrowth of the Juvenile Court Committee. One of its purposes was to control or eliminate poolrooms, bars, dance halls, theaters, and other institutions that the committee felt were breeders of crime and vice. Also in 1909 the reformers founded the Juvenile Psychopathic Institute at Hull House. Under the direction of Dr. William Healy, it became a leading center for research into the causes of delinquency. Healy's careful studies resulted in such books as *The Individual Delinquent* (1915), which rejected the theory that delinquency and crime were primarily caused by heredity. He emphasized that while delinquency had many causes, environment was the most important. In a more informal way, without the scientific evidence, Jane Addams came to a similar conclusion in her book.

Jane Addams wrote ***The Spirit of Youth,*** as she wrote most of her books, by first approaching a topic in a speech, then reworking it into an article, and finally arranging and rewriting the articles into a book manuscript. She revised constantly. The first time she gave a speech she often spoke from notes, talking quietly and calmly with a voice that could be heard easily throughout the auditorium. She illustrated her points with stories of people, sometimes pathetic, occasionally heroic, but always believable. As she gave the speech again and again, the timing became better, the illustrations sharper, until gradually she developed a polished manuscript. Usually she wrote her material out by hand (a hand that became increasingly more difficult to decipher the busier she became) before giving it to a secretary to type. Then she would cut up the typed manuscript, putting it back together again with common pins while writing in transitions and new ideas.

Jane Addams thought of herself as a professional writer and took pride in her published work. "I have always liked to write," she told a reporter, "even as a girl in school. Later when I spent a few months in Europe I took great interest in the expressive arts. I have had this feeling in everything I have written; I have not written as a philanthropist merely."[8] Her articles appeared in a great variety of magazines, and often the same basic article appeared in several different places. She asked no fee from such journals as *Charities and the Commons* or *The Public,* but from the *Ladies' Home Journal* or *McClure's* she could drive a hard bargain.

She also drove a hard bargain when it came to signing a book contract. Her books were published by the Macmillan Company, in large part because Richard T. Ely, economist, professor at the University of Wisconsin, and academic entrepreneur, had persuaded her to do a book for a series he was editing for Macmillan called the Citizen's Library. The book turned out to be ***Democracy and Social Ethics,*** published in 1902. Her next book, ***The Newer Ideals of Peace,*** appeared in the same series in 1907. As her reputation spread, Edward Marsh, the Macmillan editor, realized what a valuable property he had, and he gently prodded her through friendly letters to work on another book. His efforts paid off; in February 1909 she wrote suggesting she might have a manuscript on juvenile delinquency ready by 15 October. Marsh was delighted and offered her "a royalty of 13% on the retail price of the first 1500 copies sold and 15% on all copies sold thereafter." Jane Addams replied quickly:

> The terms you suggest are not as advantageous as those your company gave me for ***Newer Ideals of Peace.*** I have just looked over your account rendered April 30th, 1908, and find that I received 16¼ per cent upon 1112 copies of ***Newer Ideals of Peace*** and 16¼ per cent upon 497 of ***Democracy and Social Ethics,*** I am not able at this moment to lay my hand upon the original agreement, but I remember being paid an out and out sum when the manuscript was delivered. I think the sum was $100.[9]

As it turned out, she had confused 16¼ cents per copy with the percentage, which had been 13 on the previous books, but this penchant for bargaining for every dollar, for getting the best possible contract, was very much a part of her personality.

A determined pride and high professional standards motivated her as she prepared the book. It was to be composed of essays and speeches she had done over a period of two years, a speech before the National Society for the Promotion of Industrial Education, an article that had appeared in *Charities and the Commons* called **"Public Recreation and Social Morality,"** an address given for the New York Playground Association, an article that had been published in the *Ladies' Home Journal* called **"Why Girls Go Wrong,"** and some other material. In the spring and summer of 1909 she spliced the pieces together, rearranging and rewriting until she had a finished manuscript—a manuscript that, unlike some of her other work, was changed very little as it passed from typescript to galley proof to page proof. The book was published in November 1909 with two excerpts appearing in the *Ladies' Home Journal* in October and November. The Macmillan editor was not sure he liked the title of the book and was worried about confusion of copyright arising from the magazine excerpts and the book coming out so closely together, but he did appreciate the speed and efficiency with which Jane Addams worked. It had been barely nine months since she had suggested that she might have a manuscript ready for fall. Yet she could still write to a friend, "I am sending you a copy of the book which I regard with mixed emotions, one is gratitude that it is out at last, and the other regret that I did not fuss with it longer."[10]

The book was received with immediate enthusiasm. Professional reviewers, friends, sociologists, settlement workers, ministers, and ordinary citizens showered the book with praise, not only for its content but also for its literary style. And the book sold—7,000 copies during the first year and a total of 18,000-20,000 during Jane Addams's lifetime—and many more got the message through her speeches and articles. One of the reasons for the success of the book, aside from the fact that Jane Addams wrote it, was its calm, optimistic answer to the problem of juvenile delinquency. She praised the exuberance, the energy, the good intentions, the creative possibilities of young people, and argued that it was only necessary to channel this creative force in the right direction.

Perhaps the most remarkable aspect of the book, given the time that it was written, was Jane Addams's appreciation of the importance of sex and the basic erotic instincts, although she did assume that the sex drive is more important for the male than for the female. She referred to "the emotional force," the "fundamental instinct," "this sex susceptibility." Although she knew nothing of Freud, she suggested that the sex drive furnished "the momentum toward all art." She argued that this natural instinct, if repressed, served as "a cancer in the very tissues of society" and resulted in all kinds of deviant behavior. A good portion of the book is taken up with descriptions of how the modern city overstimulates the adolescent. "The newly awakened senses are appealed to by all that is gaudy and sensual, by flippant street music, the highly colored theater posters, the trashy love stories, the feathered hats, the cheap heroics of the revolvers displayed in the pawnshop windows," as well as movie theaters, dance halls, prostitution, and drugs.

The rural youth of another age, and of her memory, never had to face these temptations. In rural America the quest for adventure led to harmless pranks, but in the city the same impulse resulted in arrest and jail. She never argued for turning the clock back, for returning to the world of the small town, but rather she insisted on the need to channel and sublimate the natural drives of youth into creative and socially acceptable paths. She suggested Molière and Shakespeare to replace the cheap movie, chaperoned parties to compete with the dance halls, recreation centers and settlements to substitute for the saloon, parks and playgrounds and competitive sports to replace the spirit of adventure associated with drugs and liquor. She realized how difficult it was to find a "moral equivalent" for juvenile deliquency, and yet she revealed a certain naïve optimism in believing that her substitute would work. She is much more convincing in describing the irresistible attraction of the train, the movies, and the dance halls than in defining the alternatives. There is an assumption throughout that the lower-class urban environment of saloons, dance halls, and street life needed to be changed and made more like a middle- or upper-class neighborhood. And yet the book is amazingly free of moral superiority and puritanical preaching.

There was, however, another and more fundamental cause for the discontent of youth in the city—the industrial system which employed them for long hours in meaningless jobs. The city youth was not able to expend his energy in a worthwhile job as the rural youth could, for factory work tired only the nerves and the senses, not the body. Jane Addams understood the dullness and monotony of factory work, but her solutions seem to beg the question. She accepted the industrial revolution and realized that the machine was here to stay, but she had no great faith in technology. She wanted to control the machine so that it would not destroy the man who was forced to run it. She also wanted to preserve the art and skill of the craftsman. She put great faith in a practical industrial education to train young men and women for the real jobs they would be doing. She argued for a team spirit (for a kind of giant Labor Museum), so that thirty-nine men all working on the same product would appreciate that they were actually a meaningful part of one operation. She supported a revolt against shoddy, poorly designed products and against dehumanizing working conditions. But never did she carry her arguments to their logical conclusion and suggest that there was something fundamentally wrong with the industrial system. In the end, although she carefully documented the destruction being wrought by the factory, the best she could offer was to help adjust young people to the system and make them a little happier in the process.

Jane Addams sent a copy of her book to Vida Scudder, a Christian Socialist, an English professor at Wellesley College, and one of the founders of the College Settlement Association. After praising the "rare and lovely tenderness" of the book, Miss Scudder continued, "I rebuke myself, but I grow heavy of heart as the years pass on, 'save the children,' was our cry when the settlements started twenty years ago. Those children are men and women now, fathers and mothers and still we raise the same cry and hold the new generation under the same stupid and criminal conditions as the old. How long, O Lord how long?"[11] But Jane Addams, like most of the progressives, was more optimistic; unlike the socialists, she still had faith that the system could be patched up and made to work, that the right legislation would solve the difficulties. At the end of the book she poses the alternatives: "We may either smother the divine fire of youth or we may feed it. We may either stand stupidly staring as it sinks into a murky fire of crime and flares into the intermittent blaze of folly or we may tend it into a lambent flame with power to make clean and bright our dingy city streets." In 1972 the city's streets are still dingy, and another generation is held "under the same stupid and criminal conditions as the old." It is easy now to reject the optimism of Jane Addams and echo the cry of Vida Scudder, "How long, O Lord how long?"

Yet as one reads ***The Spirit of Youth,*** despite its romantic optimism and its occasional archaic language, one is struck by the contemporary relevance of the book. Jane Addams used "colored" rather than "black," but already in 1909 she appreciated the need for the black youngster to search for his identity in an African past. Her discussion of the drug problem sounds as if it were written yesterday. She had little faith that the machine and technology would solve America's problems, as some did in her time. She occasionally betrayed the concern for racial differences that fascinated her generation, but she avoided seeing in those differences the cause of delinquency, as Jacob Riis and others did. She referred constantly to "primitive instincts" and the "primitive spirit of adventure," but she rejected the theory of Cesare Lombroso, still popular in 1909, that the criminal is an "atavistic reversal" or throwback to a more primitive form of man. Indeed, she rejected all versions of the hereditary explanation for delinquency and emphasized the child's relation to his environment, his family, and his neighborhood, while many experts in her day were finding the cause of delinquency in race, body type, or mental deficiency.

Jane Addams did not design the elaborate theory of growth and development that has characterized the work of Erik Erikson, but she does describe young people going through an "identity crisis." She appreciated the alienation and disaffection of the young in an urban and industrial world where there is little chance for a meaningful job or sense of community, and she would have agreed with many of the points made by Paul Goodman in *Growing Up Absurd.* Although by "youth" Jane Addams meant the time of life that Kenneth Keniston calls adolescence, rather than a post-adolescent period that is the product of a post-industrial age, she would agree with him that "it is a time of turmoil, fluctuations, and experimentation, when passing moods and enthusiasms follow each other with dizzying speed. The adolescent has little lasting sense of solidarity with others or with a tradition, and little ability to repudiate people and ideas that are foreign to his commitments."[12] Most of all, Jane Addams shares with Erikson, Keniston, and Goodman a faith in the potential, in the civilizing and regenerative power of the young—that more than anything else permeates every page of her book.

NOTES

[1] *American Journal of Sociology* XV (Jan. 1910): 553. He said about the same thing in a letter to Jane Addams but added that it was "hard not to cry at certain pages." William James to Jane Addams, 13 Dec. 1909, Jane Addams Manuscripts, Swarthmore College Peace Collection.

[2] Harriet Park Thomas in *American Journal of Sociology* XV (Jan. 1910): 552-53; *New York Observer,* 16 Dec. 1909.

[3] *Leslie's Weekly,* 9 Dec. 1909; Mrs. Ethelbert Stewart to Jane Addams, Dec. 1909, Swarthmore College Peace Collection.

[4] This and the following paragraphs depend heavily on Philippe Aries, *Centuries of Childhood: A Social History of Family Life,* tr. Robert Baldick (New York, 1962); John and Virginia Demos, "Adolescence in Historical Perspective," *Journal of Marriage and the Family* XXXI (Nov. 1969): 632-38; John Demos, *A Little Commonwealth: Family Life in Plymouth Colony* (New York, 1970); Bernard Wishy, *The Child and the Republic: The Dawn of Modern American Child Nurture* (Philadelphia, 1968). See also Joseph M. Hawes, *Children in Urban Society: Juvenile Delinquency in Nineteenth-Century America* (New York, 1971), and Joseph F. Kett, "Adolescence and Youth in Nineteenth-Century America," *Journal of Interdisciplinary History* II (Autumn, 1971), 283-98.

[5] On Hall's ideas, see Lawrence A. Cremin, *The Transformation of the School: Progressivism in American Education, 1876-1957* (New York, 1961), pp. 101-4, and Nathan G. Hale, Jr., *Freud and the Americans: The Beginnings of Psychoanalysis in the United States, 1876-1917* (New York, 1971), pp. 100-109.

[6] Edward Marsh to Jane Addams, 23 Feb. 1909, Swarthmore College Peace Collection.

[7] See Allen F. Davis, *Spearheads for Reform: The Social Settlements and the Progressive Movement* (New York, 1967); and Allen F. Davis and Mary Lynn McCree, eds., *Eighty Years at Hull House* (Chicago, 1969), for the story of the growth and impact of Hull House.

[8] *New York Sun,* 30 Apr. 1910.

[9] Marsh to Addams, 15, 23 Feb. 1909; Addams to Marsh, 25 Feb. 1909, Swarthmore College Peace Collection.

[10] Jane Addams to Julia Lathrop, n.d., 1909, Swarthmore College Peace Collection.

[11] Vida Scudder to Jane Addams, 13 Nov. 1909, Swarthmore College Peace Collection.

[12] The quotation is from Kenneth Keniston, *Young Radicals: Notes on Committed Youth* (New York, 1969). For Erikson, see especially *Childhood and Society* (New York, 1950) and *Identity, Youth and Crisis* (New York, 1968).

J. O. C. Phillips (essay date 1974)

SOURCE: "The Education of Jane Addams," in *History of Education Quarterly,* Vol. 14, Spring, 1974, pp. 49-67.

[*In the following essay, Phillips identifies Addams's intellectual forebears, a group that ranges from Abraham Lincoln to Auguste Comte.*]

Perhaps as a final tribute to a nineteenth century individualism soon to be extinguished by the New Deal, Americans of the late twenties and early thirties frequently amused themselves in endless polls and competitions to find America's greatest men and women. The definitive order of greatness was never discovered, but in every poll Jane Addams did well. Included in Mark Howe's list of six outstanding Americans, she received *Good Housekeeping*'s seal of approval as the greatest living American woman. But in 1933 the National Council of Women failed her. They declared her the second greatest American woman. First was Mary Baker Eddy.[1] Jane Addams, who treasured such symbols of fame, may well have felt considerable pique at being so linked with the founding mother of Christian Science. The two women certainly appear very different types. Where Mrs. Eddy achieved power through establishing a church, Jane Addams, except for one brief episode, was never involved in organised religion; where Mrs. Eddy exploited the world of the spirit, Jane Addams consciously entered the grubby world of the slum; where Mrs. Eddy sought to cure bodies through faith, Jane Addams' solution was better housing, higher wages, and better garbage disposal. Later historians have reinforced the contrast. Some have viewed Jane Addams as an energetic feminist, which Mrs. Eddy decidedly was not; Christopher Lasch, in the most widely accepted interpretation, has seen Jane Addams as the first of a new class, the intellectuals, whose animus was a revolt against middle class gentility and particularly against the constrictive atmosphere of the 19th century family.[2] Mrs. Eddy for all her interest in the mind, was no modern intellectual, nor did she reject the family.

It is against such interpretations that this paper is leveled. In my view the National Council of Women may have spoken truer than they realized by joining Mrs. Eddy and Jane Addams. For Jane Addams' career was shaped by the same problem that impelled Mrs. Eddy: How did an ambitious egotistical woman in 19th century America break through the incredibly limited bounds which the domestic piety tradition had established for women. Woman's sphere was the home and family, but achievement could only be won in the society outside; woman's nature was to be self-sacrificing, where achievement seemed to require self-assertion; and woman was seen as the keeper of things spiritual, while achievement apparently had to be won in the material world. Mrs. Eddy's solution was to elevate the religious definition of women and create her own church. For Jane Addams that option was out. Not only had Mrs. Eddy already fashioned a monopoly in the field, but Darwin and the growing secularisation of society made a competing spiritual enterprise increasingly less viable. Jane Addams had to find an alternative outlet for her ambition, and the solution which she found goes a long way to explain the position of women in 20th century America. For, as the National Council of Women unwittingly revealed, it was a solution that bore haunting similarities with that of Mary Baker Eddy.

The problem as faced by Jane Addams involved three determining forces. The first was the traditional definition of woman, the ideology of domestic piety. Here her conditioning was early and severe. Born in Illinois in 1860, she was sent at the age of 17 to Rockford Seminary in her home state. Rockford was begun in 1847 by Congregational and Presbyterian pastors as a female seminary distinct from the degree-giving men's college of Beloit. Its conservative religious aims were solidly instituted by its first head, Anna P. Sill, who had come west after an awakening in the New York revivals of 1831 to sacrifice herself for Christian service. Rockford conceived of its aim as "to develop moral and religious character in accordance with right principles, that it may send out cultivated Christian women in the various fields of usefulness." Those fields were clearly prescribed. Rockford girls were to be "Christian Mothers and Missionaries for the Evangelization of the World." Christian instruction and worship was frequent and intense; and an ethic of "self-denying benevolence toward all" was firmly instilled. For those who would become mothers and wives rather than missionaries, special skills were needed. The curriculum aimed "to combine, to a limited extent, domestic and industrial training with the intellectual culture imparted by classical and literary study; realizing that the chief end of women's education is not simply to shine in society, but to elevate and purify and adorn the home." The dominant ethos of Rockford Seminary then was the domestic piety tradition. Most of Jane Addams' classmates did indeed become either mothers or missionaries; and the emotional core of its ideology—the belief in a missionary spirit of self-sacrificing altruism, the praise of motherhood and family became one of the defining terms of her future life.[3]

The second determinative influence of her life, and one that pointed in a very different direction, came from the active achieving world of men—through the example of her father. Jane Addams' mother had died in infancy, and although her father remarried when Jane was eight, she was never at all close to her stepmother. Instead, she writes of her father, "I centred upon him all that careful imitation which a little girl ordinarily gives to her mother's ways and habits." John Addams became the model, the superego for his daughter. It was a strong model. He had moved from Pennsylvania to Illinois in 1844, and through hard work and shrewd business skill had established a successful flourmill. He came to personify for Jane the activism of the West, the striving will of the selfmade man, and, in her own words, "the sturdy independence of the pioneer." In addition, John Addams was a public figure, for many years a state senator, and as an early Illinois Republican a close friend of Abraham Lincoln. As a child Jane was very conscious of the two pictures of Lincoln in her father's bedroom, and his carefully kept packet of letters from Lincoln each beginning "My dear double D'ed Addams." "For one or all of these reasons," she writes, "I always tended to associate Lincoln with the tenderest thoughts of my father." In her mind the two Illinois pioneers fused into a powerful image and example of Civil War heroism, of public-spirited achievement.[4]

In the context of Rockford Seminary in the 1870's the force of her father's example was crucial. It gave her the strength to resist the evangelical pressures of Rockford. John Addams never joined a church and he never had Jane baptised. But he did teach Sunday school, and it was he who first drew his daughters into "the moral concerns of life." Her father became in a sense, both Jane's priest and her God. It was his wrath, not God's, that she feared when she committed some childish misdemeanour. Her father's code of ethics became her religion.[5] The challenge of Rockford's Christian indoctrination brought this to consciousness. In her letters to her friend Ellen Gate Starr, written while at Rockford, she agonizes over her religious state. She knows that she ought to believe in Christ but finds she cannot. "I have been trying an awful experiment. I didn't pray, at least formally, for about three months, and was shocked to find that I feel no worse for it. . . . I feel happy and unconcerned and not in the least morbid." She has to conclude that "Christ don't help me in the least," and has to make do with the creed "ever be sincere and don't fuss." Instead of reading the Bible, she turns to Carlyle, and finds in his praise of the hero a religious inspiration to search for moral perfection which accords well with her father's example.[6] Religion becames not a matter of Christian dogma, but of ethics in the service of man. This humanistic conclusion was important. It closed off church missionary work as a career option, and, of more significance, it implied a challenge to the evangelical and narrowly Christian assumptions that lay behind the domestic piety tradition.

The third great social influence in Jane Addams' life was a changing mood in women's education during the 1870's.[7] Increasingly arguments were heard that women should not simply attend seminaries for training in the social graces and the Christian virtues of motherhood. Instead they should attend degree-giving colleges and have an education that would tune the intellect. Vassar, Smith and Wellesley were the institutional expression of this new climate of opinion. John Addams, once a defender of Susan B. Anthony before the Illinois legislature and long an advocate of greater rights for women, gave cautious approval to Jane's interest in the movement. She had initially hoped to go to Smith, but once at Rockford, and very much against Anna Sill's opposition, she led the fight to transform the school from a seminary to a college. When that fight succeeded Jane Addams became Rockford's first B.A. She began to see science, that traditionally masculine subject, as the great means of expanding women's mission. She founded a scientific society, spent her vacation with her brother in pressing plants and stuffing birds, and a year after leaving Rockford presented the college with $1000 for the purchase of scientific books.[8] In her graduating essay Jane Addams took the theme of Cassandra and the female fate "always to be in the right, and always to be disbelieved and rejected." But Jane suggested a solution "There is a way opened, women of the 19th century, to convert your wasted force to the highest use . . . only by the accurate study of at least one branch of physical science can the intuitive mind gain that life which the strong passion of science and study feeds and forms."[9] Science was the path to new territories for women. Superficially this mood may appear to have offered real opportunities for women's liberation. Could not Jane Addams, guided by the active public career of her father, detached from the evangelical ethos, and armed with the weapons of intellect, launch an open attack on the whole doctrine of a women's sphere? Could not she begin to claim true equality with men? Perhaps, but hardly likely. For the more one examines this educational movement in the 1870's, the more its conservative animus becomes apparent. It was in no sense an attack on the domestic piety tradition. It was merely believed that women would carry out their spiritual and cultural mission more effectively with the aid of a true college education. Smith's motto expressed it perfectly, "Add to your virtue, knowledge." In that atmosphere then an attack on the old doctrines was never really a live option for Jane Addams. Unwittingly she slipped into a course that would be crucial for 20th century women. She would not satisfy her yearnings for an active and intellectual life through rejecting the doctrine of spheres. She would simply expand that doctrine to accommodate her growing ambition. Her attitude was summed up in a speech given at her class exhibition in 1880. The exhibition itself was seen as proof of women's new intellectual confidence, and Jane's decision to speak about it in public was seen as subversive radicalism by the earnest Miss Sill. The sense of exciting new possibilities echoes through the speech. In welcoming visitors to the first Junior exhibition, Jane Addams claims, "The fact of its being the first, seems to us a significant one, for it undoubtedly points more or less directly to a movement which is gradually claiming the universal attention. We mean the change which has taken place during the last fifty years in the ambition and aspirations of women; we see this change most markedly in her education. It has passed from accomplishments and the arts of pleasing, to the development of her intellectual force, and her capabilities for direct labor." Then, however, she continues, the modern woman "wishes not to be a man, nor like a man, but she claims the same right to independent thought and action . . . We, then, the class of

1881 in giving this our Junior exhibition, are not trying to imitate our brothers in college; we are not restless and anxious for things beyond us, we simply claim the highest privileges of our time, and will avail ourselves of its best opportunities. But while on the one hand, as young women of the 19th century, we gladly claim these privileges, and proudly assert our independence, on the other hand we still retain the old ideal of womanhood—the Saxon lady whose mission it was to give bread unto her household."[10] The "on the one hand and on the other" expressed the strained compromise achieved by Jane Addams as she graduated from college in 1881. Her father had provided her with a model of pioneer activism and an ambition for heroic public achievement of Lincolnesque proportions. From the new mood in women's education she had won a confidence that education and especially science would win new respect for the female spirit. But this larger vision was always to be contained within the narrow confines of woman's traditional sphere. Jane still clung tenaciously to the Rockford view that woman's chief obligations were to the home and family, that woman's character was spiritual and self-abnegating. It was the effort to embody these somewhat contradictory demands in some vocational form which shaped the pattern of Jane Addams' subsequent career.

Just how contradictory those demands were, was painfully revealed in the 8 years after she left college. She found herself caught between the intellectual achieving world of men, and the maternal spiritual world of women. Access to the first was harshly cut off in the summer of 1881 with the death of her beloved father. Gone was her model, her cue for achievement. And in her one brief effort at a professional career, as a student at the Women's Medical School at Philadelphia, she dropped out ignominiously after seven months of misery. Options in the female world were similarly closed off. After an operation to cure the spinal problems she had suffered from childhood, she sadly learnt that she could never have children; and three years later in 1885 she turned down the offer of marriage of her stepbrother George Haldeman. Jane would never be a wife or mother. Her very femininity was thrown in doubt. Yet other traditional female roles were tried and found wanting. Launched upon the genteel waters of Baltimore society, she found it mindless and insipid. She was too intelligent and ambitious to live as a polished adornment. Twice she set off on the grandest of grand tours in a frantic search for refinement and culture. She studied over 50 Gothic cathedrals, traipsed through endless art galleries, attended the opera, and politely practised her German, Italian and French. All this was appropriately spiritual and feminine, and it had intellectual attractions of a type, but it was so passive, so private. It provided no opportunity for the dramatic public involvement for which Jane yearned. She began to feel "a sense of futility, of misdirected energy, the belief that the pursuit of cultivation would not in the end bring either solace or relief."[11] Slowly Jane herself came to the realisation that her constant depression and invalidism was not physical, but psychological: the natural consequence of passivity, the lack of an appropriate role. Cut off by her female nature from the professions and the world of business, rejecting out of ambition and intellectual conviction the old female options of marriage, missionary work or society lady, Jane Addams found herself without a viable career. She was caught, sick and inactive, between the two worlds.

This dark night of the soul ended after 8 years in 1889 when Jane Addams and her close Rockford friend Ellen Gates Starr established the first American settlement house in the 19th ward of Chicago. She was quite frank that her basic interest in this new venture was less to aid the immigrants around her than to cure her own malaise. Ellen Starr wrote to her sister, "Jane's idea which she puts very much to the front and on no account will give up is that it is more for the benefit of the people who do it, than for the other class. She has worked that out of her own experience and ill health . . . Nervous people" concluded Miss Starr, "do not crave rest, but activity of a certain kind."[12] And this was the first great function in personal terms of Hull-House, as they called their settlement. Whether out delivering babies, or reading to children in kindergarten, or organising the community's garbage disposal, Jane found herself perpetually involved, perpetually active. Her health improved dramatically. The "mere passive reciptivity" from which she had suffered for eight years was replaced by "the solace of daily activity." Jane Addams revelled in the continual contact with poverty-stricken immigrants, for at least on a vicarious level it allowed her to share the race life, to participate in the starvation struggle. At last, she felt, she was reliving the active pioneer life of her father. Not simply were the people around her immigrants and therefore pioneers, "so like the men and women of my earliest childhood," but she herself was in a sense a pioneer in a new social frontier. Even the name "settlement" itself conjured up this vision of herself as a western frontiersman, repeating her father's initial struggle with life.[13]

Second, Hull-House satisfied in vocational terms Jane Adams' desire to use the educational skills and intellectual powers upon which she had placed such store. The Settlement she said, "is a protest against a restricted view of education, and makes it possible for every educated man or woman with teaching faculty to find out those who are ready to be taught."[14] Reading classes and university extension courses were started, and Hull-House residents conscientiously led the 19th ward through their own college program in Greek and Latin, in the Florentine painters and in Shakespeare. Julia Lathrop even dragged bewildered immigrants through Jowett's Plato. Lectures with prominent academics were instituted, a library established, and for ten years there was a summer school at Rockford. College education had discovered a use. Even Jane's trips to Europe suddenly came to have a new meaning. She had deliberately chosen residence in an immigrant area, partly to give a vocational purpose to her long and patient learning of German and Italian, and partly because her European travel would allow her to understand the people around her. Art and culture too had new uses. They could bring spiritual values to the materialistic world of the slum. The first addition to Hull-House was an art gallery, where the residents were careful to show "only pictures which combine, to a considerable degree, an elevated tone with technical excellence," and a circulating library of suitable prints was instituted. It gave Jane Addams great pleasure to know that "within a short walk from Hull-House a little parlor has been completely transformed by the Fra Angelico over the mantle and the Lucca Dell Robbias on the walls, from which walls the picture scarfs and paper flowers have fallen away." Even the tasteful decorations of Hull-House itself—its oriental rugs, its piano, its marble statues, its etchings, its corinthian pillars—could now be seen, not as the useless ostentation of cultivated women, but as things "helpful to the life of mind and soul," an infusion of spiritual values into the benighted world of the tenement house.[15] Further, through its regular lectures and public discussions, Hull-House attracted to it many of the noted intellectuals of the Anglo-American world. People like John Morley, Henry George, Fredrick Harrison, Sidney and Beatrice Webb, Ramsey McDonald, and the local Chicago luminati John Dewey, George Mead, F. L. Wright, and Clarence Darrow all visited Hull-House in the 1890s. Confident that she was bringing knowledge and culture to the people, Jane Addams could satisfy her intellectual yearnings through creating her own "salon in the slum."[16]

Hull-House gave Jane Addams an active life. It gave her an intellectually invigorating life. But most significant of all it gave her a woman's life, one that well suited the Rockford alumna. Hull-House was consciously conceived of as a home. The immigrants around her were alternatively Jane's "Family" or her "guests." All the initial activities of Hull-House were seen in these terms. First was a kindergarten and soon followed children's clubs and a day nursery. Hull-House was filled with an endless chorus of children who came to think of Jane as their new mother. A public kitchen and coffee house were started, then a public dispensery of drugs and finally a public bath house. All the facilities of the traditional home were extended into society on a public basis. The 19th ward became Hull-House's family. Even the emotional function of the home was repeated. Just as the 19th century home was seen as a warm and comforting refuge from the harsh world of business and of the city, so Jane Addams welcomed people to Hull-House on exactly such terms. Indeed in its emotional demands upon her, Hull-House called forth all the values of the maternal and missionary spirit. Settlement work was a career of altruistic service, and as Jane Addams viewed it, it required qualities of sympathy and self-abnegation. She explicitly denied that she had come into the immigrant quarters to impose her own values or control the lives of the people around her. She came simply to respond sympathetically and with natural womanly emotion to the problems which the neighborhood, her children, threw up. Working people, she said, "require only that their aspirations be recognized and stimulated, and the means of attaining them put at their disposal."[17] Jane Addams set out to be the perfect mother of her immigrant family.

In a large part however Jane Addams also saw her role as "mother superior." The religious values of Rockford and the domestic piety tradition found a natural expression in Hull-House. There is some evidence that one of the models for Hull-House was the monastery, a community of love standing out against the cruel world; there is stronger evidence that a leading example was the missionary school to which so many of Jane Addams' women friends had already given their lives. Certainly she explicitly claimed that Hull-House was in the tradition of the early Christians and embodies "a certain renaissance going forward in christianity."[18] In slightly self-conscious manner she immediately joined the local congregational church, and each evening would gather the household for prayers and bible-readings. Before long she was somewhat embarrassed to find herself officiating at funerals and confessions. But such religious activity was carried out less in the dogmatic spirit of a Christian mission than in the atmosphere of the religion of humanity. During the late 80's, probably through George Eliot's example, Jane Addams had discovered Comte and Positivism. In later years Comte's famous concept of the priesthood of intellectuals came to be significant to her, but at this point she was particularly attracted by his concept of the religion of humanity, a religion which substituted for Christian worship practical service in the cause of man. An ethic of altruism, Comte argued, would replace the egotistical values of business, and in this transformation women would play a special role as examplars and guides. Comte provided the rationalisation for a religious attitude she had learned from her father. As for so many people of this generation, so for Jane Addams, Positivism served to legitimise a move from Christianity to social service. With the ideological backing of the religion of humanity she could still conceive of her function in religious terms, as the 19th century view of women demanded, yet occupy all her energies in benevolence towards man rather than in Christian dogmatising. After several years at Hull-House explicitly Christian activities ended. The prayer meetings and bible-readings died out, and Jane stopped going to church. Her sense of feminine identity was fully satisfied through the religion of humanity.

Hull-House fulfilled Jane Addams' identity as a woman in one final sense. Hull-House was always conceived of as a women's institution. Initially there was no expectation that men would live there, and although as the settlement expanded men did take up residence, the leading and charismatic figures were always women—the two founders, Jane herself and Ellen Starr, and that trio of strong women, Alice Hamilton, Florence Kelley and Julia Lathrop. The settlement's most active supporters were nearly all rich leisured women like Mary Wilmarth, Mrs. J. T. Bowen, and Ethel Dummer, and the largest most enterprising club, and ever Jane Addams' favorite, was the Hull-House Women's Club. The settlement carried a distinctly feminine atmosphere. In more personal terms, as at the Henry Street settlement in New York, so at Hull-House there are strong indications of lesbian relationships. Jane Addams herself was clearly in love with Ellen

Starr when they set up Hull-House together in 1889. By the mid 90's she had transferred her affection to Mary Rozet Smith. Their constant companionship, Jane's frequent visits to Mary's gracious mansion in Chicago, the ardent letters and sentimental love poems, all attest to the emotional depth of their attachment. In all but name it was a marriage. The existence of such a relationship reveals strikingly how alienated Jane Addams was from the masculine world and its values; and how strongly feminine were the attitudes implicit in Hull-House.

So well had settlement work fulfilled Jane Addams' various needs—her yearning for action, her desire to use her education, and her demand for a traditional female identity—that one might have imagined her continuing the rest of her life at Hull-House as the mother of the 19th ward. What disturbed the equilibrium and led to a change in public posture was first her gnawing ambition, her continued longing to emulate her father in larger public service and greater burdens of self-sacrifice; and second the arrival at Hull-House of Florence Kelley simultaneously with the onset of the 1893 depression. Florence Kelley, though a woman with children to prove it, was no precious cultivated lady trying to bring motherhood and culture to immigrants. A cool professional with a degree in economics from Zurich, a former Marxist and translator of Engels, she brought to Hull-House the stout conviction that what the American poor needed was not more art but more food. She came committed to basic economic and social reform. This was a new thought in Hull-House which had been established to aid individuals in a neighbourhood, not cure the ills of all society. Mrs. Kelley's message was reinforced by the economic depression of 1893. As a sympathetic woman Jane Addams could not stand detached and lecture on Shakespeare while children were starving and men without work. In 1893 Hull-House became the district bureau of the Central Relief Association and Jane Addams found herself dispensing coal and food and clothes.

Under the impact of these two events, Jane Addams began to see herself in a new light. She would not merely be the spiritual mother and teacher of the 19th ward. She would also become a force for reform throughout the whole Chicago community. In serving on the Civic Federation's committee of five in 1893, Jane Addams took her first public position outside Hull-House, and similar posts soon followed. She was on the committee to aid the unemployed the same year, in 1894 she was a public mediator during the Pullman strike, and the following year served on a commission to investigate the county poorhouse. The new role as a spokeswoman for reform was immensely satisfying to Jane Addams. It was an active varied life of public service. It brought her public renown and temporarily appeased her ambition. In addition it used her intellectual talents. She became a prolific lecturer for reform causes, wrote innumerable articles, and after 1902 produced a stream of books. Her literary skills, in abeyance since her college days, were fully utilized. Further, under the influence of Florence Kelley, and after reading Charles Booth, she came to accept that reform should be based on scientific expertise. In 1893 Hull-House began an investigation of Chicago slums for the U.S. Department of Labor, and the following year Jane Addams edited *Hull-House Maps and Papers,* where statistics and facts were scientifically marshalled in the cause of reform.

It was now that the other side of Comtian Positivism attained a new relevance for Jane Addams. Comte saw the intellectual, and especially the sociologist, as the priest of his religion of humanity. Jane Addams, cooperating closely with the new sociology department at the University of Chicago and writing frequently in its periodical, *The American Journal of Sociology,* saw herself in this tradition, and so confirmed the religious self-conception which the 19th century demanded of its women. Through participating in reform based on science, Jane Addams was donning the priestly garbs of the religion of humanity. But in a more direct sense her role as apostle of reform placed Jane Addams firmly in the domestic piety tradition—for in her lectures and books it is less the appeal to science that is noteworthy than the appeal to conscience and ethical values. In the traditional 19th century view the woman as wife and mother had a peculiar responsibility to uphold the morals of her family. She must lead her husband and children to salvation. It is in such terms that Jane Addams sees her new role. Her family has grown from the 19th ward to the Chicago community and eventually to all American society, and within that enlarged family Jane is the conscience, the moral beacon, to whom falls the female mission of leading all to social salvation.

Her series of books between 1902 and 1912 reveal how firmly Jane Addams retains the assumptions of the domestic piety tradition.[19] As a writer her stance is always that of the self-abnegating woman. With remarkable powers of negative capability, she is able to crush her own prejudices and sympathise with figures as diverse as the union workman, the domestic servant, the immigrant woman or the industrial boss. Each in turn becomes the host to her self-sacrificing imagination. Her mode of analysis is never a crude economic approach, for that would be to recognise the importance of the male business world. It is always a subtle evocation of other people's psychological attitudes and needs. Where others, for instance, interpreted the Pullman strike as a clear case of open class conflict, Jane Addams avoided such terms, and instead saw it as a problem of family psychology. Bringing to the issue her cultured female sensitivity, she saw Pullman as a Lear embittered at the ingratitude of his children.[20] And when she comes to pass judgement Jane Addams' appeal is to the conscience, to the individual ethics of the situation, and never to mere efficiency or economic productivity.

If we turn from her literary mode to the main burden of her message, her acceptance of the old female values are equally apparent. Her constant plea is for a universal change of heart, a semi-religious awakening that will usher in a new code of ethics. New laws and new institutions must await a "religious enthusiasm, a divine fire to fuse together the partial and feeble efforts at 'doing good' into a transfigured whole." And the new social ethic, when it arrives, will be peculiarly feminine in character. It is the old ethic of altruism, of benevolent self-sacrifice. It will arise, she says, not in consequence of some cold theory, but through the "natural promptings of the heart."[21] Her model is always the spontaneous goodness of the mother within the family. As the mother responds intuitively to the afflictions of her children, so society will respond to others less fortunate. Female emotions, not the masculine mind, will always be the source of the new compassion. Those few institutions in the modern world which Jane Addams praises as vanguards of the new order are those that embody traditional female values—the unions, not for their class consciousness or economic ideas but because "trade unionism has the ring of altruism about it"; striking workers because of their "manifestation of moral power"; the poor for their "ready out-flow of sympathy."[22] Her chief targets of abuse are those institutions retaining the traditional values of the male world—commercial greed, militarism and prostitution which she sees as "sexual commerce," the sacrifice of noble womanhood to the monied greed of men.[23] In addition she joins the growing chorus of contemporary criticism levelled at Social Darwinism, but not because of its intellectual weaknesses, as out of moral revulsion. She cannot accept its masculine principles of assertive self-interest and rank materialism. She finds it indecent for a woman charity worker to "talk always of getting work and saving money." Her most pungent and lasting social criticism is levelled at paternalism. With deftness she exposes the pretensions of those 19th century philanthropists who tried to do "good 'to' people rather than 'with' them."[24] But here again her chief animus is anti-male. What she objects to about paternalism is its assumption of self-assertion, of aggressive individualism. What she wants is less paternalism and more maternalism—rule by self-abnegating mothers.

Jane Addams' devotion to the traditional values of women is most strikingly apparent when we realise how much of her writings and almost all of her direct participation in institutional reform were concerned with the defence of the family. In 1893 she cooperated closely with Florence Kelley and Governor Altgeld to push through the first Illinois factory legislation. Its provisions were seen as a shield for the protection of the orderly family. Tenement-house work was restricted in the hope that home and labor would be clearly separated, and the home fulfill its true function as a restful retreat from the cruel world of business; women's work was limited to 8 hours a day with the aim that women would have opportunity for their true vocation as mothers and wives; and the labor of children under 14 was prohibited in the expectation that they would remain safely protected within the family's loving circle. In her writings Jane Addams showed particular concern for the domestic servant, isolated as she was from her family; and for the prostitute whose misfortune not only subverted family order but was usually caused by lack of parental control.[25] And appalled at anarchy in the immigrant family, where the children as natives to the new land frequently became the guides to their foreign parents, Jane Addams set up the labor museum at Hull-House. It was intended to show off the parents' traditional skills, and thus regain for them their children's respect. Family order would be maintained.[26] Rarely did Jane Addams press for better wages and hours for men, or for health insurance, but when she did, it was always in the hope that the male would be able to support the family unaided. Believing that "the maternal instinct and family affection is woman's most holy attribute," Jane's enduring mission was to provide the poor and the immigrant with the middle class Anglo-Saxon family circle.[27] Indeed the family always remained for Jane Addams society's most precious institution, which could never be sacrificed for any claims of selfhood or ambition. In ***Democracy and Social Ethics,*** she wrote, "The man, for instance, who deserts his family that he may cultivate an artistic sensibility, or acquire what he considers more fullness of life for himself, must always arouse our contempt. Breaking the marriage tie as Ibsen's 'Nora' did, to obtain a larger self-development, or holding to it, as George Eliot's 'Romola' did, because of the larger claims of the state and society, must always remain two distinct paths . . . The family as well as the state we are all called upon to maintain as the highest institutions which the race has evolved for its safeguard and protection. [The family's] obligations can never be cancelled. It is impossible to bring about the higher development by any self assertion or breaking away of the individual will."[28] If the action of Ibsen's Nora in slamming the door in her husband's face is accepted as the classic feminist act of the 19th century, then no clearer indication could be found than this, of Jane Addams fundamentally anti-feminist animus.

While Jane Addams' central hopes for reform always resided implicitly in the triumph of motherhood and family sympathy, yet this was only made fully explicit when she came to argue for women's suffrage in the early 20th century. Her arguments for the vote were never on the grounds of natural rights, or of a claimed equality with men. Rather the reverse. Attempting to give scientific validity to her belief in the innate difference of men and women, she turned to the work of Paul Geddes and William Thomas who posited a fundamental contrast in the cell structure of the two sexes. The male cells, they argued, were katabolic, hungry and aggressive; the female cells were anabolic, reproductive and nurturing, patient and passive. Women should be allowed the vote, said Jane Addams, precisely because the state now needed such peculiarly female anabolic qualities. While the city's chief problems were military defence or economic growth, then a male franchise was only right and proper. But now the city's concerns were the education of children and the cleaning of streets. Ruling a city, she argued, was now "enlarged housekeeping," and women, the traditional housekeepers, should take over. "The men of the city" she wrote, "have been carelessly indifferent to much of this civic housekeeping, as they have always been indifferent to the details of the household." What society desperately needed to cure its problems were women's nurturing qualities and domestic skills.[29]

This idea was most dramatically seen during Jane Addams' participation in the 1912 Progressive campaign. As her claims for the virtues of womanhood had grown more explicit, so her personal arena had widened. At first her extended family had been merely Hull-House and the 19th ward. Then in the mid 90's as she adopted the role of social reformer, it became the city of Chicago. Now in this campaign, her personal responsibility had widened to the nation. Driven by ambition and a desire for public service, and imbued with an increasingly apocalyptic vision of the triumph of domestic piety throughout the nation, she came to see herself as the great representative of American womanhood, mother of the American family and saint of the religion of humanity. For her the social welfare planks of the Progressive platform and the promise of female suffrage were inseparably connected. "One is the corollary of the other," she wrote, "a program of human welfare, the necessity for women's participation."[30] Both together promised a semi-religious awakening, the triumph of the old female values of altruism, self-sacrifice and motherhood. She was incredibly active throughout the crusade—on the platform committee, the seconder of Theodore Roosevelt at the convention, and a tireless campaign worker travelling hundreds of miles to speak for the cause. Throughout she conceived of the campaign less as an effort to elect candidates, for she was always sceptical about Theodore Roosevelt, than as an educational campaign, a religious crusade to convert America to a new social ethic. For her the "Jane Addams chorus" at the convention singing "Onward Christian Soldiers" was central to the campaign's meaning. Her personal satisfaction was immense. Her desire to emulate her father in public service was temporarily appeased; in lecturing and platform writing her intellectual talents were used to the full; and in the promise of the campaign she believed herself witnessing the triumph of Rockford's values throughout the nation.

But her will to achieve was not yet quite satisfied. The onset of the Great War brought new challenges. It challenged first her long-held belief in the potential of intellect. Now rational debate had been replaced by primitive tribal violence. Even John Dewey her close friend and philosophic guide had abandoned the critical spirit for involvement in war. It was a challenge too to her sense of community, her feeling of public recognition. Now as war mania overtook the nation she felt isolated and lonely. But above all it was a threat to her womanhood. Believing that the female spirit of nurture was unutterably opposed to the male spirit of militarism, Jane Addams had long been a pacifist. Peace she always claimed, "was not merely an absence of war but the nurture of human life."[31] The ethic of peace was the ethic of social reform, and as America prepared for war, she saw both causes being sacrificed. Isolated and depressed she slipped into invalidism.

Slowly however she began to realise that war was an opportunity not a defeat for woman's pacifist nature. A new vision began to possess her. Could not her family responsibility be extended yet again—this time from the nation to the whole world; and could not she, Jane Addams, lead a worldwide triumph of feminine values which would abolish war forever? Domestic piety in the person of Jane Addams would sweep the world to eternal salvation. In 1915 she founded the Women's International League for Peace and Freedom. Its two conditions of membership were a belief in women's suffrage and pacifism. A conference was held at the Hague, and Jane Addams was despatched on a mission to convert the world's leaders to peace and social altruism. In meetings with European cabinets, in a papal audience, in a conference with President Wilson, Jane Addams stood for the new international conscience. She was redeeming womanhood personified. In 1919 a congress of women was called to coincide with the Versailles peace conference. Led by Saint Jane, the congress called not for new institutional guarantees such as a League of Nations, but for "a great spiritual awakening in international affairs."[32] Jane began to develop a complete ideology to explain the meaning of her place in human destiny. Women, she argued, had been responsible for the first great advance in human civilisation, the move from a nomadic warring state to a settled peaceful agricultural existence. Primitive women long ago compelled by the maternal instinct, she said, "made the first crude beginnings of society by refusing to share the vagrant life of man because they insisted upon a fixed abode in which they might cherish their children." And it was women who had first opposed human sacrifice in religion. Now women might compel another human advance. "There might be found an antidote to war in woman's affection and all-embracing pity for helpless children."[33] In Jane Addams' eyes the leading expression of the new international ethic was Herbert Hoover's Food Administration which had been organised to feed the starving peoples of Europe after the war. Jane Addams quickly volunteered her services, and began to travel the nation speaking to women on its behalf. Now the role of efficient housewife became endowed with apocalyptic implications. If the American mother could save food in her kitchen then food would be available for the hungry of Europe. Competitive commerce might be replaced by a humanitarian sympathetic commerce in food. "I believed," she wrote later, "that a genuine response to this world situation might afford an opportunity to lay over again the foundations for a wider, international morality, as woman's concern for feeding her children had made the beginnings of an orderly domestic life."[34]

The great symbol of this international ethic for Jane Addams was bread. The book she wrote in 1920 was called ***Peace and Bread in Time of War.*** In her travels through America she would frequently revive the anthropological myth that women were the first grain farmers, and would allude to the corn spirits: "These spirits are always feminine and are usually represented by a Corn Mother and her daughter."[35] The choice of bread as symbol of international salvation was no accident. It revealed how perfectly the campaign of 1919-20 fulfilled all Jane

Addams' deepest needs. For bread had been her father's livelihood. He had been a flour-miller. She recalled as a child "a consuming ambition to possess a miller's thumb," and in 1919 "I used to remind myself that although I had had ancestors who fought in all the American wars since 1684, I was also the daughter, granddaughter and great granddaughter of millers."[36] In urging the women of the world to save bread, Jane Addams had finally outstripped her father. But that was not all. The motto of her Rockford class of 1881 was "Breadgivers," and its letter-head a sheaf of wheat, in recognition of "the old ideal of woman-hood—the Saxon lady whose mission it was to give bread unto her household." Jane Addams herself in that speech at the opening of her class's junior exhibition had reminded her friends, "our destiny throughout our lives should be to give good, sweet, wholesome bread unto our loved ones."[37] By 1919 the size of the family and the number of loved ones was on rather a different scale from her imaginings in 1880, but her posture, her ethical stance was still that of the Rockford alumna, the nurturing mother, the self-sacrificing woman. Finally the Christian symbolism of bread is almost too obvious to be mentioned, and that Jane Addams was aware of it, we may be certain; and here again it confirmed her within the traditional female role—that of the missionary, the religious guide and exemplar. Jane had become the Christ, not of Christianity but of the religion of humanity.

In a purely personal sense then, Jane Addams' career was a success. She had achieved a life of activism and public service way beyond that of her father. In international renown she approached even her beloved Lincoln. The Nobel Prize in 1931 was just payment of the world's dues. Her education and intellectual talent had opened new opportunities as she had so ardently wished. Ten books and some 500 articles attested to the value of a college education. Yet all had been achieved within the confines of the domestic piety tradition that Rockford had so firmly implanted. It is true that Jane Addams redefined the institutional expression of that tradition. Motherhood and family expanded out of the home into the 19th ward, the city, the nation, and eventually encompassed the world. And woman's religious function became service to man rather than service to God. But she never challenged the basic assumptions of the ideology, nor the doctrines of a separate woman's sphere and a distinct female nature. If anything she strengthened the ideas by giving them some scientific validity. And it is this inability to question the central tenets of the piety tradition which produced ultimate failure in all but a narrowly personal sense.

To the women whose cause she so fondly espoused, Jane Addams' contribution was disastrous. The generation of which she was the charismatic figure was a crucial generation for the place of women in American society. It was the first generation which had received a college education; it was the first generation which followed Darwin and the consequent secularisation of social values; and it was the first generation which had the vote and could participate fully in the political life of the nation. It was also a period, in which as Robert Wiebe has observed, the occupational structure and status hierarchy of 20th century urban society was being established.[38] Roles were fluid, the professions young and relatively open. The possibility was there for the women of that generation to strike out on a new path—the path of equality with men within the new professional structure. But Jane Addams, as the leading figure of this generation helped close off that option. The path she chose was destined to have a no exit sign at its entrance. The road to sainthood could not be trod by more than one woman a generation, and Eleanor Roosevelt was soon to ascend the saintly steps as Mrs. Eddy had done in an earlier era. Liberation in the end required more than an expansion of domestic values into the world, however bold and ingenious that expansion might be. It required an acceptance of self-assertion and ambition, and an acceptance of the grubby material secular world outside. It required a few more self-committed Noras and rather fewer self-sacrificing Romolas.

And even in the reform movements of her day Jane Addams failed. A new international ethic did not sadly sweep the world. Wars are still with us, children still starve. Female suffrage in 1920 ushered in Harding and normalcy, not the maternal state; and when a new order of a kind emerged after 1932 it was on the heels of failure by Jane Addams' great moral example, Herbert Hoover. Female values and the religion of humanity were vain hopes in a world of laws, institutions, and economic interests. Even Hull-House, Jane Addams' greatest institutional legacy, now stands gaunt and isolated amid the refuse of Chicago's urban renewal, a sad memorial to a noble woman.

NOTES

[1] James Webber Linn, *Jane Addams, a Biography* (New York, 1937), pp. 382, 399.

[2] e.g. Penina Migdal Glazer, "Organizing for Freedom," *The Massachusetts Review,* 13 (Winter-Spring 1972): 29-44; Christopher Lasch, *The New Radicalism in America* (New York, 1965), pp. 3-37.

[3] Information on Anna Sill from H.M.G[oodwin], "Biographical" in *Memorials of Anna P. Sill,* (Rockford, 1889), pp. 5-20; *Linn* p. 44; John C. Farrell, *Beloved Lady* (Baltimore, 1967), p. 30. On the later careers of Jane Addams' friends, Winifred E. Wise, *Jane Addams of Hull-House* (New York, 1935), p. 76.

[4] Jane Addams, *Twenty Years at Hull-House* (New York, 1910), p. 25; Jane Addams, *My Friend, Julia Lathrop* (New York, 1935), p. vi: *Twenty Years* p. 38.

[5] *Ibid.,* p. 19.

[6] Jane Addams to Ellen Gates Starr, Rockford, January 29, 1880; Jane Addams to Ellen Gates Starr, Cedarville,

Illinois, August 11, 1879; Jane Addams to Ellen Gates Starr, Rockford, November 22, 1879 (all in Starr Ms., Box 1, Sophia Smith Collection, Northampton, Mass.).

[7] On this theme see especially John P. Rousmaniere, "Cultural Hybrid in the Slums: The College Woman and the Settlement House 1889-1904," *American Quarterly,* 22 (Spring 1970): 45-66.

[8] *Twenty Years* pp. 52, 57-8.

[9] Quoted in *Wise* p. 77.

[10] Jane Addams, "Breadgivers," *Rockford Register* April 21, 1880.

[11] *Twenty Years* p. 64. See also Jane Addams to Ellen Gates Starr, Cedarville, Illinois, September 3, 1881, in Starr Ms., Box 1.

[12] Ellen Gates Starr to Mary Blaisdell, February 23, 1889, in Starr Ms., Box 1.

[13] *Twenty Years* pp. 74, 87.

[14] Jane Addams, "The Subjective Necessity for Social Settlements" in Henry C. Adams (ed.), *Philanthropy and Social Progress* (New York, 1893), p. 10.

[15] Jane Addams, "Appendix" in *Hull-House Maps and Papers* (New York, 1895), p. 210; Jane Addams, "Art-Work Done by Hull-House," *Forum* 19 (July 1895): 615; *Hull-House Maps and Papers,* p. 211.

[16] This felicitous phrase is Jill Conway's in "Jane Addams: an American Heroine," *Daedalus* 43 (Spring 1964): 761-780.

[17] Jane Addams, "Objective Value of a Social Settlement," *Philanthropy and Social Progress* p. 56.

[18] "Subjective Necessity," p. 17.

[19] The books are: *Democracy and Social Ethics* (New York, 1902); *Newer Ideals of Peace* (New York, 1907); *The Spirit of Youth and the City Streets* (New York, 1909); *A New Conscience and an Ancient Evil* (New York, 1912).

[20] Jane Addams, "A Modern Lear," *Survey* (November 2, 1912): 131-7 (partially included in *Democracy and Social Ethics* pp. 137-177).

[21] *Newer Ideals* p. 22; *Democracy and Social Ethics* p. 26.

[22] *Ibid.,* pp. 148, 20.

[23] *Newer Ideals* passim; *A New Conscience,* passim.

[24] *Democracy and Social Ethics* pp. 31, 154.

[25] *Ibid.,* pp. 102-136; *A New Conscience,* passim.

[26] e.g. *Twenty Years* pp. 171-2.

[27] Jane Addams, "The Settlement as a Factor in the Labor Movement," *Hull-House Maps and Papers* p. 186.

[28] *Democracy and Social Ethics* pp. 76-9.

[29] *Newer Ideals* p. 182.

[30] Jane Addams, *The Second Twenty Years at Hull-House* (New York, 1930), p. 33.

[31] *Ibid.,* p. 35.

[32] Jane Addams, *Peace and Bread in Time of War* (New York, 1922), p. 153.

[33] Jane Addams, *The Long Road of Woman's Memory* (New York, 1916), p. 127; *Peace and Bread* p. 83.

[34] *Ibid.,* p. 81.

[35] *Ibid.,* p. 77.

[36] *Twenty Years* p. 25; *Peace and Bread p.* 76.

[37] "Breadgivers," *Rockford Register* April 21, 1880.

[38] Robert H. Wiebe, *The Search for Order* (New York, 1967).

James Hurt (essay date 1979)

SOURCE: "Walden on Halsted Street: Jane Addams' Twenty Years at Hull-House," in *The Centennial Review,* Vol. 23, 1979, pp. 185-207.

[*In the following essay, Hurt examines* Twenty Years at Hull-House *as a work of literary self-examination.*]

I

It may seem somewhat wrong-headed to attempt to examine Jane Addams' ***Twenty Years at Hull-House*** as a work of art, since a major theme of the book is a condemnation of art for its tendency to numb us to living reality. Addams quotes William Dean Howells approvingly—"Mr. Howells has said that we are all so besotted with our novel reading that we have lost the power of seeing certain aspects of life with any sense of reality because we are continually looking for the possible romance"[1]—and an early turning point in the book is her horrified realization that her romantic reading has so aestheticized her that she has watched a gory bullfight with no sense of the reality of the suffering involved. It is this realization that spurs her to renounce the pursuit of "culture" and plunge into the reality of Chicago slum life.

And yet a distrust of art is not incompatible with its creation, especially in American literature, and ***Twenty Years at Hull-House*** challenges comparison with another masterpiece of American literature just as profoundly skeptical of literature, Thoreau's *Walden.* In many ways, Addams' project of 1889 recalls Thoreau's of half a century before. Like him, she finds herself increasingly discontent with the received culture and withdraws to a "sacred" space physically and emotionally outside it. She establishes herself in a house which comes to symbolize her self, the world, and the boundary between the two. And here, alone with nature, she returns to the basic questions of life: What is indispensable in life? What is our place in Nature? What is the relationship between the individual life and the life of the race? How should we live our lives? Like Thoreau, too, she writes a book which does not merely report her quest but becomes synonymous with it. For Jane Addams, in 1889, "nature" is not the woods and water of Walden Pond, but the teeming human life of South Halsted Street. The terms of the quest, though, are similar, and like Thoreau, she finds, paradoxically, that it carries her through a renuciation of art to a redefinition and reaffirmation of it.

Twenty Years at Hull-House is even structured much like *Walden.* The first five chapters are chronological narrative, covering Addams' life up to 1889, when she founded Hull-House. They present, Addams writes, "influences and personal motives with a detail which would be quite unpardonable if they fail to make clear the personality upon whom various social and industrial movements in Chicago reacted during a period of twenty years. No effort is made in the recital to separate my own history from that of Hull-House during the years when I was 'launched deep into the stormy intercourse of human life' for, so far as a mind is pliant under the pressure of events and experiences, it becomes hard to detach it" (xviii). The remainder of the book, eighteen chapters, abandons chronology to deal with a series of topics concerning the activities of Hull-House. But these are not merely a series of discrete essays, any more than Thoreau's similar sections are ("Reading," "Sounds," "Solitude," etc.). Each deals with the same fundamental questions as they apply to a different area of activity. The book thus has a kind of spiraling structure, turning around a series of fixed points but rising to a higher level of understanding each time.

II

The first four chapters of Addams' book are far from a straightforward chronological account of her early years, as a comparison with a biography like James Linn's will show.[2] They rather consist of a series of crucial memories, "spots of time" in Wordsworth's sense, some of them trivial from an objective point of view but all of them significant in the development of her sense of the world.

The first such memory is of "horrid nights" as a child when she could not sleep because she had told a lie. She would eventually leave her bed and gather her courage to go down the stairs, past the front door (always unlocked because of her father's "Quaker tendencies"), and across the wide and black expanse of the living room to her father's bedroom, where she would confess her fault. He would say that "if he 'had a little girl who told lies," he was very glad that 'she felt too bad to go to sleep afterward,'" and she would return, comforted, to her room and bed.

In this first chapter of "Earliest Impressions," Addams is frank in pointing out that they all center around her father. Her mother died before Addams was three, and her father did not remarry until she was eight, and so she "centered upon him all that careful imitation which a little girl ordinarily gives to her mother's ways and habits" (25). The father, John Huy Addams, had moved from Pennsylvania to Cedarville, Illinois, in 1844. There he prospered as a miller, helped bring a rail-road into the county, raised a military company in 1861, the "Addams guards," and served eight consecutive terms as state senator.

Although Addams remembers that her father seldom offered advice, she stood in awe of his uprightness and rectitude. He was known, while a state senator, as a man so upright that he had never even been offered a bribe, and Addams recalls that years later, when a group of Chicago businessmen offered a large donation to Hull-House if the residents would stop promoting a sweatshop bill, how humiliated she felt that she had not radiated the same incorruptibility as her father. To the reader, it does not seem that the elder Addams' Quaker righteousness was accompanied by a great deal of warmth or love, however; its keynote was the rather self-centered virtue of "mental integrity." On one occasion, Addams asked her father to explain what was meant by "foreordination." He replied that neither he nor she had the kind of mind that would ever understand foreordination very well, but that "it was very important not to pretend to understand what you didn't understand and that you must always be honest with yourself inside, whatever happened" (27). She associates this with a later crisis in boarding school when he told her, "mental integrity above everything else" (28).

The memory of the midnight confessions is very suggestive in terms of the contrast between her father's rather forbidding code of "mental integrity" and the encompassing humanitarianism which was to become Addams' own faith. Certainly her father's comfort seems cold indeed, and fits into a pattern in these early pages of a sensitive child seeking love and receiving kindness and generosity, but not what she seeks. Perhaps Margaret Tims is correct in speculating, "Was it this fact—the inability to find accord, in this overwhelming 'sympathy,' with the one most dear to her—that caused the later diffusion of her deep affections to embrace the whole of humanity rather than any other individual being?"[3]

This first chapter also vividly recalls what it was like to grow up in a natural, rural setting. Addams is precise in describing her childhood perception of nature: "much too unconscious and intimate to come under the head of aesthetic appreciation or anything of the sort." She and her stepbrother liked the wind-flowers because they were said to be born of the wind rather than because they were beautiful, and though the call of the whippoorwill "aroused vague longings," they did not feel any particular beauty in it. Addams' insistence that her stepbrother's and her perception of nature was not "aesthetic" in any way sounds a major note in the book. To Addams, the basic task in growing up, and indeed of living, is to learn to confront reality, and to do this one must reject or discard all the barriers we put up to distance ourselves from reality and to enable us to manipulate reality without experiencing it directly. Such barriers include all theories, all ideals, and all systems of belief. "Beauty" is one of the falsest and most insidious of these ideals, and one of the most tempting ways to evade experience is to aestheticize it. Later, Addams is to modify this position and discriminate between art as comforting deception and as bracing truth, but at this point, it is important that children, in a "primitive" relationship with nature, experience it immediately and without distancing it as "beauty."

Chapter 2 is structured as freely as Chapter 1, abandoning strict chronology in favor of a loosely related series of reminiscences and observations on "the influence of Lincoln." The elder Addams was a friend of Lincoln, and Addams remembers a thin packet of letters he kept in his desk marked "Mr. Lincoln's Letters," all beginning, "My dear Double-D'ed Addams." What Lincoln came to mean to Addams unfolds directly through the memoirs and anecdotes of the chapter. First, the memory of Lincoln was always bound up with her father, because of the two men's friendship, the packet of letters, and the two pictures of Lincoln that always hung in the father's house. "For one or all of these reasons I always tend to associate Lincoln with the tenderest thoughts of my father" (p. 38). Second, Lincoln's character came to epitomize an intertwined faith in self-government and in the people. One aspect of Lincoln's participation in the common experience was the connection he maintained all his life with his old neighbors in Sangamon County, and Addams found this a useful model for immigrant children who were ashamed of their origins and who "counted themselves successful as they were able to ignore the past" (p. 42). Lincoln's "marvelous power to retain and utilize past experiences" enables him to maintain a continuity between the simplest, earthiest experiences and the most lofty, a continuity Addams desires for herself as much as for the immigrant children.

Addams, in her identification of Lincoln with her father, never explicitly says what is nevertheless implicit throughout the chapter, that Lincoln's values represented an advance upon her father's. Lincoln went beyond her father's "mental integrity above all else" to embody an ideal of love for one's fellow man. "He made plain, once for all, that democratic government, associated as it is with all the mistakes and shortcomings of the common people, still remains the most valuable contribution America has made to the moral life of the world" (p. 45).

But even Lincoln does not fully embody the humanitarianism Addams is slowly progressing toward, and both the virtues and the limitations he represents are suggested in the most extended episode of the chapter, a visit to the state capitol of Wisconsin. The passage demonstrates very clearly Addams' method in the book; the episode is ostensibly a trivial one and nothing "happens" in an external sense. But the internal action is firm and clear and constitutes an almost mystic revelation for Addams, a kind of epiphany in Joyce's sense of the word. The family goes to the state capitol in Madison, sixty-five miles north of Cedarville, to see Old Abe, the "war eagle" mascot who had been carried throughout the War by the Eighth Wisconsin Regiment. But when at last they stand before the war eagle, Addams finds that she is less interested in the eagle than in the rotunda of the capitol itself.

> But although Old Abe, sitting sedately upon his high perch, was sufficiently like an uplifted ensign to remind us of a Roman eagle, and although his veteran keeper, clad in an old army coat, was ready to answer all our questions and to tell us of the thirty-six battles and skirmishes which Old Abe had passed unscathed, the crowning moment of the impressive journey came to me later, illustrating once more that children are as quick to catch the meaning of a symbol as they are unaccountably slow to understand the real world around them. (p. 36)

Around the dome of the rotunda is a mural of marching figures: "soldiers marching to death for freedom's sake" and "pioneers streaming forward to establish self-government in yet another sovereign state" (p. 37). As she looks up at the frieze, she is still aware of Old Abe sitting below and identifies him with Lincoln:

> But through all my vivid sensations there persisted the image of the eagle in the corridor below and Lincoln himself as an epitome of all that was great and good. I dimly caught the notion of the martyred President as the standard bearer to the conscience of his countrymen, as the eagle had been the ensign of courage to the soldiers of the Wisconsin regiment. (p. 37)

This memory is followed by another from thirty-five years later when Addams, revisiting Madison to receive an honorary doctorate, lifted her eyes again and saw the capitol dome, which again appeared "as a fitting symbol of a state's aspiration even in its high mission of universal education" (p. 37).

Implicit in this episode, though never formulated, are the seeds of Addams' feminism and pacificism. She lifts her eyes from the masculine and militaristic symbol of the eagle and focuses instead upon the people on the frieze. They are divided into groups of life and death: pioneers streaming westward to establish freedom and soldiers "marching to death for freedom's sake." Old Abe, the seedy, almost comic double of Lincoln, is a symbol, but of what? Immediately, perhaps, of the vision that sent thousands of men to their deaths for "freedom," but ultimately not just of war but of "all that was great and good" including more peaceful goals such as education.

The following chapter, "Boarding School Ideals," similarly contains a number of slight anecdotes which, like the visit to "Old Abe," advance the argument of the book not so much logically as symbolically, by encapsulating the entire theme in a small episode. At one time, Addams writes, she and her classmates at the Rockford Female Seminary,

> tried to understand De Quincy's marvelous *Dreams* more sympathetically by drugging ourselves with opium. We solemnly consumed small white powders at intervals during an entire long holiday, but no mental reorientation took place, and the suspense and excitement did not even permit us to grow sleepy. About four o'clock on the weird afternoon, the young teacher whom we had been obliged to take into our confidence grew alarmed over the whole performance, took away our De Quincy and all the remaining powders, administered an emetic to each of the five aspirants for sympathetic understanding of all human experience, and sent us to our separate rooms with a stern command to appear at family worship after supper "whether we were able to or not." (p. 48)

In isolation, this seems no more than an amusing anecdote, but in context, the situation of five idealistic girls attempting to achieve "sympathetic understanding of all human experience" by drugging themselves with opium is a sardonic epitome of life at the Rockford Female Seminary.

The pious idealism which dominated the Seminary was, Addams says, the result of the prominence of missionaries among its founders and leaders and of the "glamour of frontier privations" that had been thrown around those who started this early experiment in female education in the West, so that "the first students, conscious of the heroic self-sacrifice made in their behalf, felt that each minute of the time thus dearly bought must be conscientiously used. This inevitably fostered an atmosphere of intensity, a fever of preparation which continued long after the direct making of it had ceased, and which the later girls accepted, as they did the campus and the buildings, without knowing that it could have been otherwise" (p. 47). The tone of the institution was summed up in an absurd quotation from Aristotle, by way of Boswell's *Johnson,* which hung in the common room: "There is the same difference between the learned and the unlearned as there is between the living and the dead."

Jane Addams at fifty finds this slogan comically priggish. Jane Addams at seventeen was only intermittently troubled by the attitude it expresses, and throughout the chapter Addams handles delicately the tension between her adolescent and mature selves. The students at the Seminary were for the most part thirsty to drink at life's waters, but at every approach they retreated, with the encouragement of their mentors, into a defensive and alienating sentimental idealism. The prize Greek oration Addams delivered at the Junior Exhibition, for example, contained both a realistic concern with social evils and an automatic defense, through "culture" and "idealism," against confronting them directly. "The oration upon Bellerophon and his successful fight with the Chimera contended that social evils could only be overcome by him who soared above them into idealism, as Bellerophon, mounted upon the winged horse Pegasus, had slain the earthly dragon" (p. 48). And the class took the Anglo-Saxon word for "lady," translated as "breadgiver" as its motto and the poppy as its flower, because poppies grew among the wheat, "as if Nature knew that wherever there was hunger that needed food there would be pain that needed relief." "We must have found the sentiment in a book somewhere," the older Addams comments ironically; "of course none of us had ever seen a European field, the only page upon which Nature has written this particular message" (p. 49). Even the girls' concern for human hunger and pain is distanced and realized through literary symbols; surrounded by Illinois cornfields, they look past them to symbolic European fields, encountered "in a book somewhere."

These early chapters of ***Twenty Years at Hull-House*** constitute a series of plateaus in the young Addams' continuing search for a full confrontation with reality. Each presents a liberating insight and a partial creed, which is nevertheless brought into question in the succeeding chapter and, if not negated, integrated into a broader view of things. The first chapter presents sympathetically Addams' father's creed of "mental integrity above everything else," which in the following chapter is measured against and subsumed by Lincoln's social idealism. Now Lincoln's views (or Addams' version of them) are examined in turn and brought into question as Addams gropes toward a still fuller and more unmediated encounter with reality. She finds the moral idealism of Rockford Seminary merely narcotic; it takes the natural curiosity and vigor of youth, especially female youth, and strips it of its strength by teaching it to "soar above" hard reality into the safe regions of piety and culture.

Addams remembers that, on leaving Rockford, she and her friends "vowed eternal allegiance to our 'early ideals,' and promised each other we would 'never abandon them without conscious justification,' and we often warned each other of the 'perils of self-tradition.'"

Addams concludes the chapter by pointing out that whatever the dangers of "self-tradition," she certainly did not escape them, for it took her eight years to arrive at a life plan. "During most of that time I was absolutely at sea so far as any moral purpose was concerned, clinging only to the desire to live in a really living world and refusing to be content with a shadowy intellectual or aesthetic reflection of it" (p. 59).

It is this eight-year period that Addams treats most elliptically, omitting most of the crucial external events that occurred or deemphasizing them radically in favor of concentrating on a handful of apparently trivial incidents that nevertheless carried her spiritual development forward to the point at which she moved to Hull-House.

The external events are easy enough to learn from the standard biographies, such as Linn's. In the summer after Addams was graduated from Rockford, her father died suddenly of a ruptured appendix. Despite her shattering grief, she enrolled in the Woman's Medical College in Philadelphia in the autumn. She collapsed at the end of one term with severe back pains, apparently partially emotional in origin. After a rest cure in a Philadelphia orthopedic hospital, she planned to enroll at Smith College, but again collapsed and spent six months bedridden at her stepmother's home. Her stepbrother, a surgeon in Iowa, operated on her back, correcting its curvature. As she was recovering from the operation, her brother Weber suddenly went insane and had to be placed in a hospital. In 1883, she and her stepmother sailed for Europe, where they spent nearly two years. In 1885, she and her stepmother moved to Baltimore, where her other stepbrother, George, was studying at Johns Hopkins. With the enthusiastic encouragement of the second Mrs. Addams, George proposed marriage to Jane but was refused. Soon afterward, he began a slow decline into an insanity from which he never recovered, living in institutions or as a recluse in Cedarville for the rest of his life. In the fall of 1887, Addams and a friend named Sarah Anderson returned to Europe, where they stayed for a year. On this trip, Addams formulated her idea for Hull-House and within a few months of her return had moved to South Halsted Street, where she remained for the rest of her life.

Very little of this history appears in ***Twenty Years at Hull-House,*** and what does appears in the most matter-of-fact way. It is tempting to draw connections between these traumatic events and Addams' decision to renounce her former life and withdraw to a life of service to her fellow man. Adams does not deny such connections but also does not admit that such considerations in any way "explain" her decision.

> The long illness left me in a state of nervous exhaustion with which I struggled for years, traces of it remaining long after Hull-House was opened in 1889. At the best it allowed me but a limited amount of energy, so that doubtless there was much nervous depression at the foundation of the spiritual struggles which this chapter is forced to record. However, it could not have been all due to my health, for as my wise little notebook sententiously remarked, "In his own way each man must struggle, lest the moral law be come a far-off abstraction utterly separated from his active life" (p. 61).

III

The chapter which traces these spiritual struggles is entitled "The Snare of Preparation" and is centered around half a dozen comparatively trivial incidents which encapsulate Addams' spiritual growth, of which three are most prominent: a visit to East London to see the regular Saturday night sale of decaying fruit and vegetables, a visit to Ulm Cathedral, and an afternoon at a bullfight.

The experience in London occurred early in the first trip abroad (in November, 1883, as we know from other sources). She was taken with a small party of tourists to Mile End Road, in East London, where two huge crowds were gathered around two hucksters' carts full of spoiling fruit and vegetables, left over from the Saturday sales. The food was being auctioned off for farthings and halfpennies; as Addams arrived she saw the auctioneer contemptuously fling a cabbage to a successful bidder, who immediately sat down on the curb and devoured it, dirt and all. The scene was nightmarish; the memory was branded on Addams' mind of "myriads of hands, empty, pathetic, nerveless and workworn, showing white in the uncertain light of the street, and clutching forward for food which was already unfit to eat" (p. 62).

Addams became obsessed with the subject of poverty and for the next two years was "irresistibly drawn to the poorer quarters of each city." The old yearning to experience "reality" now took the form of a split perception of a world outwardly happy and prosperous and another wretched and impoverished: "I carried with me for days at a time that curious surprise we experience when we first come back into the streets after days given over to sorrow and death; we are bewildered that the world should be going on as usual and unable to determine which is real, the inner pang or the outward seeming" (p. 62).

The obsession with poverty was accompanied by a strong revulsion from "culture." At the moment of looking down on the auction from her London bus, she had thought of DeQuincy's "Vision of Sudden Death," in which he finds himself unable to form the words to warn two lovers in the path of the mail coach in which he is riding because his mind is entangled in trying to remember a line from the *Iliad.* It is an appropriate analogy but a cruelly ironic one since she feels she has been paralyzed by thinking about a literary work in which the author is paralyzed by thinking about a literary work. "In my disgust it all appeared a hateful, vicious circle which even the apostles of culture themselves admitted, for had not one of the greatest among the moderns said that 'conduct, and not culture is three fourths of human life'" (p. 64).

Addams' disgust is especially directed against herself as a woman. In Europe, she saw about her dozens of American girls in pursuit of "culture" but cut off by their training from any genuine sense of life. Their mothers, from a generation immersed in the problems of ordinary living, frequently made real connections with the life around them, sharing household lore with their hostesses, while the daughter was "only at ease when in the familiar receptive attitude afforded by the art gallery and the opera house. In the latter she was swayed and moved, appreciative of the power and charm of the music, intelligent as to the legend and poetry of the plot, finding use for her trained and developed powers as she sat 'being cultivated' in the familiar atmosphere of the classrooms which has, as it were, become sublimated and romanticized" (pp. 64-65).

The main elements of Addams' fully developed feminism are implicit in this melancholy description of the first products of women's education in America. Educated, these young women were denied the opportunity to employ their education in the real world. As Addams explained in her 1892 lecture, **"The Subjective Necessity for Social Settlements,"** reprinted as Chapter VI of ***Twenty Years at Hull-House,*** an important motive in founding Hull-House was to offer an outlet for the desire to serve felt by such young women. But her reconsideration did not merely consist in a plea for educated middle-class women to be given something useful to do; it involved a radical rethinking of woman's nature itself. At Rockford Seminary, as throughout middle-class America, it was held that women were by nature passive and unsuited to active participation in public life, that their moral natures were finer than men's and hence should be cultivated and refined, and that the aim of woman's education was to prepare her to enter her "natural" place, the home. Addams was later to dispute explicitly each of these points. Historically, "woman's place" was not the home but the field; man's "primordial" role was that of warrior, woman's that of tiller of the soil. She was by nature inclined toward the active life, and to turn her impulses toward active service to pious "idealism" and her inclination toward the outside world back into the home was to engender frustration and waste.

What gave Jane Addams such a perspective on her culture? She was, after all, one of the young women she described—with a genteel education, by nature intensely idealistic but with no real involvement in active life, and on a protracted European tour in avid pursuit of "culture." (In describing her fascination with Rome, she comments that, "in spite of my distrust of 'advantages,' I was apparently not yet so curbed but that I wanted more of them" (p. 67). What enabled her to rise above this situation, to criticize it, and ultimately to reject it?

In the first place, Addams' own position seemed almost a parodic exaggeration of that of the young American ladies on the Grand Tour. They were passive; she was condemned to spend months at a time in bedridden isolation. They were paralyzed by moral earnestness: her "wise little notebook" translated her every action into general moral terms. They were doomed to the home; she was constantly being pushed toward an unwanted marriage with her stepbrother. Perhaps the very extremity of Addams' situation forced her to objectify it, to analyze it, and to see it as an extension of the general dilemma of women of her time and class. Addams' recurring preoccupations seem to have equally subjective bases. Her obsessive preoccupation with the plight of the poor after that shattering experience in London seems, in context, to be a rather obvious displacement of her own recent personal grief. And her long-standing similarly obsessive drive to discard all "shadowy reflections" and to confront "reality" seems likely to derive from a yearning to recover the edenic joy of her early relation to her father, especially in the light of her preoccupation with "primitive" or "priordial" relationships.

Whatever the exact dynamics of her "spiritual struggles" during the period this chapter covers, it seems clear that they amounted to the kind of prolonged adolescent identity crisis Erik Erikson has described the young Luther as undergoing in which previous psychological structures disintegrate in a chaos out of which a new identity eventually emerges.[4]

The gradual end of this crisis was marked by a series of integrative experiences described at the end of "The Snare of Preparation." One of the most crucial was a visit to Ulm Cathedral; though treated very briefly and rather noncommittally here, it provides one of the major images of the rest of the book. "One winter's day," she writes, "I traveled from Munich to Ulm because I imagined from what the art books said that the cathedral hoarded a medieval statement of the Positivists' final synthesis, prefiguring their conception of a 'Supreme Humanity'" (p. 71). The carvings at Ulm depicted Greek philosophers as well as Hebrew prophets, and one stained glass window, among others showing ancient saints and Christian symbols, showed Luther nailing his theses to the door at Wittenberg.

The visit is described no further, but it apparently had a transforming impact on Addams at the time. She sat up half the night, writing page after page in her "smug notebook," in "a fever of composition cast in ill-digested phrases from Comte." The elder Addams describes her youthful fervor with amused irony and a touch of embarrassment, but observes that the jumbled notes set forth a hope for a "cathedral of humanity" that would be "capacious enough to house a fellowship of common purpose" and points out that one of the earliest seeds of Hull-House lay in this experience in Ulm Cathedral.

The climax of this chapter, and of the first section of the book, however, is a description of a visit to a bullfight in Madrid in 1888. The bullfight was carried out in "the most magnificent Spanish style," and after her companions had left in disgust at the bloodshed, Addams stayed on, fascinated by "the sense that this was the last survival of all the glories of the amphitheater, the illusion that the riders on the caparisoned horses might have been knights at a tournament, or the matador a slightly armed gladiator facing his martyrdom, and all the rest of the obscure yet vivid associations of a historic survival" (p. 73). At the end of the bullfight, she realized that insulated by such romantic idealizations, she had watched, with comparative indifference, five bulls and many more horses killed. At first she thought little about it and merely told her disapproving companions that she had not thought much about the bloodshed. But when she was alone that night, she was overcome by the horror of what she had done: "I felt myself tried and condemned, not only by this disgusting experience but by the entire moral situation which it revealed" (p. 73). As Addams indicates, she had already conceived of her "dreamer's scheme" of moving into an urban slum, but she had never mentioned it to anyone. Now, the day after the night of self-loathing and self-reproach following the bullfight, she laid out the plan to her friend Ellen Starr and was greatly relieved that it was received not as a "golden dream" but as an exciting and realistic possibility. They immediately made plans to return to the United States, go to Chicago, and put the plan in effect.

"The Snare of Preparation" is the most intensely personal chapter in ***Twenty Years at Hull-House.*** It covers a period of crushing losses, a series of physical and mental breakdowns, and a prolonged episode of confusion and paralysis. And yet it is not in the ordinary sense confessional or even autobiographical; we must turn to other sources even for the bare chronology of Addams' outer life during this eight-year period. The chapter rather focuses on Addams' inner development, and even this it treats not directly but through a series of symbolic incidents which, whatever their effect at the time, in retrospect form a coherent progression. To describe this progression in mythic terms is to do violence to the quiet understatement of Addams' account, but the chapter does present a descent into the underworld, a confrontation with demonic forces, the acquisition of a gift for mankind, and a return to the world bearing that gift. Mile End Road is a vision of hell which gains much of its infernal horror by parodically inverting the qualities of the edenic Cedarville of Addams' childhood, its sunlight becoming smoky darkness, its rural peace becoming urban squalor, and the bread of Addams' miller father becoming a rotting cabbage. But from the pain of the prolonged crisis Mile End Road epitomizes gradually comes the healing gift of insight into the true nature of the "culture" which, rooted in human misery, at the same time shields us from confronting it. The formulation of this insight and the beginning of the return to the world is encapsulated in the epiphanic experience in Ulm Cathedral with its vision of a "cathedral of humanity." And the entire spiritual experience is recapitulated at the bullfight when Addams views the microcosmic bullring with equanimity, insulated by her "culture" against its horrors, recoils in self-disgust, and determines to return to the world to translate her insight into practice.

IV

After the turbulent spiritual struggles of "The Snare of Preparation," the account of the founding of Hull-House in the following chapter, "First Days at Hull-House," seems almost anticlimactic. The story is told simply and matter-of-factly; the motives for establishing the settlement have been so thoroughly described earlier, the actual establishment seems almost inevitable. And much of this sense of inevitability results from the fact that Hull-House itself is not only a house but the climactic symbol in a series of architectural embodiments of Addams' spiritual life.

Addams and Ellen Starr went to Chicago in January, 1889, to find a suitable place to put their plan into execution; it took them until September to find the right neighborhood and house and actually take up residence there. Addams' first view of Hull-House was enveloped in a semi-magical quality very appropriate for a place which was to become so closely synonymous with her own identity. One Sunday afternoon in early spring, on her way to a Bohemian mission, she passed "a fine old house standing well back from the street, surrounded on three sides by a broad piazza which was supported by wooden pillars of exceptionally pure Corinthian design and proportion" (p. 77). She was so struck by the house that she went the next day to visit it, but was unable to find it again though she searched for several days. Three weeks later, she and Starr decided to locate the settlement as near as possible to the junction of Blue Island Avenue, Halsted Street, and Harrison Street, and when they went there, they found the house Addams had searched for. Built in 1856 for Charles J. Hull, it had become in succession a home for the aged and a second-hand furniture store and, when Addams and Starr found it, it was being used as a warehouse for a nearby factory. They were able, however, to sublet the second floor and what had been the large drawing-room on the first floor. Upon the expiration of the factory's lease the following spring, the owner, Helen Culver, gave the settlement a free leasehold of the entire house and later gave them the use of the land upon which were built the twelve other buildings which by 1910 made up with the original mansion the Hull-House settlement.

The simple idea which formed the heart of the project was that Addams and Starr were not moving onto Halsted Street as benefactors or social workers, but simply as neighbors. This policy was eminently sensible; it gains emotional richness and depth through details that suggest that in Hull-House Addams is seeking to recover her childhood home, and not only to recover it but to remake it along the lines of her own expanded view of human life and human relationships. When she describes her almost mystic sense of recognition when she first sees Hull-House, we are bound to recall not only her father's house in Cedarville but her childhood declaration to her father, when she first saw a poor neighborhood, that "when I grew up I should, of course, have a large house, but it would not be built among the other large houses, but right in the midst of horrid little houses like these" (p. 21). And when she recalls that on their first night in Hull-House, in their excitement they forgot to lock or even to close a side door opening on Polk Street only to find everything undisturbed the next morning, we are bound to wonder if this was not an unconscious tribute to her father's "Quaker tendencies" which led to his principled policy of never locking his doors.

But Hull-House is not merely a recovery of childhood security and of paternal values for Addams. It stands at the end of a series of symbolic buildings which have led her to a vision which far transcends the elder Addams' rather cold and narrow creed of "mental integrity above everything else." The paternal home at Cedarville has been supplanted first by the rotunda of the Wisconsin state capitol, with its symbolic message of a common humanity that takes precedence over individual heroism, and then by the cathedral at Ulm, with its suggestion of a "cathedral of humanity." The three symbolic buildings that anticipate Hull-House suggest home, state, and church, each dominated by father-figures; Hull-House is to incorporate something of all three, transformed and delivered over to the power of woman as bread-giver and peace-maker.

V

As Addams points out in her preface, the remainder of the book after the first five chapters abandons chronology to take up a series of topics connected with life and work at Hull-House. The power of these later chapters lies in the vividness and concreteness with which Addams describes the people and events at Hull-House. What readers are likely to retain in their memory is a series of sharply etched vignettes. Many are heart-rending, such as that of the thirteen year old girl, employed in a laundry, who swallowed carbolic acid because she despaired of repaying a three dollar loan (pp. 149-150), or the old German woman who, when county officials tried to take her to the poorhouse, "had thrown herself bodily upon a small and battered chest of drawers and clung there, clutching it so firmly that it would have been impossible to remove her without also taking the piece of furniture. She did not weep nor moan nor indeed make any human sound, but between her broken gasps for breath she squealed shrilly like a frightened animal caught in a trap" (p. 119). Or the Bohemian immigrant who beat his wife during his regular bouts of drinking and finally committed suicide in a fit of delirium tremens. Employed as a coal shoveller in Chicago, he had been a master goldsmith in the old country and his wife could sometimes calm the "restless fits" that preceded his drinking bouts by giving him a bit of metal to work on (p. 178). Others are wryly comic, such as the Italian mother whose five-year-old child regularly came to kindergarten drunk after a breakfast of bread soaked in wine; after a visit from a Hull-House resident the mother reformed and soaked the child's bread in "an American drink"—whiskey (p. 84).

This wealth of anecdote is unified by the distinctive voice of Addams herself. The "personal motives" of the earlier chapters are abandoned in the later ones in favor of a clear-eyed account of what actually went on in the neighborhood of Hull-House. And yet, paradoxically, our sense of Addams' personality is even stronger in these later, ostensibly more "objective" sections. The turbulence of the formative years has subsided; the woman who emerges is settled in her identity, unflinching in her power to confront every level of reality, and indefatigable in building a fully human community in an unlikely setting. It is extraordinary to read of the areas of experience this delicate, genteel product of the Rockford Seminary deals with quietly, calmly, and efficiently. Early in her days at Hull-House, she delivered an illegitimate baby when the doctor was late in arriving and "none of the honest Irish matrons would 'touch the likes of her'" (p. 88). She confronts drunken wife-beaters, corrupt municipal officials, and slave-driving employers, she deals with child-prostitution, narcotics peddling, and child abuse, and she gets an appointment as a garbage inspector in order to clean up the streets of the neighborhood. And her account of these experiences is invariably modest, undogmatic, and self-deprecating. She had learned at Hull-House what the girls at Rockford Seminary failed to learn: to walk in the "obscure paths of tolerance, just allowance, and self-blame" (p. 38).

The details of the chapters are also unified by a small cluster of persistent principles, the most important of which is the supremacy of experience over theory. The restless yearning of the youthful Addams to strike through the veils of idealism, aestheticism, and gentility and confront naked reality now takes the mature form of a deep distrust of all abstractions and an insistence that truth can be arrived at only through the concrete and the fully experienced. The "idea" that resulted in Hull-House was not an idea at all but an action, to move into a city slum and do whatever work came to hand without preconceptions or theories, and Addams quotes with approval an early statement of her own:

> Those who believe that Justice is but a poetical longing within us, the enthusiast who thinks it will come in the form of a millennium, those who see it established by the strong arm of a hero, are not those who have comprehended the vast truths of life. The actual Justice must come by trained intelligence, by broadened sympathies toward the individual man or woman who crosses our path; one item added to another is the only method by which to build up a conception lofty enough to be of use in the world. (p. 55)

The limitations of such a view of the relation between theory and experience are obvious. Its power and persuasiveness in ***Twenty Years at Hull-House*** result from the fact that it is an "earned" view; whatever its general validity, it has followed from a profound spiritual struggle and its resolution, and it can generate the kind of achievement the later chapters of the book document.

The same may be said of the most powerful unifying elements in the later chapters, the recurring symbols. They are rooted in Addams' childhood experiences and gain their richness from these sources in her early life. The most important of these is the house itself, but almost equally important are hands and bread. As the house recalls the paternal home, hands and bread recall the father's grain mill and his flattened "miller's thumb" which Addams had envied so much as a little girl.

We recall Addams' father's strong hands, worn with honorable and fulfilling labor, when Addams visits the vegetable auction in East London and carries away an indelible impression of "myriads of hands, empty, pathetic, nerveless and work-worn, showing white in the uncertain light of the street, and clutching forward for food which was already unfit to eat":

> Perhaps nothing is so fraught with significance as the human hand, this oldest tool with which man has dug his way from savagery, and with which he is constantly groping forward. I have never since been able to see a number of hands held upward, even when they are moving rhythmically in a calisthenic exercise, or when they belong to a class of chubby children who wave them in eager response to a teacher's query, without a certain revival of this memory, a clutching at the heart reminiscent of the despair and resentment which seized me then. (p. 62)

Throughout ***Twenty Years at Hull-House,*** hands carry a double symbolic significance. They suggest a reverence for labor, especially "hand-labor," but frequently they also inspire a "clutching at the heart" when they lie empty and idle, denied the dignity of work. Thus she describes with loving care the skillful hands of the drunken goldsmith when he can take up a piece of metal again or those of a young Russian immigrant in law school attempting to conceal his former occupation as a silversmith when one night he suddenly sat down at a bench in a crafts group and took up a piece of silver (p. 260). In her account of her visit to Tolstoy in 1896, she is powerfully attracted by his mystic faith in the redemptive power of hand labor and by his fidelity and that of his family in practicing it alongside the peasants. Addams' reverence for hand-labor, however, is most fully expressed in the establishment of her Labor Museum. One day she saw an old Italian woman sitting in a doorway and patiently spinning a thread with a primitive stick spindle, and it occurred to her that a museum of technology might not only stimulate respect by immigrant children for their parents' skills, but perhaps even more important, provide a historical context and a source of pride for factory workers through seeing the "inherited resources of their daily occupation" (p. 172). The Labor Museum was a spectacular success and eventually grew to include not only textiles but pottery, metals, and wood as well, an elaborate demonstration of reverence for the achievements of the human hand.

Bread forms a recurring symbol in the book even more persistent than hands. The miller's daughter came to see the giving of bread as an almost mystic act of human solidarity and perhaps the basic "primordial" function of woman. Even the girls at Rockford Seminary felt its power when they adopted wheat and poppies as their class symbols, as bloodless and literary as the symbols were to them. Later, a fundamental step in the Americanization of Italian women in the Hull-House neighborhood was to learn how to abandon the communal oven of Italian villages and bake bread at home. Tolstoy's reverence for bread impressed her powerfully, and although she came to reject his doctrinaire program, upon leaving Russia and recrossing Europe, she experienced an almost mystic vision of the holiness of bread:

> A horde of perplexing questions . . . pursued us relentlessly on the long journey through the great wheat plains of South Russia, through the crowded Ghetto of Warsaw, and finally into the smiling fields of Germany where the peasant men and women were harvesting the grain. I remember that through the sight of those toiling peasants, I made a curious connection between the bread labor advocated by Tolstoy and the comfort the harvest fields are said to have once brought to Luther when, much perturbed by many theological difficulties, he suddenly forgot them all in a gush of gratitude for mere bread, exclaiming. "How it stands, that golden yellow corn, on its fine tapered stem; the meek earth, at God's kind bidding, has produced it once again!" (p. 196)

It is equally characteristic that she should be caught up in Tolstoy's lofty ideas and resolve to spend two hours every morning in Hull-House baking bread and that she should subject the plan to the scrutiny of realism and give it up upon reaching Chicago. "The half dozen people invariably waiting to see me after breakfast, the piles of letters to be opened and answered, the demand of actual and pressing human wants—were these all to be pushed aside and asked to wait while I saved my soul by two hours' work at baking bread?" (p. 197)

The paradox of ***Twenty Years at Hull-House,*** like that of *Walden* in some respects, is that an attitude so profoundly skeptical of art could produce a book which belongs to such a high order of art. The solution to the paradox, of course, lies in the shifting definitions of art. Addams discriminates between these definitions in her account of the theatre at Hull-House and in the process implicitly describes the kind of art her own book exemplifies. The theatre at Hull-House was originally established as an alternative to the commercial theatre which the young people of the neighborhood regarded as their "one opportunity to see life":

> The sort of melodrama they see there has recently been described as "the ten commandments written in red fire." Certainly the villain always comes to a violent end, and the young and handsome hero is rewarded by marriage with the daughter of a millionaire, but after all that is not a portrayal of the morality of the ten commandments any more than of life itself. (p. 266)

The Hull-House theatre was established to provide theatre that did not serve as a barrier to reality but as an avenue to it, to serve "not only as an agent of recreation and education, but as a vehicle of self-expression for the teeming life all about us" (p. 267). The theatre, which eventually achieved considerable brilliance, presented everything from historical and religious pageants to Greek tragedy, the great moderns, and original plays on local subjects. Addams eventually came to see the theatre as an instrument not of illusion but of truth:

> I have come to believe, however, that the stage may do more than teach, that much of our current moral instruction will not endure the test of being cast into a lifelike mold, and when presented in dramatic form will reveal itself as platitudinous and effete. That which may have sounded like righteous teaching when it was remote and wordy will be challenged afresh when it is obliged to simulate life itself. (p. 270)

In this account of the theatre, Addams recapitulates the action of the entire book—the impatience with idealized versions of reality, the drive to move through them, and the final confrontation with genuine experience. And her description of the theatre as it can be at its best could be applied with equal justice to ***Twenty Years at Hull-House***: not an idealized treatment of reality, not even a way of "teaching," but a way of knowing, of testing versions of reality and discarding those that are false until we arrive as close as may be to "life itself."

NOTES

[1]Jane Addams, *Twenty Years at Hull-House.* Signet Classic edition (New York: New American Library, n.d.), pp. 216-17. Further page references to *Twenty Years at Hull-House* are all to this edition and appear parenthetically in the text.

[2]James Weber Linn, *Jane Addams* (New York: Appleton-Century, 1935).

[3]Margaret Tims, *Jane Addams of Hull House, 1860-1935* (New York: Macmillan, 1961), p. 18.

[4] Erik Erikson, *Young Man Luther* (New York: Norton, 1958). Addams' experiences between 1881 and 1889 constitute a classic Eriksonian "moritorium." See, especially, *Young Man Luther,* pp. 98-104, for a general description of such periods of identity diffusion and ultimate reintegration.

Stuart J. Hecht (essay date 1982)

SOURCE: "Social and Artistic Integration: The Emergence of Hull-House Theatre," in *Theatre Journal,* Vol. 34, No. 2, May, 1982, pp. 172-82.

[*In the following essay, Hecht reviews the history of the Hull-House Theatre, including political clashes over its administration.*]

Chicago's Hull-House Theatre developed specifically to combat the corrupting influences of urban tenement life. In 1889, Jane Addams and Ellen Gates Starr purchased a mansion in the city's rough Southwest section and there created the "Hull-House" settlement, a social and educational center for the largely immigrant community. The neighborhood reflected the worst of late 19th century urban conditions. Hull-House served a patchwork of ethnic neighborhoods riddled by poverty, crime, and social problems caused by efforts to acculturate. Jane Addams saw Hull-House as an educational forum, a place for the exchange of ideas and knowledge among the classes for the purpose of bridging social divisions caused by industrialism. This study will examine the process by which theatre emerged as an instrument for social rehabilitation.

Paintings, statues and other works of art filled the newly opened settlement house. Art was an intrinsic part of founder Ellen Starr's social philosophy. Starr began programs in the arts at Hull-House as a direct means of overcoming the problems of industrialism. Though influenced by Ruskin, Carlyle and others, her ideas sprang most directly from the English artist and social philosopher William Morris. His ideal was the medieval community in which craft guilds assured a healthy social position for art and beauty. This was not possible in modern industrial society where machines made work drudgery and products "rubbish." Morris believed that industrialism could be fought by making good art available, not only to an elite, but to the public at large. Morris' own art sought to develop well designed products for everyday use. His projects ranged from bookbinding to designing wall paper.[1]

Like Morris, Starr believed that direct worker participation in the product led to individual expression, and therefore to art. Industrialization, however, prohibited the worker from contributing to the final product and thereby making it, in part, his own. Instead he became an extension of the machine, toiling to produce pre-planned products. Starr juxtaposed art against the machine. Increased mechanization meant decreased artistic expression and, it followed, only increased artistic expression could combat the evils of mechanization. Starr equated the death of art with the loss of personal happiness and freedom. She therefore saw one of the settlement's major tasks as that of restoring art to workers' lives.[2]

Ellen Starr's convictions greatly influenced Jane Addams. Addams also blamed the poor quality of urban life on industrialism and recognized the practical value of art in the improvement of conditions. However, where Starr acted upon theory, Addams acted upon practical experience. On her early visits to Halsted Street, site of Hull-House, Addams witnessed the popular appeal of theatre:

> One of the conspicuous features of our neighborhood, as of all industrial quarters, is the persistency with which the entire population attends the theater. The very first day I saw Halsted Street a long line of young men and boys stood outside the gallery entrance of the Bijou Theater, waiting for the Sunday matinee to begin at two o'clock, although it was only high noon . . . Our first Sunday evening in Hull-House, when a group of small boys sat on our piazza and told us "about things around here," their talk was all of the theater and of the astonishing things they had seen that afternoon . . . it was difficult to discover the habits and purposes of this group of boys because they much preferred

> talking about the theater to contemplating their own lives, so it was all along the line; the young men told us their ambitions in the phrases of stage heroes, and the girls, so far as their romantic dreams could be shyly put into words, possessed no others but those soiled by long use in the melodrama . . . Nevertheless the theater, such as it was, appeared to be the one agency which freed the boys and girls from that destructive isolation of those who drag themselves up to maturity by themselves, and it gave them a glimpse of that order and beauty into which even the poorest drama endeavors to restore the bewildering facts of life.[3]

Unfortunately, the examples found in five-cent theatres, melodramas and vaudevilles were, to Addams, grossly unrealistic and, so being, inadequate. Addams decided that the theatre's power lay in its ability to provide models of moral behavior and social conduct otherwise not available to poor urban dwellers.[4] Her attitudes were shared by William Dean Howells who, in a 1902 letter to Addams, wrote: "I am not sure, however, that anything so false as the old melodrama can be the beginning of good. The very soul of morality is concerned in aesthetic truth; and I doubt if the delight of the poor, or even the rich, in an impossible picture of life, can be wholesome for them. They can get the same effect from gin or whiskey."[5] Jane Addams believed that if the quality of drama were improved then the theatre's potent influence on slum life could be used for social good. A fine drama, one consistent with the workers' lives and experience, would serve as a healthy standard for social conduct and moral behavior. Furthermore, Addams saw the theatre as a place where the validity of accepted social "truths" could be tested by their believability on the stage. With these convictions in mind she campaigned for the institution of dramatics at Hull-House.

It was necessary for Addams to insist on the establishment of dramatics. Art and music activities were part of the Hull-House educational program from the beginning; dramatics had to be introduced gradually. While many residents of the neighborhood regularly attended the theatre, they resisted the sponsorship of dramatics at Hull-House. The reputation of actors and actresses suffered from traditional social prejudice. Local parents feared that actual participation in dramatics would lead to careers in theatre.[6]

Jane Addams fought vigorously for the benefits of dramatics, and her insistence and personal influence eventually gained results. Acceptance was won by degrees. As early as April, 1890, dramatic readings were given in the Hull-House drawing room. Then, in October of 1890, Ellen Starr began a class in Shakespeare. This in turn led to classes in Greek tragedy, begun in June, 1892. After art and music programs had been formalized by the middle of 1893, almost four years after the settlement's founding, the Hull-House Students' Association announced that it had a distinct "Dramatic Section" which was planning its first production for that November.[7] Acceptance and support for neighborhood participation in theatre was established.

Hull-House, from the start, had offered social clubs to the local community as an alternative to street life. While each club was sponsored by a Hull-House resident, activities were generally determined by the interests of the club members. By the mid-1890s, dramatic entertainments were a regular feature of many clubs' activities. Often the then monthly *Hull-House Bulletin* would review such productions, the critic being an appreciative and encouraging Jane Addams. One such review noted that "the costumes were varied and attractive; those of the ladies unusually dainty and the men's make-up in good keeping throughout. In selection, as well, this play was perhaps the best of the season, for the humor was subtle and refined and the plot well-sustained."[8] Addams's attention to artistic considerations set an example for other productions to follow. In so doing she established the initial dramatic standards for Hull-House theatre.[9]

In October, 1896, responding to the growing demand for theatre, a Mr. Hervey White was appointed resident in charge of Hull-House Dramatics. His task was to assist the various clubs with their dramatic efforts. However, his role was soon overshadowed by the arrival of another young resident. Walter Pietsch was a recent graduate of Cornell University where he had had extensive training in theatre. By day Pietsch worked as an advertizing executive, but he gave his evenings to Hull-House. Pietsch began helping the high school age members of the Henry Learned Club prepare scenes from Shakespeare's *As You Like It.* It was presented in June, 1897, and the success of the production was so great that encore performances were presented in the wealthy Chicago suburbs of Kenilworth and Winnetka.

The suburban invitations were probably due more to the fact that the performers were from Hull-House than to any artistic accomplishment. *As You Like It* demonstrated to its influential "North Shore" audiences the great human potential the working class, immigrant population possessed. It also propagated belief in the Hull-House settlement's ability to realize such otherwise untapped potential. Thus dramatics could justify economic and political support for Hull-House and for social reform. It would not be the last time the Hull-House Theatre would be used to promote the value of Hull-House settlement work.[10]

The success of *As You Like It* won for Walter Pietsch Miss Addams's complete support and he soon replaced Hervey White as Hull-House Dramatic director. The *Hull-House Bulletin* of October 1, 1897, announced plans for establishing a formal Hull-House Dramatic Association. Pietsch's goal for the new group was to improve the overall quality of Hull-House theatre by choosing only the best performers from the various Hull-House social clubs: "Instead of drawing from the limited talent of one organization, here was material to be selected from eight to ten clubs, aggregating some hundred and fifty to two hundred young people of both sexes."[11] The selection of what Pietsch called an "all star cast" was agreed upon by Jane Addams during the summer of 1897.[12] In October a committee of qualified residents evaluated and selected sixteen performers.[13]

Selecting a few from the many contradicted Jane Addams's conception of the social group. Clubs had been conceived as open to all, to embody democratic principles. However, the selection process which determined membership in the Hull-House Dramatic Association was restrictive. Rejection meant non-membership. It was the first instance of a conflict between artistic standards and the purely social objectives of the settlement.

During the summer of 1898 Pietsch again conferred with Jane Addams. The two agreed that while Pietsch worked to improve the artistic standards of dramatic production Addams would raise funds to build an auditorium for Hull-House. Pietsch's objectives proved difficult to attain because his actors were not committed to his goals. Since the actors had remained members of their original social clubs, dramatics had to compete with social club activities for their time and attention. Rehearsals were missed and, at times, roles were dropped unexpectedly. Gradually, however, Pietsch was able to make his actors accept the artistic standards for which he was striving. Thus educated, the actors took the initiative and began devoting their attention to play production. Old affiliations were dropped as common artistic objectives proved the stronger social bond. The quality of their performance did improve and, by November 1899, the Hull-House auditorium was completed.[14]

Pietsch resigned in 1900 for personal reasons.[15] After a year's hiatus in which little dramatic work was done, Addams replaced Pietsch with Mrs. Laura Dainty Pelham. Pelham had been an actress, a soubrette touring the Chautauqua circuit before getting married and settling in Chicago. She brought to Hull-House dramatics professional theatre experience and standards along with a driving personality and mind. Under her direction the Dramatic Association was reorganized into an ensemble of fifteen members. Because Hull-House attracted influential visitors, its theatre benefited. The poet Yeats spoke to them, and veteran actor Joseph Jefferson III outlined a plan for their development.[16] Following Jefferson's suggestions, the group presented a series of light comedies in order to develop acting experience and technique. However, their first production was a melodrama, *A Mountain Pink* by Morgan Bates and Elwyn Barron. A Pelham vehicle when she was acting professionally, *A Mountain Pink* brought the Hull-House group great popularity in the community as well as much-needed capital. They followed with comedies by Gilbert and by Pinero. By 1905 they were able to perform such plays as Shaw's *You Never Can Tell,* and *Ibsen's Pillars of Society,* plays leaning towards Social Realism.[17]

Social Realism became the cornerstone of Hull-House theatrical activity. It was central to the social and artistic philosophies of Jane Addams and Hull-House. In 1902 Addams wrote that the Hull-House theatre had been given over to the people. She went on to emphasize that it took time to determine what constituted suitable plays for the local audiences.[18] Hull-House settled on Social Realism and, in so doing, provided a "healthy" alternative to the "cheap" theatre Jane Addams so despised. The dramas of Shaw and Ibsen, given in 1905, and later productions of plays by such dramatists as Galsworthy and Hauptmann all reflected the urban industrial condition. They brought actual tenement life to the stage to educate the audience in social and political ills. Jane Addams realized that such a message held much more power when presented by the tenement dwellers themselves. As she had supported the performances of *As You Like It* before the wealthy North Shore audiences some ten years earlier, Addams now supported the Dramatic Association's attempts to draw audiences from wealthy Chicago areas beyond the Hull-House neighborhood. By doing so Social Realism might garner further support for social reform.[19]

Both Addams and Pelham wanted those neighbors who came to the settlement to recognise Hull-House's theatre as representing their own lives and concerns. Toward this end Jane Addams encouraged working-class participants to help write such dramas. Most revealing is the case of Hilda Satt, a young immigrant interested in both labor unions and writing. A Hull-House resident had written a novel, entitled *The Walking Delegate,* which depicted organized labor's struggle against corruption. Addams wanted the book dramatized and asked Satt if she would do it. After completing her adaptation, Satt worked with Pelham at making the drama stageworthy. The play was successfully presented by the Hull-House Players in August of 1912. Addams along with much of the Hull-House community attended the performance and, as Satt later noted, awarded the playwright flowers.[20]

The Hull-House Players, then, used production to demonstrate their social concerns. Maurice Browne noted his impressions of a Hull-House production of Galsworthy's *Justice* in 1911. Significantly, he had to travel through the Halsted Street slum to get to the settlement theatre. After this performance Browne recorded Pelham's views on Hull-House drama and social reform: "She was asked at the close of the performance by a wealthy Chicago woman if she were not afraid of stirring up dissension among the classes; she answered, 'I don't know—I'm trying to,'"[21]

By 1911 the Hull-House Players had earned national recognition. Known as a group of immigrants working at their various jobs during the day, rehearsing and performing during the evening, their amateur ranks included a cigar maker, a school teacher, and two stenographers. Presenting Social Realism on a non-profit basis, they were free to innovate. Because the commercial theatres considered dramas of social concern too risky to present, Hull-House Theatre became, inadvertently, a mecca for serious modern drama. They gave Chicago premieres, and often American premieres, of works by Shaw, Galsworthy, Lady Gregory and Synge, among others.

Laura Dainty Pelham introduced the new Irish drama in 1912 just as Ireland's Abbey Players came to Chicago as part of their American tour. After seeing each other's productions a friendship formed between the two groups. Their association led to the Hull-House Players' visit to Ireland and England the following year. In order to earn the money needed for their visit, the Players offered an ambitious season of plays, including Masefield's *The Tragedy of Nan,* Yeats's *The Land of Heart's Desire,* and *The Jackdaw* by Lady Gregory. Percy MacKaye, then visiting Hull-House, studied a long rehearsal and gave the Players advice and encouragement. These plays were presented throughout Chicago and enough money was earned to fund their summer visit overseas.[22]

The events which followed the Irish tour demonstrate both the strengths and limitations of Hull-House's use of theatre. The Players return to America met with acclaim and attention. They had not performed on the tour; it was only intended as a visit. However, their story, that of slum-dwellers befriended by the Abbey, combined with the diligence with which they worked to earn the funds necessary for such a journey, brought them much publicity. Articles appeared in the various Chicago newspapers, and *Theatre Magazine* published a profile of the group.[23] Unfortunately, publicity over the tour affected the Players. They returned to Chicago and began preparing the 1913-1914 season of plays, but all was not well within the group.

An artistic dissatisfaction emerged, one caused by the Players' newfound sense of self-importance. In June of 1914 a committee of Hull-House Players issued a report recommending changes in the group's orientation and structure. They wanted to ensure a high artistic standard of production, something they felt lacking in their 1913-1914 season. Influenced by the Irish players they wanted to perform a greater number of American dramas. However, the central complaint of the Players was Laura Dainty Pelham's outdated style of direction:

> . . . [Today] the standard of acting demanded is higher, the finish and the polish must be greater, the staging more in harmony with the production. Crudities of acting and mounting that five years ago passed muster because they were "naturalistic" to-day writhe under the reviewer's lash. No longer are good intentions accepted for good productions. The public, our public, is insisting, not only that plays that are worth while shall be given, but that the manner of giving shall also be worth while . . . This means work—individual work—team work—not only the accurate projection of each character vocally, but the fusing of every part, every line, every property, every setting into one composite whole.[24]

The Players hoped to achieve an artistically coordinated production style by giving themselves a greater say in the artistic decision of the group.[25] Intentional or not, the recommended reforms challenged the artistry and authority of Laura Dainty Pelham.

The attempt at constitutional change was quickly squelched by Pelham. She pencilled in "corrections" which, while agreeing to present more American dramas, otherwise aborted the revisions. Pelham thus prevented the Players from wresting artistic control from her.[26] Sure of her position, in June Pelham left for Europe, not to return until September. However, the dissenting Players were not through fighting. In July, with Pelham safely overseas, the actors issued a press release announcing a playwriting contest in which they would perform the winning plays. Plays were to be sent, not to Hull-House, but rather, to one of the Players' business address.[27] This was the first step in the Players' rebellion.

In August the full extent of the actors' revolt emerged. A second press release announced the appointment of a Mr. Harold Heaton as new director of the Hull-House Players. Again, the announcement came from the Players, not from Hull-House. Heaton was a retired actor who had acted in William Gillette's production of *Sherlock Holmes,* and most recently worked as a cartoonist for a Chicago newspaper.[28] He had no association with Hull-House. In mid-September a third press release announced that the Hull-House Players were opening their 1914-1915 season with four one-act plays "of native authorship," the contest winners. It also noted that a "labor play" was planned for November.[29] The one-acts were performed, significantly, on the Hull-House stage, and met with mixed reviews, but it was too late. Pelham returned from Europe and put an end to the revolt. The rebelling members left the group, one eventually acting for Maurice Browne at his Chicago Little Theatre.

Though Pelham encouraged many of the Players to remain, the ensemble was broken. Furthermore, judging from subsequent programs, there were no efforts to recreate an ensemble. Perhaps Pelham feared such group unity. The Players were to continue on well past Laura Dainty Pelham's death in 1924 under the direction of Mr. Maurice Cooney, but they were never again to achieve the level of artistic success which had led to their Irish visit. Fortunately, at the time of the Players' revolt, other Hull-House dramatic activities were developing which were to make their own artistic and social contributions.

The conflict between Pelham and the Players was intense because each faction was convinced of its own validity. Pelham's position is simple and clear. She had made the Hull-House Players a nationally recognised theatre troupe. Pelham's association with Hull-House gave her unique opportunities—free use of a stage, contact with influential theatre people—but it was she who made the most of those opportunities. Pelham had carefully developed the group, albeit starting from a plan outlined by Joseph Jefferson. She had kept them artistically innovative through fine play selection, and she had arranged the fateful meeting with the Abbey Players. The Hull-House Players were her creation. That the group should suddenly question her craft as well as her authority appeared to be nothing less than disrespect and ingratitude. Their "constitutional revisions" were, in her eyes, a theatrical power struggle, and she would not relinquish what she had worked so long to achieve.

The Players originally thought it possible to stretch the bounds of their club's activities without breaking with either Pelham or the settlement. What began as an effort at constitutional revision only later became a desperate campaign for organizational power. Pelham's inflexibility provoked them to revolt. Once Pelham left the country on vacation the rebelling Players attempted to put their reforms into effect.[30] And yet their actions were done hastily, apparently without Hull-House support. They seemed anxious to demonstrate their revolt's legitimacy through constructive action—and to succeed before Pelham returned from Europe. It was a desperate series of moves, suggesting that they knew once Pelham returned their cause would be lost. Yet they wanted to prove that they, not Pelham, deserved Hull-House's support.

The Players appealed to the settlement because they had faith in Hull-House and in Jane Addams's sense of justice. There was good reason for them to think so. As stated earlier, Addams worked to help the immigrant find a voice, a sense of identity and, eventually, control over his own life. It was a personalized form of social rehabilitation. Arts were used, in part, to provide working-class autonomy. By 1914, the Hull-House Players had learned to equate artistic expression with individual expression. They had successfully realized Addams's ambitions. It is, then, ironic that Hull-House, while recognizing the Players' artistic accomplishment, proved unable to accept the social equivalent of that accomplishment.

Ideologically, replacing Pelham would have been consistent with Addams's beliefs. Given the relationship between artistic and individual expression, a poor production reflected badly on the performers themselves. When Laura Dainty Pelham revealed her artistic limitations, the Players felt that she should relinquish her absolute control. The implication is that if she had remained artistically innovative and reputable then she would have remained acceptable to the Players. However, because they were dissatisfied with her work and frustrated by her inflexibility, they sought artistic autonomy. They did not seem aware that their struggle for artistic authority was also an attempt at collective autonomy. Since Pelham's limitations hindered the group, and since she would not surrender her control over them, a conflict was inevitable. Certainly, given Addams's beliefs, it seemed Hull-House would recognise that Pelham stood in the way of the Players' development and would support their takeover of the group.

Why did Hull-House favor Laura Dainty Pelham over the Players? It appears, because the settlement let the rebelling Players use the stage for their production of one-acts, that Hull-House was at first unaware of the changes in that group's organization. If this is true then it is certain that when Pelham returned from Europe she informed Hull-House of the changes and that Hull-House was quick to support her over the Players. Pelham did have support within the settlement, having participated there for some fifteen years, many of those years as president of the Women's Club. However, Jane Addams was immune to political pressure from within the settlement. It might be possible that Addams backed Pelham in much the same manner that a school principal would back a teacher against an unruly class. However, the kind of institutional attitude implied does not correspond with the close individual attention and involvement which made Hull-House so effective in the neighborhood.

The explanation for Hull-House's decision lies in the limitations imposed by its own ideological commitments. Hull-House was a social institution. It used its theatre program as a practical means of applying its social philosophy. Hull-House dramatics were formed from a unique balance between social and artistic objectives. Still, art was a means, not an end in itself. The constitutional revisions suggested by the Players' committee aimed to preserve the balance between the social and the artistic. However, Pelham's resistance forced them to demonstrate their legitimacy strictly in artistic terms. Whether it was true or not, Hull-House saw the "rebels" as seeking support for a purely artistic endeavor, something which the settlement, with its commitment to social goals, was unable to accept. Because the Players failed to demonstrate their social function, Hull-House supported Pelham. This is ironic as the Players had developed the very sense of self-worth that Hull-House tried to foster in its neighboring community. That sense of self-worth, however, when expressed artistically, took the Players beyond the settlement's limited social orientation.

The balance of the social and the artistic, which maintained the Players prior to their conflict with Pelham, worked to establish the group's historical significance. Social Realism was a blend of sophisticated drama and social reform. The Hull-House Players embodied that formula. Operating out of a settlement they created a new kind of American theatre, similar to one already flourishing in Europe. Like Antoine's *Théâtre Libre* the Players were a small ensemble, performing on an intimate stage, specializing in innovative, serious drama. In so doing they may well have been the first American Little Theatre.

The Hull-House settlement's use of theatre led to common objectives for both the professional theatre and for a developing social settlement theatre movement. In a 1911 issue of *Theatre Magazine,* Maurice Browne used the Hull-House Players as a model of American theatrical potential. He criticized commercial theatre managers and pointed to the Players as responding to a public demand for fine drama.[31] Because of the Hull-House precedent Browne felt encouraged to open his Chicago Little Theatre in 1912, often considered to be the first professional Little Theatre in America.[32] By this point the Hull-House "Little Theatre" had been in existence for over ten years.

The settlement house theatre movement also fostered the development of American Little Theatre. The same conditions which had created the theatre at Hull-House created a similar theatre at New York's Henry Street settlement several years later. Henry Street's founder, Lillian Wald, shared Jane Addams's beliefs, and the two were in constant correspondence. John Collier, writing in *The Survey,* a national social work publication, presented the Hull-House and Henry Street settlement theatres as models for other communities to follow. He wrote of a need for a "people's theater," one which could embody and express the life and needs of its community. Because of this need, Collier advocated further support of such regional theatre throughout the country, always tied to the people.[33] According to Collier, a national theatre must evolve out of the communities themselves. Maurice Browne, on the other hand, urged professional theatre in response to the neighborhood demand for fine drama. Out of the balance between social and artistic objectives, the basis of Hull-House theatre, came the differing visions of Collier and Browne. While Browne's influence continued to grow, Collier's optimism would be short-lived.[34]

Paul Kellogg, editor of *The Survey,* privately wrote in 1928 that the time had come for the settlements to stop focusing their support on the arts, dramatics included. His concern was that emphasis on artistic pursuits had interfered with the primary social action function of the settlement.[35] Thus the same dilemma which in 1914 had prevented Hull-House from supporting the Players in their controversy with Pelham, also aborted the national settlement support for dramatics.

NOTES

[1] William Morris, "Art Under Plutocracy" and "Useful Work Versus Useful Toil," in *Political Writings of William Morris,* A. L. Morton, ed. (Berlin: Seven Seas Publishers, 1973) pp. 57-108.

[2] Ellen Gates Starr, "Art and Labor," in the book written by the Hull-House residents entitled *Hull-House Maps and Papers* (New York: T. Y. Crowell & Co., 1895) pp. 167-79.

[3] Jane Addams, *Twenty Years at Hull-House* (New York: Macmillan Publishing Company, 1938) pp. 383-5.

[4] Jane Addams, *The Spirit of Youth and the City Streets* (New York: Macmillan and Co., 1910) pp. 82-3: also "What the Theatre at Hull-House Has Done For the Neighborhood People," *Charities,* 29 March 1902. p. 284.

[5] William Dean Howells, Letter to Jane Addams, 9 April, 1902, Swarthmore College Peace Collection Jane Addams Papers/Series 1. Hereafter cited as *SCPC.*

[6] Jane Addams, *Twenty Years at Hull-House,* p. 385; also Robert A. Woods and Albert J. Kennedy, *The Settlement Horizon* (New York: Russell Sage Foundation, 1922) p. 156.

[7] First mention of Hull-House dramatics is found in Jane Addams' Diary, September 1889-December 1890, *SCPC;* information on early Hull-House classes found in the Hull-House Scrapbook, vol. 2. Jane Addams Memorial Collection/the Library/University of Illinois, Chicago Circle Campus pp. 1, 21 and 32. Hereafter cited as *JAMC.* By mid-1894 Starr's Shakespeare class had evolved into a set reading group, the Hull-House Shakespeare Club. Julia Marlowe was an honorary member and would attend its meetings when visiting Chicago.

[8] *Hull-House Bulletin,* 1 March 1897, *JAMC.*

[9] Addams was the primary author of the *Hull-House Bulletin,* the sole official publication of the settlement during its first seventeen years. Hers were the only reviews printed in the *Bulletin,* Just as the *Bulletin* set the direction and tone for settlement policy, so too did it try to set an example for all settlement activity, including the theatre.

[10] There is no record of whether contributions were actually given to Hull-House as a result of these performances. However, Hull-House developed strong support from influential families living in such affluent sections of Chicago.

[11] Albert D. Phelps, "How the Hull-House Players Fought Their Way to Success," *Theatre Magazine,* November 1914, p. 230.

[12] Walter G. Pietsch, Letter to Jane Addams, 7 March 1928, *SCPC,* Series 1, supplement.

[13] *Hull-House Bulletin,* 1 December 1897, *JAMC.*

[14] Phelps, pp. 229-39.

[15] Pietsch. His letter says that he was getting married and could no longer give the time needed to direct settlement dramatics.

[16] Laura Dainty Pelham. "The Story of the Hull-House Players," *Drama Magazine,* May, 1916, p. 250. This is one of the few records of Yeats's talk and it is unfortunately vague: "His talk mystified us greatly, and it was many years before we came to understand his point of view, which now seems very clear." Pelham does however clearly state the groups' indebtedness to Jefferson.

[17] Pelham, pp. 251-2; also the *Hull-House Bulletin,* all issues from *Autumn 1900 to 1905-1906, JAMC.*

[18] Jane Addams. "What the Theatre at Hull-House Has Done," pp. 284-5.

[19] Pelham, pp. 251-2; also Addams *Spirit of Youth,* pp. 82-4, 159.

[20] Hilda Satt Polacheck, *I Came a Stranger,* pp. 127-152. Unpublished MS. *JAMC.*

[21] Maurice Browne, "The Hull-House Players in 'Justice'," *Theatre Magazine,* September 1911, pp. 19-22.

[22] Pelham, pp. 255-7; also, Elsie F. Weil, "The Hull-House Players," *Theatre Magazine,* September 1913, p. 19.

[23] Weil, pp. 19-22.

[24] The Hull-House Players, *Report of Special Committee On Constitutional Revision and Policy,* 10 June 1914, *SCPC,* p. 3.

[25] Ibid. pp. 9-22.

[26] Walter Shellinger, unfinished MS on Hull-House Theatre, in possession of Northwestern University Theatre Department, n. pag.

[27] *Chicago Evening Journal,* 18 July 1914, quoted in Shellinger.

[28] *Chicago Evening Post,* 28 August 1914, quoted in Shellinger.

[29] *Chicago Evening Journal,* 11 September 1914, quoted in Shellinger.

[30] The text of the *Report to Special Committee on Constitutional Revision and Policy* clearly links the Players interest in performing new American plays with their own desire for a greater artistic say in the group. It is therefore telling that the first indication of their rebellion was a newspaper announcement calling for new native dramas.

[31] Browne, p. 90.

[32] Maurice Browne, *Too Late to Lament* (Bloomington: Indiana University Press, 1956) p. 128.

[33] John Coilier, "The Stage, a New World," *The Survey,* 3 June 1916, pp. 251-60.

[34] See Kenneth Macgowan, *Footlights Across America* (New York: Harcourt, Brace and Company, 1929): also Constance D'Arcy Mackay, *The Little Theatre in the United States* (New York: Henry Holt, 1917).

[35] Clarke A. Chambers, *Seedtime of Reform* (Minneapolis: University of Minnesota Press, 1963) p. 128.

Ellen Condliffe Lagemann (essay date 1985)

SOURCE: "Jane Addams: An Educational Biography," in *Jane Addams on Education,* edited by Ellen Condliffe Lagemann, Teachers College, Columbia University, 1985, pp. 1-43.

[In the following introduction to her book on Addams's influence on education, Lagemann offers a review of Addams's own education and growth as a thinker.]

In September of 1889, Jane Addams moved to an immigrant slum neighborhood on the West Side of Chicago. With Ellen Gates Starr, a close college friend, she had rented the top floor of the former Charles J. Hull mansion in order to live and work with the poor. The social settlement that was established in this way, which was called Hull House, quickly became a vital neighborhood center as well as a meeting place for men and women from all walks of life and from all over the world. It provided a variety of services to the people of its neighborhood, among them a day nursery, a savings bank, a medical dispensary, and a kitchen that sold hot meals to workers in nearby factories. It sponsored innumerable clubs for children and college extension courses for office and factory workers. It helped to organize a Working People's Chorus and a Paderewski Club (for the musically inclined), a Nineteenth Ward Improvement Club, and a Working People's Social Science Club, where non-neighborhood scholars, journalists, ministers, and politicians could meet and debate with neighborhood people. As it became known that Hull House was "on the side of the Unions," the settlement also became a center for trade-union organization, a headquarters for striking workers, and a place where strikers and employers could talk and find help in mediating their differences.[1]

To support Hull House and to explain its program and philosophy to the general public, Jane Addams devoted a great deal of time to public speaking and writing. At the settlement, in collaboration with increasing numbers of other residents, she tried to understand and find ways to alleviate the immediate daily problems of the people of the Hull House neighborhood. Then, in her public statements, she set forth what had been learned at Hull House and how this pertained to larger, more general, and often better known social problems and principles. The result was not only an institution that was suffused with a truly humane spirit of inquiry, but also a corpus of writings in which many aspects of turn-of-the-century American society were wisely and constructively criticized, and the nature and social implications of democracy, incisively explored.

Central to the view of democracy that Addams developed during the forty-four years she lived at Hull House was a vision of a society in which all individuals, regardless of gender, ethnicity, race, or economic status, would have the opportunity fully to express and to develop their talents, interests, and ambitions. Addams believed that democracy required true reciprocity and free accommodation between different individuals and groups, and she was convinced that this could only be achieved in a society where social goods like freedom could be guaranteed to the individual because they were guaranteed to all. Addams's view of democracy was, of course, based on a view of human nature. She recognized the existence of self-interest and potential conflicts of interest, but she also held the optimistic belief that all human beings were adaptable and capable of responding to new experiences and environmental change. Not surprisingly, therefore, her view of democracy was built on the insistent conviction that all people could be led to see that they had a self-interest—a self-interest that was also a common social interest—in the protection and fulfillment of the interests of others. Education was the basis for democracy as Jane Addams understood it, and her writings offer insights into education that remain profound.

Addams viewed education broadly. She believed that it included more than purposeful teaching and learning within a formally organized instructional setting. Hence, in her writings she tended to approach education by considering the consequences, in terms of behavior, social sensibilities, and attitudes toward self and others, of existing and possible patterns of social relationship and of available and needed opportunities for meaningful work, recreation, growth, and renewal. She focused on whether and how social relationships (domestic, familial, occupational, political, intergenerational, and intergroup) allowed and promoted free expression for all parties. She queried the degree to which such relationships offered chances to develop a fuller understanding of how one's job, social status, or immediate personal dilemma was related to the historical traditions and social systems of which it was a part. And she raised questions about whether and how such relationships supported and fostered the self-esteem, awareness, energy, and curiosity that were necessary to well-being and continuing growth.

In her writings, Addams also described the variety of impulses manifested by people of different ages—the impulse to imagine and play so evident in young children, the impulse to make idealistic commitments so prevalent among young adults, and the impulse to nurture and teach so important for mature men and women. And she explored the ways in which these impulses were or might be channeled so as to add to personal strength and competence, and thus serve socially productive ends. By inquiring into the social and developmental outcomes of everyday situations and activities, Addams was able to bring both the experiential and the deliberately pedagogical aspects of education into view.

Addams also wrote often of formal education, and placed a high priority on the improvement and the extension of public schooling. But she was convinced that just as the full realization of democratic ideals would require more than the granting of the franchise to all citizens, so, too, would reliance upon education as a basis for community, and hence for democracy, require more than fuller opportunities for school learning. In consequence, she could admire what she referred to in an early speech as "the dream of transcendentalists that each New England village would be a university," while also maintaining that study alone could not provide the active engagement in community concerns that would foster the mutuality upon which real democracy had to be built.[2] Such mutuality required a regard for others and an awareness of the necessity of defining one's personal interests with reference to collective, social interests, Addams believed; and as she learned at Hull House, such mutuality could be achieved only if culture and politics had vital meaning to all people.

Given these beliefs, it is not surprising that the reform of culture and politics became one of Jane Addams's preeminent goals. At Hull House, she rather quickly became convinced of the importance of linking culture and politics to popular wishes, needs, and activities. She decided, in other words, that culture and politics would have greater value if they were related to the contemporary experience of diverse groups of people than they would if they were based solely on classical or elite standards of beauty, conduct, and morality. This early insight had a profound influence on Addams's thought. It led her to argue and work for fundamental changes in a great variety of institutions as well as in many established patterns of belief. It led her to hope that formal education could be organized so as to contribute to the individual's capacity to engage with others in community affairs, thereby identifying and advancing the common interests that would foster gradual yet continuous social reform.

It was as a result of her experience at Hull House that Jane Addams became a student of democracy and of education. The entire corpus of her writings is significant for many reasons. Those of her writings that deal with education may be most valuable for the clarity with which they suggest the range of experiences from which education may be derived. Even more, perhaps, than did John Dewey, Jane Addams came to see ever more clearly that schooling should be, not an end in itself, but a means to other, broader educational opportunities. She believed that individually and socially enhancing life experiences were the vital sources and telling marks of a society in which democracy was a way of life, and not merely a rhetoric or a political creed. It was a desire to find educational opportunities of this broad experiential kind for herself and for others that took Addams to Hull House in the first place and that desire continued to give direction to her thought.

II

How, then, did Jane Addams acquire the interests, ideals, and ethical commitments, as well as the social capacities, intellectual skills, and personal ambitions, that were evident, first, in her move to Hull House and, then, in her ability to formulate from her experience there a highly empirical social philosophy that was at once original and rooted in the circumstances of her day? At least in part, the answer lies in the education she herself received at home and in college and from the study, travel, and seemingly aimless living that marked her immediate postcollege years.

Jane Addams was twenty-nine years old when Hull House was established. She was born on September 6, 1860, in Cedarville, a small, northern Illinois town not far from Freeport. Her parents had migrated there from Pennsylvania sixteen years earlier and had prospered. Her father, John Huy Addams, a miller by trade, had quickly become a prominent citizen. He was a founder of many community institutions—the church, the school, the library, and even the cemetery—as well as a leading subscriber to the first rail-road, which he had helped to bring to Cedarville. In addition, he was one of the organizers and the first president of the Second National Bank of Freeport. A Whig who turned Republican when that party was formed in 1854, he also served in the state senate for sixteen years.

As a child, Jane Addams was aware of her family's standing. She knew that her family's two-story, brick house was unusually large. And she knew, more importantly, that her father was a "dignified person," a "fine man."[3] Of her mother Jane could be equally proud, though Sarah Weber Addams died when Jane was two. She had responded to a call to help deliver a neighbor's baby—having herself borne eight children (four of whom died)—even though she was again pregnant at the time. On the way home, she had fallen and gone into premature labor. The baby had died within minutes of birth, and Sarah Addams, within a week. Although Jane Addams did not write of the circumstances surrounding her mother's death, she had a vague memory of the event and knew that her mother had been described in an obituary as a woman "with a heart ever alive to the wants of the poor," who would be "missed everywhere, at home, in society, in the church, in all places *where good is to be done and suffering relieved.*"[4]

If knowledge of her mother's character helped to mold Jane Addams's character, intimate acquaintance with her father's personality and values was certainly a source for all that she would be. Many of the recollections she included in ***Twenty Years at Hull-House,*** her first autobiography, were tinged with an interest in developing a logical plot line for her life. One must be skeptical, therefore, of certain of her claims—such as the one that, at the age of seven, in response to the sight of the "horrid little houses" surrounding her father's mill, she became determined that when she grew up she would have "a large house . . . in the midst of horrid little houses."[5] Possible retrospective embellishments notwithstanding, Addams's recollections convey a strong sense of connection to her father that is entirely believable, largely because her memories of her childhood are so incisively embroidered with commentary on the sources of his educational influence over her.

Having lost her mother and come to adore her father, who seems also to have adored her, Jane Addams apparently took her father as her chief childhood model. Imitation is the "sincere tribute . . . which affection offers its adored object," she observed in ***Twenty Years at Hull-House.*** She had "centered upon" her father, she explained, "all that careful imitation which a little girl ordinarily gives to her mother's ways and habits." Not surprisingly, therefore, the welcome she later extended to all people at Hull House was not different from the welcome her father had extended to her as an "ugly, pigeon-toed little girl, whose crooked back obliged her to walk with her head held very much upon one side." Having taken herself to be so misshapen (a perception others had not shared), she had been unable to "endure the thought that 'strange people' should know that my handsome father owned this homely little girl." But her father had not joined in her fear. One day, when he had gone out of his way to acknowledge their relationship in a crowded street—"with a playful touch of exaggeration, he lifted his high and shining silk hat and made me an imposing bow"—she happily saw "the absurdity of the entire feeling."[6]

John Addams's example also encouraged his daughter to study zealously as a young girl. "I was consumed by a wistful desire to apprehend the hardships of my father's earlier life," she wrote later. As her father had done as a miller's apprentice, she therefore spent the early hours of each day reading. She wanted to "understand life as he did."[7] The intellectual habits that were established in this way would subsequently be no less important than the social sympathies that similarly resulted from the modeling and imitation between father and daughter that was a constant feature of Jane Addams's early life.

Of course, John Huy Addams also shaped his daughter by means other than example. Jane Addams remembered going to her father with all her "sins and perplexities" and recalled with affection the gentleness with which he always interpreted her concerns. Through open, matter-of-fact interchange, John Addams shared with her his beliefs about equality and freedom and the commonalities that could exist between people of different nations. He helped her to understand that "you must always be honest with yourself inside." And he trained her to see the importance of individual conduct to the realization of one's espoused ideals.[8]

John Addams was not the only important person in Jane Addams's childhood. She had three older sisters (one of whom died at the age of sixteen), an older brother, and after 1868, when John Addams married Anna Haldeman of Freeport, a strong, beautiful, somewhat domineering, ambitious, and cultivated stepmother. James Weber Linn, Jane Addams's nephew and biographer, wrote that Anna Haldeman Addams "was what in those days was called 'accomplished.'"[9] She played the guitar and the piano and was a voracious reader. She brought a new style to the Cedarville household—elegant furniture, silver for daily meals, more frequent visitors, witty conversation, and dramatic readings from Shakespeare. She offered her youngest stepdaughter constant tutelage in the social graces and cultural pursuits that were so much a part of late-Victorian definitions of "the lady."

Anna Haldeman Addams also brought her two sons to Cedarville after her marriage. Harry, the elder son, subsequently married one of Jane Addams's older sisters; George, the younger, became Jane's constant companion. A bright and adventuresome boy, George Haldeman helped Jane learn to play. A serious student who was fascinated by biology, he also interested her in nature study and science. From Anna Haldeman Addams, Jane gained a lasting appreciation for music and art; with George Haldeman, she experienced what she would later describe as "the companionship which children establish with nature . . . [an] identification with man's primitive life and . . . with the remotest past."[10] Even more than her relationships with her Addams siblings, those with her stepmother and stepbrother had an enduring impact on her, but neither was as educationally or emotionally significant as the relationship she had with her father. It was primarily from her father that Jane Addams acquired strength of character, moral idealism, and an inclination for a deliberate life.

This inclination was already apparent when, reaching the age of seventeen, Addams decided that she would go to Smith College in Northampton, Massachusetts. Smith was one of the new Eastern women's colleges. It opened in 1875, and like Vassar (which was founded in 1861) and Wellesley (which also opened in 1875), it offered women a collegiate education similar to the education men could receive at colleges like Yale, Princeton, and Harvard. Smith awarded the bachelor's degree and in the eyes of many was regarded as a daring and risky experiment. In the year after it was founded, Edward H. Clarke, a Harvard Medical School professor, published a study called *Sex in Education* that heightened the controversy already surrounding the advisability of higher education for women. Going beyond arguments concerning the irrelevance of higher education to a woman's capacity to fulfill her "natural" and socially sanctioned roles as a wife, mother, teacher, and nurse—an exemplar of selfless service and virtue at home and abroad—Clarke argued that the mental exertion necessary for collegiate study would cause women to break down, physically and emotionally, and might even lead to sterility.[11]

In spite of arguments such as Clarke's, John Addams favored advanced study for women, although he did not concur in his daughter's decision to go to Smith. Rather, he insisted that she go to Rockford Seminary, which was close to the town of Cedarville and of which he was a trustee. Originally chartered by the Presbyterian and Congregational conventions to offer academic and religious training to young women in the upper Mississippi valley, Rockford resembled Mount Holyoke Seminary (founded by Mary Lyon and opened in 1837) in that the standards it maintained were more like those of an academy than those of a men's college, the difference being that the standards of a men's college were more uniformly rigorous and classics-oriented than those of an academy. But Jane Addams's older sisters had studied at Rockford, and, as a result, despite her continuing wish to go to Smith, she was enrolled at the seminary as a freshman in the fall of 1877.

During her four years there she studied Greek, Latin, German, geology, astronomy, botany, medieval history, civil government, music, American literature, Bible, evidence of Christianity, and moral philosophy, as well as taking part in debating and literary activities and in the seminary's daily rounds of work and prayer, which were modeled on those of Mount Holyoke. In addition, she quickly became a leader among the approximately fifty other young women who were enrolled at Rockford at the time. A classmate remembered that "we never speculated as to why we liked to go to her room so that it was always crowded when the sacred 'engaged' sign was not hung out. We just knew that there was something 'doing' where she was, and that however mopey it might be elsewhere there was intellectual ozone in her vicinity."[12]

Most important of all, though, it was at Rockford that Jane Addams began to express considerable independence of mind and to articulate an aspiration to pursue feminist ideals. More than many of her peers, Addams was determined to resist the intense pressures to have a religious conversion that were still pervasive at the seminary, which for all intents and purposes was still a training school for missionaries. She therefore found subtle ways to disagree with and even to oppose the rigid and zealously religious headmistress, Anna P. Sill, who, Addams claimed, "does everything for people merely from love of God, and that I do not like."[13] As the speaker for the class of 1881 at their Junior Exhibition, the first such celebration in the seminary's history, Addams announced:

> The fact of its being the first, seems to us a significant one, for it undoubtedly points more or less directly to a movement which is gradually claiming the universal attention. We mean the change which has taken place during the last fifty years in the ambition and aspirations of woman; we see this change most markedly in her education. It has passed from accomplishments and the arts of pleasing, to the development of her intellectual force, and capabilities for direct labor. She wishes not to be a man, nor like a man, but she claims the same right to independent thought and action. . . . As young women of the 19th century, we gladly claim these privileges, and proudly assert our independence, on the other hand we still retain the old ideal of womanhood. . . . So we have planned to be 'Bread-givers' throughout our lives; believing that in labor alone is happiness, and that the only true and honorable life is one filled with good works and honest toil, we have planned to idealize our labor, and thus happily fulfill Woman's Noblest Mission.[14]

Addams's speech, though avowing traditional notions of female service, challenged the conventional views of educational purpose held by the redoubtable "Miss Sill." It said nothing of piety and it claimed autonomy and independent thought as appropriate educational goals for women.

The habit of study that Jane Addams first developed in imitation of her father's systematic reading enabled her to excel academically at Rockford. And the tendency to self-direction, also nurtured by her father's example and teaching, enabled her to select for herself from among the ideals she was offered those she would, and would not, accept as her own. Like others of her classmates, Addams was plagued at times by questions of purpose. "That one should study, that one went to college for that purpose, was to our unsophisticated minds a simple self-evident fact, not debatable," a friend wrote of a group of which Jane Addams was a part. "Our only problem was study to what end?"[15] Such uncertainties notwithstanding, it was at Rockford that Addams began at least vaguely to identify what she wanted from life. While still a student there, Addams wrote to her close friend Ellen Gates Starr, who had left the seminary after a year to become a teacher, first in Mt. Morris, Illinois, and then at the Kirkland School for Girls in Chicago: "There is something in being in a big city, in giving somewhat as well as taking all the time, in gaining the ability not to move in ruts, that will give a self-reliance and an education a good deal better than a boarding school will."[16] Equally telling was her announcement in her senior essay that what women needed to gain was "what the ancients called *auethoritas* [sic], right of speaker to make themselves heard. . . . Let her not sit and dreamily watch her child," she wrote. "Let her work her way to a sentient idea that shall sway and ennoble those around her."[17]

At Rockford Jane Addams obviously began to formulate the ambitions she would finally act upon when she moved to Hull House and to recognize the sense of identity and destiny with other women that would serve as a continuing theme of her social criticism. But the seminary did not prepare Addams for a suitable adult role or satisfy her intellectual hunger. After graduation she continued to consider enrolling at Smith College. To go to Smith would signify even greater independence of action and even further commitment to the development of "intellectual force" than had four years at Rockford; and that accomplishment, recognized with the bachelor of arts degree, would be a further step toward the achievement of an authoritative, as opposed to a submissive and pleasing, woman's voice.

Jane Addams never did go to Smith, however. (She ultimately received the bachelor of arts degree from Rockford when that institution began granting such degrees in 1882.) When she returned to Cedarville after graduation, her father and stepmother still opposed her plan to study in the East; and in August of 1881, while on a trip to northern Wisconsin with his wife and Jane, John Addams died suddenly of a ruptured appendix. For eight years thereafter, his daughter endured bouts of deep depression and ill health, and was, for the time being, paralyzed in her ability to act on her previously formed ambitions.

During those eight years, Addams read Ruskin, Tolstoy, Goethe, George Eliot, and Hawthorne. She studied art and architecture, French and German. She took two extended tours of Europe, served as a companion to her stepmother, and helped to care for her nieces and nephews. For a brief time, she attended the Woman's Medical College in Philadelphia, but gave up the effort because of severe back trouble. Her stepbrother George Haldeman proposed marriage, but Jane refused him. She regarded George as a valued friend, but not as a potential husband; and doubtless, too, she was aware, as were other early women college graduates (fewer of whom married than did non-college women), that marriage would end all hopes for a life of more than traditional feminine concerns.

Only intermittently during this period did Addams marshall the energy and interest that had been so much in evidence during her college years. The children at a Baltimore mission where she worked for a brief time stirred her, as did the poverty she observed in Europe. She enjoyed writing frequent soul-searching letters to Ellen Gates Starr and keeping a journal. She immersed herself in art, even falling "in love with the gothic" on her second trip to Europe.[18] And in May of 1888, she excitedly left the continent for London to attend the World Centennial Congress of Foreign Missions. While there, she read *The Children of Gibeon* and *All Sorts and Conditions of Men,* two Walter Besant novels in which wealthy women devote their lives and fortunes to the poor; she visited the workshops and classes of the People's Palace; and she met Canon Samuel A. Barnett, who had established a mission in the Whitechapel section of London in 1884.

Called Toynbee Hall, Barnett's mission was unusual. It served as a place of residence and work for Oxford men, rather than for Church of England clergymen. It resonated with the ideas of John Ruskin, who was then lecturing at Oxford, as well as with those of the (Marxist) Social Democratic Federation, William Morris's Socialist League, and the Fabian Society. As a living shrine to liberal versions of the social gospel, which linked social reform to religious duty, Toynbee Hall had become a frequent stopping place for young American idealists. By 1888, it had already helped to inspire Stanton Coit, an Amherst graduate, to establish the Neighborhood Guild (later renamed the University Settlement) in New York, and Vida Scudder, Jean Fine, and Helen Rand, all Smith graduates, to establish the College Settlement Association, which eventually sponsored settlements in New York, Boston, and Philadelphia.[19] Jane Addams described Toynbee Hall as "a community for University men who live there, have their recreation and clubs and society all among the poor people, yet in the same style [as] they would live in their own circle." Its attraction was tremendous. "It is so free from 'professional doing good,'" she wrote, "so unaffectedly sincere and so productive of good results in its classes and libraries so that it seems perfectly ideal."[20]

From London, Jane Addams wrote with verve to her sister of her interest in missions. Soon thereafter, she convinced Ellen Gates Starr to join with her in a plan to establish a settlement in Chicago. Fourteen months later, the two took up residence in the old mansion on Halstead and Polk Streets that would become Hull House. The decision to establish a settlement ended Addams's despond. It brought into clearer focus all that she had learned at home, at Rockford, and in Europe. It helped her clarify her religious stand; and it enabled her to see a way in which she might combine her wish to be of service to others—a "Bread-giver"—with her equally urgent wish to use and to gain influence—authority—through the powers of her mind.

Although she had managed to withstand Anna P. Sill's efforts to win her conversion and had not worried over theological matters to the extent that Ellen Gates Starr and others of her Rockford peers had done both before and after graduation, Jane Addams was nevertheless a religious person and was concerned about her lack of firm religious faith. Church services had been a constant feature of her childhood, and spiritual queries had been among the "sins and perplexities" with which she had so earnestly approached her father, who, as she well knew, had been a deeply devout if rather private and personally guided believer. Religious questions concerning the meaning of faith, the nature of afterlife, and the definition of sin, holiness, and love had also suffused all of the art and literature Addams had studied. Quite naturally, therefore, she had wanted to be a believer, although she had not been able to reconcile that wish with her determination to follow her father's admonition to "always be honest with yourself inside." But in London, at Toynbee Hall, she saw what religion could mean, not as inherited dogma or abstract faith, but as a source for a truly liberating social and personal creed.

Years before her visit to Toynbee Hall, Addams had written to Starr: "You long for a beautiful faith, an experience. . . . I only feel that I need religion in a practical sense, that if I could fix myself with my relations to God and the universe, and so be in perfect harmony with nature and deity, I could use my faculties and energy so much better and could do almost anything."[21] The social gospel that was preached and practiced at Toynbee Hall allowed her to do that. In 1885, after her first trip to Europe, Addams had joined the Presbyterian church in Cedarville, although she seems to have done so without sure, deep, personal commitment. However that may be, in deciding to open a settlement Addams embraced religion. During the early years at Hull House, her speeches were filled with allusions to "salvation" and "Christ's message"; and just before moving there, she went so far as to say that in comparison to a College Settlement Association settlement she hoped that Hull House would be "more distinctively Christian and less Social Science."[22] Statements such as these may indicate that Addams had not yet learned to express her moral commitments without reference to conventional religious terminology, or that she was, at least for a time, religious in a doctrinal sense. Regardless, by putting to rest the question of whether she was or was not a believer, Addams freed herself to ask the questions that would eventually lead her to enduring conviction: to the belief that religion was a matter of ethics and discipline, a means of aligning individual private action with the ever changing requirements of social need.

In deciding to establish a settlement, Addams also resolved the occupational dilemma she had wrestled with for at least eight years. In college, she had yearned for the right to freedom of expression, but had never gone so far as to demand access to traditionally male occupations. To be sure, after graduation she had considered a career in medicine, but she had given that up and had neither found, nor, more importantly, actively sought, an alternative profession. To have done so would have been difficult. Most college women of Addams's generation married and devoted themselves to domestic duties. Those who did not tended to go into teaching. Even at the turn of the century, only some 6 percent of the nation's medical students, 2 percent of its theological students, and 1 percent of its law students were women.[23] Statistics aside, Addams seems to have wanted a different kind of challenge than she would have been likely to find in an established profession. She had refused a chance to teach at Rockford. She was disinclined to provoke direct confrontation with convention, which entrance into a "male" profession would almost certainly have brought. She was searching for challenge, but not for the challenge of a learned craft. What Jane Addams wanted was a demanding, socially valuable, and stimulating way of life.

Marion Talbot, a founder of the Association of Collegiate Alumnae, who later became dean of women at the University of Chicago, wrote in 1931 that a college woman of the 1880s had to determine after graduation how best to "fit herself into her community and play the part in its life and program which was at once her interest and evident obligation."[24] Her statement reflected the frustration she and others had felt as they struggled to surmount a disarticulation between their college experiences and their postcollege opportunities. Addams, too, had suffered from this situation, but beginning with her visit to London in 1888, she began to see a way out of the problem she shared with other women of her social status and educational background. In the urban slum, there were people suffering from squalor, poverty, and disease—people with what Addams later called "objective" social need. Among college women like herself, there was also need, a "subjective" need for opportunities—educational opportunities—that would make it possible to relate learning to life. Somewhere, she sensed, there had to be a "fit" between the needs of these two different but not entirely dissimilar groups of people. Moreover, searching for that "fit" could in itself provide a vocation, and in turn would bring an end to the aimless living she so despised.

As a result of her visit to London, then, Addams realized that she need not choose between existing vocational alternatives. She could reject both the possibility of a professional career and the possibility of a domestic career and still fulfill her wish for an independent, exciting, and socially responsible life. As was true of her discovery that there was a religion she could believe in, this insight was liberating. It enabled Addams to surmount the occupational dilemma that had previously stymied her. It transformed what had been the burden of unusual educational advantage into an opportunity for new experience. And it pointed Addams toward understanding that study unrelated to opportunities for work and service resulted in learning without instrumental value. In deciding to found a settlement, Addams recognized the social sources of a personal dilemma and in so doing was able to shift the focus of her thought and energy from self-analysis to the analysis of the society in which she lived. She had always been prone to severe self-criticism, as the negative and idiosyncratic self-image she had held as a child certainly showed; and she would always remain vulnerable to painful self-doubt—even going so far on one occasion as to wonder how she could have fallen so low, and become so different from her father, as to have been offered an unsolicited bribe. That notwithstanding, her recognition that other people, especially other young college women, had unmet needs and ambitions not different from her own enabled Jane Addams to overcome the paralysis that had resulted from her acute personal sensitivity and to begin to see that personal experience could and should be a source both for social inquiry and for social action.

III

Moving to Hull House was a happy and energizing turning point in Jane Addams's life. The move marked the culmination of a long and painful search and, in refocusing the questions that Addams could put to her experience, made it possible for her to continue her education in the broad experiential sense that she wrote of so well. It took time, though, and a good deal of observation, conversation, reading, and thought, before Addams would emerge as the settlement leader and social philosopher she would eventually be. The intellect, combined with down-to-earth practicality, sympathy, and shrewdness, that made Addams a leader among those of her contemporaries who also established or joined settlements—by 1900 there were more than 100 settlement houses in the United States and, by 1910, over 400—were called forth by developments at Hull House, especially during the early years.[25]

When Hull House first opened, its activities were based on the presumption that life could be improved by sharing the advantages of learning with people who had not had the opportunities for study associated with a secure, American middle-class way of life. Acting on this presumption, Jane Addams and Ellen Gates Starr introduced themselves to their neighbors by inviting a number of neighborhood women to Hull House to hear them read George Eliot's novel *Romola;* and they continued, at first, to try to communicate in similarly quasi-didactic, quasi-philanthropic ways. The pleasure they felt when the reproductions of classical art that they lent were hung on tenement walls tells much about their initial belief in the value of "uplift."

Such presumptions notwithstanding, the Italian, Bohemian, Polish, and Russian Jewish immigrants who came to the settlement talked of their own interests and of their need for day care, health services, and garbage removal. Their requests made it clear to Addams that, if Hull House were to be the kind of neighborhood center she wanted it to be, sharing "culture" would not suffice. Over time, therefore, the Hull House program broadened, becoming less pretentious and more practical in its aims. Formal cultural and instructional activities did not disappear, but they were increasingly designed in a more collaborative fashion and were combined with efforts to investigate and alleviate neighborhood health, housing, and environmental problems. Writing of the program that had evolved by 1895, Jane Addams said: "All the details were left for the demands of the neighborhood to determine, and each department has grown from a discovery made through natural and reciprocal relations."[26]

Early developments at Hull House reflected Jane Addams's willingness to renounce the social and cultural sensibilities of her stepmother's set as well as her continuing recoil from the kind of single-minded missionizing that Anna P. Sill had exhibited at Rockford. They also reflected her renewed sense of connection with the example of her father. Indeed, the respectful humility and strength that Addams was to attribute to her father in ***Twenty Years at Hull-House*** were the very same qualities that were emerging in her as a result of her experience in Chicago. Most of all, however, the approach and the activities that began to take root at Hull House during the 1890s reflected the influence upon Jane Addams of the extraordinary circle of colleagues she found through her work. Addams's early Hull House colleagues helped her to make sense of the lives and problems of her neighbors and to put her acute powers of observation and analysis to use in conveying to others the nature and social significance of life in an urban, industrial, immigrant slum.

At the start, of course, Ellen Gates Starr was Addams's chief confidante and intellectual resource. The two women had shared a close, supportive friendship since 1877. But there were differences between them; and, as other people joined them at Hull House, they began to grow apart. Far more than Addams, Starr was a person who found real solace in religion and who relished the aesthetics of culture and craft. This is not to say that she did not share Addams's social sympathies or that she drew back from political activism. In fact, she was more likely than Addams to be found actually marching in a picket line with striking workers. But Starr did tend to be more otherwordly than practical, and while she was increasingly drawn to the beauty of High Church Episcopalianism and to a Ruskinian interest in art, Addams was increasingly drawn to the more secular, hard-headed pragmatism that was brought to Hull House by women like Julia Lathrop and Florence Kelley.[27]

Lathrop came from an Illinois background much like Addams's. She, too, had studied at Rockford, although she had gone on from there to Vassar and after college to read law in her father's law office while serving as his clerk and secretary. She moved to Hull House in 1890 and soon thereafter was made a member of the Illinois Board of Charities. Later on, she helped to establish the first juvenile court and the Immigrants' Protection League. When the (federal) Children's Bureau was established in 1912, she became its first chief. In all these activities, Lathrop worked with Hull House residents, and throughout her life she and Addams remained close friends.[28]

Jane Addams claimed, in the biography she called ***My Friend, Julia Lathrop,*** that Julia Lathrop had "an unfailing sense of moral obligation and unforced sympathy" and that there were many stories she could tell that would show Lathrop's "disinterested virtue." Once, for example, she and Julia Lathrop were called to deliver the illegitimate baby of a neighbor whom no one else would help. Addams had apparently told Lathrop after the incident that she wondered if Hull House residents should let themselves be drawn into midwifery. Lathrop had responded with indignation. "If we have to begin to hew down to the line of our ignorance," she had said, "for goodness' sake don't let us begin at the humanitarian end. To refuse to respond to a poor girl in the throes of childbirth would be a disgrace to us forevermore. If Hull House does not have its roots in human kindness, it is no good at all."[29] In relating this story and others like it, Addams acknowledged that Lathrop had helped her to see that it was not for her to choose what services Hull House would offer. Hull House had to be ready to meet whatever needs its neighbors presented.

Florence Kelley also never let Addams forget the importance of responsiveness, although that was not her signal contribution either to Addams or to the settlement. According to James Weber Linn, who knew all the early residents at Hull House, Kelley was "the toughest customer in the reform riot, the finest rough-and-tumble fighter for the good life for others, that Hull-House ever knew."[30] By the time she moved to Hull House in 1891, Kelley had been married, had had three children, and was in the midst of a divorce. More to the point, she was far more set in her views than were the other residents.

A Quaker from Philadelphia who had graduated from Cornell and studied at the University of Zurich, Kelley was a socialist who believed in "the necessity of applying the power of the *state* to prevent the modern industrial system from destroying its own workers, particularly women and children."[31] She had translated Friedrich Engels's writings into English and worked in Chicago as a special agent for the State Bureau of Labor Statistics before being appointed Chief Factory Inspector by Governor John Peter Altgeld. By the time she left Hull House in 1899 to become executive secretary of the National Consumers' League, the settlement was far more involved in industrial questions than it had been earlier or, according to Addams, might ever have become without Kelley. In addition, thanks to Kelley Hull House became a center of social research. Prone to tease Addams, as no one else dared to do (though her son and others insisted that she "approved of her unreservedly"), Kelley prodded Addams to re-think her initial hope that the settlement should be "more distinctively Christian and less Social Science."[32] As Allen Davis has rightly argued, "more than any other single person she was responsible for making Hull House a center for reform, rather than a place to study art and hear lectures on Emerson and Brook Farm."[33]

With Julia Lathrop, Florence Kelley also encouraged Addams's emergence as a writer. Before Lathrop and Kelley moved to Hull House, Addams had already begun her career as a public speaker, lecturing widely in and around Chicago to church groups and women's clubs. But it was in response to Lathrop's prodding that Addams sold her first two major articles—two talks she had given to the School of Applied Ethics in Plymouth, Massachusetts—which were published in the *Forum* in 1892. And it was through Kelley that Addams met Richard T. Ely, whom she referred to later as her "sociological grandfather."[34]

A well-known professor of economics, Ely played an important part in turn-of-the-century efforts to move economics and social science in general from abstraction to empiricism and from a conservative laissez-faire perspective to one that was more in line with reformist, Christian Socialist leanings. In addition to being active in the Chautauqua movement, he helped to found the American Economic Association and taught at Johns Hopkins University until he joined the faculty of the University of Wisconsin in 1892.[35] Hull House embodied many of the ideals Ely espoused. He was convinced and in turn convinced Kelley, who convinced Addams, that investigations at Hull House could result in a sociological survey on a par with Charles Booth's pioneering study of life in a London slum, which had been published in seventeen volumes between 1891 and 1903 as *Life and Labour of the People in London.* The outcome was *Hull-House Maps and Papers,* published in 1895. In addition, Ely arranged for Addams to lecture at the University of Wisconsin and then, in 1902, to have the lectures published as part of a Chautauqua adult education series. Entitled ***Democracy and Social Ethics*** and, according to her nephew, thought of by Addams as a sociological text, the lectures became her first book.

There were many other people during the early years at Hull House who played important roles in Addams's development. Among these, Mary Rozet Smith was especially significant for the emotional support she provided Addams within the context of a longstanding relationship of great closeness and mutual affection; and Louise de Koven Bowen was important, not only for the friendship she offered, but also for the money she gave to support new Hull House projects and buildings. Many faculty members from the University of Chicago (founded three years after Hull House opened) also found their way to the settlement, offering help with clubs and classes and, in some instances, educating Addams as she also educated them. George Herbert Mead, the psychologist who began the development of the field of social interactionism, became one of Addams's valued intellectual comrades. So too did sociologist W. I. Thomas, whose classic study *The Polish Peasant in Europe and America* (coauthored with Florian Znaniecki) helped to legitimate the scholarly use of personal documents. It was his famous dictum—"If men define situations as real, they are real in their consequences"—that helped to inaugurate inquiry into the sociology of knowledge.[36] In addition to Mead and Thomas, the educator and philosopher John Dewey became one of Addams's most notable and valued friends.

Dewey first visited Hull House in 1892 when he was considering leaving the University of Michigan to accept a position offered him by the first president of the University of Chicago, William Rainey Harper. Immediately thereafter, he wrote to Addams of his belief that she had "taken the right way." In the years that followed, he visited Hull House frequently, to participate in Julia Lathrop's Plato Club or simply to talk with Addams. When the settlement was incorporated in 1895, he became a member of its board of trustees, remarking later that he and the other trustees had served primarily to tell Addams, "You are all right: go ahead."[37]

The relationship that grew up between Addams and Dewey was enhanced by personal regard. Dewey's daughter Jane Mary Dewey was named for Jane Addams and Mary Rozet Smith, and Addams gave the memorial service address for Dewey's son Gordon, who died at the age of eight.[38] But the relationship was primarily based on a mutually influential exchange of ideas. Dewey's daughter claimed that her father's "faith in democracy as a guiding force in education took on both a sharper and deeper meaning because of Hull-House and Jane Addams."[39] And Addams claimed in turn that Dewey had provided her with philosophic insights that she found vital to the translation of her early intuitive beliefs into a more fully elaborated understanding of relationships between inquiry and action and personal and social ideals. He taught us "a method," she remarked in 1929. "In those years when we were told by the scientists, or at least by the so-called scientists, that the world was in the grasp of subhuman forces against which it was absurd to oppose the human will, John Dewey calmly stated that the proper home of intelligence was the world itself and that the true function of intelligence was to act as critic and regulator of the forces which move the world."[40]

Jane Addams's acquaintance grew with the years, and she learned a good deal from many different people as well as from her increasing involvement in Chicago politics and in reform causes throughout the nation and the world. Addams served on the Chicago School Board. She seconded Theodore Roosevelt's nomination as the presidential candidate of the Progressive Party in 1912. She was a member of the first executive committee of the National Association for the Advancement of Colored People, a vice-president of the National American Woman Suffrage Association, and a founder of the American Union Against Militarism, from which emerged both the Foreign Policy Association and the American Civil Liberties Union. She was elected chairman of the Woman's Peace Party in 1915, and in 1919 she became the first president of the Women's International League for Peace and Freedom, having presided over the 1915 International Congress of Women at The Hague from which the League originated.

All of these efforts, especially those for woman suffrage and international peace, found their way into Addams's writings. But it was of her experience at Hull House that she wrote most often and from her experience there that she derived her most profound insights into education. The life of her Hull House neighbors, filtered through the values and ideals of her childhood, always gave focus to what Jane Addams did and said. She had had a keen and well-trained mind when she moved to the settlement, and she had been eager to find ways to use it to serve others. But her capacity to understand the social implications of her own experience and that of others was greatly enhanced by the informal tutelage she received from her fellow workers, especially during the 1890s.

IV

After her move to Hull House, Jane Addams increasingly achieved public renown. Although she endured considerable hostility during World War I as a result of her pacifism, even being portrayed by some as a "red" radical of questionable loyalties, she was widely admired and respected throughout her career. During her early decades at Hull House, she was described by journalists as altruistic, benevolent, and kind; and after the militarist hysteria of the First World War had abated, and especially after she was awarded the Nobel Prize for Peace in 1931, she was frequently portrayed as a kind of secular saint. To many of her contemporaries, as to many people since, Jane Addams was female virtue and generosity incarnate, an "American heroine," the "benevolent lady."

Certainly deserved in some ways, Addams's reputation was nevertheless more stereotypic than accurate. Although she was, indeed, gentle, empathetic, and giving, she was also capable of great strength, even of toughness, and had a powerful mind. What is more, if she managed to identify and to meet "objective" social need, she also managed to recognize, analyze, and avow "the subjective necessity" for her actions. Finally, while deeply committed to effecting concrete, practical, and immediate improvements in the life circumstances of men, women, and children in Chicago and elsewhere, she was also committed to demonstrating the role and power of ideas in promoting more fundamental and lasting social change.

Fully recognized and appreciated for her deeds and for her goodness, Jane Addams was not equally recognized and appreciated for her ability to analyze and criticize the society in which she lived. Her writings were praised as incisive, but they were often reviewed as the writings of a woman. "No other book by a woman shows such vitality, such masculinity of mental grasp and surefootedness," the economist Edwin Seligman said of ***Democracy and Social Ethics*** when it appeared in 1902.

The jurist Oliver Wendell Holmes agreed. Jane Addams is a "big woman who knows at least the facts," he wrote. She "gives me more insight into the point of view of the working man and the poor than I had before."[41]

Comments such as these, which today might suggest overt and even purposeful gender-related discounting, at the time primarily reflected the still pervasive influence of notions having to do with female capacities and gender-distinct "spheres." From at least the early nineteenth century, it was generally assumed in the United States that women had special nurturant qualities and virtues, and that these made them especially able to offer love, sympathy, comfort, and succor to members of their families and others in need. Logically, in light of this, a woman's "sphere" was presumed to encompass only those worlds where the heart, as opposed to the mind, was most needed. The home, the sickroom, the elementary classroom, and other places where humane services and tenderness were provided were considered her special preserve. All this, as Jane Addams knew full well, made "breadgiving" seem as "natural" for a woman as it made the assertion of mind—authority—seem "unnatural." To the extent, then, that reviews of Addams's books tended to praise her achievements as not only rare but anomalous, they both reflected and perpetuated presumptions of "sphere."

If traditional interpretations of female capacities skewed interpretations of Jane Addams's work, magnifying its benevolent aspects while masking and demeaning its closely related intellectual side, so too, and equally significantly, did changing perceptions of what did and did not fall within the perimeters of legitimate social science. As a thinker, Addams was more like a nineteenth-century "amateur" social scientist than she was like a twentieth-century "professional" scholar. She subscribed to nineteenth-century convictions having to do with direct, causative relationships between social progress and the general dissemination of knowledge, although she added ideas that were both feminist and radical to this traditional rationale for social science.

Addams was convinced that public consciousness and public policies were integrally related, and she thought both were in need of fundamental change. They had to be suffused, she believed, with what she and her contemporaries of both sexes took to be female concerns—concerns about the health, welfare, and education of children and immigrants, the excluded and the poor. More important still, she insisted that closer links needed to be developed between inquiry and action. Only when inquiry and action were joined, Addams argued, would there be achieved a fuller, more overtly avowed, and actually lived recognition of the rootedness of social ethics in the individual conduct and ideals that defined personal experience. Only with thoroughgoing moral reform, she insisted, would changes in law and in economic and social institutions eventually result in greater justice and enfranchisement for all.

Jane Addams's understanding of the relationship that ought to exist between social need, social inquiry, and social action, as well as her view of the intellectual, institutional, and moral reorientation that would have to take place to achieve this, were not idiosyncratic at the turn of the century. Her views were shared by many other women, especially those who subscribed to a "social feminist consciousness"; and they were also shared by prominent male reformers and social scientists, including Richard T. Ely, her "sociological grandfather," and the University of Chicago faculty members who had been among her early Hull House colleagues.[42] During the 1890s, when the variety of reform impulses that slowly coalesced into the progressive movement were just beginning to be expressed, Addams's views enjoyed a relatively wide and androgynous support.

In the decades that followed, however, as the evangelicism and optimism of early progressive protest became increasingly intertwined with a respect, even a reverence, for science, expertise, and professionalism, Addams's views became more and more marginal and began to lose their earlier and wider cross-sex appeal. Much was involved in this change of attitude, the notable development of relevance to this discussion being the increasing acceptance of sociology, psychology, and other once-intertwined branches of social science as distinct, university-based, professional fields of scholarly research.

This trend toward specialization within social science was nowhere more evident than at the University of Chicago. The university established the nation's first department of social science in 1892, including within it at the start sociology, anthropology, and a motley array of applied and reform-oriented subjects called "sanitary science." Then, in 1904, sanitary science was moved out of this department and placed in a newly created department of "household administration." At the same time, the university established training in social work.[43]

In addition to being the first in the nation, the Chicago department of social science was for many years paradigm setting. Developments at Chicago were widely influential. As a result, the new departmental lines drawn there created divisions, not just at Chicago, but also elsewhere, between theoretical, "objective," academic social research, on the one hand, and more reformist, political, and applied social work, on the other. The structural and intellectual divisions thus created were soon compounded by gender divisions that rapidly took on hierarchical status distinctions as well. Sociology, which came increasingly to be dominated by men, was more and more seen as a source for insights to be tested and applied by "social workers," most of whom were women; and settings for "social work," including social settlements like Hull House, were more and more seen as places to which (male) university sociologists might send students to collect data, which the sociologists and not the social workers would then analyze in a university laboratory and elaborate into theory.[44]

Early-twentieth-century developments in sociology, such as those at the University of Chicago, were not dissimilar from roughly contemporaneous developments in other fields of social science, which for a time had been areas of study that were relatively open to women.[45] Such developments, when accompanied by an increase in gender segregation in undergraduate study, played a crucial role in introducing the notion of gender-distinct spheres into the burgeoning early-twentieth-century world of the university. The introduction and institutionalization within the university of gender-distinct spheres and the transmission through university teaching and research of expectations related to these spheres reinforced more general expectations about gender-related capacities, and thus helped further to define, and limit, the way in which Jane Addams's writings were received.[46] Although Addams herself never fully concurred in the judgment, her views became increasingly associated with the professional practice of female altruism—put otherwise, with professional social work—and conversely, increasingly disassociated from the professional study of sociology, which was dominated and controlled, not only through university departments, but also through journals and the American Sociological Association, by men.[47]

In some ways, of course, this division lessened the influence that Addams's writings might otherwise have achieved. But the increasing fragmentation and professionalization of social science did not have only negative consequences for Addams's work. By isolating Addams and other women reformers and social scientists, these developments helped to join them ever more closely in informal female networks that sought and achieved any number of significant policy innovations, ranging from the establishment of the (federal) Children's Bureau in 1912 to the passage of New Deal labor legislation.[48] Equally important, these trends may have had the somewhat ironic effect of enhancing Addams's ability to identify and articulate what she believed. At least during her early years at Hull House, much that she said about settlements and settlement work took the form of dissent from increasing admiration for abstract, "objective," scholarly knowledge. Thus, in an 1899 paper read before the American Academy of Political and Social Science, she presented the social settlement as a potential corrective to what she still called "the college":

> As the college changed from teaching theology to teaching secular knowledge the test of its success should have shifted from the power to save men's souls to the power to adjust them in healthful relations to nature and their fellow men. But the college failed to do this, and made the test of its success the mere collecting and dissemination of knowledge, elevating the means into an end and falling in love with its own achievement.[49]

Similarly, in a 1904 speech on immigration delivered at the University of Chicago, through criticism of "the scholar" she implied what the settlement worker should do. Beginning with a polite nod to scholarly contributions to "the field," she went on to say:

> To let the scholar off with the mere collecting of knowledge, or yet with its transmission, or indeed to call his account closed with that still higher function of research, would be to throw away one of our most valuable assets. . . . The scholar has furnished us with no method by which to discover men, to spiritualize, to understand, to hold intercourse with aliens and to receive of what they bring.[50]

Statements such as these show that Jane Addams was deeply concerned with formulating views of knowledge, research, and reform, as well as views of their proper relation, that were in many ways different from those that prevailed.

Because Jane Addams's writings embodied these views and therefore pertained directly to the immediate circumstances of her world, they sometimes present particular situations and advocate specific changes of policy that have little direct relevance to social problems today. But to let that detract from their more fundamental value would be to ignore their more essential and enduring message. Jane Addams's writings assert the belief that abstract social values like justice, freedom, equality, and peace are concretely defined by daily actions and beliefs. They urge the possibility that progress toward greater justice, fuller freedom, more complete equality, and a lasting peace may be achieved, if, through social experimentation, study, and discussion, men and women become ever more cognizant of the shared consequences and social aspects of their lives. Addams's writings are those of a moralist and an idealist: of a person who never doubted that there could be values upon which all people would agree, and who never renounced the conviction that ideas might lessen and in time even modify the pervasiveness and debilitating effects of poverty, powerlessness, and social class. Addams's writings may be criticized for the biases they reveal, but they pose a key question of liberal, democratic social philosophy: the question of how, through education and experience, all people can be more fully empowered to pursue their separate, reciprocal, and common goals. It is the significance of that question as well as the astuteness of her reflections upon it that make Jane Addams's writings worth reading still.

NOTES

[1] This description of the Hull House program is taken from Jane Addams, "Hull-House: A Social Settlement," appendix in *Hull-House Maps and Papers* (New York: Thomas Y. Crowell, 1895), pp. 207-230. Later descriptions may be found in Jane Addams, *Twenty Years at Hull-House* (New York: Macmillan, 1910) and *The Second Twenty Years at Hull-House* (New York: Macmillan, 1930).

[2] Jane Addams, "The Subjective Necessity for Social Settlements," in *Philanthropy and Social Progress,* ed. Henry C. Adams (Thomas Y. Crowell, 1893), p. 8.

[3] Addams, *Twenty Years at Hull-House,* p. 7.

[4] Quoted in James Weber Linn, *Jane Addams: A Biography* (New York: D. Appleton-Century, 1935), pp. 22-23.

[5] Addams, *Twenty Years at Hull-House,* pp. 3-5.

[6] Addams, *Twenty Years at Hull-House,* pp. 11-12, 7-9.

[7] Addams, *Twenty Years at Hull-House,* pp. 12-13.

[8] Addams, *Twenty Years at Hull-House,* pp. 13 and 15.

[9] Linn, *Jane Addams,* p. 30.

[10] Addams, *Twenty Years at Hull-House,* pp. 17-18.

[11] Edward H. Clarke, *Sex in Education; or, A Fair Chance for the Girls* (Boston: J. R. Osgood, 1873). For a general discussion of the development of collegiate education for women as well as opposition to it see Thomas Woody, *A History of Women's Education in the United States,* 2 vols. (1929; reprint, New York: Octagon Books, 1966), vol. 2, chap. 4.

[12] Quoted in Linn, *Jane Addams,* p. 47.

[13] Quoted in Allen F. Davis, *American Heroine: The Life and Legend of Jane Addams* (New York: Oxford University Press, 1973), p. 14.

[14] Jane Addams, "Bread Givers," *Rockford Daily Register,* April 21, 1880; reprinted in *Jane Addams: A Centennial Reader* (New York: Macmillan, 1960), pp. 103-104.

[15] Quoted in Linn, *Jane Addams,* p. 51.

[16] Quoted in Davis, *American Heroine,* p. 14.

[17] Quoted in Davis, *American Heroine,* p. 22.

[18] Quoted in Davis, *American Heroine,* p. 48.

[19] Allen F. Davis, *Spearheads for Reform: The Social Settlements and the Progressive Movement 1890-1914* (New York: Oxford University Press, 1967), pp. 8-14.

[20] Quoted in Davis, *American Heroine,* p. 49.

[21] Quoted in Davis, *American Heroine,* p. 17.

[22] Quoted in John C. Farrell, *Beloved Lady: A History of Jane Addams' Ideas on Reform and Peace* (Baltimore: Johns Hopkins University Press, 1967), p. 61.

[23] Woody, *A History of Women's Education,* vol. 2, pp. 360, 369, and 370.

[24] Quoted in Joyce Antler, "The Educated Woman and Professionalization: The Struggle for a New Feminine Identity, 1890-1920" (Ph.D. diss., State University of New York at Stony Brook, 1977), pp. 137-138.

[25] Davis, *Spearheads for Reform,* p. 12.

[26] Addams, "Hull-House: A Social Settlement," pp. 208.

[27] *Notable American Women,* s.v. "Starr, Ellen Gates."

[28] *Notable American Women,* s.v. "Lathrop, Julia Clifford."

[29] Jane Addams, *My Friend, Julia Lathrop* (New York: Macmillan, 1935), pp. 49 and 53.

[30] Linn, *Jane Addams,* pp. 138-139.

[31] Linn, *Jane Addams,* p. 137.

[32] Linn, *Jane Addams,* p. 138.

[33] Davis, *American Heroine,* p. 77. For Kelley's life see *Notable American Women,* s.v. "Kelley, Florence"; Dorothy Rose Blumberg, *Florence Kelley: The Making of a Social Pioneer* (New York: Augustus M. Kelley, 1966); and Josephine Goldmark, *Impatient Crusader: Florence Kelley's Life Story* (Urbana: University of Illinois Press, 1953).

[34] Quoted in Davis, *American Heroine,* p. 102.

[35] Richard T. Ely, *Ground Under Our Feet: An Autobiography* (New York: Macmillan, 1938).

[36] Mary Jo Deegan and John S. Burger, "George Herbert Mead and Social Reform: His Work and Writings," *Journal of the History of the Behavioral Sciences* 14 (1978): 362-373; and "W. I. Thomas and Social Reform: His Work and Writings," *Journal of the History of the Behavioral Science* 17 (1981): 114-125.

[37] Quoted in Davis, *American Heroine,* pp. 97 and 109.

[38] Jane Addams, "Gordon Dewey," in *The Excellent Becomes the Permanent* (New York: Macmillan, 1932), pp. 61-69.

[39] Jane M. Dewey, "Biography of John Dewey," in *The Philosophy of John Dewey,* ed. Paul Arthur Schilpp, 2d ed. (La Salle, Ill.: Open Court Publishing, 1951), p. 30.

[40] Jane Addams, "A Toast to John Dewey," *Survey* 63 (1929): 203-204.

[41] Both reviews are quoted in Davis, *American Heroine,* p. 128.

[42] Ellen Condliffe Lagemann, *A Generation of Women: Education in the Lives of Progressive Reformers* (Cambridge, Mass.: Harvard University Press, 1979), pp. 154-160; Benjamin G. Rader, *The Academic Mind and Re-*

form: The Influence of Richard T. Ely in American Life (Lexington: University of Kentucky Press, 1966), pp. 28-129; and Rosalind Rosenberg, *Beyond Separate Spheres: Intellectual Roots of Modern Feminism* (New Haven: Yale University Press, 1982), pp. 28-53.

[43] Steven J. Diner, "Department and Discipline: The Department of Sociology at the University of Chicago, 1892-1920," *Minerva* 13 (1975): 514-553; and Rosenberg, *Beyond Separate Spheres,* pp. 43-51. Social work training began in 1903 in the Institute of Social Science; was reorganized under the auspices of the School of Civics and Philanthropy in 1907; and was finally transferred to the School of Social Service Administration in 1920.

[44] Rosenberg, *Beyond Separate Spheres;* and Mary Jo Deegan, "Women in Sociology: 1890-1920," *Journal of the History of Sociology* 1 (1978): 11-34.

[45] Rosenberg, *Beyond Separate Spheres;* Margaret W. Rossiter, *Women Scientists in America: Struggles and Strategies to 1940* (Baltimore: Johns Hopkins University Press, 1982); and Dorothy Ross, "The Development of the Social Sciences," in *The Organization of Knowledge in Modern America 1860-1920,* ed. Alexandra Oleson and John Voss (Baltimore: Johns Hopkins University Press, 1979), pp. 107-138.

[46] Ellen Condliffe Lagemann, "Looking at Gender: Women's History," in *Historical Inquiry in Education,* ed. John Hardin Best (Washington, D.C.: American Educational Research Association, 1983), pp. 251-264.

[47] Addams believed that social work embodied natural, historically female concerns, a belief that led her to suffragism (see, for example, Jane Addams, "Woman Suffrage and the Protection of the Home," *Ladies' Home Journal* 27 [1910]: 21, as well as comments throughout *Newer Ideals of Peace* [New York: Chautauqua Press, 1970]). She saw formal training for social work as an advantage that her "pre-efficiency" generation had not had: Jane Addams, "How Much Social Work Can a Community Afford: From the Ethical Point of View," *Proceedings of the National Conference of Social Work* (1926), pp. 108-109. She also feared, however, that the natural, emotional, and ethical aspects of social work might be lost with increasing professionalization: Linn, *Jane Addams,* pp. 111-112; and Farrell, *Beloved Lady,* p. 139. On the isolation of women sociologists from their male colleagues see Mary Jo Deegan, "Early Women Sociologists and the American Sociological Society: The Patterns of Exclusion and Participation," *American Sociologist* 16 (1981): 14-24.

[48] Nancy P. Weiss, "The Children's Bureau: A Case Study in Women's Voluntary Networks" (Paper delivered at the Second Berkshire Conference on the History of Women, Bryn Mawr, Pennsylvania, 10 June 1976); and Susan Ware, *Beyond Suffrage: Women in the New Deal* (Cambridge, Mass.: Harvard University Press, 1981).

[49] Jane Addams, "A Function of the Social Settlement," *Annals of the American Academy of Political and Social Science* 13 (1899): 339-340.

[50] Jane Addams, "Recent Immigration, a Field Neglected by Scholars," *University Record* (Chicago) 9 (1905): 246-247.

Herbert Stroup (essay date 1986)

SOURCE: "Jane Addams," in *Social Work Pioneers,* Nelson-Hall, 1986, pp. 2-28, 281.

[*In the following excerpt, Stroup presents Addams as a pioneer in developing the framework of social welfare in America.*]

Jane Addams, the founder of famed Hull House, a pioneer in the settlement house movement in the United States, and the Nobel Prize recipient for peace in 1931, was born in a red brick house in Cedarville, Illinois, in the fall of 1860. Within the house lived busy people who knew moderate worldly success and who were secure in their homey integrity and virtue. The Addamses were a successful family.

Jane Addams claimed that her father was one of the most important influences on her life. Certainly he did make an incisive impression upon her. He came from English stock that had settled in Pennsylvania under the leadership of William Penn. He was born in Sinking Springs, Pennsylvania, in 1822, and while he was attached historically to the Quakers, he did not practice that religion after he left Pennsylvania and settled with his new wife in Illinois. In Cedarville, he attended two churches, each on alternate Sundays. He was a generous contributor to both churches, and he urged his family to be devoted and loyal to some church. But he did not talk much about his religious views. Once Jane asked her father, "What are you? What do you say when people ask you?" With a twinkle in his eye, he responded, "I am a Quaker."

"But that isn't enough to say," his persistent daughter replied.

"Very well," he added, "to people who insist upon details, as someone is doing now, I add that I am a Hicksite Quaker." Try as she may, Jane could not induce her father to explain further.[2]

John Addams was a man of strict conscience. When he was a member of the Illinois legislature, Abraham Lincoln wrote him about a certain measure: "You will of course vote according to your conscience, only it is a matter of considerable importance to me to know how that conscience is pointing."

Jane's father was one of the leading citizens of Cedarville and nearby Freeport. He won the financial respect of the people of both places because of his reputation as a shrewd and careful investor. He had come to Cedarville with about $3,000, and in time, he owned two thriving mills—one for flour, the other for wood. These he managed so well he was able to secure a dependable income that allowed him to devote some of his time to community improvements and to politics. In the winter of 1846, he was prominent in the organization of a convention in Rockford to urge the creation of a railroad to be called the Galena and Chicago Union. He worked with the convention until funds were obtained to make the idea an actuality.

In his work for the railroad, John Addams got to know many of the people in his part of the state, and this came in handy later when he ran for the state legislature. He was a member of the legislature during the Civil War and was a good friend of Lincoln. Jane Addams recorded the fact that the only time she knew her father to cry was on the death of Lincoln.

Sarah Addams, Jane's mother, was a devoted wife and mother. She, too, tended to idolize her husband. She was intensely interested in charitable activities, and it was her interest reflected through others after Sarah's untimely death that encouraged Jane to think of the poor. In the obituary written for Sarah Addams, the following line gives insight into the character of the woman: "Mrs. Addams will be missed everywhere, at home, in society, in the church, in all places where good is to be done and suffering relieved." No wonder that Jane felt the plight of the poor!

Jane's arrival into the family was a welcomed event. She was the eighth child. Her sister Martha died at sixteen; three of the other children died in infancy; only four reached maturity. In her autobiography, Jane Addams emphasized her "ugliness," but this view was contested by many who knew her in her youth. It is true that she was small, frail, and pigeon-toed, and had a slight curvature of the back, which caused her to hold her head slightly on a slant. Intensely introspective, she spent many hours debating her conduct. She was an avid reader and devoured many of the classics of Western intellectual tradition at an early age. In social activities she mirrored her father's behavior, being reserved and rather intellectual.

Sarah Addams died when Jane was only two, and her death was a severe blow to the family. Mary, the oldest daughter, assumed the female headship of the family, and life continued under her direction. John Addams was serving in the legislature much of the time and gave the children considerable responsibility. By the time Jane was eight, John married again. His second wife was Anna Hostetter Haldeman, the widow of a Freeport miller. She had two sons: the elder was studying in Europe, but the younger son, George, came to live in the Cedarville homestead. Jane and George developed a close friendship.

George and Jane attended the local school in the village. George was mainly interested in "nature study," and while Jane had little regard for science, she was agreeable enough to help George in his various pursuits. Jane was chiefly drawn to Latin and English literature. One of her teachers was Samuel Parr, who later became a professor of Latin at the University of Illinois.

When she was not quite seventeen, Jane was graduated from the village school and looked toward college. She had hoped to attend Smith College in Massachusetts, but her father had different ideas. He wanted her to go to Rockford Seminary (later called Rockford College) for her basic college training and then to take advanced study abroad. He also apparently wished to have his daughter closer to home than she would be at Smith. Jane finally agreed to attend Rockford, even though she knew that it stressed "professing religion" more than she desired and it also did not award degrees.

About fifty students attended Rockford Seminary in 1877, and the cost for one year was about $300. Ellen Gates Starr, from Durand, Illinois, who later worked with Jane as a devoted friend and influential leader in her own right, was a member of the class of 1881, along with Jane. Jane was especially drawn to Ellen because of Ellen's appreciation of the beauty of religion. Jane was interested in religion, but more as truthful poetry than as dogma. Ellen was also witty, intellectual, and outgoing. The course of study at Rockford Seminary included Greek, Latin, natural science, ancient history, literature, mental and moral philosophy, and French. Addams studied music also in her first year, but gave that up because she felt she had no special talent, and substituted mathematics.

Perhaps as important as the courses she took was the discipline of student life that was imposed upon the student body by Miss Sill, the president of Rockford. Miss Sill, a Presbyterian, felt that people's lives should be run according to a definite plan, and she did not believe in wasting time. Even the walks that the students took were part of a plan engineered by Miss Sill, she believed that a one-hour walk each day should be a part of every student's routine. In all pursuits she was methodical and painstaking. While Jane was not constituted to emulate Miss Sill, she did learn the value of organization and purpose.

Jane differed with Miss Sill on the subject of degrees. She believed that the seminary should become a college that granted degrees to its graduates. Her opinion was important, for she was the daughter of one of the trustees of the seminary (another reason Jane attended Rockford) and a man who was eminently successful in business and in politics. (It was said that John Addams had refused the Republican nomination for governor of Illinois.) Jane also created support for her idea by organizing a small band of students who agreed with her. In order to show the intellectual prowess of women, she delivered a commencement address in Greek—another sign to her that the seminary was ready to grant degrees. But she did not win her battle until the year after she was graduated, when the seminary became Rockford College. She was granted a degree at that time without further study.

Jane Addams was active in the social life of the college. She joined a newly formed association that discussed the latest scientific findings of the times and she had a reputation as a debater. In 1881 she was sent to Jacksonville as the seminary's delegate to the Interstate Oratorical Contest. There were nine contestants. One was Rollin Salisbury of Beloit College—a friend of Jane—and another was young William Jennings Bryan. Neither of these men won the contest, but neither did Jane, who finished "exactly in the dreary middle." After the contest, she induced a friend, Annie Sidwell, to remain long enough in Jacksonville to visit the state institutions for the blind and the deaf and dumb.

Jane turned her hand to literary enterprises during her college days. She early became connected with the *Rockford Seminary Magazine,* a student publication. For several years, she contributed articles, and in her senior year, she became editor-in-chief.

Seventeen students were graduated in Jane's class in 1881, and Jane was the valedictorian. When she was told that she would deliver an address at the commencement, she turned to the salutatorian of her class, who was her friend, and said, "Nora, when we speak, we must say something." Her talk was serious, well composed, and thoughtful of the broader issues of the period. Indeed, throughout her life, whenever she was called upon to speak, she tried to "say something."

According to her own account, "It required eight years—from the time I left Rockford in the summer of 1881 until Hull House was opened in the autumn of 1889—to formulate my convictions even in the least satisfactory manner, much less to reduce them to a plan of action."[3] Rockford had opened many vistas of thought and action to Jane, and she did not know how she might consolidate them and begin a concerted effort toward the fulfillment of a consistent pattern of ideals. As an added factor in her confusion, her father died in the summer that she graduated. In his passing, she lost one of the most powerful influences in her life.

The death of her father increased Jane's determination to attend medical school. In the fall of 1881, she set out from Cedarville for Philadelphia to become a student at the Women's Medical College. For seven months she worked at her medical studies with considerable zeal and secured high marks for her efforts. But the strain was too much, and her health broke down, forcing her to return to Cedarville. At home, she tried to forget her health and her father's death by studying intensely. But, this course of action only proved more harmful to her health, and the following winter she was forced to spend about six months in bed.

In the spring of 1883, Addams was advised to spend some time in travel to relax and to regain her strength. Eagerly she planned a trip to Europe with her stepmother. After making a number of stops on their way east, the pair set sail on the *Servia* on August 22, 1883. One of the celebrities on board was novelist Henry James. In England they visited the places Jane had read about in her studies; but in her diary, she shows a preoccupation with the poor. One entry pertaining to Blarney castle reads as follows: "Owner said to have income of thirteen thousand pounds a year; ordinary man six shillings a week; could not kiss the Blarney stone, though the castle is very beautiful."

Leaving England, Jane and her stepmother traveled to the Continent, stopping for short periods in Holland, Germany, Austria, Italy, Greece, Switzerland, and France. They visited the great monuments of culture and spoke with leaders in many walks of life about their problems. Wherever she went, she noted the conditions under which the poor lived, sought solutions to their problems, and she studied. She was impressed by the "positivism" of Auguste Comte and thought for a time that it offered a compromise to the religious and social questions that puzzled her.

The two years that Jane Addams spent in travel were not to bring solace to her searching mind. She looked everywhere for comfort and singleness of purpose, but found none that satisfied and returned to the United States still perplexed as to what her life work should be. One insight she did gain during her trip through Europe was that learning is not enough. She saw that the practice of charity surpassed the acquisition of knowledge.

> I gradually reached a conviction that the first generation of college women had taken their learning too quickly, had departed too suddenly from the active, emotional life led by their grandmothers and great-grandmothers; that the contemporary education of young women had developed too exclusively the power of acquiring knowledge and of merely receiving impressions; that somewhere in the process of "being educated" they had lost that simple and almost automatic response to the human appeal, that old healthful reaction resulting in activity from the mere presence of suffering or of helplessness; that they are so sheltered and pampered they have no chance even to make "the great refusal."[3]

Despite what she said, Jane probably did not deserve the condemnation she brought to female college graduates. Through her European experiences, she saw clearly the need for "that simple and almost automatic response to the human appeal." Nor was she correct when she evaluated the lives of some of the women of her own and previous generations. Her generation of women possessed many notable leaders who contributed not only to acquiring knowledge but also to the practice of good will. But the impact of the idea of the need for social action had profound effect upon Jane's life, for it impelled her to discover a way that she could help the unfortunate.

Addams did not regain her health completely during her travels, so on returning to the United States, she spent a brief time in Cedarville. Then she joined her stepmother in Baltimore, where George was attending Johns Hopkins University. Jane helped her stepmother give parties and teas and other social functions, but she found no pleasure in her activities. In fact, she felt that the social occasions were a great waste of time and energy. She found the university men to be dull and uninspired, and she became depressed because she longed for work that would help people. In the summers of 1885 and 1886, she returned to Cedarville, the scene of her happy childhood. Here she tried to regain her lost composure.

She found a solution to her problems, at least for a time, in religion. Jane Addams joined the Presbyterian church when she was twenty-five, and her decision brought her great peace of mind. She was not interested in the dogmas of any particular religious group and did not wish a "canned" theology. Instead, she wished to be part of an on-going movement that stood for the humanitarian values that were so appealing to her and many others in her time. She felt that she owed membership to some Christian church; the Presbyterian happened to be the most suitable at the time. (She joined the Congregational church, now the United Church of Christ, when her life had become centered in Hull House.) In religion and humanitarianism, Jane Addams found a focus for her life—the service of the poor.

It was difficult for Jane to decide on the exact way to practice her new found faith. There were many possibilities. She already had had some experience applying her faith in everyday life. She had entered into a partnership with a young college man from Cedarville and bought a sheep-raising farm, but this she abandoned after she saw that the sheep were maltreated (at least to her way of thinking). She also maintained various personal philanthropies, for example, she gave $1,000 to Rockford College for books. She had been made a member of the board of trustees as her father had once been. And she helped several young men through college by paying part of their expenses. She also assumed responsibility for the care of the children of her oldest sister. (She wrote to Ellen Starr: "I am busy with the children. Esther [a niece] has been driving me crazy with questions about John the Baptist, and Weber [a nephew] has had his sled stolen, and is railing at the world with a power of invective that I have never heard equaled."[4]

In 1887, Ellen Starr decided to travel to Europe and urged Jane to join her. The idea appealed to Jane. She hoped not only to have a good time, but also to discover some means by which she might share her life with those in need. On December 14, 1887, she set sail from Hoboken, New Jersey, joined Ellen in Munich, and the two went on to Rome to spend the winter.

In the spring, Jane went to Madrid along with four friends. Their tour included a bullfight, and when her friends left the arena because of the brutality, Jane stayed to see five bulls killed. She was drawn to the activity because of its callousness and at the same time repelled because of her idealism. This seems to have been a significant experience in her life because the very next morning she approached Ellen Starr with the idea of establishing a "big house" right in the middle of "horrid little houses" as a means of bringing help to the poor. Ellen was enthusiastic about the idea, and from this experience, Hull House was conceived. Its birth had to wait until Jane and Ellen discovered the work of Canon Samuel Barnett in the East Side of London.

Toynbee Hall had come into existence only four years prior to Jane Addams' visit. Barnett was its first warden, or "head resident," and it was the first settlement house. Its staff was composed of university men, mainly from Oxford, who lived in the slums of London (Whitechapel) to learn conditions firsthand and to contribute to the improvement of life there with their own personal and financial resources. Toynbee Hall had already made its contribution to American life, for it was the model that Edward Denison (with the help of others) had used on the East Side of New York City in his founding of the University Settlement. It was this idea of the settlement house that Jane Addams also finally used. She believed that what Barnett had been able to do for the poor people of London she might attempt for the poor people of Chicago. She had found her mission, the purpose that she had struggled to find for so many years.

When Addams returned to the United States early in the summer of 1888, she immediately took steps to set her business affairs in order and to plan for her settlement. Until January of the following year, she was busy with preparations. She even took up bookkeeping in order that her idealism might be supported by practical methods. When she finally arrived in Chicago, it took her five months to locate a suitable house. She searched everywhere for the right place. She wanted to be in a section of the city where there was intense social and personal need and she needed a physically suitable house. The two were not easy to find in combination, but she found what she wanted one day, number 335 South Halsted, and she made up her mind to buy it.

Charles J. Hull, an early resident of Chicago, had built his house when the neighborhood was young. It was a two-story, brick house, set back from the street, and it seemed perfect as a settlement house. Addams' joy was complete when she learned that she could rent it and remodel it to suit the activities of a settlement.

On September 18, 1889, Addams, along with Ellen Starr, who helped her with the plans and activities, and Mary Keyser, who was responsible for the housework, took up residence at Hull House. Gradually, visitors from the neighborhood came to look in on the work in progress. Many of them could not understand how anyone would choose voluntarily to leave a pleasant environment to live on Halsted Street amid such poverty and need. Those who visited were often helped on an individual basis;

others were interested in forming groups for the achievement of various ends.

In the first weeks of Hull House, Starr started a reading "party" of George Eliot's *Romola.* A group of young women came once a week to hear Starr read, and sometimes the members were invited to stay for a meal. The response of the neighbors was slow until they realized that the institution existed for them and that there would be no attempt to force any sort of views upon them that they did not like. Some initially considered Hull House as a "mission station" with the purpose of converting them. Others thought that there must be some "catch" to the House and its open door. But, in time, the word was passed among the residents of the neighborhood that Hull House stood for a genuinely humanitarian ideal.

The doors of Hull House were never locked, though Addams had two experiences with burglars who entered her room at night. On the first occasion, her nephew was asleep in the next room. Addams said to the man, "Don't make a noise." He was startled and started to leap toward a window. "You'll be hurt if you go that way," she said. "Go down by the stairs and let yourself out." And he did. The second burglar was an amateur. Addams told him to leave quietly and to come back the next morning at nine o'clock and she would try to get him some work. He met his appointment.[5]

During the first year, about fifty thousand individual visits were made to Hull House. Addams was acquainted with most of the people who came. Of course, she and Ellen Starr were not able to handle so many people and activities by themselves, so from time to time, women with ability and training volunteered their services to Hull House. Some had general interests and talents and others were able to help with specialized groups.

Addams spent time not only in Hull House but also visiting the homes of the neighborhood in order to interpret the work she was doing to those who had not heard of it or who were skeptical of its aims. She also was responsible for raising money to maintain the programs, as the funds that she (and the other residents) contributed were not sufficient to carry the whole burden. She was responsible, too, for the bookkeeping, and she actively studied the community, for she believed that social research is one of the important adjuncts to settlement work. All of these responsibilities kept her busy many hours of each day. Her physical condition at this time was much improved, and she found the strength for myriads of large and small obligations.

Hull House was a center for children's activities of various kinds. One of the first groups established was a kindergarten. In many instances, the children who came responded quickly to the programs arranged for them; but sometimes they adhered to special cultural ways learned in their homes. Thus, one of the principal goals of the kindergarten was to break down the social barriers that existed among children of different nationalities and races. In the main, the kindergarten was a success, as it not only helped the children to perceive the broader implications of their behavior, but also gave Hull House a way to establish relationships with the parents.

For older children, Hull House offered clubs and special interest groups. The staff discovered early that children like to form their own special groups and provide for their own leadership (with some direction from the staff). Some groups were formed around social relationships; other groups formed for an activity, such as sports, music, literature, painting, enjoyment of art, and discussion of current affairs. In time, the boys' activities became so numerous that a special five-story building was erected to house them.

On her first New Year's Day at Hull House, Jane Addams initiated a custom that became an annual tradition—the "Old Settlers' Party." Those who formerly lived in the neighborhood were asked to return to tell of their experiences. Some of the "old settlers" had risen in social status far beyond their beginnings, and their presence at the parties provided the people of the neighborhood with an incentive for their own advancement. The parties also gave an opportunity for "old settlers" to revive friendships. As the parties continued, former staff members who had been closely connected with the development of the House returned to renew old acquaintances.

Hull House was a refuge for individuals who had no other place to turn in time of trouble. One child, for example, was lodged at the House until he could return to live with his parents. His mother didn't want him because he had been born with a cleft palate. On another occasion, a new bride took shelter in Hull House because her husband beat her during their first week of marriage. Such cases of personal need were multiplied many times over in the course of the years. While Hull House was not conceived to be an agency that granted services to individuals on the same bases that other social casework agencies did, the staff could not ignore the cries of the suffering.

An investigation of the sweatshops in the neighborhood revealed to Addams and her co-workers that, especially in the busy season, the women workers paid little attention to their families. These women had to work long hours in order to make their small wages. Often, they were too tired to cook meals, even when they could buy the food. During the day, when their children were at loose ends, these women would provide a few pennies for their offspring to buy lunch at a candy store. In order to meet the needs of these families and others, Hull House began a public kitchen, which later became its Coffee House. The Coffee House was considered one means of centering the social life of the community so far as informal recreation was concerned; but, according to Addams, the fact that it did not offer beer made it somewhat less effective than the saloons.

Not all of the efforts of Hull House were directed at delivering services; Addams believed that people should be helped to help themselves as much as possible. The Cooperative Coal Association, which led a vigorous life for about three years, represented an attempt to help people help themselves through cooperation. The association helped families to finance their fuel needs at a saving. At one point before it closed, the association's gross receipts were between $300 and $400 a day. Dividends usually were given in coal rather than cash.

A further example of cooperation showed even greater success. A group of women who worked in a factory near Hull House went out on strike, but they were worried because they were unable to pay board and anticipated being thrown out of their rooms. At a meeting held in Hull House, one of the girls asked, "Wouldn't it be fine if we had a boarding club of our own, and then we could stand by each other in a time like this?" As a result, Addams investigated the possibilities of starting a boarding club. She found that the idea was basically sound, so she rented and furnished two apartments. After the first month, the women were able to assume the responsibility for the payment of the rent, and the club was a small success. By the time the third year had rolled around, the club had fifty members, who occupied all six of the apartments in the original building of the club. Afterwards, the Jane Club, as it was called, secured its own quarters.

The campaign for the Jane Club building aroused an issue that tested the ethical philosophy of Addams and her coworkers. When the needs of the club were made known, persons of means were found who were willing to have a share in the project. One man offered $20,000 to the building fund, but he had a reputation for underpaying the workers in his establishment and for other suspect practices. It was difficult for Addams to decide whether to accept or reject this generous offer, but in the end she told the man she could not take his money, knowing as she did of his reputation. Later she had some doubts about the practicality of her decision, but she never changed her rule, even though, through the years, it cost her considerable income for Hull House.

Over and over again, it was necessary for Hull House to provide services to individuals who came asking for immediate help. Hull House dealt with many categories of need. Addams felt especially responsible for women who had "gone astray" and who came to the House as one of the last havens available. Often, they were young and were living under intense economic and family handicaps. Addams tried to do what she could to give them shelter and to guide them toward a more stable life. Sometimes she felt her efforts were thwarted by well-intentioned people. In one instance she placed a woman in a job at a Sunday school of a church on the grounds that the new environment might aid her, but the church members learned of her background and refused to have her.

Hull House dealt with other cases of individual need. On occasion, women who had been deserted by their husbands came for information and support, and the House guided them to the existing welfare and court facilities in the city that could help them. The House also provided information for families in need of medical attention and other personal services.

Many people in the district required material support in times of unemployment and because of chronic poverty, but it was not possible for Hull House to meet all their needs. At times, the House did provide direct material assistance, but its funds were too meager for any sustained effort in this direction. The staff tried to tell individuals where employment could be secured or how changes could be made in employment in order to improve income, and sometimes budgeting advice was given. The Charity Organization Society and the Visiting Nurse Association had not been born in the earliest years of Hull House, but when they came into existence there was cooperation between them.

In the summer of 1895, Addams was appointed to a commission to investigate conditions in the county poorhouse. This commission was responsible to the mayor of Chicago and was formed because of rumors that the inmates of the poorhouse were badly treated. Neighbors of Hull House came forth to document these rumors with firsthand information. As a result of the study, Addams realized how inadequate the public measures were for the support of the poor and how lacking in responsiveness the governmental machinery and personnel were to the widespread problems of the poor. The resultant report helped define higher standards for poorhouses.

A kindergarten was one of the first features of Hull House; it met the needs of families who otherwise would have been unable to care adequately for their children. Addams also established a day nursery, one of the first in this country. It proved in its operation that daytime care of children is one way to offer support to poor families. The day nursery was first maintained in a little cottage on a side street near Hull House; later, the Children's House was established for the nursery and for other children's activities.

It was natural that, where there were so many social and personal problems, there would be discussions about the means for relief. Hull House early realized that its role in the neighborhood made it responsible not only for certain welfare activities, but also for discussions of means of changing the conditions that brought about the problems. For a time, Hull House offered public discussions of social issues. Experts in the various social philosophies and schools of thought were brought to Hull House to address large audiences. It was realized in time, however, that large meetings were not entirely adequate. Smaller clubs of men and women in which the individual members had an open opportunity to express themselves were then formed. These clubs taught a degree of tolerance to the members and brought to the realization of most that the problems with which they dealt were not capable of easy solution. No attempt was made to limit the kinds of social remedies that could be offered at these meetings.

One of the products of these meetings was the Hull House Social Science Club, which aimed to study social problems in a scientific manner. In some ways it was a parallel development to the modern social science of sociology. Through the club and the other meetings, Hull House gained a reputation for social radicalism. Wherever Addams went, however, she tried to make the point that the settlement, as such, maintained no particular opinion in social matters, but did believe that it had a responsibility to see that its neighbors had a chance to discuss all points of view.

Addams was aware that Hull House could not hold itself aloof from the labor conditions of the neighborhood. Many facets of this problem were attacked. A logical starting point was to oppose the use of children in the sweatshops of the area—surely the conscience of the community (mainly that of the employers) could be touched in regard to the conditions that adversely affected children. But this supposition was not entirely true. Employers were not responsive to the ethical claims of the director of Hull House.

The conditions that affected child laborers were as deplorable as they were common. Children as young as four years old helped their mothers in sewing. Some children were in poor health, and some were motivated to suicide as a consequence of the entanglements of early labor. One girl of thirteen, employed in a laundry at work that required the strength of a man borrowed $3 from a companion that she could not repay unless she told her parents and gave the companion a whole week's wages, so she committed suicide.

There was at the time no legal recourse against employing children in all sorts of work, since the existing child labor legislation pertained only to the use of children in mines. Mrs. Florence Kelley, one of the first residents of Hull House, became especially interested in this problem. She told the Illinois State Bureau of Labor of the conditions she found on visits through the Hull House part of Chicago and suggested that what was discovered there was probably in effect elsewhere. The chief of the bureau saw the need for an investigation and appointed Kelley as head of a special committee to undertake the research and make recommendations. The results of the committee's work became embodied in the first factory law in Illinois. The legislation regulated sanitary conditions and fixed fourteen as the minimum age for workers. In every way it helped to raise the standards of working conditions, and was especially beneficial in eliminating child labor—at least in its more formal and widespread form.

The passage of the factory legislation was not accomplished solely by the report of the committee appointed by the Illinois State Bureau of Labor. That committee provided the ideological instrument by which the legislation was achieved, but agitation and support were required from those who were affected by the conditions and from their friends. This meant that Hull House had to arouse public opinion not only in its own neighborhood but also throughout the city and, indeed, the entire state. The Trades and Labor Assembly, a central labor body in Chicago, was also interested in the legislation and used its influence. Representatives of Hull House, the Trades and Labor Assembly, and other interested organizations went to the state capital to lobby for the enactment of the legislation. Although it passed, it was only a beginning. Kelley was appointed as the first factory inspector, and with her worked a staff of twelve inspectors who helped enforce the law.

Chicago politics in the last decade of the nineteenth century were characterized by laxity and corruption. Since 1868, a broadminded citizen, Lyman J. Gage, had been trying to form a "voluntary association of citizens for the mutual counsel, support, and combined action of all the forces for good," and by 1893, he succeeded in creating the Civic Federation. Jane Addams had a principal share in its establishment and maintenance through the years of its effectiveness, and even the governor, Peter Altgeld, supported it. Among its membership ranked prominent persons of Chicago from various fields of activity: Cyrus McCormick, Marshall Field, Albion Small, Graham Taylor, and many others. The federation accomplished much good in Chicago and in Illinois. One of its main efforts was the attempt to employ arbitration in labor disputes.

Jane Addams was the secretary of the Civic Federation Committee on Industrial Arbitration, and under her guidance, a system of voluntary arbitration boards was sponsored by the state legislature. Governor Altgeld asked the legislature for "such legislation as will enable the parties to the dispute, alone or with the aid of a county judge, to select their own board in each case so that there may be no question about its impartiality, on the one hand, and no unnecessary salary paid on the other."[6] The legislature, however, turned down the request of the governor and appointed a standing board of three salaried members, one an employer, one a workingman, and a third who was neither. Massachusetts had such a board, and its success was fairly well known. But the board in Illinois did not function effectively because, where labor unions were strong, there was no willingness on their part to arbitrate disputes they felt they could win without arbitration. The same held for employers. The board failed mainly through disuse. Industrial relations were not yet ready for impartial arbitration.

The problem of garbage disposal illustrates Jane Addams' willingness to consider almost any problem affecting the welfare of her neighbors and her acquiescence to perform the most menial of duties. The Hull House Women's Club had reported that garbage collection procedures in Chicago were almost nonexistent. (This opinion, of course, was more widely held than just the membership of the Women's Club!) Every family in the neighborhood suffered. The collection of the garbage was given over to private companies on a contract basis, and this contract, like others, was a victim of political preferment and graft. In 1894, as a result of careful calculation, Addams made a bid for the business of collecting the garbage. Her bid was thrown out on a technicality, but due to the publicity that followed, Addams was appointed as the garbage inspector for the ward at an annual salary of $1,000. This was the only paid position she ever held. That the work was not easy is told graphically by Addams:

> The position was no sinecure whether regarded from the point of view of getting up at six in the morning to see that the men were early at work; or of following the loaded wagons, uneasily dropping their contents at intervals, to their dreary destination at the dump; or of insisting that the contractor must increase the number of his wagons from nine to thirteen and from thirteen to seventeen, although he assured me that he lost money on every one and that the former inspector had let him off with seven; or of taking the careless landlords into court because they would not provide the proper garbage receptacles; or of arresting the tenant who tried to make the garbage wagons carry away the contents of his stable.[7]

The complete list of Addams' political activities and nonpolitical efforts would be too long to include here. Indeed, many of her works extended far beyond the horizons of that neighborhood. Before she had lived her life, the entire world was aware of her humanitarian perspectives and zeal.

Addams became interested in the nationality groups that made up the neighborhood around Hull House. She was eager to have them come together to know each other, because she believed that some of the misunderstandings between peoples were due to the fact that there were no means for an interchange of cultural values. Addams did not believe that persons with foreign backgrounds should strive to lose their special heritage, but she also believed that, in some instances, the culture of the parents harmed their children. She knew that "the faithful child is sometimes ruthlessly imposed upon by immigrant parents who, eager for money and accustomed to the patriarchal authority of peasant households, held their children in stern bondage." She worked against such cultural restrictions, but there were more positive aspects to her activities with immigrants and their children. At first she provided space at Hull House for families and groups of the separate nationalities. Later she tried to bring the various nationalities together at one time. She was fairly successful in this, although there were many problems that militated against the full success of this idea.

By her travels through the Hull House neighborhood, Addams learned of the handwork of different ethnic groups. She realized that a collection of the various tools, especially those brought from the Old World, would represent an important and appealing collection. Therefore, she founded the Labor Museum, which at first consisted of one room in Hull House. In time, many rooms held the "story of work" as it was to be found in Chicago. One of the Hull House trustees, Julius Rosenwald, later founded the Rosenwald Industrial Museum, which carried Addams' idea much further than she was able to with the relatively meager resources of Hull House.

Juvenile delinquency was always a concern of Hull House. One of the strong reasons for the establishment of the House was to reduce the juvenile delinquency rates. By its manifold activities, the House provided a place in which boys and girls who might otherwise have been roaming the streets could assemble in peace and with sanction. Hull House stood as a symbol of constructive help to bewildered and needy young people. Addams was also interested in creating a juvenile court by which young offenders could be separated from hardened criminals in treatment and where steps could be taken at an early point to prevent the further development of criminal tendencies. She was not alone in this struggle. Mrs. James Flowers, chairman of the Chicago Civic Federation's Department of Philanthropy, was the principal leader in the fight, and Addams gave Flowers every help that she could. Legislation finally established the Juvenile Court in Chicago on July 1, 1899, and a committee was appointed at the same time to see that the law actually worked. Julia Lathrop, a resident of Hull House, was the first chairman of that committee. The first probation officer provided by the law was Alzina P. Stevens, also a resident of Hull House. The juvenile court conception began in Illinois and spread to practically all of the states. Its worth has been proven over and over again.

The settlement house idea grew rapidly in Chicago as elsewhere. There was something about it so practical in its helpfulness, so genuine in its social concern, and so hopeful that persons from all ranks of society responded to it. Perhaps two of the most notable co-experiments in the settlement field in Chicago were the Chicago Commons and the University Settlement. Chicago Commons was established by Graham Taylor, who had come to the Chicago Theological Seminary in 1893 to open the first department in any American theological seminary devoted to the social interpretation and application of religion. He knew of the work that Samuel Barnett had done in London and also of Jane Addams' work in Chicago. He came to feel that the settlement was one of the best ways for expressing social Christianity. Therefore, he founded the Chicago Commons, which became in time one of the most notable of the settlements in the United States.

The University Settlement was founded by several persons attached to the University of Chicago. Albion Small, founder of the first department of sociology in an American university, was greatly interested in establishing a settlement. George Vincent and William Rainey Harper, also of the university, were co-sponsors with Small of the University Settlement. When plans were laid for its creation, the founding group looked about for a director, and they chose Mary McDowell, then a resident at Hull House.

The settlement house idea spread quickly through the United States. Today, there are more than eight hundred settlements, neighborhood houses, and community centers located throughout the United States. They are coordinated through the National Federation of Settlements and Neighborhood Centers with national headquarters in New York City. The federation was founded in 1911 by Jane Addams and other pioneer leaders, and Addams served as its first president. The federation assists its members with the many and varied problems with which they are confronted as they seek to meet the changing needs of people living together in the urban centers of the United States.

Hull House had only two residents at its start, Addams and Starr. By the end of the first ten years, there were twenty-five men and women. Some settlements accepted only men or only women residents, but Hull House was a pioneer in the use of both. Some of the residents of Hull House achieved considerable prominence on leaving for other occupations. Ellen Starr achieved a measure of fame because of the work she did at Hull House. Julia Lathrop, like Addams and Starr, attended Rockford College. She was born in Rockford, Illinois, and spent one year at the college before she went to Vassar, from which she was graduated. After a period as resident in Hull House, she became the first head of the Children's Bureau of the United States government. Florence Kelley contributed to the development of Hull House with her own strong talents of leadership. She was mainly interested in protecting children, women, and labor generally from harsh employment and living conditions. Her work as head of the National Consumers' League represents thirty years of forceful social challenge for the common good.

The physical plant of Hull House also grew with the years. The original house was constantly busy with the life of the neighborhood, and almost the whole block surrounding Hull House was taken up with other buildings of the expanding settlement. Within the buildings were various specialized functions, some of which had been created for the first time in any settlement. As Hull House grew, it was no longer possible for Addams to assume full responsibility for its maintenance, so she arranged for a board of directors, which helped her in establishing policy and raising the money required for running the settlement. More and more, Addams became the executive of a large enterprise.

In 1901, Jane Addams became one of the central figures in the frenzied aftermath of the assassination of President William McKinley by Leon S. Czolgosz. Soon after the president had been killed and his assassin identified as an "anarchist," the federal government sent out a call to all localities to apprehend known anarchists. Quite a few people were incarcerated at that time, including Abraham Isaak, who was known by Addams to be "a quiet, scholarly man, challenging the social order by the philosophic touchstone of Bakunin and Herbert Spencer." She had met him once at Hull House some years previously when Prince Peter Kropotkin visited the settlement. When Isaak was placed in the jail under City Hall and not permitted to communicate with the outside world, the Russians of the Hull House neighborhood came to Addams to protest his treatment. The following day, a Sunday, Addams met with Mayor Dunne and asked that he not yield to the panic and that Isaak be given a lawyer. The mayor was unwilling to do this, but he allowed Addams to see the man. She reassured Isaak that he had friends who were working on his behalf. In time, a lawyer was secured, and Isaak was released, for he had no connection with the slaying of the president. Addams' stand for justice in this and other similar cases brought her to the attention of many who admired her for her courage.

After her work at Hull House had received popular acclaim, Addams was appointed to the school board and served in that position from 1905 to 1909. In her own estimate, she played "a most inglorious part" as a member of the board, that of the middle road between two extremes of philosophy, a "part" rarely well received. The "conservative" elements in the city claimed that she had sold out to the "radicals," while the "liberal" elements claimed she was responsive to the "reactionaries." Certainly, whatever her real contribution, she pleased practically no one. While she always included her position as garbage collector in *Who's Who in America,* she never mentioned her service on the school board. The issues that engaged the board are not relevant here, but it is important to see that Addams rarely was a "party" person. She liked to think things through to her own conclusions without feeling obligated toward any person or group. On more than one occasion, her independent stand aroused public antagonism.

Participation in many responsibilities of social leadership greatly enhanced Addams' reputation nationally. She became the first woman president of the National Conference of Charities and Correction (now known as the National Conference of Social Welfare). In her presidential speech, she illustrated her broad humanitarianism, her deep patience with entrenched wrong, and her quiet optimism for the better world that she believed was shaping. In June 1909, Yale University presented her with an honorary doctor's degree, the first such degree ever offered a woman by Yale. Newspapers hailed her as one of the great women leaders. Smith College, to which her affections had early been turned, granted her a doctor's degree in the fall of 1909. In the procession with her was the mayor of the town, Calvin Coolidge. Many urged her to run for the U. S. Senate and other positions of public responsibility. Surely, she had achieved a popular acceptance that surpassed that of almost any other woman of her time. Her name became a byword for social welfare and social justice.

Jane Addams was a strikingly effective speaker. The oratorical flair she possessed in college was developed through years of experience. She was in demand as a speaker on many occasions and in many places, some far from home. Addams was also a writer of considerable power. She had always felt that research and writing were a part of the settlement house idea. At the end of the first five years of Hull House, Addams and the other residents published a book entitled *Hull House Maps and Papers.* The maps were taken from data gathered for the U.S. Bureau of Labor, and the papers treated various subjects of interest in the neighborhood. Later, when Addams was better known, she wrote articles and books that influenced many people. Her articles were found in such journals as *American Journal of Sociology, International Journal of Ethics, North American Review, Forum,* and *Atlantic Monthly.* Her books included ***Democracy and Social Ethics,*** 1902; ***Newer Ideals of Peace,*** 1907; ***The Spirit of Youth and the City Streets,*** 1909; and ***Twenty Years at Hull House,*** 1910. While all of her books were widely read, the most popular was ***Twenty Years at Hull House.*** In it Addams described her life in terms that were simple, appealing, and forthright. As in all her writings, she drew heavily on particular incidents, the sort that might well be forgotten by those less sensitive to people and their behavior.

In her writings, Addams commonly stressed the primary value of the home in shaping children's personalities. She believed that homelike qualities were to be cherished and furthered and that social institutions existed in large part for the full development and enrichment of the family. She did not make excessive claims for individual morality and independence, but believed that democracy entailed the restraint of individual tendencies for the benefit of the whole. She felt that democracy, in its basic sense of equality of opportunity, required much more social control than most people believed. Addams also believed that the virtue of a person is expressed to the degree to which that person is willing to contribute to the welfare of others, often at his or her own expense. Self-giving became a fundamental tenet of her personal philosophy, and in her own life, she exemplified the virtue.

In regard to the problems of youth, Addams stressed the view that some delinquency is due to a spirit of adventure that is basic to the growing-up process. She claimed that, in times past and in simpler societies, means existed by which children might express their need for adventure in relatively harmless ways, but that this was not true for our complex social order. "To set his feet in the worn path of civilization is not an easy task, but it may give us a clue for the undertaking to trace his misdeeds to the unrecognized and primitive spirit of adventure corresponding to the old activity of the hunt, of warfare, and of discovery."[8] The great need for the character development of youth, according to Addams, is the discovery and establishment of patterns of behavior that will be harmless or constructive while meeting the individual's need for adventure.

Addams was concerned with women's rights, an interest stemming from her days at Rockford College, where she met women who were convinced that they should have equal rights with men. The first step in the development of social equality for women was the winning of the right to vote. Addams used many of the traditional arguments in support of this cause, but she also suggested original ones. For example, she said that women needed to vote for the benefit of their children; it devolved upon women to defend the existing rights of children and to extend their advantages through political means. If women could vote, she declared, they would enter politics more actively and directly, and political participation on the part of women would increase family welfare. But Addams did more than argue about suffrage. She joined those organizations that were working toward the extension of the rights of women and played a leading role in several of them.

The presidential campaign of Theodore Roosevelt attracted Jane Addams, and to it she devoted her time and energy. She was a "progressive" by nature. She had few illusions about the "perfection" of Roosevelt, yet she knew that she must take sides in an imperfect situation. Even beyond the campaign, Roosevelt kept in touch with her, sometimes sending her newspaper clippings he thought she might have missed.

The Nobel Peace Prize was awarded to Addams and to President Nicholas Murray Butler of Columbia University in 1931. This prize was given her for her many years of devoted activity in the cause of peace. Jane Addams will remain as one of the most effective pacifists that the present century has known. Her message was not always well received, but she struck a chord for reason and ethics that has not been muffled to this day.

The source of Addams' pacifism is difficult to appraise. Some have suggested her Quaker background, but her Quakerism was casual at best, and she had no genuine or continuing contact with the Friends for the larger part of her life. The Friends with whom she was associated (the Hicksites), moreover, were not especially noted for their pacifism, as were the more orthodox Friends.

Probably the teachings and personality of Jesus had a considerable influence on her espousal of pacifism. Addams was not a traditional Christian. She found fault with many aspects of the work of the churches, and she never attained a great degree of theological astuteness. On the other hand, she was deeply impressed with the purely spiritual and social implications of the life and teachings of Jesus. Certainly her use of reason enabled her to achieve a pacifist position. Addams did on occasion refer to the rightness of the claims of the Gospels, but more often, she asserted that Truth itself was on the side of peace. She argued that war destroys more than human life, and she believed that national interests are never served by the waging of war. War does not alleviate intergroup tensions, according to Addams; it only intensifies attitudes of conflict.

Jane Addams was not an isolationist. She believed in international goodwill and mutual aid and that what happens elsewhere in the world is relevant to our own national and personal interests. Americans should cooperate, even at the cost of sacrifice, with all of the peoples of the world. Her lack of isolationist sentiment placed her in a different camp from those who advocated a hands-off policy in regard to the rest of the world.

Addams was a great admirer of Tolstoy, and especially liked his *My Religion,* which she reread many times during her life. Addams admired Tolstoy's religious philosophy and his insistence on practice. She believed that she had shared this philosophy by her activities at Hull House, as indeed she had. During her 1896 trip to Europe, she visited Tolstoy in Russia. It was a momentous occasion for Addams. Tolstoy, however, was critical of her. After he heard her description of Hull House and its activities, he took hold of her full sleeve and remarked that there was enough cloth in it to make a dress for a little girl. When he learned how she managed to support herself, he condemned her for being an "absentee landlord." This was disconcerting, and for a time Addams struggled with the insights Tolstoy had given her regarding her motivation in social work. She concluded that Tolstoy was "more logical than life warrants." Though she never lost her love of his teachings, especially his acceptance of nonviolence, she could not embrace all of his ideas.

Addams delivered a series of lectures at the University of Wisconsin in 1906, which were published as ***Newer Ideals of Peace.*** The volume was well received, although it provoked some to call her a traitor. She also was one of the featured speakers at the National Peace Congress held in 1907; she extended her ideas for peace at that congress. The congress of the following year increased her hopes that war was of the past and that peace had come in permanent form.

Her hopes were crushed with the start of the First World War. All of the gains that had been achieved were wiped away. Many of the peacemakers were saddened, and some turned to the war with a pathetic reversal of conviction. Addams felt all was not lost, since the United States had not yet entered the conflict. Among the women of the country, Addams took the lead for peace. In January of 1915, Addams was elected the chairman of the newly formed Women's Peace party. She also was the head of the National Peace Federation, which was organized to coordinate the efforts of many organizations working for peace in various parts of the country. The platform of the Women's Peace party was similar to Woodrow Wilson's "Fourteen Points."

In 1915, a meeting of women was held in Amsterdam, with representatives attending from twelve belligerent and neutral countries. The meeting was held to plan an international congress of women interested in peace, which was held at the Hague in April 1915. Jane Addams presided. Thus, she became the head of the Women's International League for Peace and Freedom. The assembled women advocated a Society of Nations, general disarmament by international agreement, and a series of proposals as the basis for a just peace. At the suggestions of Rosika Schwimmer of Hungary, two delegations were sent to the heads of fourteen governments and to the pope to present a concrete plan for an early peace: the creation of a commission of neutrals to offer continuous mediation to the belligerents. The delegations included Jane Addams and Emily Greene Balch (who was awarded the Nobel Prize for Peace in 1946 for her international activities, being the second woman ever to have received the award).

But, even these efforts were to no avail. The war came and spread despite the work of Addams and millions of others who supported various peace organizations. When war came, Addams protested against many of its events and requirements—conscription, for one. She castigated the failure of the national leaders to mediate peacefully the problems being fought over. She supported conscientious objectors. Nothing that she did or said, however, was taken as an offense by the great bulk of Americans, and certainly she and her ideas were well received, under the circumstances, by the political leaders in Washington.

After the war ended, Addams helped arrange for the second meeting of the International League, which took place in Zurich. Representatives of sixteen nations were present, including those of the conquered countries. Addams again was the head of the meeting. While the league did not influence the making of the peace at every turn, it did make itself felt throughout the world as a moral force. The league met annually six times before Miss Addams resigned as its president in 1929. In that time she had created an effective instrument of maintaining goodwill on an international basis. It was largely because of her work with the league that she was given the Nobel Prize for Peace.

The Women's International League for Peace and Freedom continues today its historic purposes. Its international headquarters are in Geneva, although it has "national sections" in many countries, including the United States. It conducts special missions (to China, the Middle East, Africa, and elsewhere), publishes a quarterly on the subject of its activities and the cause of peace, and maintains international summer schools. The league also raised money through its sections and members in many countries to erect an apartment house for the resettlement of thirty-two refugee families in the town of Spittal-Drau, Austria. This international memorial was dedicated to Jane Addams in the summer of her centennial in 1960 and is known as the Jane Addams Refugee House.

The closing of the war and the meeting of the league gave Addams a chance to rest. A trip around the world took her nine months, and when she returned, she was welcomed as a hero. Once back home, she began her work again at Hull House. In the 1920s, she devoted considerable time and effort to the problems of her neighbors, especially immigrants and their children. Her work, however, was not without strain, for she was sixty years old in 1920.

Addams did not support the Prohibition Amendment during the 1920s. She believed that the problem of alcoholism should be met through education. She also did not believe in the use of force to change personal behavior. Some of her friends were surprised that she did not champion Prohibition, especially since she had been so close to the negative results of alcoholism in the Hull House neighborhood, but she remained steadfast in her conviction that legislation was not the means to solve the problem.

In 1929, when Jane Addams was sixty-nine, Hull House held a fortieth anniversary celebration of her leadership. At the celebration were outstanding citizens from many different places and walks of life. Some previously had been residents of the neighborhood. Others were related to Addams in her worldwide activities for human betterment. All gratefully added their thanks to the celebration.

In February 1931, Addams was voted one of the twelve "greatest living women in America" by a popular women's magazine. In the same year, she attended the fiftieth anniversary of her graduation from college. Her words of practical wisdom were remembered by the graduates that year. In October 1965, Jane Addams was honored by being included, along with Orville Wright, Oliver Wendell Holmes, and Sylvanus Thayer, in the New York University Hall of Fame for Great Americans.

Addams died on May 21, 1935. She had been suffering for some years with several maladies; her heart was weak (which curtailed work in the latter years), and she had cancer. As the hearse containing her body moved through the streets of Chicago, a policeman stopped traffic and spoke to the driver.

"Is it her?" he asked, respectfully.

"Yes," said the driver.

"She goes in peace," said the policeman.

She was buried in Cedarville where, in her childhood and youth, she had known peace.

Hull House continues to serve its neighborhood in Chicago today, although the neighborhood and the House have greatly changed from the days of Jane Addams. The new urban campus of the University of Illinois is a principal factor in the neighborhood, and Hull House has been restored to its original size physically, the third story, for example, having once been removed. Jane Addams' agency of social welfare remains as a vital monument to her life's efforts to serve the poor of many backgrounds in the middle of a vibrant city.

NOTES

[1] A statement by Professor Charles E. Merriam in James Weber Linn, *Jane Addams: A Biography* (New York: D. Appleton-Century, 1936), p. 189.

[2] Jane Addams, *Twenty Years at Hull House* (New York: Macmillan, 1911), p. 16. The Hicksite Quakers are the "liberal" branch of the Friends, taking their name from Elias Hicks, a pioneer leader of "liberal" Quakerism.

[3] Ibid., p. 64.

[4] Ibid., p. 71.

[5] Linn, *Jane Addams,* pp. 83-84.

[6] Ibid., p. 163.

[7] Addams, *Twenty Years at Hull House,* pp. 285-86.

[8] Jane Addams, *The Spirit of Youth and the City Streets* (New York: Macmillan, 1909), p. 53.

Philip Abbott (essay date 1987)

SOURCE: "Reforming: Charlotte Perkins Gilman and Jane Addams," in *States of Perfect Freedom,* The University of Massachusetts Press, 1987, pp. 157-81.

[In the following excerpt, Abbott compares and contrasts Addams's autobiography with that of a feminist writer and contemporary, Charlotte Perkins Gilman.]

The autobiography would seem to be the ideal structure for feminist political theory. The historical subjection of women has taken the form of what John Stuart Mill called "bonds of affection." When a woman looks to identify the sources of her oppression she looks not only at the factory and its boss but also at the family and its bosses, the father and husband. For the feminist, the personal is political in a way that is fundamentally different from the experience of other writers.

This perspective can permit an understanding of the origin of politics and liberal society that the male writer can never appreciate in an autobiographical sense. For the feminist, childhood is not an escape from the demands of liberal society but rather a source of her subjection. A woman's remembrance of childhood as a state of nature is gothic but it is not its anarchic violence that she remembers. Rather it is an ordered subjection. There are, of course, many variations in this theme of childhood as a memory of bondage, as a world of "free" boys and "captured" women and girls. The autobiography can reveal the range of human experience in a way that conventional political theory cannot. There are permissive as well as overbearing fathers, homes without fathers, homes run on matriarchal principles, homes with brother and sister treated alike. But the weight of both female experience and tradition teaches the autobiographer to come to the conclusion that childhood remembered as "idylls of innocence and redemption" is a male "idealization."

But what are the consequences of this view of childhood as a state of bondage, of the effort to demythologize the origins of one's self? One result, I think, is that the autobiography, despite its penetrating analysis of social institutions, suffers from a fundamental confusion of the personal and the political, of the public and the private. In part this confusion is the consequence of patriarchy in the context of a liberal society. The autobiography simply reflects in refracted ways the burdens of social structure. The burdens here can be heavy indeed. If the self of a woman is in part the result of these institutions of bondage, then she must fashion a new identity. But a liberal society takes autonomy as, if not a given, at least the responsibility of each self. Once patricide has been committed in a psychological sense, where does a woman find her new identity? Certainly not in relation to a husband and children; that choice would involve the kind of generational reconstruction of patriarchy that the feminist wishes to break. In general, the answer to this problem lies in the feminist conception of reform. In fact, the autobiography as a positive act involves the attempt to find a new self through political action. New communities must be built, so says the feminist autobiographer, and her life is offered as an exemplar of reform. But if the recognition of sisterhood is a revolutionary act requiring devotion and commitment, what precisely is the nature of the feminist's obligation? If the construction of a new identity is the duty one sister has toward another, then is personal self-improvement an act of service and community building? Is self-aggrandizement selflessness? Is egoism an act of altruism? Is reform of the self political reform? Not all feminists have conflated the personal with the political in such a way, but the problem always remains ready to be answered in this fashion. There are ways out; there are ways in which it is possible to convert personal troubles into new and genuinely collaborative visions, and the autobiography is indeed the structure that can permit that kind of selfconsciousness. That road is suggested by Jane Addams. The other and more traveled route is taken by Charlotte Perkins Gilman and many others. The source of the confusion of the personal with the political may rest with the injustice of patriarchy itself but it also lies with the confusion that bonds of affection are really bondages.

"MY MOTHER WAS A BABY-WORSHIPER"

Are fathers the concealed enemies of daughters? Does family structure determine consciousness? The memories of Charlotte Perkins Gilman and Jane Addams reveal how complex an affirmative response to this question can be. Gilman's father abandoned his family; Addams's mother died when she was two years old. For Gilman "the word Father, in a sense of love, care, one to go to in trouble, means nothing to me." Her father was only "an occasional visitor, writer of infrequent but always funny drawings, a sender of books, catalogues of books, lists of books to read, and also a purchaser of books with the money sadly needed by his family." Addams, on the other hand, cannot recall many experiences apart from her father. Her memories form a "single cord" of "supreme affection" and a "clue" to which she clung in the "intricacy of the mazes" of "the moral concerns of life." Much of her childhood involves memories of attempts, "so emotional, so irrational, so tangled with the affairs of the imagination," to express her "doglike affection" for her father.

A fatherless childhood, for Gilman, did not create a childhood independent of the consequences of paternal power. The Perkins' matriarchal family moved nineteen times in eighteen years, fourteen of them from one city to another. Gilman's memories of childhood are "thick with railroad journeys, mostly on the Hartford, Providence and Springfield; with occasional steamboats; with the smell of 'hacks' and the funny noise the wheels made when little fingers were stuck in little ears and withdrawn again, alternately." She resented bitterly the sets of clothes she had to wear on these trips so that the number of suitcases could be kept to a minimum. Her mother refused to give up waiting for the return of her husband. She longed to see him before she died: "As long as she was able to sit up, she sat always at the same window watching for the beloved face. He never came."

The father who deserts his family exacts economic punishment through his absence. But for Gilman this exercise of paternal power affected all familial relationships. Mary Perkins avoided showing any sign of affection toward Charlotte so that her daughter would not later suffer from the same kind of bond that she had. When nursing, her mother would push aside the infant's hands. Charlotte was never hugged or kissed. Later she discovered that her mother would wait until she was asleep and then quietly caress her. The young daughter would use pins to keep herself awake, carefully pretending to be asleep until her mother would arrive, "and how rapturously I enjoyed being gathered into her arms, held close and kissed."

Charlotte was a victim of her father, and she was further victimized by the withdrawal of maternal affection, itself the result of her mother's victimization. What was the source of Charlotte's mother's suffering? Her life was "one of the most thwarted" Gilman had ever known. The young Mary Westcott was the "darling of an elderly father and a juvenile mother." She was "petted, cossetted, and indulged." She was "delicate and beautiful, well educated, musical . . . femininely attractive in the highest degree." There were always lovers, "various and successive." One man proposed to her at first sight. But Mary Westcott was a "childlike" woman. Even at seventeen she would excuse herself from gentleman callers to go upstairs to put her dolls to bed. Finally, after many engagements broken, renewed, and rebroken, Mary married at the age of twenty-nine. From this point, her life was lived in tragic contradiction: "After her idolized youth, she was left neglected. After her flood of lovers, she became a deserted wife." The "most passionately domestic of home-worshiping housewifes," she was forced to live with a succession of relatives. After a "long and thorough musical education," she was forced to sell her piano when Charlotte was two. Mary was a "baby-worshiper"; two of her four children died in infancy.

Through all these ordeals, Charlotte's mother remained absolutely loyal and as "loving as a spaniel." She was devoted to her children and "in her starved life her two little children were literally all; all of her duty, hope, ambition, love and joy." But there was to be no consolation even her. Mary could only really care for babies. As her children grew older, "she increasingly lost touch with them, wider and wider grew the gulf between. . . ."

Biblical injunction ("the sins of the fathers . . .") and psychiatric theory both confirm what all of us, including Charlotte Perkins Gilman, know autobiographically: families replicate themselves. But the young Gilman was determined not to become another victim. She must reconstruct a personality that avoided her mother's errors, a personality that would be beyond the reach of paternal power.

Charlotte Perkins Gilman's critique of her mother becomes the basis for her self-measurement and the basis of feminist reform. Mary Perkins was dependent first upon her husband, then upon the good will of relatives. She was a devoted mother but "love, devotion, sublime self-sacrifice" were not enough even in a "child-culture." Mary Perkins lacked knowledge. The descendant of Lyman Beecher and subsequent generations of "world-servers" could only serve and then would lose touch with them because of her limited knowledge of the world. She would embrace Swedenborgianism. But Charlotte regarded these meetings of coreligionists as proof of her mother's intellectual inadequacy. The Swedenborgians would sit around a table "floating and wallowing about in endless discussion of proofless themes and theories of their own . . . interminably talking on matters of religion and ethics."

Charlotte Perkins Gilman's formal education is limited largely as a result of her mother's position. She attended seven different schools and estimated that she had received only about four years of education. But she ferociously initiated her own system for self-education, which has all the earmarks of Franklin's plan. First there is the attempt, undertaken with great enthusiasm, to develop a philosophy of everything, which became the central characteristic of her later writings. The young Charlotte wrote her father for a list of books, "saying that I wished to help humanity . . . and where shall I begin." She read widely in history and anthropology and joined the Society for the Encouragement of Studies at Home. Armed with "the story of life on earth," Charlotte set out to "build her own religion." The result, achieved after consideration of God, evil, death, and pain was stated in a single maxim: "The first duty of a human being is to assume right functional relations to society—more briefly, to find your real job, and do it.'" God had a plan for the human race that was revealed in some evolutionary "telic force," and Gilman's task was to discover her role in this process. For that she needed her own plan: "And I set to work, with my reliable system of development, to 'do the will' as far as I could see it."

Charlotte Perkins Gilman described herself as a "philosophic steam engine." She believed that she had invented her own praxis. "My method was to approach a difficulty as if it was a problem of physics, trying to invent the best solution." In order to develop the energy necessary to carry out her plan, she invented her own system of "physical culture." She adopted her own style of dress (short, light garments), which included inventing a new kind of bra. She walked five miles a day and started an exercise class for women. She redecorated her stuffy room by taking a window out of its casing and installing a leaf from a dining-room table to keep out snow. On some mornings, Gilman proudly recalls, her wash bowl had ice so thick that she could not even break it with her heel. As a result, her health was "splendid": "I never tired. . . . When asked, 'How do you do it?' it was my custom to reply, 'as well as a fish, as busy as a bee, as strong as a horse, as proud as a peacock, as happy as a clam.'"

But the plan included more than a regimen for physical fitness. She worked on methods of "the turning of consciousness from self to others." She began with "minor self-denials." "I would gaze at some caller of mother's and consider what, if anything, I could do for that person; get a footstool, a glass of water, change a window-shade, any definitely conceived benefit." These efforts, however, were "too slow, too restricted." Charlotte "devised a larger scheme." She discovered a crippled and blind young girl and arranged to meet her. The girl laughed bitterly when young Charlotte asked, "Will you do me a service?" But Charlotte explained: "You see, I don't think about other people, and I'm trying to learn. Now I don't care anything about you, yet, but I'd like to. Will you let me come and practice on you?" The practicing included reading to the "unhappy creature," bringing her flowers, buying a small present. When Charlotte learned second-hand that the girl had said that Charlotte Perkins was "so thoughtful of other people," she recalls exclaiming, "Hurrah!, another game won!" With the victory over selfishness assured did Charlotte continue her visits to the young girl? Here the autobiographer is silent. We do not know if she moved on to other projects to acquire new virtues.

Like Franklin before her, Charlotte Perkins Gilman had created a new personality as an act of will. And like Franklin's, this new person entailed political implications. All of the newly acquired freedoms of both individuals were replicable. Franklin had avoided the narrow horizons of a tradesman as well as the dissipated life of a journeyman. Charlotte Perkins Gilman, at least up to this point, had not become like her mother. She was independent, educated, and primed to dedicate her life to service beyond the confines of the family. But when it had become time to marry, she could not simply find a "helpmate."

After many delays, she married Charles Walter Stetson in 1884. A year later Katherine was born. She was "angelic," "the best," "a heavenly baby." Charlotte Stetson had a "charming home; a loving and devoted husband; an exquisite baby, healthy, intelligent and good; a highly competent mother to run things; a wholly satisfactory servant—and I lay on the lounge all day and cried." "That baby-worshipping grandmother" had to come to take care of the baby because Charlotte has become a "mental wreck." No plan, no amount of will, could bring Charlotte Stetson out of her "growing melancholia." She, "the ceaselessly industrious, could not mop a floor, paint, sew, read, even hold a knife without suffering from sheer exhaustion." But worse than the inexplicable weariness was a sense of shame: "You did it yourself! You had health and strength and hope and glorious work before you—and you threw it away! You were called to serve humanity and you cannot serve yourself."

On a doctor's advice, Charlotte Stetson went West to Utah to visit her brother and from there to California to visit friends. As soon as the train moved she felt better. A month later she went home and the symptoms returned almost immediately. In 1887 she and her husband were divorced and Charlotte Gilman went to California. "After I was finally free . . . there was a surprising output of work, some of my best." Later she returned the young Katherine to her father.

In San Francisco, Charlotte Gilman begins the second reconstruction of her personality. She starts another plan with the realization that at thirty-five she is "a failure, a repeated, cumulative failure." She had published a collection of poems, worked on a small newspaper which had folded in twenty weeks. But the basis of Gilman's livelihood and of her new personality as well was the public lecture. She would speak before women's groups, church gatherings, and Nationalist Clubs. *The Living of Charlotte Perkins Gilman* is filled with accounts of the reactions to her lectures, including records of the donations that followed the talk: "lectured in Brooklyn . . . $20.25"; "spoke" in Kansas City on "'The New Motherhood.' Successful. Stayed to dinner. Stupid evening—the men afraid of me. $10.00"; "I spoke in a little church in Madison, Kansas, and on Thursday, . . . went to Eureka. . . . Friday I spoke twice, $17.00; again visiting the Addisons, and preaching the next day in the Congregational church—$4.00"; "in Bedford, Iowa, with a friend's friend, and an address—$5.45, and so back to Chicago."

This constant movement provided the structure for her new self. Gilman described herself as "propertyless and desireless as a Buddhist priest." She replicated the endless travels of her childhood, not as a mother dependent upon the charity of relatives but as a free independent woman who was dedicated to the emancipation of mothers. She had freed herself of "the home." In a visitors' book in Los Angeles she proudly signed, "Charlotte Perkins Stetson. At Large." The airy, belligerent confidence achieved by the first plan had returned: "'Don't you feel very much at sea?' someone asked. 'I do. Like a sea gull at sea.' And when inquiring friends would ask, 'Where do you live now?' my reply was, 'Here.'" Charlotte Gilman was again "as happy as a clam." But there were, on Gilman's own admission, two selves, her "outside life" in which there was "a woman undergoing many hardships and losses" and an "inside" self that was a "social inventor, trying to advance human happiness by the introduction of better psychic machinery."

Gilman is not the first reformer whose activity was impelled by psychic needs. What is instructive here in terms of American political thought is that her conception of her "real" self, the self that holds together her personality, is understood by her to be her social self. The "outside" self, the self that is existential and finite, the self that suffers and has longings, is epiphenomenal. Seen in light of Gilman's political theory, feminism promises to "free" women by abolishing those institutions that are responsible for the maintenance of this outer self.

One of the most puzzling aspects of feminism is its formation as sets of small local groups and its political agenda that promotes bureaucratic organization. Gilman's autobiography reveals how this happens and as such provides us with a complete feminist political theory. Let me recapitulate the theory as autobiographically presented thus far. Gilman's growing up is influenced by the consequences of patriarchy. With great effort she is able to conceive, and to a limited extent live, a life independent of male control. Marriage and motherhood, however, threaten this effort, an effort made at considerable psychic cost. After all, Gilman had had to deny first her father and then her mother, and this brings about a breakdown. She recovers, however, by denying her husband and her daughter and traveling to California, that land of "swift enthusiasms." Her new personality, now twice reconstructed, is formed through an identification of the only nonpatriarchal communities she can find, voluntary associations composed in part by likeminded women. Service to these groups is her "real" self, the other self becomes a recurring ghost of doubts about her independence. Thus Gilman can never really identify with the suffrage movement or socialism. "My main interest was in the position of women. . . . economic independence" was "far more important than the ballot."

But how does one translate the transient nature of the voluntary association to a firmer basis? Must Gilman travel forever, like Thoreau had considered, to maintain her real self? One alternative, offered by Addams, would be to give the voluntary association some structural permanence by linking it to traditional institutions and presumably transforming both in the process. But Gilman could not take that path. She turned down an offer to direct a settlement. When she finally did give up her "at-large" identity, by renting a flat late in life, she notes the "insidious drugging effect" of a home. She still attempted to avoid the insidious effects of "spending one's time waiting on one's own tastes and appetites, and those of dear ones" by recurrent lecture trips. Her sense of a "real" self depended upon continual contact with these groups as if her personality was strewn across the country in clubs and associations, which in a sense it was. There was also the possibility that the groups who paid her to present visions of new structures might become like her mother's Swedenborgian groups, "floating and wallowing about in endless discussion. . . ."

Thus Gilman's life work—her service, her fame, and her livelihood—is devoted to the presentation of structures that will abolish the home and the "outer" self and replace it with surer nonpatriarchal institutions than voluntary associations. Gilman's feminism, and that of others who followed her, seeks to destroy the very kind of relationships that have really made women's emancipation possible. Sisterhood is, above all, a set of personal relations, relations built upon a personal community of common experience and common goals. Can this vision be realized in sets of bureaucratic institutions? Gilman says they must.

This paradox in feminist thought can be illustrated by briefly comparing Gilman's autobiographical short story, "The Yellow Wallpaper" to her *The Home.* "The Yellow Wallpaper," written during her first years in California, is a moving fictional account of her own breakdown. It tells the story of a young middle-class wife and mother who suffers so from the bonds of affection that her personality disintegrates before the eyes of the reader. The story concludes with a doctor's prescription that the woman cease all intellectual efforts and focus what little energy she has on her family. Of course this regimen only serves to sink the young woman to deeper levels of depression; the swirls she sees on the wallpaper of her bedroom begin to float and undulate uncontrollably, as does her conception of her self. The story suggests the woman's need to experience a community of equals beyond her family. But then look at Gilman's solution to the yearning for sisterhood. In *The Home* she insists that she offers no "iconoclastic frenzy of destruction" but only a "pruning" of a "most precious tree," but she portrays the home in what is actually a much more negative light. She looks at it as an institution that has thus far resisted "social evolution." The sentimental attachment to the home is traced to two ancient twin gothics, a sexual contract (bodily submission in exchange for protection) and religion. Today our conception of religion is monotheist, we no longer need household gods. Harems have been abolished in civilized societies, but for the man the home is still his "private harem—be it ever so monogamous—the secret place where he keeps his most private possession."

Division of labor characterizes modern work but women still labor like their ancestors. They cook, clean, nurse, educate. Women must rise to the "higher plane" of evolution for which they are fit. Water and sewage used to be taken care of on an individual household basis but now there is "an insidious new system of common supply of domestic necessities." If water and sewage have come to be "fully socialized," why not food, housekeeping, nursing, and education? The endless repetition of kitchens could be replaced by cooked-food supply companies. In anticipation of modern children's rights theorists, Gilman asserts that children must be recognized as a "class" with "rights guaranteed by the state." Every baby is better off with a "good trained nurse." The housewife ought to enter the world of productive work, pay her substitute and contribute to the "world's wealth."

Of course, in a sense, *The Home* perceived changes in the structure of families and family life that were in process and Gilman simply carried them to what she saw as a logical conclusion. The language that chronicles the development of the new home of the future is that of the progressive's interpretation of evolution. The present structure of families is "irrational" in the sense that performance of its functions is wasteful and erratic. Both good wholesome food and babies are produced by families almost by happenstance. Gilman's assertion that bakers' bread is always better than homemade captures the spirit of the entire essay. But what is most important is that the new home constructed by Gilman is modeled on her conception of her "real" self. Life is service but service abstractly conceived. And who can fail to detect the element of retribution and scorn for women behind the measured arguments of progressive reform? In fact, the home conceived by Gilman has all the characteristics of Marx's description of crude communism. Marx had warned that in the first stage of revolution the workers seek to "destroy everything which is not capable of being possessed by all as private property." "The category of laborer is not done away with but extended to all men." The community becomes the universal capitalist; private property becomes "universal private property." Transpose women for proletariat, service for universal private property, and one sees Gilman's recommendations as a feminist version of crude communism. A woman must become a "free cook, a trained cook, a scientific cook." "For profit and for love—to do her duty and to gain her ends—in all ways, the home cook is forced to do her cooking to please John. It is no wonder John clings so ardently to the custom." Notice the depiction of the future: "Never again on earth will he have a whole live private cook to himself, to consider, before anything else, his special tastes and preferences. He will get better food, and he will like it." What brings Gilman to advocate this "thoughtless" communism is certainly in part what she calls the "sexuo-economic" structure of the family. But instead of attacking a gender-based system in which acts of personal sacrifice, love, and service are a perversion of the ideal of personal relationships, to be replaced perhaps by mutual acts, she seeks to destroy personal relations themselves. Who can adequately serve, she asks, under "direct pressure of personal affection?" "It is very, very hard to resist the daily . . . demands of those we love." That "outer self" is finally destroyed by Gilman in her home of the future, and only the real self remains. The personal is indeed political for Gilman and she transcends the latter by destroying the former.

"Sweet Dessert in the Morning"

If Charlotte Perkins Gilman's conception of self and political theory was the result of efforts to overcome patriarchal power asserted through the denial of bonds of affection, Jane Addams's struggle is centered around the consequences of the benevolent father. Addams's devotion is complete, so complete that she seeks to be her father. She was obsessed by the disparity in their physical appearances. She remembers herself as an awkward, homely child who so dreaded the thought that "strangers" would see the incongruity between her and the dignified man in the great frock coat that she would walk to church with her uncle. She longed to attain some physical likeness, even if it meant acquiring burns on her hands similar to those that her father had suffered during his early work as a miller.

Father Addams (he is never named in the autobiography) was also the major employer in Cedarville (he owned two mills) and the Addams house was the largest in the town. In antebellum Cedarville paternal authority was complete. The young Jane associated the mill with her father's activities and "centered upon him all that careful imitation which a little girl ordinarily gives to her mother's ways and habits." Of course, Jane Addams would learn that she could never completely imitate her father. We can even leave the Freudian implications of this observation aside. Jane Addams could not become the "self-made man" that her father was; she could not be a member of the legislature; she could not be a soldier in the "Addams Guard." But her sense of estrangement was even greater. She was born too late to be a member of even the last postwar generation of middle-class, small-town Protestant elites. America was turning away from men of "entrepreneural appetites and republican zeal," men who admired Lincoln and Mazzini and in coalition with the Protestant clergy would work for a genteel reform. New elites, robber barons and city bosses, would serve the people and be models of "careful imitation."

Jane Addams was thus doubly estranged, first as a result of her gender and second as a result of her class. Paternal authority was, of course, generally responsible for her predicament. She was a daughter and she was a daughter of the outdated middle class. Later in life, Addams was to understand an aspect of her dilemma. The liberated women of her day were liberated from the home, but then they were also liberated from the positive elements of their class and gender. They had "departed too quickly from the active emotional life led by their grandmothers and great-grandmothers. . . . somewhere in the process of 'being educated' they had lost that simple and automatic response to the human appeal, that old healthful reaction resulting in activity from the mere presence of suffering or of helplessness." They could not imitate their mothers. Nor could they imitate their fathers. A vague desire for service in the world has no outlet. "The girl loses something vital out of her life to which she is entitled. She is restricted and unhappy; her elders, meanwhile, are unconscious of her situation and we have all the elements of a tragedy."

These truths, this awareness of estrangement, are autobiographically learned. Addams had entered college but it took her eight years after her graduation "to formulate my convictions in at least a satisfactory manner. . . ." During that time she had been "absolutely at sea so far as my moral purpose was concerned." She had suffered through two major crises during this period. In 1881 her father died. Addams experienced the kind of estrangement that no political theory can ever remedy.

She does not directly discuss the loss but she gives an account of the grief she had felt at the death of the family nurse many years before: "As I was driven home in the winter storm, the wind through the trees seemed laden with a passing soul and the riddle of life and death pressed hard; once to be young, to grow old and to die, everything came to that, and then a mysterious journey out to the Unknown. Did she mind faring forth alone?" The father was dead but the daughter was alive and in imitation of him. Addams herself tried to fare forth alone in life. She enrolled at the Women's Medical College in Philadelphia but developed a severe spinal condition that left her "literally bound" to bed for six months. An operation helped but the procedure made it impossible to have children. Jane Addams had a nervous breakdown, "traces" of which haunted her long after her work had begun at Hull House. She attempted to find solace in religion. Theological speculation only worsened her depression. Baptism into the Presbyterian church helped somewhat. She "longed for an outward symbol of fellowship." She visited some farms in the West where she had invested some of her inheritance in mortgages. The expectation had been pastoral but instead she witnessed "starved hogs," "despair" and children "not to be compared to anything so joyous as satyrs, although they appeared but half-human." She immediately sold her shares. In the summers Addams lectured to women's groups and took courses in European art history. She wintered in Europe although the trips always failed to raise her spirit.

In 1887 she finally did undergo a conversion. She witnessed a bullfight. The entertainment does not horrify her and, on the contrary, "the sense that this was the last survival of all glories of the amphitheater, the illusion that the riders on the caparsoned horses might have been knights of a tournament, or the matador a slightly armed gladiator facing his martyrdom, and all the rest of the obscure yet vivid associations of historic survival, had carried me beyond the endurance of any of the party." Later that evening she came to see the reality of this "disgusting experience and the entire moral situation which it revealed." The next day she made up her mind to carry out her plan for a settlement for the poor, "whatever happened." No longer would she be tied to the "ox-cart of self-seeking," her "passive receptivity" had come to an end; she was finished with the "ever-lasting 'preparation for life.'"

The account of the bullfight, at first reading, offers a puzzling conversion. In the months preceding the occasion Addams had witnessed far more horrifying sights. She had seen children that looked only "half-human," the poor fighting for food "which was already unfit to eat." What the bullfight had achieved and the sights of urban poverty had not was a realization that her search for culture was a futile quest. She had attempted to find personal meaning in sight-seeing and collecting objets d'art. The application of this cultural knowledge to the bullfight so disgusted her that it produced a conversion and sense of commitment that church membership or the medical profession could not. But, most important, Addams told a whole generation of middle-class women that "somewhere in the process of 'being educated' they had lost that old healthful reaction resulting in activity from the mere presence of suffering or of helplessness." Their lives were incomplete because the pursuit of education had only added to their class ennui. Their lives were unsatisfactory because they were "smothered and sickened" with social advantages. It was like eating a "sweet dessert the first thing in the morning." Jane Addams knew these assertions were true because she had lived them. Likewise she knew the truth of the solution. After the bullfight experience, Addams's life became a totally public one. Service had been justified as an alternative to class boredom, as a kind of relief from personal problems.

Up to this point the autobiographical lessons of Addams and Gilman are fundamentally the same. Both women's identity had been determined by paternal authority. Both suffered as a consequence. Both fought bravely to discover an independent self. Both failed, only to finally succeed in reconstructing a personality beyond paternal power through dedication to service. But Addams's solution is different from Gilman's in very basic ways. Her life of service, her leadership in the settlement movement, her political theory, are not based upon an abolition of the "outer self" but upon a recognition of the personal as the basis for human community, however stunted and tortured this aspect of people's lives has become.

The central focus of Addams's teaching is based upon her image of immigrants as a "household of children whose mother is dead." Addams saw in the immigrant what she saw in herself, for she too was an immigrant, herself adrift from parental power, from the security of her class and the sorority of her forebears. In nearly all her analyses of political and social life she was able to capture the nature of the immigrant's estrangement and at the same time to discover aspects of her life that deserved to be preserved, even treasured, as that estrangement was overcome. In a sense, Addams had developed a praxis of social life, an achievement that Gilman, or for that matter, American liberal reform in general, never attained.

Addams included her essay **"The Subjective Necessity of Social Settlements"** in her autobiography. She had openly promoted the settlement house as a solution to personal problems. Youth, "so sincere in its emotion and good phrase and yet so undirected, seems to me as pitiful as the other great mass of destitute lives."

Christopher Lasch has argued that the essay exposes Addams's motives as a reformer. Addams's efforts to help the poor were motivated not by the outrageous conditions of the city and still less by feelings of class guilt. What animated Addams's entry to public life was her desire to avoid a sense of ennui. But to this, Addams readily admits. It becomes the central thesis of her autobiography. The important question here is how Addams sought to overcome her personal problems and what she saw as the same problems that troubled middle-class women.

The early stages of Hull House did exhibit an attempt to simply enlarge the audience of middle-class women. There were teas, discussion groups, and art appreciation classes. But the young volunteers soon provided the sorts of services that the residents needed. They washed newborn babies, prepared the dead for burial, nursed the sick, minded the children, provided shelter for battered wives. Hull House was a dynamo of invention. Some efforts were, of course, unsuccessful. Addams confessed that she was never able to find a social alternative to the saloon. One of these attempts deserves special attention because it illustrates Addams's concern with estrangement and its transcendence through the expansion of social life. Addams had been concerned over the estrangement between immigrants and their children. Why, she asked, "should that chasm between fathers and sons, yawning at the feet of each generation, be made so unnecessarily cruel and impassable to these bewildered immigrants?" The Italian mothers who came to Hull House despaired over the "loss" of their "Americanized children." Walking down the street she had noticed "an old Italian woman, her distaff against her homesick face, patiently spinning a thread by the simple stick spindle so reminiscent of all southern Europe." The woman's face brightened as Addams passed by and she held up her spindle for her to see and yelled that after she had spun out some more yarn she was going to knit a pair of stockings for her goddaughter. Addams was so struck by the moment that she decided to set up a labor museum at Hull House. She invited immigrant women to demonstrate their crafts. Lectures were arranged to illustrate the industrial history. The museum afforded parents the opportunity to be teachers, "a pleasant change from the tutelage in which all Americans, including their own children, are so apt to hold them."

The museum also had its impact on Addams herself:

> In some such ways as these have the Labor Museum and the shops pointed out the possibilities which Hull-House has scarcely begun to develop, of demonstrating that culture is an understanding of the long-established occupations and thoughts of men, of the arts with which they have solaced their toil. A yearning to recover for the household arts something of their early sanctity and meaning arose strongly within me one evening when I was attending a Passover Feast to which I had been invited by a Jewish family in the neighborhood, where the traditional and religious significance of the woman's daily activity was still retained. The kosher food the Jewish mother spread before her

> family had been prepared according to traditional knowledge and with constant care in the use of utensils; upon her had fallen the responsibility to make all ready according to Mosaic instructions that the great crisis in a religious history might be fittingly set forth by her husband and son. Aside from the grave religious significance in the ceremony, my mind was filled with shifting pictures of woman's labor with which travel makes one familiar; the Indian women grinding grain outside of their huts as they sing praises to the sun and rain; a file of white-clad Moorish women whom I had once seen waiting their turn at a well in Tangiers; south Italian women kneeling in a row along the stream and beating their wet clothes against the smooth white stones; the milking, the gardening, the marketing in thousands of hamlets, which are such direct expressions of the solicitude and affection at the basis of all family life.

Addams was no narodnik. ***Twenty Years at Hull House*** contains its share of comments on what Marx had complained of as the "idiocy" of village life. But it is precisely these liberal antipathies toward the pre-modern world that make Addams's sentiments so important. She knew the value of literacy, hygiene, and economic mobility as much as any American but she would not forsake these peasant women nor cut their children adrift from their own autobiographical past in the name of liberal emancipation.

In all of her essays Addams strove to find the element of sociability beneath the disintegrative aspects of immigrant life. She was willing to search for social functions in institutions she abhorred. She noted that the city machine, for all its corruption and systematic greed, provided important personal relationships for displaced urban people. The aldermen gave presents at weddings and christenings, bought "tickets galore" for benefits for widows, distributed turkeys at Christmas. Addams asked, "Indeed what headway can the notion of civic purity, of honesty of administration, make against this big manifestation of human friendliness, this stalking survival of village kindness?" These were not the "corrupt and illiterate voters" of which the reformers complained. But neither was Addams prepared to defend a system that ultimately must be judged as one that exploits a "primitive" people. If men of "low ideals and corrupt practice" win the hearts of the people because they stand by them in basic ways, then "nothing remains but to obtain a like sense of identification before we can hope to modify ethical standards."

No institution could agitate Addams's middle-class progressive morality more than the "gin palaces" of Chicago. These huge dance halls were places where youth gathered in which "alcohol was dispensed, not to allay thirst" but to "empty pockets." The places confused "joy with lust, and gaiety with debauchery." But Addams knew that these "lurid places" were a reflection of the modern city. Daily labor had become "continually more monotonous and subdivided." Children had been gathered "from all the quarters of the earth as a labor supply for the countless factories and workshops." Young girls were valued for the products they manufactured. Society did not care for "their immemorial ability to affirm the charm of existence."

Progressive reformers had been able to see two cities in Chicago, one that was represented by the old class of wealth and status and one that was represented by the poor immigrant. But Addams was able to see two cities from the vantage point of the settlement. The new economic structure had convulsively produced a new class ripped from traditional culture. The young people who walked through the city streets after a day in the factories would have attended a dance on the village green or a peasant festival had they not been gathered from across the country and the world to "work under alien roofs." The city "sees in these girls only two possibilities, both of them commercial: first, a chance to utilize by day their new and tender labor power in its factories and shops, and then another chance in the evening to extract from them their petty wages by pandering to their love of pleasure." But Addams saw another city among the poor and displaced which was not economic in character although it had been perverted by the commercial hegemony over all aspects of urban life. The gin palace was meeting, albeit in a "pathetic" way, basic social needs. Addams's description captures this second, and submerged feature of the city:

> As these overworked girls stream along the street, the rest of us only see the self-conscious walk, the giggling speech, the preposterous clothing. And yet through the huge hat, with its wilderness of bedraggled feathers, the girl announces to the world that she is here. She demands attention to the fact of her existence, she states that she is ready to live, to take her place in the world. The most precious moment in human development is the young creature's assertion that he is unlike any other human being, and has an individual contribution to make to the world.

She continues her story of the girl as she enters the palace and young men "stand about vainly hoping to make the acquaintance of some 'nice girl.'" "They look eagerly up and down the rows of girls, many of whom are drawn to the hall by the same keen desire for pleasure and social intercourse which the lonely young men themselves feel." Of course, Addams knows well that these desires may conclude in only a one-night stand but she is able to see that closing of the palaces without providing some substitute only destroys an outlet, however imperfect, for social life. "Even the most loutish tenement-house youth vaguely feels this, and at least at rare intervals reveals it in his talk to his 'girl.'"

It is, I believe, Addams's discovery of this social aspect of the new city that permitted her to make a connection between the personal and the political quite different from that made by Charlotte Perkins Gilman. For Addams affirmed herself (her "outer self"), fractured and threatened as it had become in her own youth, through an appreciation of the struggles of the displaced. Their estrangement was also hers, but more positively, their victories over anomie and economic exploitation were hers as well. Two incidents, minor in themselves, illustrate Addams's development in this regard. She had been called to come quickly to the house of an old German woman who was resisting resettlement to the county infirmary. She found a "poor old creature" who had "thrown herself bodily upon a small and battered chest of drawers and clung there, clutching it so firmly that it would have been impossible to remove her without also taking the piece of furniture." She looked like "a frightened animal caught in a trap" and despite the assurances of Addams and a group of neighborhood women, she would not move. Addams concluded:

> To take away from an old woman whose life had been spent in household cares all the foolish belongings to which her affections cling and to which her very fingers have become accustomed is to take away her last incentive to activity, almost to life itself. To give an old woman only a chair and a bed, to leave her no cupboard in which her treasures may be stowed, not only that she may take them out when she desires occupation, but that her mind may dwell on them in moments of revery is to reduce living almost beyond the limit of human endurance.

There is in Addams a frank assessment of the intrinsic value of possessions; these were after all "foolish belongings." But the utility of things owned is not the standard of measurement. This old woman saw the dresser and its contents as a means by which she could retain a conception of herself. From that realization on, Addams found that the old women whom she began to invite to Hull House as a vacation from the poor house had many "shrewd comments on life" and made "delightful companions."

A second incident occurred shortly after Addams had started her settlement. It is not mentioned in ***Twenty Years at Hull House*** but is reported autobiographically in an essay. A "delicate little child" had been deserted in the Hull House nursery. Addams had been able to find that the infant had been born ten days before in the Cook County Hospital but she could not locate the "unfortunate Mother." After a few weeks the child died and Addams made arrangements for burial by the county. A wagon was scheduled to arrive at eleven o'clock. At nine, Hull House was the scene of protest by neighborhood women. They had taken up a collection "out of their poverty" to pay the costs of a funeral. Addams is able to see two moralities encapsuled in the situation. Her first reaction was defensive. After all, "we instanced the care and tenderness which had been expended upon the poor creature when it was alive." The infant had received the attention of a skilled physician and trained nurse. Where, Addams asked "the excited members of the group," were you when the baby was alive? "It now lay with us to decide that the child should be buried, as it had been born, at the county's expense." Unstated in Addams's defense is the accusation that the community had abandoned an illegitimate child and that the "professional" thus has assumed proprietary interests over those whom it serves. But her remarks are prefaced by confession of the "crudeness" of her position: "We did not realize that we were really shocking a genuine moral sentiment of the community. . . . We were only forgiven by the most indulgent on the ground that we were spinsters and could not know a mother's heart." There is certainly a note of self-deprecation in the concluding response, but Addams is more concerned that sentiments in "the mother's heart" were a collective overlay of biological function. "No one," she insists, "born and reared in the community could have possibly made a mistake like that."

Addams's development of a praxis between the personal and political achieves the status of political theory in her analysis of the Pullman strike. Her essays and the autobiography are always focused upon the problems of women. Men never receive the same empathetic efforts that characterize her accounts of children, young women, mothers, and widows. There is certainly an appreciation for "the sorry men" who "for one reason or other" have "failed in the struggle of life." But the emphasis is on "heroic women" who must deal with drunkards, domestic violence, and deserting husbands. The Pullman strike provided Addams with the opportunity to examine the nature of paternal authority.

George Pullman represented an alternative to the rapacious capitalist of the post-Civil War era. He had created a model company town for his workers. Successive wage reductions led to workers' pleas for arbitration. This Pullman refused. When railway employees would not work on Pullman cars, there were dismissals and then a massive strike which was broken by President Cleveland's deployment of federal troops to Illinois. The strike was broken. Many historians regard the strikers' defeat as a setback that would require labor generations to overcome. The Pullman strike had briefly showed the power of the labor movement (the railways west of Chicago had been shut down) and the American middle class was badly frightened. After all, had not Pullman spent large sums of money to provide his workers with modern plumbing and even a park, a theater, and a church? Is this, they asked, the reward for benevolent paternalism?

Addams, who was clearly sympathetic to the workers but also skeptical of the value of strikes, used Shakespeare's story of King Lear as the basis for her analysis of the incident. Pullman was a modern Lear and the strikers Cordelias. Shakespeare had described a domestic tragedy; Pullman had created an industrial one. Addams was struck by the "similarity of ingratitude suffered by the indulgent employer and an indulgent parent." The lesson of Lear had "modified and softened her judgment" of the workers.

"A Modern Lear" is a neglected masterpiece because it shows how the connection between the personal and political can be made. This, after all is said, is the goal of all American political thought. Addams never tells us that Pullman like Addams is an example of paternal authority: "The minds of all of us reach back to our early struggles. . . ." We all know what it might be like to kill our father: "We have all had glimpses of what it might be like to blaspheme family ties. . . ." We all have suffered from the bonds of paternal will: "The virtues of one generation are not sufficient for the next. . . ." The Lear analogy enabled Addams to see the character of her own struggles as a woman, but it also allowed her to appreciate the struggles of men against paternalism in the industrial sphere. The Pullman strikers may not have agreed that their position was analogous to daughters, but Addams saw a resemblance between them and the workers who first petitioned and then struck out against paternal authority and risked the charge of "ingratitude." Here were for Addams the counterparts to the "heroic women" of Halsted Street. These men were "self-controlled and destroyed no property." They were "sober and exhibited no drunkenness even though obliged to hold meetings in the saloon hall of a neighboring town."

This is not to say that the rejection of paternal authority presents no moral ambiguities. "Cordelia does not escape our censure. Her first words are cold, and we are shocked by her lack of tenderness. Why should she ignore her father's need for indulgence, and be so unwilling to give him what he so obviously craved?" So too the claims of the workers will consist of "many failures, cruelties and reactions." But Addams insisted that paternal authority, those bonds of bondage, must eventually be accommodated. Pullman and Lear were "tragic" examples of paternal authority. They had forgotten the nature of their trust. Lear had "ignored the common ancestry of Cordelia and himself." He could see Cordelia only in terms of signs of fidelity that he demanded. Likewise, Pullman's town became only "a source of pride and an exponent of power": "We can imagine the founder of the town slowly darkening his glints of memory and forgetting the common stock of experience which he held with these men."

Bonds of affection need not always be arbitrary exercises of power. The "family claim" (which Addams had also herself overcome autobiographically) must be "tested" by a commitment to a larger life. The daughter must pass this test by asserting her individuality and so must the father by realizing that the child can fulfill the family claim in all "its sweetness and strength" by enlarging it. The "adjustment of the lesser and larger implies no conflict." In all the affairs of society consent must eventually temper paternal power:

> The man who insists upon consent, who moves with the people, is bound to consult the feasible right as well as the absolute right. He is often obliged to attain only Mr. Lincoln's "best possible," and often have the sickening sense of compromising with his best convictions. He has to move along with those whom he rules toward a goal that neither he nor they see very clearly till they come to it. He has to discover what people really want, and then "provide the channels in which the growing moral force of their lives shall flow." What he does attain, however, is not the result of his individual striving, as a solitary mountain climber beyond the sight of the valley multitude, but it is underpinned and upheld by the sentiments and aspirations of many others. Progress has been slower perpendicularly, but incomparably greater because it is lateral.

Unlike Gilman, Addams taught that there must always be parents, that the "outside self" is the "real self," and that the realization of the one depends upon the affirmation of the other.

Jean Bethke Elshtain (essay date 1990)

SOURCE: "A Return to Hull House: Reflections on Jane Addams," in *Power Trips and Other Journeys: Essays in Feminism as Civic Discourse,* The University of Wisconsin Press, 1990, pp. 3-12.

[*In the following excerpt, Elshtain offers a critique of Addams's career from a feminist standpoint outside the traditional left-wing framework.*]

From a standpoint of jaded modern sophistication, the story of Jane Addams at first seems a tale of old-fashioned do-goodism fired by the charitable impulses of a "lady" who wound up fashioning an overpersonalized approach to social problems. Such naive forms of social intervention, the sophisticate might continue, inevitably gave way to professionalism, social workers who neither require nor need even be aware of the complex inner wellsprings of their own motivation but who act, instead, from the realization that there is a job to be done. The primary question is how most efficiently to do it—to "manage" a "client" population. To see Hull House and Jane Addams simply as an instance of noblesse oblige suited, perhaps, to its day but quickly eclipsed by the welfare state and the abstract demands of justice is not so much to oversimplify—though it is to do that—but to pretty much miss the boat altogether. For Jane Addams was up to something else.

A second layer of distortion that partially obscures Jane Addams's life and work reflects our changing constructions of American womanhood. The chaste and the maternal intermingled in Addams, always Miss Addams, sometimes Queen Jane. Hers was a symbol overtaken in epochs that witnessed, successively, flappers, WACS and Rosie the Riveters, the feminine mystique, feminist protest, sexual liberation, rampant consumerism, demands for "self-actualization" and the (apparent) final triumph of secular and technological world views. A life of unforced chastity infused with a deeply felt maternalism is a combination that we find difficult to understand, even more difficult to respond to. We no longer see the world, as Addams did, through the prism of duty and compassion, social responsibility and witness-bearing; life as a Pilgrim's Progress. Perhaps this as much as anything else dates her and fixes her in our eyes as a remote figure.

Having said all this, I shall try, nevertheless, to see her once again, rethinking her as both a theorist and symbol.

Briefly, however, it is worth surveying the received wisdom of Addams as a social thinker. Views of her long ago congealed. Nearly all commentators, with few exceptions, find her work derivative. Allen F. Davis, her most recent biographer, endorses the view that Addams is "more important as a publicist and popularizer" than as an original thinker.[1] Daniel Levine, author of *Jane Addams and the Liberal Tradition,* concurs: Addams is "not an original thinker"; rather, she was a "publicist" alive "to the currents of the day."[2] Addams fares little better in a number of influential social and cultural histories. Henry Steele Commager, in *The American Mind,* mentions her in no capacity.[3] Ralph Henry Gabriel's classic standard, *The Course of American Democratic Thought,* contains one scanty reference to Addams. In his discussion of progressivism, Gabriel gives the progressive kudos for transcending both the agrarian parochialism of the populists and "the humanitarianism of such urban reformers as Jacob Riis and Jane Addams" in the name of a more cosmopolitan, less personally humanitarian stance.[4] In *Age of Reform,* Richard Hofstadter characterizes **"The Subjective Necessity for Social Settlements,"** an early and important Addams essay, as "fine and penetrating" and Addams herself, he declares, embodies "the most decent stream" in the Progressive moment given her keen awareness of the deracination attendant upon industrialization.[5]

One important exception to cursory notices on Addams is Christopher Lasch's introduction to *The Social Thought of Jane Addams* and his chapter devoted to Addams in *The New Radicalism in America.* Lasch sees Addams as "a theorist and intellectual—a thinker of originality and daring."[6] Though he is critical of the anti-intellectualism he finds in some of her work, particularly in those discussions of education that extolled "applied knowledge," Lasch's serious consideration of Addams as a social theorist of continuing importance is instructive, and it is one on which I shall build.[7] I do so in an effort to recover and restore Addams's commitment to an interpretive social theory that bears within it the seeds of cultural and political criticism.

Jane Addams was forty-five years old when she began ***Twenty Years at Hull House,*** the first volume of her autobiography. Published in 1910, it was to be her most successful book; eighty thousand copies were published during her lifetime. ***Twenty Years*** stands out among her nearly dozen books and her many essays and occasional pieces as, perhaps, her finest sustained effort.[8] Her gifts as a thinker of rare insight and a writer of unusual descriptive powers are here abundantly displayed. Already a celebrated public figure when she penned her own story, her autobiography sealed that public persona. To her biographer, Davis, ***Twenty Years*** captures Addams in the self-conscious process of casting her public image in a heroic mold, "at least," Davis equivocates, "acquiescing in the public image of herself as a self-sacrificing saint, and friend of the down-trodden." Davis goes on to scold Addams for refusing to "come clean" about her "administrative talent and her ability to compete in a man's world that actually made her a success"[9]—an injunction wholly out of touch with Addams's own sensibilities and her moral location.

But Davis's judgments, those of a sympathetic but partially debunking observer, show how difficult it is for the sensibilities of the present to get inside the world as Jane Addams understood it. That difficulty is manifest, for example, when the fact that Addams deployed various literary conceits and fictional conventions popular in her era serves as the basis for Davis's additional claim that there is little difference, in principle, between ***Twenty Years*** and the other tales of the self-made person who overcomes all obstacles to achieve fame and success. If Addams's story were just one more example of the pluck and luck *genre,* we would long ago have ceased to pay it any mind, whether as personal history or as social commentary. These judgments by a biographer highlight a general problem that emerges when our historic hindsights are so finely attuned to contemporary abuses of "publicity" that we blind ourselves to the deeper discursive tradition that—in this case—***Twenty Years*** embodies.

What I call to mind here is story-shaped history that aims to edify. "Jenny" Addams viewed her world through the prism of Christian symbols and injunctions, purposes and meanings. These gave her world its shape—a narrative form involving the use of instructive parables in the conviction that the moral life consists in "the imitation of Christ," not in abstract obedience to a formal model of moral conduct. From the book's opening passages, Addams traces her life as a singular narrative, a *particular* story but one that forms as well part of the greater American story. Addams quotes herself (from an 1889 journal entry): "In his own way each man must struggle, lest the moral become a far-off abstraction utterly separated from his active life."[10] Life, she declares, is a quest, and a life of virtue lies within reach if one emulates exemplary individuals. For Jenny, Mr. Lincoln early became her secular saint, a figure with whom she explicitly, self-consciously, and unwaveringly identified until her death. Lincoln was the standard by which she took the measure of her own existence.[11]

Just as she had an ongoing connection to Lincoln, in ***Twenty Years*** Addams invites her reader into a particular identification with herself. For Addams, each human life was instructive. She evokes the desire of the young girl to please her "handsome father" trying to understand life "as he did," including the sense he conveyed through his attachment to the Italian patriot Joseph Mazzini of the "genuine relationship which may exist between men who share large hopes and like desires, even though they differ in nationality, language and creed."[12] As a child, Addams claims, she recoiled from adult attempts to patronize her by isolating her from life's experiences, being already (at least from hindsight) convinced that ethics "is but another word for 'righteousness,' that for which men and women of every generation have hungered and thirsted, and without which life becomes meaningless."[13]

If the child, from the standpoint of the mature adult, can, through reminiscence, instruct that adult on childhood; if the rebellion of youth is forged and shaped so long as there "is something vital to rebel against"—adults revealed with their flaws but their dignity intact—the social bond is strained but unbroken and the power of empathetic reflection is affirmed. "Even if we, the elderly," she writes, "have nothing to report but sordid compromises, nothing to offer but a disconcerting acknowledgement that life has marked us with its slow stain, it is still better to define our position."[14] ***Twenty Years*** is her attempt, mid-life, to define and to clarify her own position so that others might emulate or challenge written in the conviction that "truth itself may be discovered by honest reminiscence."[15]

In this sense ***Twenty Years*** represents the culmination of Addams's early social thinking and sets the agenda for her work to come.[16] All the characteristics of her philosophy are present: her repudiation of abstract systems in favor of a social theory open to experience; her sense of moral seriousness and struggle; her rejection of "feverish searches" after culture that cultivated a life of pale aestheticism in favor of a life of action, for "action is the only medium man has for receiving and appropriating truth."[17] To this one must add her powerfully conveyed image of human solidarity, "which will not waver when the race happens to be represented by a drunken woman or an idiot boy."[18] That was the starting point from which she derived a politics whose end was social change through the ever-deepening processes of social democracy.

Several apparent paradoxes in Addams's thought come to the surface—double convictions that set her apart from unambivalent celebrants of the progressive faith. One such double commitment lies in her battered but never repudiated belief in progression towards more inclusive and pacific social forms, on one hand, and her equally unwavering recognition and depiction of the pathos of those lives swept up, as so much human debris, by imperious waves of industrialization, on the other. When Addams celebrated progress she did so as an expression of liberal faith and given a particular reading of history. But when she told the story of history's victims she did so from the point of view of those victims, from inside their despair, their often stupefied not-being-at-home in a strange new world that forced many into silence, madness, or self-destruction.

Addams's ambivalence about the world industrialization had wrought is rooted in her social morality and compelled as well by her commitment to a social theory anchored in the detailed consideration of particular cases. No social abstraction has authenticity, she argued, unless it is rooted in concrete human experience. Her immersion in the particular, her ability to articulate wider social meaning through powerful depictions of individual suffering or joy, hope or despair, sets her apart from all who write abstractly about experience. One example must suffice to evoke the human suffering the early wage-labor system trailed in its wake and to illustrate Addams's descriptive powers. Addams pens an unforgettable word portrait of a single suffering woman, one human story beneath—or beyond—the facts of the matter. She writes:

> With all the efforts made by modern society to nurture and educate the young, how stupid it is to permit the mothers of young children to spend themselves in the coarser work of the world! It is curiously inconsistent that with the emphasis this generation has placed upon the mother and upon the prolongation of infancy, we constantly allow the waste of this most precious material. I cannot recall without indignation a recent experience. I was detained late one evening in an office building by a prolonged committee meeting of the Board of Education. As I came out at eleven o'clock, I met in the corridor of the fourteenth floor a woman whom I knew, on her knees scrubbing the marble tiling. As she straightened to greet me, she seemed so wet from her feet up to her chin, that I hastily inquired the cause. Her reply was that she left home at five o'clock every night and had no opportunity for six hours to nurse her baby. Her mother's milk mingled with the very water with which she scrubbed the floors until she should return at midnight, heated and exhausted to feed her screaming child with what remained within her breasts.[19]

Addams's project, with this vignette, is a task at once ethical and political. Her theory of morality opposed abstract appeals and the repetition of formulae. It was her conviction that only a tug upon our human sympathies and affections could draw us into an ethical life and keep us there. This life has no final fixed reference point but evolves as an ongoing engagement with competing human goods and purposes. "Pity, memory, and faithfulness are natural ties with paramount claims,"[20] claims run roughshod over in the preceding story. To override these claims, those Addams called "the family claim," or in some manner to reconstruct and transform the terms and boundaries of moral life, powerful countervailing forces, "the social claim," must be at work.[21] The tragedy of the scrubwoman is that she has no choice at balancing out these competing claims: She is simply forced against her will into ill-paid labor by economic necessity, compelled to deny the needs of her child but denied as well the opportunity to make her way in the larger scheme of things.

A human ethic, then, is embedded in life as lived. Because that life is complex, not simple; because human motivations are a dense thicket, difficult to cut one's way through; because one often has to choose between two goods, not between a clear-cut case of good versus evil, our ethics must be similarly complex. What spares Addams from a slide into thorough-going relativism or, alternatively, a leap into high-handed moral preachment, is her dual commitment to empathetic understanding as the surest route to social truth and to a compassion that eschews judging human beings by their "hours of Defeat."[22] These two—understanding that demands of the social observer a sympathetic attempt to convey the nature and meaning of the experiences of others, and a compassionate awareness of our human tendency to "backslide"—lie at the core of Addams's social theory and her apostleship of nonviolent social change.

Human nature being "incalculable," there can be no final, fixed human definition—neither fallen man, nor economic man, nor any other one-dimensional substitute for infinitely varied human life. What staves off anarchy and flux is that rootedness provided by Addams's social ontology, the ground of her discourse. She gives prescriptive force to a human solidarity that links us, across societies and through time; that has its base in "widespread and basic emotional experience" central to a human condition but allowing a wide berth for individual particularity and cultural diversity. As individuals and societies we can come to know ourselves, Addams suggests, *only* to the extent that we realize the experience of others. Cultures as well as individuals would fall into stagnation and dullness without the terms of perspicuous contrast offered by those different from themselves.

This brings us, in a sense, to the starting point—to the establishment of Hull House itself. That experiment was never intended primarily as a charitable institution or as a possible solution to the assorted evils of uncontrolled industrialization. Addams's "subjective necessity" compelled the genesis of Hull House and precluded any simple account of its purposes or her own. Hull House aimed explicitly to meet the needs of Addams and others like her to put their beliefs into practice, to lead lives of action. She and her comrades needed Hull House and that is why it was created—to open up a life of humanitarian action to young women "who had been given over too exclusively to study."[23] To serve but in serving to reveal oneself. Without an understanding of this double edge, Hull House cannot be seen for what it was: an attempt to put into practice "the theory that the dependence of classes on each other is reciprocal."[24] This reciprocity "gives rise to a form of expression that has peculiar value."[25] "It is not," she declared, "philanthropy or benevolence, but a thing fuller and wider than either of these, as revelation that, to have meaning, to be made manifest, must be put into terms of action."[26]

Placed alongside Addams's rich exploration of her own complex motives, the prose of the Hull House charter sounds remarkably prosaic: "To provide a center for a higher civic and social life; to institute and maintain educational and philanthropic enterprises, and to investigate and improve the conditions in the industrial districts of Chicago."[27] She and her companions learned quickly "not to hold preconceived ideas of what the neighborhood ought to have, but to keep ourselves in readiness to modify and adapt our undertakings as we discovered those things which the neighborhood was ready to accept."[28] "Those things" were diverse, and Hull House quickly turned into a social space, a particular sphere, that encompassed drama classes, play groups, music societies, well-baby clinics, nutritional courses, day nurseries, and an immigrant arts and crafts museum to reveal the skill and pride of immigrant parents and grandparents to Americanized children often ashamed of them. To this one must add the "Working People's Social Science Club" and Hull House's own social scientific investigation of conditions in the district ranging from housing to hygiene, medicine to transportation, employment to child care, prostitution to truancy. In ***Twenty Years,*** Addams details this diversity and an exhilarating sense of shared adventure. She resisted attempts to structure Hull House rigidly or to homogenize its many activities. The firmness of her commitment to social interpretation, to politics as the chief way people in a complex, heterogeneous society reveal themselves to one another, shines through. But what also emerges is the tension between providing a forum where immigrant cultural diversity and dignity could be displayed and preserved and studying this population or that through the methods of the new social science and in the sure conviction of historic progress.

We, from our standpoint, are aware of the decline of the Hull House model as the state has taken over more and more benevolent functions and we are immersed, in a way Addams was not, in a social era that is almost totally dependent on officials and experts. Given this, our assessment of Addams and her "subjective necessity" will depend in part on our approval or dissent from our own era. Whatever that assessment, there is great poignancy in Addams's summary of the idealistic convictions that dignified Hull House: "At that time I had come to believe that if the activities of Hull House were misunderstood, it would be either because there was not enough time to fully explain or because our motives had become mixed, for I was convinced that disinterested action was like truth or beauty in its lucidity and power of appeal."[29]

Criticism of the progressivist spirit and faith that Jane Addams shared, if not uncritically, is by now well known: the stress on social hygiene and "more wholesome" pursuits; the promotion of better methods of "social adjustment," wavering, in Addams's case, between bitter indictments of a brutal industrial order and efforts to make that society work better by smoothing over some of its roughest edges and helping people to adjust to industrial machinery and to a social world indifferent to their welfare.[30] With other progressives, Addams turned to the state to ameliorate social distress, to embody a social-wide commitment to compassion, constituting the state as a Hegelian embodiment of the highest ethical imperatives. But Addams's suspicions of the state grew after World War I, and she eventually concluded that any state founded on nationalism and militarism was incompatible with genuine social progress, perhaps even with democracy. She also held apparently contradictory views on play and pleasure as well, celebrating play as free and spontaneous, on the one hand, and calling for its organization and control on the other.[31] There are tensions embedded in her celebration of the settlement as "a place for enthusiasms," an attempt "to interpret opposing forces to each other," and her stress upon adjusting these same individuals to industrial life. The lacunae in her thinking often leave one stranded; paradoxes and tensions threaten to implode her arguments from within. But in ***Twenty Years*** she holds it all together, grasping firmly to the thread of empathetic understanding made manifest in her potent characterizations of the plights and purposes of others.

The honesty of this early vision shows us Addams at her best. This is an Addams concerned with the kind of story America will tell the world. Will it be a tale of power and conquest through arms? Or will it be the story of a decent and free industrialized democracy? Will there be room for many diverse stories or will one grand narrative swallow up all "lesser" tales? Perhaps even Addams's politics of class cooperation is less disingenuous than it appears at first glance. We all know the problem: How can there be class reciprocity and mutual recognition in the face of vast disparities of power and privilege? Given that Addams was no advocate of quiescent social suffering, what did she have in mind by repudiating politics as preeminently a power struggle? It is clear that disparities of power *and* the politics that flow from a power-grounded obsession concerned her. Within such a power system, the politics available to those least well placed often results in romantic, suicidal gestures or a smoldering resentment that sees politics as the means to get what "they" have now got. As an advocate of nonviolent social change, Addams urged face-to-face (or arbitrated) debate, even confrontation, so that each side could see and hear the other. What to us sounds hopelessly naive may, in fact, offer a compelling alternative to power politics-as-usual. Whether we are open to Addams's arguments will turn, in part, on how we evaluate later movements for nonviolent social change and what space, if any, we see for moral suasion, for the power of disinterested moral action to touch and to persuade people—even one's adversaries.

There is, then, much to question and to challenge in Addams's social thought but there is also much to learn, particularly about how to do social theory from the "inside out." But ***Twenty Years at Hull House*** also retains its freshness after more than seventy years because it invites us to reflect on welfare state liberalism, on the difference between Addams's participant-interpreter and the bureaucratic case worker; between a social science that views the world through the lens of functionalist givens and an interpretive approach alive to the sights, sounds, and smells of everyday human existence. That a "Jane Addams" is unlikely to come into being in our society at this time tells us much about ourselves. It signifies how deeply we are sunk in instrumental reason and technocratic bureaucracy. It indicates how entrenched is the conviction that nearly all constraints on the pursuit of personal pleasure are unacceptably limiting. For Jane Addams recalls another world. The fact that contemporary America would not provide the social soil to nurture her points to our loss of a particular civic culture and the ideal of that culture. Paternalistic, hypocritical, and stifling as that world could be, especially for young women, it nevertheless instilled in many of its young the conviction that a *human* life is one lived with purpose, dignity, and honor.

To see in the dissolution of the way of life that sustained such beliefs and practices *only* our collective liberation from irrational constraints is no longer tenable. Jane Addams helps us to take the measure of what we have lost as well as what we have gained. We cannot simply call up or go back to the civic culture of an earlier time, whether through individual will or social polity. But we can at least try to understand what forms of community make lives such as Jane Addams's possible. Rereading Jane Addams renews our acquaintance with a writer of great clarity, one gifted with the capacity to convey deep human emotion without mawkishness or cheap sentimentality. In this way she deepens our empathies and stirs us to an awareness of human limits and vulnerabilities.

Though Jane Addams has had her day, she has yet to receive her due.

NOTES

[1] Allen F. Davis, *American Heroine: The Life and Legend of Jane Addams* (New York: Oxford University Press, 1973), xi. Addams is not among the many women rediscovered in our time and restored to her presumed rightful place in history by feminist social historians and political thinkers. Outside the mainstream feminism of her day, Addams remains an ambivalent figure for contemporary feminists, one not easily appropriated to any particular cause save that of antimilitarism.

[2] Daniel Levine, *Jane Addams and the Liberal Tradition* (Madison, Wis.: The State Historical Society of Wisconsin, 1971), x.

[3] Henry Steele Commager, *The American Mind* (New Haven: Yale University Press, 1959).

[4] Ralph Henry Gabriel, *The Course of American Democratic Thought* (New Haven: Yale University Press, 1956), 360.

[5] Richard Hofstadter, *The Age of Reform* (New York: Vintage, 1955).

[6] Christopher Lasch, ed., *The Social Thought of Jane Addams* (Indianapolis: Bobbs-Merrill, 1965), xv, and *The New Radicalism in America 1889-1963* (New York: Vintage, 1965). The chapter devoted to Jane Addams is entitled "Jane Addams: The College Woman and the Family Claim," 3-37.

[7] Interestingly, John J. McDermott, editor of *The Philosophy of John Dewey* (Chicago: University of Chicago Press, 1981), states that much of Dewey's "range of in-

terests" in addressing public issues "can be traced to Jane Addams and her work at Hull House in Chicago." This appears in footnote 13 to the "introduction," xxxiii. McDermott here counters the received view that Addams is, at best, a pale, derivative Deweyite who popularized a simplified version of his philosophy. The story of Addams as an intellectual influence on Dewey has yet to be told. This lacuna no doubt reflects Dewey's stature as a philosopher and his seminal influence. But my hunch is that the somewhat condescending treatment of Addams as a thinker has other roots. One may be the fact that her role as social activist and interpreter rather than career academic meant she never acquired the automatic legitimacy we accord to credentialed scholars; in fact her interpretive, storytelling social theory is easily viewed as personalistic and subjectivist by those who prefer bloodless abstractions; and no doubt, by the presence of the old-fashioned sexist canard that posits a tacit Manichean dualism between man the thinker and woman the feeler.

[8] I worked from three published editions of *Twenty Years at Hull House* at various points: a 1968 edition published in New York by Macmillan; a New American Library paperback published in 1960; and the one-volume combined edition of *Twenty Years at Hull House* and *The Second Twenty Years at Hull House,* the final installment of Addams's autobiography, published originally in 1930, republished as part of *Forty Years* by Macmillan in 1935, the year of Addams's death.

[9] Davis, *American Heroine,* xi. Addams could never have seen herself reflected from the mirror as a tough-minded *realpolitiker.* This is not a piece of dissimulation; instead, it is her honest awareness of the fact that the trajectory of her life and the response of a particular public at a particular time to her evocations of moral suasion were of a piece. Given that Addams repudiated a power definition of politics, a repudiation fully compatible with a realistic assessment of who has force, who controls, who manipulates, etc., for her to have embraced a tough-minded, calculating image of herself is unthinkable.

[10] Addams, *Forty Years at Hull House,* 66.

[11] I do not see the American chauvinism Davis covers in *Twenty Years,* which most often includes a heavy dose of arrogance towards other ways of life. As a social activist Addams resisted overidentifying her public life with a narrow nationalism that might preclude criticism of state policy. She broke openly with the mission of America to "make the world safe for democracy" in World War I. This undercuts, at least in part, Davis's collapse of Jane Addams's personal calling with America's mission.

[12] Addams, *Forty Years at Hull House,* 66.

[13] Jane Addams, *Democracy and Social Ethics* (New York: Macmillan, 1902), 1.

[14] Addams, *The Second Twenty Years,* 6.

[15] Ibid.

[16] Her first published book was a collection, *Democracy and Social Ethics.*

[17] *Twenty Years* (Macmillan ed.), 122.

[18] Ibid., 126.

[19] Ibid., 174-75.

[20] Ibid., 247.

[21] Addams implies but never develops fully a theory of the child's developmental emergence as a moral being. She recognizes that early neglect may lead the individual to remain forever impervious to life's gentler aspects, and that compelling a child to complete tasks beyond his or her "normal growth" is cruel and often disastrous. She poses a concept of sublimation, urging that blind appetite be transformed into worthy psychic impulses by the moral motives. For Addams, child development was a *Bildung,* an evolving education of the heart.

[22] Jane Addams, *A New Conscience and an Ancient Evil* (New York: Macmillan, 1912), 137. This attack on prostitution and paean to chastity is described by Walter Lippman as a "hysterical book." It is not one of her finest efforts.

[23] Jane Addams, *Twenty Years* (Macmillan ed.), 85.

[24] Ibid., 91.

[25] Ibid.

[26] Ibid., 121-22.

[27] Ibid., 111-12.

[28] Addams, *Forty Years,* 132.

[29] Ibid, 150-51.

[30] See Lasch, *The New Radicalism,* 157. Addams's ambivalence is also traceable to the fact that she saw in the social forces of industrial production a political potential for the spread of industrial democracy.

[31] Discussion of aesthetic impulses and the necessity of social space for free play are themes that run through her work.

Ursula Lehmkuhl (essay date 1990)

SOURCE: "The Historical Value and Historiographic Significance of Jane Addams' Autobiographies 'Twenty Years at Hull-House' and 'Second Twenty Years at Hull-House,'" in *Reconstructing American Lit-*

erary and Historical Studies, St. Martin's Press, 1990, pp. 285-97.

[*In the following essay, Lehmkuhl treats Addams's two Hull House books as historical narratives and examines them in the context of Charles A. Beard's "new history."*]

Since the late 1960s, when literary critics discovered the autobiography as a literary genre, much has been written on the literary qualities of autobiographical writings in order to prove the literary significance and value of autobiographies. These endeavours were quite successful if one looks at the long list of scholarly literature on autobiography written since the 1970s. They were successful not only in proving the autobiography's literary significance and in integrating this genre into the canon of literary studies but also in supporting historians who questioned the value of autobiography for historical research—a value that since Dilthey was, at least for "Geistesgeschichte," an undeniable fact.[1] The loss of the autobiography's significance for historical research went along with a "Paradigmenwechsel" in historiography which, like the new interests in literary criticism, resulted mainly from the political events of the late 1960s. Structural analysis and quantification replaced narration as the main mode of historiographical presentation. Categories like subjectivity and intuition or "Einfühlung" into the historic subject, which Dilthey claimed were a means to come to terms with evaluating actions or a certain kind of behaviour,[2] were denounced as interpretative arbitrariness.

Today the political conditions that shaped literary criticism and historiography in the late 1960s and 70s have changed. In the social and political climate prevailing in most western democracies new philosophical and sociological concepts have been formulated which question such notions as progress, sense and history. Neo-structuralism, postmodernism, or posthistoire—to name just three of the many expressions for the new theories[3]—have opened up new perspectives. At the same time, the social significance of historiography has declined. "Alltagsgeschichte" or Micro-History tried to increase the attractiveness of historiographical writing to a broader audience by looking for new modes of presentation; this often involved a return to the simple form of narration. In turn, this has been criticized by those who still adhere to structural analysis as a dangerous form of social romanticism which neglects critical aspects of history.

Confronted with these developments, it not only seems necessary to rewrite literary history but also to rethink the function of historiography.[4] Looking at the problems and questions facing our profession today, I would like to develop some propositions concerning how the profession might react to current challenges; I will argue historically by examining an historical subject, the autobiographies of Jane Addams, ***Twenty Years at Hull-House*** and ***Second Twenty Years at Hull-House.*** I will first put forward some arguments for characterizing Jane Addams' autobiographical writings as historical as opposed to fictional accounts. Thereafter I will examine her presentational techniques and discuss the advantages and disadvantages of her mode of presentation. My argument is that one should integrate Jane Addams' autobiographies into the tradition of new history with which Charles A. Beard was closely identified and therefore take them as historical rather than fictional accounts. Accepting the fact that her autobiographies have to be taken as historiography one might look at her historiographical method which uses narration without abandoning totally meta-reflections or theoretic-philosophical consideration as a way out of the deadening effects of overemphasized theoretization.

I

Arguing against the fictionalisation of autobiographical writing in 1977, Robert Sayre stated that autobiographies offer the student of American Studies broader and more direct contact with American experience than any other kind of writing.[5] He proves his argument by pointing to a fact already mentioned that autobiographies have been the subject of literary criticism only since the early 1970s.[6] However, he stresses the point that the character of autobiographies—documentary or fictional—is nevertheless difficult to determine.[7] Autobiographies are history in that they are source materials, which contain and interpret facts, preserve the past, and draw lessons from it. They are literature in that they must please and entertain as well as teach. Like both history and literature, they must select and narrate. They have to organize their materials, address an audience and, in more subtle ways, find links between the actor-writers who are in them and the readers, then or generations later, who must be engaged, drawn in.[8]

Pointing out economic, social and political controversies which influenced current and historical facts and circumstances was an aim followed especially by progressives, journalists and professionals from about 1900 onward. They wrote critically on subjects such as monopolies, immigration, the shame of the cities, modern marriage, women's suffrage, and so on. These intellectuals often conveyed their experiences and ambitions using the autobiographical genre.[9] Since autobiographies are meant to pinpoint the individual's role on the stage of history,[10] the significant increase in the number of autobiographies written during the era of "Progressivism"[11] must be interpreted as expressing the changed concept of self and civilization in America during that period.[12]

Reflecting this significant historic development in America, autobiographies as history and documentary have an ultimate value no novel, drama, or fiction can ever have. These autobiographies widened the areas of public trust, breaking down the old restrictive civilization with its dangerous assumption that it alone offered a rewarding life.

One of these progressive autobiographies is Jane Addams' two-volume account ***Twenty Years at Hull-House*** and ***Second Twenty Years at Hull-House.*** She writes about the origin of the idea of settlement, as well as about developments in contemporary world politics such as the First World War. She also reports about social opposition and reflects on her experiences at Hull-House, Chicago. Although the purpose of both books is to relate the history of Hull-House Chicago, the first American social settlement, both books have a sharply autobiographical character since Jane Addams' own career was so closely intertwined with Hull-House. This and the fact that both books are written in the first person singular induced me to call them autobiographies. Jane Addams herself did not designate them as such; indeed, the author herself felt compelled to make apologetic remarks in her introductions—probably so as not to let the subjective character of her account become too prominent.[13] Jane Addams' description of the first steps in realizing the concept of social settlement was supposed to help other projects to overcome their initial difficulties. She writes:

> Because settlements have multiplied so easily in the United States I hoped that a simple statement of an earlier effort including the stress and storm, might be of value in their interpretation and possibly clear them of a certain charge of superficiality.[14]

Jane Addams' autobiography explicitly takes the reader into account. She gives her narration a special function: that of enabling the reader to get an accurate inside-account of the beginnings of social settlement in the United States.[15]

As has become a frequent practice in current historiography, Jane Addams reflects about the plot she has chosen. She deplores the necessity of abandoning chronological order in favor of a topical account; she justifies this by arguing:

> . . . during the early years at Hull-House, time seemed to afford a mere framework for certain lines of activity and I have found in writing this book, that after these activities have been recorded, I can scarcely recall the scaffolding.[16]

Through coping with the social challenges of every-day life at Hull-House, Jane Addams had gained insight into social contexts which she tries to communicate to the reader by means of using deliberately selected evidence from her experience. The system chosen becomes itself subject of her preliminary reflections. She notes how hard it has been to determine which incidents and experiences should be selected for recital; she points to her fear that although she might give an accurate report of each isolated event she might yet give a totally misleading impression of the whole, solely by the selection of the incidents.[17]

While the problematization of the subjective selection of the events described in the preface to ***Twenty Years at Hull-House*** focuses on the text and its degree of objectivity, the introduction to ***Second Twenty Years at Hull-House*** disassociates itself from the actual text to continue the legitimization of the content of her book on a philosophical meta-level. With her account Addams would like to point at one of the few incentives which really motivate human conduct. In her opinion, it was such a motive which promoted her work at Hull-House. The history she writes about her settlement project is meant as an effort to define this motive as well as to illustrate it.[18] For this reason her history is based on deliberately selected stories that should serve as an explanation for the experiences of her every-day life at Hull-House. She explains to the reader:

> If conclusions of the whole matter are similar to those I have already published at intervals during the twenty years at Hull-House, I can only make the defense that each of the earlier books was an attempt to set forth a thesis supported by experience, whereas this volume endeavors to trace the experiences through which various conclusions were forced upon me.[19]

One of these conclusions drawn from her experiences is the gender-specific function of narration that Jane Addams describes in ***Second Twenty Years at Hull-House*** and which I would like to elaborate, both to give an example of the stories that form the history of Hull-House and to point to one detail in Jane Addams' autobiographies that reflects the documentary value of her account.

In ***Second Twenty Years at Hull-House*** Jane Addams reports about the "Devil Baby at Hull-House."[20] This chapter deals with the rumor that a devil-baby was cared for in Hull-House. The imaginary creature attracted numerous visitors who all wanted to see it, so that they would be able to talk about it. Jane Addams does not narrate this story to entertain the reader between more serious chapters dealing with Progressivism or the First World War. By reproducing the story, Jane Addams tries to demonstrate a special functional pattern that characterizes the narration of mystical horror stories.

The Devil Baby, so the rumor has it, was the result of the punishment of a blasphemous deed and sinful words of a man in the presence of his pregnant wife. Because of the wicked conduct of her husband the woman gave birth to a devil-like creature. This story, Jane Addams writes, had a social function especially for two groups of women. For older women, who by seeing the baby would become centers of attention in their neighborhoods, the narration was a means of regaining social interest and would thus help them to become less lonely. Secondly, Jane Addams writes, this story was a favourite of younger women who had to cope with uneducated and inconsiderate husbands. With the example of the Devil Baby, Jane Addams felt, they hoped to be able to make their husbands believe that uncouth behavior would be punished by a divine force. In this context the narration of the story had a social control function. The chapter of the Devil-Baby points to the relevance of story-telling as a female means of social or marital control in this specific historical context of female social interaction. Looked at from a scholarly point of view, the documentary character of Jane Addams' autobiographies becomes obvious. They give evidence of social and political patterns prevailing during the first decades of this century. The female interactional behavior mentioned by Jane Addams might prove a worthwhile field of research either in historically oriented sociology or gender studies.

In addition, Jane Addams' autobiographies have to be categorized as historiography because of the detailed explanation she gives of how the emplotment of her account took place. If one accepts Käte Hamburger's proposition that the crucial distinction between "autobiography" and "fiction" is not to be found in comparing what is written to the "world outside" but that the distinction seems to exist only inside the writer's own head,[21] it is obvious that we have to speak of historiography when considering Jane Addams' books. The autobiographies not only rest on fact; Jane Addams' writing was meant to be historiography.

II

The question of the form of historiography that Jane Addams uses is both historical and systematic. We all know the changes that have taken place in the modes of presentation in historical studies. Which modes existed, and how and when they changed is an historical or diachronic question. The systematic question refers to a set of problems which can be traced in each of the historiographical cases marking the historical development of historiography. The systematic question aims at the relationship that exists between the different modes of presentation and the story being told in this particular way. Both perspectives have to be considered in analyzing Jane Addams' presentational techniques.

In accordance with Jane Addams' intention, narrative elements dominate in both books. The narration is guided by a certain set of ideas, which help to explain the chain of events and the manifold experiences. As Jane Addams explains in the introductions, this selective approach is applied during the conceptualizing stage as well as in formulating the message of the text.

Jane Addams' history of Hull-House is a sequence of intentionally selected stories. The characteristics of the single story correlate with the description developed by Hayden White in his "Metahistory":

> . . . like "chronicle" "story" refers to "primitive elements" in the historical account . . . both represent processes of selection and arrangement of data from the unprocessed historical record in the interest of rendering that record more comprehensible to an audience of a particular kind . . . Historical stories trace the sequences of events that lead from inauguration to (provisional) terminations of social and cultural processes.[22]

However, unlike a simple story, Jane Addams' mode of narration is not chronological; rather it is guided by systematic aspects, which are related to the history of Hull-House by special relevancy. For the reader, the reason for the sequence of the single chapters appears to be not always convincing. There are chapters which could also be found in scholarly historical studies like "Social Service and the Progressive Party," "Aspects of the Woman's Movements" or "Immigrants under the Quota." These chapters are followed by others whose content may be categorized as a fairy tale story-telling. This characterization especially applies to the already mentioned second chapter of ***Second Twenty Years at Hull-House*** which deals with "The Devil Baby at Hull-House." However, it is exactly the selective character of her history which makes her autobiography, from a sociological point of view, an historical rather than a fictional document. The structure and functional meaning of narration in ***Twenty Years at Hull-House*** and ***Second Twenty Years at Hull-House*** correspond to the theory that is developed by the sociology of knowledge to explain the social function of history.[23] Using the premise that narration, the telling of stories, is a prerequisite for the organisation, transformation and communication of experience, the sociology of knowledge argues that people are always involved in stories. We experience our world in such a way that we perceive and select our experiences with regard to the possibility of forming them into a story. We judge experiences of our every-day life as relevant or significant by whether they can be arranged into stories; in turn, by being arranged experiences gain a concrete meaning in the course of time. Inversely, when there are events that we perceive as being of a special relevance we try to arrange them into a story and integrate them into the over-all history of our life. The narrative structure of the story connects the beginning and the end not only as a factual course of events but as a conceptual configuration. The way stories are formed in a coherent history provides the background for a meaningful, structured continuity of the life of the person who is telling this particular history.[24]

Jane Addams started her work at Hull-House without a social theory or ideology;[25] however, during the years of her work she did form a kind of theory in order to explain to herself her experiences and to use the theoretical conclusions to select the experiences to be written about in her autobiography. This leads to the question of whether she formulated a coherent set of social ideas that could be labeled a social theory. The answer is negative. There is no explicit social theory that directs the argument and the narrative of her two books. However, there are theoretical or philosophical reflections related to the story being told. These short passages reveal her thinking and her moral demands. In this respect, her philosophical reflections depend on the historical discourse. The stories perform the function of explication and illustration of philosophical insights. Beyond this, to a certain extent the narratives in ***Twenty Years at Hull-House*** and ***Second Twenty Years at Hull-House*** reflect how her philosophical ideas have developed.[26]

The interrelationship between Jane Addams' daily social practice and her philosophical ideas is without doubt one reason for the marked action-oriented quality of her reflections. Another reason is her dedication to John Dewey's pragmatism.[27] Philosophical considerations are worthless if they are not adaptable to social action.

The way her philosophical ideas are integrated into the text makes for a successful combination of analytical and narrative elements. Inspite of her presentational mixture the liveliness of the narration remains so distinct that one sometimes feels as if one were reading a fictional text rather than an historical account. How can one explain the lively historiograhical style which prevails in both volumes? One reason for the liveliness is the close relationship between knowledge and personal experience in Jane Addams' subject matter. In scholarly historiography this relationship normally does not exist. In most cases there is a deep gap between the historian and his/her subject, resulting from the distance of time and content. This distance frequently deadens the presentation of history.[28]

The loss of liveliness in historical narration has already been described and criticized by Walter Benjamin in his essay *Der Erzähler*.[29] In developing his criticism, Benjamin uses an argument similar to the one which Charles Beard uses in a passage quoted later in this article. Walter Benjamin characterizes historical narration as a narrative neutral point, because historiography tends to become more and more mere knowledge and is thus purified from subjective breaks resulting from personal experience. In this context, Walter Benjamin deplores the crisis of narration as a crisis of the formation of experiences, a crisis from which Jane Addams' narration does not suffer because she is so personally involved in her subject matter.

Although Jane Addams uses narration extensively as a mode of presentation she does not narrate for narration's sake. Nor does she neglect the message emanating from the conclusions she draws from her experiences. She employs narration as an act of constituting sense or meaning. Narration utilized in this way has not only a secondary function of mere representation, but performs a primary function, that of constituting elementary frameworks for meaningful action. The work of Jane Addams demonstrates that the division between narration and discourse (analysis) as modes of presentation, a division that has been discussed ever since Droysen published his *Historik*,[30] simply does not exist as an either-or. Both modes of presentation are interconnected and neither can be used independently of the other. Differing from the modern, often scientifically oriented historiography in which the accumulation of facts to prove an historical argument is the historian's main occupation, Jane Addams as a non-professional historian uses rhetoric and even poetry. Jane Addams writes history according to the classic ideal of historiography which has been increasingly superseded by structural and quantifying starting points in social history. She narrates, however, without losing a critical perspective and without abandoning personal opinions and subjectivity.

The content and mode of Jane Addams' historiographical account of the history of Hull-House reflect conceptual demands formulated by scholars representing the "New History." In 1912 James Harvey Robinson, a Columbia colleague of Charles Beard, complained that historians seemed to justify facts for their own sake.[31] Mere namelisting and an emphasis on extraordinary events destroyed perspective, even when the narrative was told in an interesting manner. He argued that the question of whether the fact or occurrence was one which would aid the reader in grasping the meaning of any period of human development or the true nature of any momentous institution was the only true principle of selection.[32] This, however, is exactly what Jane Addams' concept of selection was.

> Because settlements have multiplied so easily in the United States I hoped that a simple statement of an earlier effort, including the stress and storm, might be of value in their interpretation and possibly clear them of a certain charge of superficiality.[33]

Not only the selective approach but selection as such corresponds to Beard's views on history which are elaborated in his presidential address, "Written History as an Act of Faith," delivered before the American Historical Association at its meeting in Urbana, Illinois, in late December 1933. Citing Benedetto Croce he characterized history in the following way:

> . . . history is contemporary thought about the past . . . but it is history as thought, not actuality, record, or specific knowledge, that is really meant when the term history is used in its widest and most general significance.[34]

Like Robinson and Beard, Jane Addams does not consider her account as something to learn from; instead she tries to give insights that render her picture of the situation as real as possible in order to prevent misleading interpretations by future historians. This also corresponds to the demands of the historians representing the "New History." They reject the idea that reliable "lessons" can be learned from past events. Such beliefs assumed that conditions remained sufficiently uniform to give precedents a perpetual value. Actually modern conditions changed so rapidly that it would be risky to apply past experience to solve current problems.[35] The historians of 1900-1920 who sought economic determinants for history felt the pragmatic urge to make history serve society by curing its social ills. It was not enough to commemorate the past. One needed to apply the current lessons of the Industrial Revolution, experimental science, finance capitalism, and materialist factors to history rather than depend upon ineffectual idealistic conceptions.[36] Like scholars who represented one thread of a collective development which also included the legal realism of Holmes, the economic institutionalism of Veblen, and the instrumentalism of John Dewey,[37] Jane Addams was aiming at "reality." All these scholars attempted to come more closely to grips with reality, especially with reality in the course of change.[38] Their research constituted the academic counterpart of muckraking in journalism and the realist and naturalist writing of authors engaged in a literary revolt.[39] Although these scholars and journalists maintained a critical perspective on social and political developments—current or historic—they did not question narration as the presentational technique able to convey their critiques to a broader audience.

III

To return to the starting point of this paper: I argued that Jane Addams' autobiographies have to be considered as historiography able to combine analytical and narrative elements in a quasi-ideal way. Jane Addams' autobiographies are more than just a recital of her career. They are an inside-story of at least three aspects characterizing Progressivism: the concept of social settlement, the women's suffrage movement and pacifism. Jane Addams' work can be identified as owing much to the Columbia School and as such provides an argument against the short-sighted condemnation of narration characterizing the discussion about the "new" histories of our time. Although we all have realized that learning from history, that the concept of "historia magistra vitae," is obsolete and even dangerous, learning from historic forms of historiography may be something different. Perhaps Jane Addams can teach us to give faith to the narrative form that Beard and his contemporaries considered an unquestioned element of historiography—although they took nearly everything else belonging to traditional historical writing as anachronistic. Narration is a historiographical mode which is necessarily connected with history, which constitutes history and as such should not be antagonized from the ambition of putting the results of historical research into analytical frames.

NOTES

[1] Wilhelm Dilthey, *Pattern and Meaning in History,* New York: 1962; Roy Pascal, *Design and Truth in Autobiography,* Cambridge: 1960.

[2] Wilhelm Dilthey, "Die Methoden der Geisteswissenschaft," in Hans-Ulrich Lessing, ed., *Texte zur Kritik der historischen Vernunft,* Göttingen: 1983, pp. 256-266; Jörn Rüsen, "Geschichtsschreibung als Theorieproblem der Geschichtswissenschaft. Skizze zum historischen Hintergrund der gegenwärtigen Diskussion," in R. Koselleck/H. Lutz/J. Rüsen, eds., *Formen der Geschichtsschreibung, Theorie der Geschichte. Beiträge zur Historik* 4, München: 1984, pp.14-35.

[3] See Manfred Frank, *Was ist Neostrukturalismus?,* Frankfurt a.M.: 1984.

[4] See Jörn Rüsen, "Wie kann man Geschichte vernünftig schreiben? über das Verhältnis von Narrativität and Theoriegebrauch in der Geschichtswissenschaft," in J. Kocka, Th. Nipperdey, eds., *Theorie und Erzählung in der Geschichte, Theorie der Geschichte.Beiträge zur Historik 3, München:* 1979, pp. 300-333.

[5] Robert F. Sayre, "The Proper Study—Autobiographies in American Studies," *American Quarterly* 29, 1977, 241.

[6] R. F. Sayre, "The Proper Study," 242.

[7] See James M. Cox, "Autobiography and America," in J. Hillis Miller, ed., *Aspects of Narrative, Selected Papers from the English Institute,* New York/London: 1971, p. 146; Louis A. Renza, "The Veto of the Imagination: A Theory of Autobiography," *New Literary History* 9, 1977/78, 1-26; Darrel Mansell, "Unsettling the Colonel's Hash 'Fact' in Autobiography," *Modern Language Quarterly* 37, 1976, 115; Francis R. Hart, "Notes for an Anatomy of Modern Autobiography," *New Literary History* 1, 1969/70, 485.

[8] R. F. Sayre, "The Proper Study," 242.

[9] See e.g. Robert Stinson, "S. S. McClure's *My Autobiography:* The Progressive as Self-Made Man," *American Quarterly* 22, 1970, 203-212.

[10] James M. Cox, "Autobiography in America," pp. 144-45.

[11] See Louis Kaplan, *A Bibliography of American Autobiographies,* Madison: 1962. Unfortunately there exists no special bibliography for women's autobiographies for the first half of this century. For the period after 1945 Patricia K. Addis filled this gap. Patricia K. Addis, *Through a Woman's I: An Annotated Bibliography of American Women's Autobiographical Writings 1946-1976,* New Jersey: 1983.

[12] See Milan James Kedro, "Autobiography as a Key to Identity in the Progressive Era," *History of Childhood Quarterly* 2, Winter 1975, 391-407; Robert F. Sayre, "The Proper Study," 254.

[13] With this she refers to that tendency in historiography that disapproves autobiographies as source material arguing that they are too subjective. See Robert F. Sayre, "The Proper Study," 21; Jane Addams, *Second Twenty Years at Hull-House,* New York: 1930, p. 9.

[14] Jane Addams, *Twenty Years at Hull-House,* New York: 1910, p. VIII.

[15] Jane Addams, *Second Twenty Years,* p. VIII.

[16] Jane Addams, *Second Twenty Years,* p. IX.

[17] Jane Addams, *Second Twenty Years,* p. VII.

[18] Jane Addams, *Second Twenty Years,* pp. 8-9.

[19] Jane Addams, *Twenty Years,* p. IX.

[20] Jane Addams, *Second Twenty Years,* pp. 49-79.

[21] Käte Hamburger, *The Logic of Literature,* Bloomington: 1973, pp. 312, 328-29.

[22] Hayden White, *Metahistory. The Historical Imagination in Nineteenth-Century Europe,* Baltimore/London: 1973, pp. 6-7.

[23] See Alfred Schütz, *Collected Papers, II. Studies in Social Theory,* The Hague: 1964, pp. 56-61; Thomas Luckmann, "Lebensweltliche Zeitkategorien, Zeitstrukturen des Alltags und der Ort des historischen Bewusstseins," in B. Cerquilini, H. U. Gumbrecht, eds., *Diskurs der Literatur- und Sprachhistorie,* Frankfurt a.M.: 1982.

[24] Alfred Schütz, Thomas Luckmann, *Strukturen der Lebenswelt, Vol.1,* Frankfurt a.M.: 1979, pp. 73-78; E. Husserl, *Vorlesungen zur Phänomenologie des inneren Zeitbewusstseins,* Halle: 1928; H. U. Gumbrecht, "Uber den Ort der Narration in narrativen Gattungen," in E. Lämmert, ed., *Theorie des Erzählens,* Stuttgart: 1983.

[25] Jane Addams, *Twenty Years,* p. VIII.

[26] See Ursula Lehmkuhl, "Jane Addams: Theorie und Praxis einer Sozialreformerin," *Amerikastudien* 33, 1988, 439-457.

[27] Anne Firor Scott, "Jane Addams," in Edward T. James/ Janet Wilson James/Paul S. Boyer, eds., *Notable American Women 1607-1950. A Biographical Dictionary, Vol. 1,* Cambridge: 1974, p. 19: "Perhaps her closest intellectual affinity was with the pragmatism of William James and John Dewey."

[28] See Karlheinz Stierle, "Erfahrung und narrative Form. Bemerkungen zu ihrem Zusammenhang in Fiktion und Historiographie," in J. Kocka/Th. Nipperdey, eds., *Beiträge zur Historik 3,* pp. 85-118; G. Devereux, "Zeit: Geschichte versus Chronik. Sozialisation als kulturelles Vor-Erleben," *Ethnopsychoanalyse,* Frankfurt a.M.: 1978.

[29] Walter Benjamin, *Der Erzähler. Betrachtungen zum Werk Nikolai Lesskows,* Frankfurt a.M.: 1955.

[30] J. G. Droysen, "Historik," in R. Hübner, ed., *Vorlesungen über Enzyklopädie und Methodologie der Geschichte,* Darmstadt: 1960, pp. 273-275.

[31] James Harvey Robinson, *The New History: Essays Illustrating the Modern Historical Outlook,* New York: 1912.

[32] Harvey Wish, *The American Historian. A Social-Intellectual History of the Writing of the American Past,* New York: 1960, p. 268.

[33] Jane Addams, *Twenty Years,* p. VIII.

[34] Charles A. Beard, *Written History as an Act of Faith,* El Paso: 1960, p. 1. Beard continues: "It is thought about past actuality, instructed and delimited by history as record and knowledge—record and knowledge authenticated by criticism and ordered with the help of the scientific method."

[35] H. Wish, *The American Historian,* p. 268.

[36] H. Wish, *The American Historian,* p. 265.

[37] Richard Hofstadter, *The Progressive Historians. Turner, Beard, Parrington,* New York: 1968, pp. 182f.

[38] I.e. they are not aiming at "objectivity" but they tried to approach reality as closely as possible. See for a theoretical explanation of the difference between "objectivity" and "reference to reality" Hans Ulrich Gumbrecht, "Das in vergangenen Zeiten Gewesene so gut erzählen, als ob es in der eigenen Welt wäre. Versuch zur Anthropologie der Geschichtsschreibung," in R. Koselleck/H. Lutz/J. Rüsen, eds., *Beiträge zur Historik 4,* pp. 485-487.

[39] R. Hofstadter, *The Progressive Historians.*

Harriet Hyman Alonso (essay date 1992)

SOURCE: "Nobel Peace Laureates, Jane Addams and Emily Greene Balch: Two Women of the Women's International League for Peace and Freedom," in *Journal of Women's History,* Vol. 7, No. 2, Summer, 1995, pp. 6-26.

[*In the following essay, which was first presented at a conference of the Norwegian Nobel Institute in 1992, Alonso compares and contrasts the career of Addams with that of another radical pacifist and Nobel laureate, Emily Greene Balch.*]

In November, 1895, Alfred Nobel, wealthy inventor and entrepreneur, signed his last will and testament. In it, he stipulated that the major part of his estate be converted into a fund and invested, the interest to be used for prizes in five areas he wished to promote, one of which was peace.[1] Nobel's interest in the peace cause centered around his passionate friendship with Baroness Bertha von Suttner, the founder of the Austrian Peace Society.[2] Nobel envisioned the prize as a tribute to the woman or man who did the most for obtaining peace in Europe. Little did he imagine that it would become one of the most pretigious and lucrative awards in the world.[3]

In the spring of 1992, eighteen peace historians gathered at the Nobel Institute in Norway to probe the question, "How has the Nobel Peace Prize been accepted in the laureates' own nations?" My assignment was to enlighten the group on the two women from the United States who won the prize: Jane Addams (1931) and Emily Greene Balch (1946).[4] Each received the honor for her work with the Women's International League for Peace and Freedom (WILPF). Addams was already a well-known Progressive Era reformer when she was named a Nobel laureate and is well placed in U.S. history. Emily Greene Balch, however, was and still is virtually unknown in the land of her birth. Why, I wondered, was this so? Both women came from similar backgrounds, lived through the same eras, and embraced many of the same causes. They worked together in WILPF and other organizations to ward off U.S. participation in World War I, faced similar harassment during the Red Scare of the 1920s, and worked together in the international search for world peace during the interwar years. After Addams died in 1935, Balch continued working with WILPF until her death in 1961.

Three factors may explain the inconsistency in the two women's reputations: 1) Addams is best known for her work in the settlement house movement, an extension of the domestic sphere and traditionally occupied by women, whereas Balch chose peace activism as a career, thereby entering the world of international affairs, a sphere traditionally closed to women. Addams's social work, in other words, did not generally threaten the status quo, whereas Balch's peace work did. 2) Addams did not criticize the nation's capitalist ideology while Balch openly declared herself a socialist, allying with political groups which U.S. policy makers disfavored. Throughout her career, Balch challenged the basic economic principles of capitalism. 3) Addams received the prize during a time of relative peace while Balch received it during the early Cold War years. The public's view at the time was that Addams's work mirrored government policy, whereas Balch's reflected clearcut opposition. A comparison of these women's lives and careers offers more insight into the matter.

THE EARLY YEARS

Jane Addams and Emily Greene Balch had much in common during their early years. Their upbringing and education led to a similar desire to end poverty and war. The two women were born just six years apart to upper middle-class parents—Addams on September 6, 1860, and Balch on January 8, 1867.[5] Both women had industrious, politically liberal fathers and traditional Victorian-era mothers. Addams's father, John Huy Addams, a prosperous Illinois miller and banker, was heavily involved in community affairs. An opponent of slavery, he met and befriended many influential figures, among them, Abraham Lincoln. Balch's father, Francis Vergnies Balch, a graduate of Harvard University, volunteered to fight in the Civil War, and served as secretary to the abolitionist U.S. senator, Charles Sumner. Returning to Boston, he devoted the remainder of his life to practicing law. Addams's mother, Sarah Weber Addams, concentrated on her role as wife and mother, and died when Jane was only two years old. Five years later, her father married another traditional woman, Anna H. Haldeman. Balch's mother, Ellen Maria Noyes Balch, also devoted herself to her domestic sphere, even though she had worked as a teacher before her marriage. She died when her daughter was seventeen years old.

Both Addams and Balch received Progressive Era private school educations which fostered their liberal attitudes towards reform. From 1877 to 1881, Addams attended the Rockford Female Seminary in Illinois and then enrolled in the Woman's Medical College of Pennsylvania, only to decide within the first year that medicine was not her calling. The death of her father and her own poor health stemming from childhood spinal tuberculosis disrupted her education. However, two trips to Europe after her recuperation pointed her to a future as a social reformer and pacifist, especially after she visited the London settlement house, Toynbee Hall in 1887/1888. As a result, in February 1889, Addams and her close friend, Ellen Gates Starr, rented the decaying Charles J. Hull mansion in the slums of Chicago and turned it into Hull-House. Within four years, the settlement house boasted an array of clubs and functions, a day nursery, gymnasium, dispensary, playground, and a cooperative boarding house for single working women known as the Jane Club. In addition, lobbying efforts and public campaigns instituted by such Hull-House workers as Florence Kelley and Alice Hamilton resulted in the passage of Illinois' first factory inspection act (1893), the establishment of its first juvenile court (1899), and investigations into city sanitary and health conditions.

Hull-House made Jane Addams famous. Her work in the settlement led to her election in 1909 as the first woman president of the National Conference of Charities and Correction (later known as the National Conference of Social Work) and in 1911, as the first head of the National Federation of Settlements, a position she held until her death. In 1912 as a respected public figure, Addams was invited to second Teddy Roosevelt's nomination for President on the Progressive Party ticket, and she proceeded to campaign vigorously for him. Logically, she also stood for woman suffrage. From 1911 through 1914, she held the position of first Vice-President of the National American Woman Suffrage Association and became involved in the International Woman Suffrage Alliance. In other words, Hull-House, the epitome of the concept of "social housekeeping," took Jane Addams into the public sphere, making her into a political force even though, as a woman, she did not hold even the most basic political power—the right to vote.

Balch's advanced education took place at Bryn Mawr College. Entering in 1886, she discovered the field of economics and her interest in using economic theories to address social issues. After graduating in 1889 with an A.B. degree, Balch traveled to Paris to study political economy at the Sorbonne. In 1893, the results of her research were published by the American Economic Association as "Public Assistance of the Poor in France." Unhappy with the lack of hands-on work her studies in France had offered, Balch returned to the United States, where, for a short while, her career somewhat mirrored that of Jane Addams. In 1893 Balch, Vida Scudder, and a few other Massachusetts women founded Denison House, a settlement house in Boston. Unlike Addams, however, settlement house work itself did not stimulate Balch, whose prime interest turned towards a career as a college professor of women students. This decision, which marked her first divergence from the career path followed by Addams, resulted in her more isolated and politically radical life. Teaching and researching moved Balch to the political left. In 1906, ten years after she accepted a position at Wellesley College, she publicly declared herself a socialist. Immediately aware of the possible implications of her stance, she wrote in her journal: "Within the year I have decided to call myself a socialist and accepted [re]appointment at Wellesley only on condition of the president knowing this. It will lead to some misunderstanding, of course, but I hope to some better understanding too."[6] In spite of her fears, by 1910, with the publication of *Our Slavic Fellow Citizens,* a comprehensive analysis of an immigrant community, Balch had established herself as a sound scholar and received a five-year reappointment as professor and chair of Wellesley's Department of Economics and Sociology.

Balch's professional choices, although different from those of Addams's, reflected their common concerns. Both were devoted to improving society by addressing the issues of class, race, gender, and ethnicity within the United States. Both traveled in similar social circles. Both preferred the company of women, and neither married nor had children. In addition, each was forging her way as an independent, professional woman within the acceptable spheres of settlement house work and teaching in a women's college. However, these early years would lead both to venture into one area largely unacceptable in the United States—the movement against war and militarism.

WORLD WAR I

Addams's settlement house work and Balch's studies on immigrant experiences opened their lives to people from other cultures and to the fact that many types of people could live together in peace. This taught them that wars were usually caused by governments and generally scorned by the average person. In turn, each woman's vision expanded from her immediate work to include international affairs. Jane Addams had initially shown her disdain for war by becoming a member of the Anti-Imperialist League, founded to protest the results of the Spanish-American War of 1898. At that time she openly deplored the racist and imperialistic implications of the war, stating that patriotism and duty had to be separated from war mongering. Addams clearly felt that people's consciences would dictate the end of political intrigue and the initiation of a peaceful world based upon sound universal moral principles.[7]

By 1902, Addams had begun to formalize her ideas in print. In ***Democracy and Social Ethics*** she stated that popular support for war would gradually disappear once the larger society developed the type of collective social morality she had found existed in the crowded immigrant tenement quarters surrounding Hull-House. "In this effort toward a higher morality in our social relations, we must demand that the individual shall be willing to lose the sense of personal achievement, and shall be content to realize his activity only in connection with the activity of the many."[8] Later opponents to Addams's peace work would use these ideas to label her a "socialist," when in fact, she never proposed an end to capitalism. She merely supported a caring, cooperative society. Five years later in 1907, Addams produced another tract entitled ***The Newer Ideals of Peace*** which further illustrated her growing political sophistication. In it she introduced the idea that the world needed to substitute "nurture for warfare," and that nurturing was a perfect role for women. The "newer humanitarianism" Addams proposed depended upon women's presence in the political forum as well as the home. Women needed the vote in order to take "a citizen's place in the modern industrial city" and, hence, the world.[9]

Since both Addams and Balch had declared their pacifist leanings in 1898, both were naturally distraught when war erupted in Europe in August 1914. As Balch later recalled: "When the World War broke out in 1914, my reaction to it was largely a sense of tragic interruption of what seemed to me the real business of our times—the realization of a more satisfactory economic order . . . Now all the world was at war, one hardly knew for what—for reasons of ambition, prestige, mutual fear, of frontiers and colonies. None of the war aims seemed very relevant to progress, in any important sense."[10] Immediately, both women joined the movement supporting complete U.S. neutrality. As early as September 1914, Addams, Balch, and other social work professionals, such as Lillian Wald, Crystal Eastman, Roger Baldwin, and Paul U. Kellogg, organized the American Union Against Militarism (AUAM). Their main concern was that war would harm their efforts to improve interethnic relations and also result in fewer monetary donations for settlement house work. Initially, the AUAM supported neutrality and anti-preparedness, but once the United States entered the war, it attempted to protect the civil liberties of conscientious objectors and other war dissenters. Addams and Balch supported the work of the AUAM throughout the war, but their hearts, souls, and physical energy took them in a slightly different direction, one which eventually led to each receiving the Nobel Peace Prize.

At the urging of two European suffragists, Emmeline Pethick-Lawrence of Great Britain and Rosika Schwimmer of Austria-Hungary, who believed that President Woodrow Wilson could be an effective mediator, Jane Addams, on behalf of several U.S. suffragists including Emily Greene Balch, called a meeting of representatives from prominent women's organizations. Held from January 9 to 11, 1915, in Washington, D.C., the conference resulted in the formation of the Woman's

Peace Party, which in 1919 became the U.S. Section of WILPF. A uniquely feminist group, the Woman's Peace Party sought to empower women. The "Preamble" of its founding document, for example, proclaimed that women had "a peculiar moral passion of revolt against both the cruelty and waste of war," and were fed up with the "reckless destruction" caused by men in powerful positions. Women wanted "a share in deciding between war and peace," and that share included equality in all aspects of public and private life.[11]

Within a year, under Addams's leadership, the eighty-five Woman's Peace Party charter members had grown to 512. By February 1917, the organization reached a peak membership of 25,000, and even though numbers of women dropped out after the United States entered the war in April 1917, in December 1917, the organization still included 200 local branches and affiliated groups. However, while U.S. women were organizing locally, both Addams and Balch cast their eyes upon Europe where in April 1915, they and forty-five other U.S. women joined over one thousand European women, largely suffragists, from both neutral and belligerent countries at a meeting at The Hague. As the proceedings of the congress made clear, the women not only wanted peace through mediation, but also equality with men. The concluding document stated: "The International Congress of Women is convinced that one of the strongest forces for the prevention of war will be the combined influence of the women of all countries. . . . But as women can only make their influence effective if they have equal political rights with men, this Congress declares that it is the duty of the women of all countries to work with all their force for their political enfranchisement."[12]

The congress also created two delegations to visit national leaders in an effort to promote mediation. Jane Addams, Aletta Jacobs of the Netherlands, and Rosa Genoni of Italy met the leaders of England, Germany, Austria-Hungary, Italy, France, Belgium, the Netherlands, and Switzerland. Emily Greene Balch, Rosike Schwimmer, Chrystal Macmillan of England, and Cor Ramondt-Hirsch of the Netherlands visited Denmark, Norway, Sweden, Russia, and also the Netherlands. From May to August, the two groups paid a total of thirty-five visits to leaders of both neutral and belligerent nations, asking each directly if he would like to see the war mediated.

Addams returned home as the first President of the newly formed International Committee of Women for Permanent Peace of which the Woman's Peace Party was the U.S. Section. Upon her arrival, she addressed a mass meeting in Carnegie Hall where she revealed her dismay that stimulants such as alcohol were being used in battlefields to enable men to kill each other. Addams added that many young men told her they did not want war and considered the older men responsible for it.[13] The press lambasted Addams, claiming that she was aiding the Germans by spreading such propaganda, and for several years to come both the press and the U.S. government portrayed her as an unpatriotic subversive out to break the nations' sons' fighting spirit. Bad press, however, did not cause Addams to lose her fine reputation as a social reformer nor did it prevent her from trying to achieve an end to the war through neutral mediation. From July to December 1915, she paid six visits to President Wilson. However, her confidence in his possible role as mediator dwindled as Wilson turned towards a policy of military preparedness, and then, in 1917, to war.

Throughout the war years, the U.S. Woman's Peace Party remained intact but not very active. The organization, fearful of membership decline and government persecution, took the position that the U.S. Congress had followed correct constitutional procedures to enter the war; therefore, the most that Woman's Peace Party members could do was to make plans for postwar peace work. The national office in Chicago remained open, but Addams found it an unpleasant place to enter. "If a bit of mail protruded from the door it was frequently spat upon, and although we rented our quarters in a first class office building on Michigan Boulevard facing the lake, the door was often befouled in hideous ways."[14] In an effort to search for new and more acceptable ways to work for peace, Addams volunteered for Herbert Hoover's federal Department of Food Administration. She traveled to many states, urging women to conserve food and to help increase its production. This work related closely to Addams's belief in women's responsibility to nurture the world and thereby create a healthier, more politically responsible population. As she later stated: "I firmly believed that through an effort to feed people, a new and powerful force might be unloosed in the world and would in the future have to be reckoned with as a factor in international affairs."[15]

In May 1919, while world leaders gathered in Versailles to write the treaty which officially ended World War I, the women who had met at The Hague in 1915 reconvened and formed the Women's International League for Peace and Freedom.[16] Their new constitution pledged the organization's support for "movements to further peace, internationalism, and the freedom of women."[17] Headquarters was established in Geneva, the seat of the League of Nations. Jane Addams became President and Emily Greene Balch, the first Secretary-Treasurer.

Even though Addams's and Balch's World War I peace work followed similar paths, Balch's journey took her into more politically radical waters. Throughout the war years her work with the American Union Against Militarism and the Woman's Peace Party increased her reputation as a national and international peace movement leader. Like Jane Addams, she became an elder stateswoman, a figure of wisdom and common sense. It was during this time that Balch's peace work became her profession. At first she merely intended to spend her sabbatical leave in New York City working for peace, not knowing that she would never return to academia. In New York City, the organizations Balch encountered were quite different from those in Massachusetts. Rather than middle-aged white Progressive reformers, they consisted largely of thirtyish feminists and socialists who lived in Greenwich Village and associated with artists and writers such as John Reed, Susan Glaspell, and Eugene O'Neill. The leading figures of the New York branch of the Woman's Peace Party were lawyers Crystal Eastman and Madeline Zabrisky Doty. Being a socialist herself, Balch seemed to have no problem working with the New York women. Addams, on the other hand, often claimed that their aggressive protest activities gave the national Woman's Peace Party a bad name.

Balch's other peace activism in New York led her to efforts which Addams preferred to avoid as much as possible. These groups (the American Neutral Conference Committee [1915], the Emergency Peace Federation [1917], and the People's Council of America for Democracy and Terms of Peace [1917]) each evolved from the preceding one, and each reflected a stage of U.S. policy towards the war, namely, neutrality, preparedness, and war. These three groups attracted an assortment of women and men—pacifists, socialists, feminists, and labor leaders—whose political stands became more leftist as the war came closer. The People's Council was formed after the United States declared war, and government leaders portrayed it as unpatriotic, even traitorous, for its stands included open support of the Russian Revolution, an end to war, justice for conscientious objectors, and elimination of poverty and labor exploitation.[18]

Unlike the Woman's Peace Party (or WILPF), the People's Council became obsolete once the war ended. Balch once again turned her emphasis towards international pacifist-feminism. In 1919, she joined Addams in Zurich for the founding meeting of WILPF. As Britisher Helena Swanwick reported, on the final day of the conference Balch rose to her feet, raised her right hand and, inviting all present to join her, pledged to do everything she could to bring about a permanent peace. Swanwick wrote, "I have never witnessed or imagined so remarkable an affirmation. Such scenes can, of course, be staged, but only intense feeling can cause them to occur spontaneously as this did."[19]

THE POST-WORLD WAR I RED SCARE

Both Addams and Balch were personally harassed for their political views—whether it be for supporting peace, woman suffrage, Bolshevik Russia, workers' rights, or the elimination of poverty.[20] While the Woman's Peace Party office in Chicago was vandalized and Addams was maligned by the press, Balch also experienced her first serious personal blow as a consequence of her peace activism. In 1919, after several appeals from Balch, the Board of Trustees of Wellesley officially refused to reappoint her. Apparently, they questioned her loyalty and were upset by her affiliation with the People's Council.[21] Balch had taught at the school for twenty-one years, but at the age of fifty-two found herself unemployed and having no immediate job prospects.

Other Red Scare events affected both women. In January 1919, for example, Archibald Stevenson, a New York lawyer employed by the Military Intelligence Division of the War Department, testified before the Overman senate subcommittee. Stevenson produced a list of sixty-two names of people whom he labeled "dangerous, destructive and anarchistic."[22] Addams and Balch were both on the list which the newspapers dubbed, the "Who's Who of Pacifists and Radicals." The Lusk Commission of New York State also singled out Addams and Balch in 1920 in its report on "Revolutionary Radicalism." This report accused Addams of using both the national and international women's peace movements to foster her socialistic views. Balch's activities for the People's Council were attacked. Using Council documents and correspondence, which the state officials had confiscated from the group's office, the Lusk report contained an entire chapter on the organization, describing its activists as "crafty" agents of Germany and/or Russia intent on overthrowing the U.S. government.[23]

Balch avoided some of the Red Scare heat by leaving the U.S. to take a salaried position as Secretary-Treasurer for the international WILPF offices in Geneva. Addams, while maintaining her home base at Hull-House in Chicago, also traveled a great deal throughout Europe, to Mexico, Hawaii and to several nations in Asia from 1919 through 1929, the years she was International President of WILPF. In all parts of the globe, people knew of her work at Hull-House and with WILPF and greeted her warmly, while at home many people shunned her. During the first half of the 1920s, the press and such patriotic organizations as the American Legion and the Daughters of the American Revolution (DAR) constantly attacked Addams. The DAR actually expelled Addams from membership, claiming that WILPF was part of a "world revolutionary movement" out "to destroy civilization and Christianity . . . and the government of the United States."[24] Addams noted that the DAR sent out a dossier on her and other individuals that was "a curious mixture of truth and fiction, and of sinister interpretations of simple situations."[25]

In 1923 the U.S. government issued a document known as the "Spider Web Chart." Allegedly prepared by Lucia R. Maxwell, a librarian of the Chemical Warfare Services of the War Department and the signer of the document, with the approval of Brigadier General Amos A. Fries, the chart contained criss-crossed lines linking individual women to organizations tinted from red to violet. WILPF was red, signifying its subversiveness. Several versions of the chart included the names of both Addams and Balch. Using the pages of *PAX,* the WILPF organ, Balch protested the Spider Web Chart, citing that it was "evidently related to the fact that women have succeeded in carrying through certain reforms . . . and that they seem likely to effect other social advances."[26]

Carrie Chapman Catt, the former President of the National American Woman Suffrage Association, also protested Red Scare activities, especially the DAR's attacks on Addams. Catt wrote an open letter to the DAR, citing Addams as "one of the greatest women this Republic of ours has produced. She has given her life to serve others. She knows no selfish thought. You slap her on the right cheek; she only turns the left. Sticks, stones, slanders, you cast upon this highest product of American womanhood and not a protest passes her lips. She is the kind of Christian who might have been thrown to the lions and would have gone cheerfully."[27]

Although both Addams and Balch faced open hostility from some quarters within the United States, they were also highly regarded by others, especially as the Red Scare died down and peace sentiment grew. By 1928, when the U.S. Congress ratified the Kellogg-Briand Pact, peace had become popular, and Addams something of a hero.

THE INTERWAR YEARS AND THE NOBEL PEACE PRIZE

From 1919 to 1935, Addams continued her constant and diligent work for both Hull-House and WILPF, but her health was deteriorating. Her physical weaknesses did not prevent her from traveling around the world in the 1920s (especially to avoid harassment) nor from speaking out about postwar conditions. Concerned by the conservative trend within the United States which not only hindered free speech but also discouraged the younger generation from becoming involved in controversial issues, Addams hoped to ease the stifling climate by helping to found the American Civil Liberties Union in 1920, an outgrowth of the Civil Liberties Bureau of the American Union Against Militarism.

Addams also hoped that a more nonviolent climate could foster freedom of speech and enhance political and economic changes in the world. In 1921 at the third WILPF international congress in Vienna, she proposed the adoption of Mohandas Gandhi's ideas into the organization's practices. She spoke continuously about Gandhi throughout the 1920s, hoping that his example would lead to a world of nonviolence rather than militarism. In the meantime, Addams supported all international treaties, conferences, organizations, or proposals which might lead to universal peace.

Loyal supporters submitted Addams's name to the Norwegian Nobel Peace Prize Committee in 1916, 1924, 1928, 1929, 1930, and 1931. Apparently, she wanted the prize very much and allowed various campaigns to be launched on her behalf. Balch, in particular, supported Addams's wish to show her critics that her peace work was indeed valuable and respected, especially outside the United States. Finally, in December, 1931, Addams shared the prize with Nicholas Murray Butler of Columbia University. By this time she was the Honorary President of the international WILPF but too ill to be very active. Addams received the news of her honor in a bed at Johns Hopkins hospital in Baltimore, where she awaited surgery for the removal of an ovarian cyst. The news could not have come at a better time. As Mary Rozet Smith, her close friend and companion, wrote to Addams's nephew, "The Nobel Prize really was a grand stimulant. While we were waiting for those three dreary days before the operation . . . , hundreds of telegrams and letters poured in and kept your Aunt Jane entertained. She was naturally greatly pleased by the award."[28] Along with all the messages came "a lovely box of flowers from the White House," where Addams's old Food Relief colleague, Herbert Hoover, resided as President.[29]

Several of the letters Addams received expressed impatience with the Nobel Committee for taking so long to honor her and then for making her share the prize with such a politically conservative man. Paul Kellogg, editor of *Survey,* the social workers' magazine, wrote that the Nobel "people" had been "blind" for such a long time that it was "good to learn" that they had at long last "opened their eyes," and Alfred E. Smith, ex-governor of New York, wrote that it was "especially a cause for congratulations when a woman's name is added. . . . We are proud that it is an American woman."[30] A *New York Times* editorial reiterated this sentiment, adding, "It is a recognition that in international affairs man's cause is woman's as well as woman's man's."[31] In addition, in a feature story on Addams in its Sunday magazine, *The Times* mentioned that although Addams had been scorned previously, the award had made her into a "heroine."[32]

Addams must have been very pleased with the hundreds of letters, cards, and gifts she received, and moved by the numerous requests for money. After all, 1931 was one of the worst years of the Great Depression. She probably enjoyed the letters from younger people most. One eighth-grader wrote that he had been composing a biographical essay on her when he learned that she had won the prize and that she was in the hospital. Still, he hoped that Addams would find the time and energy to send him her autograph.[33] By this time, Addams had become a popular figure for school children's essays and reading, although the peace part of her work was usually deemphasized or omitted. Still, she had become a role model for the next generation of progressives. As one seventeen-year-old high school student wrote, "As an advocate of peace and a great humanitarian you have long been the idol of we young would-be philanthropists who so often say, 'If I had a million dollars, I'd give it to charity.'"[34] In fact, that was exactly what Addams did. Her share of the prize, approximately $16,480, was donated to the international WILPF organization with the stipulation that if WILPF disbanded, the "investment in toto" would revert to the Foreign Service Committee of the Society of Friends.[35]

Addams received many other honors from 1931 to 1935. Besides the Nobel Peace Prize, 1931 brought her Bryn Mawr's M. Cary Thomas Prize and the *Pictorial Review* award "to the woman who in her special field has made the most distinguished contribution to American life."[36] Each award of $5,000 was donated to Hull-House to help those unemployed in the neighborhood. The same year she was ranked first on several lists of "America's Greatest Women," including one sponsored by *Good Housekeeping Magazine.* In 1932, she was named second in a contest run by the National Council of Women for the twelve greatest U.S. women of the century. (Mary Baker Eddy, founder of the Christian Scientists, was named number one.) In the next few years, Addams received numerous honorary degrees, including ones from Northwestern University, the University of Chicago, Swarthmore College, Rollins College, Knox College, the University of California, and Mt. Holyoke.

In 1933, Addams suffered a severe heart attack. Two years later she was diagnosed with cancer of the colon, dying that year, on May 21, 1935. For two days her body lay in state at Hull-House, where as many as 2,000 people an hour paid their respects. She was then buried in her hometown of Cedarville, Illinois. Jane Addams quickly achieved prominence in U.S. history.

Balch was deeply saddened by her co-activist's death. She had long considered Addams a dear friend, even though a study of their correspondence seems to indicate that the friendship was more professional than personal.[37] On an undated scrap of paper she wrote, "I am thankful to have known and worked with Jane Addams and that she loved me so much more than I deserved or could repay. Help me not to dwell on my loss. Help me to enjoy her still. To learn from her and be glad of her and do what is in me to do, as she did, living to the full her great soul."[38] Balch most certainly felt the need of Addams's guidance as she faced some of the most troubling issues of the day—the growth of fascism in Europe; the persecution of so many people, including fellow pacifists and suffragists; the question of U.S. neutrality, and, of course, the quickly approaching Second World War.

From 1922 on, Balch divided her work between international WILPF and its U.S. section, holding important offices on both sides of the Atlantic.[39] In the mid-1920s she traveled for WILPF to North Africa, the Middle East, and Central Europe. Most importantly, in 1925 a WILPF task force of five women and one man spent three weeks in Haiti examining the effect of the United States' ten-year military occupation on the living conditions of the native population. The team produced a report, entitled *Occupied Haiti,* which Balch edited in 1927. A graphic indictment of the U.S. government representatives' and military's behavior, *Occupied Haiti* cited the suspension of Haitians' civil liberties, self-determination, and access to adequate health care, education, and public services.[40] A later investigation by President Herbert Hoover reiterated the WILPFers' conclusions. As a result, U.S. troops were withdrawn in 1934.

During the interwar years, Balch wrote many papers on disarmament, the internationalization of aviation, the 1931 situation in Manchuria, the need to reform the League of Nations, and a plea for mediation to end the Spanish Civil War. Within WILPF, especially in the United States, however, her attention centered on the issues of isolationism and, hence, neutrality. Balch felt that the United States needed to resist the expansion of fascism and aggression through nonviolent methods derived from cooperative international effort. She endorsed economic sanctions against fascist nations and believed that neutrality was "impractical, amoral" and selfish in that it encouraged people to turn their backs on other nations' problems as long as they, themselves, were not harmed.[41] Debate over neutrality within the U.S. section was intense, and eventually Balch lost, for in its desire for group coherence and for the avoidance of war, the national board supported the various acts passed by Congress establishing the so-called "New Neutrality" in the 1930s.

Balch, herself, admitted that even the U.S. declaration of war against Japan in December 1941, caused her to go through "a long and painful mental struggle," never coming to a "clear and consistent conclusion." The attack on Pearl Harbor, she claimed, would make it difficult for any nation not to enter a war, "given the existing degree of development of mankind and its failure to have ready any effective and generally understood technique for constructive, non-violent *action.*" During the conflict, Balch found herself, on one hand, refusing to buy war bonds while, on the other, contributing to the Community War-Funds, which gave out "peaceful social aid."[42] During the war, Balch, as did the U.S. Section of WILPF, concentrated on social, not military, concerns. She spoke out against U.S. internment of Japanese-American citizens and worked for their future relocation to friendly communities and monetary compensation for their losses. She spoke out regarding the persecution of Jews and pressed for the U.S. government to accept refugees. She also supported the establishment of the United Nations and for WILPF's recognition as an NGO (non-governmental organization) which it was granted in 1948.

In 1946, the Nobel Peace Prize was awarded jointly to Balch and John Mott, leader of both the Student Christian Movement and the YMCA. The idea to nominate Balch originated with Mercedes Randall, a peace activist since World War I, an active leader in the U.S. section of WILPF, and Balch's future biographer. Along with her husband, a Columbia University professor, Randall led a well-organized and orchestrated campaign which utilized philosopher and educational leader, John Dewey, to recruit support. The Randalls' campaign was extremely effective, especially considering that Balch had never been nominated before. This was her euphoric response to the flattering letters sent on her behalf: "It is as good as going to one's own funeral without having to die first (which I don't at all want to do, till I am more played out than I am now.)"[43]

Eighty when she received the telegram of the good news, Balch, like Jane Addams, was ill and in the Wellesley-Newton Hospital with a bronchial infection. She was unable to go to Oslo to accept the prize in person, a fact which she, as a professional pacifist, greatly regretted because she would be unable "to make full use of this extraordinary opportunity for publicity favorable to our work."[44] However, she did receive many letters and cables, sometimes reaching twenty or thirty a day, a far cry from Addams's hundreds. Many were from friends and colleagues, and from various national sections of WILPF. Neither President Harry S Truman nor any other prominent U.S. figure sent congratulations or gifts. Like a few of the people asked to nominate her who declined, *The New York Times* also welcomed her honor with lukewarm enthusiasm. The editorial of November 16 lamented the fact that the prize had not been given to the international leaders responsible for forming the United Nations.[45] Like Addams, Balch did not keep the proceeds from her prize. Of the approximately $17,000 she received, $10,000 went to international WILPF. Five thousand was placed in a bank for a European colleague who had worked for WILPF. The final $2,000 was used for her 1948 trip to Oslo to present her Nobel lecture and to hire a secretarial assistant to help her with this presentation.[46]

The lecture Balch presented in Oslo in 1948 was entitled "Toward Human Unity or Beyond Nationalism." In it, she stressed her lifelong belief that the needs of humanity, not national pride, should be the values emphasized in the post-World War II nuclear-age. Included in these were the preservation of personal freedoms, the establishment of democracies in every nation, and the removal of violence from institutions such as prisons, families, religion, and government. Extolling Gandhi's use of nonviolence as a political tool, Balch ended the talk by praising the founding of the United Nations with the hope that it would provide a way for the world to develop and mature peacefully.[47]

From 1946 to 1956, when she entered the Vernon Nursing Home in Cambridge, Massachusetts, Balch continued to travel and give lectures. She addressed atomic age issues and tried to press for more openness between the United States and the Soviet Union and China. Once she retired from active life, she had time to read and welcome visitors, but largely she felt that her existence had become "duller than ditch water."[48] For Emily Greene Balch, her career as a peace activist had presented many trials and tribulations, but it had been a life full of challenge and excitement. Towards the end of her life, she still maintained the bittersweet feeling so prevalent in her writings. One of the last entries in her journal read: "I am bringing my days to a close in a world still hag-ridden by the thought of war, and it is not given to us in this new atomic world to know how things will turn out. But when I reflect on the enormous changes that I have seen myself and the amazing resiliency and resourcefulness of mankind, how can I fail to be of good courage?"[49] Balch kept up that courage until her death, on January 9, 1961, at the age of ninety-four.

CONCLUSION

The Nobel Peace Prize, one of the most prestigious awards in the world, actually did little to enhance either Jane Addams's or Emily Greene Balch's reputations and place in U.S. history. The United States has not been a nation which traditionally exalts peace advocates. Military men make up many of our national heroes. It is their stories children study in school, their images we see on statues, and their lives novelists and filmakers romanticize. Women usually do not even make the list. However, there are specific reasons why Addams is well known whereas Balch is not. Addams was a lifelong social reformer. Hull-House was key to her fame. Her work there reflected those concerns considered socially acceptable for women. In addition, all her other political work stemmed from her commitment to social work—helping the poor survive and improve their lot, and making the broader society and government respond to their needs. Addams's peace work evolved from her belief that people from different cultures *could* work together and learn to understand each other from their common roots and experiences.

In addition, the documents reveal that Addams was also a unique and gentle person. Balch's own remembrance of Addams in 1943 demonstrates this point:

> Of all my experiences the greatest and dearest was the being privileged to know Jane Addams. It is as impossible to evoke her for those who did not have the happiness of knowing her as to evoke the fragrance of a ripe strawberry or of a water-lily for someone who has never smelled one. She was so utterly unlike anyone else that I have known—so utterly real and first-hand; so subtle, so simple and direct; so free from any preoccupation with self, as free from asceticism as from self-indulgence; full of compassion without weakness or sentimentality (though she grew up in a sentimental generation), loving merriment while carrying the world's woes in her heart—both the many which pressed upon her in immediate personal shape at Hull-House and those of the nameless, unseen millions whose fates are part of our own personal fate. A great statesman, a great writer, one of the world's rarest spirits, how can I or anyone evoke her?[50]

Many people around the world acknowledged that special nature that characterized Jane Addams.

Emily Greene Balch was a different kind of person with a different life journey. Addams once stated that of all the hundreds of people she had known in every part of the world, she knew "none that was as good as Emily Balch."[51] As "good" as she was, Balch operated within a small elite world. Rather than working on a grassroots level, she chose the ivory tower of the academy until 1918, and then ensconced herself within WILPF. Unlike Addams, she did not live with the poor nor did she do settlement house work. As a consequence, Addams was known and loved by thousands of average people; Balch was admired by the same small group of educated, politically active women who also loved Addams. In this sense Hull-House was the basis of Addams's local and international stature; the Nobel Peace Prize was just the icing on the cake.

For Balch the prize should have been the key to making her name a household word and to vindicating her life's work. It might have done so had she received it at a different historical moment and if she had not allied herself solely with the peace movement, a movement traditionally scorned by most people who feel that peace activists threaten the status quo.[52] Addams received the prize in 1931, at the peak of a very rare time in U.S. history, a time when a sincere interest in world peace existed for both representatives of the government and the people, as the ratification of the Kellogg-Briand Pact in 1928 attests. When Addams won the prize, peace was a popular, even honorable, cause. Within a few years, this would change. Therefore, winning the Nobel Peace Prize in 1931 added to Addams's already inestimable reputation.

In constrast, Balch had the dubious honor of winning the prize in 1946, a year in which the Cold War and the nuclear arms race were intensifying. In addition, anticommunism was also gaining force, making the peace cause not only unpopular but appear treasonous. Peace became equated once again with a communist plot to demasculinize, disarm, and destroy the U.S. government. Balch, who had openly embraced the ideas of socialism, was not likely to be extolled in such a political climate. The effects of the McCarthy era lasted beyond Balch's death in 1961, especially with U.S. involvement in Vietnam. Even though the Nobel Peace Prize enhanced Balch's standing within the relatively small world of WILPF, it did little to endear her to the U.S. public.

Comparing the experiences of Jane Addams and Emily Greene Balch sheds light on the peculiar dynamics of achieving prominence in U.S. history. For women, working with the poor, the ill, or the homeless is acceptable and even honorable, reflecting society's traditional desire to reinforce conventional gender roles, especially selflessness and nurturance which undergird values associated with mothering. Work on the international level, especially in the diplomatic arena, is considered inappropriate and, at times, even treasonous, reflecting society's aversion to assertiveness in women and fear of women displacing men in top-level, decision-making positions. In this sense, the theory of "separate spheres" rings true. Jane Addams is remembered for her "woman's work" even though she expanded the notion of women's sphere, whereas Emily Greene Balch is virtually ignored because she crossed that line of appropriate female behavior and stepped into the public sphere itself.

NOTES

I would like to thank the following: Karl Holl, and the Norwegian Nobel Institute, especially Geir Lundestad, Director, and Anne C. Kjelling, Head Librarian, for graciously organizing and sponsoring the June 24-28, 1992, conference, "The Meaning and Acceptance of the Nobel Peace Prize in the Prize Winners' Countries," for which this paper was originally written; historian Irwin Abrams and the two anonymous readers for the *Journal of Women's History* for their most astute and helpful comments; and Fitchburg State College for a Graduate Research Grant and a Harrod Lectureship which enabled me to do further research on Addams and Balch. The original conference paper has been published in Karl Holl and Anne C. Kjelling, ed., *The Nobel Peace Prize and the Laureates: The Meaning and Acceptance of the Nobel Peace Prize in the Prize Winners' Countries* (Frankfurt am Main: Peter Lang GmbH, 1994).

[1] The other areas were literature, physics, chemistry, and physiology or medicine. For more on the man and his will, see Nils K. Ståhle, *Alfred Nobel and the Nobel Prizes* (The Nobel Foundation, The Swedish Institute, 1978).

[2] For a detailed account of Alfred Nobel's passion for Bertha von Suttner, see Brigitte Hamann, *Bertha von Suttner: Ein Leben fur den Frieden* (Munich: R. Piper GmbH and Co., 1986). An English translation of this work is currently under contract with Syracuse University Press.

[3] The laureate is chosen by a committee of five appointees of the Norwegian Parliament. In 1993, the award was worth $825,000 (U.S. dollars).

[4] To date, only nine women have won the prize. They are Bertha von Suttner of Austria (1905), Jane Addams of the United States (1931), Emily Greene Balch of the United States (1946), Mairead Corrigan and Betty Williams of Ireland (1977), Mother Theresa of the former Yugoslavia (1979), Alva Myrdal of Sweden (1982), Sung San Suu Kyi of Burma (1991), and Rigoberta Menchu Tum of Guatemala (1992).

[5] There are many volumes which offer the basics about Jane Addams's life. I relied heavily on the following: Anne Firor Scott, "Jane Addams," in *Notable American Women, 1607-1950: A Biographical Dictionary,* ed. Edward T. James, et al. (Cambridge, Mass.: The Belknap Press of Harvard University Press, 1971); Allen F. Davis, *American Heroine: the Life and Legend of Jane Addams* (New York: Oxford University Press, 1973), Jane Addams, *Twenty Years at Hull-House* (New York: New American Library, 1981; reprint of New York: The Macmillan Company, 1910); and the Jane Addams Papers: Swarthmore College Peace Collection (henceforth noted as JA: SCPC). Since Jane Addams hyphenated the name Hull-House, I have followed that practice in this article.

Balch's life is based on: Barbara Miller Solomon, "Emily Greene Balch," in *Notable American Women: The Modern Period: A Biographical Dictionary,* ed. Barbara Sicherman and Carol Hurd Green (Cambridge, Mass.: The Belknap Press of Harvard University Press, 1980); Mercedes M. Randall, *Improper Bostonian: Emily Greene Balch, Nobel Peace Laureate, 1946* (New York: Twayne Publishers, 1964); and the Emily Greene Balch Papers: Swarthmore College Peace Collection—Scholarly Resources Microfilm Edition (henceforth noted as EB: SCPC).

[6] December 31, 1906 journal entry, Reel 18, Box 19, Folder 2, EB: SCPC.

[7] I hesitate to use the term, "Christian ethics" here as neither Jane Addams nor Emily Greene Balch referred to religion in their peace work or writings. Addams, born into a Quaker family, affiliated with a Presbyterian church in 1885. Balch, born into a Unitarian family, became a Quaker in 1921.

[8] Jane Addams, *Democracy and Social Ethics,* edited by Anne Firor Scott (Cambridge: The Belknap Press of Harvard University Press, 1964; reprint of New York: The Macmillan Company, 1907), 275.

[9] Jane Addams, *The Newer Ideals of Peace* (New York: The Macmillan Company, 1907), 26.

[10] Emily Greene Balch, "Working for Peace," *Bryn Mawr Alumnae Bulletin* 13 (May 1933): 12 (as cited in Randall, *Improper Bostonian,* p. 135).

[11] "Woman's Peace Party Preamble and Platform Adopted at Washington, January 10, 1915," Subject Files 463, Rosika Schwimmer/Lola Maverick Lloyd Collection, Rare Books and Manuscripts Division, The New York Public Library, Astor, Lenox and Tilden Foundations (henceforth noted as S/L: NYPL).

[12] "Program from the International Women's Congress, April 28, 29, 30, 1915," Series A, Box 3, Folder 2, Women's International League for Peace and Freedom/ U.S. Section, 1919-1959 Papers: Swarthmore College Peace Collection-Scholarly Resources Microfilm Edition (henceforth noted as WILPF/US: SCPC).

[13] Jane Addams, "The Revolt Against War," reprinted from the *Survey,* July 17, 1915, Subject File 464, S/L: NYPL.

[14] Jane Addams, *Peace and Bread in Time of War* (Silver Springs, Md.: National Association of Social Workers, 1983; reprint of New York: The Macmillan Company, 1922), 127-128.

[15] Jane Addams, *The Second Twenty Years at Hull-House, September 1909 to September 1929* (New York: The Macmillan Company, 1930), 144.

[16] Because the U.S. Congress never ratified the Versailles Treaty, President Warren G. Harding had to sign a separate treaty with Germany in 1921.

[17] "Report of the International Congress of Women, Zurich, May 12-17, 1919" as cited in Marie Louise Degen, *The History of the Woman's Peace Party* (New York: Garland Publishing, 1972; reprint of Baltimore: The Johns Hopkins Press, 1939), 232.

[18] For more on Balch and the People's Council, see Harriet Hyman Alonso, "A Shared Responsibility: The Women and Men of the People's Council of America for Democracy and Peace, 1917-1919" (M.A. thesis, Sarah Lawrence College, 1982); and Frank L. Grubbs, Jr., *The Struggle for Labor Loyalty: Gompers, the A.F. of L., and the Pacifists, 1917-1920* (Durham, N.C.: Duke University Press, 1968).

[19] Helena Swanwick, *I Have Been Young* (London, 1935), 318 (as cited in Randall, *Improper Bostonian,* 276).

[20] For a detailed account of the government's surveillance of WILPF, see Joan M. Jensen, "All Pink Sisters: The War Department and the Feminist Movement in the 1920s," in *Decades of Discontent: The Women's Movement, 1920-1940,* ed. Lois Scharf and Joan M. Jensen (Boston: Northeastern University Press, 1987), 199-222; and Harriet Hyman Alonso, *Peace as a Women's Issue: A History of the U.S. Movement for World Peace and Women's Rights* (Syracuse: Syracuse University Press, 1993).

[21] Emily Greene Balch to President Pendleton, April 3, 1918, EB: SCPC.

[22] *The New York Times,* January 25, 1919, 1: 4, 4: 4.

[23] Clayton R. Lusk, Chairman, *Report of the Joint Legislative Committee Investigating Seditious Activities, Filed April 24, 1920 in the Senate of New York: Revolutionary Radicalism: Part I: Volume I* (Albany, N.Y.: J.B. Lyon, 1920), 967-1111.

[24] Addams, *Second Twenty Years,* 181.

[25] *Ibid.,* 182.

[26] Emily Greene Balch, "Statement of Facts Concerning the Women's International League in Regard to Certain Misrepresentations," *PAX,* no date, Reel 33, WILPF/US: SCPC.

[27] Carrie Chapman Catt to the [Daughters of the American Revolution], 1927, Carrie Chapman Catt Papers: Rare Books and Manuscripts Division, The New York Public Library, Astor, Lenox and Tilden Foundations.

[28] Mary Smith to Stanley, December 16, 1931, Reel 23, JA: SCPC.

[29] Ferdinand Hansen to Marburg Clinic, December 14, 1931, Reel 22, JA: SCPC.

[30] Paul Kellogg to Jane Addams, December 19, 1931; Alfred E. Smith to Jane Addams, December 12, 1931, Reel 22, JA: SCPC.

[31] *The New York Times* editorials, December 11, 1931, 26: 2.

[32] Eunice Fuller Barnard, "Jane Addams: Bold Crusader for Peace," *The New York Times Magazine,* Sunday, December 30, 1931, 8.

[33] Douglas Osterheld to "Miss Addams," December 11, 1931, Reel 22, JA: SCPC.

[34] Morris Osofsky to Jane Addams, December 10, 1931, Reel 22, JA: SCPC.

[35] Signed statement by Jane Addams, no date, Reel 45, "Nobel" file, JA: SCPC.

[36] Cited in *Notable American Women.*

[37] In my fourteen years as a researcher of women's peace activism, I have not encountered any hint of a deep friendship between these two women. In fact, the one thing I have noted is that Addams addressed letters to "Dear Emily" while Balch began hers, "Dear Miss Addams." I think it is likely that even though Addams and Balch worked for WILPF for many years, their friendship did not extend beyond this professional level for several reasons: Balch lived and worked in Boston or New York whereas Addams spent most of her time in Chicago or at her summer cottage in Bar Harbor, Maine; Balch was not a part of the Hull-House community where Addams had her support network; and Balch did not share Addams's main work—that of Hull-House.

[38] Undated scrap of paper as cited in Randall, *Improper Bostonian,* 324.

[39] From 1928 to 1933, Balch was president of the U.S. Section; from 1929 to 1931, she was also on the U.S. executive committee. From 1934 to 1935, she accepted a second term (without pay) as international secretary-treasurer. In 1937, she was named honorary president of the international.

[40] Emily Greene Balch, ed., *Occupied Haiti* (New York: Garland Publishing Company, 1972; reprint of New York: The Writers Publishing Company, 1927). The report is especially interesting in light of current events between Haiti and the United States.

[41] Emily Greene Balch, "A Foreign Policy for the W.I.L." appended to Branch Letter 70, February 28, 1939 as cited in Barbara Solomon, "Dilemmas of Pacifist Women, Quakers and Others, in World Wars I and II," in *Witnesses for Change: Quaker Women over Three Centuries,* ed. Elisabeth Potts Brown and Susan Mosher Stuard (New Brunswick, N.J.: Rutgers University Press, 1989), 137.

[42] Emily Greene Balch, draft of "Personal History," 1945, as cited in Randall, *Improper Bostonian,* 340-341.

[43] Emily Greene Balch to J. H. and M. M. Randall, Reel 12, January 30, 1946, Box 13, Folder 6, EB: SCPC.

[44] Emily Greene Balch to Friends, November 19, 1946, Reel 12, Box 13, Folder 6, EB: SCPC.

[45] *The New York Times,* November 16, 1946, 18: 2.

[46] "Dispatch No. 407," December 13, 1946, Reel 2, Box 3, Folder 4, EB: SCPC. I have been unable to trace the name of Balch's WILPF friend who received the $5,000 donation.

[47] Emily Greene Balch, "Toward Human Unity or Beyond Nationalism," Nobel lecture delivered at Oslo, April 7, 1948, Reel 2, Box 4, Folder 4, EB: SCPC.

[48] Cited in Randall, *Improper Bostonian,* 443.

[49] Journal as cited in *ibid.,* 445.

[50] Emily Greene Balch in *Four Lights,* 3 (June 1943) as cited in *ibid.,* 325.

[51] Dorothy Detzer Denny to Barbara Miller Solomon, January 27, 1979, Reel 2, Box 3, Folder 8, EB: SCPC.

[52] For more on peace movement history, see Harriet Hyman Alonso, *Peace as a Women's Issue;* Charles Chatfield, *The American Peace Movement: Ideals and Activism* (New York: Twayne Publishers, 1992); and Charles DeBenedetti, *The Peace Reform in American History* (Bloomington: Indiana University Press, 1980.)

Louise W. Knight (essay date 1992)

SOURCE: "Jane Addams's Views on the Responsibilities of Wealth," in *The Responsibilites of Wealth,* edited by Dwight F. Burlingame, Indiana University Press, 1992, pp. 118-37.

[*In the following essay, Knight presents Addams's views on charity, both as a member of a wealthy family and as a humanitarian seeking to raise funds.*]

The title of this paper is in a sense offered tongue in cheek. While the theme of this book, "The Responsibilities of Wealth," captures a point of view held by Andrew Carnegie and other late nineteenth century philanthropists, it does not reflect the view of their contemporary, Jane Addams. She rejected the belief that an individual's wealth defined his or her responsibilities to the poor. Herself a woman of inherited wealth, Addams gave careful thought to the moral aspect of the relations between the classes, but her conclusions went in another direction.

A better phrase to describe Addams's views might be "the responsibilities of being human." In her life's work as the head of the Chicago settlement house, Hull House, as a national leader in social reform, and as a world leader for peace, she tried to honor the Judeo-Christian tenet that every individual merits equal respect. Her reform agenda thus rejected distinctions based on class and race and promoted social justice. She saw the gap between the ideal of equality and the reality, a gap even larger in her day than in our own, and fought to narrow it.

Her ideas about philanthropy were built on this philosophical foundation. Without denying the usefulness of money to accomplish good work, she rejected the materialism that overvalued such achievements. She sought, along with her colleagues in the settlement house movement, to instigate a "new philanthropy" by calling for the creation of cross-class social relations as a means to motivate people to desire the improvement of society.[1] Diverse social relations, Addams believed, would also bring benefits to the individual. In particular, they would benefit the wealthy, who lived in the greatest isolation from other classes.

Addams's claim that philanthropy would benefit the philanthropist was not new. Traditional philanthropy, while stressing the benefits to the poor as its first motive, acknowledged that the rich would gain in virtue from the encounter. This was based on the condescending assumption that the rich were morally superior to the poor. Uninterested in questions of sin and virtue and uncomfortable with assumptions of class superiority, Addams made a different case—that through cross-class relations philanthropists could gain knowledge of themselves and the common humanity that they shared with the poor. They could also improve their philanthropy.

Not surprisingly, she developed these ideas out of her own experience. As a single woman, she found that a life consisting of the company of family and friends and regular doses of cultural enrichment was too narrow, leaving her feeling isolated and dissatisfied with her uselessness and ignorance of the broader human world. Her first reason for founding Hull House, she always said, was to enrich her own life and give it meaning. Her desire to help the poor, also strong, came second in her mind. The benefits were to be mutual. Once she came to understand her own needs, she made it part of her life's work to guide others of wealth to make the same discoveries.

I. CLASS DIFFERENCES

It is no coincidence that Addams founded Hull House and Carnegie published his essay "Wealth" in the same year, 1889. The decade of the 1880s had seen a rising concern in both England and the United States about the distance between the classes and the misery of the poor. Stimulated in part by such books as Henry George's influential *Progress and Poverty* (1879), citizens of these countries viewed the intensifying forces of industrialization on both sides of the Atlantic and the mounting wave of European emigration to the United States as developments which required new approaches. The period was, in Addams's words, one of "widespread moral malaise in regard to existing social conditions."[2] Carnegie and Addams each attempted to respond in his or her own way with a new theory of philanthropy.

Like others, Addams was deeply troubled by the gulf between the classes. The gulf was material, of course, but it was also social. In both England and the United States in the 1880s, the rich (and the middle classes) and the poor viewed each other with hostility. Then, as now, the rich scorned the poor for their lack of moral fiber. For their part, the poor hated the rich for their greed and lack of compassion. In his novel *Sybil, or Two Nations,* Benjamin Disraeli, England's prime minister when the decade of the eighties opened, characterized this gulf of understanding in vivid terms. The rich and poor, he said, "are as ignorant of each other's habits, thoughts, and feelings, as if they were dwellers in different zones or inhabitants of different planets."[3]

Acknowledging the existence of class differences has always made Americans uncomfortable. In Jane Addams's day, when the upper class felt confident enough in their moral superiority to the "lower class" to call it by that name, this discomfort was still felt. "We do not like to acknowledge," she wrote, "that Americans are divided into 'two nations,' as her prime minister once admitted of England, . . . even if we make that assumption the preface to a plea that the superior class has duties to the inferior."[4]

Class was a confusing riddle for Addams. While she inherited wealth, she was the daughter of a self-made man who had arrived on the Illinois frontier with few resources. Although her small hometown in the northern part of the state had a class structure (her father soon became the richest man in town), it was egalitarian in spirit. The culture she absorbed in school was imbued with class prejudices, but her family history taught her that class was an achieved status and that any superiority it brought with it was also achieved. For Addams, as an inheritor of wealth rather than the creator of it, the question was how to merit the wealth her father had earned.

II. THE YEARS LEADING TO HULL HOUSE

Addams wrestled with this question during the eight years between her graduation from college and her bold act of founding Hull House. Her first plan had been to care for the poor through a career in medicine. The year after her graduation from college, despite her father's unexpected death, she enrolled at the Woman's Medical College in Philadelphia, but her own health failed, forcing her to withdraw.

The loss of her only career goal left her vulnerable to the "family claim," as she was later to describe it. Yet the life of culture, wide reading, and travel that the family claim imposed on her also appealed to her, feeding as it did her love of learning. With her stepmother's full approval, she pursued a life of family visits and travel abroad. She was the perfect daughter of the upper class.

As the years passed, she became increasingly unhappy. Her education had given her high ideals of service but her life offered no outlet for their expression. The difficulty, she finally formulated, was "the assumption that the sheltered, educated girl has nothing to do with the bitter poverty and the social maladjustment which is all about her, and which, after all, cannot be concealed, for it breaks through poetry and literature in a burning tide which overwhelms her; it peers at her in the form of heavy-laden market women and underpaid street laborers, gibing her with a sense of her uselessness."[5]

Adding to her misery was her inability to find a way to express her sense of "human fellowship."[6] From her experience, sympathetic temperament, and wide reading, she was developing the conviction that, as one of her favorite authors, George Eliot, put it, "human nature is lovable."[7] In his essay on "Man the Reformer," another of Addams's favorite authors, Ralph Waldo Emerson, pointed out the missed opportunities: "See this wide society of laboring men and women," he wrote. "We allow ourselves to be served by them, we live apart from them and meet them without salute in the streets. We do not greet their talents, nor rejoice in their good fortune, nor foster their hopes."[8]

Other authors she read—Mazzini, Ruskin, Arnold—were imbued with this same ideal of the lovability of human nature, as was the philosophy of positivism, which she encountered in Comte's works. Yet, in the end, it was the idea's original source, the faith of the early Christians, that inspired her the most and Christ who became her model. In 1887, she returned to Italy to undertake a study of the Catacombs.[9] A year after founding Hull House, she was to write, "It seems simple to many of us to search for the Christ that is in each man and to found our likeness on Him—to believe in the brotherhood of all men because we believe in His."[10]

During this second trip, as she traveled and watched people from all walks of life go by, she found herself wanting to act on these feelings of brotherhood. Still the rules of her class held her back. A waiter who brought her breakfast one morning at a hotel became the focus of her longing; her memory of the encounter became to her a symbol of her inability to bridge the class gulf: "You turn helplessly to the waiter [but] feel it would be almost grotesque to claim from him the sympathy you crave because civilization has placed you apart."[11]

As the clash between her ideals and her conduct intensified, she became even more "pitifully miserable."[12] In the end, she viewed her decision to found Hull House as, in part, an act of desperation. She had become disgusted with her life of culture and observation and determined to find a way "to learn from life itself."[13] She had decided that "whatever perplexities and discouragement concerning the life of the poor were in store for me, I should at least know something at first-hand and have the solace of daily activity."[14] She would also be free of the tyranny of the family claim and its emotionally closed world.

Her desire to help the poor, initially expressed in her application to medical school, remained. But that motive had been reshaped by the realization, reached over the eight years, that she also needed to help herself. She had decided that the poor had what she sought: generosity, gaiety, hospitality, courtesy, and kindness in their human relations with each other.[15] She knew that she had culture and organizing abilities to offer the poor; now she knew as well that they had much to offer her.

Ellen Starr, writing to her sister a few months before she and Addams moved into Hull House, stressed that point. "Jane's idea, which she puts very much to the front and on no account will give up, is that [the settlement] is more for the people who do it than for the other class. She has worked that out of her own experience and ill health."[16] As Addams put it, "the dependence of classes on each other is reciprocal."[17]

During this period, she read about Toynbee Hall in London, the world's first settlement house, and was drawn to its innovative approach to bringing the classes together in social relations. At Toynbee, middle and upper class college-educated young people, called residents, shared a comfortable home in a poor neighborhood, earning their livelihood during the day in the city and spending their free time getting to know their neighbors in the evenings and weekends. Clubs, classes, and cultural events grew out of these relations, in response to the needs of the neighborhood. Local political reform and union organizing soon followed. However, the philosophy of the settlement was not simply one of service. Toynbee's founder, Canon Barnett, stressed that the residents benefited as much from their social relations with their neighbors, as their neighbors benefited from knowing the residents.

This philosophy struck a chord in Addams. A visit to Toynbee Hall in 1888 convinced her that she wanted to found a settlement too. Here, at last, was something she could do. With her friend Ellen Starr, she moved to Hull House, a fine old mansion in a rundown district of Chicago, in September 1889. She was twenty-nine years old. She and Starr had no plan, but intended to get to know their neighbors and see what activities might evolve. Addams saw the settlement simply as "an effort . . . to insist that a life is not lived as it should be unless it comes in contact with all kinds of people. We should endeavor, in addition to our individual and family [lives], to live a life that will bring us into a larger existence, and connect us with society as a whole."[18]

III. THE HUMANITY OF THE POOR

As she met and talked with the working poor, her neighbors, she listened carefully, trying, as she later advised Hull House residents, to "empty her mind" of preconceived ideas and to truly learn what the lives of her neighbors were like.[19] The stories were gripping. She heard terrible tales of small children crippled by accidents that occurred when they were home alone while their mothers were at work. One had fallen out of a third story window, another had been burned. A third had a curved spine from being tied to the leg of the kitchen table, no doubt to keep him from burning himself or falling out of the window.[20]

She learned of the pressures on those who could find no regular employment and no steady income. When one man, who Addams knew had been able to earn only twenty-eight dollars in the preceding nine months and was thirty-two dollars in debt, told her casually one day that he had sold his vote for two dollars, Addams fell silent, unable to criticize his betrayal of democracy because she knew he had been tempted in ways she never had been.[21]

Addams and Starr had only been living in Hull House for a few months when they began to learn about the harsh realities of child labor. Several little girls refused the candy the two women offered them at Christmas because they had spent the last six weeks working fourteen-hour days in a candy factory and could not bear the taste or sight of it. In the neighborhood Addams and Starr found mothers and daughters at home sewing mounds of clothing for a few cents an hour. One four-year-old child pulled out basting threads hour after hour, sitting on a stool at her mother's feet.[22]

From these and many other stories and experiences, Addams learned that the poor were, on the whole, neither lazy nor immoral but simply trapped in a cycle of "toilsome and underpaid labor."[23] She met among them intelligent people of many talents and found herself forced to discard old assumptions about the stupidity of the poor. "It is a mistake," she pointed out, "to believe that all poor people are dull and lacking in intellectuality. People are poor because they have no ability to make money, but this may or may not be accompanied with ability in other directions."[24] The apparent "intellectual and moral superiority" of the upper classes, she concluded, rested on "economic props which are, after all, matters of accident."[25]

Hull House pursued practical solutions to the problems their neighbors faced. A day nursery and a kindergarten were opened in the first year, where, for a small fee, working mothers could place their pre-school children. To address the problems of low factory wages and cyclical unemployment in certain industries, Hull House encouraged workers to organize into unions and fight for better working conditions. To prevent the employment of young children, the House lobbied successfully for a new state law banning the practice.

Jane Addams preferred these types of solutions because they left her neighbors' dignity intact. Sometimes a gift of money, the usual form of charity, was necessary in an emergency, but she knew the more important gift was respect, because people prized it more highly than charity.[26] She felt that "contempt was the greatest crime one could commit against one's fellow man."[27] Determined not to condescend, she identified other motivations for her efforts, motivations that went beyond the usual ones of noblesse oblige and service.

A case in point was her views on the difficult subject of gratitude. Her wealthy friends like Louise deKoven Bowen viewed gratitude for their good work as the only payment they required of the poor. In this they felt noble. But Addams soon deflated them. In complaint one day Bowen told Addams, "I have done everything in the world for that woman and she is not even grateful." Bowen recalled that Jane Addams "looked at me quizzically and said, 'Is that the reason you helped her, because you wanted gratitude?'"[28] For Jane Addams, gratitude was not the point. She was helping them because they, like her, were part of the human race. This sense of fellowship left "no room for sensitiveness and gratitude."[29]

Addams's belief in "the solidarity of the human race" may have been inspired by literature and Christianity initially but life at Hull House deepened her understanding, as it also deepened the understanding of the other residents. One of them, Grace Abbott, learned on one occasion just what "solidarity" meant to Addams in practical terms.

An old Frenchman from the neighborhood was a chronic visitor to Hull House. He had, in his poverty and old age, been assigned by the county to the poorhouse in Oak Forest, a nearby suburb, but refused to go. Instead, he would regularly sit on the sofa in the Hull House reception room, "when and as it suited him," as Edith Abbott, another resident, described it. She felt that he should no longer be allowed to come to the crowded, busy room; his presence was a nuisance. She was also frustrated by his recalcitrance, since she sat on the charity district committee for Cook County that had assigned him to the poorhouse.

At Abbott's urging, Jane Addams politely asked the old man to go to the Infirmary, as the poorhouse was called, but he refused again. "Miss Addams," he said firmly, "it is a poorhouse. It is not a place for higher life." Addams, unwilling to evict him, let him remain, his dignity intact. He "continued to sit in our reception room," Abbott recalled, "as long as he was able to get there."[30] One senses in Abbott's telling of the story that, at the time, she did not have the patience required to practice such respect, and that she knew it. She told the story many years later—an indication that she did not forget the lesson provided by Addams's example.

Through such experiences among the neighbors of Hull House, Addams and the other residents learned, as she had hoped, "from life itself," that "the things that make us alike are stronger and finer than the things that make us different. Human nature is essentially the same in a Chicago tenement or a Kansas farm."[31] Before moving to Hull House, Addams had imagined this was true. Now she knew it.

IV. THE HUMANITY OF THE WEALTHY

Jane Addams's views toward the wealthy were the same as her views toward the poor. The amount of money they controlled did not cause her to respect them more or less. Thus, although she regularly and effectively raised money for Hull House from her wealthy friends, she did not view them as being defined by their wealth. Emily Balch, a settlement and peace activist colleague of Addams, recalled that while Addams, "like the rest of us, liked some people and did not like others," she "never judged anyone as a member of any class or the bearer of any sort of label." Balch tells of "a wealthy woman [who was] very lonely because her family and old friends disliked her 'radical' interests while her labor friends seemed chiefly concerned with the money she could contribute. [She] told a friend, with tears in her eyes, that 'Miss Addams is interested in rich people too.'"[32]

As a wealthy person herself, Jane Addams was not intimidated by the wealth of others. This no doubt made it far easier for her to see them simply "as human beings." More remarkable was her ability to sympathize with them in their failings. She might have condemned them for lacking the fellow-feeling she believed in and practiced daily but there is no trace of anger in her writings regarding the wealthy as a class, only perplexity at their motives and sadness at their inability to break free.

One wealthy person she particularly studied was George Pullman, the millionaire owner of Pullman Car Company. He was one of the wealthiest men in Chicago, and, in his treatment of his striking workers, one of the cruelest. Deeply troubled by his actions, Addams pondered the reasons for his behavior in the months following the massive Pullman Strike. She decided that, while he had worked hard to be a generous benefactor to individuals in need, in her opinion, he gradually had lost "the power of attaining a simple human relationship with his employees," having forgotten "the common stock of experience which he held with his men."[33] "Successful struggle can often end," she wrote in another context, " . . . in a certain hardness of heart."[34]

Pullman shared with many other wealthy people a strong individualism and sense of being different. The rich, Addams knew from personal experience, tended not to have much group feeling. Indeed they had little ability to sympathize with people of their own class, let alone with those outside it. In one of her most remarkable essays, the "Introduction" to her first book, ***Democracy and Social Ethics,*** she pondered the reasons behind the short horizons of her well-read and well-traveled class.

People are not selfish, she decided, because they choose to be. Rather they are content to be ignorant. "We do not blame selfish people for [having] the will which chooses to be selfish," she wrote, "but for [having] the narrowness of interest which deliberately selects its experience within a limited sphere."[35] This has unfortunate consequences. Their judgments about society are impaired and their interest in broader society nil, except to the extent their own self-interest is at stake.

The solution was for people to mix "on the thronged and common road" of life, "where all must . . . at least see the size of another's burdens."[36] A broader set of experiences, she argued, would result in a "social perspective" and "sanity of judgment" that would be "the surest corrective of opinions concerning the social order and . . . efforts . . . for its improvement."[37] This would not only help them become more effective philanthropists; it would also bring meaning to their lives. Towards the end of this insightful essay, she put the challenge to her reader. "We are under a moral obligation," she wrote, "in choosing our experiences, since the result of those experiences must ultimately determine our understanding of life."[38]

Years earlier, during her second year at Hull House, she had put the same challenge even more directly to the women of her class who formed the membership of the Chicago Woman's Club. She told them in a talk, "We need the thrust in the side, the lateral pressure which comes from living next door to poverty."[39] She then reviewed the collective ground of their shared class lives, reminding them that "cultivation is self-destructive when shut away from human interests." With youthful brutal frankness, she noted that the "misdirected young life [of an upper-class young woman] seems to me as pitiful as the other great mass of destitute lives. . . . It is hard to tell which is most barren."[40] One wonders if a few of her audience did not squirm in their seats. This was perhaps not her most successful recruitment speech for Hull House. She was to learn soon enough how to couch her message in less stark terms.

By such speeches but primarily through personal contacts, she drew the wealthy and middle classes to Hull House. While some had had previous experience doing charity work with the poor, for others, as Kathleen McCarthy has noted, "the pungent sights and sounds of the West Side tenements were more foreign than the Egyptian bazaars and Parisian cafés which they visited with increasing regularity."[41] The lack of contact between the rich and poor so typical of the 1880s was a relatively new phenomenon. Before the Civil War, the rich had visited the poor with charity baskets and moral advice.[42] The settlement house movement, radical in its claim that social relations between rich and poor were a good thing, was, in its attempt to put the rich and poor back in touch with each other, a modern version of this older practice.

Beginning even before Hull House opened its doors, Addams had remarkable success in interesting and involving both the rich and the upper middle classes in the settlement and its neighborhood. An early friend was the architect Allen B. Pond, who helped her find the building that became Hull House and who was quick to embrace her philosophy that the rich could benefit from knowing the poor. In a church newsletter, Pond sought to spread the word: "Each of the lowest gets out of life, misery notwithstanding, something which he of the 'upper classes' has failed to discover," he wrote in 1890.[43] Pond, with his brother Irving, designed all of Hull House's buildings, while also serving as a trustee and secretary of Hull House Association from the board's founding in 1895 until his death in 1929. According to his brother, Allen's friendship with Addams "greatly influenced the trend of [his] future activity outside his profession."[44] Allen Pond became a leading citizen of civic and social reform in Chicago, with a particular interest in low-income housing and municipal reform.

Another early wealthy friend of Hull House was William Kent, whom Jane Addams had first met in 1890, when he was a young man. A Yale graduate from a wealthy family, Mr. Kent had inherited from his father a block of tenement houses located across the street from Hull House that were as run down and neglected as any in the district. In a speech that was reported in the press, a Hull House resident took him to task for his heartlessness, with the happy result that he stopped by Hull House to defend himself and found himself, after talking with Jane Addams, turning over the tenements to Hull House to manage. That experiment failed, but, when the buildings were torn down and replaced with a new neighborhood playground, Mr. Kent and Hull House were equally pleased with the fruits of his philanthropy.[45]

Years later, however, what Kent most remembered and sought to record was what he had learned from Jane Addams about the poor. "The great difference in our points of view," he wrote, "was that Miss Addams had discovered and keenly realized that these people [his tenants] were human beings and filled in varying degrees with the same virtues and vices as other people. . . . She had learned that dirt was not . . . an article of faith [with the poor] but a by-product of poverty."[46] Kent became a volunteer at and a donor to Hull House, and served on the board of trustees. He applied the education he gained there in his subsequent careers as a Chicago politician and senator from California.

Among the wealthiest of Hull House's close friends was Louise deKoven Bowen. Daughter of a leading Chicago family and wife of a well-known businessman, Bowen was both rich and socially prominent. Serious-minded, she had been interested in charity work and helping the poor as a young mother, before she came to Hull House in 1896. Yet what she learned there was eye-opening: "My whole acquaintance with Hull House opened for me a new door into life. . . . I have made many good friends among working people and have come in contact with problems and situations about which I would have otherwise known nothing."[47]

Like Pond and Kent, Bowen was struck by the realization of the humanity she shared with the poor. "It was most interesting to realize," she recalled, "that although the people I met at Hull House lived a life far removed from the kind I led, yet, after all, we are all cast in the same mold, all with the same emotions, the same feelings, the same sense of right and wrong, but, alas, not with the same opportunities."[48]

Bowen came to believe firmly in the value of the settlement house's work, especially in its function as a bridge between the classes. "I began to feel that what was [most] needed . . . was an acquaintance between the well-to-do and those less well off. Until [this can happen], there will always be difficulties and there will never be that sympathy which should exist."[49] She was president of the Hull House Woman's Club for many years and a founder of the Juvenile Protection Association, which worked with the courts to address the special needs of youth defendants. She poured her wealth generously into Hull House, primarily to support her particular interests in boys and the Hull House Woman's Club. She financed two Hull House buildings, one for each group, and every year helped Jane Addams bail Hull House out of its annual debt. Like Pond's, her commitment to Hull House was whole-hearted and long-term. She joined the Hull House Association board in 1903 and served until 1944.[50] In her life, her understanding of the poor, and her philanthropy, Bowen pursued the pathway that was Addams's vision. Bowen did not allow her wealth to prevent her from following Jane Addams's admonishment to "hook yourself fast with your whole mind to [the] neighborhood."[51]

Addams's wealthy friends were enthusiastic capitalists. Their experience at Hull House did not change this, but, motivated by their growing realization that the poor were victims of a harsh environment, several of them found themselves viewing corporations' treatment of their employees in a new light. Indeed, in cases where they themselves owned stock in a company that was mistreating its employees, they began to feel partially responsible for the grievances of which they were now learning. Bowen, who learned of the dangerous working conditions at the Pullman Company from Hull House resident Alice Hamilton in 1911, felt compelled as a major stockholder to write the company's president and ask him to review the situation and meet with her to discuss solutions. Eventually she succeeded in prompting the company to make the needed improvements. She undertook a similar effort with International Harvester, persuading that company to cease employing women all night and to provide women with a living minimum wage.[52]

The principle that the corporations had an ethical responsibility to treat their employees well was also applied in reverse. Like other social reformers of the day, Jane Addams and her Hull House friends believed that a corporation that treated its employees badly should not be permitted to assuage its conscience by making gifts to Hull House to benefit those same employees. This was the concept of "tainted money."

When such a situation arose, it provided a Hull House trustee, major donor and businessman William Colvin, with an education. He had found a factory owner who was willing to give $20,000 to support the construction of a new building on Hull House land for the Jane Club, a cooperative housing club for working girls. But when Mr. Colvin brought back the news of the gift and revealed to the residents the name of the donor, he was soon informed of the man's cruel employment practices. He came to see that, as Jane Addams described it, "it would be impossible to erect a clubhouse for working girls with such money." Persuaded of this new way of looking at things, Mr. Colvin, with some embarrassment, had to tell the factory owner that he must now refuse the gift he had just solicited from him.[53]

The lesson Colvin learned was not unanticipated. Addams often warned people not to be alarmed if they found their ethical standards broadening as they became acquainted with the real facts of the lives of their neighbors.[54] This, too, was part of what Hull House was all about.

V. THE BENEFITS TO THE PHILANTHROPIST

Most of Hull House's major donors were active volunteers in one or more Hull House activities; as a result, their volunteer work shaped, informed, and fueled their philanthropy. Not surprisingly, their monetary gifts to Hull House reflected the wisdom they had gained: the typical Hull House project was designed as much as possible to address the root causes of problems, rather than treat short-term symptoms.[55]

Addams viewed this grounding in reality as essential to effective philanthropy. She wrote, "A man who takes the betterment of humanity for his aim and end must also take the daily experiences of humanity for the constant correction of his process. He must . . . test and guide his achievement by human experience."[56]

By such knowledge the donor could avoid the twin pitfalls of "indiscriminate giving," on the one hand, and "the stern policy of withholding" on the other. The first occurs, she wrote, when the donor, viewing matters from a distance, is filled with mercy; giving motivated solely by kindness "has disastrous results." The second comes from a single-minded commitment to justice, again when the donor is viewing matters from a distance, and produces in the donor a "dreary lack of sympathy and an understanding that the establishment of justice is impossible." Recalling the biblical injunction to love mercy and to do justly, she concluded, "It may be that the combination of the two can never be attained save as we fulfill the third requirement—'to walk humbly with God,'" which to her meant "to walk for many dreary miles . . . in the company of the humble."

As a long-time resident of Hull House, she did not romanticize the experience. She knew it would offer not "peace of mind" but "the pangs and throes to which the poor human understanding is subjected whenever it attempts to comprehend the meaning of life."[57] Part of the pain came from the new self-knowledge philanthropists would gain—self-knowledge that was vital to their effectiveness.

Addams believed that they could only succeed if they could recognize in themselves the humanity they saw in the poor. The philanthropist, she wrote, "must succeed or fail in proportion as he has incorporated that experience [of humanity] with his own [human experience]." If he does not, conceit and arrogance follow. "His own achievements," she wrote, "become his stumbling block, and he comes to believe in his own goodness as something outside himself. He makes an exception of himself, and thinks that he is different from the rank and file of his fellows."[58]

Jane Addams often spoke of the transformational power of the first-hand knowledge of the lives of the poor that her friends were gaining. Ever the philosopher, she liked to describe the process abstractly. "We are under a moral obligation in choosing our experiences, since the results of those experiences must ultimately determine our understanding of life." But the advantages went beyond understanding; they included redemption, both for the individual and society. "The subjective necessity for social settlements," she wrote, "is identical with that necessity which urges us toward social and individual salvation."[59]

Although she inherited wealth, Jane Addams did not, after some struggle, permit her wealth to dominate her life. She chose instead to travel the "thronged and common" road that she came to believe every person should travel, where people could "see each other's burdens" and discover what they shared as human beings.[60]

She believed that the individual who sought such experience would benefit and so would society. Like many before and after her, from Plato to Robert Bellah, Addams held that there was an intimate relationship between the moral character of a people and the nature of its political and social community. The exploration of the meaning of life was, among other things, a civic responsibility.

In her view, to undertake such an exploration, not to dispense their wealth properly, was the important task facing the rich, or, indeed, any human being. The responsibilities of the wealthy were the responsibilities of the poor: to be active, involved members of the human community. She did not discount the power of money but she knew its limits, having explored them as a young woman. "We forget," she wrote, "that capital cannot enter the moral realm."[61] Like Ruskin, she held that "there is no wealth but life," that life is the most important wealth that humanity has to share.[62]

Today's philanthropists have much to gain from considering Addams's views on the "responsibilities of being human." Too often we of the wealthy and the middle classes have no contact with the people whom we support with our philanthropy, preferring simply to send our checks across town. Or, if we volunteer, it is only to raise money from others of our class, not to participate in the programs that serve the working poor, the unemployed, and the dropouts. Ignorant of how hard the poor work and the extent to which their lives are shaped by forces beyond their control, we too quickly condemn them for their lack of work ethic and self-discipline and for their failure to climb out of poverty.

Disrespecting and distrustful of the poor, we design our philanthropy accordingly. The policies of the states and the federal government toward the poor, those policies representing a major arm of modern philanthropy, reflect our biases. Exhortation, social science research, and dramatic news stories have made little dent in the class assumptions of the voters. True welfare reform remains politically out of reach.

Cross-class social relations may be part of the answer. Although the idea sounds Victorian, it needn't. One is cheered to note that Morton M. Kondrake of *The New Republic* recently suggested it. He wrote, "If there is ever to be a consensus again [in the United States] behind efforts to help the poor, it will have to come—or at least is most likely to come—from sustained human contact between middle-class voters (and rich people too) and individual poor."[63]

Today cross-class relations are as elusive as ever. Most of us in the middle and upper classes live and work in what Robert N. Bellah and his colleagues have termed "life style enclaves." Like Addams, we are isolated in our class. Still, like her, we can escape through our volunteer work.[64] We can follow our gifts of money across town, to the charities of our choice. For the sake of both the country and ourselves, more of us need to travel the "thronged and common road."

NOTES

[1] Jane Addams, *Twenty Years at Hull House with Autobiographical Notes* (New York: Macmillan Company, 1910), p. 123.

[2] Jane Addams, "A Book That Changed My Life," *Christian Century* 44 (October 13, 1927), p. 1196.

[3] Benjamin Disraeli, *Sybil, or Two Nations* (New York: Thomas Nelson and Sons, 1940), p. 85.

[4] Jane Addams, "A Function of the Social Settlement," *Annals of the American Academy* 13 (May 1899): 33.

[5] Addams, *Twenty Years,* p. 73.

[6] Ibid., p. 17.

[7] George Eliot, *Adam Bede* (New York: Viking Penguin, 1986), p. 229. In her unpublished speech, "Outgrowths of Toynbee Hall," delivered in December 1890, Addams acknowledges Eliot as a passionate advocate for humanity (p. 8). Jane Addams Peach Collection, Swarthmore College.

[8] Ralph Waldo Emerson, "Man the Reformer," in *America's Voluntary Spirit, A Book of Readings,* ed. Brian O'Connell (New York: The Foundation Center, 1983), p. 51.

[9] Addams, *Twenty Years,* p. 77.

[10] Jane Addams, "Outgrowths of Toynbee Hall," p. 8. Jane Addams's religious motivations were initially and remained far more central to her work than has been generally recognized. But that is a topic for another essay.

[11] Addams, *Twenty Years,* p. 117.

[12] Addams, "Outgrowths," p. 4.

[13] Addams, *Twenty Years,* p. 85.

[14] Ibid., p. 88.

[15] Addams, "Outgrowths," p. 13.

[16] Ellen Starr to Mary Blaisdell, February 23, 1889, Star Papers. Sophia Smith Collection. Smith College, Northampton, Mass.

[17] Jane Addams, "The Subjective Necessity for Social Settlements," *Philanthropy and Social Progress,* ed. Henry C. Addams (New York: Thomas Y. Crowell & Co., 1893), p. 1.

[18] Jane Addams, "Hull House as a Type of College Settlement," *Proceedings, Wisconsin State Conference of Charities and Corrections* (1894), p. 97.

[19] Several of her colleagues in the settlement house movement recalled observing her listening to her neighbors throughout the 1890s. When Graham Taylor, who founded the Chicago Commons Settlement, first began visiting Hull House in 1893, he wrote (Graham Taylor, "Jane Addams: The Great Neighbor," *Survey Graphic* 24 [July 1935]) that he "almost always found her listening" to one or more of her neighbors (p. 338). Mary Simkovitch, who founded the Greenwich House Settlement in New York City, described (Mary Simkovitch, *Memorial Service for Jane Addams* [National Conference of Social Work Memorial Service: June 1935]) her as "always in that listening attitude of mind of 'what is it?'" (p. 6).

[20] Addams, *Twenty Years,* p. 168.

[21] Jane Addams, "Ethical Survivals in Municipal Corruption," *International Journal of Ethics* VIII (April 1898), p. 284.

[22] Addams, *Twenty Years,* p. 198.

[23] Addams, "Outgrowths," p. 11.

[24] Jane Addams, "The Settlement," *Proceedings of the Illinois Conference of Charities* (1896), p. 57.

[25] Addams, "A Function," p. 32.

[26] Lillian Wald, paraphrasing Jane Addams in "Afterword" to *Forty Years at Hull House* by Jane Addams (New York: The Macmillan Company, 1935), p. 432.

[27] Alice Hamilton, *Exploring the Dangerous Trades* (1943; repr., Boston: Northeastern University Press, 1985), p. 59.

[28] Louise deKoven Bowen, *Growing Up with a City* (New York: Macmillan Company, 1926), p. 87.

[29] Jane Addams, *Democracy and Social Ethics* (New York: Macmillan, 1902), p. 154.

[30] Edith Abbott, "Hull House Years," a chapter in an unpublished biography of Grace Abbott by Edith Abbott. Grace and Edith Abbott Papers, p. 29; Special Collections, Regenstein Library. University of Chicago.

[31] Addams, "The Settlement," p. 58.

[32] Emily Greene Balch, *Beyond Nationalism: The Social Thought of Emily Greene Balch,* ed. Mercedes M. Randall (New York: Twayne Publishers, 1972), p. 206.

[33] Jane Addams, "A Modern Lear," in *The Social Thought of Jane Addams,* ed. Christopher Lasch (New York: The Bobbs-Merrill Company, 1965), p. 112.

[34] Jane Addams, "Municipal Administration," *The American Journal of Sociology* X (January 1905), p. 444.

[35] Addams, *Democracy,* p. 10.

[36] Ibid., p. 6

[37] Ibid., p. 7.

[38] Ibid., p. 9.

[39] Addams, "Outgrowths," p. 3.

[40] Ibid., p. 6.

[41] Kathleen D. McCarthy, *Noblesse Oblige: Charity and Cultural Philanthropy in Chicago, 1849-1929* (Chicago: The University of Chicago Press, 1982), p. 31.

[42] Ibid., p. 18.

[43] Scrapbook I, p. 5. Jane Addams Memorial Collection. University of Illinois at Chicago Library. University of Illinois at Chicago.

[44] Irving Pond, chapter 7, ms. autobiography, p. E-17. The Irving Pond papers. Archives, American Academy of Arts and Sciences, New York.

[45] Addams, *Twenty Years,* pp. 289-291.

[46] William Kent, "Jane Addams," pp. 13-14. The William Kent Family Papers. Yale University Library, Yale University.

[47] Bowen, *City,* p. 92.

[48] Ibid., p. 94.

[49] Ibid., p. 93.

[50] *Notable American Women, The Modern Period,* s.v. "Louise deKoven Bowen."

[51] Addams, "Hull House as a Type of College Settlement," p. 97.

[52] Bowen, *City,* pp. 165-166; Louise deKoven Bowen, *Speeches, Addresses and Letters of Louise deKoven Bowen, Reflecting Social Movement in Chicago* (Ann Arbor, Mich.: Edwards Brothers, Inc., 1937) ed. Mary E. Humphrey, I, p. 168.

[53] Addams, *Twenty Years,* p. 138.

[54] H. F. Hegner, "Scientific Value of the Social Settlements," *American Journal of Sociology* III (September 1897), p. 176.

[55] Addams, *Democracy,* p. 9.

[56] Ibid., p. 176.

[57] Ibid., p. 70.

[58] Ibid.

[59] Addams, "Subjective Necessity," p. 26.

[60] Ibid., p. 6.

[61] Jane Addams, *The Excellent Becomes the Permanent* (New York: Macmillan, 1932), p. 45.

[62] John Ruskin, *Unto This Last* (New York: Crowell & Co., 1872), p. 125.

[63] Morton M. Kondrake, "Just Say Yes," *The New Republic* 200 (April 24, 1989), p. 12.

[64] Robert N. Bellah; Richard Madsen; William M. Sullivan; Ann Swidler; and Steven M. Tipton, *Habits of the Heart: Individualism and Commitment in American Life* (New York: Harper & Row, 1985), p. 75.

Linda Schott (essay date 1993)

SOURCE: "Jane Addams and William James on Alternatives to War," in *Journal of the History of Ideas,* Vol. 54, No. 2, April, 1993, pp. 241-54.

[*In the following essay, Schott contrasts the pacifism of William James with the much more radical anti-war views of Addams.*]

On the evening of 7 October 1904, some 500 members of the Universal Peace Congress attended a banquet in Boston. An evening of good food and conversation culminated in talks by nationally prominent peace advocates. The speakers that night included, among others, two individuals who had figured prominently in the anti-imperialism movement after the Spanish-American War: the well-respected and widely-known philosopher from Harvard University, William James, and one of the most prominent women in the United States and founder of the Hull House social settlement in Chicago, Jane Addams. Their talks differed in specifics but shared a common purpose. Both tried to articulate an alternative to the psychological allure of war.[1]

Doing so seemed particularly necessary, for the United States had recently begun to modify its traditional isolation from foreign affairs. In the last decades of the nineteenth century the United States had worked to consolidate its influence in Latin America and the Pacific, and it had acquired its first formal colonies as the result of victory over Spain in 1898. Furthermore, these developments were approved and encouraged by the man who became president in 1900, Theodore Roosevelt. An advocate of foreign intervention and the use of military force, Roosevelt, as well as other like-minded contemporaries, worried that as the United States became industrialized and urbanized, its citizens were growing too accustomed to comfort, security, and leisure. To counteract this development, he advocated a renewed appreciation of militarism and violent conflict.[2]

Roosevelt's views did not, of course, stand unchallenged. Soon after the end of the Spanish-American War the peace movement in the United States grew tremendously, with forty-five new peace organizations appearing between the years 1901 and 1914. Most of these advocated international law, arbitration, and international trade agreements as means to maintain the peace between nations. Led usually by members of the economic elite, these new peace organizations brought unprecedented respectability and influence to the peace movement.[3]

To these peace activists and to many other Americans, war seemed anachronistic; surely nations in advanced stages of civilization would never resort to such a barbaric means of solving their disagreements. Yet these same activists had to admit that if war looked like the nadir of civilization from their perspective, from another perspective it looked like the apex: individual citizens stirred to acts of heroism and selflessness for the good of their fellow human beings or for an abstract principle. Would heroism and selflessness gradually fade away if war—its memory, its experience, and its prospect—became a relic of less civilized eras?

This was the question with which Addams and James struggled when they appeared before the Universal Peace Congress in 1904. That night was not the first time that Addams and James had expressed their thoughts on this topic, however, and it would not be the last. Both went on to refine their ideas and present them in more detail, Addams in 1907 in her book, ***Newer Ideals of Peace,*** and James in 1910 in his essay, "The Moral Equivalent of War."

James's essay quickly became famous and received much attention from his contemporaries as well as from historians. Furthermore, James's essay is often cited as the model for public works programs such as the Civilian Conservation Corps, the Peace Corps, and the Job Corps. Addams's book, on the other hand, although well-received by her contemporaries, has only occasionally received serious comment by historians and has been completely ignored as a model for public programs.[4] In spite of the similarity of their topics and the familiarity of the authors with each other's works, only rarely have historians compared the alternatives to war posed by Addams and James.[5]

It is the purpose of this article to make such a comparison and, further, to argue that nineteenth-century gender roles account for the differences in the alternatives Addams and James envisioned. Historians have often described gender roles in the nineteenth century as characterized by "separate spheres." According to the prescriptive literature of the time, women were to inhabit the private world of home and family while men worked in the public sphere of politics and business. Women were supposedly suited for their role by particular personality traits; they were thought to be passive, submissive, pious, and nurturing. Likewise, men were also supposed to have certain traits that suited them for their role; they were to be aggressive, rational, and dominant.

Historians have also rightfully questioned how widely accepted this ideology was, especially among poorer families in which the wife (and often the older children) as well as the husband worked outside the home, and who had less exposure to the literature and institutions propagating this ideology. Among the middle and upper classes, however, it is clear that this ideology was quite influential.[6] Since these are the classes to which Addams and James belonged, it should not be surprising that at least some of the tenets of this pervasive ideology made their way into the alternatives to war proposed by Addams and James.

William James, born in 1842, grew up on the east coast in a privileged family. He parents provided him with excellent educational opportunities and encouraged him to pursue diverse intellectual interests. Guided and occasionally pressured by his father, James studied first art, then science, and finally philosophy and psychology. His studies often took him to Europe where he sought out the leading scholars in his areas of interest. Such travel and contact with the best minds provided James with an excellent education; yet he was still discontent, unhappy, and often ill. He suffered periodically from what would most likely now be labeled depression but which was then most often diagnosed as neurasthenia—a common complaint of the upper class in the late nineteenth century. James's condition eventually improved, but only after he began a career he believed was meaningful, teaching physiology at Harvard in 1872.[7]

Jane Addams, born in 1860, also grew up in a privileged family, although not one located in the intellectually stimulating environment of the east coast, but rather in the midwest. Addams's family also provided her with a good education, although not what she desired. She wanted to attend Smith College in Massachusetts, but her father insisted that she stay closer to home. Thus she entered the Female Seminary in Rockford, Illinois. This school combined domestic and religious instruction with a good liberal arts education. Addams flourished at Rockford but after graduation entered a period of depression, illness, and lack of direction. Trying to overcome this state of inactivity, she traveled to Europe. It was on the second of two journeys there that Addams reputedly decided on her life's work, which was the opening of a social settlement house. With that decision in 1889, Addams found meaningful work and escaped the depression that had plagued her before.[8]

Addams and James, then, came from similar backgrounds and had similar experiences as they pursued their educations and careers. Furthermore, they associated professionally and read each other's books.[9] Thus it is not surprising that Addams and James shared similar philosophical perspectives; their ideas are particularly similar on issues of war and peace. Their mutual dislike of philosophical abstraction and their shared belief in the importance of cultural pluralism led them to oppose the imperialistic policies being pursued by the United States at the turn of the century, especially when those policies led to war.

Both James and Addams criticized the use of abstract terms and phrases and stressed the need for specificity. James, for example, made this point clearly in his critique of the German philosopher Hegel. In his essay "On Some Hegelisms" James criticized Hegel for being totalistic and abstract. He argued that this approach caused Hegel to lose contact with reality. Hegel posited a thesis and an antithesis that resulted in a higher synthesis, but James denied the validty of that position: in reality, "We cannot eat our cake and have it; that is, the only real contradiction there can be between thoughts is where one is true, the other false. When this happens, one must go forever; nor is there any 'higher synthesis' in which both can wholly revive."[10] For James a "true philosophy must clear itself from . . . smugness. It must keep in touch with the *character* of reality."[11]

Addams held a similar view. It was time to abandon "the eighteenth-century philosophy upon which so much of our present democratic theory and philanthropic activity depends," Addams wrote, and to substitute for it "the scientific method of research" that deals with "real people." She noted that the "eighteenth-century humanitarian" had insisted upon "the rights of man," but that he had "loved the people without really knowing them." It was up to her generation, she believed, "to dissolve 'humanity' into its component parts of men, women, and children and to serve their humblest needs with an enthusiasm which, so far from being dependent upon glamour, can be sustained only by daily knowledge and constant companionship."[12]

Addams believed that when one avoided abstraction, one was much more likely to notice and respect individuals; this was the philosophical root of her pluralism. Furthermore, living in the culturally diverse community surrounding Hull House had doubtlessly convinced Addams of the importance of respecting cultural differences. As she stated repeatedly, she believed that the immigrant community provided a model for all peoples: "Because of their difference in all external matters, in all of the nonessentials of life, the people in a cosmopolitan city are forced to found their community of interests upon the basic and essential likenesses of their common human nature."[13] Thus the immigrants Addams observed were able both to appreciate each others' differences and to see what each shared as well. That kind of tolerance and understanding, Addams believed, was vital to life in the twentieth century. Without it people were likely to stereotype others and to assume their inferiority. That action then led to the belief that the other group could not "be appealed to by reason and fair dealing" but must be dealt with violently, using "brute force" or the "methods of warfare."[14]

James's pluralism likewise emerged from his appreciation of individual differences and similarities. "Why may not the world be a sort of republican banquet . . . where all the qualities of being respect one another's personal sacredness, yet sit at the common table of space and time?" he asked.[15] James also emphasized that each person needed to learn to empathize with what he called "the vital secrets" of others. This was not always easy to do, as his own experience taught him. In his essay, "On a Certain Blindness in Human Beings," James related that while traveling through a rural area, he had been struck by the ugliness of the area's small farms, most of which had only recently been scraped from the hillsides. Of course the local farmers did not think their farms ugly; in fact, James realized, what he perceived as ugly was to the farmers a sign of progress, hard work, and perseverance.[16] Thus considering the farmers' point of view not only broadened James's own outlook but increased his respect and admiration for those farmers.

In addition to their shared dislike of abstraction and belief in the importance of pluralism, Addams and James were also strong opponents of United States imperialism, believing that it was a natural outgrowth of abstraction and lack of pluralism and that it was a violation of traditions that made the United States exceptional among nations. James, for example, indicted Theodore Roosevelt for his "imperialist abstractions" illustrated by phrases such as "the white man's burden" or "America's destiny." James believed that these abstractions prevented Roosevelt and his followers from empathizing with the Filipinos as fellow human beings who might want to govern themselves and also from seeking to understand the true motives of the United States.[17]

Addams, too, condemned American imperialism, noting that one never knew at exactly what cost one imposed one's culture upon another. Although most European states had imposed themselves upon parts of Africa and Asia, she thought that the United States should act differently. Addams wanted the United States to say "We will trust the people although they are of a different color, although they are of a different tradition from ours." She thought that by doing so, the United States might "nourish them into another type of government, not Anglo-Saxon even. Perhaps we shall be able to prove that some things that are not Anglo-Saxon are of great value, of great beauty."[18]

The dislike of philosophical abstraction, the belief in cultural pluralism, and the strong criticism of imperialism combined to commit Addams and James to abolishing war, completely if possible but, if not, at least as an instrument of policy for the United States. Necessary to the abolition of war was an understanding of why, when a nation declared war, its citizens participated willingly. Addams and James put much effort into answering that question, and both concluded that the people of a nation did not support war because of economic need or a sense of nationalism. Rather, they believed, ordinary people found war psychologically attractive: it appealed to a basic human desire for self-sacrifice and adventure.

Addams expressed this view in a preliminary form at the Universal Peace Congress in 1904. In her address to the Workingmen's Public Meeting on October 5, she stated that "the thing that is incumbent on this generation is to discover a moral substitute for war, something that will appeal to the courage, the capacity of men, something which will develop their finest powers without deteriorating their moral nature, as war constantly does."[19] In an address that same day to the Public Meeting of Women, Addams emphasized her belief that it was vital for nations, as well as individuals, to have a will for "self-surender" or "self-forgetting."[20] Finally, in yet another address two days later, Addams expressed her belief that people also seemed to have a "spirit of adventure."[21] These needs had often been fulfilled, for men at least, by going to war for some supposedly noble cause, but that route of fulfillment was not, in Addams's view, appropriate to a civilized society.

Addams did not believe that these needs had to go unfulfilled. Rather, she would tell the young man yearning for sacrifice and adventure "that adventure is not only to be found in going forth into new lands and shooting"; there were equivalent pleasures waiting in the modern city. These equivalent pleasures included "the nourishing of human life" and "the bringing of all the world into some kind of general order and decent relationship one with another." Addams believed that if she and her listeners could persuade their "fellow*men*" of the challenge of these alternative causes, then their "childish notions of power," their "*boyish* ideas of adventure," and their "veritable rabble conceptions of what pleasure and *manliness* and courage consist in, w[ould] fall away from them as the garments of a child are dropped off from his growing form."[22]

Thus Addams stressed that what she believed were basic human desires and needs—the desire for adventure and the need for selflessness—could be satisfied through efforts to nourish human life and relationships. Furthermore, Addams's choice of words foreshadowed the clear connection she would later draw between being male and being warlike; it was most important to persuade *men,* she believed, that actions other than war could fulfill these human desires and needs.

James also explained his views on the psychological attractiveness of war to the Universal Peace Congress, but his initial comments must have made the banquet's organizers wonder if they had selected the wrong speaker. James began by acknowledging what he called "the rooted bellicosity of human nature." This characteristic of human nature meant that "The plain truth is that people *want* war." War was "the final bouquet of life's fireworks"; war was "human nature at its uttermost"; war was "a sacrament." If war were ever abolished, James believed, "a deadly listlessness would come over most men's imagination of the future." "In such a stagnant summer afternoon of a world," he asked, "where would be the zest or interest?"[23]

Hearing these statements, it must have been hard for the members of the Universal Peace Congress to believe James was an opponent of war; he sounded rather like a more eloquent version of Teddy Roosevelt. As James continued his talk, however, his listeners no doubt breathed a sigh of relief as it became clear that it was not war he was favoring after all, only the opportunities provided by war for self-sacrifice and adventure. Because James believed most people did not realize that they sought these goals and not war itself, he thought it impractical to work for the abolition of war—what he called a "radical cure." In fact one should "Let the general possibility of war be left open . . . for the imagination to dally with. Let the *soldiers* dream of *killing,* as the old *maids* dream of *marrying.*" What could be done at this point was to try to develop some kind of "preventive medicine," some way to "cheat" men's desire for war by giving them other opportunities for self-sacrifice and adventure. What this alternative would be James was not yet sure. All he could offer at this point were general suggestions: electing "peace men" to office, educating national leaders about peace, increasing the emphasis on arbitration of international differences, and fostering "rival excitements" and "new outlets for heroic energy."[24]

This last suggestion was at least new, but he gave no details about how it could be accomplished. That would come in his 1910 essay.

James's comments thus showed that he agreed with Addams's belief in the importance of selflessness and adventure, but his comments also showed that his ideas differed from Addams's in crucial ways. First, James's choice of words implies that the yearning for adventure and self-sacrifice that he had previously seemed to say was a human characteristic, was really a male one. He wanted the possibility of war to remain an option, but for men only: "let the soldiers dream of killing." Women's desire for adventure and self-sacrifice, he implied, was best fulfilled by the "dream of marrying." Thus while Addams was envisioning men participating in the traditional work of women—nurturing human life and relationships—James envisioned men and women staying securely in traditional roles.

Second, James's comments that night also illustrated that there were some differences between his and Addams's views on human nature. Although both thought that humans sought self-sacrifice and adventure, James further argued that bellicosity was part of human nature; it was destructive for it to result in war, but it would need some kind of outlet, some "equivalent" of war. Addams, on the other hand, saw bellicosity not as a fundamental part of human nature but as just one method humans had used to satisfy their desire for self-sacrifice and adventure. Thus Addams sought a peaceful rather than a bellicose method, a "substitute," for satisfying those human desires.

The differences between Addams and James became even clearer by the time they published their ideas: Addams in ***Newer Ideals of Peace*** (1907) and James in "The Moral Equivalent of War" (1910). In her book Addams analyzed war as a limiting experience that was inappropriate to modern life; in his essay James saw war as an ennobling and unifying experience that, in its modern form, had unfortunately become too destructive of human and material resources. Furthermore, Addams envisioned, as an alternative to war, a moral community in which people of all types and classes worked together for the common good; James proposed conscripting young men for public works projects.

In ***Newer Ideals of Peace*** Addams explained her substitute for war more completely than she had done previously but did not change its essence. Once again Addams criticized war as inappropriate to modern life. Defenders of war, she wrote, argued that it "stirs the nobler blood and the higher imagination of the nation and thus frees it from moral stagnation and the bonds of commercialism." To Addams, however, to take that position was "to borrow our virtues from a former age and to fail to utilize our own."[25] She admitted that in the past warfare had "done much to bring men together" and to open the "channels of sympathy through which we partake of the life about us."[26] In the modern world, however, war would not have this effect, she believed, because the military tended to make men too passive, too willing to be ordered and disciplined. By emphasizing these qualities instead of nurturance and empathy, the military confessed its "totally inadequate conception of the value and power of human life."[27]

Addams believed that the "channels of sympathy" to others could be better stimulated through what she called "the substitution of nurture for warfare."[28] Addams herself sometimes had trouble explaining exactly what she meant by this phrase,[29] but what she meant essentially was that instead of competing against others for resources, people should cooperate to increase resources and improve living and working conditions for all. Addams believed that this new ideal was growing most rapidly in the modern city. There, Addams wrote, "Men of all nations are determining upon the abolition of degrading poverty, disease, and intellectual weakness with their resulting industrial inefficiency, and are making a determined effort to conserve even the feeblest citizen to the State."[30]

The modern city exhibited this development best, Addams believed, because it was there that people from all nations lived and worked in close proximity; and it was these people who were leading the way to a peaceful world. As Addams put it, "It is possible that we will be saved from warfare by the 'fighting rabble' itself, by the 'quarrelsome mob' turned into kindly citizens of the world through the pressure of a cosmopolitan neighborhood." These immigrants had discovered that ethnic differences meant little in the face of common challenges; so Addams hoped all people might acknowledge their common humanity, help each other, and "give up war, because we shall find it as difficult to make war upon a nation at the other side of the globe as upon our next-door neighbor."[31] Furthermore, these residents of the inner city were members of the working class, and as such, Addams believed they understood the importance of producing instead of destroying, of nurturing each other instead of competing.[32]

The other group that Addams believed clearly understood the importance of production and nurturing was women—women of all classes and countries. For centuries, Addams wrote, women had taken care of children, the elderly, and the infirm; had prepared their food and clothing; and had maintained their shelter. In a rural, agrarian society, women had performed these tasks relatively independently, seeking assistance only for the most onerous jobs; but in the modern city it was impossible for them to fulfill these tasks alone. As soon as a mother's children stepped outside the house or apartment, they entered a world governed by the standards of cleanliness and safety of other people. As soon as a woman purchased processed foods, she lost control over the quality of ingredients and workmanship. Men, Addams believed, were "carelessly indifferent" to these issues, "as they have always been indifferent to the details of the household." The logical solution was to allow women a role in public affairs.[33]

But how would this contribute to a peaceful world? Addams, influenced by the ideology of "separate spheres," believed that just as women's traditional work had been to nurture, men's traditional work had been to compete, whether for individual or national gain. She did not believe, however, that this was a good system; rather, it was one that glorified war and minimized women's accomplishments. Thus she wanted to integrate women, whom she believed understood the importance of nurturing others, into a public world that she believed was currently dominated by the competition of men.

Furthermore, Addams knew that women had already begun to figure in the public world in crucial ways. They had become increasingly organized and active in the late nineteenth century, often arguing, as did Addams, that women's "maternal" values were needed in the public realm as well as within the home. Whether in women's clubs or the temperance movement, in universities or settlement houses, in the suffrage movement or in labor organizations, women had become visible and powerful to an unprecedented extent.[34] In Addams's view, then, women performed important, challenging work; and now was the time for everyone to acknowledge its importance to the public sphere and to realize that it need not be just women's work.[35] Thus Addams believed that people's desire for adventure and self-sacrifice could be fulfilled through an active, dynamic caring for others; and to move society in that direction she looked not to the traditional leaders of society—white, generally wealthy men—but to the poor immigrant workers of the inner city and to women. Both in this respect and in the specifics of her proposed alternative to war Addams differed pointedly from James.

James's complete proposal for a "moral equivalent" of war came in an essay in 1910, a proposal that was both briefer and more specific than Addams's.[36] James set out to develop the ideas suggested at the end of his 1904 address to the Universal Peace Congress, that it was possible to provide an alternative to war by fostering "rival excitements" and "new outlets for heroic energy." His specific proposal would not come until the end of his essay, however; at the beginning he focussed on trying to bridge the gap that he saw between the "peace-party" and the "war-party." James suggested that it was so hard to get these two groups to understand each other because there were "certain deficiencies in the program of pacifism which set the militarist imagination strongly, and to a certain extent justifiably, against it." He then tried to explain the views of the war party before proffering his own plan.[37] His explanation deserves analysis, for it betrays some of the assumptions that made his final proposal much less inclusive than Addams's.

First, James assumed that women should not participate in the public sphere. This is clearly evident in his explanation of the views of the so-called war party. He began this explanation by pointing out that people he considered "reflective apologists for war" defended war as "an absolute good," as "human nature at its highest dynamic." Unlike opponents of war, these individuals were not discouraged or horrified by the destruction of war; rather, James wrote, they saw it as "a cheap price to pay for rescue from the only alternative supposed, of a world of clerks and teachers, of co-education and zo-ophily, of 'consumer's leagues' and 'associated charities,' of industrialism unlimited, and feminism unabashed." This characterization of a world without war shows that James believed that the apologists for war were anti-women and anti-feminist. After all, women were beginning to take over teaching and clerking as professions and had worked for coeducation for decades; they were among the major supporters of animal protection, consumer's leagues and charities; and at least some were committed to the feminist demand for equality in all areas. James also made it clear that he was not just explaining the position of the apologists for war, he agreed with this position. If the trends toward a warless world (and a public role for women) continued, James believed the militarists would likely say, "Fie upon such a cattleyard of a planet!" It would not be just the militarists who felt this way, James added, for "So far as the central essence of this feeling goes, no healthy-minded person, it seems to me, can help partaking of it."[38]

James's second assumption was related to the first: he was convinced that the "martial virtues"—which he identified as "intrepedity, contempt of softness, surrender of private interest, obedience to command"—were "absolute and permanent human goods."[39] James believed that in a warless world where women played prominent roles, these virtues would gradually vanish. One reason humans had not freed themselves from the allure of war, he wrote, was that they were unwilling "to envisage a future in which army-life, with its many elements of charm, shall be forever impossible, and in which the destinies of peoples shall nevermore be decided quickly, thrillingly, and tragically, by force, but only gradually and insipidly by 'evolution.'" A second reason was an unwillingness "to see the supreme theater of human strenuousness closed, and the splendid military aptitudes of men doomed to keep always in a state of latency and never show themselves in action." War might indeed be horrible, but to talk of its horror would never convert people to pacifism because advocates of war did not deny the horror. Rather, they said that war was worth the horror; for "taking human nature as a whole, its wars are its best protection against its weaker and more cowardly self."[40]

Thus James made clear that his sympathies lay with the war party. To him, its members were more realistic and provided an alternative to a world softened by women's public participation. On the other hand he could not reconcile his sympathies with the war party with his philosophical reservations about war and imperialism. Thus he came, not altogether happily, to propose "a moral equivalent of war"—one that he hoped would preserve the psychological benefits of war while avoiding its material and human destruction.

Crucial to James's proposal as to that of Addams's was getting individuals to participate in some kind of collective effort, for James believed that such an experience endowed people with dignity and selflessness. He did not believe as Addams did, however, that voluntary service to the modern city could provide his moral equivalent: "The only sentiment which the image of pacific cosmopolitan industrialism is capable of arousing" he wrote, "is shame at the idea of belonging to *such* a collectivity."[41]

What then would constitute his moral equivalent of war? James suggested that the nation institute a period of mandatory national service for "the whole youthful population." This service would require that youths sacrifice part of their lives, probably two to three years, for the good of the nation. They would spend their time not warring against each other or the youth of other nations but against nature—building roads and bridges, mining coal, clearing forests. As they did so, "the military ideals of hardihood and discipline" would be inculcated in them; they would have "the childishness knocked out of them"; and they would return to society "with healthier sympathies and soberer ideas."[42]

Two important points emerge from a close examination of James's proposal. First, although he stated that his plan would apply to all youth, his comments make it clear that it is intended for young men only. Among the virtues bestowed on youth by his plan were that it would "make the women value them more highly" and make them "better fathers" of the following generation. He was presumably not interested in making young women into fathers nor in making them more valuable to other young women. Second, although he explicitly included young men from all economic classes, his plan was tailored to the needs of the affluent. It was they, not members of the working class, who had most likely lost contact with what James called "the permanently sour and hard foundations" of life and with hard physical labor.[43]

James's "moral equivalent," it appears, was designed to maintain a society dominated by wealthy men, a society in which women stayed in the private sphere and the poor went unnoticed. It stands in stark contrast to Addams's "moral substitute," which lauded the work of women and the poor and asked the traditional leaders of society to renounce competition, militarism, and war and experience the pleasure that came from nurturing others.

Thus it is apparent that Addams's and James's alternatives to war were circumscribed by both the assumed and actual gender differences of that period. As a wealthy white male, James benefitted, in ways that probably rarely if ever occurred to him, from a society that favored wealthy white men. To his credit, he tried to reach out and understand those who were not of his class and gender, but he was never completely successful. His failure was clearly evident in "The Moral Equivalent of War," written during the last year of his life.

Although Addams shared many of the privileges of the upper class with James she was a woman and as such knew what it was like to be outside the dominant group. She was able to use that experience to help herself develop a more inclusive vision of society. She also used her understanding of women's traditional role. Having grown up in a time and place that emphasized that women were responsible for nurturing others, she became convinced of the importance of that job. As she became more educated and experienced, she came to believe that women could and should do more than nurture others, yet she never lost the sense that nurturing others was important, valid work. Thus Addams developed a social vision in which traditional women's work and values were made priorities of all people. James, on the other hand, grew up with the belief that men should be strong, hardy, and intrepid. Little in his life substantially challenged these beliefs, thus they remained basic to his understanding of the world. In ways that neither he nor Addams completely realized, nineteenth century gender roles and definitions were fundamental to their philosophical systems and to the alternatives to war they posed.

NOTES

[1] *Official Report of the Thirteenth Universal Peace Congress* (Boston, 1904), 261-62; 267-68.

[2] T. J. Jackson Lears identified this strain of antimodernism in *No Place of Grace: Antimodernism and the Transformation of American Culture, 1880-1920* (New York, 1981), chapter 3.

[3] Charles DeBenedetti, *The Peace Reform in American History* (Bloomington, 1980), 79. For an overview of the peace movement in the United States in the late nineteenth and early twentieth centuries, see also Charles Chatfield, *For Peace and Justice: Pacifism in America, 1914-1941* (Knoxville, 1971); Charles DeBenedetti, *Origins of the Modern American Peace Movement, 1915-1929* (Millwood, N.Y., 1978); Sondra Herman, *Eleven Against War: Studies in American Internationalism, 1898-1921* (Stanford, 1969); C. Roland Marchand, *The American Peace Movement and Social Reform, 1898-1918* (Princeton, 1972); and David S. Patterson, *Toward a Warless World: The Travail of the American Peace Movement, 1887-1914* (Bloomington, 1976).

[4] Charles Moskos, *A Call to Civic Service: National Service for Country and Community* (New York, 1988), 9, notes that James is usually seen as the originator of the idea of national service but does not mention Addams's plan. John Whiteclay Chambers II, *The Eagle and the Dove: The American Peace Movement and United States Foreign Policy, 1900-1922* (2nd ed.; Syracuse, 1991), 14, also cites James's plan as the precursor of public works programs.

[5] Allen Davis does so in *American Heroine: The Life and Legend of Jane Addams* (New York, 1973), 143-47. See also Sondra Herman, *Eleven Against the War: Studies in*

American Internationalism, 1898-1921 (Stanford, 1969), 127.

[6] On the ideology and the reality of "separate spheres" for different economic classes and ethnic groups see Sara M. Evans, *Born for Liberty: A History of Women in America* (New York, 1989), especially ch. 4-6.

[7] On James's struggle to find meaningful work and its importance to him, see Howard Feinstein, *Becoming William James* (Ithaca, 1984), esp. 316-29.

[8] On Addams's struggle to find meaningful work as it resulted in her decision to found Hull House, see Allen Davis, *American Heroine,* especially Chapter 3. Addams was also sensitive to the importance of meaningful work for others. In *Newer Ideals of Peace* (New York, 1907), 147, she noted that the real problem with factory work was that "the intricate subdivision of factory work, and the lack of understanding on the part of employees of the finished product, has made an unnatural situation, in which the worker has no normal interest in his work and no direct relation to it."

[9] For example, Addams wrote in *Twenty Years at Hull House* (New York, 1910), 308, that James had given "hearty assent" to her idea of a moral substitute for war in 1904. James had also written to Addams to praise both *Democracy and Social Ethics* (1902) and *Newer Ideals of Peace* (1907). See James to Addams, 17 September 1902, in Frederick J. Down Scott (ed.), *William James: Unpublished Correspondence, 1885-1910* (Columbus, 1986), 293-94, and James to Addams, 12 February 1907, *ibid.,* 433-34.

[10] "On Some Hegelisms," in *The Will to Believe and Other Essays in Popular Philosophy* (New York, 1907), 293.

[11] *William James: Public Philosopher* (Baltimore, 1990), 139.

[12] *Newer Ideals,* 28-29. Mary Jo Deegan also noted Addams's dislike of abstraction in *Jane Addams and the Men of the Chicago School, 1892-1918* (New Brunswick, N.J., 1988), 33. Some contemporary feminist scholars also see women as more oriented toward the concrete and away from the abstract; for example, Sara Ruddick, *Maternal Thinking: Toward a Politics of Peace* (Boston, 1989), 95-96, and Carol Gilligan, *In a Different Voice: Psychological Theory and Women's Development* (Cambridge, 1982).

[13] *Newer Ideals,* 16.

[14] *Newer Ideals,* 150. On Addams's pluralism see Daniel Levine, *Jane Addams and the Liberal Tradition* (Madison, 1971) and Deegan. Although I do not agree with her analysis, Rivka Shpak Lissak, *Pluralism and Progressives: Hull House and the New Immigrants, 1890-1919* (Chicago, 1989), argues that Addams was actually an agent of social control who only unintentionally paved the way for a more pluralist view of society in the 1930s.

[15] "On Some Hegelisms," 270.

[16] "On a Certain Blindness in Human Beings" in *William James: The Essential Writings,* ed. Bruce Wilshire (New York, Publishers, 1971), 327-28.

[17] Cotkin, 139. James's writings show some inconsistency on this point, as in his address to the Universal Peace Congress, where he excused the wars of "civilized" nations against "uncivilized" ones as "pecadilos," not "absolute crimes against civilization" (*The Official Report of the Thirteenth Universal Peace Congress,* 268-69).

[18] *Official Report,* 121-22.

[19] *Official Report,* 145.

[20] *Official Report,* 122.

[21] *Official Report,* 261.

[22] *Official Report,* 261-62; emphasis mine.

[23] *Official Report,* 268.

[24] *Official Report,* 267-68; emphasis mine.

[25] *Newer Ideals,* 26-27.

[26] *Newer Ideals,* 213-14.

[27] *Newer Ideals,* 220.

[28] *Newer Ideals,* 26.

[29] *Newer Ideals,* 224 and 237.

[30] *Newer Ideals,* 236.

[31] *Newer Ideals,* 18-19. Such comments occur repeatedly throughout this work.

[32] Addams stated this view most forcefully in her address to the Workingmen's Public Meeting in 1904; see the *Official Report,* 146.

[33] *Newer Ideals,* 182-84.

[34] For a summary of women's activities in the late nineteenth century, see Evans, *"Maternal Commonwealth" in the Gilded Age, 1865-1890,* ch. 6.

[35] *Newer Ideals,* 206-7. For a more detailed explanation see my *Women Against War: Pacifism, Feminism, and Social Justice in the United States, 1914-1941* (Ph.D. diss., Stanford University, 1986). See also Ruddick, 80-81, Deegan, 229-30, on Addams's views as "cultural

feminism"; the chapter on Addams in Herman; and C. Roland Marchand, *The American Peace Movement and Social Reform, 1989-1918* (Princeton, 1972), ch. 7.

[36] James's essay was written as a pamphlet for the American Association for International Conciliation and later published as an article in *McClure's* and in *Popular Science Monthly.* See Davis, *American Heroine,* 140-47.

[37] James, "The Moral Equivalent of War," *William James: The Essential Writings,* 352.

[38] "Moral Equivalent," 353. Later in this essay, James again singles out feminism for criticism, commenting on in a book written by General Homer Lea, an American adventurer and soldier of fortune who shared Theodore Roosevelt's love of war and belief in the importance of martial virtues; see John P. Mallan, "Roosevelt, Brooks Adams, and [Homer] Lea: The Warrior Critique of Business Civilization," *American Quarterly,* 9 (1965), 216-30.

[39] "Moral Equivalent," 358, voicing a sentiment shared by many antimodernists. See T. J. Jackson Lears, *No Place of Grace,* ch. 3.

[40] "Moral Equivalent," 355-56.

[41] "Moral Equivalent," 357 (emphasis in the original), a clear, but unnamed reference to Addams's plan for a moral substitute for war. James had often expressed admiration for Addams, her writing, and her work, as in his letter to Addams after reading *Newer Ideals of Peace* (*Selected Unpublished Correspondence,* 433-34); his attitude had apparently changed by 1910.

[42] "Moral Equivalent," 359.

[43] *Ibid.,* I am indebted to Cotkin for this analytical point. Cotkin also notes (149-50) that James's plan ignored older men who presumably were already confirmed belligerents. Gerald Myers does not agree that James's plan is essentially elitist, but I find his analysis unconvincing. Myers (602) includes the interesting point that James encouraged his two eldest sons to work in the summer for the U.S. Forestry Service. See Myers, 602. Neither Cotkin nor Myers notes that women were completely excluded from James's plan. This exclusion is noted in Jane Martin, "Martial Virtues or Capital Vices? William James's Moral Equivalent of War Revisited," *Journal of Thought,* 22 (1987), 32-44.

Francesca Sawaya (essay date 1994)

SOURCE: "Domesticity, Cultivation, and Vocation in Jane Addams and Sarah Orne Jewett," in *Nineteenth-Century Literature,* Vol. 48, March, 1994, pp. 507-28.

[*In the following essay, Sawaya compares the nonfiction portrayal of a household in* Twenty Years at Hull-House *with a fictional one in the work of Sarah Orne Jewett.*]

In her preface to the 1893 edition of *Deephaven* Sarah Orne Jewett describes her call to vocation some twenty years earlier as having arisen out of her "dark fear that townspeople and country people would never understand one another."[1] She felt as a "younge writer" (p. 3) that "the individuality and quaint personal characteristics of rural New England" were being "swept away" (p. 5) by the rise of "fast-growing . . . cities" (p. 1), which had not only "drawn to themselves . . . much of the best life of the remotest villages," but which also in summer had sent to the country "the summer boarder" (p. 2) or tourist. "Grave wrong and misunderstanding" between rich "timid ladies" and laboring "country people" ensued. Jewett attempted to remedy this misunderstanding in her writing: "There is a noble saying of Plato that the best thing that can be done for the people of a state is to make them acquainted with one another" (p. 3). She tried to offer an "explanation" of the country to the city, in order to defuse the tension between the two, a tension so extreme that it threatened to divide the nation.

Three questions arise here about Jewett's formulation of her work. Why does she rewrite the classic pastoral division of city and country as that between tourist and laborer? Further, why does she see the tension between this tourist and laborer as a "misunderstanding," a kind of failed communication, rather than as a conflict of interest? And last, why does she imagine herself as a mediator between the two, introducing one to the other?

Jewett was not alone in envisioning a division between city and country in post-Civil War America. Nor was she alone in seeing this division as threatening. Historians have long argued that while the "agrarian myth"[2] continued to dominate political rhetoric after the 1870s, in reality the countryside was increasingly marginalized by and dependent upon the urban metropolis. Because statistically the countryside was being emptied of its population, the fact of its decline and the fears it created must be (and usually are) recognized in relation to Jewett's work. But while this shift in regional dominance is of central importance in her work, it provides necessary but not sufficient information for answering the above three questions.

To understand why Jewett describes the division between city and country the way she does, we must look at how her work involves itself in a larger progressive discourse about woman's labor at the turn of the century. Like many women of the progressive era, Jewett inherits from the nineteenth-century "cult of domesticity" the idea of separate spheres in which woman is figured as a single class who, through the home, would provide compensation for man for his alienated labor and would unite the fragmented and competitive masculine American society in an oasis from itself. But, at the same time, Jewett substantially modifies this idea about domesticity by combining it with new ideas about woman's role as a consumer of culture, an individual who has "leisure, culture, grace, social instincts, artistic ambitions," as Henry James described this new woman, or who experiences "vicarious leisure," as Thorstein Veblen said.[3] In Jewett's writings, woman's ability to reform and unite a divided nation through the home is backed by a newfound knowledge about the (supposedly) unifying power of art, of culture.

Criticism about Jewett has tended to ignore her relation to progressive politics and has seen her work as regional pastoralism or feminist realism—in either case divided from the nation or society at large in a hermetically sealed and pure universe. In particular, feminist criticism, which has done so much to revitalize the study of Jewett's work, has tended to rely on transhistorical notions of "woman" and "feminism" to read her work. Josephine Donovan, for example, claims that Jewett produced "an authentically female-identified vision," while more recently Margaret Roman argues that Jewett's successful women characters "exist independently of the Victorian society that attempts to enclose them."[4] While the individual insights feminist critics bring to Jewett's work are very useful, these transhistorical claims do a disservice both to Jewett's work, which they flatten, and to feminism more generally. Jewett's writings recount and reflect the politics of her day and of her situation—her racism, nativism, and class snobbery—and to argue for her transhistorical authenticity as a feminist is to ignore these issues in her work.

In this essay I will show how Jewett's notions about regional misunderstanding and her role as mediator are part of a progressive discourse about woman's labor. By reading Jewett's *The Country of the Pointed Firs* (1896) with Jane Addams's ***Twenty Years at Hull-House*** (1910), I hope to demonstrate that Jewett's regionalism and feminism are not separable from the politics of the day but rather interact with those politics, and more important, that woman's role in society—no matter how described—must be read in relation to the society against which it often defines itself or against which it has been defined.

What was it that led Jane Addams, a college-educated heiress from "the pastoral community"[5] of Cedarville, Illinois, to found Hull-House in the center of one of Chicago's slums? Further, what is it that Hull-House expressed to women of Addams's generation to cause thousands of them to flock to settlement homes throughout the country?[6] While Addams links the founding of Hull-House to her childhood experience with rural democracy and to her education at one of the first women's colleges, she describes the formative moment for her as occurring during a visit to Europe. In a continuation of her college education and in "preparation" (p. 60) for a nondomestic career for which she is filled with "enthusiasm" and "driving ambition" (p. 52), she travels to Europe "in search of culture" (p. 64). One day she is taken by "a city missionary" to London's East End with "a small party of tourists" so she can "witness the Saturday night sale of decaying vegetables and fruit" to the impoverished "masses" (p. 61). Because of the "moral revulsion" (p. 66) she experiences, Addams becomes afraid of wandering about London, "afraid to look down narrow streets and alleys lest they disclose again this hideous human need and suffering" (p. 62). She realizes that her desire for education, her search for culture, is indicted by the poverty she sees:

> For two years in the midst of my distress over the poverty which, thus suddenly driven into my consciousness, had become to me the "Weltschmerz," there was mingled a sense of futility, of misdirected energy, the belief that the pursuit of cultivation would not in the end bring either solace or relief. (p. 64)

However, Addams does not simply reject her education and cultivation in this formative moment. As it is through her "search [for] culture" that she discovers poverty, so it is only *through* culture that she can understand poverty. Her "painful" view of the "masses" leads her to remember De Quincey's "The Vision of Sudden Death," which in turn reveals to her that "we were . . . lumbering our minds with literature that only served to cloud the really vital situation spread before our eyes" (p. 63). So while her first response to the "unlovely" masses is to avoid seeing them, her second response is to look everywhere for them, to be "irresistably drawn to the poorer quarters of each city" (p. 62). She sees poverty through the lens of her cultivation and searches for it as feverishly as she did for culture.

These two contradictory responses toward poverty in this crucial moment of vocation, both centered around "culture," need to be explained, since they become integral to Addams's vocation and to the philosophy behind Hull-House. In her first response Addams finds the pursuit of cultivation futile; she rejects it as a "snare" (p. 60), especially for women. It is "American mothers and their daughters who cross the seas in search of culture" (p. 64), not American fathers and sons. While she had traveled to Europe because she believed that education would liberate women from their domestic lives, education now becomes to Addams that which prevents women's involvement in the world outside the home. And subsequently, Addams imagines a domestic role for women as the solution:

> I gradually reached a conviction that the first generation of college women had taken their learning too quickly, had departed too suddenly from the active, emotional life led by their grandmothers and great-grandmothers[,] that the contemporary education of young women had developed too exclusively the power of acquiring knowledge and of merely receiving impressions; that somewhere in the process of "being educated" they had lost that simple and almost automatic response to the human appeal, that old healthful reaction resulting in activity. . . . (p. 64)

In this first response to poverty, Addams associates the past with activity, with labor that is natural, almost instinctual ("simple and almost automatic response"). The present, by contrast, is associated with passivity, with an experience of reality so mediated that it has become unreal ("merely receiving impressions"). To remedy her alienation in the present she must return to the past; from culture, she must return to nature.

A central paradox of Hull-House, then, is that an intentionally reactionary rhetoric, inextricably tied to an imagined biological truth, is used in the service of a progressive political agenda.[7] The lady's useless and alienated leisure can only be remedied by a return to labor, because labor is instinctual. Thus, Addams argues, "young people" (p. 91), especially "young girls" (p. 93), "bear the brunt of being cultivated" and "have been shut off from the common labor by which they live which is a great source of moral and physical health" (p. 91). "There is something primordial," Addams says, in how these young people "long" to work, a longing that is biological:

> We all bear traces of the starvation struggle which for so long made up the life of the race. Our very organism holds memories and glimpses of that long life of our ancestors which still goes on among so many of our contemporaries. . . . (p. 92)

In order to express the "life of the race," however, labor needs to be preindustrial. Addams's plan for Hull-House follows this understanding of the bodily need for preindustrial labor:

> I gradually became convinced that it would be a good thing to rent a house in a part of the city where many primitive and actual needs are found, in which young women who had been given over too exclusively to study might restore a balance of activity *along traditional lines* and learn of life *from life itself*. . . . (p. 72; emphasis added)

Addams suggests not only that observing the "starvation struggle" returns one to life, but also that preindustrial, "traditional" labor does. By laboring in the house, women will discover their own nature; and we can thus understand the significance of Hull-*House*. The House is a "Settlement," an oasis of civilization in the middle of a territory not yet reached by civilization, but it is also a nostalgic escape from civilization, a return to the labor of one's grandmother. Food, child care, and facilitation of social events are the primary activities at Hull-House (though later less traditionally female activities became important), while the residents of the area are described as neighbors and friends.

Appropriately, Addams's Hull-House Labor Museum, which depicts preindustrial forms of labor, becomes a crucial means by which she can create relationships with her "neighbors," particularly her female neighbors. The idea for the Labor Museum arises out of a walk she takes where, "perturbed in spirit, because it seemed so difficult to come into genuine relations with the Italian women [in her neighborhood]," she decides to "devise some educational enterprise" that will provide "a dramatic representation of the inherited resources of . . . daily occupation" (p. 172). Addams specifically emphasizes her "yearning to recover for the household arts something of their early sanctity" (p. 175), to show "the charm of woman's primitive activities" (p. 176). Around this representation of older forms of labor women will unite, just as they do around and in Hull-House. Because of the natural instinct to labor and because of the universality of domesticity, the similarities between Addams and her female "neighbors" will outweigh their differences.

But if labor generally, and preindustrial domestic labor specifically, are to Addams the bodily inheritance of humanity and thus the great ameliorative force between classes and "races," the Labor Museum also reveals Addams's second response to poverty—a belief in the power of culture and of representations to unify disparate groups. In the moment when Addams formulates her desire to recover the sanctity of woman's "primitive activities" as a solution to poverty, her mind fills "with shifting *pictures* of woman's labor *with which travel* makes one familiar" (p. 175; emphasis added). That is, the very leisured and cultivated existence she has castigated and is resisting becomes her model for the active laboring life she praises and wants to live. By this I mean that not only do her leisured travel experiences create her view of the significance of labor, and not only does she see a museum as a form of communication between cultures, classes, and generations, but also that the traveler and the museum-goer are her models for understanding differences. Thus, Addams recounts how the Hull-House "Social Extension Committee" attempts, by giving a party, to bridge the "distinct social 'gulf'" between Irish-American and Italian neighbors. Afterward one of the members of the committee tells Addams "I am ashamed of the way I have always talked about 'dagoes.' They are quite like other people. . . ." Addams comments on this:

> To my mind at that moment the speaker had passed from the region of the uncultivated person into the possibilities of the cultivated person. The former is bounded by a narrow outlook on life, unable to overcome differences of dress and habit, and his interests are slowly contracting within a circumscribed area; while the latter constantly tends to be more a citizen of the world because of his growing understanding of all kinds of people with their varying experiences. We send our young people to Europe that they may lose their provincialism and be able to judge their fellows by a more universal test, as we send them to college that they may attain the cultural background and a larger outlook; all of these it is possible to acquire in other ways, as this member of the woman's club had discovered for herself. (pp. 249-50)

It is the cultivated person who is able to discern and understand differences disinterestedly, and while it is "possible" that such disinterest can be acquired elsewhere, the museum visitor and the tourist represent the exemplary forms in which understanding can be attained. Culture is what "lumber[s] our minds" (p. 63) *and* is also "an understanding of the long-established occupations and thoughts of men, of the arts with which they have solaced their toil" (p. 175), an understanding of the universal that results in the ability "to interpret opposing forces to each other" (p. 167).

Having traced Addams's description of her call to vocation to two contradictory models of woman's sphere, one, domesticity, that she links to the past and the other, education, to the present, we might usefully ask why she feels compelled to use both of them in her solution to her vocational crisis, and how they might function for her. At a pragmatic level the answer seems clear. Women flocked to settlement houses in America because few professional avenues were open to them, and those that were open limited their advancement. The settlement house enabled middle- and upper-class women to work outside the home and to involve themselves in the social issues of the day. It also gave them an acceptable rhetoric with which to describe their activity.[8] They were "neighbors" and "friends," cultivated and humane ladies, not professional social workers, economists, or sociologists; they were, as Addams calls them elsewhere, "public housekeepers."[9]

In fact, the women argued that this unprofessionalism was exactly what made them effective. Not only did it create a truer and more democratic relation with the poor,[10] but it also made them more disinterested, better able to understand social problems and to create solutions for them. Their belief in their unique effectiveness reveals more clearly than "pragmatic" explanations can that the two contradictory models of woman's sphere actually work together: the cultural claims of the education model are inflected with the claims to virtue and authority of domesticity. The sphere of woman (upper-class woman, that is), as Addams experiences it in her European travels, is a kind of cultivated leisure. While this cultivation is at first castigated and replaced by its figured opposite, domesticity, it still remains, taking on the characteristics ascribed to domesticity. Cultivation becomes the glue that binds society together, just as in "the cult of domesticity" the home was the universal glue that would bind the competitive and fragmented American society together. Thus, in the final pages of ***Twenty Years at Hull-House,*** Addams argues that to make American society stable, culture must be accessible to all. It is the "profound conviction" of the Settlement

> that the common stock of intellectual enjoyment should not be difficult of access because of the economic position of him who would approach it, that those "best results of civilization" upon which depend the finer and freer aspects of living must be incorporated into our common life and have free mobility through all elements of society if we would have our democracy endure. (p. 310)

Along with being a neighbor and a friend, the rich and educated settlement worker also dispenses culture to the poor and uneducated. Because of her education she understands and can explain cultural as well as political differences and so becomes an "interpreter" (p. 170) of truths. Addams even theorizes a neutral interpretive power and neutral activity that is based on an idea of pure cultural value and that will have the same "universal" acceptance as pure cultural value has. The settlement worker, she says, should have "nonresistance or rather universal good will" and perform "disinterested action" that would be "like truth or beauty in its lucidity and power of appeal" (p. 115). While the idea of pure cultural value is clearly not unique to women or to the time period, Addams's insistence that such value can transcend history and differentiations, and can be neutral, coincides with and contains the claims to authority of domesticity.

The settlement worker in particular is modeled on the figure of the tourist, the educated tourist who knows pure cultural value and understands the "language" of the foreign country. Thus one of the first major projects of Hull-House was the publication of a book called *Hull-House Maps and Papers* (1895). The maps, made for the United States Bureau of Labor's investigation into "the slums of great cities" (p. 117), delineate the different ethnic neighborhoods and list the occupations and salaries of individuals in them. While the papers treat a variety of concerns, the map is a crucial metaphor for the project as a whole. It assumes that a guide through and an explanation of different areas will provide enough knowledge of the problem to precipitate change. Making the problem visible is understanding and solving it. And in Addams, domestic ideology is implicit in her high valuation of tourism. A man's "predatory instinct" makes him "carelessly indifferent" to what he sees, while women, "traditional housekeepers,"[11] grounded in a realm of natural and unalienated labor, see and know what to do.

A novel without tension, confrontation, or denouement, and in which the main activity is visiting, Jewett's *The Country of the Pointed Firs* may seem to have little to do with the problem of vocation for women at the turn of the century. But it is through the activity of visiting that the book's thematic conflict between city and country reveals itself; and it is through the vocation of the text's narrator—a writer and summer visitor from Boston—that this conflict is defused. Just as Addams attempts to claim through her gender a position for herself as a political arbiter, to represent herself as a neutral interpreter of conflicting interests, so Jewett in this text attempts to claim a neutral and trans-historical position for her writing. This claim inheres in Jewett's understanding and depiction of woman's relation to work. Like Addams, Jewett combines the discourse of the "cult of domesticity" with woman's new role as leisured consumer of culture. While imagining domesticity as a human instinct, Jewett sees culture as transcending even the universality of instinct, and hence woman as uniquely able to understand, interpret, and finally overcome differences. I want briefly to spell out the differences between city and country that the novel depicts. Next, I will describe the ways Jewett's text and narrator are figured as defusing these conflicts.

During one of the most ecstatic moments of community in *Pointed Firs*—the Bowden family reunion—the narrator suddenly makes explicit all the differences between city and country, between herself and the rural inhabitants, that until now she has left implicit. At the same time, and in a typical gesture, she works to contain and deny the differences she herself explicates:

> As the feast went on, the spirits of my companion [Mrs. Todd] steadily rose. The excitement of an unexpectedly great occasion was a subtle stimulant to her disposition, and I could see that sometimes when Mrs. Todd had seemed limited and heavily domestic, she had simply grown sluggish for lack of proper surroundings. She was not so much reminiscent now as expectant, and as alert and gay as a girl. . . . It was not the first time that I was full of wonder at the waste of human ability in this world, as a botanist wonders at the wastefulness of nature, the thousand seeds that die, the unused provision of every sort. . . . More than one face among the Bowdens showed that only opportunity and stimulus were lacking,—a narrow set of circumstances had caged a fine able character and held it captive. One sees exactly the same types in a country gathering as in the most brilliant city company. You are safe to be understood if the spirit of your speech is the same for one neighbor as for the other.[12]

The differences between city and country inhabitants are many. From the narrator's citified perspective, Mrs. Todd is "sometimes" "limited and heavily domestic" because she lacks "proper surroundings"; that is, she is stuck in "a narrow set of circumstances"—the countryside. The narrator's belief that Mrs. Todd and many other Bowdens are "caged" by their rural surroundings is inextricably tied to a distinction between classes. The narrator's experience of the city is also an experience with "the most brilliant city company." While she claims that "one sees exactly the same types" in the country as in an upper-class city gathering, such a claim paradoxically suggests that this is not obvious, since she must state it. If the "spirit" of the words one uses is the same, the words themselves are not. Finally, that the narrator is able to generalize in such a fashion about the limitations of rural life means that she has choices Mrs. Todd and the others lack. She can see that the country is confining because she knows something that is not confining. In comparison to the sometimes "sluggish" Mrs. Todd (with her mental as well as her physical immobility), the narrator has money and the mobility it brings, mobility translated as the leisure to travel, to be cultivated and educated, and to understand differences.

The narrator also links city and country to different temporalities. Under even the "subtle" stimulation of the reunion, Mrs. Todd becomes "expectant" and "alert" rather than "reminiscent." The countryside is associated with memory and the past, the city with the rush and bustle of the present. While memory is usually highly valued in *Pointed Firs,* here the narrator suggests that living in the past is an act of necessity. She gives Mrs. Todd's usually reminiscent state a negative connotation and makes the words "limited," "sluggish," and "heavily domestic" synonymous, implying that the "domestic" labor that Mrs. Todd does and that is characteristic of the past is part of the problem of "narrow" circumstances. Meanwhile, the narrator metaphorically links herself to a profession not traditionally associated with women. She compares herself to "a botanist" in her wonder at "the waste of human ability in this world." She is beyond the "heavily domestic" worldview of past generations of women and can see the world from a broad and scientific perspective.[13] The movement from the limited to the objective and universalistic also resonates with another division in the book, that between the region, with all its individual peculiarities, and the nation. The narrator, representing the nation, depicts scientifically the activities and thoughts of the idiosyncratic region. The rural characters speak in dialect that the narrator records precisely, and *as dialect,* within the national language she uses to tell the story.

It is here, in the movement of narrative agency from the individual case study (Mrs. Todd), to a more universal perspective ("the waste of human ability"), and finally to a directive (how one should talk to people from the country), that we can see how the narrator attempts to deny or contain the differences between city and country that she herself has explicated. The reunion passage starts in the first person, compares the first person to a third person (the botanist), becomes the impersonal third person (one), and then uses a second-person plural to direct the actions of the reader as well as (presumably) to explain the actions of the narrator. First the narrator presents herself as a subjective agent in the story with her own opinions and interpretations, then as a kind of objective agent, and then as an agent integrated into a community of agency (the community that reads her book). This movement from a specific to a more general narrative agency occurs continually in the book, and to understand its significance we need to understand the narrator, who moves between these different agencies.[14]

We learn almost all the facts that we ever learn about the narrator in the first chapters of the book. She is from Boston and is wealthy, leisured, and well-traveled, and thus discovered Dunnet Landing "two or three summers before in the course of a yachting cruise" (p. 2) (she has so much leisure she cannot exactly remember when). She is condescending about the simplicity and ignorance of the Landing, a simplicity and ignorance that she also romanticizes so that at her return she discovers "the same quaintness of the village with its elaborate conventionalities; all that mixture of remoteness, and childish certainty of being the centre of civilization of which her affectionate dreams had told" (p. 2). In addition, she is an independent career woman, a "single passenger" (p. 2) traveling to Dunnet Landing on her own, looking for "seclusion and uninterrupted days" (p. 6) in order to write. While the other characters' names and backgrounds are presented, hers are not. In other words, all that we learn about the narrator and her existence outside of Dunnet Landing underlines her distinction from the village and its people. The very privacy in which her history is enclosed separates her from the villagers, whose personal histories are described in detail.

Nonetheless, from the moment she arrives, the narrator attempts with more and more facility to bridge the divisions between herself and the community by taking part in its activities and interests while also remaining exactly what she is—a wealthy, leisured traveling lady. These attempts correspond with her two methods for defusing conflict in the book: involvement in the community's labor (particularly domesticity) and cultivated perception of that labor. For the narrator, involvement in the community entails first of all that she learn *how* to involve herself in it, how to empathize with the people in it. While the narrator's empathy does not evolve in clearly defined stages, she seems to become accretively more empathetic under Mrs. Todd's guidance. As the book progresses the narrator no longer needs to ask Mrs. Todd about the meaning of actions but rather begins to understand actions on her own, even begins to visit people on her own.

What the narrator learns particularly to understand *through* her involvement in the community is the universal nature of domesticity. As the narrator visits from house to house she shows us the way that the houses and housekeeping of various individuals reveal their common, as well as their individual, histories. The house (and family) becomes the bond that unites everyone despite their differences. So it is at the Bowden reunion, where the narrator has given us the most explicit description of division, that she also gives us the most explicit description of unity through domesticity. She describes the "old Bowden house" as standing "low-storied and broad-roofed, in its green fields as if it were a motherly brown hen waiting for the flock that came straying toward it from every direction" (p. 159). The old house stands in the midst of the natural world as a unifying point, the mother/creator around which all the "straying" individuals "from every direction" gather. More specifically, as in Addams, domesticity represents a part of the biological makeup of all individuals:

> The sky, the sea, have watched poor humanity at its rites so long; we were no more a New England family celebrating its own existence and simple progress; we carried the tokens and inheritance of all such households from which this had descended, and were only the latest of our line. (p. 163)

The semicolons between sentences suggest that the ideas are equivalent and explain each other. Nature has watched so long that the individual "household" has become an expression of nature, and the "family" inherits its household through nature. Even the narrator, who is not a Bowden, becomes part of the now unified flock ("we") by the universality of the household. Just as in ***Hull-House*** Addams argued that the desire to do domestic labor is the physical trace of "the starvation struggle" left on our bodies (p. 92), so the narrator of *Pointed Firs* learns that domesticity is the body, a universal case for the individual soul: "a man's house is really but his larger body, and expresses in a way his nature and character" (p. 192).

The repeated description throughout the text of the house as a shell, as a body that encases the individual, underlines what is at stake in such an understanding of domesticity. The narrator writes of how she lives in Mrs. Todd's "quaint little house with as much comfort and unconsciousness as if it were a larger body, or a double shell, in whose simple convolutions Mrs. Todd and I had secreted ourselves" (p. 86). In the precolonial and colonial period the home was frequently described as a shell in which women resided, protected and excluded from the world, and so this simile associates the home with preindustrial society.[15] But there is also a biological implication. The self (individual) is a secretion of the universal body (home). The statement reads, in a double body that stands interchangeably for both domesticity and nature, that Mrs. Todd and the narrator are joined.

While the narrator learns from her involvement in the community that domesticity is nature, that it is the universal body of humanity, however, involvement is shown in the end to be less efficacious in overcoming differences than are the narrator's own cultivated perceptions as a wealthy, leisured traveling lady. Cultivation, as in Addams, coincides with but also contains domesticity. The necessities of the situation reveal that involvement can only be temporary; domesticity finally cannot override difference. Thus, in the narrator's second return to Dunnet Landing for William's wedding, she returns to her shell metaphor, describing her "odd feeling of strangeness" in "the little rooms" of Mrs. Todd's house: "It was like the hermit crab in a cold new shell" (p. 284). While the narrator does readjust to the rooms, her readjustment shows that for her the shell (both nature and domesticity) is a temporary body in and out of which she can slip. And as the story of Joanna Todd's "Shell-heap Island" warns, domesticity by itself can lead to monomania, insanity, and death (a pile of cast-off shells).[16]

What supersedes domesticity (the body), then, is the perception of domesticity that the narrator brings to the situation because she is leisured, wealthy, and nondomestic. Her understanding of culture entails a universality that goes beyond the body. Repeatedly, in the midst of mundane activities and a generally muted narrative, come highly charged comparisons between the people and activities of Dunnet Landing and high culture.[17] Returning to the Bowden reunion, for example, we can see how the narrator's understanding of the universality of domesticity is framed by her larger understanding of high culture:

> we might have been a company of ancient Greeks going to celebrate a victory, or to worship the god of harvests in the grove above. It was strangely moving to see this and to make part of it. The sky, the sea, have watched poor humanity at its rites so long; we were no more a New England family. . .
> (p. 163)

The reference to the "ancient Greeks" links the reunion to a civilization that has long been associated with timeless thought. The reunion is a kind of instinctual drive, but such a drive comes from the "ancient Greeks" and so transcends culturally the mortality of the body. Similarly, the reference underlines the narrator's own transcendence of the merely domestic or natural. She can empathize with the residents of Dunnet Landing in part because of her experiences elsewhere. The reference is meant to reveal how the perception of universality, the perception of a cultivated tourist, is sufficient for dealing with the divisions depicted in the book.[18]

The fact that the narrator is a leisured tourist (the opposite of the residents of Dunnet Landing) is figured paradoxically as the greatest force linking her to its citizens. While her knowledge of high culture reveals her status, the way she figures herself telling the story does so even more clearly. The cipherlike quality of the narrator works much as the idea of pure artistic value does in Addams. The narrator, with no name and no history, is figured as a thoroughly cultivated *and* thoroughly neutral witness, a kind of perfect tourist: while observing the villagers' "normal" talk and activities, she reveals nothing about herself that would interfere with that talk or those activities. Taking in a view, then, is the *form* in which her perception of the community occurs; she transcends difference and social conflict by observing them.

Thus, in the logic of the text, the most profound moments of transcendence occur when the narrator and the villagers observe views together (particularly domestic views). For example, when the narrator tours Green Island with Mrs. Blackett and Mrs. Todd, the three women at first view the scenery separately. But this separate viewing gives way when the "house [is] . . . just before us," and, for no given reason, the narrator then switches to a description of a unanimity of viewing:

> There was just room for the small farm and the forest; we looked down at the fish-house and its rough sheds, and the weirs stretching far out into the water. As we looked upward, the tops of the firs came sharp against the blue sky. (p. 59)

As the description continues, the narrator switches back to what the "I" can see, emphasizing the moment when all three perceived together, looking downward and then upward to see in a theologically weighted moment what lies below and above. Later in this section Mrs. Blackett shares the "quiet outlook" from her bedroom with the narrator, and, *because* of that shared viewing, even the separation caused by language breaks down: "I looked up [from the view, to Mrs. Blackett], and we understood each other without speaking" (p. 84).

Returning again to the Bowden reunion, we can understand an odd image that follows the narrator's cultivated celebration of the universality of domesticity. The narrator writes of the Bowden family and herself: "We could see the green sunlit field we had just crossed as if we looked out at it from a dark room, and the old house and its lilacs standing placidly in the sun" (p. 164). The house in question is lit up in contrast to the surrounding darkness. It becomes a focal point that unifies all, that enables all to see together. From the midst of nature, which itself is understood as a "room" in a house, they see "the" house that unifies them; they see together. The narrator describes the scenery in terms of what "we" see, even as a shared simile of what "we" see ("as if we looked out"), suggesting that the unanimity expressed by the event of the reunion is also a unanimity of perception, feeling, and emotion. All separation is nullified in the reunion; each becomes all: "Each heart [was] warm and every face [shone] with the ancient light" (p. 156). And it is through the unanimity of what *we see* that this is expressed.

The cipherlike quality of the narrator, then, is part of the same way in which the "I" just as easily becomes the "one," "you," or "we" in the novel, or the way narrative agency shifts continually from the specific to the general. That is, in the book, the manner in which reality is perceived by a tourist, as a "view," is the way transcendence of difference can occur; the manner in which the narrator is not an "I" with a personal history but rather a purely observing "eye" means that she is figured as imagining beyond the limitations of personality. In fact, the last chapter of the 1896 edition is called "The Backward View." In this chapter the narrator views not only the death of the New England past ("the islands and the headland had run together and Dunnet Landing and all its coasts were lost to sight" [p. 306]) but even her own death ("So we die before our own eyes; so we see some chapters of our lives come to their natural end" [p. 303]). The ability to understand objectively, through seeing "timeless" cultural representations (in this case a chapter in a book), enables the narrator to transcend even her own mortality, to encompass the natural within the cultural.

We can return now to our questions of why Jewett might have seen "misunderstanding" between city and country as so threatening and why she saw the solution to this "misunderstanding" as being simply a matter of introducing one to the other. Like Addams, Jewett saw and was part of the "status revolutions"[19] in region, class, and gender in turn-of-the-century America. Like Addams, she had grown up with representations of an American democracy based on rural, small-town life, on hierarchies of class, and on separate spheres of the sexes; and, also like Addams, she had recourse to these representations in attempting to understand and address contemporary issues. But even in using the outmoded representations, she invoked new models. While the house with women at the head was imagined by these upper-class, progressive feminists as a site where national unity could be achieved, it was a new kind of house, a house that reflected these women's experience of education and leisure. Unity based on the home became also unity based on transhistorical cultural values. These women imagined themselves as hostesses at a kind of national soiree, able, because of their gender and newfound access to culture, to introduce to each other the disparate and frequently opposed social groups that made up American life.

Jewett's writings, then, are no more classic pastoral representations of a dying region than they are feminist in some essential sense. Part of a new movement to revise the meaning and use of the home, to insert women and their labor into the "world," Jewett's pastoral regionalism and feminist realism are written in the language of the "national" progressive debates of the day, debates that changed not only the meaning of women's work but also, as Hull-House reveals, the meaning of social activism more generally. By writing her texts about the regional into the national, the domestic into the world, Jewett does not reverse the hierarchies of the national culture any more than Addams does. Nonetheless, she does attempt to create a new relation between margin and center. She herself explains this dynamic perfectly in her local history "The Old Town of Berwick" (1894). Writing of village life after the Revolutionary War, she says,

> The importance of the village, and its connection with the world outside, can be measured by the manner of its housekeeping; and no one can enter Judge Chadbourne's house or the Hamilton house at the Lower Landing . . . without seeing at once that people of refinement and cultivation had planned them and lived in them with elegance and hospitality. The best life in such a town as this was no more provincial in early days than it was in Salem or Boston, and the intercourse and sympathy between people of the same class in New England was more marked than at any other period.[20]

On the one hand she recounts Berwick's history because it "is so locally important and interesting" (p. 598); on the other hand she recounts it because the specific and local history of Berwick is not subordinate to or outside of national history but part of it. Additionally, she realigns this relation of local to national history in terms of the relation of the house to the world. It is through housekeeping, she argues—just as it is through the region—that one can read and understand the world.

NOTES

[1] *Deephaven* (London: Osgood, McIlvaine and Co., 1893), p. 3.

[2] The term is Richard Hofstadter's in *The Age of Reform: From Byron to F.D.R.* (New York: Vintage Books, 1955).

[3] See James, *The Complete Notebooks of Henry James*, ed. Leon Edel and Lyall H. Powers (New York: Oxford Univ. Press, 1987), p. 73; and Veblen, *The Theory of the Leisure Class: An Economic Study of Institutions* (1899; New York: New American Library, 1953), pp. 56, 60.

[4] Donovan, *New England Local Color Literature: A Woman's Tradition* (New York: Frederick Ungar Publishing, 1983), p. 99; and Roman, *Sarah Orne Jewett: Reconstructing Gender* (Tuscaloosa: Univ. of Alabama Press, 1992), p. 17.

[5] Henry Steele Commager, foreword to Jane Addams, *Twenty Years at Hull-House, with Autobiographical Notes* (1910; New York: New American Library, 1938), p. vii.

[6] Women dominated the settlement house movement in America from its inception. See Allen F. Davis, *Spearheads for Reform: The Social Settlements and the Progressive Movement, 1890-1914* (New York: Oxford Univ. Press, 1967); and Judith Ann Trolander, *Professionalism and Social Change: From the Settlement House Movement to Neighborhood Centers, 1886 to the Present* (New York: Columbia Univ. Press, 1987).

[7] T. J. Jackson Lears uses *Twenty Years at Hull-House* and Addams's work to discuss his concept of antimodernism in relation to what he calls the "Arts and Crafts ideology" of late-nineteenth-century America (see *No Place of Grace: Antimodernism and the Transformation of American Culture, 1880-1920* [New York: Pantheon Books, 1981]). Lears argues that, because Addams and the other Arts and Crafts ideologues sought personal fulfillment through premodern work rather than new ways to improve the degrading and alienated forms that modernized labor was taking, they capitulated to "capitalist cultural hegemony" (p. 80). While Lears's analysis is extremely helpful, one issue that his analysis does not explore is that of leisure: how premodern labor became an object of quest for the leisured bourgeoisie, an object to be kept "other" to the self, as well as to be—as he argues—forcefully integrated into one's life. A related issue he does not discuss is that of gender. While Addams's ideas do indeed seem to fit Lears's concept of antimodernist sentiment, Addams links her alienation to her exclusion from the "work of the world," and she wants to return specifically to domesticity.

[8] Because one of the main concerns of the settlement house was shaping public opinion, it was important to relay a safe and inoffensive image to the public. This desire to influence and mold public opinion can also be tied to domestic ideology, and in *Professionalism and Social Change* Trolander argues convincingly that because women settlement workers censored their feminism, a movement originally led and dominated by women became one led and dominated by men (see pp. 57-65). See also Davis, p. x.

[9] Jane Addams, "Women and Public Housekeeping" (New York: National American Woman Suffrage Association, 1913).

[10] In *Neighborhood: My Story of Greenwich House* (New York: W. W. Norton, 1938), Mary Kingsbury Simkhovitch writes that "the realism of the settlement, its

understanding that, before any help can be given, the situation *must be felt,* realized and understood *at first hand,* was sound" (p. 39; emphasis added). Later she criticizes as unsound the sociologist's method (p. 102). See also Addams, *Hull-House,* pp. 123-25.

[11] Addams, "Women and Public Housekeeping."

[12] Sarah Orne Jewett, *The Country of the Pointed Firs,* ed. Willa Cather, vol. 1 of *The Best Short Stories of Sarah Orne Jewett: The Mayflower Edition* (Boston: Houghton Mifflin, 1925), pp. 173-74.

[13] The use of the term "botanist" at this moment underlines the narrator's belief in her larger worldview. A few pages before she has described Mrs. Todd's ideas and expressions as "nothing if not botanical" (p. 167). Here she appropriates the role of botanist from Mrs. Todd in order to describe Mrs. Todd herself.

[14] See Sivagami Subbaraman's "Rites of Passage: Narratorial Plurality as Structure in Jewett's *The Country of the Pointed Firs," The Centennial Review,* 33 (1989), 60-74, for a formalist account of the text's "multiple voices" (p. 62).

[15] See Julie A. Matthaei, *An Economic History of Women in America: Women's Work, the Sexual Division of Labor, and the Development of Capitalism* (New York: Schocken Books, 1982), p. 49.

[16] For a different reading of domesticity in *Pointed Firs,* see Ann Romines, "Domestic Troubles," *Colby Library Quarterly,* 24 (1988), 50-60.

[17] The high culture comparisons are frequently Greek. Thus, for example, Mrs. Todd is a "sibyl" (pp. 10, 289); "grand and architectural, like a *caryatide*" (p. 46); "a large figure of Victory" (p. 61); "Antigone alone on the Theban plain" (p. 78); has wisdom that "belong[s] to any age, like an idyl of Theocritus" (p. 93); is an "oracle" (p. 139); is "Medea" (pp. 209, 290); is cousin "to the ancient deities" (p. 259).

[18] The references also make an appeal to us as educated readers, to see how the limited and narrow lives the narrator depicts are nevertheless universal.

[19] See Hofstadter, *The Age of Reform,* p. 143.

[20] "The Old Town of Berwick," *New England Magazine,* n.s. 10 (1894), 600.

Marianne DeKoven (essay date 1994)

SOURCE: "'Excellent Not a Hull House': Gertrude Stein, Jane Addams, and Feminist-Modernist Political Culture," in *Rereading Modernism: New Directions in Feminist Criticism,* edited with an introduction by Lisa Rado, Garland Publishing, Inc., 1994, pp. 321-50.

[*In the following excerpt, DeKoven draws parallels between the lives and of Addams and Gertrude Stein.*]

An enormous gulf would seem to divide Jane Addams's immigrant Chicago from Gertrude Stein's expatriate Paris; Jane Addams's social work and politics from Gertrude Stein's writing and art. But the terms of the first opposition, immigration and expatriation, suggest at least a symbolic mutuality, and it will be my purpose here to investigate, within a particular historical context, the parallel mutuality of progressive politics and avant-garde art.[1] Gertrude Stein and Jane Addams opened remarkably similar spaces: borderlands that served as powerful mediations, if not resolutions, of the contradictions of gender, politics and culture in the early twentieth century.

These borderlands were at once the feminist-modernist spaces opened by these two women's lives and works, and, at the same time, materially incarnated as or in actual houses. Stein and Addams reinvented not only the Angel but also the House she must sanctify. Addams's reputation is perhaps more firmly associated with Hull House than Stein's is with 27 rue de Fleurus, but Stein's was originally founded on her salon in the atelier of that house. She became famous as the guru of the Steins' remarkable collection of modernist paintings well before her writing received any meaningful notice. I will begin, therefore, by discussing the significances of the parallels between the political culture each woman created in her house.

I

Women are supposed to occupy houses. Stein and Addams both worked from within the house, literally and metaphorically, to change its politics. These changes were palpable, but at the same time palatable, to most of the agents policing gender at the turn of the century, in large part because the umbilical cord connecting the woman to the house was not severed.[2] Neither Stein nor Addams led a life or adopted a persona that would force the general public to name or even really recognize their radical revisions of acceptable feminine scripts. Stein presided over a salon in an atelier attached to the house she occupied first with her older brother and then with her "companion"—what could be less unusual for a woman of her class and education? Addams ventured farther out than Stein on a visible political limb, but carefully, carefully.

Perhaps the most important borderland Addams forged occupied the ground between traditional charitable work and movements for radical social change. To begin, she worked within the already established social settlement movement; Toynbee Hall in London was her primary inspiration.[3] Though her impetus in joining that movement was precisely to avoid the genteel do-goodism of upper-class ladies' charitable work, her activities were perceived and categorized in relation to that safe, familiar feminine role (Davis, *Heroine*).[4] For example, in an 1889 article entitled "A Chicago Toynbee Hall," appearing, crucially, in the feminist publication founded by Lucy Stone, *Woman's Journal,* Leilia G. Bedell writes:

> It is evident to every one that she [Addams] goes into the work from no desire for notoriety, for she is the physical expression of modest simplicity itself; nor as an employment for remuneration, for she gives not only her time but generously of her means, of which she possesses sufficient to place her beyond the need of remunerative occupation. . . . Miss Addams' rarest attraction—although possessing a generous share of physical beauty—is her wonderful spirituality.

These remarks are painfully governed by the confining codes of genteel feminine stereotype Addams had finally shed in founding Hull House: the emphasis on the modest body, or the embodiment of modesty; the dissociation from the masculine world of "remuneration" concomitant with the assurance of upper-class independent income; the "generous share of physical beauty"; and most important, the absolving "spirituality." One wonders whether Bedell was, either consciously or semiconsciously, providing a protective camouflage for Addams's feminism.

Although she objected to the language of this article, particularly its emphasis on her spirituality (Davis, *Heroine* 60), Addams took care throughout her career at Hull House to annex the assistance and remain in the good graces of Chicago's upper-class charitable establishment, especially of women's organizations such as the Chicago Woman's Club, which endorsed her work enthusiastically. She was determined to "use everything," as Stein said in a different context.[5] She saw no contradiction between establishing an upper-middle-class home—establishing it *as* her home, as a new bride would—and locating that home in the slums for the purpose not just of going out among the lowly as the great lady come to improve their lives, but explicitly for the purpose of inviting the neighbors in, with books around the rooms and fine china visible on the sideboard. As she says in ***Twenty Years,*** "probably no young matron ever placed her own things in her own house with more pleasure than that with which we first furnished Hull-House" (78). It is not just that this nesting provided her with an acceptable feminine niche, literally a home base, which it did. More than that, it allowed Addams to satisfy her own need to play some version of the feminine role for which she was raised and trained while at the same time revising, rewriting that role from within in accordance with the "unfeminine" ambitions also instilled in her by her contradictory upbringing and training. This structure of simultaneously deploying and reconfiguring an old social or literary text is characteristic of feminist-modernist political culture, as it is characteristic, as I have argued in my book *Rich and Strange: Gender, History, Modernism,* of modernism itself.

I would like to digress at this point from Stein and Addams in order to summarize briefly one version of that analysis of modernism, because it provides the historical-theoretical basis for the arguments I am making in this essay. Perry Anderson locates the modernist historical moment at the conjuncture of "a still usable classical past, a still indeterminate technical present, and a still unpredictable political future" ("Modernity" 106). For my purposes here, that "still usable classical past" includes the rigid Victorian gender binary along with the great heritage of Western high art, as well as the moribund artistic academicism that Anderson mainly has in mind. The "still indeterminate technical present," which Anderson associates with "mass consumption industries" just in their earliest stages at the turn of the century, provides the context for the opening of public space to women as consumers, an opening Stein and Addams, and many other public women in this period, were able to use differently, to redefine women's movement into the public sphere in more radical terms.[6] Finally, the "still indeterminate political future" encompasses what Anderson describes elsewhere as the "profoundly ambiguous possible revolutionary outcomes" of "the downfall of the old order," and also as the "imaginative proximity" throughout the modernist period of "a violently radical . . . rejection of the social order as a whole," the "apocalyptic light" of nascent social revolution (105), phrases all of which I find profoundly suggestive for my argument here.

Stein and Addams, like most other modernists, were both at once entranced and terrified by that apocalyptic light. It allowed them to see their way to an entirely different order of gender at the same time that it revealed to them the void beyond the limits of some version of the old order. It was Kate Chopin's "light which, showing the way, forbids it" (14); both Stein and Addams managed to convert that formula for defeat into its more enabling obverse: It became the light which, forbidding the way, shows it. While Anderson is primarily concerned with proletarian revolution, it is crucial to recognize that the egalitarian forces generating this apocalyptic light in their promise or threat of imminent revolution in this period were just as much feminist as they were socialist. It is also crucial to remember that this promise/threat of egalitarian revolution was what Fredric Jameson has called the "political unconscious" of modernism.

Stein's atelier at 27 rue de Fleurus, like Hull House and unlike the standard Parisian salon (as represented, for example, by Proust), was permeable to its environment, nonselective, open to heterogeneous penetration from outside the house and the social circle it would normally define. James R. Mellow begins *Charmed Circle,* his popular account of what he calls "Gertrude Stein and Company," with an imagined new visitor arriving at the salon on a Saturday evening, greeted by the ritual question "De la part de qui venez-vous"; by whose invitation do you come? Mellow continues,

> Because anyone was admitted to the weekly at homes at the rue de Fleurus, the question was a mere formality. As likely as not, however, the guest might be forced to stammer "But by yours, Madame." For Gertrude Stein . . . was frequently in the habit of meeting interesting people, inviting them to her home—and promptly forgetting that she had. (13-14)

Stein not only allowed anyone in, she actively but very casually recruited new people. The embracing, egalitarian openness of Stein's salon was diametrically opposite to the exclusivity of the conventional salon, defined as superior, selective and elite precisely by means of regulation of admission, enforced by exclusion of the unworthy.[7]

This nonselective openness was crucial to Stein's own representation of her salon, clearest in *The Autobiography of Alice B. Toklas.* Much of the book is structured by recollection of who came to the Saturday evenings in each period. The salon functions not only as a device of narrative ordering, but also literally as a narrative home base from which the anecdotes that are the primary substance of the book depart and to which they return. Just as the dedefined social space of the salon itself was anchored by the atelier, the paintings, the regular Saturday evening, and the obligatory but emptied-out question, "De la part de qui venez-vous?", this very freewheeling, nonlinear, associative narrative is anchored by repeated return to the salon.

Stein's account of the inception of the salon reveals the deep imbrication of both her own writing, and also the social and intellectual relationships that grew out of her art collecting, with her life in that house. "Little by little," she says, "people began to come to the rue de Fleurus to see the Matisses and the Cézannes, Matisse brought people, everybody brought somebody, and they came at any time and it began to be a nuisance, and it was in this way that Saturday evenings began" (*Autobiography* 41). Comfortable regulation of domestic life in the house that contained the remarkable paintings produced the Saturday evening salon.

It was not only domestic life, however, that the random visitors disrupted. Immediately following "it was in this way that Saturday evenings began," Stein says, "it was also at this time that Gertrude Stein got in the habit of writing at night. It was only after eleven o'clock that she could be sure that no one would knock at the studio door" (41). Stein wrote in the studio—the space of the salon was also the space of her working life. When the Saturday evenings began, she was working on *The Making of Americans,* as she puts it "struggling with her sentences, those long sentences that had to be so exactly carried out" (41). It was in this period, approximately 1906 to the war, that her work most radically and definitively broke with all known literary convention. Even though the Saturday evenings presumably ended those unwelcome interruptions, her habit of writing at night persisted, as she says here, "to the war, which broke down so many habits" (41). After a detailed description of what it was like to write at night, going to sleep as the birds awoke, comes a one-sentence paragraph, "So the Saturday evenings began" (42).

In the voice of Toklas, Stein summarizes the significance of the Saturday evenings for both of them as well as for this narrative: "But to return to the beginning of my life in Paris. It was based upon the rue de Fleurus and the Saturday evenings and it was like a kaleidoscope slowly turning" (89). The kaleidoscope is at once circular and nonhierarchical. Again, "everybody brought somebody. . . . It was an endless variety. And everybody came and no one made any difference" (123-24). Within that endless variety of people who came and made no difference, class distinctions are further undercut. In fact, the point of this passage is that aristocrats and even royalty had begun to arrive but Stein was not impressed, as she "sat peacefully in a chair and those who could did the same, the rest stood" (124). "As I said," she says, "the character of the Saturday evenings was gradually changing, that is to say, the kind of people who came had changed. Somebody brought the Infanta Eulalia and brought her several times" (123). The combination of "somebody" and "brought her several times" deflates the importance of "the Infanta Eulalia," as does the impatient cabman of the unnamed "roumanian princess" mentioned a few paragraphs later. It is the cabman rather than the princess who stars in this anecdote: "Helene came in to announce violently that the cabman would not wait. And then after a violent knock, the cabman himself announced that he would not wait" (123).

Since both the egalitarian openness of Hull House and also the fact that it was at once private and public, Addams's home and the site of her lifework, are so firmly established that they need not be demonstrated here, I will only clarify the parallel to 27 rue de Fleurus by discussing the unusual heterogeneity of both the residents of Hull House and also of the neighborhood groups that used it, and also by pointing to the same-sex relationships at the center of the lives of both houses.

Toynbee Hall in London's East End, Addams's inspiration, was far more homogeneous in its residential population than Hull House. It was inhabited, as Addams herself said in a letter to Alice Hamilton, by "University men who live there, have their recreation and clubs and society all among the poor people, yet in the same style they would live in their own circle" (June 14, 1888, quoted in Davis, *Heroine* 49).[8] Her primary purpose in this description was to praise Toynbee Hall for its freedom from what she calls "professional doing good"—a freedom derived from the way in which its inhabitants integrate their normal lives into the lives of the poor instead of descending from a great height in order to perform charity upon them.

One of Addams's alterations of the Toynbee model involved the nature of the lives so integrated. The founding residents of Hull House were of course Addams herself and her closest friend, Ellen Starr. While Addams was never part of the kind of lesbian bohemian subculture in which Stein and Toklas were able to live as lovers, acknowledged at least to a "charmed circle" of knowing friends, and it is most likely that Addams's two primary romantic friendships, with Ellen Starr and later with Mary Rozet Smith, never became overtly erotic, it is nonetheless the case that relationships with female partners were crucially enabling for the lifeworks of both women, and also were literally at the heart of the houses where those lifeworks transpired and in which they were to a large extent incarnated. Jane Addams would not have been able to found Hull House without the support, encouragement and active collaboration of Ellen Starr, any more than Gertrude Stein would have been able to make her miraculous leaps into the literary unknown without the support, encouragement and active collaboration of Alice Toklas.

Unlike the "University men" of Toynbee Hall, the first residents of Hull House were all women, though quite early on a men's residence was added (***Twenty Years*** 115).[9] In addition to being therefore "coed," Hull House was exemplary in the diversity of its residents (Davis, *Heroine* 74-75). Residents brought to Hull House a wide variety of backgrounds and social-political agendas. Addams herself emphasizes that diversity in her account of the earliest residents of Hull House:

> The group of Hull-House residents, which by the end of the decade [the '90s] comprised twenty-five, differed widely in social beliefs, from the girl direct from the country who looked upon all social unrest as mere anarchy, to the resident, who had become a socialist when a student in Zurich, and who had long before translated from the German Engel's *Conditions of the Working Class in England*. . . . (145-46)

The diversity of the residents consisted not only in their political beliefs but also in the nature of their contributions to Hull House. Ellen Starr herself lived her life in the arts. Her commitment as cofounder of Hull House was to make the arts accessible to the community, and in doing so she made the arts as central to the neighborhood work of Hull House as was its work in areas of social reform.

The resident Addams mentions as having translated Engels was Florence Kelley, a professional social investigator who, according to Allen F. Davis, was "responsible for making Hull House a center for social reform, rather than a place to study art and hear lectures on Emerson and Brook Farm" (*Heroine* 77). Davis concedes that "both kinds of activity remained," but claims that Kelley "helped redress the balance" in favor of social reform. Note the valorization of social reform and the condescension toward the study of art and toward lectures on Emerson and Brook Farm evident in Davis's formulation.[10] However, Addams gives both lectures and Brook Farm a prominent place in her saga of the founding of Hull House. They were both the province of "a charming old lady who gave five consecutive readings from Hawthorne to a most appreciative audience, interspersing the magic tales most delightfuly with recollections of the elusive and fascinating author. Years before she had lived at Brook Farm as a pupil of the Ripleys." This woman, who "gaily designated herself" Hull House's "'first resident,'" came to Hull House, according to Addams, "because she wished to live once more in an atmosphere where 'idealism ran high'" (***Twenty Years*** 83). Addams continues, concerning the Hawthorne readings, "we thus early found the type of class which through all the years has remained most popular—a combination of a social atmosphere with serious study" (83). The study and practice of art and literature within a congenial "social atmosphere," aspects of Hull House a male historian like Davis trivializes implicitly as feminine, were crucial to Addams's lifework in ways that might elude the dominant discourses of social science.[11]

Social work and social science have claimed Hull House, rightly and understandably, for the politics of social reform. A look down the index of ***Twenty Years*** under "Hull-House," however, yields a much more diverse, polymorphous, uncategorizable sense of the uses to which Hull House was put and of the groups that defined those uses, a heterogeneity far more striking even than that of the Hull House residents. Here are some of the entries under "Hull-House," of which there are over seventy: "first Kindergarten at, first coffee house at, Cooperative Coal Association, art at, day nursery at, reputation for radicalism, unions organized at, and law enforcement, playground of, post-office at, pleasures at, art exhibitions at, studio at, shops at, concerts at, chorus, music school, theater, college extension, summer school, gymnasium, military drill at, economic lectures at, University Extension at"; under "Hull-House Buildings," "Butler Gallery, Music School, Theater and Gymnasium," and under "Hull-House Clubs," after the obvious boys', children's, men's, working people's, and women's clubs, the "Dramatic Association" and the "Shakespeare Club." Clearly, literature and the arts were crucial activities at Hull House, just as Addams says they were in her chapter devoted to "The Arts at Hull House" in ***Twenty Years,*** and as she also indicates in this poignant statement from her chapter on "Early Undertakings at Hull-House": "Life pressed hard in many directions and yet it has always seemed to me rather interesting that when we were so distressed over its stern aspects and so impressed with the lack of municipal regulations, the first building erected for Hull-House should have been designed for an art gallery. . . ." (***Twenty Years*** 113).[12]

As upper-middle-class American women, both Addams and Stein were raised and trained to be conspicuous consumers of culture and genteel promulgators of the arts. As college-educated American women, both Stein and Addams were at the same time imbued with the feminist ambitions of the earliest generations of women in higher education for work in the public sphere. Each woman forged her own complex mediation of these two excruciatingly contradictory feminine trajectories.

II

The biographical parallels between Jane Addams and Gertrude Stein are clear and important. Addams, born in 1860, was fourteen years older than Stein, who was born in 1874; Addams was Quaker and then Protestant while Stein was Jewish; Addams's father was a successful businessman who was also very involved in public life while Stein's was exclusively a successful businessman. Those strike me as the most apparent differences between the backgrounds of the two women. The similarities are much more salient. Each was the youngest child in a large family. Both families were dominated by powerful, charismatic fathers, with whom each daughter identified in ways both enabling and inhibiting.[13] Addams's mother died when she was quite young (two and a half), while Stein's, whom she represents fictionally as passive and ineffectual,[14] died after a long illness when Stein was fourteen. Both Stein and Addams grew up in relatively rural, relatively Western outposts—Addams in Cedarville, Illinois (a frontier town when her father settled there), and Stein in Oakland, California, about which she later memorably said "there is no there there." Both women were precocious, clearly exceptionally intelligent, but for both of them college was a somewhat accidental destination.

Addams wanted badly to go to Smith, the preeminent women's college at the time, but was not allowed by her father to do so because he insisted that she remain closer to home. She went instead, as her older sisters had, to Rockford Seminary in Illinois, at that time on its way to becoming a full-fledged women's college modeled after Bryn Mawr, but still also strongly influenced by its original purpose as an institution for training in Christian submissiveness and feminine domesticity. Stein attended the Harvard Annex, which later became Radcliffe College, but only because her brother Leo was at Harvard at the time, and Gertrude went wherever Leo went. Both women had powerful, transforming intellectual awakenings in college, both women were very successful academically, and both graduated determined to pursue a medical career, within the feminist context of the new possibilities opening for women of lives in the public sphere. Both women failed to complete their medical education, and that failure coincided with extended periods of depression, self-doubt, paralysis of will, and quasi-psychosomatic illness. Both women then emerged from these periods of despair by means of finding at once ways to work and ways to live in a primary relationship with another woman. The ways they found to work allowed them to reconcile some version of traditional femininity with some version of the brave destiny they acquired in college.

Stein and Addams were both propelled into their different but similar inventions of feminist-modernist political culture by resolving for themselves, in very different ways, contradictions inscribed in their lives by the tangled relationships among higher education, high culture, femininity, feminism and the public sphere at the turn of the century. In order to understand how this resolution worked itself out for Stein, we will need to piece together excerpts from several of her texts. For Addams, we need only look at her consecutive chapters in ***Twenty Years*** entitled "Boarding-School Ideals" and "The Snare of Preparation."

Toward the end of "Boarding-School Ideals," her ironically titled chapter on her experience at Rockford Seminary, Addams brings into focus the contradictions it will take her eight painful years to resolve (as she herself says, "it required eight years—from the time I left Rockford in the summer of 1881 until Hull-House was opened in the autumn of 1889—to formulate my convictions even in the least satisfactory manner, much less to reduce them to a plan of action" [59]). The first step in this revealing textual sequence is the story of what her schoolmates considered her disappointing performance in the "intercollegiate oratorical contest of Illinois" (Interstate Oratorical Contest, Davis, *Heroine* 21), to which she and her friends "succeeded in having Rockford admitted as the first women's college" (53). This anecdote is located in relation to what Addams calls "the new movement of full college education for women," which inspired her and her cohort with "a driving ambition . . . to share in this new and glorious undertaking" (52). She connects this glorious undertaking very explicitly to the suffrage movement, by claiming that her companion in the study of mathematics, which the two women undertook in the service of their college's scholastic standing, "has since accomplished more than any of us in the effort to procure the franchise for women" (53). However, Addams distances herself subtly from the "glorious undertaking" in ways that reveal her fear of turning her back on sanctioned femininity, a fear that, in equipoise with radical desire, characterized feminist-modernist political culture in general.

Addams's account of being chosen Rockford's orator is strongly tinged with resentment of what she paints as an unfeminine feminist fanaticism. She says,

> When I was finally selected as the orator, I was somewhat dismayed to find that, representing not only one school but college women in general, I could not resent the brutal frankness with which my oratorical possibilities were discussed by the enthusiastic group who would allow no personal feeling to stand in the way of progress, especially the progress of Woman's Cause. I was told among other things that I had an intolerable habit of dropping my voice at the end of a sentence in the most feminine, apologetic and even deprecatory manner which would probably lose Woman the first place. (***Twenty Years*** 53)

She came in fifth, "exactly in the dreary middle," as she puts it, having lost to no less a man than William Jennings Bryan, "who not only thrilled his auditors with an almost prophetic anticipation of the cross of gold, but with a moral earnestness which we had mistakenly assumed would be the unique possession of the feminine orator" (53). She is satisfied with her performance, she does not insist on winning, but her friends are sorely disappointed, "much irritated as they contemplated their garlands drooping disconsolately in tubs and bowls of water" (54). Forced to stamp out traces of her "feminine, apologetic and even deprecatory manner" in the service of Woman's Cause, she loses to a great man who prevails partly by means of a feminine strength. Water, the feminine element, wrecks the garlands that would crown an unfeminine victory.[15]

Not surprisingly, given these fierce contradictions, Addams collapsed almost immediately after her graduation. The rise of feminism coincided exactly, as we know, with the hystericization and invalidization of women,[16] and the first generations of college-educated women, as among the most visible of the New Women, were prime targets of this form of debilitation (Davis, *Heroine* 25). Addams roused herself enough from her mysterious nervous prostration to enroll at the Women's Medical College in Philadelphia the following fall, in spite (or perhaps also because) of her father's sudden and devastating death in August. She had decided at the end of her four years at Rockford that she would "study medicine and 'live with the poor'" (***Twenty Years*** 57). Medical school was very explicitly a way into masculine science and officially sanctioned masculine public efficacy. Science, as she wrote in her graduation speech on the tragedy of Cassandra, would allow woman, "always . . . in the right and always . . . disbelieved and rejected," to "grow accurate and intelligible" by means of "eyes accustomed to the search for truth" (57). Further, as Addams does *not* say, medical school would provide access to, and feminist appropriation of, precisely the disciplinary, repressive power over women's hystericized bodies being deployed at this time to suppress the New Woman.

Medical school, perhaps not surprisingly given how much was at risk, was even more of a disaster for Addams than it would be for Stein. After just a few weeks of feeling bored and ineffectual, Addams collapased again.[17] This time she was delivered into the hands of S. Weir Mitchell, that bogeyman in the lives of so many women in this fraught space of feminist modernism. Mitchell's notorious rest cure left Addams "literally bound to a bed in my sister's house for six months," a chilling and unelaborated statement, during which time, when she was at last allowed to read and write, she produced notebooks that struck her as she wrote ***Twenty Years*** as having been written in "deep depression when overwhelmed by a sense of failure" (60-61).[18]

Addams sees this period in her life as the originary moment of "the spiritual struggles which this chapter is forced to record," the chapter entitled "The Snare of Preparation," recounting the story of the years leading up to the founding of Hull House. The thesis of this chapter is that "the pursuit of cultivation,"[19] as she calls it—the passive and conspicuous consumption of European high art that was the expected occupation of a college-educated woman who has succumbed to nervous prostration and was then sent abroad to recover—in fact brings only "a sense of futility, of misdirected energy" (***Twenty Years*** 64). "I gradually reached a conviction," she says,

> that the first generation of college women had taken their learning too quickly, had departed too suddenly from the active, emotional life led by their grandmothers and great-grandmothers, that the contemporary education of young women had developed too exclusively the power of acquiring knowledge and of merely receiving impressions. . . . (64)

She goes on to describe "American mothers and their daughters who had crossed the seas in search of culture." The mother could establish "real connection with the life around her" . . . "using her inadequate German with great fluency" in "exchanging recipes with the German Hausfrau, visiting impartially the nearest kindergarten and market," responding directly and unselfconsciously to "the mere presence of suffering or of helplessness" (64). The daughter, on the other hand, "was critical and uncertain of her linguistic acquirements, and only at ease when in the familiar receptive attitude afforded by the art gallery and the opera house" (64).

In a telling substitution, the daughter's college education, which in Addams's case had inspired her to enter the masculine public sphere of science, becomes instead a sheltered, passive, almost cloistered life of social uselessness, self-cultivation, and conspicuous consumption of high culture. Where Addams blames the distorted expectations engendered by higher education, we might much more readily blame upper-middle-class grooming for the marriage market, and in fact resocialization away from the expectations of entry into the public sphere young women acquired precisely from their college educations.

Such an analysis does not occur to Addams. Instead, she repudiates her college education and retreats nostalgically, safely, to Victorian femininity, albeit a version of it that emphasizes active engagement in the welfare of the community rather than Christian submissiveness and cloistered domesticity.[20] She gives herself here an ideology of femininity that allows her to break free of the antifeminist reterritorialization of the college-educated woman without provoking retaliation, and to lead a new social movement under cover of a relatively conservative gender self-definition, one that at the same time accomodates her own resistance to the kind of feminist single-mindedness she rues in her debate narrative.

This self-definition, in its repudiation of a passive self-cultivation and acquisition of high culture, ostensibly involves a repudiation of art and literature as ends in themselves. Addams sets up a binary of art and literature versus social engagement; as she puts it, "the paralyzing sense of the futility of all artistic and intellectual effort when disconnected from the ultimate test of the conduct it inspired" (***Twenty Years*** 67):

> This, then, was the difficulty . . . the assumption that the sheltered, educated girl has nothing to do with the bitter poverty and the social maladjustment which is all about her, and which, after all, cannot be concealed, for it breaks through poetry and literature in a burning tide which overwhelms her; it peers at her in the form of heavy-laden market women and underpaid street laborers, gibing her with a sense of her uselessness. (65)

In her account of her stay in London, she locates the epiphany of her visit to the East End as a geographic and symbolic opposition to the futility of her West End life of passive acquisition of high culture. However, just as the arts were always crucial to the work of Hull House, the visit to the East End enacts not a narrative of anti-art but a narrative of both a different kind of art and also a different relation of art to the feminine. The official culture Addams and her cohort were supposed to acquire was precisely the moribund academicism Perry Anderson identifies as the residual social formation determining the conservative boundary of the historical space of modernism. Further, women were passive consumers, not producers, of this academicism. Addams's experience in the East End inspired her to produce a modernist moment of narrative, and her years of culture-vulturing led her to formulate a modernist view of art.

The story of what Addams saw in the East End is for her a story of hands.[21] She has been taken with a small group by a missionary to witness a Saturday midnight auction of rotten fruit and vegetables which could not be sold legally otherwise. It is a scene of horror for Addams, and it stays with her as symbolic of the human wretchedness she will commit her life to ameliorating. She sees a man buy a rotten cabbage and, "when it struck his hand, he instantly sat down on the curb, tore it with his teeth, and hastily devoured it, unwashed and uncooked as it was" (***Twenty Years*** 61-62). But it is not the obviously memorable dehumanization of this man that comes to symbolize to her the mission she will undertake. Rather, "the final impression was not of ragged, tawdry clothing nor of pinched and sallow faces, but of myriads of hands, empty, pathetic, nerveless and workworn, showing white in the uncertain light of the street, and clutching forward for food which was already unfit to eat" (62). In its symbolic abstraction, its synecdoche (hands stand for both suffering bodies and suffering humanity), its eerie, penetrating yet detached horror, its power as an objective correlative of Addams's response to poverty, this is a piece of modernist writing. Quite literally, "bitter poverty . . . breaks through poetry and literature in a burning tide," (62) not because poetry and literature deny or stand in opposition to bitter poverty but because they can most powerfully represent it.

Later in this chapter, Addams discusses her response to the paintings of Albrecht Dürer. She says she sees them "in the most unorthodox manner, merely as human documents" (66). However, in seeing "merely a human document," what she finds in Dürer is not something opposed to or different from art. Instead, again, she sees a modernist art rather than the academicist high culture she was supposed to be acquiring. As she says,

> I was chiefly appealed to by his unwillingness to lend himself to a smooth and cultivated view of life, by his determination to record its frustrations and even the hideous forms which darken the day for our human imagination and to ignore no human complications. (***Twenty Years*** 66)

Complication, frustration and dark, hideous imaginative forms, as opposed to smoothness and cultivation, sound to me like elements of certain kinds of modernist art practice, for example expressionism, or at least of the ideology of the late-nineteenth-century realism and naturalism that were modernism's precursors.[22]

Modernist versions of art enabled Addams to retain her strong connection to art and literature while repudiating feminine upper-middle-class passive self-cultivation and consumption of high culture. Similarly, Addams created, by means of Hull House, borderlands of mediation between traditional upper-class feminine charity work and radical or progressive feminist and socialist movements for political change. While ostensibly repudiating art and embracing politics, and while ostensibly rejecting her college education in favor of an earlier, Victorian feminine model of social engagement, Addams found a feminist-modernist space in which art, politics, and the ambitions for work in the public sphere she acquired in college could coalesce in new ways.[23]

Gertrude Stein's trajectory was, as we have seen, remarkably similar to Jane Addams's, yet also neatly opposite to hers. Both women went from the optimism and ambition of college through the failure of medical school and a subsequent period of depression and inertia, and finally emerged into a productive life based on forging new mediations or borderlands of engagement with traditional femininity, new art forms, women's entry into the public sphere, and possibilities of radical social change. But where Addams ostensibly rejected art in favor of politics, Stein ostensibly rejected politics in favor of art. Yet, as I have argued in *Rich and Strange: Gender, History, Modernism,* feminism and egalitarian politics in general were a powerful if displaced and ambiguous motive force in Stein's radical writing.

Like Addams's, Stein's story begins with a violent reaction against her successful career in higher education. Stein set her 1904-05 story *"Fernhurst"* one of her earliest works, written just before she met Alice Toklas, at a women's college based on Bryn Mawr. She describes the college and its graduates in language remarkably similar to Addams's account of the futile lives of college-educated women:

> I have seen college women years after graduation still embodying the type and accepting the standard of college girls—who were protected all their days from the struggles of the larger world and lived and died with the intellectual furniture obtained at their college—persisting to the end in their belief that their power was as a man's—and divested of superficial latin and cricket what was their standard but that of an ancient finishing school with courses in classics and liberty replacing the accomplishments of a lady. Much the same as a man's work if you like before he becomes a man but how much different from a man's work when manhood has once been attained. . . . I have heard many graduates of this institution [the fictional

> Fernhurst] proclaim this doctrine of equality . . . mistaking quick intelligence and acquired knowledge for practical efficiency and a cultured appreciation for vital capacity and who valued more highly the talent of knowing about culture than the power of creating the prosperity of a nation. . . . Had I been bred in the last generation full of hope and unattainable desires I too would have declared that men and women are born equal but being of this generation with the college and professions open to me and able to learn that the other man is really stronger I say I will have none of it. (3-8)

Like Addams, Stein blames her failure not on the powerful social forces working against women's success in the public sphere but on the desire to attain that success, and the confidence in her ability to do so, that she acquired at college. Stein ends her account of Philip Redfern, an idealistic but failed professor at Fernhurst, with a judgment remarkable in its reflection of Jane Addams's dilemma:

> This was the end of Redfern's teaching experience—for the rest of his days he lived the difficult life of a man of letters who aspires to be an effective agent in the actual working of a boisterous world. Such lives are hard in the living and for the most part poor in result. He plunged deeply into the political life of his time and failed everywhere. (47)

Even a man, if he associates himself with the cause of higher education for women, becomes enmeshed in the contradictions it generates between the life of culture and the life of political action.

Like Jane Addams, Gertrude Stein assimilated her failure at medical school and her subsequent inertia and depression by blaming and repudiating both her college education and the self-confident ambition, nurtured by feminism, it instilled in her.[24] In *The Autobiography of Alice B. Toklas,* she gives a very complex, ambiguous account of her career at Johns Hopkins Medical School, where she had gone on the advice of her mentor at Harvard, William James, so she might follow in his footsteps in the study of psychology: "for psychology you must have a medical education, a medical education opens all doors, as Oliver Wendell Holmes told me and as I tell you" (80), Stein has James say to her. In going to Hopkins, Stein was quite explicitly acquiring a patrilineage of male greatness in the public sphere: Oliver Wendell Holmes, William James, Gertrude Stein. Stein did well, by her own account, in the first two years, but in the second two years she became bored, "frankly openly bored." Stein claims she dropped out after failing one course; in fact, she failed four courses.[25] As she tells it, the story is again remarkably similar to Addams's: Where Addams passed the requisite exams for her first year but used the advice of an authoritative male doctor as her official "sanction" for leaving medical school after her collapse, Stein claims the professor in question would gladly have given her another chance at passing his course, since all the big men thought she was brilliant and wanted her to finish, but she took the opportunity this failure gave her to get out, just as Addams had taken the opportunity offered by the doctor's advice.

Two sets of comments in the *Autobiography* within this narrative of the medical school failure are most relevant to my concerns here. One is Stein's notorious repudiation of feminism:

> There was great excitement in the medical school [at the news of her failure]. Her very close friend Marion Walker pleaded with her [to finish her degree], she said, but Gertrude Gertrude remember the cause of women, and Gertrude Stein said, you don't know what it is to be bored. (82)

She then says she had seen Marion Walker again "only a few years ago," as she writes in 1932, and they "disagreed as violently about the cause of women as they did then. Not, as Gertrude Stein explained to Marion Walker, that she at all minds the cause of women or any other cause but it does not happen to be her business" (83).

The other set of comments concerns Stein's sense of the relationship of her experience at medical school to her career as a ground-breaking modernist writer. At the end of her last year at Hopkins, when she was generally bored and failing, she had the opportunity to "take her turn in the delivering of babies and it was at that time that she noticed the negroes and the places that she afterwards used in the second of the *Three Lives* stories, Melanctha Herbert, the story that was the beginning of her revolutionary work" (82). A page earlier, she had associated her arrival in Baltimore at the beginning of her medical education with having a "servant named Lena and it is her story that Gertrude Stein afterwards wrote as the first story of the Three Lives" (81). The feminist ambition for masculine-style success in the public sphere that sent Stein to Hopkins, but that failed her, was converted into literary ambition to do revolutionary work based on childbirth and the lives of black and working class women. Both the overt feminism and any overt radical politics that Stein repudiated returned in the form of the subject matter of her pioneering modernist work, *Three Lives,* and then, as I have argued elsewhere,[26] in the form of form itself—the radical, antipatriarchal, culturally subversive literary forms she invented in the 1910s and 1920s.

At the end of her life, successful and possibly reconciled to the feminist context of her early academic success, Stein wrote a fairly adoring play about Susan B. Anthony called "The Mother of Us All." And even in the *Autobiography,* a sequence of juxtaposed recollections reveals an association in Stein's mind between feminism and the launching of her career with the publication of *Three Lives.* On a trip to London to negotiate that publication with John Lane, Stein says first that she began reading the *Daily Mail* because she liked to read about the suffragettes, and then, further down the same page, that John Lane made an appointment with her to sign a contract for

Three Lives because he has, as he says, "confidence in that book" (144).

The *Autobiography* bears some remarkable similarities to ***Twenty Years at Hull-House.*** Both autobiographies use deep-structural distancing devices in order to promote their authors' reputations and publicize their achievements by the very means used to deprecate them. Stein's device of course is to write the autobiography of herself as if it were the autobiography of her lover, so that it is in another's voice that she extols her own genius. This device also allows her to avoid altogether the appearance of claiming for herself sufficient importance to be the subject of an autobiography. Addams structures her book, as her title indicates, as the story of Hull House rather than the story of Jane Addams, but, of course, the point is that one is essentially the same as the other. She uses self-deprecation throughout the book to make possible this chronicle of her remarkable success. Both books are episodic, anecdotal, partly achronological. These are casual forms for new feminine modes of public autobiography, producing the informal story of the great woman, not the official history of the great man.[27]

There is a further, quite specific parallel: In both books, strongly gender-marked scenes of looking and not looking at the violence of the Spanish bullfight coincide with moments of career-altering revelation. The force of that revelation is only implicit in the *Autobiography,* though explicit in ***Twenty Years.*** In the chapter on their lives from 1907 to 1914, after Toklas had moved in with Stein and before the war, Stein describes the crucial trip to Spain during which she began to forge the most powerful, vibrant experimental writing style she ever invented, the style I have called "lively words." It was this style that culminated in *Tender Buttons.* Again, it is necessary to read the juxtaposition of recollections in order to understand the significance of the passage. First, Stein says "we finally came back to Madrid again and there we discovered the Argentina and bull-fights" (118). The Argentina was the flamenco dancer who was the subject of Stein's great poem "Susie Asado." Bullfights are therefore connected immediately to her new writing and to the lesbian desire associated with one of its most successful instances.

Stein and Toklas as Toklas goes on to say, went to see the Argentina "every afternoon and every evening. We went to the bull-fights. At first they upset me and Gertrude Stein used to tell me, now look, now don't look, until finally I was able to look all the time" (*Autobiography* 118). Two paragraphs later, we hear that it was in Spain that "Gertrude Stein's style gradually changed. She says hitherto she had been interested only in the insides of people, their character and what went on inside them, it was during that summer that she first felt a desire to express the rhythm of the visible world" (119). Able to claim the masculine gaze—to look at the Argentina and at the bullfight as a man would, fearlessly, with confidence and desire—Stein is able to initiate Toklas into the gaze and then to align it with a powerfully subversive new style of writing the "rhythm of the visible world." The public sphere has opened out again for Stein; she could not enter it as a great man like William James or Oliver Wendell Holmes, but she can enter it now as a great experimental writer, as long as Toklas is there with her.

Addams presents her experience of the bullfight in much more equivocal terms. At the end of that pivotal chapter on "The Snare of Preparation," Addams finds herself in Madrid, with a group of friends including Ellen Starr, some twenty-five years before Stein and Toklas. She goes to a bullfight, where, as she says, "greatly to my surprise and horror, I found that I had seen, with comparative indifference, five bulls and many more horses killed" (***Twenty Years*** 73). She did not even notice that her friends had long since left in what she calls "faintness and disgust." "I finally met them in the foyer," she continues, "stern and pale with disapproval of my brutal endurance" (73). She claims that it is her ensuing self-loathing, her horror at her ability to enjoy this bullfight, that "made quite clear to me that I was lulling my conscience by a dreamer's scheme" for founding a settlement house, and that pushes her to take the first steps toward the realization of her plan. The very first step consists of discussing the plan with Ellen Starr. I would argue that it was precisely her ability to watch the bullfight, not her disgust at her ability, that empowered her to take that step. Like Stein, she saw that she could function as a man would.[28] She therefore could have access to the public sphere, as long as her partner would go there with her, and as long as no one knew.

III

I do not know whether Stein read ***Twenty Years at Hull-House.*** It's quite possible that she did, because she claims she read everything. Addams's book, published in 1910, had just come out when Stein and Toklas made that momentous trip to Spain in 1912. I wish I knew whether Stein had the book with her on that trip. I do know, however, that Stein knew of Hull House. The penultimate section of "Objects," the first part of *Tender Buttons,* is a very short piece entitled "It Was Black, Black Took," which I will quote in full:

> Black ink best wheel bale brown.
>
> Excellent not a hull house, not a pea soup, no bill
> no care,
>
> no precise no past pearl pearl goat. (476)

This is one of the most obscure pieces in *Tender Buttons.* Unlike even the pieces before and after it, which are equally radical in their destruction of the conventional sense-making function of symbolic language, it offers very little access to the interpreting reader.[29] The pieces before and after are loaded with puns and with strongly emotive, suggestive verbal juxtapositions. "It Was Black, Black Took," by contrast, is cool, detached, offering access, if any, only through its submerged illusion to

Lord Jim—"It was black, black" is Jim's description of the squall that overtakes the renegade *Patna* officers in their ignominious lifeboat—and through the self-referentiality of its black, black, black ink. The repeated negation, "*not* a hull house, *not* a pea soup, *no* bill *no* care, *no* precise *no* past," functions almost to erase this piece as it is written. But the second line of the piece begins with the word "excellent,"[30] and ends with the almost readable "pearl pearl goat," suggesting (to me at any rate) the pearls that were his eyes, the sea change in the realm of the empowered sexuate maternal feminine that enabled modernism and that modernism brought about.[31] The string of negations suggests perhaps that "hull house" is part of the mundane universe of pea soup, bills, and cares, and that "excellent" connects to the negation of that universe. However, "precise" and "past" seem to belong to a different realm, at least linguistically, from pea soup, bills and cares, and perhaps "hull house" occupies precisely the position in this piece that I have argued it occupies in its historical-cultural moment, a position of mediation between the mundane, ordinary and known, on one hand, and on the other the realm of powerful historical gender transformations.

I would argue in general that, at the current juncture in feminist scholarship, we ought to expand our sense of the connections between feminism and modernism: to move beyond analyses of women modernists, their separate tradition and their complex relations to canonical male modernism in order to include a much broader historical provenance and a much wider range of cultural work. Exemplary in that expansion is a recent article in the journal *differences* by Janet Lyon entitled "Militant Discourse, Strange Bedfellows: Suffragettes and Vorticists Before the War." In this article, Lyon demonstrates the influence of suffragist rhetoric and political practice on the development of the vorticist manifestos and of *Blast* itself. In comparison to bedfellows as strange as those, Jane Addams and Gertrude Stein, and my argument here for the congruence of the feminist-modernist political-cultural spheres they invented, may perhaps seem less unlikely.

NOTES

[1] The historical affiliations of avant-garde art and left politics have been explored most fully, of course, by the Frankfurt School theoreticians and their chroniclers. See especially Aaron, Anderson et al., eds., Jameson, and Lunn.

[2] For a powerful literalization of that umbilical cord, a prime representation of the woman's relation to the house in the turn-of-the-century feminist imaginary, see "The Yellow Wallpaper," in which the protagonist ends literally tied by a rope to the marriage bed. Gilman's remarkable story resonates throughout the material that concerns me here.

[3] Davis, *Heroine* 57; Addams, *Twenty Years* 74.

[4] See Walkowitz, 59, on the influence of women's charitable work on Samuel Barnett and his founding of Toynbee Hall.

[5] Stein says in "Composition as Explanation": "Continuous present is one thing and beginning again and again is another thing. These are both things. And then there is using everything. . . . A continuous present and using everything and beginning again. . . . In the first book [*Three Lives*] there was a groping for a continuous present and for using everything by beginning again and again" (518). By "using everything," Stein means undoing the censorship of consciousness that produces coherence and consistency of characterization in realist fiction. What she promulgates here is akin to stream of consciousness, though Stein's version is much more abstract, stylized, and focused on time-sense rather than the psyche. The connection to Addams comes in the embrace of contradiction, the renunciation of consistency.

[6] See Walkowitz, 46-50, for an analysis of this phenomenon most directly relevant to my argument here.

[7] For an analysis of this egalitarian openness as a primary motive force in her writing, see *Rich and Strange,* chapter 6, 198-201.

[8] See Walkowitz, 59-60, on Toynbee Hall's elitism.

[9] See Walkowitz, 59, on Toynbee Hall's exclusion of women.

[10] Davis expresses a more explicit contempt for Hull House art practices in *Spearheads* (40-43), finding them "unrealistic," and disparaging a popular Hull House art exhibit because its viewers were primarily women and children.

[11] See, for example, Levine and Linn.

[12] Chapter 11 of *The Second Twenty Years* is entitled "Play Instinct and the Arts." In it, Addams argues that the "power of unfolding human life which is implicit in the play instinct" (358) is an antidote to the reification of factory life, and is also necessary for the cultivation of the imagination of common purpose on which democracy must rest. See also the Ruskin- and Morris-influenced Starr, "Art and Labor"; Saarinen, who says "Jane Addams looked at the arts without the myopia of either the sociologist or the esthete . . . from the beginning the arts had an important place at Hull-House" (172); and Elshtain, who notes that "discussion of aesthetic impulses and the necessity of social space for free play are themes that run though [Addams's] work" (183 n.31).

[13] "The frequency, passion and extent of Gertrude Stein's treatment of her father in her writings all indicate his ineradicable primacy in her imagination" (Bridgman 10). The opening chapter of *Twenty Years* reveals the centrality of Addams's relationship to her father in the construction of her ambivalent self-image—her idealization of

and identification with him coupled with her fear of his disapproval and her sense of unworthiness.

[14] See especially Stein, *The Making of Americans.*

[15] Davis, *Heroine,* notes the way Addams plays down this episode almost apologetically in a letter to her father, while sounding "confident and full of enthusiasm" (21) about it in a letter to her sister Alice.

[16] See for example Bernheimer and Kahane, eds., Foucault, and Showalter.

[17] "The long illness inevitably put aside the immediate *prosecution* of a medical course, and although I had passed my examinations creditably enough in the required subjects for the first year, I was very glad to have a physician's *sanction* for giving up clinics and dissecting rooms and to follow his prescription of spending the next two years in Europe" (*Twenty Years* 60, italics added). Addams retreats from the dangerous position of female medical student to the safe position of female patient. See also Hotaling for an analysis of Addams's strategic narrative deployments of illness in *Twenty Years.*

[18] Note again the remarkable parallels to "The Yellow Wallpaper."

[19] For an ironic treatment of upper-middle-class feminine self-cultivation, see Stein's "Miss Furr and Miss Skeene."

[20] Addams had given a speech at Rockford foreshadowing this move, advocating for women a fusion of the new independence with the ancient "saxon" womanly role of "breadgiving" (Davis, *Heroine* 20).

[21] "The [East End] slum street acquired [for female charity workers] the ludic qualities traditionally associated with the city center; it became an improvisational site for strange encounters with unforgettable characters" (Walkowitz 57).

[22] In a similar vein, Elshtain refers to Addams's "rich exploration of her own complex motives" (9) in *Twenty Years,* and describes Addams's view of human life as "complex, not simple . . . a dense thicket, difficult to cut one's way through" where "one often has to choose between two goods, not between a clear-cut case of good versus evil" (8).

[23] See Walkowitz, "Contested Terrain: New Social Workers," on women's charity work *as* entry into masculine public space.

[24] See Blankley, 196-97, for evidence of Stein's early adherence to feminist principles, particularly in a speech she gave in Baltimore in 1898, visibly influenced by Charlotte Perkins Gilman's *Women and Economics,* advocating higher education for women and endorsing the New Woman. See also Stimpson's powerful analysis of the biographical determinants, particularly her lesbianism, of Stein's repudiation of the New Woman ideal.

[25] See Bridgman 360; these events occurred in 1901.

[26] See my *A Different Language* and *Rich and Strange.*

[27] The feminist study of women's autobiography is of course a burgeoning field. See for example Benstock, ed., and Smith and Watson, eds.

[28] See Walkowitz on "The Glorified Spinster and the 'Manly Woman,'" 61-68.

[29] Ruddick (213-14) makes a valiant attempt.

[30] In a noteworthy coincidence, Addams collected her memorial essays in 1932 under the title *The Excellent Becomes the Permanent.*

[31] I refer here to the central argument of *Rich and Strange.*

WORKS CITED

Aaron, Daniel. *Writers on the Left.* New York: Oxford UP, 1961.

Addams, Jane. *The Excellent Becomes the Permanent.* New York: Macmillan, 1932; rpt. Freeport: Books for Libraries Press, 1970.

———. *The Second Twenty Years at Hull-House, September 1909 to September 1929.* New York: Macmillan, 1930.

———. *Twenty Years at Hull-House.* New York: Macmillan, 1910.

Anderson, Perry, et al., eds. *Aesthetics and Politics.* London: New Left Books, 1977.

———. "Modernity and Revolution." *New Left Review* 144 (March-April 1984): 96-113.

Bedell, Leilia G. "A Chicago Toynbee Hall," *Woman's Journal* XX (May 25, 1889).

Benstock, Shari, ed. *The Private Self: Theory and Practice of Women's Autobiographical Writings.* Chapel Hill: U of North Carolina P, 1988.

Bernheimer, Charles, and Claire Kahane, eds. *In Dora's Case: Freud-Hysteria-Feminism.* New York: Columbia UP, 1985.

Blankley, Elyse. "'Beyond the Talent of Knowing': Gertrude Stein and the New Woman." *Critical Essays on Gertrude Stein.* Ed. Michael J. Hoffman. Boston: G.K. Hall, 1986. 196-209.

Bridgman, Richard. *Gertrude Stein in Pieces.* New York: Oxford UP, 1970.

Chopin, Kate. *The Awakening.* 1899; rpt. New York: Norton, 1976.

Conrad, Joseph. *Lord Jim.* 1900; rpt. New York: Norton, 1968.

Davis, Allen F. *American Heroine: The Life and Legend of Jane Addams.* New York: Oxford UP, 1973.

———. *Spearheads for Reform: The Social Settlements and the Progressive Movement, 1890-1914.* New Brunswick, NJ: Rutgers UP, 1984.

DeKoven, Marianne. *A Different Language: Gertrude Stein's Experimental Writing.* Madison: U of Wisconsin P, 1983.

———. *Rich and Strange: Gender, History, Modernism.* Princeton, NJ: Princeton UP, 1991.

Elshtain, Jean Bethke. "A Return to Hull House: Reflections on Jane Addams." *Essays on Feminism as Civic Discourse.* Madison: U of Wisconsin P, 1990. 3-12.

Foucault, Michel. *The History of Sexuality, Volume 1.* Trans. Robert Hurley. New York: Random House, 1978.

Gilman, Charlotte Perkins. "The Yellow Wallpaper." 1892; rpt. Old Westbury, NY: The Feminist Press, 1973.

Hotaling, Debra. "The Body of Work: Illness as Narrative Strategy in Jane Addams's *Twenty Years at Hull-House.*" *A/B: Auto/Biography Studies* 6:1 (Spring, 1991): 33-39.

Jameson, Fredric. *The Political Unconscious: Narrative as a Socially Symbolic Act.* Ithaca, NY: Cornell UP, 1981.

Levine, Daniel. *Jane Addams and the Liberal Tradition.* Madison: State Historical Society of Wisconsin, 1971.

Lewis, Wyndham, ed. *BLAST* 1 and 2 (June 1914, July 1915).

Linn, James Webber. *Jane Addams: A Biography.* New York: D. Appleton-Century Co., 1935.

Lunn, Eugene. *Marxism and Modernism: A Historical Study of Lukacs, Brecht, Benjamin and Adorno.* Berkeley: U of California P, 1982.

Lyon, Janet. "Militant Discourse, Strange Bedfellows: Suffragettes and Vorticists Before the War." *differences* 4:2 (Summer 1992): 100-133.

Mellow, James R. *Charmed Circle: Gertrude Stein and Company.* New York: Avon, 1974.

Ruddick, Lisa. *Reading Gertrude Stein: Body, Text, Gnosis.* Ithaca, NY: Cornell UP, 1990.

Saarinen, Aline B. "The Arts." *Jane Addams: A Centennial Reader.* New York: Macmillan, 1960. 171-188.

Showalter, Elaine. *The Female Malady: Women, Madness, and English Culture, 1830-1980.* New York: Pantheon, 1985.

Smith, Sidonie, and Julia Watson, eds. *De/Colonizing the Subject: The Politics of Gender in Women's Autobiography.* Minneapolis: U of Minnesota P, 1992.

Starr, Ellen Gates. "Art and Labor." *Hull-House Maps and Papers.* rpt. New York: Arno Press and *The New York Times,* 1970. 165-179.

Stimpson, Catharine. "The Mind, the Body and Gertrude Stein." *Critical Inquiry* 3:3 (Spring 1977): 489-506.

Stein, Gertrude. *The Autobiography of Alice B. Toklas.* New York: Random House, 1933.

———. "Composition as Explanation." *Selected Writings of Gertrude Stein.* Ed. Carl Van Vechten. New York: Random House, 1946. 511-523.

———. "Fernhurst." *Fernhurst, Q.E.D., and Other Early Writings.* New York: Liveright, 1971. 1-49.

———. *The Making of Americans.* New York: Harcourt, Brace, 1934.

———. "Miss Furr and Miss Skeene." *Selected Writings.* 561-568.

———. "The Mother of Us All." *Last Operas and Plays.* New York: Vintage, 1975. 52-88.

———. "Susie Asado." *Selected Writings.* 549.

———. *Tender Buttons. Selected Writings.* 459-509.

———. *Three Lives.* 1909; rpt. New York: Random House, 1936.

Walkowitz, Judith R. *City of Dreadful Delight: Narratives of Sexual Danger in Late-Victorian London.* Chicago: U of Chicago P, 1992.

FURTHER READING

Biography

Davis, Allen F. *American Heroine: The Life and Legend of Jane Addams.* London: Oxford University Press, 1973, 339 p.

A critical biography which examines Addams's intellectual roots and offers an appraisal of her significance.

Linn, James Weber. *Jane Addams: A Biography*. New York: D. Appleton-Century, 1935, 457 p.

Linn, Addams' nephew, had her full cooperation and access to all her papers in his preparation of this authorized biography.

Meigs, Cornelia. *Jane Addams: Pioneer for Social Justice*. Boston: Little, Brown, 1970, 274 p.

A biography of Addams as a woman of action who changed her environment and era.

Criticism

Baxter, Edna M. "Jane Addams." In *Women Leaders*, Vol. II of *Creative Personalities*, edited by Philip Henry Lotz, pp. 1-10. New York: Association Press, 1946.

In a style written for young readers, with discussion questions at the end of the chapter, Addams's life as a "creative personality" of great impact is examined.

Brieland, Donald. "The Hull-House Tradition and the Contemporary Social Worker: Was Jane Addams Really a Social Worker?" *Social Work*, Vol. 35, No. 2 (March 1990): 134-38.

Brieland examines Addams's contribution to social work with descriptive statements developed by a task group of social work leaders, and investigates the question of whether her activities would qualify as social work according to these later definitions.

Commager, Henry Steele. "Jane Addams at Hull House." In *The Search for a Usable Past, and Other Essays in Historiography*, pp. 270-81. New York: Alfred A. Knopf, 1967.

Biographical sketch of Addams that explores her influences and impact.

Cottler, Joseph. "The Good Neighbor: Jane Addams." In *Champions of Democracy*, pp. 259-84. Boston: Little, Brown, 1936.

Examines the foundations of Addams's dedication to the poor and to achieving unity among immigrants of many nationalities.

Deegan, Mary Jo. *Jane Addams and the Men of the Chicago School*. New Brunswick, NJ: Transaction Books, 1988, 352 p.

Deegan examines Addams as a sociologist, and juxtaposes the primarily female-led work of Hull House with that of its neighbor, the influential and male-dominated University of Chicago sociology department.

Farrell, John C. *Beloved Lady: A History of Jane Addams' Ideas on Reform and Peace*. Baltimore: Johns Hopkins Press, 1967, 272 p.

Farrell's doctoral dissertation—which he died before completing—examines Addams's worldview within the framework of the development of American progressive thought.

Felton, Keith Spencer. "Let There Be Light: The Genesis of a Social Conscience in the New Century (Jane Addams and Alice Hamilton, M.D.)." In *Warriors' Words: A Consideration of Language and Leadership*, pp. 9-20. Westport, CT: Praeger, 1995.

An examination of the political rhetoric used by Addams and her friend and fellow reformer Hamilton.

Hagedorn, Hermann. "Jane Addams 1860-1935." In *Americans: A Book of Lives*, pp. 161-80. New York: John Day, 1946.

In a biographical form that juxtaposes Addams' story with that of other famous Americans of her era, Hagedorn evaluates Addams as a philanthropist, pacifist, and philosopher.

Kent, Muriel. "Jane Addams: 1860-1935." *Hibbert Journal*, Vol. 35 (January 1937): 279-90.

Writing from a British and leftist viewpoint, Kent examines Addams's life, based on James Weber Linn's biography.

Lasch, Christopher. "Jane Addams: The College Woman and the Family Claim." In *The New Radicalism in America*, pp. 3-37. New York: Alfred A. Knopf, 1965.

Explores the personal and intellectual roots of Addams's radicalism.

Levine, Daniel. *Jane Addams and the Liberal Tradition*. Madison, WI: State Historical Society of Wisconsin, 1971, 277 p.

Presents Addams as a key figure in the development of the American welfare state. An extensive bibliography.

MacLeish, Archibald. "Jane Addams in Chicago." In *A Continuing Journey*, pp. 337-42. Boston: Houghton Mifflin, 1968.

An appraisal of Addams as one of several great figures offering direction to a world plagued by the uncertainties of nuclear war, totalitarianism, and other threats.

Meiklejohn, Donald. "Jane Addams and American Democracy." *The Social Science Review*, Vol. XXXIV, No. 3 (September 1960): 253-64.

A review of the background to Jane Addams's thoughts on democracy with a view toward what guidance she would give the maintainers of that democracy a generation after her death.

Morris, Lloyd. "The Woman Takes Over." In *Postscript to Yesterday: America: The Last Fifty Years*, pp. 32-63. New York: Random House, 1947.

An examination of the transformation of women's roles in the first half of the twentieth century, due in part to technological changes, with Addams as a leading figure.

Sherrick, Rebecca. "Their Father's Daughters: The

Autobiographies of Jane Addams and Florence Kelley." *American Studies* Vol. 27, No. 1 (Spring 1986): 39-53.

A comparison of the closely related life stories of Addams and Florence Kelley, who came to work at Hull House in 1891.

Tims, Margaret. *Jane Addams of Hull House: A Centenary Study*. New York: Macmillan, 1961, 166 p.

An examination of Addams's life and thought, focusing on the development of Hull House.

White, Morton and White, Lucia. "Pragmatism and Social Work: William James and Jane Addams." *The Intellectual Versus the City,* pp. 144-58. New York: New American Library, 1964.

Presents Addams as part of a movement to rescue American urban life from decay.

Ion Luca Caragiale

1852-1912

Romanian playwright, short story writer, translator, and journalist.

INTRODUCTION

Caragiale was one of Romania's preeminent playwrights and among the most important literary figures in his country's history. Though he earned his living variously as a journalist, translator, and prose writer, he is best known for plays such as *O scrisoare pierduta* (1884; *The Lost Letter*), in which he satirized the vanity and smugness of the bourgeoisie. Caragiale enjoyed a few minor successes during his lifetime, but his work was often plagued by government censorship and even legal woes, not to mention a generally tepid response from the public. By the middle of the twentieth century, however, critics had recognized him as a writer of great insight.

Biographical Information

Caragiale came from a family well acquainted with the stage: his father, a lawyer, had once worked as an actor, and two uncles remained in that profession. Born in the tiny village of Haimanale, Caragiale attended school in the larger nearby city of Ploesti, and at age sixteen moved to Bucharest. From 1868 to 1870, he studied under his uncle Costache, an established actor, and in 1870 went to work with the other uncle as a prompter at the National Theatre. Also in that year, his father died, leaving Caragiale to take care of his mother and sister. During the next three decades, Caragiale—of whom it was said that "he made more reputation than money"—struggled to support his family, which grew in number when he married. Meanwhile Caragiale worked at a variety of jobs, including as a tutor and a journalist. His first literary successes came in 1873 with the publication of humorous stories in the journal *Ghîmpele,* followed by his well-received translation of a collection of poetry by Dominique-Alexandre Parodi in 1876. In 1879, when he was twenty-seven, Caragiale saw the production of his first play, *O noapte furtunoasa sau numaral 9* (*A Stormy Night, or Number 9*), which met with minor success. Five years later, he reached the peak of his career with the enthusiastic popular and critical reaction to *The Lost Letter.* However, his foray into tragedy with *Napasta* (1890) was not well-received, and Caragiale even had to go to court over the work because a critic accused him of plagiarism. His spotty resumé as a breadwinner grew in tandem with his frustrated career as a playwright: Caragiale held another string of jobs, including one as proprietor of a beer garden, between 1881 and 1904. In the latter year, however, he received an inheritance and moved to Berlin. There he spent the remaining eight years of his life, during which time he wrote a number of short stories and sketches but no further dramatic works.

Major Works

Caragiale's reputation rests chiefly on four of his eight plays, all published between 1879 and 1885. In *A Stormy Night, or Number 9,* the city father Dumitrache has entrusted his right-hand man Chiriac to spy on his wife, who he is certain is having an affair. She is, as the audience discovers—only her lover is Chiriac himself. Meanwhile the wife's sister's lover goes to visit the sister, but because of an upside-down nine (which looks like a six) on the house number, winds up inside Dumitrache's house instead. He nearly gets himself killed by both Dumitrache and Chiriac before the sister identifies him, and her explanation convinces Dumitrache that his wife has remained faithful to him after all. *The Lost Letter,* generally considered Caragiale's greatest work, also makes use of romantic intrigue with a political hue. Stepan Tipatescu, a candidate for office in a small-town election, discovers that his opponent has obtained an old love letter that he wrote to another man's wife. In vain Tipatescu attempts to persuade the opponent, Catavencu, to give up the letter. But when the government announces its support for a third candidate, Tipatescu withdraws himself from the race and puts his support behind Catavencu. In the meantime, Catavencu manages to lose the letter, which passes through the hands of the town drunk to Zoe, the woman to whom Tipatescu had originally written the letter. By the end of the play, the opponents are reconciled, and the government's candidate wins. Caragiale's other two significant works, *Conul Leonida fata cu reactiunea* (1880; *Mr. Leonida and the Reactionaries*) and *D'ale Carnavalului* (1885; *Carnival Scenes*), follow the pattern established by *A Stormy Night* and *The Lost Letter*: biting political satire in the case of the first, and romantic intrigue in the latter case.

PRINCIPAL WORKS

O noapte furtunoasa sau numaral 9 [*A Stormy Night, or Number 9*] (drama) 1879
Conul Leonida fata cu reactiunea [*Mr. Leonida and the Reactionaries*] (drama) 1880 [first publication]
O scrisoare pierduta [*The Lost Letter*] (drama) 1884
D'ale Carnavalului [*Carnival Scenes*] (drama) 1885
Napasta (drama) 1890
Pacat (short stories) 1892

Note si schite (short stories) 1892
Moftul român (short stories) 1893
Sketches and Stories (short stories and sketches) 1979

CRITICISM

E. D. Tappe (essay date 1952)

SOURCE: "The Centenary of I. L. Caragiale," in *The American Slavic and East European Review,* Vol. XI, 1952, pp. 66-76.

[*In the following essay, Tappe presents an overview of Caragiale's career, highlighting his most prominent works and the chief characteristics of his writing.*]

When Rumanians are asked, "Are there any great comic writers in Rumanian literature?" there can be no question that most of them think first of Caragiale. If I were asked, "Who is the most original of Rumanian writers?" I should be tempted to answer likewise: "Caragiale!" Perhaps what I should really mean is that his writing is exceptionally vivid and vital, so that through him Rumania, and especially Bucharest, of the late nineteenth century lives in the imagination with an intensity and individuality such as that, for example, with which another great comic writer, Mark Twain, has endowed the Mississippi Valley of a slightly earlier period.

Ion Luca Caragiale was born on January 29, 1852, in a Wallachian village not far from Ploesti. His father was one of three brothers who were all connected with the theater, but had left the stage years before, divorcing his actress wife and marrying a country woman. While I. L. Caragiale was still a small boy, the family moved into Ploesti, and it was there that he went to school.

In 1868 he left for Bucharest to study declamation with his uncle, Iorgu Caragiale, and to be prompter to his company. After his father's death in 1872, he combined the job of prompter and copyist with that of proofreader for two newspapers. Thus he was initiated in his teens into a life of poverty and hard work. In 1877 he began to write for the Conservative paper *Timpul,* of which his friend, the poet Eminescu, had just become editor. For a while, in 1878, Caragiale, too, was on its editorial staff. But it was the production of his verse translation (from the French) of Alexandre Parodi's classical tragedy, *Rome Conquered,* which first attracted attention to his literary gifts. That imposing figure, Titu Maiorescu, professor, critic, and politician, approved of him and introduced him to the literary circle *Junimea* ("Youth"), over which he presided at Jassy. No doubt it was Maiorescu's influence which later procured him an inspectorship of schools (1881-84).

Caragiale's period of productivity as a playwright lasted a little over ten years. The comedy, ***O Noapte Furtunoasa*** (***A Stormy Night***) was first performed in 1879; ***O Scrisoare Pierduta*** (***A Lost Letter***) marked the zenith in 1884; and the period closed with the drama ***Napasta*** (***False Witness***) in 1890. For a few months in 1888 Caragiale was Director-General of the National Theater, but was not a success. It was then that he married. The financial responsibilities of married life made his position—and he was never economical—still more difficult than before; an irregular income from journalism was not enough. Nor did his sarcasm and irritability help matters; to offense thus given may be attributed to a very large extent not only the refusal of the Rumanian Academy on two occasions to award him a prize for his writings, but also his inability to get a good job and keep it.

From 1889 to 1904 his struggles for a decent livelihood were continuously frustrated. Among the expedients he tried was running a tavern, and at another time, a station buffet. Only for two years (1899-1901) did he hold a minor post as a civil servant. To add to his troubles he became involved in a lawsuit against an unscrupulous critic who accused him of plagiarism. From this period of fifteen years date most of his stories and sketches.

In 1904 his luck turned. He obtained a share of a long-disputed inheritance. At once he removed with his family to Berlin, where there were greater opportunities for cultural activities, and especially for going to concerts. Though he made occasional trips to Rumania, he continued to reside in Berlin for the rest of his life. He died unexpectedly on the night of June 9, 1912.

Most of Caragiale's best-known work consists of short sketches, two or three pages long. These are normally scenes of contemporary Rumanian life, sometimes in the capital, sometimes in the provinces. Very often they are about clerks and their wives, the life not of the more fashionable parts of Bucharest, but of the *mahala* (the "suburb," if only one could divest that word of its specific associations in modern English). Sometimes they are about Caragiale's own world of journalism, about his acquaintances, about the people he meets in trains. He is continually making fun of pretentious ideas voiced by fools or humbugs; of the petty ambitions and quarrels of provincial life; of the folly of women who spoil their children or their lapdogs; of the absurdities of journalism; and so on. Sometimes the fun consists as much in parody as in ridiculous situations. For example, there is the delightful series of **"Telegrams"** about a scandalous incident in a provincial town, which starts with the prefect of the local police smacking the face of an ex-M.P. at the Central Café. Here a great deal of the fun lies in the combination of the style of official telegrams with the melodramatic exaggeration of the whole affair by the senders. Another parody of official jargon is a series of letters about the supply of firewood for a provincial girls' school. Incidentally, Caragiale published literary parodies in prose and verse. His facility in this line is illustrated by the following story. On one occasion, in a literary circle, the poet Iosif asked him how it was that Bolintineanu had written verse so prolifically. Caragiale told him to take a piece of paper, and then dictated impromptu a parody of Bolintineanu's verse, thirty-six lines long. "You see," said he, "it's not difficult. The fact is, Bolintineanu could write a poem in twenty-five minutes, and assuming that he only worked six hours, that means sixteen a day."

How much as a rule in these sketches the effect is made by dialogue, and how comparatively little by narrative and description! That is very characteristic of Caragiale—who was a dramatist and came of a theatrical family—and it contributes very largely to the liveliness and concreteness of his work. The habit of driving home his points by repeating key phrases, and especially of sharpening the outline of his characters by giving them clichés which they constantly repeat, serves him as well in his sketches as in his comedies. Just as in the comedy ***A Lost Letter*** Trahanache, the chairman of many committees, cannot be thought of apart from his mannerism, "Just a moment!" (*Ai putintica rabdare!*), so in the sketch **"O Lacuna"** (**"A Gap"**) Mache is forever identified with his "Stop it, Lache!" *(Lasa, Lache!),* and Lache with his "You're dreadful, old boy, really you are!" *(Esti teribil, monser, parol!).*

Such sketches as **"Petitie"** (**"An Application"**) are practically dramatic dialogues. In fact, some of them have actually been put on the stage with some success. Their resemblance to the mimes of Hellenistic literature in the third century B.C. has been noted by Zarifopol, the editor of the definitive edition of Caragiale's works; he compares them to the Mimes of Herondas. And surely Caragiale might well have written the Fifteenth Idyll of Theocritus, *The Women at the Festival.* Indeed, his sketch **"At Peles"** is strongly akin to it in spirit and observation: Madam Piscopescu is at her toilet before lunching with the King and Queen, her mother assists while her husband waits impatiently outside.

Generally speaking, Caragiale's sketches are comic, while his stories are serious. But naturally there are notable exceptions to this. The sketch **"O Reparatie"** (**"An Act of Redress"**) describes a visit to a little monastery in the hills. A bear has been robbing the apple tree. The monks' servant, a dumb, half-witted, epileptic gipsy, had tried to stop him the previous day, but the bear had knocked him flat. Now the gipsy lies in wait, and as the bear mounts the stile, the gipsy cracks it over the head with his staff. Both fall dead, the bear with its head broken, the gipsy overstrained by his effort. The monastery bell, tolling for vespers, reëchoes his knell among the wooded hills. Here Caragiale, who normally was preoccupied with human idiosyncrasies and not notably fond of nature, contrives to give his little sketch of a thousand words an extraordinary atmospheric charm. Conversely, in **"Doua Loturi"** (**"Two Lottery Prizes"**) he writes a story of ten thousand words on a theme contrived to display the irony of fate in a comic light. Lefter Popescu, a minor civil servant, has mislaid two lottery tickets, each of which has gained the first prize in its own lottery. Under the strain of this situation, all the worst side of him comes to light. He harries his wife, he bullies an old-clothes woman because he fancies that a coat which his wife let her have, had the tickets in one of its pockets, he stays away from the office to carry on the hunt. At last, when he is compelled to go back to work under threat of dismissal, he finds the tickets there, and in triumph sends in his resignation. When he reaches the bank to draw the prize money, the banker points out that he has in one lottery the ticket which won first prize in the other—and vice versa. "If I were one of those self-respecting and respected authors," continues Caragiale, "I should finish my tale thus." And there follows a mock-pathetic description of Madam Popescu years later as an old nun and Popescu himself as a little old man murmuring, "Vice-versa! . . . Yes, vice-versa!" "But," says Caragiale, "as I am not one of those authors, I prefer to tell you frankly: after the row at the bank, I don't know what happened to my hero and Madam Popescu." This ending has been criticized as an artistic irrelevancy which should have been pruned away. But there is a good deal to be said for the gently frivolous conclusion to a story which was otherwise on the point of getting itself taken too seriously.

Caragiale reaches the highest level of his powers in the story **"Kir Ianulea,"** one of his latest works. Here he has taken Machiavelli's *The Marriage of Belphegor,* which itself, we are told, can be traced back to ancient India, and has expanded it into a *nouvelle.* What in Machiavelli's version is not much more than a study becomes in Caragiale's hands a finished painting. He sets the tale in eighteenth century Wallachia under the Fanariot regime, a very happy choice because he could depict a Levantine scene most convincingly. Aghiuta, an imp, is sent upon earth by the King of Hell to find out the truth about women, since all the men who arrive in Hell lay the blame for their perdition upon their womenfolk. He is under orders to marry and live with his wife for ten years. He puts on the likeness of a man in his prime, and choosing Bucharest for his activities, settles down there in the guise of a Greek merchant with the name of Kir Ianulea. He marries a young woman named Acrivita, who is a beauty, but proves to be a shrew. Not only does she make his life intolerable with her tantrums; she also ruins him with her extravagance. On the verge of bankruptcy he runs away, and being hidden from his creditors by a certain Negoita, rewards him as follows. Whenever Negoita hears of a woman being possessed by the devil, he may be sure that it is Kir Ianulea, or rather Aghiuta, who has entered into her. Aghiuta will depart from her at Negoita's bidding, and the latter will naturally receive a suitable reward from her grateful relations. At his first case Negoita asks a fairly modest reward. The spirit reproaches him and tells him that he will only have one more chance, but that the patient will be the wife of the governor of Craiova. Of course, Negoita's fortune is made. Unluckily, Aghiuta proceeds later to enter into the daughter of the reigning Prince, who summons Negoita to cure her. Negoita, though well aware that the spirit will be angry this time, cannot refuse to go. He is greeted with fury by Aghiuta, speaking through the possessed Princess, but has the brilliant idea of announcing that he will bring Acrivita to assist him in the exorcism. The spirit at once departs appalled, and Negoita is showered with wealth and honors. Aghiuta returns to Hell, defeated and exhausted, and as a reward for his labors, asks only for rest and that Acrivita and Negoita may go to Heaven so that he may never see them again.

This tale is told by Caragiale with many pleasing details, and many minor characters are touched in with an admirable economy of strokes. Here, illustrating one aspect of his humor, a blend of the ruthless and the absurd, is an extract from the cock-and-bull story which Kir Ianulea tells his housekeeper about his past.

> When I was in my seventh year, my parents felt a longing to make a pilgrimage; and so, procuring some money, they took me with them and we went on muleback as far as the port of Salonica. There we boarded a large ship which was waiting with sails spread for a wind, to make southwards to Jaffa. Presently the expected wind began to blow, the canvas filled, and we sailed. For three sunny days and moonlit nights we kept straight ahead without any trouble. According to the custom we were fasting. About the third day, for our midday meal, we ate beans and radishes. What was the result? About the time of vespers my parents began to clap their hands to their bellies and wail horribly: "I'm dying! I'm dying!" The captain, seeing them writhing and curling up in deadly pain, quickly sent for a papist monk who had boarded the vessel with us, a learned man who was skilled in the care of disease. Before the monk arrived, the patients had begun to turn livid and could scarcely tell him what they had eaten—beans and radishes. The monk asked again: "I understand, my children. But you must tell me, did you eat beans and radishes or radishes and beans?" My mother replied in a faint voice: "Radishes and beans." "Ah, that's bad!" said the monk. And he gave orders to rub their bellies with rough tow. But they rubbed in vain till they took the skin off; for while the moon was rising, first my father and immediately after him my mother passed away. What was I, a child, to do? I followed the captain and the monk about, weeping, and I heard them talking as follows. Said the captain: "Father, if it's cholera, I'm done for; they won't let me enter port for forty days, and my cargo will be spoiled. I shall be left a poor man." But the learned man replied: "It is no more cholera than I am a nun. It is a sort of disease which is particularly prevalent among Eastern Christians during Lent. People make a mistake—men are like that, subject to error—they eat radish first and then beans. The radish, you see, directs its strength upwards, and the bean exerts its force in the opposite direction; one pushes, the other resists. The struggle begins with great speed in the entrails, spasm after spasm, until there is an entanglement of the bowels and the stomach bursts. Then the patient dies of *hurduharismus*—that is the name the Greeks give to this fearful disease." "Is it infectious?" "Not at all; don't be alarmed." . . . They wrapped my parents decently in some clean sheets and lit a wax candle at their heads. Another Greek monk read the burial service, and early in the morning, as the sun showed above the waves—"eternal rest" . . . one! two! three! . . . and they cast them into the deep.

The other story in which Caragiale reaches his highest level is **"Mânjoala's Inn."** This story of the Rumanian countryside of the nineteenth century is a masterpiece of delicate irony. The hero is riding to his betrothal. He stops to rest the horse at the inn, run by a widow, Marghioala. She charms him into lingering, but at last he breaks away. Caught in a storm, he loses his way and in the end finds himself back at the inn. There he succumbs to the fascination of Marghioala and has to be removed forcibly by his future father-in-law. The story must be read and re-read for the subtlety of its detail to be fully appreciated. With delicious irony every indication that his hostess is a witch draws from the hero a rationalistic interpretation. Even at the end, when years later they hear that Marghioala has perished in a fire which destroyed her inn, the hero greets with scepticism his father-in-law's assurance that she was a witch. The descriptions of the ride, the inn, the storm, are remarkably vivid. Nowhere else, I think, does Caragiale create with such sustained delicacy.

In these stories **"Kir Ianulea"** and **"Mânjoala's Inn"** we have seen Caragiale treating the supernatural, and from that it is a short step to the macabre and the gruesome. These he treats most notably in the story **"An Easter Candle."** The Jewish landlord of a lonely country inn is terrified of a brutal ruffian whom he has dismissed and who has threatened to come back on Easter Eve. Late on Easter Eve a band of robbers, led by the ruffian Gheorghe, try to make a hole in the door and break in. The Jew, his wits sharpened by the extremity of his terror, traps Gheorghe's hand in a noose as he completes the hole, and the other robbers run away. When the villagers return from the midnight service, they find the corpse of the robber trapped in the door with the hand burned off. The Jew explains that he is now a Christian—for he has lit a candle to Christ! In all this there is something of Edgar Allan Poe, whose stories *The Mask of the Red Death* and *A Cask of Amontillado* Caragiale translated into Rumanian from Baudelaire's French version. The frightful tension of the Jewish innkeeper as the robbers bore through the door to break into his lonely inn is as skillfully depicted as that of the victim of the Inquisition in Poe's *The Pit and the Pendulum.* But the scenery is not the fantastic scenery of Poe; it is the naturalistic background of a Moldavian village in the marshes. The element of the monstrous and unnatural in the psychology links this tale with the play ***False Witness,*** though the process whereby the menace of the robber Gheorghe acting on a mind already excited by terrifying memories is more credible than the cold-blooded vindictiveness of Anca. Though the revolting brutality of the whole tale may not be emphasized beyond what is artistically necessary, it is nevertheless unpleasant reading. Unpleasant reading too, and without such artistic justification, is the story **"Sin" ("Pacat"),** in which Caragiale deploys lurid descriptions of bloodshed, unnatural cruelty and other horrors, without creating an impressive whole.

Allied to these tales, **"An Easter Candle"** and **"Sin,"** in theme and psychological treatment, and contemporary with them, is Caragiale's only serious play ***Napasta,*** a word with the double meaning of "unjust accusation" and of "disaster," which I have translated ***False Witness.*** It is a drama in a setting of peasant life. Anca suspects her second husband, Dragomir, of having murdered her first husband, Dumitru, in order to marry her. Nine years after the murder, the woodcutter Ion, who had been unjustly accused of it and sent to the mines, escapes, half-witted as a result of his sufferings, and by chance calls at their house for something to eat. Anca becomes increasingly certain of Dragomir's guilt. When Ion kills himself during one of his mad fits, Anca talks to Dragomir as though *he* had killed Ion. Dragomir, thoroughly demoralized, allows her to extort from him the confession that he did kill Dumitru, and Anca hands him over to the authorities as the murderer of Ion. "False witness for false witness!" are her last words to him as the curtain comes down. This two-act drama has a classical simplicity of structure and unity of time and place. The plot is ingeniously constructed and the whole development logical. And yet there is something unsatisfying about the play. Perhaps this would disappear on the stage, and a fine actress might be able to make Anca's calculated revenge convincing. But I do not feel that Caragiale succeeded in making his audience believe in this persecution, as for instance, Strindberg makes us believe in the equally monstrous hounding of the husband by his wife in *The Father.*

Of Caragiale's comedies I propose to consider the best, ***A Lost Letter.*** The scene is a provincial town. Just before an election, a letter from Tipatescu, the prefect of police, to Zoe, the young wife of Trahanache, chairman of innumerable committees, falls into the hands of an unscrupulous newspaper editor, Catavencu. Although Trahanache implicitly trusts his wife and friend, Catavencu blackmails them all by threatening to publish the letter unless they throw over their parliamentary candidate Farfuridi, and nominate him instead. They are prepared to agree, when a telegram from Bucharest imposes an outsider, Dandanache, as the candidate. Before the public meeting at which the nomination is to be announced, Trahanache discovers a forgery committed by Catavencu; so, enabled by this to counter the blackmail, he announces the nomination of Dandanache. When Zoe sends for Catavencu and proposes to give him his forgery in exchange for the prefect's indiscreet letter, she finds that he has lost it. It is then handed to her by the same Drunken Citizen that originally let it fall into Catavencu's hands. Finding Catavencu at her mercy, Zoe forgives him, and a general reconciliation takes place at the reception in honor of Dandanache.

The striking thing about this comedy is its detachment. Our sympathy is not given to any character or set of characters, nor yet, despite their corruption, are we revolted by any. The prefect Tipatescu is hasty and violent, Zoe is heartless, and both are selfish. The amiable Trahanache is fatuously trusting. Catavencu is a scoundrel, though his demagogic gifts fascinate us. The policeman Ghita is dishonest and unprincipled, even if likeable. Dandanache is not only fatuous but a blackmailer. The Drunken Citizen is a complete sot. And the reconciliation of all these people in the finale is remarkably cynical. Yet as a whole the comedy is delightful and leaves no unpleasant taste behind. The fact is that Lamb's words on Congreve apply remarkably closely: "Judged morally every character in these plays . . . is alike essentially vain and worthless. The great art of Congreve is especially shown in this, that he has entirely excluded from his scenes—some little generosities on the part of Angelica perhaps excepted—not only anything like a faultless character, but any pretensions to goodness or good feelings whatsoever." Substitute Zoe for Angelica, and this last sentence fits ***A Lost Letter*** admirably. "Whether he did this designedly," continues Lamb, "or instinctively, the effect is as happy, as the design (if design) was bold. I used to wonder at the strange power which his *Way of the World* in particular possesses of interesting you all along in the pursuits of characters, for whom you absolutely care nothing—for you neither hate nor love his personages—and I think it is owing to this very indifference for any, that you endure the whole." That description might have been written of ***A Lost Letter.***

While engaged in writing the play, Caragiale is said to have asked his friends' advice as to who was to win the election, Farfuridi or Catavencu? One friend answered: "Both!" Some time later Caragiale said to him: "I have made them both win, as you jokingly suggested . . . but in the person of one man, Agamita Dandanache, who is more of a fool than Farfuridi and more of a cad than Catavencu. That is the dramatic climax, the surprise *dénouement,* which I had been after for two months and couldn't find!"

It is easy to imagine the splendid vivacity with which ***A Lost Letter*** must sparkle in actual performance. The public meeting of Act III, with its uproar and interruptions, and the contrasted speeches of the incoherent bungler Farfuridi and the fluent demagogue Catavencu, is skillfully worked up to the climax when the candidate's name is announced, and the curtain comes down on a general riot. Once more Caragiale has a surprise in store for us, in Zoe's clemency toward Catavencu, and the finale must surely be exhilarating as the music of the band draws nearer and nearer, until the electors pour onto the stage, and the reconciliation takes place to the clinking of champagne glasses.

What now are the characteristics of Caragiale's writings? In the first place, his comic spirit is what one would call "astringent." It is the antithesis of that of Alphonse Daudet or James Barrie. The tender, caressing, arch humor of such writers is quite foreign to him, and would no doubt have been repugnant. On the other hand, he lacks the indignation of satirists of morals and the partisan bitterness of political satirists. He is curiously detached in his outlook. We have noticed this particularly in ***A Lost Letter.*** But as it is the secret of ***A Lost Letter***'s success, so perhaps it is the secret of ***False Witness***' failure. In the tragedy the audience must feel in sympathy with at least one of the main characters. Neither Anca nor Dragomir engage our sympathy, and so ***False Witness*** remains a study in abnormal psychology rather than a tragedy. It is interesting to see in the half-witted convict, Ion, the one type of character for which Caragiale does seem to show a sympathetic emotion, a sort of indignant pity for the unfortunate whose weakness of intellect or character gets him pushed around by the harder and more capable members of society. Ion is, in fact, the tragic counterpart of the Drunken Citizen in ***A Lost Letter.***

Caragiale's ironic detachment is not to be understood as indifference. But indignation did not blind him, nor did it tempt him to sacrifice the values of art to those of propaganda. His attitude to his creations has been well pointed out by D. Murarasu in placing side by side two antithetical remarks of Caragiale about his own characters: "I loathe them!" and "See what dears they are!"

The other main characteristic of Caragiale's work is the fascination which the cruel and the monstrous have for him. We have noticed it already in ***False Witness*** and in the tales **"An Easter Candle"** and **"Sin."** But it is often to be seen in his comic work too. Sometimes it is ruthless in the manner of Harry Graham's *Ruthless Rhymes;* sometimes, like the stories of Saki, it is more sinister. The extract given above from **"Kir Ianulea"** illustrates his light-hearted ruthlessness, and so does a tale which he had heard in his childhood from a Ploesti barber and which he retells with the title of **"Pastrama Trufanda"** (**"Prime Salted"**). A Turk, Yussuf, to oblige a Jew, Aaron, takes a sack of salted meat with him on a trip to Jerusalem. Tempted by the appetizing smell, he eats or sells it all. On his return he explains to the Jew and offers to pay for it. The Jew is appalled. When his father had died, expressing a wish that his remains might moulder away in the soil of Palestine, Aaron for motives of economy had salted the flesh and entrusted it to Yussuf to save the cost of transport!

We have seen Caragiale's treatment of the cruelty of fate in **"Two Lottery Prizes."** Subtly connected with this is his love of the unexpected twist. In the story, **"Inspection,"** the cashier Anghelache behaves in a peculiar manner just before his accounts are due to be audited. He disappears and presently he is discovered to have committed suicide. We await the result of the audit—and the accounts are found to be in order! "Why should Anghelache have committed suicide?" Caragiale used to say to his friends with a chuckle; "I don't know myself!" Not only the unexpected twist, but also the unsolved enigma appealed to his sense of the ironic.

At the age of thirty Caragiale must have seemed destined to a long and successful career as a writer of comedies. Yet his last comedy appeared in 1884. Next, he was occupied with his tragic creations, **"An Easter Candle," "Sin,"** the drama ***False Witness,*** and so on. Then, once more, the comic began to prevail, but this time in the form of sketches and tales. The best of these mostly date from the last decade of the nineteenth century; **"Mânjoala's Inn,"** for instance, was published in 1898-1899. He reached his highest level once more in **"Kir Ianulea,"** published in 1908. What he would have made of a projected comedy, reintroducing characters from ***A Stormy Night*** and Catavencu from ***A Lost Letter,*** as he imagined them to have developed in the twenty-five years or so since their first appearance, we cannot know. But it is probable that he could not have equalled his own previous achievement in that line, and that he was wise to end his career as a writer with the posthumously published **"Abu-Hasan,"** which, like **"Kir Ianulea,"** is an old tale retold. Thus, the man who at thirty-two was the author of the best of Rumanian comedies forsook the stage and became a master of story-telling. At the very least, **"Kir Ianulea"** and **"Mânjoala's Inn"** deserve to rank among the classics of the world's literature.

Ileana Popovici (essay date 1972)

SOURCE: "Two Visions of 'A Lost Letter'," in *Romanian Review,* Vol. 26, No. 3, 1972, pp. 103-108.

[*In the following essay, Popovici compares two productions of* A Lost Letter, *the standard rendering at the I. L. Caragiale National Theatre in Bucharest and an alternative version mounted at the Lucia Sturdza-Bulandra Theatre in 1971.*]

Every culture possesses in its classical zone, icy cold peaks to which pilgrimages are undertaken, and burning hot sources, permanently connected with present-day circumstances by all manners of bridges and channels. For Romania, ***A Lost Letter,*** a comedy of manners by Ion Luca Caragiale—a playwright and prose writer, a basic author due to the conception and means through which he asserts the specific national, comic spirit—is a burning-hot source of this kind.

The life of this play is a somewhat odd phenomenon; acted almost permanently, it draws full houses—from schoolchildren to pensioners, who listen to a text they know by heart, whisper the spoken-cues beforehand, looking forward to the sallies of humour, watching for the punches, fully enjoying some nuance of the interpretation, as only music fans weigh the virtuosity of an instrumentalist. In their turn, the actors deal with it as with a great score, and its tackling is a foolhardy attempt and a certificate of maturity.

The fact that a play written at the end of the last century, in the solid traditional manner of a realistic satire, can give birth to and keep up so strong a theatrical myth, is in itself exceptional. It is not in any case justified by *the subject,* by the originality of the plot: in the thick of elections which absorb the public life in a little provincial town, a love letter sent by the prefect to his mistress—the wife of his best friend—is found, then stolen and negotiated like a political weapon; the lady's husband is an influential person locally, far older than she, an honest-minded cuckold with all the advantages resulting from a cunning credulity and a sort of idyllic boorishness. Then follow threats, arguments, a ludicrous muddle leading inevitably to a compromise: but the usual bourgeois electoral farce has an unexpected dénouement: the headquarters of the party oblige them to elect as deputy a contemptible, almost senile non-entity, but who in his turn wishing to secure the electoral mandate, had commited the same kind of blackmail with another compromising letter. What had seemed only an innocent vaudeville imbroglio revealed its character of complex artistic radiography. Constructed perfectly, the comedy combines picturesque, amusing episodes connected with the trajectory of the troublesome letter, until it reaches the woman it was addressed to, with an image of the social and human existence, achieved with extraordinary vigour. ***A Lost Letter*** is endowed with a miraculous power of synthesis and expression; every word, every scene is an image of the world it depicts, a blend of vulgarity and pathos, of good-naturedness and abjection, of upstartism and demagogy, from which the ridiculous and at the same time terribly real personages take shape, so full of vitality, so concentrated that they have lost their character of fiction and have become human prototypes. And their spoken cues have penetrated into current speech, having become set phrases. The extraordinary amusing character of the text is unfortunately difficult to translate, but for the Romanian spectator it has lost none of its evocatory resonances. The special pungency of the language, both vulgar and affected, the penetration of the rudiments of journalistic cant, high-sounding and empty, the borrowing of bookish "mannerly" elements, mark the beginning of a modern concern for the language. As nothing has become old fashioned in this work, ***A Lost Letter*** is the supreme masterpiece of Romanian dramaturgy.

A letter of such cultural importance was bound to be given a performance worthy of it. Since 1948, on the academic-type stage of the I. L. Caragiale National Theatre of Bucharest, numerous generations have made their apprenticeship as spectators repeatedly watching the staging, now classical too, directed by Sica Alexandrescu, today the doyen of Romanian stage managers. His performance is a concert in which, at every stand there is a reputed soloist purposing to give to every retort the expressiveness of an aria of bravery. The cast of great actors—with few exceptions the same as 20 years ago—have polished to perfection every nuance, every intention, lending the structure of the performance the transparence of crystal. In the minds of audiences, the characters have identified themselves so perfectly with the appearance, gestures, and inflections of the voices of actors Alexandru Giugaru, Costache Antoniu, Radu Beligan, Ion Fintesteanu, Marcel Anghelescu—the illustrious gallery of People's Artists, which younger actors (Carmen Stanescu, Dem Radulescu) have joined, fitting in perfectly—that for a time, it seemed daring that any other scenic image could be suggested.

And now this daring idea has become one of the events of the 1971-1972 season: at the Lucia Sturdza-Bulandra Theatre, Liviu Ciulei (an accomplished artist, stage manager, scenographer, actor, one of the creators to whom the Romanian theatre owes, essentially, its explosion of modern thinking) has achieved, with a perfectly faithful observance of the text, a new version.

While in the "classical" staging, the entire *mise en scène* is subordinated to the speech, setting off its quintessential function, the new staging attempts to drill deeper into the life strata deposited in the play. The scenographer's and stage manager's vision go deep into the environment; it brings into relief the relations between the personages, it portrays them carefully, noting their habits, with regard to the theatrical process itself. The actors of the cast (a team of brilliant comedians, at the height of their creative force: Toma Caragiu, Octavian Cotescu, Petre Gheorghiu, Rodica Tapalaga, Dem Radulescu, Stefan Banica) are of the age of the personages they act. The stage manager requires their behaviour to be exact and varied—he makes them react properly and vividly to the situation, to their partners' cues. The scenography too has freed itself from tradition and gained genuineness: the prefect's dwelling, for example, is filled with a jumble of ill-matched things of lamentable provincial elegance, in inevitable bad taste. The setting off of the implicit truth of the play and the force of revelation of the performance succeeds in transfiguring a well-known thing into a surprise. The spectator does not feel he is hearing the personages speak, but that he sees them live. The lovely adulterous lady who risked being compromised by the publication of the letter is no longer so ethereal and helpless, she struggles with the energy of a lioness to escape danger. She obliges both her husband and her lover to act in her interest and she actually succeeds in managing all the affairs of the district, which she had always known how to influence. The two rivals for the seat of deputy in the Chamber join the electoral struggle with might and main; they unscrupulously use any means that can serve their interests—lies, blackmail, forgery; the public meeting at the townhall where each of them state their "political programme," uttering solemn nonsense and pretending to be patriotic, is a real arena. The personage whose duty is to solve the conflict, the half-witted deputy the government wanted elected, is interpreted by Liviu Ciulei as a reject of the cosmopolitan aristocracy, with a vacant look quite incapable of grasping the elementary facts of a situation, but at the same time dreadfully cunning, and giving himself the airs and arrogance of an influential politician, snobbish and contemptuous. Through the personages the play is lent its original vitality. The brilliant verbal cover, with its piercing effects is not dealt with for itself, it does not disguise the conflict, on the contrary, it brings out its acuity. The finale of the performance, the popular demonstration when the elections come to an end, with the traditional get-togethers and speeches delivered on such occasions, is the climax of the new interpretation; the stage managing organized a huge banquet on the stage: bitters and snacks are served and traditional dishes whose strong flavour floods the house, glasses are clinked while a brass band plays deafeningly; the people hug one another, in a sham atmosphere of fraternization.

It is a metaphor of rare suggestive force of bourgeois petty politics, with its whole train of demagogy, inconstancy, profittering, with unassimilated West-European influences and rudimentary Machiavellisms. The comical frenzy is thus paired with a sarcastic projection, bitter and lacking illusions.

Keen theatre-goers have got a new interest now: they go from one performance to the other, they analyse, compare, form their preferences, agree or not with the new vision, find it hard to give up some well-known familiar image, choose one nuance from one performance, another from the other. And they are captivated by the vigorous acting of Toma Caragiu, Octavian Cotescu, Petre Gheorghiu, by the vivid images of the *mise en scène,* by the acidly ugly scenery of the new staging; sometimes they are faithful to the traditional interpretation, to the classical portraits, to their unshakeable perfection. This friendly artistic contest occasioned by the dramatist's anniversary will bring increased renewing force to the Romanian theatre and to the power of discernment and taste of audiences.

The two performances are a homage to the classical values, productive for modern culture, a living culture in perpetual motion.

Valentin Silvestru (essay date 1987)

SOURCE: "Studies and Essays: Caragiale's Day," in *Romanian Review,* Vol. 41, No. 6, 1987, pp. 55-67.

[*In the following essay, Silvestru discusses critical response to Caragiale's works during his lifetime and traces the growing acceptance of his works among international and Romanian audiences of the twentieth century.*]

The national and international area of spreading of I. L. Caragiale's work, the amount of studies devoted to him and the fact that his plays are untiringly present in the theatres, have all imposed the currency of a new term: CARAGIALEOLOGY. A literary-dramatical society of applied studies, set up in Craiova will probably contribute also to establishing this term, whose pronunciation sounds rather forbidding, but has the same *raison d'être* as the already established Shakespeareology, Brechtology or Eminescology.

About a century after I. L. Caragiale's literary début one may say that two essential attitudes have manifested themselves towards his writings. For about seven decades, this gigantic and singular creation had to be defended by the broad circles of the public opinion—headed by the great scholars of Romania—against detractors of all kinds, ranging from quasi-anonymous journalists to venomous brethren of some prestige, against misunderstandings, misjudgments and misconstructions, against the declared hostility of political clans as well as against the dulled hostility of an adverse social group, against the official enmity involving fundamental institutions. In the last thirty years or so, the main attitude has been that of innovating continuous and maximum capitalization, in defiance of (set) interpretations and of the establishment of immutable traditions regarding Caragiale shows, as well as in defiance of depreciating, minimizing sequellae.

What have been the reproaches, brought vehemently and tenaciously against this genius whose entering upon the arena of letters and arts inaugurated a new realistic trend, laid the foundations of modern Romanian satire as well as an exceptional national landmark along the road of the world's great comedy? He was reproached with being no patriot. On 14 April 1890, when the dramatist I. L. Caragiale submitted nearly all of his productions for the stage (written within a decade) to the Romanian Academy, with a view to the latter's prize, twenty of its members decided, against barely three, that I. L. Caragiale could not be awarded the prize because first of all he had "to learn how to respect his nation, and not to mock it," as the secretary of that institution, Dimitrie A. Sturdza declared in public. In 1902, probably with similar arguments, the same secretary again determined the rejection of Caragiale for the prize. The charge of lack of patriotism, grossly ignoring the nature and goals of satire, its specific way of acting in the sense of the requirements for society's development and for the people's edification, reverted again and again along the years, from the same source of every ignominy, which is aggressive and authoritative stupidity, heavily hurt in its pride by the exposure of laughter. This kind of stupidity manifested itself most violently from the very début of the dramatist who remembered that the very next day "A patriotic newspaper denounced me to all true Romanians for a traitor who exposes our petty miseries to the foreigners. On the second performance I was hooted and hissed and threatened by some patriotic members of the Civic Guard in Theatre Square. It was some young officers that saved me from the mob's fury. But the play was eliminated from the National Theatre's repertoire."

Caragiale was constantly and ruthlessly reproached with immorality by people who cynically and dishonestly mistook the vulgarity of thinking and behaviour of Caragiale's personages with the way of thinking and living of the very man who had rendered them immortal as comic characters. After the première of his comedy ***A Stormy Night,*** most critics were scandalized by his having hurt public morality. Horrified, the critic of the *Românul* (Frederic Damé) confessed he was "ashamed" of relating what was taking place in the comedy and, stifled with fury, perorated like this: " . . . That he should invite us to the theatre with our wives, with our children, in order to test to what extent an audience may listen to the crudest obscenity without blushing, seems to me to be going rather too far." The furious critic considered that the young playwright "accepted to defile his own profession." The anonymous critic of the newspaper *Binele public* considered indecent and impudic "Veta's infatuation, her scene with her lover Chiriac, the latter's attitude, the curtain falling right when Chiriac embraces

Veta, the fact that her husband himself finds Chiriac's necktie in her bed,"—these and other things causing the brave chronicler, with an eye on the stage and another in the house, to note that "among the ladies shining bright in the boxes . . . there were many who hid their genteel faces with the fans they handled so elegantly."

Even the prosewriter Ioan Slavici, a friend of Caragiale's—while admitting in the *Timpul* that the comedy displays "People whom we do meet in Bucharest suburbs, true things which indeed occur with us nearly everyday, an unworthy way of living but, in the last analysis, a kind of life we ourselves share"—immediately commented very pudically "Such beings as Veta and Chiriac . . . can hardly—or rather never—have their place in a comedy." And Slavici publicly advised the playwright to expurgate "a few rather bold passages."

On the other hand, the *Telegraph* declared that Caragiale's comedy was imbued with "the most perfect type of lascivious immorality, displaying on the stage the most abject vices of society." It was indeed amazing how the critics failed to note that immorality—a reality—was satirized, therefore condemned, therefore repudiated! The reproach made a long career (For instance Iacob Negruzzi, in his *Dictionary of the Youth Literary Society*—published after Caragiale's death, characterized the Romanian genius but lapidarily, mainly by the label: "A pessimistic, sceptical and cynical youth") and one can hardly say his reproach has yet been buried very deep.

Critics contested Caragiale's thorough knowledge of realities and denied his capacity as a playwright, his skill for the well-made comedy, which nowadays sounds like an absurdity. Nevertheless, even Ioan Slavici believed about ***A Stormy Night*** that "Viewed as a comedy, it is no more than stage movements written with greater or smaller talent, some of them below any serious criticism." In Caragiale's other major comedy ***The Lost Letter,*** the *Liberalul* discovered "a rudimentary plot, that is one developing along a well-known and almost rusty road." The *Telegraph* in its turn was decreeing: "Mr. Caragiale lacks the art of a dramatist and that of a man of letters." After the first night of Caragiale's next play ***Carnival Scenes,*** the *Românul* was overindignant and concluded that the farce was "written in a corrupted language, loaded with all the banalities and absurdities at the turnpike of the city." The critic of the *Râsboiul* noted that Caragiale "was in poor luck even while sprinkling salt on the dialogues and dreadfully hasty in writing the play generally." The critic of the *România liberâ* thought that "the dramatist chooses a few types from the rabble and in a few scenes causes aspect rather than the deep character to surface," which meant that Caragiale could only have a superficial perception of reality. The criticism in the *Doina* noted that "misunderstandings and mistakes succeed each other and are knotted together so fast, the plot is so crowded that the spectator's attention is soon wearied and he can hardly follow the complications he witnesses." In the *Vointa,* D. C. Ollanescu-Ascanio, a historian and a man of letters chronicled his own "disappointment" because "neither things of interest nor emotions, nor even some crafty seed for laughter can be found in this farce called ***Carnival Scenes***—definitely a very sad and wilted carnival."

Most critics complained that "people cannot laugh" or "we didn't laugh."

Caragiale's drama ***The Bane*** (or rather: ***Wrong for Wrong***—translator's note) was subject to the hardest criticism, charging the author with ignorance of life, the lack of truthfulness of its characters, the fallaciousness of the plot; it was sententiously affirmed that "the peasants are not true to life," "the plot is unbelievable," "Dragomir's psychic states are all wrong," "the finale lacks logic," "Anca is no peasant woman," etc. Caragiale, who had been threatened with a hiding, then had seen one of his plays mangled, another one withdrawn after two performances alone, was now forced—to cap it all—to reply to a trumped up charge of plagiarism and to defend his honour as a writer in court.

Naturally enough there have always been also honest attempts at criticizing what seemed to lack perfect fulfilment, explainable controversies, fertile doubts perhaps even various hierarchies and classifications, but fundamental adversity elicited an essential attitude of defence. The playwright's defence was assumed in various ways and at various times by Romania's great critics: Titu Maiorescu, C. Dobrogeanu-Gherea, G. Ibraileanu, Paul Zarifopol, Pompiliu Constantinescu, Serban Cioculescu, Tudor Vianu, Perpessicius, George Calinescu, as well as by writers or scholars ranging from Eminescu, Delavrancea, Goga, and Iorga to Camil Petrescu, Liviu Rebreanu, Arghezi and Mihail Sebastian. It is to be noted, however, that any article or study regarding Caragiale's plays, sometimes even regarding short fiction, his journalistic contributions or his own person, were polemic in their nature and struck a distinctive note of speech for the defence in a trial that has not yet been concluded.

The last three decades have brought about an essential change in Caragialeology, the reception of his works being achieved gradually but fully, the essential issue being that of its exhaustive restoration, in the spirit in which it was written, as a monumental asset of our national culture and as an artistic testimony of exceptional political efficiency in the revolutionary upheaval of society.

The essential contemporary attitude in matters of Caragialeology is the permanent capitalization on his work in the present times, through better connections with the thinking and tastes of our own epoch, against the stagnant tendency to turn previous models into fetishes and for routine productions. The first and most significant gesture was the innovating revival of Caragiale's comedies at the National Theatre, thus reimposing them strongly upon the public consciousness: they have drawn categories of spectators who had not been sensitive to this work, or to the theatre generally.

The second decisive gesture was the printing of Caragiale's complete works in a critical edition edited by Serban Cioculescu, Alexandru Rosetti, Liviu Calin (with an introductory study by Silvian Iosifescu) which at the same time included a sui generis history of each play. Then monographic, analytic, historical and comparative books on Caragiale have appeared in turn, signed by Serban Cioculescu, Silvian Iosifescu, Stefan Cazimir, Ion Roman, B. Elvin, Ion Constantinescu, Alexandru Calinescu, Mircea Tomus and others. Collective volumes of studies were published on the occasion of various anniversaries, recollections about the man and the writer have been published by those who knew him, followed by a general bibliography (1948-1962) and, more recently, a selection from criticism *I. L. Caragiale interpretat de . . . (I. L. Caragiale Interpreted by . . .)* as well as numerous studies. We now have at our disposal the director's notebooks of producer Sica Alexandrescu, the testimonies of great actors in our own days as well as of recent producers who have staged revivals of late. Contemporary criticism has given particular attention to the revival of each play, so that all performances since 1949 are accompanied by ample files, even of performances outside Bucharest. Respect for the original text is unanimous and full, discussion always bears on the quality of the staging in relation to the exigences of the work and of audiences. A criterion which frequently appears in critical considerations is the modern spirit of the staging or, as a controversial issue, the confirment within imagistic and verbal clichés.

With the assertion of Romanian culture abroad in post-war times, the attitude of making the most of Caragiale's work has irradiated towards other areas of the world; he has been discovered in many centres of practically every continent, through local performances or tours of Romanian companies; Caragiale has gradually but definitively joined the gallery of great world dramatists. He has been included in *Lexikon der Weltliteratur* (Dr. Gerhardt Steiner, VEB, Leipzig, 1965), *Histoire des spectacles* (Encyclopédie de la Pléiade, Guy Dumur, Gallimard, Paris, 1965), *Theater Geschichte Europas* (Vol. 3, Heinz Kindermann, Otto Müller Verlag, Salzburg, 1974). In *Storia universale del teatro dramatico,* (Unione Tipografica Editrice Torinese, 1964), Vito Pandolfi makes the following remarks: "The Romanian theatre reached the level of art with I. L. Caragiale . . . We must once more note how the vigorous blossoming of a national spirit always blends with the most direct and lively expression: the theatre. Between ***The Inspector General*** and ***Rabagas, The Lost Letter*** admirabily rounds off—with a theatrical game of irresistible comic vivacity—the picture offered by the European society in its relationships with political institutions."

Foreign criticism has also been interested in the author on the occasion of each important performance. The Romanian spectacle given at the Théâtre des Nations in Paris in June 1956 was praised by all the French press, French writers and artists alike asserting in writing, over the radio and television that they had the revelation of a masterpiece and of a genius. The specialized archives preserve encomiastic reviews written in Holland, Italy, the Soviet Union, Finland, Chile, Greece, Turkey, Germany, Japan, Peru and it is highly probable that there are earlier or newer testimonies which have not yet reached us.

But the considerable extension of historical and critical studies only partly satisfies the need for a theatrical interpretation of Caragiale's drama. In this respect, a decisive contribution has been made by producers and actors, not so much by literary or drama critics. There has been the ever keener requirement for new answers to questions regarding Caragiale's stageworthiness, the nature of his characters and of the relationships between them, the comic theatrical methodology. The re-evaluations in the middle of this century, due to Sica Alexandrescu, restored to us the comic peculiarities and the authentic historical condition of Caragiale's types, offering us a standard. Among the stage versions of some sketches or plays, those produced by Valeriu Moisescu, Lucian Pintilie or Liviu Ciulei have revealed to us—with new vigour,—the comic power of generalization and the psychological as well as sociological condition of Caragiale's personages, suggesting new standards to us. Thanks to one of those productions, ***Carnival Scenes*** obtained a different status also among specialized literary commentary: one has ceased to encounter the old-fashioned formula, in the spirit of rudimentary schoolbooks—"it is Caragiale's poorest comedy."

Such re-evaluations, to which are added praiseworthy, highly personal productions staged in Iasi, Craiova, Brasov, Cluj-Napoca, enjoying the adhesion of vast audience, require a new discussion on the question of how topical Caragiale's work is. It used to be said that his types are ephemeral; that the mobiles of his satire are short-lived; that the political situations and the social ambience are sure to be obfuscated in the process of historical development. And yet reality demonstrates that this grandiose œuvre increases its appeal as time passes and continues to be perceived as topical by each generation. In what does this topicality consist? Is there a constant ratio between the satirical outlook on the world in Caragiale's plays and our own critical view of the prolongations of that world in the contemporary universe? Does the topical virtue of Caragiale's comedies reside in types? Or is it explained by the penetrating scrutiny of social mechanisms, in full accord with our present-day outlook on past realities? Or is it the fact that the social universe, the political aspect, the scathing criticism of old institutions and the structure of life are deeply encrusted into psychological categories of classical realistic orientation—the thinking and language bordering on caricature, the comical behaviours giving expression to the character's fundamental non-conformity with reality?

If I am not mistaken, it was Professor and critic Garabet Ibraileanu that used to remark at the beginning of the century that with Caragiale the suburb itself is a psychological category . . . If we could give an unhesitating answer to our last question, it would mean that the Caragialean scenic modality discovered in the '60s and

'70s, generated a new and ample possibility for knowing and accepting plays through performances. They can hardly become obsolete, in very much the same way as Aristophanes, Molière, Gogol or Goldoni's comedies do not become stale but, depending on the way they are staged, they may appear either out of date and pointless or, on the contrary, fresh and pithy, actually linked to topical realities, particularly from the characterological point of view.

An assertion which recurred several times—and still recurs today—is that, in Caragiale's work, we have to do with a whole world of bland idiots, creatures who look sweet in their harmless patriarchialism, ridiculous nincompoops, endowed with a gift for conversation and confession, essentially kind though foul-mouthed occasionally, decrepit yet picturesque, etc. But after all isn't this world in the last analysis rapacious and ferocious? For instance scrutinizing not so much the personages' irrascibility, but rather the latter's specific manifestations, we may note that most characters in Caragiale's comedies are highly aggressive and practise thrashing as a favourite means for solving disputes. In ***The Lost Letter,*** from policeman Ghita Pristanda's confession to Zoe we learn that the prefect Tipatescu often beats him in his anger, as if the policeman were just a stupid servant; moreover, in a fit of anger, prefect Tipatescu seizes the Intoxicated Citizen by his collar while during his secret encounter with his enemy Catavencu he behaves so threateningly that the latter, who knows the official fairly well, thinks it wiser to take refuge behind the furniture. "I'll break his bones," "I'll shoot him dead," "I'll burn him to death," are threats which do not seem mere asseverations since at a certain moment Ipatescu even picks up a walking-stick from a corner and "turns wrathfully, on Catavencu hissing: 'I really don't know what keeps me from, bashing your head in! You scoundrel! You have to surrender that letter to me, you have to tell me where the letter is . . . or else I'll kill you like a puppy!' *(He rushes at Catavencu but the latter goes round the table and the sofa, upturns a few chairs and tries to make an escape out of the window)*" and so on. In ***A Stormy Night,*** the main character, the merchant Dumitrache Titirca has got into the habit on his return home of beating his apprentice Spiridon every night either because the latter is found awake or because he is found asleep. A sample is actually offered us on the stage, and Titirca's foil Ipingescu participate in the thrashing with exalted urges, overjoyed at by the scene. In ***Carnival Scenes,*** the barber Nae Girimea, having caught the pharmacist with the faked customer's card, "gave him a good talking-to, not using many other words than *swine* and *ass,* boxed his ears several times and kicked him out of the shop" as his journeyman narrates. Pampon questions his maid servant by first boxing her ears and then he beats Cracanel savagely (the latter narrates the clash: "I hardly had time to reply, sir, when slap! dash! pop! he boxed my ears four times; and he crushed my hat, sir, and cast it away"); then, finding Cracanel in the barber's shop again, Pampon "is about to seize him," while the former runs in terror around the furniture and shouts at the top of his voice "Help! police! guards!" Later on, reconciled and united in their grief over their mistresses' betrayal, they ill-treat the Probationer in the carnival ball-room, "catch him and start pouncing on him," mistaking him for the seducer they had been seeking. Their mistresses, Didina Mazu and Mita Baston have a dreadful skirmish in the dark, pulling each other's hair and scratching each other savagely ("they both shriek and clinch each other, foaming at their" mouths, the stage directions tell us).

And returning to ***A Stormy Night,*** the journeyman Chiriac, who is also a sergeant in the Civic Guard promises his superior, Titirca, that he would "seize" Take the Cobbler for the "exercise" this operation being foreseen as not quite delicate. Zita's ex-husband Ghita Tircadau is a notorious rowdy, he carries a long dagger in his walking-stick, preparing to molest his former wife at any moment. It is therefore easy for us to picture what the gallant Rica Ventuarino would have gone through if, being caught by his pursuer he had not been recognized by Ipingescu as the latter's favourite journalist. An interesting suggestion offered by a production of ***A Stormy Night*** (Bacau, 1976) conveyed the sensation that the young journalist was forced into a shotgun wedding that very moment. Actually come to think of it, he can hardly be supposed to have paid that visit at night—incidentally at the wrong address—for a formal proposal . . .

In ***Carnival Scenes*** Mita Baston has bought vitriol for the purpose of disfiguring her faithless lover Nae Ghirimea—and she actually carries out her threat, only the chemist has fooled her selling her violet ink, which she is not aware of on throwing the liquid at the man's face. Soon afterwards she seizes Girimea's razor, struggles with him and then attempts to cut her own throat.

Collective fights are famous: the one taking place on the stage in the third act of ***The Lost Letter*** is followed by the turmoil at the "encyclopaedic society" (merely narrated) where the members of the "Romanian Economic Aurora" fight so badly that they even break the skull of priest Pripici.

As a rule, everything starts from some banal mistake or misunderstanding, sometimes even from a practical joke or ends in a joke; but violence, cruelty, the inclination to exterminate one's enemy or at least to maim him, are realities. Perhaps a synthesis of such inclinations is to be found in the monologue **"April Fool"** which begins with a practical joke: "We'll just have a good laugh at Mike the Poltron, so what, after all?" As it turned out "I saw his brain mingled with hair and foamy blood." So that, in Lucian Pintilie's production of ***Carnival Scenes*** at the Bulandra Theatre in Bucharest, when the ball comes to a halt the music stops and the masks gather threateningly around the suspected philanderer and Pampon puts his hands into his broad belt to pull out his claspknife, we realize that a crime is about to be committed or is quite probable. In ***Uncle Leonidas Facing the Reaction,*** the terror of the title character who barricades himself against a possible assault of the rioters is not entirely unexplainable it becomes ridiculous only later on, when we learn that it had all been a false alarm.

The fact that such inclinations or events have been treated superficially—even nowadays—the error being revealed in anticipation, the false appearance being disclosed too soon, the aspect of brutality being polished off and choleric extremities being edulcorated, can hardly conceal the essential cruelty. As a matter of fact the living models of these bland characters went so far as to try and lynch Caragiale, they demanded his arrest (even in written petitions!), they summoned him in Court for imaginary guilts, they took his plays off the bills, they denied him the rewards he deserved, they persecuted him everywhere, having him dismissed from the minor job he held at the State Monopolies Administration, from that of a school inspector, from the management of the National Theatre, from an editorial job, eventually driving him even into exile. One could hardly say that his characters, so true to life, behaved inconsistently to their creator . . .

It is asserted that a general kind of bonhomie is involved, residing in chats in the drawing-room and in the coffee-house, here and there with a flash of cunning, soon divulged even by the person who practises it. But a close investigation of the texts points rather to harsh cunning which disguises the most shameless interests in the fine clothes of "principles." The distilled formula, enounced by the personages themselves—or by the author—is diplomacy, while the crude formula is "traducement" (i. e. betrayal) the plot proper consisting in intrigue ("and then we'll sap the right honourable as we very well know how.") Such are Caragialean expressions of the characters' *transactional conscience*—as a critic has styled it.

Many of Caragiale's personages feel an imperious urge to cheat or betray, no matter whom, taking as their credit that they master the science of "traducement". Adulterous couples hold a prominent place. But even the most naïve characters—because of age or of lack of experience—start along this road as soon as they can: the young apprentice Spiridon fools Rica Venturiano for the sake of a tip, the journeyman Iordache mystifies the customers who enter the barber's shop, Zita tries to hoodwink her elder sister Veta into going to the night club again in order to secure the apprentice Spiridon as a courier for her love messages; the women in ***Carnival Scenes,*** Mita and Didina betray out of habit, thus joining the list of women who have inflicted "seven cases of betrayal" upon the unfortunate former volunteer Cracanel; the policeman Pristanda tries to cheat even his superior, prefect Tipatescu, in counting the flags displayed for the parade ***(The Lost Letter)***; in ***Carnival Scenes*** another policeman, Nae Ipistatul cheats the others with his self-managed "lottery," the Probationist is horrified at the possibility for his elder brother in Ploiesti to discover his nasty tricks. Then in Caragiale's ***Sketches and Moments,*** Mita, Mr. Mandache's wife, "traduces everybody with her diplomacy," even the chief editor of the *Romanian Trifles;* Uncle Stasache's Acrivita traduces her husband by presenting her lover with a brilliant, a young hypnotizer diddles Caliopa "the typically Romanian woman" by stealing her valuables after he had left her "in a trance"; Dick tries to take in Mick, inventing all sorts of slander at his expense but ascribing it to another friend (**"Friends"**), the Newcomer in the sketch **"Trains"** sadistically pulls the leg of the two belated customers in the alehouse, by giving them details of intimacy between his wife and his station master, only at the end disclosing the fact that they are brother and sister. Another character mystifies himself in order to better undergo the ordeal of his wife's delivery of a child; and between this personage, who deliberately deceives himself, and Uncle Leonidas, who has the enormous ambition of "traducing" the government itself (by not levying any taxes, by paying monthly wages "to say nothing of the pension" and to cancel all debts through a "mortuary law") there is a very ample scale, which includes political lies, electioneering, gerrymandering, demagogic explosions, terrible infamies planned or even carried out in cold blood—at all times in the name of some "ideal". Therefore, caught in the whirl of an intrigue which he makes nothing of but which he fears, Farfuridi (a minor character in ***The Lost Letter)*** appears justified to burst out in exasperation: "Let there be treason, if warranted by our Party's interests, but let us be clearly told about it!"; that is he is indeed ready to betray everything, everywhere, at all times, merely on condition he is not pushed aside from sharing the truth—or else why should there be treason, if not in order to obtain some advantage?

Candour is usually a simulacrum of perfidiousness and when characters try to dissimulate it, they adopt sly, temporizing interrogation. When his two political acolytes (in ***The Lost Letter)*** corner him, the prefect Tipatescu ingenuously questions them: "Which Party? Which Catavencu?" And his whole talk with the latter—termed by him "the nihilist"—is but a subtle game of questions. It is no bickering between two petty cheats, but a dishonest negotiation between two sharks. They are provincial skarks, yet their greed is very high, they aim at high government functions or even estates.

They are rather sly, all these candid characters, haunted by the demon of interrogation: sometimes their cunning is very accurately calculated and when Caragiale himself was telling the critic Dobrogeanu-Gherea that Trahanache was aware of his wife Zoe's cuckolding him with Tipatescu although he pretended to be ignorant of it, this was due to Trahanache's being "a devilishly artful Greek." All protagonists of ***A Stormy Night***—with Titirca's exception—know that the latter's wife Veta is on intimate terms with journeyman Chiriac, but they all pretend not to know anything of it. In the Paris production of ***The Lost Letter*** (directed by Marcel Cuvellier at the Théâtre de Poche in 1955), Trahanache appeared as well informed on his wife's love intrigue, but suggested in various ways that it suited him to preserve the status quo, which brought him only advantages and no disturbance of the spirit; in this way the lack of morality of this world was endowed with one more characterizing note, severe and essentially comic.

The above considerations are strengthened by Caragiale's own perspective on the evolution of his characters—as suggested by planning a new play *Titirca, Sotirescu & Comp.* in which their rapacity was to manifest itself at the level of an upper social status.

An outlook on Caragiale's characters can hardly overlook their literary-dramatic structure or the satirical essence of the comic element, or the way in which the characters real models acted upon Caragiale's colossal work. Such a complex system of comparisons and relationships is imposed upon us by the profound realism and by the civic, moral and political condition of his comedy. In his time, as well as later on, the comedy was a test for the degree of moral health or unhealthiness of society, it generated adhesions as well as extreme adversities, function of a more general creed and a general frame of mind.

In order to explain all this better, our famous dramatist and prose-writer left us also a sketch entitled **"Yes and No"**—a confession in the form of a fable—as conclusive as possible:

> You are of course acquainted with the poor jade of the watercarrier who brings you your supply of water: the wretched animal, as modest as it is brave, never got bored with ambling from the watercarrier's house up to the well in Filaret suburb and thence to another house and then back to Filaret and then . . . Well, to cut a long story short, the job that any watercarrier's horse is called upon to discharge.
>
> So far, there is no outstanding moment in the life of the noble animal. But things may change once in a while. One day the watercarrier himself may fancy to reach his home sooner. Yet the nag refuses to move faster. It would sooner die than change its slow amble. It knows how to go at a pace, not at a trot, and not for the world would it change its pace, or its way either.
>
> The watercarrier first speaks honeyed words to the jade, pats her neck, calls her by her name, urges her gently; it is all in vain. Losing patience, he whips her lightly; the nag starts hopping on the spot and refuses to move on; she may hop so many times as would be enough for she to cover a league, yet she does not budge from the spot.
>
> Seeing the obstinacy of the beast, the watercarrier thinks of another device: laughing, he starts tickling the horse's ear, hoping to move her in this way. But then the old nag is seized with a fit of fury: she starts snorting, kicking, straddling her legs, retching, coughing and taking ridiculous leaps, actually threatening to break the shafts of the water-cart.
>
> May God protect you from an old crock when personal dignity moves it to revolt!
>
> Well, do you think that there are jades only harnessed to watercarts? No! Do you want jades, true jades, the most ornery ones? Seek them in literature. As soon as you try to take your jade off the beaten track, as soon as you ask it—tickling it as you can—to walk at another pace than the one known to the old crock—it starts hopping, kicking, straddling its legs in order to assert its personal dignity.
>
> Just try to waste a joke on such a noble animal! The animal won't take it and is sure to stage a ridiculous demonstration to you.
>
> May one joke?
>
> Yes and no.
>
> One may—when in the presence of sane people.
>
> One may not—when one has to do with sick people.
>
> One may—with jolly, good-natured people.
>
> One may not—with morose and aggrieved people.
>
> One may—with witty people.
>
> One may not—with witless people.
>
> One may—with literary and artistic people.
>
> One may not—with literary and artistic crocks.

What could we add—paraphrasing the dubitative conclusions of this juicy and pithy prose-piece? "I kept silent and I endured"—the author wrote in moving prophesy—"hoping that my own day will eventually come." Well, his day has come, things have changed radically, Caragiale's work careers gloriously at home and abroad; so that to the question "Can one laugh nowadays together with I. L. Caragiale?" we have every reason to answer: Yes, one may—and even heartily. He remains—and shall remain—as the literary historian George Calinescu defined him: "A great artist, the creator of a total world, with its own institutions and language, with every string of human life, from the tragical one to the grotesque one."

Florin Manolache (essay date 1987)

SOURCE: "Between Minitext and Maxitext," in *Romanian Review,* Vol. 41, No. 6, 1987, pp. 67-77.

[*In the following essay, Manolache examines Caragiale's narrative style.*]

> " . . . *take me for a sea-trip, timely and wisely.*"
>
> I. L. Caragiale, **"A Few Opinions"** (1896)

The note which Caragiale made on the manuscript of a story ("N.B.: Great attention should be paid to whatever may be suppressed—that is as much as possible") was for a long time considered a key to his writing. Actually to our surprise we discover "two Caragiales" at this level too, for one of the many instances of the Caragiale vs. Caragiale situation lies in the author's placing himself half way between a minimum and maximum of literary expression. In this respect, Caragiale is the first Romanian writer to have left us a considerable number of theoretical pages and remarks on the main theme of the "text contour" of a play or prose piece.

By *text contour* we understand the recurrence rate and distribution patterns of the basic units of literary texts: plot, description, information, image, the portrait, general considerations, stage directions, the dialogue or the scene, the maxims and aphorisms, and even spells of silences and pauses.

A text contour model must start with a minitext (one using the smallest possible number of basic units (texts tending to become zero-narrative) and go as far as a maxitext (one in which all possible units are represented). The first type includes only the elements indispensable for the existence of a certain literary genre (personage, plot, scene), while the second, associates to them at least one more temporal basic element (general considerations, descriptions, maxims, etc.). The model could also be constructed as a continuous string of generative text units or as a progression whose terms are—among others—sentences, items of information, anecdotes, sketches and the ten-minute play, the short story, the novel or the drama.

The two types of texts, at the hypothetical extremities of this model range, were described by Quintillian in Chapter VIII of his *On the Training of an Orator:*

> Undoubtedly, whoever says that a city was conquered, includes in that expression whatever happens in such cases, though this expression which is in fact a short announcement does not find its way to our feelings. If, on the contrary, he develops what is included in this expression alone, there will appear before us the flames invading houses and temples, the noise of falling roofs, the hubbub and turmoil in which shouts and shrieks of people are blended; we shall see some people running for their lives, others embracing for the last time, women and children crying, as well as the old people who curse their fate which has kept them alive to reach that day; then, the sacking of sacred as well as lay sanctuaries, the soldiers who run for loot this way and that and those who beg not to be robbed; people bound hand and foot and driven away by the enslaver; the mother who tries to keep her baby back and, wherever the booty is tempting enough, the haggling between the conquerors themselves. Although, as we have already said, the term of "conquest" includes all this in itself, enouncing the whole, we do say less by it than by enumerating every detail.

All texts approaching the first narrative formula may be called texts of the "veni-vidi-vici type."

Starting from Boileau, the Romanian writer Ion Ghica, in a letter to his friend, the poet and dramatist Vasile Alecsandri (1819-1881) offers a comic example of an author of non-fictional texts who tends to illustrate the type of zero-narrative communication:

> When writing, Boileau was in the habit of cutting off three words out of four . . . The late high steward Draganescu went even farther then Boileau in matter of sacrifices: he had his secretary re-read aloud so many as ten times what he had dictated to him. For instance: "It is with brotherly love that I am bowing to you, honourable steward."
>
> "Come, quill driver, read out", Draganescu used to say when the sentence had been written. On the first reading, he asked the clerk to cross out the beginning. "It is with brotherly love", because the boyar he was addressing did not deserve brotherly love. On the second reading he ordered the clerk to cross out the words "I am bowing to you" under the pretext that it was not meet and proper for him, a high steward, to stoop to bowing before a lower boyar. And, eventually, on the third reading, he also crossed out the words "honourable steward" being still angry that the voivode had elevated that petty squire to such a lofty rank. Such was high steward Draganescu's correspondence throughout his life!

On the contrary, texts at the other extremity of our range of models risk to lose their finite character through the author's ambition to emulate the registrar's office and reality. This category of texts includes Laurence Sterne's *Tristram Shandy* in which, however, the narrative proves incapable to catch up with reality although the narrator may have assumed precisely that aim. Writing in a year a novel about one day of his existence the novelist lags 364 days behind and the more he writes the more he has to recover.

What interests us in connection with these two ideal types of texts does not refer to the relation between plot and story, a ratio which is shown by the above examples to be conversely proportional (a minimal story would correspond to a maximal plot and vice-versa), but to the author's preference for certain kinds of text elements and, naturally enough, to the way in which the latter uses them with a view to giving his text a certain contour.

In Caragiale's case, the relation between minitext and maxitext decisively involves the relationship between fiction and drama, for these two genres, observing different conventions, resort to the word or to the basic elements of the text in a different manner and ascribe a different signification to the expressive role of blanks.

In point of text contour, the relation between fiction and drama may be examined either from the dramatist's angle or from that of a novelist (prosewriter), or else, more impartially, from the relatively objective angle of literary theory.

In one of the earliest European works on the modern theory of fiction *(Die Rolle des Erzählers in der Epik),* Käte Friedemann, Oskar Walzel's pupil, resorts to the ideal case of two texts by Zola, using the same epic material (the crime in *Thérèse Raquin),* in the two systems which concern us—drama and fiction—to check the different functions of description as a basic element of the literary text.

This comparison reveals a difference of genre conventions, not one of value or quality. Indeed, out of the objective differences of point of view (the most important of which is the presence or absence of the *mediator* in fiction and in drama, respectively) primarily results the "preference" of the two literary forms for certain basic elements of the text (description or portrait for fiction and discussion or dialogue for drama); in the second place the phenomenon of contamination or of borrowing some specific forms which change from one genre to another (dialogue in fiction and narrative in drama) in the form of the "messenger's report"—the most typical narrative elements in a play.

Closer to us in time and pursuing the prosewriter's point of view, in *Die Logik der Dichtung,* Käte Hamburger cites a few examples of writers for whom drama is inferior to the novel precisely because it allegedly offers us a simplified image or a summarization of life.

Thus, Hugo von Hofmannstahl imagines (in an essay of 1902) a dialogue in which the novelist Balzac reproaches the theatre with "narrowing reality"; in much the same way, Thomas Mann, in *Versuch über das Theater* (1908) considers that drama offers us an artificial and inaccurate image of life.

In Romania, the historian Nicolae Iorga (1871-1940) upheld at the end of the 19th century the idea that the theatre had become "a secondary genre," "doomed to perish because of the triumphant competition provided by the novel;" the same idea was expressed by the novelist Duiliu Zamfirescu (1858-1921) in his letters to the critic Titu Maiorescu (1840-1917) after the writer and philologist Bogdan Petriceicu Hasdeu (1838-1907) in his well-known study of 1863 "The Movement of Letters in Iasi" had asserted the opposite, namely that the drama was superior to the novel and to history proper.

Without trying to demonstrate the existence of a tendency categorically underrating fiction or of some aversion of the dramatist to the novel, in Caragiale's case we can detect an obvious partiality to the theatre and to its stricter laws during the period of the great comedies, of his tragical stories and even of his comic "moments." In his "critical investigation" of 1878, this partiality took the form of a comparison between the "plan of a drama" and "the plan of a story" and concluded that drama was more concise, its parts more closely linked and that, all in all, it was the more coherent of the two:

> In a story, catastrophes occur and are strung independently, having no further kinship between them than their belonging more or less to the same subject—very much like a rosary: the beads themselves being independent of each other are only strung and brought together on the same thread; we may cut the thread wherever we like and leave as many beads drop as we like and yet, if we knot the thread again, the rosary will still be a rosary, though with fewer beads. On the other hand, the plan for a drama must be different: here, incidents hang on each other, flow out of each other, are woven into each other for the same end, that is for preparing the great catastrophe, the conclusion or the denouement—exactly as organic cells depend on each other and are woven into each other in order to make up organs of the body which all together work for the same and, i.e. for the constitution or the economy of the being: in this case we no longer can—as in the case of rosaries—cut or maim the organs wherever and whatever way we like, without thus destroying the being or at least shattering all its economy.

By comparison with the drama and with the latter's ideal economy, one may infer that fiction is characterized by prolixity and, in favour of that hypothesis one might also bring a definition of the novel given in Caragiale's lecture **"The Romanian Letters and Arts in the Second Half of the 19th Century"**; through rhetorical questions, overstatement and an agglomeration of contrary epithets, as marks of irony, the Romanian writer offers a definitely negative definition of a genre not yet consolidated in Romanian letters at the time: "The novel? But the novel is like itself, not of an individual but of a whole society, with its entire array of troubles, inclinations and urges, devotions, mean actions, of love, hate, wickedness, goodness, envy, admiration, of baseness, sublimity, brutality, etherealness, selfishness and selflessness, in a word, every variation of which the human soul is capable in its well-known virtuosity."

Even if we leave aside the bad impression that may have been left on truly refined readers by the amount of trash translated overnight and claiming the status of a novel, Caragiale's attitude may have been motivated by at least two states of things: the old classicist prejudice, considering the novel a minor genre, and the Romanian narrative production—rather precarious in quality up to the end of the 19th century.

Anyhow, if we confine ourselves to the theatre alone, whenever he has to choose between two dramatic texts, Caragiale prefers the short one (realistic or classical) to the loose and rambling (romantic) one; the same applies to his own plays, which he compresses ***(The Bane*** or ***Wrong for Wrong)*** deleting whole scenes or an entire act ***(Carnival Scenes, A Stormy Night).*** Out of *Hernani* "you may cut four fifths to the advantage of the play itself and particularly of well-trained audiences—and *Hernani* will remain *Hernani;*" the romantic drama *Ruy Blas* is repudiated because of its "enormous tirades" and if Shakespeare had done like Victor Hugo when Othello went desperate, then the Moor "confronting the audience . . . and assuming a dignified pose" would have been forced to deliver "a long tirade," first enumerating all the sufferings of his soul then all imaginable tortures by which he plans to punish the wretched Desdemona!" But then, "all comparison between the state of his soul and the Tartar's tortures, all rhetorical curses, all rhetorically ringing threats would have caused us to shrug and exclaim: 'This Moor is not jealous like a self-respecting Moor, he is only an Oriental bragadoccio!'

Even more obvious seems to be Caragiale's preference for "concision" in prose. Perhaps also under the influence of the dramatist's logic, in the phase of the "sketches" and "moments" the prosewriter reduced to a minimum—if he did not entirely eliminate—descriptions of nature, images, portraits, maxims, the narrator's general considerations or comments, which he frequently replaces by short remarks, very similar to stage directions. As his contemporary, critic Paul Zarifopol, noted, when Caragiale did make digressions, their subject is only the narrative technique and, additionally, the reader's "training" in the spirit of narrative discipline. Thus, in a spectacular theoretical digression included in his short prosepiece **"A Tale"**, Caragiale uses the allegory of the "cross-eyed man", an image eloquent of the prolix narrator who complicates the "roads" of the story, forcing the reader to ramble at the risk of getting completely lost: ". . . And then, when I tell you, as far as my abilities help me do my trade, I would not like to have at least one of you go through the experience of a cross-eyed man whom a stray traveller asked one evening which way to turn in order to reach a certain place sooner, and the cross-eyed man pointed one way: but the traveller asked him 'Tell me true, man, for I am keen on arriving there before nightfall; which way shall I go? Where you point to me with your hand or where you look with your eyes? . . . !"

Of course, we must distinguish between prolixity itself—that is "swelling up" the plot—and the technique of multiple game strategies. For, in the latter sense, Caragiale often behaved like the "cross-eyed" man in the story, pointing to the reader one way "with his hand" and another way "with his eyes", i.e. banking on the possibility of building a system of expectation in the reader, alternatively fulfilled and frustrated. But the "cross-eyed man" in **"A Tale"** is the narrator who writes for the sake of writing, the "double" negative, perhaps a nightmare of Caragiale, the "cobbler" who vainly increases the size of the text only in order to put in additional "pretty" or "fanciful" seaming:

> . . . shall I do like other story-tellers? Instead of briefly showing you what misfortune befell the woman, shall I start telling you what that misfortune of a certain empress in bygone times looks to me like nowadays? But the heart of that mother may be likened—for whoever has time to waste as a reader, paper and ink to waste as a writer—to a lofty tower which a terrible earthquake ruins at one shake turning the proud building which until a moment ago had soared up, its gilt top tearing the blue canopy into a slumped heap of broken stones, scattered without further reason than the insanity of blind chance . . . or shall I liken it to a poor tender and frail rose, just blossomed forth, which the hostile blizzard has cruelly wrested from its slender stem, crushing it dead, its delicate petals torn, into the rabid, tempestous, downrushing stream? . . . or shall I liken it rather to a bold flint rock, which the ruthless lightning split in a moment, from its brow to its root? Or, even stronger: shall I liken it to a sturdy oak-tree which the worthless axe . . . etc., etc.?
>
> To which one would like me to compare the empress's heart? To one, to two of them or to all three of them? I could do it anyway, only to please you . . . that is for the sake of words I have tried to invent a story for you. But you shouldn't believe that. As far as I am concerned, I deliberately seek words by which to tell you the *story* as I imagine it, as fast and as clear as I can.

Very much as in the case of drama, where Caragiale's method appeared as a reaction to the earlier romantic current or to contemporary melodramas, in the case of his prose, narrative concision and understatement are not only a personal approach, but also an ironic comment on a literary fashion which fostered a whole "industry" of popular novels, Zolaesque novels or, specifically in Romania—sentimental, idyllic stories of rural life: "One knows the method—we are inclined to call it a mania, but for its being deliberate—of the great French writer to take a very simple frame, a commonplace plot, and to crowd upon it a colossal, would-be 'documentary' superstructure, which he keeps turning, twisting and upsetting on all sides and facets, multiplying it in such a way that, out of a story which—with all its necessary machinery—would not take more than 40 pages, he manages to produce a 400-page volume." (Caragiale's article **"The Zola-Bibescu Case of Plagiarism"**).

With such theoretical views, the writer first reaches the formula of "moments" and "sketches," the *tour de force* of concision in **"The Mosi Fair"** (**"Table of Contents"**) and especially in **"Telegrams"** with its arresting technique of "stroboscopic" sentences of the type "Prosecutor absent town nunnery binge nuns" (Caragiale's friend, professor I. Suchianu asserted that such a sentence could easily be turned into "a whole novelette of monastic manners"; in the second place, Caragiale develops a steady bantering tone in his parodies, whose main theme is precisely prolixity.

In the sketch **"The Romanian Nation"** (1899), the recipe for quickly drawing up press columns consists in using information from a Viennese newspaper, over which one pours "much deluted fantasy soup, then the description of the locality, historical notes and statistical data, most of it derivated from an old though excellent—in its time—conversation guide book." In **"The Poet's Share"** (1909) God is exasperated at the writer's consuming too much ink and paper, while in **"A Christmas Chronicle . . ."** (1907), the narrator ironically simulates envy in the face of a short-story of 100 pages "foolscape, covered with clean small handwriting . . . :" "Oh! why cannot my pen too run without stumbling over such vast, immense white fields? . . . Why can't I too overcome the candour of several reams of paper at one stroke of the pen? . . . Why, my cruel Weird Sisters, why is my dry hand incapable to pour so many generous torrents and cascades of prose?"

Up to a point, perfectly eloquent is also the situation of Caragiale's translations, almost invariably shorter than the original: for instance the story of "The Unrestrained Curious Man" in Cervantes' *Don Quixote* (with Caragiale's title being **"The Curious Man Punished"**). As is known, the text had been translated into Romanian by Ion Heliade Radulescu (1802-1872) after Florian's French version (in the publication *Curier de ambele sexe,* of February/March 1881 and in the daily *Timpul* of March 1881). Caragiale certainly knew the latter's complete translation, since he contributed **"Theatrical Recollections"** to the same issue of the *Convorbiri* while being still a sub-editor at the *Timpul;* Zarifopol assumes that in 1911, when he published **"The Curious Man Punished"** in the daily *Românul* of Arad, Caragiale made use of a French intermediate.

Accepting the hypothesis that the Romanian translation had proceeded from a text of the same proportions as the original, and not from an abridged translation, then his version is about one fourth of Cervantes' novella, from which Caragiale condensed or deleted adjectives, repeated qualifications and forms of address, general considerations on the philosophy of existence, together with the narrator's rhetorical and moralizing interventions, the rather numerous digressions, quotations or allusions to certain contemporary works, the fables or parables, the story-teller's mediation between the reader and the narrative, all clichés of allegorical expression (that of the besieged fortress as an equivalent of a woman's virtue, that of the navigator and the port at sea, etc.), the love sonnets and the other verses, the anticipations that may diminish the tension of the story, the lengthy dialogues similar to theatrical tirades and frequent comparisons with mythological, historical or epic heroes.

If we divide Cervantes' text into sequences considered by us "translatable units" (sentences, lines of dialogue, comments, letters and messages, verses, fables, allegories, etc.) then out of a total of about 150 such units, Caragiale eliminated approximately 50 and condensed the others in order to obtain his own much more concentrated version. To put it in a nutshell, the translator gave up only the non-temporal elements, orienting Cervantes' novella towards dialogue and action, making it the size of a minimal text based on some minor event, but with a moral attached to it.

Nevertheless, in Caragiale's *œuvre* one can also find the reverse situation that of preference for broad contexts, and this alternative ought not to be explained only by the relation between the primary text (as a rule an anecdote or a tall tale) and the definitive work. As a matter of fact, Caragiale himself fought shy of a possible reduction of his narrative approach to preference for the minimal context, establishing a distinction between the prosewriter's logic and the dramatist's logic on the one hand and the useless prolixity of the narrative strategy on the other hand:

> "But then, would you like to cut the short-story to the proportions of a three-line news-item, and the novel to the strict form of a police inspector's report?' 'Not at all, but take me for a sea-trip timely and wisely'." (**"A Few Opinions"**)

The earliest visible "deviations" from the controlled thrift of the theatre and from the telegraphic style of the old anecdotes and tall tales, may be recorded in Caragiale's short-story **"A Taper for Easter"** which critic Constantin Dobrogeanu-Gherea thought "too short"; also in **"A Sin",** which poses every problem connected with the hesitation between the short-story and the novel or between the short-story and the play. As a matter of fact, both narratives may be analysed as texts which, over the close-knit logic of the theatre, the prose-writer superposed the logic of the short-story programmer, using descriptions and collateral episodes and indulging in considerations like those about the human souls and the celestial bodies (in **"A Sin"**) or in the digressions of a fly on the marble top of a table—an episode in which people have seen a spectacular enrichment of the narrative technique in Romanian literature.

Doubtless, however, the most obvious alternation of strategies appears in **"Ker Ianulea"** which, as Caragiale himself warned us, had its starting point in Machiavelli's novella "Belphegor the Arch-Devil or "The Story of the Devil Who Took a Wife to Himself." This time, the Romanian writer uses exactly the reverse method of that employed in the translation from Cervantes. Now the original is nearly four times shorter than the Romanian version, in which nearly all units of Machiavelli's text were dilated and completed with numerous new episodes, with customs specific to suburban life in the 18th century Phanariot rule in the Romanian Lands, with the two juicy anecdotes on the disease called "Hurducharisoms" and on the hag who orders the devil to stretch "a kinky hair" of hers or with the image—like a faded print of old Bucharest, in which one can barely make out Manuc's Inn, the Coltea Tower, Silverknife Street, the Metropolitan Church and the Vineyards up Filaret Hill. The tendency for "expanding" the text does not seem to come to an end even after the completion of the story, for, as we know from Caragiale's own correspondence with Zarifopol, the writer, instead of abridging the text, as he was to do with the Spanish original of **"The Curious Man Punished"** at a certain moment wanted to introduce exactly what he was to eliminate from Cervantes: verses in the form of a song by the early Romanian poet Costache Conachi. Nevertheless, he eventually gave up the project.

The alternative of the broad context in **"Ker Ianulea"** and as a matter of fact, also in **"Special Pastrami"** or **"Abu-Hasan"** was all the more spectacular as it manifested itself parallel to the new series of sketches published in the daily *Universul* (1909) and the stage of the short style of "moments" and the heavily cut translation from **"The Curious Man Punished."** That was why, the idea of transformation or evolution in Caragiale's art of a narrator ought to be taken with a grain of salt anyhow completed with the more plausible hypothesis of different or double strategies which enrich his work without requiring the integration of its various components into a hierarchic schema, with "positive" and "negative" terms.

Seen in a perspective which is only apparently chronological, Caragiale's work seems to "evolve" between a maximum of *blanks* (or a minimum of text) in the case of his drama, sketches and moments and a minimum of such elements (which means a maximum of text) in the short-stories of 1909. As a matter of fact, Caragiale permanently alternated his text-plans according to necessity and genre. The idea of evolution after a while becomes irrelevant, since it cannot include a single continuous thread of experience or literary expression. For the relation between the "sketch" entitled **"Telegrams"** for instance and the short-story entitled **"Ker Ianulea"** is not a relation of the type 1,2,3 . . . n., in which each term is quantitatively superior and has a more varied text contour than the term preceding it. *Blanks* in "1" do not become full spots in "n", but on the contrary: what is missing in "1" (for instance in **"Telegrams"**) may be quite easily filled in by any writer, while all narrative elements in the spots that might have been left blank in "n" (for instance in **"Ker Ianulea"**)—could only be filled in by Caragiale himself. Therefore **"Ker Ianulea"** is neither the maximum variant of Machiavelli's short-story nor a translation proper, but an "adaptation" and, in the last analysis, an original text, written on the basis of a previously drawn up plan or script.

In Caragiale's case, the succession (poetry), comedies, moments, sketches, tales and stories, or—to put it differently—the selection of different literary alternatives, with a different text contour developed along a maximal or minimal context, can be ascribed not so much to a chronological evolution of taste, of the author's own literary theories or of personal readings, as it has been asserted, but to a highly accurate knowledge of the specific features of literary genres and to his observing the principle of suiting literary means to each species or genre. In actual fact, this is a paradox of Caragiale's career, because, while the mixture of forms in the "Well-established" area with those in the "peripheral" area of a culture is accepted unreservedly, the mixture between drama and fiction and especially poetry never exceeds the proportions of what is strictly necessary.

As a matter of fact, when Caragiale was a fully mature creator and the aesthetician Mihail Dragomirescu passed criticism on him for the absence of descriptions of nature and of lyricism from his prose Caragiale answered him, in a letter of November 1907, advocating the rational utilization of nontemporal elements (which he called delectable entertainment), depending on the specific features of the genre and even on the special strategy for a class of texts.

> And now please allow me to write a brief personal apology. You are accusing me that in my writings I do not show enogh love for the paysage, for the still life, or enough lyricism either. I for one (not that I should like to contradict you systematically) believe that I may not have too much, very much or much of all this, yet I believe I have enough; moreover, I believe that in art, above enough one does not need anything. The picturesqueness of animated as well as still life, very much like lyricism, in themselves—or at least that is what I think—form the object of other arts than that of story telling; and thus I only think of them as helpers to the latter, whose object is the most interesting phenomenon *quant à nous:* circumstance arising out of the particular way of being of so many souls and minds, on the whole similar to ours.
>
> As a child, I read an old translation of the *Theogony,* where Mnemosina's daughters were described like this: 'They reside on Mount Olympus and they praise in their songs the wonderful feats of the immortal gods; and they know the past as well as the present and they tell the future, and with their masterly music they enliven the entire array of gods.' And since then all of them have remained dear to me. They are good sisters; when necessary, they lend each other their graces and attributes; and the one who has lent these attributes to one of her sisters stands aside and allows that sister of hers to sing and to dance, without tripping her cothurni: she has lent assets to her in order to help her, of course, not to trammel her up; to strengthen her particular prestige, not to usurp it. That is how they help each other; now one, now another, in turn learning or amusing themselves, amazing the mortals—each of them in her turn shines with the full charms of the entire divine choir.
>
> Now, what shall I say without exceeding what is *enough?* . . .
>
> I believe that in my work there are enough instances of inter-assistance of the amusement. But, of course, in order to find it somebody—an amateur, to say nothing of the critic—must seek it. Or to use the language of shoemakers, one does not easily see the seam of the sole, unless it has been sewn in white thread. Yes, my dear friends, I am but an old cobbler: I sew for the sake of the sole not for the sake of the seam.

Al. Calinescu (essay date 1987)

SOURCE: "Caragiale and 'Rhetoric'," in *Romanian Review,* Vol. 41, No. 6, 1987, pp. 78-88.

[*In the following essay, Calinescu discusses the theoretical principles underlying Caragiale's drama and fiction.*]

Let us begin by resuming one of Caragiale's well-known texts:

> Oh, sacred rhetorics!
>
> It is most piously that I remember the highly elevated *Cours francais de rhétorique,* the first udder from which I sucked the milk of literary science.
>
> A wonderful book! And what joy I experienced in learning that the principles and method of my very old French course, in its n'th edition, this time in

> our mother tongue, keeps feeding as nourishingly as of old, the intelligence of the younger generations of Romania, who dedicate their lives to literary duty.
>
> Out of this old course, still green and full of sap, whose empire cannot be usurped by any innovation, we have been learning numberless kinds of styles: the clear style, the terse, pompous, light, grandiose, simple, sublime, pathetic, majestic, adorned and even the florid styles and so many others. And it is from the same course of lectures that we have learnt what figures of speech or tropes are—how we call the taking of the whole for a part and of the part for the whole, of the man for his place of origin, of the place for the man, etc., well, to put it in a nutshell, all the subtle formal differences between the hundreds if not thousands of ways in which man expresses his thoughts.

Commentators have interpreted this passage as an unequivocal condemnation of rhetoric. But a first question arises immediately: what kind of rhetoric is involved? Caragiale's text is dated *between* the appearance of the last great manuals of rhetoric (Dumarsais, Fontanier) and the emergence of stylistics as a discipline. It was the period of the transmission—and distortion—of rhetoric through schoolbooks, apparently represented also by this mysterious *Cours français de rhétorique* to which he refers. Secondly, Caragiale's texts have been correlated with the numerous passages in which the writer ridicules rhetoricity, taken derogatorily as grandiloquence, pomposity, exaggeration; which once more causes us to drift from the initial objectives of rhetoric (though this semantic glide, this decadence of the term is no less significant for the evolution of the discipline).

Caragiale has two objects in view: the classification of styles and the classification of figures of speech. As his literary practice points out, our writer "felt" the figures of speech as aberrations. There are but few "serious" comparisons or metaphors: with Caragiale figures of speech are enormous and ridiculous; epithets are almost always predictable, therefore considered clichés and denounced as such: many testimonies—from the writer himself or from those who were intimate with him—converge in pointing out his aversion to the abusage of adjectives, in which he saw a distinctive mark of romanticism (another *bête noire* of our writer). As regards the problem of styles, things are more intricate, for here is how Caragiale's text continues:

> There was an excellent school for tailoring in my course with that classical motto: *le style c'est l'homme,* and I learnt from it how to cut all sorts of clothes, how to sew them, to embroider them, to patch them up if need be, to repair them and to clean every spot on them; and yet I never learnt for whose practical use are meant those wonderful and distinguished clothes; not knowing my customer, it goes without saying that I could not learn how to take his measurements. So I learnt tailoring without for a moment thinking that it is an art whose purpose is to clothe someone's body.
>
> So, when I became I journeyman and wanted to get some work on my own account, when a customer came up to me—meaning an idea—to commission from me a coat enabling it to appear in the world, I just picked up at random from the heap of clothes, and pulled over the fair curly head of a young prince, the loose cape of an unwashed pilgrim, then an imperial purple mantel on the back of a cranky and lanky harlequin, and covered the lofty shoulders of a young Caesar, with the motley cloak of a hunch-back clown.
>
> And I released them into the world like this; and the world, which judges people by their clothes, as the wise Nasr-ed-din-Hodja says, gave alms to the royal child, worshipped the harlequin and hooted and hissed my young Caesar!
>
> Successfully! . . . But why?
>
> Because there is one style alone which my elevated French course forgot to teach me, one style alone: the adequate style, precisely the one I needed, the only one that can be called style, properly speaking.
>
> There is only one.
>
> I don't know who once said by way of a joke that it was the easiest thing in the world to carve a statue. You only need a block of stone; inside it, in its very heart there is an Apollo imprisoned like a living kernel waiting for the wooden nutshell to break. Well! You only need to break that shell and to release the captive . . . So you pick up a chisel and a hammer and step by step you carve out the useless cover, fragment by fragment and there is Apollo emerging, victorious and brilliant. You must only take care not to let your chisel go too deep and harm the kernel.
>
> Now you can bring out Apollo guarding his flocks and lighting the primitive shepherds of Thessaly, driving his chariot, defeating the serpent or playing on his seven-string lyre after having sacrificed the bold satyr; you can therefore bring out a simple, majestic, thundering or sublime Apollo—all this being merely a matter of style.
>
> "All right (quoth I, who have learnt the French course in rhetoric by heart) I know in how many ways Latona's sun may appear to me, I know all the styles, there is but one little thing that I don't know: how to carve the statue."
>
> "If you don't know, go and learn!" my jokester answers me. "You'll see (if you indeed have the calling to learn) that you needn't know all styles: you only have to know one style—the adequate style, which comprises all of them, in order to adapt them to any intention whatsoever, according to necessity."
>
> So what the French course was pointing out to me as different styles, were in fact the variations of attributes of one and the same style,—attributes which ought to be kept locked up in the wardrobe and put on only in case of need. Woe to the man

> who gets the coat wrong; that one will incur the same punishment as I got when I released into the wide world my young prince, my harlequin and my Caesar, all in the wrong attire.

Therefore adequacy was the fundamental principle of Caragiale's so-called anti-rhetoric. The principle to which the writer insistently reverts in his text **"A Few Opinions"**. He says there that in a living organism, organs are not independent, but intercondition themselves in order to maintain the balance and coherence of the entire complex (we must admit that the idea is typically structuralistic, *avant la lettre);* likewise, in the work of art there must be "fitting" between intention and expression, or else the result is a monster. The work exists through its structure:

"Therefore, very much as life in Nature can only clothe a structure of intimate size, proportions and relations, within the same intimate economy, subject to the empire of necessity, in much the same way artistic intention must—for its own existence and maintenance—don a form of expression, a material structure of absolutely necessary size, proportions and relations of intimate economy." According to Caragiale, to master style means to harmonize your own melodic invention with the movement of the "eternal prelude" of the world and of the soul. There must be adequacy, harmony between language and thinking: "Never has thinking a worse enemy than words, when they are not obedient and loyal servants . . ." (Caragiale, ***Works,*** Volume, V, 1938, pp. 83-84).

But, returning to **"A Few Opinions,"** let us note the ample digression on such expressions as "it fits him", "it misfits him,"—synthesizing the writer's conception of adequacy. The examples provided by Caragiale are no less significant: to the ham actor in the "straight theatre" he prefers the clown at the circus ("they fit each other"); to the marble statue, carved by all the standards of realism that dominated 19th century sculpture, Caragiale prefered the little gingerbread doll bought at a cheap price in the fair; a monumental historical painting by Makart abounding in "realistic" details (Caragiale says: "no historical mole is absent from any face") is held by him inferior to a cartoon describing a dog contest. Important in this case is also the fact that all examples of adequation are taken from the marginal arts—*de bas étage*—opposed to the conventionalism of "official" art.

Caragiale was the first Romanian writer considerably to broaden the concept of art—in the most modern spirit. Therefore "it fits or it misfits." But this is the way in which Caragiale restores the key principle of great ancient rhetoric, before its crisis and decline: adequacy, functionality. Moreover, the metaphors used by Caragiale in order to illustrate the necessity for adequation—the human body, the clothes covering the body—recall, occasionally in a downright surprising manner, the metaphors used for the same purpose by Aristotle, Cicero or Tacitus (for instance, in Aristotle's *Rhetoric* we find the following passage: "We ought to see whether a purple tissue suits a young man, what kind of material suits an old man, as it is impossible for the same attire to fit both of them." Here is a passage from Tacitus' *Dialogue on Orators:* "It is much more convenient to clothe your speech even in a coarse toga than to dress it gaudily, like a courtesan." And with Cicero, in his *Orator,* we find a similar idea: "Very much as about some women it is said that they use no fard, and that sits them well, in much the same way, the precise style is likeable, even without ornaments.")

Let us then point out this curious assertion in Caragiale's article **"Is the Theatre Literature?"** Caragiale says that since the theatre is also speech, it ought not to be considered a literary genre because "in this light, the theatre seems to be more closely related to the oratoric art" which, quite unexpectedly, relegates the theatre to the sphere of rhetorics (let us repeat, classical rhetoric, which covered the functionality, efficiency and adequacy of the discourse.) Last but not least, one has to make it clear that while refusing rhetoricity, Caragiale did not in the least mean that it was easy to write prose, an undertaking within anybody's reach, because fiction could be free of any secrets and could therefore do without rhetoric. On the contrary, it is common knowledge that the writer had earned a reputation (sustained by himself) of a *forçat de la plume,* that he laboured on certain texts with Flaubertian obstinacy. Like Flaubert, Caragiale tried to impose the idea that a prose writer has to face numberless dificulties in his struggle for mastering language and for building sentences. Flaubert was the first French writer to have the ambition of raising prose to the dignity of poetry, pointing out that it was as difficult to write prose as to write verse. Caragiale (not very much in love with poetry, actually) went one better: he considered prose harder to write than poetry, whose secrets may be discovered by learning a handful of rules, while prose is more intricate than is shown by any treatise on rhetorics:

> The technique of versification, at first sight very difficult, is definitely much easier than that of prose. In modern languages, syllabic verse has barely two or three rules: respect for the natural accentuation of words, the number of syllables and the accuracy of rhymes—rules that any intelligent school-boy can grasp and apply. Then, one may write quantities of quite decent verses whitout much thinking, if their appearance is more or less accomplished. In prose, however, one can hardly go along such a line. If prose fails to clothe some thoughts, it immediately sounds hollow to the mind of a current reader, it immediately denounces itself as worthless. Besides, precisely for the man who thinks, who therefore has something to say, the technique of prose conceals hundreds if not thousands of secrets, whose subtlety easily defies even the most refined course in rhetorics. It is an art which—for those who do not know it—appears as easy and as natural as learning common speech, but, for those who are acquainted with at least a few of its secrets, it remains a permanent desideratum. Whoever has but once penetrated its difficulties, must have become convinced that he can never

triumph fully over them (**"Good Reading,"** ***Works,*** Volume IV, page 286).

Therefore, an important role in Caragiale's aversion to normative, didactic rhetoric (actually also in the obviously unjust condemnation of poetry) is played also by his vanity as a prose writer.

What happens to the other "styles" (besides the adequate one) mentioned by Caragiale in **"A Few Opinions"**? Far from driving them out of his literary practice, our writer used them insistently, thus offering us genuine exercises in style. As professor and esthetician Tudor Vianu noted, in the course on rhetoric evoked by Caragiale "the style appears as set, codified, structures, apt to be proposed to our choice, like any other thing made before we came into the world. The ancient rhetorical wisdom teaches us that there are clear as well as terse styles, pompous as well as light, grandiose, simple as well as sublime, pathetic, majestic, adorned and even florid. It is enough to choose the style of your own work in order to find, in the respective column, the norms guaranteeing it for you." (Tudor Vianu, *The Art of Romanian Prose Writers,* 1941, p. 125). It is precisely what Caragiale did: he resorted to those imaginary columns (in a sort of Mendelejeff's periodical table of styles) and proposed to us stylistic variations, exercises on given themes and in manners "imposed from the outside." No less important is the fact that this exploration of the possibilities offered by speech and manners is made through peripheral, marginal genres (particularly on the border between literature and journalism)—the results being the emphasis, thickening and vehement denunciation of the manner. Or, from another angle, as Pierre Kuentz puts it: *"C'est dans la marginalité que se réalisent les opérations rhétoriques ou, plus exactement, c'est dans la marginalisation qu'elles se soutiennent"* ("L'enjeu des rhétoriques", in *Littérature,* 18, p. 3).

Another idea obsessively recurrent with Caragiale is that of compositional motivation. The way he puts it coincides with the way in which it has been tackled by modern poetics. Presumably, the writer first has an acute awareness of the proliferating, infinitely catalysable nature of the text (and of the sentence). The romantic drama is also rejected because it includes numberless redundant passages.

In Caragiale's short fiction, the (otherwise numerous) "fillings" exist only through the writer's parodistic intentions: otherwise—it was noted a long time ago—descriptions, digressions, a.s.o. are eliminated—whence the dramatic effect of many of his sketches and "moments" (his critic and editor Paul Zarifopol very accurately noted that "the artist simply does not know how to get rid of words, in order to show as directly as possible the figures which suffer from the slowness and abstract dryness of words."—"The Public and Caragiale's Art"). The essence of the work lies in its internal coherence and logic; decisive is the construction, the way in which the architecture of the work is achieved. Here is, along this line, the testimony provided by one of his sons, the poet Luca Ion Caragiale: "He proved to me that Macbeth was a masterpiece of dramatic art. The architectural construction is offered to you from the very beginning. Macbeth's fate is sealed from the very first scene and, perfectly knowing what is going to happen, you are only interested in the purely artistic side of the work, *the way* it is going to happen" (reproduced in *Caragiale,* "Critical Library" Eminescu Publishing House, Bucharest, 1974, p. 22). The work must lie under the sign of equilibrium, of the concordance between its inherent laws and what it proposes to embody: "Let the mirror be imperfectly spherical, irregular in shape, distorted, wavy, stained in various ways, as such it will preserve at all times the same kind of reflexion—there will always be an equilibrium, a constant ratio between what is reflected and the way it is reflected" (Caragiale, ***Works,*** Volume IV, p. 47; this sentence actually contains the fundamental thesis of the new sociological criticism descending from Lukacs and represented for instance by Zéraffa, who studies the consonance between the structures of novels with Balzac, Joyce, Kafka, etc. and the social structures represented in the respective novels). Such is therefore the fundamental and infallible criterion: "To put it briefly, is (the work) logical in its relation to itself? For, if we are interested in something else than its own logic, then we may lose our way and never find it again." (*Ibidem,* p. 462).

From this, up to discussing compositional virtualities, the possibilities available to the creator, out of which he is to choose the adequate one, the aberrant versions which may be reached through transgressing the motivational norm—there is only one more step to take. Well, taking it, Caragiale replaces classical rhetoric and poetics through *poietics.* He placed himself at the very heart of the work, in the very centre of the process of manufacturing, producing, establishing the work; he adopted the angle of (in his own words) "a practitioner" of literature, which he judges from inside.

Let us first analyse one example of a current illogical, unjustified version of a work: commenting upon Barbu Stefanescu Delavrancea's drama *Sunset*—much praised for the logic and symmetry of its construction and for the accuracy of the mediaeval fresco—Caragiale wrote: "But the eye of a person unaccustomed to such things is sure to require from the brilliant, ample frescoes, spicy miniature details—*'pompadours';* is always going to pretend from a heroic tragedy an ingenious melodramatic plot—some infant kidnapped out of its cradle and drowned during the prologue but found retrieved in his old age and saved in the epilogue ('Thank you, my Lord!')—or some letter written before the first act which all personages are seeking everywhere, and the main hero can hardly give up the ghost until he swallows the . . . lost letter by the end of the fifth act; or the same reader will wish for the gratuitous piercing of a soul which has appeared as round and whole as the sun . . ." (***Works,*** IV, p. 464). Caragiale concluded his article with a quotation from Goethe which is also most representative of the theory of compositional motivation: the poet, Goethe says subordinates the nature of his characters to the effect which he wants to obtain; thus, if he had represented Egmont, in keeping with historical truth, as the father of many children, his behaviour would have appeared most unlikely: the personage Egmont is a different Egmont, "in harmony with my practical intentions." There is in this assertion of Goethe's—endorsed by Caragiale—an emphatic underlining of the principle of the intrinsic verisimilitude of the work of art: we find here again a fundamental principle of Aristotle's *Poetics,* taken over and synthesized by Boileau in a famous dictum (very seasonably) quoted even nowadays in certain debates on the theme of realism: *"Le vrai peut quelquefois n'être pas vraisemblable."*

Very much like Lessing in his *Hamburg Drama* and *Treatises on the Fable,* Caragiale made experiments in potential literature: proceeding from a given theme, from a certain subject, he imagined the various possible modalities of treating the subject, of *"mise en texte."* There are two significant examples in the above quoted **"A Few Opinions."** In a first stage, Caragiale reduced the plot to a minimum (he used the term "fable") of two plays sharing some elements—*King Lear* and Schiller's *The Robbers*—after which he developed the plot along two different lines, later comparing the resulting versions. Naturally enough, they are the directions followed by Shakespeare and Schiller, yet it is important that, by adopting the standpoint of the creator who has to make a choice out of several possible developments, Caragiale remade the road covered by each author, checking the validity of the solutions through referring them to the motivational criterion. Thus, Shakespeare lets his characters do what they can, while Schiller obliges them to tell us what they are like. Caragiale praises Shakespeare for having his personages act by their nature, and condemns Schiller for his interventions (extolling, criticising or admiring his heroes) as well as for the abuse of tirades, so that in *The Robbers* Caragiale identifies "a continuous torrent of exterior affirmations, devoid of any interior confirmation."

Yet, in a higher stage, Caragiale imagines things in an absolute manner, indeed inventing versions. He submits to us the plot (the minimal narrative) which is going to be developed and the work appears—to resume Étienne Souriau's expression—*Un monstre à nourrir.* The next fragment from **"A Few Opinions"** offers a wonderful example of poietic research, of investigating, exploiting and analysing the virtualities of the literary discourse:

> One author tells us the story of two friends, sworn brethern, who quarrel, hate each other, fight and kill each other—for a woman, that goes without saying.
>
> It is an old story; but that does not matter: if the story teller is an artist, we shall listen to it once again with delight, very much as we always listen to a song we have known from our infancy, provided it is well sung—beautiful things never age.
>
> Let us see.

The artist first shows us what close links there had been, ever since grammar school, between the two friends, Peter and Paul; how they had never failed in their mutual devotion and esteem; how one had saved the other from death at the peril of his own life, and so on, and so forth . . . But here is how Peter, jealously in love with a woman, Kate, came to be suspicious of Paul.

The woman was a woman like any good woman: she was no fool to struggle hard in order to dispel his suspicions; moreover, through ambiguous smiles, through deliberately clumsy protestations, through ostentatiously delicate tears, she systematically nurtured those suspicions. The woman mastered her art to perfection: as long as a man has his fears and doubts, he is easier to hold in hand. She knew that a good friend of the man who loved her was always a great danger for her empire; therefore, a quarrel between the two friends, the removal of the importunate one, was an indispensable triumph for the woman's policy—a policy of peaceful and unquestioned domination. In order to reach that triumph, the woman had a whole arsenal of weapons; she may vainly break all of them, except one—the supreme one, absolutely unfailing.

So Kate started talking to Peter only about Paul: Paul now and Paul then; Paul here and Paul there; Paul is nice, witty, agreeable, waggish, *charmant.* Peter started losing his temper. But here is Paul coming in: Kate can hardly keep back a cry and a gesture of satisfaction. Although Paul says he is in a hurry, she does not allow him to leave: he must by all means dine with them. During the dinner, Peter finds fault with the servants, is about to break a plate on the cook's head, while Kate and Paul keep laughing and telling each other all sorts of pretty nothings. In the evening, at supper, she tells Peter she regrets not having invited Paul to join them. She has lost her appetite and she is in a pensive mood, staring vacantly; she drums her fingers on the table; she sighs; she stands up; she is impatient; she starts crying all of a sudden, without being able to give any reason. Then, she rises from table altogether and goes to sleep sobbing. Well, after all, a whole area of alarming symptoms. Overnight she keeps writhing in her bed, oppressed by a nightmare; she groans, she yells and Peter hears her uttering a name between her clenched teeth . . . Terrible! Oh! Paul!"

Now Paul's fate is sealed. Peter has had a few bickerings with his friend now and then; but this time he must mark the break with full pomp. They meet. Peter, frowning sullenly, invites him, according to their habit, to have a glass of beer together in a quiet pub, because "he's got something to tell him." . . . Hard and violent accusations on one side . . . protestations of innocence on the other; and, as the discussion became more heated:

"Scoundrel! Traitor! . . . For my woman . . ."

"Blockhead! for a . . ."

Then Peter stands up straight, picks up his mug of beer, lifts it over the forehead of his old friend and,

A line of dots.

And? . . . And? . . . I ask myself worried to death.

We must say (the author continues) that Peter was one of those passionate natures which at the bottom of their soul carry more reasons for agitation than the world can drive out: they are like the sea. Look at it under a clear sky, under the oppressive haze of the equator, when not even the lightest breath of wind blows above it, look at it how it starts seething; it boils up and down, it swells, it heaves enormous; it writhes, it grinds round, ever harder, ever faster, the vast anarchy of billows over billows! We have killed the gods! Neptune is now dead! There is nobody to settle it, to quiet it down by one frown, by one sign alone. Look at this satanical turmoil arisen out of the blue! Listen to that bellow which causes the very skies to shake! Sailor, don't waste here your time which is so precious for saving your soul! Let alone the ropes of your sails and raise a prayer: the deep keeps calling you impatiently! The terrible hurricane is at its height! But who? Who has started it with such terrible commands? The sea itself. The sea which tortures itself out of its own deep restlessness. That is what the soul of the passionate man is like.

"What beautiful style! How wonderful! How wonderful!" you will say. "Here is a model of pompous, grandiose, sublime style."

"I must confess," I will answer, "that I have not read a course in rhetoric for a long time. Perhaps in your official rhetoric such a thing is called sublime style; but please allow me to call it, with all due respect for you . . ."

"To call it what?"

"Poor style."

"But why? This is the style of all famous poets, like Victor Hugo, Schiller, Lamartine, the Romanian Bolintineanu . . ."

"Even if it were the style of Saint John the Golden-Mouthed still it is what I call it."

"But why? I can't understand."

"Precisely because you can't understand! . . . You must have forgotten that while we have been watching together the splendid panorama of the sea, merely for the sake of a commonplace, hackneyed comparison, you have forgotten that, far from that impressive spectacle, in the dark corner of a beer-house, our friend Petru is holding his mug of beer over the forehead of his would-be rival. You are not noticing, because your attention has been diverted, that the two old friends are in this way condemned to stand for a long time in the same attitude, like Canova's statuary group *Theseus Killing the Minotaur,* because the author has another thirty pages or so of digressions—which modern criticism calls psychological analysis."

"But then, would you like to reduce the short story to the size of a mere three-line news item and the novel to the strict form of a police report?"

"Not at all; but please take me a sail at sea timely and wisely. All the seascapes and all your banal ingeniousness in likening for my benefit the torment of the human soul to that of the billows, are perfectly gratuitous for you, null and void for me. What I want to hear is the mug breaking on Paul's head . . . You're taking me away from that through a worn out artifice; you brutally check a gesture that is already in progress; you take me on a trip to the equator, artificially starting another movement, with an entirely different rhythm, and while I tremble for the fate of Paul, cornered in a tight place, you are trying to have me lament the fate of a sailor lost in the desert of the billows. But what am I after all? What is my head for you to play with it like a child with a ball, which he stupidly throws at all the walls, now hitting it with his hand, now kicking it? Just listen to that! In order to have me call your style sublime, you're trying to make me take a mug of beer for Damocles' sword and a beer-house for the labyrinth, to mistake Peter for Theseus and Paul for the Minotaur!"

Well, definitely no! I cannot call *sublime* the style that wants to fool me in this way sublime: I call it something else.

The first question that Caragiale is trying to answer here, after having submitted the plot schematically is: how to "fill" the text, or, to put it differently, how to alter the text, how to "textualize" the main data of an epic conflict. To this question, the writer immediately adds a second one, equally important: how to avoid unjustified "fillings", redundant, parasitical digressions. The model of "pompous" style," which Caragiale rather abusively assimilates to "psychological analysis," is in fact a digression which arbitrarily checks the plot, suspends action, therefore dealing a blow also at the level of narrative temporality. The moral: one has to delete whatever is superfluous. Then Caragiale's imaginary interlocutor fears such a thinning out for the text, fears that the short-story or the novel would be reduced to the proportions of news in brief or of verbatim reports: this is a major statement, for the idea of the possibility to summarize a narrative text has been exploited by modern literary theory also in the other sense, hence the thesis of derivation of literary forms from the so-called "simple form" (cf. André Jolles, *Einfache Formen,* 1930). And then does not Caragiale himself tell us in his sketch **"A Very Lucky Man"**: "*I was just thinking* what an eventful though serene novel could emerge from a *study on the life of this typical happy man* . . . ?" (our italics, A.C.) As regards the issue of fillings, Caragiale's sentence is unequivocal: digressions must be made "timely and wisely" . . .

We are coming across this *poietic* practice also in Caragiale's literary texts. Let us quote the end of his sketch **"Two Lottery Tickets:"** "Should I be one of those authors who respect themselves and are consequently very much respected by the readers, I would conclude my story like this . . . (. . .) but . . . as I am not one of those authors, I prefer to tell you frankly: after the row made in the banquer's house, I simply do not know what further happened to my hero and to Mrs. Popescu."

By laying bare the method, Caragiale at the same time makes potential literature, capitalizing on two of the possible ways of "closing" a text: "Should I be an author like . . . I should do like this . . ." This is a *poietic* modality of understanding literature. His wish to go beyond rhetoric, which he considered compromised by having abandoned the principle of adequation, turned Caragiale into our first *poietician,* on the plane of both theory and literary production proper.

Valentin F. Mihaescu (essay date 1987)

SOURCE: "A Game of Love or of Chance?," in *Romanian Review,* Vol. 41, No. 6, 1987, pp. 89-95.

[*In the following essay, Mihaescu analyzes love relationships and the impact of chance in* A Stormy Night.]

> "RICA VENTURIANO": Oh, I am sorry, I apologize, but neither I am to blame, nor you, or Madam Zita either: The blame lies with the number plate on the gate . . . Madam Zita had written to me she lived at number 9 . . . I saw number 9 on the gate and I entered (*He talks sotto voce with Zita, Veta and Chiriac*).
>
> DUMITRACHE TITIRCA (*speaking to Nae Ipingescu*): That's right. It's the builder who did it to me: he plastered the wall at the gate and nailed number 6 upside down; tomorrow I must by all means have him set it to rights, for fear of another conflict happening to me."

In I. L. Caragiale's ***A Stormy Night,*** these words are exchanged in the ninth scene of the second act, that is very close to the final curtain. Up to that moment, the spectator knows everything about the stormy night unfolded in the house of Dumitrache Titirca the Evil-Hearted, a timber merchant and a captain in the civic guard. But what has happened so far at number 6 which was turned into number 9 (by mistake, Dumitrache "thinks")? With almost imperceptible subtlety the author introduces and causes to cross each other, two series of events. The first series includes whatever is seen, is known, is offered by the author in packing of such transparence as not to arouse suspicions among modern audiences. To put it in a nutshell, Veta, Dumitrache's wife, maintains adulterous relations with Chiriac—the merchant's trusted man—innocently delegated by the same merchant to watch very vigilantly and "as closely as possible" over his honour as a family man. Therefore, the classical triangle, stable enough (it has been going on for a year), whose balance is however about to be upset through the intervention of Rica Venturiano, an archive clerk, a student of law and a journalist. Venturiano "sympathizes" through letters (carried to and fro by Spiridon, an apprentice in Titirca's house) and through an exchange of sheep's eyes made at the "Iunion" coffee-house with Zita, the sister-in-law of Dumitrache, who does not know the truth but suspects Veta, although unaware of the truth and suspected also by Chiriac, also ignorant of of the truth, who "accepts"—isnt it? the cuckold's honour of a family man. But the imbroglio is clarified—from Dumitrache's angle—when the police inspector Nae Ipingescu, Dumitrache's political friend, recognizes Venturiano (at a moment when his very life was in danger) as the columnist of the liberal journal *The Voice of the National Patriot* (the year is 1879), admitted by the two coffee-house politicians as "one of ourselves, a son of the people." Now the balance has been restored: Rica is going to marry Zita, Veta is patching it up with Chiriac, Dumitrache goes to bed with . . . his intact honour as a family man, while in the morning the builder Dinca is going to turn number 9 to its true position as number 6.

But is that so? Is ***A Stormy Night*** merely an illustration of the theme of the cuckolded husband, treated as an "imbroglio" and spiced by the often caricatural linguistic humour? Well, there is all this, but not only this. Because, into the information supplied by the events in the series that I should like to call *transparent* and into the messages included, which programme the interpretation of the dramatic text, the author inserts another series—*discreet,* I should say—of insinuating, insidious information, similar to those subliminal publicity inserts of a few fractions of a second, with belated though lasting effects. One has already demonstrated that in Caragiale's *œuvre,* nothing is redundant or fortuitious, everything has a meaning and a purpose, and that is why each word or even the signs marking silence must be regarded with the utmost attention. And, at the same time, with the utmost precaution, because Caragiale "plays" with his reader (spectator), misleading him, annoying him, then meeting him half way, only to abandon him the next moment. The writer very thriftily doses the information, occasionally reducing it to infinitesimal details. For instance, the text of ***A Stormy Night*** begins with what we might consider an ordinary stage direction regarding the decor: "A suburban room. Door upstage to corridor; windows on both sides of it. Wooden and wicker furniture. Doors downstage right and upstage: another door in the backround left. Leaning against the window bottom left, *a civic guardsman's rifle with its long bayonet hanging by*" (our italics—V.M.). Later on, we are going to learn that the gun is used by Chiriac. But what is the use of this gun in the decor of the political chat between Dumitrache and Ipingescu, during which the former also expresses his worries regarding his honour as a family man? Apparently, no use at all, when we first read the play. But on re-reading it (i.e. knowing the events in the transparent series) we immediately realize that it is a metonymy, whose function it is to enhance humour by licentious allusions. It is the symbol of adultery, the emblem under which the talk unfolds from the very beginning significantly enough; during it, Dumitrache confesses his fear that Rica Venturiano (for the time being an unknown person whom Dumitrache calls the "vagabond") makes attempts on his honour of a family man. Caragiale calls our attention to the fact that the gun now has *"its long bayonet hanging by it"* (our italics—V.M.) but in the fifth scene of the second act, when Chiriac urges Dumitrache and Ipingescu to start a chase after the unfortunate Rica whose ill-luck has brought to number 6 instead of number 9 (therefore to Veta instead of Zita, the woman he is actually courting), the stage direction is as follows: "Chiriac rushes to pick-up his rifle, *which now has its bayonet attached.*" (Our italics—V.M.). *With the bayonet hanging by it,*" as opposed to *"with the bayonet attached to it":* what does this opposition mean? In the former case, the relations between Veta and Chiriac are temporarily suspended, as the lover suspects his mistress of betrayal. The bayonet is attached to the gun only after the scene of their reconciliation, prolonged up to about eleven before midnight, when Chiriac "rushes to pick up the bayonet of his gun," while Veta "rushes at him to wrest the bayonet from him." Moreover, the woman confesses to her lover, trying to convince him of the innocence, that even at the "Iunion" public house she had only been obsessed by . . . his gun: "You know that it had rusted inside and you had started unloading it with that iron rod. I could hardly take my thoughts off that gun. I was pondering: 'Suppose the gun goes off in his hands. God forbid!'"

In his book *Les structures anthropologiques de l'imaginaire,* Gilbert Durand called attention to the fact that the sword (but what is a bayonet if not a variant of the sword?) is a symbol of masculinity, virile at that. Naturally, Caragiale had no possibility to become acquainted with Durand's work, but the anthropological structures of the imaginary were not Durand's creations, only the pre-existing matter studied by him. Therefore, Caragiale knew what he knew and knew it very well, handling symbols with infinite subtlety. Yet, it is not only this kind of information (suppose we call it illicit, destined for the careful reader) dosed with utmost precaution and thrift, but also the information which the characters themselves hold about each other. Depending on the quantity and particularly on the quality of that information, one can define the characters' behaviours as well as the pertinence of their speeches, on a scale ranging from stark stupidity up to ineffable subtlety. We may say that none of the personages in ***A Stormy Night*** is aware of the entire "scenario" but only with partial truths. Being totally engrossed in her feelings for Chiriac, Veta does not notice Zita's "idyll" with Rica and for that very reason risks to ruin her great love and to compromise the stability of her marriage. Chiriac himself, otherwise very much abreast of whatever happens in Dumitrache's family, is in his turn unaware of Zita's love and (crudely taking over the information supplied by his boss and interpreting it wrongly), comes to suspect his otherwise faithful mistress Veta. Zita on the other hand lives in the artificial universe of romances—of adventures and passion—and,—being under the spell of young Venturiano's epistolary style—ignores her sister's relationship with Chiriac. The apprentice Spiridon carries the *billets-doux* of Rica and Zita and, although he never states it in so many words, he seems to know a lot about Veta and Chiriac. There are at least two sequences in the play which justify this supposition: in the fifth scene of act one, Spiridon delivers a soliloquy confessing to the spectators on the one hand his fear and loathing of Mr. Dumitrache Titirca and, on the other hand, his warm feelings for Veta and Chiriac, whose names and deeds he always evokes *together:* "Man! This master of ours is the devil himself! That was no dullard who nicknamed him 'Titirca the Evil-Hearted'! Why has he got this down on me? Really! My poor lady and uncle Chiriac! They are my luck, they can occasionally wrest me from the devil's hands, for if I were to depend on Titirca the Evil-Hearted alone, my own bones would be in danger! He would crush them all! "Beyond possible kindheartedness, though not supported by further evidence or speeches—what else if not the intention to repay his discretion in this way, determines the lovers to save poor Spiridon repeteadly?

And then, at the end of scene IV of the second act, when Dumitrache accompanied by Ipingescu catches sight of the importunate Venturiano's shadow in Veta's room and rushes in, resolved to avenge the compromised honour of a family man with his sword, the following dialogue takes place:

> SPIRIDON *(crying):* Ouch, master, ouch! But what have I done, to you, master? How am I to blame if I fell asleep?
>
> IPINGESCU *(in an awesome voice, to Spiridon):* Why are you not present when we call your name on the roll?
>
> (. . .)
>
> SPIRIDON: Ouch! Woe to me! *(He weeps)*
>
> DUMITRACHE TITIRCA: Shut up! Where is Chiriac?
>
> SPIRIDON *(escaping to a corner of the room):* I don't know . . .
>
> DUMITRACHE TITIRCA *(making a pass at him, while Spiridon runs to the opposite corner):* But you do know how to eat and to sleep, don't you?
>
> SPIRIDON: He is asleep in his own room, master.

When taken unawares and at close quarters, Spiridon first hesitates whether to supply the violent Dumitrache with the information required by the latter. He hesitates because he is not sure whether Chiriac has reached his own room or is still lingering in Veta's in that prolonged reconciliation. Spiridon is playing for time, polarizing Dumitrache's attention and wrath, being convinced that the shouts would give a warning to Chiriac, if the later were still in Veta's bedroom. It is only after his shouts, his hemming and hawing that Spiridon gives the answer required from him, formulated as he wishes things to be and as they eventually came out.

Therefore Spiridon is in the know (or else the above-mentioned speeches would be meaningless) but for the time being he is holding his tongue, in gratitude to his protectors.

Rica Venturiano is the caricature of the journalist intoxicated with and made dizzy by words, in his turn rendering other people intoxicated and dizzy through the fustian of his own articles—a bizarre mixture of neologisms and vernacular, of confusions and demagogy. His role in the play is that of mixing up things, actually of justifying the title of Caragiale's comedy. Without Venturiano, the night in Dumitrache Titirca's house would have been . . . perfectly wound: the captain in the civic guard would quietly have concluded his nightly round, while Veta and Chiriac would have enjoyed two more hours, Spiridon would have enjoyed his sleep, Zita would probably have read *The Dramas of Paris* for the fourth time. As it was, however . . . beyond the significance of the events whose protagonist he was, Venturiano's function in the play is also set off through an almost imperceptible detail, insinuated by the author as if by chance. Speaking about Ghita Tircadau, Zita's former husband, from whom he had eventually "divorced" her ("because he never ill-treated her sir, at least with one kind word"), Dumitrache Titirca concluded: "Well, Sir, if the husband is not *levent,* what kind of a home could it be?" Therefore Tircadau had not been levent—i.e. generous, magnanimous and, at the same time, valiant, as this old Turkish word meant. On the other hand, Rica Venturiano signed his articles by abbreviating his name to R. Vent.—which in Romanian can also be read *revent.* Therefore, Tircadau was not *levent,* while Venturiano was *revent,* which is another word for rhubaro, i.e. a purgative.

Indeed, Rica Venturiano caused "honourable" people to go out of their usual patterns, to become violent.

Particularly subtle, very special is Ipingescu's attitude. From his speeches one might take it, at a first, superficial level of the interpretation, that the police officer was merely Dumitrache's mechanical echo, inclined to accept and to approve anything, without understanding anything of anything. His stereotypical word *"Raison"* gives his interlocutor full confidence, while sparing himself the effort of thinking for himself. When nevertheless he does that effort (in reading out and commenting upon Rica Venturiano's article in the newspaper), the result is a terrible confusion, in spite of the apparent logic that only Dumitrache Titirca can still accept. Ipingescu knows nothing about Zita's love affair with Rica, while about Veta's relations with Chiriac, his opacity is only surpassed by the cuckold's own credulity. Well, it seems so, but it is not so! When "read" through the grid suggested by the discreet series of events, the personage emerges much more complex than at first sight. From a certain point onwards, a few of his speeches force us to be rather cautious regarding his so called stupidity: Dumitrache narrates to Ipingescu the scene that had taken place at the "Iunion", the exchange of glances between the *"employé"* Rica and Veta (as the maniac of family honour thinks) followed by a narrative of their return home, escorted by the insistant "vagabond," "ne'er-do-well" and "ragamuffin." When Chiriac's voice is heard off, heralding his entrance, Ipingescu stops Dumitrache's narrative: "Here is Chiriac coming. He shouldn't hear about it." But why "shouldn't Chiriac hear about it? Because Ipingescu is aware of the latter's affair with Veta and wants to preclude any reason for suspicion! And then, when Dumitrache imparts to Ipingescu his project of settling money on Chiriac to facilitate his marriage, Ipingescu answers insinuatingly: "But what does your honourable wife say?" And, last but not least, when Dumitrache, in the street, wishes good night to Chiriac, who is holding Veta in his arms, Ipingescu adds with feigned candour: "And sweet dreams, honourable gentleman!" Ipingescu is abreast of everything and makes fun at the credulousness of Dumitrache, who has remained impenetrable to his allusions. Or, at least, such is the point of view of Ipingescu, whom we suspect of chuckling jubilantly in his sleeve. Yet, he is taken in, very much as the other characters are taken in, and as the reader (or spectator) is about to be taken in.

As we have been able to notice so far, each character knows something about the others—sometimes quite a lot. The only one who appears as a perfect idiot, impervious to the signals coming to him from all sides, seeking outside what is actually taking place under his very nose, is Dumitrache Titirca. He savagely punishes Spiridon for sleeping at various hours, for smoking in secret, while he praises Chiriac for watching vigilantly, "as closely as possible" over Dumitrache's conjugal honour. Dumitrache does practically everything in order not to see what is obvious to everybody else: Spiridon tells him that Veta is sewing the épaulettes of Chiriac's uniform, but to Dumitrache it seems the most natural thing in the world: Chiriac insistently urges him to go out sooner to do his nightly round, and Veta conveys to him the same message, scarcely disguised, ("She said you ought to come earlier tonight as she felt too lonely at home"), but the merchant sees nothing dubious in all that, on the contrary, he takes it for concern and love for his own person; Ipingescu makes all sorts of allusions to him but the man remains impassive; he finds a necktie in his wife's bed, but when Chiriac appeases his worry, reassuring him with the words: "Never mind! Bring it over, master. It's my own scarf, don't you recognize it?" Dumitrache's answer is astounding (and it elicits Ipingescu's last "Raison"—rather disconcerned this time): "Oh, God bless you, brother, why didn't you tell me so?" (philosophically, to Ipingescu): You see, that's how a man may be blinded with fury!"

What is unnatural, "topsy-turvy"—like number 6 turned into 9—seems to Dumitrache the most natural thing in the world. But does it actually *seem so?* Or, does he want *to take things like that?* If Dumitrache were a true idiot, the comic effect would be enormously diminished, for the other personages' "tricks" played on him would no longer have any justification. Innate, pathological stupidity does not give rise to laughter, but to sympathy if not to tears. That is why, let us assume for a moment that Mr. Dumitrache Titirca knows everything and turns a blind eye on the "manipulation" for reasons which are as yet mysterious. Do inacceptable inadvertencies appear in the dramatic text in this way? Hardly.

At the end of scene VIII of the second act, Spiridon promises Rica Venturiano to get him out of the trouble into which he had fallen. The next scene begins with a stage direction of particular importance for what we are out to demonstrate: suddenly, in the room on the left one hears a few slaps and Spiridon's yells. "There follows the scene when Rica is caught by Ipingescu and Chiriac. There is one thing alone to be inferred from this: that Spiridon could not withstand Dumitrache's "treatment" and betrayed Venturiano. But, if this is true, then why should we not assume that under similar circumstances Spiridon had revealed to Dumitrache the content of the *billets-doux* between Zita and Rica? Therefore, from a certain moment onwards, Dumitrache is perfectly aware of the object of Rica's affection, yet he pretends to suspect Veta revealing his "fears" both to Chiriac and to Ipingescu. Why does he do this? One interpretation alone is acceptable: because Dumitrache has long been aware also of Veta's liaison with Chiriac. He is aware of it and he puts up with it (we will see why) yet does not want those involved or the suspicious Ipingescu to know that he knows. It would be much too compromising and his "honour of a family man" would go to the dogs. But Dumitrache is indeed a stickler not so much for his *pundonor,* but for something much more precious in his own system of values: the *appearance of honourableness.*

That is why, through all his behaviour, he eliminates any possible suspicion on the part of Veta and Chiriac, while he dominates Spiridon through violence and threats (*this* is the real cause of the more or less groundless thrashings given to the boy); on the other hand, to Ipingescu, whose allusions he understands perfectly but ignores deliberately, he offers this "imbroglio". For Ipingescu it must be clear, when the knot is unravelled, that Dumitrache's honourable marriage has not for a moment been threatened from the outside.

As regards Veta's relationship with Chiriac, which Dumitrache knows Ipingescu to be aware of, the merchant acts the great scene of—let's say—the necktie. Definitely, he could easily have pretended not to have found it at all. But in this way, he would have allowed Ipingescu's suspicions to continue, together with the latter's consequent ascendency and upleasant allusions during their talks. The self-assurance with which Chiriac tells the truth (an attitude which certainly Dumitrache has stimulated for a long time, at his moment banking on a prompt reaction), to which is added the merchant's incredible feigned naivety do take the expected effect upon the ironist Ipingescu. He is reduced to saying "Raison!" as a personal conclusion, in the finale, this time however, without any connotation, but only expressing full agreement with his better skilled friend.

In ***A Stormy Night,*** the games of love (Veta-Chiriac and Zita-Rica) are programmed efficiently and supervised rigorously by Mr. Dumitrache Titirca, a past master at combinations, while the game of chance (number 6 turned into 9) is in fact merely an ingenious stratagem of the same, meant to cancel any shadow cast upon the honourableness of his home. In the morning Dinica, the builder, is going to amend the "error," the best—and especially the most moral—of possible worlds returning to its natural course. From the wings, Caragiale winks at the spectator who is now his safe ally.

Stefan Cazimir (essay date 1987)

SOURCE: "Classicism and Realism," in *Romanian Review,* Vol. 41, No. 6, 1987, pp. 95-104.

[*In the following essay, Cazimir discusses Caragiale's reliance on classical literary principles and the realistic presentation of character in such works as* A Stormy Night *and* A Lost Letter.]

The attempt to define by a terse formula the essence of Caragiale's view of man invariably resorts, in the most penetrating exegesis, to invoking classicism as the proximate genus and realism as the specific difference. Yet another survey of his œuvre confirms this opinion, supporting it with several considerations on Caragiale's way of conceiving of the situation of types in space and time, on their degree of stability and *pregnantz* as resulting from such determinations, on the more general aspects of their affective and moral moulding, and lastly, along a somewhat secondary line of thought, on the author's attitude to his own creations, on the distinct tonality of Caragiale's laughter.

The whole comic *oeuvre* of Caragiale points with negligible differences between one segment and another, to his "fixist" conception of character. A more careful definition of the latter would note that evolution—only retrospectively admissible as a finite process of character crystallization—in general precludes the hypothesis of later changes. Relating the moral structure of the characters to the diagram of their movement on the social scale, one can see that the most markedly outlined figures were captured at the time of a final situation-character concretion. Master Dumitrache, to quote George Calinescu, "no one can imagine as a speculator. His condition is fixed and so is Pristanda's, who by definition cannot get out of his 'fixed pay' condition, without becoming structurally altered." Some could say that the author thought differently for twenty five years later he depicted Titirca as a ruling-party senator, big landowner and capitalist, and oil magnate. But the lack of success of Caragiale's Berlin project illustrates the flimsiness of its groundwork, flagrantly emphasized by the parallel rise of all the characters: Chiriac, Sotirescu is a ruling-party deputy, Spiridon Ionescu a deputy, doctor of law from Liège University, owning a motorcar and race horses, Nae Ipingescu a county prefect—all three being big landlords and capitalists, oil magnates, etc. Schematic and unconvincing, this removal into an Eldorado of men whom ***A Stormy Night*** had fixed between the bounds of satisfied mediocrity, with no inclination for grand-scale arrivism, is a demonstration *per contrarium* of the principle of indestructible solidarity between character and social condition. Further evidence is the less expressive delineation of those characters that age or profession places in transition stages. Compared with Titirca or Zaharia Trahanache, with Ipingescu or Pristanda, Chiriac and Tipatescu are evanescent figures. One obvious consequence in such cases is the scarcity of comical effects, these being—to the extent that they do occur—connected with the conjuncture rather than with the essence.

Sketches like **"Tempora"** . . . or **"Hard, from Hand to Mouth."** . . . , apparent deviations from the law of character immutability, merely go to confirm it indirectly. From the brave tribune who, for years on end leads "the generous university youth" and its anti-government demonstrations to the stage of "any impudent police inspector, regular scoundrel, shameless knave, savage brute and man-eating butcher" we see the hierarchical rise rather than the evolution of Coriolan Draganescu. Outwardly contradictory, these two facets are closely connected beneath, ultimately providing the comical turn of the story. Generalizing broadly, we could also mention the stages in the humbug's ideology: "From primary school to high school leaving—an anarchist. From high school leaving to the first college examination—a socialist. From the first college examination to graduation a progressive. From graduation to job-finding—a liberal. From job finding to retirement—a conservative." In all these forms of manifestation, the humbug's essence remains unchanged.

Constant formulae, which some have accused of schematism without denying their impact, are actually just another expression of character fixity, as seen notably from Caragiale's specific manner of using this age-old device. In Plautus or Molière, no matter how effective, characteristically, the formula is born and disappears within a single scene ("Sine dote?", "Qu'allait-il faire dans cette galère?", "Le pauvre homme!", etc.) Labiche extends the life of formulae to the length of a whole play ("Mon gendre, tout est rompu!" "Embrassons-nous Folleville!"), but their strict dependence on the texture of the plot deprives them of any more lasting significance. Caragiale's formulae, instead, are more wide-embracing. They are not mere momentary expressions but accompany the characters over an indefinite length of existence and implicitly guarantee their structural consistency. Similar conclusions can be drawn from conflict-solving, in a spirit totally different from the sudden, facile conversions to which his forerunners' comedies—supported by foreign models too—had so often resorted. Far from altering the moral profile of the character, the finale of Caragiale's plays subjects it to a last check and reinforcing, and vigorously projects it into a surpriseless future. It is on this conception on character stability essentially refusing all flexibility, that the basic mode of defining them through actions stands, by devising situations that can bring them under revealing pressure. Self-important Master Dumitrache is placed in a state of alarm as to his spot of maximum sensibility, theorist Leonida is faced with circumstances defying his power of explanation, placid Trahanache is confronted by several occasions for indignation, zealous Intoxicated Citizen is baffled by a number of hindrances on his path to duty. Once the artistic goal has been achieved by an adequate determination of the substance, the characters are restored to their original state of balance. To judge by Caragiale's approach the best way to bring out a character is to place him in vexing situations.

Caragiale's adherence to classicism—no doubt, in an expanded sense of the concept—must also be viewed from other angles too, such as that stressing the great importance attached by him to the technical aspect of literary art, his constant emphasis on the formal scruple, his considering expression a reality consequent on the content and possibly diverging from it. However ironical generally, the author's intended answer to those who sent him manuscripts asking for certain plastic-surgery operations contains some enlightening lines: "In principle, by rectifying or, to put it differently, by repairing a piece of poetry, one understands, quite naturally, changing only the material side, that is the wording, rather than the thinking, the poetry itself. Similarly, when one calls upon a tailor to have a misfitting coat corrected, one does not ask to have the body reshaped but only to have a badly cut coat adjusted to the body, such as it is in shape." The writer's youngest son, Luca Ion Caragiale, gives us some complementary details: "In his youth, at Iasi, he had frequented the Junimea circle and there he had established a strong, much-cherished link with Vasile Pogor. With Pogor, he had talked about style. Pogor had been reared to the aesthetic dogmas of French classicism, and Caragiale too had grown familiar with them. Caragiale mocked the cold style of the French classics, but, after all, his own aesthetic rules were not too far removed from Boileau's. 'Tout doit tendre au bon sens' was his principle also. Clarity and conciseness were to him the true qualities of style." The writer's literary practice, cultivating the tragic and the comic alike, adds to the above his respect for the classical precept of genus separation: "Le comique, ennemi des soupirs et des pleurs./N'admet point en ses vers de tragiques douleurs."

Against the background of such views and positions, the placing of Caragiale beyond the bounds of orthodox classicism can be more clearly realized. His "fixist" conception of character blends with his dynamic view of society, based directly on the example of Romania, whose overall image had been greatly changed in the nineteenth century: "Our parents tell us incredible stories about the state of public life in their youth, as if they talked of things that happened five hundred years ago; people still young can very well remember the time of their childhood, with no railways and when only two or three cities in the country had their centres lit up with tallow candles or rudimentary oil lamps." The aesthetic consequences of this world-view are often important to Caragiale. He demands of artistic representations to observe the unity between the generally human, unchanging in its essentials, and the specific tune and place colour: "although man will be man and mankind will be mankind anywhere and at any time, yet the customs, thoughts and feelings will differ just as do places, times and people." Literary genres like satire, drama and the novel "will preserve the passing social physiognomies of various periods." The writer praises the sketches of D. D. Patrascanu for depicting valuable figures of human comedy in the local Romanian garb. While postulating the pervasion of the artistic creations by the social-historical concrete, Caragiale rejects its being brought down into the contingent and any improvised actualizations. The initiave taken by a group of actors to lend the heroes in ***The Lost Letter*** the physiognomies of some politicians of the day justly bring forth the writer's indignation, as he saw in his comedies "not mere buffooneries meant to incidentally ridicule real persons, but works of art aimed at more lastingly depicting ideal types."

Undoubtedly, between a moving-world concept and one of static character there cannot be perfectly peaceful coexistence. When the former tries to restrain the latter, my effort will be made in vain (see Caragiale's plans for the comedy *Titirca. Sotirescu & Co.)* Aggravation of this virtual contradiction can however be averted by presenting the individuals in accordance with the time-unity rule. In the historical film produced by Caragiale the heroes change with the setting and thus the feeling of social evolution, illustrated with unique force in the global approach to the work, remains without notable consequences on the plane of individual lives.

As an entity taken from under the sway of becoming, the heroes increase their force as memorable representations of the *milieux* and times that produced them. Caragiale's path is not quite unlike that formerly followed by Molière, a playwright belonging more to the classical age than to classicism as such, who took enough liberties at the expense of dogmatic spirits. (An unmistakable departure from the classical doctrine can also be seen in the language used by Molière's heroes, geared to their social environment and thereby open to a wide variety of sources.) As is well known, with the author of *Le Bourgeois gentilhomme* the comedy of character and of manners draws towards a synthesis repeatedly achieved in his masterpieces. An organic communion is thus established between the generality of inherent tendencies of human nature and the historically determined mode of the way they start and manifest themselves, a communion that analysis no longer can dissolve. In its subsequent evolution, French comedy could not retain or retrieve this close unity, because of a variety of factors. As noted by Lanson, "Molière quite involuntarily helped to accredit a false idea born of a superficial study of his plays: the idea of a comedy of characters without any treatment of manners, with an elevated, restrained comicality, allegedly representing the higher form of comedy. . . . On the other hand, those not having such lofty ambitions would no longer attempt to lend a moral sense or universal value to manner depictions." [G. Lanson, *Histoire de la littérature française,* 14th revised edition, Paris, 1918, p. 530.] Significant in this respect are also the views of Diderot, who called for replacing character study with investigating the social conditions and ultimately advocating a comedy of vocations. The eighteenth-century theories could not, however, find any viable embodiments and then comedy had to traverse a period of precariousness, between indifference on the part of most romanticists and the artisan skill of vaudeville writers. The nineteenth-century comedy of manners, with its keen interest in the social and moral problems of the day, was born under the auspices of Balzac's novels. The new trend was not unconnected with the awareness that characteriological study had been exhausted. "L'homme moral est déterminé," wrote A. Dumas *fils,* "l'homme social reste à faire." (Preface to *Le Fils naturel).*

The particular circumstances attending the growth of Romanian comedy offered Caragiale a favourable position. For the French dramatists of the mid-century the golden age of comedy was already a matter of the past. With us, the comic character had only reached the embryonic stage, and the comedy of manners, in a fertile existence of several decades, had the characters' moral structure at the level of sketchy, labile forms. The legacy of the forerunners, never felt to be a burden, pointed, on the contrary, to an unachieved synthesis and to the conquest of still unatained perfection. In terms of exploring the contemporary realities, Caragiale carried on and completed the work of his predecessors, in agreement, also, with some wider tendencies of European literature. His keen perception endows each separate type with attributes intensely characteristic of the place and time that produced him. Caragiale's heroes bear the indellible mark of the surroundings where they were born and live, and transplanting them to another *milieu* seems impossible. The character is not dressed in period costume but inwardly moulded by his social condition. Outside his conditioning the self-importance of Master Dumitrache, the ambition of Catavencu and the servilism of Pristanda would remain empty concepts, without any support. In this sense we may presume to believe that Caragiale's creative approach starts from the manner to reach the characters, that, in other words, without the global intuition of a frame of existence, the men peopling it could not have come into being. This impression is also based on Caragiale's masterly sureness in drawing the supra-individual traits. The most general of them is the characters' belonging to changing times, with many novel, surprising aspects likely to seduce or confuse one, at any rate to impose an attitude and thus help define the characters and achieve a deeper motivation of the comic effects.

With determining consequences for the inalterable vitality of his types, Caragiale's eyes are wide open to the concrete picturesqueness of human actions, which he eagerly recorded—witness his biography and work alike. "I occasionally happened," recalled Ioan Slavici, "to be with Caragiale in the same coffee house or restaurant, or at some celebration when lots of people came in, stayed and went out, and hours passed with no word between us.

Still we felt very fine together. One of his perfect pleasures was to watch those passing about him, to scrutinize their faces, to capture gestures and attitudes—a pleasure of mine also, to the present day. He would nadge me now and then, or wink at me and whisper, 'Did you get that?' and we understood each other to perfection. 'Why,' he would also say, 'nature works to pattern, she casts every one in a different way. This has one oddity, that another, each in his distinct manner, you never tire watching them and getting heaps of fun.'" In view of such remarkedly eloquent lines, the concept of Caragiale's classicism needs must take another correction. "All the pleasure of a classical mind," wrote G. Calinescu in *The Sense of Classicism,* "lies in never coming across novelty, in perpetually sticking to the typical. But, no doubt, the world of the particular will quite often bring new appearances. Faced by them, the classical mind has a feeling of contradiction . . ." Caragiale, on the other hand, far from feeling annoyed by unusual forms, derived from contemplating them a state of exultancy that passed into his world with undiminished freshness. To capture the image of Mr. Leonida at the height of his dramatic stupefaction, of Pristanda perched on Catavencu's fence, of the coffee-house keeper wearing his Civil Guard coat over the five-inch longer apron into which he now and then blows his snivelling nose, one must possess the eye and pen of a Daumier in his unique *Croquis d'expression.*

Hegel saw the ideal character as resulting from the fusion of three capital elements: richness, determination and firmness. The first involves associating the dominant trait with several others so as to turn the hero into a real, complete man, capable of acting in a variety of situations, under a variety of aspects. Determination adds the imperative of a fusion between the several qualities so as to form an indivisible whole rather than merely remain juxtaposed. The highest goal is consistency and firmness, enabling a character to retain the unity above all contradictions or fluctuations. There is no other work in Romanian literature better suited to answer to Hegel's postulates than the comic *œuvre* of Caragiale, notably his comedies. Anticipating by some critics, the only observation could refer to richness, if taken in a quantitative sense. True, the writer builds his heroes out of a few traits, but this is only found out analytically, for in terms of the action the elements included are precisely those required by a convincing vigorous presence, ultimately synonymous with substantial vitality. Caragiale may sometimes define a character summarily but never mutilates him, never makes him unstable, unequal or expressionless. Possessing the virtue of identity in the highest degree, he confirms himself by every sentence however unexpected it may be. His unflinching consistency, organically and unostentatiously maintained, seems devoid of rigidity and cannot be reduced to a general concept. This is more remarkable as one essential tendency of the comic lies precisely in a character's generality, unthinkable without some concessions to schematism.

In achieveing the organicity of Caragiale's heroes a major role is played by the relationship established between character and temperament, the latter integrating the inner structure in a sensorially perceptible reality. This calls for some general considerations, for the heroes' belonging in one large family is vividly felt here, which once more proves the author's unitary approach. The emotional type of Caragiale's heroes points to a prevalence of excitation over inhibition, hence to a notably greater consumption of nervous energy than needed. One much exploited source of the psychological comic is making an affect do duty for a passion. Overwhelming though superficial emotional reactions assume, during their brief evolution, the garb of profound, irresistible feelings. But one moment suffices to give them the lie. From a deadly foe of Cracanel, Pampon instantly turns his protector, willing to wipe away his tears with touching gentleness: "Don't cry any more, it isn't done by a volunteer like you . . ." Transferred into politics, the meridional spirit of noisy quarelling followed by equally noisy reconciliations lend to such pieces of opportunism of an inimitable naturalness: "*Trahanache:* And so you're one of ours, aren't you, my dear? Good show, I'm very glad. *Catavencu:* Venerable Mr. Zaharia, in circumstances like these *(moved)* the little passions must vanish. *Trahanache:* Well said! Good show! Bless you!" Knowing how much importance it deserves, people are not upset by violence: "We contented ourselves with taking the *agent provocateur* to the police station to be kept there till the rage blows over." Similarly inconsistent is the threatened suicide, undermined by its very repetition: "Mrs. Zamfira Popescu changed the subject because Portia, who was a highly sensitive being, had repeatedly threatened with suicide at moments of downheartedness"; "I told him, 'Lae, she's not your type', but he, madly in love. . . . nothing doing, would never listen to me and said he'd kill himself if I refused to let him"; Poor Mita is in despair because Octavian told her frankly that if he failed to get his remove he would shoot himself." In certain situations one will note the contribution of bookish models to the emergence of affective complexes and their verbal expression. We have to do with a false romanticism born of unconsciously mimicking poses drawn from epigonic literature. Throughout the comic *oeuvre* of Caragiale passions are noted for their ridiculous, ephemeral character. As aesthetician Mihail Ralea points out, the heroes would never commit murder or other crimes just to indulge a desire: "They will make a great fuss and boastfully display their carnival fate, but actually they are 'bons enfants', jovial and quite good-natured." This is indeed a major characteristic. The heroes' self-pride almost invariably includes a false notion of their own emotional capacity. In fact it is a mole-hill turned mountain that quickly reverts to its real size. In his tragic writings, Caragiale took a different course and depicted tenacious hatred and implacable revenge blended with desperation, madness and death. Through this strange symmetry, his *œuvre* seems to reveal an intimate law governing the genetic processes in a way alien to all deliberation.

The morals of Caragiale's heroes are a heatedly discussed problem. Some commentators agree in investing these heroes with a monstruous selfishness" (G. Ibraileanu);

they have "a solid instinct of self-preservation," are "selfish in their adaptability," the women in their turn appearing to be "vulgar, hypocritical and selfish" (Pompiliu Constantinescu); the characters in ***A Stormy Night*** are "obtuse, selfish, uninterested in the outside world unless it comes into immediate contact with their real interests" (I. M. Sadoveanu). A more nuanced position is taken by G. Calinescu who, while pointing out the heroes' instinct of individual self-preservation, which accounts for their manifest cowardice, does not fail to notice their fatalism, which entails a limitation on this selfishness. Reviewing the elements of the *œuvre,* one must admit that the impulse in question, no matter how typical of a large number of cases, cannot be viewed as general and absolute. Master Dumitrache's concern about the success of Zita's marriage; Veta's pity for Spiridon and even for the unknown nocturnal guest, Trahanache's delicacy in sparing his wife's blushes, or his indignation at his friend being slandered, to say nothing of Pristanda, who can be fully exonerated from selfishness—all these are just a few examples worth noting.

With special reference to Ibraileanu's opinion, it must be said that selfishness is too deeply rooted in every one of us to be useful in motivating our hatred of those afflicted with the same infirmity. Caragiale's heroes remind us of a hateful social order, but no one can actually say they too are hateful. It is only a mechanical identification of the heroes and situations with their real prototypes that leads to the false conclusion that the ridiculous blends with the detestable. In fact, Caragiale's peculiar vision consistently aimed at removing the hateful and thus give rein to laughter. For many of his heroes vice is a medium of existence, but it does not result from a conscious option, nor does it entail an understanding of guilt. In this modelling of the heroes' morals we find the most profound expression of Caragiale's irony. With some exaggeration arising from his well-known moral rigorism, Slavici was able to grasp this particular aspect: "In comedy we laugh at the foibles of innocent people. In Caragiale's comedies we are tempted to laugh at the ugliest passion, of morally dead people who can only end up in the cemetery, in prison, or in the lunatic asylum. 'Nonsense', the master used to say, 'in other times and places (this could really happen—S. C.); in this country of ours falsehood, cowardice, vile intriguing, seduction and adultery are just as many funny trifles at which everyone laughs heartily.' *And he would laugh at those who laughed.*" I stressed the last sentence for its synthetic virtues. And this brings us back to the question of the innocence of Caragiale's heroes, a trait that considerably facilitates placing them under the auspices of the comic. It should be noted here that some heroes display a guilty innocence, if one may put it so, that is a kind of innocence born of long-standing familiarity with wickedness, which is no longer perceived as such. It is at such innocence that Caragiale's irony is chiefly directed, at the taking of bland, good-natured attitudes in the face of detestable phenomena. The author's leniency is as Slavici most pertinently remarked, a malicious reflex of the heroes' own leniency towards themselves: "You must forgive and love me," Catavencu asks the prefect, "because we all love this country, we are all Romanians—more or less honest ones!"

Caragiale's attitude to his own creations rules out the hostile impulse ascribed to him by some exegeses. Quite undoubtedly, the dramatist was deeply dissatisfied with the unjust social order, he was particularly indignant at the mockery of bourgeois democracy, at "the chasm between reality and appearance." He rebelled against the social environment, but in the individuals he saw the inevitable products of determining circumstances and did not refuse them his superior understanding. "After the toast proposed by Brezeanu [the actor who played the Intoxicated Citizen on the first night—S. C.]," Caragiale commented on the finale of ***A Lost Letter*** "a good-natured man cannot leave the theatre without being reconciled to, even without feeling sympathy for the distinguished lady of the world and for the pub-debased drunkard, two erring, strayed, guilty creatures, God knows for what reasons, but nice, whatever hypocrites might say, undoubtedly nice." Sympathy for the hero is a more general disposition with Caragiale, generally blended with irony, in the multiple nuances the latter may assume. The blending of sympathy and irony takes us into the core of the writer's comic art, perfectly consonant with the style of his human actions, as so many contemporary records have preserved for us.

To infer from the social conditions of a period the temperament of its artists is a most regrettable piece of schematism. The circumstances evoked by Caragiale's writings may have the bitterest substratum, yet his laughter is not constricted but clear and powerful, a laughter of invincible moral strength. Only a man could laugh thus who had grasped the transcience of that wrong social order, its inability to destroy the perennial values of our national life. The timbre of Caragiale's laughter should not be confused with the colour of the thoughts it inspires for the simple reason that the timbre is unique and the thoughts are many, capable sometimes of changing and evolving under the impact of an indefinite number of factors. What remains unchanged is his *œuvre*'s power to stimulate thinking—the surest mark of its inner earnestness. There are few authors in world literature who can be admired for the same generous laughter allied to the same substantial profoundness. "In our short toilsome lives," Caragiale maintained, "merrymaking is not so frivolous, after all, as some sages, grumblers and hypocrites would have us believe."

The common paradox of the comic author's sadness is so old that we owe it some respect. The attempt to apply it to Caragiale (Delavrancea and Vlahuta are among those who have made it) seems less fruitful than any other. "The Caragiale's," Paul Zarifopol tells us, "were a dynasty of people with a genius for laughter . . . The habitual guests of the Caragiale family were able to know at first hand the vocation for laughter as an art and the sense of the comic as a basic instinct." A more recently found record goes to confirm the above. On April 28,

1852, writing to her husband with the usual pride of young mothers, Ecaterina Caragiale noted, as a striking trait of their first-born, a permanent inclination to laugh: "God had given us a blessed child; his kindness is extraordinary, now he's got used to water and he'll utter no sound till I bath him, and then he'll laugh very, very gaily, he'll even wake up laughing and babbling." Those are words that no one, under the sign of fate, can read without emotion. It was the birth of the loudest and most richly echoing laughter ever heard within Romania's boundaries.

FURTHER READING

Criticism

Barbuta, Margareta. "The Fiftieth Anniversary of the Death of I. L. Caragiale/Le Cinquantenaire de la Mort de I. L. Caragiale." *Le Théatre dans le Monde/World Theatre* XI, No. 4 (Winter 1962-63): 363-69.

Reviews events in Romania and elsewhere commemorating the fiftieth anniversary of Caragiale's death; in English and French, with photographs.

Feraru, Leon. "Opere, Tomul III, Reminiscente si notite critice, Editie îngrijita de Paul Zarifopol." *The Romanic Review* XXV, No. 1 (January-March 1934): 70.

A favorable review of Paul Zarifopol's third volume (in Romanian) of an edition of works by Caragiale.

Tappe, E.D. "Opera alese (Ausgewählte Werke)." *The Modern Language Review* LII, No. 2 (April 1957): 291.

Unfavorably reviews a German-language selection of Caragiale's works, which he finds was made with Marxist, rather than literary, criteria in mind.

The following source published by Gale Research contains further information on Caragiale's life and works: *Contemporary Authors,* Vol. 157.

Val Lewton

1904-1951

(Born Vladimir Ivan Leventon) Russian-born American producer, screenwriter, novelist, poet, and nonfiction writer.

INTRODUCTION

Considered a brilliant producer of B-movie features, Lewton is primarily known for the series of low-budget horror films he created in the early 1940s. Beginning with 1942's *Cat People* and ending with *Bedlam* four years later, Lewton's creative and critically-acclaimed motion pictures were said to have revived the flagging horror genre by injecting it with a renewed psychological intensity. Critics have since generally focused on Lewton's innovative use of shadow to create an encircling mood of terror in his pictures, a now staple method of the contemporary horror film.

Biographical Information

Lewton was born on May 7, 1904 in Yalta, Russia. His mother brought him to the United States when he was seven years old, and he was granted citizenship while still a child. Lewton attended Columbia University in New York City, and later began his career as a writer and as an employee of the publicity department at MGM studios. One of his earliest works, a book entitled *The Cossack Sword* (1926) caught the attention of film producer David O. Selznick, whose staff Lewton joined in 1933. While a script editor for Selznick for nearly a decade Lewton penned several novels, most of them published under the assumed names H. C. Kerkow, Cosmos Forbes, or Carlos Keith. In 1942 Lewton left Selz-nick to join RKO as a producer—part of a new low-budget film studio designed to compete with Universal's like division. It was during the years 1942 to 1946 that Lewton—teamed with such directors as Jacques Tourneur, Mark Robeson, and Robert Wise—created a string of nine successful B-grade horror flicks, each shot over a period of about a month for approximately $150,000 apiece. In 1946, after his work on the last of these was complete, Lewton left RKO and continued his career as an independent producer. He made three more movies outside the horror genre with various studios before his death from a heart attack on March 14, 1951.

Major Works

While he wrote an assortment of novels and nonfiction, Lewton's primary artistic contribution remains his collection of nine horror pictures produced in the 1940s. The first, *Cat People*, plays upon the theme of lycanthropy, and features a young New York fashion designer who claims to possess the ability to transform herself into a large, deadly feline. *I Walked with a Zombie* (1943) demonstrates Lewton's literary imagination. Its story is a version of Charlotte Brontë's *Jane Eyre* set in the West Indies, and follows the activities of a young woman hired by a planter to look after his catatonic wife. The wife's nightly walks lead the natives to believe she is under a spell of voodoo, and is a member of the living dead. The setting of *The Leopard Man* (1943) is small-town New Mexico, where the locals suppose a leopard is the cause of several murders that in reality are the work of a psychopath. Lewton returns to Manhattan for *The Seventh Victim* (1943), a tale of satanic worship set in Greenwich Village. *The Curse of the Cat People* (1944) is a psychological thriller that explores the imaginary fantasy world of a seven-year-old girl. Derived from a story by Robert Louis Stevenson, *The Body Snatcher* (1945) takes place in nineteenth-century Scotland and recounts the activities of two unseemly men who supply doctors and medical students with fresh cadavers for anatomical research. *Isle of the Dead* (1945) features a woman buried alive, while *Bedlam* (1946), Lewton's final horror film, visits the notorious London insane asylum of the same name.

PRINCIPAL WORKS

Panther Skin and Grapes (poetry) 1923
Improved Road (novel) 1925
The Cossack Sword [also published as *Rape of Glory* and *Sword of the Cossack*] (novel) 1926
The Green Flag of Jehad (nonfiction) 1926
The Theatre of Casanova (nonfiction) 1927
The Women of Casanova (nonfiction) 1927
Manual and History of Cosmetics [as Sidney Valentine] (nonfiction) 1930
The Rogue Song (screenplay novelization) 1930
The Fateful Star Murder [as H. C. Kerkow] (novel) 1931
The Unemployed Working Girl in the Present Crisis (nonfiction) 1931
Four Wives (novel) 1932
No Bed of Her Own (novel) 1932
Where the Cobra Sings [as Cosmo Forbes] (novel) 1932
Yearly Lease (novel) 1932
A Laughing Woman [as Carlos Keith] (novel) 1933
Rasputin and the Empress (screenplay novelization) 1933
This Fool Passion [as Carlos Keith] (novel) 1934
Cat People [producer; directed by Jacques Tourneur] (film) 1942
The Ghost Ship [producer; directed by Mark Robson] (film) 1943
I Walked with a Zombie [producer; directed by Jacques Tourneur] (film) 1943
The Leopard Man [producer; directed by Jacques Tourneur] (film) 1943
The Seventh Victim [producer; directed by Mark Robson] (film) 1943
The Curse of the Cat People [producer; directed by Robert Wise and Gunther von Fritsch] (film) 1944
Mademoiselle Fifi [producer; directed by Robert Wise] (film) 1944
Youth Runs Wilds [producer; directed by Mark Robson] (film) 1944
The Body Snatcher [producer; directed by Robert Wise] (film) 1945
Isle of the Dead [producer; directed by Mark Robson] (film) 1945
Bedlam [producer; directed by Mark Robson] (film) 1946
My Own True Love [producer; directed by Compton Bennett] (film) 1949
Please Believe Me [producer; directed by Norman Taurog] (film) 1950
Apache Drums [producer; directed by Hugo Fregonese] (film) 1951

CRITICISM

Joel E. Siegel (essay date 1973)

SOURCE: "The Seventh Victim: The 'Haunted Eyes' of Jean Brooks—Val Lewton, 1904-1951," in *Val Lewton: The Reality of Terror,* The Viking Press, 1973, pp. 7-100.

[*In the following excerpt, Siegel discusses Lewton's career and the production histories of his films, from* Cat People *through* The Curse of the Cat People.]

It is generally nonsensical to speak of producers as creators when, in all but a few cases, they were the enemies of creation. One of the exceptions was Lewton who, though credited only as producer, was unarguably the artistic creator and prime mover of his films. Apart from his last, troubled productions, Lewton's films were easily identifiable by their attention to detail, their unusually literate screenplays, their skillful, suggestive use of shadow and sound. Although his production unit at RKO was fully democratic, with each member having a full say on artistic matters, Lewton's eleven RKO films constitute an uncommonly personal body of work.

Lewton contributed a great deal to the screenplays of his films, from the original story-lines, which were often his, through the various drafts and revisions; and he always wrote the final shooting scripts himself. Lewton employed writers, although he really did not need them, for several reasons. As a literary man, he enjoyed the company of writers, and as a chronic dawdler, he often could not get projects into gear without some external stimulus. He would select a writer to work up one of his ideas and then, trained by his work at M-G-M publicity and his years at Selznick, he would take the writer's work, determine its strengths and reshape, often remake, the story to take advantage of its possibilities. It would be grossly unfair to conclude that Lewton's writers did not make important contributions to his films, but a look at the subsequent credits of those writers will show that none ever managed to match the quality of the work he did for Lewton.

Lewton never took screen credit for the writing of his films. When, at the end of his tenure at RKO, he was forced to take a writing credit, he used the old pseudonym Carlos Keith. He explained this apparent modesty in a note to his mother and sister. 'I have to laugh at both your ignorance of the "moom picture industry" as she industrates [*sic*]. I am and have always been a writer-producer. That does not always mean more money. The reason I do not ordinarily take credit for my very considerable work on my own scripts is that I have a theory that if I take credit, whenever I rewrite another writer's work, I can very properly be suspected of rewriting merely to get such credit.' So although it was not in Lewton's nature to impose his will upon his co-workers, he was able to maintain control over his films by participating in their writing as well as taking care to choose collaborators who were sympathetic to his personality and vision. Obviously Lewton proved to be a lasting influence on his directors. Years after the producer's death, each has attempted a return to making modest, Lewtonesque psychological suspense films—Jacques Tourneur in his excellent *Night of the Demon,* Robert Wise in the visually distinguished *The Haunting,* and Mark Robson in the unfortunate *Daddy's Gone A-Hunting.*

The first member of the new unit was selected not by Lewton but by the studio; nevertheless she became an important part of his early days at RKO. Jessie Ponitz, an attractive, outgoing young woman, was a member of the studio stenographic staff and had been working as secretary to a producer. Because she knew the studio so well, she had been assigned to help Lewton get acquainted with the lot and its facilities. Mrs Ponitz, who is now executive secretary to. Walter Mirisch of the Mirisch Corporation, was instantly affected by Lewton's gentleness, shyness and sensitivity, and became quite protective of him in the short time they worked together. Once Lewton told her, following a visit from some studio executives, 'It is extremely difficult for me to even shake hands with people.' As she recalls it, this was not so much a fear as a dislike of physical contact. It is paradoxical that Lewton, who gave so much of himself to others, who was emotionally so vulnerable, so accessible, could not stand being touched or patted on the back.

His associates throughout his career were aware of Lewton's aversion and respected it. However, they did once manage to play a rather spectacular practical joke on him. After the completion of shooting on one of his last RKO movies, there was the customary party. Some of the cast and crew managed to talk Jane Russell, who had been a sensation in *The Outlaw* in her Howard Hughes-designed bra and was under contract to the studio, into taking part in their prank. Just as the party was in full swing, Miss Russell appeared, in a rather Outlawish dress, and began slowly advancing towards Lewton. Those in on the joke saw to it that a path was cleared between the actress and the puzzled producer. As Miss Russell, arms clasped behind her back, slowly and slinkily manoeuvred herself towards Lewton, he heard her huskily murmuring, 'Look, no hands! No hands!'

Mrs Ponitz's feeling for Lewton increased when the unit actually began functioning and she was made to feel a key participant in their first project. 'Val always rewrote everything that his writers turned in; the last draft was always his. As his secretary, I would type up the final script before it was sent out to be duplicated. Val spent a great deal of time talking over the effectiveness of the characterisations and situations in the screenplays. He often asked me for my advice, making me feel as though I was contributing much more than I actually was. When he asked for your opinion, you felt that he seriously wanted to hear what you had to say. You felt so much a part of the picture he was making. It was the same with everybody else; there was a great sense of collaboration, although it was really, and finally, Val's work. Afterwards, when you saw the finished movie on the screen, you felt that it all had something to do with you.'

The first writer chosen for the production unit was DeWitt Bodeen. The two men had met in 1941, while Lewton was still at Selznick. A production of *Jane Eyre* was in the works, and Lewton recalled having seen a play Bodeen had written about the Brontës called *Embers at Haworth.* Bodeen, who was then working as a reader in the RKO story department, was borrowed on Lewton's recommendation and signed on to serve as research assistant to Aldous Huxley, who was writing the *Jane Eyre* screenplay. It was Lewton, not Huxley, who supervised Bodeen's work, and a mutual respect grew out of their frequent discussions. When Lewton finally decided to accept the RKO offer, he told Bodeen to keep him in mind when the Selznick research job was finished.

Jacques Tourneur, director of the first three Lewton pictures, had known and admired the producer for a number of years. Tourneur, son of the great director of silent films, Maurice Tourneur, arrived in Hollywood in 1935 after directing four films in France, and signed a contract with M-G-M to direct shorts, something of a step backward in his career. For several years he toiled away on Pete Smith Specialties and John Nesbitt's *Passing Parades* until he was finally given a feature called *They All Come Out,* a semi-documentary about penitentiaries, cosponsored by the Department of Justice. Shortly after completing that film, Tourneur was assigned to direct the second unit of Selznick's *A Tale of Two Cities,* on which Lewton was also working, tightening the screenplay and checking for period authenticity. The two men had similar tastes, particularly a love of sailing, and quickly became friends, often spending boating weekends with their combined families. Tourneur went on to make several low budget movies in the early Forties, and then, when Lewton was setting up his unit at RKO, was called in to direct.

The final member of the initial Lewton group was editor Mark Robson. Robson had served as cutter for Orson Welles during the Mercury Theatre heyday at RKO, the period that produced *Citizen Kane* and *The Magnificent Ambersons.* When *Citizen Kane* failed at the box-office and its director went to South America to work on the *It's All True* project, everybody associated with Welles was 'punished' by the studio. Many of those who could not be fired were demoted to working for the B-unit. Joseph Breen, former head of the censor board and RKO production head prior to Koerner, recommended Robson to Lew Ostrow, head of the B-unit, who in turn assigned him to work as cutter for the Lewton horror unit. Robson, well schooled in film technique, was expected to advise

Lewton on any cinematic matters about which the producer might have questions.

In the years to come, other people would join this unit—directors Robert Wise and Gunther Von Fritsch, writers Ardel Wray and Josef Mischel, and secretary Verna De Mots. But in those first, pleasant days, only Tourneur, Robson, Bodeen and Mrs Ponitz sat in Lewton's office, listening to him spin stories, drinking Russian tea with strawberry jam, exchanging theories about film suspense and visual beauty, and awaiting word from Koerner's office as to what their first assignment would be.

TOM GRIES: *I learned a great secret about film producing from Val. He always told me not to spread a small budget over five or six sets—instead pick the location where most of the action will be played and make that a real showpiece. Then make do with the rest of the scenes. One elaborate set makes a film look much richer than it deserves to look. Val was a very careful man; he knew how to spend money and how to put it on the screen. When I began directing television, all of the things he told me about producing low budget pictures were extremely helpful.*

In an article for *Films in Review,* DeWitt Bodeen recalls the genesis of Lewton's first and probably most famous film, ***Cat People***:

> Val departed for RKO two weeks before I'd finished my work at Selznick's, and when I phoned him, as I had promised, he quickly made arrangements for me to be hired at RKO as a contract writer at the Guild minimum, which was then $75 a week. When I reported for work, he ran off for me some U.S. and British horror and suspense movies which were typical of what he did *not* want to do. We spent several days talking about possible subjects for the first script.
>
> Mr Koerner, who had personally welcomed me on my first day at the studio, was of the opinion that vampires, werewolves and man-made monsters had been over-exploited and that 'nobody has done much with cats.' He added that he had successfully audience-tested a title he considered highly exploitable—***Cat People***. 'Let's see what you two can do with that,' he ordered.
>
> When we were back in his office, Val looked at me glumly and said: 'There's no helping it—we're stuck with that title. If you want to get out now, I won't hold it against you.'
>
> I had no intention of withdrawing, and he and I promptly started upon a careful examination of the cat in literature. There was more to be examined than we had expected. Val was one of the best-read men I've ever known, and the kind of avid reader who retains what he reads.
>
> After we had both read everything we could find pertaining to the cat in literature, Val had virtually decided to make his first movie from a short story, Algernon Blackwood's *Ancient Sorceries,* which admirably lends itself to cinematic interpretation and could easily be re-titled ***Cat People.*** Negotiations had begun for the purchase of the screen rights when Val suddenly changed his mind.
>
> He arrived at his office unusually early and called me in at once. He had spent a sleepless night, he confessed, and had decided that instead of a picture with a foreign setting, he would do an original story laid in contemporary New York. It was to deal with a triangle—a normal young man falls in love with a strange foreign girl who is obsessed by abnormal fears, and when her obsession destroys his love and he turns for consolation to a very normal girl, his office co-worker, the discarded one, beset by jealousy, attempts to destroy the young man's new love.

As Lewton's sister was later to recall, the story-line was inspired by some French fashion designs Lewton had seen. The fears which were to plague the young woman had to do with her sense of being descended from a race of Serbian women who, stemming from a tradition of animal worship in the Middle Ages, had the ability to change into vicious cats whenever their passions were aroused. There were several reasons why Lewton decided to drop the Blackwood story and invent his own. *Ancient Sorceries* would have required a foreign, period setting, and Tourneur argued that for an audience to experience terror it must be able to identify with characters of its own world and time. And, as if this advice were not reason enough, the fear of cats, like the uneasiness at being touched, was deeply ingrained in Lewton's complex nature and may well have compelled him to invent a story in which he could give his fear substance.

Although it is not possible to trace this phobia back to its origin in Lewton's experience, documented evidence as to its existence pre-dates the ***Cat People*** script by many years. In 1934, while crossing the United States by train for the first time to work on the *Taras Bulba* treatment, Lewton kept a journal of his thoughts and experiences. The following entry was headlined 'Albuquerque': 'My sleeping habits on a pullman seem to have become fixed. I have difficulty falling asleep—doze first, then drop abruptly into a deep, dreamless sleep which seems, on waking, to have lasted a moment but actually extends for eight or nine hours. I always wake at a stop and am awakened by a dream. This morning I dreamt that a house cat jumped on my shoulders and began to claw me. I woke. The person in the berth above was stirring. Evidently some atavistic instinct to guard against a beast leaping from above brought on the dream and had wakened me.'

Ruth Lewton remembers another incident which took place while her husband was working for Selznick. He did his best writing at night and often worked so late that Ruth would be forced to go to bed without him. One night she was suddenly awakened by the piercing screams of a neighbourhood cat. A moment later the door of the bedroom opened, her husband entered and stood silently at the foot of the bed. 'The cat's scream frightened him and he didn't want to have to face it alone. He had a folk fear—an atavistic kind of fear of something going way, way back. Of course, he knew better—he was a very intellectual man and not a superstitious person—and so he was both frightened and fascinated by his fear. Maybe the source of it all can be traced back to the fairy-tales told him by his Russian peasant nurse. The old nurse, like many others of her calling, used to control her charges by frightening them half to death. She was strongly aided by the Russian fairy-tale tradition which makes the Brothers Grimm seem like very tame stuff. In the Russian Little Red Riding Hood, for example, the wolf is split open down the front and dies all covered with innards and gore.'

After presenting his ideas to Bodeen, Lewton spent a week with the writer working up a two-page story-line which detailed the characters and action of ***Cat People*** more specifically. The obsessed girl was to be a Balkan-born dress designer called Irena Dubrovna who lived and worked in Manhattan. Lewton had seen and admired the French actress Simone Simon in William Dieterle's *All That Money Can Buy,* the movie version of Benet's *The Devil and Daniel Webster.* Miss Simon, a star in France in both theatre and films, had been brought to Hollywood in 1938 to make a much-publicised debut in Irving Cummings' *Girls' Dormitory* for 20th Century-Fox. Her career as an American film star had not been as successful as she had hoped, and after completing her part in the Dieterle film at RKO, Miss Simon returned to France. Making inquiries around the studio, Lewton discovered that Miss Simon's services might be obtained rather inexpensively; and after reading a rough draft of the screenplay, she cabled back her acceptance. With the key role cast, Lewton sent Bodeen home to work up the finer points of the story-line, instructing him not to return until he had a completed story—a long short story, as if he were writing for magazine publication rather than for the screen. After a time, Bodeen returned with the completed story, and the entire unit—Tourneur, Robson, Jessie Ponitz and Bodeen—went to work on it.

During these script sessions, a number of story-points were established which would become hallmarks of Lewton's productions. Each of the central characters was to have an occupation and was to be shown at work during the course of the movie. This was not merely an attempt to break away from the Hollywood convention of presenting characters with elaborate but unspecified means, nor yet just an attempt to add the required plausibility to a supernatural story; it was part of Lewton's respect for the characters in his films as human beings. The humans in horror movies are traditionally puppets, glorified reactors. The heroine screams, the hero tries to save her, the scientist mumbles discount metaphysics about Man daring to enter God's realm, and the Negro, pop-eyed and stuttering with fright, runs through a closed doorway, leaving behind his silhouette. In the Universal-type chillers, only the monsters were permitted recognisably human emotions—e.g., the lovely scene between the monster and the little girl in James Whale's *Frankenstein.*

Though planned as supernatural thrillers, and as such not primarily involved with the intricacies of human relationships, Lewton's films always managed to suggest a sense of an everyday life existing around and beyond the particulars of the story being told. Homes and apartments looked as if somebody had been living in them before the movie started; characters wore only the styles and qualities of clothing that their counterparts would in real life. (Verna De Mots, Lewton's secretary after Jessie Ponitz, recalls discussing where in Los Angeles a particular female character would buy her clothes, and then going off to that store to purchase the wardrobe.) It was, partly, this uncommon respect for the look and texture of daily life that led James Agee to write of Lewton: 'I think that few people in Hollywood show in their work that they know or care half as much about human beings as he does.' In ***Cat People***, Irena Dubrovna was shown doing fashion sketches (Miss Simon had a knack for sketching which Lewton was quick to employ), and her husband Oliver was a draughtsman for a ship-designing firm, in whose offices several of the key sequences were staged.

From the ***Cat People*** story conferences there emerged something of a formula which would recur in Lewton's subsequent pictures. He described this to an interviewer from the *Los Angeles Times:* 'Our formula is simple. A love story, three scenes of suggested horror and one of actual violence. Fadeout. It's all over in less than 70 minutes.' The calm, everyday sequences were to alternate with suspense sequences of ascending terror, resulting in a climax which would bring the two moods of the story together. 'We tossed away the horror formula right from the beginning. No grisly stuff for us. No masklike faces hardly human, with gnashing teeth and hair standing on end. No creaking physical manifestations. No horror piled on horror. You can't keep up horror that's long sustained. It becomes something to laugh at. But take a sweet love story, or a story of sexual antagonisms, about people like the rest of us, not freaks, and cut in your horror here and there by suggestion, and you've got something. Anyhow, we think you have. That's the way we try to do it.'

Lewton had provided Bodeen with several of the key shock sequences—Irena's rival being stalked by some unseen beast as she crosses a Central Park traverse at night, and the sudden appearance of a huge cat while Oliver and his friend are working late on a special project. To these, Bodeen added the final suspense sequence—one of the most terrifying in screen history—in which Irena's rival for Oliver's affections is menaced by a beast while swimming at night in a darkened, deserted swimming-pool. Bodeen got the idea from Tourneur's experience of having nearly drowned while swimming alone at night. In all of these sequences the horror is implied and never explicitly shown. Lewton felt that the absence of *specific* menace permitted each member of the audience to project his own innermost fear, to make connections with the fears of his own life. Eschewing the studio-made monsters characteristic of the Universal movies, Lewton's films dealt with realistic horror situations based upon some universal fear or superstition—fear of the dark, the unknown, madness, death.

Lewton particularly enjoyed devising moments in his films which would cause audiences to gasp with terror. His name for these moments of sudden shock was 'busses.' The term derives from the Central Park sequence of ***Cat People***. Jane Randolph, crossing the park late at night, hears footsteps following her. She stops under a street lamp and looks back into the darkness. The noises stop; she sees nothing. As soon as she walks beyond the circumference of lamplight, the footsteps begin again, and she hurries to the next lamp-post. At the moment when audience tension is at its height, a bus coasts into frame, simultaneously applying its pneumatic brakes in order to let off passengers. The unexpected appearance of the bus, sight and sound interrupting an already tense scene, invariably lifted theatre audiences several inches out of their seats. Lewton explained how he came up with 'busses' in an interview for *Liberty* magazine. 'To find ever new "busses" or horror spots, is a horror expert's most difficult problem. Horror spots must be well planned and there should be no more than four or five in a picture. Most of them are caused by the fundamental fears: sudden sound, wild animals, darkness. The horror addicts will populate the darkness with more horrors than all the horror writers in Hollywood could think of.' He amplified the point in a *Los Angeles Times* interview: 'I'll tell you a secret: if you make the screen dark enough, the mind's eye will read anything into it you want! We're great ones for dark patches. Remember the long walk alone at night in ***Cat People***? Most people will swear they saw a leopard move in the hedge above her—but they didn't! Optical illusion; dark patch.'

Lewton himself used an atmosphere of darkness to test the effectiveness of a screenplay on his staff. He would begin telling the story, and as the action grew more frightening, would snap off the lights around his office and continue the story in darkness. Charles Schnee used this and other Lewton working techniques in his screenplay for Minnelli's *The Bad and the Beautiful*; in particular, in an episode in which Kirk Douglas, a film producer, comes up with darkness as the solution to a sleazy low-budget movie he's making about people turning into cats. However, the ruthless, egocentric character Douglas portrays had nothing at all to do with Lewton, as some may have supposed. Schnee had combined dozens of snippets of Hollywood gossip and lore in the creation of his enjoyably over-ripe melodrama about Hollywood insiders.

With the major problems of the screenplay ironed out and the leading actress signed, there were still a number of matters to take care of. Irena's husband and her rival were still to be cast. Lewton had noticed a young actor bicycling to the RKO lot every morning. He discovered that the actor was Kent Smith, a Broadway performer who had been under contract to RKO for nine months without having appeared in a picture. Although Smith would be expensive—his nine-month salary would be charged against the ***Cat People*** budget—Lewton felt that his air of solidity, even stolidity at times, would make the draughtsman a plausible character who would aid in suspending audience disbelief in the farther reaches of the screenplay. Another contract player, dark, attractive Jane Randolph, was selected to play Smith's co-worker who consoles him when his wife begins acting up. Tom Conway, Russian-born like Lewton and George Sanders' brother, was cast as the psychiatrist, Dr Judd. Lewton always referred to Conway, who had been starring in RKO's 'Falcon' series, as 'the nice George Sanders'. Elizabeth Russell was cast for her unforgettable bit as a cat-woman who 'recognises' Irena in a cafe, and Alan Napier, a close friend of Lewton's, was assigned a small character role.

As production time for ***Cat People*** drew closer, Lewton gathered, or was assigned, the rest of his company. The director of photography was to be Nicholas Musuraca, a specialist in shadowy, low-keyed shooting (which, in addition to heightening suspense, also served the purpose of obscuring the economic limitations of the film) who was to work on many of Lewton's other RKO pictures. The producer and his team scoured the lot for existing sets which they could use, since the allotment in the budget came to little more than $10,000—hardly enough to do more than re-dress standing sets. The Central Park setting, complete with zoo, had been used in a number of RKO films which called for Manhattan locales, notably several of the Astaire-Rogers films and a Ginger Rogers comedy. The magnificent staircase built by Orson Welles for the Amberson house was used in the brownstone where Irena had her apartment. These sets were dressed with Lewton's meticulous attention to detail and period consistency. As Bodeen points out, feline references were sprinkled throughout the sets: 'the statue of Bubastis in the museum sequence; the tiger lilies in the florist shop window; the cat's claws on the base of the bathtub when Simone tries to cleanse herself of guilt after murdering the lambs; the cats in the Goya reproduction hanging over her mantle when she tells the hero of her past.' Once, while the sets were being prepared, Tourneur did a sketch of a very small, innocent-looking kitten. Lewton loved the sketch and had it set in the middle of an outsized mat with an inscription from the ***Cat People*** screenplay: 'A cat is a frightening thing.'

At last, on 28 July 1942, shooting began on Val Lewton's first production (officially known as RKO Production 386) under Tourneur's direction. Almost immediately there was the threat of catastrophe. On the morning of the fourth day of shooting, Lew Ostrow, head of the B-unit, called Lewton into his office. Ostrow had just come from a screening of the first three days' rushes and had not liked what he had seen. He informed Lewton that he had decided to replace Tourneur with one of the studio contract directors. Lewton put in a panicky call to Koerner's office to see if he, Ostrow's superior, could prevent Tourneur's dismissal, only to be informed that Koerner was in New York and would not be returning until the next morning. Lewton somehow managed to talk Ostrow into keeping the director until Koerner could be consulted. The next day, Koerner looked at the rushes and called Ostrow to tell him that Tourneur was doing fine and was to be left alone. After that, there was little trouble. Shooting went smoothly and almost without incident, if only because the schedule was so short; so much had to be done in so little time that there was no room for temperament. Again departing from Hollywood custom, Lewton retained DeWitt Bodeen as dialogue director, feeling that whenever possible the writer should be on set when his screenplay went into production.

Only on one other occasion did the front office interfere. As Lewton conceived it, no cat was to be shown until the last few frames of the film. The presence of the beast was only to be suggested by sound and shadow, so that audiences could never be sure whether Irena's fears were imaginary or had some terrifying basis in fact. Ostrow, however, decided that a black leopard had to appear in the draughting-room sequence, and after seeing the rushes told Tourneur to reshoot the scene with a cat while the set was still standing. Technically, Tourneur complied; a drugged leopard was brought on to the set and the sequence was redone. However, Tourneur managed to shoot the scene so ambiguously (the only light in the room emanating from the top surfaces of the designing tables) that viewers could still not be sure what they were seeing. Almost all obvious traces of the leopard were obliterated by Robson in the cutting-room, so the front office was, for the first of what would be many times, outsmarted. In the swimming-pool sequence, Tourneur, again instructed that the cat's presence had to be clearly indicated, came up with another solution. The menacing shadows on the walls around the indoor pool, suggestive forms reinforced by growling noises on the soundtrack, were made by the director's fist moving in front of a diffused spotlight.

Shooting ended on ***Cat People*** on 21 August 1942. The film had been completed ahead of schedule at a total cost of $134,000. While the post-production work of editing and scoring continued, the Lewton unit scarcely had time to worry about the success of its first effort. The next project, ***I Walked With a Zombie***, was due to begin production in less than two months, and the third, ***Leopard Man***, two months after that. There were story conferences, casting sessions, and set and costume designs to approve. Working hard at their pre-established schedule, Lewton and his associates had little reason to suspect, even dream, that ***Cat People***, approaching the time of its first previews, would prove to be one of the least expected, most astonishing popular successes in American film-making.

MARK ROBSON: *His was a divided character. On one hand, he was an insecure man who tended to chop himself down, and yet he was a proud man too. He knew he was good and still he had a habit of pleading poverty. The stories of his pictures are not half so important as the experiments and innovative effects he tried and his ideas about shock and beauty in motion pictures. He loved beauty but disliked camera preciousness. He was a man of great likes and dislikes and a man of even greater loyalty to his people; in his eyes, they could do no wrong.*

In the course of his life, he transformed himself into an Old Greenwich gentleman—that's what he really wanted to be. He tried to live up to all of the great American myths—the sailor, the athlete, the hunter. My image of him was one of a very tolerant human being who was the most human Protestant ever devised by man. His sympathy for the underdog was boundless and he very often created jobs in his films for actors and writers who had fallen upon hard times.

In a way, I think he was a man who needed an enemy. He was often unsure of himself and tended to be self-destructive. In difficult situations, he had a nervous habit of stammering. He wasted time and seldom could accomplish anything without the pressure of a deadline on his head. His nervousness and his need to push himself too hard contributed to the decline of his health.

Everyone in the Lewton unit attended the first preview of ***Cat People***, held at the Hillstreet Theatre, a downtown Los Angeles movie house frequented by a distinctly roughneck clientele. Lewton was extremely apprehensive. Several weeks before, he and Tourneur had run the completed film for their studio bosses, and after the screening nobody would speak to them. Only Lew Ostrow stayed behind, to criticise the film for its lack of horrific content. For a man who was terrified of being without a job, this was an extremely important evening. DeWitt Bodeen recalls what happened at that first public screening:

> The preview was preceded by a Disney cartoon about a little pussy-cat and Val's spirits sank lower and lower as the audience began to catcall and make loud mewing sounds. 'Oh God!' he kept murmuring, as he wiped the perspiration from his forehead. The picture's title was greeted with whoops of derision and louder meows, but when the credits were over and the film began to unreel, the audience quieted, and, as the story progressed, reacted as we had hoped an audience might. There were gasps and some screaming as the shock sequences grew. The audience accepted and believed our story, and was enchanted.

The trade paper reviews, appearing appropriately enough on Friday, 13 November 1942, were all mildly favourable; there was reason to suppose that ***Cat People*** would do all right, but no hint of the tremendous popular response it would receive. The New York newspaper reviews were not particularly encouraging when ***Cat People*** opened at the Rialto Theatre, a famous chiller showcase, on 7 December, backed up by a particularly lurid advertising campaign. Reviewers for the *Times, Herald Tribune, Sunday News* and *World-Telegram* all went thumbs down; the *Sun, Sunday Mirror, Journal-*

American and *PM* were more positive, if not really enthusiastic. The Los Angeles reviews were somewhat better when the film opened on 14 January at the Hawaii Theatre on Hollywood Boulevard, supported by a Warner Brothers' dud called *The Gorilla Man.* But a number of reviewers from various women's clubs had very definite feelings about ***Cat People***. 'Fantastic and unhealthy,' said the University Women; 'Weird and unbelievable,' said the Business and Professional Women; 'Morbid and unconstructive,' chimed in the Parent-Teachers Association; and Zeta Phi Eta, a speech arts honorary fraternity, condemned the film as 'a horrible idea, unethically treated.' Such reviews were nearly success enough for Lewton, who delighted in them.

In spite of the mixed reviews, word-of-mouth was very good and audiences flocked to see ***Cat People*** wherever it played. The film that theatre bookers had expected would run no longer than a few days was held over week after week. It played so long at the Rialto that a number of newspaper reviewers went back for a second, more favourable look. In Hollywood, ***Cat People*** played a record thirteen-week engagement at the Hawaii, where *Citizen Kane*'s first run lasted only twelve weeks. By the time the film's general release was completed, it had earned enough money to save RKO which, in deeper financial trouble than ever before, had been forced to pinkslip many of its employees. Although the studio has now been out of existence for nearly seventeen years, the owners of its records, RKO General Tire, will not release any of the financial files, making it impossible to quote an exact figure on how much ***Cat People*** grossed. Bodeen says $4,000,000; almost every published estimate exceeds $2,000,000.

As soon as it appeared that ***Cat People*** was going to be a sleeper, Lewton and his staff were suddenly the talk of the studio. Bodeen's old contract was replaced by a long-term pact at a higher salary. Tourneur was given an RKO director's contract with provision for his promotion to A pictures as soon as he had completed three films for Lewton, plus a bonus of $5,000. There was no salary boost for Lewton, but doors began to open to him that had been closed before. Of all the plaudits, none pleased Lewton more than a telegram from his old boss, David Selznick, which read: 'I feel that ***Cat People*** definitely and at one stroke establishes you as a producer of great competence and I know no man in recent years who has made so much out of so little as a first picture.'

After this success, the Lewtons decided that the time had finally come to put down roots in Los Angeles and buy a house. In 1943, real estate prices, particularly along the ocean where they wanted to live, were incredibly low. Many coastal home-owners quite seriously believed that they would awaken one morning to find the Japanese entrenched in their front yards. Actor Jack Holt, who had appeared in ***Cat People***, was one of those who were frightened of a Japanese invasion and was extremely eager to sell his ranch-style house on Corsica Drive between Brentwood and Pacific Palisades. Holt had built the house himself, and it was something of a showplace with its pine-panelled living-room, suite of maids' rooms, four-car garage, and acres of surrounding land rich with fruit trees and one hundred rose bushes. The actor was so anxious to unload the house that he threw in most of the furnishings—china, crystal, linens, even blackout curtains—all for the selling price of $15,000. Lewton, whose salary at RKO was quite modest, was able to raise $5,000 as a down payment and moved in immediately. Friends who used to visit remember the house, where the producer lived until the time of his death, as a particularly warm and charming place, where the conversation was always lively and amusing.

The Lewtons never really lived a Hollywood social life; they seldom went out and almost never to the bigger parties or nightclubs. At home, they preferred small dinner parties and sailing excursions to larger gatherings, and yet the house was always filled with friends. The Tourneurs were frequent guests, and Ring Lardner, and Fred Zinnemann, and economist Josef Mischel, who would shortly become one of Lewton's writers, and Mark Robson, who sometimes brought over a friend from the RKO editing department, Robert Wise. Alan Napier, the British character actor, who appeared in ***Cat People*** and three subsequent Lewton pictures, was a special friend. He and his wife Gypsy were often invited on sailing parties on the *Nina.*

However, long before the ***Cat People*** success was known, Lewton and his cohorts had completed two more films and several new members had been added to the unit. Jessie Ponitz's husband, whom Lewton liked and had presented with one of the Boy Scout pocketknives he always carried, was drafted and in Officer's Training at Fort Benning, Georgia, and Jessie resigned to be with him. Her successor was Verna De Mots, a more subdued but even more devoted young woman, who served as Lewton's secretary almost until the time of his death. Verna had come from Iowa to attend U.C.L.A. until the Depression put an end to her studies. She had worked in the short subject department at RKO for nine years, and immediately before her assignment to the Lewton unit, had been assisting a contract writer at the studio. Like Jessie, Verna felt that Lewton was not really appreciated or respected by his superiors:

> His film, ***Cat People***, saved RKO when it was practically bankrupt, but they didn't show much appreciation. Charles Koerner kept on dreaming up those outrageous titles to stick him with. They didn't understand this man at all or what it was he was trying to do. But his movies cost practically nothing to make, so they let him go ahead, although they really wanted more conventional horror pictures. I remember only once did he protest one of Koerner's decisions by insisting that his ***Cat People*** had been a big success. Koerner replied, 'The only people who saw that film were Negroes and defense workers.' That's just one example of the sort of thing he was up against. One night, when Mr Lewton and I were working on the ***Youth***

> ***Runs Wild*** script, he got a phone call from Sid Rogell, who replaced Lew Ostrow as head of the B-unit. Rogell had a brilliant idea which he said couldn't wait until morning. Why not, he suggested, give the judge in the story a butler? It would give the picture more class. After that call, Mr Lewton couldn't write another word. That was the kind of mentality he was forced to deal with.

Another new member of the unit was Ardel Wray, a young woman who had been involved in a Young Writers' Project at RKO and whose work had attracted Lewton's attention. Miss Wray started her association with Lewton on what is perhaps his most finished, most haunting film, ***I Walked With a Zombie***. Even before shooting commenced on ***Cat People***, Koerner told Lewton that his second project would be based on an article called 'I Walked With a Zombie' by columnist Inez Wallace, which had appeared in the *American Weekly* magazine. Mark Robson remembers that Lewton's face was white and his manner impossibly gloomy when he returned from that meeting with Koerner. He spent the rest of the day in a grumpy, irritable mood. His associates dreaded his arrival the next morning, but Lewton came in unusually early and in an inexplicably gay mood. He called his staff together and announced that in the guise of a zombie chiller, he would make a West Indian version of *Jane Eyre.* He would use the Brontë story-line: a young girl leaves home to work for a strange, satanic man whose wife suffers from a bizarre, incurable mental illness. Curt Siodmak, brother of the director Robert Siodmak and a novelist whose books include *Donovan's Brain,* was assigned to work on the screenplay with Miss Wray. Again Jacques Tourneur would direct and Mark Robson edit.

Miss Wray remembers the preparation of ***I Walked With a Zombie:***

> We were all plunged into research on Haitian voodoo, every book on the subject Val could find. He was an addictive researcher, drawing out of it the overall feel, mood and quality he wanted, as well as details for actual production. He got hold of a real calypso singer, Sir Lancelot he was called—a charming, literate, articulate man. He, in turn, found some genuine voodoo musicians. I remember they had a 'papa drum' and a 'mama drum,' that the crew on the set were fascinated by them, and by one particular scene in which a doll 'walks' in a voodoo ritual. They managed a concealed track for the doll, and it was effective. I particularly remember that doll because Val sent me out to find and buy one 'cheap.' Everything had to be cheap because we really were on a shoestring. That was another thing about Val—a low budget was a challenge to him, a spur to inventiveness, and everyone around him caught the fever. Anyway, I got a rather bland-faced doll at a department store, cheap, and by the time she had been dressed in a soft grey robe, and her hair had been combed out to the appropriate 'lost girl' look, she, too, was somehow transformed.
>
> I don't think I can explain the particular kind of togetherness (a concept not dear to me) that Val managed then. You can't call it teamwork, because that implies a kind of hearty I'll-be-quiet-while-you-talk-and-then-you'll-be-quiet-while-I-talk situation—all wrong. It wasn't cosy. I can't speak for the others, but certainly I went home to my own life every night, though sometimes pretty late. (We'd work late, go to dinner at the Melrose Grotto, back to the studio, work some more, then walk out enjoying and talking about the eerie, half-sinister quality of an empty lot at night.) And it wasn't a meeting of the minds, in the sense that everyone agreed about everything. There were some pretty rugged disagreements. But it was togetherness, all right—really ideally, in a work sense . . . more like theatre. It was a small, close unit, comparable to today's independent. There wasn't too much Upstairs interference, except on the everlasting budget problem. And, if I'm not remembering falsely, some Upstairs fears that sock-it-to-them was being sacrificed for 'arty stuff.'

Shooting on ***I Walked With a Zombie*** started on 26 October 1942 with a somewhat more impressive cast than for ***Cat People***. Frances Dee, that darkly beautiful and unusually intelligent actress who never quite managed to fit into any of the standard Hollywood slots, was to play Betsy, the young Canadian nurse who leaves her home to attend the sick wife of a plantation owner on San Sebastian in the West Indies. Tom Conway was the Rochester-like Holland. James Ellison, filling out his last obligation as an RKO contract player, was top-billed as Conway's brother, and Edith Barrett was cast as the mother. Sir Lancelot made a strong impression, singing a calypso ballad of his own devising which was woven into the story, and Christine Gordon, as Holland's afflicted wife, was especially effective in her non-speaking role. (The wife was called Jessica, Lewton's farewell tribute to the departing Mrs Ponitz.) Darby Jones made an equally silent and iconographically effective contribution as a zombie. The art direction by Albert D'Agostino and Walter Keller magically evoked the West Indies, and Roy Hunt's photography was superb. Shooting ended on 19 November and the trade reviews, appearing in early March, were enthusiastic.

In late April, when ***I Walked With a Zombie*** had its first public screenings, the newspaper reviewers were unanimous in their praise. Perhaps Lewton's masterpiece, it is one of those exceedingly rare movies which manage to summarise everything that is artistically valid about a Hollywood genre and then go on to transcend the genre itself. ***I Walked With a Zombie*** does for horror movies what Sam Peckinpah's *Ride the High Country* does for the Western, and the Gene Kelly-Stanley Donen *Singin' in the Rain* for the musical. Tourneur prefers it above all the films he has made, and Ruth Lewton considers it her favourite among her husband's productions.

However, there was still the problem of the title. As Mrs Lewton says: 'I would never go to see a movie called ***I Walked With a Zombie*** unless somebody dragged me there.' It is perhaps characteristic of Lewton's career that this film, one of the rare pieces of pure visual poetry ever to come out of Hollywood, was seen by hardly anybody but the bloodthirsty chiller fans who frequented theatres like the Rialto in New York. Later, through the efforts of critics like James Agee and Manny Farber, readers of magazines like *The Nation* and *The New Republic* were alerted to the very special quality of Lewton's productions.

Lewton's third assignment was a shade more prestigious—a novel by suspense writer Cornell Woolrich called *Black Alibi.* Koerner, never one to overlook a past success, retitled the property ***The Leopard Man.*** Ardel Wray was given sole responsibility for the screenplay this time, and Lewton asked her to take on some of the pre-production work as well. '***Leopard Man*** had a New Mexico background. There was no hope of location shooting or even a second unit for backgrounds, so Val handed over to me his very good camera and sent me to Santa Fe to take pictures of whatever exteriors I thought might be useful to use, set-wise. This, although he knew that I had never taken any pictures more elaborate than Brownie camera snapshots and had no other qualifications either for the job. I don't know why he trusted me with this—faith and desperation, I guess. I was in mortal terror of the camera. First day there I took pictures frantically, of anything and everything, and took them to a shop for development, then waited a couple of days, as I recall, to see if I had gotten anything at all, let alone something useful. Miraculously, probably because it was a nearly foolproof camera, it was all right. From the pictures I took there, we worked out the sets. Another instance of Val's genius for improvisation.'

Shooting on ***The Leopard Man*** began on 9 February 1943. Once again Tourneur directed and Robson edited. As with the ***I Walked With a Zombie*** casting, the male lead, Dennis O'Keefe, was fulfilling the last part of an RKO contract; the leading lady, Margo, was an intelligent, brunette actress who had never quite managed to find her niche in Hollywood pictures. The supporting cast included Jean Brooks and Isabel Jewell, whom Lewton was to use again.

The Leopard Man was a departure from the Lewton formula in several important respects. It was not a supernatural story: though the Woolrich novel has its unearthly overtones, these turn out to be red herrings—inventions of a deranged killer designed to mask his activities. It was Lewton's first try at a straightforward murder story, and for the first time he included several sequences of explicit bloodshed. In an episode which haunts the memory, a little Mexican girl returning from the store where her mother has sent her to buy food is clawed to death while trying to get someone to open the door. Although the violence is mainly suggested—after the child's shuddery walk home, the attack itself is shot from *inside* the house so that we can only hear what is happening—the fact of the child's death is revealed by a rivulet of blood trickling under the door. As several of the more perceptive New York reviewers observed, the sequence is so strong that it turns out to be too much for the better interests of the film, leaving the remainder of the story as anti-climax. There were two other fairly explicit homicides as well, again a departure from the Lewton formula of suggest, don't show. Not too long after the film's release, Lewton admitted to an interviewer from *Coronet* magazine that ***The Leopard Man*** had been a miscalculation. 'We knew we were right from the start. It took only one more picture to convince us of that. Now we're right back in the groove.' Like the other two films, ***The Leopard Man*** had a shooting schedule of less than a month, cost no more than $150,000 to produce, and proved an extremely lucrative venture for RKO.

The Leopard Man was completed in early March; the next film, ***The Seventh Victim***, was not scheduled to go into production until May. Lewton's experiment had been successful. In spite of the poverty row budgets and the awful titles, he had managed to make the kind of film he believed in and had proved that the public would recognise and respond to quality in low-budget movies. The next group of films would involve new talent and fresher, more ambitious themes. In less than a year, Lewton had scored the kind of success that becomes an instant part of Hollywood mythology. He entered his second year as a producer with everything in his favour, a position he would never quite manage to achieve again.

JACQUES TOURNEUR: *We complemented one another, never argued. We sailed together often but nothing extraordinary ever happened; we just relaxed and made a point of never discussing films. Usually he was easy-going and between pictures tended to put on weight. He never got drunk or arrested or ran around or did anything crazy. We worked so well together. At the time it appeared beneficial for both of us to split up but now I realise that it was a mistake.*

RKO broke up the Lewton-Tourneur partnership after the completion of ***The Leopard Man***, on the dubious premise that since the producer and director had worked so well together, they would work twice as well separated. As promised, Tourneur was promoted to A pictures, the first being *Days of Glory,* a war story set in Russia which featured Gregory Peck in his first film role. Today, regretting the separation, Tourneur says: 'We had a perfect collaboration—Val was the dreamer, the idealist, and I was the materialist, the realist. We should have gone right on doing bigger, more ambitious pictures, and not just horror movies.'

In fact, Lewton had been planning his escape from the restrictive horror genre for some time. The titles he was assigned prevented his films from being taken seriously. As he once wrote to his sister, 'You shouldn't get mad at the New York reviewers. Actually, it's very difficult for a reviewer to give something called ***I Walked With a Zombie*** a good review.' Lewton often managed to get past the opposition of his superiors by writing dummy screenplays which would secure him the necessary actors and properties without really letting the front office know what the film would be about. He attempted a trick of this kind, unsuccessfully, as his breakaway from horror movies:

> One trick under my belt is that I'm going to sneak over a comedy on them. They've given me a silly title, *The Amorous Ghost*, and I plan to make a comedy of it, a comedy in which Casanova, because he never made any woman unhappy, is allowed to return to earth for a twelve-hour visit. In this time he goes to a masquerade, meets a lovely but very forthright modern girl and is so desirous of her that much to his and her amazement when he is snatched back to the other world, he finds that he has brought her with him. His world is an eighteenth-century conception of heaven, a little Fragonard masterpiece, as charming and as unreal as it can be. From then on, the story takes several directions; the comedy theme, which is a sort of Yankee in King Arthur's Court affair, with a young modern girl shooing away the eighteenth-century wolves, and the dramatic story, which is concerned with the modus operandi of the girl's return to this world, a sort of Orpheus and Eurydice theme. I know this sounds mad, but I've been rehashing the plot so much today with the writer, a German refugee and formerly director of the Dresden State Theatre, Leo Mittler, that I'm weary of it. I've given you enough of the plot to give you the central idea. Tom Conway, who played Holland in ***Zombie***, will play Casanova, and I'm looking for a girl. (In a letter to his mother and sister, 11 May 1943.)

With Tourneur gone, Lewton was forced to find a director for the next picture on his schedule, a suspense original called ***The Seventh Victim*** to be scripted by DeWitt Bodeen. He chose Mark Robson, who had been working with him since he arrived at RKO and had been plumping for advancement from the cutting-room to directing. Robson had obtained his first studio job while still an undergraduate at U.C.L.A.; he continued in films while studying law in the evenings, working himself up through the system from set director to assistant cutter to cutter. He and Lewton had something more than a working friendship; Robson was a constant guest at the Lewton home, and at one time, as Nina Druckman recalls, was so under her father's spell that he talked and gestured exactly like him. Lewton treated Robson with the tenderness reserved for a son and felt pleased to be able to help him advance his career. As he observed in a note to his mother, 'I gave the direction of ***Seventh Victim*** to the young cutter who did the editorial work on the other pictures, Mark Robson, and he's doing a beautiful job—almost as well as Jacques. This makes me very happy as I'm extremely fond of him.'

Bodeen's ***The Seventh Victim***, again written in short story rather than screenplay form, dealt with an orphaned girl in Los Angeles who is marked as the seventh victim of a murderer and must discover his identity to save herself. While Bodeen was in New York enjoying a studio-paid bonus vacation and researching Washington Irving and Tarrytown legends for a future film, Lewton decided to scrap the Bodeen story and replace it with one of his own devising. The new ***Seventh Victim*** was to be about devil worship in Manhattan. Charles O'Neal was brought in to work up the Lewton story-line about an orphaned schoolgirl who goes to New York in search of her older sister, only to discover that the sister is a member and intended victim of a cult of Greenwich Village devil-worshippers. While O'Neal was working, Lewton was called to attend a meeting of studio executives. At this gathering, he was praised for the success of his first three productions and told that a promotion would be forthcoming. After his current slate of productions was completed, Lewton was to be advanced to A-producer status. He was naturally delighted by the news and immediately set about planning for his first big-budget film. Several weeks later, Lewton announced some of the properties he was considering and stated that Mark Robson would be the director of his first A feature.

The studio bosses were outraged at the idea of entrusting a major production to an untried director and presented Lewton with an ultimatum—either no Robson or no A-producership. Ever loyal to his co-workers, Lewton thereupon refused the promotion and went ahead with his plans to turn ***The Seventh Victim*** over to Robson. He realised that his only chance for artistic control over his productions depended upon his remaining with the B-unit where the films were so inexpensive that the front office seldom felt the need to meddle. Later in his career, Lewton was to know the frustration of trying to work without sufficient decision-making authority.

As successor to Tourneur, Robson recognised that he had his work cut out for him. '***I Walked With a Zombie*** was the best of Val's films, an absolutely beautiful movie. Jacques is a rare talent with a magnificent eye. It was his misfortune to come up in the period when the virtuosity of the actor had come to predominate and the public started to lose interest in the visual elements of films. His is an extraordinary talent and ***Zombie*** is one of the most exquisite films ever made. Jacques was promoted to *Days of Glory* and all at once he was a big-time director. Val could no longer afford him and, since I had been in on all of the conferences from the very beginning, he turned to me.'

The Seventh Victim introduced another newcomer: a twenty-year-old actress named Janet Cole, who had been discovered by Selznick agent Leon Lance at the Pasadena Playhouse, was selected to play the orphaned heroine. Miss Cole, who changed her name to Kim Hunter just before shooting began, was supported in the film by a number of Lewton veterans chosen from what was rapidly becoming a private stock company. Tom Conway was starred again, along with Jean Brooks, Isabel Jewell and Ben Bard, from the ***Leopard Man*** cast. Elizabeth Russell, the elegantly feline menace from ***Cat People***, turned in a memorable cameo as a consumptive beauty preparing to go out on the town for a final fling. Chef Milani, of bottled salad-dressings fame, played an Italian chef. Once again Nicholas Musuraca was director of photography and Roy Webb supplied the musical score.

The Seventh Victim rivals ***I Walked With a Zombie*** as Lewton's masterpiece. The bizarre tale is told with tiny, impressionistic strokes which combine to form a haunting vision of isolation and despair, a superb illustration of the Donne epigraph, 'I run to Death, and Death meets me as fast, and all my Pleasures are like Yesterdays.' A comparison with Roman Polanski's recent and over-praised *Rosemary's Baby,* a movie which treats the same subject, sets the many excellences of Lewton's film into bold relief. The producer had provided his fledgling director with an extensively annotated screenplay, filled with carefully detailed atmospheric touches recalled from his own bachelor days on Perry Street. (The sequence in which two men prop up a dead man in a subway car, attempting to pass him off as a drunk, stems from a similar incident which Lewton once observed in Greenwich Village.)

Perhaps because it was the first Lewton film with a reasonably intelligent title, ***The Seventh Victim*** did not do quite so well at the box-office as his previous pictures. RKO hardly helped matters with its suggestions as to how this poetic little film might best be promoted. Example: 'On a small table in your lobby, display a statue, a bust and head of a woman. Wherever the skin shows on the statue, mould small spots out of chewing gum or candle grease to resemble goose pimples. Place a card nearby reading "Even this marble developed goose pimples after seeing ***The Seventh Victim***".'

Lewton promptly assigned Robson a second film, ***The Ghost Ship***, which was scheduled for production in early August 1943. This new film was predicated upon an unusual set of circumstances and demands. RKO had built a huge ship set for a film directed by Lew Landers, and, hoping to squeeze a bit more out of its investment, instructed Lewton to come up with a story which would utilise the impressively detailed set. At the same time, he was ordered to make sure the leading role would be suitable for Richard Dix, who had one remaining contractual obligation to the studio. Lewton worked up the story and assigned it to his old mentor and friend Donald Henderson Clarke, who had moved to Hollywood and was trying to establish himself as a screenwriter. ***The Ghost Ship*** co-starred Russell Wade and Edith Barrett, with such Lewton alumni as Ben Bard and Sir Lancelot in supporting roles.

It opened to indifferent reviews, and had just managed to play out the first engagements when serious legal problems developed. Some months before, two men had dropped off an unsolicited story and play at Lewton's office, and Verna De Mots, following usual studio procedure, returned the manuscripts to the writers. Shortly after the ***Ghost Ship*** première, the men brought a law suit claiming that Lewton had appropriated crucial elements of their work. Although Lewton's story had nothing in common with the submitted material (except for those essentials which all stories in that genre share), the claimants were able to prove that Lewton could have had access to their work. Lewton described the case in a letter to his mother and sister, dated 26 August 1945:

> A plagiarism case on ***The Ghost Ship*** is to be tried tomorrow and although the plaintiffs are obviously wrong and have no merit in their case, it is the kind of racketeering which is very hard to guard against and we all have to be very much on our toes in the court room or the case may go against us despite the most obvious sort of innocence. The studio wanted to settle out of court, as the plaintiffs are suing for fifty thousand dollars but were willing to settle for seven hundred. I refused, as I have a deep-seated moral feeling that such persons should not be allowed to get away with their little practices, even if it is much more convenient to let them get away with it. It will cost the studio and myself three or four times as much to defend as to settle, but I feel it is a small price to pay for a really clear name.

Ironically, Lewton did not clear his name in the suit. He and RKO lost the court case and were forced to pay damages of $25,000 plus court costs. Lewton was shocked at being convicted of an act which he did not commit. As part of the judgment, ***The Ghost Ship*** was withdrawn from theatrical exhibition, and has since been seen only in infrequent and presumably illegal television airings.

Shooting on ***The Ghost Ship*** had ended on 28 August 1943. Two days earlier, shooting commenced on one of the producer's greatest popular and critical successes, ***The Curse of the Cat People***. Once again Charles Koerner had come up with a tawdry title designed to cash in on the ***Cat People*** success, and once again Lewton was powerless to do anything about it. But that fact did not prevent him from using the title as a cover for his attempt to make a film quite beyond the scope of the thrillers he had previously produced. After weeks of fighting and resisting the idea of a ***Cat People*** sequel, Lewton finally sat down and wrote his own story, a fascinating study in child psychology, about a lonely little girl who invents an imaginary friend to supply her with the love and understanding that her parents are too limited and unperceptive to provide. DeWitt Bodeen developed Lewton's idea, adding elements from his Tarrytown research, and Lewton reassembled the key members of his ***Cat People*** cast to convince the studio that they were going to get another supernatural chiller. Simone Simon would reappear as Irena, the imaginary playmate, dead long before the story begins, whose photograph serves as the child's inspiration for what her invented friend looks like. Kent Smith was again Oliver Reed, Irena's former husband, now remarried to his sympathetic co-worker, Jane Randolph, and moved to Tarrytown suburbia. Of course, the relationship of these characters to their previous incarnations was rather tenuous at times, but the repeat casting and his acceptance of the title were sufficient to free Lewton to make this unusually sensitive and delicate film.

The subject material of ***The Curse of the Cat People*** provides some important insights into Lewton's curious, paradoxical nature. Much of his desire to make the film, and his skill at handling such an unusual and uncommercial theme, stems from his own insecure, repressive and highly romantic childhood at Who-Torok, geographically close to the film's Tarrytown setting. Ruth Lewton has described her husband as a man who, as a youngster, was forced to retreat from reality into an insubstantial world of his own creation and who never quite made it all the way back to reality. At least two sequences in the film are based upon events from his own life. Early in the film, nobody attends the child's birthday party because she has placed the invitations in the cleft of a tree, which her father had once told her was a magic mailbox. Lewton himself had once been instructed to mail invitations to his sister Lucy's birthday party and had made the same mistake, unable to separate fact from fantasy. Later, in the sequence where Irena teaches the child arithmetic, she uses the courtly, enchanting number-stories that Lewton had invented to educate his own children. One was a tall princess; two, a prince who kneels before her on one knee, and so forth. Most significant of all, this tale of a troubled child, so incisive that it has been frequently screened for students of child psychology, was created by a man who was almost totally incapable of recognising and handling the needs of his own sensitive, insecure little daughter.

Other Lewton regulars, including Elizabeth Russell and Sir Lancelot, were cast, along with Julia Dean, who was especially charming as a senile actress. Six-year-old Ann Carter turned in an astonishingly precise and decidedly unmoppety performance as the child, Amy. Nicholas Musuraca was director of photography, and Robert Wise was signed on to cut the film. Because Robson's schedule on ***The Ghost Ship*** overlapped with the start of ***The Curse of the Cat People***, Lewton had chosen a second new director, a young man with documentary film training named Gunther Von Fritsch.

Fritsch was taken off the picture about halfway through. RKO officially announced that he had been drafted, but Robert Wise recalls that those were not the actual circumstances of Fritsch's departure:

> Gunther wasn't drafted. ***The Curse of the Cat People*** was to be his first feature and I was his editor. A shooting schedule was set up for eighteen days but he fell so far behind that after the eighteen days were used up, he was still only halfway through the screenplay. Val tried and tried to get Gunther to pick up the tempo, but it was his first big job and he was just too nervous to move any faster. One Saturday morning, I got a call from Sid Rogell, who was then head of the B-unit. I had done some second unit work for Rogell and had been after him to let me direct. Rogell told me that I was to replace Gunther on Monday morning. Gunther and I had planned to do some extra night footage that very evening and I knew he had not yet been told of his dismissal. I couldn't bring myself to go to work with him under those conditions and I called Val to ask his advice. 'Look,' he said, 'if it's not you, it will be somebody else. You're not pushing Gunther out.' So I took over the picture on Monday morning and brought it in by early October. When I arrived on the set that first day, Val gave me a copy of Shaw's *The Art of Rehearsal* which I've kept with me ever since.

The Curse of the Cat People lacked all of the blood and guts that the studio had expected. Some retakes were ordered, like the insertion of a shot of two boys chasing a black cat up a tree, and a number of small but artistically crucial details were cut. The most damaging of these excisions was a shot of Amy looking at a picture book illustration of a Sleeping Beauty princess dressed in a medieval gown. When the imaginary friend appears, she is dressed in this same garment, so the omission of the preparatory sequence makes her garb seem inexplicable, even laughable. (Manny Farber commented upon the 'burleycue discordancy' of this 'amazing garment', and James Agee described Miss Simon's first appearance as 'in a dress and a lascivious lighting which make her facade look like a relief map from *What Every Young Husband Should Know*.')

Still, in spite of the meddling, ***The Curse of the Cat People*** managed to emerge from RKO without too much disfiguration and it proved to be one of Lewton's most highly acclaimed films. Agee named it, along with Lewton's subsequent ***Youth Runs Wild***, the best fiction film of 1944, Joseph Foster in *The New Masses* found it a charming picture and remarked that he could not 'for the life of me understand why RKO should have presented the film under such discouraging auspices'—i.e. the misleading title and showcasing in horror theatres like New York's Rialto. (Lewton had tried to persuade the studio to change the title to *Amy and Her Friend*, but to no avail.) John McManus of *PM* also deplored the awful titling of what he considered 'one of the nicest movies ever made.'

The Curse of the Cat People was the film which finally convinced even the most sceptical critics and moviegoers that Lewton was a film-maker to take seriously, even to treasure. It was his first production with 'serious' subject matter, and on the basis of its theme alone it merited a great deal of attention and applause. Probably no Hollywood film-maker ever managed to achieve anything quite so fine while working at so low a level on the economic scale. Still, ***The Curse of the Cat People*** is not aesthetically one of Lewton's very best productions; it is probably more worth doing than any of the others, but it is not done half so well as ***I Walked With a Zombie*** or ***The Seventh Victim***. Manny Farber, writing in *The New Republic*, provided a fair appraisal of the film's weaknesses and its special virtues: '***The Curse of the Cat People*** lacks sufficient life in the significance of its insights into reality, and the playing, which is on the stiff, precarious side of naturalism, doesn't compensate for this sterility with enough vitality to make it an artistic dream movie.

But it has so much more dignity than the other Hollywood films around that it seems at this moment inordinately wholesome.'

As usual RKO decked out the film with moronic promotional taglines like 'The Black Menace Creeps Again!' and 'Sensational Return of the Killer-Cat Woman.' One wonders whether anyone in the studio's publicity department had ever bothered to take a look at what they were promoting. Once again there were the bizarre suggestions for exhibitors. 'Stencil paw prints leading to your theatre.' 'Send out a small group of men and women wearing cat masks to walk through the streets with cards on their backs reading "Are cats people?" Schedule their routes so that they appear before the gates of defense factories when the various shifts are changing.'

But once again, Lewton's film was recognised through all of the chiller trappings as a work of sensitivity and grace, and this time not only by film critics. On 7 September 1944 the film was used by the Hollywood Writers Mobilization and the Los Angeles Council of Social Agencies as the highlight of a seminar devoted to the treatment of children in films. Lewton and Wise appeared and were praised not only for the soundness of the film's psychological content but also for the 'intelligent and unselfconscious' handling of the Negro servant. Such use of Negro characters was a distinguishing feature of Lewton's productions, from the black waitress in the ***Cat People*** cafe to the Negro man Friday in his last film, ***Apache Drums***. His films are free of both the racial caricature typical of Hollywood in the Thirties and Forties, and the patronising special pleading of more recent pictures like *The Defiant Ones* and *Guess Who's Coming to Dinner?*. Lewton was simply a film-maker who, above all else, respected the human dimensions of the materials he handled, and so it is hardly surprising that his are among the very few American films which treat the black man with individuality and dignity. Shortly after the Los Angeles seminar, Lewton was again invited to appear with his film, this time by Dr Fearing, head of the Child Psychology Clinic at U.C.L.A., who wanted his students to see the picture and discuss with Lewton some of the problems it raised. At one point, Dr Fearing praised Lewton's use of Amy's tight-lipped half-smile, observing that in his treatment of children with similar emotional problems, the same reticent smile appeared again and again. But Lewton, more the yarnspinner and B movie miracle worker, refused to take credit for this particular touch. Little Ann Carter, he explained, had lost one of her front teeth during shooting, and since there was not enough time or money to have the tooth replaced, she was instructed to act with her mouth shut for the rest of the filming.

JAMES AGEE: *The best fiction films of the year,* ***The Curse of the Cat People*** *and* ***Youth Runs Wild****, were made by Val Lewton and his associates. I esteem them so highly because for all of their unevenness their achievements are so consistently alive, limber, poetic, humane, so eager toward the possibilities of the screen, and so resolutely against the grain of all we have learned to expect from the big studios. But I am afraid there is no reason to believe that the makers of these films, under the best of circumstances, would be equipped to make the great, and probably very vulgar, and certainly very forceful revolutionary pictures that are so desperately needed. Indeed, I suspect that their rather gentle, pleasing, resourceful kind of talent is about the strongest sort we can hope to see working in Hollywood with any consistent, useful purity of purpose; and the pictures themselves indicate to what extent that is frustrated.* (In *The Nation*, 20 January 1945.)

William K. Everson (essay date 1974)

SOURCE: *Classics of the Horror Film*, The Citadel Press, 1974, pp. 179-87.

[*Everson was an eminent film historian, collector, and educator. In addition to the work excerpted here, his other scrupulously researched and enthusiastically written books include* A Pictorial History of the Western Film (*1969*), The Detective in Film (*1972*), *and* American Silent Film (*1978*). *In the following excerpt, he discusses* The Body Snatcher, Cat People, Night of the Demon (*which, though directed by Jacques Tourneur—arguably Lewton's most distinguished collaborator—was neither produced nor written by Lewton*), *and* The Curse of the Cat People.]

Val Lewton produced nine horror films for RKO Radio, all of them aiming at horror by suggestion, rather than statement, and employing intelligent writers (DeWitt Bodeen in particular) and new, young directors, still fresh and full of enthusiasm. ***Cat People*** was the first, and probably the best, even though it has been so acclaimed in later years that those coming upon it now for the first time must inevitably be disappointed. One of the perennial problems of "B" pictures is that critics see so few of them; when they do stumble across a good one, they lose all sense of proportion, and extol the film for virtues and intentions which need the sense of surprise and discovery for those virtues to remain intact. A ***Cat People*** elevated to the level of *The Picture of Dorian Gray* no longer retains the same sense of initiative; but to encounter a ***Cat People*** on the budgetary and commercial level of a *Mad Ghoul* is stimulating and rewarding.

The great material of ***Cat People*** is all concentrated in its second half, and the literate but very slow first half makes one wonder (at first) what all the shouting was about. The Lewtons were always interesting, though their standards were somewhat uneven. ***The Leopard Man*** had a terrifying opening and brilliant individual moments, but a weak climax and sets too often revealed the paucity of budget. Despite its well conveyed atmosphere of claustrophobic evil, ***The Seventh Victim*** didn't quite come off, and ***The Ghost Ship*** seemed to be striving too hard to turn a psychological melodrama into a horror film, just *because* it was a Lewton production. ***The Curse of the***

Cat People . . . and the others—Tourneur's ***I Walked with a Zombie*** and Robson's ***Isle of the Dead*** and ***Bedlam*** (defeated by its own pretentions and enlarged budget, but still offering some beautifully bizarre moments and some fine low-key photography)—are all much better known.

Sadly, theatrical exhibition of these films in recent years has been virtually non-existent, and a whole generation of moviegoers has grown up knowing them only from television—which, in many cases, is not knowing them as they were at all. Apart from the damage done to such carefully constructed films by breaking them up for commercials, they have been seriously hurt by cutting. The one sequence that is directly responsible for ***Cat People***'s being considered a classic—the beautiful and chilling episode in the swimming pool—is almost invariably cut from TV prints, not only because it is a dark sequence that does not register well on television, but also because, while it is a key sequence, it is a little unit in itself. It *can* be cut *in toto* without leaving a jagged edge. Since other (though less dynamic) sequences make the same plot point, continuity is not impaired—even though the overall power of the film is dealt a death blow.

The Body Snatcher, however, is quite certainly the equal of ***Cat People***, and possibly its superior, but strangely enough, it is one of the least respected. Even now it is regarded mainly as an example of early Robert Wise, not as a significant film on its own. In England, though audiences at the time were not aware of it, it was carefully trimmed of some of its grimmer scenes. It was still a good film, since it depended more on dialogue and characterization than on visuals, yet it received a very lukewarm reception from the critics, with such phrases as "fair" and "misfire thriller" cropping up with regularity. Perhaps one of its problems was that it *sounded* like a horror film. For box office reasons, Boris Karloff and Bela Lugosi were given the best billing, another misleading suggestion that it was "blood and guts" of the old school, and regardless of the fact that it was Henry Daniell who really had the lead, with Karloff in the top supporting role.

Despite the fact that its very theme indicates more "physical" horror than many of the other more psychologically motivated Lewton films, ***The Body Snatcher*** is one of the most literate and restrained of all horror films. There are the odd shock effects, to be sure (and so well edited that they remain effective and achieve their attention-grabbing ends even on repeat viewings), and a climax of pure nightmare quality, but the film's finest achievement is the image of latent malevolence created by Karloff as the cabman/grave-robber, acquiring bodies (initially from graves, later more directly) for medical school usage. As a sort of out-side-the-law Uriah Heep, kind to children and his horse, yet persecuting a basically decent man above his own station purely for the sense of power and perverted self respect it gives him, Karloff is superb. How sadly he was wasted in routine horror roles. His dialogue here is beautifully written to begin with, and equally well delivered. That excellent actor Henry Daniell is somewhat overshadowed by Karloff, yet his performance, too, is first-rate, and it is good to see him in a leading role for once.

The whole film reflects all the care, photographic excellence and production ingenuity (not least, in the utilization of sets from bigger pictures) that distinguished the best of the Lewtons. Just how good a film ***The Body Snatcher*** really was is emphasized by a comparison with one of the Hammer blood baths from the early 60s—*The Flesh and the Fiends*—likewise dealing with the days (and profession) of Burke and Hare, but with far less taste and subtlety.

For all of its restraint, ***The Body Snatcher*** still came up with one of the grimmest climaxes of any horror film. Having stolen the body of a woman from a fresh grave, Dr. MacFarlane (Henry Daniell) is driven to madness by his conscience. Careening along in his coach at the height of a thunderstorm, he becomes convinced that the corpse has changed into that of Gray, the cabman (Karloff), whom he had killed earlier. As he stops to examine the body and make sure, a lightning flash (and a sudden tracking shot into a closeup) reveals the chalky-white face of Karloff. In a panic, Daniell whips up the horses, and the emaciated corpse of Karloff, still half encased in its shroud, slumps over him in an unholy embrace, the sound track repeating an earlier threat of Karloff's ("You'll never get rid of me!") as the coach plummets off a cliff. Subsequent examination of the two bodies reveals that the stolen corpse was, of course, still that of the woman. Yet that one classic image of terror that has invaded all our nightmares at one time or another, to be in the embrace of a dead person, is such an overpowering one that the "rational" explanation of hallucination doesn't altogether settle all doubts.

Apart from being a good horror film, ***The Body Snatcher*** is a disturbing one, since the "villains" are both fascinating and even likeable, and the villainy itself is perpetrated for a worthwhile end. The ambiguous, semi-mystical literary quote, with which Lewton liked to end his films, provides a last minute note of upbeat optimism, but certainly doesn't dispel the effectiveness of what has gone before.

. . . . .

Jacques Tourneur, son of Maurice Tourneur—perhaps the greatest pictorialist director of the silent screen—started as an editor, and established himself as a director of note with ***Cat People*** and ***I Walked with a Zombie***, the first two of the nine intelligent horror films that Val Lewton produced for RKO Radio in the early 40s. Other subsequent directors included Mark Robson (who edited ***Cat People***) and Robert Wise (an editor on *Citizen Kane*).

Tourneur's importance to the Lewton unit has often been underrated by critics, although his skill was quickly recognized by Hollywood and he was soon promoted to commercially more important properties. His initial, bigger films reflected some of the pictorial eloquence of his father, and the quality of understatement that was a characteristic of the Lewton films. His big 1946 Western, *Canyon Passage*, contained only short, spasmodic moments of violence and action, and much of its savagery was merely suggested, while a good deal of traditional action took place off-screen. When, years later, Val Lewton was to produce a Western himself (***Apache Drums*** for Universal), it was fairly obvious that he had seen, remembered and emulated Tourneur's stylized approach. By the early 1950s however, Tourneur, still commercially reliable, seemed somewhat *passé* in terms of an original and recognizable directorial style. Then, along came *The Night of the Demon*, which he made in England, to show that in the intervening sixteen years he had lost none of his old cunning.

Considered together, the two films provide an interesting contrast in styles. Both films are related in that they spin tales of the supernatural, and both have a methodical skeptic as the hero. When he is convinced—and scared—despite all the logic he can muster, so is the audience. The utilization of the whole arsenal of film grammar is basically the same in both films: some of the most telling effects are achieved by shock cuts of sound, or picture, or both; or by the delaying or accelerating of *anticipated* scenes, so that the audience is caught off guard.

But in terms of overall design, the two films are quite different. ***Cat People***, with its totally manufactured variation on the Werewolf theme, eschews all of the standard effects of fog, creaking doors, trick photography, and monstrous changeovers. Working on Lang's old premise that nothing that the camera can show can possibly be as horrible as what the mind can imagine, it shows nothing—and suggests all. (Only once is an actual leopard shown in a supernatural context; Lewton fought against it, but was overruled. However, it does little damage, as the scene can still be interpreted as a subjective imagining on the part of the trapped hero and heroine.) The backgrounds are modern, normal, and unspectacular, unglossy studio reconstructions of New York's offices, museums, Central Park Zoo, and environs. The people are ordinary, even dull and pompous. While the moments of horror are ambiguous and fragmented, the film leaves one with the deliberately uneasy feeling that the only explanation must be an acceptance of the supernatural. The episode in which the heroine, swimming in a darkened hotel swimming pool, is menaced by the unseen presence of the Cat Woman—or by a real leopard—is not only a classic episode of economical screen terror, it works on a second level too, since its symbolic imagery is essentially Freudian. With its basically realistic setting, and its logical use of light, shadow, and distorted sound, it is a perfect example of the Fritz Lang *modus operandi*, of turning the everyday into a black, nightmare world of unseen menace.

The Night of the Demon, likewise intelligently scripted, goes to the other extreme of *showing* its Monster. Luckily, its Demon is such a lulu that it lives up to the fearsome descriptions of it (something that most movie Monsters do not). Tourneur, in later interviews, claims that it was never his intention to show the Demon, that he had wanted to follow the pattern of his Lewton films and merely suggest it, and that its graphic physical depiction was included at the insistence of the producer, who wanted real meat in his film. Tourneur made no such protests at the time of release, however, and one wonders whether these latter-day protestations are entirely genuine. Certainly the construction of the film, and the scenes in which the Demon's presence is undeniably felt, even when not visible, leave no doubt at all as to the creature's existence. The whole point of the film, in fact, is not that horrors can be created within the mind, but that some horrors are so unthinkable that the mind must deny them in order to retain its sanity. The final line of the film—the time-honored, "There are some things it is better not to know!"—comes after a materialization of the Demon, which is ambiguous only to those who want it to be ambiguous.

Tourneur, like Lang, takes his thrillers seriously. There is some humor in *Night of the Demon* in the person of the villain's slightly dotty mother, dabbling in the charades of seances, while her son (another screen incarnation of Aleister Crowley, and extremely well played by one-time rugged, outdoor hero Niall MacGinnis) is the evil central force in a malestrom of witchcraft, conjuring up demons, giant cats, and sudden storms, to demonstrate his powers. But she is there primarily to illustrate the impotency of normalcy against such total evil, just as Hitchcock's master criminals in *Saboteur* and *The 39 Steps* were surrounded by loving wives and families. There is a kind of mordant humor in ***Cat People***, too, but it is mainly in the writing of Bodeen. The psychiatrist who thinks to effect a cure by simply telling his patient to go home and lead a normal life is a little hard to take seriously! And the vivacious Negro waitress, who seems to serve her customers according to their personalities—Bavarian Cream for one, and, somewhat contemptuously, "The apple pie for *you*" to the cloddish hero—underlines in a very lighthearted way that everyone is, in a sense, a captive of his own destiny, type-cast by life. But there is no constant undercurrent of humor, as there always is with Hitchcock. He, for example, would doubtless have extracted some visual humor from the disturbing scene in which the Cat Woman enters a pet store, only to have the normally docile cats and birds screech in terror until the whole store is in an uproar. Tourneur means you to believe in and take seriously all that he is showing you. When he borrows, significantly it is more from Lang than from Hitchcock.

Much of *Night of the Demon* takes place at night, and two sequences in a deserted forest are very reminiscent of the climactic chase from Lang's *The Testament of Dr. Mabuse.* Even drab old Clapham Junction Station—one of the most unpromising of locations—seems almost to take on the fatalistic characteristics of one of Lang's unreal way-stations between life and death. Tourneur's inability to spoof (or more likely, his lack of interest in so doing) was shown by his much later Karloff-Rathbone-Lorre horror satire *Comedy of Terrors*, which, in Tourneur's hands, emerged as leaden burlesque.

Night of the Demon, which borrowed many touches and individual moments of cutting from the earlier ***Cat People***, increased and sustained its pattern of chase and suspense. It is undoubtedly a better (and more genuinely frightening) film than ***Cat People***, and, more importantly, it is the last genuine horror "classic" that we have had. In the 16 years that have elapsed since it was made, one or two films have come close to it—most particularly, *Burn Witch Burn* (its similarity stressed by its British release title, *The Night of the Eagle*)—but none have quite equaled, let alone surpassed it. In time, it may well prove to be not only the apex, but the climax to the *genre* of "thinking" horror films introduced by Val Lewton over a decade earlier.

The Curse of the Cat People was handicapped by the double misfortune of a title that tried to pass off a fairy story as a horror yarn, and by being touted as a sequel to the original ***Cat People***. As such, it could hardly fail to disappoint the traditional horror fanciers, nor could it reach those who would most appreciate it, and its distribution was slight. Apart from reemploying some of the same characters, it is really only the vaguest kind of sequel to the original. Indeed, to explain how a malevolent supernatural Werecat could become, after death, a kindly and protective spirit friend to the child of her former husband, the original writer (Bodeen) had to insert several explanatory lines of dialogue which falsified and distorted the events of the original. In only one sense was there real continuity: the father (Kent Smith in both films), originally an unimaginative dullard, proved to be even less successful as a father than he had been as a husband. His attitude throughout is one of stupid condescension, and even at the film's fadeout, he is still lying to his much more imaginative daughter.

The menace in ***The Curse of the Cat People*** (which contains neither curses nor Cat People) is nebulous and deliberately vague. Nothing more horrifying occurs than the hair-raising telling of the "Headless Horseman" legend to a frightened child by a half insane, old actress—and the disturbed child's later belief (when lost on a country road at night) that she is about to encounter the ghost. Yet the moments of terror, built by imagination out of nothing—as the majority of a child's fears are—reach heights equal to those of the scratching from within the coffin in ***Isle of the Dead***, the sealing up alive of Karloff in the asylum walls in ***Bedlam***, the sudden stopping of the bus with the catlike hiss, in ***Cat People***, or the sobbing in the deserted village and the terrifying journey to the Voodoo village in ***I Walked with a Zombie***. And, as in all good fairy tales, poignancy and beauty walk hand in hand with fear. It would be exaggerating to say that ***Curse of the Cat People*** approaches the beauty of Cocteau's *Le Belle et la Bête*, or Autant-Lara's *Sylvie et le Fantome*, but it does have the same kind of beauty.

One suspects that no one was quite sure whether this film should have been complete fantasy or complete horror film. The film was also not helped by a split directorial credit; Gunther Fritsch started the film, and relinquished to Robert Wise when he was called to service with the Army. The effects of compromise and indecision show. Certain scenes were shot a number of ways. In one version of the climax, for example, the ghost of the former Cat Woman played a far more positive and melodramatic role, including the unlocking of a jammed closet door to enable the child to hide from the crazed woman who seeks to kill her. In the final release version, this element was eliminated and fairy tale magic won out over prolonged suspense, a preferable solution. Despite the occasionally uneven quality throughout, one feels that this is one of those rare cases where the fussing was justified, and where the final version was not a "butchery" of what might have been.

Steve Jenkins (essay date 1981)

SOURCE: "Val Lewton: Curse of the Critics?" in *Monthly Film Bulletin*, Vol. 48, July, 1981, p. 148.

[*In the following essay, Jenkins summarizes the critical reception of Lewton's films, examining the various positions taken regarding the relation of the producer to his films.*]

> American producer, former writer, notable for a group of low-budget, high quality horror films made for RKO in the Forties. . . . Later films unremarkable. (Leslie Halliwell, *The Filmgoer's Companion*)

The above 'definition' is a neat guide to Val Lewton's accepted place and significance in film history and criticism. He is considered primarily responsible for the particular qualities discernible within a group of generically locatable films produced within a definable Hollywood context (history, studio). Working with sympathetic collaborators, and with strict financial constraints, the creative producer turned pulp titles into low-budget poetry, stamped with the seal of 'quality.'

The writings of Manny Farber and James Agee in *The Nation* and *New Republic* helped form this picture, but also revealed 'Lewton' as a figure constructed in order to grind particular axes. For Agee, Lewton "and the rest of his crew . . . have a lot of taste and talent and they are carrying films a long way out of Hollywood". It was "startling to see such a film as ***Youth Runs Wild*** coming out of a Hollywood studio". Watching the work of Lewton's actors and technicians "you would hardly think they had ever heard of Hollywood, much less wanted to go there". They became "one group of men working in Hollywood who have neither lost nor taken care to conceal the purity of their hopes and intentions". Agee's championing of Lewton as producing work "resolutely against the grain of all we have learned to expect from the big studios" was echoed by Farber who, writing after Lewton's death, criticised the industry which never considered his films Oscar-worthy, which "in acclaiming people like Ferrer, Mankiewicz and Holliday . . . indicated its esteem for bombshells who disorganise the proceedings on the screen with their flamboyant eccentricities and relegate the camera to the role of a passive bit player". Lewton was a key figure in Farber's 1952 tirade against "the present crowd of movie-goers, particularly the long-haired and intellectual brethren, (with) a taste for precociously styled, upper-case effects and brittle sophistication . . . and whose idea of good movies is based on an assortment of swell attitudes". This audience once performed a "function as press-agents for movies that came from the Hollywood underground" (e.g. Lewton's), but had been led astray by the "snobbism" of the critics.

Farber was the more perceptive as regards the surface qualities of the films (***The Leopard Man*** "shows a way to tell a story about people that isn't dominated by the activity, weight, size and pace of the human figure"), but it was Agee's fantasy of the man of taste transcending 'the system' that survived. Whether it was *Sight and Sound*'s 1951 obituary ("Lewton experimented with the tastefully macabre"), or Joseph McBride in the January/February 1976 issue of *Action* ("The tradition of taste and subtlety Lewton established in the genre proved highly influential on later film-makers"), the image held. Lewton's RKO work, with ***Mademoiselle Fifi*** and ***Youth Runs Wild*** (both praised by Agee) conveniently forgotten, neatly plugged a gap in chronological histories of the horror film, coming between the Thirties Universal 'classics' and the Fifties science-fiction cycles. Assumptions about genre became a way of defining Lewton's personal sensibilities, almost by default. Thus, David Robinson in *The Times* (17.8.73): "Above all one is struck in these little films by the taste and tact Lewton was able to deploy. What made him unique as a master of horror was that he never resorted to the crude visualisation which characterised the films made at Universal".

Joel Siegel in his book *Val Lewton: the Reality of Terror* (1972) bolstered the opposition between Lewton (the artist) and the studio front office (the system) through an accumulation of biographical detail. But *Sight and Sound* had already hinted at a problem in 1965: "Clearly this ('Lewton') is a case of that mysterious and problematic animal, the producer *auteur* who prints his taste and his personality on his films whoever happens to direct them". This 'animal' was soon threatened with extinction by film culture's investment in the director-as-author, and it was Robin Wood (*Film Comment*, Summer 1972) who, rather hesitantly, championed Jacques Tourneur against his producer. Describing Lewton's work as "at once a demonstration of the limitations of the auteur theory and its vindication", Wood opposes Wise's ***The Body Snatcher*** as "a potential masterpiece (a *producer's* film cannot be more than potential)" to ***Cat People*** and ***I Walked with a Zombie*** which "should be regarded as group achievements (but) under Tourneur their implicit poetry reaches sensitive visual expression". 'Lewton' was dealt another blow by the auteurist/Tourneur thrust with Paul Willemen's *Notes Towards the Construction of Readings of Tourneur* (1975) which dismissed Siegel's book as "gossip, plot synopses and the kind of 'criticism' one tends to associate with fan magazines and publicity handouts". Thereafter, the producer's name was completely repressed from his account of 'Tourneur', a name "used as a formula to designate a particular activity of reading/writing, a practice of textual production".

While this abandonment of 'Lewton' in favour of auteurist textual analysis is historically understandable (writings on the producer essentially amounting to endless repetition of the same ideas of taste, subtlety, making the best of limited financial resources, etc.), it is hardly desirable. The producer's name was/is at least the basic signifier of a specific production context and as such should be useful. In this respect, it is interesting to look at contemporary trade press reviews of Lewton films, examples here being taken from *Motion Picture Herald, Kine Weekly* and *Today's Cinema.* It is immediately apparent that almost everything subsequently written about Lewton was said by the trade at the time. The films are distinguished from the "conventional thick-ear thriller" by "restrained directorial treatment" in which "all the tricks of light and sound are used to produce an effect of menace and eeriness", resulting in something "a cut above the average horror picture". At the same time, the films' evident aspirations towards 'art' (the most obvious sign of Lewton's input) are firmly dealt with: "The director, Jacques Tourneur, definitely has ideas and imagination, but in trying to convert a conventional creepy to something a little more intelligent he falls between two stools . . . lacks the power of the popular thriller without rising to the heights demanded by the connoisseur". More aggressively: "We prefer our thrillers straight and we think the industrial masses share our views".

This leads to the significant fact of the trade papers' reluctance to classify these products as horror films, a crucial element in the critical attempt to establish Lewton's 'difference.' Other terms abound: "melodrama", "psychological thriller", "dual personality melodrama", "out-of-rut-thriller", "supernatural melodrama", "murder-mystery melodrama", "high falutin' thriller", "suspense film", "pseudo-thriller", "psychological melodrama", etc. This plethora of labels (concentrating on melodrama) hints at a way out of the Lewton critical impasse. In his article "Out of What Past? Notes on the B-Film Noir" (*Screen Education*, Winter 79/80), Paul Kerr suggests that "By the end of the 1930s . . . double bills were beginning to contrast the staple A genres of that decade . . . with a number of Poverty Row hybrids, (including a mixture of) melodrama and mystery". This "hybrid quality", a description which certainly fits Lewton's work, is seen by Kerr not only "in terms of studio insecurities about marketing their B product", but also as pointing forward to the "cross-generic quality of the *film noir* . . . perhaps a vestige of its origins in a kind of 'oppositional' cinematic mode" (Farber's "underground"?).

If one sees 'Lewton' in a *noir* spectrum reaching from, say, *Stranger on the Third Floor* (1940) to *Out of the Past* (1947), both RKO and both photographed by Lewton regular Nicholas Musuraca, the visual style becomes unreadable as a simple sign of the producer's radical reworking of the horror genre. The ideological significance of that style, and of 'Lewton' as a construct, is thrown into question. Which is not to replace 'horror film' with *'film noir'* as a catch-all phrase coherently binding a body of work beneath a particular name, but rather to suggest the illusoriness of coherence. The Lewton unit worked in conditions of relative autonomy within RKO, but the work it produced was subject to a battery of constraints, pressures and influences (a complex field that Kerr concisely maps out) which have so far been effectively ignored by Lewton admirers, except insofar as they suit the ideology of hero worship. Essentially, 'Lewton' remains to be deciphered.

Christopher Palmer (essay date 1981)

SOURCE: "Write It Black: Roy Webb, Lewton and Film Noir," in *Monthly Film Bulletin*, Vol. 48, August, 1981, p. 168.

[*In the following essay, Palmer examines composer Roy Webb's contributions to Lewton's films.*]

Film noir attracted some outstanding individual scores from composers generally better known for their work in other contexts: Hans Salter's *Phantom Lady*, Max Steiner's *The Big Sleep*, Miklós Rázsa's *Asphalt Jungle*, David Raksin's *Force of Evil.* But Roy Webb, one of the least fêted and most underrated of all Hollywood composers, displayed a particular talent for translating both horror and violence, and their more subtle and far-ranging nuances, into musical terms—largely through a wide spectrum of modern harmonic resource and an intuitive understanding of the atmospheric properties of orchestral colour.

Webb was born in New York in 1888 and attended Columbia University. While there, he was asked to take charge of a sixteen-year-old boy who was already an outstandingly gifted melodist, but who needed help to put his ideas down on paper. Nearly sixty years later, Richard Rodgers paid a warm tribute to his former teacher in his autobiography *Musical Stages.* While still at Columbia, Webb made his début on Broadway conducting the musical *Wildflower*, and this led eventually to a full-time career as a Broadway musical director. A colleague and close friend at this time was Max Steiner, later to become an important figure in Hollywood film music and greatly to influence Webb's style as a composer in his early years. In fact, both Steiner and Webb, neither in the first instance composers, both reared in a tradition of operetta and musical comedy, later found themselves faced in Hollywood with the necessity of creating dramatic, symphonic music of a kind with which they had previously had little experience.

Webb arrived in Hollywood in 1929 and spent virtually the remainder of his working life in the employ of RKO. Not, however, until the development of the *noir* cycle in the Forties did he begin to evolve the personal style epitomised in his score for Dmytryk's 1944 version of *Farewell, My Lovely.* Webb's feeling for atmospheric nuance—for mutedly dissonant harmonic colours and sparely evocative textures—stands the nocturnal, metropolitan setting of the film in excellent stead. But Webb was pre-eminently the composer of Val Lewton's horror pictures: ***Cat People*** (1942), ***I Walked with a Zombie, The Leopard Man, The Seventh Victim*** (1943), ***The Curse of the Cat People*** (1944), ***The Body Snatcher*** (1945) and ***Bedlam*** (1946). As developed through harmony and timbre, Webb's 'horror' music is the precise aural equivalent of Lewton's half-heard sounds, half-seen shadows, and atmospheric lighting.

It is quite possible that in a close-knit team such as existed at RKO (Webb worked alongside cinematographer Nicholas Musuraca, who was a specialist in this particular idiom, and with art directors Albert D'Agostino and Walter Keller, and editor Mark Robson), the work of one member of the team would be influenced by that of another and begin to assume some of its characteristics. One of the more positive aspects of the studio system was that it encouraged this type of artistic cross-fertilisation. (On the other hand, it did not provide for any closeness of collaboration between director and composer since the former would, in the normal course of events, be already engaged on another picture by the time the latter was called in.) Lewton is known to have put his personal stamp on almost every aspect of his productions, and it is more than likely that, having discerned Webb's gifts in the treatment of musical chiaroscuro, Lewton requested him specifically (normally Webb, as RKO's premier composer, would not have been assigned to B-pictures).

The musical *leitmotif* in ***Cat People*** is particularly interesting in that the idea came from actress Simone Simon who plays Irena, the Cat Woman. She sang a little French nursery tune ("Dodo, l'enfant do") to Webb, who agreed that it could usefully serve as the thematic basis of the score. [In a footnote, Palmer notes: "This traditional tune was also playfully used by Debussy in 'Jardins sous la pluie' (the third of his *Estampes* for piano), and in the piece in *Children's Corner* entitled 'Jimbo's Lullaby.'"] First heard over the credits, it is hummed by Irena to Oliver (Kent Smith) in one of their early scenes together, and is then used in many subtle variations, haunting the film just as Irena is increasingly haunted by the fear that she will turn into a cat and kill the man she loves. It is most horrifyingly transformed at the climax, when Irena murders her psychiatrist Dr. Judd (Tom Conway). The very sweetness and innocence of the original tune intensifies the dark horror of the harmony which distorts it: the tune turns into a monster along with Irena.

Both Simone Simon and Webb showed unconscious foresight in selecting this particular tune, for it fits with singular aptness into ***Cat People***'s sequel ***The Curse of the Cat People***, a delicate and poetic fantasy of childhood (*pace* the title). Other musical survivors of the earlier film are the main title music (*in toto*), Irena's theme, and the sinister four-note cat motif—which, incidentally, Webb could not resist quoting and extensively developing in Wellman's superb *Track of the Cat* made some ten years later. This film owes not a little to Lewton's prototype inasmuch as the monster is never actually seen, only suggested. Remarkable in this respect is the way the music identifies itself both with the characters' fear of the cat and with the elemental forces of nature which it in turn symbolises.

In ***The Curse of the Cat People***, the music's responsibility is to turn quite another kind of fantasy into reality. "Dodo, l'enfant do" is all important during the first scene in the garden when lonely little Amy (Ann Carter) first wishes for a 'friend' to love and understand her. The screen darkens, showers of petals rain upon the garden and the tune, scored with a gentle translucent beauty, tells us not only that the friend has arrived but also (if we remember the music from ***Cat People***, of course) who she is. The result is that when Simone Simon actually appears for the first time, we have been aurally prepared for her, and can revel in the magical variations in harmony and orchestral texture to which Webb submits his theme. Another musical sleight-of-hand is in the Christmas scene when carollers are singing "Shepherds shake off your drowsy sleep"; Irena appears to Amy and sings the French carol "Il est né, le divin enfant" which, miraculously, is woven in counterpoint with the English.

In view of the essentially lyrical, musical (in the widest sense) qualities of Lewton's films, it is scarcely surprising that they lend themselves so readily to actual music. His masterpiece, ***I Walked with a Zombie***, has been described by Tom Milne (*Focus on Film*, No. 7, p. 53) as "a nightmarishly beautiful *tone-poem* of voodoo dreams, dark moonlight and somnambulist ladies in floating white" (my italics); and Joel Siegel (*Val Lewton: the Reality of Terror*) refers to the walk to the Houmfort in the same film as "a *symphony* of graceful movement". The latter sequence, being so 'musically' self-contained, does not need the support of actual music; indeed one of the virtues of Webb's handling of Lewton's films is that, at a time when over-scoring was the rule rather than the exception, his placing or 'spotting' of music is so judicious.

In ***The Seventh Victim***, the music is notable both for the sympathy it engages for Mary (Kim Hunter) and the feckless poet Jason (Erford Gage) and for its evocative, intimidating power in the scene of Mary's night-walk through a deserted Greenwich Village. The music embraces and enhances all the elements—nameless fears and forebodings, sudden alarms, the distant merriment of an acting troupe—and finally explodes in a climax of racing panic. Elsewhere in the film, as in ***I Walked with a Zombie*** and ***The Ghost Ship***, it is above all the atmospheric properties of Webb's music—its ebb and flow of *Stimmung*—that brings these 'tone-poems' to their rare pitch of perfection.

The special qualities of Webb's Lewton scores contributed greatly to the distinction of his work on other RKO films of the 1940s now recognised as masterpieces of their kind: Siodmak's *The Spiral Staircase, Out of the Past* (directed by Lewton's favourite, Jacques Tourneur), *Crossfire*, Hitchcock's *Notorious, The Window.* Of course he dissipated his gifts in over-productiveness: this was another fault endemic in the studio system (the total number of films with which he had to do exceeds 300). Other titles on which he worked include *Bringing Up Baby, Journey into Fear, Hitler's Children, The Enchanted Cottage, The Locket, I Remember Mama, Mighty Joe Young, Clash by Night, Marty* and finally *Teacher's Pet.* After RKO disbanded in the mid-Fifties, Webb still worked occasionally as a freelance for other studios. Only the disastrous Bel Air fire of November 1961, in which his home and studio were burnt to the ground, put a permanent stop to his activities.

George Turner (essay date 1982)

SOURCE: "Val Lewton's Cat People," in *Cinefantastique*, Vol. 12, No. 4, May-June, 1982, pp. 23-7.

[*In the following essay, Turner describes the production history of* Cat People.]

The great days of the horror film had become wistful memories. By the early '40s only an occasional worthwhile chiller emerged from the morass the genre had become. And these few films served only to keep alive the hope that a successor to James Whale and Tod Browning would herald a rebirth.

Finally, a new master of horror did appear. A man who opened new directions for the horror genre by purposely going against the established grain, throwing out the old, stale conventions, and producing something *new.* From producer Vladimar (Val) Lewton's first picture, ***Cat People***, he started a small renaissance that breathed new life into the stagnant pond that horror films had become, bringing with him a cadre of talented men whose influence went far beyond the atmospheric horror films made at RKO.

Of course, in the film industry renaissance doesn't happen because of artistic need, but because of money. And Lewton's horror unit was born as a consequence of the periodic management shakeups at RKO. Such upheavals were due to the failure of expensive productions to make money for the studio.

Charles Koerner, a former theater executive, was appointed production vice-president early in 1942. A glance at the ledger sheets convinced Koerner that the company was losing money on many of its high budget features, but making healthy profits on the so-called "B" pictures—those made on budgets below $150,000. He also noted that a rival studio, Universal, was making so much money from horror pictures that the front office referred to them as "Midas productions." Koerner decided to establish a new production unit which would specialize in the making of low-budget horror films built around exploitable titles that could be audience tested in advance.

At a Beverly Hills dinner party, Koerner met Lewton, a Russian-born novelist and publicity writer who was a story editor and research director for David O. Selznick and had been for the past eight years. Burly and good humored, a natural raconteur, Newton impressed the studio chief as a man who could put together a good show. Following his instincts, Koerner offered Lewton a job as horror specialist and Lewton accepted.

In March, 1942, Lewton went on the RKO payroll at $250 per week. He delighted in informing his friends that he was listed on the studio roster as an "ass. prod." His immediate superior was executive producer, Lou Ostrow.

At first Koerner and Lewton worked on adapting published literary works and looked at Algernon Blackwood's *Ancient Sorceries.* Lewton was impressed with Koerner's taste, but later he revised his opinion. Koerner had been to a party and someone there suggested that werewolves and vampires had been overdone in films, but "nobody had done much of anything about cats." Abandoning the Blackwood tale, Koerner came up with a title: ***Cat People***. Lewton found the title depressingly lurid, but kept his opinion to himself.

Finding an acceptable work to fit the title was not as easy as thinking up the name. Lewton spent months looking at stories including Ambrose Bierce's *The Eyes of the Panther* and Margaret Irwin's *Monsieur Seeks A Wife*, which he noted down as "a fetching little tale about a man who meets two sisters that are not really women, but cats." Finally, Lewton dropped all pretense of adapting a published literary work and roughly outlined an idea of his own.

This embryonic version opens in a snow-covered Balkan village being invaded by a Nazi Panzer division. By day the inhabitants seem somnolent and unconcerned by such a threat; by night, however, these same individuals change into great cats and turn against their captors. A girl from this village flees to New York and falls in love, but she can't escape her heritage.

Lewton initially planned for the girl never to speak directly. "I thought we might let our cat-girl only speak in long shots," he said. "You hear the murmur of her voice, you never hear what she is saying and, if it is necessary to give her words meaning to the audience, I think we can always contrive to have some other character tell what the girl said." This idea was not popular with the decision-makers.

Also, the projected ending was quite unlike the one eventually filmed. "Most of the cat/werewolf stories I have read and all the werewolf stories I have seen on the screen end with the beast gunshot and turning back into a human being after death," Lewton wrote. "In this story I'd like to reverse this process. For the final scene I'd like to show a violent quarrel between the man and woman in which she is provoked into an assault upon him. To protect himself, he pushes her away, she stumbles, falls awkwardly, and breaks her neck in the fall. The young man, horrified, kneels to see if he can feel her heart beat. Under his hand black hair and hide come up and he draws back to look down in horror at a dead, black panther."

While many of these initial ideas didn't survive, important elements of the final version were suggested. Lewton wrote that he wanted "a man, possibly a doctor, who always gives the scientific or factual explanation for any phenomena that occurs, brushing the supernatural aside, and yet, who is always proved wrong by the events on the screen. This device, I hope, will express the audiences' doubts even before they are fully formulated in their minds and quickly answer them, thus lending a degree of credibility to the yarn, which is going to be difficult to achieve."

Another idea envisioned early in the production and later seen on the screen, was the scene in which Oliver takes Irena (Simone Simon) into a pet store. "Here," wrote Lewton, "I'd like to show the chattering fear that arises upon her entrance. At the very height of the uproar, I would like to have a little black cat come down the center aisle of the store, very calmly, and rub affectionately against the girl." (In the film, the cat is as frightened as the other animals.)

Lewton's desire to avoid typical horror film situations led him to drop the Balkan sequence entirely, opting instead to present the entire story in the context of modern, workaday settings. As he stated in a studio press release in 1944, "the characters in the run-of-the-mill weird films were usually people very remote from the audiences' experiences. European nobles of dark antecedents, mad scientists, man-created monsters, and the like cavorted across the screen. It would be much more entertaining if people with whom audiences could identify were shown in contact with the strange, the weird and the occult. We made it a basic part of our work to show normal people—engaged in normal occupations—in our pictures."

Ostrow, Lewton's direct superior, was not particularly sympathetic to Lewton's ideas of cinema. He gauged Lewton as too pretentious and fussy to succeed as a producer of popular entertainment—a view shared by many others at the studio. Fortunately, Koerner liked most of the ideas and only his intervention saved ***Cat People*** from being reshaped along conventional lines.

As soon as the basic story idea was given a reluctant go-ahead by Ostrow, Lewton sent for DeWitt Bodeen, a playwright working as a research assistant at Selznick-International, who became the first screenwriter of the group. "Before Val departed for RKO," said Bodeen, "he asked me to call him as soon as my work for Selznick was completed. I phoned him two weeks later and he made arrangements for me to be hired as a contract writer at the Guild minimum of $75 per week. I had never written for the screen before."

Bodeen, now 74, lives in Woodland Hills, and is the only member of the Lewton team credited on Universal's new ***Cat People*** remake, for the original story. Universal sent Bodeen a copy of the new script. "It follows the original fairly closely as to the incidents," he said, "but of course it is very modern and very, *very* sexy. I didn't really like that part, but I'm glad they gave me a credit, and I plan to see it."

For a week, Lewton and Bodeen read all the literature about cats they could unearth. They also screened numerous successful horror films, mostly made by Universal, with the idea of eliminating as many cliches of the genre as possible. At last Lewton turned his notes over to Bodeen and had him construct a 50-page story, not in treatment or script form, but one written as though for publication in a magazine.

Bodeen produced a first-person narrative written from the point of view of Alice, a woman in love with the cat girl's husband. He brought many important elements to the basic story, including what proved to be an outstanding sequence wherein Alice is menaced by a shadowy, cat-like presence in a hotel swimming pool. The idea sprang from a personal experience: Bodeen had almost drowned once when swimming alone.

Jacques Tourneur, son of the great French director, Maurice Tourneur, was hired by RKO at Lewton's instigation. After working in France and America on various features and short subjects, he met Lewton while both worked on staging the French Revolution sequences for the Selznick *MGM* epic, *A Tale of Two Cities* (1935). By 1942, Tourneur's career was stagnant and he was only too happy to join Lewton's horror unit.

The next member of the team was film editor Mark Robson. Robson was one of the studio's top editors, not the sort generally relegated to B productions but, as he explained: "I was Orson Welles' editor on *Citizen Kane*, and that picture cost a lot of time and money it didn't recoup. Management tended to blame all of RKO's financial troubles on Orson, and those of us who worked with him had to share the blame."

Being exiled to the horror unit proved a good break for Robson, however. He was brought into all pre-production and story sessions from the first and made important contributions. He also had experience as a second unit director, which proved an asset. As the production neared realization, Lewton wrote to Koerner that "If I were asked to name one single factor, beyond the director's work, which helped me most with ***Cat People***, I would name Mark's work. Jacques says of him that he cuts like a director, which, from a director, is praise indeed."

The neophyte producer received valuable help from a fellow "B" movie producer, Herman Schlom, who was one of RKO's leading experts in making slick, economical melodramas. Schlom explained to Lewton the many ways of cutting preproduction costs, particularly in the planning of sets.

The government had imposed a strictly enforced wartime limit of $10,000 on set construction, making it necessary to utilize standing sets almost exclusively. There was, fortunately, a great deal to choose from at RKO, which in addition to the Hollywood studio had use of the big 40-acre backlot and stages at RKO-Pathe (now Laird International Studio) in Culver City and the RKO ranch at Encino.

Lewton said it was from Schlom that he learned to lavish greater care in dressing one or two major sets and skimping by on the rest. Accordingly, the main action focuses on the cat girl's studio apartment, the exterior of which was a brownstone front on Pathe's venerable New York street. The marvelous stairway, used a few months earlier for Orson Welles' *Magnificent Ambersons* and still standing on a Pathe sound stage, was altered by adding an adjacent elevator cage from the scene dock. The Central Park settings were familiar to lovers of the Astaire-Rogers musicals and some offices and stairways were left over from the 1941 comedy, *The Devil and Miss Jones.*

A standing cafe set was dressed as a coffee shop for one sequence, a pet store for another and a Serbian cafe for a third. Wild walls set up with props from the scene docks made up most of the sets that couldn't be redressed. Unit art director Walter Keller so artfully disguised these sets as to obscure any suggestion of "hand-me-down" origins. They were smothered in appropriate decor by set decorator Al Fields, who combed the property department and prop rental houses for items significant to the development of the characters as well as the story.

Casting was an important aspect of the plan to avoid horror film conventions. "I'd like to have a girl with a little kitten-face like Simone Simon, cute and soft and cuddly and seemingly not at all dangerous," Lewton wrote to Ostrow. "I took a look at the Paramount picture *The Island of Lost Souls* and after seeing their much-publicized 'panther woman,' I feel that any attempt to secure a cat-like quality in our girl's physical appearance would be absolutely disastrous." Bodeen recalled that "Val told me from the first to write the part of Irena around Simone Simon. He seemed confident that he would be able to get her."

A leading star in her native France, Miss Simon had made a number of films in the United States, but never achieved the popularity her sponsors at 20th Century-Fox had anticipated. Lewton sent the actress a copy of the first draft script while she was appearing on stage in Chicago and she quickly accepted at rather generous terms.

For the ambiguous character of psychiatrist Dr. Judd, first visualized as a sinister European called Mueller, Lewton's first choice was the German actor Fritz Kortner, who would, he believed, "add a great deal of menace and a certain conceited continental quality that would make audiences dislike him." As the script developed, however, he decided to cast against type and have the character be a young and handsome Britisher. Likeable Tom Conway, a contract player who had recently succeeded his older brother, George Sanders, as star of RKO's popular *Falcon* series, was available and proved an apt choice.

Kent Smith, a successful Broadway leading man, who signed an RKO contract in 1941, had been in Hollywood for nine months without appearing in anything except some Army training films. Lewton saw Smith as he commuted to the studio every day on his bicycle and decided he might be an ideal Oliver, the film's quiet-man hero. Smith's sympathetic portrayal launched a long, solid film career.

Jane Randolph, also a contract player, was chosen for the second woman role because she was *not* the ingenue type usually favored for such parts. Tall and efficient-looking, she epitomized the modern career women who had come to the fore since the beginning of World War II. The other actors, even down to the bit players, were handpicked by Tourneur and Lewton from the contract list and casting catalog. The most striking small role is that of the cat-like woman who appears in only one scene—an unforgettable cameo by the statuesque Elizabeth Russell.

Cinematographer Nick Musuraca had been typed for some years as a photographer of Western and action pictures before he was assigned to ***Cat People***. Musuraca's work for Lewton (for whom he shot five horror films altogether) established him as a master of highly dramatic lighting. His distinctive technique is now celebrated as the quintessential *film noir* style. After making a string of similarly atmospheric films, including *The Spiral Staircase* (1945). *The Locket* (1946) and *Out of the Past* (1947), he complained bitterly that he had become typecast again, this time as a mystery expert, and would like to shoot more "normal" pictures for a while.

Despite Lewton's determination to eschew the usual conventions of horror films, the lessons of the masters were not lost upon him. More innovations in sound recording technique were introduced in mystery and horror films than in the more readily accepted mainstream works. Lewton was adamant that dialogue should be used only when the story could not be advanced through the combination of visual image and natural sound.

When the cost accounting office demanded to know why John Cass's recording crew worked an extra three days on ***Cat People***, it was explained that they spent one day at Gay's Lion Farm recording the growls and roars of the big cats and two days at the indoor swimming pool of the Royal Palms hotel recording reverberation effects. A vocal effects actress, Dorothy Lloyd, was hired to create the cat noises. The studio bosses regarded all this unusually extravagant for a "B" picture.

Unwilling to settle for the pastiche musical scores normally assembled for low budget pictures, Lewton conferred with musical director Constantin Bakaleinikoff and composer Roy Webb long before the screenplay was underway. Webb was brought into the story sessions to contribute ideas for linking visuals with music. Like most film composers, Webb was accustomed to being consulted only after the photography was completed. He later said that by being involved in the planning he was able to provide a more effective score.

"We were searching for a lullaby theme suited to a story about cats," wrote Lewton, "something with a haunting, memorable quality somewhat like the short bit from 'Anitra's Dance' which was used so memorably in the German picture *M.* And we wanted a little strain of music to be sung or hummed by the heroine, to have a cat-like feeling and a sinister note of menace." Unfortunately, none of the compositions considered had the qualities Lewton wanted.

Then one day on the set, Simone Simon sang for Lewton a traditional French lullaby she remembered from childhood, *Do, Do, Baby Do.* Webb agreed that it would make an ideal *leitmotiv* for the film. A Russian writer, Andrei Tolstoi, was hired to translate the lyrics into Russian and coach the actress in the proper pronunciation and delivery.

Although the stringent budgets of "B" films did not permit a great deal of visual effects work, Vernon Walker's excellent camera effects department made important contributions to the production. Veteran technical artist Al Simpson, after reading a request from Lewton for changes in a matte painting, scribbled a note to his boss: "Getting damned hard to please these 'B' producers."

Linwood Dunn, chief of the optical department, composited a beautifully crafted dream montage of graceful, animated art deco panthers, and diffused images of Tom Conway in ancient armor brandishing a sword, a crucial image in the story. He also supplied special transitional wipes that were deliberately soft edged and uneven so as to resemble amorphous shadows crossing the screen.

The most memorable optical effect shows Simone Simon beginning to change into a cat after being kissed by Tom Conway. It had been decided to avoid any scenes showing an actual metamorphosis from woman to panther, but upon viewing the sequence Tourneur and Lewton agreed that the closeup of the baby-faced actress backing away from the camera failed to convey sufficient menace to justify the following cut of Conway recoiling in horror. "There was no preparation of any kind for the effect, otherwise it would have been easy," Dunn said. "I made her darken by a complicated application of density manipulation and masking."

Principal photography for ***Cat People*** was completed in 24 days with a budget of $118,948, quickly revised to $141,659 after shooting began. The picture was actually brought in *under* budget at $134,959. Ostrow wanted to fire Tourneur after viewing the first three days of rushes, but once again Koerner supported Lewton and the production proceeded smoothly.

Some of the department heads grumbled about Lewton's fastidiousness, which extended even to the credit titles. He insisted that the writing credit be changed to "Written by . . ." instead of "Original Screen Play by . . ." because it would make a "smoother and more tasteful" title card. Having cleared this point with the screenwriters guild, he had the writer's card moved from its customary position (preceeding the technical credits) to appear between the producer and director credits. Lewton believed the writer should receive equal recognition with the director and producer.

Lewton also insisted upon opening and closing the film with literary quotations—an uncommon delicacy even among the more pretentious films of the time. The film is prefaced by a quote from a work supposedly by Dr. Louis Judd, *The Atavism of Fear*: "Even as fog continues to lie in the valleys, so does ancient sin cling to the low places, the depressions in the world's consciousness." Instead of the traditional end title, a quotation from John Donne's Holy Sonnet V appears: "But black sin has condemn'd to endless night / My world, both parts, and both parts must die."

The preview was a great success—much to the amazement of most of the studio executives. It was decided, however, that the panther, which had been represented in the original version only by indistinct shadows, must be shown in the sequence where it threatens Oliver and Alice in his drafting room at work. Trainer Mel Koontz and his panther were brought back for one day of filming. Through clever staging by Tourneur and cutting by Robson, the three obligatory cuts of the cat seem almost imaginary, yet are sufficiently palpable to satisfy the demands of the more literal minded.

Cat People proved to be a big money maker, outgrossing much bigger pictures in many cities. It also received wide acclaim within the industry. David Selznick, in a letter to Koerner, said, "I wish that other studios were turning out small budget pictures that were comparable in intelligence and taste with Lewton's first film."

But the film is not totally flawless; there are occasional clumsy moments and the Lewton-Tourneur team is a bit too continental to put over the idea of ordinary working people with complete conviction. It is a classic, nevertheless, both for its own intrinsic value and, as a turning point in the genre, with its effectively macabre style that relied on suggesting the presence of the monster without actually showing it. This technique has been often imitated, but rarely improved upon.

While it is a story of good versus evil, it is hardly as simplistic as that. Irena is driven to evil by forces beyond her control, as are the central characters in all of Lewton's horror films. The title character of Lewton's ***The Leopard Man*** states the case perfectly as he watches a ball dancing in the jet of a fountain: "We know as little of the forces that move us and move the world around us as that empty ball."

Simone Simon captures Irena's ambivalent nature very well. Her natural child-like charm is disarming. She conveys quickly that she is fear-ridden, but it is only gradually that she betrays any hint of the sinister. Kent Smith and Jane Randolph are sufficiently down-to-earth to create a realistic ambience that makes the fantasy more believable. Conway is a convincing Dr. Judd, a role that could have been inexplicable if less skillfully played.

Both Musuraca's photography and Keller's sets are perfectly keyed. Interiors have the kind of delicate shadings found in fine etchings, with rich shadows and striking highlights. The exteriors are also strong on atmosphere, with change of seasons clearly defined, from the Indian summer beginning through the rain, snow and mist of winter.

The use of sound is equally creative. The distant noises of the omnipresent zoo animals, the terrifying echos in the swimming pool, the clacking of high heels during a chase through the park, the sudden hush as the pursuit becomes a silent one, the rustling of leaves in darkness, the nerve-jarring hissing of air brakes on a bus at the instant one expects a deadly panther to leap into the scene—these are sounds cunningly married to the visuals to inspire unease, fear, suspense and shock. The bus gag proved so successful that Lewton used it in other films and whether the intruder was a train, a horse, a tumbleweed or an Apache warrior, Lewton always called it a "bus."

Roy Webb's music conveys an undercurrent of menace without becoming obtrusive, adding immeasurably to the gathering atmosphere of dread. It meshes perfectly with Musuraca's photographic style (the teaming was often repeated). The deployment of Irena's childish song as counterpoint to a heavily dramatic theme is ingenious.

The subtleties of the film are too numerous to catalogue. There are, for example, the cat images that permeate the scenes. The most prominent prop in Irena's apartment is a folding screen upon which is painted a handsome art deco panther slinking through the jungle, a motif introduced earlier as a title background. A Goya print in which cats appear hangs in the apartment, and there are tiger lilies in a florist shop window. And there is a nice moment when Alice, shuddering because she senses she is being watched, explains that "A cat just walked over my grave." Perhaps some of the psychological fear that dominates ***Cat People*** derives from the fact that Lewton himself had what he called "an atavistic fear of cats."

Lewton went on to produce 10 more pictures for RKO, all but two of them in the horror genre. All were distinctive; several approached perfection. They were: ***I Walked with a Zombie, The Leopard Man, The Seventh Victim*** and ***The Ghostship (1943); The Curse of the Cat People, Youth Runs Wild*** and ***Mademoiselle Fifi (1944); Isle of the Dead*** and ***The Body Snatcher (1945);*** and ***Bedlam*** *(1946)*. All were predicated like ***Cat People*** on "intelligence and taste" and, as the titles suggest, all were exploited in the most lurid manner. Lewton was thoroughly disenchanted with RKO by the mid-'40s, and after Koerner died of leukemia, he realized he could never achieve his ambitions there.

Unfortunately, he was never satisfied with his work again. During stints at Paramount and MGM, he produced what he considered his worst pictures and an attempt to form an independent company failed after a series of disagreements. Only for his last production, a Technicolor western called ***Apache Drums*** (1951), did he get back to the formulas he established with his RKO films, using suspense, terror, psychological insight and artistry to great effect. He died in March of 1951 while engaged on preproduction work for the Stanley Kramer Company.

The other members of the RKO horror unit went on with long and illustrious careers. Tourneur, who directed two other Lewton films ***(I Walked with a Zombie*** and ***The Leopard Man)***, directed a total of 28 pictures. Mark Robson and Robert Wise, who both started as editors, eventually directed films for Lewton. Wise directed ***The Curse of the Cat People, The Body Snatcher*** and went on to direct *The Day the Earth Stood Still* and *The Andromeda Strain.*

DeWitt Bodeen was promoted after writing ***Seventh Victim*** and ***The Curse of the Cat People***, and contributed scripts for many successful pictures, including I *Remember Mama* (1947) and *Billy Budd* (1962). Though it reteamed Kent Smith and Simone Simon, ***The Curse of the Cat People*** was an oblique followup to the original with a totally different slant, a poetic fantasy centering on Oliver's little daughter, who conjures up Irena as a benign, imaginary playmate.

"I think it's overrated," said Bodeen of the followup. "Val and I had a dispute over it because he completely rewrote the ending I'd done. I think his ending ruined it. [Lewton's ending suggests Irena's spirit is purely imaginary.] I wanted it to be more supernatural, more of a horror story. Lewton resented being considered a horror specialist, I think. But it was what he did best."

In a 1944 press release, Lewton summed up his approach to the horror film in one short paragraph. He was speaking of ***The Seventh Victim***, but the formula applies to ***Cat People*** as well:

"This picture's appeal, like that of its predecessors, is based on three fundamental theories," he said. "First is that audiences will people any patch of prepared darkness with more horror, suspense and frightfulness than the most imaginative writer could dream up. Second, and most important, is the fact that extraordinary things can happen to very ordinary people. And third is to use the beauty of the setting and camera work to ward off audience laughter at situations which, when less beautifully photographed, might seem ludicrous."

By these means was Val Lewton able to dramatize man's natural fear of the unknown, of things that can't be seen but only imagined. Through the resources of the cinema he expressed the universal, primitive fears and superstitions that survive in all of us.

J. P. Telotte (essay date 1982)

SOURCE: "The Horror Mythos and Val Lewton's *Isle of the Dead,*" in *Journal of Popular Film and Television*, Vol. 10, No. 3 Fall, 1982, pp. 119-29.

[*Telotte is a film scholar and educator whose well-respected books include* Dreams of Darkness: Fantasy and the Films of Val Lewton (*1985*) *and* Voices in the Dark: The Narrative Patterns of Film Noir (*1989*). *In the following essay, he discusses the ways in which Lewton's horror films—specifically* Isle of the Dead—*embody and transform fundamentally mythic notions about the individual's relation to the world.*]

> We return to Greece in order to rediscover the archetypes of our mind and of our culture. Fantasy returns there to become archetypal. By stepping back into the mythic, into what is nonfactual and nonhistorical, the psyche can reimagine its factual, historical predicaments from another vantage point.
>
> —James Hillman, *Re-Visioning Psychology*

Myths, Claude Lévi-Strauss hints, have both creative and destructive functions. On the one hand, they provide man with "a logical model capable of overcoming a contradiction" in his culture, while on the other, they act as "instruments for the obliteration of time," effectively blasting away our preconcern with that cultural present and a personal history, and replacing it with another, ahistorical mode of thinking [Claude Lévi-Strauss, "The Structural Study of Myth," in his *Structural Anthropology*, translated by Claire Jacobson and Brooke Schoepf, 1967; and "Overture," in his *The Raw and the Cooked*, translated by John and Doreen Weightman, 1969]. While myth helps us cope with our problems, then, it does so at the price of ego reduction, as it enjoins a way of thinking that removes man from his singular, historical identity, even as it regenerates the larger and continuing human community of which he is a part. In the popular mythology of the movies, this dual function probably surfaces most clearly in the horror genre. As Stuart Kaminsky notes [in *American Film Genres*, 1974], its subjects are "mythic presentations of universal concerns and fears," and its form derives from the shocks and surprises which can be suddenly revealed in every shadow or innocent appearance. Moreover, it helps us resolve or bear with cultural problems in what seems a most ego-threatening way, its most beneficial effects deriving from the manner in which it challenges the way we think about ourselves and our world. Val Lewton understood this mythic underpinning particularly well and used it to create a singular body of horror films, beginning with ***The Cat People*** (1942) and culminating with his last RKO production, ***Bedlam*** (1946). The best of the Lewton unit's films foreground their genre's basic mythos and thereby reveal not only those underlying archetypal concerns of the horror film, but also a manner of thinking about man and his world which lies at the core of all myth.

It is the particular way the Lewton works mirror and transform this horror mythos which distinguishes them from the normal run of such genre pieces. Most horror films place the viewer within a realm that is deceptively quotidian, and through a series of jolting encounters with previously unseen terrors, they then suggest a need for greater awareness and caution as one goes about his daily affairs. Some monstrous presence typically serves as a catalyst, embodying our anxieties or serving to visualize what Robin Wood terms "our collective nightmares," thereby enabling us to cope with them "in more radical ways" than our consciousness might otherwise countenance ["Return of the Repressed," *Film Comment*, July-August 1978]. The Lewton films differ mainly in their consistent focus on the internal and intangible rather than on what lies threateningly "out there," as they reveal the manifestly inadequate mental picture his characters have of their world, yet their reluctance to reformulate that perspective in light of their obvious limitations. Irena Dubrovna of ***The Cat People***, for instance, a Serbian immigrant living in New York, finds herself even in the midst of that model of modern civilization still beset by the legend that, when emotionally aroused, her people can change into murderous cats. As a result, she isolates herself, projecting a fearful animistic universe in which she attempts to live regardless of the consequences. A clear counterbalance to this depiction of a mind paralyzed by legend occurs appropriately in this film's sequel, ***Curse of the Cat People***, wherein Irena's husband Oliver suffers from a similarly debilitating but rationalist perspective. He repeatedly tries to reason his daughter Amy out of her recurrent fantasies—which she uses to fill the human gaps in her world—and his denial of that fantasy life nearly leads to disaster. In the characters of Irena and Oliver we see the two poles around which most of the Lewton films circled, the superstitious and the rational, two methods of thinking about and structuring the world man inhabits, though neither truly commensurate with the human experience.

An examination of the various ways in which the Lewton films depict man thinking about his world and attempting to formulate its threatening presences does, I believe, lead us back to the fundamental strategies of the horror film and help us to better understand why these entries in the genre are so highly regarded. Underlying the mythos of horror is a natural and probably even necessary desire in some way to account for that which defies explanation, and so render it less threatening to the human community. We do this through what might be termed "mythic thinking," that is, the tendency "to build up structures by fitting together events" which otherwise seem meaningless [Lévi-Strauss, *The Savage Mind*, 1966]. It does not represent an attempt to deny mystery or ambiguity, but rather to ascribe a name to that perceived openness and thus draw the namer—man—into its mysterious realm. And since, as Joseph Campbell points out, the basic elements of myth "are not manufactured; they cannot be ordered, invented, or permanently suppressed. They are spontaneous productions of the psyche, and each bears within it, undamaged, the germ power of its source" [*The Hero with a Thousand Faces*, 1956], mythic thinking actually admits man's limitations, acknowledging that the most fundamental mysteries really lie *within*, sourced in the psyche itself. It, therefore, affords a basic means of dealing with that monstrous presence, more precisely the absence or void which lies at the center of the self, upwelling from time to time to remind us of how tentative our place in the world remains.

In contrast, our rational thinking attempts to vanquish all trace of the unknown, the mysterious, and hence the frightening, first by denying that internal enigma, and then by enclosing the world and the self within a secure, humanly imposed order. Historically, we have sought to dispel the mythic with reason, to evaporate mythic thought into the solutions of science, psychology, or anthropology; and one of the horror film's projects has always been to respond to this tendency, through the monstrous presences it fashions reasserting the existence of the mysterious and uncontrollable. This rational thinking afforded the Lewton films their most consistent target, one which was probably hit most accurately in ***Bedlam***, wherein an insane asylum's inmates are shown to be, for all their infirmities, more humane and understanding than those people of the Age of Reason who created this institution to hold them. By persistently projecting our rational tendency against the horror film's mythic backdrop, the Lewton films successfully evoke the very essence of the genre; they conjure a vision of those most elemental and powerful forces in man and his world which, despite our modern efforts, still deny appeasement and disconcertingly confront us with our very human limits.

Isle of the Dead (1945) brings together both the rational and superstitious impulses of the earlier films, contrasting them with the perspective afforded by mythic thought. Like ***The Cat People***, it announces in an opening epigraph a concern with the place of myth in human consciousness: "Under conquest and oppression the people of Greece allowed their legends to disintegrate into superstition; the goddess Aphrodite giving way to the Vorvolaka. This nightmare figure was very much alive in the minds of the peasants when Greece fought the victorious war of 1912." This signpost links the early twentieth-century events with which the narrative is concerned to Western man's classical cultural heritage—his inheritance of tragedy and philosophy, of Dionysian and Appollonian impulses—and also to a crucial shift in his manner of thinking. In the course of Western history, the film suggests, a mythic way of thinking about the world and our place in it has decayed and been transformed into the extremes of a fearful superstition and a proud rationalism which places man, with all of his violent capacities, at the center of this world—from which point he futilely asserts an ability to explain and control all around him.

Despite that decay, a tension lingers here, as the opening close-up of the victorious General Pherides (Boris Karloff) washing his hands reveals. While cleaning, he listens as Colonel Tolopedes (Sherry Hall) explains his regiment's failure in the recent battle, and he then hands the Colonel a pistol with which he may kill himself to "honorably" resolve the matter. This harsh response hints at Pherides' reasoned pragmatism, a concern only for results; it is, he admits, "my way, the only way I know." Overlaid on this cause-effect consciousness, however, is a mythic resonance, that sanitary impulse suggesting a sort of ritual cleansing. In refusing the Colonel's pleadings, Pherides invariably resembles a modern Pilate, denying personal responsibility for the scapegoat-like punishment of his "friend." We, thus, immediately glimpse two systems of thought at work, the modern and the mythic, the latter persisting to color the way we perceive even the most common actions, even while its opposite is almost violently affirmed.

In this violent world individual and general destruction are decreed by man himself, and for a cause that is never made clear. René Girard theorizes that such a tendency to violence inheres in the human spirit, and that the primary function of myth and ritual is to exorcize such impulses before they rend man's world apart. In this way the human community is effectively "engendered by" its myths since they represent a shared response to that impending threat and foster a "cultural unanimity" in its expulsion [*Violence and the Sacred*, translated by Patrick Gregory, 1977]. What the rampant violence in ***Isle of the Dead*** might suggest is a deterioration of that mythic consciousness and the return of those dangerous forces, formerly projected into an animate universe, to reside in the self. The plague which breaks out following this recent battle and which becomes the film's central focus, then, might be seen as a self-induced affliction due to those violent impulses going unchecked by mythic representation. In fact, in discussing the plague as a recurrent literary motif, Girard terms it an archetypal affliction and "a disguise for an even more terrible threat that no science has ever been able to conquer" ["The Plague in Literature and Myth," *Texas Studies in Literature and Language* 15, 1974]. In essence, he suggests that we view it as "a generic label for a variety of ills that affect the community as a whole and threaten or seem to threaten the very existence of social life. It may be inferred from various signs that inter-human tensions and disturbances often play the crucial role." In ***Isle of the Dead*** the plague serves as a telling transformation of the monsters of horror film tradition; here they go disguised, wearing the masks of men, and fragile indeed, the film suggests, are the cultural ties which may hold those masks in place.

A lethal atmosphere, therefore, naturally rises from that Greek victory and threatens to spread, to visit its violence on the larger community yet untouched. As the General reminds, "The horseman on the pale horse is pestilence. He follows the wars" and threatens to render these human "accomplishments" meaningless: "If it isn't stopped, our victories on the field will mean nothing." That vain preconcern man has with giving *meaning* to all his actions, especially the most senselessly violent, is a common target of Lewton's films, and it is immediately scored here. Pherides and Oliver Davis (Marc Cramer), correspondent for the *Boston Star*, tour the battlefield, and as they discuss the plague's threat amid the grotesque, corpse-littered landscape, any sense of meaning behind this violence quickly vanishes. Even that sanitary impulse glimpsed in the film's opening has been pushed to an extreme and transformed here as Dr. Drossos (Ernst Dorian), his death cart piled high with corpses, hurries about cleaning up the battlefield to prevent the plague's spread. This new "enemy" which Pherides and Drossos must now combat functions as an emblem of that innate human violence which has been unleashed in the war; it is an invisible threat replacing those traditional monsters of the horror genre in order to better point up the specifically human "tensions and disturbances" prevalent here. Unable—or unwilling—to recognize this fundamental connection, General Pherides simply assumes he can control the plague, just as he controls his army, and through his army, his enemies. By the proper application of force—physical and mental—he feels he can enclose his world in his own ordained meaning and keep those upwelling violent forces in check.

Wherever he goes, though, so too goes the plague, constantly challenging that modern consciousness which has put aside myth and its implicit admission of society's fragility. Together with Davis, the General travels to a nearby island to visit his wife's grave, only to find that the plague has followed him. Appropriately, this island cemetery is a place at once redolent of myth, yet a reminder of the decay into which it has fallen. When

Pherides and Davis arrive, for example, they are met by an imposing statue of Cerberus, watchdog of the ancient gods and guardian of the gates of Hades. It seems an appropriate sentry for the island, though Davis sees in it something more, a likeness to his companion, whom he has earlier derisively described as "the watchdog" of Greece; "There's another watchdog for you," he now chides the General, who disavows the similarity, reminding Oliver that Cerberus "only guards the dead; I have to worry about the living." The statue subsequently becomes a haunting presence, a key transitional device whose grimacing heads remind us of Pherides and his menacing aspect and serves to cast a more threatening light on his supposedly beneficent watchfulness and protective militarism.

At the same time, the island's very history bespeaks that widespread loss of mythic consciousness. The General cannot find his wife's body in its crypt because the original inhabitants have long since plundered the island's tombs and burned the disinterred bodies. This impiety resulted from the intrusion of the modern world with its new system of values and rational perspective on life and death. Upon beginning his research in the area, the Swiss archaeologist Albrecht (Jason Robards, Sr.) offered the islanders money for any artifacts they might turn up, and they obligingly put aside any lingering reverence for their ancient gods, as well as those cultural taboos against violation of the dead, to pillage the ancient sites. That step precipitated an even greater falling off, seen in their subsequent plundering of all the island's tombs in search of other prizes. Too late Albrecht realized that "unwittingly I had turned good, simple people into graverobbers," who in turn abandoned their island when no more easy riches were to be found. Only his housekeeper Madame Kyra (Helene Thimig) remains from that broken community, and she lives within her own fallen world of superstition. Without the bond of myth apparently, only science and superstition, two equally incommensurate perspectives, survive in this fragmented world. It is on such a stage that we then witness the effects of that mythic decay on the people who have sought sanctuary from the war, that man-made plague: the British consul St. Aubyn (Alan Napier) and his wife (Katherine Emery), their servant Thea (Ellen Drew), the tinware merchant Robbins (Skelton Knaggs), as well as Albrecht, Kyra, the General, Davis, and later Dr. Drossos. Through them, we see how man, once deprived of his myths, attempts to cope with visitations like the plague—not by recognizing its human source and letting that original "mistake" run its course, not by simply acknowledging man's impotence in the face of an enigmatic and powerful nature, but by stubbornly defying that inexorable force, termed Fate by the ancients, and asserting his own control through his rational powers. In the ongoing breakdown of human society seen here, ***Isle of the Dead*** demonstrates our feeble capacity for controlling that world we inhabit, as well as the fragility of that human community in the face of its own internally generated corrosive forces.

Control is, of course, the General's obsession and the characteristic which most keeps him apart from the island's civilian inhabitants. Before the war, we learn, Pherides collected taxes from the peasants with field artillery, firing on his own people because "the laws" dictated it, and in his eyes anyone "who is against the laws of Greece is not a Greek" and is, therefore, dangerous. The argument advanced by the peasant girl Thea, that "laws can be wrong and laws can be cruel, and the people who live only by the law are both wrong and cruel," seems irrelevant to him. Denying his own peasant background, Pherides sees himself as part of a new order, a Greece which has left behind the ancients and their divine pantheon; "These are new days for Greece. We don't believe the old, foolish tales anymore," he explains. Like Oliver Reed of ***The Cat People*** and ***Curse of the Cat People***, he describes the old legends as "nonsense," and in their place substitutes a totally rational system, putting all faith "in what I can feel, and see, and know about." In place of the gods and their powers, he pays homage to that rational perspective which he so rigidly imposes on his world with no regard for its human consequences, and certainly without recognizing the horrors and carnage it effects.

With the advent of the plague, that dominating conceptual framework with which Pherides overlays his world is cast in stark relief. He simply assumes control, declares himself the "watchdog" for this small, heterogeneous society, and decrees that "no one may leave the island." In effect, he declares war on the plague, treating it as he would an enemy. To his new "army" he commands that through Dr. Drossos "we will fight the plague," and that they "had better believe in the doctor. He's the only one who can save us." The proclamation of the myth of modern medicine further underscores that attempt to abrogate to man the primordial power of myth to explain and control his environment. Like another Greek leader whose realm was besieged by plague, King Oedipus, Pherides looks only to his own rational powers for a means of overcoming that cultural affliction, and it is the ultimate weakness of that resource which the film, like Sophocles' play, then demonstrates.

What ***Isle of the Dead*** suggests is not that reason is inherently evil or dangerous, but that, given absolute and unquestioned power, it can easily become a threatening, even self-destructive force. To this end the film emphasizes an intimate connection between the General and Drossos, first by a form transition linking the two characters, and second through a similarity in their actions. Following the announcement that the plague has hit the island, the image of Pherides dissolves into that of Drossos, clinically describing the disease's symptoms. The General then reinforces the authority of science and the other the force which assures its sway—as he directs the people: "The doctor will tell you what to do and I will see that you do it." The doctor's measures, though, amount to little more than distraction and sanitation, neither of which affects the progress of the plague. He explains that "the disease is transmitted by fleas. Their bodies have an eighty percent moisture content. The hot wind from the south literally burns them away. If the sirocco blows, all danger will be over in twenty-four hours." To remind the people of their need for a favorable breeze, he then raises a pennant, a device which, he admits, is meant to distract them from a situation over which they all ultimately have no control: "Better to watch the wind and hope that it changes than to watch each other and have no hope at all." His sanitary precautions have little more effect, since they simply involve washing after every contact with another person. In fact, the medium shot which shows him washing his hands, demonstrating this precaution, only underscores his similarity to the General by recalling the film's opening, while it also points up the essential futility of these actions. When Drossos warns against any personal interaction and suggests that they wash afterwards, both Madame Kyra and Albrecht protest, the former reminding him that "you cannot wash away evil," and the latter holding that the plague is the work of the gods and thus immune to human precaution; "The doctor can use his science; I'll pray to Hermes," he asserts. Those sanitary measures are, in any case, immediately undercut as the General, after washing, reaches out to shake hands with Albrecht, who immediately calls his attention to this violation of his own rules. It is Drossos' subsequent death by the plague, though, preceded by his admission that the ancient gods "are more powerful than my science," which most clearly completes the questioning of this rational perspective.

The injunction against contact with others also underscores the breakdown of the human community which inevitably accompanies the plague, since that precaution dictates isolation from anyone who might be a carrier of the disease. It is an approach which forces each person to view the others with suspicion—an attitude especially marked in the case of Madame Kyra who suspects the girl Thea of being a vorvolaka and thus the cause of their affliction. As the opening epigraph states, Kyra's superstitions signal a first step in the decay of myth and suggest as well the flaw in the modern, rationalistic view espoused by the General and Drossos. As Girard and others note, mythic consciousness enjoins community by embodying a threat in an external figure, against which communal unanimity can be mustered. Both Kyra's superstitious mind, seeing in Thea "an evil for which the gods punish us mortals," and that rational, "sanitary" perspective create separation and fragment the community; only the stated reasons for that isolation differ. Given this context, we can perhaps better understand why Pherides, weakened by the plague and Kyra's harpings, so easily slips into her superstitious way of thinking and also threatens Thea. As Oliver warns him, there is a subtler danger here, lodged not in the plague but within man, especially the way in which he conceives of his world: "There is something here more dangerous than septicemic plague—more dangerous as far as Thea is concerned—and that's your own crazy thoughts about her." More precisely, it is that desire for control, for a closure of ambiguity, which is firmly lodged in man's mind and which takes shape in those rational and superstitious attitudes alike.

Ironically, it is precisely because she looks so healthy and beautiful, so "full of life" as Mrs. St. Aubyn notes, that Thea is suspected of being a vorvolaka and carrying into their midst "a contagion of the soul." When death and decay seem the order of the day, life itself can become suspect, largely because its almost miraculous flourishing in that context seems to defy understanding. This persistence of the inexplicable again points up the weakness in those rational and superstitious attitudes, as we see when Pherides inquires how he is different from the others in his reaction to the plague; Oliver explains that the others "sort of take it, accept it, but you're fighting it. It seems to me you're fighting something bigger than the plague, wrestling with something you can't see. Kyra too." That "something bigger" is his almost consuming desire to explain away troubling uncertainties, to dispel any unsettling complexity from the human realm. As a result, though, both Pherides and Kyra risk becoming themselves a source of violence by dredging up from within an obsessive and dangerous force; as Mrs. St. Aubyn cautions the General, "Evil breeds evil and in the end it will be you yourself who will suffer."

Of course, it is always the victim who first suffers, in this case Thea who is constantly watched and accused. Kyra stays awake at night hoping to catch her in some "evil," and after Drossos fails him, Pherides too watches and attempts to isolate Thea from the others, especially Oliver who is in love with her. Once planted, that seed of suspicion takes such deep root that it even undermines Thea's view of herself, bringing her to question her possible influence on Mrs. St. Aubyn's poor health. Despite her mistress' reassurance that she is "good . . . kind and generous. How can anything bad come from goodness?" Thea fears she could harbor some evil which her conscious mind cannot detect, and when Mrs. St. Aubyn slips into a death-like trance, she honestly wonders, "It is my fault?" In her troubled state, we see once more the fragility of reason, how easily it can be turned against the self, questioning all that is not consciousness. If we recall the film's opening commentary on the degeneration of Aphrodite, the goddess of love and beauty, into the vorvolaka, a figure of life-draining evil, we might also understand how Thea helps point up that mythic decay which haunts the narrative. Almost an embodiment of Aphrodite, Thea—whose very name means "goddess"—is a beautiful young girl who brings the possibility of love into this death-filled world; yet she is eyed suspiciously for her beauty and life. Man has here come to such a state that beauty can be thought a thing of evil, love can be denied, and the human spirit can be suspected of being sinister and potentially threatening simply because that fear of the unknown and compulsion for rationalism remain strong.

The name Aphrodite, we might also recall, derives from the Greek word for "foam" or "surf," and literally means "born from the foam." It is an appellation which helps to link a number of the film's themes, especially that of mythic decay, the suspicion of Thea, and those recurrent scenes of washing, a few of which we have already noted. After each victim of the plague is buried, for instance, we always see the ritualistic cleansing carried out, despite its rather obvious futility. To show how compulsive this action becomes, a series of symbolic shots is inserted at the height of the plague's onslaught; it is of many hands scrubbing in a pool of dark swirling water, in fact, a montage of washing hands intercut with several shots of the surf crashing on the island's rocky cliffs. These shots evoke that association to Aphrodite and, thus, ironically comment upon this urge for sanitation, for those shots of the surf evoke in the mythic consciousness the goddess of love and the power of life which both she and the water from which she was born represent. With that association forgotten, however, water becomes affiliated with sterility and the people see in their world a place hostile to love, beauty, and life. Only after many deaths, including the doctor's, is the ineffectual nature of that washing made clear and the attitude behind it called into question. Appropriately, it is Albrecht, the scientist whose experience has converted him to a mythic consciousness, even spurred him to pray to Hermes, god of healers, for aid, who finally announces that this washing "does no good" and that "it would serve our purpose a great deal more to join in prayer." What he essentially affirms, of course, is the fundamental power of "belief," especially a communal belief, to bring some fellow comfort into this threatened and threatening world; hence, his comment that "To believe, to pray, even if only to some pagan god, so long as belief is there, it brings comfort." This simple philosophy hints at the very essence of what I have termed mythic thinking, as it suggests man's need—and his capacity—to locate some hope or assert a communal strength in the face of a disconcerting, even chaotic moment; even in the avowal of human limitation, a comfort can be found.

The alternative to such a mythic view, it seems, is to lodge that threat, that dangerous violence which appears to haunt man, solely within the self, through reason or a suspicious superstition effectively transforming the self into some threatening presence. In attempting to exorcize monsters from our thoughts and world, the film implies, we always run the risk of becoming that sort of monstrous, disintegrative force we fear. As the film *Forbidden Planet* illustrated, uncontrollable "monsters from the Id" ever stand ready for liberation into a world that is hardly a match for them. What ***Isle of the Dead*** underscores are two equally threatening forms that monstrousness may take: first, its inherently self-destructive nature, and second, its disintegrative influence on the community itself.

General Pherides clearly demonstrates the former danger, as his authoritative, self-assured rationalism gradually gives way to a superstitious and clearly dangerous mania. Of course, casting Boris Karloff in the role almost automatically prepares us for such a frightening transformation, since he brings resonances of his earlier monster portrayals; his role here simply seems doubled, as if he were playing both Frankenstein and his creation. After trying "everything—every *human* remedy," all to no avail, Pherides turns to Kyra's superstitious explanations; his reason, pushed to its limits in seeking to maintain control, becomes unreason. Consequently, when the plague strikes him and thus underscores his helplessness, the General, keeper of "the laws," can try to murder Thea as a solution. The particular form of the plague which has struck and precipitated his delirious state seems carefully selected to comment on this circumstance. Bearing no visible signs other than a change in behavior which marks its final stages, the septicemic plague essentially eats away at the vitals, specifically the blood stream. As its etymology suggests, it is a kind of cancerous rotting from within, which hints at an internal danger to which man is prone, a self-destructive violence or decay he may set in motion with the eventual abandonment of a mythic consciousness.

A correlative danger naturally accompanies this degeneration of mythic unanimity, namely the loss of community. The island society, like Pherides' army, is being decimated by the plague, and even the spirit of community is eroding. Each person eyes the others suspiciously, wondering who might be carrying the sickness that could bring him death. In Mrs. St. Aubyn we see the most subtle example of this decay. She refrains from burdening the others with her fears of premature burial resulting from a history of catalepsy, so only her husband and Drossos know of the problem. When both of them die, she is left essentially alone with her fears, isolated from the others who have their own, more immediately pressing anxieties with which to cope. When such a trance occurs, therefore, it is mistaken for but another visitation of the plague, and Mrs. St. Aubyn is buried like the others—mute testimony to the frailty of the modernist view which cannot even discriminate between life and death. Her interment alive, of course, only completes that ongoing pattern of isolation and eventual destruction of the ego which naturally accompanies a loss of community.

Mrs. St. Aubyn's premature burial also points up one of Lewton's subtler revisions of the traditional horror formula. While the genre typically evokes some monstrous presence or external threat to embody its elemental dangers and drive home its cautionary message, the consul's timid wife assumes that role here. Driven mad by her interment, she is transformed into just the sort of murderous being that usually haunts such films. And if, as suggested, the plague and accompanying violence here correlate to a degeneration of mythic thinking, then the victims of her murderous rampage are most appropriate, demonstrating the sort of ironic justice which pervades classical legend and literature. Seizing one of the artifacts Albrecht has been studying, a version of Neptune's trident, Mrs. St. Aubyn stabs both Kyra and Pherides, the latter just as he attempts to kill Thea. That mad but timely wielding of Neptune's weapon accomplishes much: it visits the ultimate power of the mythic world upon those who have gainsaid it, reaffirms its powerful presence, and demonstrates how we often generate from within—not only from our innate capacity for violence, but also from our fear of it—our own monsters, every bit as dangerous as those which typically inhabit this genre.

That trident, we might also remember, is employed by the great "earth-shaker" to stir the oceans, creating waves and storms which might buffet mankind—the like of which we saw in the repeated shots of crashing waves on the island's coast. Its use here, then, hints at a continuing and powerful mythic presence in this world, even if it often goes unseen or denied by those who prefer to put their faith in what they "can feel, and see." Certainly it is force which reserves the last say with those who, like the General, see themselves as modern "earth-shakers."

Mrs. St. Aubyn's subsequent death elaborates upon this mythic motif, for after killing Pherides and Kyra, she rushes outdoors, hair streaming in maenad-like frenzy, and plunges from a cliff into the sea, back to Neptune's world, as it were. We view this sudden climax in what is easily the film's most careful composition. Mrs. St. Aubyn enters a perfectly balanced frame, to the left the remains of an ancient temple, a single doric column marking its margin, and to the right a wooded area with an old, gnarled tree rising from its edge. Between these almost archetypal signs of culture and nature, she rushes to her death, demonstrating thereby the tragic result when these two realms fail to come together. Without the force of myth, we understand, the psyche cannot bind the natural and the human worlds—the wild and the cultured, the superstitious and the rational—into a humanly meaningful pattern.

The film's closing images then provide eloquent testimony to the tentative reconciliation between man and his mythic heritage which this violent purging effects. As a shot of Drossos' pennant shows, the long-awaited sirocco arises, heralding the end of the plague and of the General and his reign of reason. And following Mrs. St. Aubyn's death, we see the General's dead face in close-up, frozen into a fearful stare which makes him seem all the more like a human watchdog, counterpart to the haunting figure of Cerberus. His image then dissolves into a long shot of Oliver and Thea leaving the island, their departure watched over by Albrecht on the left and the statue of Cerberus on the right; in a longer shot, Cerberus' image is then juxtaposed over that of the couple in their boat. In these various images, especially the pairing of Albrecht and Cerberus, we see a science brought back into some harmony with myth. That sense of mystery which myth points up in both man and his world, and the inexorable and unpredictable forces it recognizes therein have been affirmed with the beneficial effects which traditionally attend a culture's mythmaking. Although myth-haunted, as Cerberus' superimposed image attests, Oliver and Thea can depart from this "isle of the dead," and their love, proscribed by Pherides and Kyra, might flourish. Love and life have thus replaced war; a couple united in mutual care and mindful of their fragile happiness supercedes the individual who, in his hubris, washed his hands of human responsibility. In more archetypal terms, the Jungian *shadow*, the projected dark side of human nature, has been subsumed into a *persona* and *anima* brought into their proper harmonious relation; and this archetypal marriage has been effected and a renewed sense of community is made possible by "stepping back into the mythic" and experiencing its power.

Isle of the Dead accomplishes this psychic and communal rejuvenation largely through the repetition of two central image patterns. We have traced out the developing imagery of washing in which water comes to suggest not only life, but sterilization and a denial of human complicity. In this usage, its archetypal life-affirming characteristics are undercut, as the powers of Neptune, god of the sea, are symbolically usurped by man. This particular repetition, therefore, emphasizes the human impulse for power and control in order to reveal its inevitable consequences. The recurring image of Cerberus, on the other hand, works in a different manner. In its monstrous aspect, it stands out from the environment and, despite its stony solidity, seems to come alive as the film progresses. Its recurrent appearances, however, only haunt this world with a reminder of something permanent, not subject to change, of that mythic realm whose influence modern man seeks to deny or appropriate as his own.

The two styles of repetition which these recurring images demonstrate afford an added commentary on the theme of change and permanence here. As Bruce Kawin has shown, these forms of repetition—the developing image and the recurring image—correspond to our different ways of representing time. The former implies a "time that builds," what we might term a human sense of history, and the latter a time "that is always present, time that continues," in fact, a sort of timelessness [*Telling it Again and Again; Repetition in Literature and Film*, 1972]. The film thus develops a complementarity between these two time schemes—that of man and that of myth, that of change and of the truths which defy all change, ultimately, that of life and of death as well. The film's opening epigraph describes a sense of historical development which allows us to forget about the ahistorical or eternal verities. The final image, however, evokes a constant presence—a presence that casts the present in a new light, just as the knowledge of death does the experience of life. From this perspective the single moment fruitfully opens into a vast horizon of time—mythic time—an eternity in which man finds himself immersed as he often frustratingly tries to sift some sense from his short life. What the Lewton unit's particular horror formula demonstrates is how myth might energize the present with its presence, by transporting man from an isolated, dead world to a larger, if equally unsettling world of the living in which, with some pain and effort, he might hopefully reside.

A great appeal of the horror film, of course, is that it always seems to strike such a universal chord, revealing our common fears and awakening us not *from* but *to* our collective anxieties. If the responses the genre evokes often appear predictable or its mechanisms too easily copied, we might simply interpret this as evidence of its truly archetypal value. The Lewton films more pointedly than many works of the genre call attention to this value. In fact, they suggest that the very persistence of such archetypes in our thinking is most significant. Those mythic presences remind us of our inability to control or demystify both the world and the self, even as they point to man's capacity to find a communal comfort in the collective confrontation with mystery which he so eagerly seeks out on the movie screen.

J. P. Telotte (essay date 1982)

SOURCE: "A Photogenic Horror: Lewton Does Robert Louis Stevenson," in *Literature/Film Quarterly*, Vol. 10, No. 1, 1982, pp. 25-37.

[*In the following essay, Telotte examines the specifically cinematic qualities of Lewton's adaptation of Robert Louis Stevenson's short story "The Body Snatcher" (1895).*]

Before becoming a story editor for David Selznick and then going on to produce his famous series of B-films at RKO, Val Lewton had embarked on a writing career, working first as a reporter and then churning out a broad range of historical novels, romances, and thrillers. That literary background apparently served him well in his film work, for according to his associates he "rewrote everything that his writers turned in; the last draft [of each script] was always his" [Joel Siegel, *Val Lewton: The Reality of Terror*, 1973]. Perhaps more importantly, he made that literary atmosphere felt everywhere in his productions; as Mark Robson, director of five Lewton films, recalls, "we were sort of brainwashed, in a way—brainwashed into thinking in poetic terms" [quoted in Joseph McBride, "Val Lewton, Director's Producer," *Action*, January-February 1976]. However, that almost tangible literary quality for which the Lewton films are justly esteemed has often made for a strangely *uncinematic* evaluation of them. They have been praised as "ambitiously literary," "poetic," and have been lauded for *what they did not show*, as if their success were largely due to Lewton's prizing literary techniques over established film practices. Certainly he sought to tone down the conventional grotesquery of the horror genre in which he most frequently worked, eliminating the spectacular monsters and ghouls with which his competitors at Universal Studios had been so successful. In place of what he termed those "masklike faces hardly human, with gnashing teeth and hair standing on end" [McBride], Lewton strove for a subtler form of the grotesque; yet it was one which indeed thrived on distinctly cinematic techniques of narrative.

Lewton's adaptation of Robert Louis Stevenson's story, "The Body-Snatcher," may best exemplify what he added over and above the "literary" and testify to his mindfulness of cinematic practice. In order to bring that Victorian horror story to the screen, Lewton fully reworked the tale's structure and characterization to such an extent that, for one of the few times in his career, he took screen credit for the final script, using the pseudonym Carlos Keith, a name under which he had previously penned several novels. What he had to work from was a complex tale in which an anonymous narrator introduces an older acquaintance named Fettes and then proceeds to relate this character's past history as it was told to him. Distanced by time from the actions he reports, that narrator inexplicably breaks off his account with one horrific scene, the description of a grotesque vision or visitation once experienced by Fettes. While that frame structure involving several time periods, an intrusive narrator, and the single-effect shock ending are devices hardly alien to film narrative, they do present some obstacles in translation to the screen. Flashbacks, voice-over narration, and arresting imagery have long been the stock-in-trade of film story-telling, though each imposes limitations particularly unwelcome for the horror genre. A frame tale most often brackets the grotesque, keeping it at a less alarming temporal remove, just as a voice-over intrudes a "safe," rationalizing buffer between the audience and those horrors it recounts. The shocking image trades on film's immediate visual impact, but almost inevitably at some cost in ambiguity and complexity. The narrative effects found in Stevenson's short piece would, therefore, pose a test of cinematic skill for any adapter.

Although with far greater complexity and to more point, Henry James's *The Turn of the Screw* employs generally similar elements and narrative structure as does "The Body-Snatcher," and its famous screen adaptation, *The Innocents*, is quite effective. That film beneficially eliminates both the framework and narrator of James's story, but at the end it capitulates to our curiosity, providing an objective view of one of the tale's "ghosts," and thereby fails to achieve quite the complex and troubling ambiguity of its literary source. Given far less to work with, Lewton fares somewhat better overall with ***The Body Snatcher***, creating a film perhaps less understated than *The Innocents*, but one more complex and original in conception. Partly because of monetary restrictions and partly because he well understood the cinema's persistent and effective sense of "present tense," Lewton deleted the frame from Stevenson's tale, thus avoiding the necessity of depicting two different time periods; and with that deletion went the anonymous young narrator, whose characteristics Lewton wedded to the figure of Fettes. Knowing too that grotesque visions, given their initial shock effect, cannot stand sustained scrutiny—by the camera or the human eye—that they tend to become "something to laugh at" [McBride], Lewton altered that final horrific scene as well, giving it a pointedly hallucinatory effect. In general, he turned to distinctly filmic methods of telling his story, using complex recurring images, atmospheric and metaphoric settings, paired scenes to generate ironic effect, and identifiable characters to link scenes and plot elements visually. Although Lewton often did not *show* significant actions, relying instead on the allusive potential of character and setting, those things he depicted and the manner in which he avoided showing others demonstrate the truly cinematic sense which he brought to his many horror subjects.

Stevenson's tale, for much of its length, offers scant potential for those striking images which so easily translate to the screen; its focus is rather on a particular state of mind, that of Fettes who, while working in the dissecting laboratory of Mr. K. . . .'s medical school, became "insensible to the impressions of a life thus passed among the ensigns of mortality." In retrospect, a narrator tells of Fettes' medical schooling and of his association with a fellow student, one "Toddy" MacFarlane, whose callous example further spurred his downfall: "His mind . . . closed against all general considerations. He was incapable of interest in the fate and fortunes of another, the slave of his own desires and low ambitions." At this time the bodies used in medical study were often obtained illegally—through grave robbing or even murder—and with only slight prodding from his friend, Fettes learned "to avert the eye from any evidence of crime" for the right reward. Consequently, we follow Fettes' descent into crime as he helps MacFarlane dispose of the body of Mr. Gray, a blackmailer whom he has murdered. Together they then plot to join in the lucrative "resurrection" business, digging up bodies to sell to the various medical schools. On their initial attempt, though, "some unnatural miracle," as Stevenson describes it, transforms the body of a local farmer's wife into that of Gray. With this discovery, "a fear that was meaningless, a horror of what could not be" afflicts the grave robbers, and with this single shocking discovery and the sudden intrusion of the supernatural it suggests, the narrative breaks off. Having achieved this effect, Stevenson never returns to his narrator's perspective, to the frame of his frame-tale. Rather than belabor a rather obvious moral, he simply demonstrates the horror which the unfeeling consciousness of Fettes and MacFarlane has conjured up and allows that image to stand as a striking cautionary note.

Such startling effects might seem the norm for film horror, but they are hardly conducive to any moral complexity. While Lewton's ***The Body Snatcher*** is visually rich, it is not with such grotesque images. True, he retains a version of that shock ending provided by Stevenson's tale; however, Lewton brackets that apparition of Gray within an explanatory context and takes one of his characters beyond that simple horrific confrontation. Apparently he was much less concerned with the details of individual degradation than with the various ways in which we try to cloak or explain away those frightful aspects of our natures. He thus strove to create a sense of incongruity and employed numerous ironic juxtapositions to criticize that rationality with which we often unwittingly disguise or explain away the horrors around us. Although concerned with the complexities of human psychology, Lewton was able to fashion a decidedly photogenic horror simply by concentrating attention on the context of his characters' actions. ***The Body Snatcher*** suggests, in fact, that the grotesque lurks in our own day-to-day inhumanities and is transferred from one person to another—here from teacher to pupil as he transforms that relationship between MacFarlane and Fettes. His film consequently does more than merely shock; it is an atmospheric piece in which horrors seem almost quotidian and the meaning of being human is left open to question.

As Lewton well understood, horror is most effectively presented when a norm is established against which we may measure aberrance. With the opening specifically he conjures up that appropriate context, the texture of the commonplace, through a wealth of richly detailed images of daily life nowhere found in the original story. This visual detail drew some criticism for the film, several critics seeing in it but another example of Lewton's drift from the pure horror film to the flamboyant period piece. Joel Siegel, for one, finds the opening "too detailed to suit its function," and a further demonstration of Lewton's need for a director with a more discriminating eye, one who "could select and graphically order the screenplay's abundant materials," as Jacques Tourneur did on films like ***The Cat People*** and ***I Walked with a Zombie***. While Robert Wise, the film's director, is an admitted "stickler for realism and honesty" ["Robert Wise," *Directors at Work: Interviews with American Filmmakers*, edited by Charles Neider, Irwin R. Blacker, Anne Kramer, 1970], he is hardly one given, as Manny Farber slightingly suggests, to a "delirious . . . scenic camera work" ["Val Lewton: Unorthodox Artistry at RKO," *King of the B's* edited by Todd McCarthy and Charles Flynn, 1975]. In fact, his own theory is that careful attention to visual detail more subtly contributes to a film's effectiveness by better evoking proper characterizations. "Maybe some of the details could have been a little less thorough, might have been sloughed off a bit," he allows, "but I believe that the atmosphere that's created by some of those 'unregistering' bits of detail is very pervasive and gets to the actors; it influences them, therefore it influences the whole scene" [*Directors at Work*].

That philosophy marked Wise as a director largely in agreement with Lewton, and the success of their collaboration, I feel, is actually nowhere better attested than in those highly detailed opening scenes—all carefully laid out by Lewton in his screenplay. More than merely establishing a period setting, that opening montage—shots of a road leading to a castle, the cobbled streets of Edinburgh, and an avenue leading to an imposing estate—and the following detailed scene of a single street subtly establish an important metaphor for the film, that of the various roads of life, and firmly convey a solid sense of *civilization.* The camera lingers to depict a bookstore, bootery, public house, police kiosk, and strolling shoppers, all of which suggest that here "In Edinburgh in 1831," as the opening title carefully announces, a sedate and civilized society routinely goes about its daily business. That serene atmosphere is underscored for ironic effect, though, both to establish a normalcy out of which unexpected horrors might later more strikingly emerge and to allow for a truly stark contrast to the film's closing scene—another road, but this one winding through a dark, craggy landscape as a storm rages. By that careful and parallel visual detailing, Lewton could thus move his characters from order to chaos, from all the appearances of civilization into a turbulent and threatening natural world. As we move with them, we seem to approach nearer some essential truth which his films continually explored. In Stevenson's tale that immersion into the unknown and horrific is basically a function of the narrative frame which plunges the reader into a time and place *removed* from the narrator's more "civilized" world, there to discover misdeeds and encounter that horrible apparition. For Lewton that remove would have been superfluous, for the civilized, mundane present he employs throughout the film renders the realm of horror precisely coterminous with ordinary society, thereby making that everyday world bear a greater burden than Stevenson was wont to impose, but one which more closely approximates Lewton's vision of reality. In fact, it is this attitude which closely links a "costume" picture like ***The Body Snatcher*** to his customary modern setting horror films. Here that civilized order carries the weight of those murderous actions which it has both unknowingly inspired and effectively disguised from full view.

Those opening scenes therefore prepare for a complexity which succeeding images will more fully develop. We enter a world bustling with commerce, good intentioned, and seemingly innocent, one initially evoking the typical Hollywood vision of a quaint Victorian England. At the same time, though, it is a world of frustration at the limits of human knowledge, of pain both treated and caused by the doctors of the day, and of murder for hire. The infamous Burke and Hare, who obtained specimens for the medical schools, have been caught and punished, but their spirit lingers, as the dead and living alike still prove salable commodities in the lucrative business of aiding the advance of medical science. The film thus generates a tension between that mundane surface and these darker depths, between those everyday images of civilization and that unsettling reality seldom seen or acknowledged.

Lewton fittingly dramatizes both that world's complexity and our ignorance of its nature through his central character, Donald Fettes. Stevenson's character—lacking even a Christian name—is essentially one-dimensional, but he is sharply defined; working in the dissection laboratory, he "understood his duty . . . to have three branches: to take what was brought, to pay the price, and to avert the eye from any evidence of crime." The manner in which Lewton introduces his protagonist speaks much more ambiguously, though it ultimately underscores his character's quite different naivete. We first see Fettes seated atop a fresh grave in the city cemetery, incongruously eating his lunch, heedless of those "ensigns of mortality" around him. His attitude is made clear—an important fact, since this image later finds its counterpoint in a similar view of the cabman Gray—by the appearance of an old lady visiting her son's grave. She tells Fettes of her fear that grave robbers will steal her son's body and of her disdain for the doctors who encourage that practice. Fettes is incredulous, defending the medical profession he hopes to join and assuring her that there is "not much danger here . . . I wouldn't think, not right here in the heart of Edinburgh." Rather than close the scene on this note of naive confidence, though, Lewton intrudes a questioning image. In an extreme long shot of the cemetery, metaphorically a more encompassing view than that enjoyed by Fettes, we see a mysterious carriage slowly pass the gate. It is a commonplace image, but due to the context and oblique camera angle, it seems unnaturally eerie and inspires little confidence in Fettes' statement. That feeling is soon substantiated as we learn that it is the coach of Gray, the "resurrectionist" who supplies bodies to the young man's teacher, the illustrious Dr. MacFarlane.

Gray's coach is itself a fine example of Lewton's cinematic approach, for it serves as a visual link between the introduction of Fettes and MacFarlane, and it suitably suggests the full complexity of this world. The next scene opens with that coach pulling up in front of MacFarlane's magnificent house. It brings a crippled girl, Georgina Marsh, to the doctor to request that he operate on her spinal injury. When he refuses, claiming to be "more dominie than doctor," the image of the helpless child provides an immediate emotional indictment of his cold, theoretical concerns in medicine. Even Gray initially comes across much more sympathetically than MacFarlane, as we see him bearing Georgina in his arms, helping her from his carriage and smiling as he lifts her up to pet his horse. Disarmed by that image and the seemingly genuine feelings displayed there, we almost inevitably find our next view of Gray quite jarring. That night, following Georgina's interview with MacFarlane, Gray appears as a silhouette—suggesting the darker side of his character not seen before—against the cemetery wall. There he unhesitatingly kills a small dog guarding its master's grave, which he then plunders, whistling while he "works"—and ironically it is the same grave Fettes had earlier attested to the security of. With that shift from day to night, from light to shadows, and from manor house to graveyard, ***The Body Snatcher*** effects a full transformation in our perspective, one which points up the complex and ambiguous nature of the world depicted here. Gray's carriage, as we see, by day transports the living, and by night the corpses he has stolen, while Gray himself is a figure disturbingly able to blend in with that world of common day, then prowl the cemeteries and streets at night, stealing or, if necessary, murdering to obtain those valuable specimens for the dissecting tables.

The paradoxical nature of his character is most clearly expressed in a later scene composed to recall Fettes' introduction. Gray murders MacFarlane's servant Joseph who has attempted to blackmail him, and as he sits astraddle the corpse, he strokes his pet cat and speaks lovingly to it. That incongruous composition evokes the scene of Fettes eating his lunch, oblivious to the fresh grave on which he sits, though here all notion of naivete is dispelled by the horrifying heedlessness which is implied. The discordant note thus sounded affords a key to the film's horror formula; it starts a fear that every neutral image or benevolent appearance might only mask some unseen, unimagined terror, that the clear, rational light of day might simply serve to disguise those dark, irrational elements of the human situation.

Though with more subtlety, this same approach is used to delineate MacFarlane's character. As the most eminent surgeon in Edinburgh, he presents an impeccable appearance. His house, over which the camera seems to linger pointlessly, effectively serves to visualize his true character. Before he is introduced, we see several interior shots of his home as Georgina and Mrs. Marsh enter. Angled shots and a dimly lit interior create an eerie effect, and the high angle view of mother and daughter from atop the staircase, making them seem small and insignificant, foreshadows the condescension and air of detachment which the doctor displays. The very layout of the house hints at MacFarlane's attitudes, for it suggests the doctor's tendency to compartmentalize his life. His lodgings occupy the second floor and part of the first, his office and examination rooms the remainder of the first, and his medical facility, including the dissection tables, lecture room, and storage facilities, is confined to the basement. This arrangement leads us to suspect that MacFarlane feels he can simply shut out the more unpleasant aspects of his profession with the closing of a door or figuratively hold himself above those troublesome concerns he has relegated to his basement school and delegated to his assistant Fettes and his henchman Gray.

That effort at compartmentalization, however, only reinforces a sense of entrapment which pervades the film, as it suggests how little able MacFarlane is to ever break free of that life. Even while he sleeps upstairs, for instance, Gray steals into his basement and leaves Joseph's corpse as a suitably shocking surprise which the doctor must then hurriedly dispose of to avoid a scandal. He finds himself in that situation because, on the one hand, the pursuit of knowledge forces him to traffic with men like Gray, with ghouls and murderers who obtain the bodies he needs for study. And on the other, he is haunted by his own past, especially his associations with Gray when he was a young student like Fettes and forced into unscrupulous methods of gaining the specimens his teacher wanted. As his mistress Meg explains, there has always been "the shame of the old ways and the old life to hold him back" from a glorious career. The house and Gray's continual appearances visually affirm his entrapment in that round of sordid actions and explain his warning to Fettes that, given an initial accession to evil, one cannot easily turn back: "the more things are wrong, the more we must act as if everything is right." Gradually we come to see that the essential difference between the esteemed Dr. MacFarlane and the lowly Gray is not a deeper understanding or moral sensibility, but mainly a greater ability to make things seem "right," to present a more natural and civilized appearance to the world. And it is the haunting presence of Gray which increasingly promises to collapse that fragile facade of propriety. The development of this disparity between what we see and what really is represents one of Lewton's major additions to his source, and it injects a distinctly cinematic sense of tension between those deceptive appearances and their underlying reality.

The characters of MacFarlane and Gray especially are developed far beyond Stevenson's original conception in order to suggest this tension. In their contending alter egos, they seem much like the two skeletons which MacFarlane's students arrange in fighting postures in the laboratory. As Gray tells the doctor, "you and I have two bodies, . . . very different sorts of bodies, but they're closer than if we were in the same skin." Like MacFarlane, Gray has become caught in his situation, particularly by his past association with Burke and Hare, and finds himself preyed upon by the blackmailing servant Joseph, just as he has sought to manipulate MacFarlane. Having previously accepted a bribe to hide MacFarlane's complicity in their activities, Gray now resents the fact that the doctor's *appearance* of respectability seems so much at odds with his own lowly situation. Like a bothersome conscience, then, he bedevils MacFarlane, finding in that relationship some small consolation for his station: "I'm a small man, a humble man, and being poor, I've had to do so much that I did not want to do. But so long as the great Dr. MacFarlane jumps at my whistle, that long am I a man—and if I have not that, I have nothing. Then I am only a cabman and a grave-robber."

That disparity in appearance is visually underlined by Gray's lodgings which, located in the rear of a barn on a dead-end street, contrast markedly with MacFarlane's manor. In those dark, meager quarters, he seems similarly trapped and ever reminded of his situation. When Fettes comes to Gray's place with an urgent request for a specimen, that sense of hopelessness translates into a series of telling compositions. After Fettes leaves, for instance, we see Gray in long shot, a small figure framed first in the doorway of his apartment, then, as the camera tracks back, through a viewport on his door. Diminished and confined by those multiple frames, he seems almost pitiable, yet firmly locked into that round of gruesome activities he has made his life. Fittingly, as Gray harnesses his horse in preparation for his mission, we watch him through the bars on the side of the horse stall; it is a composition which affirms this self-imprisonment, even as it suggests an internal tension, a reluctant resignation to the way of life he has entered into.

Through this visualized tension, Lewton established a truly troubling atmosphere of moral ambiguity. He could thus depict a world in which the best intentions can lead to evil deeds, and those same, apparently quite frequent misdeeds are excused or covered up by a human penchant—perhaps even a need—for rationalization. In Stevenson's story Fettes and MacFarlane are simply fellow students brought to their crimes by the lure of easy money and pleasures. As in his previous film ***The Ghost Ship***, Lewton here fashioned almost a father-son relationship between the two characters, thereby imparting to his narrative a greater moral imperative. MacFarlane, with his technical brilliance but lack of a truly humanistic sense, provides a sharp contrast to the idealistic young medical student Fettes. Both, though, display a quite similar failing. MacFarlane, singlemindedly concerned with the advance of medical knowledge, complains that "Ignorant men have damned the stream of medical progress with stupid and unjust laws. If that damn will not break, the men of medicine . . . have to find other courses." In his case, that means dealing with men like Gray and winking at their methods—including murder. Lest we judge MacFarlane too hastily, though, Lewton offers a parallel case in Fettes, demonstrating how easily and unwittingly our moral concerns can be put aside by expediency. In his zeal to help the crippled Georgina, Fettes presses MacFarlane to operate and demands that Gray quickly obtain a specimen for the doctor to study in preparation for the delicate surgery. His urgings, however, precipitate Gray's murder of a young street singer, whose body Fettes immediately recognizes. Her corpse visually drives home the moral complexity of the world Fettes inhabits; as he perceives, it is one in which murder can be accidentally—even profitably—used to promote life, where even the most humanitarian concerns can be twisted into rationales for murder and violation of the dead.

This sort of horror might seem to defy visualization, though, since it seems so integral a part of human psychology. It is what we might term an internal grotesquery that lurks beneath the proper appearance MacFarlane presents and is often displaced into the character of Gray, that alter ego he tries to suppress. Because of this tension, almost everything the doctor says ultimately imparts an ironic edge to that proper image, and he seems singularly given to an irritating rhetoric—to mouthing platitudes to justify his actions. Stevenson's original character lacks this dimension; his philosophy is distressingly simple and straightforwardly naturalistic: "there are two squads of us—the lions and the lambs. If you're a lamb, you'll come to lie upon these tables . . . if you're a lion, you'll live and drive a horse like me, . . . like all the world with any wit or courage." In the film, though, he is a figure obsessed with his sense of right, one who consistently feels compelled to *explain* himself to Fettes. On three occasions he reasons his assistant out of quitting the medical profession and into helping him with his work, pointing to "the stupidity of the people, the idiocy of their laws" as a suitable rationale for continuing in their own questionable activities. That ready ability to turn reason to such ends, however, is itself unsettling, as Lewton underscores through the image of the young street singer. In one of ***The Body Snatcher***'s most effective scenes, she disappears into a dark alley and is followed by Gray and his coach; after some moments her singing is abruptly cut off, suggesting that the cabman has done his work. When she turns up on one of his dissection tables, MacFarlane attempts to explain away her sudden death for Fettes by surmising that she may have been an epileptic who, in a fit, had fallen and hit her head. "All the pieces fit," he says, but that implausible explanation hardly convinces even the gullible young student. It simply has a jarring effect, as it undercuts MacFarlane's pretensions to a truly humanitarian concern and calls into question the rational basis for so much of his conduct.

Lewton fashions an even more pointed indictment of this ethic and MacFarlane's kind of medical practice in his depiction of the operation on Georgina Marsh. It is shown as a kind of performance in which the doctor demonstrates correct surgical procedure to his students who are admiringly gathered around, praising his technique. And after this surgery the child still cannot walk, despite the fact that, as he avows, "everything is in place." This result demonstrates to MacFarlane that there are yet things he "can't define, can't diagnose." With his philosophy thus undermined, MacFarlane goes to the public house and there drinks with Gray, the eminent doctor and the murdering cabman, for all their disparity in appearance, seeming mirror images of each other. It is ironically from Gray, that reflection of his darker side, that the doctor learns an important lesson, that "you can't build life the way you put blocks together." As that displaced ego amplifies, MacFarlane has "a lot of knowledge . . . but no understanding"; it is only "the dead ones" he knows.

That apparent failure to heal Georgina finally disillusions Fettes with his teacher, as he comes to realize that MacFarlane "taught me the mathematics of anatomy, but he couldn't teach me the poetry of medicine." With that disillusionment, the implicit father-son relationship of the two men also fails, but to good purpose. MacFarlane has been seeking more than just approval from his student all along. Childless and with a low-born mistress he is ashamed to acknowledge as his wife, the doctor seeks an extension of himself, someone who will continue his work and "see it as I see it." Lewton subtly summarizes this theme in the climactic scene which echoes another failed father-child relation already developed. Three years earlier, we know, Georgina Marsh was crippled and her father killed when his reckless driving caused their coach to overturn. MacFarlane and Fettes are now placed almost symbolically in a similar position. Having murdered Gray, MacFarlane promises that he will be "a new man and a better teacher" with that haunting presence gone, and thus convinces Fettes to join him in digging up a corpse to supply the school. Having done their "dirty work," the pair set out in a coach, the body propped between them as the doctor drives wildly through a suddenly stormy night. The metaphoric weight of the scene is fairly obvious. Fettes, at the mercy of a morally reckless "father," faces a fall just as did Georgina, though he risks a far less remediable injury, a crippling not of the body but of his sensibilities, if he follows the path laid out by MacFarlane. In a swift series of medium and close shots, we observe MacFarlane's self-control rapidly erode as the corpse repeatedly topples onto his shoulder. Finally he hallucinates that it is, in fact, the body of Gray, who has returned to haunt him. This vision, shared by

MacFarlane and Fettes, climaxes the Stevenson story, but Lewton, in keeping with his parallel tale of the Marsh family, limits this guilty vision to the doctor who is killed as the coach lurches out of control and careens over a precipice, while his student is thrown clear and saved. Fettes then holds up a lamp—symbolic of his clearer vision—to that corpse which so frightened MacFarlane and affirms that it was simply the body of an old woman. The horror which effectively frightened the doctor to death is thus revealed as a product of his own disordered mind, a projected image of that internal horror which he long tried to repress or cloak under the guise of respectability and scientific purpose.

Lewton's final addition to Stevenson's story underlines this pattern of visual revelation, dispelling that disparity between appearances and reality with which his film has dealt. In extreme long shot we see Fettes leave the site of that accident and begin walking back to town, lighting his way with that lamp he used to inspect the bodies. As he does, a rather didactic title is superimposed: "It is through error that man tries and rises. It is through tragedy he learns. All the roads of learning begin in darkness and go out into the light." That bit of moralizing affirms that the cycle of grave robbings and murders in the name of science may be halted, that Fettes at least will not follow that path laid out by this strange "father." The final image, though, more effectively conveys this message, as it harkens back to those opening shots of the cobbled, well-lighted, and bustling city streets of Edinburgh, so that these two scenes may effectively bracket and comment upon the story of MacFarlane and Fettes. While the body of the film has demonstrated the deceptive nature of those initial images of civilization, this final scene, emphasizing the dark dirt road which winds through a rough, craggy landscape, suggests some element of that truth which Fettes has discovered. In that vista he seems a small, very fragile figure, though one who, we perceive, now carries a deeper understanding of both his world and himself—a knowledge which, like the lamp he carries, hopefully will light his way along the hazardous paths he has yet to travel. This suggestive combination of light and dark, man and nature, direction and disorder makes for what is arguably the single most striking image in Lewton's films and an effective *coda* for ***The Body Snatcher***. It denotes a frightening world, though one often made so by man himself, even as it demonstrates man's ability to hold up a lamp to that darkness in which he dwells and, at least for a time, to dispel it.

The Body Snatcher provides no easy resolution for the problems it has revealed, but it does offer a complex vision of the world and a reminder of our complicity in its make-up. In this respect alone it demonstrates a great advance over Stevenson's far from subtle story. In order to adapt that tale to the screen, Lewton clearly had to make a number of changes, foremost of which was the elimination of its frame narrative; but the consistent visual richness and finely textured sense of reality which result seem more than adequate compensation. It is, finally, that very visual texture which carries the crucial weight of this film. That sense of the commonplace, of the everydayness of all we witness, could easily overwhelm what we normally think of as the material of horror; while corpses abound in ***The Body Snatcher***, they seldom appear out of place or truly shocking. Instead, they suggest those internalized, half-hidden horrors of the human situation which Lewton has sought to lay bare. What makes his film all the more effective, then, is this understated horror which seems to emerge quietly from that veneer of normalcy. As a result, Lewton has crafted a grotesquery more subtle, yet also more truly photogenic, than that found among the ghouls and monsters which so populated the genre during the 1940's. In focusing our attention on man and his actions in all their ambiguity of motivation and unintended effect, Lewton put on display those more unsettling horrors which come from within, manifestations of those ghosts with which we commonly haunt our own lives. That is Lewton's greatest accomplishment and best evidence of his true cinematic sense.

J. P. Telotte (essay date 1985)

SOURCE: "Structures of Absence: *Cat People,*" in *Dreams of Darkness: Fantasy and the Films of Val Lewton*, University of Illinois Press, 1985, pp. 21-39.

[*In the following excerpt, Telotte argues that elements of the mise-en-scene in the film* Cat People *(for example the shadows that dominate many of the scenes and the off-screen depiction of horrific events) represent a thematic concern with mythological, psychological, and philosophical notions of absence—that is, an absence that implies the presence of something too awful to imagine concretely.*]

> From seeing the bars, his seeing is so exhausted
> That it no longer holds anything anymore.
> To him the world is bars, a hundred thousand
> Bars, and behind the bars, nothing.
> —Rainer Maria Rilke, "The Panther"

While Val Lewton, like few other producers in Hollywood, generally wielded a free and creative hand in crafting his unit's films, his first production, ***Cat People*** (1942), demonstrated the typical studio distrust of any tampering with traditional and box-office-proven formulas. Alarmed by his unconventional approach to what was seen as a simple horror "programmer," and especially the substitution of little more than shadow and suggestion in place of the usual monstrous presences of the genre, the RKO front office demanded that the film be tailored to look more like the successful competition at Universal Studios; thus added footage of a menacing panther was inserted in several scenes. Although that interference was mitigated and little affected the final film, it points up the salient difference between the work of the Lewton unit and the typical horror vehicles of the era. As Curtis Harrington summarizes. [in "Ghoulies and Ghosties," *The*

Quarterly of Film, Radio and Television, Vol. 7, 1952-1953], Lewton "observed that the power of the camera as an instrument to generate suspense in an audience lies not in its power to reveal but its power to suggest; that what takes place just off screen in the audience's imagination, the terror of *waiting* for the final revelation, not the seeing of it, is the most powerful dramatic stimulus toward tension and fright." This commentary recalls Lewton's personal dislike for the "mask-like faces hardly human, with gnashing teeth and hair standing on end [quoted in Joseph McBride, "Val Lewton, Director's Producer," *Action*, Vol. II, January-February 1976] that were common to the genre. At the same time, though, it might also seem to imply that he produced simply stylish, *frisson*-evoking vehicles, master texts in the mechanism of horror with little substance at their core. The absence of the traditional and highly visual threats that characterizes ***Cat People*** and the Lewton unit's subsequent films implies more than a concern with the machinery of suspense or horror, more too than a simple admission of the imagination's power. In these works absence takes on substance, forming the cornerstone of their distinctive fantasy aesthetic.

What a film like ***Cat People*** especially demonstrates is how well Lewton and his production team—particularly director Jacques Tourneur—understood the fundamental relation between our perceptions of the world and our conceptions of its nature. Certainly, the limitations of time, money, and material necessitated that less concern be given to fashioning elaborate spectacles than to making audiences believe they had seen something unusual or nightmarish. Lewton from the first realized that monsters and what we today term special effects were quite dispensable, even in films targeted at a far from sophisticated wartime audience mainly looking to the movies for distraction, hence his comment on the use of shadows or "dark patches" into which "the mind's eye will read anything." Consequently, the ominous and ubiquitous dark patches, which became a stylistic signature of these films, shoulder a heavy structural and thematic weight. They generate a pervasive dreamlike atmosphere, that of a world in which the individual seems to have little autonomy, and they are the surest sign of our participation in this world; as James Hillman reminds, "Dreams are made by the persons in them, the personified complexes within each of us; these persons come out most freely in the night" [*The Dream and the Underworld*]. While engaging our imaginative participation, the absence marked by those dark patches speaks of a fundamental—and disturbing—relationship between man and his world: it signals a black hole or vacant meaning in the physical realm which, in spite of man's natural desire to fill it with consciousness and significance, persistently and troublingly remains open. This sense of absence, therefore, not only supplements the presence of the many quotidian, even banal elements abounding in a film like ***Cat People***, but also points up the main problem facing both the audience and this film world's inhabitants, both of whom struggle to account for the unknown, to explain away the ambiguities with which the human realm is plagued.

To be sure, absence serves a fundamental rhetorical purpose, akin to the literary convention of apostrophe, since, like the gaze of Rilke's panther, it signals something not even present. In studying what he terms "the marriage between speech and Being," Jacques Derrida observes that we typically "represent the presence in its absence" whenever "we cannot take hold of or show the thing, let us say the present, the being-present, when the present does not present itself"; we might think of absence, then, as "a deferred presence" [*Speech and Phenomena, and Other Essays on Husserl's Theory of Signs*, 1978]. But of what? It must be something that stubbornly resists signification, that we often defer from consciousness, perhaps to consign to dreams and the night. Joel Siegel [in *Val Lewton: The Reality of Terror*, 1973] simply describes this aspect of the Lewton films as the "symbolic displacement" of "drives and desires presumably too dreadful to be shown directly." However, such "drives and desires," especially Irena Dubrovna's fear of possession by an evil spirit and her growing sense that, like Rilke's panther, she is trapped in a barred-off realm, are precisely what ***Cat People***'s rhetoric foregrounds. Certainly it is what the film's characters have on their minds and are constantly discussing. In fact, one of the key concerns here, at least superficially, is whether Irena is lying about those anxieties she confides to her husband and which soon become general knowledge. A greater concern of the film is our inability to make satisfying sense of such admitted impulses. More than simply investing the environment with a threatening aspect, then, those shadows which abound in the Lewton unit's films, those black holes in the fabric of the commonplace which seem to intrude into every frame, warn of an absence lodged at the center of the self, one which we strive to defer and project onto the world we inhabit. What we fear in those disconcerting absences are, after a fashion, truly monstrous presences, but are they those of our own creation, modeled on a most disturbing anxiety—absence of meaning, of order, of any discernible difference between man and that dark, enigmatic realm in which he must live.

That sense of absence shapes ***Cat People***'s world both thematically and structurally, while it also qualifies how we perceive its characters. Irena's Serbian origins and her enduring and insistent folk beliefs show up this absence most clearly, for her untold personal history, her life as an immigrant living in the New World mecca, New York, seems simply swallowed whole by her Old World cultural background, especially the medieval legends of her homeland concerning King John and the Mamelukes, which she recounts to Oliver Reed. In effect, it is as if she has no personal history, hardly any past beyond her first encounter with Oliver. Yet those deep cultural roots which cloak her absent personal past—or render its detailing irrelevant—not only suggest a mysterious depth in her character, but also underscore a significant absence in the Americans here who seem quite divorced from history. Ironically, Irena's residence is the only one shown; it is a personalized place of her own into which Oliver moves when they are married. Not only do the other players lack such characterizing locales, but their very homelessness seems emphasized. Dr. Louis Judd, the psychiatrist, is an international traveler with no permanent home; Alice tells how she first met him on a yacht, and when in New York he stays in a hotel. Alice apparently lives in a YWCA, and, while we never see her room, only the building's lobby and basement swimming pool, the insecurity of her place is underscored by the panther attack which occurs there. Neither do we know anything about Oliver's residence, and he apparently takes his meals at a diner near his work. Consequently, the immigrant in many ways seems least rootless here, as her situation accentuates an unexamined rootlessness typifying the Americans around her.

In contrast to Irena's history-haunted psyche, Oliver Reed seems unconscious of any cultural past, and his lack of awareness, once revealed, actually becomes as troubling as Irena's accumulation of folk beliefs. He clearly knows nothing about Serbia; he has never been in love before; and he simply sees himself as "quite a nice fellow." Oliver's limited experience and understanding speak of a personal and even cultural absence that has been deferred or banished, as if to the shadows or dark patches which frequently frame the screen or fill its depths, hinting at some discomfiting presence which lingers just out of view. Besides evoking a sense of the unknown or unseen, therefore, those ubiquitous shadows suggest how much in these people's lives remains unconscious, unformulated, and unquestioned. The darkness surrounding the pool into which Alice jumps to escape attack—from she knows not what—clearly echoes this absence, as the water, casting its eerie and shifting shadows on the oppressively low basement ceiling, recalls the archetype of the unconscious, whose fears have formed a reservoir here which, once tapped, readily floods the darkness with unnameable horrors. Whether they truly exist "out there" or only arise from our own absence-haunted psyches to fill the void is never made clear.

The recurrence of such shadow imagery, like the repetition of the water/unconscious motif, renders the sense of absence in a way that, as one critic notes, practically "constitutes a dramatisation of the structure of phantasy itself" [Paul Willemen, "Notes Towards the Construction of Readings of Tourneur," *Jacques Tourneur*]. That structuring begins in the film's opening sequence when Oliver walks Irena home from the zoo where they have met and remarks on her lodgings, "I never cease to marvel at what lies behind a brownstone front." His comment not only introduces the darkly elaborate interior of Irena's apartment building, dominated by an immense winding staircase—originally constructed for Orson Welles's *Magnificent Ambersons*—which seems to thread labyrinthinely only to Irena's apartment, but also suggests a significant disjunction between immediate appearances and the fullness of reality that comes to characterize this world. In addition, their entrance into the brownstone's foyer starts a recurring pattern of entry, a motif of thresholds waiting to be crossed, of doors which wait open—or mysteriously fail to open—onto some unknown, often foreboding presence. The simple act of entrance thus becomes a traumatic, anxiety-laden event, as we see with the Cooper Building's revolving door, which several times seems to move by itself, Oliver's office door, which mysteriously closes to suggest Irena's threatening presence, and the elevator door in the same building, half-open at one point, as if waiting for Oliver and Alice, but strangely shutting when they take the stairs. These doors hint, too, at the threshold between Irena's conscious and unconscious mind, crossed tentatively under Dr. Judd's hypnotic trance and definitively in a later dream sequence, but suggested by the locked door with which Irena separates herself from Oliver on their wedding night. That door she cannot open to her husband, Robin Wood interprets, is in turn "paralleled by the cage which separates her from the panther: divided between two worlds, she is barred from access to either" ["The Shadow Worlds of Jacques Tourneur," *Film Comment*, Vol. 8, No. 2, 1972]. Unlike those other doors, though, the one in the zoo seems to mark a greater danger that lurks within, not a desire to control Irena's most dangerous impulses but a compulsion to release them; according to Dr. Judd, it represents her unconscious but insistent "psychic need to loose evil upon the world," and thus points to a dialectical struggle deep within her personality.

The most obvious structural use of absence, though, shows up in the film's visual styling, for instance, in the long tracking shots which serve less as transitions from one locale to another than as a means of emphasizing the shadowy world these characters are passing through. ***Cat People***'s most effective sequence in this regard, . . . depicts Irena, apparently transformed by her jealousy, stalking Oliver's friend Alice as she walks home after a late-night meeting with him. Parallel tracking shots of the two women traversing the dark city streets give way to a series of static shots which emphasize the patterns of light and shadows, as each girl enters and exits from the field of view. In repeating these compositions the narrative creates a pattern of expectation which primes us for the most discomfiting anxieties, not through the appearance of what we have imagined lurking beyond our view, but simply through the disruption of this pattern of presences, as happens when one woman fails to appear as expected. Confronted by an absence—really nothing at all—we draw on the surrounding shadows for some explanation, a substance to fill the sudden gap, some means of securely closing what now seems a disturbingly open world. Such an encounter leads us back within, in a preliminary vesperal motion, there to glimpse our own frailty.

What makes the sudden encounter with absence all the more effective is that it typically goes masked in images of normalcy or even banality, such as recur in the Lewton films—and for which they have at times been criticized. One such carefully calculated injection of the normal in ***Cat People*** is the precise detailing of occupation for every character. As Siegel notes, during initial script conferences the Lewton team would spend some time assigning occupations to the film's key characters and determining how each might "be shown at work during the course of the movie." Following this formula, ***Cat People*** quickly establishes that Irena sketches fashion designs, that Oliver is a draughtsman for the Cooper Ship and Barge Construction Company, and that his best friends—Alice, Doc, and the Commodore—all hold positions with the same firm. The details surrounding these characters then flesh out this sense of the quotidian, decisively distancing them from any hint of the fantastic. Oliver we first see drinking a bottle of soda pop at the zoo, where he calls Irena's attention to an anti-littering sign and, displaying his best baseball form, tosses the drawing she has discarded into a receptacle. An additional touch to this characterization is that Oliver seems to order apple pie whenever he goes to the local diner. He is, in short and by his own admission, "a good plain Americano," having simple pleasures and holding down a steady job. Despite her foreign accent Irena, too, gives every indication of normalcy; she likes to visit the zoo, lives in one of those anonymous brownstone apartment houses which abound in New York, and innocently offers Oliver a cup of tea when he escorts her home. Her rival for his affections, Alice, seems more the typical female buddy of the type popularized by Howard Hawks in this period than a romantic predator and is described simply as a "good egg" by Oliver. Even the film's minor characters are woven into this fabric of the commonplace, as we learn of the cleaning lady's matchbook collection, the zookeeper's absentmindedness, and Millie the waitress's concern with pushing the chicken gumbo on her customers. Rather than a distraction, the development of this texture provides an effective prelude to the aberrant, the strange, the lack of normalcy which people like these typically try to gloss over with details that make them seem like ordinary people. Oliver's impulsive marriage to Irena works in this way, although when she fears consummating the marriage and it begins to sour, another effect of this texture of normalcy surfaces. As Irena tells Oliver, she envies every woman she sees because "they're happy; they make their husbands happy; they lead normal, happy lives." The seemingly universal and rather formidable appearance of normalcy also suggests its opposite, breeding the most debilitating anxieties in a person who must confront the absence of such a norm in her own life.

This phenomenon of absence, though, is a necessary supplement for its opposite, the presence with which consciousness is typically concerned, so that in a film like ***Cat People*** we see absence and presence contributing to a dialectic which informs the human world. In fact, this film derives much of its unsettling effect from a series of conflicts or oppositions which echo this absence/presence matrix; between Oliver's Americanness and Irena's foreign background; between his scientific concerns and her artistic ones; between the inanimate, nonthreatening world of modern-day New York and the frighteningly animate environment in which Irena sees herself trapped; and between the different explanations offered for her anxieties, the psychological/Freudian interpretations of Dr. Judd and Irena's folk belief that she is possessed by some evil spirit. What we learn is that neither side, no single element in the dialectic adequately explains these problems. Moreover, our attention is continually called to the fact of absence as an unsettling supplement that defies systematization, articulation, and explanation. In this way the problems of understanding which always plague the human consciousness come into more immediate focus.

The most obvious element in ***Cat People***'s system of oppositions is its meeting of American and Serbian cultures, which provides the springboard for much of the film's action. In fact, Oliver's at-homeness and Irena's foreignness are played up immediately to emphasize their character differences. Both are at the zoo as the film opens, Oliver surrounded by others as he eats and drinks at a sidewalk vendor's stand, and Irena alone in the frame, isolated by her thoughts as she sketches a panther in its cage. As we later see, Oliver tends to surround himself with friends, all "good plain" types like himself; they do things together and know each other's business. Irena, on the other hand, has made no friends since coming to America, and her isolation is hardly accidental; as she confesses to Oliver, "I've stayed away from people; I've lived alone." Later, she admits that she "never wanted" to fall in love because she was afraid of the effects any commitment might have, especially the consequences due to her foreign birth and a curse that she fears follows from it. In essence, each person suggests the other side, the absence in his opposite's life: Oliver offers the love Irena has denied and fled from, while she, in her morbid fears, brings dark, unimagined possibilities into his simple, everyday existence. Oliver confesses to Alice afterward that he has "never been unhappy before. Things have always gone swell for me," and for this reason his troubled marriage is all the more perplexing: "That's why I don't know what to do about all this. I've just never been unhappy." Even as they complement each other, Oliver and Irena also reveal a lack in their lives: their equal inability to cope with an absence shown to be at the core of their being.

Their basic characteristics also suggest much of what has been omitted. Oliver is, after all, a ship designer, someone interested in figures, forms, measurements—he even seizes upon a T-square to ward off Irena when she has apparently been transformed into a menacing panther at one point. And Alice can tell when something is troubling him by his mathematical miscalculations: "That's the third wrong figure you've given me," she notes just before he confides his marital problems to her. His abiding interest in ships, extending to the models he brings into Irena's apartment after they are married and those he admires in the museum scene, subtly combines with the film's recurrent water imagery—most often associated with Irena—to sketch out the place of the unconscious in his everyday life. Oliver's concern, like that of his friends, is with vehicles enabling one to float over and thus avoid any dangerous immersion in that unconscious realm where unknown and potentially threatening forces contend. In contrast to his scientific and rational perspective, Irena takes the artist's outlook. She views reality through her imagination rather than conforming the imagination to a hard and fast reality as Oliver does. Her introduction clearly emphasizes this trait, as we see her sketching a panther in the zoo but repeatedly ripping up her attempts, not because they fail to capture her subject, but because they do not express what she feels inside, which is some deep, unarticulated impulse from her cultural past. As we see, Irena is not simply tracing out the cat's appearance, but depicting it, as if a dream image, transfixed with a large knife. In her distinctly imaginative way she responds to a recurrent threat stirring within her; figuratively she tries to kill off that haunting force. In keeping with this introduction Irena proves prone to dreams, visitations from the unconscious which Oliver little comprehends, as we see in his mocking response to her fears of the cat people legend of her birthplace: "Oh Irena, you crazy kid." Her very constitution dramatically distances her from his supremely practical, commonsense world. It is not just her deep-rooted fears or even the drawings and paintings which decorate and personalize her apartment, but her perfume, her singing, her great fondness for the night ("I like the dark; it's friendly," she tells Oliver), and the pleasure she finds in the screams of the cats in the nearby zoo ("To me it's the way the sound of the sea is to others, natural and soothing. I like it," she notes) that distinguish her personality and underscore its immersion in everything that Oliver's lacks.

Because of this difference in their personalities, yet another disjunction seems so marked, that between the largely inanimate view of the world which Oliver, Alice, and Dr. Judd maintain and Irena's animate vision. Her world seems fully alive, filled as it is with flowers, animals, and wild sounds; its ruling deity could easily be the cat goddess Bubastis, shown juxtaposed to Irena as she stands on a museum staircase. This animate perspective lets her see the world as much more threatening than it seems to Oliver. The unexpectedly fierce reaction of a pet kitten to Irena and a canary that dies of fright when she tries to play with it both hint at a menacing, almost predatory aspect in her and signal a blurring of distinction between the human and animal. Her folk belief in a race of cat people, who are inexplicably turned into murderous felines when their emotions are aroused, naturally accords with this animistic view. Oliver, however, has no such dreams to haunt his nights, so he simply terms Irena's notions "nonsense." In his experience everything can be "got at"—measured, studied, or manipulated—and fears of the unknown are considered the stuff of "fairy tales," as he says, or products of mental problems that should be dealt with by the proper medical authorities.

In fact, Oliver and several other characters here, like proper denizens of the modern, rational world, readily defer to the experts, in this case, the psychiatrist Dr. Judd—first of a long line of wrong-headed, even dangerous doctors in the Lewton films—whom Alice suggests could help Irena. And his involvement underscores a related dialectic at work in ***Cat People***, that between modern psychology and Irena's folk belief in evil possession. Oliver admits his own inability to solve Irena's problems and offers a suggestion that directly reflects his quite limited perspective: "There's something wrong and we have to face it in an intelligent way. We don't need a King John with fire and sword. We need someone who can find the reason for your belief and cure it. That's what we need—a psychiatrist." In his simplistic, almost ludicrous response, reflecting Oliver's naive faith in the world of science, we glimpse the popularized notion that psychology's primary purpose, as Hillman explains, is to interpret dreams, "to bring them over into the dayworld, shall we say rescuing or 'reclaiming' (Freud's own metaphor) the dream from its underworld madness." In response to Irena's plea for help and her "feeling there's something evil in me," however, Judd with his clearly Freudian perspective can only suggest that her troubles may stem from some early, half-remembered experience: "These childhood tragedies are inclined to corrode the soul, to leave a canker in the mind. We'll try to repair the damage." While she recognizes that dark, ineffable force within and realizes that "whatever is in me is kept in, is harmless, when I'm happy," Judd and Oliver both presume that there is no real absence, no depth in the personality that cannot be plumbed and brought to light. To them it is simply a case of uncovering the truth or finding the right events in the past which have fostered Irena's present neurosis. In short, they see her disease as no more than a disease awaiting cure.

As in many of the films produced by the Lewton unit, however, that dis-ease seems lodged in a human history that the individual attempts to deny in vain. In this instance, Irena readily admits that the legend of the cat people remains a living reality for her people in Serbia, that it "haunts the village where I was born"; and her chance meeting in a Serbian restaurant with a woman who "looks like a cat" only demonstrates how completely she feels bound by that cultural heritage. It is an intangible bond, not always present to her consciousness, as we several times note when she attempts to go routinely about her daily activities. Subtly, though, it influences her every action—her sketches, home decorations, pets, and her relationships with Oliver and Judd especially. Judd's solution, like Oliver's, is simply to annihilate that troubling past: "You keep going back to the mad legends of your birthplace. Forget them. You surround yourself with cat objects, pictures. Get rid of them. Lead a normal life," he tells Irena. And after a fashion he is right, that Irena's history-haunted psyche prevents her from living in the present, but his own view, shared by Oliver, that history should simply be denied existence, that myths have no substantial hold on us, and that absence cannot affect the present if we choose to gainsay its influence is itself shortsighted and signals a failure to understand the depths of the human psyche. Presence clearly has a time component, that of the present, but so does absence, which bears upon the past and future, both of which should help to cast a more comprehensive and revealing light on the immediate situation. For a person can live neither in a constant present nor in another time than his own; the human world, marked as it is by memories, hopes, and present concerns, demands that we merge these various time schemes to live our lives.

Neither this time relationship nor the other dialectical structures in the narrative are reconciled, however. The potential for happiness promised in the wedding of Oliver to Irena—of the complacent American to the mysterious foreigner—vanishes as their marriage goes unconsummated; Oliver turns to Alice—almost his mirror image—for affection; and Irena fully abandons herself to her fears of cat possession and attacks Oliver, Alice, and finally Judd. The possible combination of the scientific and the artistic, the rational and the imaginative, issues not in a kind of humanism, a happy combination of two complementary ways of seeing and understanding the world, but in a fundamental struggle, as each seeks to deny the validity of the other. Dr. Judd's treatment of his patient predictably brings no cure, not even a proper understanding of her problem; if anything, his treatment only exacerbates Irena's trouble and precipitates the film's tragic conclusion. Even Irena recognizes why Judd's approach to her problem is of no avail: "You're very wise; you know a great deal. Yet when you speak of the soul, you mean the mind, and it is not my mind that is troubled." Meanwhile he sees in her fears "hallucinations" that "approach insanity," nothing less than "a deterioration of the mind, an escape into fantasy—and it's dangerous." Finally, the inanimate and animate views of the world meet not in a more coherent perspective, not in a mythic view of man and his place in the world, such as the Lewton unit fashioned in their later ***Isle of the Dead***, but in an anthropomorphism gone wrong, a tendency to project our fears and anxieties into the absence felt around us. As the bus technique, which made its debut in this film, demonstrates, it is often because of such anxieties that our world grows so dark, objects begin to assume menacing shapes, shadows take on dangerous substance. At the same time ignorance of those dark possibilities or the belief that they are simply "bad dreams" that need to be brought into the light of day and rational understanding can be every bit as dangerous and debilitating and can certainly prevent one from ever truly understanding himself, much less others. It is the tension between these vying powers that creates the main threat here and generates a sign of that absence which the psyche typically and stubbornly seeks to deny.

Unable to locate a counterbalance, that tension is effectively subsumed within the individual as a self-destructive force, a maelstrom drawing him—though almost with a kind of relief, ***Cat People*** suggests—to oblivion. When faced, like Rilke's panther, with a world that seems totally barred from her, Irena plunges further into her primitive cat people belief and its realm of evil, as she fears that if she "were to fall in love and if a lover were to kiss her, take her into his embrace, she would be driven by her own evil to kill him." This fear, despite what Carlos Clarens and others suggest, represents not a "repressed lesbianism" at work [Clarens, *An Illustrated History of the Horror Film*, 1968; and Siegel], but an unconscious fear of the self's opposite. Neither is it an attraction for mirror images of the self—as her more than physical recoil from the Serbian woman who calls Irena "my sister" demonstrates—as much as an anxiety at what happens when a psyche surrenders itself wholly to that opposite. Of course, as Irena's statue of King John with his sword impaling a cat and the sword cane with which Judd later stabs her imply, male sexuality does at times seem threatening; yet Irena does not find it totally frightening, or so the drawing she makes in the first scene suggests. Indeed, she seems to long for that sexuality, for absence to assume a masculine and authoritative shape. Her dream of Judd as a modern-day knight in armor, bearing before him a long, drawn sword, explicitly emphasizes this point. Through that symbolized sexuality, if she could only embrace it, Irena might vanquish the fears which beset her.

The only forms that opposite takes, however, are Oliver and Judd, the one too immature for a proper sexuality, the other too detached and self-concerned to perceive its full importance for his patient. When his marriage fails to meet his naive expectations, Oliver can only turn to Alice—who shares his commonsense, day-world view of things—for an almost motherly consolation and admit, "I don't know what love really is." In contrast, Judd's growing sexual attraction to Irena eventually comes to stand in the way of his diagnostic and therapeutic roles, while his coldly rational attitude precludes any real sympathy for her. As he readily admits, he has "never believed" any of her stories. In this way he serves as a comment on the extremes of Freudian psychology, particularly its manner of explaining the sense of absence which haunts all human consciousness. As Hillman explains, the basic thrust of the Freudian project is "interpretation," a drive "to take the *via regia* of the dream *out* of the nightworld," its proper place. The film's opening epigraph—"even as fog continues to lie in the valleys, so does ancient sin cling to the low places, the depressions in the world consciousness"—is attributed to Judd himself and his fictive book *The Anatomy of Atavism*, but it seems almost a paraphrase of Freud, particularly his *Civilization and Its Discontents*. And his initial approch to Irena's troubles suggests the classic manner of Freudian analysis, as Judd seeks to tap the id through hypnosis and dream interpretation to determine the source of her problem, which he identifies not with her folk beliefs but with her libido and the sexual dysfunction in her marriage. The folklore he interprets as a disguise for some deep secret, a trauma resulting from her father's mysterious death in the forest when Irena was a child or some other childhood experience too long repressed by the superego. That libidinal cause, he is certain, can be located, examined, and treated to permit her to function sexually and thus save her marriage. When his attempts to determine that cause fail, he responds with his own sexuality, embracing and kissing her, only to evoke the very cat-persona his theories have denied, liberating that violent impulse he has simply seen as an instance of sexual repression. To what he determines to be a biological problem, he reacts biologically himself, with a peculiar but undeniably biological revenge the result—Irena's transformation into the panther which mauls and kills him, despite the protection afforded by his phallic sword cane. In this mutually destructive encounter we might see a dramatization of what Jung was to describe as the fundamental limitation of the Freudian approach: it "is limited to the task of making conscious the shadow-side and the evil within us. It simply brings into action the civil war that was latent, and lets it go at that" [*Modern Man in Search of a Soul*, 1953].

In its manifest inability to cope with Irena's terror, Judd's perspective only underscores the persistence and power of certain archetypal forces, what Hillman terms "underworld images," which provide an alternative account of human consciousness. The cat imagery is obviously pervasive here, extending even to the tiger lilies employed in one scene and the claw-shaped feet on Irena's bathtub; that animal motif, we might recall, "is usually symbolic of man's primitive and instinctual nature," its constant appearances normally signaling "that an instinct has been split off from the consciousness and ought to be (or is trying to be) readmitted and integrated into life." In Jungian terms this imagery suggests the shadow element of the psyche, the dark element in human nature which must find a proper balance with the persona and anima if one is to live happily, without a disabling dread of that dark realm within. In Irena's case that integration is denied by her husband, her psychoanalyst, and even society—all refusing to acknowledge what they cannot see. The general attitude is that cats are only animals, to be kept in boxes at the pet store or cages in the local zoo, to be used as pets, mousers, or visual attractions, and they have no business running free; in such situations they might well be run over by a car, as indeed happens at the film's end when Irena frees the zoo's panther. Modern society, rational and ordered as it is, free from anxieties about the unknown and the superstitions of folklore, clearly allots no place for shadows in its makeup.

As Jung was to remind, however, there are undeniable "deeper spiritual needs" in man which psychology, at least of the kind practiced by Judd, can never touch, a depth of human nature upon which the scientific perspective casts no light. A final dialectic, measured by the film's opening epigraph and its closing title, underscores this mystery. The former, as we previously suggested, simply dismisses anxiety as an atavism, a residue of man's religious taboos, and thus a dream of humanity in general from which we must be awakened. It is an explanation, however, which seems most ironic in light of Judd's failure and death. In contrast, the closing epigram is poetry of an emphatically spiritual sort, a quote from one of John Donne's Holy Sonnets: "But black sin hath betrayed to endless night / My world, both parts, and both parts must die." While the two passages similarly speak of "sin" and of the "night" and "fog" which shroud humanity, their implications are quite different. For Judd, "sin" is simply a primitive sensation which unnecessarily haunts those who will not emerge from the "low places" of their cultural past and cast a modern, rational light on their anxieties. For Donne, in contrast, the very word "sin" bears an almost archetypal meaning and deeply moral value, as it refers to a primordial Fall that still casts its dark shadow over man, reminding him of his frailty and inevitable end. It affords a sobering yet necessary perspective, since it admits the tragic nature of the human story, though in acknowledging the absence with which man must live, it opens onto a more truthful vision and holds out the possibility for some meaning.

If there is truly sin, if there is a "sickness unto death" such as Kierkegaard suggested in describing the most fundamental human sense of absence—absence of the divine presence—then there also exists the hope of coming to oneself. Kierkegaard [*The Sickness Unto Death*, 1954] posited that the very "possibility of this sickness is man's advantage over the beast, and this advantage distinguishes him far more essentially than the erect posture, for it implies the infinite erectness or loftiness of being spirit." In effect, a sense of absence, of this human "sickness," is what differentiates man from animal, keeps him from becoming no more than a violent cat person. In the shift from the opening epigram to the film's last statement, then, we can glimpse the revision of human perspective which is at work in this story. It is one that, the film's makers may have felt, modern America particularly needed. At the same time, creating such a new perspective is the fundamental process in "soul making," as Hillman describes it. Seen in such contexts, the notion of a "cat people" seems especially suggestive, implying a threat that haunts man as a direct result of his Fallenness. The film's final shot, of an empty panther cage in the background and Irena's lifeless body in the foreground, emphasizes this point, for it hints at the imprisoning nature of life, as well as the one sure release from it—death. For Oliver and Alice who view this spectacle and note that Irena "never lied to us," it also serves a cautionary purpose, like a collective dream from which they have simultaneously awakened. It reminds them of the otherness they originally dismissed as the product of her "overworked imagination," while it also reaffirms both the existence and unseen power of absence.

Cat People affords a prototype of the world which the Lewton films consistently evoked. It is a perfectly open, if not openly perfect realm which its characters inhabit, that is, its bounds are unmarked, its depth unmeasured, though largely because it is a human world, distinguished by the same troubling ambiguity, the same property of absence as is man himself. The Lewton films draw their structure and imagery from this fundamental substance. They indeed offer mainly shadows, dark patches, half-opened doorways—all threatening absences somehow bracketed on film by the most mundane of presences; however, as Derrida cautions, "the absence of an object" should hardly be seen as indicating "the absence of meaning." In fact, the opposite occurs as those enigmatic elements evoke common human lacunae, dark patches from within the self.

The studio heads did force an element of presence on ***Cat People*** in the form of insert shots of a real panther to supplement the shadows and suggestion which originally distinguished the film. As Tourneur notes with some satisfaction, though, despite orders to reshoot one scene, "I shot it so that you couldn't really be sure what you were seeing. That's the only way to do it. In the swimming pool sequence, the cat was my fist. We had a diffused spotlight and I used my fist to make shadows against the wall" [Siegel, "Tourneur Remembers." *Cinefantastique*, Vol. 2, No. 4, 1973]. This bit of directorial trickery only amplifies the suitably knotted interworkings of presence and absence in this and the subsequent Lewton films, as absence not only stands in for a presence—shadows evoking a cat—but even masquerades as itself, through the silhouettes cast by the director's hand, which make us guess at the substance of what we have seen. The resulting *mise en abîme*, as contemporary critics would term it, an abyss of ambiguity, pervades the subsequent films and injects that degree of complexity which distinguishes them from other narratives in the genre. In short, it represents the very structure of what we have termed a vesperal film. The discomfiting twists and turns, the dark patches that mark the meeting of presence with absence, as ***Cat People*** effectively demonstrates, dwell in man's psyche and, consequently, always inscribe their ambiguous patterns on the stories we tell of it. What the Lewton unit sought to do was to map those dark patches where possible and to put us on that track of the cat which leads within.

J. P. Telotte (essay date 1986)

SOURCE: "Val Lewton and the Perspective of Horror," in *Forms of the Fantastic: Selected Essays form the Third International Conference on the Fantastic in Literature and Film*, edited by Jan Hokenson and Howard Pearce, Greenwood Press, 1986, pp. 165-74.

[*In the following essay, Telotte discusses the ways in which the horror in Lewton's films comes from the undermining of individuals' perceptions of the world.*]

The modern horror classic *Night of the Living Dead* concludes with the protagonist, Ben, survivor of a night of terror, suddenly shot down, as he is mistaken for one of the zombie flesh eaters inexplicably threatening society. Despite the sense of inevitability that clings to the scene, the conclusion is unsettling, particularly since his death occurs just as normalcy seems restored, and it is at the hands of his fellow man, trying to rid his world of those horrors. Ben is simply the victim of a certain "distanced" perspective, as he is glimpsed through the telescopic sight of a rifle; a product of the modern, technological mind, here employed rather irrationally to "kill" the already dead. I recount this scene because it effectively dramatizes a fundamental motif of the horror genre, occurring in both its modern realistic form and that older concern with monsters and an "otherness" that seems to reside threateningly outside of us, in the dark, ever ready to interrupt our normal world.

In this scene a man is confused with a monster, and in the process, that insecure self and the threatening other so clearly become one that our own sense of normalcy is radically disrupted, our view of the human realm disoriented. The means by which this identity is established—that distorted perspective, through a mechanism—insinuates a central thrust of the genre, for *Night of the Living Dead*, like the recent *Halloween*, Hitchcock's *Psycho*, and especially the films produced by Val Lewton, is implicitly concerned with a transformation that occurs when we view the world and our fellow man in an improper way, as if through a telescope. That distanced perspective, such films suggest, interprets life itself as an otherness against which we must guard; that form of vision, consequently, becomes a sort of murderous glance, which ultimately transforms the viewer into just the sort of monstrous presence he so deeply fears. In light of the recent trend in horror films to manipulate audience perspective, allying it, as the opening of *Halloween* so effectively does, with that of a killer or maniac at large, this motif seems especially worthy of exploration.

Not only the horror film, but most forms of the fantastic actually operate within the structure of this perceptual encounter with the unknown. As Tzvetan Todorov explains [in *The Fantastic: A Structural Approach to a Literary Genre*, 1975], fantasy narratives "essentially concern the structuring of the relation between man and the world. We are, in Freudian terms, within the *perception-consciousness* system." Despite the great capital it makes from our immediate responses, then, the horror film through its disconcerting images functions in more than a merely gratuitous, anxiety-producing manner; rather, it challenges the way in which we consciously perceive—or, through repression mechanisms, fail to perceive—our world. This confrontation, as R. H. W. Dillard argues [in "The Pageantry of Death," *Focus on the Horror Film*, edited by Roy Huss and T. J. Ross, 1972], can work "instructively," like a medieval morality play, teaching us to accept "the natural order of things and . . . to cope with and even prevail over the evil of life." Or, as Robin Wood contends [in "The Return of the Repressed," *Film Comment*, July-August 1978], such films may serve to visualize our dreams, "our collective nightmares," whose imaging on the screen empowers us to cope with subconscious fears "in more radical ways than our consciousness can countenance." At the same time, of course, this perceptual emphasis invests the genre almost automatically with a metacinematic character as well, by clearly reminding us that what we see is essentially a way of seeing, a perception impressed upon us by the manipulative imagination of a narrator or filmmaker, seeking to bring our conscious and unconscious visions and fears together on the screen, as if in a kind of psychological therapy.

No single body of horror films demonstrates a greater mindfulness of this perceptual encounter than that produced by Val Lewton for RKO in the 1940s. In place of what Lewton described as those "masklike faces hardly human, with gnashing teeth and hair standing on end" [quoted in Joseph McBride, "Val Lewton, Director's Producer," *Action*, January-February 1976], the stock-in-trade of his competition at Universal, he demonstrated in films like ***Cat People, I Walked with a Zombie***, and ***Isle of the Dead*** the great effectiveness of controlling perception. As Curtis Harrington pointed out, "Lewton had observed that the power of the camera as an instrument to generate suspense in an audience lies not in its power to reveal but its power to suggest; that what takes place just off screen in the audience's imagination, the terror of *waiting* for the final resolution, not the seeing of it, is the most powerful dramatic stimulus toward tension and fright" ["Ghoulies and Ghosties," *Quarterly of Film, Radio and Television*, Vol. 7, 1952-53]. This notion of perceptual control suggests that what we naturally perceive is essentially not dangerous, or at least not truly frightening; rather, it is the withholding of vision or its manipulation that instills dread by filling our imaginations with that that is not-life, only darkness itself, the shadows and boundaries that mark off for both the film characters and movie audience the normal world of light and life. At the same time, it implies that human beings' greatest terrors reside not necessarily within their world, contiguous with their normal environment, but possibly within the mind, which by turns represses them or projects them into that surrounding negative space of darkness and boundary, and which, prodded by its rational demand to know all, to understand and explicate the world around, too readily fills all shadows with visions of its own devising, mirror images, in fact, of that voracious instinct to grasp all things—save the self. That play of light and dark, the seen and the unseen, then, is more than simply atmospheric in Lewton's shadow-filled, low-key lit films, and by extension, more than merely a conventional trapping of horror. From those dark realms—the city streets of ***Cat People*** and ***The Leopard Man***, the cane fields in ***Zombie***, the back alleys of Edinburgh in ***The Body Snatcher***—monsters truly are born; but they take shape from our own inability to dispel the darkness—physical and intellectual—within which we dwell, as Lewton reveals how that very incapacity can, after a fashion, make Frankensteins of us all, creating our own twisted versions of life, as we attempt to fill up the surrounding void with images of our compulsions, "monsters from the id," as the film *Forbidden Planet* well termed them.

All of Lewton's horror films seek to sidestep our usual concern with monsters or external threats, while at the same time they clearly establish the sort of atmosphere that seems to breed and promise such menacing shapes, prompting us to look for killer cats or zombies in the shadows. In point of fact, though, their central concern is the sort of perspective we bring to that world, a perspective that, if unintentionally, lends a shaping hand to an environment that is neither malevolent nor benevolent, simply ambiguous, unknowable, yet the home of creatures who require knowledge. The greatest threats in the Lewton films, consequently, prove to be those authoritarian and supremely rationalistic figures, such as Dr. Galbraith of ***The Leopard Man*** and Dr. MacFarlane of ***The Body Snatcher***, who, despite their great learning, ultimately turn out to be the chief horrors of their landscapes. ***Isle of the Dead*** probably most fully develops this horror formula, Lewton's legacy to the genre, for it establishes as a central motif that compulsion to watch over and hence control the human realm; from this impulse there naturally follow tragic consequences, including the literal transformation of man into murderous monster.

The very title of ***The Leopard Man***, like the earlier ***Cat People***, underscores this problem of transformation at the core of the film, although it also automatically misleads audiences accustomed to more conventional horror films. ***The Leopard Man*** details a series of similar grisly murders, attributable to two quite different causes: one, an escaped leopard who kills out of fear and hunger, as a product of his natural instincts; the other, one of those "men with kinks in their brains," as he is described, who murders out of some inexplicable mental aberration. The latter is so clever, however, so able to divorce his conscious and unconscious selves, that he nearly succeeds in placing the blame for his own irrational, animalistic actions on that escaped cat. Through this paralleling, then, ***The Leopard Man*** points up the presence of a monstrous, bestial element in man that often goes cloaked or unacknowledged, but that can easily surface to render one something less than human and a threat to others.

The human transformation this film recounts begins innocently enough, although in a fashion that underscores the improper mode of vision accompanying, even precipitating the problem. The leopard is originally unleashed on society when a publicity stunt backfires. In order to create an effective spectacle, the nightclub entertainer, Kiki Walker, rents a leopard to help her make an entrance on opening night; in fact, she even plans to wear a particular black dress that she feels will make her look "just like" that dangerous cat. This implicit recognition of a kinship between the human and animal, of a certain bestial force that might be externalized and rendered symbolically, opens onto a greater complexity when Kiki finds she is unable to control the leopard because of its great strength and the fact that, as the local museum curator explains, such animals "are unpredictable; they're like frustrated human beings." Our initial introduction to Kiki, as we see her staring into a mirror, concerned with the image she will present to her audience, suggests that she is concerned largely with appearances and thus gives little thought to the potential danger she might unleash on others. It is that selfish perspective, however, that seems prevalent here and that precipitates that almost willful transformation wherein Kiki makes herself look like the leopard; the subsequent escape of that dangerous beast and the string of murders that follows symbolically denote the threat implicit in a mode of vision that detaches the self from all others.

Most fittingly, it is the person who seems most detached from these events, Dr. Galbraith, curator of the local museum and, ironically, the sheriff's expert consultant on the "cat murders," who turns out to be the killer. Perhaps not even fully conscious that he is speaking of himself, Galbraith can clinically dissect the possible murderer, explaining that he would "be a hard man to find . . . especially if he were clever. He'd go about his ordinary business calmly, except when the fit to kill was on him." In his case, the reasons for that murderous instinct go largely unexplained, are simply deferred by Galbraith's own comment on how little we know "about the forces that move us, and move the world around us." That a scientist could so easily fall prey to these violent, animal instincts, undergo such a complete transformation, and yet so effectively hide those irruptions of the unconscious, though, seems an unsettling enough comment on our normal rational pretensions. Rather than simply leave us with this iconic commentary on the darker possibilities of the self, the film depicts a similar transformation in the character of Raoul Belmonte, boyfriend of one of the murder victims. As Galbraith finally confesses to the murders, we watch Raoul's reaction, and in close-up see his eyes as they take on a frightening gleam, similar to that previously noted in close-up shots of the leopard. His sudden murder of Galbraith does, of course, represent a kind of justice, but it ultimately affords a discomfiting glimpse indeed of how easily those transformations can occur and that sense of humanity become lost.

If the metamorphosis lying at the core of ***The Body Snatcher*** is less radical than that of ***The Leopard Man***, it is for that reason probably more disconcerting. This adaptation of a Robert Louis Stevenson story describes the problems of the medical profession in nineteenth-century Scotland, focusing especially on the many obstacles to the advance of medical knowledge in that era. The eminent Dr. MacFarlane, a surgeon and teacher of distinction, explains for his student assistant, Donald Fettes, how "ignorant men have dammed the stream of medical progress with stupid and unjust laws. If that dam will not break, the men of medicine will have to find other courses. As for me, I'll let no man stop me when I know I'm right." That rhetoric reveals much about the speaker, particularly MacFarlane's headstrong and self-righteous attitude, which allows him to place himself above the law in all questions of scientific research and application. While he voices a plea for the liberal attitude necessary for the advance of human knowledge, then, he also points up the underlying reason for such repressive laws, as a check to the possible dangers that may surface from that Faustian desire for knowledge that seems to haunt all men. MacFarlane's subsequent reminder to Fettes, that "if you're a real man and want to be a good doctor, you'll see it as I see it," suggests the dangerously autocratic nature of that point of view he maintains, as well as the will to transformation that subtly moves it, seeking to work its way upon others—as we saw after a fashion in the conclusion of ***The Leopard Man***.

MacFarlane's plea for more liberal laws and a more tolerant perspective on the quest for knowledge springs from his difficulties in obtaining bodies for dissection and instruction in his medical school. To his mind, a human corpse is nothing more than a potential object of study, and a municipal council that disputes that view and regulates access to the dead he sees as demonstrating "the stupidity of the people, the idiocy of their laws." Having worked this initial transformation of the human body in his own thinking, then, he need take only a short step to transgress those "stupid" laws and contract with Mr. Gray, an old acquaintance, to rob graves and attain cadavers by any means possible—and with no questions asked. When a small girl, Georgina Marsh, needs spinal surgery so that she might walk, MacFarlane delegates to Fettes the task of obtaining a similar specimen so that he might perfect his technique before performing the delicate operation; and his student goes to Gray, as he normally does, to place an order. With no appropriate corpses available, Gray simply murders a young street singer to accommodate his customers. It is a poor bargain indeed, that one girl must die so another might walk—murder thus facilitating medical research—and it precisely points up the danger in MacFarlane's abdication from a true concern for others in his work. At the same time, of course, this episode also hints at the sort of gradual and almost imperceptible transformation the teacher has already begun to work in the consciousness of his pupil, eroding his humanistic ideals and prompting him to wink at the actions of his confederates; as Fettes later notes, MacFarlane started him on "a road that led to knowledge, not to healing." It is a knowledge that, given free reign, can eventually transform an individual, as we see when MacFarlane himself becomes a murderer, killing Gray when that henchman tries to blackmail him, and then excusing his act by noting that with him out of the way, "I'll be a new man and a better teacher." That "new man," however, is no better than a ghoul, as he presses Fettes to assist him in stealing bodies from the graveyard; "We can do our own dirty work," he informs his student with some satisfaction.

The flawed perspective that underlies this transformation is particularly underscored in the film's final scene, in which MacFarlane and Fettes return from exhuming the body of an old woman. As they ride off with their prize, the corpse repeatedly topples onto the doctor's shoulder, and he gradually begins hallucinating that the body is actually that of Gray, returned to haunt him. Confronted by this imagined sign of his crimes, a long-repressed guilt suddenly unleashed on his consciousness, MacFarlane seems to go mad and drives his carriage over a precipice. Fettes, thrown clear of the careening coach, then inspects the wreck, holding up a lamp (symbolic of his own clearer vision) to the corpse that had so frightened his tutor, and affirms that it was indeed simply the body of an old woman. The guilty vision that effectively frightened MacFarlane to death, we understand, was an image of his own distorted perspective, a projection of that internal horror he had long denied and repressed under a guise of respectability and scientific purpose.

With ***Isle of the Dead***, the faulty perspective precipitating such human transformations becomes the key motif, literally framing the tale with its various formulations. It first takes shape in the character of General Pherides, known as "the watchdog" of Greece and the "guardian of his country." As the film opens, the general summarily court-martials a subordinate, ordering him to take his own life, despite the fact that he is an old friend. Immediately established is the general's desire to maintain order in his army by closely overseeing every action. The other emblem of that dangerous perspective is the recurring image of Cerberus, literally the watchdog of the ancient gods, guarding the gates of Hades, which here takes the form of a statue that greets all who land on the island where the story's main action occurs. A similarity between these two figures is immediately established when the war correspondent, Oliver Davis, notes for the general, "There's another watchdog for you." Pherides disavows the likeness, though, and points up his own belief in the correctness of his perspective, reminding Oliver that Cerberus "only guards the dead; I have to worry about the living." Like the general, however, the figure of Cerberus seems ever present, watching over the action of the film, serving as a key transitional device, and providing the narrative's closing image. What those recurring shots of that mythic watchdog suggest is just how closely death lingers in this world, and how hellish human beings can make their environment by misfocusing their perspective on it and fellow human beings.

Vision for the general, we understand, is associated with warding off danger and preserving the laws of his homeland. What he sees around him is a world of chaos, of constant threats he must notice as soon as they take shape in order to counter them. One form this attitude takes is his rigid enforcement of the law, even to the point of collecting taxes from the native villagers with field artillery; he could fire on his own people, he admits, because the law dictated it, and anyone "who is against the law of Greece is not a Greek." While Pherides earnestly keeps watch, then, it is through a transforming filter, the conceptualizations afforded him by a rigid and inhuman system of laws that so clouds his true perceptions that he can deny the very nationality of his countrymen.

The advent of a truly invisible threat, the plague, as a consequence of the general's latest military victory serves both to underscore this attitude and to illustrate effectively its danger. In fact, with the plague comes a literal transformation in the general's character, from protector to destroyer, which serves to comment upon the perspective he brings to this world. Although of peasant origins, Pherides sees himself as a representative of a new order, a Greece that has abandoned the ancients and their superstitious ways; "These are new days for Greece. We don't believe the old, foolish tales anymore," he boasts. In place of those myths he describes as "nonsense" the general pays homage to a rational perspective, putting his faith totally "in what I can feel, and see, and know about." When the plague strikes, therefore, he turns to modern science, embodied in his subordinate, Dr. Drossos, to halt its spread and keep it from devastating his army. All that Drossos can counsel, however, is sanitary precautions and patience while the disease runs its course. Since a favorable wind might rid them of the fleas that spread the plague, the doctor does raise a pennant, in part to keep track of the wind's shifting direction, but more to distract the vision of those under his quarantine; as he readily admits, it is "better to watch the wind and hope that it changes than to watch each other and have no hope at all." What Drossos thereby admits is the complexity and even futility of that watching process, an activity that simply transforms human beings into potential victims of the devastating and uncontrollable forces they unwittingly evoke.

When Drossos's precautions fail to stop the plague's progress—the disease even taking his life—Pherides gradually returns to the long-repressed fears and beliefs of his folk heritage. From that collective unconscious, Madame Kyra, the old housekeeper, dredges up a superstitious explanation for the disease: the notion that a *vorvolaka*, or evil spirit inhabiting a human form, has brought about this affliction. Since, as he notes, "everything—every *human* remedy" has failed, Pherides embraces this explanation and turns his attention to the servant girl, Thea, who, in the midst of the plague, inexplicably remains healthy, beautiful, and, as one character notes, "full of life." Pherides and Kyra, therefore, mount a constant watch over Thea, even at night while she sleeps, in hope of catching her in some evil act; he justifies the transformation he has worked on her character by asking her if "a *vorvolaka* in human form can remember the evil that she did at night," and he vows that "until I know, I must watch you." That constant surveillance and the suspicion it denotes deeply affect Thea, undermining her view of herself, even bringing her to question whether she has, in fact, become possessed by such an evil influence. Consequently, the general's watching, initially prodded by his desire to save his fellow human beings, becomes less a protective activity than an injurious one, as he isolates Thea from the others, especially Oliver who is in love with her, and forces her into a desperate self-doubt, as she too lives in fear of those forces lingering beneath her consciousness, threatening even those she loves. Because of the perspective the general brings to his world, then, a human being has arrived at such a state that the beautiful can be thought a disguise for evil, love can be denied, and the human spirit can be suspected of the most sinister motivations.

What the narrative repeatedly underscores is just how much remains invisible, though, and thus how unavailing that watchfulness must ultimately prove to be. When the British Consul, St. Aubyn, dies, his wife asks for some proof, since, she asserts, "the breath can stop; the heart can stop. It still doesn't mean death." Visible signs, she knows from experience, can be most deceptive, for there is a history of catalepsy in her family, of trance-like states that give the illusion of death; consequently, she has always feared being buried alive. When she is apparently stricken with the plague, though, that sanitary impulse precipitates a hurried burial, and she is entombed alive, a symbolic reminder of the dangers of our limited perspective and of that mode of vision the general has brought to bear on those around him—a vision that readily sees death even in life, pestilence in the natural order, and danger in the harmless. The darkness in which all of the subsequent action takes place serves only to emphasize the difficulty of those visual judgments Pherides so precipitately makes, while allowing for the note of irony Lewton injects by repeatedly depicting Thea carrying a lamp or candle to dispel that darkness in which those around her dwell, enabling them to see circumstances all the more clearly.

In his discussion of this plague motif in literature, René Girard points out its archetypal characteristic and suggests that we should see in its narrative recurrences "a disguise for an even more terrible threat that no science has ever been able to conquer" ["The Plague in Literature and Myth," *Texas Studies in Literature and Language*, Vol. 15, 1974]. The shape of that threat appears most clearly here in the final transformation Pherides undergoes when he is himself stricken by that disease he has sought to ward off. Taunted by Madame Kyra that "you stayed your hand and now the plague punishes you," he decides to murder Thea, believing that he will thereby vanquish the *vorvolaka* she harbors within and appease the anger of the ancient gods. In effect, he becomes with this decision precisely the sort of evil and threatening spirit he seeks to remove from this human realm. Transformed into a raving maniac, he stalks Thea, only to be stopped at the last moment by the intervention of Mrs. St. Aubyn, who has escaped from her premature entombment where she has apparently undergone a similar transformation. In her own madness, then, she kills both Pherides and Kyra, visits their fears upon them, before throwing herself off a cliff. Oliver earlier warned the general of a danger far greater than the plague: "There is something here more dangerous than septicemic plague . . . and that's your own crazy thoughts." His point is simply that human beings often become their own worst enemy, harboring within the potential for their own destruction, their own monstrous shape or madness, usually repressed or lost in the unconscious, but waiting to be evoked. Fittingly, the particular form of the plague that strikes and elicits that delirious state in which the general can attempt murder is an internal disease with no visible marks, other than, as the doctor notes, a change of behavior in its final stages. Septicemic plague, it seems, eats away at the vitals, particularly the bloodstream, and etymologically suggests a rotting from within. In short, it seems carefully selected to denote the sort of internal, cancer-like danger to which we are prone, an internal violence that defies watchfulness and points up our own complicity in those threats that often seem to erupt in our world.

Lewton ends ***Isle of the Dead*** with a most telling juxtaposition, one that underscores the connection between that failure of vision and the terrible events that accompany it. A close-up of the dead Pherides's face, his eyes open and staring, still keeping their frightful vigil, even in death, dissolves to a long shot of Oliver and Thea leaving the island, taking their love out of this land of the dead so that it might prosper. Their departure, however, is haunted by these events, as a close-up of the statue of Cerberus is superimposed, the three snarling heads of that monstrous watchdog recalling the dangers of a vision whose only purpose is to control life.

That final image well sums up this genre's concerns with both internal and external threats, with human anxieties and those monstrous presences that often provide the objective correlatives for our vague and unformulated fears. One of Lewton's great achievements, in fact, was that he consistently managed to dramatize how interwoven these concerns ultimately are, how fully the unconscious must influence the conscious world. Like the more conventional examples of the genre, his films explore that very common fear we have of otherness, but at the same time they reveal how it may prompt us to distance ourselves from other people and to abdicate participation in that human realm we necessarily inhabit. Nietzsche's warning in *Beyond Good and Evil* that "whoever battles with monsters had better see that it does not turn him into a monster. And if you gaze long into an abyss, the abyss will gaze back into you" hints at just this sort of transformation to which we are prone when we lose an essential human perspective, the ability to look within as well as without. An improper mode of vision, such as the sort that enables us to abdicate our human responsibility or see in our fellow human beings that otherness we almost instinctively fear, in the end engenders that very monstrousness from which we initially and naturally recoil.

What the horror film in its various formulations has ideally sought to do is to prod us into a more comprehensive perspective, to engender, as it were, a morality of seeing. Recent work in the genre, it has been suggested, has essentially abdicated that moral function by forcing an identification between the audience and some aberrance, through a subjective camera placing a "killer's center of consciousness in the audience" [Roger Ebert, "Why Movie Audiences Aren't Safe Any More," *American Film*, March 1981]. Even if poorly controlled and misguided, though, that effect derives from and points back to a most important impulse in the horror genre. A major legacy of the Lewton films, more recently found in the work of Hitchcock, Brian DePalma, and John Carpenter especially, is to call attention to that frame of reference to which we normally and unconsciously cling, a framework that allows us to see marked distinctions between the self and a threatening otherness, but that may also blind us to a similar duality within the self. Our experience of the horror film clearly prompts us to perceive the world differently when we emerge from the theater, to find a new potential—both a frightening and an exhilarating one—in that world we normally inhabit. This is one transformation we sorely need, though, for the ways in which we see the world and the self are mutually dependent. Those formulas that help to foster that vision, consequently, serve a vital function, promising to make us more human, if paradoxically by forcing us to recognize a monstrous potential within.

FURTHER READING

Criticism

Bansak, Edmund G. *Fearing the Dark: The Val Lewton Career*. Jefferson, N. C.: McFarland & Company, 1995, 571 p.

Biography of Lewton that primarily focuses on his major films of the 1940s.

Clarens, Carlos. "Horror, the Soul of the Plot." In *An Illustrated History of the Horror Film*, pp. 111-17. New York: Capricorn Books, 1967.

Overview of Lewton's films. Clarens considers Lewton as a maverick producer in the context of the otherwise seedy horror-film genre of his day.

Telotte, J. P. *Dreams of Darkness: Fantasy and the Films of Val Lewton*. Urbana: University of Illinois Press, 1985, 223 p.

Contains critical evaluations of Lewton's major productions.

Oscar Micheaux

1884-1951

(Born Oscar Devereaux Michaux) American director, producer, screenwriter, and novelist.

INTRODUCTION

Micheaux was a pioneering African American filmmaker, among the first in the American motion picture industry. With the early success of his novel *The Homesteader* (1917), which he adapted into a film two years later, Micheaux was able to write, produce, and direct approximately forty-eight films over the next three decades in both silent and sound formats. Spurred by a desire to depict African Americans in non-stereotypical roles, Micheaux created his motion pictures with all-black casts and featured in them the genres of mainstream film: western, detective mystery, romance, and melodrama. His works, however, failed to achieve acceptance outside of the African American community during his lifetime, and today Micheaux is primarily remembered for his bold efforts in a white-dominated industry rather than for the content of his films themselves.

Biographical Information

Micheaux was born on his father's farm near Metropolis, Illinois, on January 2, 1884. As a youth he spent a great deal of his leisure time reading, notably the works of Booker T. Washington, whose philosophy of diligence and hard work was to make an impression on him. After graduating from high school at the age of seventeen, Micheaux left southern Illinois and headed to Chicago. There he worked a series of menial jobs and became a Pullman train porter, a vocation that occupied him until 1904. At this time Micheaux decided to purchase and farm a piece of land in South Dakota. He would later record this period of his life in his autobiographical novel *The Conquest: The Story of a Negro Pioneer* (1913). After its publication Micheaux alighted upon the idea of selling his story door-to-door, which he did successfully in the American South. This later period of his life offered the source for his second work, *The Forged Note: A Romance of the Darker Races* (1915). A third novel, somewhat less autobiographical but still based on his South Dakota farm life, *The Homesteader* caught the attention of the Lincoln Motion Picture Company, representatives of which approached Micheaux offering to make the story into a film. Micheaux liked the idea but wanted to direct the picture himself. Their refusal led him to create his own company, the Micheaux Film Corporation. Active until the 1940s, the company allowed Micheaux to write, direct, and produce an assortment of silent and "talkie" films. These works were played in black ghetto movie-houses and earned him considerable success, although he never achieved mainstream critical approval. In the 1940s Micheaux wrote several more novels, produced his final film *The Betrayal* (1948), and conducted speaking tours of the South in support of his works. It was during one of these promotional visits to Charlotte, North Carolina, that Micheaux died in 1951.

Major Works

Both Micheaux's novels and his motion pictures feature themes relating to race and race relations, such as interracial love, prejudice, and censure. His autobiographical novel *The Conquest: The Story of a Negro Pioneer*, details the life of Oscar Devereaux, a young black man who leaves the racially-divided city to pursue a utopian dream as a farmer in South Dakota. Though he falls in love with a white woman, Devereaux marries a member of his race, only to find that marriage thwarted by her father and his dream of being a homesteader melodramatically crushed by the forces of nature. Micheaux revived this story of his real-life experience in South Dakota in his considerably more successful novel (and later film) entitled *The Homesteader*. Its protagonist, the solitary and aloof Jean Baptiste—unlike Devereaux—finds his dream on the American plains. After *The Homesteader* Micheaux turned his attention to film for the next two decades, producing a variety of works in many genres—some of them cautionary tales, others uplifting, and a few that depict the racial stereotypes he intended to denounce. *God's Stepchildren* (1938) looks at group of light-skinned blacks who endeavor to pass as whites in order to succeed in American society. *Underworld* (1936) is a gangster story; while the 1939 sound version of *Birthright* dramatizes the racial prejudice inflicted upon a recent African American Harvard graduate by both blacks and whites.

Critical Reception

Although popularly successful in the milieu of black film during his life, Micheaux and his works fell into relative obscurity in the years following his death in 1951. Several decades later he has received considerable recognition for his ground-breaking efforts as an African American filmmaker, including a posthumous lifetime achievement award granted by the Director's Guild of America in the 1980s. Today, however, only about a dozen of his estimated forty-eight films still exist, and these have been frequently cited for their uneven writing and low production values. Additionally, scholars who have studied Micheaux's work conclude that his pieces demonstrate an assimilationist ethic rather than a strident desire to eradicate racial prejudice and intolerance through example.

Nevertheless, Micheaux continues to be valued as a pivotal figure in the early motion picture industry and as a vital inspiration to contemporary African American filmmakers.

PRINCIPAL WORKS

The Conquest: The Story of a Negro Pioneer (autobiographical novel) 1913
The Forged Note: A Romance of the Darker Races (autobiographical novel) 1915
The Homesteader (novel) 1917
The Homesteader (film) 1919
The Brute (film) 1920
Symbol of the Unconquered (film) 1920
Within Our Gates (film) 1920
Deceit (film) 1921
The Gunsaulus Mystery (film) 1921
The Dungeon (film) 1922
Uncle Jasper's Will (film) 1922
The Virgin of the Seminole (film) 1922
The Ghost of Tolston's Manor (film) 1923
A Son of Satan (film) 1924
Body and Soul (film) 1925
Marcus Garland (film) 1925
The Spider's Web (film) 1926
The Broken Violin (film) 1927
The Millionaire (film) 1927
Easy Street (film) 1928
Thirty Years Later (film) 1928
When Men Betray (film) 1928
Wages of Sin (film) 1929
A Daughter of the Congo (film) 1930
Darktown Revue (film) 1931
The Exile (film) 1931
Black Magic (film) 1932
The Girl from Chicago (film) 1932
Ten Minutes to Live (film) 1932
Veiled Aristocrats (film) 1932
Ten Minutes to Kill (film) 1933
Harlem after Midnight (film) 1934
Lem Hawkins' Confession (film) 1935
Swing (film) 1936
Temptation (film) 1936
Underworld (film) 1936
Miracle in Harlem (film) 1937
God's Stepchildren (film) 1938
Birthright [sound version] (film) 1939
Lying Lips (film) 1940
The Notorious Elinor Lee (film) 1940
The Wind from Nowhere (novel) 1944
The Case of Mrs. Wingate (novel) 1945
The Story of Dorothy Stanfield, Based on a Great Insurance Swindle, and a Woman (novel) 1946
The Masquerade: An Historical Novel (novel) 1947
The Betrayal (film) 1948

CRITICISM

Hugh M. Gloster (essay date 1948)

SOURCE: "Negro Fiction to World War I," in *Negro Voices in American Fiction,* The University of North Carolina Press, 1948, pp. 23-100.

[*In the following excerpt, Gloster briefly assesses* The Conquest, The Homesteader, *and* The Forged Note.]

Avoiding both pride and bitterness in his treatment of interracial subject matter, Oscar Micheaux writes somewhat autobiographically of the experiences of an enterprising Negro in Chicago, the South Dakota farm lands, and the urban South. His first novel, ***The Conquest: The Story of a Negro Pioneer*** (1913), based largely on the author's own life and dedicated to Booker T. Washington, relates the experiences of Oscar Devereux in Illinois and South Dakota. In the latter state Devereux, after acquiring a homestead and becoming a prosperous farmer, falls in love with a Scottish girl but evades matrimony because of the racial barrier. Later marrying Orlean McCraline, daughter of a Negro preacher of Chicago, he finally leaves her because of frequent disagreements with her father.

In ***The Conquest,*** for the first time in American Negro fiction, a leading colored character appears in the role of a pioneer; and settlement in the Northwest is proposed as an approach to the alleviation of racial tension in the South. Admitting that the black man suffers injustice in the United States, Micheaux nevertheless asserts that this "should be no reason why the American Negro should allow obvious prejudice to prevent his taking advantage of opportunities that surround him." Recommending the Northwest as an area where the Negro might work out a successful future, the author continues:

> . . . for years I have felt constrained to deplore the negligence of the colored race in America, in not seizing the opportunity for monopolizing more of the many million acres of rich farm lands in the great Northwest, where immigrants from the old world own many acres of rich farm lands; while the millions of blacks, only a few hundred miles away, are as oblivious to it all as the heathen of Africa are to civilization.

In didactic chapters entitled "Where the Negro Fails" and "Progressives and Reactionaries" Micheaux advances opinions concerning the shortcomings and leadership of his race. He affirms that "the greatest of all the failings" of his people, both ignorant and educated, is the lack of "that great and mighty principle which characterizes Americans, called the initiative." In amplification of this idea, he says:

> Colored people are possible in every way that is akin to becoming good citizens, which has been thoroughly proven and is an existing fact. Yet they

> seem to lack the "guts" to get into the Northwest and "do things." In seven or eight of the great agricultural states there were not enough colored farmers to fill a township of thirty-six sections.
>
> Another predominating inconsistency is that there is that "love of luxury." They want street cars, cement walks, and electric lights to greet them when they arrive.

In an evaluation of the two conflicting schools of Negro leadership, Micheaux expresses a preference for the racial platform of Booker T. Washington:

> The Progressives, led by Booker T. Washington and with industrial education as the material idea, are good, active citizens; while the other class, distinctly reactionary in every way, contend for more equal rights, privileges, and protection, which is all very logical, indeed, but they do not substantiate their demands with any concrete policies; depending largely on loud demands, and are too much given to the condemnation of the entire white race for the depredations of a few.

A further examination of Micheaux's views on the Washington-DuBois controversy reveals, however, that he is not altogether in agreement with the views of the Tuskegee educator. He proposes the Northwest for Negro settlement, while Washington advised the black man to remain in the South. In addition, Micheaux is incorrect in the observation that DuBois was not a leader of the anti-Washington movement and that this movement did not gain momentum with the passing of the years.

The Forged Note: A Romance of the Darker Races (1915), largely autobiographical like ***The Conquest,*** is also a trail-blazing novel in its treatment of the experiences of a Negro writer in selling his own book in the urban South. Sidney Wyeth, author of a novel called *The Tempest* (really ***The Conquest***), and Mildred Latham are promoting the sale of *The Tempest* among colored people in Southern cities. Wyeth goes to Attalia (Atlanta) and Effingham (Birmingham), while Mildred works in Memphis. At the close of the novel the couple, reunited in New Orleans, set out for South Dakota, the part of the country that Wyeth prefers and calls home.

Much of ***The Forged Note*** is direct criticism of Negro life in the urban South, "wherein people and environment are so different from the rest, that a great problem is ever at issue." Though aware of prejudice and persecution, Micheaux is chiefly concerned with the black man's own delinquencies. For example, one character in the book makes the following comment concerning the colored population of Effingham:

> "These Negroes in Effingham are niggers proper. They think nothing about reading and trying to learn something; they only care for dressing up and having a good time."

A further indictment of Negroes, especially the leaders of the race, is given in an article which Wyeth contributes under the following headline to a Southern daily newspaper:

> Negro Says Race Faces Dreadful Conditions, Due to Lack of Leaders. Says Selfishness Is So Much the Order That There Is No Interest Whatever Toward Uplift. Professional Negro the Worst.

A sordid picture of the criminality and profligacy of colored Memphians is painted for Mildred by a minister:

> "The city has a preponderance of ignorant, polluted people among the Negroes. They flock into this town from all around, and represent the low, polluted, and depraved element of our race. They settle about the levee district, spend their earnings for the worst whiskey, give the remainder of their time to gambling and all kinds of vice, and murder is the natural consequence."

Though indicating the degeneracy of Negro life in Southern cities, Micheaux offers no panacea and fails to exhibit the optimism and enterprise which characterize ***The Conquest.***

Except for an intensification of the theme of intermarriage and a more detailed analysis of the main character's difficulties with his Negro wife because of her father's interference, ***The Homesteader*** (1917) is quite similar to ***The Conquest.*** The novel is an account of the love of a Negro farmer of South Dakota for the daughter of a neighbor who has recently migrated from Indiana. When the lovers are brought together in a driving snowstorm, the author comments:

> But what he was yet to know, and which is the great problem of our story, the girl, his dream girl, Agnes Stewart, happened to be white, while he, Jean Baptiste, The Homesteader, was a Negro.

Although strongly attracted to Agnes, Baptiste concludes that their marriage could not be consummated in the United States since

> . . . *between him and his dream girl was a chasm so deep socially that bridging was impossible.* Because she was white while he was black, according *to the custom of the country and its law,* she could never be anything to him. (Italics by Micheaux.)

Moreover, he feels that such a union would not be for the best interests of the girl and himself:

> But to marry out of the race to which he belonged, especially into the race in which she belonged, would be the most unpopular thing he could do. He had set himself in this new land to succeed; he had worked and slaved to that end. He liked his people; he wanted to help them. Examples they needed, and such he was glad he had become; but if he married now the one he loved, the example was lost; he would be condemned, he would be despised by the race that was his. Moreover, last but not least, he would perhaps, by such union

bring into her life much unhappiness, and he loved her too well for that.

For these reasons, therefore, Baptiste decides to marry a woman of his own race and eventually weds Orlean McCarthy (note the similarity of the name to that of the wife of the hero in ***The Conquest***), a Chicago minister's daughter, whom he carries to his homestead in South Dakota. The Reverend McCarthy succeeds in alienating his daughter's affections and causing her to sell property which her husband had given her. After Orlean, tormented by conscience, commits patricide and suicide, Baptiste is accused of a double murder but is later acquitted because of findings of a detective hired by Agnes. Baptiste and Agnes are brought together through the use of *deus ex machina,* a device frequently used in American fiction to solve the difficulties of interracial romance. Returning to South Dakota, Baptiste learns that Agnes has Negro blood and marries her without anxiety concerning American mores and law.

Though unimpressive in technique, Oscar Micheaux's novels introduce characters and settings far removed from the well-trod paths of American Negro fiction. The problem of intermarriage, the cardinal interest in ***The Conquest*** and ***The Homesteader,*** is left dangling in the former work but is solved in the latter through the hackneyed device of revealing that the supposedly white heroine is a mixed-blood. ***The Conquest,*** which attempts to defend the program of Booker T. Washington, proposes Negro migration to the Northwest as a means of improving race relations in the South. In ***The Forged Note*** the author missed an unusual opportunity to probe the life of the Southern urban Negro. With all their inadequacies, however, Micheaux's novels stand in contrast to much of the complimentary fiction produced by many Negro writers before the World War.

Janis Hebert (essay date 1973)

SOURCE: "Oscar Micheaux: A Black Pioneer," in *South Dakota Review,* Vol. 11, No. 4, Winter, 1973-74, pp. 62-9.

[*In the following essay, Hebert discusses Micheaux's novels as socio-historical artifacts that offer unique glimpses of South Dakotan life during the times in which the works were written.*]

During the spring of 1905, a unique homesteader appeared in Gregory County, South Dakota who became the object of much attention and gossip, for as the homesteader himself claimed, he, Oscar Micheaux, "was the only colored man engaged in agriculture . . . from Megory [Gregory] to Omaha, a distance of three hundred miles." Today, attention is again being directed toward Micheaux, not only because he was a black homesteader, but because he recorded his South Dakota experiences in two novels, ***The Conquest: The Story of a Negro Pioneer*** published in 1913 and ***The Homesteader*** published in 1917.

Most of what is known about Micheaux's background and his experiences in Gregory County exists in these two novels and the memories of those Gregory County pioneers who knew him. According to both sources, Micheaux spent his childhood about forty miles from Cairo, Illinois, but being more interested in people than in his father's small farm, he began working in the cities of Illinois, at one point as a shoe-shine boy.

Micheaux left Illinois when about eighteen and became a Pullman porter, a fact which later amused his homesteading neighbors. As one of these neighbors recalls, "You can't find a better metaphor than a Pullman porter pushing a plow. He must have gone through the agonies of hell. However, he must have got the hang of it because he used eight horses pulling a binder with a seeder on behind. Harvesting and seeding at the same time was an innovation all his own.

However little Micheaux's experiences equipped him for farming they did increase his awareness of the opportunities available to black people, for while he was a porter, he heard rumors that the eastern part of the Rosebud Reservation in South Dakota was to be opened for settlement. To Micheaux, the prospects here looked inviting because as he says [in ***The Conquest***], "I concluded on one thing, and that was, if one whose capital was under eight or ten thousand dollars, desired to own a farm in the great central west, he must go where the land was new or raw and undeveloped. He must begin with the beginning and develop with the development of the country." And so, while he missed the actual opening of Gregory County in the spring of 1904, he did purchase a relinquishment southeast of Gregory that fall.

The location of this particular relinquishment, however, has brought into question Micheaux's real motives regarding the purchase. In ***The Conquest*** and ***The Homesteader,*** Micheaux claims that he was not only sincerely interested in farming, but that he was also very successful in it. He comments [in the former], "When I broke out one hundred and twenty acres with such an outfit as I had, as against many other real farmers who had not broken over forty acres, with good horses and their knowledge of breaking prairie, ... I began to be regarded in a different light. . . . I was not called a free-go-easy coon, but a genuine booster for Calias [Dallas] and the Little Crow [Rosebud]." On the other hand, one of the pioneers who knew him says that Micheaux purchased this particular piece of land for speculative purposes, basing his purchase on rumors that the railroad would soon pass through Dallas, a small town in a section adjoining Micheaux's land. "Micheaux's game was trying to outfox the railroad, and his farming efforts merely a front." (The railroad by 1904 had gone as far west as Bonesteel, thirty miles east of Micheaux's claim and was in the process of extending farther west.) "The railroad no doubt put out decoy plans and survey to throw the land speculators a curve. From Bonesteel they first said they were going to the northwest and then said to the southwest. After they got everyone touted off, they put her right down the middle. Micheaux got sucked in on the southwest route."

Whatever Micheaux's intentions may have been, the railroad was routed about three miles north of his claim, and he did turn to farming and begin to consider his future as a permanent resident of the area. Of special concern to him were the prospects for obtaining a wife. There were, of course, no young black women in the area, and although Micheaux became very close to a young white girl who was his neighbor, he admits, "when the reality of the situation dawned on me, I became in a way frightened, for I did not by any means want to fall in love with a white girl. I had always disapproved of intermarriage, considering it as being above all things, the very thing that a colored man could not even think of. That we would become desperately in love, however, seemed inevitable." Remembering that he had relatives in Chicago who might be able to help him find a black wife, Micheaux went there several times. Finally, he did meet a young black girl willing to leave the lights of Chicago for a life on the prairie. She was Mildred, the daughter of a minister in one of the leading Negro churches.

While describing his experiences while courting Mildred, Micheaux is very careful in ***The Conquest*** to inform his readers that he is cultured, and this often pretentious concern leads him into several digressions relating to his experiences in Chicago. In regard to a play which he and Mildred attend, he offers this criticism. "The next play we attended suited me better as, to my mind, it possessed all that 'Madam X' lacked, and instead of weakness and an unhappy ending, this was one of strength of character, and a happy finale. It was 'The Fourth Estate,' by Joseph Medill Patterson, who served his apprenticeship on the *Chicago Tribune.*"

While Micheaux's attitude as expressed here is certainly unimportant in terms of the plot of ***The Conquest,*** it does reveal a certain aspect of his character, an aspect which was most disagreeable to his future father-in-law. Nevertheless, despite his dislike for Micheaux, the minister did permit the couple to marry and return to South Dakota.

During the time that Micheaux was in Chicago, progress was continuing on the frontier. The town of Dallas, having been ignored by the railroad, was literally moved piece by piece to five miles west of Gregory. In this position, it for a time realized its desire of being the western terminus, but this glory was short-lived as in 1908, Tripp County was opened for settlement, and the railroad again moved westward.

Micheaux again was not far behind. Upon his return from Chicago, he made arrangements for his wife to establish a claim in Tripp County. Since his farm was in Gregory County and she was required by terms of her claim to establish residency there in Tripp County, the couple was separated much of the time. Mildred, of course, began writing letters to her family in Chicago, and it was not long before the minister began interfering in his daughter's marriage. As previously mentioned, the minister and Micheaux disagreed on many subjects, but they primarily fought over Micheaux's belief [expressed in ***The Forged Note***] that "the Negro did not put forth the effort he could and should, from an industrial point-of-view, for his ultimate betterment." The minister, accustomed to being a dominant figure undoubtedly felt threatened because he could not exercise control over the ideas and actions of his adventurous son-in-law. Within a year or two after his daughter's marriage, the minister went to South Dakota, coerced Mildred into signing her husband's name on a check, then cashed it, and took her back to Chicago.

Despite his efforts, Micheaux could not get Mildred to return to South Dakota, and it was during the next few years while he was alone on the homestead that Micheaux began writing ***The Conquest,*** a description of the events of his life up to that time. Shortly after, he wrote ***The Forged Note*** which deals with Southern blacks, but then again returned to his South Dakota theme in ***The Homesteader.***

At this point, knowledge of Micheaux as an author and as a homesteader becomes very vague. Other pioneers in the area seem only to agree that "he had borrowed money everywhere he could and skipped out without a trace owing a lot of people." In fact, it was not until nearly thirty years later that the name of Oscar Micheaux drew the attention of his former neighbors, and then it was not merely attention, but surprise. In 1940, a local newspaper noted that at a meeting in Chicago, Ernest Jackson, who had been active in founding Dallas, and later Winner, South Dakota, reported the following for the interest of those who may have remembered Oscar Micheaux. "(He) told about the present abode and prosperity of Mr. Micheaux. He stated that he had risen high in the movie producing industry, and that two-thirds of the movie houses in the Negro district of Chicago continuously show 'Oscar Micheaux Productions.' He lives in New York and drives to Chicago in a 16-cylinder car with a white chauffeur. He weighs over three hundred pounds" ["Negro Who Homesteaded in Rosebud Now Big Man in U.S. Movie Pictures," *Sioux Falls Argus Leader,* 4 March 1940].

Micheaux again came to life in a 1970 issue of the *New Yorker* [18 April] which stated that "***God's Step Children,*** a melodrama filmed in 1938 for black audiences by the black director Oscar Micheaux, who died in 1951, was shown in New York the other day . . . at the Jewish Museum." According to the article Micheaux directed between twenty and thirty films, which were created to make money and generally involved stereotyped characters. The article gives a very negative review of the movie, but one of Micheaux's leading men is said to have emphatically stated, "I think Micheaux was a genius."

Genius or not in the film industry, Micheaux also continued writing novels; these again were directed primarily to black readers. The *Black Yearbook 1947* lists the following three novels: ***The Wind From Nowhere*** (1942), ***The***

Case of Mrs. Wingate (1944), and ***The Story of Dorothy Stanfield*** (1946), and further comments that "Dealing with sensational themes such as Negro-white marriage, the stage type of woman, black Nazis, and the Negro's shortcomings, these novels present as few other works today the attitude, the thinking, the prejudices, and to a certain degree the turn of phrase of the Negro man-in-the-street. Micheaux knows intimately the psychology of the mass-Negro and he exploits it effectively in his novels. But he too suffers from many technical deficiencies. For this and other reasons there has been a tendency among critics to 'dismiss' Oscar Micheaux as a writer."

Whatever evaluations have been made concerning Micheaux's later work, for those persons interested in literature of Midwestern settlement, evaluation should be primarily concerned with his two early novels, ***The Conquest*** and ***The Homesteader.*** The merit of these two novels may perhaps best be determined by two investigations, the first concerned with their historical validity and the other concerned with their expression of a black man regarding his role as a homesteader.

Although, as earlier mentioned, Micheaux sometimes related quite vaguely his intentions and relationship to the history being made around him, he does give a reasonably accurate account of the area's development. In ***The Conquest,*** he has changed the names of the actual towns and people, but one needs only to read a history of the area to identify the places and people with certainty.

Micheaux is perhaps the most valid and most interesting in describing the development of towns and railroads; the relocation of Dallas, the ensuing battle between the new Dallas and Gregory, the founding and death of Lamro in Tripp County, which gradually moved itself to become a part of the railroad town, Winner, and the confusion and lawlessness which entered these towns whenever there was a land opening.

With regard to people, Micheaux goes into little detail except when speaking of the Nicholson brothers, actually the Jackson brothers, who, through their political connections, greatly influenced the development of Dallas and Winner, and whose names are generally associated with the large and successful Mulehead Ranch. Another interesting historical character whom Micheaux does mention is the "Oklahoma" grafter, Numemaker from Bonesteel, who deceptively and unscrupulously helped Micheaux select his first team. "He finally persuaded me to buy a team of big plugs, one of which was so awkward he looked as though he would fall down if he tried to trot. The other was a powerful four-year-old gelding, that would have never been for sale around Oristown [Bonesteel] if it hadn't been that he had two feet badly wire cut." But as later events show, Micheaux didn't learn much from his dealings with this grafter, for he traded three or four times before he finally got a team that was worth anything.

While Micheaux's perception of the people he dealt with may have been weak, his perception of incidents occurring around him was quite vivid, and he relates for his readers some of the more interesting ones such as the prairie fire in Dallas, the death of Jack Sully, and the story of Rattlesnake Jack. The latter of these indicates the way a small incident can be blown up into a headline story. According to an Omaha newspaper, Rattlesnake Jack, who was a woman, killed eighty rattlesnakes in her little shanty in Gregory County. "The Omaha newspaper printed the story illustrated with a picture of a beautiful girl in a leather skirt, riding boots, and cowboy hat, entering a sod house and being greeted by a monstrous snake. . . . For a few brief weeks or even months, the Gregory area was boasting a character as important as Calamity Jane or Poker Alice" [*Gregory Times-Advocate,* "Fifty Years in the Rosebud Country of South Dakota," 7 January 1954]. However, as historical records show and Oscar Micheaux notes, while in the article, "she was also credited with having spent the previous winter alone on her claim and rather enjoyed the wintery nights and snow blockade," she actually "had spent most of the previous winter enjoying the comforts of a front room at the Hotel Calias . . . she had no horse, and as to the eighty rattlesnakes, seventy-nine were myths, existing only in the mind of a prolific feature story writer for the Sunday edition of the great dailies. In fact, she had killed one small rattler with a button."

This perception of actual events was not something Micheaux simply developed on the prairie, but seems to be a quality he had always possessed, and in his novels, he does relate most events with accuracy. In addition, Micheaux was a keen observer of various types of people and his frequent comments on them form a partial picture of his self-expression in the unique role of a black homesteader.

As previously noted, one of Micheaux's main concerns throughout his early novels as well as in his later work is the role of the black man in a predominantly white society. Time and again, Micheaux repeats the idea that while black men are in a bad situation and have some legitimate complaints, they often don't take advantage of opportunities available to them. Through his many experiences as a porter he "learned the greatest of all the failings were not only among the ignorant class [of blacks] but among the educated as well. Although more agreeable to talk to, they lacked that great and mighty principle which characterizes Americans, called 'the initiative'. Colored people are possible in every way that is akin to becoming good citizens, which has been thoroughly proven and is an existing fact. Yet they seem to lack the 'guts' to get into the northwest and 'do things'".

This obvious statement of "See, I am better than most blacks" is quite in keeping with what is known of Micheaux's character, but considering the fact that his later work was directed almost exclusively to black audiences, the following attitude appears somewhat incongruous. "By reading nothing but discussions concerning the race, by all but refusing to accept the success of the white race as an example and by welcoming any racial disturbance as a conclusion that the entire white race is bent in one great effort to hold him—the negro, down, he can not very well feel the thrill of modern progress and is ignorant as to public opinion."

Micheaux also expressed himself in relation to another minority group with which he came into contact, the American Indian. Here his attitudes, whether based on experience or hearsay, are quite narrow. In ***The Homesteader,*** he digresses from his main plot to include a chapter on how the Indians shot up the town when a Dallas bartender refused to serve them, and in ***The Conquest,*** he mentions that "The Indians were always selling and are yet, what is furnished them by the government, for all they can get. When given the money spends it as quickly as he possibly can, buying fine horses, buggies, whiskey, and what-not. Their only idea being that it is to spend. The Sioux Indians, in my opinion are the wealthiest tribe. They owned at one time the larger part of southern South Dakota and northern Nebraska, and own a lot of it yet. Be it said, however, it is simply because the government will not allow them to sell."

While there is certainly room for argument in many of Micheaux's statements, his novels are none the less valuable, for an informed reader immediately realizes that he is simply one man expressing one point-of-view, from a position that is certainly unique. Taking this into consideration then, there can be little argument concerning the fact that Oscar Micheaux experienced several interesting years as a South Dakota homesteader, and has left us two valuable accounts to add to the literature of settlement in the Midwest.

Arlene Elder (essay date 1976)

SOURCE: "Oscar Micheaux: The Melting Pot on the Plains," in *The Old Northwest: A Journal of Regional Life and Letters,* Vol. 2, September, 1976, pp. 299-307.

[*In the following essay, Elder examines the historical information contained in Micheaux's published works about the westward expansion of the United States.*]

When the Department of the Interior opened up land on the eastern part of the Rosebud Reservation in Gregory County, South Dakota, in 1905, the most unusual homesteader to stake his claim was the young Afro-American, Oscar Micheaux, a former Pullman porter from Illinois. Micheaux's ambition and daring seem to have fascinated his German, Swedish, Irish, Assyrian, Russian, Danish, and Austrian neighbors; there can be no doubt that he was deeply involved in his own accomplishments. He told of his homesteading experience in an autobiography, ***The Conquest, the Story of a Negro Pioneer*** (1913), and again in two novels, ***The Homesteader*** (1917) and ***The Wind From Nowhere*** (1941).

Micheaux's story of his life on the South Dakota Prairie is doubly significant. First, it represents an American ideal at the turn of the century—the movement west and the opening up of the country. More interesting for the student of cultural pluralism, however, is Micheaux's self-conscious emotional division between personal ambition, marked by intense frontier individualism, and his hope of being not only a racial representative but a leader of his people and a model for them. Reflective of this paradoxical self-image is the contrast he establishes between the City and the Wilderness as he develops his theme of the West. This symbolic juxtaposition also serves as the organizing principle for his discussion of race.

Like the writings of other regionalists, Micheaux's books provide a wealth of topographical, historical, and political information. He gives details about the methods of holding lotteries to settle the country (first choice of a homesite going to the holder of the first number pulled from a pile by a blindfolded child); the astonishing way new towns sprang up almost overnight on the prairie; and the way two-story buildings in the town which boomed a few months before would be sawn in half and both parts moved to the next settlement boosted by the local businessmen, who had themselves started from nothing and flourished overnight. He enlightens us on the condition of the Indians, especially the social history of families of "breeds" like the Amoureaux who were ranchers, owners of great herds of cattle and much land, and "high moguls in Little Crow society." He emphasizes the importance of the railroad in making or breaking the fortunes of the towns and farms in its path; and he skillfully describes the appearance and unusual features of the new country, frequently described as "the hollow of God's hand." Despite Micheaux's interest in local color, however, his real subject is himself. The introduction to his autobiography states: "This is a true story of a negro who was discontented and the circumstances that were the outcome of that discontent."

The West, the Wilderness, represents to him, as it does to his German and Swedish neighbors, all that is new and promising for the future. Here, he says in his book, is "unbroken prairie all about him; with its virgin soil and undeveloped resources. . . . Here could a young man work out his own destiny." His own growth is intrinsically linked with the growth of the country; a young man starting out with few resources, he explains, "must begin with the beginning and develop with the development of the country." The prairie is the "land of raw material, which my dreams had pictured to me as the land of real beginning. . . ."

Micheaux, like his fictional counterpart in ***The Homesteader,*** Jean Baptiste, was the only Black man to settle on the Rosebud after its opening; and he was one of the few settlers with sufficient foresight, frugality, ambition, determination, and industry to survive the dreadful winters on the prairie, the scarely less dreadful summers, and the plagues of prairie fires and drought. A list of his virtues would sound remarkably like Ben Franklin's, and he had the same trouble with "humility." This connection with one of America's founders, whose own *Autobiography* emphasizes the pleasure and possibility of rising from "poverty and obscurity . . . to a state of affluence and some degree of celebrity in the world," is apt, for Micheaux dedicates his own story to that Black Ben Franklin, Booker T. Washington.

Micheaux's story, despite its hopeful premise of participation in the American Dream, is one of increasing isolation. The loneliness is not only that physical solitude imposed by the darkness which steals up swiftly, imperceptibly, on the plains, or by the snow which sweeps "into huge drifts or long ridges," forming "one endless, unbroken sheet of white frost and ice," isolating individuals within their flimsy shacks, locking them within their sod houses, covering over the fences and roads man uses as marks and guides for his presence on the earth, and threatening the lone man in the wilderness with perceptual distortion as well as physical extinction. More significantly, Micheaux comes to realize his emotional and psychological isolation from his people. Late in his autobiography, he observes:

> Before I had any colored people to discourage me with their ignorance of business or what is required for success, I was stimulated to effort by the example of my white neighbors and friends who were doing what I admired, building an empire; and to me that was the big idea. Their parents before them knew something of business and this knowledge was a goodly heritage. If they could not help their children with money they at least gave their moral support and visited them and encouraged them with kind words of hope and cheer. The people in a new country live mostly on hopes for the first five or ten years. My parents and grandparents had been slaves, honest, but ignorant. My father could neither read nor write, had not succeeded in a large way, and had nothing to give me as a start, not even practical knowledge.

Micheaux notes the two distinct factions in Afro-American political and social thought at that time, factions which he characterizes as Progressives and Reactionaries. Classifying himself with the former, he explains: "The Progressives, led by Booker T. Washington and with industrial education as the material idea, are good, active citizens; while the other class distinctly reactionary in every way, contend for more equal rights, privileges, and protection, which is all very logical, indeed, but they do not substantiate their demands with any concrete policies; depending largely on loud demands, and are too much given to the condemnation of the entire white race for the depredations of a few." While Micheaux agrees that the Black man has been discriminated against, his own powerful sense of self-sufficiency and individualism prevents him from identifying with a people whom he characterizes as unable to "feel the thrill of modern progress and . . . ignorant to public opinion." As his story progresses, it becomes increasingly apparent that despite his desire to inspire and lead other Blacks into the glories of settling the plains, Micheaux actually defines himself in contrast to them.

Shortly after leaving home as a very young man, he starts his first bank account, and his view of it as opening the door for a literal and imaginative flight from his race is instructive:

> The little twenty-dollar certificate of deposit opened my mind to different things entirely. I would look at it until I had day dreams. During the three months I spent in Eaton I laid the foundation of a future. Simple as it was, it led me into channels which carried me away from my race and into a life fraught with excitement; a life that gave experiences and other things I had never dreamed of. I had started a bank account of twenty dollars and I found myself wanting one of thirty, and to my surprise the desire seemed to increase. This desire fathered my plans to become a porter on a Pullman car.

After working several months on irregular runs that take him to all the major cities east of the Mississippi, he is put on a steady run to Portland, Oregon. Micheaux makes much in his books of the importance of the railroad in developing the Midwest. By the vagaries of its hitting one town and missing another, the fortunes of western entrepreneurs and prairie towns are made or lost. It is clear that the railroad serves as a "civilizing" force in his own life, as well, and those of his fictional counterparts. By working as a porter, he sees most of the country from Boston to Portland; he learns about farming and sheep-raising from the western sheepmen he encounters on return runs from Chicago; he becomes familiar with the features of the country where he is later to locate his claim. His inquisitiveness, which he shows as having been a burden to his family when he was growing up, now provides him with the basis for his acquisitiveness.

Moreover, once he moves onto the Rosebud, he sees his unique presence there as another opportunity to prove himself. Although he spent time on farms as a child, he was never very fond of or good at farm work; and his struggles to get started in South Dakota provide the few humorous passages in his autobiography:

> I had left St. Louis with two hundred dollars in cash, and had drawn a draft for five hundred dollars more on the Chicago bank, where my money was on deposit, and what did I have for it? One big horse, tall as a giraffe; two little mules, one of which was a torment to me; a sod house; and an old wagon. As I faced the situation there seemed nothing to do but to fight it out, and I turned wearily to another attempt, this time with more success. Before I had started breaking I had invited criticism. Now I was getting it on all sides. I was the only colored homesteader on the reservation, and as an agriculturalist it began to look mighty bad for the colored race on the Little Crow.

He trades one bad mule for another bad mule: "I learned afterward the trader had come thirty-five miles to trade me that mule. . . . I soon had the enviable reputation of being a horse trader. Whenever anybody with horses to trade came to town, they were advised to go over to the sod house north of town and see the colored man. He was fond of trading horses, yes, he fairly doted on it." His white neighbors keep waiting for him to sell out "and 'beat it' back to more ease and comfort":

> This is largely the opinion of most of the white people, regarding the negro, and they are not entirely wrong in their opinion. I was quite well aware that such an opinion existed, but contrary to expectations, I rather appreciated it. When I broke out one hundred and twenty acres with such an outfit as I had, as against many other real farmers who had not broken over forty acres, with good horses and their knowledge of breaking prairie, acquired in states they had come from, I began to be regarded in a different light. At first I was regarded as an object of curiosity, which changed to appreciation, and later admiration. I was not called a free-go-easy coon, but a genuine booster for Calias and the Little Crow. I never spent a lonesome day after that.

His acceptance among the white homesteaders, however, is offset by his rejection among the Blacks he knows in Chicago. "One of the greatest tasks of my life," he reports, "has been to convince a certain class of my racial acquaintances that a colored man can be anything." When more land opens up for settlement, lengthy advertising circulars are printed and distributed to lure settlers. Micheaux "gave the name of not less than one hundred persons, and sent them personally to many as well. I wrote articles and sent them to different newspapers edited by colored people, in the east and other places. I was successful in getting one colored person to come and register—my oldest brother."

As the West, the Wilderness, represents success and the future of the country to Micheaux, the City is linked irredeemably in his mind with the plight of his less ambitious brothers. The City is Chicago, the great "hog-butcher" of the plains, the home of thousands of Blacks at the turn of the century. On its South Side, he is trapped once again by the backwardness, improvidence, insecurity, ignorance, and cramped spirits he went on the road to escape. Consistent with the sexual tension central to the American slavery experience, the dichotomy between the City and the Wilderness is reinforced by the two women with whom Micheaux becomes romantically involved: Orlean, his Black wife, who is inescapably rooted in the sterile soil of Chicago's ethnic mentality, and the artistic, appreciative, hard-working, ambitious, and, unfortunately, white Agnes, whom he meets on the plains.

Micheaux's portrait of Chicago, "the Mecca for southern Negroes," is unusual, for most early Afro-American fiction writers focus upon Harlem as the goal of the turn-of-the-century urban migration. "Always the freest city in the world for the black man," Micheaux explains, "Chicago has the most Negroes in the mail service and the civil service; more Negroes carry clubs as policemen; more can be found in all the departments of the municipal courts, county commissioners, aldermen, corporation counsels, game warden assistants, and so on down. Indeed, a Negro feels freer and more hopeful in Chicago than anywhere else in the United States." Such freedom and hope appear illusory and limited to the homesteader, however, when he compares them to the opportunities the Wilderness offers. Unfortunately, he cannot convince many others that they can do as he did. His brother-in-law expresses the general attitude of Chicago Blacks when he states, "that colored people had been held in slavery for two hundred years and since they were free they did not want to go out into the wilderness and sit on a farm, but wanted to be where they could have freedom and convenience. . . ."

In an attempt to alleviate his increasing loneliness and isolation, Micheaux decides to marry. Despite his firm resolve not to, he falls in love with the daughter of a Scots homesteader. His reason for not pursuing the relationship, which is reciprocal, reveals both his dependence upon white good will and his racial loyalty. He marries a Black girl from Chicago, but because of her immaturity, her preacher father's interference, and the general attitude of her family and friends that she is throwing her life away out in the wilds, the marriage fails.

Much more interesting than the details of his actual marriage are the imaginative uses to which Micheaux puts it in ***The Homesteader.*** In the novel, the timid wife of the autobiography turns into a she-devil who attacks Micheaux in a hysterical rage, as though punishing him for attempting to move beyond the confines of his racial experience. After striking him with all her force, scratching at his eyes, and abusing him so furiously that he sinks, with "no effort to protect himself," to the floor, "she suddenly raised her foot and kicked him viciously full in the face. This seemed, then, to make her more vicious, and thereupon she started to jump upon him with her feet. . . ."

If Micheaux envisions himself martyred by his race for his individualism, he indulges in an amazingly violent and melodramatic way of avenging himself. Orlean, stunned finally by her realization of what her attack on Jean Baptiste means and aware, as only Micheaux was really aware, of the chaos and sterility her rejection of him guarantees, stabs her father, whom she blames for her predicament, and then kills herself.

Having dispatched the Blacks to their bloody ends, Micheaux turns his attention back to Agnes, the Scots girl. His resolution of this relationship is another example of pure wish-fulfillment. Incredibly, he secures for her a previously unsuspected Black ancestor so that his hero can follow "The Custom of the Country—and its law" and still, as in real life he was unable to do, obtain his dream-girl. In his autobiography, Micheaux admits, "I would have given half my life to have had her possess just a least bit of negro blood in her veins . . . ;" in his fiction, he provides her with barely that "least bit." She certainly does not share the insecurities of the rest of their race. On the contrary, she is artistic and, because of her experience as a homesteader's daughter, every bit as ambitious and determined to succeed as he. She even saves his life twice.

If Agnes is Micheaux's fantasy girl (she too has had dreams from early childhood about the faceless, dark man who would totally alter her life), ***The Wind From Nowhere,*** essentially the same story as in the earlier works, extends the racial fantasy to include representatives of those Blacks Micheaux dispatched in ***The Homesteader.*** Martin Eden and his racially-mixed Deborah go east from the prairie, where

> unfortunate families of their race had been forced on relief. They selected from them the worthy and industrious ones, brought them hither and permitted each to buy and pay for out of earnings, ten acres of rich, deep plowed land. And with each purchase they supplied a cow, a horse, chickens and pigs. Each family then grew its own food. The women were able to make their pin money from eggs and chickens and milk; the men were given work in huge food product factories and manganese alloy plants that were built, where they were given a few days work each month. Twenty-five years hence, a great Negro colony will call the Rosebud Country home and be contented, prosperous, and happy.

The utopia of socialism comes, then, to replace the rugged individualism of Micheaux's early self-image and definition of America's promise. Only through a kind of benevolent paternalism can he now imagine the mass involvement of his people in the hope of the Wilderness.

The paradoxes of the personal and racial tensions in Micheaux's books render them fascinating testaments to the Black identity struggle at the beginning of the twentieth century as well as illuminations of the Afro-American experience in a section of the country seldom examined in this regard, the rural and urban Midwest. The Black pioneer's perception of his visibility among European immigrants in the Wilderness and his invisibility among his own people on Chicago's South Side results in one of our literature's most revealing views of the Black's dual role as "America's metaphor" and her scapegoat.

Henry T. Sampson (essay date 1977)

SOURCE: "The Micheaux Film Corporation; Oscar Micheaux," in *Blacks in Black and White: A Source Book on Black Films,* The Scarecrow Press, Inc., 1977, pp. 42-55.

[*In the following essay, Sampson presents a historical overview of Micheaux's filmmaking career.*]

> The appreciation my people have shown my maiden efforts convinces me that they want racial photoplays depicting racial life, and to that task I have concentrated my mind and efforts.
>
> —Oscar Micheaux (1920)

Undoubtedly the most successful of all black-owned independent film production companies which produced films about black people and employed all-black casts was the Micheaux Film and Book Corporation, which later became the Micheaux Film Corporation. This company, founded in 1918, was the only black-owned company which continued to produce films through the 1920's and 1930's. This company was established by one of the most colorful characters in the history of American films, Oscar Micheaux. During the 21 years between 1918 and 1940, Micheaux produced and distributed nationally and in Europe over 30 black-cast films, many of which were based on books which he wrote himself. Until recently, Micheaux has received very little recognition by film historians, but among his contemporaries who knew him he was considered to be a skilled entrepreneur, an astute businessman and a man who was sensitive to the needs of the black film audience. From an analysis of the responses of black film audiences to his films, Micheaux concluded that they did not care for propaganda as much as they did for a good story. Although he recognized that a strong story line was a key ingredient for a successful film, Micheaux also felt that his films should depict accurately the social, economic and political conditions under which the black man existed in America. Although perhaps not intended as such, some of his films can be considered as protest films. They were, in any event, considered at the time, by both whites and blacks, to be quite controversial.

Micheaux was born in Metropolis, Illinois in 1884. Not much is known about his parents and early childhood, although it is known that he had a brother, Swan Emerson Micheaux. The extent of his formal education is uncertain, but in his youth he worked as a Pullman porter and a farmer. Later, as a young man, he was a rancher. In 1909, at the age of 25, Micheaux purchased a homestead in South Dakota and after five years had successfully expanded his holdings to 500 acres.

During his period as a rancher in South Dakota, Micheaux conceived and wrote a book titled ***The Homesteader*** which he eventually published in 1914 or 1915. In 1915 he established the Western Book and Supply Company, headquartered in Sioux City, Iowa. Micheaux worked hard traveling about the countryside around Sioux City selling his book, primarily to white farmers and businessmen. ***The Homesteader*** was based on his experiences as a rancher and the characters in it were Negro substitutes for the white persons with whom he had been in contact. The book was fully illustrated and sold for $1.50 per copy.

In 1918, Micheaux's book came to the attention of George P. Johnson, then General Booking Manager of the black-owned and operated Lincoln Film Company of Los Angeles, California. From his office in Omaha, Nebraska, Johnson contacted Micheaux regarding the feasibility of letting Lincoln Film Company produce ***The Homesteader.*** Micheaux responded favorably to this proposition and in May 1918 traveled to Omaha and lived in Johnson's house for two days while discussing the details of the contract. Eventually, contractual papers were drawn up and ready to be signed, but Micheaux insisted that as part of the agreement he would go to Los Angeles and supervise the filming of the story. On the basis of Micheaux's lack of film experience, Johnson and the other directors of the Lincoln Motion Picture Company decided that they could not go along with the deal, and hence it fell through. This is the set of circumstances that launched Oscar Micheaux into a career of film production.

In 1918, Micheaux organized the Micheaux Film and Book Company with offices in Sioux City and Chicago, Illinois to produce the film ***The Homesteader.*** Using his considerable skills as a businessman and salesman, Micheaux sold stock in his corporation to the white farmers around Sioux City at prices ranging from $75 to $100 per share. Eventually enough capital was secured to produce ***The Homesteader*** as an eight-reel film starring Charles Lucas as the male lead, and Evelyn Preer and Iris Hall, two well-known dramatic actresses who at the time were associated with the Lafayette Players Stock Company.

In 1920, Micheaux's brother Swan joined him as Manager of the Micheaux Film and Book Company. Swan was later promoted to Secretary and Treasurer and General Booking Manager. In 1921, the company announced a cash dividend of 25 per cent. Also in 1921, in order to take advantage of better studio facilities and the availability of more talented actors, the company established an office in New York City. The distribution and financial office remained in Chicago under the supervision of Swan Micheaux and Charles Benson, formerly with the Quality Amusement Company. Tiffany Tolliver and W. R. Crowell, operating out of a branch office in Roanoke, Virginia, were in charge of the distribution of the company's films in the east. The distribution of films in the southwest was done by A. Odams, owner of the Verdun Theatre in Beaumont, Texas. Production of the film ***Deceit*** was begun at the Esste Studios in New York, June 6, 1921.

The first controversial film produced by Micheaux was ***Within Our Gates*** (1920), controversial because it contained a scene involving the lynching of a Negro in the south. The film was shown for the first time in Chicago at Hammon's Vendome Theatre. Before that, however, the picture had been turned down by the Chicago Board of Movie Censors because it was claimed that its effect on the minds of the audience would result in a race riot similar to the one which had occurred in Chicago a year earlier. The picture was given a second showing at the Censor Board, and a number of prominent people, including a representative of the Association of the Negro Press, were called in to see the picture in its entirely and express their opinions on the effect the film might have on public sentiment.

Opinion was divided after the showing. Those who objected pointed out that because of the previous race riot, showing the film would be dangerous. Others who approved argued that because of the existing conditions of the time, the lynchings and handicaps of ignorance, it was time to bring such issues before the public. Among those who argued forcefully for the film were Alderman Louis B. Anderson and Corporation Counsel Edward H. Wright. These men, with the endorsement of the press, prevailed, and a permit to show the film was finally granted.

Those who objected, however, did not give up. They visited churches and protested at length against the showing. Among the most vigorous protesters were blacks, many of whom had not seen the picture. The protests against the film continued right up to the day of the opening of the film. That morning a committee was appointed from the Methodist Episcopal Ministers' Alliance, consisting of both whites and blacks. This committee visited the Mayor of Chicago and the Chief of Police, but without avail. The picture opened to a packed house.

Within Our Gates was shown at the Loyal Theatre in Omaha, Nebraska on August 9, 1920. It had taken two months to get approval from the Omaha Censor Board.

The majority of people who objected to the film had never seen it. One reaction from a movie reviewer who had reads as follows:

> Preliminary reading of the outrages perpetrated in the south opened the scene of ***Within Our Gates*** at the Pickford last week, Friday, when I dropped in to see the picture released in its entirety. You see the chickens out of doors and the good mother of a progressive family all enacted most naturally. Discussions which show the colored race had never practiced anarchy and there never was a slacker and Theodore Roosevelt's picture seen on the outside of the Literary Digest which opened to readings of great value seen in the movies by reflection. You do not see much in evaluation of the south but you see a minister of the submissive to Massa Charles type who agrees with everything that the white man says and you see singing and shouting and old time religion and the tedious church collection. You see the white man who claims the black child laid at his doorstep by the mother because it is his own and he later gives the mother some money. The lynching attempt leads to the boy who dreams he is lynched. You see him hung up in the vanishing illusion. It is quite natural and effective. Attempted burning at the stake in another scene only shows fire. There is nothing in the picture but what is true and lawfully legitimate.

Many theatres in the south refused outright to book the film because of its "nasty story." The white manager of the Star Theatre in Shreveport, Louisiana, refused to book the picture on advice of the Superintendent of Police in New Orleans who stated that " . . . the present Manager of the Temple (Theatre) stated that he had witnessed this picture demonstrating the treatment during slavery times with which the negroes were treated by their masters, also show the execution by hanging of about nine negroes for absolutely no cause and that it is a very dangerous picture to show in the south."

The controversy caused by ***Within Our Gates*** did not deter Micheaux from making another picture with similar theme, ***The Gunsaulus Mystery,*** in 1921. This eight-reel film was based on a murder case in which Leo Frank was convicted of the crime. The movie was filmed in New York studios and starred Evelyn Preer, Dick Abrams, Lawrence Chenault and L. DeBulger.

In a letter dated May 5, 1919, Oscar Micheaux offered George P. Johnson, then General Manager of the Lincoln Motion Picture Company and employee at the Omaha Post Office, a position as General Manager, providing that Johnson could be transferred to the Chicago Post Office and work on a part-time basis at a salary of $50 per month. Johnson decided not to accept Micheaux's offer.

The Dungeon, a seven-reel feature, was produced by Oscar Micheaux in 1922. The *Chicago Defender* openly criticized Micheaux for using light-skinned actors and not advertising the film as a "Race" production. In a column which appeared in the July 8, 1922 edition of the *Chicago Defender,* D. Ireland Thomas stated:

> The advertising matter for this production has nothing to indicate that the feature is colored, as the characters are very bright; in fact almost white. 'The All-Star Colored Cast' that is so noticeable with nearly every race production is omitted on the cards and lithographs. Possibly Mr. Micheaux is relying on his name alone to tell the public that it is a race production or maybe he is after booking it in white theaters.

Micheaux released ***Son of Satan*** in 1924. The film was reviewed by D. Ireland Thomas, black owner of the Lincoln Theatre in Charleston, South Carolina. In a column appearing in the January 31, 1925 edition of the *Chicago Defender,* Mr. Thomas commented:

> It was a very good picture and comes nearer to having an all-star cast than any other Race picture that I have noticed. The cast includes Andrew S. Bishop, Lawrence Chenault, Emmet Anthony, Edna Morton, Monte Hawley, Shingzie Howard, Ida Anderson, E. G. Tatum and others. Some may not like the production because it shows up some of our race in their true colors. They might also protest against the language used. I would not indorse this particular part of the film myself, but I must admit that it is true. We have got to hand it to Oscar Micheaux when it comes to giving us the real stuff. This is all the criticism that I could find and I am a hard critic when it comes to Race pictures, and like Sylvester Russell, I do not want to see my Race in saloons or at crap tables. But it is not what the public clamors for that makes the coin jingle. We naturally expect good acting from Andrew Bishop, Lawrence Chenault, E. G. Tatum, Shingzie Howard, Edna Morton and Ida Anderson. I was very much impressed with the clever acting of Monte Hawley. I like his pleasing appearance and I predict a great future for him if he is given a chance. Just one more word before I finish, I wish to praise the work of E. G. Tatum in this production, it stood out strong. His acting greatly helped to put the picture over—but as I said before we expect it from him. I remember him way back in the Ebony Comedy company's days when he did good work also.

On March 1, 1927, Swan Micheaux resigned his position with the company to become manager of imported films of the Agfu Raiv Film Corporation of Berlin, Germany, with offices at 729 Seventh Avenue, New York City. After a year in this job he left this company to become the Vice President and General Manager of Dunbar Film Corporation, with offices at 440 Lenox Avenue, New York City.

Micheaux produced two versions of the film ***Birthright,*** the first a silent picture in 1924 featuring Evelyn Preer, J. Homer Tutt, Salem Tutt Whitney and Lawrence Chenault. The second version was a sound picture released in 1939 and featured Ethel Moses, Alec Lovejoy, and Carmen Newsom. J. A. Jackson, whose column appeared in the *Baltimore Afro-American,* reviewed the silent version and stated in a column appearing in the January 25, 1924 edition of the *Afro-American* that

> The photoplay is good, the scenes well selected, the continuity carefully done, the atmosphere carefully created and maintained, and Micheaux has a film of which he may well be proud.
>
> Every school teacher, every Negro who has purchased property in the south, all who have ever had a contact with the police and deputy sheriffs or constables in the southern states, every returned soldier, and every pretty colored woman who has or does live in a southern state will find some big truth that a personal experience or observation can confirm.

Micheaux was married in 1929 to Alice Russell, an actress who appeared in a number of his films and had a leading role in ***God's Stepchildren.*** The couple set up a home in Montclair, New Jersey, but both Micheaux and his wife did a lot of traveling around the country in the interest of the company. Although not an official member of the company, Mrs. Micheaux took charge of the office after Swan left the company.

Micheaux operated the company with a limited staff, primarily as an economy measure. He did all of the work himself. He wrote scenarios, supervised filming and did the bookkeeping; in short, he did everything. Micheaux pictures took about an average of ten days to shoot and cost from $10,000 to $20,000. Micheaux usually obtained his actors from around the New York City area, frequently using actors of the Lafayette Players Stock Company. However, in several instances when filming on location he employed local talent. For example, *The House Behind the Cedars,* written by Charles W. Chestnutt, was filmed on location in Roanoke, Virginia. In this film he made generous use of local talent as extras. One of the familiar persons used was William "Big Bill" Crowell, who was at the time a popular fraternal leader in the state of Virginia. Other cast members included Shingzie Howard, Lawrence Chenault and Douglass Griffin.

Evelyn Preer, a member of the Lafayette Players Stock Company, was featured in many Micheaux films, as were Mercedes Gilbert, and Julia Theresa Russell, a sister-in-law of Micheaux.

In February 1928, the Micheaux Film Corporation, with offices at 200 West 125th Street, filed a voluntary petition of bankruptcy in the U.S. Seventh District Court. The petition listed the assets of the company as $1,400 and liabilities as $7,837.

In the latter part of 1929, the company reorganized with new capital and was incorporated as a new company under the laws of the state of New York. At the time of reorganization, the officers were Oscar Micheaux, President; Frank Schiffman, Vice President; and Leo Bracheer, Treasurer.

Shortly after reorganization, Micheaux produced and directed ***A Daughter of the Congo*** in 1930 and his first "all-talkie" film, ***The Exile,*** in 1931. The cast which Micheaux assembled for ***The Exile*** included Charles Moore, Eunice Brooks, George Randol, Lorenzo Tucker, Nora Newsome, Stanley Morell, Inez Persaud, A. B. Comethiere, Norman Reeves, Lou Vernon, Carl Mahon, and a number of singers and dancers from "Blackbirds," "Brown Buddies," Connie's Inn, and the Cotton Club appeared in cabaret scenes in the picture.

Both pictures met with some negative reaction. Micheaux was accused of perpetuating the "high yaller fetish" in ***A Daughter of the Congo.*** Theophilus Lewis, in an article which appeared in the April 16, 1930 issue of the New York *Amsterdam News,* stated that:

> The first offense of the new film is its persistent vaunting of intraracial color fetishism. The scene is laid in a not so mythical republic in Africa. Half of the characters wear European clothes and are supposed to be civilized, while the other half wear their birthday suits and some feathers and are supposed to be savages. All the noble characters are high yellows; all the ignoble ones are black. Only one of the yellow characters is vicious, while only one of the black characters, the debauched president of the republic, is a person of dignity.
>
> Even if the picture possessed no other defects, this artificial association of nobility with lightness and villainy with blackness would be enough to ruin it. It is based on a false assumption that has no connection with the realities of life, as Mr. Micheaux could have been convinced by five minutes reflection of the progress of his race.

The Exile had a successful premiere in New York City, but the first showing in Pittsburgh was halted mid-way through the showing. The action was taken by two members of the Pennsylvania Board of Censors, both women. Their reason for stopping the showing was that it did not carry the seal indicating that it had been passed by the State Censor Board. There was some speculation at the time, however, that the real reason for stopping the picture was that it contained scenes showing a Negro making love to a "near-white" woman. In a scene near the end of the picture (which the Censor Board members did not see) it is revealed that the woman actually had one per cent "Negro" blood. Another scene in the picture shows a white man trying to take advantage of the woman and being soundly thrashed by the Negro who comes to her rescue. It was at this point that the picture was stopped. In reaction to the halting of the film, an article in the *Pittsburgh Courier* stated in part that

> The refusal to allow the running of ***The Exile*** brings clearly to mind the furor created by the running of *The Birth of a Nation,* a race-hating and mob-inciting film if ever there was one, and the apathetic attitude of the Board of Censors in connection with this film. It's all right for a picture to arouse race hatred, apparently, if the victims of the mob's spirit are Negroes, and now they're making a 'talkie.' Negroes all over the country will watch with a great deal of interest just what action the Board of Censors of the Keystone State will take in this film.

The background of ***The Exile*** is Chicago, at a time when blacks migrating from the south were pushing wealthy white property owners off South Parkway.

Micheaux produced two pictures in 1936, ***Temptation*** and ***Underworld.*** Each picture cost about $15,000 to produce, of which approximately $2000 was allocated for salaries to the actors. The minor actors were paid about $10 per day and the principals received from $100 to $500 per picture. All of the money, including production costs, was paid before the pictures were completed. For these two pictures, Micheaux used professional singers and dancers instead of trained dramatic actors. Most of the performers were nightclub stars instead of stage artists because, Micheaux claimed, he could depend on the former being available in one city at least until the picture was completed. Micheaux also stated that the big problem was getting the artists to work on time in the morning. This was a serious matter because the technicians, who were paid by the hour, would be standing around waiting for the performers to appear.

The picture ***God's Stepchildren,*** released in 1938, was probably the most notable of Micheaux's productions. The film was unique in that most of the important scenes were shot in a friend's home in front of a staircase where Micheaux found optimum lighting conditions.

God's Stepchildren had its world premiere at the RKO Regent Theatre, 116th Street, New York City; it was withdrawn after a two-day run and was later prohibited from being shown at any RKO Theatre in the country. The announcement of the ban followed previous announcements, made prior to each showing by Oscar

Micheaux, that the objectionable parts of the picture had been deleted.

One scene which caused many of the patrons to get up and walk out of the theatre showed an actor, playing the part of a white man, knocking down a young girl and spitting upon her because she had revealed that she had "colored blood" in her veins. Among those groups protesting the picture were the Young Communist League and the National Negro Congress. A clipping from a New York City newspaper reads, "the picture creates a false splitting of Negroes into light and dark groups. It slandered Negroes, holding them up to ridicule."

In 1940, Micheaux produced ***The Notorious Elinor Lee,*** and announced that Negro aviator Col. Hubert Julian ("The Black Eagle") was joining the company as co-producer. The film had its world premiere in Harlem, complete with gold-engraved invitations, floodlights, a carpeted sidewalk, police, and Col. Julian as master of ceremonies in formal dress, top hat, white silk gloves and a flowing cape.

Not much is known about the activities of the company after the release of ***The Notorious Elinor Lee*** in 1940. The last known activity of Micheaux was in 1948 when he wrote and directed the film ***The Betrayal*** for Astor Pictures. The film was based on Micheaux's book, ***The Wind from Nowhere.*** Other books by Micheaux include, ***The Case of Mrs. Wingate, The Masquerade, The Story of Dorothy Stanfield,*** and ***The Forged Note.***

Perhaps the best summary of Oscar Micheaux's approach to film production is given in a signed article he wrote for the *Philadelphia Afro-American.* It appeared in the January 24, 1925 edition, and is presented here in its entirety.

> Unless one has some connection with the actual production of photo plays, it is impossible fully to recognize the tremendous scope which the motion picture embraces. The completed picture is a miniature replica of life, and all the varied forces which help to make life so complex, the intricate studies and problems of human nature, all enter into the physical makeup of the most lowly photo play.
>
> The mastery, therefore, of the art of production, for indeed it is an art, is no small attainment, and success can only be assured when assisted by the most active encouragement and financial backing. The colored producer has dared to step into a world which has hitherto remained closed to him. His entrance into this unexplored field, is for him, trebly difficult. He is united in his themes, in obtaining casts that present genuine ability, and in his financial resources. He requires encouragement and assistance. He is the new-born babe who must be fondled until he can stand on his own feet, and if the race has any pride in presenting its own achievements in this field, it behooves it to interest itself, and morally encourage such efforts.
>
> I do not wish anyone to construe this as a request for the suppression of criticism. Honest, intelligent criticism is an aid to the progress of any effort. The producer who has confidence in his ideals, solicits constructive criticism. But he also asks fairness, and fairness in criticism demands a familiarity with the aims of the producer, and a knowledge of the circumstances under which his efforts were materialized.
>
> I have been informed that my last production, ***Birthright,*** has occasioned much adverse criticism, during its exhibition in Philadelphia. Newspapermen have denounced me as a colored Judas, merely because they were either unaware of my aims, or were not in sympathy with them. What then, are my aims, to which such critics have taken exception?
>
> I have always tried to make my photoplays present the truth, to lay before the race a cross section of its own life, to view the colored heart from close range. My results might have been narrow at times, due perhaps to certain limited situations, which I endeavored to portray, but in those limited situations, the truth was the predominant characteristic. It is only by presenting those portions of the race portrayed in my pictures, in the light and background of their true state, that we can raise our people to greater heights. I am too much imbued with the spirit of Booker T. Washington to engraft false virtues upon ourselves, to make ourselves that which we are not. Nothing could be a greater blow to our own progress.
>
> The recognition of our true situation, will react in itself as a stimulus for self-advancement.
>
> It is these ideals that I have injected into my pictures, and which are now being criticized. Possibly my aims have been misunderstood, but criticism arising from such misunderstanding, only doubles the already overburdening labors of the colored producer.
>
> If I have been retarded by the unjust criticism from my own race, it has been amply made up by the aid of the Royal Theatre, which from the very beginning, has encouraged the production of colored photoplays, and in the face of burning criticism, has continued to foster my aims, and help place my organization on a strong footing.
>
> It is only by constructive criticism, arising from an intelligent understanding of the real problem, however, that the colored producer can succeed in his efforts and produce photoplays, that will not only be a credit to the race, but be on a par with those of the white producer.—[Signed] Oscar Micheaux.

Oscar Micheaux died in Charlotte, North Carolina in 1951 at the age of 67.

Chester J. Fontenot (essay date 1982)

SOURCE: "Oscar Micheaux, Black Novelist and Film Maker," in *Vision and Refuge: Essays on the Literature of the Great Plains,* edited by Virginia Faulkner, University of Nebraska Press, 1982, pp. 109-25.

[In the following essay, Fontenot discusses the history and major themes of Micheaux's most important novels and films.]

Oscar Micheaux, who lived from 1884 to 1951, was a black novelist and movie producer who believed that one solution to the problems that plagued black urbanites was for them to abandon the cities and to look to the Great Plains as a place where they could build an alternative society. Similarly, according to Micheaux, black southerners could homestead in what he called the Great Northwest (northern Great Plains) instead of following Booker T. Washington's philosophy of economic and moral betterment and staying in the South. Drawing upon his own experience as a settler on the Rosebud Reservation in South Dakota from 1909 to 1914, Micheaux delineated the process of blacks freeing themselves from urban decadence in each of his seven novels, but especially in ***The Conquest*** (1913), ***The Forged Note*** (1915), and ***The Homesteader*** (1917).

Not only was Micheaux the first black writer to portray a black leading character in the role of a pioneer, he was also the first black film maker. He produced at least forty-five movies and organized private corporations to distribute both his films and his books. Micheaux tried to present a realistic picture of black urban life in contrast to that which then emanated from Hollywood studios. Instead of emphasizing the carnal or gutter instinct of black people, he tried to portray the problems of the black middle class. Although he has been criticized for casting light-skinned people as actors in his films for imitating white society, and for using black people as plastic models, he sought to offer meaningful alternatives to the negative images created by the American film industry.

My purpose in this essay is to discuss Micheaux's three major novels and analyze briefly some of the things he attempted to do in his films. His significance for the study of Afro-American literature and films is clear enough. His philosophy is important because it led him to break through propagandistic notions about the social and political situation of Afro-Americans and because he moved black people from the category of subhuman creatures incapable of carrying out the most ordinary human functions to one of a dignified people whose problems are much like those of white Americans.

The stereotyping of black people in films as subhuman has a long history. In 1905, *Fights of Nations* and *The Wooing and Wedding of a Coon* showed blacks as childlike lackeys who were meant to be ridiculed. In 1907, *The Masher* told the story of a ladies' man who chased anyone remotely resembling a woman, but whose advances were always rebuffed; finally, he succeeds with a veiled lady, only to discover that she is a black woman. In 1910 and 1911, slapstick comedies—*Pickaninnies and Watermelon, Chicken Thief, Coon-Town Suffragettes, How Rastus Got His Turkeys, Rastus and Chicken, Rastus in Zululand*—stereotyped blacks as so completely illiterate that "they did not have to respond when demeaned because they were always unaware of what was being done" [Donald Bogle, *Toms, Coons, Mulattoes, Mammies, and Bucks,* 1973]. The Sambo films, which appeared between 1909 and 1911, also offered stock racist black characters. In 1910, after the release of *Uncle Tom's Cabin,* came several films which characterized blacks as faithful slaves often so loyal to their masters that they would voluntarily offer themselves for sale rather than see their masters agonize over gambling debts. The image of Uncle Tom as faithful slave was developed in such films as *The Dark Romance of a Tobacco Can* (1911), *For Massa's Sake* (1911), *The Debt* (1912), and *Slavery Days* (1913). Their enormous appeal to white audiences encouraged Hollywood producers to film stories of miscegenation, dealing with the tragic mulatto. For example, *The Nigger and the Octoroon* (1913), attached shame and degradation to even the smallest measure of nonwhite blood, thereby implying that being black was somehow subhuman [Peter Noble, *The Negro in Films,* 1948].

The acceptance of antiblack images in American films probably can be explained by the willingness of white Americans to see confirmed in visual images their belief that black people were subhuman. The Hollywood film industry, which had begun its quick rise to prominence, saw a chance to gain an economic foothold in American society by exploiting the tremendous mythmaking potential of motion pictures. Motion pictures exert a considerable influence on an audience partly because film is mimetic; that is, a film attempts to capture a selected version of reality. Since we see only what is selected for us by the camera, films unfold a story by narration. The camera gives the film an authorial presence much like that found in fiction; the movements of the camera constitute style. Like novels, films can render anything which can be perceived. A film presents speech through "techniques more vivid but conceptually equivalent to those of language. Just as the formal identity of fiction depends on the existence of narrated description as well as dialogue, so the formal identity of film is dependent upon its ability to describe experience through the medium of cinematography as well as to make statements about language" [Charles Thomas Samuels, *Mastering the Film and Other Essays,* 1977].

Micheaux understood the mythmaking potential both of novels and of films, and made use of these media in his attempt to create an alternate set of cultural referents for Afro-Americans. Since his films were based largely on his first three novels, a description of their plots is appropriate here.

Writing autobiographically about his life in western South Dakota, Micheaux invented three personae: Oscar Devereaux, Jean Baptiste, and Sidney Wyeth. In ***The Conquest*** Oscar Devereaux sets out to establish himself as a homesteader in South Dakota and to conquer the Northwest. A good deal of the story told in ***The Conquest*** is repeated in greater detail in the story of Jean Baptiste in ***The Homesteader.*** In ***The Forged Note*** the hero is Sidney Wyeth, who has written a novel; he goes to Attalia (Atlanta) to promote its sale, sees the decadence of black urban life, and meets and marries a black woman. In each novel the protagonist is a black pioneer who sets out to create a new society free of the restrictions and distortions of life in urban areas. Viewed in this light, the novels represent an attempt to create a mythology, to construct an alternate set of values to that already existing in black urban society, and to depict this new mythology in a manner which would be accessible to black people in general.

Micheaux's mythology is thematic: ***The Conquest*** and ***The Homesteader*** stress the importance to black Americans of avoiding at all costs interracial marriage and of abandoing the cities for the Great Northwest; ***The Forged Note*** offers a critique of the most damaging aspects of black urban life. In writing these novels Micheaux wanted to reorder the cultural mores of black Americans, to transmute the decadence he found into a solid moral and intellectual cornerstone upon which black Americans could build a society free of the existing pitfalls.

The hero of ***The Conquest,*** Oscar Devereaux, is an enterprising young black man, determined to show that black people can do anything they want to do. Leaving his family at the age of sixteen, he takes a job paying $1.25 a day in a car-manufacturing company, where he meets a black minister, the Reverend McIntyre, described as a "fire-eating colored evangelist." Devereaux decides that the religious fervor of the black church is unproductive and ultimately antithetical to self-determination. After spending about two years in the car-manufacturing plant, he leaves for an all-black town. He gets a job boiling water in a coal mine for $2.25 a day, but since he sees no opportunity for advancement he moves on to Carbondale, Illinois, where his sister teaches school. She introduces him to a beautiful black girl, Jessie Ross, with whom he later becomes involved. Moving on again, this time to Chicago, he works part time at the Union Stockyards for $1.50 a day. Dissatisfied with this situation, he goes to nearby Joliet to work in the steel mills. Here he is employed at the coal chutes at $1.50 per twenty-five tons of coal shoveled, but the work is much too severe for him. Returning to Chicago, he is swindled out of two dollars by an employment agency, and goes next to Eaton, where he works in a barbershop shining shoes. He takes on a second job working on a farm, but quits after one hard day of pitching hay with a sixteen-year-old girl and a second day of shucking oats with a twelve-year-old boy, a fourteen-year-old girl, and the farmer's wife. Concluding that manual labor is not for him, Devereaux finds employment with the Pullman Company on a parlor car that runs through summer resorts in southern Wisconsin. Eventually he becomes porter of his own car, the Altata. With his friend Wright he devises a scheme for swindling fares on the train. When his share of the profits amounts to $2,340, he goes west.

At this point, the plot begins to take shape. Devereaux hears about Oristown, South Dakota, a town on the edge of the Little Crow Reservation. Parts of the reservation are to be opened to settlement; would-be settlers are to draw lots for homesteads. Since there are only twenty-four homesteads available and about ten times that many people have placed their names in the lottery, it appears to Devereaux that his chances of obtaining a homestead are very remote—he holds number 6,540—and he starts back to Chicago. En route he learns that it is possible to buy a relinquished claim. Heartened by this news he returns to Oristown and finally succeeds in purchasing a relinquishment for $375. Being new to the Great Northwest and ignorant of its ways, Devereaux is an easy mark for horse-traders, who sell him their poorest stock at high prices, and for merchants, who sell him defective farm equipment. Nonetheless, he manages to turn over ten to twelve acres per year, winning the respect of his white neighbors. The greatest hardship he suffers is the lack of female companionship; there are almost no eligible black women in South Dakota. Since he wants to maintain racial loyalty, he visits Jessie Ross in Carbondale and declares that he loves her.

Upon his return to South Dakota, Devereaux buys a neighboring homestead for three thousand dollars, but the acquisition of the additional land leaves him little time to court Jessie. During the period between their last meeting and his next trip to see Jessie, he meets and falls in love with a twenty-year-old Scottish girl, but decides against marrying her because of the color barrier. Still determined to find a suitable wife, Devereaux again seeks out Jessie Ross, but he is too late; during his long absence she has married someone else. His quest for a wife appears to be ended when he makes the acquaintance of Orlean McCarthy, the daughter of a black minister whom he had met when visiting Jessie. After a brief courtship he persuades Orlean to return to South Dakota with him and get married, but her father wants them to abide by social custom and be married in Chicago. Devereaux goes to Chicago to win her back, but is unsuccessful.

The story of ***The Conquest*** is rendered in more detail in ***The Homesteader.*** In this novel Oscar Devereaux becomes Jean Baptiste, the Scottish girl is called Agnes Stewart, and Orlean McCarthy retains the same name. The plot moves quickly into thematic categories. In an overly sentimental scene Baptiste and Agnes meet and fall in love, but before Baptiste can make up his mind to marry her he recalls the story of a black man who married a white woman and ended up claiming to be Mexican, not black. The recollection of this story impels Baptiste to give up the idea of marrying Agnes. Committed to marrying within his race, he goes to Chicago, meets Orlean McCarthy, and embarks upon a fiery courtship. We learn that her father, the Reverend McCarthy, is sexually promiscuous and that he has plotted to keep Orlean from marrying Baptiste. But his scheming is thwarted: Baptiste marries Orlean and takes her to live on his homestead. He buys the neighboring homestead for his bride, but the purchase is challenged by the townspeople. When news of their problems reaches the Reverend McCarthy, he visits Baptiste and Orlean, who is now pregnant, and starts to plant the seeds which will eventually destroy their marriage. After McCarthy returns to Chicago, Baptiste leaves the homestead for a few days and during his absence the baby is born dead. Orlean's father seizes the opportunity to break up the marriage and takes Orlean back to Chicago.

Baptiste and Orlean do not see each other for a year; then they are reunited in Chicago and he hopes that she will return with him to the homestead. When he gets into an argument with her father, Orlean attacks Baptiste viciously and he allows her to beat him up. Back in South Dakota Baptiste faces a drought and is soon in deep financial trouble. He loses his own land but is saved by his sister's homestead, which is not in his name and thus is not legally subject to foreclosure. In the face of adversity, Baptiste resolves to become a writer. He has a book published and sets up a publishing house.

Now Micheaux launches his criticism of black urban society. Baptiste engages Irene Grey, a mulatto woman to whom he once wrote letters, to help him sell his books. He is impressed by her and her father, Junius N. Grey, known as the Negro Potato King, and sees in them the prototypes of the black race. The juxtaposition of Irene and Junius Grey with Orlean and the Reverend McCarthy is significant, for Baptiste perceives that the oppression of the black people is not wholly the fault of the whites; contributing factors are the inability to read and the generally decadent nature of urban black people. In particular, Baptiste criticizes black Baptist ministers like McCarthy for their lack of education. Moreover, he attributes much of the conflict between Orlean's father and himself to different ideologies: Baptiste is a follower of Booker T. Washington, while the Reverend McCarthy subscribes to the ideas of W. E. B. Dubois. McCarthy uses his ideology so effectively that he alienates Orlean from her love for Baptiste, causes her to sell the homestead Baptiste has given her, and unwittingly sets up a situation which ends in her committing patricide and suicide. Baptiste is accused of the double murder but is acquitted, thanks to a detective who succeeds in solving the case. He is then reunited with Agnes Stewart, who has become an established songwriter. They discover that she is a mulatto, resolving the tension created by the prospect of interracial marriage, and become man and wife.

The interwoven theme of these two novels is most clearly seen in Micheaux's exposé of the vices of black urban life. He contrasts the harsh reality of that life—violence, racism, lack of education, unemployment, black-on-black crime—with the utopian environment of the Great Northwest. In ***The Conquest*** and ***The Homesteader*** Micheaux sets up the first parts of his mythology: loyalty to the black race (dramatized in the rejection of interracial marriage) and black settlement of the Great Northwest.

In ***The Forged Note*** Micheaux itemizes the destructive elements of black city life. Devereaux / Baptiste is reborn as Sidney Wyeth, the black author of a novel called *The Tempest.* In order to increase sales Wyeth travels to several cities hiring agents who will promote the book. In Atlanta his eyes are opened to the degradation of black life in the cities, a situation which he blames on the failure of blacks to read black literature (or, for that matter, much of any literature). From Atlanta he goes to Effingham (Birmingham), where illiteracy is even more rampant. He comments that "these people considered literature, as a whole, dead stock. More than sixty thousand in number, the demand among them for books and magazines was insufficient to justify anyone's running a place for such a purpose. It was not large enough to justify either of the Negro drug stores carrying periodicals in stock, even those that were carried by all white drug stores, excepting those in districts occupied and patronized by the colored people." Black people seemed to be more interested in establishing an all-black park than in building a library in a black community. Wyeth sees a great part of the corruption of youth as stemming from lack of interest in education, but he does not blame blacks entirely. He believes that civilization is an artificial construct which does not permit the individual to grow from his own potential. In this sense Micheaux is almost Rousseauesque. He thinks the Great Northwest will allow black people to build an alternate society which will annihilate the social and racial distinctions that are the foundation of urban society. This seems to indicate that Micheaux does not adhere strictly to Booker T. Washington's philosophy, for Washington believed that blacks should remain in the South and try to gain an economic foothold, while Micheaux sees the South as corrupt and beyond redemption. The alternative, then, is to leave both artificial worlds—the North and the South—and settle in a region untainted by American racism.

The faults of black leaders are personified in Micheaux's characterizations of black ministers. Orlean's father, the Reverend McCarthy, is guilty of much worse offenses than hypocrisy; he uses the office of the church for his own benefit. Mildred Latham, the black woman whom Sidney Wyeth falls in love with and marries, is tormented by the knowledge that her father took five thousand dollars of his church's money and used it to be made a bishop. The ranks of black leadership comprise uneducated ministers, a few teachers who also share a dislike of black literature, and a couple of self-styled politicians. Wyeth becomes so disgusted with black leaders that he is responsible for the appearance of the following headline in a black southern newspaper: "NEGRO SAYS RACE FACES DREADFUL CONDITIONS, DUE TO LACK OF LEADERS. SAYS SELFISHNESS IS SO MUCH THE ORDER THAT THERE IS NO INTEREST WHATEVER TOWARD UPLIFT. PROFESSIONAL NEGRO THE WORST."

Hugh M. Gloster writes that in ***The Homesteader,*** "though indicating the degeneracy of negro life in Southern cities, Micheaux offers no panacea and fails to exhibit the optimism and enterprise which characterize ***The Conquest***" [*Negro Voices in American Fiction,* 1948]. This statement indicates a misreading, for while it is true that in ***The Conquest*** Micheaux does not condemn black urban life to the extent that he does in ***The Homesteader*** and ***The Forged Note,*** it is not because he is more optimistic in the earlier novel. Rather, he is investigating a different aspect of the mythology he is trying to construct. The purpose of ***The Conquest*** is to show that the black race can determine its own destiny, that it can leave behind the moral decadence of cities, and that it can build a more suitable society in the Great Northwest. Speaking through the voice of Oscar Devereaux, Micheaux says: "For years I have felt constrained to deplore the negligence of the colored race in America, in not seizing the opportunity for monopolizing more of the many million acres of rich farm lands in the great Northwest, where immigrants from the old world own many acres of rich farm lands, while the millions of blacks, only a few hundred miles away, are as oblivious to it all as the heathen of Africa are to civilization" (p. 204).

In contrast, ***The Forged Note*** is Micheaux's attempt to lead the black reader from the decadent world of black urban life to the liberated life of the Great Northwest. He chooses to do this through focusing on the evils existing in black southern life and pointing to some possible reasons for their coming into existence. True, he does not offer a panacea for the problems he exposes, for ready-made solutions are as artificial as the civilization whites have imposed upon blacks. Like Voltaire's Candide, the black race must learn to work toward a realistic goal, not an abstract one such as that described in the ideology of W. E. B. Dubois. The process of ridding the black race of the weaknesses which prevent natural growth goes through several stages: rejection of interracial marriage, acceptance of moral responsibilities, and embracing education through literature.

Micheaux's efforts to popularize his novels led him into film making. Since 1913, when he established the Western Book and Supply Company in Sioux City, Iowa, Micheaux had been able to reach a large audience. In 1918 George P. Johnson, general booking agent of the black-owned-and-operated Lincoln Film Company of Los Angeles, read ***The Homesteader,*** and through the company's Omaha office got in touch with Micheaux to see about the possibility of producing it. At a meeting in Omaha in May 1918, Micheaux signed a contract with Johnson which provided that he would go to Los Angeles and watch the filming of his novel. But Micheaux's desire to supervise the filming and his total lack of experience in directing led to the cancellation of the contract.

In the latter part of 1918 Micheaux formed the Micheaux Film and Book Company, with offices in Sioux City and Chicago. As he had done previously, when he established the Western Book and Supply Company, Micheaux sold stock in the new company to white farmers around Sioux City and finally amassed sufficient capital to make an eight-reel film of ***The Homesteader.***

Subsequently, he produced more than forty-four black-cast films nationally, some of which were also distributed in Europe. They achieved such wide distribution partly because of Micheaux's refusal to indulge in propagandizing. In his view, black people did not want racial propaganda of the sort that characterized many films produced by Hollywood and by some white independents. He believed that a good story was what they wanted, and a good story must mirror reality, reflecting accurately the social, economic, and political conditions common to the lives of American black people. Though some of his productions may be considered protest films, he did not see film solely as a political instrument. The mythology which he stressed attempted to combat the unrealistic images of black people created by Hollywood producers, images which Donald Bogle identifies as toms, coons, mulattoes, mammies, and bucks [*Toms, Coons*].

In an article published in the *Philadelphia Afro-American* (24 January 1925), Micheaux discussed his approach to film making. Film, Micheaux observes, is an art which requires an extraordinary amount of "encouragement and financial backing," neither of which he had been able to obtain in abundance. A black producer dares to "step into a world which has hitherto remained closed to him. His entrance into this unexplored field, is for him, trebly difficult. He is united [*sic*] in his themes, in obtaining casts that present genuine ability, and in his financial resources." Micheaux's comments on the extra difficulties confronting black film producers were not meant to shield his own work from criticism. "I do not wish anyone to construe this as a request for suppression of criticism," he states. "Honest, intelligent criticism is an aid to the progress of any effort. The producer who has confidence in his ideals solicits constructive criticism. But he also asks fairness, and fairness in criticism demands a familiarity with the aims of the producer, and a knowledge of the circumstances under which his efforts were materialized."

Many of Micheaux's critics apparently feel no need to respond to his plea to take into account the exceptional difficulties under which he labored or to consider his films from the point of view of their creator's conscious intention. Disregarding these two factors, they are too willing to write off his productions as second-rate underground films, comparable to Hollywood C-grade productions. After Micheaux released a seven-reel feature, ***The Dungeon,*** D. Ireland Thomas, writing in the *Chicago Defender* (8 July 1922), castigated him for using light-skinned actors and for not giving the film "race" promotion: "The advertising matter for this production has nothing to indicate that the feature is colored, as the characters are very bright [*sic*]; in fact almost white. 'The All-Star Colored Cast' that is so noticeable with nearly every race production is omitted on the cards and lithographs. Possibly Mr. Micheaux is relying on his name alone to tell the public that it is a race production or maybe he is after booking it in white theaters."

D. Ireland Thomas's criticism of Micheaux is typical of that of the majority of his critics. Even those who temper their comments with a tribute do so by way of an apologia. An article in the *Baltimore Afro-American* (24 July

1921) exemplifies this sort of qualified praise. It attacks race movie fans for their failure to develop separate criteria for evaluating black-produced films. And since the development of race films was in an embryonic state in 1921, harsh criticism from the audience was a threat to the survival of the new genre: "Moving pictures cannot be made without money. These pictures are shown in houses catering to colored patrons only. From them must come the means that will determine whether the industry will live. To bear with such men as Oscar Micheaux and other pioneers today means bigger and better race pictures tomorrow."

Some critics did evaluate Micheaux's works from the perspective of his conscious intention, but—ironically—it was partly because of such criticism that several of his films were nearly banned from public showing in Chicago and Philadelphia. In the previously cited 1925 article, Micheaux wrote that his intention was to "present the truth, to lay before the race a cross section of its own life, to view the colored heart from close range." He believed that "it is only by presenting those portions of the race portrayed in my pictures, in the light and background of their true state, that we can raise our people to greater heights. I am too much involved with the spirit of Booker T. Washington to engraft false virtues upon ourselves, to make ourselves that which we are not."

The false virtues of which he speaks are usually portrayed in his films as vices associated with black urban life. It is important to realize that many of the stereotypes Micheaux was fighting were propagated by black as well as white producers and writers. Micheaux's depiction of black people was also in striking contrast to the images popularized by the writers of the Harlem Renaissance. Many black writers of the 1920s tended to glorify the black lower class (pimps, whores, pushers, and so on), and to denigrate the black middle class as imitation white people. Moreover, black writers who attempted to reverse negative images of black people by elevating the "dregs of society" (to paraphrase Frantz Fanon) to "humanly" status insisted that the low-life characters they created were representative of black culture.

Micheaux was not alone in his criticism of the tendency to place one aspect of black life on a symbolic level intended to represent the whole; George Schuyler also made a critical analysis of the reversal of images by black writers. To my knowledge, however, Micheaux was the only black artist to present his critique through the medium of cinema. Unlike those black writers of the Harlem Renaissance who stigmatized black middle-class people as plastic replicas of white society incapable of sustaining African and Afro-American cultural traditions, Micheaux portrayed the black middle class as real people who were well educated, whose moral standards were high, and who were strongly motivated to achieve success. However, the methods by which members of that class attempted to better themselves often led them to commit dishonest or criminal acts, even murder. The plots of many of Micheaux's films center on realistic problems of the black middle class.

While Micheaux's emphasis on plot derived in part from his belief that black people wanted a good story, he had to depend on story because he lacked the technical ability to create special effects and the financial resources required to stage massive, spectacular action scenes. He usually did all the work on his productions, except for minor tasks: he wrote the scenarios, supervised filming, and handled the bookkeeping. His pictures took an average of ten days to shoot and usually cost ten to twelve thousand dollars. The most remarkable thing about Micheaux's career both as a novelist and as a film maker was his ability to work within stringent limitations. He rarely would reshoot a scene, no matter how badly it turned out, and as substitutes for a studio he used the homes and offices of his friends.

Quite often Micheaux would grant a theater manager first rights to show his films in return for the money to make them. In quest of such a deal, he would visit prospective patrons accompanied by several actors. The actors would perform a couple of scenes for the theater manager and Micheaux would extol the importance and marketability of the script.

In 1920 Micheaux's brother, Swan, joined him as manager of the Micheaux Film and Book Company; later he was promoted to secretary-treasurer and general manager. In 1921, when the corporation had a 25 percent cash dividend, it opened an office in New York, where facilities were better and casting easier; however, the distribution and financial office remained in Chicago under the supervision of Swan Micheaux and Charles Benson. Tiffany Tolliver and W. R. Crowell distributed the Micheaux films in the East from a branch office in Roanoke, Virginia, and A. Odams, owner of the Verdun Theatre in Beaumont, Texas, was the distributor for the Southwest. Lack of money forced Micheaux to file a voluntary petition in 1928. At this time the Micheaux Film Company listed assets of $1,400 and liabilities of $7,837. Yet Micheaux's perseverance, combined with the ingenuity of Alice Russell, an actress he married in 1929, soon got him back in business. Having obtained new money, he reorganized the company in the latter half of 1929, incorporating it under New York state laws.

Between 1918 and 1931 Micheaux produced twenty-seven films, most of them silent. His first all-sound feature was ***The Exile*** (1931), another adaptation of ***The Homesteader.*** Between 1931 and 1940 he produced and directed sixteen all-sound features. His last known film activity was writing and directing ***The Betrayal*** (1948), adapted from his novel ***The Wind from Nowhere.*** It opened to poor reviews in a white movie theater in downtown New York. Three years later, in 1951, Micheaux died at the age of sixty-seven in Charlotte, North Carolina.

Although Micheaux operated independently, a good many of his critics seek to equate his productions with those Hollywood made for blacks. Eileen Landry writes [in *Black Film Stars,* 1973] that Micheaux's stories were "often typically Hollywood—adventures, melodramas, mysteries—starring black actors. There was little 'ethnic truth' to these films; Micheaux gave his audiences a 'black Valentino' and a 'sepia Mae West.' And he perpetuated many white stereotypes; his heroes and heroines were usually light-skinned and fine-featured, his villains darker and more negroid. While some of his films dealt with the problem of being black, this was never from the point of view of the ghetto dweller or sharecropper; his subjects were the black bourgeoisie."

The same sort of comments have been made by those among Micheaux's critics who fail to place his books and films within the parameters of his conscious intention. Such criticism also omits from consideration the strongest characters Micheaux created—black pioneers. For it was through the creation of the black pioneer as an individual able to collapse the distinction between race and class that Micheaux made his most lasting contribution to black literature and films. The black pioneer is freed from the artifices of "civilization" and is allowed to fulfill his own potential through a process inherent in his cultural history.

Oscar Micheaux is emblematic of the black pioneer as a symbol of black achievement. The character was derived from experiences he himself had lived through. His films explore various aspects of the problem of being black in a racially oriented society from the point of view of black goal-oriented behavior. Central to the mythology he constructed in his novels and popularized in his films is the emphasis on abandoning metropolitan black areas and moving to the Great Northwest, where black men and women could build a civilization based on their own cultural ethos. Micheaux's impact on black film is widely recognized, even though its nature is debated. His film making stands as a symbol of the race pride he sought to instill in black people through his emphasis on the values of the black middle class.

Donald Bogle (essay date 1985)

SOURCE: "'B'. . . for Black," in *Film Comment,* October, 1985, pp. 31-46.

[*Bogle is the author of* Toms, Coons, Mulattoes, Mammies, and Bucks *(1973), a study of the representation of African Americans in movies. In the following essay, he discusses Micheaux's place in the history of African American filmmaking.*]

The heroine of Oscar Micheaux's 1937 film ***God's Step Children*** is Naomi, a high-toned, light-skinned black girl who wants to be white. She frets, pouts, plots, whines, and, well, *just plain acts up,* turning her tiny black community topsy-turvy. Finally, Naomi does everyone a great service; she throws herself into the river and, like a nasty stain on her race, is washed away. For white moviegoers during the Depression, Naomi's trials and tribulations passed unnoticed. But for black audiences, Naomi's was a lopsidedly caustic and cautionary morality tale about cultural roots and loyalties, racial heritage and pride. It was only one of many such narratives told in a long forgotten branch of American movie history: race movies, independently produced films with all-black casts, made outside Hollywood, in an attempt to merchandise mass dreams for black America.

America's race movies—from the early years of the century to the late Forties—first turned up as a kind of alternative cinema, made in response to the general movie fare of the time, all those crude, corny, insulting, racist little ditties with titles that just about said everything: *The Dancing Nig* (c. 1907), *For Massa's Sake* (1911), and the Rastus series (*How Rastus Got His Turkey, How Rastus Got His Pork Chops, Rastus and Chicken*). In the early years of the 20th century, all a black audience could expect to see of itself was a shocking parade of stereotypes stumbling across the screen. Naive, doltish toms. Feisty mammies. Contorted comic coons. Worse, the roles were almost always played by white actors in blackface.

The same was true, of course, of even D. W. Griffith's *The Birth of a Nation.* More than any other movie in history, Griffith's 1915 Civil War epic, with its images of marauding Negro troops, power-mad mulattoes, and lusty black bucks, sent shock waves through black America, galvanizing its leaders into an uproar of protest and action. The NAACP launched a formal protest movement against the picture, setting up picket and boycott lines. And soon there appeared a group of independent black filmmakers—Emmett J. Scott, the brothers George and Noble Johnson, and the legendary Oscar Micheaux—who scrambled for money (from the black bourgeoisie or white backers) and quickly formed production companies, determined to make all-black films that stressed black America's achievements. Their first films—*The Birth of a Race* (1918), *The Realization of a Negro's Ambition* (1916), *Trooper of Troop K* (1916), and ***The Homesteader*** (1919), all initially serious tributes to black endurance and ambition—were important mainly because they proved that black cinema could exist.

Afterwards scores of other film companies (Reol Productions, The Unique Film Company, The Norman Film Manufacturing Company, The Frederick Douglass Film Company), some black owned, others white controlled, sprang up in places as diverse as Jacksonville, St. Louis, Philadelphia, Chicago, and New York, often using the abandoned studios of mainstream film companies that had fled to California. Their low-budget films, frequently crude and misshapen, were shown at segregated theaters in the South, at big city ghetto movie houses in the North, and on occasion, at black churches, schools, and social gatherings—almost anyplace where it was possible to reach a black audience. Before this movement of independents ended, approximately 150 such companies had come into existence. Hundreds of films had been produced. And race movies themselves had undergone two distinct phases and points of view.

Sometimes plodding, sometimes didactic, sometimes deliriously disjointed, some of the early race films were, quite frankly, terrible. A movie like *Spying the Spy* (1917), produced by a white-owned company (Ebony Pictures), was almost as stereotypical as any Hollywood product, with a bug-eyed lead character called Sambo Sam.

But others offered rousing, optimistic stories of black derring-do. *The Bull Doggers* (1923) featured Bill Pickett as a cowboy performing feats of heroism and honor. *The Flaming Crisis* (1924) focused on a tough black newspaperman falsely accused of murder, fighting to prove his innocence. *The Flying Ace* (1926) spotlighted a daring black aviator who, in midair, rescues a fair black damsel in distress. In these films, black Americans saw themselves incorporated into the national pop mythology, and a new set of archetypes emerged: heroic black men of action. Whether cowboys, detectives, or weary army vets, many of the early characters were walking embodiments of black assertion and aggression, and, of course, they gave the lie to America's notions of a Negro's place.

But the early race films touched on other matters, too. Among the most interesting were those that were high-minded statements on the nature of black life in America or on the racial dynamics—divisions and tensions—within the black community itself. Nowhere was a race theme more apparent than in the 1927 production *Scar of Shame*. Produced by The Colored Players of Philadelphia, this slow-moving and melancholy film told the story of an ill-matched marriage between a young, black concert pianist and a poor, lower-class, young black woman. Secretly ashamed of his wife, the young man keeps her hidden from his socially prominent middle-class mother. Through a series of likably implausible plot maneuvers, the two part. He begins life anew and falls in love with another woman, only to meet up with his wife again. She still loves him but knows she can never be his equal. Socially—despite both being black—they are of different worlds. Despondent, the wife commits suicide and frees him to marry the other woman, his social equal. Melodramatic but effective, *Scar of Shame* was a surprisingly eloquent statement on the class and color caste system that existed within the black community. Though Hollywood would never have touched, least of all understood, the subject, the film reached and moved black audiences in a personal, intense way that Hollywood never did.

Of all the early black filmmakers, the most important (and one of the few to work in both silent and sound pictures) was the indefatigable producer/director Oscar Micheaux (1884-1951). A charismatic showman with a dash and flair he no doubt felt befitted a motion picture director, Micheaux was dedicated to his own concept of black cinema (a heady mix of subliminal social messages and sheer entertainment) and perhaps also to the creation of his own personal legend. He had once been a Pullman car porter, then a farmer in South Dakota, and by 1915, a self-published novelist. Within a few years, he turned to film, his fervid enthusiasm for moviemaking eventually carrying him to Chicago and later New York.

Early on, Micheaux realized (and relished) the importance of promotion. He is said to have toured the country to publicize one film and at the same time to seek financing for his next, often stepping out of cars and into meeting halls as if "he were God about to deliver a sermon." "Why, he was so impressive and so charming," said Lorenzo Tucker, an actor who appeared in several Micheaux films, "that he could talk the shirt off your back." On his tours, Micheaux approached white Southern theater managers and owners, often persuading them to show his black films at special matinee performances for black audiences or at special late shows for white audiences interested in black camp. Micheaux's shrewd promotional sense kept him in business, enabling him to produce, direct, and write, by some counts, almost 30 films from 1919 to 1948.

Micheaux's features were similar to Hollywood's, only technically inferior, resembling B-movies of the period. Lighting and editing were usually poor, and the acting could be dreadful—ranging from winging it to grandstanding. Often a scene was shot in a single take, as the camera followed an actor through a door or down a hallway. Since he was forced to shoot scenes so rapidly, he seldom had time (or money) to do retakes. Consequently, an actor might flub a line, then just pick up the pieces of his sentence and keep on going.

The action in Micheaux's films sometimes centered around one set. In ***God's Step Children,*** several key scenes occurred in front of a staircase. Filming in the home of a friend, Micheaux discovered that the staircase area offered the best lighting angles, and thus he worked his big scenes around it. Oddly enough, his limitations—the uncontrolled performances and the lived-in look of some sets—endowed his films with a strange realism. One half expects to hear Micheaux call "Cut" and to see the actors walk away from the camera or talk about how they're actually making a movie.

Intertwined in all his films is the consciousness of how race is a force in black life. Just as Negro newspapers and magazines took major news stories and reported them from a black angle, Micheaux took the typical Hollywood script and gave it a black slant. ***Underworld*** (1937) was a gangster film with a black gangster (he's the recent grad of a good colored college, who's gotten himself mixed up in Chicago's crime world) and a black gun moll. ***Daughter of the Congo*** (1930) was an African adventure story with a colored cavalry officer bent on rescuing a young Negro girl lost in the savage tropics. ***Temptation*** (1936) was a sophisticated sex drama in the DeMille vein.

On occasion, Micheaux focused exclusively on race as subject, as in ***Birthright*** (1924), the story of a young black Harvard graduate who returns to his home town in Tennessee bent upon founding a colored school to "uplift the race." Naturally, he encounters opposition, some of which comes from his fellow blacks, who agree with white Southerners that education ruins a Negro. In its own corny and sly way, ***Birthright*** made a definite plea for black unity while satirizing the old-style turncoats and toms. Micheaux liked this material so much that he remade the film in 1939.

Micheaux also gave his actresses vivid, important roles. Several of his films were also "women's pictures," with independent, strong-willed heroines. ***God's Step Children*** was part woman's film, part race-theme movie, its heroine Naomi punished with death perhaps precisely because of her free-wheeling independence.

Oscar Micheaux's greatest contribution is often viewed by some contemporary black audiences as his severest shortcoming. That his films reflected the interests and outlooks, the values and virtues, of the black bourgeoisie has long been held against him. Though his films never centered on the ghetto, few race movies did. They seldom dealt with racial misery or decay. Instead, they concentrated on the problems facing black "professional people." Then, too, his leading performers—as was typical of race films—were often close to the white ideal: straight hair, keen features, light skin.

To appreciate Micheaux's films one must understand that he was moving as far as possible from Hollywood's jesters and servants. He wanted to give his audience something "to further the race, not hinder it." Often he sacrificed plausibility to do so. He created a deluxe, ideal world where blacks were just as affluent, just as educated, just as "cultured" as their white counterparts. Oddly enough, as such, they remain a fascinating comment on black social and political aspirations of the past. And the Micheaux ideal Negro world view popped up in countless other race movies. His films likely set the pattern for race movies in general.

The audience for black films grew rapidly (particularly between 1915 and 1923; eventually there were about 600 theaters on the race-movie circuit). But a number of unfortunate events halted this burgeoning black industry. Distribution problems proved hard to lick. When talkies came in, many companies lacked the capital to keep up production and to acquire the new sound equipment. The release of the big-studio black musicals, *Hearts in Dixie* (1929) and *Hallelujah* (1929), spelled disaster for the small independents. Then the Depression killed many off.

Curiously, during this period (from the mid-Thirties through the war and postwar years), independent black films for black audiences underwent a significant change: They were made almost entirely by white filmmakers. Such men as Ted Toddy, Jack and Bert Goldberg, and Robert Savini, heading such companies as Herald Pictures, Astor Pictures, and Jubilee, eventually moved into the market.

During this second phase of the independents, there were some interesting films, among which *The Emperor Jones* (1933), starring Paul Robeson, was one of the best of the lot. In 1938 National Pictures released *The Spirit of Youth,* dramatizing the meteoric rise of a black boxer. Joe Louis played the central character, a figure closely related to the champ himself. As might be expected, Louis' acting was wooden. But what a hero for black audiences. In 1940, veteran Hollywood actor Clarence Muse also was able to co-write and star in *Broken Strings,* technically one of the better made features of the period. Spencer Williams, too, with white backers, directed two highly idiosyncratic films that touched on the black religious experience: *The Blood of Jesus* (1941) and *Go Down Death* (1944). Williams wrote the scripts for several other films, including *Harlem On the Prairie* (1939) and also directed *Juke Joint* (1947) and a raunchy black version of *Rain* called *Dirty Gertie from Harlem, USA* (1946). Ironically, Williams is best remembered today for his role as Andy Brown on TV's *Amos 'n Andy.*

For the most part, though, the producers of the later race movies were determined to make slick and glossy products that resembled typical Hollywood fare: black westerns, mysteries, boy-meets-girl stories, and gangster pictures. Concentrating more on entertainment unencumbered by weighty messages about race, the new features nonetheless—simply because of their all-black casts—could never leave the race issue behind. Thus the new leading players, whether dapper Ralph Cooper as a smooth-as-silk doctor in *Am I Guilty?* (1940) or Herbert Jeffrey as a spiffy cowboy immaculately dressed in tight riding clothes and fancy silver spurs and guns in *Bronze Buckeroo* (1938), remained indelible black middle-class heroes, still promoted as an ideal for the black masses.

Pepped-up and faster moving, escapist and high-spirited (some reflecting the optimism of the postwar era), the later films often featured musical stars or introduced new personalities. Lena Horne, dewy-eyed and giddy, no doubt caught up in the excitement of making her first film, was the plump but very pretty ingenue in *The Duke Is Tops* (1938). Endearingly lovely and fresh in *Ebony Parade* (1947), Dorothy Dandridge became one of black America's great cultural icons of the Fifties when she starred in Otto Preminger's *Carmen Jones* (1954) and *Porgy and Bess* (1959). Then she committed suicide. Count Basie, Cab Calloway, Dizzy Gillespie, The Mills Brothers, Nat "King" Cole, and jazz vocalist Helen Humes all performed for the later race-movie cameras.

So, too, did entertainers who, having endured the Hollywood grindstone for years, needed a break and a breath of fresh air. Stepin Fetchit, Nina Mae McKinney, Mantan Moreland, Bill "Bojangles" Robinson, and Louise Beavers were launched as genuine stars in their race movies with roles tailor-made for them. Ironically, Fetchit was cast as the same shufflin', dimwitted soul he'd always played, but with a twist. In the all-white environment of his Hollywood features, Fetchit was a talented black comic yanked out of his cultural context; this man who had started in black vaudeville, performing for black audiences, was clowning it up for whites. In his all-black films, he's simply an oddball funnyman in a world full of diverse black images.

The later independents also made a place for a figure Hollywood seemed to have no use for at all: the unabashed, unchangeable, raunchy or rowdy ethnic star who wasn't about to clean up his or her act (to tone down cultural differences or smooth out rough ethnic edges) to please a large white audience. Thus Jackie "Moms" Mabley, Dusty "Open the Door, Richard" Fletcher, Dewey Pigmeat Markham, and the great rhythm-and-blues star Louis Jordan did star spins in such films as *Killer-Diller (1948), Boarding House Blues* (1948), *Fight That Ghost* (1946), and *Look Out Sister* (1946).

In Louis Jordan's black films, Hollywood clearly missed something else. When the big studios did employ Negro entertainers, the black stars usually performed during an "interlude" when the white stars might rush off to a nightclub or party for some fun. Thus in *Rhapsody in Blue* (1945), Hazel Scott suddenly appears in a European supper-club sequence, singing George Gershwin's "The Man I Love," in French and English. Scott's innate poise and dignity and her skilled performance evoke an enigma: She's a blazing symbol, a sophisticated black woman at home in the most continental of settings, yet we sense Hazel Scott's isolation, so completely cut off is she from everything else in the film.

But isolation or star alienation are the last things one sees in the old race movies. In *Caldonia* (1945), *Beware* (1946), and *Reet, Petite, and Gone* (1947), not only did Louis Jordan have a chance to jam with his Tympany Five group but he was the star as well: As Jordan moves from boy-meets-girl plot mechanics to musical sequences and then back to the plot, the pictures give a portrait of the Negro performer who's also a person with some semblance of an offstage life, with cultural connections and roots he can always return to.

Perhaps that's where so many of the later race films (as well as some of the more socially conscious earlier ones) succeeded best: as fundamental celebrations of cultural roots and communal spirits—and also as pure, undiluted celebrations of black style. Such movies as *Broken Strings, Boy! What a Girl!* (1946), *Sepia Cinderella* (1947), *Bronze Buckeroo,* and scores of others introduced a new rhythm to American cinema. Vocal inflections and intonations set the ears abuzz. The manners, gestures, postures, surprising double takes, swift interplay and communication between the characters is a world unto itself, capturing, despite whatever other distortions or failings, a segment of black American life and culture.

By the late Forties, race movies were on their last legs, victims of changing attitudes within black America and of the major studios' budding interest in blacks as vehicles for the metaphor of American justice. In 1949, Hollywood released a series of problem pictures, *Home of the Brave, Pinky, Lost Boundaries,* and *Intruder in the Dust,* all of which dealt with a new view of the Negro and his role in American life. The old race movies could not compete with the technically well-made Hollywood products. Moreover, the black audience had an altered vision of itself.

Following World War II, black America, aware that black G.I.s had fought abroad for the freedom of whites only to return home to find economic slavery, had become increasingly more vocal about the nation's racial codes and divisions, its injustices and inequities. It sought a different kind of movie product, too, considering the racially hermetically sealed worlds of the race movies passé. In the Fifties, during the rise of the civil rights movement, black audiences preferred to see Sidney Poitier in *No Way Out* (1950), *Edge of the City* (1957), and *The Defiant Ones* (1958), which promoted the then acceptable themes of racial integration and cultural assimilation—and which also, despite serious compromises, touched on the conflicts between black and white. The latter was something race movies had rarely done. So they faded away.

Today, many of the old films have vanished or been destroyed. Surviving films are often dated, mangled, and sweetly naive, yet they remain vivid cultural artifacts, comments on black America's past fantasies, obsessions, attitudes, and aspirations, a rare glimpse of the way black America was once willing to look at itself. And sometimes, as in some of the films of Micheaux, of the direction in which black America once hoped to see itself move.

Bell Hooks (essay date 1991)

SOURCE: "Micheaux: Celebrating Blackness," in *Black American Literature Forum,* Vol. 25, No. 2, Summer, 1991, pp. 351-60.

[*Hooks is a major contemporary feminist and Afrocentric literary critic. In the following essay, she discusses the ways in which Micheaux's films "work to transgress boundaries, offering perspectives, 'takes,' on black experience that can be found/seen in no other cinematic practice during his day." Specifically, she examines the depiction of sexuality in the film* Ten Minutes to Live.]

Conceiving of his work in independent filmmaking as counter-hegemonic cultural production, Oscar Micheaux worked doggedly to create screen images that would disrupt and challenge conventional racist representations of blackness:

> I have always tried to make my photoplays present the truth, to lay before the race a cross section of its own life, to view the colored heart from close range. My results might have been narrow at times, due perhaps to certain limited situations, which I endeavored to portray, but in those limited situations, the truth was the predominant characteristic. It is only by presenting those portions of the race portrayed in my pictures, in the light and background of their true state, that we can raise our people to greater heights. [Micheaux, in the *Philadelphia Afro-American,* 24 January 1925]

Though Micheaux aimed to produce a counter-hegemonic art that would challenge white supremacist representations of "blackness," he was not concerned with the simple reduction of black representation to a "positive" image. In the spirit of oppositional creativity, he worked to produce images that would convey complexity of experience and feeling, arguing that, "before we expect to see ourselves featured on the silver screen as we live, hope, act, and think today, men and women must write original stories of Negro life." Though he did not conceive of his work as documentation, as though all he hoped to make the camera do was mirror life, he did want black folks to see images on the screen that were not stereotypes or caricatures. Micheaux endeavored to go beyond the realm of the ordinary, and it is this vision that gives his films an element of intrigue and delight that fascinates.

Ironically, his use of melodrama has been misunderstood by contemporary viewers, who believe this style undermines the cinematic capacity to convey complexity. Micheaux did not suffer from an error of insight. Laura Mulvey explores the subversive possibilities emerging from the location of melodrama, drawing on Peter Brooks's *The Melodramatic Imagination:*

> Peter Brooks shows how the melodrama's aesthetic strength lies precisely in its displacement of the power of the word. This "low cultural" form could reflect on human struggle with language and expression and thus influence the development of romantic theatre. The aesthetics of the popular melodrama depend on grand gesture, tableaux, broad moral themes, with narratives of coincidence, reverses and sudden happy endings organized around a rigid opposition between good and evil. Characters represent forces rather than people, and fail to control or understand their circumstances so that fate, rather than heroic transcendence, offers a resolution to the drama. . . . While the aesthetics of melodrama evolved for a non-literate audience, the style throws doubt on the adequacy of speech to express the complexities of passion. . . . A whole terrain of the "unspeakable" can thus be depicted. ["Melodrama Inside and Outside the Home," in her *Visual and Other Pleasures,* 1989]

Micheaux used melodrama in precisely this way, and approaching his work from this standpoint enables the contemporary viewer to see more clearly how his films work to transgress boundaries, offering perspectives, "takes," on black experience that can be found/seen in no other cinematic practice during his day. Critic Marilyn Jimenez [in an unpublished manuscript] says of Micheaux's films:

> There is in them the true mark of the "auteur," the unmistakable stamp of a personality, the obsessions of a visionary: this all generally under the surface, for the distinctive mark of a Micheaux film is the relationship between text and subtext, between what the film says and what it really says. In so doing, Micheaux, more than any other filmmaker, embodies the ancient characteristic of black artistic creation: the trope of reversal, the use of "indirections to find directions out."

Micheaux, fascinated by what I will call "a politics of pleasure and danger," focused on both racialized sexual politics as they informed the construction and expression of desire within black heterosexual couples, as well as interracial sexual bondings. Though he was involved in a romantic liaison with a white woman in South Dakota, Micheaux felt marriage to her was tantamount to a betrayal of his race. A constant theme in his films, desire, expressed sexually, becomes a site where loyalty and solidarity are tested. Much of his work explores passions aroused in response to acts of betrayal. Attempting to express and convey the particular forms desire and courtship take within a racial context of color caste, a society in which black male and female sexuality is constructed as dangerous, threatening, Micheaux's work "exploits" conventional constructions of good and bad sexuality as he simultaneously "toys" with the idea of transgression.

The 1932 Micheaux film ***Ten Minutes to Live*** problematizes the location of black heterosexual pleasure within a rigid color caste system that makes the desired object the body most resembling whiteness. Challenging assumptions that whiteness/light skin should be interpreted as signifying innocence in a series of narrative reversals, the question of who is good or bad is rendered far more complex than the issue of color. Calling into question the Western metaphysical dualism which associates whiteness with purity and blackness with taint, the subtext of Micheaux's seemingly simple melodrama interrogates internalized racism and the color caste system.

Superficially, ***Ten Minutes to Live*** conforms to the cinematic paradigm already set by Hollywood and gives his audience a bad guy. Addressing the black public's need to have race movies reproduce aspects of that white mainstream cinema which denied their presence, Micheaux incorporates into his work familiar melodramatic narratives. Just as the white "master" narratives of cinema insisted that plots be structured around conflicts between good and evil, this became the usual ground of conflict in race movies. Responding to what Clyde Taylor [in "The Master Text and the Jeddi Doctrine," *Screen,* Vol. 24, No. 4, 1988, pp. 96-104] calls an insistence on "the sense of the presence and identity of corruption" which then "embodies the need for a menacing Manichean adversary." Micheaux used this model to generate suspense, that cinematic tension that fascinated audiences.

Ironically, even though ***Ten Minutes to Live*** interrogates the audience's need for a "bad guy," Micheaux structures the film's opening scenes so that they stimulate the audience's interest in identifying a villain. First, we are shown the image of a distressed black woman, the glamourous Letha, boarding a train. A male voice-over poses the question "What mystery here? Why has this beautiful girl been put on the spot?" The film proceeds to explain the scenes we have just seen. Initially jolted into a state of defamiliarization, the audience sees images that they know but whose meaning in the film's context cannot be discerned. Micheaux works to establish film as a site for the production of narratives that are structured to be more compelling than ordinary life: After all, race movies were, like their Hollywood counterparts, about business; audiences had to be captivated so that they would return to see more. Using the camera to disrupt fixed notions of subject and place, to create an aura of intrigue, Micheaux aggressively insists that viewers be "glued to their seats" if they want to solve the mystery. (His shooting of this scene is really technologically spectacular when viewed within the context of early film production.) Disrupting the audience's capacity to "read" familiar signs, Micheaux delights in the pleasure of manipulation, excessively subordinating everything to the narration. Though a race man, eager to work for the uplift of black people, he refused to accept the notion that black cultural production should simply be a response to white representations of blackness and, thereby, only portray blackness in a positive light. Insisting on diversity and complexity of image, his films set an example.

After the train scene, which opens the film in the middle of the story, strategically shifting the focus away from linear narrative, Micheaux breaks with convention and lets the audience know from the onset who the villain is. Identified by a snapshot from a police blotter, he, Marvin, is described as "40, deaf and mute—but cunning, formerly an actor known on the stage as the 'escape' king due to his ability to pick any lock, open any door . . . lost his voice and hearing about 5 years ago and developed strange hallucinations." Though appearing to "identify" the bad guy, this description does not really say what crimes have been committed. Presented as official information even though it says nothing specific, this representation undercuts the stereotype of the black male as criminal, hinting at the possibility that all representation is subject to manipulation (Marvin as actor), and that nothing is as it appears.

Unable to speak or hear, Marvin must rely solely on sight as a means to perceive reality. Concurrently, since he has no voice (a symbolic mirroring of the voicelessness of black masculinity in racist culture during the 1930s), he must think and feel through the body. Richard Dyer's critical assessment of Paul Robeson calls attention to the way representations of black folks in the white imagination are a "site where the problem of the body is worked through":

> Representations of blacks . . . function as the site of *remembering and denying* the inescapability of the body in the economy[:] . . . on the one hand, the black body as a reminder of what the body can do, its vitality, its strength, its sensuousness; and yet, simultaneously, the denial of all that bodily energy and delight as creative and productive. . . . [*Heavenly Bodies: Film Stars and Society,* 1986]

Conversely, in order to subvert the negation of the black body that is imposed by white supremacy, representations by black people claim that creative potential, glorifying it. Even though the fair-skinned, handsome Marvin is the bad guy, his body is constructed as the object of a desiring black female gaze. Challenging dominant cinematic practices that position woman as the objects of male gaze, Micheaux acknowledges female desire, exploiting it to create interest in Marvin's character. His body is excessively objectified, all the more so because he does not speak. Asserting a masculine presence that is profoundly physical, embodying a sense of threat and menace, he is a seductive villain.

Micheaux both critiques and celebrates this black male physicality. Beginning his professional life as a Pullman porter, respectable employment (the train scene represents the inclusion in the film of his personal history), Marvin is identified with that organization of black men who militantly resisted racist discrimination in the work force. Yet Micheaux knew all too well that it was easy within a racist society for black men to fall into disrepute, to end up like Marvin on the chain gang. It is only when the film is about to end that we learn from a letter Marvin's mother writes rebuking him for persecuting the beautiful Letha that he has been on the chain gang, a site where white domination over the black male body is expressed by excessive exploitation of blacks' physical labor. Many chain gangs composed solely of black men did the arduous labor on railroads—laying tracks, making repairs. Micheaux inclusion of these historical references (that would have been immediately understood by his audience) situate representations of black male "criminality" in a social and political context, contesting notions of inherent biological propensity toward evil perpetuated in racist ideology—and in white cinema.

Even though Marvin is a sympathetic character, he is depicted as dangerous, exhibiting all the characteristics of "the demon lover." He has returned to old haunts to kill the woman who betrayed him by turning him over to the authorities. Robin Morgan's description of "the deadly hero" in *The Demon Lover* [1989] could be a profile of Marvin:

> Valorous, abnegating his own selfhood and severed from that of others, disconnected from a living logic and the pathos of emotional commitments, recognizing only the redeeming ecstasy of a tragic death, *the hero already lives as a dead man.* As a dead man he is fearless, because as a dead man he is unconquerable by any life force.

Throughout ***Ten Minutes to Live,*** Marvin resurfaces as though from the dead. His inability to speak, to communicate, reinforces the sense that he has no ties with the human community, as it is language that affirms this bonding. Able to express himself to others only by writing, he terrorizes Letha by sending her threatening messages, "death warrants," to let her know that she is his prey, hunted by an old love who intends to show no mercy. Inverting the popular myth of embittered, revengeful womanhood betrayed and scorned by man, Micheaux implies that it is really the black male, personified by Marvin, who will be betrayed and manipulated.

In keeping with his critique of a color caste that sees fair-skinned black women as more desirable and worthy of love, Micheaux's "vamp" Charlotte could pass for white. Jewish American actress Theda Bara, whose real name was Theodosia Goodman, brought the image of the vamp to Hollywood and popularized it. Woman as "vamp" was depicted as an adventuress—alluring, enticing, dangerous. Vamp was short for vampire; she had the power to seduce and destroy men. In *Girls on Film* [1986], Julie Burchill critically examines the cinematic portrait of woman as vamp, emphasizing that this character was often portrayed as dark, in contrast to white:

> The vamp was a beacon and a blessing in the cinema, the apex of what a woman on the screen can be. The vamp was beautiful *and* strong; she made helplessness, which previously and ever since has been the desirable norm for girls on film, look insipid and uninspiring. She came from nowhere and she walked alone. The vamp was rhapsody and a revolution.

Micheaux offers his viewers images of woman as "vamp" and as helpless damsel in distress in ***Ten Minutes to Live*** via his juxtaposition of the characters Charlotte and Letha. Again as though to counter the racism of mainstream cinema, his vamp is the fair-skinned white-woman-look-alike.

Marvin's inability to distinguish between Charlotte and Letha, to know which woman is vamping and betraying him, is Micheaux's way to once again problematize the question of representation and our capacity to know reality via the senses. How can we judge good and evil if so much that appears to be one thing is really the other? His answer, of course, is to sharpen and intensify one's capacity for perception, to learn to be more aware. Employing diverse images of black womanhood, Micheaux encourages audiences to resist the urge to construct a totalizing vision of woman, one that sees the female as embodying all that is evil, licentious, and morally corrupt. An advocate of rights for women, Micheaux created a space in cinema in which black women could be portrayed as desiring subjects; he countered the demeaning images of black femaleness in Hollywood cinema. In his films, black women's bodies are celebrated: Plump or thin, light or dark (though they are never "too" dark), they are sensual and desirable.

Careful in ***Ten Minutes to Live*** to distinguish between the image of woman as the "vamp" who uses her body as a seductive weapon to exert power over men and the representation of a liberated image of the sensual/sexual black woman who is at home in her body, Micheaux remains one of the few filmmakers to portray black women's bodies in a manner that does not invite a phallocentric, violating gaze. Without allying himself with idealized representations of "innocent" womanhood, he portrays Letha as a virtuous woman who is also glamorous, and therefore desirable. Annette Kuhn offers this account of glamor's allure:

> Glamour is understood generally to imply a sense of deceptive fascination, of groomed beauty, of charm enhanced by means of illusion. A glamourous/glamourised image then is one manipulated, falsified perhaps, in order to heighten or even to idealise. A glamourous image of a woman (or an image of a glamourous woman) is peculiarly powerful in that it plays on the desire of the spectator in a particularly pristine way: beauty or sexuality is desirable to the extent that it is idealised and unattainable. ["Living Dolls and 'Real' Women," in Kuhn, et al. *The Power of the Image: Essays on Representation and Sexuality,* 1985]

Micheaux employs this notion of glamor in his representation of Letha. One of longest scenes in ***Ten Minutes to Live*** shows Letha returning to her bedroom in a boarding house to change clothes. There, fully made-up, gazing at herself in the mirror of her vanity table (all images that identify her as using cosmetics to create glamor), attired in beautiful lingerie and dressing gown, she dresses for an evening out. Unself-consciously adorned, Letha maintains an aura of naïveté even though she is not innocent. That aura is not disrupted by the presence of Marvin, who has entered her space, violating her privacy, for she does not know that her integrity is threatened until the front door slams as he escapes.

Fully adorned, the glamorous Letha meets her current, dark-skinned male admirer Anthony in a nightclub. She shows him another terrorizing message from Marvin, one that says she has only "ten minutes to live." That they should go nightclubbing when her life is endangered seems outrageously melodramatic, yet Micheaux's tactic is always to reproduce an image of the real in the context of the bizarre. Intrigue requires a combination of the ordinary and the fantastic. In his films, nightclubs are the perfect settings to introduce this mixture, representing as they do sites of transgression, existing on the boundaries of morally sanctioned social life. Seeing nightclubs as non-hegemonic, non-homogenous spaces where class/caste barriers were crossed in the realm of pleasure, Jimenez comments:

> The song-dance sequences in black films lifted the film out of social reality, relieved the tensions of having to maintain racial consciousness, and broke the chains of unrealistic, narrative developments. The nightclub was a play-space, a dystopia, not a space that was no-where, but a dis-associated, discontinuous real.

In ***Ten Minutes to Live,*** Micheaux includes a song-and-dance sequence in the nightclub scene that at first glance seems in no way connected to the suspenseful drama. It is, however, as much a clue hinting at the film's subtext as any other scene in the movie.

In the nightclub Letha talks quietly to Anthony, encouraging him to wait, even though they are waiting for death. He replies, "Are you mad to think I'm going to sit here and let you, the woman I love, the woman I've always loved, be killed by this madman?" This melodramatic, passionate declaration and its underlying eroticism can be expressed in the nightclub setting, since the sexual tension it arouses, the desire, can be displaced onto the dancers. Letha and Anthony's passionate talk is interrupted by the master of ceremonies' announcement: "And now we introduce you to a little bit of the jungle—'Spirit of the Jungle.'" Suddenly, skimpily dressed black women of all sizes and varying shades appear and begin to dance. Their body movements resemble those of Josephine Baker, calling attention to their breasts, legs, and asses. Yet this display does not evoke pornographic gazes from folks in the nightclub; it is presented not as exposure of taboo sexuality but as comfortable expression of bodily delight. Like Baker, Micheaux saw the black body as a site where nakedness, eroticism was not considered a shameful reality to be hidden and masked.

Though Phyllis Rose's biography of Josephine Baker [*Jazz Cleopatra: Josephine Baker in Her Time,* 1989] assaults her life and work, now and then it offers tidbits of useful information. This is particularly so in passages that address Baker's theorizing of the body and its relation to eroticism. Attempting to describe Baker's sense of the body, particularly the rear end, and documenting Baker's words, Rose comments:

> She handled it as though it were an instrument, a rattle, something apart from herself that she could shake. One can hardly overemphasize the importance of her rear end. Baker herself declared that people had been hiding their asses too long. "The rear end exists. I see no reason to be ashamed of it. It's true that there are rear ends so stupid, so pretentious, so insignificant that they're good only for sitting on." With Baker's triumph, the erotic gaze of a nation moved downward: she had uncovered a new region for desire.

Rose lacks the knowledge of black culture that would have enabled her to decode the subtext of Baker's comments, as well as an informed perspective on race that would have enabled her to understand that "asses" have always been eroticized in black sexual iconography, that within black folk culture the asses that are ridiculed and mocked are those of whites, called by names like *ironing-board butts.* Hence, only the gaze of the white segment of the nation was transformed by Baker's assertion of bodily passion in dance.

Though associated with the "jungle," all the dancers in Micheaux's sequence are light-skinned, some light enough to pass. Yet by connecting this image with a jungle experience, Micheaux affirms an unbroken diasporic bond with Africa that has not been severed by assimilation. Atavism, as expressed in this dance routine, glorifies the connection to Africa. As Dyer puts it, atavism is often rooted in "the idea of the black race as a repository of uncontaminated feelings." Though Dyer acknowledges that the atavistic image in the white imagination is similar to that in black folk culture, as a "sign" it has different meanings in the black context. In the black imagination, atavism was primarily connected to a counter-hegemonic sense of history wherein the African past white supremacy had taught blacks to despise was revered, seen as a site for "the recovery of qualities and values held by one's ancestors."

After the dancers evoke an atavism that is about ancestor acknowledgment, Letha emphasizes her familial legacy. She explains to Anthony that she has received spiritual guidance from her mother in a dream:

> Last night, I dreamed of mother, my poor dear mother, who is dead. She came to me in my sleep and told me not to run away. "Be calm, my baby. Place your trust in God. Something terrible is going to happen. Have faith, my daughter. Have faith."

Trusting in the wisdom of her mother, Letha refuses to listen to either the patriarchal voice that threatens her or the one that encourages her to flee, offering to Anthony a paradigm for romantic love that is rooted in trust.

Contrary to the Freudian conceptualization of subjectivity wherein, as Jane Gallop describes it [in *Thinking through the Body,* 1988], "universal ambivalence toward the mother is made up of a universal primary attachment to the mother as nurturer and universal disappointment in the mother," Micheaux's drama suggests that only by maintaining connection to the mother is one not tainted by suspicion, that the adult child receives the mother's unmediated wisdom and guidance. Both Letha and Marvin are rescued after they listen to the mother's voice. The possibility of disappointment rests not with the mother, but with the child, who may lack the ability to recognize "truth," and therefore reality. Marvin's mother informs him that Charlotte is the vamp who has betrayed him for monetary rewards even as she castigates him for being a "fool."

As in other Micheaux films that have feminist implications, his representations of maleness in ***Ten Minutes to Live*** challenge the patriarchal construction of masculinity as powerful and all-knowing. The men in the film lack insight. They can only apprehend the world fully, grasp the true nature of reality, by learning from women. Letha and Marvin are spiritually renewed when they listen to the mother's voice. Escaping after he has revenged himself against Charlotte, Marvin writes a note of apology to Letha. This expression of regret enables him to reconnect with the human community. His representation as "villain" is mediated by his confession of wrongdoing.

Ten Minutes to Live exploits all the conventions of simplistic melodrama even as it interrogates on multiple levels issues of representation. Nothing appears on the screen to be as simplistic as it often seems in everyday life. The capacity of individuals to discern good and evil, to distinguish that which is desirable and that which threatens, is interrogated. Micheaux lets the audience know how easily perceptions can be manipulated. Representing the ultimate villain, Charlotte, who is white enough to pass, in contrast to the romantic, trusting lover Anthony, who is dark-skinned, Micheaux subtly urges black spectators to reevaluate the internalized racism that leads them to respect white or light skin and devalue blackness. Simultaneously, he urges us to claim the past, symbolized by the body of the mother—the mother tongue, the mother land. It is a call for a celebration of blackness in all its diversity and complexity—for that level of collective self-recognition that brings clarity, and insight, that allows for reunion and reconciliation.

Pearl Bowser and Louise Spence (essay date 1996)

SOURCE: "Identity and Betrayal: 'The Symbol of the Unconquered' and Oscar Micheaux's Biographical Legend," in *The Birth of Whiteness: Race and the Emergence of U.S. Cinema,* edited by Daniel Bernardi, Rutgers University Press, 1996, pp. 56-80.

[*In the following essay, Bowser and Spence discuss the interrelationships between what is known about Micheaux's life, the ways in which he mythologized his life in his creative works, and the significance of his novels and films as documents of the African American social experience.*]

> ***The Symbol of the Unconquered,*** the latest and the best of the Micheaux productions, will open a six day showing at the Vendome Theater on Monday January 10th [1921]. This feature has been creating a wonderful amount of comment all over the East and is one which should be seen by everybody. The story is a clean-cut one and the action is full of speed, interesting and exciting. It tells of the struggles of a young man to retain possession of a piece of valuable oil land against tremendous odds, which includes [*sic*] everything from intimidation at the hand of his neighbors to a narrow escape from death for him at the hands of the Ku Klux Klan. A love story of beautiful texture lends added interest and some red-blooded scrapping and hard, hard riding furnishes the picture with the amount of exciting action required to make the blood tingle through your veins at high speed.
>
> —*The Chicago Defender,* 1/8/21
>
> It is claimed the touch of the romance woven in ***The Homesteader*** is coincident with the author's own life but this is still a matter of conjecture.
>
> —*The Half-Century Magazine,* April 1919
>
> My color shrouds me in. . . .
>
> —Countee Cullen

Seventy-two years after its 1920 premiere at the Vaudette Theater in Detroit, a print of ***The Symbol of the Unconquered,*** Oscar Micheaux's tale of mistaken identity, romance, and adventure in the West, was repatriated to the United States from the Belgium national film archives (Cinémathèque Royale/Koninklijk Filmarchief) with French and Flemish intertitles. ***The Symbol of the Unconquered*** is one of only three of Micheaux's silent films that have "survived" thus far. Though his career spanned thirty years, approximately twenty-five features—more than half of his total output—were produced in the first decade (1918-1929). These films were tools to express his personal view of the African American experience. In his desire to have his life be an example for others, Micheaux fostered certain aspects of his personal vision, made artistic use of his personal history, and dramatized particular motifs. He created a biographical persona composed of selected actual and imaginary events that continues to exist and exert influence today, even though many of his films are lost and forgotten.

In his silent films, Micheaux chose themes that were contentious or explosive in their time. By responding to such contemporary social issues as concubinage, rape, miscegenation, peonage, and lynching, he created a textured and layered expressive response to the social crises that circumscribed African American life. ***Within Our Gates,*** for example, unveils the lynch mob, exposing its members as ordinary townfolk: men, women, and even children who participate in hunting down and hanging a Black family. ***The Symbol of the Unconquered*** unmasks the Ku Klux Klan. In ***The Gunsaulus Mystery*** (1921), a reworking of the Leo M. Frank case, a man is wrongfully accused of the murder of a white woman. Promotion for ***The Dungeon*** (1922) touted the film as dealing with the then-pending Dyer anti-lynching bill. ***The Brute*** (1920) condemned racketeering and the abuse of women. Passing is the central theme of ***The House Behind the Cedars*** (1925); ***Body and Soul*** confronts hypocrisy and corruption in the ministry; and racially restrictive real estate covenants are challenged in ***Birthright*** (1924).

These films generated heated debate and were subject to censorship by official censor boards, community groups, and individuals such as local sheriffs and theater owners. For instance, a police captain in New Orleans ordered a Race theater to discontinue showing ***Within Our Gates*** because in his opinion the lynching scenes would incite a riot. The Virginia State Board of Motion Picture Censors rejected the full version of ***The House Behind the Cedars*** for "presenting the grievances of the negro in very unpleasant terms and even touching on dangerous ground, intermarriage between the races."

Micheaux sometimes defied the censor board by showing a film without submitting it for a license or without eliminating offensive passages and, on occasion, would use the controversy over a film in one town to promote it in other locations, advertising, for example, the "complete version" of ***Within Our Gates.*** For its run in Omaha, an article in a local newspaper announced the forthcoming showing as "the Race film production that created a sensation in Chicago" and "required two solid months to get by the censor board." Censorship became the plot of his 1921 film ***Deceit.***

The silent features now extant (***Within Our Gates*** [1920], ***The Symbol of the Unconquered*** [1920], and ***Body and Soul*** [1925]), along with his novels, promotional materials, and personal papers, illuminate the degree to which Micheaux used his self-constructed social identity, political point of view, and status as African American entrepreneur to create, promote, and shape the reception of his works. This "biographical legend," to borrow from Boris Tomashevsky, was not only the way that Micheaux made expressive use of his biography, it also validated the racial experiences of his audiences and gave credibility to his role as a successful filmmaker and novelist. During the first decade of his career, Micheaux developed a public persona as an aggressive and successful businessman and a controversial and confident maverick producer—an image that was to sustain him for the next twenty years, although little of the work after his first sound picture, ***The Exile*** in 1931, would seem to justify it.

Micheaux, son of former slaves, was the product of a generation of African American migrants who left the land in search of "the freedom of life and limb, the freedom to work and think, the freedom to love and aspire" [W. E. B. DuBois, *The Souls of Black Folk,* 1903]. In his semi-autobiographical novels ***The Conquest: The Story of a Negro Pioneer by the Pioneer*** (1913) and ***The Homesteader*** (1917), he tells of venturing forth from his home in southern Illinois in 1901, in search of a career at the age of seventeen. Heading north to Chicago, he supported himself at odd jobs, shining shoes, bailing water in a coal mine, laboring in a factory, the stockyards, and as a Pullman porter. While working as a porter, Micheaux was able to save enough money to set up an agrarian enterprise, a homestead on the Rosebud Reservation in Winner, South Dakota. His novels suggest that, like many of his white immigrant neighbors who made land purchases based on the prospects of the railroad extending westward, he hoped to turn a profit on the value of his holdings. However, in order to acquire title to the land, it was necessary to build a house on it and till the soil. He wrote of preferring selling the family crop to working in the fields as a boy and knowing little about farming. Undeterred by lack of experience, he taught himself the rudiments of Great Plains farming, a process he described in painful detail, including purchasing mules, getting the right equipment to break the prairie, and turning the sod over day after day. He also reflected on the need, as the only "colored man" engaged in agriculture on the Reservation, to demonstrate to his neighbors that he was an honest, hardworking Negro determined to succeed. Bent on disproving the widely held belief that "the negro," when faced with the hardships of homesteading, would opt for the "ease and comfort" of the city, Micheaux broke-out three times as many acres as his neighbors.

Working hard for five years, Micheaux amassed more than five hundred acres by the time he was twenty-five. He approached homesteading with the same philosophy he was later to apply to his book and movie businesses: independence, persistence, and a willingness to take risks. One chapter of ***The Conquest,*** in a writing style that differs from the rest of the novel, digresses to report the history of two towns, detailing the townsfolk's speculation on the routes of the railroad's expansion. Although the "objective reporting" of the details and key players obviously attempts to distance Micheaux from those speculators, it is given such prominence in an otherwise personal story that one cannot help but wonder what role he had in the scheme. Indeed, the image of Micheaux as land speculator seems more in tune with Micheaux-the-entrepreneur than with Micheaux-the-homesteader. In his own words, he "was possessed with a business turn of mind." In ***The Homesteader,*** for example, he boasts about how, after writing "his life story" and having a publisher reject it, he financed ***The Conquest*** himself. With borrowed money for a suit and a trip to Nebraska, he struck a deal with a printer there and then raised money for the first payment by preselling copies of the book to his neighbors in South Dakota.

Although Micheaux acquired a large holding and claimed to have been successful at farming wheat and flax, his career as a farmer ended sometime between 1912 and 1913. He tells of liens on his homestead and struggling to pay interest and taxes so he would not lose his land. Many homesteaders who had settled with great optimism were forced to abandon their claims because of a prolonged drought. Foreclosures were so common, they "occasioned no comment" [*The Chicago Defender,* 28 October 1911]. In his next novel, ***The Forged Note*** (1915), he refers nostalgically to the Rosebud Reservation and returning to the land. By 1916 Micheaux had moved to Sioux City, Iowa, where he published a third novel, ***The Homesteader,*** and sold his earlier works through his firm, The Western Book Supply Company.

In 1918 George P. Johnson, general booking manager of the Lincoln Motion Picture Company of Los Angeles, initiated a correspondence with Oscar Micheaux, now an author, publishing his own books and selling them door-to-door. Johnson wrote to The Western Book Supply Company about his discovery of ***The Homesteader*** in a *Chicago Defender* advertisement and inquired into the film rights to the book. His brother and founder of the company, the actor Noble Johnson, reviewed Micheaux's novel and suggested that parts of it—the interracial romance, most likely—were too controversial for them to deal with, adding, "It is a little too advanced on certain subjects for us yet and unless we would change [it] so decidedly that it would hardly be recognizable, we could not expect much support from white houses."

There followed a rapid exchange of correspondence over three months between Micheaux and George P. Johnson, with Johnson initially trying to convince Micheaux that he had more expertise in "the movie game" and promising that he could mold it "into a first-class feature." Micheaux, just as he had approached learning to farm by inquiring from others, was probing for information from the Johnsons. At the same time, he was already constructing a grandiose persona by maintaining that his 500-page novel should be a big picture, at least six reels, not the Lincoln Company's usual two- or three-reel product. He was also apparently convinced that, far from being a detriment to profitability, the controversial nature of such themes as interracial marriage was a very good selling device and should be exploited: "Nothing would make more people as anxious to see a picture than a litho reading: SHALL RACES INTERMARRY?"

With no movie experience at all, Micheaux ultimately decided to produce ***The Homesteader*** himself, incorporating under the name of Micheaux Book and Film Company. Bragging to Lincoln that he was able to raise $5,000 through a stock subscription in less than two weeks, he went on to produce an eight-reeler, the longest African American film at that time, and advertised it as "Oscar Micheaux's Mammoth Photoplay." The theatrical debut of the film was promoted as "Passed by the Censor Board despite the protests of three Chicago ministers who claimed that it was based upon the supposed hypocritical actions of a prominent colored preacher of the city!"

With the release of ***The Homesteader*** in February of 1919, Micheaux joined the growing number of small companies producing films exclusively for African American audiences. By the end of 1920, Micheaux had released his fourth feature, ***The Symbol of the Unconquered,*** "A Stirring Tale of Love and Adventure in the Great Northwest," like ***The Homesteader,*** a wilderness story. The frontier, for Micheaux, is the mythic space of moral drama and the site of opportunities seemingly free of the restrictive and discriminatory laws and social arrangements of the rural South and the urban metropolis, where the characteristic model of economic expansion is entrepreneurship. His first novel, ***The Conquest,*** set in Gregory County, South Dakota, celebrates the enterprising individuals: homesteaders, merchants, bankers, and real estate dealers involved in commercial clubs, land booms, and speculating on the route of the railroad. The hero of ***The Symbol of the Unconquered,*** a man of the frontier, self-willed and self-motivated, is another articulation of Oscar Micheaux's biographical legend. Accumulating wealth through hard work and self-denial, he is almost a metaphor for the spirit of individualism. In a 1910 article in *The Chicago Defender,* Micheaux quoted Horace Greeley, "Go west young man and grow up with the country," and although he wrote about openings for doctors, lawyers, laborers, and mechanics, he posited the future of the West with agricultural possibilities, calling farmlands "the bosses of wealth." For Micheaux, the land openings along the Frontier provided the opportune moment for the Negro to "do something for himself." Detailing the participation of the Race in agriculture, he wrote of fewer than "300 Negro farmers in the ten states of the Northwest [and] more opportunities than young men to grasp them" [**"Where the Negro Fails,"** *The Chicago Defender,* 19 March 1910]. Although such an image made him seem unique, enlarging his legend as a "Negro pioneer," Micheaux was one of many thousands of African Americans, since emancipation, who saw the frontier as the land of hope where one could realize one's own destiny.

The appeal of the West spoke strongly to many Americans as both a symbolic and actual place offering an unspoiled environment in "the hollow of God's hand" for individuals to fill with their own virtue, where social conventions and distinctions prove less important than natural ability, inner goodness, and individual achievement. Real estate promoters, railroad advertisements, news stories, dime novels, traveling shows, and movies mythologized the frontier as the site of freedom, wealth, and independence, capturing the imagination of a multitude of African Americans determined to put the residues of slavery and racial barriers behind them. Micheaux's hero in ***The Symbol of the Unconquered,*** Van Allen, a gentlemanly frontiersman in a buckboard riding the prairies of South Dakota, embodied the Western hero, self-sufficient and calmly rugged. Race theaters, not unlike white houses, featured Westerns as an important part of the programming in the late teens and twenties. Edward Henry, a projectionist throughout the 1920s in a Black theater in Jackson, Mississippi, recalled, "When you go back, William S. Hart was one of the big men. . . . All you had to do was just put his name out there; [you] didn't have to put any pictures or anything, just William S. Hart, Wednesday, and they'd be coming. . . . William S. Hart, Tom Mix . . . as I say, just open the door and stand back. The crowds'll come in."

The great antagonist in ***The Symbol of the Unconquered,*** however, was not hostile elements, menacing outlaws, or "savage" Indians, as in most white Westerns, but the Ku Klux Klan. And Micheaux capitalized on that. Despite a climate of racial violence and intimidation, he advertised the film's premiere in Detroit as, "SEE THE KU KLUX KLAN IN ACTION AND THEIR ANNIHILATION!" When it played in Baltimore, the *Afro-American* ad exhorted, "SEE THE MURDEROUS RIDE OF THE INSIDIOUS KU KLUX KLAN in their effort to drive a BLACK BOY off of valuable Oil Lands—and the wonderful heroism of a traveler to save him!" [31 December 1920]. Another reference to the KKK (apparently quoting from Micheaux's press release) appears in *The Chicago Whip:* "night riders rode down upon [the hero] like ghosts with firey torches intent upon revenge" [15 January 1921]. And a *New York Age* review headlined, "KKK Put to Rout in PhotoPlay to be Shown at the Lafayette [Theatre]," called attention to "[t]he viciousness and un-Americanism of the Ku-Klux-Klan which . . . is beginning to manifest itself again in certain parts of the United States. . . . [The film] is regarded as quite timely in view of the present attempt to organize night riders in this country for the express purpose of holding back the advancement of the Negro" [25 December 1920].

Promotion for ***The Symbol of the Unconquered*** addressed the Black spectator and underscored the protest nature of the film. However, to think of the Klan as the singular antagonist is to reduce the complexity of Micheaux's representation. The hero, the homesteader Hugh Van Allen (played by Walter Thompson), is echoed by Driscoll (played by Lawrence Chenault), the villain who is also out to improve his lot. Both characters are speculators who have migrated to the Northwest in pursuit of bigger and better opportunities. Although Driscoll is motivated by the same drives as the hero (indeed, as Micheaux himself), he acts in unscrupulous ways. He advances his standing, not by hard work and self-denial, but through coercion and deception. Through Driscoll and his cohorts, Micheaux exposes the economic origins of whitecapping; Driscoll, a light-skinned man passing for White, is the leader of a gang of greedy misfits plotting to intimidate Van Allen and drive him off his valuable oil lands. It is Driscoll's participation in the Klan, his use of the same forces of intimidation that he would experience if his true racial identity were known, that disturbs the equilibrium of any clear-cut binary opposition.

Why does Micheaux superimpose the image of the KKK over an interracial band of thieves, swindlers, and connivers (including a former clergyman)? Is Driscoll the resurrected Eph from ***Within Our Gates,*** a betrayer, albeit in a more complex form? Driscoll's racial ambiguity allows him to pass, but the darker complected Eph must rely on a charade of obsequious behavior to gain white acceptance. Micheaux appropriated the stereotype to comment on the aspirations and social behavior of those who kowtow to Whites. Eph's wearing of the servile mask and his loyalty to his master represents his way of negotiating racism; however, as the mob turns on him, it is clear that his shield is precarious; in the end, he is just another "nigger." Driscoll, on the other hand, not only wants to be White, but in order to achieve whiteness, he assumes the posture of the oppressor; in order to ward off the terror of the other, Driscoll himself becomes a terrorist. He counters racism with hatred, turns that hatred on the Race and, by extension, on himself. Both Eph and Driscoll deny their solidarity with the group. Eph in trying to secure his own "privileged" position among the Whites in the big house, separates himself and betrays a fellow Negro. Driscoll, by internalizing negative perceptions of blackness, isolates himself and betrays the Race. Micheaux criticized the social behavior of both characters and both get their just desserts.

Van Allen's triumph over hatred is even sweeter because he has overcome Driscoll's "self-hate," as well as the nightriders, the symbol of racial oppression and intimidation. The unmasking of hatred is as much a part of the film as the violence perpetrated in the name of hatred.

We think of Van Allen as Micheaux's surrogate, and in the character of Van Allen, Micheaux was dreaming and redreaming his own ambitions and desires. In the epilogue, Van Allen's good deeds are rewarded: He becomes prosperous from the oil on his land and discovers that Eve Mason (played by Iris Hall), a neighboring homesteader, is, despite her looks, really a Black woman, and thus a suitable wife. In ***The Conquest,*** Micheaux writes of his experiences homesteading and falling in love with his neighbor's daughter, an unnamed young Scottish woman of strong character and "anxious to improve her mind," attributes he clearly admired. One of the least verifiable facts of the author's life, this interracial romance is a recurring theme and rhetorical trope in his films and novels. Micheaux replays this love, or the possibility of it, in much of his work. In ***The Conquest,*** although he never acts on his feelings, he conveys a sense of anxiety about even considering it: To pursue an interracial relationship would be to call into question his loyalty to the Race.

This type of titillation—and concession to popular mores—is more developed in his novel ***The Homesteader.*** The main character, the Negro pioneer Jean Baptiste, deciding not to marry the woman he loves (whom he believes to be Caucasian), cites, *"The Custom Of The Country, and its law,"* and goes on to note that such a marriage "would be the most unpopular thing he could do . . . he would be condemned, he would be despised by the race that was his." However, in this book (and in his later films and novels) Micheaux provided a happier ending: The hero discovers that his love is not White after all and marriage becomes possible.

Clues to the true racial identity of the woman, who seems to be an inappropriate love interest for the hero, emerge in different ways in these works. In ***The Exile*** (1931), for example, the heroine is described as a White woman by another character early in the film. The audience gets essential narrative information as she does: We share her curiosity when she examines her physical appearance before a mirror, but do not know for certain that she is Black until the heroine does, in a final scene.

On the other hand, the audience knows more than the characters do in ***The Betrayal*** (1948), the film version of Micheaux's 1943 novel, ***The Wind from Nowhere*** (another reworking of his biographical legend). The film opens with a scene of an elderly Black man explaining his granddaughter's lineage; however, the heroine is not present in that scene and does not know that the gentleman is her grandfather. By carefully tracing the character's origins, Micheaux informs the audience that the heroine herself is unaware of her true racial identity and therefore is neither deceitful nor disloyal. Consistently in all these works, it is the Micheaux-like male hero who struggles for much of the story with the political and moral dilemmas of such a marriage. His is the noble fight. In ***Thirty Years Later*** (1928), it is the man who is unaware of his ancestry; however, he *also* fights the noble fight, and when he finds out his origins, the hero becomes proud of the Race and marries his love.

Micheaux's treatment of miscegenation in such films as ***The Homesteader, Within Our Gates, The Symbol of the Unconquered, A Son of Satan, The House Behind the Cedars, Thirty Years Later, Birthright, The Exile, Veiled Aristocrats, God's Stepchildren, The Betrayal,*** and all seven of his novels, are ambitious reworkings of the conventions of melodrama from a point of view within the Black community—a resourceful reconfiguration of the genre. By centering the African American experience, he offered a bold critique of American society. To understand the scope and complexity of this critique, we must see it as a political enterprise that both codified the values of the time and attempted to mold them.

Although mistaken identity was a common convention of nineteenth- and early twentieth-century melodrama—the ill-suited lover who turns out not to be ill-suited after all (not a sibling, a pauper, a moral indigent, etc.)—the reversals in Micheaux's stories more often involve the potential transgression of the social taboos and legal prohibitions against miscegenation.

Miscegenation threatens definitions of race, challenging the idea that racial identity might be "knowable." By blurring the dichotomy on which whiteness depends, miscegenation throws into disarray the basis of white supremacy, Black "inferiority." As Toni Morrison has pointed out, it is by imagining blackness that whiteness "knows itself as not enslaved, but free, not repulsive, but desirable, not helpless, but licensed and powerful" [*Playing in the Dark: Whiteness and The Literary Imagination,* 1992].

Rather than suggesting a radical new way of seeing or attempting to create a new narrative space for representation, in ***The Symbol of the Unconquered*** (as in much of his other early work), Micheaux worked within the hardened conventions and presuppositions of "the Negro problem" text, melding the plots and conventions of the sentimental melodrama with Western settings and characters. He was "crafting a voice out of tight places," as Houston Baker wrote of Booker T. Washington's use of minstrelsy [*Modernism and the Harlem Renaissance,* 1987]. Often invoking the novel *Uncle Tom's Cabin* in his promotional material (print ads, trailers, etc.), Micheaux seems to have admired not only the enormous social impact (and commercial success) of Harriet Beecher Stowe's work, but also its evangelical piety and moral commitment.

Many of his characters represent sociological and moral forces rather than psychologically individuated people, and function as models to prove what can be accomplished through hard work and industry. At the beginning of his career, striking out on his own and settling on the land, Micheaux was influenced by Booker T. Washington's philosophy, "not of destruction, but of construction; not of defense, but of aggression; . . . not of hostility or surrender, but of friendship and advance"; where self-help, one's "own efforts," and "usefulness in the community" were the "surest and most potent protection." ***The Conquest,*** a success and adventure story about a Black pioneer in the West, was dedicated to "The Honorable Booker T. Washington," and many of his other books and movies aimed to galvanize the spirit of success through examples of individual achievement. In ***Body and Soul,*** Micheaux used Washington's image as a visual tag to identify characterological traits. Sylvester, the industrious inventor, is introduced in a shot that frames him with a portrait of Booker T. Washington. In the 1910 *Defender* article referred to earlier, Micheaux wrote that he was "not trying to offer a solution to the Negro problem, for I don't feel that there is any problem further than the future of anything, whether it be a town, state or race. . . . It depends first on individual achievement, and I am at a loss to see a brilliant future for the young colored man unless he first does something for himself." The hero of his film ***The Millionaire*** (1927), a soldier of fortune, who as a youth possessed "great initiative and definite purpose," returns to the community as a rich man. Explaining why Jean Baptiste foreswears marriage with his White neighbor in ***The Homesteader,*** Micheaux wrote, "He had set himself in this new land to succeed; he had worked and slaved to that end. He liked his people; he wanted to help them. Examples they needed and such he was glad to have become; but if he married now the one he loved, the example was lost." Micheaux stated in ***The Conquest*** that one of his greatest tasks in life was "to convince a certain class of my racial acquaintances that a colored man can be anything." Mildred Latham, the love interest of the homesteader, author, and itinerant book peddler in ***The Forged Note,*** admires the hero as "a Negro pioneer . . . [who] blaze[d] the way for others."

However, Micheaux's racial uplift, which was so important to counter accusations of "inferiority," challenged White definitions of race without changing the terms. Others in this period—Sterling Brown, Langston Hughes, and Zora Neale Hurston, for example—questioned those very terms, demanding new definitions of Race from within Black America. Hurston's work recodifies both language and story by bringing out the richness of oral culture, the African American vernacular, and folk tales. Hughes wrote of his own use of Black culture, "Jazz to me is one of the inherent expressions of Negro life in America: the eternal tom-tom beating in the Negro soul—the tom-tom of revolt against weariness in a white world, a world of subway trains and work, work, work; the tom-tom of joy and laughter, and pain swallowed in a smile" ["The Negro Artist and the Racial Mountain," *The Nation,* 23 June 1926]. Hurston and Hughes, and other New Negroes, saw themselves as reclaiming images of blackness, an attempt, as Alain Locke put it, to build Americanism on Race values [*The New Negro: An Interpretation,* 1925].

Like Hurston, Hughes, and Brown, Micheaux spoke as a Negro; the "blackness" of the author is a strong presence. However, because of his sense of personal responsibility and uplift, he saw himself as an instructive voice and an empowering interpreter of Black life *for* the community. Van Allen in ***The Symbol of the Unconquered,*** as the title implies, is an expression of Oscar Micheaux's optimism for the Race. Like Micheaux's biographical legend, Van Allen is the adventurous entrepreneur, an achiever, loyal to the Race, persistent and brave in the face of adversities.

Ironically, however, today Van Allen is one of the least provocative characters! Driscoll, on the other hand, is so overdrawn that he borders on the horrific—almost uncanny. "Uncanny" because he is at once so evil and so familiar. The act of passing is not uncommon or automatically condemned by the Black community. Rather, it is Driscoll's attitude of superiority, seeing Blacks as subhuman and taking pleasure in their misfortune, that is so wicked and well known—both a betrayal and a surrender. In his hotel, he refuses a room to Abraham, a Black traveling salesman (played by E. G. Tatum), and leads him to the barn. When Eve arrives from a long journey exhausted and hungry, Driscoll at first thinks the light-skinned woman is White; but, as she is about to register, he looks into her eyes and "sees" her true identity. His initially genial behavior turns to hatred; he denies her a bed in his hotel, sending her to the hayloft. During the night, Eve, awakened by a storm and frightened when discovering that there is someone else in the barn, falls from the loft and runs out into a driving rain. Driscoll, watching from his bedroom window as she struggles in the storm, takes sinister joy in her suffering. Surrounded by an aura of shimmering whiteness (in white nightshirt and sheets, lit as if he were aglow), he thrashes his arms in triumph.

What is so disturbing about Driscoll is his assumption of the posture of the oppressor *and* his terror of discovery. He sees both his true identity in Eve's pale face and the possibility of being unmasked. In ***The Conquest,*** invoking a story from his experiences as a homesteader in South Dakota, Micheaux wrote about the children of a wealthy mixed-race family who were passing and lived in fear of other members of the Race, dreading "that moment of racial recognition." Driscoll's own racial identity is exposed early in the film by his mother, a darker skinned lady, as he is proposing to a White woman. In this scene, the terror of racial recognition and the odiousness of racial terror come together as Driscoll attacks his own mother because she is Black.

Later, in a barroom scene, there is a fist fight between Van Allen and Driscoll, supposedly over a horse deal turned sour. The fight scene is introduced by a close shot of both Driscoll and Van Allen framed in a mirror. Driscoll looks up and recognizes Van Allen. Perhaps he sees Van Allen as the horse-trade victim he has been mocking. Or is this that moment of racial recognition? Perhaps Driscoll sees his despised self in Van Allen, his own blackness. Driscoll pulls a gun threatening Van Allen; but Van Allen wrestles the gun away from him and they fight. After being beaten by Van Allen and declaring, "I'll get my revenge!," Driscoll is thrown out of the bar with a swift kick in the butt by the same traveling salesman whom he had refused to serve in his hotel. Is this a matter of a Black man getting the better of a "White" man or is it intra-racial censure?

Lawrence Chenault's performance style throughout the film—his chalky makeup; outlined eyes; arched eyebrows; tense, often flailing, arms and hunched shoulders; the rigidity of his body and the vehemence of his gestures—expresses a man driven by fear. Driscoll's self-loathing and terror of discovery provoke his attack on Van Allen; having failed, he uses the Klan as a personal instrument of revenge. It is because his life is so tenuous that he is so vicious. Reflecting on the South Dakota mixed-race family, Micheaux wrote, "What worried me most, however, even frightened me, was, that after marriage and when their children had grown to manhood and womanhood, they . . . had a terror of their race." They looked upon other Blacks with a dread of discovery. Such a discovery would expose not only their racial identity, but also a life of deception, threatening social and psychological upheaval. For Driscoll, race is the unspeakable, the stranger entering the gate, menacing his whiteness. Identity, to borrow from James Baldwin, "would seem to be the garment with which [he] covers the nakedness of the self" [*The Devil Finds Work,* 1990].

The Competitor magazine [January-February, 1921] praised ***The Symbol of the Unconquered*** as making a significant thrust at the "more than 500,000 people" in America who are "passing for white." *The Daily Ohio State Journal* in 1909 wrote of thousands of people passing in Washington, D.C. alone: "Those who just occasionally pass for white, simply to secure just recognition, and the privileges the laws vouchsafe an American citizen, should not be censured harshly. An unjust discrimination, a forced and ungodly segregation drives them to practice deception. . . . But it is an awful experience to pass for white. At all times fear—the fear of detection—haunts one. . . . Those who turn their backs upon their own color, own race and own relatives to live a life of fear, of dread, and almost isolation just to pass for white seven days in the week, while regarded with utter contempt by their colored race, really ought to be pitied, when it is known how heavy is the burden they carry, and how much they suffer in silence."

Micheaux exploited these concerns in the script for the 1938 film, ***God's Stepchildren.*** Andrew, the white husband of the young woman who is passing, upon discovering his wife's "streak" says, "You aren't the first to try this, Naomi. No, it has been tried since the days of slavery and even before that; but they can't get away with it, so you see you can't get away with it, for sooner or later, somewhere, some time after a life of fear and exemption you will be found out, and when you are they'll turn on you, loath you, despise you, even spit in your face and call you by your right name—Naomi, Negress."

The Black press often covered both well-known interracial marriages and court cases of people attempting to prove that they were Negro in order to counter charges of miscegenation. Stories of Whites not being able to discern what is obvious to a Black person were part of the popular discourses of the time. It was thought quite funny that for Whites, race was not so much a matter of color and appearance as mannerisms and deportment. Helen M. Chesnutt, in her biography of her father [*Charles Waddell Chesnutt: Pioneer of the Color Line,* 1992], tells of the family entering a restaurant while traveling and after being seated, seeing the manager "bearing down" upon their table; they immediately began speaking French . . . and the man retreated.

Lester Walton, in an article entitled "When is a Negro a Negro to a Caucasian?," asked, "[B]y what standard do they differentiate as to when is a Negro a Negro?" and laughed about vaudevillian John Hodges ("Any colored person can tell what John Hodges is") trying to eat at a restaurant and telling the waiter that he is not a Negro, but an English Jew, and getting served. In another article [in *The New York Age,* May 1913], Walton tells the story of the White manager and cashier at the Fifty-ninth Street Theatre in New York who were discharged because "they mistook a young lady of color to be of the white race and proceeded to speak disrespectfully of their ebony-hued employer [William Mack Felton]." Walton mused, "One of the amusing features of the so-called Negro problem is the inability of the white people to recognize hundreds and hundreds of colored people who have gone on the other side of the color line. To us there is nothing so ludicrous as to observe one known as a violent Negro hater walking arm-in-arm or sitting at a table eating with a person of color, the radical Caucasian indulging in an erratic outburst of abuse on the Negro to the unconcealed delight of the colored person."

In 1925, the wealthy White New York socialite, Leonard "Kip" Rhinelander, took his new wife, Alice Jones Rhinelander, to court to dissolve their marriage when he found out that she had "Negro ancestry and concealed the fact from him during their courtship" [(Norfolk) *Journal and Guide,* 28 November 1915]. Mrs. Rhinelander denied any deception, insisting that anyone could tell she was a Negro. The trial made the front pages of the Black weeklies. Micheaux used the notoriety of the Rhinelander case to promote ***The House Behind the Cedars,*** his 1925 adaptation of Chesnutt's story of passing. But even without mentioning it in his ads, such popular discourses on crossing the "color line" certainly would have influenced the way audiences understood Micheaux's films. Press coverage, folk sayings, blues songs, verbal exchanges are all part of the spectatorial experience. As Tony Bennett and Janet Woollacott put it [in *Bond and Beyond: The Political Career of a Popular Hero,* 1987], "a text . . . is never 'there' except in forms in which it is also and always other than 'just itself,' always-already humming with reading possibilities which derive from outside its covers."

Because Driscoll's true racial identity is established early in the film, audiences watch his vileness, knowing he is Black. In his mask, he so rejects blackness that, turning his anger on the Race, he becomes an assault on the audience. The defeat of the vengeful character at the end of the film must have given the audience a moment of relief and joy—an assault on the oppressor. Likewise, the scene in the bar where he is kicked in the butt by the traveling salesman, one of the gestures that clustered around the "Tom" character in minstrelsy, offers vicarious pleasure in his humiliation. Driscoll's downfall and the apocalyptic renewal of the ending is a victory not only for Van Allen, but for the audience as well, putting to rest notions of Black "inferiority." What visions of their own radical anger and omnipotence might the audience have experienced through the hero!

Driscoll is both a vehicle to explore interracial relations and, as a person of mixed blood (the product of historical miscegenation), an expression of those relations. The question of color is a recurring interest for Micheaux. However, it's not a simple infatuation with color, nor is it simply a narrative contrivance—that is, the melodramatic trope of someone being not what he or she seems. It's far more complex than that. Although he was often accused of casting by color, he criticized the color-caste system within the community as destructive social behavior. And although he created a star system of fair-skinned performers (Iris Hall, Shingzie Howard, Evelyn Preer, Lawrence Chenault, Carman Newsome, Lorenzo Tucker, etc.) chosen for their "look" and potential appeal to audiences, he didn't necessarily associate these "looks" with certain qualities, such as "goodness." In ***Body and Soul,*** Paul Robeson plays both the hero and the villain with no change of make-up, and the scoundrel, Yellow Curley, is played by Lawrence Chenault (who also plays villains in other films where the shade of one's skin is not part of the story). In ***The Symbol of the Unconquered,*** Walter Thompson playing the hero, a rugged outdoorsman, acquires his swarthy complexion with dark make-up. Carl Mahon, who did not think of himself as an actor, felt that Micheaux cast him in romantic leads because of his "exotic looks," the combination of dark skin and straight hair. In several of Micheaux's films—***The Symbol of the Unconquered, The House Behind the Cedars,*** and ***God's Stepchildren,*** for examples—we would argue that he is not reproducing "color prejudice," but criticizing it.

For Micheaux the problem of miscegenation is not the mixing of the races but the disloyalty that comes from trying to hide one's racial identity. Sylvia, in ***Within Our Gates,*** who is the offspring of the plantation owner's brother, is adopted by Black sharecroppers and is raised as one of their own. She sees herself as a Black woman. As a person of mixed blood, Sylvia is not automatically an outsider, someone different, a point of division. In a medium long shot of her family around a table, there are a variety of skin colors. The storyline is not "about" skin color per se; it is "about" the rape of Black women by White men.

Although much of Eve's backstory in the only surviving print of ***The Symbol of the Unconquered*** seems to be missing, Eve, like Sylvia, is comfortable with who she is and is not trying to pass. In an interview around the time of the film's release, Micheaux said, "There is one thing aside from [making] the story interesting that I strive to demonstrate in all my pictures and that is, it makes no difference what may be a person's color, or from where a person comes, if the heart is right, that's what counts, and success is sure" [*The Competitor,* January-February 1921]. Eve is not only a Black woman but a Race woman. It is through a letter commending her for her service to the Race that Van Allen discovers her true identity.

In ***The Betrayal,*** Micheaux's final film, Martin Eden (the character's name, like Eve's, associates him with a pastoral innocence) tells the story of a mixed-race family in South Dakota with many children who would pass their father off as an "old colored servant who helped to raise them" when visitors came to call. One of the brothers was dark. Drafted into the army and assigned to a colored unit, unhappy with being unable to serve in a White regiment, "he stood before a mirror in his tent one night, took a German Luger that he had acquired—and blew his brains out."

Although some contemporary critics have accused Micheaux of "Race hatred," it might be more fruitful to look at his work as adamantly depicting the diversity of Black life as he saw it. His works criticized certain attitudes, behavior, and conduct as detrimental to the future of the Race. Among the great diversity of characters criticized are gamblers, womanizers, people without ambition, and blind followers of the faith. As Bell Hooks put it [in "Micheaux: Celebrating Blackness," *Black Looks: Race and Representation,* 1992], "[H]e was not concerned with the simple reduction of black representation to a 'positive' image." In his 1946 novel ***The Story of Dorothy Stanfield,*** Micheaux described his surrogate, the book publisher and motion picture producer Sidney Wyeth with the following: "Wyeth is an intense race man; and while he can and does criticize the Negro in his books . . . , he is for his people at all times, regardless the circumstances."

There are characters who hate the Race—Driscoll in ***The Symbol of the Unconquered*** is a clear example; Naomi in ***God's Stepchildren*** is another. Like Driscoll, Naomi abandoned her family in order to pass for White. The scene of discovery is once again a scene of maternal devotion; however, contrary to Driscoll's, Naomi's is a scene of love not hate. It is her pained reaction upon seeing her small son on the street that gives her away. Driscoll has no loving ties to anyone; Naomi is defeated by both her love and her self-loathing. Condemned by her betrayal, she quietly sinks into the murky river to end her suffering. In the film's final shot, the words "As ye sow, so shall ye reap" are superimposed over her hat floating on the surface of the water.

The most Micheaux-like character in ***God's Stepchildren*** is Jimmy, Naomi's morally upright foster brother. Like Micheaux, Jimmy worked as a railroad porter and saved money to buy a farm. In a scene where he tells his fiancée Eva his plans, she asks, "Why is it that so many, most all of our men, when they go into business it's got to be a crap game, a numbers bank or a policy shop? Why can't they go into some legitimate business, like white people?" Jimmy replies, "They could, but they made no study of economics. Their idea of success is to seek the line of least resistance. The Negro hates to think. He's a stranger to planning. . . . For that is the failure of our group. For we *are* a failure, you know. . . . [I]t seems that we should go right back to the beginning and start all over again. That's what I've decided to do. . . . I'm going to buy a farm and start at the beginning." A similar pastoral image appears in Booker T. Washington's *Up from Slavery* where he wrote about wishing he could "remove the great bulk of . . . people into the country districts and plant them upon the soil, upon the solid and never deceptive foundation of Mother Nature, where all nations and races that have ever succeeded have gotten their start—a start that at first may be slow and toilsome, but one that nevertheless is real." If one accepts Jimmy as a voice of Micheaux, Micheaux is once again adapting Booker T. Washington's attachment to the land, philosophy of meritorious work, and proving one's self to the outside world. Twenty-five years before Jimmy's speech, Micheaux declared his own decision to seek a homestead, going West to "the land of real beginning" [***The Conquest***].

However, unlike Washington, Jimmy's criticism of the work attitudes of urban Blacks suggests an acceptance of the mythical figure of the shiftless "coon," incapable of learning or achieving, holding the Race down. In the 1910 *Defender* article quoted earlier, Micheaux himself confessed, "I return from Chicago each trip I make, more discouraged year after year with the hopelessness of [the young Negro's lack of] foresight. His inability to use common sense in looking into his future is truly discouraging. . . . The trouble with the men of our race is that they want something for nothing."

In his biographical legend, Micheaux was working to disprove these kinds of stereotypes. The portrait he paints of himself is one of ambitious well-laid plans, initiative, and persistent hard work. In ***The Conquest*** he comments on planting more acres than than his neighbors: "At first I was regarded as an object of curiosity, which changed to admiration. I was not called a free-go-easy coon, but a genuine booster for Calias and the Little Crow." It is almost as though Micheaux felt that in order for him to rise, he had to uplift the Race, and a criticism of negative behavior would help to advance his cause. Although not an essentialist position (Micheaux clearly felt that, with education and guidance, people could change), the rub is, of course, that the character on whose back he builds his own legend of success must be held in contempt for the comparison to work.

Jean Baptiste, in ***The Homesteader,*** a more clearly autobiographical character than Jimmy, "had confidence in education uplifting people; it made them more observing. It helped them morally":

> He had studied his race . . . , unfortunately as a whole their standard of morals were not so high as it should be. Of course he understood that the same began back in the time of slavery. They had not been brought up to a regard of morality in a higher sense and they were possessed with certain weaknesses. He was aware that in the days of slavery the Negro to begin with had had, as a rule only what he could steal, therefore stealing became a virtue. When accused as he naturally was sure to be, he had resorted to the subtle art of lying. . . . So with freedom his race had not gotten away from these loose practices. They were given still to lustful, undependable habits, which he at times became very impatient with. His version was that a race could not rise higher than their morals.

With the arrogance of the self-taught and self-made, Micheaux projects himself as upright and highly moral; he also sets himself apart from others as a superior and righteous person. Part of the means by which he built the appearance of success included singling out those of the Race whom he characterized as immoral or without ambition and perseverance and censuring them for impeding the progress of the Race, and therefore holding *him* back. When he says there's no Negro problem, just the problem of individuals, he was acting on the premise that individual acts affect the entire group, a dynamic imposed by a racist system. That was his "burden of Race." By setting himself up as a model of one who had risen above the prevalent notion of the Negro as "inferior," he was inadvertedly reinforcing the very attitude he imagined he was overcoming—the notion that the morality, ambition, and abilities of the Negro was "the problem." Col. Hubert Fauntleroy Julian, associate producer of two of Micheaux's films, was still using these same discourses in 1940. Describing ***Lying Lips*** in *Time* magazine [28 January 1940], he said, "It's about a beautiful girl who is led astray because she wants beautiful things. . . . You see, I am trying to build up the morals of my race."

The Symbol of the Unconquered sets up a moral opposition between individual attitudes and behavior (such as the denial of racial identity in order to assert personal power and privilege) and the well-being of the group. Driscoll is the moral instrument through which Micheaux offers direction on social aspirations. Van Allen is both a stand-in for Oscar Micheaux and a means through which Micheaux builds his biographical legend, his legend of success. The working title of ***The Symbol of the Unconquered*** was ***The Wilderness Trail.*** The name change is both affirming and challenging, a call to collective consciousness—very much like the title and long patriotic speech at the end of ***Within Our Gates.*** These films are a part of a continuous recoding and reshaping of Racial identity, African American solidarity, and the individual.

Richard Grupenhoff (essay date 1988)

SOURCE: "The Rediscovery of Oscar Micheaux, Black Film Pioneer," in *Journal of Film and Video,* Vol. 40, No. 1, Winter, 1988, pp. 40-8.

[*In the following essay, Grupenhoff provides a historical overview of Micheaux's life and career.*]

The stars on the sidewalks of Hollywood Boulevard are dedicated to those who have achieved a measure of fame in the entertainment industry. But one of the most recent stars honors a film director few people have ever heard of, and even fewer have seen any of his films. Unveiled in February 1987, that new star belongs to Oscar Micheaux, a rather obscure and engimatic individual who was, nevertheless, the most prolific and consistent independent black filmmaker in the United States between 1918 and 1948. During that time he produced, directed, edited, and distributed approximately 40 feature-length black cast films for all-black audiences. Yet, for the past 40 years Micheaux's achievements (as well as the achievements of black independent film production as a whole) have gone virtually unrecognized.

A renewed interest in Micheaux's life and work has recently surfaced, however, and the Directors Guild of America has taken a leading role in reviving Micheaux's name. The Directors Guild was instrumental in getting Micheaux's star placed on Hollywood Boulevard, and in May 1986, the Directors Guild celebrated its Fiftieth Anniversary by bestowing its "Golden Jubilee Special Directorial Award" on Micheaux for his pioneering efforts during the early days of black filmmaking.

Even though he was the most important black filmmaker in the first half of this century, Micheaux left few traces behind when he died in 1951. A rather flamboyant and gregarious public person, Micheaux was guarded and secretive about his personal life. No full-length biography of Micheaux has yet been published, and until recently little was known about his family background, the disposition of his records and estate, or his filmmaking methods and techniques. What little we know about him has had to be pieced together from the revelations he made about himself in his autobiographical films and novels, and from new information gathered in recent interviews with his last living relatives and with friends who knew him.

I first became familiar with Micheaux while conducting research for a biography on Lorenzo Tucker, once known to black moviegoers as "The Colored Valentino," and one of Oscar Micheaux's leading men from 1927 to 1937. (It was Micheaux who first dubbed Tucker "The Colored Valentino.") Some basic detective work led me to find Micheaux's last living blood relative, Verna Louise Crowe, of Pasadena, California, who provided me with memories about Micheaux's background and family, and with photographs and letters that help to fill in parts of the puzzle of Micheaux's life.

Born on January 2, 1884 in Illinois, some 40 miles above Cairo on the Ohio River (***The Conquest***), Oscar Micheaux was the fourth son of the marriage between Calvin Swan Micheaux and Belle Goff, who had 11 children in all (Crowe). In the late 1880s the family moved to nearby Metropolis, Illinois, and it was there that Oscar was raised. A bright, independent, and strong-willed child, Oscar Micheaux usually avoided most childhood games and was always off working on some project of his own, a behavior that earned him the nickname "Oddball" [From a personal interview with Lylas Keyes, 2 April 1985]. Years later Micheaux wrote about his early childhood and his realization that for the rest of his life he would be his own man.

> My father complained of my poor service in the field and in disgust I was sent off to do the marketing—which pleased me, for it was not only

> easy but gave me a chance to meet and talk with many people—and I always sold the goods and engaged more for the afternoon delivery. This was my first experience in real business and I found that from that time ever afterward I could always do better business for myself than for anybody else (***The Conquest***).

By the time he was a teenager Micheaux was a free-thinker prone to disagree with the prevailing conventional wisdom, and he would counter discussions about the miserable plight of blacks with arguments for self-improvement and success that were to become his standards for the rest of his life.

> Another thing that added to my unpopularity, perhaps, was my persistent declarations that there were not enough competent colored people to grasp the many opportunities that presented themselves, and that if white people could possess such nice homes, wealth and luxuries, so, in time, could the colored people. "You're a fool," I would be told, and then would follow a lecture describing the time-worn long and cruel slavery, and after the emancipation, the prejudice and hatred of the white race, whose chief object was to prevent the progress and betterment of the negro . . . and I became so tired of it all that I declared that if I could ever leave M——pls [sic] I would never return. More, I would disprove such a theory (***The Conquest***).

Micheaux finally did leave home in 1901 at the age of 17, and went to live for a short time with his brother in Chicago, where he worked briefly as a stockyard hand and as a coal hauler. Then he got a job as a Pullman porter, and for the next three years he traveled by rail throughout the United States. By 1904 he had saved enough money to buy a relinquishment on a homestead located on the edge of Indian territory in South Dakota. By 1907 Micheaux, who was then 23, had parlayed his original investment into a considerable tract of land.

On a trip to Chicago in 1909 Micheaux witnessed a performance of a minstrel show, and was so taken by it that he decided to begin a career as a writer by turning out short observational pieces and reviews for local newspapers. The following year he fell in love with the white daughter of a nearby homesteader, but realizing that public opinion would be opposed to their marriage, he married instead a black woman from Chicago whose father was a preacher. According to Micheaux, the father-in-law cheated him out of his property and ruined the marriage (***The Conquest***). Micheaux quit farming and became a professional writer, publishing his first novel, ***The Conquest: The Story of a Negro Pioneer, by the Pioneer,*** in 1913.

A rambling and uneven work, ***The Conquest*** is a fictionalized version of Micheaux's early economic success and marital difficulties, events that would be re-told again and again in his later films and novels. In effect, the novel is an autobiographical self-vindication of Micheaux's first 30 years, containing many of the early hopes and desires that were to guide him for the rest of his life. ***The Conquest*** is dedicated to the black champion of self-improvement and economic independence, Booker T. Washington, and it contains one of Micheaux's primary goals: "One of the greatest tasks of my life has been to convince a certain class of my racial acquaintances that a colored man can be anything."

Micheaux sold his first novel door-to-door to his white neighbors and in nearby towns. With the revenues from this book he formed his own publishing company, and soon wrote and published a second novel, ***The Forged Note*** (1915), and a third, ***The Homesteader*** (1917), which was a reworking of the events depicted in ***The Conquest.*** It was this one-man cottage-industry pattern of writing, publishing, and door-to-door marketing of his books that Micheaux was to copy with the films he produced in the years that followed.

When Micheaux began making films in 1918 there were very few all-black films being produced. For the most part the only black images to be seen on American movie screens were the stereotypes that white producers and directors had coopted from earlier entertainment forms and from the popular cliches of blacks current in the dominant white society.

The stock stereotypes of black characters that evolved in turn-of-the-century white-produced films included those all-too-familiar characterizations of the shiftless fool, the brute, the comic female pickaninny, the faithful servant, the unfortunate mulatto, and the wise old mammy. Indeed, the early images of blacks in film mirrored the attitudes of white society in general: blacks were "subhuman, simple-minded, superstitious and submissive" [Daniel Leab, *From Sambo to "Superspade": The Black Experience in Motion Pictures,* 1975].

At the time, the most significant film containing negative depictions of the black race was D.W. Griffith's *The Birth of a Nation.* Released in 1915, *The Birth of a Nation* was a landmark production from the perspective of early cinema aesthetics, but it also depicted a bleak and racist view of the Reconstruction Era. The screening of the film touched off a storm of controversy that was to last for years. Rather than quiet its critics, however, the screening had an opposite effect, for it helped to solidify a growing black consciousness that had been pioneered by such leaders as W. E. B. Du Bois.

The power of the motion picture as a new medium for education had already been realized by 1915, and its potential as a polemical tool had been made blatantly apparent by *The Birth of a Nation.* Recognizing Griffith's genius as a filmmaker, Du Bois suggested that the answer to *The Birth of a Nation* was not for blacks to condemn its shortcomings, but rather to create a film aesthetic of their own. Consequently, after 20 years of being stereotyped in negative roles by white producers, blacks decided that the only way they were going to achieve positive images of blacks in films was to form production companies of their own. The rise of all-black cast films made by black producers for segregated black audiences came as a response to the white producers' demonstrated unwillingness to represent blacks in other than pejorative stereotypes. White discrimination was, paradoxically, one of the causes for the rise of independent black filmmaking.

All-black cast films produced exclusively for segregated black audiences ("race movies," as they came to be known), actually began around 1913, two years before *The Birth of a Nation.* It was then that black showman William Foster outlined the economic and educational aspirations of black filmmakers: to make money and to redeem the black race by showing it in its true condition (Leab).

The first successful black production company to make feature films about blacks in positive roles was the Lincoln Motion Picture Company of Los Angeles. Formed in 1916, Lincoln was headed by a handsome, light-skinned black actor named Noble Johnson, and that same year the company produced its first two-reeler feature short, *The Realization of a Negro's Ambition,* with Johnson as its star. The film was "the first feature film produced in the United States which featured blacks in dramatic, non-stereotypical roles" [Henry T. Sampson, *Black in Black and White: A Source Book on Black Films,* 1977].

By 1918 at least eight film production companies were engaged in producing race movies, and over the next 30 years more than 150 companies would be formed for the same purpose. Yet of this number only 75% would actually produce one or more films, and only 33% would be totally owned and operated by blacks. Limited by lack of capital, technical sophistication, and distribution networks, these companies simply could not compete with Hollywood. The most they might hope for were the marginal profits they could gain from screening their films to segregated black audiences in the urban areas of the north and midwest, and in the small southern towns where screening facilities existed for black audiences.

In early 1918 George Johnson, the brother of Noble Johnson and the Omaha-based distributor of the Lincoln Motion Picture Company's films, read ***The Homesteader*** and suggested to Noble that the novel might be worth developing into a film dramatization. The Johnsons contacted Micheaux and began negotiating with him for the rights to the novel. In a letter to the Johnsons dated May 18, 1918, Micheaux agreed to allow them to film the novel, under the condition that the three of them form a new production company for the purpose of making the film, with Micheaux as president, Noble Johnson as vice-president, and George Johnson as secretary. The Johnsons, however, were not about to relinquish the control of their production to this upstart prairie novelist, and the deal fell through.

Undaunted, Micheaux combined his book company with film production, and called it The Micheaux Book and Film Company. He financed his first production by selling stock in the company at $75 a share to the same farmers who had bought his books. Then he set about teaching himself how to make films, and within a year he surpassed all the black filmmakers who had preceded him by producing the first full-length feature film with an all-black cast, ***The Homesteader*** [Bernard L. Peterson, Jr., "The Films of Oscar Micheaux: America's First Fabulous Black Filmmaker," *The Crisis,* April 1979].

Following ***The Homesteader,*** Micheaux produced a controversial film entitled ***Within Our Gates*** (1920), that contained a realistic scene of a lynching in the south. Initially rejected by the Chicago Board of Movie Censors for fear it might cause a race riot, ***Within Our Gates*** was eventually allowed into general release.

Moving to New York City to take advantage of the talented black actors performing in Harlem, Micheaux became a production dynamo, turning out in quick succession over 20 silent films, shooting them in the spring, editing them in the summer, and distributing them in the fall and winter. Included among these films were: ***Symbol of the Unconquered*** (1920), a film with a strong anti-Ku Klux Klan stance; ***Deceit*** (1921), about rural blacks who come to the big city and pass as whites; ***The Gunsaulas Mystery*** (1921), about a black man unjustly accused of murdering a white woman; ***Birthright*** (1924), which concerned black achievement in the face of white prejudice; and ***Body and Soul*** (1924), about black religious leaders and gamblers who exploit the black community. This last film is the only one of Micheaux's silent films still available for screening, preserved perhaps because it starred Paul Robeson in his first film. This film, and about eight sound films, are all that remain of Micheaux's work.

It is true, as many critics claim, that by Hollywood standards Micheaux's films were often technically inept and poorly structured, although it must be remembered that Micheaux produced each film on a budget of about $15,000, whereas Hollywood's budgets were then approaching a million dollars. It is also apparent that Micheaux gave little consideration to the formal conventions of film art that had recently been developed by his contemporaries Porter and Griffith. Micheaux was not a film artist, nor was he a meticulous craftsman; at best, he was a novelist working as a filmmaker.

Micheaux approached the business of motion pictures from the perspective of a pre-corporate, turn-of-the-century farmer and frontiersman. His life as a home-steader trained him to learn and perform all the different yet essential tasks that needed to be done in order to insure survival and success. Micheaux brought this rugged individualism to his filmmaking. He taught himself the craft and performed most of the tasks himself. He was the producer, writer, director, lighting director, editor, and distributor of almost all of his silent films.

Constantly working under the limitations of low budgets and time constraints, Micheaux was apparently willing to sacrifice quality for quantity. The handful of films that remain for viewing indicate that Micheaux was not concerned with the elements of film art; rather, he was intent on moving the actors through the scene and getting the film made. Lorenzo Tucker recalled that while Micheaux was excellent in preparing and arranging a shot, the work of directing actors did not come easy to him. In fact, Micheaux's usual practice was to direct while lying on a couch and swallowing handfuls of Argo starch directly from the box. "It soothes my aching stomach," he would say (Tucker).

Micheaux rarely granted actors a chance to rehearse a scene once it had been blocked for the camera. Tucker, whose theatrical background had taught him the importance of rehearsals, would often ask Micheaux for time to rehearse, but Micheaux, well aware that time meant money, would refuse.

> He would get frustrated and yell at me, "You young actor! I don't know what I'm going to do with you. What's the matter, Tucker, you can walk, can't you? And you can talk, can't you? Well, then, let's shoot the scene!" (Tucker).

Micheaux's attitude about second takes was even more tightfisted. If an actor forgot a line while the camera was rolling, Micheaux sometimes let it pass and printed the scene. Hardly ever would he shoot a scene over. As a concession to an actor he might begin the next shot from the point where the mistake was made—at times from the middle of a sentence. Later edited without benefit of a cutaway, the result was a jump cut. In one of Micheaux's early sound films, ***The Girl From Chicago*** (1932), one can hear Micheaux's off-camera voice cuing the actor as the actor, in turn, gestures for Micheaux to be quiet. Micheaux's films are filled with these strange, revealing moments in which we are able to see both the character and the actor behind the character in self-conscious behavior. Critic J. Hoberman called Micheaux's directing a kind of "*ipso facto* avant-gardism."

> To call Micheaux's work problematic is to say the least. His films were made on a shoestring and are characterized by a surreal degree of corner-cutting. He seemed to be oblivious to the laws of cinematic continuity. . . . Micheaux's actors ran the gamut from B-movie competents to would-be matinee idols, to utter amateurs. Thus, most of his big dramatic moments are played to utter cross-purpose. Left stranded by their director—in scenes grossly overextended—Micheaux's performers strike fantastic poses or stare affectingly into the camera, revealing their individual personalities. Thirty years before Warhol, Micheaux approached a mise-en-scene "degree zero" [J. Hoberman, "A Forgotten Cinema Resurfaces," *Village Voice,* 17 November 1975].

Why didn't Micheaux spend more time and money on his films? According to Lorenzo Tucker, Micheaux was first and foremost a businessman who knew better than anyone through on-the-job research what the black film market would bear. The margin he was working under would not allow him to raise his standards and make a profit, too. Tucker said that Micheaux would laugh when he saw other producers spending too much money to hike up production values, knowing that even though the film might be better crafted, the box office just wasn't there to make the film profitable. A strange approach to making a film, perhaps, but obviously the black film market did not operate in the typical Hollywood fashion. In any case the fact remains that Micheaux outlasted every one of his competitors, so he must have known something about marketing and distribution.

Oscar Micheaux was the quintessential self-taught grass roots filmmaker, and that fact is perhaps partly responsible for his naive approach to cinema technology and for his rather parochial sense of visualization and mise-en-scene. Yet his rural background infused Micheaux's films with a rugged individualism and a refreshing outspokenness. In the decades when Hollywood (and white society at large) insisted upon stereotyping blacks as Uncle Toms, Mammies, and Stepin Fetchits, Micheaux presented a positive image of blacks in films that dealt honestly and openly with the social and economic issues they were forced to face on a day-to-day basis.

Rarely, if ever, did Micheaux depict members of his race in a negative light. That is not to say that his films lacked negative behavior. Micheaux's films were often melodramatic, and as such presented a world of good versus evil, with its obvious heroes and villains. ***The Girl From Chicago*** (1932), for instance, is a tale of exploitation, greed, and murder. ***Swing!*** (1936) is a proto-feminist critique of middle-class black male behavior. Still, while there are negative characters in Micheaux's films, there are no negative stereotypes held up to ridicule.

In ***The Exile*** (1931) Micheaux addressed the issue of race and blood. In one of the film's central scenes Micheaux grapples with the dilemma of light-skinned blacks. A white neighbor boy visits the cabin of the light-skinned hero, Jean-Baptiste, and the boy tells Jean-Baptiste that a new farm family has moved in nearby, headed by a Scotsman named Jack Stewart, who has two sons and a pretty daughter.

> Jean-Baptiste: They're white, I suppose.
>
> Boy: Yes. Ain't that funny?
>
> Jean-Baptiste: What's funny?
>
> Boy: Your asking me if they're white people. What difference does that make? Anyway, you're not all colored, are you?
>
> Jean-Baptiste: Yes, brother. All colored.
>
> Boy: Aren't you sort of mixed—got some white blood in you?
>
> Jean-Baptiste: If you're part white and part colored, it's all the same. You're considered all colored.

It is a simple scene, yet in a few lines of dialogue Micheaux was able to pinpoint an important distinction.

To be black in America did not simply mean that one had black skin. Anyone, even light-skinned enough to be recognized as white, was considered tainted and consequently inferior to whites as long as there was black blood flowing in their veins. No Hollywood films dared to deal so openly with such issues in 1931.

By 1940 Micheaux had made all but his final film. Realizing that his films were now neither popular nor profitable, Micheaux returned to novel writing. During World War II he wrote, published, and distributed novels that sold rather well. In 1947 he took some of his profits and struck a deal with Astor Pictures to make one more film, ***The Betrayal.*** By this time, however, he was suffering from painful arthritis, and walking and writing became very difficult. Still he managed to shoot the film on location in Chicago. On January 7, 1948, Alice B. Russell, Micheaux's wife and an actress in some of his films, wrote a letter to Oscar's sister, Ethel, who lived in Great Bend, Kansas. The letter was rather personal, especially in its description of Micheaux's debilitating illness. But it also provides us with an insight as to how he struggled to put together his final film.

> My dear sister Ethel,
>
> Just a note to let you know we are thinking of you and we hope and pray that you are getting along all right.
>
> Things are just so-so with us right now. Dad [Micheaux] has arthritis all over his body, but he keeps going. I have to help him put on his clothes and take them off. And I have to help him take a bath. His hands are slightly swollen and he can't grip or hold anything tightly, but as I said, he keeps on working. It is better for him to keep busy as long as he can, because he is so restless he couldn't stand not being able to go when he wanted to go.
>
> Last spring, Dad saw that the Book business was going down, so he decided that he would try to get back in Pictures as soon as possible. Therefore, he took all his little money and went to Chicago last summer and made a big Picture. He took me along to help him. We came back home in November with the Picture. He has been busy cutting it since and finished last week. He must get $500.00 which he is working on now and then he will start matching the negative so he can get a print for screening, then he will start booking the Picture and he hopes to be ready to play by April. He has already made up some of his advertising matter. I'm enclosing a Program. So you can see dear, he is doing a big job. And he is doing it alone. Isn't that wonderful?
>
> I thought we were going to visit you last year, but we didn't get there. Maybe we will sometime soon, I hope. Take good care of yourself and try to keep well. Dad's books are still selling, but nothing like in the past. Write when you can.
>
> With love, as ever
>
> Alice

Unfortunately for Micheaux, ***The Betrayal*** was not a success, and he was finished as a filmmaker. By 1949 the arthritis had confined him to a wheelchair but, even though he must have been in a great deal of pain, he continued to travel from city to city selling his books. He was on the road when he died in Charlotte, North Carolina in 1951.

For some unknown reason Micheaux's body was not shipped back to New York to his wife, Alice B. Russell. Instead, it was sent to Micheaux's sister, Ethel, who buried him in the family plot in Great Bend, Kansas. To this day, 37 years later, Micheaux's grave remains without a tombstone.

Micheaux was always aware of the criticism leveled against his films, and more than once he replied with an appeal for understanding of what he was trying to do. In the January 24, 1925 edition of the *Philadelphia Afro-American* he summarized his work.

> I have always tried to make my photoplays present the truth, to lay before the race a cross section of its own life, to view the colored heart from close range. My results might have been narrow at times, due perhaps to certain limited situations, which I endeavored to portray, but in those limited situations, the truth was the predominant characteristic. It is only by presenting those portions of the race portrayed in my pictures, in the light and background of their true state, that we can raise our people to greater heights (Sampson).

FURTHER READING

Criticism

Creighton, Alan. Review of *The Case of Mrs. Wingate*, by Oscar Micheaux. *Canadian Forum* 25 (June 1945): 75.

Recounts the plot of Micheaux's 1945 novel *The Case of Mrs. Wingate* and comments on its theme: "the position of the Negro in America."

Cripps, Thomas. "Black Underground" and "Meanwhile Far Away from the Movie Colony." In *Slow Fade to Black: The Negro in American Film, 1900-1942*, pp. 170-202, 309-48. Oxford: Oxford University Press, 1993.

Summarizes Micheaux's life and studies his films. Cripps characterizes Micheaux as "the exemplar both of persistence and of failure in the face of unyielding barriers."

Diawara, Manthia, ed. *Black American Cinema.* New York: Routledge, 1993, 324 p.

Includes three essays on Micheaux: "'Twoness' in the Style of Oscar Micheaux" by J. Ronald Green; "Fire and Desire: Race, Melodrama, and Oscar

Micheaux" by Jane Gaines; and "Oscar Micheaux: The Story Continues" by Thomas Cripps.

"Black America's Rich Film History: From Oscar Micheaux to Spike Lee." *Ebony* XLVIII, No. 4 (February 1993): 154-60.

Mentions Micheaux's "breakthrough movie, *The Homesteader*" as the first black-directed film.

Gehr, Richard. "One-Man Show." *American Film* (May 1991): 34-39.

Surveys Micheaux's films and career, and offers an estimation of critical reaction to his work.

Green, J. Ronald, and Neal, Horace, Jr. "Oscar Micheaux and Racial Slur: A Response to 'The Rediscovery of Oscar Micheaux.'" *Journal of Film and Video* 40, No. 4 (Fall 1988): 66-71.

Examines the presence of "racial stereotypes and ridicule" in Micheaux's films.

Hoberman, J. "Bad Movies." *Film Comment* (July/August 1980): 7-12.

Cites Micheaux's motion pictures for numerous faults.

———. "White Boys: Lucas, Spielberg, and the Temple of Dumb." *The Village Voice* XXIX, No. 17 (5 June 1984): 1, 63-64.

Includes a brief account of Micheaux's 1936 feature *Swing*.

Sampson, Henry T. "The Micheaux Film Corporation; Oscar Micheaux." In *Blacks in Black and White: A Source Book on Black Films*, pp. 42-55. Metuchen, N.J.: The Scarecrow Press, 1977.

History of Micheaux's film company and its major productions.

Young, Joseph A. *Black Novelist as White Racist: The Myth of Black Inferiority in the Novels of Oscar Micheaux.* New York: Greenwood Press, 1989, 181 p.

Studies Micheaux's ideological framework, including his "tragic vision," belief in the "ideal of assimilation," and "negrophobia."

The following source published by Gale Research contains further information on Micheaux's life and works: *Dictionary of Literary Biography*, Vol. 50.

Kenji Miyazawa

1896-1933

Japanese poet, short story writer, and essayist.

INTRODUCTION

A Buddhist writer who abandoned traditional Japanese forms in his verse, Miyazawa is remembered for his intensely personal poems, which feature an idiosyncratic mix of ethical idealism, humor, agrarianism, and Buddhist piety. Self-trained in traditional, highly-structured *tanka* poetry, Miyazawa was among the first poets in Japan to exploit the possibilities of the free verse form, most notably in his *Haru to shura* (*Spring and Asura*). Juxtaposing images from science, religion, and the rugged environment of his native Honshu, he created works he called "imagery sketches," which explore themes of selflessness, compassion, and the ultimate unity of all sentient creatures. In addition, Miyazawa is recognized for his many short stories, ostensibly written for children. Akin to his poetry in vision and theme, these tales range in subject matter from comic satire to metaphysical meditation.

Biographical Information

Miyazawa was born in Hanamaki, Iwate prefecture on the northern Japanese island of Honshu. A poor farming region, Iwate was Miyazawa's home for the majority of his life and the inspiration for much of his poetry. Demonstrating an early interest in the natural environment, he attended an agricultural high school, and later worked for a time in his father's pawn shop on Honshu. While still young, Miyazawa formed a devout interest in Mahayana Buddhism, focusing his studies particularly on the *Lotus Sutra*, one of its sacred texts. After high school he traveled to Tokyo to further his learning with the Nichiren Buddhist sect, and began to write poetry and children's stories. Some of his verses were published in national literary magazines, but Miyazawa remained largely unknown in Japanese literary circles. In 1921 news of the prolonged illness of his sister Toshiko prompted him to return to Iwate; Miyazawa later chronicled his intense sadness at her passing in the poem "Last Farewell." He remained on Honshu for the remainder of his life, returning to Tokyo only on occasion, as in 1924 to publish several of his poems. In addition to composing more works of poetry and fiction, he devoted his everyday existence to the destitute farmers of the Iwate prefecture. As a teacher of natural science and agriculture he instructed them in soil improvement, crop rotation, and other modern forms of cultivation. During this period, Miyazawa is said to have undertaken a rigorous schedule of work while allowing himself only meager nutrition, a combination that eventually destroyed his health. He died of pneumonia in 1933, with plans to publish a collection of short stories, and more of his approximately 1200 poems.

Major Works

Unpublished during his lifetime, Miyazawa's essay "Agrarian Art" is thought to outline the basic tenets of his aesthetic theory. In it, he seeks to combine the ideals of artistic beauty with the earthy agricultural ethic of hard work demonstrated by the impoverished farmers of his native Iwate region. A philosophical idealist and devout Buddhist, Miyazawa focused his writing on the transcendence of the phenomenal world through the humble ideals of compassion, selflessness, and equality. His poetry—written in both the classical Japanese style and a modern, colloquial idiom—is considered to be at once highly personal and spiritually transcendent, as it depicts the beautiful landscape of the Japanese countryside alongside his inner feelings of despair, self-pity, and elation. Miyazawa's collection *Spring and Asura* features a variety of these poems, as well as satirical and humorous pieces in free verse. Its companion volume is *A Future of Ice* (1989), a collection of previously unpublished poems translated into English. This later work contains Miyazawa's most widely-known poem—written while he was sick and preparing to die—"November Third." Bearing many similarities to his poetry, but often more comic and light-hearted, Miyazawa's short fiction has been collected in two English editions, *Winds from Afar* (1972) and *Night of the Milky Way Railway* (1991). Visionary and poetic, "Night of the Milky Way Railway," the title story of the latter collection, follows young Giovanni on a fantasy trip into the afterlife instigated by the mysterious disappearance of his classmate Campanella. Critics see this work as demonstrative of Miyazawa's belief in the fluidity of time and ultimate unity of the cosmos. Other tales of note include "A Biography of Gukibudori," whose protagonist, like Miyazawa in his later years, dedicates his life completely to the welfare of others, and "Oppel the Elephant," a satire on blind capitalism.

Critical Reception

Miyazawa's works were almost completely unknown during his lifetime; he was able to publish only a handful of his free verse poems as *Haru to shura* by financing the entire run himself. Yet soon after his death in 1933, Miyazawa was elevated to the position of cultural hero, known to many Japanese as "the saint of northern Japan." Likewise his famous poem "November Third" is familiar to many in his native country who otherwise know nothing about him. By the second half of the twentieth century, Japanese scholars had begun to devote considerable attention to his poetry and fiction, an interest that was carried across the Pacific to the United States in the 1960s with the appearance of several of Miyazawa's translated poems in Gary Snyder's *Back Country*. In the ensuing decades further translations of Miyazawa's writings have appeared, making Miyazawa's comic, spiritual, and idiosyncratic works accessible to audiences outside Japan.

PRINCIPAL WORKS

Haru to shura [*Spring & Asura: Poems of Kenji Miyazawa*] (poetry) 1924
Winds from Afar (short stories) 1972
A Future of Ice: Poems and Stories of a Japanese Buddhist (poetry and short stories) 1989
Night of the Milky Way Railway (short stories) 1991

CRITICISM

John Bester (essay date 1972)

SOURCE: A foreword to *Winds From Afar,* by Kenji Miyazawa, translated by John Bester, Kodansha International Ltd., 1972, pp. 7-9.

[*In the following foreward to his translation of Miyazawa's children's tales entitled* Wings from Afar, *Bester summarizes the "charm and inventiveness," humanism, and "intense nostalgia for innocence" that characterize Miyazawa's short stories.*]

Of the sixteen tales translated [in ***Winds from Afar***] six have appeared previously in a small volume entitled ***Winds and Wildcat Places.*** The previous collection was produced essentially as a book for children. In increasing the number of stories and publishing them in the present format, the aim has been not only to create a definitive edition of the best of Miyazawa but also to produce a book that can be enjoyed at least as much by adults as by children.

To do this implies a considerable confidence in the value of Miyazawa's children's stories. To translate works such as these forty years after their author's death and from a language as remote as Japanese suggests that they have acquired a kind of classic status.

Such a status has in fact long since been achieved in Miyazawa's own country. His place in modern Japanese literature is secure. Learned papers are published on him, and new editions continue to appear. His work does not seem to date, for it is read now by a generation quite different from Miyazawa's.

One obvious reason for this is that although his writing is very much a product of the northern country district of Honshu where he lived his short life, his appeal relies basically on qualities unrelated to any particular society or country. The same is true, of course, of most classic children's stories, and in this sense Miyazawa's work easily avoids the barriers that inevitably blunt our response to much in Japanese literature. More important here, though, is the question of what, in the positive sense, Miyazawa offers the adult reader in other countries.

The most obvious elements in Miyazawa's appeal are the charm and inventiveness of his tales. They are all good stories. They have the humor and inconsequentiality, the ability to evoke a world of their own, the absence of theorizing, and the satisfying sense of inevitability that everyone expects of children's stories. With engaging freedom, the choice of characters ranges from wildcats to elderly generals to dustpans. And as most good children's stories do, they comment ruefully on moral questions and the realities that precede and underlie the adult world.

But it is in the way Miyazawa's work, consciously and unconsciously, reflects that world that his special qualities begin to assert themselves. The realm that his characters inhabit is not a cozy middle-class world, but neither do his shapes and shadows harbor barely concealed Freudian horrors. His settings are northern without nordic morbidity. He avoids insipidity without falling into the grotesque. In his cautionary tales he disposes of his villains with satisfying heartlessness, but there is little sadism. Without sentimentality, his world achieves a peculiar sweetness and light.

That Miyazawa was aware of the everyday foibles and stupidities of humanity is clear, of course, from the element of fable in his work. The three episodes of **"The Spider, the Slug, and the Raccoon,"** though humorous, have an unusually sharp element of satire. That he also knew enough of human relationships to have developed a remarkable compassion for their well-meaning blunderings is clear from that moving little tragi-comedy, **"Earthgod and the Fox."**

Yet still more essential in Miyazawa than this humanism is an intense nostalgia for innocence, for the childlike state that precedes all such things as society and morality. This nostalgia, together with the sensitivity towards nature with which it is so closely linked is, above all, what gives his work its special flavor. The harking back to innocence is not so much a retreat into childhood as a reaffirmation of certain aspects of our relationship with the universe about us. When, as in **"The Kenju Wood,"** this theme of innocence is fairly explicit, it can come close to sentimentality (even though this particular story has a special poignancy in today's polluted world). In other tales, however, it is treated more subtly, while in some—especially in that small masterpiece of economy, **"A Stem of Lilies"**—it acquires a peculiarly radiant, almost religious intensity.

And here we come close to the heart of Miyazawa's appeal. A similar quickening of the poetic imagination, triggered in most cases by the author's response to nature, occurs sporadically throughout the whole of his work. Basically, it is the strength of his feeling for nature that makes him unique. For Miyazawa, nature is all movement and color. His word-painting, simple though it is, has a freshness of palette, a sense of rediscovery, and an almost unnatural sensitivity that calls to mind some Impressionist pictures. With all this goes a sense of immense space—of distant hills, winds from afar, and infinite depths to the heavens. Not only is his work free of coziness and claustrophobia: he seems positively to go out to meet the loneliness of the universe.

Time and again, this awareness of nature transmutes something quite ordinary into poetry. **"The Dahlias and the Crane"** would be no more than a charming cautionary tale if it were not also a miniature prose-poem showing the year slipping inexorably from late summer into autumn. **"The Fire Stone"** might be a routine morality without its recurring images of nature. **"Wildcat and the Acorns,"** superficially one of the more "childlike" of the stories, has a morning freshness that complements the character of the boy Ichiro. And the whole of **"The Red Blanket"** is a kind of set-piece that magically evokes the passage of a snowstorm from the first uneasy stirrings in the sky, through the height of the blizzard, to the serenity of the sun's return.

Yet this is not quite all. Here and there, in these stories, one is struck by a strength of feeling that borders on ecstasy. It is as though Miyazawa's nostalgia for innocence was accompanied by a longing for complete absorption into the universe, a longing whose intensity is heightened to the point where the only outlet it can find is in ritual. Nowhere is this more clear than at the end of **"The First Deer Dance,"** where the sense of quivering joy goes far beyond what one would expect in a tale that, superficially, is no more than an imaginative reconstruction of the origins of a folk dance. In **"The Nighthawk Star,"** the return to nature finds a different (perhaps slightly more facile) form when the unhappy nighthawk attains release in an almost Christian style apotheosis. In **"The Bears of Mt. Nametoko,"** the hunter forced by circumstances into the destruction of other creatures is finally reconciled with his victims and reabsorbed into the universe in a scene of brooding grandeur that has the mystery of some primeval rite.

But once this element is perceived, it is found recurring, in less obvious ways, again and again throughout the stories. A sunset becomes a ceremony; the bellflower tolls the indifference of nature to its creatures; the seasons parade past, and man gazes in awe at the solemn procession of the stars. Miyazawa takes us back, not to the nursery but to somewhere freer, more timeless, and more indifferent to ourselves. From time to time, in these seemingly slight, utterly charming tales, he reaches out towards the essence of wonder and the heart of poetry. It is those moments that give them their substance and set the seal on their value for anyone, in any country, who will respond.

Burton Watson (essay date 1973)

SOURCE: An introduction to *Spring & Asura: Poems of Kenji Miyazawa,* translated by Hiroaki Sato, Chicago Review Press, 1973, pp. xv-xix.

[*In the following introduction to Miyazawa's collection of verse* Spring and Asura, *Watson notes the pervasive presence of Buddhist ideals—selflessness, compassion, and the oneness of the universe—in Miyazawa's life and poetry.*]

Those who with a happy frame of mind
Have sung the glory of the Buddha,
Even with a very small sound, . . .
Or have worshipped,
Or have merely folded their hands, . . .
Or have uttered one 'Praise be!'—
All have reached the state of buddhahood.

So declares the *Saddharmapundarika* or *Lotus of the Wonderful Law,* one of the most important sutras or scriptures of Mahayana Buddhism. It is a text to which Kenji Miyazawa paid special reverence, and both his life and his poetry were dedicated to the active expression of its teachings.

Kenji Miyazawa was born in 1896 in Iwate prefecture, an impoverished farming region of northern Japan. As a child he displayed great interest in minerals and wild life, and went on to major in agricultural studies in high school and to take part in various agronomical surveys and research activities after graduation. It was in his high school days likewise that he first manifested an unusual devotion to Buddhism, first undergoing a period of Zen training and later becoming a follower of the Nichiren Sect and a devotee of its principal object of veneration, the *Lotus Sutra,* reciting from the text morning and evening.

For a time he worked in his father's pawn shop, and later attempted to support himself in Tokyo by doing various literary chores, at the same time writing poems and children's stories and pursuing his studies on his own in the Ueno public library. The critical illness of his younger sister Toshiko brought him back home to Iwate in 1921. With the exception of brief trips to the capital, he remained there until his death in 1933, unmarried, living a life marked by extreme frugality and hard work.

These later years were dedicated to improving the spiritual and material lives of his neighbors in the farming towns and villages of Iwate. He taught natural science and other subjects in the local schools, composed songs and wrote and produced plays for his pupils and fellow townsmen, taught them to perform ritual dances and play musical instruments, and entertained them with his phonograph records. He instructed them in practical matters of soil improvement, fertilizers, and crop rotation, operated a free counseling service on agricultural affairs, and consulted with local weather stations and meteorological observatories on ways to prevent or alleviate the floods, droughts, and cold and wind damage that so often afflicted the area. At one point he ate so sparingly and drove himself so hard that he was laid up for three years with pleurisy. His last job was that of engineer with a local rock-crushing company, working to improve methods of refining calcium carbonate and lime. He died of pneumonia at the age of thirty-eight, affirming on his deathbed his unbounded faith in the *Lotus Sutra.*

Miyazawa was a rapid and prolific writer, turning out a large number of children's stories and other prose works, as well as poems, some written in classical Japanese and cast in traditional forms, others in a freer form and employing a simple, colloquial style. It is the works of this last category that concern us here, the collection of free-verse poems known as ***Spring & Asura.*** Only the first part of the collection appeared in Miyazawa's lifetime, a small group of poems printed at the author's expense in Tokyo in 1924. The remainder of the poems was published in the years immediately following his death, when his works gradually gained the recognition they had been denied during his lifetime. The entire collection contains something over twelve hundred poems; many were left untitled and are identified by the number of the work in the collection as a whole.

Miyazawa looked on his poems as expressions of his religious convictions and ideals, on poetry itself as a form of religion. Underlying his poems and other writings is the world concept of Mahayana Buddhism, particularly as it is expounded in the *Lotus Sutra.* The fundamental doctrine of that text (as may be seen from the quotation at the beginning of the introduction), is the immediate accessibility of buddhahood to the sincere believer, no matter how humble or hampered by circumstance, as well as the compassionate aid extended to all creatures by the bodhisattva, the potential buddha who chooses to remain in the phenomenal world in order to assist other creatures to the realization of buddhahood. Miyazawa's own life of selfless service to his neighbors, along with his passionate and hauntingly beautiful poems and stories, represent and attempt, in so far as the human condition allows, to approximate this bodhisattva ideal.

A second fundamental concept of Buddhism, the equality and ultimate oneness of all beings and objects in the phenomenal world, finds expression in his poetry in an attitude of compassion and tenderness toward even the lowliest forms of life and a sense of mystic and intensely personal identity with the universe and all that makes it up. His skyscapes in particular manifest a kind of Vedic reverence for the forces of nature and an inexhaustible joy in the celebration of winds, clouds, and the constantly varying lights of the atmosphere.

Overt references to Buddhist belief are to be found scattered throughout Miyazawa's poetry, to the *Lotus Sutra,* object of his veneration, to the so-called six realms of existence into which unenlightened beings are repeatedly reborn, or to the Tushita Heaven, paradise of the bodhisattva Maitreya, to which he prayed that his dying sister Toshiko might be transported. To this extent, and in its underlying philosophy, his poetry is conventional and rooted in the age-old Buddhist traditions of the Japanese past. In its imagery, however, his poetry breaks totally from the stereotypes of the past. In place of the Indian landscape with its elephants and tropical birds that is a fixture of the sutras and other early works of Buddhist literature, he shows us the green-bladed rice paddies and snowy mountains of his native Iwate; while the lapis lazuli, emeralds, and other fabulous gems that in the ancient scriptures symbolized the splendor and multifariousness of creation are in his writings transformed into the minerals, metals, and chemical compounds which he himself worked with and knew from daily experience. All the varied elements of his knowledge, both technical and commonplace, book-learned and experiential, are treated with equal honor and reverence by him, and are ranged side by side in indiscriminate and joyous profusion. The juxtaposition of levels and categories of diction that results is like nothing that I am familiar with in the work of any other poet, east or west.

Such a conglomeration of diction may at first encounter strike one as bizarre, even surrealistic, and yet one should not suppose that the aim is merely to startle and arrest. Because Miyazawa, through his studies, happens to know the precise scientific term for a particular chemical substance or meteorological phenomenon, he takes the same delight in naming it that he takes in naming the trees of the hillside or the grasses of the field, as a more traditional poet might do. He celebrates not just the picturesque or conventionally beautiful elements of the scene around him, but all the dharmas or phenomena of existence, without prejudice or partiality. In this sense, his works may in fact be called a poetry of universal affirmation.

The seventy-three poems in Mr. Sato's selection are representative of the entire span of Miyazawa's poetic career, beginning with works that appeared in the first section of ***Spring & Asura*** that was published in 1924 and ending with those written shortly before his death. At the same time they succeed in conveying an excellent impression of the breadth and variety of subjects treated in Miyazawa's free-verse poems. There are works dealing with the poet's friends and family, including the famous **"Last Farewell"** to his sister Toshiko; sketches, sometimes with a satiric bite, of local officials and entrepreneurs, and portrayals of the hard pressed farmers whose sorrows he shared and did his best to assuage. There are poems that reflect his abiding interest in music and his passion for Japanese prints; poems about fertilizer, factories, ailing draft horses and doomed irises; about a hemorrhaging tooth that can't be stopped and a mysterious enemy named Kuma; and poems that simply extol the rivers, birds, uplands and vast light-struck skies of the Japanese countryside that Miyazawa saw each day and couldn't rest until he had written about.

Few of these free-verse poems of Miyazawa, so far as I am aware, have been translated into English. The Bownas and Thwaite *Penguin Book of Japanese Verse* (1964) contains a translation of Miyazawa's best known poem, **"November Third"** (Bending neither to the rain / Nor to the wind"), a homiletic piece written when he was ill in Tokyo and expecting to die. So great is its popularity in Japan that it is printed on cloth and hung in sampler fashion: almost any Japanese, though he may know little else about Miyazawa, can identify it as the work of "the saint of northern Japan" and recite it by heart.

In the 60's the distinguished American poet and translator Gary Snyder produced translations of eighteen of Miyazawa's poems, published in his *The Back Country,* the finest and most extensive selection of Miyazawa's work at that time available to the English reading public. With Snyder's striking and deeply sympathetic renditions, Miyazawa for the first time became a poet of international importance.

It is no easy task to follow in Snyder's footsteps, as I myself learned in making translations from the Chinese poet Han-shan, whom Snyder had previously translated. Mr. Sato's Miyazawa selection, of course, is by far the most voluminous to appear to date in English. In addition he has, it seems to me, been extraordinarily successful in capturing and bringing over both the sharply observed, often dazzling imagery of Miyazawa's poetry, and the relaxed, almost prosy matrix in which it is characteristically set. Miyazawa's free-style poetry, totally divorced from traditional Japanese forms and, so far as I know, uninfluenced by foreign models, is lumpy and jarring, inset with difficult Chinese compounds, terms borrowed from Sanskrit, English or German, and even bits of local Tohoku dialect, deliberately spaced on the page in ways that Mr. Sato has been careful to suggest in his translation. And yet—to return to a point already made above—as though to point up the essential commonness and universality of the statement, Miyazawa has enclosed his astonishing assortment of terms and images within the simple vocatives and declaratives of everyday Japanese. Mr. Sato in his translation has with great taste and fidelity rendered both the strangeness and the simplicity of Miyazawa's poetry, both its intense individuality and its passionate concern for transcendent values and the celebration of all the manifold aspects of creation. He has made it possible for Miyazawa to speak not only to his neighbors and countrymen, but to readers of English as well, a step toward the universal call to all sentient beings that Miyazawa no doubt visualized as his ideal.

Makoto Ueda (essay date 1983)

SOURCE: "Miyazawa Kenji," in *Modern Japanese Poets and the Nature of Literature,* Stanford University Press, 1983, pp. 184-231.

[*In the following essay, Ueda studies Miyazawa's literary style, creative process, aesthetic theory, and poetic vision.*]

Secluded from the mainstream of modern Japanese verse, Miyazawa Kenji (1896-1933) was almost totally unknown as a poet during his lifetime. He published few poems in magazines of nationwide literary reputation, and for his one published book of poetry and single collection of children's stories he shouldered all publication costs himself. After his death, however, his works soon gained a large following of people from all walks of life. Six different periodicals have been founded by different groups exclusively to study his works. Although literary critics still find it difficult to place him in the history of modern Japanese poetry, his faithful readers could not care less, nor could his posthumous publishers. Five different editions of his complete works have been published, the latest matched in its comprehensiveness only by Sakutaro's among modern poets.

The charms of Kenji's poetry are manifold: his high idealism, his intensely ethical life, his unique cosmic vision, his agrarianism, his religious faith, and his rich and colorful vocabulary. But ultimately they are all based in a dedicated effort to unify the heterogeneous elements of modern life into a single, coherent whole. Kenji stood in solitary opposition to all the other major poets of his time, who as modern intellectuals suffered one or another kind of dichotomy within the self. By training he was an agricultural chemist, and he considered it his heaven-sent work to mingle with farmers in the open fields and to give them expert advice on soil conditioning. He was also a devout Buddhist of the Hokke sect who wanted to propagate the teaching of the Lotus Sutra as widely as possible. He was a man of science, religion, and poetry; yet his mental energy was of such a centripetal nature that he could unify them all. Furthermore, that mental energy was not satisfied until it took a physical form in daily life. Kenji was a whole man, and therein lies the basic charm of his poetry.

IN SEARCH OF THE GALAXY WITHIN

Kenji wrote many works directly or indirectly touching on the nature of literature. A story called **"The Dragon and the Poet,"** for instance, presents his concept of poetry in the form of a Buddhist parable; several fairy tales, such as **"Grape Juice"** and **"A Night in the Oak Grove,"** reveal what he thought of the origin of poetry, music, and dance; and an aphoristic essay entitled **"Agrarian Art: An Outline"** sums up the idea of art he came to conceive in his later years. Most significant of all, however, is the prefatory poem to ***Spring and Asura,*** the only collection of verse published during his lifetime. Here he directly addressed his prospective readers and explained his concept of poetry, which he knew was radically different from the prevailing ones. He wanted a reader to digest his preface before venturing into the anthology, and we too shall begin our discussion with this poem.

The poem, appropriately called **"Proem,"** consists of five stanzas. The first reads:

> The phenomenon called I
> is a blue light
> coming from the temporary, organic AC lamp
> (a synthesis of all transparent spirits).
> With the landscape and with everybody
> it incessantly blinks
> yet never stops glowing:
> a light
> from the karmic AC lamp
> (the light remains, the lamp vanishes)

The stanza metaphorically defines a poet: he is a light shining out across, or rather with, the landscape. But that light is from an AC lamp, a lamp whose constant glowing is in fact an incessant blinking, although so little time elapses between each blink that we are not aware of the light's other truth, the darkness.

Despite its imagery from modern technology, the stanza portrays the poet from a Buddhist perspective. Both the significance of the karmic AC lamp and its Buddhist background are made clearer in one of Kenji's fantasies for children, **"A Night on the Galactic Railway."** In the story, young Giovanni is grieving over the disappearance of his schoolmate Campanella. At that point, a pale-faced man appears, wearing a large black hat and carrying a dictionary. After telling the boy how knowledge of history and geography changes through the ages (an impermanence not unlike what Giovanni has just experienced in the loss of his friend), the scholar raises one finger and then lowers it. In the next instant,

> Giovanni saw that he and his thoughts, along with the train, the scholar, the Milky Way, and all else, glowed brightly, faded out, glowed again, faded again, and when one of the lights glowed there spread out the whole wide world with all its history, but when it faded there was nothing but empty darkness. The blinking grew faster and faster, until everything was back as before.

Giovanni's vision seems a comprehensive view of fundamental reality. As he himself, his thoughts, his surroundings, and all of human history in turn glow, then fade to empty darkness, they come to be like the AC lamp. In faster and faster alternation, he sees both the fundamental emptiness underlying all phenomena and the transitory existence of himself and all the world fuse into samsara, the stream of appearances comprising repeated births and deaths that is reality as we ordinarily know it, "everything . . . back as before." Giovanni's vision reveals the unity of phenomenal world and empty darkness in the ongoing process of constant transformation or change.

To return to the **"Proem,"** the "temporary, organic AC lamp" seems a comparable vision of a reality that is at once plenum and void. It is explicitly linked to the Buddhist concept of karma, the accumulation of deeds, intentions, and events that continually works itself out through the cycles of cosmic history and thus powers the revolutions of samsara. Yet the poet's spiritual essence (at one with all other "transparent spirits" in the absolute mind that contains and creates all beings), although it at present seems determined by the organic lamp of the karmic world, is finally independent of samsara in the absolute mind that forms its ultimate reality, along with that of all other creatures: "the light remains, the lamp vanishes."

In the second stanza and throughout the rest of the poem, Kenji gives his own twist to this Buddhistic image of self and world in the manner in which he conceives of its realization in time and in his poetry. He continues:

> These have come from a period of 22 months
> that I feel lies in the direction of the past.
> By bringing paper and mineral ink together
> (it blinks with me
> and is felt simultaneously by everybody)
> I have preserved until now
> each chain of shade and light
> in these imagery sketches.

The key phrase here for describing Kenji's poetry is "imagery sketches," a phrase Kenji considered important enough to print as a subtitle on the cover of ***Spring and Asura.*** He deliberately avoided using the term "poems," since he felt his sketches were different from ordinary poems. In a letter to a friend he wrote, "What I have published in ***Spring and Asura,*** what I have written between then and now, all of those are definitely not poetry. They are no more than rough sketches of images I have drawn on various occasions in preparation for a certain project in psychology, which I would very much like to complete, although I do not have time to undertake a full-scale study." What Kenji called "imagery sketches," then, differ from ordinary poetry in two ways. First, they are not finished products but rough drafts, and since they have not yet received the poet's finishing touches, they are closer to the immediate thoughts and sensations in his mind. Second, Kenji's imagery sketches, besides recording what lies in his mind, also duplicate what lies in the minds of everyone else. His presupposition is that the imagery sketches he draws portray what is common to the human race in general, since like all people he is but a transitory creation out of the pure and absolute mind that is true reality.

This second point is elaborated in the third stanza, since Kenji apparently felt a need for further explanation:

> From these, men and the galaxy and asura and sea urchins
> as they eat cosmic dust or breathe air or seawater
> may each think up a fresh cosmology,

but ultimately all is a mental landscape.
These scenes, clearly recorded,
are the records of scenes as they were.
If they show the void, it is the void as it was
and is shared to some degree by all people.
(For everything is within me, within my inner
everybody
and likewise within everybody else.)

The stanza's first line reminds us that although the Milky Way and sea urchins possess different habits and follow different life cycles, they are one with men in being manifestations of the cosmic mind, the primal reality of the cosmos. Kenji's sketches are not, then, depictions of external objects as observed by the poet but records of internal images and sensations that reflect this greater mind. There is no borderline between the subjective and the objective, nor is there a division between man and inanimate things. Imagery sketches are the records of this nondivisive consciousness.

The fourth stanza, a long one, reintroduces the element of time:

However, it is theoretically conceivable
that these seemingly accurate verbal records
made amid the piles of massive, bright time
in the alluvial epoch of the Cenozoic era
have already changed their structures and qualities
in what to them is a momentary blink
(or asura's one billion years)
and yet neither my printers nor I
have noticed the change.
For we sense our own emotion
and see a landscape or a person
only through the faculties common to us all.
Likewise, what we know as records or history or
geology
probably is, with all its numerous data,
nothing more than what we feel
(within the karmic limits of time and space).
Perhaps in two thousand years
a new geology proper to that age
will unearth plenty of proper evidence for the
past.
Everyone may think two thousand years ago
a transparent peacock filled the blue sky.
New bachelors of science may excavate splendid
fossils
from the ice nitrogen zone
glittering at the top layer of the atmosphere
or discover gigantic footprints
of an invisible man
in the Cretaceous sandstone.

The time referred to is cosmic time, hence the use of many geological terms. Human life, which is part of the life of the universe, must be measured against cosmic time, as both geologists imply and Buddhists say it should be. Seen in this perspective, imagery sketches are extremely fleeting things, as evanescent as a blink of light. Nevertheless, they are made by a man who has transcended human time, who is well aware of the limits of human faculties. They are significant, and insignificant, for those reasons.

The fifth and final stanza consists of just three lines, which cryptically bring the poem to its conclusion:

All these problems
inherent in the nature of imagery and time
will be pursued within the fourth dimension.

"The fourth dimension" is one of Kenji's favorite phrases; in **"Agrarian Art"** and elsewhere he repeatedly used it to describe his artistic ideal. In art, the "fourth dimension," which Kenji roughly associated with time, is the source of fluidity, an ability to change through time as reality does. As he said in **"Agrarian Art"**: "The four-dimensional sense adds fluidity to a static art." Kenji must have considered an awareness of time and temporal change to be the basis of that fluidity, for he also said, "The huge drama of human life moves along the axis of time and creates an everlasting, four-dimensional art." Thus, in being imagery sketches the 73 verses in ***Spring and Asura*** are the tentative records of a man who was clearly aware of the fleeting nature of his vision. Ordinary poems are three-dimensional: they are snapshots of nature, portraits of people, depictions of sentiments, and the like. On the other hand, Kenji's verbal sketches are four-dimensional, since they are aware of their own change through time.

To summarize, Kenji's concept of poetic mimesis as expressed in the **"Proem"** is characterized by two features. First, the reality represented in poetry is conceived neither as external reality mirrored in the poet's mind nor as internal reality expressed through metaphors, but as cosmic reality rooted in a Buddhist vision of the ultimate unity of all creatures in being manifestations of an absolute and all-pervading consciousness. Second, the reality thus represented is four-dimensional in the sense that it is not a framed picture or a piece of finished sculpture but a slice of infinite space and time.

Kenji reiterated his idea of cosmic reality in other writings. It appears, for instance, in a letter to his brother, in which he wrote, "When I forget my existence in the wind and the light, when I feel the world has turned into my garden, or when I am entranced to think that the entire galaxy is myself, how happy I feel!" Once he expressed such happiness in a short lyric called **"A Grove and Thoughts"**:

Look! You see?
Over there, drenched in the fog,
there is a small mushroom-shaped grove.
That is the place where
my thoughts
swiftly drift
and one by one
dissolve.
Butterburs are flowering everywhere.

The communion between man and his surroundings is not a one-way street. The grove, and all other beings on earth, respond to the poet in turn. So Kenji implied when he said in a note, "I am interested in the clouds and the wind not only for their scenic beauty, but because they provide a source of new strength for man, an endless source of strength." In the preface to his collection of children's stories, ***The Restaurant of Many Orders,*** Kenji recalled, "I received all these stories of mine from the rainbow and the moonlight as I was in the woods, on the fields, or alongside the railway. Honestly, I could not help feeling these things when I passed near the green oak forest in the evening all by myself, or when I stood shivering in the mountain wind of November." In some of his stories he cited examples of a poem's emerging from a cosmic awareness shared by all things. In **"Grape Juice,"** for instance, a youngster named Seisaku hears a song coming from afar, but he cannot tell whether the singer is the sky, the wind, or a little child standing in the field; apparently it is something within all three. In **"A Night in the Oak Grove,"** Seisaku ventures into the woods, from which a song is coming, and he finds that oak trees, owls, and a human painter all sing similar songs. In **"A Spring Day at Ihatove School of Agriculture,"** a song is sung by the sun in the sky, and the author has even provided its melody in musical notation. To a person who can hear, poetry comes from all things in the universe, as they all share in the cosmic mind.

The relationship of poetry and this cosmic awareness is reiterated in the story **"The Dragon and the Poet,"** where it is connected with the idea that there is a progressive trend in cosmic history. The story outlines how a budding poet named Surdatta wins a decisive victory over a poet of great reputation, Alta, at a song contest. Surdatta himself does not know how he composed his winning song; all he remembers is that he seems to have heard it in his sleep one windy day when he dozed off on a headland. But the older Alta knows the creative process better and explains it to the younger poet in a song of his own:

> No sooner have the wind sung and the clouds
>   echoed and
>   the waves resounded
> than you sing their song, Surdatta.
> You are a prophet who envisions
> a model of truth and beauty for tomorrow's world
> after which the stars yearn and the land shapes
>   itself
> and who eventually makes the world become so.
> You are an architect, Surdatta.

Here again is the idea that a song—or a poem—expresses an impulse or an awareness shared by the wind and the clouds as well as the poet, and here too is the idea that the world and all it contains are constantly changing through time. But Kenji also suggests that the changing cosmos has a direction and purpose, and that the change is for the better. The poet, in singing out the cosmic mind, conveys a sense of progress.

In Kenji's view the purpose thus expressed is that of universal reality, not the individual poet. In an advertisement he wrote for ***The Restaurant of Many Orders*** he said, "These stories are designed to provide materials for building a new, better world. But that world is entirely a development of this world, a ceaseless, wondrous development unknown to me. Definitely it is not a sooty, misshapen utopia." In his opinion, most utopian stories are products of authors' individual imaginings, reflecting their personal idiosyncrasies. But the stories collected in ***The Restaurant of Many Orders*** are based on the cosmic mind, and hence on the cosmic will at work to perfect the world.

The clearest expression of Kenji's idea of cosmic will appears in what seems to be a draft of a letter to an unidentified acquaintance:

> There is one problem I can never pass over. Is there such a thing as cosmic will deigning to lead all living things to true happiness? Or is the world something incidental and sightless? If confronted by this choice between what is known as religious faith and what is known as science, I would by all means select the former. The universe has a great many stages of consciousness, and the final one is endeavoring to lead all living things away from all delusions and toward ultimate happiness.

Kenji, an avid reader of the Lotus Sutra, may have associated the highest stage of universal consciousness with the compassionate bodhisattva, who strives to lead all beings to the pure bliss of the Buddha's Paradise, "away from all delusions and toward ultimate happiness." Here he sees a similar ideal embodied, not in a specific religious figure, but in the movement of cosmic history as a whole.

Kenji does not seem to have believed that poetry always reflects universal consciousness in its last stage of supreme happiness. By and large, his own poetry reflects various prior stages. The title of his anthology, ***Spring and Asura,*** is symbolic; "spring," denoting the most beautiful time of the year, alludes to the last and highest stage, whereas "asura" refers to one of the lower phases. (In Mahayana Buddhism, an asura is a demonlike creature suffering from such delusive passions as arrogance, suspicion, and jealousy in one of the four spheres occupying the space between heaven and hell.) In **"Spring and Asura,"** the title poem of the collection, Kenji described himself as such a creature, tears streaming from his eyes, who restlessly roams the idyllic countryside on a radiant April day. The poem's speaker is aware of universal consciousness, but he has not yet reached its final stage.

Three representative poems pin down more exactly Kenji's idea of mimesis. I will start with a simple one:

> **"Politicians (Opus 1053)"**
>
> Over there, and here too
> everybody wants to make a fuss
> and get treated to a drink.
>   Fern leaves and the clouds.
>   The world is so cold and dark.

But before long
those fellows will
rot
and flow away in the rain,
leaving only the silent green ferns behind.
"That happened in the coal age of man,"
Some transparent geologist will record.

This is not among the best of Kenji's poems. The satire is too simple, and a facile, escapist attitude is implied. Nonetheless, the poem clearly shows the nature of his cosmic awareness, since it regards reality from a standpoint that transcends human time and recognizes a slow progress on the universal scale. The human perspective and resulting anger presented in the first three lines are replaced by a cosmic perspective as the poem progresses, and the anger is thereby sublimated.

The next poem is more famous and more complex. I shall quote its longer version:

"Flower of Karma"

Over the moisture of night forlornly blending with
the wind
and above a black grove of pines and willows
the sky is filled with dark petals of karma.
Having recorded the names of gods
I shiver violently with cold.
Oh someone, come and assure me
that there will arrive a radiant world
where millions of great men are born
and live together without defiling one another!
A heron is crying in the distance.
Will it stand on the cold marshland
throughout the night, its red eyes burning?
As dewdrops fall from pine trees
a few lonely clusters of stars
emerge afresh from the western clouds.
By coincidence a pair
join their rays to form a yellow plume,
while the rest, a large bushy shadow,
show an obscure white shape.

Here again the imperfections of human reality are implied, and they are viewed from the standpoint of a poet who can identify the gods. Transcending the limits of human time, he envisions the great accumulated mass of actions past, present, and future spread out like petals across the night sky, and in it he recognizes the force determining the course of people's lives. But, in contrast to **"Politicians,"** in this poem the poet is not sure whether time will eventually bring forth a radiant world. By chance a person may attain luminous harmony with others, as a few of the stars do, after coming out of the clouds of suspicion. Yet most of mankind may be like the heron that keeps crying throughout the night. A sense of a higher level of consciousness is still present in the poem, but there is no longer certainty of cosmic progress.

Kenji must have wondered about the ways of overcoming such doubts. His answer is implied in some of his later poems, such as this one:

"Opus 1063"

These are modest fences like the Ainu's.
Yes,
the mulberry tree by their house
was stripped down to the letter Y
and yet they could not make a living.
Last April
the water was black in the rice paddies
as eddies of dark air
incessantly fell from the sky
and crows
noisily flew by.
It makes me wonder.
Though the field is full of sharp-edged gravel
and overgrown with horsetails and mugworts
they till it, those women clothed in black,
while rearing their babies,
patching together the rags from older children,
cooking, doing duties for the village,
shouldering the whole family's discontents and
desires,
with no more than a handful of coarse food
and six hours' sleep nightly all the year round.
They also clear a bamboo grove
and make an acre of farmland
in exchange for eight yen's worth of fertilizer.
In this area
if they sow two bushels of buckwheat they harvest
four.
It makes me wonder:
Aren't these people
comparable to those modern heroes—
the many revolutionaries chained in prisons
or the many artists starved by their luck?

Again, in the final lines a broad perspective of time and history forms the background for the comparison of peasant women to reformers and artists from a standpoint that transcends current, imperfect human reality. Yet the dominant emotion is admiration for those women courageously battling against adverse natural and human circumstances. They are farming in northeastern Japan, where neither the climate nor the soil is favorable, and their attempts to raise silkworms on mulberry leaves, or to cultivate rice in the paddies, all too often end in disaster because of circumstances beyond their control. Their fields have such poor soil that only the sturdiest of weeds, horsetail and mugwort, can grow, yet they are too poor to afford much fertilizer. Still they keep working hard to improve their farms and to change their lives by even a tiny bit. For them, it does not matter whether the world is changing for the better or for the worse; they try to make a positive contribution in a small way. In that sense they can be compared to revolutionaries who endeavor to reform society and to artists who envision a model of truth and beauty for a future world.

Here Kenji's concept of poetry merges with agrarianism. For him, ideal poetry unifies theory and practice, dream and reality, the imaginative capacity to conceive an ideal and the physical energy to work toward it: a farmer is an artist, and an artist should be a farmer. His **"Agrarian Art"** begins:

We are all farmers, with a rigorous schedule and exhausting work.
We seek the way to a more radiant, vital life.
Among our forefathers there were some who did so.
Scientists' proofs, mendicants' tests, and our intuitions all form a common base for our discussion.
No one person can attain happiness until the entire world does.
Self-awareness evolves in stages: first the individual, then the community, and then the society and the universe.
Isn't this the way the ancient sages trod and preached?
The new age points toward a world with a single consciousness, a single living thing.
To live a righteous and sturdy life we must become aware of, and respond to, the galaxy within us.
Let us seek happiness for the world. Such seeking is itself the way.

Here is Kenji's ultimate poetic, which has been absorbed into something larger than poetics. Natural science, which provides objective proof, religion, which provides human test cases, and poetry, which provides intuitive insight, are brought together to contribute to progress at personal, global, and cosmic levels. Kenji's poetic gains its identity by losing it.

ALL POEMS ARE TENTATIVE

To the north of the city of Morioka in northeastern Japan is a plain known as Ippongi. One fine day Kenji walked across it, and the experience resulted in this poem:

"Ippongi Plain"

Suddenly the pine grove brightens
and opens a field before me, showing
an endless expanse of dead grass aflame in the sun
and a row of hydro poles, with white insulators, gently
extending almost as far as the city of Bering.
The sky of clear ocean blue
and cleansed human wishes—
Larches regain their youth
and I hallucinate the call of a transparent lark.
Green Nanashigure Hills
rise and fall in my mental landscape too.
A cluster of willow trees
are the willows along the Volga.
Hiding in the heavenly malachite bowl,
clay-colored Yakushi Peak points harsh and sharp.
Snow in the crater contours its wrinkles
and Kurakake's sensitive ridges
let nebulae rise toward the blue sky.
(Say, Oak,
is your nickname really
Mountain Tobacco Tree?)
What a blessing
to stroll for half a day
on the grass, under such a bright canopy!
To obtain it, I would be willing to be crucified.
Isn't it like a rendezvous?
(Say, Mountain Tobacco Tree,
if you keep doing that awkward dance
you may be mistaken for a futurist.)
I am the beloved of the woods and fields.
When I make my way through the reeds
green messages, coyly folded,
slip into my pockets.
When I walk in a shady forest
crescent-shaped lipmarks
cover my elbows and trousers.

The poem reveals an early stage of the verse-writing process as conceived by Kenji, even though its persona cannot, of course, be considered identical with Kenji himself. It begins in a sudden brightening, as a landscape unexpectedly appears beyond the dark woods. The poet emerges and surveys the scene, and as he does so ordinary external reality, such as the line of hydro poles, begins to be transformed in his act of perceiving it. This transformation becomes in effect hallucination, visual and aural, for the city of Bering is imaginary and not even the lark's invisible call, let alone its body, is actually transparent. As his physical eyes sight the Nanashigure Hills in the north of Ippongi Plain, the eyes of his imagination glimpse Siberian hills that he has never seen.

In the second half of the poem, he communicates with trees and plants. Using human language, he addresses an oak tree, which happens to be shaped like an object in a futurist painting. Nature seems to respond to him, too: reeds slip their messages into his pockets as he passes, and trees, helped by the sun, print their kisses on his clothes. As he perceives the things around him, he at once transforms and communes with them: in the act of seeing the shadows of pine needles as the marks of lips or the blades of reeds as messages, he shares with these fellow beings, both in their eternal flux and in a cosmic awareness, the ecstasy of a fine day.

For Kenji, then, the first step in verse writing is to submerge oneself in one's surroundings, particularly natural surroundings. "Communicate with the wind, and obtain energy from the clouds" was his advice to would-be agrarian poets. He seems to have thought that such oneness must be attained on a preconscious level, presumably because the conscious mind makes distinctions between different objects. "Unless it flows out of the subconscious," he said, "what you have is frequently powerless or false." The young poet Surdatta in **"The Dragon and the Poet,"** who sings out the song of the wind, the clouds, and the waves, conceives the song in his sleep and does not himself know how he arrived at it; he has communed with all things while unconscious. A similar experience is told by the narrator of **"The First Deer Dance"**:

> Then, from between the bright, frizzled clouds in the western sky, the evening sun shed its crimson rays aslant on the moss-covered plain, making plumes of pampas grass waver like white flames. Exhausted, I fell asleep there. Then the rustling wind gradually began to sound like human words,

eventually telling me about the true spirit of the deer dance, which is still performed in the Kitakami mountains and plains.

In Kenji's view, a storyteller, like a poet, is a medium: he does not speak his own thoughts, but allows the cosmic mind to speak through him.

However, the poet must immediately record his visions in words; otherwise his memory of the experience will fade away. Kenji habitually kept a notebook with him, whether at home or outdoors, in which he jotted down whatever came to mind. Some of his notebooks have been preserved, and they give clues to the second stage in his creative process.

We have, for instance, a notebook with a black leather cover that Kenji used around 1928. He wrote down all kinds of things in it: names, dates, a study schedule, mathematical formulas, and letters of the English alphabet. On two of its pages he scrawled in a hurried hand:

already
I am a feverish
  forlorn salt lake
along the shore
  many miles of
   jet-black
lepidodendron
  groves extend
must I
  until the reptiles
change into birds
  keep
   oozing up?

Without other evidence, there is no way of knowing the exact circumstances that prompted Kenji to scribble these words. The contents of the note suggest that while lying sick with fever he had a dream or vision in which he became a salt lake in prehistoric times. Immediately afterwards, he jotted down these fragmentary words.

Kenji seems to have wanted to polish his wording almost as soon as he had finished initially setting it down. Using the same pencil, he erased the word "already" and changed "I am" to "I have turned into." Then, some time later, he copied the jotting in another notebook, making revisions as he did so. There it reads:

Now my chest
has turned into a feverish, forlorn salt lake.
Along the shore, miles and miles of
jet-black lepidodendron groves extend.
And I wonder: Must I
until the reptiles change into birds
keep lying like this?

After copying this version, Kenji inserted the word "still" between "lying" and "like this" in the last line.

The third draft is written on a sheet of manuscript paper, and the handwriting is much neater, although the poem still shows the traces of revision:

Now my chest
is a feverish, forlorn salt lake
on whose shore, for full five hundred miles,
a jet-black lepidodendron grove extends
and I wonder—must I
until the reptiles change into some birdlike form
keep lying
still?

Kenji apparently intended to publish this version. He placed the manuscript among other poems he wrote around this time, inserted them all into a binder, and put on the cover a label reading "During an Illness," a collective title for all the poems.

The first of these three drafts is like a personal note, syntactically looser and semantically more vague than the other two. The second version tries to focus the images more sharply. Thus "already I am" is revised to "my chest has turned," and "oozing up" is changed to "lying like this" and then to "lying still like this." The third draft continues the process. The vague "miles and miles" turns into a more precise phrase, "five hundred miles"; the personal "lying like this" is transformed into "lying still," explaining to the reader what "like this" means. The changes of "has turned" to "is" and of "birds" to "some birdlike form" are probably intended to emphasize the slowness of evolutionary time. "Is" expresses the length of time the poet experiences that state, for the change is so slow he does not experience it as change; "some birdlike form" emphasizes the many stages of evolutionary development—the reptiles turn, not to birds, but to some lower form gradually developing toward a bird. The third version expresses the poet's original experience in a way that is easier for the reader to understand.

In another example of Kenji's verse-writing process, the initial note is even more fragmentary:

child eating a melon while walking
          sun resides on the castle field
                    bird
mother gathers plumes of pampas grass
  pine grove

The note, scrawled in light pencil on a page of a notebook, gives the date as August 1918. Other evidence shows that at this time Kenji was working as an assistant to a professor at a local agricultural school who had been commissioned by the county government to do soil research on farms in the area. When he made the note, Kenji was probably on a field trip to a farm. Having poetic inspiration but no time to compose a poem, he jotted down the essence of his impressions in his notebook.

Some time later he drafted a poem from the jotting. The earliest surviving version is written in pencil on a sheet of manuscript paper:

Over a manifold pine grove
a flock of birds swiftly passes,
and off the mountains in the clear wind

white clouds of autumn coil.

The child with a black snow-skirt
eats a melon,
and the mother, gathering red plumes
of pampas grass, walks across the field.

It seems that Kenji, on completing this draft, crossed out the initial note in red ink. He crossed out this first draft, too, when he came up with a new version. The second draft is written on the back of the paper on which the first appears:

A child with a black snow-skirt
eats a melon, walking:
off the mountains in the clear wind
white clouds of autumn coil.

Doesn't she want a melon herself?
The young mother of the child,
absorbed in gathering red plumes
of pampas grass, comes across the field.

Kenji further revised the poem and eventually published it in a local women's magazine on November 15, 1932. The published version was entitled **"Mother."** It retained the first stanza intact, but changed the second to:

Doesn't she want a melon herself?
The mother, still young in age,
amuses herself by gathering red plumes
of pampas grass as she crosses the field.

Apparently the poem was a favorite of Kenji's, for he placed it at the very beginning of ***One Hundred Poems in Classical Japanese,*** a poetry anthology he compiled in August 1933. The version in the anthology is virtually the same as that published in the magazine.

The three drafts of the poem **"Mother"** reveal something of Kenji's art in polishing a poem. One can gather from the initial note, fragmentary as it is, that the core of the poet's experience was contemplation of a scene: a child eating a melon and a young mother plucking pampas plumes in a wide expanse of landscape that included the sun, a field, birds, and a pine grove. The first draft tries to capture the communion with the scene the poet seems to have felt, but it is not successful because there is too wide a gap between the two stanzas. The first stanza is merely a landscape sketch, with no suggestion of correspondence between man and nature. The second draft corrects the situation by placing a child in the center of the landscape: both the child's snow-skirt and the coiling clouds anticipate the coming winter. The new second stanza is linked more closely with the first through its revised first line, which makes the mother similar to the child by implying that she might want a melon, too. We cannot tell whether she does or not, however, for she is "absorbed," caught up in communion with another aspect of the landscape. In the third draft, Kenji chose to emphasize the new link by making the mother still more childlike. He revised the stanza's second line to place stronger emphasis on her youthfulness and changed "absorbed" to "amuses herself"—her action in picking the plumes becomes like a child's play. This final version presents a happy vision of the two walking across the autumn field, their gaiety and self-absorption dispelling any hint of melancholy in the signs of coming cold.

The second stage in Kenji's creative process, as illustrated in these two examples, may not seem significantly different from what other poets do at a similar stage in their verse writing: he attempted to clarify his initial inspiration and to communicate it more fully. Kenji was different, however, in that for him there was no such thing as a finished poem. His clearest statement of this point appears on the cover of ***One Hundred Poems in Classical Japanese,*** where he wrote, "I regard the current revision as the definitive version at that particular time." The statement is dated August 22, 1933, just one month before his death. Kenji undoubtedly knew he was dying, and he did not know how much more time he had to revise the poems intended for the anthology. That did not bother him, however, because he considered each poem's current version to be the final draft *at that time,* and he wanted to convey this belief to his family and to others who would take care of the manuscripts after his death. Indeed, many of his manuscripts show the marks of continual revision up to his final days.

The belief that no poem is ever final can be seen at work in ***Spring and Asura,*** too. Kenji personally oversaw this anthology's publication, occasionally even helping the publisher with details of printing. When the book appeared he was quite pleased with it and gave copies to a number of his friends and acquaintances. Yet he went on revising the poems after publication, just as he had before it. In at least three surviving copies of ***Spring and Asura,*** Kenji wrote down post-publication revisions. The first copy includes some three hundred amendments; the second, approximately ninety; and the third, ten. To be sure, many poets want to revise poems after publication, but how many would take the trouble to revise an anthology in four hundred places if they had no plans to publish a second edition? Kenji thought the poems printed in ***Spring and Asura*** were merely "the definitive version at that particular time," the time of publication. They continued to metamorphose after publication, just as they had before it.

Kenji's unique conception of the creative process is related to his idea that art is four-dimensional. In his view, art has to be fluid, for human life—and the life of everything else—flows along the axis of time. A poem has to move along that axis, too, even after it is printed, and even after its author is dead. The verse-writing process has to be open-ended because the poem itself exists in time and people "rewrite" it whenever they read it. Toward the end of **"Agrarian Art"** Kenji declared, "An eternal incompletion is itself a completion." That idea applies to the creative process, too.

WE CREATE NEW BEAUTY

In **"Agrarian Art,"** Kenji made some strong statements about aesthetic beauty. Deploring the corruption of art and religion in modern times, he said:

> Nowadays, men of religion and art monopolize the sale of truth, goodness, and beauty.
>
> We cannot afford these, nor do we need them.
>
> Now we must start along a new, authentic path and create beauty of our own.
>
> Of course, agrarian art will have beauty as its essence, too.
>
> We create new beauty. Aesthetics keeps moving on.
>
> It will expand boundlessly until the very word "beauty" perishes.

These statements indicate that Kenji was dissatisfied with the aesthetic effects created by contemporary works of art. No doubt he saw these works as becoming progressively isolated from the lives of ordinary people; yet their creators claimed truth, goodness, and beauty as their own elite and exclusive property. He had no use for such art or for the rarefied productions of a modernist avant-garde. Instead, his goal was to infuse life and art with a single spiritual awareness—a single understanding, acceptance, and grateful fulfillment of man's place in the universe. In life, this would take the form of a simple and selfless dedication to one's work and one's fellow human beings; in art, it would take the form of a new beauty, whose connection with life would grow until finally the two would become indistinguishable, and the very concept of beauty as a separate phenomenon would disappear.

Kenji seems to have had ideas about the new kind of beauty he wanted agrarian art to create, but he had not formulated them well enough to commit them to writing. Apparently he discussed the subject publicly around the time he wrote **"Agrarian Art."** One of his comments was recorded by a young man who in February 1926 heard Kenji give a lecture entitled **"Agrarian Art: An Introduction."** According to him, Kenji wrote the main points of the lecture on the blackboard but discouraged the audience from copying them down, saying that his thoughts had not yet been finalized. Of aesthetic effects, he wrote, "Features of poetry in the new age: it must be sound (hope, determination to progress, resistance to corruption, emphasis on being social and productive)." The comment, fragmentary though it is, points toward Kenji's concept of the "new beauty" he urged his fellow agrarians to create in the years to come. In a word, the new beauty yields the impression of being "sound," and its ingredients are aspiration, will to progress, hatred of wrongdoing, and a positive contribution to society. The connotations of these terms become clearer in the context of Kenji's other comments and his poems touching on the subject.

It is easy to see that a poem expressing hope produces a sound, healthy impression. Contemporary Japanese free verse, dominated by a school of which Hagiwara Sakutaro was a leader, must have seemed misguided to Kenji, as it frequently embodied aspects of modern pessimism. Kenji would have no part of this. He chose to believe in a cosmic will that would eventually direct all living things to true happiness, and he felt verse composed by a poet of the new age should reflect that optimism. Indeed, when Kenji was asked where such a poet should start, he answered, "First of all, hold a great hope for the world."

Kenji's poem **"Snow on Kurakake"** embodies such hope:

> All I can depend on
> is the snow draping Kurakake.
> Since the fields and the woods
> are either fuzzy or dusky,
> though it is a snowdrift
> as blurry as yeast,
> I hang my last faint hope
> on the snow covering Mount Kurakake.
> (An old-fashioned faith)

Kurakake is a high mountain located near Kenji's hometown, but it was also part of his mental landscape. As Kenji looked around, people looked "fuzzy" or "dusky," with pallid faces and a gloomy appearance. He could see no ideology, religion, or art in contemporary Japan that promised salvation; the only encouraging sight was a mountain towering in the distance, capped with pure, white snow. The mountain was remote, but he could hang his hope on nothing else. Such a state of mind seemed to him to be the kind of faith cherished by people of older times, when religion was a more important part of life. The poem, despite its largely dark imagery, does leave a positive, wholesome impression because of the poet's refusal to lose hope in a hopeless world.

The second ingredient of soundness, "determination to progress," can be considered an extension of hope or a restatement of it in more practical terms. It is not enough to stand by and hope; one must work actively to realize one's aspirations. As we have seen, Kenji urged his readers, "We seek the way to a more radiant, vital life" and "Let us seek happiness for the world." Elsewhere in **"Agrarian Art"** he called out to his fellow farmers, "Oh, friends, let us join our righteous forces together and transform all our farms and all our lives into a magnificent, four-dimensional art." Of course, in Kenji's view determination to progress should not be an individual assertion but part of the cosmic will. Yet as he realized later in life, one cannot identify oneself with that will without making an effort to do so.

Many of Kenji's literary works embody such a determination. One of his finest stories for children, **"A Biogra-**

phy of Guskobudori," is a good example, as it traces the life of a man who devoted his life to helping others. Also belonging to this category are some of the finest poems of his later period, such as **"Rice-Farming Episode"** and **"The Gentle Breeze Fills the Valley."** Here I will cite **"To My Students,"** a poem drafted in 1926 or 1927, when Kenji had just resigned from a teaching position at Hanamaki School of Agriculture.

> Dear students:
> When the dark blue horizon swells upward
> do you feel like submerging yourselves in it?
> You must become the many-shaped
> mountains on the horizon.
>
> Don't you feel this
> transparent clean wind
> coming from your wondrous new world?
>
> With a black flower called *sakinohaka*
> a revolution will soon be here.
> It is a ray of light sent to us,
> a southerly wind already decided on.
>
> Do you want to endure a slave's life
> and keep serving an age that leads you by force?
> No, you must create a new, stalwart age.
> The universe is ceaselessly changed by us.
> You must go a step further
> than using up all the energies of nature
> like the tide and the wind;
> you must try to form a new nature.
>
> Copernicus of the new age:
> set this galaxy free
> from the oppressive law of gravity.
>
> Marx of the new age:
> reform this world that moves on blind impulse
> and give it a splendid, beautiful system.
>
> Darwin of the new age:
> board the *Challenger* of Oriental meditation
> and reach the space beyond the galaxy.
> From there, send us a purer, deeper, more accurate
> geology and a revised biology.
>
> All that labor on the farm
> performed as if driven by an impulse:
> through a cool and transparent analysis
> elevate it, together with
> its dark blue shadow,
> to the level of dance.
>
> New poets:
> obtain new, transparent energy
> from the clouds, from the light, from the storms
> and suggest to man and the universe the shapes
> they are to take.

In bidding farewell to his students, Kenji described in lucid terms what he wanted them to do in the coming years. Underlying the poem is his optimistic view of cosmic progress, but he also urged his students to work actively to create a better age. "The universe," he declared, "is ceaselessly changed by us." The piece is filled with his confidence in human capabilities, and as a result it produces the kind of positive, vigorous impression he wanted from a poem.

Now it is easy to understand why "resistance to corruption" was the third ingredient of poetic beauty as conceived by Kenji. "Corruption" probably included all the political, social, and moral evils that seemed to him to obstruct the progress of mankind. He wanted poetry to criticize those evils. "Religion, after tiring itself out, has been replaced by modern science, but science is cold and dark," he said. "Art, having gone away from us, has degraded itself." In his view, contemporary religion and art had lost the critical spirit they should have. He wanted poetry, his type of poetry, never to follow suit.

Resistance to corruption is more directly manifest in Kenji's stories for children than in his poetry. For example, **"Oppel and the Elephant,"** describing how an agricultural entrepreneur takes advantage of a gentle elephant, attacks the capitalist exploitation of labor; **"The Spider, the Slug, and the Raccoon,"** which recounts the destinies of three graduates from a school in the woods, criticizes modern laissez-faire society and its educational philosophy; and **"The Restaurant of Many Orders,"** in which two game hunters from the city narrowly escape being served up at a dinner table in a wildcat's restaurant, satirizes the aggressive, warlike civilization of modern industrialized countries. Kenji did not write such overtly satirical works in verse; yet, as we have seen, such poems as **"Politicians"** do contain elements of social satire.

Another example embodying social criticism is the following untitled poem, of which I will cite only the opening section:

> Two or three more times
> I must glare at Kosuke.
> In the shrill wind blowing off the mountain snow
> he ordered all the villagers to come out
> and had them cut cedars, chestnut trees, and
> whatnot
> to erect two poles amid the willows on the canal's
> edge
> and three more along a cliff shaded by the
> grove—
> those unneeded hydro poles
> for unneeded electric light.
> Now, to thank the electricians
> he says we'll have a celebration.
> He says we'll drink in the grove;
> he says all the dignitaries are invited;
> he says I'm one of them too.
> What! I'm not like you.
> Rambling about in a group all day,
> you say this hole isn't deep enough or that pole
> looks slanted
> as if you were performing an important service
> when in fact you are just loafing.
> I'm not one of you.

The poem so far is a fierce invective against Kosuke, a representative of an electric company, and against the kind of civilization he stands for. In the rest of the poem, however, the attack is blunted as the poet becomes more reflective and thinks of his own imperfections. In general, Kenji seems to have been too self-conscious and too gentle-natured to write bitingly satirical poems. His spirit of criticism was more constructive than destructive.

Indeed, being constructive was the fourth element of sound, wholesome poetry as envisioned by Kenji. His term for it was "emphasis on being social and productive." In the same lecture he referred to "true poetry," saying, "It must be the prime energy for production, capable of helping one to recover one's strength and complete one's labor." **"Agrarian Art"** contains such statements as "Set your gray labor aflame by means of art" and "It [agrarian art] always affirms actual life and tries to heighten or deepen it." There he also said, "No one person can attain happiness until the entire world does." Evidently Kenji believed that all people, including poets, should be directly concerned with the welfare of society and should work constructively to improve it. In his view, therefore, poetry should inspire all workers toward the aim of ultimately bringing about an ideal society. In other words, sound poetry should concern itself with social issues and should incite its readers to productive action.

At this point Kenji's poetic seems to approach that of socialism. Indeed, **"To My Students"** includes lines suggesting his belief in a coming revolution. **"Oppel and the Elephant"** also appears to support a proletarian revolution, and in another of his stories, **"The Polano Plaza,"** some laborers who have been exploited by a shrewd capitalist finally succeed in setting up a cooperative factory of their own. However, in the context of all his writings such works are in the minority. As Kenji himself wrote in a letter, "Our age must as a matter of course move toward proletarian literature, but my writings somehow do not clearly follow that course." His idea of revolution and social reform was too idealistic and dreamy to motivate the kind of social criticism socialist critics would want. On the other hand, that dreamy idealism helped keep his poetry from becoming propaganda.

Examples of poems that try to be social and productive are more abundant in Kenji's later poetry. **"Opus 1063,"** in praise of peasant women, is a good example; another shows Kenji himself as a farmer:

"Clearing the Wild Land (Opus 1017)"

When we at last finished clearing
all the thorn bushes
the sun was shining brightly
and the sky was hollow and dark.
Taichi, Chusaku, and I
felt like dropping on the bamboo grass
and sleeping like logs.
The stream carried nine tons of needles a second;
a large flock of herons flew toward the east.

Taichi and Chusaku are typical names of farmers, and the poem portrays Kenji toiling side by side with them and sharing their hard work and fatigue. The sturdy thorns indicate the poor quality of the soil, as well as the difficulty of clearing it. Yet the three are not discouraged, and by sheer hard work they complete the project. The poem calls to mind one of Kenji's remarks in **"Agrarian Art"**: "We are all farmers," he said, "with a rigorous schedule and exhausting work."

One of the most famous poems in modern Japan, written by Kenji, falls into the same category. It is untitled and was written only 22 months before his death:

Neither rain
nor wind
nor snow nor summer's heat
will affect his robust body.
Free of anger
and desire
he will always keep a calm smile.
A quart of brown rice, miso
and some vegetables will be his daily food.
In all things
he will not think of himself
but will observe, hear, and understand well
and will not forget.
Living in a small, reed-thatched hut
under pine trees in the field,
he will go to tend
a sick child in the east
or carry a bundle of rice plants
for a tired mother in the west
or try to dispel the fear
of a dying man in the south
or stop a trivial quarrel or lawsuit
of people in the north.
He will shed tears if a drought comes
and trudge disconsolately if the summer is cold.
Called a bum by all
he will be praised by no one
and will bother no one.
I should like to become
such a man.

The poem has attracted a great deal of attention because it is believed to represent the image of an ideal man Kenji held in his last years. Because of its intense idealism and lucid diction, it has been a staple of Japanese textbooks for many years, but of late it has become an object of controversy. The militarist government advocated a similar self-abnegating spirituality in its propaganda during the war years, and this has been the basis for some critics' disparaging remarks. Kenji's ideal man takes too passive an attitude, others say, when he does nothing more than shed tears in a time of drought and trudge disconsolately in a cold summer. Those critics, however, overlook Kenji's basic stand as a man of morality and religion. The reform he had in mind was more religious and moral than political and social, and the social reform he talked of was of a nonviolent nature. He would rather be a bum who was praised by no one than a revolutionary hero who hurt others in the course of attaining a worthy aim. He would do everything within his power to help others, but he knew some things were beyond his control, and when they happened he would grieve with other victims. Whether or not such an attitude is too passive is a matter of opinion; from Kenji's own point of view, the poem's implications are sufficiently "social" and "productive."

The foregoing examples show how various ingredients in Kenji's poetry contribute to a "sound" emotional effect. It must be conceded, however, that many of his poems do not produce such an effect. **"Spring and Asura"** and many of his elegies for his sister, for example, although they are not morbid like many of Hagiwara Sakutaro's poems, show anxiety, irritation, or grief. **"Flower of Karma"** and the untitled poem beginning "Now my chest," both already cited, are cases in point. To quote another example:

> **"Opus 1087"**
>
> What a coward I am!
> Because those rice plants were beaten down by the
> rain at dawn
> I have been working with abandon
> to help drown my woe.
> Yet again
> the black death
> floats up in the west.
> Last spring,
> wasn't that radiant love itself?

This is a poem not of hope but of lost hope. The poet, an expert in soil conditioning, had advised farmers on fertilizing farms in the spring and had been delighted to see the rice plants growing well. Then a rainstorm came one morning in late August, beating down all the plants and ruining any hope for a good harvest. The poem implies no determination to progress, no resistance to corruption, no positive desire to make a contribution to society; its total impact is far from what one might call "sound." Its implications of frustration, worry, and self-doubt reveal the other extreme of Kenji's poetry.

In talking about the nature of poetry, however, Kenji completely ignored this darker side. He preferred to look at what poetry could do, rather than what it was doing for him. Part of the reason for this may be that when he discussed the nature of poetry he was usually addressing someone, whereas when he wrote poetry he wrote it for himself. But his attitude must also be related to his basic mental outlook. He was an idealist, and when he talked about the beauty of poetry he did so in terms of ideals rather than reality.

VARIATIONS ON 7-5

"Poetry is a rhythmical language that spontaneously flows out from the innermost part of the soul. . . . The sound, the melody, the tone, the wording, all come out automatically." According to a student's note, Kenji said something to this effect in one of his lectures. In keeping with his conception of poems as imagery sketches and his idea that the creative process begins with the submersion of self in natural surroundings on a preconscious level, his idea of poetic form seems to have centered on spontaneity: a poet, in touch with the cosmic mind, instinctively and automatically sketches his inner vision. The touchstone of this half-conscious singing out is the rhythmical language in which it occurs: the course of Kenji's poetic development shows that he came to consider a flow of strongly rhythmical language to be the essence of poetic form. Unlike Hagiwara Sakutaro, he seems to have been less concerned with an individualized rhythm and shape for specific poems than with rhythmical language per se. From his initial involvement with experimental tanka through his move to free verse, his prosody remained quite regular, and it grew more so in the course of his career. Thus the form of his poems comes to echo their content: as imagery sketches they portray slices of the infinite continuum of time and space; as variations on 7-5, they are slices of the rhythm echoing throughout all previous Japanese poetry—above all, through popular marches and songs.

Kenji stated explicitly his emphasis on the basically musical nature of poetic language in an apologetic letter written home to his father in 1926 during a three-week stay in Tokyo, where he was indulging his enthusiasm for classical European music by taking daily organ lessons. "You may wonder," he wrote, "why I have to pain myself unnecessarily to learn music. But I need it badly, as it is a foundation for the language of literature, especially of poetry and children's drama." The link between poetry and children's drama may indicate that he was thinking primarily of rhythm, since in the East as in the West, children's literature tends to be marked by a strongly rhythmical quality.

There was room for individual variation in the poetic rhythm, however, as his story **"The Dragon and the Poet"** makes clear. The young poet Surdatta, now knowing how he composed his contest-winning song, is tormented by the suspicion that he may have unconsciously stolen it from a wise old dragon. He remembers that when the song came to him in his sleep he was on a headland where the dragon lived. But the dragon, when hearing Surdatta's misgivings, reassures the young poet:

> Surdatta, that song is yours as well as mine. . . . At that time I was the cloud and the wind. And you were the cloud and the wind, too. The poet Alta would probably have sung the same song if he had meditated then. But, Surdatta, Alta's language would have been different from yours, and yours from mine. The same thing can probably be said about rhythm, too. For this reason that song is yours, and it is also ours to the extent that it belongs to our spirit that controls the clouds and the wind.

Here Kenji implies that the spirit moving all poets is the same, but that it takes different forms when different poets verbalize it. Each poet has his own individuality, which colors sound, melody, tone, and wording, resulting in a mode of expression uniquely his own.

Kenji began his career as a poet by writing tanka, and he used that form almost exclusively until he was 24 years old. He was a prolific tanka poet: a collection of tanka he himself compiled contains more than eight hundred poems. In choosing the 31-syllable form, he may have been influenced by the examples of Yosano Akiko and Ishikawa Takuboku. Many middle-school students who aspired to literary fame in those days wrote tanka; even Hagiwara Sakutaro wrote in that form as a secondary school student. For the young Kenji, Takuboku's influence must have been particularly great. Takuboku had been born near Kenji's hometown, had attended the same secondary school, and had published poems and essays in local newspapers. It must be more than coincidence that Kenji began writing tanka seriously in January 1911, several weeks after the publication of *A Handful of Sand.* "Various Kinds of Poetry," Takuboku's essay eloquently advocating the merits of tanka—his kind of tanka—had been published at about the same time. No explicit proof of Kenji's indebtedness to Takuboku has been preserved, but in theme, imagery, diction, and style his tanka have a good deal in common with those in *A Handful of Sand.* The most convincing evidence of direct influence is that he consciously manipulated the length of lines and their appearance on the page, as did Takuboku. In practice Takuboku wrote only three-line tanka, but Kenji used two-, three-, four-, and five-line forms, following closer in fact to what the older poet preached in theory.

A couple of Kenji's tanka will illustrate Takuboku's influence. The first was written in 1914, the year Kenji graduated from middle school and began to help in his father's pawnshop on a full-time basis. His nose was operated on for ozena in the spring, and the resulting complications kept him in the hospital for more than a month.

> My friends'
> matriculation tests must be soon.
> Having been ill, I dig up
> a small lily.

Compare this with a poem from *A Handful of Sand*:

> The day when all my friends seem superior to me,
> I bring home a flower
> and cherish my wife.

Both tanka portray a young man comparing himself with his friends and suffering from an inferiority complex; in an effort to overcome his feelings, he pays attention to a flower, something outside of competitive human society. The two poems use similar themes, materials, and images, except that the bachelor Kenji could not refer to a wife. Also, both verses look like fragments of a diary, recording the poet's emotion of the moment. Of course, Kenji also utilized the multi-line form characteristic of Takuboku's tanka.

As another example, here is a tanka Kenji composed in 1915:

> Dokugamori Woods,
> Mount Nansho, and the rest of the range
> suddenly leap up and hang over my forehead.

This can be traced back to another poem in *A Handful of Sand*:

> I think of an October morning
> when Mount Iwate's
> first snow closed in over my eyebrows.

Although Takuboku's tanka records a recollection rather than an immediate experience, the center of interest in both poems is a colossal mountain towering above the poet, who for an instant feels both awe and a sense of purification. Again, both poems use the multi-line form.

Other tanka by Kenji also suggest his indebtedness to Takuboku. Indeed, many resemble the older poet's not only in form but also in that they record the emotions the poet experienced from day to day, in sharp contrast to most contemporary tanka, which copied nature in the way advocated by Shiki. Kenji even grouped poems by date of composition when he compiled his tanka anthology, so that the collection looks almost like a diary. Thus Takuboku's theory that poetry should be a diary, that it should record the poet's thoughts of the moment in the fragmentary way they come to mind, may have laid the foundation for Kenji's own later theory of imagery sketches.

In 1921, at the age of 24, Kenji almost completely stopped writing tanka and then slowly began to write free verse. The fact that his later tanka include many rensaku, or sequential compositions, may evince an increasingly urgent need for a verse form longer than 31 syllables. A rensaku collectively entitled **"Andersen's Swan,"** for instance, is a sequence of ten tanka, but because each tanka has a varying number of lines—from two to five—it looks more like a free-verse poem consisting of ten stanzas. Its first tanka especially, which contains five lines of three, two, seven, five, and fourteen syllables, does not look like a tanka at all. From this type of tanka to free verse, the distance is very short. In a sense, Kenji's shift from tanka to free verse had already been determined when he began to emulate Takuboku by allowing the needs of each poem to dictate its line divisions.

On the other hand, Kenji seems to have carried the rhythm of traditional poetry into his free verse, and the 7-5 pattern is basic to a considerable number of his "imagery sketches." For instance, the line-by-line syllabic scheme of **"Clearing the Wild Land,"** a nine-line poem cited earlier, is:

> 7
> 7-7
> 7-5
> 7-5
> 7-5
> 7-5
> 8-7
> 7-5-9
> 7-7

The basic rhythm of seven and five syllables is so distinct that one is tempted to view the poem as several tanka glued together or as a variation on rensaku. Likewise, the 52 lines that constitute **"Spring and Asura"** include sixteen 7-5 lines (and variations), eighteen 5-7 lines (and variations), and seven 7-7 lines. **"Green Blades of Spears,"** another poem in ***Spring and Asura,*** presents an extreme case: it is neatly divided into seven parts by a one-line refrain, each part consisting of four lines with the syllabic scheme:

7-7
7-5
7-7
7-5

The rhythmic pattern is so regular that one feels hesitant to call it free verse. Most of Kenji's imagery sketches show the 7-5 scheme less markedly than do these examples, but many of them have one or two 7-5 lines or variations at a crucial spot in the poem, thereby providing a rhythmic undercurrent for the entire piece.

Kenji's predilection for the 7-5 syllabic pattern links his work to the rhythm of the traditional Japanese song, utilized in popular Buddhist hymns as well as in folk songs and songs for children. One of the strongest popular uses of this rhythm is in marching songs. When Kenji himself wrote a marching song in a story called **"Hydro Poles on a Moonlit Night,"** he used the 7-5 pattern for its basic rhythm; he did the same when he wrote a school song for Hanamaki School of Agriculture, clearly keeping in mind that the song would be used to accompany students' marches. Being the basic rhythm of a march, the 7-5 pattern conveys a sense of progress, comradeship, and exaltation; Kenji, who wanted his poetry to produce a "sound" impression, may have exploited this effect in his free-verse poems. Perhaps he hoped that the march rhythm would help a poem move forward in time and space, as it were. The rhythm can be used for laborers' processions, too, and its popular valence can make it seem a "workers' rhythm."

Kenji would have denied consciously using a syllabic scheme, however, for he believed that the language of poetry was spontaneous. He would have insisted that the language of his free verse automatically had the basic 7-5 rhythm. For him, that was probably true: the rhythm sometimes flowed out even when he wrote prose, as in some sections of such stories as **"Tales of Zashiki Bokko"** and **"General Son Ba-yu and Three Physicians."**

Kenji was sensitive not only to the rhythm of a poem but also to the aural effect of the individual words used in it, and he made some interesting remarks on the subject. According to a student of his, for instance, he once said in a lecture that a poem loaded with consonants sounds rough. In the same lecture he arranged the five vowels of the Japanese language according to degree of tonal brightness: the order was, from the brightest to the darkest, "a," "i," "o," "e," and "u." On another occasion, when he offered critical comments on a children's story written by a friend, he observed that Rirura, a name given to one of its characters, sounded too smooth to fit the ill-natured character of the child. His suggestion was to change one of the three "r"s to either "m," "s," or "h." In his own story **"Windflowers,"** the narrator observes that *okinagusa,* the usual Japanese word for a windflower, does not have aural qualities that suggest the gentle, youthful beauty of the flower; he prefers its alternate name, *uzunoshuge,* whose tonal qualities suggest to him the black petals, pale green leaves, and gleaming pappi of a windflower. In yet another revealing example, an idyllic poem called **"A Picture of Flowers and Birds: July,"** Kenji presents a young man and his sister standing on the edge of a river and enjoying the scenery on a summer day. The sister notices a bird that has alighted on a power line and points it out to her brother, who responds:

"Oh, that's a kingfisher.
A kingfisher, you know—the one with crimson
eyes.
Say, Michia, this is another hot day, isn't it?"
"What is Michia, brother?"
"That's his name.
'Mi' refers to the smoothness of his back;
'chi,' to the way his bill is pointed;
and 'a' makes it a pet name."

Here Kenji has coined a name for the kingfisher purely on the basis of the aural effects produced by three syllables. This example, together with the others cited, shows that Kenji's imagery sketches included not only visual images but auditory ones as well.

Kenji's preference shifted from imagery sketches in the colloquial language to shi in classical Japanese as he grew older. Especially in the last five years of his life, largely a period of illness, he liked writing poems in the classical language. There is no doubt that he thought quite seriously about those verses, for he called them shi, and not the modest-sounding imagery sketches. Even as he lay dying, he continued to revise, copy, and compile them into two anthologies entitled ***Fifty Poems in Classical Japanese*** and ***One Hundred Poems in Classical Japanese.*** He died before he had time to finish compiling a third. All in all, the poems he wrote in this form total more than three hundred.

Many of those poems are adaptations of imagery sketches or tanka he had written earlier. It appears that the ailing Kenji, lying in bed, took out old manuscripts and reworked them. One example is a free-verse poem he wrote in July 1926:

"Opus 728"

As the rainshower pours down
a smoke of dust rises.
 In the billowing steam
 I, all alone, am angered at my work.
  Dead leaves of fern,
  wild roses' roots,

and busily scurrying ants
around their collapsed castle.
The cedar trees hang streams of rain
and send faint, white splashes.

Kenji crossed out this poem, presumably when he made the first draft of a shi some time later on the margin of the manuscript. He then copied the final draft on a new sheet of paper:

"Rainshower"

As the rainshower pours down, the tilled ground
sends up a smoke of dust.

In the lukewarm steam a person stands,
his figure dark with groundless anger.

When wild roses' roots have been washed
and ants scurry around their nest

the cedar trees hang banners of water
and splashes faintly extend.

The most obvious difference between the two poems is in form. **"Rainshower"** is more deliberate and formal, a quality that is even more evident in the original because it is written in classical Japanese. The sense of immediacy present in the language of the earlier poem is all but gone, for better or for worse. It has been replaced by the strong rhythm of a well-regulated prosody: the second poem consists of four stanzas, each with two lines of an identical 7-5 syllable pattern. No wonder Kenji had to change "I" to "a person" in the latter poem, placing greater distance between the poet and the experience depicted. In it, the poet's anger is neatly framed.

"Rainshower" typifies the prosody of Kenji's poetry in classical Japanese. The form he considered standard had four stanzas, each consisting of a couplet, with each line consisting of seven and five syllables. Many pieces in ***Fifty Poems in Classical Japanese*** and ***One Hundred Poems in Classical Japanese*** are written in this form, and the others can be seen as variations on it. Kenji's predilection for this form can also be surmised from a note entitled "A Study of Four-Couplet Poetry in Classical Japanese," apparently an outline for a projected essay with that title:

1. Introduction. The Fixed Verse Form in Classical Japanese. A Poem in Four Couplets. Its History. Imayo. Toson, Yau, Hakushu.
2. Beginning, Development, Change, and Conclusion in a Four-Couplet Poem.
3. Prosody. Composition of a Line.
4. Rhyme.

Sketchy though it is, the note suggests Kenji's idea of his favored verse form in classical Japanese. The sequence of four couplets had precedents in the Japanese poetic tradition, its origin going back to the imayo of the late Heian period. Several modern poets before him had experimented with the form, too. He conceived the poem's structure in terms of the time-honored method of development used in classical Chinese verse, the first couplet constituting a "beginning," the second a "development," the third a "change," and the fourth a "conclusion." He gave no further explanation of prosody or rhyme, but he clearly regarded these as important elements of shi. The reference to rhyme is odd, for Japanese poetry had never utilized that device in its long history. No extant shi by him has a distinct rhyme scheme, either.

Kenji's poems in classical Japanese have usually been ranked lower than his free verse. They have been described as less fresh, less vigorous, and less original, and this has been attributed to the fact that the poet, confined to bed, had no new experience to stimulate his mind, no new images to sketch. However, Kenji's poems in classical Japanese sound more melodious than his imagery sketches. The 7-5 rhythm, which was submerged in his free verse, appears openly and resounds throughout his shi. Perhaps Kenji thought of these works more as songs than as poems. He wanted them to be read less by literary critics than by the general public, for whom free verse was still an import, whereas the 7-5 pattern was easy and familiar. In allowing that strong, popular rhythm, anchored by the four-couplet form, to prevail in his last poems, Kenji was true to his desire to be both a Buddhist poet and an agrarian artist—he was attempting to write poems that would sing out of the minds of ordinary people, as well as out of the cosmic mind of wind and clouds and trees.

ART IN A TURNIP FIELD

Roughly speaking, Kenji's view of the use of poetry evolved in three stages. At first he expected a good deal out of literature, linking it with religion and envisioning much usefulness for it at both personal and social levels. Then he came to admire a farmer's life so highly that art began to seem a luxury. In later years he tried hard to resolve the dichotomy between art and manual labor, as is evident in **"Agrarian Art."** One cannot, however, clearly demarcate the three periods; it is more accurate to say that elements of the three co-existed to varying degrees, on the whole moving in the general direction of a dialectical synthesis of labor and art.

At the personal level, verse writing early functioned as a means of relieving loneliness for Kenji. His early tanka are full of insecurity, uneasiness about the future, self-accusation, unfulfilled desire, causeless anger, gloom, and even despair. Writing poetry seems to have been one of the few, if not the only, means he had to vent those emotions. A tanka he wrote in 1916 is typical:

Steel pen, steel pen,
steel pen: all alone, you
move on the barren moor
of my doubts.

The picture is brighter in **"A Biography of Guskobudori,"** his pseudoautobiography, in which the hero is described as feeling so lonely in childhood that he sings songs and scribbles words on tree trunks in the woods. Yet the idea that poetry relieves loneliness remains. Kenji's most direct statement of it appears in a letter he wrote to a friend in 1932. Referring to his motive for writing poetry, he said, "I have not been writing imagery sketches to please the public. It is all because I could not bear loneliness, because I could not resist my desire to own something beautiful. If a handful of readers were to completely share my feelings and say a few words to me to that effect, that would be about all I hope for."

Although it may sound as though Kenji were writing verse only for himself, significantly he mentions his hope for "a handful of readers" to share his feelings completely. He was not blind to the social functions of poetry, and the preceding quote shows his awareness that poetry can serve as a means of uniting people. In general, he stressed the social functions of poetry more than its personal uses, and we have seen him presenting a particular kind of social function in an early story, **"The Dragon and the Poet,"** in which Surdatta is praised for his ability to envision a model of truth and beauty for tomorrow's world. This story shows the main drift of Kenji's early views on the function of poetry: he saw the poet as a prophet, an architect, a seer—as a moral leader like a man of religion.

From early youth Kenji seems to have seen literature as allied to religion. It is widely assumed that he began writing free verse and juvenile literature seriously in 1921, after a high-ranking Buddhist priest named Takachio Chiyo advised him against entering the priesthood, explaining that in the Hokke sect a believer was expected to try to reach a higher level of faith while following his line of business. The priest further suggested that if Kenji felt gifted as a poet, he should pursue that art until his faith in Buddhism manifested itself in his poems without conscious effort. Kenji seems to have taken the advice to heart. The words "Through Reverend Takachio's advice, creation of literature for the Flower of the Law" are recorded in one of his notebooks, and a letter from the same year declares: "The religion of the future is art. The art of the future is religion."

In what sense can poetry serve as a religion? Kenji's answer would have stressed poetry's ability to widen our perspective. The kind of poetry collected in ***Spring and Asura*** helps a person to transcend the human and merge with the true mind, the single, shared consciousness that is reality. It helps a person know his true self and experience his true place in the scheme of things.

Unfortunately, Kenji could not unwaveringly keep his belief in such a lofty view of poetry. Especially in his later years, he doubted poetry's capabilities more and more. A devaluation of poetry is already evident in a preface he wrote for his unpublished second collection of imagery sketches, entitled *Spring and Asura II.* Toward its end he entreated magazine editors not to press him for more poetry after they read the collection. Explaining why he disliked such solicitations, he said, "Incompetent man though I am, I have a farm to till, and in winter I have to set up an 'office' with jute sacks at various places and advise rice farmers on fertilizing. My head is filled with thoughts about those works, which are somewhat more humble than such declarations as 'Let us march on full stride' or 'Let us make a pledge,' and so on." Although he did not deny the value of poetry, Kenji implied that he personally attached equal or even higher importance to other things that were generally considered lower than poetry in the hierarchy of human activities. Foremost among those other things were farming and helping people to farm. To Kenji, poetry began to look less meaningful because a poet merely promised without making the physical effort to fulfill his promise.

Kenji's misgivings about the capabilities of poetry came to take more direct expression in later years. An extreme case is his poem **"Love and Hate for Poetry,"** an imagery sketch that he published in a magazine in 1933. The poem is about an electrical engineer on a night shift at a hydroelectric plant. As he sleepily watches over the gauges on the master panel, there appears before him a sweet-voiced woman whose body is made of ice and through whose chest show three radiant hearts. The engineer, who apparently has a complex about art, recognizes her as Poetry and strikes up a conversation:

> "Just as I suspected,
> you have three hearts, don't you?"
> As the engineer sadly mutters,
> the beautiful lady, heaving her chest in pride, says
> "How could anyone write a play
> without three or four hearts?"
> That angers the engineer.
> "What is a play anyway?" he asks.
> "Because of your petty education
> and silly vanity
> those children in the field out there
> cannot buy
> little red pants or even a pair of socks.
> At the year's end, the heads of their families
> must go to the market for fish and medicine
> and roam the streets, sighing,
> until the night falls.
> Who is the master artist
> deserving that kind of sacrifice?
> Where is the work of art
> rivaling that kind of sacrifice?
> If what is known as art
> remains an imitation, a fake
> or a place of refuge for incompetents and cowards
> for ever and ever,
> we should smash it to pieces!"

When the engineer realizes that his words have been a bit too violent, it is too late. The shocked lady collapses to the floor and disintegrates, whereupon the engineer's vision vanishes, too.

In **"Love and Hate for Poetry,"** Kenji criticized poetry for ignoring current social conditions, and thus helping to create them. Yet Kenji must have felt a certain affection for his Lady Poetry, since the engineer belatedly regrets having blasted her, and the poem's title includes the word "love" as well as "hate." The later Kenji loved poetry so long as it presented a vision of beauty and truth mankind could seek, but he had to reject it when it did little or nothing to actualize that vision.

Kenji tried hard to resolve the dichotomy between art and life, between vision and reality, in his later years. His endeavor was twofold: on the one hand he attempted to transform real life into art, and on the other he tried to bring art close to the life of workers. In other words, he attempted to bring art and life together by reorienting each toward the other. His attempt to see art in a worker's life has already been glimpsed in **"Opus 1063"** and **"To My Students."** It took even more direct expression in the following poem:

"Third Art"

As I ploughed the field for turnips,
a stocky, gray-haired man
sneaked up behind me
and asked what I planned to sow.
Red turnip seeds, I answered.
The man, saying a turnip field
should be ploughed like this,
quietly stretched out his hand
for my hoe
and drew a curved furrow with it.
Stillness ringing in my head,
I stood there vacantly
as if entranced by a magic potion.
There were the sunshine, the wind,
our two shadows cast on the sand,
and a stream gleaming in the distance.
Yet I was in a trance, wondering
what brushstroke in black ink
or what fragrance of a sculptor's chisel
could ever surpass that furrow.

Here the old farmer is identified as a master artist who uses a hoe for his paintbrush and the earth for his canvas. His art is that of the Third Estate, or "third art." By extending the meaning of art to include the consummate skill of an experienced laborer, Kenji was attempting to unify life and art.

On the other hand, Kenji tried to bring art into laborers' lives, for he felt that too many workers never knew the enjoyment afforded by beautiful things. That feeling is expressed in such poems as this:

"Opus 739"

In the dense fog the hands are freezing.
  The horse's thighs tremble, too.
Toss me the rope. The rope!
  The plumes of pampas grass are loaded with
    frosty dew.
  Would that sunrise be soon!
A pheasant is crowing. A pheasant
appears to be in your house.
  Striding through the vacant house,
    looking for food
    and crying. Isn't that a pheasant?

The poem, written in 1926, depicts farmers working in the field on a chilly autumn morning. On the dusky farm before sunrise, their minds are occupied with work and with their wish for the sun to bring some warmth. Kenji, however, wants them to think of a pheasant, a beautiful bird that symbolizes art. He believed the farmers would get a bit of relief from their hard work if they could divert their minds to things of beauty from time to time.

Kenji's twofold approach to a synthesis of art and life found its definitive expression in **"Agrarian Art."** The title of the essay suggests its purport, a unification of art and farm life; that unification is attained when all artists become farmers who physically till the land and all farmers become artists who are sensitive to the beauty of nature and of their own work. As has been noted, Kenji criticized contemporary artists for monopolizing beauty, an old, unproductive kind of beauty. In the same essay he had this message for artists:

> Look at those long-haired ones sipping coffee,
> their faces vainly waiting for something.
>
> Burn up all your worries and merge with the soul
> of all that exists.
>
> Communicate with the wind, obtain energy from
> the clouds.

And he had this message for farmers:

> Set your gray labor aflame by means of art.
>
> Here is our ceaseless, pure, and happy creation.

He explained, "Labor is something instinctive. It is not always pain. It is always creation. Creation is always a pleasure. When a person sacrifices his humanity and enslaves himself for productivity, it turns into pain." Ultimately, Kenji was trying to restore humanity to art as well as to workers' lives, making it the basis of both. Of course, in his vocabulary "humanity" had unusually large connotations, including the cosmic mind that man shares with all other beings. Agrarian art as conceived by Kenji was based on this kind of humanity; it should enable all men to join together in a common spirituality and a shared work.

Such a view of the use of art is open to criticism when seen against the backdrop of contemporary society. In the first place, Kenji's identification of a higher type of art with agrarian life is too limited in scope, for labor is not limited to farm labor. Life on a farm provides more opportunities for the artist to merge with nature and to receive creative energy from it than does life in a factory. But Japan had already begun transforming herself from an agrarian into an industrial nation, and Kenji appears to have regarded that fact too lightly. Second, he was too optimistic in his expectations for the role of art in agrarian life. He thought art would relieve the hardships of peasant life, but he seems to have overlooked the fact that the main cause of those hardships was the existing social order, which heavily favored landlords. Poetry might bring emotional relief, but it could not cure social inequities. Takuboku eventually found that out, but to the last Kenji does not seem to have felt it of paramount importance.

Be that as it may, Kenji's vision of the use of art remains an attractive ideal. Long after his death Japan has not yet solved the problems that concerned him. Many artists still suffer from a dichotomy between art and life, as evidenced by the life and death of the novelist Mishima Yukio (1925-70). Like Kenji, Mishima in later life came to recognize that art was powerless to improve existing conditions. Earlier he had tried to create the kind of art that would positively contribute to the spiritual well-being of his countrymen, but in the last phase of his career, he seems to have given up hope that art could make an active contribution to social welfare. Other novelists, like Abe Kobo (*b.* 1924), have written extensively about alienation, a prevalent problem in contemporary, urbanized Japan, and have tried to find some way to facilitate meaningful communication between individuals. Kenji's poetry, and his idea of poetry, address these and other problems that are still vital today. His solution requires an idealistic and spiritualistic belief beyond the grasp of many, but his proposal of uniting through art with both the world and one's fellow humans is appealing. And the honesty, sincerity, and intensity with which he made that proposal are exceptional, moving all who read his biography and his writings. He not only conceived a unique view of poetry; he lived it.

J. Thomas Rimer (essay date 1988)

SOURCE: "The Poetry of Miyazawa Kenji (1896-1933)," in *A Reader's Guide to Japanese Literature,* Kodansha International, 1988, pp. 145-47.

[*In the following essay, Rimer examines several poems from* Spring and Asura *that demonstrate Miyazawa's style and personal vision.*]

Matsuo Basho made famous the north country of Japan in his *haiku* journal *The Narrow Road to the Deep North,* in which he characterized the particular poetry of that area, still remote and mysterious for so many Japanese. Miyazawa Kenji (1896-1933), one of the greatest of the modern poets, has through his brilliant and idiosyncratic poetry become the modern gatekeeper to the elusive beauty of the north and to the traditions harbored there, which he evoked through the powerful expressiveness of a self-trained and highly original spirit. Like Basho, Miyazawa seemed throughout his life to be on a quest. A sense of freedom and urgency runs through much of what he wrote. His poetry is at once mystical and earthy.

Miyazawa seemed an unlikely candidate for the literary life. Born in the northern town of Hanamaki in Iwate Prefecture, he studied agriculture with an eye to alleviating the plight of the poor farmers in his area. After a brief stay in Tokyo, where he had gone to further his studies of Nichiren Buddhism, Miyazawa returned to the north country to be present during the final illness of his beloved sister, Toshiko, about whom he wrote some of his most moving poetry. Taking a job at a local agricultural high school, he began to work to improve the lot of the farmers in the region, both in terms of their immediate livelihood and of their broader cultural concerns. Self-denial and overwork, however, led to the poet's early death. Miyazawa was looked on as a kind of saint by the local people, who deeply appreciated what he had done for them during his lifetime. It is doubtful if many would have read or appreciated his poems and touching children's stories, which became widely circulated only after his death.

Spring & Asura (***Haru to shura***) contains most of Miyazawa's major poems and reveals an astonishing depth of religious conviction, conveyed in an often exhilarating exuberance of language. Miyazawa's commitments to Buddhist belief caused him to place the Lotus Sutra, a central scripture in the Chinese and Japanese tradition, at the center of his meditations. The metaphysical underpinnings provided by this great sacred text run like a thread through his sensibility as expressed in his poetry. Miyazawa's images, however, are altogether his own and lend an invigorating freshness to his verse.

> The hard keyura jewels hang straight down.
> Twirling, shining, the creatures keep falling.
>
> Truly, they are the angels' cries of grief,
> clearer than hydrogen—
> haven't you heard them
> sometime, somewhere?
> You must have heard their cries
> stab heaven like icy spears.
> —(trans. Hiroaki Sato)

Even when his poetry is simple and deeply personal, it resonates with the forces of nature.

> The blizzard drives hard
> and this morning, that catastrophic cave-in
> . . . Why do they keep blowing
> the frozen whistle?
> Out of the shadows and the frightening smoke
> a deathly pale man appears, staggering—
> the horrible shadow of myself
> cast from a future of ice.
> —(trans. Hiroaki Sato)

For Miyazawa, knowing and doing must be one in order for man to find his place in nature.

> The new age points toward a world with a single
> consciousness, a single living thing.
> To live a righteous and sturdy life we must
> become aware of, and respond to, the galaxy

within us.
Let us seek happiness for the world. Such seeking
is itself the way.
—(trans. Makoto Ueda)

Even readers who may be resistant to the metaphysics of Miyazawa's personal vision will be moved by the verse he wrote concerning the death of his sister. The poet's fierce affection, his vulnerability to her death, bring him close to the reader, in a kind of awkward embrace.

Toshiko,
now so close to death
you asked for a bowl of clean snow
to brighten me for the rest of my life.
Thank you, my brave sister,
I too will go by the straight way
(Get me some snow, Kenji)
In your delirious fever, panting,
you asked me for the last bowl of snow
that fell from the sky,
the galaxy, the sun, the atmospheric strata
. . . Between two pieces of granite
sleet makes a solitary puddle.
I stand on them, precariously,
keeping the pure, white two-phased balance of
snow and water
and get for my gentle sister her last food
from a glowing pine branch
laden with cold transparent drops.
—(trans. Hiroaki Sato)

Despite the intensity of such moments in his poetry, however, Miyazawa on the whole strikes a powerful note of affirmation, not in terms of his individual ego or his accomplishments as a poet, but rather an affirmation of the healing power of the great forces of Nature to which he found access, and in which, he insisted, we are all, perhaps unwittingly, involved. It may be because the poet's writings can provide the reader with a means of entering Miyazawa's own "deep north" that he has become a sort of cultural hero in Japan. While Miyazawa's poetry is often resistant to quick comprehension, and his juxtapositions of images are often easier to feel than to understand, the totality provides a special species of spiritual clarity, one that is virtually unique.

Geoffrey O'Brien (essay date 1989)

SOURCE: "A Man For All Seasons: Miyazawa Kenji Cultivates His Garden," in *The Village Voice,* Vol. 34, No. 49, December 5, 1989, pp. 75-6.

[*In the following review, O'Brien details the sources, imagery, mood, and themes of Miyazawa's poetry.*]

The Japanese poet Miyazawa Kenji, who died in 1933 at the age of 37, became a culture hero on the strength of a single brief poem written toward the end of his obscure and voluntarily impoverished life. **"November 3rd"**—an unpublished notebook entry probably intended more as a prayer than a poem—sketches a portrait of an idealized ascetic, "neither yielding to rain / nor yielding to wind," "without greed / never getting angry / always smiling quiet- / ly / eating one and a half pints of brown rice / and bean paste and a bit of/ vegetables a day / in everything / not taking oneself / into account," and concludes:

someone
like that
is what I want
to be

Revered as a religious utterance, exploited in the 1940s as a wartime morale booster promoting self-sacrifice, and memorized by every subsequent generation of schoolchildren, **"November 3rd"** remains universally familiar in a way that no poem has been in the West since Kipling's "If" or Kilmer's "Trees." The world it evokes, a world of thatched huts and drought-stricken fields, sickly children and rice farmers with bent backs, might appear anachronistic when set against the Japan of computer graphics and advanced robot technology—unless you take a bus into the mountains and see landscapes and faces lifted in act from a Miyazawa poem.

In his own way Miyazawa came close to realizing the saintly ideal set forth in **"November 3rd."** The son of a pawnbroker in northern Japan's Iwate Prefecture (a backward region afflicted with chronic crop failures), he converted in adolescence to the Nichiren sect of Buddhism. Taking as his guide the *Lotus Sutra,* which teaches the availability of buddhahood for all sentient beings, he dedicated himself to the welfare of the local farmers, becoming a one-man educational and agricultural missionary, encouraging local cultural traditions, teaching crop rotation and soil improvement, and exploring methods of flood and drought prevention. In the meantime, as his translator notes, "he forced himself, unscientifically to subsist on a poorer diet than even the local people were accustomed to, and ruined his health."

Such a career clearly lends itself to hagiography, and it is somewhat ironic that Miyazawa has been claimed in turn by militarists, Buddhists, modernist aesthetes, and most recently (so Gary Snyder tells us) the Japanese Greens. All these claims occurred after the poet was safely dead: for Miyazawa was not the sort of person ever to become a leader or spokesman. He was a strange mix of humility and irascibility, whimsy and anguish, and the self-imposed deprivations of his life contrast mysteriously with the exuberant profusion of his writing. His poems—he wrote several thousand in both traditional and modern forms—range from epigrams to an 800-line free-verse notation of a journey on foot, from comic monologues to metaphysical reveries, from scientifically precise landscapes to fervent devotional outpourings, while his children's stories express sometimes surprisingly violent and tragic themes through a cast of animals, stars, and gods.

The scope and variety of Miyazawa's work is amply displayed in ***A Future of Ice,*** a revised and expanded follow-up to Hiroaki Sato's 1973 translation ***Spring & Asura.*** It forms part of a series of books (most of them, unfortunately, out of print) in which Sato has single-handedly set about making available the work of Japan's leading modern poets. The whole series is admirable, but this is the best of all, a full-scale portrait that clearly establishes Miyazawa as one of the most distinct poetic voices of this century.

He was one of the most private as well. A single self-published collection in 1924 was his only gesture toward making his poetry public, his life was lived apart from literary circles, and he thought of his writing more in religious than in aesthetic terms. This makes the vigorous modernity of his style all the more surprising.

Miyazawa wrote at a time when Japanese poetry, after a millennium or so of being confined to effusions of no more than 33 syllables, was branching out with gusto into vers libres. But much of this work had a borrowed tone, heavy with Parnassian and Symbolist echoes, and imbued with lugubrious self-pity. Miyazawa—for whom self-pity was never a mild emotion, but something closer to self-torture—nevertheless cultivated a bright, sharply defined, often comic diction, hurling incongruous elements together and letting them find their own unexpected unity.

Miyazawa gave the overall title ***Spring & Asura*** to all his poetry in modern forms. An *asura* is a demon, inhabiting one of the six Buddhist realms of existence, and the opposition of restless demon and vegetative landscape makes a fitting ideograph for Miyazawa's poetry, where consciousness erupts into its surroundings and mind does not merely contemplate the world but actively constructs it. Yet mind is also a construct:

> The phenomenon called "I"
> is a blue illumination
> of the hypothesized, organic
> alternating current lamp
> (a compound of all transparent
> ghosts)
> a blue illumination
> of the karmic alternating current
> lamp
> which flickers busily, busily
> with landscapes, with everyone
> yet remains lit with such assuredness
> (the light persists, the lamp lost).

Self, the organizing principle of consciousness, is fragmentary. The "I" of Miyazawa's diaristic voice charts its own disintegration into its compound elements: lava slopes, mineral deposits, parched reeds, foreign scientific terms, Sanskrit mantras, imaginary vistas of China or Italy or Russia, apparitions of Buddhist saints and demons, abstract patterns of line and color. (The expertise with which Miyazawa breaks down the world in his poems ties in curiously with his employment, in the last years of his life, as engineer for a local rock-crushing company.) The wonder is that this disintegration of self leads not into a void but into an ecstatic fullness: "Out of the gray steel of the imagination / akebi vines entwine the spider web, / wildrose bush, humus marsh," begins the title poem **"Spring & Asura,"** one of Miyazawa's most energetic flights:

> At the bottom of the light in April's
> atmospheric strata,
> spitting, gnashing, pacing back and
> forth,
> I am Asura incarnate
> (the landscape sways in my tears) . . .

He is devotional without ever being didactic. Despite the orthodoxy of his religious beliefs, one never gets the feeling that Miyazawa is limiting himself to what he ought to say. On the contrary, there is a nakedness and spontaneity leading to constant surprise. In the poems concerning the death of his sister Toshiko in November 1922—including three written on the day itself—the grief is palpable and unpredictable in its manifestations. The death scene continues to well up in poems written the following year, along with visions of Toshiko assuming other forms: "Two large white birds fly / calling to each other sharply, sorrowfully / in the moist morning sunlight. / They are my sister, / my dead sister." Elsewhere, as the wheels of a train squeak noisily and a moth crawls under a ceiling lamp, he writes: "My feelings are warped with sorrow / and I can't help thinking of her, hidden somewhere."

In the wake of her death Miyazawa's poetry seems to toughen, mournful subjectivity hardening into mineral edge—"The sea is rusted by the morning's carbon dioxide"—and the poet taking a critical tone toward his own spiritual aspirations: "Why do you try to grasp firmly in the human / what is obtainable only in religion? / . . . Come now, wipe your tears, collect yourself. / You must not love in so religious a manner." Feeling, however intense, is not privileged over other levels of experience; it is a vehicle, not an end in itself. Many of Miyazawa's poems begin at a level of keyed-up emotion where someone else's would end, and extend a mood of turmoil in almost leisurely fashion, as if the poet were sufficiently at home in his own anxieties to feel out the space around them and take notes on the view.

His images suggest not so much the contents of his self as what remains after self has been exhausted. The world articulates itself in hard jabbing lines: "The flock of crows is zinc scrap in dilute sulfuric acid." "Pale-blue sap oozes from the severed root." "The gray light avalanched in the distance." In the later poems the world enters more and more, bringing with it a varied population of animals (pigs, snakes, horses, insects) and humans whose doings are chronicled with almost novelistic density. A disheveled landlord, having loaned back the rice he's received as rent, goes off hunting to feed himself: "But when he manages to haul back a bear, / they say, 'He killed the mountain god / so this year's crop is poor.'" A young doctor begins to integrate himself into village life, and Miyazawa suddenly sees him as he will be in a few years: "By the time this doctor finally comes to feel / just as the villagers do . . . / he'll have fallen behind in new techniques / and at the lecture of the county doctor's society / he'll curl up small, a perpetual listener." The hallucinatory center of his poetry is framed by a broad, even humorous picture of the surrounding community. He is not apart from the world, but consciously alone in the midst of it, with all his senses operating.

The human is chiefly evident in the monologues spoken by a series of bureaucratic or academic personae: **"The Landscape Inspector," "Mr. Pamirs the Scholar Takes a Walk," "The Prefectural Engineer's Statement Regarding Clouds."** Even in translation—or at least in translation as accomplished as Hiroaki Sato's—it is possible to gauge the juxtaposition of formulaic, ritually self-deprecating official language and the rugged, unresponsive landscape in whose midst it is spoken. Not surprisingly, the comedy has a bitter aftertaste, most memorably in **"An Opinion Concerning a Proposed National Park Site,"** where the poet suggests turning his volcanic surroundings into a theme park embodying the Buddhist underworld:

> Now, set up a Hell here.
> Make it charming in the Oriental
> fashion.
> Put up a red fence of spears
> with a scattering of dead trees to
> terrify them . . .
> As a finale, blast off real shots
> electrically
> from two field cannons
> hidden this side of the mountain.
> The moment they think, Here we go!
> they'll find themselves in the real
> Styx.

In fact where he is—"this prefecture where there's nothing to eat"—is a lot tougher than Hell: "Over there on the frozen riverbed / a naked baby was found abandoned." The flights of fantastic invention always return to their source. What separates Miyazawa's poetry most strikingly from his modernistic contemporaries in Europe and America is its immersion in actual hunger and actual labor. The imminence of drought or flood and the murderous difficulty of procuring sustenance can be felt in every line.

In the later poems, physical work is the abiding and obsessive theme, not work on behalf of some idealized nation-state or political program but for bare survival. The anguish is no longer metaphysical but practical: "I'm filled with anxieties about the manure / I threw from the horse cart and left on the slope yesterday." He monitors weather and growth as if vigilantly surveying the movements of a potential enemy: "I calculate again and again / the number of days before the delayed rice takes root, / the number of days before bifurcation, and the time when the ears will come out."

The real threat of starvation makes for the force of **"The Breeze Comes Filling the Valley,"** a cry of triumph that, in the face of an anticipated crop failure and despite a violent flood of rain, "because of the slight differences in seedling preparation / and in the use of superphosphate, / all the stalks are up today." The triumph is only temporary, tentative—there will always be another season to worry about—but for the moment Miyazawa allows himself an instant of pure elation:

> I went home late at night.
> But in the end I did not sleep.
> And, look,
> this morning the east, the golden rose, opens,
> the clouds, the beacons, rise one after another,
> the high-voltage wires roar,
> the stagnant fog runs in the distance.
> The rice stalks have risen at last.
> They are living things,
> precision machines.
> All stand erect.
> At their tips, which waited patiently in the rain,
> tiny white flowers glisten
> and above the quiet amber puddles reflecting the
> sun
> red dragonflies glide.

This plenitude—literal, not metaphoric—is after all only another moment of reality, no more privileged than the others that Miyazawa recorded. Yet on the day of his death six years later, this tanka was the last poem he wrote: "Because of an illness, crumbling / this life— / if I could give it for ripening rice / how glad I would be."

Hiroaki Sato (essay date 1998)

SOURCE: Introduction to *A Future of Ice: Poems and Stories of a Japanese Buddhist, Miyazawa Kenji,* North Point Press, 1989.

[*In the following essay, which is a revised version of an introduction originally published in 1989, Sato provides an overview of Miyazawa's life and work.*]

Miyazawa Kenji (1896-1933)—here his and other Japanese names are given the Japanese way, family name first—is probably the only modern Japanese poet who is deified. A good part of the deification may come from a piece called **"November 3rd."** Opening with the phrases

> neither yielding to rain
> nor yielding to wind
> yielding neither to
> snow nor to summer heat

and ending with

> called
> a good-for-nothing
> by everyone
> neither praised
> nor thought a pain
> someone
> like that
> is what I want
> to be

it describes in simple, moving words the poet's wishes to do good for others while remaining humble and obscure himself.

"November 3rd" was found posthumously, written in a pocket notebook Miyazawa is thought to have used beginning in late 1931, two years before his death. Though the text is broken up into lines, considering his approach to versification at the time, it is likely to have been meant more as a prayer than a poem. Yet as early as 1942, the Japanese government, then in the early stage of the Pacific War, used it as a propaganda piece, apparently deciding that it would help inculcate the sacrificial spirit in the general populace. A few years later Tanikawa Tetsuzō, a well-known philosopher and the father of the poet Tanikawa Shuntarō (b. 1931), called it the "noblest" Japanese poem of modern times, while describing the poet as the only man of letters before whose grave he would want to genuflect. Since then, **"November 3rd"** has not only been used in school textbooks, but printed on an assortment of souvenir products.

The deification of Miyazawa may also derive from the way he lived. The aggressive promotion of the man as a saint by his surviving family members and others confounds much of his belief and action. But there seems little doubt that Miyazawa was profoundly concerned about the plight of the peasants of his region, Iwate, which was then known as the "Tibet of Japan" for its unaccommodating climate, topography, and soil, and for its frequent crop failures. A devout Buddhist of an activist sect founded by Nichiren (1222-1282), a firebrand polemicist who taught in essence that a true believer in the *Saddharma-pundarika* or *The Lotus of the Wonderful Law* must work for universal salvation through action and deed, Miyazawa, after studying and teaching at two agricultural schools, put his knowledge to practical use. And for the few years after he began helping the peasants learn modern, scientific farming methods, he forced himself, unscientifically, to subsist on a poorer diet than even the local people were accustomed to, and ruined his health, his body already infested by tuberculosis. One thing that makes this story ennobling, if you will, is the fact that as the first son of a well-to-do businessman, albeit a pawnbroker of used clothes, Miyazawa did not have to do any such thing. Furthermore, for religious reasons he led an ascetic life and remained unmarried.

Should, however, **"November 3rd"** and a bare biographical sketch, such as I have just given, create an image of Miyazawa as the sort of pious wimp you would want to avoid, that would be most unfortunate. Miyazawa was no weak-kneed murmurer of ineffectual pieties. He compared himself to an *asura,* in Buddhist belief the contentious, sometimes malevolent giant who ranks between the human and the beast, a sort of perpetually dissatisfied trouble-maker. In ***Haru to Shura*** (***Spring & Asura***), the title poem of his first book of poetry, published in 1924 at his own expense, he put it this way:

> how bitter, how blue is the anger!
> At the bottom of the light in April's atmospheric
> strata,
> spitting, gnashing, pacing back and forth,
> I am Asura incarnate. . . .

Miyazawa thought this image of himself as an *asura* important enough to use the title ***Spring & Asura*** for three unpublished collections of his poems. And the picture of Miyazawa that emerges from his poems is a man who is entranced by the things that happen around him, and eternally restless.

He frequently took long walks, day and night, furiously scribbling in his notebook with a pencil hung from his neck on a string. As a result, a great many lines of his poetry and, indeed, a good many of his poems are detailed descriptions of things observed. So, for example, **"Koiwai Farm,"** a poem of more than 800 lines, is largely a catalogue of what he saw and thought as he walked one day from a railway station to a Western-style farm established by three entrepreneurs in 1891.

His fascination with what happened around him and his delight in describing observed things rarely produced trivial or merely curious pieces. He was, for one thing, blessed with a singular, almost hallucinatory imagination. As the critic Yoshimoto Ryūmei has noted, Miyazawa's writings are so attractive because of "the extraordinarily free placement of the eyes." In one moment, the scope is as sweeping and grand as if seen by "the eyes attached to a body giant enough to reach the top of an exceptionally tall building"; in the next instant, it is as microscopically detailed as if seen by "the eyes attached to the head of a crawling, minute insect." Here, for example, is the opening of **"Annelid Dancer,"** in which Miyazawa is believed to describe a mosquito larva:

> (Yes, it's water sol,
> it's opaque agar liquid)
> Sun's a golden rose.
> A red, tiny wormy worm,
> draping itself with water and light,
> is dancing a solitary dance
> (Yes, *8γe6α*
> in particular, arabesque ornate letters)
> the corpse of a winged insect
> a dead yew leaf
> pearly bubbles and
> a torn rachis of moss. . . .

Miyazawa also had a highly developed sense of drama and humor, as exemplified by such dramatic monologues as **"The Prefectural Engineer's Statement Regarding Clouds,"** which begins:

> Although mythological or personified description
> is something I would be ashamed to attempt,
> let me for a moment assume the position of the
> ancient poet
> and state the following to the black, obscene
> nimbus. . . .

These qualities, when blended with a Buddhist vision and a belief in science that was tempered by a fine sensibility, created a unique poetic world that is at once intense and light, joyful and moving. It is a world yet to be matched by another Japanese poet, ancient or modern.

As might be expected, Miyazawa in real life was often frustrated in trying to carry out his good intentions among the peasants. This may be discerned from ruefully comic poems, such as **"The Hateful Kuma Eats His Lunch,"** and other more straightforward pieces. Many peasants no doubt valued his new agricultural knowledge. But many also regarded him as an obnoxious do-gooder who intruded into their centuries-old ways of doing things. Though he himself didn't say so explicitly, it is thought that he was beset with a sense of failure toward the end of his life. Some say that what appears to be, at least on the surface, innocuous pieties in **"November 3rd"** in fact hid Miyazawa's admission of defeat—although others say that those "pieties" are the ultimate expression of Buddhist sincerity as Miyazawa understood it.

Still, Miyazawa maintained a resilient soul. An outstanding manifestation of this is the poem entitled **"Pictures of the Floating World,"** whose sensuality may seem so uncharacteristic of this determinedly ascetic poet. He wrote it after seeing a wood-block print exhibition in Tokyo in 1928. Indeed, he had a life-long interest in this genre of art, including the pornographic subsection of it called *shunga,* which actually dominated the genre. Once he wrote an essay on the technical aspects of print-making. Another time, in 1931, he composed advertisement copy for prints to help a friend start a new business.

Miyazawa began writing poems in the traditional 5-7-5-7-7-syllable *tanka* form at age fifteen, in 1911. He continued to write mainly in this form until 1920, when he put together a "tanka manuscript" of 735 pieces. In preparing it he recast, for some unstated reasons, what were originally poems written in the standard single-line format into poems of one to six lines.

> In the autumn wind
> deep in my head a tiny bone
> must have splintered:
> there was that sound.

Such lineation of the tanka, normally regarded as a "one-line poem," began with the publication, in 1910, of *Nakiwarai* (Crying, Laughing) by Toki Aika (1885-1980), who broke up every piece in the book into three lines. The practice was followed by some notable poets, among them Ishikawa Takuboku (1886-1912), who would become the best-known writer of three-line tanka. Miyazawa's lineation was much freer and might have influenced the later development of this poetic form had the manuscript been published. However, even though many of the pieces had appeared in school magazines and other places, he strictly proscribed the publication of the manuscript. This he did probably with the thought, at least initially, of revising the pieces, as he evidently continued to do for a few years. Then, perhaps, other things began to preoccupy him. In any event, the two poems he wrote several hours before his death are also in the tanka form:

> Within these ten square miles: is this in Hinuki
> alone?
> The rice ripe and for three festival days
> the whole sky clear
>
> . . . . .
>
> Because of an illness, crumbling,
> this life—
> if I could give it for ripening rice
> how glad I would be

Not long after putting together the tanka manuscript Miyazawa switched to free verse. In between, he wrote a group of poems called "Winter Sketches," which are regarded as transitional pieces.

Free verse became the accepted standard in Japanese poetry during the 1910's with the appearance of such books as *Dōtei* (Journey) by Takamura Kōtarō (1883-1956), published in 1914, and *Tsuki ni Hoeru* (Howling at the Moon) by Hagiwara Sakutarō (1886-1942), published in 1917. Miyazawa continued to write in this format to the end of his life, although in 1928 he also began writing *bungo-shi,* which employed syllabic patterns and literary rather than colloquial language. The reasons for his reversion, if it was such, are obscure, and of the 262 *bungo-shi* he composed, only a handful rival his free verse in strength and intensity. Toward the end of his life he also wrote some haiku and even a few sequences of *renga,* linked verse. But these, too, are not remarkable.

In addition to poetry, Miyazawa wrote a good many short stories, mostly for children. The best of these stories, written from 1918 to the year of his death, are characterized by the same qualities that make his poetry stand out: keen power of observation, imagination, Buddhist vision, and a sense of humor. Many are stark, at times brutal. And even when compassion is the theme, the resolution of the conflict is usually realistic and credible. One of the three stories I have translated . . ., **"The Ground God and the Fox"**describes a cthonic deity who kills a foppish fox out of sheer jealousy for the animal's flirtation with a beautiful birch tree whom he loves.

The two other stories, **"The Nighthawk"** and **"The Bears of Nametoko,"** deal with the Buddhist precept *(kai)* against killing or taking life and the inevitable sufferings and pain that arise when you try to live up to it. To conclude this introduction to a poet who, during his lifetime, remained a largely obscure local writer but is now recognized as one of the three or four greatest poets—and surely the most imaginative spinner of children's stories—of twentieth-century Japan, it may be worth noting how Miyazawa decided to observe an important precept of his faith and pursue vegetarianism. In a long letter he wrote to a friend, on May 19, 1918, he said:

> In spring I stopped eating the bodies of living

things. Nevertheless, the other day I ate several slices of tuna sashimi as a form of *magic* with which to "reestablish" my "relationship" to "society." . . . If the fish, while being eaten, stood behind me and watched, what would he think? . . . .

Suppose I were the fish, and suppose that not only I was being eaten but my father was being eaten, my mother was being eaten, and my sister was also being eaten. And suppose I were behind the people eating us, watching. "Oh, look, that man has torn apart my sister with chopsticks. And while talking to the person next to him, swallowed her, thinking nothing of it. Just a few moments ago her body was lying there, cold. Now she must be disintegrating in a pitch-dark place under the influence of mysterious enzymes. We have given ourselves up; our precious lives, which should be treated with reverence, are being sacrificed, but we haven't won a thimbleful of pity."

FURTHER READING

Criticism

Khan, Robert Omar. "Heaven and Hell." *The San Francisco Review of Books* 16, No. 2 (Fall 1991): 58-9.
Includes a positive assessment of Miyazawa's children's story collection *Night of the Milky Way Railway.*

McKinney, Meredith. "Poems of Miyazawa Kenji: Notes and Translations." *Overland* 69 (1978): 8-10.
Overview of Miyazawa as a writer who "strove to bring religion and science together." Contains English translations of seven of Miyazawa's free verse poems.

Naff, William E. Review of *Spring and Asura: Poems of Kenji Miyazawa. Journal of the American Oriental Society* 98, No. 3 (July-September 1978): 300-01.
Surveys the major elements of Miyazawa's life and thought that inform his poetry, such as Buddhist compassion and the ideals of agrarianism.

Sato, Hiroaki. Introduction to *A Future of Ice: Poems and Stories of a Japanese Buddhist* by Kenji Miyazawa, pp. xiii-xvii. San Francisco: North Point Press, 1989.
Notes the "keen power of observation, imagination, Buddhist vision, and . . . sense of humor" Miyazawa displays in his poetry and short stories.

Smith, Larry. Review of *A Future of Ice: Poems and Stories of a Japanese Buddhist. Small Press* 8, No. 2 (April 1990): 36.
Comments on the authenticity and humble simplicity of Miyazawa's verse.

Strong, Sarah M. Introduction to *Night of the Milky Way Railway*, by Kenji Miyazawa, pp. xi-xiii. New York: M. E. Sharpe, 1991.
Summarizes young Giovanni's extraterrestrial train ride into the afterlife in Miyazawa's *Night of the Milky Way Railway.*

Yasuda, Kenneth K. Review of *Spring and Asura: Poems of Kenji Miyazawa. The Journal of Asian Studies* XXXIV, No. 2 (February 1975): 535-38.
Offers a brief account of Miyazawa's life and literary works.

The following source published by Gale Research contains further information on Miyazawa's life and works: *Contemporary Authors,* Vol. 157.

Joseph Pulitzer

1847-1911

Hungarian-born American journalist.

INTRODUCTION

Pulitzer was among the most influential and well-respected figures in American journalism. As the owner/editor of the New York *World* he is remembered both for his association with "yellow journalism"—newspaper sensationalism of the 1890s designed to promote circulation—and for his editorial crusades to expose the corruption of big business and government. An innovator in the field of newspaper journalism, Pulitzer is credited with the addition of Sunday supplements, fashion sections, comic strips, and profuse illustrations to the medium. Additionally he is celebrated for his philanthropic activities, most notably his creation of the esteemed prizes for journalistic and literary excellence that bear his name.

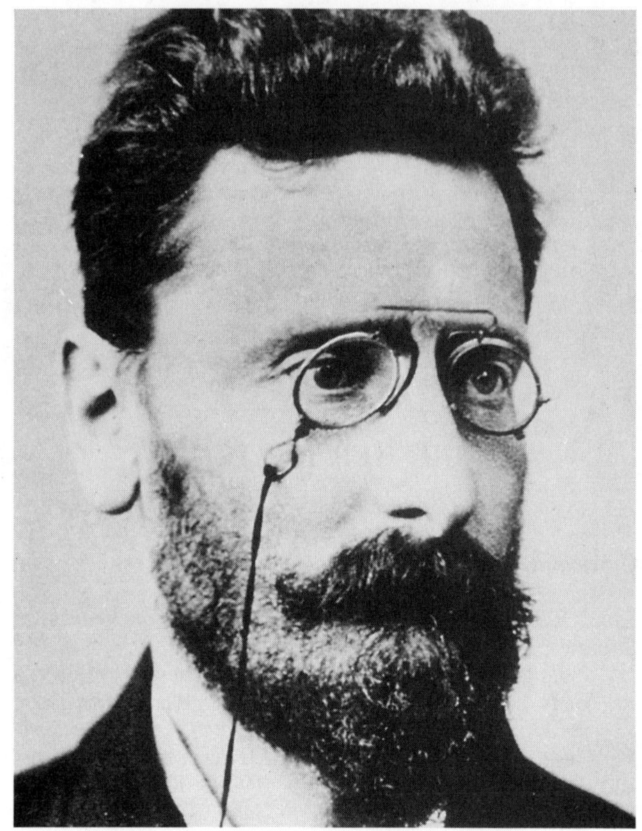

Biographical Information

Pulitzer was born on 10 April 1847 in Mako, Hungary to parents of German-Jewish extraction. Schooled in Budapest, he later emigrated to the United States in 1864 under the auspices of a general recruitment for the Union army. He jumped ship upon his arrival in New York harbor, but later joined the army as a member of the First New York Cavalry regiment. Seeing only a brief tour of combat duty during the Civil War, Pulitzer mustered out in 1865 and, unable to find employment in New York City, traveled to St. Louis, Missouri. He was granted American citizenship in 1867, and obtained a job as a reporter with the *Westliche-Post*, a German-language newspaper in St. Louis. His growing interest in local politics at this time led to a successful bid for a Republican seat in the Missouri state legislature in 1869. Retaining his position as a reporter, and later as managing editor and part owner of the *Westliche-Post* while in office, Pulitzer sold his interest in the daily in 1871 and embarked upon a tour of Europe the following year. He returned to America in 1874 and purchased another German paper in St. Louis, the *Staats-Zeitung*, but quickly sold it and turned his interests to the study of law. Two years later Pulitzer, who had maintained his regard for politics and was now active with the Democratic party, passed the bar. In 1878 he bought the St. Louis *Dispatch*, and merged it with another newspaper to form the *Post-Dispatch*. Ownership of this successful daily occupied Pulitzer until 1883, when he returned east and acquired the failing New York *World*. With clever management, Pulitzer quickly made the newspaper into one of the strongest in the nation. His primary competitor during this era was William Randolph Hearst, owner and editor of the New York *Journal*. The rivalry between the two shortly proved the impetus for the period of so-called "yellow journalism" in the 1890s. Carrying sensational journalism to its extreme and catering to the steadily growing demands of the nascent consumer age, Pulitzer and Hearst waged a battle for circulation that culminated in the *World*'s editorial support for the Spanish-American War of 1898. One year prior to this, Pulitzer's poor health and weakening eyesight, however, had forced him to forsake his daily editorial duties, which in 1890 he placed in the hands of an executive board. Still extremely active in defining the role of his paper, Pulitzer changed its focus over the next decade. Advocating the principles of democracy and the rights of workers in his editorials, he turned the *World* into a highly-respected publication. Pulitzer maintained his daily contact with the paper, making himself known throughout the country and acquiring substantial wealth for himself, until his death from pneumonia on 29 October 1911.

Major Works

As the owner and editor of the New York *World* and several other newspapers, Pulitzer produced no works save for the many editorials he wrote to appear in his publications. These writings are nevertheless considered significant as they represent Pulitzer's at times enormous impact on public opinion in America in the late nineteenth and early twentieth centuries. Among the crusades he championed in the pages of the *World* were against the corruption of such businesses as Standard Oil, Bell Telephone, and the Pacific Railroad Company. Additionally he was often cited for his impassioned plea to the American public, asking them to contribute funds for the construction of a pedestal to support France's gift of the Statue of Liberty in 1885. Near the end of his life Pulitzer also dictated a memorandum that set aside $2.5 million of his personal wealth for the creation of a school of journalism at Columbia University and for the establishment of the famed Pulitzer Prizes, awarded annually since 1917 to outstanding American writers of journalism, fiction, history, biography, and poetry.

Critical Reception

Pulitzer's biographers have noted his enormous contributions to the field of journalism, and have studied his well-publicized eccentricities, such as his obsessive regard for accuracy and his desire for absolute silence. Also, many have commented on his unbending management style and numerous attacks on political and industrial corruption in the name of democracy and the American people. More recently, Pulitzer's social influence has become the source of some critical interest, particularly in the work of Janet E. Steele, who has observed the correspondence of his journalistic style with "the emergence of a value system that increasingly celebrated consumption, leisure, and self-indulgence" in American society.

CRITICISM

Will Irwin (essay date 1911)

SOURCE: "Yellow Journalism," in *Highlights in the History of the American Press,* edited by Edwin H. Ford and Edwin Emery, University of Minnesota Press, 1911, pp. 267-99.

[*In the following excerpt, Irwin discusses Pulitzer's influence during the era of "yellow journalism" that flourished in the late nineteenth-century.*]

The seeds of yellow journalism, so called for want of a better name, sprouted at St. Louis and San Francisco during the eighties; they came to fruition in New York, thrashing-floor for changes in journalism, during the early nineties. In the decade which preceded the full flowering of Hearst and Pulitzer, however, a change in the spirit of newspaper publication had crept in by way of the business office—a change which prepared the ground for this new seed. From a rather humble professional enterprise, the newspaper had become a great "business proposition," holding infinite possibilities of profit.

Dana, Medill, Greeley, Godkin, even Bennett, adopted their vocation from that mixture of motive and chance which leads a man into any profession; they certainly reckoned the chance of getting rich very slightly among possibilities. But the field for newspaper circulation grew, . . . and with it grew the perfection of swift mechanical processes. By 1891 a quadruple Hoe press would print, fold, cut, paste, and count 72,000 eight-page papers an hour. The linotype, or mechanical typesetting machine, climax of delicate mechanism, was not yet perfected; that was to come just after the yellows made their start. Our publishers had facilities, therefore, to handle any imaginable increase in circulation. It was necessary only to enlarge basement spaces and increase the number of presses. And now big retail business discovered the newspaper as a salesman. Yankee advertising had been a jest of Europe for a half-century long, before experience proved that for most commodities advertisement in a regular and respectable periodical pays better, dollar for dollar, than advertisement by circular or sign-board.

THE NEW SALESMANSHIP

In the same period the retail dry goods business, consistently an advertiser since the first newspapers, began to concentrate in department stores and to drag into these great emporiums other forms of retail business, such as hardware, jewelry, and groceries. With their bargain days, their special offerings, designed to attract customers to the store, their advertising became a matter of news. They did not now announce, as in 1810: "We offer prints and calicoes at lowest prices," but: "Special today: A hundred dozen pairs of ladies' lisle hose, worth 75 cents, at 49 cents." For this form of publicity the newspaper was the only possible medium except privately distributed circulars; and a circular, as experience has shown, is usually thrown into the ash-can, while a newspaper notice, surrounded by matter which commands some respect, is kept and read. Newspaper and periodical advertising grew from tiny beginnings to a great force of distribution. Where the senior Bennett's old *Herald* got its advertising revenue by hundreds of dollars, the junior Bennett's *Herald* of the eighties got it by tens of thousands. There came, then, a gradual shift of power from the editorial rooms to the business office.

The stalwart old-time newspaper proprietor, who had entered the editorial game for love of it, still held his paper to editorial ideals, though he grew rich incidentally. McCullagh of the *St. Louis Globe-Democrat,* it is remembered now in these changed days, would not let a business office man come on to the editorial floor, lest his staff become commercialized. There remained, however, a multitude of lesser souls who yielded to the temptation of the flesh-pots and trained their eyes solely on commercial possibilities. Their advertising solicitors raked the city for copy; the less scrupulous coerced advertisers by a species of blackmail—"You advertise with us and we'll leave you alone." Above all—and this is where the commercial movement ties up with "yellow" journalism—they were ripe and ready for any method which would serve to extend circulation and therefore make their advertising space more valuable.

During the seventies, a young German-American, a pest to his fellows with his truculence, a blessing to his employers with his news sense and his vigorous writing, shuttled back and forth between the German and English newspapers of St. Louis. Joseph Pulitzer had been a soldier of bad fortune for some years before he entered journalism; he had served as coachman, as waiter, as common laborer, as private in the burial squad which laid away the dead after the St. Louis cholera epidemic; and he had learned the common man's attitude toward life and the news. His fellows of the police stations in his early journalistic days remember him as a restless, inquiring youth, ready to try almost any experiment with life, if he might learn thereby what was inside the sealed envelope: above all, as a man with his own opinions, ready to back them with fist and tongue. He rose; he did his turn at Washington, where his writing attracted the attention of Dana; and he might have taken service with the *New York Sun.* He preferred the power of the game to its art, however; and in 1878 he raised money to acquire the *St. Louis Post-Dispatch,* an obscure paper, dying of inanition.

WHAT PULITZER FOUND

It is not true, as some assume, that Pulitzer founded yellow journalism then and there. What he did discover—and that is only one element in yellow journalism—was the means of fighting popular causes by the news. The process was not wholly original with him; the *New York Times* had smashed the Tweed Ring by publishing plain accounts of their corrupt transactions. Perhaps, however, Pulitzer was first to go out systematically and find evil before evil obtruded itself on public notice. He had a conservative community to serve. In such an atmosphere certain set and old injustices always flourish for lack of popular opposition. Pulitzer scratched this surface and showed what lay beneath. He made himself the bugaboo of the big cinch; he made his organ such a champion of popular rights that to this day the humble citizen of St. Louis who has a grievance tends to write to the *P.-D.* before he employs a lawyer. That was the kind of journalism which Pulitzer brought to the hospitable-minded metropolis when, in the middle eighties, he bought the *New York World.* . . .

. . . . .

Joseph Pulitzer had been fighting his way on the *New York World* with the sensational, militant style which he perfected in St. Louis. He took personal charge of the *World* in 1884. Within two years he had attacked so many things which the other newspapers had not perceived as copy, or had not dared to touch, that he was disputing circulation with Bennett the Younger and Dana. By the end of the decade the *World* was altogether the most reckless, the most sensational, and the most widely discussed newspaper in New York. He has been several men, all extraordinary, in the course of his career, this Pulitzer; nothing so impresses one who regards him in the light of a historic character as the manner in which his able, penetrating, highly energized mind has shifted its point of view. In that stage he was a creature of infinite recklessness and incredible suspicion. By mental habit he scratched every fair surface to find the inner corrupt motive. Journalism, it appears, bounded his ambition; that was one secret of his extraordinary freedom from control. Had he cared for political position, for pure financial power, the history of American journalism in the past twenty years might have been very different. Within that narrow limit he, like the silent, cold, light-eyed young man experimenting out on the Pacific Coast, had the passion for leadership. "If you should put Hearst in a monastery," said one of his early associates, "he would become abbot or die." The gods cut Pulitzer off the same stripe.

The Sunday supplement was by this time an integral part of metropolitan journalism. As early as the Civil War period, the newspapers had been giving space on Sunday mornings to entertaining matter bearing only indirect relation to the news. When, with the development of the rotary press, they were able to print large issues by eight-page sections, the most advanced journals began to add one of these sections on Sunday mornings as a kind of catch-all for routine semi-news matter, like notes of the fraternal orders and women's clubs, and mild write-ups of picturesque features of city life, together with such embellishment of fiction and beauty hints as they could afford. S. S. McClure, breaking into the world of print at about that time, made a fortune from his idea of selling the best current literature to newspapers for simultaneous publication on Sunday mornings, the famous McClure Syndicate.

PULITZER FINDS THE MAN

Pulitzer, like the rest, published a supplement. Although by 1891 he had brought his Sunday circulation up to 300,000 copies, the *World* did not show so great a proportionate increase over daily circulation as the *Herald* or the *Sun;* and Pulitzer worried and tinkered over it. In 1891, H. H. Kohlsaat, then part owner of the *Chicago Inter Ocean,* saw in Paris the rotary color presses of the *Petit Journal.* Printing in colors, be it known to the layman, had hitherto been done almost exclusively on slow, flat-bed presses, fed by hand, not from a roll or web. It had been thought impossible to the swift rotary press. When Kohlsaat returned to Chicago, he had Scott build him a color rotary on the European model. This would not handle whole sections, but only small inserts; Kohlsaat used it mainly for premium World's Fair views and the like. Pulitzer, alert to anything new, sent a man to see this press. The report was favorable. He consulted the Hoes, who informed him that they were already manufacturing color rotaries for small sheets. As a costly experiment, he ordered a rotary, turning out full-size pages in three colors and black. With this the *World* printed colored cartoons and beauty pictures on the outside pages of one Sunday section.

The process was costly and infinitely troublesome; and the dash of color had no visible effect upon the Sunday circulation. At the end of the year the heads of the department sent a round-robin to Pulitzer, who was fighting blindness in Europe, begging him to drop it. "The very building groaned," says an old executive of the *World,* "when the boss cabled back ordering us to put a new man in charge of that section, and use the color pages for funny pictures, like *Puck* and *Judge.*"

Already, Pulitzer had found his editor for the Sunday supplement. Morrill Goddard, a young city editor "with a dynamo inside," had developed a faculty for getting "features" out of the news. Against his earnest protests, Pulitzer sent him over to the Sunday supplement. Once established at his new desk, Goddard, like Hearst, set out, naked-eyed, to find what the common mind wanted. An instinct quite extraordinary, considering that Goddard is a ripe scholar, led him to it; within the year he was running in that supplement what we now call "yellow journalism" as distinguished from "sensational journalism."

Pictures first—for ten grasp with the eye to one with the mind. He brought the size of pictures up from one column to two, to five; and, finally, the first "seven-column cut" made its appearance in his Sunday *World.* Then reading matter so easy, with the startling points so often emphasized, that the weariest mechanic, sitting in his socks on Sunday morning, could not fail to get a thrill of interest. "Economy of attention"—that, unconsciously to him probably, made up his whole formula. Nothing which called for any close attention; something which first caught the eye and then startled, tickled, and interested without wear on brain tissue. For subject-matter he clung close to the news, choosing and expanding the bizarre, the startling, the emotional, though the item occupied only a line in the daily paper. When such subject matter failed, he was capable of making history yellow. Did a treatise on *The Man in the Iron Mask* appear, Goddard, taking the publication of this book as an excuse, would rush into print a page of the *Iron Mask,* with nightmare pictures, three inches of "snappy" introduction "playing up" the mystery, and two or three "box freaks" distributed among the pictures, giving learned opinions by great historians. So he played on still another popular weakness; he made his readers believe that they were on the royal road to learning.

One of Goddard's old associates has given his formula for a page in a yellow Sunday supplement. "Suppose it's Halley's comet," he says. "Well, first you have a half-page of decoration showing the comet, with historical pictures of previous appearances thrown in. If you can work a pretty girl into the decoration, so much the better. If not, get some good nightmare idea like the inhabitants of Mars watching it pass. Then you want a quarter of a page of big-type heads—snappy. Then four inches of story, written right off the bat. Then a picture of Professor Halley down here and another of Professor Lowell up there, and a two-column boxed freak containing a scientific opinion, which nobody will understand, just to give it class."

THE "SECTIONAL VIEW"

From the smallest opening, Goddard would develop a road to popular interest. He and Andrew E. Murphy, his assistant, used to walk home to their lodgings in Washington Square, talking newspaper as they went. "Have you noticed," said Murphy one night, "how the crowd stops to watch the picture in that drug-store window? It's nothing but a cheap chromo. What's the reason?" This was indeed the crudest kind of chromo—it represented "sponge fishing on the Florida coast." Goddard studied it a long time. "I have it," he said that night. "It's a sectional view. You can watch the ships above and the shark eating the diver below at the same time. Let's try it." And the Sunday magazine of the *New York World* had a "sectional view," first of its kind, in the next issue. This bit of prospecting opened a paying streak. A hundred others ended in blind pockets, and Goddard abandoned them at once.

And just when the comic section and the Sunday magazine of the *World* were beginning to bear fruit in increased circulation, Hearst bought the *New York Journal* and broke into the metropolis—"with all the discreet secrecy" some one has said, "of a wooden legged burglar having a fit on a tin roof." He brought his Chamberlains and McEwens, his Hamiltons and Winifred Blacks; brought his own sensational, ruthless style of journalism; brought also the Hearst millions and the steady profits of the *Examiner.* He began to win over the Pulitzer men by offers of increased salary; Goddard was one of the first whom he lured away. Forthwith, the yellow supplement burst out on the *Journal.* A carnival of bids and counter-bids for men followed. Newspaper salaries, in the sensational division, went up never to fall back to their old level; newspaper desks became tenancies of a day.

Some one met "Cosey" Noble, Hearst man, in a restaurant. "What are you doing now, Noble?" he asked. "When I left the office," Noble replied, "I was city editor."

BRISBANE GOES TO THE JOURNAL

Arthur Brisbane, a graduate of the *New York Sun,* was then a kind of factotum on the *World.* He admired the Goddard discoveries in journalism, and had maintained, against Pulitzer's own pride of invention, that the supplement, and not the colored comics, was responsible for the steady rise of Sunday circulation. When Goddard went over to Hearst, Pulitzer made Brisbane his Sunday editor. At once this section went still further in audacity, so that Goddard, to maintain the pace, had to outdo even himself. The Sunday *World* had 450,000 circulation when

Hearst appeared. By 1897 Brisbane had raised it to 600,000. And now the yellow flood flowed over from the Sunday magazine to the daily paper. "What are you fellows doing?" asked Pulitzer and Hearst, in effect, of the managing editors and city editors. "The Sunday is going ahead; you are standing still." Having no great discovery of their own to stimulate circulation, the editors of the daily paper imitated the Sunday supplement. Into their own product they brought this fake, shallow, supersensational method, this predigested information, this striving for hitting effect at any cost.

Sensational newspapers tremble always with office politics. In 1897, after the club boycott on yellow journalism, Brisbane found his position on the *World* fading away from him. Hearst, meantime, had established a circulation for his morning *Journal* (later called the *American*), and was making inroads on the *World* with his Sunday paper; but the evening paper lagged at little more than 100,000 a day. Brisbane, who had already received bids from across the street, approached Hearst with a proposition. "I'll take charge of your evening paper at a hundred dollars a week," he said, in effect. "But I'll expect a dollar a week raise for every thousand I add to the circulation." Hearst accepted.

Brisbane, with a free hand, started to make an evening newspaper on the plan of a yellow supplement. He invented the job-type head—half the front page devoted to two or three smashing words, blaring forth sensation. He went further and devised that trick headline wherein the first and third lines, in immense type, proclaim a sensation, while the interlarded second line, in small type, reduces the whole head to a commonplace meaning ("WAR Will Probably be DECLARED," for example). Then fortune filled his sails. He took the evening *Journal* late in 1897. On February 14, 1898, the *Maine* was blown up in Havana Harbor. There followed six months of rumors of war, preparation for war, and, finally, war. Never had a sensational editor such an opportunity. In heads which occupied sometimes three-quarters of the page, the *Journal* blazoned forth the latest rumors. In smashing, one-sentence-to-the-paragraph Brisbane editorials, it bellowed at the Government the mob demand for vengeance on Spain. In one year the *Journal* touched the million mark; and Brisbane was earning, by his agreement, $50,000 per annum. It is said that the agreement was in form of a short note, and that Hearst might have broken it had he gone to law. But he paid gladly, personal liberality being one of his virtues. And liberality was wisdom, for Brisbane has been a gold-mine to his employer.

There followed the climax of the yellow craze, an episode in social history which we may yet come to regard with as much amazement as the tulip craze in Holland or the Mississippi Bubble. Now did the *World* and *Journal* go insane with violent scareheads, worded to get the last drop of sensation from the "story" and throw it to the fore; now did they make fact out of hint, history out of rumor; now did they create, for their believing readers, a picture of a world all flash and sensation; now did they change their bill day by day like a vaudeville house, striving always for some new and startling method of attracting a crowd. Now they hunted down the criminal with blaring horns, so playing on the mob weakness for the thief chase; now, with the criminal caught and condemned and sentenced, they howled for his reprieve, glorified him in hysterics, so availing themselves of the old mob sympathy for the victim of the law, mob hatred for the executioner. Now they dressed out the most silly and frivolous discussion of the day with symposiums of solemn opinion from prominent citizens; now they went a step further in audacity and headed an interview from Bishop Potter or Chauncey M. Depew "By Bishop Potter" or "By Chauncey M. Depew," as though these eminent citizens were real contributors. Now they discovered the snob in all humanity and turned reporters, artists, and—after the half-tones became possible—photographers loose on "Society." The Four Hundred of New York, largely a newspaper myth, was the target for this army. Their doings, with the follies emphasized, bedecked column after column, daily and Sunday, of hysterical slush. Life, as it percolated through the *World* and *Journal,* became melodrama, the song of the spheres a screech.

PULITZER SHIFTS GROUND

Suddenly the *World* dropped the whole game; changed almost in a week from yellow to merely sensational. This came almost coincidentally with those three months in a dark room from which Pulitzer emerged almost totally blind. There are those who believe that Pulitzer, had he retained his sight, would have drawn a string of yellow newspapers across the country as Hearst has done. I prefer to think, as do his best old counselors, that Pulitzer perceived the end of this madness; that he came to one of his sudden transformations in point of view. This blind man sees further into his times than any other American journalist; he must have known that it could not last. Change he did in the spring of 1901, so that now the worst one can say of the evening *World* is to call it a little sensational and rather silly, while his morning *World* is possibly the freest and most truthful popular newspaper in New York. . . .

. . . . .

SOME YELLOW VIRTUES

I have shown how Pulitzer brought to New York, as the nucleus of yellow journalism, the method of finding and fighting public evils through the news. This method the yellow newspapers perfected with their growth in general efficiency. They learned how to fight; they taught the method to other newspapers. Their period of greatest power was also the period of unchecked corporation abuses, of alliance between bad ward politics and bad high finance. The ten-cent magazine, with its healthful "muck-raking," had not yet arrived. These blatant voices, husky with much bawling, were almost the only voices raised, for a decade long, against such principles as Mark Hanna typified.

Again, like the French philosopher, they "brought philosophy from the library and the cloister to dwell in the kitchen and the workshop." A parade of learning, of scientific and philosophical knowledge, was always among their little tricks. They gave it to their readers predigested, the sensational detail to the fore, with an eye always on "economy of attention"; but they did hammer the big principles home, I believe, to people who could have accepted them in no other form. Their "stories" were an edge of interest for the wedge of knowledge. So always philosophies first reach the bottom of popular intelligence. Had we an accurate and critical record of early Christianity, we should find, probably, that after its first pure flow the people in general accepted its picturesque superstitions before they grasped its spirit; and the Darwinian theories had been mentor to the laboratories for a quarter century before the mob believed that Darwin taught anything except the bizarre idea—which he never did teach—of man's descent from the monkey.

Oswald Garrison Villard (essay date 1923)

SOURCE: "The New York World, A Liberal Journal," in *Some Newspapers and Newspaper Men,* Alfred A. Knopf, 1923, pp. 42-62.

[*In the following essay, Villard summarizes the editorial history of Pulitzer's newspaper the* World.]

A monument to Joseph Pulitzer the New York *World* unquestionably is. It is even more than that; it is really a monument to the idealism of the many men from Central Europe who came to America as to the promised land, so joyous at having turned their backs upon the falsities, the hypocrisies, the military autocracies of the Continent that they brought to America a devotion quite unsurpassed by any native born. Theirs was a far keener appreciation of the true principles of a democratic society and of the fundamentals of American idealism than is held by nine-tenths of the college graduates of today who claim admittance to the Sons of the Revolution. True, Mr. Pulitzer was not like three others who left their mark upon American journalism—Carl Schurz, Oswald Ottendorfer, and Henry Villard—a product of the Revolution of 1848. He belonged to a later generation of immigrants and did not cross the ocean as a result of that idealistic uprising which would have liberalized Germany and spared the world its greatest agony had it succeeded. But the fact is nevertheless that New York owes what is today its most liberal English-language daily to a simple Jewish-Hungarian immigrant of humblest origin, who came to this country friendless and unknown with so little money it is a question whether he would not have been excluded had the laws been what they are today. If men like Congressman Johnson, who are now so bent on excluding all aliens from America in pursuit of the narrow, selfish, nationalistic dogma of "America for those who are already here," could ever be brought to measure the contributions of some of the thousands who came penniless to these shores in foul-smelling steerage quarters, they would surely be shamed into something different. They would at least have to concede that the morning *World* is today one of the few remaining assets in the field of journalism in which Americans with ideals can take pride.

Yet it does not begin to approximate what it ought to and so easily could be. The fact that the *World* is and always has been a creature of compromise is responsible for this. Nothing could be finer than the vision of its purpose, which Joseph Pulitzer published when he purchased it in 1883, and which it now daily carries under its "masthead" on the editorial page:

> An institution that should always fight for progress and reform, never tolerate injustice or corruption, always fight demagogues of all parties, never belong to any party, always oppose privileged classes and public plunderers, never lack sympathy with the poor, always remain devoted to the public welfare, never be satisfied with merely printing news, always be drastically independent, never be afraid to attack wrong, whether by predatory plutocracy or predatory poverty.

His platform, dubbed radical, demagogic, socialistic, and altogether upsetting (in the lack then of the easy epithet of "bolshevist"), called for the taxation of luxuries, inheritances, large incomes, monopolies, all the special privileges of corporations, as well as a tariff for revenue only, and the reform of the civil service—most of the taxation proposals are now law.

At the beginning of Mr. Pulitzer's ownership the *World* (which was originally founded as a one-cent religious daily!) proceeded to touch even lower depths of journalism than had the *Herald* under the elder James Gordon Bennett. Mr. Pulitzer played far more directly to the base passions of the multitude than Mr. Bennett, yet his was a moving vision of a great daily of the working masses among which he had himself toiled, suffered, and almost starved, until his feet reached the road to renown and to riches. It was by this appeal to the basest passions of the crowd that Mr. Pulitzer succeeded; like many another he deliberately stooped for success, and then, having achieved it, slowly put on garments of righteousness. I am old enough to remember that forty years ago in New York it was impossible to find the *World* in any refined home; it was regarded much as Hearst's *Evening Journal* is today. It was the *World* as well as the *Journal* which Mr. Godkin had in mind when he wrote in the *Evening Post* some twenty-four years ago that "a yellow journal office is probably the nearest approach, in atmosphere, to hell existing in any Christian state, for in gambling houses, brothels, and even in brigands' caves there is a constant exhibition of fear of the police, which is in itself a sort of homage to morality or acknowledgment of its existence." If this language seems preposterously strong today it was pretty well justified at the time by the devilish work done both by the *World* and the Hearst press in bringing on the war with Spain. Then Mr. Pulitzer was willing to outdo Hearst in shameless and unwarranted sensationalism lest Hearst inflict on his papers irrevocable injury. That chapter in the *World's* history is not one to be read with satisfaction today by any one connected with it. To the eldest generation of intellectual New Yorkers the *World* is still anathema; to them it connotes only sensationalism and a journalism utterly without principle.

But like Mr. Bennett's *Herald,* the *World* grew more conservative with time, because its permanence was established, because Mr. Pulitzer himself grew older, and because he and his family came to a social prominence in which a more sober appearance and less sensationalism in their chief newspaper had their merits. It is undoubtedly true also that the change lies in part in our own altered vision. A first page which horrified New York in 1880 would seem tame and commonplace today. As Pulitzer outdid Bennett so did Hearst's yellowness make the *World's* seem merely a sickly pallor. Nevertheless the *World* has been for decades under the spell of Mr. Pulitzer's constant admonition to his editors to hold its popular following. In modern slang, he wanted a "high-brow" editorial page embodied in a "low-brow" newspaper. This Pulitzer policy has long exerted an unfavourable influence upon the *World* and caused it to lose the great opportunity of becoming the newspaper of the thoughtful middle-classes which Mr. Ochs and his *Times* seized—to the community's loss, for the liberal editorial page of the *World* would accomplish great good in thousands of homes in which the dull reactions of the *Times's* editorial writers do harm. For decades, and long, long after the *World* was rich enough to buy the best of paper and ink, it kept to its poor ink and newsprint in craven fear apparently, lest, if it presented a front page as clear and typographically handsome as that of the *Times* or the *Evening Post,* the toiling masses who rush downtown on the East Side elevated railways or surge across the bridges would abandon it. Only within the last few years has the *World* slightly spruced up its appearance without as yet, however, so improving it as to become the formidable rival to the *Times* that it ought to be in the most influential quarters of the city. One hesitates to put one's own opinions against those of the able business men who builded, with Mr. Pulitzer, the newspaper's success, yet I have a very strong feeling that as the *Manchester Guardian* has a large labour following, so the *World* could years ago have improved its appearance and yet held a labour constituency had it so desired, or had its editors and owners had the vision and the necessary courage. I am emboldened to believe that this is not a wholly mistaken theory of mine by the fact that the *World* is now turning in a new direction. It has not only improved the quality of its ink and paper; through the addition to its staff of Messrs. Walter Lippmann, F. P. Adams, and Heywood Broun it is reaching out for a new group of readers since those gentlemen, for all their merits, will not appeal to the masses. After all, the workers are best drawn to a daily like the *World* by a friendly, understanding, appreciative, and just editorial attitude toward the aspirations of labour. Even now, I think, the *World* could cut deeply into the *Times's* field; but something still keeps the management from bettering the paper other than slowly—too slowly for quick results. The insiders believe that they have exchanged about 90,000 new readers for a similar number of the old following lost. It is interesting to note that the circulation of the *World* was 382,087 on October 1, 1922, and 392,387 on April 1, 1923; it was 395,495 in October, 1912, when the price was, however, only one cent instead of two. It sank to 346,289 in 1918.

The apparent duality of editorial aim is everywhere in evidence. Alongside excellent and worthwhile reporting there are still occasional vulgarities, often lapses of omission, and much poor recording of events, as in labour matters; alongside admirable foreign correspondence, notably in the Sunday issue, appear crude and sensational articles bent on keeping up the large Sunday sales. The *Times* sells nearly 600,000 copies on Sunday without that abomination known as the "Sunday Comic"; the *World* sticks to its distinctly inferior supplements of this type. But the most striking illustration of the dual aim is, after all, its relationship to the other daily published under the same roof and owned by the same persons, which hides behind the reputation of the morning *World.* The *Evening World* is the black sheep of the family, about whose whereabouts and mode of life one does not inquire too carefully. Like others of questionable repute, this denizen of Park Row lives for the moment and the hour. It is of the earth earthy, although it, too, has been growing more respectable. It profits largely by its mode of life and it has even been rumoured that the proceeds of its lack of high character have at times been of generous reinforcement to the purse of the more respectable member of the family.

So it is of the latter that one thinks when one talks of the New York *World.* When Senators and Congressmen rise, as they frequently do, to speak with admiration of the courage and outspokenness of the *World* they mean, of course, the morning edition. The *Evening World* rigidly continues the original Pulitzer policy of playing down to the masses; the morning edition slowly but steadily worms itself into politest society and does so in part by calling to its service the pens of men like Frank A. Vanderlip, H. G. Wells, A. G. Gardiner, Joseph Caillaux, André Tardieu, George N. Barnes, and Maximilian Harden and many another writer of world-wide fame. Indeed, the most reliable foreign correspondence is to be found in its columns. In the perusal of no other New York daily does one rest so safe in the belief that its correspondents are writing what they think, untrammelled either by editorial inhibitions or by subconscious consciousness of the paper's prejudices and policies. No other New York paper told the truth about the Ruhr invasion as did the *World.* Like the Baltimore *Sun,* the *World* gave great attention to the reporting of the Washington Conference on the Limitation of Armaments by many distinguished writers from all countries and all points of view—it brought over Mr. Wells. Yet it did not profit by this as much as it should have, again because of its appearance. It deliberately hides its own light under a bushel. The ordinary city reporting is probably done on the *World* as well as if not better than on any other New York daily, but its editors have been known to bewail, quite as if they could not correct it if they would, the shocking decadence of the modern reporter. Yet it is not the reporters' fault that every now and then there appear crime "stories" in the *World* which are not fit for print and help to debar it from many a breakfast-table upon which it ought to be. The freedom of the news columns from control by advertisers is admirably complete.

Independence is the *World's* stock in trade. To its honour be it said that it was among the first to become, with the New York *Evening Post* and the *Springfield Republican,* really independent politically. That, too, was Joseph Pulitzer's policy, and right nobly has the paper clung to it despite its natural leanings to the Democratic Party. Its championship of Grover Cleveland, its espousal of the cause of Woodrow Wilson were of enormous benefit to those two Democratic Presidents—Mr. Cleveland almost directly attributed his first victory to its support. Its refusal to accept the specious and superficial Bryan went a long way to insure that gentleman's defeats. In the local politics of New York City it has never faltered in well-doing; yet after years of battling for reform it pays its share of the price the whole press pays for its loss of public confidence by seeing the candidates it opposes, like every other reputable newspaper, overwhelmingly elected and re-elected. Despite Joseph Pulitzer's admonition to its editors "never to lack sympathy with the poor," despite the great hold it has had upon the labouring classes, the *World* has not escaped the wide criticism of New York's dailies that they are of the "kept press," and that they reflect primarily the views of the great capitalists.

Yet it has waged some tremendous fights for the people against those capitalists. It has at times, for instance, wanted to abate the Stock Exchange. It attacked its own hero, Grover Cleveland, in the matter of a national bond issue which he sold to the House of Morgan at a greater profit to them than was earned by all the bankers combined who floated the loans of the Civil War. It compelled him to convert the next issue into a popular one, thus giving the public a chance to subscribe and saving a high commission to the Government—there never was a secret bond issue after that. It has fought nobly against special privilege in the form of tariffs, subsidies, grabs, bonuses, and all sorts of raids upon the Treasury. It has not hesitated to oppose the Government in many of its overseas ventures such as the mad policy of Mr. Cleveland in the Venezuela matter. Nobody forgets like the American public and it forgets nothing so rapidly as a newspaper's good deeds. Indeed, the daily is usually judged every day afresh and a single stumble today will bring down a torrent of abuse no matter how white the record may have been for years before. So it is a fact that today the *World* does not stand so well as a champion of the people as it did two or three decades ago, and that it is the object of widespread suspicion among people who ought to be its friends and admirers. It has lost and not gained ground.

But blame for that is by no means wholly to be laid at the door of the public; the newspaper is itself at fault because its liberalism has had grave lapses, because it is not always consistent, and because it curiously lacks driving force in its efforts to ram home its views. The occasional inconsistency is doubtless partly due to the mechanics of the editorial page; it seems as if the editor on duty evenings were sometimes overruled the next day. Joseph Pulitzer in praising the alertness and promptness of expression of editorial opinion of the *Evening Post* once complained to me bitterly that he could not get his "editorial gentlemen" to write on events the day they occurred. In connection with its failure to win for its usually sound, wise, and admirably expressed views the attention and influence they deserve, it is to be noted that Henry Watterson did Mr. Frank I. Cobb, the *World's* chief editor, the disservice to characterize him as the greatest editorial writer of this generation. Comparisons are still odious, if only because they set people to measuring and judging. Clear, cool, able, forceful in the presentation of his views, excellent user of English, Mr. Cobb has never equalled Rollo Ogden at his best before the World War gravely tarnished the latter's liberalism and he took his plunge into the dull senescence of the *Times's* editorial page. Once Mr. Ogden wrote with a passion for justice and righteousness which no one equalled after the retirement of his exemplar, Edwin L. Godkin. It was Mr. Ogden's fiery pen as much as any one's which made the McKinley Cabinet counsel one morning during the Spanish War whether it should not have the editors of the *Evening Post* and *Springfield Republican* indicted for treason; it was his pen which with a single stroke punctured the dangerous Hearst boom for the Presidency in 1904. That particular quality of passion Mr. Cobb lacks; nor does he somehow use as effectively as might be the weapon of reiteration which was one of the deadliest in Mr. Godkin's arsenal. There is, in other words, often a failure to follow through the stroke.

Perhaps the point can best be illustrated by a really great editorial which Mr. Cobb published, double-leaded, in the *World* on December 5, 1920, entitled "An Antiquated Machine." To it was devoted the entire editorial page of that issue. Had it appeared in one of the weeklies which are called radical it would have been denounced as dangerously revolutionary. Had it been printed in the conservative *Tribune* or *Times* it would have created a national sensation. For it declared the truth that our Constitution is outworn, our scheme of government hopelessly antiquated and inefficient, our Congressional system as if planned to exclude the best minds of the country "except by accident." "The cold inexorable fact," Mr. Cobb wrote, is that "the Congressional system is no longer adequate to the political necessities of 105,000,000 people. The failure of government is largely the failure of that system, and until the legislative machinery is modernized the affairs of government are bound to go from bad to worse no matter what party is in power or what its policies or promises may be. An ox-cart cannot do the work of an automobile truck, and an ox-cart does not cease to be an ox-cart when it is incorporated into the Constitution of the United States." But Mr. Cobb did not stop there. "We talk much of representative government in the United States, but we have no representative government." The political, social, and economic conditions of 1920, he pointed out, "bear little relation to the political, the social, and the economic conditions of 1787, yet the American people are trying to make a governmental machine which was constructed under the conditions of 1787 function under the complex conditions of 1920 and are bitterly complaining because they do not get better results"—a sentiment which is as if lifted bodily from the creed of the wicked *Nation.* Then behold this dangerous iconoclasm:

> During the first half of the nineteenth century the United States remained the model of all nations seeking self-government. It is no longer the model. Of all the new republics that came into existence as a result of the Great War, not one of them has fashioned its machinery of government after that of the United States. All of them have adopted the British parliamentary system as adapted to the uses of a republic by the French. All of them have rejected congressional government in favour of parliamentary government. All of them have made their government directly and immediately responsible to the people whenever an issue arises about which the will of the majority is in doubt or in dispute. In consequence all these governments have become more democratic than that of the United States, more responsible to public opinion and more responsive to public opinion than that of the United States, and more closely in touch with the general political sentiment of the country than that of the United States.
>
> Instead of remaining the leaders in the development of democratic institutions, the American people have lagged behind. They cling obstinately to most of the anachronisms of their Constitution although they are wholly indifferent to the great guaranties of human liberties embodied in the Bill of Rights. They retain a legislative system that time has made obsolete; but they have forgotten all about the principles of local self-government which was at the foundation of the republic, and they have equally forgotten all about the rights of the minority which are at the foundation of all freedom. While holding to the letter of their Constitution, they have so far perverted its spirit that the United States is now the one country among the great civilized nations in which the will of the people can never be definitely ascertained, in which it can never definitely be put into effect, and in which it can be successfully overruled whenever a political cabal is organized for that purpose.
>
> Every intelligent American citizen knows that the machinery of government is breaking down. He knows that the public confidence in government is at the lowest ebb. He knows that government has ceased to function in harmony with either the political or economic necessities of the people, that it is rapidly becoming a thing apart from the actual life of the country and in a great degree indifferent to the life of the country. It is a huge, clumsy machine that requires a maximum of energy to produce a minimum of results, and those results are often worse than no results at all.

Surely an editorial so startling and revolutionary—the only one in more than two years to which the *World* devoted its entire editorial page in one issue—ought to have brought down on the *World* the wrath of 100 per cent patriots, of every one of the multitude of worshippers of things as they are. The society for the preservation of the Constitution, whose headquarters are in Washington, ought to have solemnly resolved that the *World* was a traitor to its country. The American Legion ought to have risen in its wrath to point out the truth that if the *World* had published such an editorial during the war Mr. Cobb and Mr. Ralph Pulitzer would have gone to jail—many went for saying less. Wall Street ought to have removed all its financial advertising from the *World,* and the New York State Chamber of Commerce should at least have demanded that Mr. Cobb be finger-printed. None of these things happened; indeed, so far as it was possible to ascertain without having subscribed to the clipping bureaus, the editorial attracted surprisingly little attention—do not editors read the Sunday *World,* or do they prefer to golf? Or is it due to the absence in the editorial of the passionate ring of the reformer who must be heard no matter what the price? Certain it only is that the Constitution and our legislative system did not rock as they should have. More seriously, how has the *World* followed up this magnificent beginning? Has it, after the manner of Joseph Pulitzer at the time of the secret bond deals, made itself known throughout the country as the ardent, flaming exponent of the growing demand that the strait-jacket of an outworn Constitution under which we live, and upon which our highest officials spit as and when they choose, shall be changed? On the contrary, I venture to assert that 98 per cent of the faithful readers of the *World* are unaware of its views on this subject; they have certainly not had it drilled into them day by day, or week by week, how grave the national emergency is which is set forth in that leader. No, the *World* is not living up to the great opportunity which here offers itself to make the public realize whither we are drifting, and to lead the country toward gradual reforms without which we shall some day have an overturn as far-reaching as the Russian.

But there is still another vital reason why the *World* does not lead as it once did. The *World's* editors were of those liberals who failed utterly to see that when liberalism strikes hands with war, liberalism withers if it does not die. The *World* supported Woodrow Wilson because he proclaimed in his "New Freedom" largely the *World's* own gospel of social and political reform. Today the progressive movement in America which looked so hopeful in the first three years of Wilson's Administration is flat on its back, every reform cause is checked when it is not dead. The "New Freedom" reads like a travesty today; or like a note out of the long dead past. It bears no relation whatever to current political action, and no one more than the *World* bewails the political reaction of the hour—a reaction which was as inevitable after the war as the following of night upon day, which the *World* itself did its full share to create. Far-sighted editors truly steeped in democratic liberalism would have foreseen this; Mr. Pulitzer would certainly never have been taken in by such phrases as the "war to end war" and "making the world safe for democracy" and the rest of the war humbug whose falsity and hypocrisy have been and are hourly being demonstrated by every event from Paris to the Ruhr. In vain in the sight of so experienced a bird would those nets have been spread.

But the *World* and Mr. Cobb differed but little from the ordinary run of dailies and editors. They were silent or mildly protested while liberalism was done to death; while every right that American citizens were guaranteed was trampled underfoot with the consent and approval of the great prophet of liberalism, Woodrow Wilson. During the greater part of the war the *World* ran with the herd and was as rabid and poisonous as the rest. Only long after the mischief was done and all danger to the protestant was over, when the new chains, not yet broken, had long been welded upon us in place of the "New Freedom," did Mr. Cobb speak—bravely, eloquently, ably, persuasively, effectively. But the *World* ought to have suffered for assenting to the eclipse of political independence, the muzzling of the press, the denial of the famed historic American right to one's conscience at any and all times, and it has suffered.

Nor can it soon recover from this unpardonable lapse from the principles of its founder. How can the masses be expected to rise to a leader who falters and keeps silence when the enemy is most powerful and in control? To its blind faith, too, in its idol, Mr. Wilson, must be attributed some of the *World's* vagaries in regard to the League of Nations. It seems incredible that it really swallowed so many of the pro-League arguments because, democratic methods being its specialty, it ought to have resented most strongly the undemocratic character of the League. Last of all American newspapers should the *World* have given currency to the idea that, if we had entered the League, the whole history of the last three and a half years in Europe would have been different, that all would have gone as happily as a marriage bell. For that totally ignores European economic conditions and the fact that the infamous Treaty of Versailles is at the bottom of the present rapid collapse of Europe, and that the League is hopelessly woven into the texture of the treaty. Far more defensible is the contrary belief that if the United States were in the League, under a Harding and a Hughes, this country would have thrown its weight to the imperialists of Europe, especially to the French. Surely if Lloyd George could make no headway against the French policies there is little to make us believe that the United States could or would have done so.

A final illustration of the *World's* limping anti-imperialism is that after so bravely fighting against American conquest of the Philippines, it only recently discovered our bloody imperialism in Santo Domingo and Haiti. Yet the principle at stake and the menace to our own political and moral welfare are the same. One can only add again that the *World* limps far less than others, that it does often see some things where others are totally blind. But it was sad to see it using the alleged Kipling interview deliberately to arouse bitterness against England, and a worthless interview with the contemptible, brainless Ludendorff to increase ill-will in the United States against Germany and to play Germany and France off against each other again. This is treason to the old *World*. Can it be a deliberate policy of a recent accession to the managerial staff?

One word more: From all accounts there is much democracy in the *World's* inner organization. With this the modesty and self-effacement of the Pulitzer brothers, Ralph and Joseph, must be duly recognized. Whether because of good taste or for other reasons, they have, thank fortune, never utilized their positions to secure political office, or to plaster their names all over their papers after the manner of Hearst, or to feather their nests. They have, if an outsider can judge aright, given free play to their editors. The shortcomings of the *World* are not due to its being controlled either by business considerations, or by any selfish dominance of the owners. It remains the nearest approach to a great liberal daily which we have in America and as such its owners and editors are deserving of high praise.

Don C. Seitz (essay date 1924)

SOURCE: "The Portrait of an Editor: Joseph Pulitzer," in *Highlights in the History of the American Press*, edited by Edwin H. Ford and Edwin Ford, University of Minnesota Press, 1924, pp. 284-99.

[*In the following essay Seitz offers a largely anecdotal look at Pulitzer's career as owner/editor of the New York* World.]

Joseph Pulitzer was tall—six feet two and a half inches in height—but of a presence so commanding as to make his stature seem even greater. His hair was black and his beard a reddish brown. A forehead that well bespoke the intellect behind it shaded a nose of the sort Napoleon admired; his chin was small but powerful and of the nutcracker variety, such as the portrait of Mr. Punch affects. To conceal this he always went bearded after he was thirty. His complexion was as delicate and beautiful as that of a tender child. His hands were those of genius, with long, slender fingers, full of warmth and magnetism. The eyes before they became clouded were of a grayish blue. Always weak, they never lent much expression to the face, yet his visage was animated and attractive. Temperamentally, his was the type of the poet and musician; yet, while adoring music, he professed to care little for verse and rarely read it. However, he appreciated the singers in his native tongue and, I have often thought, really repressed his poetic instinct for fear it might be considered a weakness.

The nose vexed him. If there had been any way of modifying its prominence, he would have greatly rejoiced. But it was the delight of cartoonists, chief of whom was his friend, Joseph Keppler. When idling together in the cafés of St. Louis, Keppler would rack his brains for an idea and, failing to find one, would remark: "Well, Joey, there's only one thing left to do. I'll go back to the office and draw your nose"—which he invariably did to the great disgust of the subject.

His days after his withdrawal from active work were monotonously regular: morning hours spent with his secretaries over the papers and mail, a drive before luncheon, then an hour of reading and repose, after which he rode in a carriage or on horseback, saw visitors from five o'clock to six, went to bed for a brief rest, dressed for a seven-thirty dinner, left the table about nine, listened to a little music, and was read to sleep by one of his secretaries.

Just as old King Frederick William of Prussia, father of Frederick the Great, was always hunting Europe over for tall men to recruit for his Potsdam Grenadiers, Mr. Pulitzer, who resembled his Majesty in many ways, was forever hunting readers and secretaries. Ballard Smith, while London correspondent, and after him Frederick A. Duneka, David Graham Phillips, and James M. Tuohy, all English representatives in the order named, were on perpetual assignment. The secretaries in office were frequently set to finding other secretaries, and George Ledlie, his general and personal representative, had a permanent commission to find "the right man." Alfred Butes, a clever young Englishman, came closest to filling all the requirements. He had been in Africa with General Francis de Winton, was an accomplished stenographer, wrote an excellent hand and, above all, was most discreet. He penetrated more deeply in his employer's confidence than any of the other young gentlemen; indeed, he was destined to become a trustee of the vast estate and to receive a handsome legacy, although he forfeited these honors in 1907 to join Lord Northcliffe in a secretarial capacity.

The duties of the secretaries were very exacting, and the position was irksome except to men of sympathetic temperament and to lovers of good living. Most of the secretaries were English, although occasional Americans served with individual success. But the life palled on these lighter temperaments and they required frequent furloughs.

Mealtimes were play hours. At the table, liberty of speech was the rule and the guests and secretaries had full freedom to express themselves without regard to the feelings of the host. Sometimes the fire became pretty hot and Mr. Pulitzer would retreat to have his dessert and coffee alone. Violent disputes about music, literature, politics, history, and art were the rule, with not infrequent assaults upon his own opinion and the ways of the *World*, tempered by anecdotes and good stories. He loved table-talk of this sort. "Tell me a good story" was his most frequent greeting to a guest. It was hard to set him to "reminiscing"; but when he did venture back over the traveled road, the tale was worth hearing.

He was always interesting, seldom companionable, taking all he could from the minds of others, but rarely giving much back, his method being to dispute and to reap the benefits of an aroused defense. Thus he became a great hunter for facts. Often at luncheon or dinner, when a free-for-all conversation took place, some remark would arouse a dispute over accuracy of statement. If the question could not be settled by someone at the board, he would command a charge on all the reference books at hand and there was no rest until the doubt was cleared up. The waiters were often prohibited from serving more food until this happened. The facts found, he would listen intently to their reading and they remained in his mind forever. The best of dinners would be much improved for him if there had been added a satisfying fact-hunt. He would puff his cigar, pat the pile of reference books lovingly with his graceful hands, and smile in deep content.

Mr. Pulitzer read omnivorously. He was always buying books. One of his great griefs over the fire that destroyed his Fifty-fifth Street mansion was the total loss of his library. He was not a "collector" in any sense, but loved his volumes for what they contained. Like most of us who were fed educationally on Homer in our youth, Mr. Pulitzer reserved the *Odyssey* as a treasure to be enjoyed in riper years. He had long looked forward to the celebrated episode of the wooden horse. Coming to the event, he found it described in seven rather dull lines. "I was so d——d mad," he remarked, "that I could have kicked Homer!"

His speeches during the Greeley campaign were all made in German, his familiar tongue. When he came to stump for Tilden, he employed English. This was not an easy task, for he thought in German and had to translate as he talked. To facilitate clearness of expression he laboriously wrote out his addresses in English and committed them to memory. When he spoke in later years, after coming to New York, he had acquired the habit of thinking in English, and when asked to make an address in German during the Nicoll campaign, found it very difficult. In his after years of retirement he took up German again and used it faultlessly, cultivating the language, through skilled readers, from the best books in German literature.

He loved art and music, a taste reflected in the great benefactions made in his will to the Philharmonic Society and the Metropolitan Museum of Art. When sight grew dim, as with most blind people, music became a solace. The piano appealed to him especially and he heard great players whenever possible. Now and then Paderewski would pay him a visit and there would be a carnival of piano playing. The strings were next. His winters on the

Riviera were made happy by the splendid orchestra maintained at Monte Carlo by the Prince of Monaco. He frequented the opera, but the social noises usually drove him home early. The group of secretaries always included one excellent pianist whose duties were by no means light and whose slightest error in technique met with instant and fierce rebuke.

Like Napoleon his omnivorousness and great curiosity gave him a tremendous appetite. He was most insistent about his meals; ate often and heavily, frequently awakening in the night to satisfy his hunger with an extra meal. He was fond of luxury—always craved and secured the best. This was from no vainglory of extravagance, but was an inborn instinct, which he almost always managed to gratify even when poor. The best vintages came to his table, the finest moselles, champagnes, and burgundies; yet he drank little, rarely more than a single glass. He loved to be warm, to sleep well, to be comfortably housed, and to have at his command good books. In his later years he spent at least twelve hours of the day in bed. His afternoon nap was the trial of his valet and the terror of fellow travelers. Rooms had to be kept vacant above, below, and on either side of him at hotels; and the White Star Line, upon whose steamers he usually made his European voyages, kept his good will for many years by maintaining a huge drugget, made of manila rope, which was spread upon the deck so that the footsteps of the idlers on the promenade deck could not jar his slumbers in the stateroom below.

This desire for silence became almost a mania. The great house, Chatwold, at Bar Harbor, had added to it in 1895 a huge granite pile, called by some of the humorous inmates the "Tower of Silence." It was provided with specially constructed walls and partitions designed, unsuccessfully, to shut out all noise. The new city mansion, on East Seventy-third Street, New York, built in 1902, failed to provide soundproof quarters in spite of much planning by the architects, McKim, Mead & White. Indeed, his own rooms seemed to be haunted by noises, among them a strange knocking that nearly drove him frantic. After experts had failed, I discovered the trouble. In building the house, a living spring which could not be suppressed was found in the cellar. It was fed into a sump-pit; this in turn was emptied by an automatic pump, operated by electricity, which started when the water reached a certain level. By a rare fatality the pump had been placed so that the drum of the heating system acted as a sounding board and spread the incidental vibrations through the house, centring most loudly in Mr. Pulitzer's bedroom. The pump was shifted under the sidewalk, but he abandoned the room and built a single story annex in the yard, with double walls packed with mineral wool. The windows were guarded by triple glass; ventilation was by the fireplace chimney. He was sure that the jar of early morning whistles found its way to his ears by this opening. Silk threads were stretched across it to break the sound. Three doors were hung in the short passage from the main house, the floor of which was on ball bearings to prevent vibrations. The room was so still as to be uncanny.

Behind the "Tower of Silence" at Chatwold was a little balcony overhanging a rock-lined canyon through which Bear brook went babbling to the sea. This was his favorite resting-place. Here he would sit in the cool of the morning, or in the grateful shade of the afternoon, listening to the surf breaking almost under his feet, and gaining a tranquillity denied him elsewhere in the clatter of life.

The entourage came at times to be skeptical about Mr. Pulitzer's sensitiveness to noises, but rarely dared to experiment. Once, when the *Liberty* was in dock at Marseilles, a local carriage was hired by Norman G. Thwaites, then secretary, for a morning's ride. Mr. Pulitzer joined him with Harold S. Pollard, his reader and companion. Hardly had the equipage reached the park when a wheel began squeaking outrageously. Mr. Thwaites nerved himself for an explosion. None came. Instead Mr. Pulitzer remarked sweetly: "There must be a great many birds in this park, Thwaites." Thwaites had not seen any but he agreed that it was quite possible as there were plenty of trees.

"Tweet-tweet, tweet-tweet," went the wretched axle. "Really, now," said he, "can't you hear them singing? It is very delightful."

His olfactory nerves, like the nerves of his ears were abnormally sensitive. Perfumes he especially abhorred. On one occasion while at Cap Martin, a luckless British medico, who had come from London to be surgeon of the *Liberty,* for the first time in his life loaded his pocket handkerchief with patchouly. By mischance a whiff of this reached Mr. Pulitzer before the candidate was presented and roused him to fury. The doctor was taken below by a valet and deodorized before the patient could be examined; but the incident so unsettled the professional man that he declined the berth.

His love of chess was cherished as long as his fading sight made playing possible. He had a special set of chessmen made, of large size, to render them plainer to his fading vision. In time it became impossible to employ even these. During the early days of his exile, when at Beaulieu, Arthur Brisbane sought to allay the tedium by reviving Mr. Pulitzer's interest in the seductive game of draw poker with a pack of very large cards. All went well until Arthur's winnings at a sitting ran up to five hundred dollars. Mr. Pulitzer paid up but discontinued the diversion. Long afterward Joseph Junior chanced to remark that he had taken up the game for amusement—carefully adding that the "limit" was always twenty-five cents, and that he found it entertaining. "I don't know about that, Joseph," remarked his father, doubtfully. "I am afraid you will find it a rather dangerous accomplishment."

He loved horses and rode with the grace and freedom of one born to the saddle. Always in good weather, at home or abroad, an afternoon ride was the rule. As he became more blind, the pace was always a sharp trot or a canter but his seat was secure and his mastery of his steed perfect. Good horses were always plentiful before the automobile drove them out of use. At one time the Chatwold stables contained twenty-six animals. He was slow in taking to the motor car, but once converted took to it amazingly. Indeed, he liked speed. To be in motion was his incessant delight. For this reason he made long and seemingly purposeless journeys. Life soon became dreary if he settled down for a time. The thought of moving cheered him up and in motion he was serenely amiable.

He was singularly delicate about being fully clad and could not bear to have any part of his person exposed to the gaze of another. His sensitiveness in this particular developed in an amusing way at Cap Martin in the spring of 1910 when, after much negotiation, the great Rodin was commissioned to execute a bust. Rodin insisted that Mr. Pulitzer in posing should lay bare his shoulders in order that the poise of the head might be correctly revealed. To this Mr. Pulitzer objected strenuously. Rodin was obdurate but it was not until he threatened to throw up the commission and return to Paris that his subject surrendered, and then only on condition that none but his immediate attendants should be admitted to the studio. This was agreed to and the work went on, the model proving very petulant and unruly and refusing to talk to Rodin, who naturally wished to put his sitter at ease and to get at least a glimpse of his mind. The contract was for busts in bronze and in marble. The bronze is a mere head with no attempt to indicate the shoulders. The marble goes further—and here Rodin had his revenge; for he laid a bit of ruching across the chest, playfully suggestive of a chemise!

As Mr. Pulitzer was troubled with asthma, his yacht, the *Liberty,* was often set in motion for no other object than to create a breeze which would pour fresh air into his gasping nostrils. "Find a breeze" was his most frequent sailing-order. He was a reckless navigator, defying harbor rules, and often taking great risks from storm and tide. Odd as it may seem, he knew nothing of the latter phenomena and had to be argued with when told it was a factor to be reckoned with when the *Liberty* had to wait outside a harbor.

Although long blind for all practical purposes, complete loss of sight had apparently come by 1910. One evening while the *Liberty* lay at anchor in Mentone, the marvelous moon of the Mediterranean came up in its fullest splendor. Mr. Pollard, the companion, thinking Mr. Pulitzer might get a glimpse of its glory, led him to the bow of the yacht and placed him where he could see to the best advantage. Mr. Pulitzer strained his eyes long in the given direction, but said sadly at last: "No use, my boy, I can't make it out."

Miss Dorothy Whitney, now Mrs. Willard D. Straight, was one of his last memories before his eyes grew dim. "You know," he once said, "before I lost my eyes I used to walk around and talk politics with Whitney. He was so very interesting. This young lady, then a little girl, would climb upon my knees and pull my whiskers. So she stays in my memory as among the last of those whom I could see. I shall always be interested in her."

As Ponce de Leon sought the Fountain of Youth, Mr. Pulitzer was forever seeking the fountain of health. Consulting doctors became a passion with him. The most distinguished practitioners in Europe passed in review, taking fees and leaving no cures behind. The entourage came to believe that seeing doctors was more of a pastime than a hope, especially after the distinguished von Nordheim, who journeyed from Vienna to Wiesbaden, was turned away with the excuse that his prospective patient was "too ill" to see him.

The search for the attendant doctor was always on, even with a satisfactory man in the entourage. He always wanted to be sure that another could be had if the incumbent should weary of his job.

This letter to the late James M. Tuohy, the *World*'s London correspondent, written March 9, 1910, from the Villa Arethuse, Cap Martin, by Mr. Pulitzer's secretary, Norman G. Thwaites, shows the system:

> MY DEAR MR. TUOHY:
>
> Mr. Pulitzer asks me to write to you at once that it may catch you before you start on your holiday. He has been ill in bed for two weeks with severe bronchial cold, reviving his old whooping cough, and is now amazingly weak and sleepless. As soon as he is able to be moved, he is planning a month's trip on the yacht, probably into the East and the Red Sea.
>
> The point is this: utterly disregarding all qualifications heretofore specified as to agreeability, conversation, knowledge of history, editorial ability, and so on, can you set in immediate motion a search for a first-rate, practical physician who would be willing to go off immediately for a month on the yacht? Mr. Pulitzer underlines three times the point that *you can drop all former requirements as to personal qualifications,* concentrating on experienced, reliable, first-class professional ability. The man need not be a specialist so long as he is able to study and diagnose Mr. Pulitzer's peculiar history and condition of nervousness, insomnia, and recently recurring complications of whooping cough.
>
> You can also dismiss the idea of permanency. Mr. Pulitzer's present plan is leave here about March 15, and to be gone till about the first of May, calling very probably at Constantinople, Athens, Egypt, and the Red Sea. The man will have nothing to do except to enjoy himself, and, apart from the study of Mr. Pulitzer's case, it ought to be an exceedingly pleasant trip for anyone.
>
> *Needless to say the man must be sea-sick-proof!!!*
>
> Mr. Pulitzer says emphatically he does not wish this matter to interfere with your holiday or to spoil it. It must not interfere with that.
>
> You will see that it is quite different from anything he has asked for before in that it distinctly eliminates the point of intellectual companionship, and asks

merely for a first-rate doctor. Mr. Pulitzer says he may stutter or be a hunchback, but of course not preferably so. This ought to make the search much easier. Mr. Pulitzer has really been very ill and ought not to go off without a serious-minded, capable physician, in whom he and Mrs. Pulitzer can have some confidence. I am sure you can understand why the present author-physician fails to inspire that feeling.

Hoping that someone may be found as soon as possible as it is entirely desirable that Mr. Pulitzer should get away at once, and with best wishes to yourself,

Yours sincerely,

NORMAN G. THWAITES

When John S. Sargent was approached to paint Mr. Pulitzer's portrait, in 1909, a shy secretary intimated that Sargent's specialty lay in divining the innermost weaknesses and powers of his sitters and putting them on canvas. Mr. Pulitzer grimly warned the painter not to spare him. "That is what I want," he said. "I want to be remembered just as I really am, with all my strain and suffering there." The picture shows the blind man seated, holding a riding crop in the one hand and resting the other lightly against his cheek—a favorite attitude. The pain and suffering of years shows on his face, blended with high intellect, energy of character, and fierceness of temper.

Mr. Pulitzer's habits of thought and his later invalidism kept him aloof from affairs. Where a Horace Greeley became personally one of the shapers of a cause, Mr. Pulitzer after the early days of his *World* ownership was in but slight touch with individuals in politics and affairs. He did not wish to be in intimate touch with or in the confidence of political leaders. I recall once mentioning the visit of an eminent Democrat to the *World* editorial rooms. His instant comment was: "I don't like that. I don't want those fellows calling at the office."

He did not care to have an inside share in moulding matters, wishing all his efforts to appear openly on the editorial pages of his newspapers. He lived most of his life apart from other men, having a feeling that his was the fate of the true journalist, that he must devote—and limit—his interest to his paper.

Discussing some passing matter, I once used the phrase "your friends." "My friends," interrupted Mr. Pulitzer ironically; "I have no friends. You fellows in the office will not let me have any."

This was in a great measure true. But the "fellows in the office" did not have any either, and he knew it and delighted in the singleness of their devotion to the *World.* There was no list of "sacred cows" in the place, nor any *index expurgatorious.* The facts had to warrant the story. That was the only rule.

Mr. Pulitzer cared little for the evening or Sunday editions of the *World,* beyond expecting them to prosper, which both did amazingly. His interest and affection centred in the six-day morning issue, which he regarded as his paper. The others were mere commercial enterprises, but the morning *World* contained his soul—and that of the establishment. He lavished money on it, leaving the evening edition to get along with a slender force, though one of much talent. In time it developed almost complete independence of him and his ideas and became what it is to-day.

The *World* was managed by its managers and edited by its editors. Mr. Pulitzer suggested freely, but ordered little. Final judgment was always with the office. He once advised me, when business manager, that I could do anything on behalf of the paper except hunt for the North Pole, or back the invention of a flying machine, both ideas seeming chimerical to him. Within less than a decade after this adjuration Peary reached the Pole and the Wrights had conquered the air. Mr. Pulitzer was still alive. Indeed, it was the *World*'s award of $10,000 to Glenn Curtiss for flying from Albany to New York that enabled that aviator and inventor to establish the great business which now bears his name.

His initiative, strange as it may appear, was not extraordinary, and he frequently showed a hesitancy that verged upon timidity in adopting policies urged upon him by the juniors. His strength lay in stimulation. Here he had few superiors. He was a man of enormous impulses curbed by great reactions, who safeguarded himself from the effects of either by carefully warning his aides not to be swept off their feet by any order he might issue; all directions from headquarters were to be tempered by judgment or fuller information which he might not possess. If a very radical ukase came, the office custom was to reply, fixing a delayed day and hour for the execution. Usually a restraining telegram came above five minutes before the appointed moment. Under his policy the virtues of the *World* were easily his own, while the mistakes and conflicts became readily the property of others.

Extravagant as he was in verbal expression, Mr. Pulitzer valued judgment that waited on facts. In one of the changes of a generation in the office, when the old heads vanished almost altogether, he caused each of the younger moulders of opinion to be given a beautiful set of gilded scales from Tiffany's—the hint was quite plain.

It was his habit always to require two men on the same job and then to let them fight it out, though often to his own discomfiture and despair. The office theory was that he liked competition and sought to gain advantage by the strivings of the one man to outdo the other. If this is correct, it never worked; either hopeless deadlocks followed or the men divided their domain and lived peacefully. There was probably something in the theory, but more in the habit of precaution which he developed early in life. He always wanted to have a second resource in hand if one chanced to fail him, and to avoid being held up by any journalist who might think himself super-valuable.

The new men on the paper were always under scrutiny and the old ones never free from the test. One day at the lunch table at Bar Harbor, in October 1899, the company was discussing the achievements of an able reporter, Charles W. Tyler, who had just done a very good piece of work. Mr. Pulitzer was complimenting Tyler highly. Professor Thomas Davidson spoke up: "I cannot understand why it is, Mr. Pulitzer, that you always speak so kindly of reporters and so severely of all editors." "Well," he replied, "I suppose it is because every reporter is a hope, and every editor is a disappointment."

His blindness caused him to test men severely. He could learn the shape of an article by touch, but the qualities of a man could be ascertained only by intellectual pressure, and this he applied so searchingly as to seem merciless. Yet it can be truthfully recorded that no survivor ever failed at his task.

To one of the young men, who afterward rose to high rank on the *World,* Mr. Pulitzer remarked: "I wish I could take your brain apart and look into it."

"I don't," the youngster said; "I am afraid you would mix up the parts and never get them in place again."

Usually each fall, after election, the *World*'s circulation dropped. Mr. Pulitzer would credit the slump to the errors of the editors during the campaign, and a shake-up almost always followed. One year there was no election, with the same result. Much puzzled, he called on me for a solution of the mystery. I proved that it was due to the shortening of the daylight hours, showing that the paper always grew in the lengthening days. Appeased, he left the staff in peace on this one count at any rate.

"Forever unsatisfied" described his temperament. He was forever unsatisfied, not so much with the results as with the thought that if a further effort had been made, a sterner command or greater encouragement given, more would have been accomplished. Curiously enough, he was most pestiferous in his urgings and drivings when all was going at its best. In times of trouble he rested his lash. Men were left unhampered in their responsibilities, seldom chided when they failed, if there was evidence that they had tried to succeed, and richly rewarded if they triumphed.

Another high quality he had: to use poker parlance—he never would "call" anyone. From the same characteristic no one could "call" him. Men who tried it were usually sorry. He had an amazing patience with human frailty and an unfailing belief in the merits of mankind.

All newspapers have periods of "flattening out," when the entire editorial force needs reinvigorating. During one of these spells on the *World,* Mr. Pulitzer was sojourning at Lakewood, New Jersey. Much disturbed, he wished to know the cause of the dullness. The business manager thought the boys were track-sore and suggested a "shake-up"—meaning a shifting of jobs, familiar to all pressworkers in the metropolis, invented, it is believed, by the younger James Gordon Bennett, who sometimes made weird transpositions in his endeavors to stimulate the staff. Mr. Pulitzer liked this kind of experiment, but this time it did not appeal to him.

"I don't think that's the reason," he said. "I think it's because nobody on the staff gets drunk. Brad [Bradford Merrill, then editorial manager] never gets drunk; Burton [city editor] lives in Flatbush—he never gets drunk; Van Hamm [managing editor] sleeps out in New Jersey—he never gets drunk; Lyman [night managing editor] he's always sober. You live in Brooklyn and never get drunk. When I was there some of them got drunk, and we made a great paper. Take the next train back to the city, find somebody who gets drunk, and hire him at once."

Returning on this strange errand, when crossing Park Row, the business manager ran into a very brilliant writer whom he had long known as a friend of the flowing bowl. He looked down-at-the-heel and depressed.

"What are you doing?" he was asked.

"Nothing," was the glum response.

"I thought you were on the *American?* What's the trouble?"

"Same old thing," was the dolorous response. "I can't let the hard stuff alone."

So he was still eligible. "Good!" cried the business manager. "I have a life job for you."

With that he dragged him into the office and nailed him to the pay roll. Supplementing this the Flatbush city editor was given two weeks' board at the Waldorf-Astoria—to get some acquaintance with New York. Curiously enough, the paper responded to the prescription and became lively again.

While severely critical of the *World* and its makers, Mr. Pulitzer could not brook the least disapproval of either from others. One day at Bar Harbor, after a period of very acrimonious faultfinding, he wound up with this blanket condemnation of the shop: "It had no head, no sense, no brains."

This passed in silence, but later in the day he broached a suggestion to which I replied that the idea had been tried by the *Herald* without success.

"Why do you mention the *Herald?*" he interrupted sharply. "They have no head, no sense, no brains!"

"Neither have we," I replied.

He reached his long arm forward and, grasping my throat, choked it vigorously and remarked reprovingly:

"Stop that! You are altogether too critical and unjust to the office!"

To compress cables and telegrams a considerable code was developed through the years, which included the names of men in the office, rivals in the profession, and others who had to do with business or politics. For himself he selected the cipher word "Andes," modestly taking the name of the second highest altitude on the earth's surface. He commonly went by the code name in office conversation. Mr. William H. Merrill, his chief editorial writer, was "Cantabo"; his treasurer, J. Angus Shaw, was "Solid"—a neat compliment; S. S. Carvalho was designated by a single syllable, "Los"; John Norris became "Anfracto"; C. M. Van Hamm, "Gyrate," illustrating perhaps the vicissitudes of a managing editor; Florence D. White was "Volema" on the wire. I was honored with three stage-names—"Gulch," "Mastodon," and "Quixotic"; Dumont Clarke, his vice-president, was "Coin," a commodity with which he had much to do; Colonel George B. M. Harvey was "Sawpit"; James Gordon Bennett came over the cable as "Gaiter," and William R. Hearst as "Gush." For William J. Bryan, two code designations were used: "Guilder" and "Maxilla," the latter possibly a delicate reference to jaw. Pomeroy Burton became "Gumbo," perhaps as he himself said because he was "so often in the soup." The code amused Mr. Pulitzer and he was forever tinkering it.

His telegrams and cables usually came unsigned save for a final word—"Sedentary"—which meant that a prompt reply was required. This usually went back in a single word—"Semaphore"—meaning "message received and understood." When in good humor and pleased he would sign personal messages "J.P.," but when his wrath was high they came signed "Joseph Pulitzer." That meant trouble. In my eighteen years of association I received three bearing the ominous full signature!

Like most successful men, he had his superstitions, and one of these was a reverence for the figure ten. He was born on the tenth of April, reached St. Louis on the tenth of October, consolidated the *Post* with the *Dispatch* on the tenth of December, 1878, and bought the *World* on the tenth of May, 1883. He made the superstition something of a fad and used the numerals always when he could. In buying his first New York house, he selected No. 10 East Fifty-fifth Street—the two fives adding another ten. Lastly he cut the price of his morning newspaper from two cents to one, on February 10, 1896, and began the interesting duel with the millions of the Hearst estate. The result of the latter experiment was not to his liking and he lost interest in the superstition in his later years. But the dates remain milestones to be remembered in considering his extraordinary career.

Perhaps his birth on the eve of the great revolutionary period of 1848, had something to do with the fact that all his life he was a passionate devotee of Liberty—liberty of action, of opinion, of government. He opposed all sumptuary legislation, all tax-law inequities, all political bossism whether of the party or its leaders, and above all war!

When some new delight came his way, he liked to pass it on to those he wished to reward or encourage. Coming from the mild and humid central Mississippi Valley, he found the New York winter chill and took to a furlined overcoat for protection. This was before the days of heated street cars or comfortable subways, and the heavy garment gave him great content. Soon the men of mark on the *World* were garbed in fur with the compliments of the owner. When his eyes grew troublesome, he secured needed shade from the flexible brim of a Panama hat. Presto, all the favorites were likewise bedecked. He had great regard for the tall silk hat and always wore one on occasions that seemed important. When the *World* passed its 100,000 mark every employee received a silk hat with Mr. Pulitzer's best wishes. He usually closed all arguments with a bet when the talk grew too strenuous, and the wager took the form of a hat—frequently *five* hats. I had a controversy once that lasted five months over the "return" rules of the *New York American.* He refused to believe my statements, but finally incontestable proof of their accuracy found him at Corfu. He cabled me to buy the hats, but stipulated that one of them must be a "crush" for the opera, knowing that I detested both. This and other winnings kept me in headgear for about twenty years at Mr. Pulitzer's expense.

The considerable fortune left by Mr. Pulitzer was enhanced by the profitable outcome of wise investments in American securities listed on the New York Stock Exchange. They were not made primarily with this intent, but to protect the *World.* When the paper began piling up money, with his customary caution he looked ahead for lean years. He wished to be securely beyond the need of borrowing from banks. So he picked out what appeared to be the soundest easily marketed securities on the list. The paper never needed his aid and the investments grew with the years and the increasing prosperity of the country. When his property was listed, but one worthless item was found, a twenty-share certificate in some long-forgotten effort to build a railroad in Missouri. Every other item had held or increased its value. Some had repaid him more than three-hundred fold!

He bought stocks in large lots—2000, 3000, and 5000 shares, always in even numbers so that the holdings might easily be carried in his memory. Some of these vast blocks were made up of Delaware, Lackawanna & Western, Lake Shore, Central Railroad of New Jersey, and like gilt-edges. They were bought at the instance of the late Dumont Clarke, president of the American Exchange National Bank, and long vice-president of the Press Publishing Company, though having no relation to the production of the *World.* To Mr. Clarke's sound judgment Mr. Pulitzer added his own with highly satisfactory results. Mr. Pulitzer had himself a fear of the influence of his growing wealth upon his views and their consequent reflection in the paper. In 1907 he sent for Frank I. Cobb, his chief editorial writer. It was during the tremors that preceded the "Roosevelt" panic. The editor was addressed in this wise: "Boy, I am, as you probably know, a large owner of stocks. Some of them are bound to be affected by public actions. I am not sure of myself when I see my interests in danger. I might give way some day to such a feeling and send you an order that would mean a change in the paper's policy. I want you to make me a promise. If I ever do such a thing swear you will ignore my wishes."

The promise was made, but no such order ever came. It would have passed unheeded had it come, so thorough was the singleness of purpose which characterized the paper. Once in a while the traffic manager of the Western Union would claim a large share of words because the owner of the *World* was one of its chief stockholders. Such visits usually increased the trade of its Postal rival. Mr. Pulitzer never mentioned his holding in the concern to anyone in the shop.

He never embarked in any enterprise for making money, confining himself entirely to the investment of earnings from his newspapers in sound securities. Yet of his talents in a financial way, Lord Rothschild once said, "If Pulitzer would devote himself entirely to finance, he could be the richest man on the globe."

His personal expenditures were enormous, probably exceeding, outside of royalty, those of any man of his time. The *Liberty* was always in commission and her operating cost, with repairs, ran close to $200,000 a year. In addition to this he maintained costly residences at Bar Harbor, Jekyl Island, Georgia, and in New York, to which was added the finest villa to be had at Cap Martin. Probably the bill totaled $350,000 a year, but it barely dented the great income from newspapers and investments. There was always a large annual surplus.

Although one of the masters of the art of attracting attention, he was singularly shy himself. He did not like to be pointed out publicly, or to be personally a centre of interest. Once at Bar Harbor I had told Mrs. Pulitzer a merry tale about him, the joke of which was on the other fellow. She repeated it to her husband. "What's this story you have been telling Mrs. Pulitzer?" he queried at luncheon. I replied that it was a good one. He was silent for a moment, then said gently: "Don't tell stories about me. Keep them until I am dead."

Don C. Seitz (essay date 1927)

SOURCE: "The Day's Work," in *Modern Essays of Various Types,* edited by Charles A. Cockayne, Charles E. Merrill Company, 1927, pp. 249-63.

[*In the following essay, Seitz recounts Pulitzer's efforts for the public good, such as his founding of the School of Journalism at Columbia University and other notable endeavors.*]

The opportunity to perform a great public service and at the same time aid in erecting a monument to the dearest longing of his soul—Liberty—arrived for Mr. Pulitzer in 1885. Commissioned by the people of France, who raised more than 1,000,000 francs for the purpose, August Bartholdi, the sculptor, had executed a gigantic figure of the goddess, wonderful in art and magnificent in conception, designed to stand on Bedloe's Island in New York Harbor, holding a torch of freedom to welcome the oppressed of all the world. A committee had been formed, of which William M. Evarts was Chairman and Richard Butler Secretary, to secure funds for the construction of a proper pedestal. The work lagged until the statue, boxed and ready in France for shipment to America, bade fair to remain there. Enough money had been gathered to lay a concrete base, but not a cent was in sight to pay for the construction of the great pedestal designed to lift the statue a hundred feet above the level of the sea. The committee had vainly sought aid from Congress to avert the shame. This failing, it announced its inability to proceed further and in effect threw up its hands. It was then Mr. Pulitzer made his first great appeal to the American public. On March 16th, he published in the *World* this effective editorial:

> Money must be raised to complete the pedestal for the Bartholdi statue. It would be an irrevocable disgrace to New York City and the American Republic to have France send us this splendid gift without our having provided even so much as a landing place for it.
>
> Nearly ten years ago the French people set about making the Bartholdi statue. It was to be a gift emblematical of our attainment of the first century of independence. It was also the seal of a more serviceable gift they made to us in 1776, when, but for their timely aid, the ragged sufferers of Valley Forge would have been disbanded and the colonies would have continued a part of the British dominion. Can we fail to respond to the spirit that actuated this generous testimonial?
>
> The statue is now completed and ready to be brought to our shores in a vessel especially commissioned for the purpose by the French Government. Congress, by a refusal to appropriate the necessary money to complete preparations for its proper reception and erection, has thrown the responsibility back to the American people.
>
> There is but one thing that can be done. We must raise the money.
>
> The *World* is the people's paper, and it now appeals to the people to come forward and raise this money. The $250,000 that the making of the statue cost was paid in by the masses of the French people—by the workingmen, the tradesmen, the shop girls, the artisans—by all, irrespective of class or condition. Let us respond in like manner. Let us not wait for the millionaires to give this money. It is not a gift from the millionaires of France to the millionaires of America but a gift of the whole people of France to the whole people of America.
>
> Take this appeal to yourself personally. It is meant for every reader of the *World.* Give something,

> however little. Send it to us. We will receive it and see that it is properly applied. We will also publish the name of every giver, however small the sum given.
>
> Let us hear from the people. Send in your suggestions. We will consider them all. If we all go to work together with a firm resolve and a patriotic will we can raise the needed money before the French vessel bearing the Bartholdi statue shall have passed the unsightly mass on Bedloe's Island that is now but a humiliating evidence of our indifference and ingratitude.

The response was instant and popular, as these excerpts from the daily files of the paper show:

> Please receive from two little boys one dollar for the pedestal. It is our savings. We give it freely.
>
> Inclosed please find five cents as a poor office boy's mite toward the pedestal fund. As being loyal to the Stars and Stripes, I thought even five cents would be acceptable.
>
> The inclosed dollar comes from a party of poor artists who dined in University Place this evening.
>
> A lonely and very aged woman with very limited means wishes to add her mite to the Bartholdi fund. Hoping that the inclosed dollar may induce multitudes all over the country to respond and that the enterprise may be very speedily accomplished is the earnest wish of the writer.
>
> A few poor fellows whose pockets are not as deep as a well but whose love of liberty is wider than a church door, hand you the inclosed $7.25 as their mite toward the Bartholdi fund. May Heaven help your good work; it seems that New York's rich men do not.
>
> I am a young man of foreign birth and have seen enough of monarchical governments to appreciate the blessing of this Republic. Inclosed please find $2 for the Bartholdi fund.
>
> I am a cash boy with a salary of $5 per month, and I contribute 50 cents to the Bartholdi fund.
>
> I am a wee bit of a girl, yet I am ever so glad I was born in time to contribute my mite to the pedestal fund. When I am old enough I will ask my papa and mamma to take me to see the statue, and I will always be proud that I began my career by sending you $1 to aid in so good a cause.

On August 11th, following, the *World* was able to announce in triumph the success of its undertaking. The $100,000 was in hand. Work had not been delayed. The money was turned over, first in a $25,000 check and later as needed, while the work went on.

General Charles P. Stone, late of the American and later of the Egyptian Khedive's army, was the engineer. When the French transport *Isere* brought the statue to New York the pedestal was ready and, as Mr. Pulitzer wrote, the nation had been "saved from disgrace."

The statue was dedicated October 28, 1886, with a great naval and civic demonstration. The sculptor was present to witness the crowning of the work. "It is as I wished," he said. "The dream of my life is accomplished. In this work I see the symbol of unity and friendship between two nations—two great republics."

How that symbol endures the world learned in 1917 and 1918, when America stepped across the sea and paid her debt to France, principal and interest, compounded a thousandfold!

President Cleveland, in accepting the statue, used these notable words:

> We are not here today to bow before the representation of a fierce and warlike god, filled with wrath and vengeance, but we joyously contemplate instead our own deity, keeping watch and ward before the open gates of America, and greater than all that have been celebrated in ancient song.
>
> We will not forget that Liberty has here made her home; nor shall her chosen altar be neglected.

As the paper prospered so famously Mr. Pulitzer wished all who had to do with it to prosper accordingly. He was always giving rewards to bright reporters and enterprising editors. Each new press as it came in was the warrant for some sort of celebration. Christmas and Thanksgiving brought turkeys for all. When the *World* passed 100,000 in circulation 100 guns were fired in City Hall Park and every employee received a tall silk hat.

He was anxious that the men should enjoy themselves and actually bought a section of the old Elysian Fields in Hoboken as a playground. It was too far off and there was little time to play, so the experiment was no great success. He then sought to use the ground as a site for a *World* village, offering to aid the men in building houses. They preferred to select their own abiding places, so the project came to nothing. He was disappointed but took some small consolation in taking shares in the *World* Building and Loan Association, keeping up his payments until everybody else had "bought out" their shares. Then he caused it to be wound up with no record of having provided a home for anybody. He evolved a number of mutual benefit plans, none of which was welcomed by the unions, who in time controlled all departments, and so gave up his efforts to uplift beyond providing a good workshop, plenty of employment and decent pay.

. . . . .

In founding the School of Journalism at Columbia University, Mr. Pulitzer was moved by an impulse to educate newspaper writers and editors up to a standard of ideals. He had long had the project in mind. In the winter of 1903, journeying to Jekyl Island, he took me along as far as Washington. As the train left Jersey City, Dr. G. W. Hosmer, chief secretary, handed me the outline of the scheme to read over and be prepared for an opinion when called upon. I was isolated in a stateroom and read the document. Before it was well digested, Mr. Pulitzer appeared, having groped his way down the car corridor. Without asking for my view, he observed by way of opening: "You don't think much of it."

"I do not," I said.

"Well, what shall I do?" he asked. "I want to do something."

"Endow the *World,*" I replied. "Make it fool-proof."

"I am going to do something for it," he replied, "in giving it a new building."

There was some further talk, all quite inconclusive. The plan underwent much modification. The authorities at Columbia were inclined to look rather doubtfully upon the proposition. Mr. Pulitzer himself had some fears as to how the suggestion would be received, coming as it did from the head and front of journalistic aggressiveness. He expected severe criticism and was quite overwhelmed at the cordial greeting that met the announcement. Of course, there were carpers. These he answered in the *North American Review* for May, 1904, replying, as he remarked introductorily, to "criticisms and misgivings, many honest, some shallow, some based on misunderstandings, but the most representing only prejudice and ignorance." He added: "If any comment . . . shall seem to be diffuse and perhaps repetitious, my apology is that—alas! I am compelled to write by voice, not pen, and to revise proofs by ear, not eye—a somewhat difficult task."

"Some of my critics," he continued, "have called my scheme 'visionary.' If it be so I can at least plead that it is a vision I have cherished long, thought upon deeply and followed persistently. Twelve years ago I submitted the idea to President Low of Columbia, but it was not accepted by the trustees. I have ever since continued to perfect and organize the scheme in my mind, and now it is adopted. In examining the criticisms and misgivings I have been anxious only to find the truth. I admit that the difficulties are many, but after weighing them all impartially I am more firmly convinced than ever of the ultimate success of the idea. Before the century closes schools of journalism will be generally accepted as a feature of specialized higher education, like schools of law or of medicine."

This prophecy came quite true. Few colleges of consequence in America are now without their departments of journalism.

The first contention he met was that a newspaper man must be born; he could not be made. This he dismissed with scorn. "Perhaps," he said, "the critics can name some great editor, born full-winged like Mercury, the messenger of the gods? I know none. The only position that occurs to me which a man in our Republic can successfully fill by the simple fact of birth, is that of an idiot. Is there any other position for which a man does not demand and receive training—training at home, training in schools and colleges, training by master craftsmen, or training through bitter experience—through the burns that make the child dread the fire, through blunders costly to the aspirant? . . . I seem to remember that Lincoln, whose academy was a borrowed book read by the light of a pine knot on the hearth, studied Euclid in Congress when near forty. But would it not have been better if the work had been done at fourteen? . . . Shakespeare's best play, *Hamlet,* was not his first, but his nineteenth, written after growth and maturity, after hard work, the experience, the exercise of faculties and the accumulation of knowledge gained by writing eighteen plays. As Shakespeare was a 'born' genius, why did he not write *Hamlet* first?"

He argued further that the brain, like Sandow's muscles, had to be developed by hard work, though admitting that in every field natural aptitude was the key to success. "When the experiment was tried of turning Whistler into a disciplined soldier," he went on in illustrating his assertion, "even West Point had to lay down its arms. Your sawmill may have all modern improvements, but it will not make a pine board out of a basswood log. No college can create a good lawyer without a legal mind to work on, nor make a successful doctor of a young man whom nature designed to sell tape. Talleyrand took holy orders, but they did not turn him into a holy man."

Sometimes in the course of his contention Mr. Pulitzer almost proved the other fellow's point, a defect that comes from breadth of view when matched in argument. Using a military analogy he went on: "The brilliant general is simply a man who has learned to apply skillfully the natural laws of force, and has the nerve to act on his knowledge. Hannibal, the greatest of all in my opinion, is called a typical example of native military genius. But can we forget that he was the son and pupil of Hamilcar, the ablest soldier of his generation, born in the camp, never outside of military atmosphere, sworn in earliest boyhood to war and hatred of Rome and endowed by his father with all the military knowledge that the experience of antiquity could give? He was educated. In his father he had a military college to himself. Can we think of Napoleon without remembering that he had the best military education of his time at Brienne, and that he was always an eager student of the great campaigns of history? Frederick the Great lost his head in his first battle. It took him years to learn his trade and finally to surpass his instructors. There is not a cadet at any military school who is not expected as a necessary part of his professional preparation to study every important battle on record—to learn how it was fought, what mistakes were committed on each side and how it was won.

"Every issue of a newspaper represents a battle—a battle for excellence. When the editor reads it and compares it with its rivals he knows that he has scored a victory or suffered a defeat. Might not a study of the most notable of these battles of the press be as useful to the student of journalism as is the study of military battles to the student of war?"

Of the need of "born" news instinct, he observed: "Certainly. But however great a gift, if news instinct as born were turned loose in any newspaper office in New York without the control of sound judgment bred by considerable experience and training, the results would be much more pleasing to the lawyer than to the editor. One of the chief difficulties of journalism is to keep the news instinct from running rampant over the restraints of accuracy and conscience."

At an historic moment in the career of the *World* he had caused great placards reading

ACCURACY
TERSENESS
ACCURACY

to be posted in its editorial rooms; he was forever insisting on these points. Compelled to be diffuse in expressing himself, as noted, he wished no such excuse for others. As he said in continuing his homily: "If a 'nose for news' is born in the cradle, does not the instinct, like other great qualities, need development by teaching, by training, by practical object lessons illustrating the good and the bad, the Right, the Wrong, the popular and the unpopular, the things that succeed and the things that do not—not the things only that make circulation for today, but the things that make character and influence public confidence?"

This last was a perpetual study which carried insistence to all his executives. "Why did the circulation go up?" he once asked me during an unexplained rise in the number of readers. I did not know. "Find out," he ordered. "It is just as important to know why circulation goes up as why it goes down." This also applied to fluctuations in advertising. On one occasion during the Russo-Japan War the "Want" advertising moved upward.

"Why?" he asked. I said I did not know unless it was due to "The virtue of the Emperor," a phrase that had come from Japan anent the cause of victories.

"What virtue?" he asked sharply. "What Emperor?"

The joke was lost. To his mind the question was, as indeed it needed to be, one of basic importance. Turning again to his critics he observed:

> They object that moral courage cannot be taught. Very true. I admit that it is the hardest thing in the world to teach. But may we not be encouraged by the reflection that physical courage is taught? It is not to be supposed that every young man who enters West Point or Annapolis, Brienne, St. Cyr or Sandhurst is a born hero. Yet the student at any of these schools is so drilled, hammered and braced in the direction of courage that by the time he graduates it is morally certain that when he takes his men under fire for the first time he will not flinch. Pride and the spirit of emulation can make masses of men do what even a hero would not venture to do alone. Is it likely that Napoleon himself would have charged in solitary grandeur across the bridge at Lodi if there had been no one to see him do it? Or would Pickett's brigade at Gettysburg have gone forward to destruction if every man in it had not been lifted out of himself by the feeling that he and his comrades were all doing a heroic thing together—a thing in which he simply could not do less than the rest?
>
> If such things can be done for physical courage, why not for moral courage? If the mind can be taught to expose the body fearlessly to wounds and death, cannot the soul be taught to cling to its convictions against temptation, prejudice, obloquy and persecution? Moral courage is developed by experience and by teaching. Every successful exercise of it makes the next easier. The editor is often confronted by an apparent dilemma—either to yield to a popular passion that he feels to be wrong or to risk the consequences of unpopularity. Adherence to convictions can and should be taught by precept and example as not only high principle but sound policy. Might not a hundred concrete examples of inflexible devotion to the right serve as a moral tonic to the student?

Answering the point that much that it was proposed to teach in his school was already taught in colleges, he agreed. But, he thought, they were overtaught for the purpose he had in mind. Things in professions were specialized, even in newspapers. "The object of the College of Journalism," he commented, "will be to dig through this general scheme intended to cover every possible career of work in life, every profession, to select and concentrate only upon the things the journalist wants and not to waste time on things he does not want."

Yet he had a broad perspective: "Historians like McMaster, [Woodrow] Wilson, and Rhodes; college presidents like Eliot, Hadley, and Angell; judges like Fuller, Brewer, and Gray—could help the work with lectures and suggestions. It is nothing new for a justice of the Supreme Court to lecture in college. Justice Story did it at Harvard, Justice Field did it at the University of California, Justices Harlan and Brewer do it now at the Columbian University at Washington. Even ex-Presidents have not thought such work belittling. Harrison lectured at Stanford and Cleveland at Princeton."

He remarked in conclusion: "Our Republic and its press will rise or fall together. An able, disinterested, public-spirited press, with trained intelligence to know the right and courage to do it, can preserve that public virtue without which popular government is a sham and a mockery. A cynical, mercenary, demagogic, corrupt press will produce in time a people as base as itself. The power to mold the future of the Republic will be in the hands of the journalists of future generations. This is why I urge my colleagues to aid this important experiment. Upon their generous aid and coöperation the ultimate success of the project must depend."

. . . . .

Besides establishing the School of Journalism at Columbia, Mr. Pulitzer in his will provided a series of prizes in the interest of letters, the drama, music, and good newspaper work, to wit:

> 1. For the most disinterested and meritorious public service rendered by any American newspaper during the year—$500 gold medal.
>
> 2. For the best example of a reporter's work during the year; the test being strict accuracy, terseness, the accomplishment of some public good, commanding public attention and respect—$1000.
>
> 3. For the American novel published during the year which shall best present the wholesome atmosphere of American life, and the highest standard of American manners and manhood—$1000.
>
> 4. For the best book of the year upon the history of the United States—$2000.
>
> 5. For the best American biography, teaching patriotic and unselfish service to the people illustrated by an eminent example—$1000.
>
> 6. For the best cartoon published during the year—$500.
>
> 7. For the best book of verse published during the year—$1000.

Three traveling scholarships of $1500 each were established for the graduates of the School of Journalism who passed their examinations with the highest honor, to enable each of them to spend a year in Europe for the study of social, moral, and political conditions and the character and principles of the European press.

An annual scholarship of $1500 was also established for the student of music in America who may be deemed most promising to continue study in Europe; also another annual scholarship of $1500, under the same conditions, to be awarded by the National Academy of Design for the most promising and deserving art student. The awards are under the control of the University authorities.

Silas Bent (essay date 1939)

SOURCE: "Pulitzer: Past-Master," in *Newspaper Crusaders: A Neglected Story,* Whittlesey House, 1939, pp. 20-42.

[*In the following essay, Bent focuses on the crusades against government and big business corruption undertaken by Pulitzer's newspapers the New York* World *and St. Louis* Post-Dispatch.]

Premier among the journalistic crusaders of this country was the elder Joseph Pulitzer. He was convinced that a newspaper should "never be satisfied with merely printing news." He stood for political independence, fearless attacks upon demagoguery, injustice, corruption, and "predatory plutocracy." If told fully, his achievements in that field alone might well fill a volume; I shall attempt no more here than to indicate their scope and the methods he employed, disregarding chronological sequence.

Two of the earlier campaigns of the New York *World,* which serve to illustrate its methods, its courage, and its power, were completed within less than a month, one upon the heels of the other. The first concerned the disputed line between Venezuela and British Guiana. Drawn by a surveyor in the employ of the British government, this boundary had never been accepted by Venezuela, and when an attempt was made to map it the President of Venezuela appealed to the United States for help. His Minister in Washington cited the Monroe Doctrine, and newspapers opposed to Grover Cleveland were aroused to ridicule his delay in acting.

Then, on December 18, 1895, President Cleveland gave out a special message, declaring that the attitude of Britain menaced our "peace and safety," and saying that if Britain did not renounce her claims an American commission would be appointed "to determine the true divisional line."

Now, the *World* had virtually forced the nomination of Cleveland and had been the chief instrument in electing him. Yet its owner at once prepared an editorial in which he said:

> Are our peace and safety as a nation, the integrity of our free institutions, and the tranquil maintenance of our distinctive form of government threatened by an extension, however unwarranted and arbitrary, of the British possessions in Venezuela? The assumption is absurd. And with it falls the structure of ponderously patriotic rhetoric reared upon it by the President.

In spite of a succession of editorials in that vein, showing for one thing that the Monroe Doctrine was in no way affected, there was an outburst of jingoism, and under its pressure both Houses of Congress adopted resolutions providing for a commission to fix the boundary and appropriating money for the task. The President's message was read in schoolrooms, former soldiers volunteered their services, and many newspapers joined the outcry. The New York *Sun,* as John L. Heaton tells us in "The Story of a Page," denounced as "an alien or a traitor" any American citizen who did not uphold the President. It demanded that the State Department reach an understanding at once with France and Russia, in order that their navies might assist by making war in the English Channel and the Irish Sea. Commenting on efforts in behalf of peace downtown, the New York *Times* said:

> Under the teachings of these bloodless Philistines, these patriots of the ticker, if they were heeded, American civilization would degenerate to the level of the Digger Indians, who eat dirt all their lives and appear to like it. We should become a nation of hucksters, flabby in spirit, flabby in muscle, flabby in principle, and devoid of honor, for it is always a characteristic of the weak and cowardly to make up by craft and trickery for their defect of noble qualities.

Said the *Tribune:*

> The message will not be welcome to the peace-at-any-price cuckoos who have been clamoring that the Monroe Doctrine is a myth, and that we have no business to meddle with affairs between Great Britain and Venezuela.

The *World* appealed by cable and telegraph to the reigning house in England and to church dignitaries there, as well as to leaders in this country. The Prince of Wales, later Edward VII; the Duke of York, who was to be George V; William E. Gladstone, Lord Rosebery, Archbishops and Cardinals replied with earnest expressions of their horror at the thought of a war with this country. Clergymen and other leaders in the United States lent their aid. The upshot was that war was averted, this country acted for Venezuela in negotiations, and an international commission laid down a modified boundary satisfactory to both sides.

High tribute was paid to the *World* and its owner. Peace societies of Great Britain arranged a meeting at which they presented a memorial of thanks, and Ralph Pulitzer read for his father an address, "The Reign of Reason *vs.* the Reign of Force," which concluded:

> However we may differ on many questions, we have common sympathies for liberty and humanity, just as we have a common language.
>
> We speak, we read, we think, we feel, we hope, we love, we pray—aye, we dream—in the same language. The twentieth century is dawning. Let us dream that it will realize our ideals and the higher destiny of mankind.
>
> Let us dream not of hideous war and butchery, of barbarism and darkness, but of enlightenment, progress, and peace.

Sir Robert Head Cook, then editor of the London *Daily News,* emphasized the service the *World* had rendered to journalism as a profession.

In provoking that crusade, Richard Olney, Secretary of State, wrote the blundering Venezuela message; in the second of these concurrent campaigns John G. Carlisle, Secretary of the Treasury, was primarily to blame. In each the *World* rebuked President Cleveland, who was responsible, obviously, for the acts of his Cabinet members.

In February of 1895 the Treasury, to replenish its gold stock, issued $64,000,000 bonds at 104½ to J. P. Morgan and Company as head of a syndicate. In a short while the bonds were selling at 120. In the following August the chief of the *World's* Washington bureau said that another and larger issue was impending, under the same terms. At once the newspaper gave sharp warning that the Treasury must not permit itself to be "cornered" again. Nevertheless, word arrived that a contract had been signed with the Morgan firm.

George Cary Eggleston tells us, in "Recollections of a Varied Life," how Pulitzer took hold of such a situation and outlined explicitly to his department heads a course of action. His instructions are set down:

> We have made our case in this matter of the bond issue. We have presented the facts clearly, convincingly, conclusively, but the Administration refuses to heed them. We are now going to compel it to heed them on pain of facing a scandal that no administration could survive.
>
> What we demand is that these bonds shall be sold to the public at something like their actual value and not to a Wall Street Syndicate for many millions less. You understand all that. You are to write a double-leaded article to occupy the whole editorial space tomorrow morning. You are not to print a line of editorial on any other subject. You are to set forth . . . the patent falsehood that the United States Treasury's credit needs "financing." You are to declare, with all possible emphasis, that the banks, bankers, and people of the United States stand ready and eager to lend their government all the money it wants at three per cent interest, and to buy its four per cent bonds at a premium that will amount to that . . .
>
> Then as a guarantee of the sincerity of our conviction you are to say that the *World* offers in advance to take one million dollars of the new bonds at the highest market price, if they are offered to the public in the open market.
>
> In the meanwhile, [E. O.] Chamberlin has a staff of men sending out dispatches to every bank and banker in the land, setting forth our demand for a public loan instead of a syndicate dicker, and asking each for what amount of the new bonds it or he will subscribe on a three per cent basis. Tomorrow morning's papers will carry with your editorial its complete confirmation in their replies, and the proposed loan will be oversubscribed . . . Even Mr. Cleveland's phenomenal self-confidence and Mr. Carlisle's purblind belief in Wall Street methods will not be able to withstand such a demonstration as that . . . If it is true that the contract with the syndicate has already been made, they must cancel it.

In reply to the *World's* queries, a mass of telegrams pledging capital for the purchase of the bonds was received. Then an editorial was printed telling specifically of Wall Street bankers and the amounts of gold they had accumulated to "invest in the speculation." It was not in fact so much a speculation as a sure-thing gambler's chicanery; but the newspaper's protest was against the "waste of ten or fifteen millions" in the transaction, and it made an appeal to the President "to save the country from the mischief, the wrong, and the scandal of the pending bond deal."

Two New York banks, in the face of these revelations, withdrew from the bond syndicate. The President yielded, and his Secretary of the Treasury, with bad grace, offered the issue to the public, although the Morgans offered six millions more than their original bid. The $100,000,000 bonds were oversubscribed more than six times. The Morgan syndicate had the small consolation of getting five millions at a fraction less than 111 while another bidder was offering 114, but that was under a special ruling by Secretary Carlisle.

No such distinguished success attended every campaign undertaken by the *World*. Its effort, for example, to break the financial and political power of E. H. Harriman was a failure. The campaign was an outcome of its long fight against Theodore Roosevelt and its exposure of contributions to his campaign fund by J. P. Morgan and Company, the Standard Oil, George W. Perkins, George J. Gould, C. S. Mellen, C. H. Mackay, E. T. Stotesbury, Chauncey M. Depew, Harriman, and others, embracing representatives of the Steel Trust, the insurance companies, International Harvester, the Coal Trust, bankers, and so on.

A letter from Harriman to Sydney Webster, a New York lawyer who was active in politics, was published in the *World* of April 2, 1907, which showed that Harriman had raised $260,000 for Roosevelt's 1904 campaign. He told Webster that this was with the understanding that Depew was to be made an ambassador, that Frank Black was to succeed him as senator, and that Harriman was to be consulted by Roosevelt about railroad recommendations in the President's message to Congress. None of these things had been done, and Harriman wanted to know where he stood.

No proof was forthcoming that Roosevelt had asked Harriman to raise the fund. The *World* said that the President had asked the financier to the White House for a talk, and Roosevelt denied it, whereupon the *World* printed the invitation to Harriman; it printed also the President's letter to him, saying "you and I are practical men." It exposed Harriman's manipulations of railroad stock. Finally Pulitzer instructed his staff:

> Put utmost vigor without violence into "Harriman must go" series—say one editorial addressed to each director, stating his character, career, moral, social, religious position, pretensions, responsibilities, etc., every second or third day. Directors alone responsible. Whole country's reputation involved. Harriman vindicates Hearst and almost justifies Bryan's State ownership; certainly helps both and even worse socialist attacks, as practical, horrible example to be pointed at railroad corruption generally. Harriman should go as railroad's worst enemy.

Later, he instructed C. M. Van Hamm, managing editor, to get biographical material on each director of the Union Pacific, one of the Harriman roads, "how he rose, what he did in a public-spirited way . . . and yet how they allow this man to be their representative, their Grand Elector, their Chosen. They are responsible, *not* Harriman." Yet Harriman remained. Perhaps his associates thought the more highly of him for the drubbing he got. At any rate, he was too well established to be ousted, although the crusade was waged with full Pulitzer persistence and vigor.

Although the crusade to oust Harriman failed of its ultimate objective, doubtless it impaired his power to dicker with Presidents and dictate to lesser political luminaries. It arose from Pulitzer's conviction that great wealth must not be permitted to impair democratic processes. From that conviction came the *World's* exposure of insurance corruption, in which also Harriman figured. Like the other crusades I have described, this was a single-handed fight.

A quarrel between James Waddell Alexander, president of the Equitable Life Assurance Society, and James Hazen Hyde, heir to the majority stock (which under his father's will Alexander controlled), revealed conditions so questionable that the *World* began a series of two hundred editorials, "Equitable Corruption." In the first of these it said that the "most astounding, farreaching financial scandal known to the history of the United States" was approaching a climax, told of stock jobbing by Jacob H. Schiff and Harriman with the insurance company, in which they were directors, and demanded a legislative investigation.

Against an investigation were arrayed powerful business interests in the City of New York, the legislature, Governor Francis W. Higgins, and the State superintendents of insurance and banking. In response to public feeling, a committee of directors was appointed and made certain recommendations, which the board rejected. The *World* continued its hammering and brought out more damaging facts. Reluctantly Governor Higgins directed the superintendent of insurance to look into the matter, and he made a report the most of which was suppressed for a time. Day after day the newspaper trained its guns on Albany until finally the Governor capitulated and advised the appointment of a legislative committee. As counsel, at the suggestion of Don C. Seitz, the committee chose Charles Evans Hughes, who became, by reason of his patience, perseverance, and skill in this investigation, a national figure.

It was shown that the big insurance companies in New York maintained what the *World* properly named corruption funds, and contributed generously to campaign chests. This resulted soon in a charge of larceny against George W. Perkins of the New York Life Insurance Company, in contributing $48,702.50 to Theodore Roosevelt's campaign and then receiving that sum from the funds of the corporation. The Court of Appeals, to which the case was carried, absolved Perkins on the ground of motive, but the Chief Justice, dissenting, said that when Perkins reimbursed himself he was as guilty of larceny as though he had taken insurance money to buy a necklace for a woman. The crusade divulged a mass of malodorous facts.

The investigating committee drew two bills to reform insurance company practices. The day after the Governor had signed the second, the *World* said:

> The law now calls it a crime for any corporation, excepting such as are organized for political purposes, to contribute to any campaign fund. No railroad, bank, trust company or manufacturing or mining corporation may hereafter lawfully give one cent to politics. Neither may any corporation maintain in Albany a secret lobby . . .
>
> But the greatest of all in its service to the community is the blow the Armstrong laws strike at the system of high finance which uses the savings of the people to convert public franchises into instruments of oppression. The prohibition of any participation by any life insurance company in syndicates, flotations, or stock speculations cuts off the great source which Wall Street promoters draw upon for speculative funds.

Conditions had been improved but not perfected. James Hazen Hyde, for example, sold his Equitable stock, which had a par value of $51,000, to Thomas Fortune Ryan, a notorious figure of the day, for $2,500,000. The elder J. P. Morgan "persuaded" Ryan, so subsequently he told a Congressional committee, to transfer the stock to him, and paid him some three millions for it. Since that day insurance companies generally have been under suspicion, and dubious practices among them have come to light. But the *World* and its owner had confidence that these conditions would be set right in time.

> The public conscience is sound [it said] . . . The force of moral ideas in the community is omnipotent. What it has done to insurance corruption it can do wherever and whenever the public safety is menaced.

Pulitzer was ill in Paris when strikers locked out of the steel mills of the Carnegie company at Homestead, Pennsylvania, were being killed by Pinkerton thugs and the Coal and Iron Police, a private force hired by the employers, and he was deeply agitated when the news began to reach him. Without his guidance, the *World* said editorially on July 1, 1892:

> Under the McKinley [tariff] Act the people are paying taxes of nearly $20,000,000 and a much larger sum in bounties to Carnegie, Phipps & Co., and their fellows, for the alleged purpose of benefiting the wage-earners. And yet there is war at the Homestead works, and the employers have enlisted Pinkerton Hessians and fortified their property that they may pour scalding water on their discharged workmen if an attack is made upon them.

Strong in his sympathy with the underdog, Pulitzer was thrown into one of the serious crises of his illness by the news and the editorials. A member of the *World* staff who was with him tried to reassure him by saying that the accounts might be exaggerated. "There have been as many men killed in this labor war," his chief retorted, "as in many a South American revolution." In that day the rights of labor were obscure, and the feudal conditions which prevailed in American industry had received little attention. The *World* continued its editorial campaign by demanding:

> Is it right that a private detective agency shall maintain a standing army, a thing forbidden even to the several States of the Union? Is it well that a body of armed mercenaries shall be held thus at the service of whomsoever has money with which to hire them?

Other newspapers, shocked at this impertinence to a big corporation, sharply critized the news editors of the *World* for the sensationalism of the stories they were printing from the war zone, and these comments were sent to the owner in Paris. Meanwhile the editorials continued:

> If force must be used to sustain the beneficiaries of protection in reducing wages and breaking down labor organizations it is better that it should be the citizen soldiery of the State, for the workmen will not resist them.

On the next day, in response to cables from Paris, the newspaper spoke in a different tone:

> There is but one thing for the locked-out men to do. They must submit to the law. They must keep the peace. Their quarrel is with their employers. They must not make it a quarrel with organized society. It is a protest against wage reduction. It must not be made a revolt against law and order. They must not resist the authority of the State. They must not make war upon the community.

That moderation of the editorial note was due to direction of the owner, but he so much preferred an editor who would take a courageous course to one who was irresolute and weak that he bore no resentment. As a fact, and as subsequent developments bore out, the editorials told nothing but the truth and actually were not incendiary. The *World* continued, indeed, to denounce Henry Clay Frick and his associates for their "appeal to Pinkerton rather than to the lawful officers of the State."

After Martin Tabert was fatally lashed by a "whipping boss" in a Florida convict camp, a score of newspapers to which telegrams were sent asking that they give publicity to the facts, ignored the request. Tabert was an underdog, he had died nearly a year earlier, and he hailed from North Dakota, which had been unable to get action. The *World,* however, immediately sent a staff man to Florida, and presently thirty-eight other newspapers were buying his syndicated articles, so that the news associations were compelled to take up the story. As a result, Florida abolished the prevailing penal system within six weeks, and forbade the use of the lash on convicts. The judge and the sheriff in the Tabert case were removed from office and the man who had beaten him was charged with murder. Once aroused by the *World* and the newspapers which followed the trail it blazed, public opinion forced action with exceptional speed, notwithstanding the influence of corporations which had profited from the leasing system and which had induced politicians to maintain it.

Corrupt business, national politics, and foreign affairs, however, were by no means the sole interest of the *World* in crusading. It forced an investigation of the gas monopoly in New York City and brought about lower rates. It was an untiring enemy of Tammany Hall, although a Democratic newspaper. Its reporters investigated hundreds of bakeshops in the city, found that many were violating the sanitary code, and forced municipal inspectors to clean them up. It exposed both the milk trust and the poultry trust, and caused scores of indictments. It revealed that rotten eggs were being sold widely for the manufacture of foodstuffs, and that the refrigerator system was utilized to control or affect prices. If it did not cure these conditions permanently, it put the public on its guard and made city officials more scrupulous and more wary. That a great deal remains to be done, with little newspaper inclination in the metropolis to take a hand, has become apparent repeatedly. It is not always true that a crusade, at least temporarily successful, creates a vacuum at that point. The *World* is dead, and it left no New York heir.

Not until 1883 did Joseph Pulitzer buy the New York *World.* He had come to this country near the middle of the century, friendless and penniless, had slept in a public park, had done the most menial work to fend off starvation, had served as a volunteer in the Civil War, and then had moved on to St. Louis, where he worked for a time for the *Westliche Post,* then edited by Carl Schurz. He was elected a member of the Missouri Legislature, and afterward helped organize the Liberal Republican Party in 1872, which nominated Horace Greeley for the presidency. Schurz refused to support the ticket, and Pulitzer, who had bought an interest in the *Westliche Post,* sold it back; then he stumped the midwest for Greeley, who was defeated. After working for a time as a Washington correspondent, he returned to St. Louis in 1878, and bought for a song successively the *Post* and the *Evening Dispatch,* which he merged. Semiliterate as an immigrant, he had spent all his spare time in reading and had educated himself; and although his accent lingered, he was a good speaker.

For a week or so the new paper was called the *Post and Dispatch,* then the *Post-Dispatch;* at the outset it stated a creed:

> The *Post and Dispatch* will serve no party but the people; it will be no organ of Republicanism, but the organ of truth; it will follow no causes but its conclusions; will not support the "Administration," but criticize it; will oppose all frauds and shams wherever and whatever they are; will advocate principles and ideas rather than prejudices and partisanship. These ideas and principles are precisely the same as those upon which our Government was originally founded, and to which we owe our country's marvellous growth and development. They are the same that made a Republic possible, and without which a real Republic is impossible. They are the ideas of a true, genuine, real Democracy.

That pronouncement struck a new note in the journalism of the midwest. Moreover, the newspaper undertook to live up to it. Never a hidebound partisan organ, it undertook to expose frauds and shams regardless of political consequences, and made powerful enemies thereby, but established itself powerfully in the affection of its public. One of its first campaigns was against rich tax dodgers. The files of the assessor's office showed understatement of property values and false inventories on the part of the wealthy, while those not so blessed in worldly goods were blessed at least with more honesty. The *Post-Dispatch* printed side by side the returns filed by the well-to-do and the poor. By this simple device it subjected civic slackers to reproach more severe than editorial comment, and the practice was corrected.

When less than a year old the *Post-Dispatch* began a crusade against protected gambling. The chief of the industry was Alanson B. Wakefield, a political luminary; the Board of Police Commissioners was politically appointed. Wakefield was indicted for perjury and sent to the penitentiary, fifty of his employees were fined, and a lottery was put out of commission. The paper fought for two years, however, before gambling was made a felony in Missouri. Meanwhile it did not neglect less sensational matters; through its influence the municipality began the purchase of lands for a beautiful park system, cleaned and repaired its streets, and erected a permanent exposition building. Twice the owner of the paper was physically attacked, but his courage was undiminished.

In 1880, while T. J. Pendergast's elder brother began building in Kansas City a political machine which was to achieve an unenviable fame (to which I shall refer presently), the owner of the *Post-Dispatch* heard that the Republicans were planning to buy Indiana in the presidential campaign. In Indianapolis we hear him, on October 9, speaking in a strain which the Pulitzer newspapers were to make familiar to the nation. Protesting against the "power of the millionaires" in elections, he reviewed the influence in Indiana of the banks, railroads, and protected industries, and added:

> We want prosperity, but not at the expense of liberty. Poverty is not as great a danger to liberty as wealth, with its corrupting, demoralizing influences. Suppose all the influences I have just reviewed were to take their hands off instead of supporting the Republican Party, would it have a ghost of a chance of success?
>
> Let us have prosperity, but never at the expense of liberty, never at the expense of real self-government, and let us never have a government at Washington

> owing its retention to the power of the millionaires rather than to the will of the millions.

Indiana had been a Democratic State, but the "power of the millionaires" lifted it over into the Republican column that year. At a banquet in New York in honor of S. W. Dorsey, who had charge of the Indiana campaign, it was said that Dorsey had been "able to save not merely Indiana, and through it the State of New York, but the nation." He admitted subsequently that some five thousand persons aided him in buying Indiana. "Each of these men," he explained, "reported what they could do . . . and how much it would take to influence people to a change of thought. We paid $20 to some, as high as $75 to others, but we took care that the three men from every township should know just what each got. There was no chance of 'nigging'."

Whenever that idealist who had spoken unsuccessfully at Indianapolis encountered the "power of the millionaires" in corrupt operation, he set himself to combat it; whenever he suspected that the ballot was being undermined, he sought to put it on an honest basis, and he handed down a tradition in the office of the *Post-Dispatch* which resulted long after his death in a political house cleaning, and in a challenge, across the State, to the power of Boss "Tom" Pendergast. The long-drawn crusade whereby St. Louis was taken out of political red ink and put on the credit side of the electoral ledger merits examination at some length because it illustrates, as the other campaigns I have discussed do not, untiring pursuit of a purpose and unwearied attention to minute detail. For the facts of this crusade I am indebted to Carlos F. Hurd, an especially gifted member of the *Post-Dispatch* staff; for the consequences in Kansas City I have drawn upon other sources of information.

Although Kansas City was but half the size of St. Louis, Pendergast bossed the State democracy as well as his local machine, and almost always named the candidate for Governor. In St. Louis, as in Kansas City, there was ballot-stuffing with a complaisant election board; and when a ward boss, making war on his overlord, added more than three thousand votes to his ward list, while the other added nearly five thousand, the unexampled inflation offered an opportunity to the *Post-Dispatch* to rivet the attention of its readers on the frauds. On July 22, 1936, it began a series of first-page broadsides which ultimately cleaned out the voting lists, gave the city honest elections, and compelled the Governor to oust the election board.

Work began with two overswollen wards. Reporters found empty brick shells with scores of ghostly voters, hotels with half a dozen names on the register and dozens on the registration lists, saloons with more votable names than there were bottles behind the bar. Their photographers pictured the walls on which were chalked the numbers of phantom citizens. The first story was enough to convince the average citizen of St. Louis; it was not enough to convince James A. Waechter, the backslapping chairman of the election board, who, when he saw a copy of the first edition containing the exposé, nodded that he had heard that sort of thing before. If anything was wrong with the registration he would take it up, of course, but just then he was busy with a case in court.

The newspaper did not wait until the chairman of the election board got through with his case in court. A special staff worked daily, in sweltering heat, studying voting lists, ringing doorbells, taking affidavits—for beside each reporter was a notary public—and turning out copy by the column. The sworn statements of election judges and clerks corroborated their findings in many instances. The investigators moved on from the river wards, where corruption was taken rather as a matter of course by the public, into staid residential districts. In a north-side area of homes, where a street had been widened, rows of dwellings had been wrecked, and the tenants had registered from the new homes to which they had moved, but their names remained on the lists at the old addresses. South and west the reporters moved relentlessly. The solid element of the city was thoroughly aroused when it found that from ten to thirty per cent of the voters in their own neighborhoods were duplicates or phantoms. There were mass meetings. Telegrams and letters poured in on the Governor.

When Chairman Waechter tried to evade a thorough examination of the rolls the *Post-Dispatch* demanded a recanvass of each of more than seven hundred precincts in the city. The election board capitulated and reported that some 46,000 registrants were "not found." But there was no time, so Waechter said, to strike those names off before an impending primary, and in most precincts judges and clerks voted them.

More broadsides in the news columns followed. A canvass was made by *Post-Dispatch* reporters of the vote on a bond issue a short time before, and the figures ran laboriously into pages of copy. Even the politicians who profited from the corruption began to perceive that the election board must go; and three days before a general election the Governor, under their pressure, announced that it had been removed "for the betterment of the public service" and because there had not been enough "diligence in supervision." In place of the members removed he appointed a new board satisfactory to the paper, and a purge of office clerks, precinct judges, and clerks, began. In their places new man power was recruited from banks, factory offices, and commerce.

It was a day-and-night job, both for members of the board and their underlings and for members of the *Post-Dispatch* staff. The outcome was the largest registration St. Louis had ever witnessed, but nobody made charges that the lists were padded. A grand jury, which indicted eleven six-man groups of election officials, and admonished the courts not to dismiss the charges on "immaterial technicalities," said in its report:

> We think it worthy of comment that, acting under

> exactly the same laws as previous election boards, with a minimum of time at their disposal to prepare for the election, the present board carried through successfully an election at which the greatest number in the history of the city voted, and this without any evidence of fraud. The reason for this was simply that these gentlemen were possessed of what might be termed honesty of purpose, and handled a most difficult situation with no other thought than the carrying out to the fullest extent of their sworn duty. These gentlemen deserve the commendation of all honest citizens.

One may fancy that Tom Pendergast observed from afar with some perturbation the pertinacity, patience, and skill of that horde of *Post-Dispatch* reporters and photographers, with their notary-public accompanyists. His local machine had proved invulnerable to similar exposures, but had never been subjected to a test so thoroughgoing. Now the Kansas City *Star* adopted on a smaller scale the methods of its greater neighbor. Two reporters began an inspection of the registration lists, and found 270,000 names, in a city with some 400,000 population; they found a funeral "parlor" with one occupant and seventeen voters; they found other registrations from vacant lots and untenanted warehouses, others who had been dead for years. They found, in brief, as far as they went, what the *Post-Dispatch* reporters had found in St. Louis. A Citizens' League was formed, to demand a grand-jury investigation.

This investigation brought 199 indictments; in the first eighty cases tried, there were fifty-six convictions, one plea of guilty, and twenty defendants threw themselves on the mercy of the court. As time went on, the sentences to the penitentiary, ranging from a month to five years, multiplied. It looked gloomy for Tom Pendergast; but it did not defeat his slate in the 1938 election. Orators for the coalition opposition charged that the town's good name was being besmirched because of stories about wide-open gambling, unregulated prostitution, and vote frauds. The outcome was merely a reduction by about one-third in the Pendergast plurality. The machine was still running, but was not in good working order.

After the election, Governor Lloyd C. Stark of Missouri declared that his administration was pledged to "eradicate the blight of crime and corruption from Kansas City," and instructed his Attorney General to oust officials who refused to assist court and grand jury proceedings. "Information from reliable sources," said the Governor, "shows that the gambling racket is carried on openly and in defiance of law and without protest from any official heads of the city's government; that houses of prostitution flourish within the very shadows of the Court House and the City Hall and the inmates solicit openly, unashamed and unafraid of official authority; that gangsters and racketeers, unmolested by official authority, ply their trade and prey, through violence and intimidation, upon citizens and business men alike."

That was but another repercussion of the *Post-Dispatch* crusade, in which the practices of the Pendergast machine had been held up as a vicious example of electoral corruption.

In long-term consequences the restoration of honest elections to St. Louis may prove to have been the most valuable of the numerous *Post-Dispatch* crusades; it was an evidence that the newspaper was still carrying on in the Pulitzer tradition, after the owner's death.

It was no easy tradition to live up to. One of the noteworthy exploits of the paper, for example, had been the exposure in 1898 of the Central Traction (street railway) bribery of municipal representatives. No action could be forced in that case, however, until 1902, when Joseph Jolk was Governor. Then the key man of the House of Delegates "combine" slipped away to Mexico. The *Post-Dispatch* sent a staff man to find him and persuade him to return. He gave State's evidence, and nine boodlers were sent to prison.

Instances of that sort had helped make the newspaper an immensely profitable enterprise. Within a few years after it was started it was netting its owner $200,000 a year. Pulitzer's success was won, I believe, through a certain art of getting close to the heart of a vast audience and through his fight for the underdog; his crusade against wealthy corruptionists was the brushwork of that art. Not long before his death, which occurred October 29, 1911, he wrote for the *Review of Reviews* an article in which he said:

> What is everybody's business is nobody's business—except the journalist's. It is his by adoption. But for his care almost every reform would be stillborn. He holds officials to their duty. He exposes secret schemes of plunder. He promotes every hopeful plan of progress. Without him public opinion would be shapeless and dumb. Our Republic and its press will rise or fall together. An able, disinterested, public-spirited press, with trained intelligence to know the right and courage to do it, can preserve that public virtue without which popular government is a sham and a mockery.

To but one of his sons did the elder transmit the strong sense of social justice and civic responsibility, the courage, and the high order of intelligence essential to a crusader of the first water. This was Joseph Pulitzer, Jr., to whom fell the management of the *Post-Dispatch.* It was under his hand that honest elections were restored finally to the city. In this and other reforms, until the middle of 1938, he had the assistance of Oliver K. Bovard, a superb executive and a crusader who had won his spurs under the elder Pulitzer. Together they made the Teapot Dome scandal so apparent that a Senate committee was compelled to investigate it, forced a corrupt Federal judge in the East St. Louis district off the bench, and brought kidnappers to justice. But it was Joseph Pulitzer's son and namesake who had the final say-so when the *Post-Dispatch* assailed the American Newspaper Publishers Association (ANPA), of which he was a member, for undermining public confidence by its mercenary attitude.

This was just before the 1937 annual meeting of the association. Editorially the newspaper said:

> The ANPA is to be likened to the National Association of Manufacturers or the American Petroleum Institute or any other coalition of business men for the purpose of advancing the fortunes of themselves and their companies. This comparison is borne out by the by-laws of ANPA, showing it was created to foster the business interests of members, to procure uniformity of usage, to settle differences, to protect members from irresponsible customers, and so on.
>
> This is the language of business; it is not the language of the newspaper profession. It is the language of men engaged in manufacturing a product; it is not the language of men engaged in the high and responsible calling of writing, editing, and interpreting the news.

The editorial continued by saying that the association had gone far afield to engage in pronouncements giving the impression that it was "grinding its own ax at public expense," and set forth a formidable list, including its condemnation of the Wagner Act setting up a national labor board and its opposal of the Copeland pure food and drugs bill. In the latter case the position "represents pressure of advertisers." It added:

> How can the public be expected to separate these activities of the men who own and manage newspapers from the responsibility to the public interest borne by writers and editors? The fact is they are inextricably joined in the public mind. Such activities cast a reflection on the whole press. They impair public trust in the disinterestedness of newspapers.

In that case the younger Pulitzer turned his batteries upon an organization of which he was a member, and held aloft the torch his father had raised more than once, that newspapers must not permit selfish interest to impair their public service. His services to the press have been marked, as well as his services to his city and his State. Among the officials of St. Louis and to a great extent throughout Missouri there has prevailed a sense that malfeasance in posts of public trust was not to be risked, with so powerful and vigilant a watchdog on guard. The newspaper has been a benison on occasion, when civic causes called, a builder as well as a scourge and a discipline. It remains a monument to the self-taught genius who made it his proving ground and the agency of his earliest triumphs over wrongs.

Janet E. Steele (essay date 1990)

SOURCE: "The 19th-Century *World* Versus the *Sun*: Promoting Consumption (Rather than the Working Man)," in *Journalism Quarterly,* Vol. 67, No. 3, Autumn, 1990, pp. 592-600.

[*In the following essay, Steele argues that the victory of Pulitzer's* World *over its competitor the New York* Sun *in the late nineteenth century "signified the erosion of traditional American values such as hard work, thrift, and self-sacrifice, and the emergence of a value system that increasingly celebrated consumption, leisure, and self-indulgence."*]

One of the most familiar dramas of late nineteenth-century journalism is that of the epic battle for circulation between Joseph Pulitzer's New York *World* and William Randolph Hearst's New York *Journal.* The role of the yellow press in aggravating what Theodore Roosevelt called the "splendid little war" with Spain has been taught to generations of journalism students as an object lesson on the dangers of sensationalism and the need for editorial responsibility.

For cultural historians, however, a much more important battle took place a decade earlier. It was not Pulitzer versus Hearst that ushered in a new era in American journalism, but rather Joseph Pulitzer versus Charles A. Dana, the editor of the New York *Sun.* At stake in this circulation war was the very definition of the reading public. Pulitzer's victory over Dana marked the creation of a consumer society; it signified the erosion of traditional American values such as hard work, thrift and self-sacrifice, and the emergence of a value system that increasingly celebrated consumption, leisure, and self-indulgence.

Metropolitan newspapers at the turn of the 20th century were unique in their relation to the culture of consumption. As the most important medium of communication that city dwellers had for learning about the abundance of consumer goods, the daily press took on an expanded identity as a vehicle for advertisers. This was evident in the development of sporting news, the women's page, and the paid advice column—as well as in the growing cooperation between newspapers and department store managers.

Yet, by the turn of the century, newspapers were not merely important vehicles for advertising new forms of mass-produced culture, they were themselves mass-produced and mass-marketed. By as early as the 1870's, newspapers had become big businesses worth several million dollars—larger than all but a few manufacturing concerns. The metropolitan press underwent a technological and managerial revolution at the turn of the century, which coincided with the breakdown of "producer" values. Both of these transitions were indicative of the broader changes in American culture that led to the creation of a consumer society.

While many historians have described Joseph Pulitzer's enticing vision of the metropolis, less attention has been paid to the values of the late 19th century newspapers that the *World* displaced. For the 15 years before Joseph Pulitzer bought the New York *World* in 1883, the paper with the largest circulation in the city was the New York *Sun,* edited by Charles A. Dana. Significantly, Dana's paper neither relied on advertisements for revenues nor devoted much space to consumer goods and leisure activities.

The competing styles of the New York *Sun* and the New York *World* (both democratic, working class newspapers) reflected the cultural orientations of their editors. The ways in which Dana and Pulitzer viewed their readers—as producers on the one hand and as consumers on the other—accounted not only for the differences in the content of the two papers, but also for the ways in which the editors used the technologies available to them. Analysis of these differences will shed new light on what may have been the most culturally significant newspaper drama of the late nineteenth century—the phenomenal rise of the New York *World,* and the partial eclipse of the *Sun.*

DANA AND THE *SUN*

When Charles Dana bought the *Sun* from Moses Beach in 1868, the paper had a strong tradition as a Democratic, working class newspaper. Founded in 1833 by Benjamin Day, the *Sun* was New York's first "penny paper." Like the imitators that would follow it, the *Sun* made money from street sales and classified advertising, rather than from subscriptions and political subsidies. Popular with the mostly Democratic working class (though nominally "independent" of politics) the early *Sun* revolutionized the definition of news, emphasizing timeliness, human interest, and sensational accounts of vice and crime.

Dana drew upon the *Sun*'s antebellum roots to create a new version of urban, Jacksonian Democracy. Ever mindful of the paper's pre-existing working class readership, Dana announced that the *Sun* would be "an uncompromising advocate of the laboring masses." This was no idle promise. On a typical day in July, 1868, the *Sun* reported on strikes by the journeymen bakers and the Singer machine iron moulders, fund raising efforts by the Coach Makers' Union, and the activities of Typographical Union #6, the union of the *Sun*'s printers. During the first year that Dana owned the *Sun,* he called for the repeal of the Conspiracy Law, an ordinance that forbade union members to act together in a manner injurious to trade. *Sun* editorials argued that workingmen combinations were no worse than those of stock market manipulators who "plunder[ed] the public." Of the two, in fact, the paper asserted that the capitalists were the "greater criminals."

The *Sun* offered its working class readers the same ideas of cooperation and self-help that had been prevalent in the 1840's: "by the concentration of a number of small sums into one definite channel, they can produce very remarkable results." The paper advocated cooperative associations of workingmen that would build housing, establish reading rooms, and provide lectures and self-help programs. It also pledged to do what it could to assist these organizations, for example embarking on a crusade to fight Sabbath laws that would close the reading rooms on the only day that most workingmen and women were at liberty to use them.

While Dana was sympathetic towards the interests of the working class, he found no serious fault with capitalism. The editor distrusted monopolies, but the only alternative he raised was greater competition. Propelled by a sentimental notion of labor as "the noblest duty of life," he argued that higher wages for labor would add to the prosperity of all.

Dana's understanding of his readers was also reflected in the *Sun*'s expanded use of the human interest story, a genre which sociologist Robert Park credited Dana's paper with developing. Dana believed his readers were interested in more than stories of vice and crime. When a 1919 anniversary issue of the *Sun* looked back on Dana's achievements, it recalled that the editor had believed the public would "enjoy a discourse upon the architecture of the tombs of the Pharaohs as much as it liked a description of the Tombs of Centre Street." The *Sun* reflected Dana's belief that an editor was obliged to print *all* the news, whether or not it would be acceptable to polite society. This contrasted sharply with the views of his peers in New York's literary establishment, who held that editors should censor and sanitize the news before they published it. In Dana's words:

> The newspaper must be founded upon human nature . . . It must furnish the [news] which the people demand, or else it never can be successful . . . by news I mean everything that occurs, everything which is of human interest . . . There is a great disposition in some quarters to say that the newspapers ought to limit the amount of news they print; that certain kinds of news ought not to be published . . . I have always felt that whatever the Divine Providence permitted to occur I was not too proud to print.

Though Dana eventually made quite a fortune at the New York *Sun*—one 1884 estimate placed his income at $150,000 annually—he remained sympathetic with the experiences and desires of his largely working class readers. This accounted for his allegiance to the Democratic party, his friendliness towards Tammany Hall, and his dislike of genteel reformers (such as Henry Ward Beecher, E. L. Codkin, and George William Curtis) who achieved a political triumph in the 1884 presidential election of Democratic candidate Grover Cleveland. Dana was convinced that the Independent Republicans (whom he named the Mugwumps) were motivated by distrust of the people, and that their crusade for reform of the civil service masked issues of ethnicity and class. As the *Sun* jeered:

> [the Mugwump] would as soon think of parting his hair elsewhere than in the middle as of voting for the 'Bobs,' Mikes,' and 'Pats' of politics. . . . He is very anxious to cast a 'clean ballot' all by himself, and wants it generally understood that he has none of the enthusiastic devotion to party manifested by the ungenteel publics . . . for Tammany Hall especially he has unutterable loathing. The thought that the 'common people' are in the majority and have as much right to vote as he has almost drives him into exile. He would have the

polls fumigated and perfumed before he entered to deposit his dainty ballot."

A PULITZER CHALLENGE

Despite the great successes of Dana's *Sun,* the paper nearly collapsed in 1884. The circulation of the *Sun* plummeted by 70,000 readers within six months, a development that caught Dana completely by surprise. While historians of journalism have generally concluded that Dana's 1884 rejection of Democratic presidential candidate Grover Cleveland caused this startling drop in circulation, Dana's bad political judgment did not alone explain the suddenly declining sales. It was the revolutionary kind of newspaper that Joseph Pulitzer was creating in the New York *World* that sent the *Sun*'s fortunes reeling.

The rapid growth of the New York *World* came at the direct expense of the New York *Sun.* Dana and Joseph Pulitzer competed for the same market in the mid 1880's. Both papers were read by the city's skilled and semi-skilled laborers, factory workers, immigrants, and small merchants. This raises an interesting question: what did the *World*'s readers find in their paper that was not available in Dana's *Sun?*

The readers of the New York *Sun* and the New York *World* may have been the same, but the two editors viewed them very differently. In 1884, Dana saw the *Sun*'s working class readers as he always had: as producers. While Dana championed the interests of workingmen, he defined those interests in the rhetoric of antebellum workingmen's associations, emphasizing cooperation and self-help. Pulitzer, on the other hand, knew that the *World*'s readers spent their leisure hours window-shopping, seeing vaudeville shows, and saving for weekend excursions to Coney Island. By defining New York's working class as consumers, with leisure time and dollars to spend, Joseph Pulitzer helped to create markets that were vital to the health of a rapidly expanding capitalist economy. The New York *World* depicted—and advertised—a city rich with excitement and commercial amusements. The paper's explosive growth was testimony to the success of this new outlook.

Pulitzer bought the *World* in 1883, paying what many considered the exorbitant sum of $346,000 for a newspaper with a circulation of about 15,000. Almost immediately, the Hungarian immigrant attracted attention by his willingness to exploit modern technology. Pulitzer recognized that New York's increasing dependence on rapid transit provided an opportunity to grab the attention of the commuter at the newsstand. Illustrations and alliterative headlines drew in new readers, and made the paper appealing even to the illiterate. Before his purchase of the *World,* newspapers had been staid, conservative-looking blanket sheets, neatly divided into columns headed by modest titles. Pulitzer caused an explosion of pictures, advertisements and headlines to rip through the New York newspaper industry. Building on the tradition of sensationalism established by penny papers like the antebellum *Sun,* the *World* published titillating stories of sex, vice, crime, and disaster. Like twentieth-century supermarket tabloids, the *World* used sensationalism as bait; the underlying message was prim enough to satisfy rigid Victorian mores.

The visual impact of Pulitzer's *World* was remarkable. Just as revolutionary was his use of the "crusade" for social justice. Though other Democratic newspapers (particularly Dana's *Sun*) had long championed the working class, Pulitzer outflanked them by transforming the *World* into a paper that was—at a glance—unmistakably the people's. Brilliantly, Pulitzer endowed traditional Democratic views with a class-based appeal. When the editor called for reform and social justice, he responded to widely-held fears of concentrated power and authority. Like Dana, Pulitzer defended both labor's right to organize, and the right of capital to run its own enterprises. In the best tradition of reform-minded journalists like Jacob Riis, Pulitzer believed he could end the problems of the poor by turning the glare of publicity onto their suffering.

Pulitzer was adept at mixing charity with self-promotion. The *World* gave Thanksgiving dinners to hundreds of newsboys, clothes and special holiday matinee tickets to needy children at Christmas-time, and summer beach excursions to the city's working boys and girls. While these charities helped to sell newspapers, that subtlety was lost on the happy beneficiaries. If competitors sneered at this as ingenious advertising, it made no difference to the *World*'s readers, who apparently found in Pulitzer's style and message heartening evidence that the newspaper really cared about them.

Pulitzer was one of the creators of an American consumer culture. The *World* offered its readers a guide to the abundance of the metropolis. Pulitzer understood and exploited the connections between text, advertisements, and illustrations. The paper would, for example juxtapose helpful articles such as the "Rage for Decollete" with sketches of the latest ready-to-wear, and advertisements pointing out where these garments could be purchased. Foreign-born readers, wanting to adapt to American ways, eagerly turned to the pages of the *World* for guidance. Many of these readers were women. Pulitzer's *World* was the first newspaper to experiment with a women's page that included society items and gossip columns. When Carrie Meeber, the Midwestern-born heroine of Theodore Dreiser's *Sister Carrie,* was invited by wealthy friends to dine at Sherry's, she knew what to expect. Like thousands of others she had, in Dreiser's words "read of it often in the *Morning* and *Evening World.*"

In short, the *World* radiated an energy and enthusiasm that shook newspaper readers out of their settled habits and made an immediate hit at the newsstand. The paper promoted itself with frequent announcements of its growing circulation. At first these additional sales came from a new market of the foreign-born who had never before purchased English language papers. But before long

Pulitzer's aggressive promotions began to threaten the established dailies.

A COMPARISON

There is an asymmetry to any comparison of the producer outlook of Dana and the consumer orientation of Pulitzer. The *Sun*'s producer orientation was reflected in the paper's political outlook; in its championing of labor organizations, producer's cooperatives, and Democratic Tammany Hall. The *World*'s consumer orientation was not reflected in the paper's political leanings, (which were only slightly to the left of the Democratic *Sun*) but rather in its advertisements, illustrations, and emphasis on leisure activities.

Dana's producerism was evident, for example, in his well-known antipathy towards advertisers. Dana considered advertising to be a waste of valuable space, arguing that a newspaper ought to be able to support itself on sales alone. It was beyond Dana's comprehension that some readers might actually *enjoy* reading ads. Dana frequently expressed the hope that one day the *Sun* would "politely decline to have any of our space used by advertisers." Despite this, approximately one-fourth of the four-page New York *Sun* was devoted to advertising during the 1870's and early 1880's. Nearly all of these were classified, and, incidently, provide a good indication of the newspaper's working class readership. Most of the advertisements were either "Help Wanted" or "Situation Wanted," and referred to domestic, skilled, or semi-skilled work. While a few theatres, dry goods retailers, and manufacturers of patent medicines advertised in the *Sun,* they were overshadowed by the classifieds.

Likewise, Dana believed that illustrations added little of value to a newspaper. As late as 1894, after newspaper illustrations had become common even in the *Sun,* Dana insisted that they were nothing but a "passing fashion." He stated, "I don't believe so many pictures are going to be required for the next century."

By the late 1880's distinctions between the *Sun* and the *World* become more difficult to find, because by then Dana—along with the rest of the New York press—had begun to imitate Pulitzer's techniques. (The group of editors who self-consciously modeled themselves on Joseph Pulitzer would soon include William Randolph Hearst, who bought the New York *Journal* in 1895.)

In 1886, Dana abandoned the *Sun*'s traditional four-page length in order to compete with the eight-page *World.* Critics claimed that at eight pages the tightly-edited *Sun* lost its characteristic brightness, and became "puffed up" with extra material such as serialized fiction and sporting news. According to the trade weekly *The Journalist,* when the *Sun* imitated the *World* and expanded its use of illustrations, the result was clumsy and haphazard.

The *Sun*'s new length and more modern look stopped the hemorrhaging of daily circulation, however. By the end of 1887 sales leveled off at 80,000. No longer willing to watch Pulitzer steal his readers out from under him, Dana reoriented his newspaper in the 1890's, and appealed to a new audience, probably the city's rapidly expanding white collar class. Abandoning its role as the workingman's "uncompromising advocate," the *Sun* grew increasingly conservative and hostile towards labor, a tendency that culminated in the paper's support of Republican Presidential candidate William McKinley in 1896.

In spite of the *Sun*'s strengthened alliance with business interests, the paper never completely lost its producer orientation while Dana was alive. For example, the *Sun* remained steadfastly loyal to the union of its own typesetters, New York Typographical Union #6. Under Dana, the *Sun* had always paid its typesetters the Union scale, at a time, according to the Union, when "the proprietor had the power to dictate his own terms." *The Union Printer,* a labor weekly, frequently quoted Dana as declaring that Union men were well worth the higher wages "because they were the most skillful as well as the most trustworthy."

Dana's continued friendliness to the workers in Typographical Union #6 was not inconsistent with his growing hostility to labor in general, given the extent to which most of his actions were determined by personal loyalty. The *Sun*'s "Chapel," or local, had been faithful to the interests of the paper's editor; he defended it in turn. This loyalty contributed to his refusal to install the linotype machine in the *Sun* offices. Furthermore, Dana liked the look of a handset page. At a Founder's Day speech at Cornell University Dana explained in 1894:

> I have never taken to [the Mergenthaler linotype] . . . because it didn't seem to me to turn out a page as handsome, in a typographical point of view, as a page set up by hand. The difference of expense is something considerable, however. I have been told by one large newspaper publisher who employs that machine that he gets his typesetting done for one-half the cost of typesetting done by hand.

In the broadest sense, Dana ran aground on the shoals of mechanization in the late 1880's and 1890's. New typesetting and printing technologies, spurred in part by the changing material underpinnings of the newspaper industry, greatly increased the relative importance of the business office. As publishing became more business-oriented, the opinions of iconoclastic individuals became a liability. For Dana, the issue of "independence" was entwined with the business organization of the newspaper. According to the memoirs of *Sun* reporter Charles Rosebault, Dana believed that the *Sun* was his paper, "the organ to express his will, his wishes, his views." As proof, Rosebault pointed to Dana's readiness to adopt editorial policies that resulted in great pecuniary loss, noting that "millions of dollars were sacrificed by the exuberant indulgence of his will." In 1876, Dana dismissed as "twaddle" the idea that the day for this kind of journalism had passed. He asserted:

> Whenever in the newspaper profession a man rises up who is original, strong and bold enough to make

> his opinions a matter of consequence to the public, there will be personal journalism; and whenever newspapers are conducted only by commonplace individuals whose views are of no interest to the world and of no consequence to anybody, there will be nothing but impersonal journalism.

Despite Dana's strong words, by the 1890's there was considerable agreement that "the day . . . of the editorial is past." The trade weekly the *Journalist* attributed this to a desire to give readers the "facts" and let them make up their own minds. What had at one time been the province of, as Dana put it, "strong" individuals with "bold" and "original" opinions, was being encroached upon by accountants, advertising salesmen, and production experts. Little wonder, then, that "virile comment" was increasingly relegated to signed columns, where it played second fiddle to the far less controversial factual reporting of the news.

The ways in which Dana and Pulitzer viewed their readers were closely connected both to the contents of the *Sun* and the *World,* and to the business strategies pursued by the two editors. In the case of the New York *Sun,* Dana's producer orientation contributed to his disdain for illustrations and advertisements, his refusal to use the linotype machines and his maintenance of a management style that rejected corporatism and the lack of independence it entailed. For most of his career, Charles Dana had been sensitive to the interests of his readers—this had been crucial to the success of the New York *Sun.* Yet the *Sun*'s circulation fell in the late 1880's and 1890's precisely because Dana lost touch with the experiences and desires of ordinary people. By contrast, Joseph Pulitzer's New York *World*—with its more vivid display of consumer goods, excitement and leisure—met with greater success among New York City's largely immigrant working class. It ushered in a new era in metropolitan journalisms and set the stage for the great circulation battles of the next decade. Not only did Pulitzer's self-promotions and crusading Democratic reforms earn readers, they were also a means of mass-marketing a product. That product was a newspaper that, in turn, promoted the culture of consumption. Pulitzer sold more than a newspaper, he promoted a newspaper that advertised a way of life.

FURTHER READING

Biography

Alexander, Jack. "The Last Shall Be First (Joseph Pulitzer)." In *Post Biographies of Famous Journalists,* edited by John E. Drewry, pp. 391-410. Athens: University of Georgia Press, 1942.

Biographical sketch that features Pulitzer's rise to notoriety and influence on the politics of his day.

Barrett, James Wyman. *Joseph Pulitzer and His World.* New York: Vanguard Press, 1941, 449 p.

Biography of Pulitzer written by the last city editor of the New York *World.*

Black, Alexander. "Four Men." In *American Husbands and Other Alternatives,* pp. 149-82. Indianapolis: The Bobbs-Merrill Company, 1923.

Includes an anecdotal reminiscence of Pulitzer.

Croffut, William A. "Journalist at Large." In *An American Procession 1855-1914: A Personal Chronicle of Famous Men,* pp. 139-53. Boston: Little, Brown, and Company, 1931.

Contains a brief examination of Pulitzer early in his career.

Juergens, George. *Joseph Pulitzer and the 'New York World.'* Princeton N. J.: Princeton University Press, 1966, 392 p.

Details Pulitzer's transformation of "the *New York World* from a moribund sheet into one of the most prosperous and influential dailies of all time."

Morris, Lloyd. "The Uses of News." *Postscript to Yesterday,* pp.217-66. New York: Random House, 1947.

Studies Pulitzer's eccentric personality in relation to the success of the New York *World.*

Swanberg, W. A. *Pulitzer.* New York: Charles Scribner's Sons, 1967, 462 p.

Biography of Pulitzer that endeavors "to show the man himself as clearly as possible" and "to illustrate his methods and achievements . . . in some of their more outstanding instances."

The following sources published by Gale Research contain further information on Pulitzer's life and works: *Contemporary Authors,* Vol. 114; *Dictionary of Literary Biography,* Vol. 23.

Frederick Winslow Taylor

1856-1915

American efficiency engineer and nonfiction writer.

INTRODUCTION

A mechanical engineer by trade, Taylor is generally considered the father of scientific management. Dissatisfied with what he perceived as a lack of efficiency among American workers, Taylor began a series of time management studies that resulted in his best-known work, *The Principles of Scientific Management* (1911), in which he set forth a system of efficient work that eventually was adopted by managers throughout the United States, most notably Henry Ford, who used Taylor's principles in his automobile factories. As the ideas outlined in the *Principles* spread from the workplace to the larger cultural sphere, Taylorism became one of the most influential social forces in twentieth-century American thought, leading ultimately to the modern phenomena of industrial engineering and mass production.

Biographical Information

Taylor was born into a wealthy Philadelphia family in 1856. His father, Franklin Taylor, was an attorney who later in life devoted his time to writing poetry, while his mother, Emily Annette Winslow, instilled in her son her own strong-willed practicality and independence. Groomed from an early age to study law at Harvard University, Taylor decided against entering his father's profession when his eyesight became troublesome, and instead began work in 1874 at the Enterprise Hydraulics Works, a pump manufacturing company in Philadelphia, where he worked as a pattern maker and machinist. In 1878 Taylor moved on to the Midvale Steel Company, working as a common laborer. In 1884 he gained the position of chief engineer and earned a mechanical engineering degree from Stevens Institute of Technology. Taylor distinguished himself in his early years at Midvale by performing experiments with cutting metals and patenting many inventions. Eventually he turned his attention to the stopwatch time studies and experiments with differential piece rates that would become the basis of his later principles. Taylor left Midvale in 1890 and became general manager at the Manufacturing Investment Company in Philadelphia. Additionally, he worked as an independent engineering consultant and continued patenting his inventions. From 1898 to 1901 Taylor worked as a consultant to the Bethlehem Steel Company in Bethlehem, Pennsylvania. There he furthered the development of what he called scientific management, performing numerous time-and-motion studies of workers as well as experiments on optimizing the effectiveness of machinery. Taylor was elected president of the American Society of Mechanical Engineers (ASME) in 1906. By then he was devoting most of his time to perfecting his system of management, and in 1910 Taylorism was formally introduced into the American workplace when Taylor gained government contracts to use his system in federal arsenals. Although Taylor had intended his system to ease tensions between employers and workers—because he had measured exactly how much work a person could do in a certain amount of time—he met with extreme opposition from organized labor, which viewed the system as dehumanizing. The issue came to a head in 1911 when workers at the Watertown Arsenal staged a strike. This event resulted in a governmental investigation of scientific management, which concluded that Taylorism was not in the best interest of workers. Business leaders and industrialists nonetheless widely adopted the system of scientific management, in particular Henry Ford, who enthusiastically implemented Taylorism in his automobile factories. The Society to Promote the Science of Management was founded in 1911 to further the cause of Taylorism throughout the industrialized world; after Taylor's death in 1915, the group's name was changed to the Taylor Society to honor what was considered his revolutionary approach to management.

Major Works

Taylor's numerous studies with workers and machinery resulted in his treatise *The Principles of Scientific Management.* Written as a guide for managers to reorganize the workplace, the *Principles* delineated a system of worker efficiency based on Taylor's time-and-motion studies and his advancement of the differential piece rate–a method of payment based on a standard rate of time and output. In Taylor's system, work was broken down into minute series of motions performed by each worker, who received detailed instructions and specifications on how to execute each task. Taylor's system accounted for every movement performed throughout the workday and left no room for unforeseen incidents. In this way, the *Principles* paved the way for the ideal of mass production in industrialized contemporary culture. Taylor originally submitted his *Principles* to the American Society of Mechanical Engineers; when he received no response, he published the work himself. Wide demand led to the 1911 publication of the work in book form by Harper and Brothers. Taylor's *Principles* drew heavily from two of his earlier papers, both published by the American Society of Mechanical Engineers: "A Piece-Rate System" (1895)–in which he reported his conclusions on the piece rate method of worker payment–and *Shop Management* (1903)–which attempted to redefine the managerial structure in factories, largely through the elimination of the position of foreman and its replacement with a planning department broken into highly specialized administrative units.

Critical Reception

Critics are quick to point out that although Taylor's influence was felt in virtually all industrialized nations, and his methods continue to affect contemporary ideas about work, his theories were rarely accepted and adopted in their entirety. Taylor's principles called for extreme specialization among workers, which many managers considered impractical and overly complex. Additionally, organized labor's campaign against Taylorism made some employers hesitant to endorse it; walkouts were common when Taylorism was introduced into factories. Some critics even contend that Taylor's ideas were not entirely original—that he appears to have borrowed heavily from an unpublished manuscript by his associate Morris L. Cooke, and that results of some of his experiments may have been more fiction than fact. Taylor's conservatism, his scorn of labor unions and what he saw as laziness among workers, and his seemingly quixotic search for perfection in the most minuscule details are frequently cited as evidence of his own feelings of inadequacy, and his principles are considered an attempt to impose order wherever he could in the turbulent early years of the twentieth century. Nevertheless, scientific management permeated twentieth-century society as it ushered in a period of mass production and industrialization previously unseen; Taylorism's wide-reaching effects were even satirized in the Charlie Chaplin film *Modern Times.* Taylorism continues to influence contemporary work, as management theories rooted in Taylor's ideas persist.

PRINCIPAL WORKS

"A Piece-Rate System, Being a Step toward a Partial Solution of the Labor Problem" (essay) 1895
Shop Management (essay) 1903
"On the Art of Cutting Metals" (essay) 1907
The Principles of Scientific Management (nonfiction) 1911

CRITICISM

Edgar V. O'Daniel (essay date 1912)

SOURCE: "Paying for Alaska," in *Political Science Quarterly,* Vol. XXVII, No. 3, September, 1912, pp. 534-536.

[*In the following essay, O'Daniel reviews the first edition of* The Principles of Scientific Management.]

In his little book [***The Principles of Scientific Management***], which grew out of a paper prepared for the American Society of Mechanical Engineers, Mr. Taylor discusses, in a general way, the principles of task management, or, to put it in the words commonly used to describe the author's theme, "efficiency engineering." Although he gives a number of examples of the actual working of the new type of management, he confines his attention for the most part to the fundamental principles underlying its methods. Much of the discussion in the newspapers and magazines has left the impression that the chief, if not the only, object of efficiency engineering is the speeding-up of the workman for the profit of the employer; and it is well that we now have a more accurate statement of its real purposes from the man who is generally recognized as its originator.

The principal object of all management, Mr. Taylor says, should be to insure maximum prosperity to employer and employee; and, "contrary to the beliefs of many, scientific or task management has for its very foundation the firm conviction that the true interests of employer and employee are one and the same; that prosperity for one cannot exist through a long term of years unless it is accompanied by prosperity for the other." There are, in the opinion of the author, three very serious obstacles to the attainment of this form of management: the attitude of the employer in desiring to secure a maximum quantity of work for a minimum amount of wage; the attitude of the employees in begrudging any profit to those for whom they work or any reasonable return on the capital invested; and the inefficiency of the workmen. This inefficiency may result either from spontaneous soldiering on the part of the employees; from a bad organization which necessitates soldiering for the self-protection of the workmen; or from the prevalence of rule-of-thumb methods of shop or works management.

Scientific management, in its attempt to overcome these difficulties, differs from other types of management chiefly in the adoption of the "task" as a "work unit" and in the more careful consideration given to the individual workmen. Under all the best forms of ordinary management which use special incentives, such as the bonus and premium systems of pay, to bring out the best initiative of the workman, the method to be pursued in doing any set task is left entirely to him. To relieve him of some of the duties for which he is not fitted and to develop his efficiency, by scientific management, on the other hand, undertakes four new responsibilities:

> (1) The development of a science for each element of a man's work, to take the place of rule-of-thumb methods.
>
> (2) Scientific selection, training, teaching and development of the workman; whereas under ordinary management he chooses his own work and trains himself as best he can.
>
> (3) Hearty coöperation with the men, so as to insure all the work being done in accordance with the principles of the science which has been developed.
>
> (4) Equal division of the work and responsibility between the management and the workmen. The management should take over all work for which it is better fitted than the workmen; whereas in the past all of the work and the greater part of the responsibility were thrown upon the men.

In showing the application of these new principles, the author gives illustrations of the actual working of the system; and as he himself says, these examples are truly remarkable—so remarkable in fact that many will not be convinced that it is possible for the individual, who supposedly has been doing a fair day's work, to increase his production to any such extent without increasing to a dangerous degree the energy expended. It is this feature of speeding-up that has been the object of the severest criticism on the part of labor leaders and others; but Mr. Taylor states very distinctly that any attempt to increase production without consideration of other vital features of task management, such as the strain on the workman, is certain to result disastrously. Objection has also been made to the efficiency movement on the ground that it has a tendency to make machines of men; but we cannot assume that training a man to do a thing in the best way is more likely to make a machine of him than permitting him to do it in the manner in which he has trained himself.

The results of scientific management, Mr. Taylor concludes, should be considered and tested with respect to three beneficiaries: the employee, who should benefit through shorter hours and higher pay; the employer, who should benefit through increased profits resulting from increased production and consequently lower cost price; and the consuming public, which should benefit through lower prices for manufactured articles brought about by the increased production.

Milton J. Nadworny (essay date 1955)

SOURCE: *Scientific Management and the Unions 1900-1932: A Historical Analysis,* Harvard University Press, 1955, 187 p.

[*In the following excerpt from his book* Scientific Management and the Unions, *Nadworny traces the history of theories of scientific management from their roots after the Civil War to the introduction of Taylor's system to American industry and discusses the adaptation of Taylor's methods by his successors, as well as union opposition to scientific management.*]

THE ORIGINS OF THE TAYLOR SYSTEM

Scientific management was fashioned during the post-Civil War era, when business enterprises were expanding in size and scope, and when the mode of industrial production was becoming increasingly complex. This development was generating a separation of the "businessman" and the "captain of industry" from the technical problems of industrial enterprises, for manufacturing was becoming highly mechanized. Automatic and semiautomatic methods of processing goods have by now become characteristic of American industry, but the period during which they were introduced and developed was one of revolutionary change in the business world.

One important result of this fundamental alteration of the character of production was the intrusion of the mechanical engineer into the vital currents of business; the mechanical engineer became a key figure in the industrial structure because he could meet the technical needs of machine production. A significant manifestation of the growing importance of the engineer was the founding of the American Society of Mechanical Engineers in 1880. The A.S.M.E. was truly the parent organization of "management engineering," and the foster parent of most of the later management societies.

At the annual meeting of the society in Chicago on May 26, 1886, the first in a long series of papers on management was presented to the membership. Two of them, Captain Henry Metcalfe's "The Shop Order System of Accounts," and Oberlin Smith's "Inventory Valuation of Machinery Plant," acquired comparatively little lasting fame; but the third, "The Engineer as an Economist," by Henry R. Towne, has gained recognition as a pioneer paper on industrial management.

In his short, suggestive presentation, Towne, the president of the Yale & Towne Manufacturing Company, did little more than challenge the members of the society to think along lines of management in addition to those of engineering. He reminded his listeners that the mechanical engineer's value to any firm was measured in dollars and cents, and it was therefore incumbent upon the engineer to look to the "economics" of his work. Towne called for more detailed analysis of elements affecting the costs of production, for the recording of experiences and methods in the field of management, and for the publication and exchange of ideas on the subject.

The discussion which followed the presentation of these three papers was lengthy and enthusiastic. The most important contribution, from the point of view of this study, was made by a thirty-year-old member named Frederick W. Taylor, Chief Engineer of the Midvale Steel Works in Philadelphia. Taylor told the assemblage that he was already using "shop order cards" similar to Metcalfe's. The cards were really sets of instructions for the worker. They informed him "what work is to be done, and how it is to be done; what order number to charge it to, and what drawings and tools are to be used, etc." He thereby revealed two fundamental elements of his management system, which was then being developed at Midvale, namely, specific, written instruction for workmen, and recordkeeping for determining and distributing labor costs.

At a meeting of the A.S.M.E. in 1889, Henry Towne, now president of the organization, returned to the subject of shop administration and one of its most prominent elements—the method of paying wages. He had devised a "gain-sharing" system for the employees of Yale & Towne under which any savings in the cost of the product, labor, and/or supplies effected by the workers were shared by the workers, the company, and the foremen. The system required some acquaintance with the costs of production, and therefore encouraged a more comprehensive attack upon both production and wage problems.

Neither gain-sharing nor its counterpart, profit-sharing, found as wide an adoption by industrial firms as did a third incentive method, the "premium plan," which was first described by Frederick A. Halsey to the A.S.M.E. in 1891. Halsey continued to fasten attention on wage methods as the source for the "solution" of production and labor problems. In doing so, he rejected both the day wage and piecework payment. Under the former, he argued, the total benefit of an increase in the rate of production accrues to the employer, hence the workers restrict their output. Under restricted production, the employer "pays extravagantly for his product." Under piecework, increased rate of production (hence increased wages) almost invariably brings a cut in piece rates by employers in order that total labor costs be lowered; the common practice of rate-cutting is again countered by the workers' restriction of output.

Halsey contended that his method eliminated rate-cutting, for premium payment would raise wages and lower unit costs at the same time. The premium plan was a "time-saving" plan: the time of a given job was known from "previous experience"; as a reward for completing this job in less than the usual time, the employee received a sum in addition to his regular hourly rate. This sum, or "premium," was usually calculated as one third of the hourly rate. For each hour saved in production, one third of the gain accrued to the employee. Any increase in the production rate under this plan could not fail to lower labor costs, since it encouraged an absolute increase in output in return for a percentage increase in wages. For example, a worker whose hourly rate was 30¢, and who ordinarily completed one piece of work every hour, would receive a premium of 10¢ for each piece completed in excess of his usual daily output. His *total* daily wage would rise while the cost per piece declined.

The novel ingredient in Halsey's plan was the element of time, although it was rather crudely employed. The same factor had greatly interested Frederick Taylor for more than a decade. It underlay the latter's whole approach to management. Four years after Halsey read his paper, Taylor delivered his first A.S.M.E. paper on management, **"A Piece Rate System, Being a Step Toward Partial Solution of the Labor Problem."** It bore two important surface characteristics. First, in deference to the dominant thinking of the time, the paper's title featured a method of wage payment; and second, it implied that such methods were but a part of the total problem.

Taylor described his own pay plan, called "the differential piece rate," which embodied two distinct rates of pay based on a combination of rewards and punishments. A high piece rate was paid to workmen who completed given assignments in the time allotted for them; in cases of failure, a low rate was paid. The low price was so small that the "slothful" could earn "scarcely a day's pay," forcing them either to work at a faster pace, or to quit. In time, therefore, this wage method could create a work force composed solely of "high grade" men, Taylor said.

Taylor's system contained two additional factors: an "elementary rate-fixing department," which conducted stop watch time studies; and "the best method of managing men." Taylor believed that the greatest obstacle to efficient production was poor management, simply because employers knew little about the elements of production. During the period in which he was employed at Midvale (1878-1890), he labored to discover what he considered an essential element in efficient shop operation: the "quickest time" in which a worker could complete a given task. The determination of that factor, he said, could create an accurate basis for setting wages. Taylor claimed to have found the key to this knowledge in "elemental time study"—breaking down a task into its component parts, or "elements," and timing these parts with a stop watch. By eliminating "unnecessary" motions by the worker and adding certain (unspecified) percentages for delays, the "quickest time" in which a job could be completed became a matter of recorded statistics. Elements common to many tasks would, of course, have the same time values; retiming these would be unnecessary.

Taylor also urged that friendly relations be established between employer and employee, and that management take a genuine interest in the welfare of the workingman. However, he pointed out that if management would merely carry out the methods he prescribed, relations between men and management would automatically be maintained on a high level. For example, there would be no need to cut rates that were based on "scientific" procedures, and thus one of the most serious causes of conflict would be eliminated.

Running through Taylor's presentation was a strong current of feeling against labor unions, which were characterized as destructive and stultifying. He claimed that his method of payment "renders labor unions and strikes unnecessary." The workers, dealt with individually and not "herded" into groups, would be better able to pursue their own individual ambitions. To Taylor, the practice of collective bargaining—"conference and agreement"—was "vastly inferior" to his own plan of "stimulating each workman's ambition by paying him according to his individual worth, and without limiting him to the rate of work or pay of the average of his class."

Until Frederick W. Taylor began broadcasting his philosophy, his discoveries, and his methods, the economics of managerial thinking was largely restricted to using wages as the means to increased worker output and reduced labor costs. Taylor suggested that the wage incentive was but a "partial step" toward these ends, but the full force of his thesis was neither felt nor understood in 1895. His "wage-conscious" audience by and large ignored the concept of a *system* of management inherent in his presentation. Taylor attempted to remedy this misdirection of attention at the 1903 meeting of the A.S.M.E. in Saratoga. There he read his famous "Paper Number 1003," which bore the title ***Shop Management.***

His earlier "rate-fixing department" was metamorphosed into an agency designed to deal with a broader job situation. Now designated the "planning department," it was to decide the order in which work was to be done, and the "route" of the work from start to finish (the sequence of individual machines, or groups of machines, to be employed in processing the job). It would also issue the written instruction cards that informed the worker of the precise method to be used or followed in completing his task. The department would administer all disciplinary action, compile all records of worker performance, analyze costs, and conduct all time studies.

In addition, Taylor proposed that one foreman should no longer be responsible for coping with all the complex and variable factors governing a worker's job. He believed the foreman's job should be functionalized (as, indeed, should all of management's activities) and reduced to its elementary segments. Usually, the foreman was required to prepare the work and the equipment for the workman, determine the proper feeds and speeds of the machines, inspect the finished product, and repair broken or damaged machine parts. Taylor proposed instead that these activities be divided among four "functional foremen," each responsible for a specific task, and each a specialist in his particular activity. In effect, this plan was one aspect of Taylor's attempt to standardize all plant methods.

Since a major objective of the Taylor system was to increase the rate of production of the worker, it was but natural that Taylor should consider time study "the foundation of scientific management." It was time study that made increased production a specific, definable goal. "Accurate time study" was the means by which the "quickest time" in which a worker could complete his task could be determined. Increased output by the worker meant increased plant production and lower costs.

There remained one other obstacle to overcome—the method of inducing the worker to cooperate in bringing management's efforts to a successful conclusion. Taylor prescribed higher wages. He felt certain that a workingman would not work at his maximum pace unless wages were increased 30 to 100 per cent, according to the requirements of the task. Throughout his life, Taylor clung to the belief that high wages was the most effective means by which management could secure the workmen's cooperation.

According to Taylor, his system had proved remarkably successful in achieving worker cooperation. He stated that no strike had ever taken place under his system. He claimed that the higher wages his system offered had, on several occasions, caused men to leave their unions. Taylor believed it to their advantage to have done so, because the restriction of output which, he alleged, was practiced by the unions was an unmitigated evil, and their other practices were not much better. Although he saw no reason why "labor unions should not be a great help to both employers and men," he insisted that they were "in many, if not most, cases a hindrance to the prosperity of both." Many times afterward, Taylor admitted the "possibility" that unions could prove valuable, but he claimed never to have seen it. In theory, they could be beneficial; in practice, they were detrimental to the best interests of employers and their employees.

In ***Shop Management,*** Taylor believed he had at last given engineers, managers, and employers an effective guide to the economic goal of lower production costs toward which they were striving. His program for the standardization of operations; the planning, routing, and scheduling of work; the revision of methods of storing materials; and the stop watch determination of the time of worker performance were practices which obviously would broaden the activities of the manager and the industrial engineer. The mere introduction of a system of incentive wages would not suffice where the objective was truly efficient, low-cost production. Taylor sought to understand and control all of the numerous factors in the manufacture and processing of industrial products.

The specifics of Taylor's system were closely bound up with, and obvious manifestations of, his own life experience. Born in Philadelphia in 1856 of well-to-do parents, Frederick Taylor had the benefit of education in Philadelphia and in France and Germany, as well as at Exeter Academy, where he stood at the head of his class. He gave up his plans for studying law at Harvard, and embarked instead on a new and unusual course: he became an apprentice pattern maker and machinist in a Philadelphia firm at the age of nineteen. It was the beginning of a long industrial career that was crowned with worldly renown and worldly success.

When Taylor's apprenticeship ended in 1878, he took a job as a laborer at the Midvale Steel Company. In six years, he progressed through the positions of gang boss, assistant foreman, and foreman in the machine shop; through master mechanic in charge of repairs and maintenance and chief draughtsman to chief engineer of the plant. (It should be noted that one of the owners of Midvale was a close friend of the Taylor family.) On his own, he took engineering courses offered by Stevens Institute of Technology in Hoboken, but he worked at home most of the time. In 1883, he received his degree in mechanical engineering.

In assuming his role as gang boss, Taylor moved to the other side of the factory fence for good. As he put it, "he was now working on the side of the management." His task was clear: he had to get a "fair day's work" out of his subordinates. He believed that the shortcomings of his shop, and every other shop in the country, were due to the fact that it was, in effect, run by the workers, not the employers. "The workmen together had carefully planned just how fast each job should be done, and they had set a pace for each machine throughout the shop, which was limited to about one third of a good day's work." The fact that he did not know what was "a good day's work" apparently did not prevent him from attempting to elicit it from the workers.

Taylor used "every expedient" to speed up the workers, such as firing the "stubborn" ones, cutting piece rates, and hiring "green hands" and training them himself. And yet, while he was applying these harsh measures, he told the workmen under him that "if he were in their place he would fight against turning out any more work, just as they were doing, because under the piece work system they would be allowed to earn no more wages than they had been earning, and yet would be made to work harder." (A shaving of the piece rates as output increased would keep their earnings fixed.) Nevertheless, Taylor tells us that the ultimate triumph was his. At the end of this "friendly war" the output of his section had been greatly increased. Soon after, he was promoted to machine shop foreman.

Taylor's new position brought greater responsibilities, and he soon began to apply himself to the broader problems of management. He notes that he recognized the drawbacks of piecework methods, and therefore resolved to devise a management program that would harmonize the interests of the workers and the employers. In contrast to his earlier attitude, he decided that the greatest obstacle to cooperation was management's ignorance of what constituted a "proper day's work," and set out to discover this "fact." The decision to determine the ingredients of a fair day's work set off a series of experiments on worker fatigue, methods of shoveling, ball-bearing inspection, pig-iron handling, and metal-cutting, which spread over a period of twenty years.

In addition, Taylor sought to create a system of management that would produce "intimate, friendly cooperation" between employer and employee. To Taylor, "cooperation" meant that management should gather in the traditional know-how of the workers and organize this knowledge into "laws" and formulas. Taylor insisted that when these formulations were made, workers could be instructed and trained to work in accordance with the "one best way" of pursuing any industrial activity. For the workmen, cooperation meant "to do what they are told to do promptly and without asking questions or making suggestions." The "cooperative" role of the management was therefore an active one, while that of the worker was of the passive kind—he had merely to obey the "laws."

After more than a decade at Midvale, Taylor decided to embark on a career as a "management consultant." Armed with his ideas on planning, research, the differential piece rate, and, of course, the stop watch, he sought to widen the influence of his management practice and ideas. Beginning with his general managership of the Manufacturing Investment Company, pulp and paper manufacturers, in 1890, the early and somewhat crude "Taylor system" was introduced into a number of firms during the decade. Taylor worked at Cramp's Ship Yard, Northern Electric Motor Company, Steel Motor & Johnson Company, Simonds Roller Bearing Company, and Bethlehem Iron [changed to "Steel" in 1899] Company, where he met with varying degrees of success. However, only Simonds and Bethlehem were mentioned later in connection with his own history of the development of scientific management. The most important training ground for scientific management was Bethlehem Steel. It was in South Bethlehem, Pennsylvania, that Taylor's experiments bore their greatest fruits, and where the system reached maturity.

In May 1898, at the instance of financier Joseph Wharton, who held a large share of Bethlehem stock, Taylor was hired to reorganize the machine shops in accordance with his own principles. His objectives, he told President Robert P. Linderman, included the introduction of a system which would guarantee prompt execution of management decisions; the curtailment of "soldiering" by the workers; the gathering of information about the qualities of cutting tools; the determination of "correct" work methods; and the increase of workingmen's wages by 25 to 30 per cent as a means of increasing production.

At Bethlehem, work was continued on the metal-cutting experiments begun at Midvale in order that the properties of steel used in cutting tools might be "codified." The purpose of these experiments, and every other experiment conducted by Taylor, was to increase specific information about all factors influencing the worker's task. One result of this activity was that the team of Frederick Taylor and metallurgist J. Maunsel White devised the process of heat-treating steel which produced so-called "high speed" steel. It revolutionized machine production in the United States by permitting greater amounts of metals to be cut at higher machine speeds. At the same time, it prolonged the life of the cutting tool. The new process brought world-wide fame and recognition, and wealth, but it temporarily overshadowed Taylor's other discoveries in the field of management.

He had, for example, conducted experiments which ultimately enabled him to increase by four times the tonnage of pig iron carried by laborers loading "pigs" in freight cars. The men were instructed as to when they should carry the pigs and when they should rest in order to avoid excessive physical fatigue. Taylor also demonstrated that the optimum load for shoveling was twenty-one pounds, which necessitated the use of different-sized shovels for different materials. Furthermore, a great deal of information was gathered on optimum feeds, speeds, depths of cut, and cutting angles of metal-cutting machines such as lathes, planers, and millers.

The metal-cutting experiments enabled Taylor and his assistants to reduce much of their information to formulas. But the great hurdle that remained was the need for solving the mathematical problems involved in the daily application of these formulas to machine work. Henry L. Gantt, Taylor's "chief assistant," had collaborated in constructing a table for determining the speeds and feeds of various machines cutting metals of differing qualities, but it was Carl Barth, a mathematician, who devised a series of slide rules that could be used by machine operators and set-up men to determine quickly and easily the proper settings. The "Barth slide rules" marked one of the great advances of the Taylor system.

Despite the advances in the refining of the new management system, Taylor found his relations with Bethlehem most unsatisfactory. His recommendations, letters, and reports to President Linderman reveal an ever-increasing number of suggestions, demands, and complaints left unsatisfied. The reluctance to carry out Taylor's directives shown by the company's lesser managers roused his ire even more. The company's top officers were apparently unwilling to go any further with Taylor's ideas than they already had. Perhaps Taylor was becoming somewhat annoying; the fact that Wharton did not come to his aid certainly did not help the engineer's cause. Finally, Linderman found a solution: Taylor was abruptly dismissed. Linderman's note, dated April 17, 1901, was hardly touching. It read, *in toto:* "I beg to advise you that your services will not be required by this company after May 1st, 1901."

Taylor claimed that he was not sorry to leave Bethlehem, but he now had to choose between continuing his work as a paid management consultant or devoting his time exclusively to spreading the gospel of his system. He chose the latter. Fortunately, he had by now amassed a sizable amount of wealth. "I cannot afford any longer to work for money," he announced in 1901. Henceforth, he would be guide and mentor, propagandist and broadcaster, eager to inform employers and managers about what he then called "task management." He had already gathered around him men with whom he had worked, and who were associated and identified with his methods of management. These men later formed the core of the scientific management movement.

The first to work with Taylor, and the most important management leader after the "father" of the system, was Henry L. Gantt, who first assisted Taylor at Midvale, and later, at Taylor's instance, became superintendent of the Simonds rolling mills. Subsequently, he went with Taylor to Bethlehem.

Sanford E. Thompson became a specialist in time study, and had extensive training in the building trades. He, too, worked at Simonds during the 1890's.

The last to join the group before 1900 was Carl G. Barth, who was teaching mathematics when he was called to Bethlehem to help solve the vexing problems encountered during the metal-cutting experiments.

One of the first tasks which Taylor undertook after his "retirement" was the writing of ***Shop Management*** for the purpose of advertising his management system. He spent more than a year of work on it. Because the paper was read to a restricted audience of engineers, its influence was for many years limited to industrial engineering circles, and even there such influence was far short of overwhelming. Nevertheless, it did achieve increasing recognition during the first decade of the new century, and was read with interest in parts of Europe.

Each year after 1903 brought more requests from businessmen for Taylor to advise them on the methods necessary to convert their shops to modern principles of management, or for him to recommend someone who was capable of introducing his methods in their shops. Taylor worked as a "consulting engineer" only during the formative, experimental period in the history of scientific management; when he was satisfied that he had finally developed a compact management system, he ceased to pursue management consulting work as a vocation and became a consultant in a broader sense. His house was always open to visitors who desired information about the Taylor system; the number of visitors increased yearly. By such means were Henry L. Gantt, Carl Barth, and, later, a few others whom Taylor trained and advised, hired to install the methods learned from the leader of this embryonic movement. The "Taylor system of shop management" was, oddly enough, generally introduced into American industries by men other than he whose name it bore.

EXPANSION AND OPPOSITION

Soon after Taylor's sudden dismissal from Bethlehem, his two chief assistants, Gantt and Barth, were also dismissed. Barth continued to experiment with metal cutting at another firm, but Gantt immediately embarked on a career as an independent management consultant.

Although his methods were based on Taylor's, Gantt's approach to his work diverged somewhat from his chief's. Taylor desired to make all shop practices conform to standardized procedures, and he objected to the installation of his methods in only part of a plant. (Rarely, however, did a firm ask to have the complete system installed). On the other hand, Gantt was quite content to go only as far as his immediate client desired. His specialty was a wage-payment method of his own design, called "task and bonus." Like Taylor, he determined the workman's production goal, or "task," and paid him a fixed bonus for reaching it. Gantt eliminated the punishment feature of the differential rate and substituted the regular day's wage in case of failure to reach the production standard. Taylor gave his unqualified blessing to Gantt's wage system, which came to be used far more widely than the rarely employed differential piece rate.

For two years, Gantt was the only representative of the Taylor system active in the consulting field. He installed routing and scheduling methods and the bonus system in two shops of the American Locomotive Company, and introduced the beginnings of such methods in two smaller firms. At each of these firms, Gantt experienced difficulties with the management because it was either reluctant to carry out his plans in the manner he desired, or was anxious to achieve instantaneously successful results. His troubles continued at the Sayles Bleacheries in Rhode Island; indeed, not until the end of the decade, when he began work at Brighton Mills in Passaic, and subsequently, at the Union Typewriter Company, did Gantt find a more friendly environment in which to operate.

While Carl Barth began his consulting work later than did Gantt, he met with more immediate success. In fact he achieved a double success, for in 1903 he began work almost simultaneously in two Philadelphia firms—the Tabor Manufacturing Company and the Link-Belt Company. These two firms became the showplaces of scientific management, where all the prescriptions of the Taylor formula were employed.

The Tabor Company was organized in 1900 under the leadership of Wilfred Lewis, a boyhood chum of Taylor's. At the request of his friend, the latter willingly supplied funds for the new company. When the firm, which manufactured molding machines, began to lose money, Taylor provided more funds on the condition that his friend adopt the methods described in ***Shop Management*** as a means of strengthening the condition of the company. Carl Barth was hired to reorganize plant methods under Taylor's general supervision.

The Link-Belt Company manufactured principally conveying equipment and belting. The chairman of the firm's board was James Mapes Dodge, son of the famous editor of *St. Nicholas* magazine, and a past president of the A.S.M.E. Dodge had earlier been impressed with "high speed" steel, and used it in his factory. He soon realized that the steel could prove most effective when it was used in conjunction with Taylor methods, especially the Barth slide rules. Thereupon, Barth was induced to divide his time between Tabor and Link-Belt, while Taylor, in his unpaid but vital role as supervisor, did the same.

To Link-Belt and Tabor came also those who had earlier worked with Taylor, among them Dwight V. Merrick, the time study man at Bethlehem. Merrick assumed similar duties at Link-Belt, where he first established his reputation as a foremost Taylor time study specialist. These plants also served as training grounds for many of the men who later became prominent in management circles, as well as for many scientific management "trainees," some of whom were paid by Taylor to learn the methods firsthand.

It was through Link-Belt that Horace K. Hathaway joined the new movement. Only twenty-six, Hathaway was hired to aid Barth in Dodge's shop, and so rapidly did he learn the techniques of task management that he was lent permanently to the Tabor Company to carry out most of the work there. By the time he was thirty, Hathaway had become Vice-President of Tabor.

During Taylor's lifetime, Link-Belt and Tabor remained the most cherished acquisitions of the scientific management movement. They served as the exhibition pieces for those who visited Philadelphia to see scientific management in action.

While gratifying progress was being made in Philadelphia, the inaugurator of "modern management" was acquiring greater recognition of his work. At the end of 1905, Frederick W. Taylor was elected President of the A.S.M.E., largely to conduct an analysis and a reorganization of the functions of the society. For this purpose, Morris L. Cooke was called in to assist.

Cooke had met Taylor through a mutual friend in 1903, when the former was general manager of the Booklover's Library, a Philadelphia firm. Cooke had an engineering background and mechanical training, and was a member of the A.S.M.E. He did not become formally associated with Taylor's new group until the project at the engineering society was undertaken. His work in revising the methods of publishing the organization's papers and *Transactions* and reducing operating costs was an effective ticket of admission to the group.

Taylor's other A.S.M.E. task was the presentation of his presidential address. He chose his metal-cutting experiments as the topic, and read his paper, **"On the Art of Cutting Metals,"** to the society in December 1906. Although the paper explained how "high speed" steel was discovered, and described the amazing results gained from its use, a thick vein of the author's management philosophy ran through it. The purpose of these experiments, Taylor explained, was to aid in determining the qualities of tools and equipment for the purpose of standardizing machine operation.

So interesting was this paper to managers and metallurgists—indeed, to a cross section of the higher echelons of industry—that it gained immediate renown here and in Europe. Unlike ***Shop Management,*** which was not translated into European languages until more than six years after its presentation to the A.S.M.E., translations of Taylor's presidential address appeared in France, Germany, Austria, and Russia as early as 1907. **"On the Art of Cutting Metals"** was Taylor's last A.S.M.E. paper.

By 1907, Taylor could once more turn his undivided attention to furthering the cause of his system. Barth was continuing to concentrate on machine shop work and increasing his clientele, which soon included the Yale & Towne, Smith and Furbush, and Erie Forge companies. At the same time Gantt expanded his field of operations from the Sayles Bleacheries to the printing firm of Williams & Wilkins (with Cooke assisting), and to the Brighton Mills, a textile firm in Passiac. In addition to following closely the progress being made by his apostles, Taylor took advantage of every opportunity to persuade management executives to employ his methods as well as his associates. The Plimpton Press, in Massachusetts, was recruited in this manner.

In the spring of 1908, Henry P. Kendall, the superintendent of Plimpton, who was later to take a leading role in the history of the management movement, signified interest in Taylor methods. Almost immediately, Taylor arranged to meet Kendall in Boston for the purpose of persuading him to adopt the system. Kendall was advised to acquire the services of Gantt, Hathaway, and Cooke, but the superintendent was not yet ready to take such action. Not until the summer of 1909 was the decision made, but only Hathaway and Cooke got the job. More than three years elapsed before Kendall showed complete satisfaction with the results of the principles of scientific management at Plimpton; but during the ensuing years the firm joined the exclusive circle of "demonstration" shops.

Throughout the decade the Taylor system of shop management increased its influence, however slowly, because of the A.S.M.E. sounding board and the practical advertising provided by the growing number of firms that employed its techniques. The growing popularity of these methods, and the financial rewards offered "systematizers," led to an influx into the consulting business of men who had few qualifications and little to offer except incentive wage systems that were designed to speed up the worker unduly in order that the burden of "efficiency" might be placed solely upon the shoulders of the employee. These quacks either did not know how to or did not care to standardize working conditions, a process so necessary to efficient operation. They began to invade the new field soon after the presentation of **"A Piece Rate System"**; as a result, Taylor was often plied with letters from employers who explained that a "Mr. Jones," who said he had worked with Frederick W. Taylor, and/or was familiar with his methods, wanted to increase the efficiency of their plants with his "Jones System." These employers wrote to find out if Mr. Jones was really as good as he said he was. Taylor invariably informed his inquisitors that only Barth, Gantt, or Hathaway were capable of introducing his methods in any shop. Nevertheless, the Taylor apostles and disciples were not the only important management consultants in the field. There were others who were neither Taylorites nor quacks; one of them was Harrington Emerson.

In 1904 an unsuccessful strike of machinists, boilermakers, and blacksmiths on the Santa Fe Railroad prodded the executives of the road to seek new methods of dealing with their employees. As a result, a new "plan" was drawn up which proposed to restore harmony in the shops by "freeing" workers from "the tyrannies of petty and arbitrary officials on one side and from individuality-destroying, union domination on the other." It was designed to encourage the employees to be more "reliable and trustworthy," and to increase wages and reduce costs. The "betterment" program was placed under the direction of Harrington Emerson.

Emerson was a well-read, cultured man who had not originally been an engineer, but who had encountered and solved engineering problems in his various vocations. He traveled around the world, taught French in a college, engaged in sundry business ventures, and ultimately settled in the field of shop management. His work on the Santa Fe brought him and his methods wide recognition.

Emerson drew on Taylor's methods of planning, routing, scheduling, and standardization for his own work. He added a few elements of his own, including graphical representation of work progress, and the "Emerson bonus plan," which found the widest employment of any of his methods. Although he based his plan on time studies, he did not seek to achieve the exactness that Taylor desired. His bonus payments began at one per cent of the worker's wage rate when the worker reached 67 per cent of the established production rate, and were gradually increased to 20 per cent when "100% efficiency" was achieved. If a worker averaged better than the production standard, which was hardly uncommon, his bonus percentage was increased in direct proportion to the percentage by which he exceeded "100% efficiency."

To distinguish his methods and philosophy from Taylor's, Emerson led the "efficiency movement," preferring the title of "efficiency engineer" to "scientific manager." Like Taylor, he emphasized the individual character of employer-employee relations. His procedures endowed benefits on the Santa Fe in the form of cost savings in the railroad repair shops. He claimed to have effected a saving of $100,000 per month in 1906 at the Topeka shop alone through more efficient use of machines and men. He believed that he could have increased the figure if the company had "permitted it."

The last important entrant into the ranks of the practitioners of "modern management" during this period was Frank B. Gilbreth, building contractor and bricklayer extraordinaire. Gilbreth had avidly devoured ***Shop Management*** when it appeared in the *Transactions,* and he subscribed wholeheartedly to Taylor's management ideas. After meeting Taylor in 1907, his respect increased to proportions that bordered on adoration. Gilbreth did construction work for many of the firms employing scientific management methods, and he was familiar with the personnel as well as the principles of the new movement, in which he was eager to join. Toward the end of 1907, he gained an opportunity to do so by permitting Sanford Thompson to take some time studies on one of his construction jobs.

In addition to their task of acquiring clients, the management engineers were at all times faced with the problem of dealing with the worker and securing his cooperation, and there is no doubt that they wanted to obtain voluntary cooperation. They saw the solution to industrial problems almost solely in terms of production: increase the rate and volume of production, and costs will decrease while wages and profits rise. Therefore, any description of the benefits which their methods would provide the workman was based on the assumption that he would increase his output. They desired to increase the worker's wage as a reward for greater production, for they were convinced that high pay would eliminate worker discontent. Furthermore, all the scientific managers shared, in varying degree, Gantt's belief that "the most important thing for the average workman is not that he shall have exceptionally high wages during times of prosperity, but that he shall have continuous employment and fair wages at all times."

Although the scientific managers proclaimed themselves the best friends the workingmen had, they never seriously deluded themselves into believing that they would be welcomed with open sinewy arms. There is little doubt that they expected worker opposition rather than cooperation. Taylor advocated undertaking all the physical changes necessary in a plant before the methods that directly affected the worker were introduced. It was necessary to standardize the conditions surrounding the work, of course, but this practice had the added advantage of permitting the shop to function along prescribed lines before the workmen could react and possibly wreck the system. Taylor expressed the belief that an increase in wages could overcome worker opposition even to the hated stop watch. "Workmen . . . are in time reconciled to time study," he wrote Sanford Thompson, "when they appreciate that the ultimate outcome of it means higher wages for themselves . . ." Nevertheless, Taylor was not completely convinced that the promise of higher wages, by itself, would really invoke harmony. He feared that unless a scientific management "expert" (one whom he designated as such) introduced the system, it was highly probable that the undertaking would result in "strikes and labor troubles."

Taylor's attitude toward labor unions was colored by his own conception of scientific management. He had no doubts about the reliability of the information gathered during his various experiments, and often announced his conviction that time study was scientific in method and result. Since "scientific facts" could not be questioned or debated, the practice of collective bargaining advocated by unions had no logical place in the new scheme of things.

Taylor disliked and distrusted organized labor, and had no doubt that any shop would fare better if the workers were unorganized. Indeed, when he recommended Gantt for a job at the Amoskeag Mills in New Hampshire (which he got), he told his associate that one of the best points in its favor was that it was a nonunion plant, hence Gantt would have "an especially good chance" for success there. Taylor was highly pleased with developments at Tabor when it "changed from a Union shop to absolutely Non-Union"—a mark of success of scientific management. In a letter to David Van Alstyne of the American Locomotive Company he summed up his attitude toward the presence of a union in any factory: " . . . be sure that it starts and remains an absolutely non-union establishment." He also threw in some advice to Van Alstyne on how to break a Molders Union local at the latter's plant. Taylor suggested that a "dummy" molding shop be set up near the company's Schenectady plant, to which all molding equipment should ultimately be sent. In addition, only nonunion labor should be hired there. With the counterfeit firm underbidding the "legitimate" factory for work, Van Alstyne could either break the union directly or transfer all molding work to the ostensibly independent shop, forcing the displacement of the unionized molders. (Four months after this letter was written, Taylor wrote Naval Constructor Holden A. Evans that he would not be "influenced in the slightest degree in employing machinists or other workmen, by the fact that they were union workmen or non union.")

Prior to 1911, Taylor had few occasions to write about or discuss the subject of trade unions in detail. Neither he nor his closest associates had systematized a shop where organized labor had any sizable membership. On the other hand, Frank Gilbreth had had practical experience in dealing with unions. He had his industrial training in the highly organized building trades, and his first step in beginning a contracting job was to contact the local unions for workers who were available, and effect agreement on wages and working conditions. Unlike Taylor, he did not wish to eradicate union influence, although at one time he believed it would happen automatically when the millenium of scientific management arrived. In the meantime, he chose to deal with unions.

The ungrateful union men responded by resisting the introduction of Taylor methods on his job in Gardner, Massachusetts, in November 1908. Gilbreth was infuriated. "I have been a Union man and I know what is good for you," he told them. Though he insisted that he was using the methods of "the best friends Union labor ever had," and promised to pay higher wages than the union rates, they remained adamant. "I will raise the pay of the bricklaying mechanics throughout the United States in spite of the pig headed, ignorant men in Gardner," Gilbreth stated. Ultimately, a compromise was effected and Taylor organizational methods were employed on that contract, but not the stop watch.

Gilbreth was practically alone among Taylor's associates who sought any cooperation with unions. He was one of the few in the scientific management movement who registered any degree of sympathy for organized labor prior to 1914. However, it was not Gilbreth, but Taylor, who set the tone for scientific management, and it was Taylor who sustained the prevailing unfriendly attitude toward unions.

The reciprocal attitude of labor toward the system of task management during the period preceding 1910 has generally been ignored in the past, because managers and students of management history believed, in Harlow S. Person's words, that "The controversy between labor and management concerning scientific management did not arise until after . . . 1911. For nearly thirty years Taylor had been developing scientific techniques in various plants, and labor had given it no attention." This thesis has been accepted at face value even by labor leaders. It has been reinforced by Taylor's oft-repeated statement, "there has never been a strike under scientific management," as well as by the reluctance of the management engineers to advertise any labor disturbances they might have experienced or incited. In addition, the absence of a single title for the system ("scientific management," or "Taylor system," gained currency beginning in 1910) has made it very difficult to follow the attitude of organized labor toward "scientific management." Nevertheless, there is evidence that the unions paid some attention to the methods identified with the new movement, often to the dismay of the consultants and the employers.

When Taylor advertised the absence of strikes under his system, he was correct in the sense that there was no organized walkout at Midvale, Simonds, or Bethlehem; or at any of the plants where Barth, Hathaway, or Cooke worked. Yet union men did leave every plant where Taylor was employed, and Emerson's methods (and, indirectly, Taylor's) precipitated a strike at the American Locomotive Company. At some navy yards and arsenals, workers objected to the application of Taylor methods, and in at least one case a strike was avoided because the objectionable practice was abandoned. However, the fact remains that during the period preceding 1911, plants which employed scientific management techniques were comparatively free from strikes.

The trade unions of the American Federation of Labor have always represented a job-wage consciousness which concentrated the objectives of the movement on employment, wages, hours, and working conditions. Of course, the fundamental objective of the union is to maintain some sovereignty over the job through recognition and collective bargaining, which are essential in making effective its demands. The union aims to protect as well as improve the conditions surrounding the job, and any threat to existing standards is usually vigorously opposed. Where recognition is granted, the opposition to the threat follows the channels of collective bargaining; if that fails, the strike is invoked. Where a union is not recognized and has not enough members in the plant to call for a strike, it resorts to a kind of paper blockade. Although the strike and the "paper blockade" were used against methods of scientific management prior to 1911, the latter was, of necessity, used most.

Because of the emphasis placed by Samuel Gompers' brand of unionism on "wages, hours, and working conditions," it is not unusual that the most prominent of these—wages—has been the cause of the vast majority of strikes that have occurred in our history. The wage is crucial to the worker, for it not only governs the economics of his mode of living, but also measures his occupational social position. In their concentration on "immediate objectives," the A.F.L. unions heightened the importance of wages and the natural interest of the worker in them. Industry encouraged this condition by a continuing downward pressure on wages, either through direct total reductions or through cutting piece rates.

Experience with piece rates had demonstrated to many union and nonunion workers that it was to their disadvantage to speed up in order to increase their wages, for when their increased production brought higher earnings, the price per piece was reduced. This meant that in order to maintain increased earnings they would have to increase their working pace further. The unions held a "lump of labor" philosophy—increased individual productivity means that less workers will be needed to produce a fixed amount of goods, and therefore an increased work pace leads to unemployment. As a result, their abhorrence of rate-cutting was matched only by their distaste for the "speed-up."

The unions were divided in their attitude toward piecework. Some demanded day wages in order to avoid the attendant evils of piecework. Others maintained that the flat day rate afforded even less protection against speeding up, since increased production under piecework resulted in increased earnings, while under day work it did not. A contemporary observer noted that, in general, "the question of acceptance or opposition to piece work turns on whether prices are reduced." Therefore, the unions struggled hard to establish some degree of control, usually through collective bargaining, over the conditions affecting the job.

Taylor, Gantt, Halsey, and the others denounced the practice of rate-cutting and attempted to devise wage methods that would make the practice unattractive to the employer. They actually fashioned variations of the piece payment method, variations which the unions uniformly opposed. Under piecework, the employee received the total price per piece for each increase in production; under the incentive methods, he received only a part of the price for each piece produced in excess of his production goal. Taylor tried to disguise his differential method by paying a "high" piece price when the production standard was reached, but actually the prescribed high rate was to be *lower* than the price per piece that was being paid prior to the introduction of the differential rate. However, according to Taylor, the combination of his higher piece rate and the production goal he set would result in a higher total wage for the employee.

All of the innovators presented schemes which included opposing elements of trade union philosophy. On one hand, they favored high wages; on the other, they demanded an increased work pace and increased production. The unions did not dissect the systems and separate the "good" elements from the "bad"; they opposed incentive systems *in toto*.

As early as 1903, the International Association of Machinists went on record in opposition to "work by the piece, premium, merit, task, or contract system." Though the union long maintained official prohibitions on its members from accepting such work, it was often powerless to prevent the imposition of such conditions. For example, a year after the unsuccessful strike on the Santa Fe, the machinists in the Topeka shop were all working under Emerson's "Individual Effort System." Where it could not use the strike to remove such conditions, the union was forced to resort to the "paper blockade" by exhorting its members to stay away from identified shops where piecework was used, and conducting a vigorous propaganda campaign against such methods.

There were other evidences of union attitudes toward the new methods of management during the years immediately following 1900. For example, Emerson was fully aware of the hostility toward the bonus system on the part of the "Union Blacksmiths" at the Topeka shop of the Santa Fe. He decided, in 1905, to "pass them by for the moment." The Brotherhood of Locomotive Engineers succeeded in resisting bonus system wages on the Santa Fe in 1906. The Molders joined these others in 1907, when the union adopted a convention resolution that condemned "the premium system . . . and kindred systems" for unduly speeding up the workers. Even pieceworking unions like the Boot and Shoe Workers and the Garment Workers resisted "bonus and premium systems."

There was no doubt in David A. McCabe's mind that the unions had given "attention" to scientific management prior to 1911. McCabe conducted a survey of union policies on methods of wage payment in 1908-1909, and on most points the unions evidenced differences in their attitudes. The closest the organizations came to unanimity was on the subject of premium and bonus methods. McCabe found that "unions almost without exception prefer the straight piece system to premium or bonus systems." Among these unions were those opposed even to the piecework system! There apparently was a crystallized union attitude toward the methods which the workers later discovered to be adjuncts of "scientific management."

Before 1911, there was but one example, except for the United States Army arsenals, of the introduction of Taylor's management methods, or variations thereof, into plants where unions were present in strength. The events precipitated by this installation dramatically contradicted Person's later analysis of organized labor's attitude before 1911 toward these management methods.

Early in 1906, Taylor received a letter from J. E. Sague, Vice-President of the American Locomotive Company, who wrote ostensibly to request information about some Tabor molding machines which his company purchased. In the letter, he mentioned a talk he had had with David Van Alstyne, the Superintendent of Motive Power on the Northern Pacific Railroad. Van Alstyne aroused Sague's interest in the Taylor system of shop management, and Sague thought it would be an excellent idea to have Taylor meet the superintendents of his firm's shops and interest them in his management methods.

The molding machines were completely ignored by Taylor. He urged Sague, as he urged every one who showed an interest in his system, to come to Philadelphia to talk about it and see it in action at Tabor and Link-Belt. He cautioned Sague that he would make no effort to help him until the higher executives of the firm understood what would be involved in applying his methods, and, of course, were ready to follow through.

Taylor did not again hear from the firm until the following winter. At that time David Van Alstyne, now a vice-president of American Locomotive, wrote for further information about the system. He visited Taylor in Philadelphia soon after, and was shown around the Tabor shop. He came away greatly impressed. Van Alstyne wanted Barth, Hathaway, or Gantt to survey American Locomotive's Schenectady plant for the purpose of estimating the cost of putting Taylor's system in operation there. Again Taylor urged that the "higher-ups" understand and sanction such procedures before any move was made. Bethlehem cast long shadows.

Taylor's caution was well grounded, for Van Alstyne discovered that his superiors were not ready to begin the program on the scale he desired. Therefore, he decided to introduce the methods "in a more moderate form." But instead of acquiring the assistance of a Taylor associate Van Alstyne called for the aid of Harrington Emerson. The system that soon appeared in the company's shops at Pittsburgh, Schenectady, Richmond, and Montreal bearing the succinct title, "Standard Time Card Dispatching and Time Study System," had the Emerson imprint. The worker's "efficiency" and bonus began at 70 per cent of task and the bonus increased to 20 per cent when the standard rate of production was reached.

In 1908, the unions began to stir, for the effects of the Panic of 1907 were easing. The molders and blacksmiths were content to accept the new system, but the boilermakers secured an agreement that exempted them from working under it. However, the unorganized machinists in Pittsburgh were seething. In September, the machinists organized a local of the International Association of Machinists, and six weeks later went on strike. Almost 350 men left the Pittsburgh shop to enforce a demand that the system be eliminated: it was too complicated to understand and too difficult to earn a bonus; moreover, the men wanted the day rate reinstalled. The executive board of the I.A.M. did not authorize the strike, because it was not informed of what was happening in Pittsburgh until the strike took place. Soon thereafter, the demonstration was called off.

In December, the company abrogated its agreement with the boilermakers in the Schenectady and Richmond plants. The union promptly struck, and the workers stayed out for three weeks. The strike was finally settled by the removal of both the Standard Time System and Van Alstyne. In the first test of strength, the unions had triumphed.

Taylor was irked and troubled by the whole episode. He believed the culprit to be Harrington Emerson, who had used his "short cut" methods, to which Van Alstyne added some of his own.

When Taylor referred to "our work" at the beginning of 1910, he was not only referring to Tabor, Link-Belt, Plimpton, and the others; he was referring to the grand new vistas that had opened during 1909 as a result of the acquisition of a new client, the United States Government. It was not a big jump from the machine shops of private industry to those of the navy yards and arsenals, and it was not surprising that the Army Ordnance Department, as well as navy yard administrators, should show an interest in the Taylor techniques.

The first government agency to use Taylor methods was the navy. In 1906, Naval Constructor Holden A. Evans, stationed at the Mare Island Navy Yard in California, asked Taylor to send him copies of his A.S.M.E. papers, which had aroused his interest. Taylor, naturally, obliged, and the constructor began to study them with an eye toward the application of their programs to his own work. A year later, the United States Navy Bureau of Construction and Repair received a request from Evans for permission to change the method of paying ship scalers (who remove rust from the hull with pneumatic hammers) from day wage to piece rate. Evans had made time studies of the workers, and he decided that they could almost double their daily work pace. He suggested a piece rate which, if the new task goal was met, would raise the scalers' income by 50 per cent. The Bureau approved the plan. As a result, Evans became, in effect, the unofficial Taylor representative on the West Coast.

On the East Coast was Admiral Casper F. Goodrich, Commandant of the Brooklyn Navy Yard. Goodrich had been associated with Taylor at the Manufacturing Investment Company during the 1890's, and their friendship grew strong during subsequent years. The Admiral introduced many reforms into navy yard administration during the term in office of Theodore Roosevelt's last Secretary of the Navy, Truman Newberry. One of these resulted in the establishment of a "Tool Steel Board," which abolished the practice of ordering steel by brand and substituted that of ordering it by specification. Thereafter, the navy yards received and worked with uniform steel, and reduced their operating costs greatly. As was true of all of Goodrich's plans for improvement, he did not submit this one until Taylor had been consulted. Indeed, Taylor had originally suggested the employment of this practice.

Taylor and Goodrich decided that the Navy Department as a whole would prove a fertile field for the operations of the Taylor system. In December 1908, Taylor visited Secretary Newberry in Washington to sell the idea. Though the Secretary made no promises, Taylor's disciples began to find employment in the yards. Hathaway was hired that very month to install a tool room at the League Island Yard in Philadelphia, and Barth was called to the Brooklyn yard to advise on standard machine shop practices.

The only grumblings that were heard at this time were those from the workers at the Philadelphia yard, who complained that the Taylor system method of "numbering and marking tools" was too complicated. More general and widespread complaints were to come later.

Before Newberry left office in March 1909, he drew up a plan to reorganize the navy yards. Based largely on "Taylor-Goodrich ideas," the plan was opposed by the officers of the line and largely ignored by the new Secretary, George von L. Meyer. For the time being, however, hope was not abandoned that the Taylor system might yet invest the navy yards.

In the Ordnance Department, the Taylor system was far more successful. In 1906, Brigadier General William Crozier, Chief of Ordnance, showed a desire to investigate the system on the possibility that it might be installed in the arsenals. An appointment was made for a meeting with Taylor in Philadelphia, but it was not kept. Nevertheless, Taylor was enthusiastic about the possibility of introducing the complete system into the government shops, although his reasoning revealed a rather startling lack of faith in his own methods. "There is no danger from strikes in Government shops," he was pleased to note; it was a poor contrast to his written statements on the system's magical immunity from labor disturbances.

To Crozier, the situation was rather delicate. His "employees" were not only organized to some extent, but they were voting members of the "corporation." He had to be certain of his ground before embarking on a new program of the proportions of Taylor's shop management system. Though he did not keep his appointment in Philadelphia, he corresponded with Taylor during the next two years. The General's interest in the system mounted, but he had to move cautiously. "My principal difficulty," he told Taylor, "is in arranging such methods of payment of workmen as will not result in pressure by the Unions upon Members of Congress for change, which the Members will find difficult to resist." Crozier understood the situation in the arsenals more fully than did Taylor; it was a situation that caused the former to be as deliberate as the other was eager. Inadvertently, Crozier had accurately forecast the course of events in the arsenals after 1910.

The first attempt to introduce any of Taylor's methods into an arsenal occurred at Rock Island, which drew its workers from two states, Illinois and Iowa, because it was located in the Tri-Cities area (Rock Island, Moline, and Davenport). The commanding officer of the arsenal, Major F. E. Hobbs, first met Taylor at Midvale when Hobbs had been an observer there for the Ordnance Department. The Major decided to institute some of the practices he had seen at Midvale. In September 1908, some time studies were begun for the purpose of establishing more "accurate" piece rates. Immediately, the workmen appealed to their Congressmen to "do something" about the infernal stop watch. That was enough for Hobbs; the project was suspended.

Earlier, at the arsenal at Watertown, Massachusetts, Taylor, Barth, and Gantt began a concerted effort to gain another client. Taylor suggested to the adjutant at Watertown that Gantt or Barth survey the arsenal and report on its needs, and soon thereafter Gantt visited the arsenal. Gantt came away with the feeling that it was "out of the question" to attempt to introduce the whole system. He did believe, however, that he could speed up production with "task and bonus." The difference between Gantt's and Taylor's approaches was immediately revealed. While Gantt was willing to apply merely the pay methods and time study, Taylor believed that it was absolutely essential to go all the way. Without the "whole system," Taylor insisted, "the workmen will surely oppose all work which tends to increase the output." Gantt continued to visit Watertown throughout the year, but no definite step was taken by Ordnance.

Finally, in January 1909, General Crozier visited Philadelphia and spent two days looking over the system in operation at Tabor and Link-Belt. He was impressed, but not completely convinced. For four months he plied Taylor with questions about the operation of the system, which the consultant patiently answered. Crozier was most interested in its effect upon the workingman, and almost all his inquiries revolved around this crucial factor.

At first, Crozier could not understand why it was necessary to pay a premium to the worker, since nothing was left to his judgment or initiative, for he simply followed orders and worked no harder than before. Taylor pointed out that under his system the workman *did* work harder, "at a continued rapid pace (even although the pace is by no means a killing one)." In return for following new methods and increasing his work pace, the employee had to be "encouraged" by extra compensation. "I can assure you," he informed Crozier, "that you will meet with absolutely no success with the task idea if you leave out this most essential feature." The mighty American dollar would quell any worker antagonism to time study also, for any opposition would cease "the moment they realize that time study means higher wages for them."

Taylor's confident assertions did not go unchallenged. Major Hobbs, still smarting from the stop watch episode four months earlier, objected to Taylor's contention that he could introduce his system "without opposition from the workmen and without contest with the trade organizations." From his own experience, and his observations at Midvale, he was certain that unions would oppose it. Taylor, of course, believed that Crozier would experience little trouble, but for good measure, Wilfred Lewis and James Mapes Dodge were called upon to reassure the General that there was nothing to worry about. Dodge saw "nothing about the system that conflicts with Trade Unionism," because there were a "number" of trade union members working in his shop, with whom he had no difficulty.

Despite his seeming hesitancy, Crozier had practically decided in January 1909 that the Watertown Arsenal should be reorganized along prescribed Taylor system lines. Major (later, Colonel) C. B. Wheeler, commandant of the arsenal, wanted Taylor, and no one else, to inspect the arsenal so that he might get a concrete estimate of the requirements for such an undertaking. Taylor declined the offer, but he suggested other candidates for the job. Although Gantt had offered his services to the Watertown officers, Taylor now decided that he did not want Gantt to "get mixed up with this." He wrote Crozier that although Gantt was the best "all-around man," he was not a machine shop specialist. He therefore suggested that either Barth or Hathaway should make the report.

Crozier complied with the suggestion, and subsequently requested the Civil Service Commission to waive its regulations to permit him to hire Barth for the job. The Commission complied, and in June 1909 Barth, joined later by Dwight V. Merrick, the time study man, began one of the most famous of all scientific management projects.

By 1910, scientific management had grown to maturity: it had acquired a set of well-defined practices and an ever widening circle of converts and clients. It had, too, its full measure of rivals and mimics; the unions were stirring against it; and it had met with disappointment and even defeat. However, this first decade of the century had proved generally successful and quite satisfactory to Taylor and his associates. But "scientific management" had not yet received its formal christening, nor had it received much popular attention. Both were provided in 1910 by the Eastern (Railroad) Rate Case and Louis D. Brandeis.

Milton J. Nadworny (essay date 1957)

SOURCE: "Frederick Taylor and Frank Gilbreth: Competition in Scientific Management," in *Business History Review,* Vol. 31, No. 1, Spring, 1957, pp. 23-34.

[In the following essay, Nadworny explains the antagonistic split in the scientific management movement between Taylorites, who favored a stop-watch method of measurement, and adherents to Frank Gilbreth's micromotion technique.]

A century has elapsed since the birth of Frederick W. Taylor, the so-called "Father of Scientific Management," and it has been almost seventy-five years since Taylor began to evolve his management system. Note has been taken, and will continue to be taken, of Taylor's contributions to management philosophy and practice and to the improvement and advancement of managerial and business efficiency. Taylor was an innovator and an entrepreneur in his field, and he had more than his share of emulators, rivals, and disciples. When Taylor died in 1915, the field of management consulting which he took a leading role in developing was much less institutionalized than it is today; the impact of individual consultants' personalities, ideas, and techniques was relatively greater than at present; and the recognition and identification of various programs and methods were rather highly personalized. The label of "scientific management" is the one with which we are most familiar today, but in 1915, and earlier, management programs were most likely to be identified with the names of the management engineers themselves, e.g., "Taylor system," "Gantt system," "Emerson system," and so forth. In such a setting, the activities, attitudes, and personalities of the outstanding leaders were bound to have great influence upon the manner in which this field of management consulting developed. A further consideration is that the rewards of a successful practitioner were twofold: (1) the psychological and social rewards of being recognized, and honored, as a leader and developer of a given line of thought and practice; and (2) the economic rewards of a successful practice. These two factors are almost inextricably intertwined in the development of the scientific management movement, as is effectively illustrated by the relationship between perhaps the two most popular and famous men in the field—Frederick W. Taylor and Frank B. Gilbreth.

By the time Gilbreth began his acquaintanceship and association with Taylor in 1907, the latter had laid almost all of the groundwork for his management system; in addition, he had ceased to perform consulting work for pay after 1903, the year in which he read his paper, ***Shop Management,*** before the American Society of Mechanical Engineers. Furthermore, he had gathered around him a group of disciples who formed the core of the scientific management movement, and all of whom worked with him at one time and received training in his methods. They were Henry L. Gantt, Carl G. Barth, Horace K. Hathaway, Sanford E. Thompson, and Morris L. Cooke. Taylor's role was an interesting one; he apparently considered himself the patriarch and protector of scientific management, and insisted that he was to certify who was qualified to be a "scientific management expert," and thereby have a decisive influence upon the methods used to introduce scientific management into various firms. He consistently warned acquaintances and potential clients that unless a scientific management "expert" (one whom he designated as such) introduced his system, "strikes and labor troubles" would be the result. According to Taylor, the number of experts was limited to Barth, Gantt, Hathaway, Thompson, and Cooke. (After 1911, Barth and Hathaway were most often recommended.)

Frank Gilbreth, on the other hand, had worked for years in the building trades as an independent contractor and builder. He was an active member of the Society for the Promotion of Engineering Education and of the A.S.M.E. Gilbreth became acquainted with Taylor's system by reading ***Shop Management,*** through contracting work he did for some "Taylorized" firms, and by permitting Sanford Thompson to take some time studies of workers on one of his construction jobs. Gilbreth's admiration for Taylor was unbounded, and he reputedly honored the spot in the Engineering Societies Building in New York where he first met Taylor in 1907. He ardently desired admission into the inner circle of the Taylor following, but the latter and his closest associates were reluctant to satisfy that desire. However, Taylor and Thompson were not above picking Gilbreth's brains for his ideas and methods, which they apparently intended to incorporate into an edition of their own book, *Concrete, Plain and Reinforced.* Yet, when Gilbreth asked for a supply of Hathaway's record-keeping blanks (evidently at no charge), the Taylorites were incensed, and they feared that Gilbreth's employment of Taylor methods in construction work was for the purpose of making "a further reputation for himself" by wrongly labeling such methods as the "Gilbreth system," rather than "Taylor system." The management engineers agreed that "Mr. Gilbreth is not a man whom it would be well to place a good deal of dependence upon unless there is something further in view," and that he should be denied access to the Taylor tools and secrets unless he were "ready to pay for it."

What the roots of this attitude were is not clearly established, but Taylor appears to have abided rather consistently by this policy, for Gilbreth supplied one valuable asset for his scientific management program: he could speak "so convincingly about modern scientific management." As a result, Gilbreth was selected by Taylor to represent the latter in describing the philosophy and program of the Taylor system to the New York Civic Forum in 1911 and the Western Economic Society in 1913. He was also commissioned by Taylor to answer letters from the readers of the latter's ***The Principles of Scientific Management.*** It was Gilbreth, too, who was the original driving force in organizing the Society for the Promotion of the Science of Management in 1910, which society was later renamed the Taylor Society. There were no dissents at this time from Taylor's contention that Gilbreth "has done our cause a very fine service," but "our cause" was not intended to include Gilbreth.

Gilbreth seems to have been oblivious to the attitude of Taylor and his disciples, and, as long as he pursued the vocation of building contractor, he was considered most useful. In 1912, however, Gilbreth turned industrial management—indeed, "scientific management"—consultant. Toleration on the part of the Taylor group turned increasingly to hostility. It is not clear whether this hostility was due to the competitive economic threat presented by Gilbreth, or to a sincere belief that his professional qualifications were low. The latter certainly had to be tempered because of the assignments Taylor continued to give Gilbreth to represent the scientific management group. At any rate, Gilbreth's first big job in this field was at the New England Butt Company in Providence, and the undertaking had the early assistance of H. K. Hathaway (who surveyed the operating procedures of the company and made some recommendations for improvement) and Hathaway-trained aides Royal R. Keely and Albert R. Shipley. Nevertheless, Taylor and his associates were skeptical of the whole project, and Taylor, himself, was sure that Gilbreth's activities would precipitate a strike at the company, for Gilbreth "had no business whatever to undertake the systematizing of a large company without having any experience in this field." Hathaway believed that there was some hope of ultimate success of the Gilbreth project, but only if Gilbreth proceeded "according to the rules"—presumably, Hathaway's and/or Taylor's rules. When Gilbreth did meet with success and approval at New England Butt, the Taylorites still refused to concede him anything. "Practically all the credit for the work at the New England Butt Company," said Hathaway, "is due [Albert R.] Shipley. . . ." The obvious pique was due, most probably, to the fact that Gilbreth was now competing rather successfully with Taylor's chosen "experts."

While the New England Butt installation was in progress, Gilbreth, probably unwittingly, broadened and deepened the competitive nature of his relationship with Taylor and his closest followers. In 1912, Gilbreth devised and began to use a technique of work measurement which he called "micromotion study," which employed a motion picture camera to record the performance of a worker on a job, with a clock calibrated in hundredths of a minute placed in viewing range. With this technique, Gilbreth could record the motions, the time, and the conditions surrounding the job. His major objective was the recording, and ultimate simplification and improvement, of the motions of the worker. His method permitted him to time both the motions of the worker and the total job, and also provided an opportunity to reproduce the performance of the worker a relatively unlimited number of times. Gilbreth subsequently devised other schemes of recording and tracing worker motions, but he considered micromotion study to be his most important contribution to scientific management.

Work measurement was, of course, one of the most significant aspects of scientific management. The Taylor program was based on the use of stop watch time study, under which the time study technician determined what the "elements" of a particular job were, and took a number of stop watch readings of each of the elements in developing data from which the ultimate time standard for the job would be developed. Taylor, himself, considered time study to be the "foundation of scientific management," and the Taylorites were primarily interested in the timing of the job. While Gilbreth was, of course, vitally interested in establishing a standard time for the job, he was perhaps more interested in analysis of work methods and patterns and in achieving economy of motions and effort, and he therefore viewed the setting of work standards from a different point of view. It is therefore not surprising that when Gilbreth described his new technique to the scientific management leader, the reaction was something less than enthusiastic. "Showed micromotion to Taylor," he noted, "and told him what it would do and told him I was surprised that he did not recognize its meaning. He said it was undoubtedly good where one was investigating the minutia of motions. He acted so that I saw he was hurt and so I changed the subject." When Gilbreth again tried to impress upon Taylor what he conceived to be the importance of micromotion study, and suggested that his own "process and combination of clocks and motion picture machine should really go with your [Taylor's] great invention of time study," Taylor suggested that Gilbreth's "photographic scheme" might enable the latter to "develop a very fine system of time study." Taylor and his disciples maintained that time study automatically included the concept of motion study, as far as they understood it, and therefore viewed micromotion study as simply another, somewhat unimportant and perhaps irrelevant, appendage to stop watch time study. There is evidence, beginning with Taylor's initial reaction to Gilbreth's description of micromotion, that the Taylor group did not understand the methodology or implications of Gilbreth's technique. As a result, they depreciated micromotion study and increased their distrust of its originator.

Up to this point, the relationship between Gilbreth and the Taylorites was a peculiar one, indeed: Taylor and his confidants distrusted and resented Gilbreth, not the least reason for which seems to be the competitive threat he presented. Gilbreth, on the other hand, apparently assumed that he had received the Taylor blessing, for all of his personal notations reveal nothing but fierce admiration for Taylor and his other associates. Gilbreth got a rather rude awakening in regard to the real attitude of the Taylor group when Taylor and Hathaway reversed the competitive pressure in dramatic fashion.

In August, 1912, Gilbreth was hired by the Hermann, Aukam Company, handkerchief manufacturers, to direct the installation of scientific management methods in its plants. His contracts were renewed every four months throughout 1912 and 1913. In March, 1914, M. C. Hermann paid a visit to Taylor to complain about Gilbreth's work, assuming, as did Gilbreth, that the latter was an acknowledged protégé of Taylor. Hermann stated that he was paying an exorbitant amount of money for the little time and the inferior assistants Gilbreth provided for the job. Taylor suggested Hathaway for the task, and an agreement was reached to the effect that the reorganization of production methods at the handkerchief works would be assumed by him. Hathaway was under the impression that Gilbreth had cancelled his fifth contract with the firm (which Gilbreth denied), but he decided to delay final acceptance until Taylor discussed the situation with Gilbreth himself.

From the time when Gilbreth left the building trade and entered into competition with Taylor's chosen disciples, Taylor had become increasingly critical and distrustful of him; by 1914, Taylor was convinced that Gilbreth did not fully grasp the techniques and implications of scientific management. The events at the handkerchief company fit well with Taylor's predispositions and suspicions of Gilbreth's professional ability; Mr. Hermann's complaints were sympathetically received. It is not surprising, therefore, that Gilbreth's side of the story made no favorable impression upon Taylor, and Hathaway got the green light. (It is interesting to note that Taylor and Hathaway had already arranged for the latter to take over the consulting work at the firm.)

Gilbreth was aroused and bitter over the action of Taylor and Hathaway, because his fifth contract with Hermann, Aukam was not due to expire until May. However, he refrained from taking any overt counteraction, apparently because he was in the midst of making preparations for a trip to Germany, where he had a sizable consulting job awaiting him. From this point on, as might be expected, Gilbreth was an acid critic of Taylor and his associates.

Hathaway's reports on Hermann, Aukam described a confused state of affairs there, which Hathaway claimed was brought about by Gilbreth's work—especially, micromotion study. These reports were broadcast by him and Taylor to the rest of the group, and it was generally agreed that, in Hathaway's words, Frank Gilbreth was "either raving crazy or a . . . fakir." The Taylorites feared that he would wreak havoc in Germany, especially since newspapers were reporting German Social Democratic protests against the "Americanization" of German General Electric by Gilbreth. Carl Barth and Hathaway urged Taylor to write friends in France and Germany and "expose" Gilbreth, but the leader of the group was reluctant to do so. "I agree with you that he might discredit the whole movement in Germany," he wrote Barth, "and yet it seems hard to write and point out his incompetence." Yet Taylor was not reluctant to give his rather bald opinion of Gilbreth to American acquaintances. He suggested to Professor Lionel S. Marks of Harvard that the latter not "lay too great a stress on the work that is being done by . . . Frank Gilbreth," because Gilbreth was interested solely in money, and was "likely to do great harm to our cause."

On his part, Gilbreth confided his own sentiments largely to his personal note file. He privately inveighed against Taylor's "bent viewpoint" and "tactless disposition." Gilbreth did not reveal when he first recognized the "absolute lack of human element" in the Taylor system, but in view of the fact that he had wholeheartedly embraced and defended the system prior to 1914, it is obvious that his dissatisfaction stemmed at least partly from a source separate from the system itself. He apparently believed that his difficulties sprang from the variations he introduced into the Taylor program, for he wryly cautioned imaginary readers of his personal notes to "make no changes from Taylor's plan whatever or you will not be able to avail yourself of Taylor's and S.P.S.M. (Society for the Promotion of the Science of Management) militia." Throughout 1915 and 1916 he refused to divulge the names of his clients to authors who requested such information for books or articles, claiming that he had to keep these names confidential, because "some people who . . . used to be my friends have made a systematic attempt to get all my jobs away from me. . . ."

Despite the strong hostility between the Taylorites and Frank Gilbreth, none of the parties involved publicly indicated the existence of this state of affairs. Taylor's death in 1915 undoubtedly deterred Gilbreth from doing so, and World War I extended his period of relative silence. Until 1920, the public, and perhaps most businessmen and management executives, knew little, if anything, of the conflict among the most famous and important leaders in the scientific management field. Had the conflict been purely personal, it might have remained confined to personal correspondence files and diaries; the fact that professional techniques and businesslike competition were also at stake increased the probability that at least some of the issues would be brought out in the open. Gilbreth and his wife took the initiative in doing so in December, 1920, when they delivered "An Indictment of Stop-Watch Time Study" at a Taylor Society meeting in New York.

The Gilbreths characterized time study as unethical, wasteful, and inaccurate, among other things, although they were careful to point out that they were not personally criticizing Frederick Taylor, "the great founder of stop watch time study." (It would, however, have been strange indeed if their audience, and readers of the Taylor Society *Bulletin,* did not construe their strongly adverse criticism of time study to be an attack upon Taylor himself, because the most popular symbol of the latter's program was the stop watch.) The Gilbreths' essential contentions were that time study did not "preserve the best that has been done," employed questionable statistical methodology in arriving at standard times, and was costly because of the inaccurate and useless data it developed. They took pains to point out that motion study was not the same as time study, nor "a part of time study," and denounced the developers and practitioners of time study for failing to "co-operate with motion study."

Obvious personal bitterness was added to professional differences when a general debate on the paper was held during the following April in Philadelphia, when, among others, Carl Barth and Dwight V. Merrick, who was Taylor's time study man as early as 1900, defended the use of stop watch time study. Barth's reference to "myself and other direct disciples of Mr. Taylor," and his "concession" that the Gilbreths had "a far more accurate time measuring device than the stop watch," were dashes of salt on some old and unhealed wounds, and served to make Frank Gilbreth's closure far more bitter than the indictment itself. Without specifically naming them, he attacked Barth, Sanford Thompson, and Merrick for defending time study because they were "interested in the profits from the sale of stop watches, time study devices or books describing stop watch time study methods." At the same time, he laid claim to his own "direct discipleship" by enumerating the occasions when he had acted as Taylor's chosen representative in describing the program of scientific management to different groups. (Despite his differences with Taylor, Gilbreth wished to bear the Taylor stamp of approval for personal and/or professional reasons.)

It would be interesting, and important, to know how businessmen in general, and potential clients of the management engineers in particular, reacted to this episode. It is possible that these latter were not Taylor Society members, or that they did not read the Society's *Bulletin.* It seems rather unlikely that there would be complete ignorance of the now-open conflict between the time study and motion study leaders in that part of the business community where there was some interest in the employment of scientific management techniques as well as scientific management consultants. What the actual effect was is not known.

For Gilbreth, of course, the issues were not resolved. He was still unhappy and displeased about the Taylor associates' lack of consideration and appreciation of him and his work. The failure of the Taylor Society, "which he started," to grant his work the recognition he believed was due it was also a sore spot. Gilbreth believed that he had no recourse but to bring his grievances into the open. "We believe we have already waited more than long enough," he told Morris L. Cooke. "The engineers of Europe and the labor unions of America have waked up to the unscientific pretensions of the proponents and advocates of the stop-watch. We refuse to be classified with those who believe that anything but the best is good enough in Scientific Management. . . . We shall continue to stand for Science in Management, even if we stand alone." He reminded Cooke of the Hermann, Aukam episode, and complained that micromotion study was "deliberately and intentionally misrepresented and belittled" by Taylor and his closest followers. All that he wanted from Cooke and the Taylor Society, he said, was a "square deal."

Apparently, he did not get what he considered to be a "square deal," for he continued to attack stop watch methods and to advertise the superiority of motion study. Gilbreth's popularity as a public speaker appears to have had some effect, because Sanford Thompson decided to take it upon himself to arrange a truce. "Is it wise," he admonished Gilbreth, "even from the sordid viewpoint of good business policy, to damn Taylor and all his works up hill and down before large audiences . . . ? You and we are working for the same end (1) to develop the science and philosophy of management, and (2) to make a darn good living." Thompson suggested that these objectives could be achieved through the employment of more "constructive" means.

Gilbreth denied he was attacking either Taylor or Thompson; "To damn your stop watch methods as being rule of thumb," he wrote, "is quite different from what you accuse me of. . . ." He charged that Thompson's partner, William O. Lichtner, had employed an unfair competitive argument by publicly stating that micro-motion studies were too expensive to use, but that no public retraction was made, despite the fact, Gilbreth suggested, that "neither of you know anything about it." Nevertheless, Thompson's admission that both he, unquestionably a "direct disciple" of Taylor, and Gilbreth were "working for the same end," was music to Gilbreth's ears. Gilbreth finally admitted that Thompson's "smooth and tactful" words had poured oil on troubled waters. Whether a real rapprochement was in the offing remains unknown, because before anything more tangible could be developed, Frank Gilbreth died suddenly.

The issues raised by Thompson were particularly vital, for when one consultant claims that another's basic technique (in this case, time study) is almost valueless at the same time that his rivals are insisting that his own method (micromotion study) is too expensive for businessmen to use economically, the demand for the services of all of them may be reduced. Thompson's reference to making "a darn good living" might be an indication that such was the case, but no evidence is at hand either to support or refute it. It remains, however, a reasonable assumption that such was the case.

Despite the death of Frank Gilbreth, the competitive nature of his relationship with the "direct disciples" of Taylor was continued by Mrs. Gilbreth. While she directed her own consulting business in the field of motion study and work simplification, she also concentrated on achieving recognition for her husband's role in the development of the scientific management movement and on gaining wider acceptance of the concept and program of micromotion study. Ultimately, both were achieved.

What has happened in the field of work measurement is that an accommodation has taken place, and both stop watch time study and motion study and its derivatives are used, either by individual firms or within the same work measurement program. It is, in a sense, a triumph for the Gilbreths, and particularly Frank Gilbreth, who, long ago, suggested to Taylor that motion study "should really go with your great invention of time study." It was not, of course, the kind of economic or intellectual triumph that Gilbreth might have desired in 1921, but rather a process of gradually increasing co-operation between the techniques and their representative practitioners, his more consistently sought goal. No doubt the absence of the leading antagonists and competitors expedited the process of accommodation.

L. Urwick and E. F. L. Brech (essay date 1959)

SOURCE: "Frederick Winslow Taylor," in *The Making of Scientific Management Volume I: Thirteen Pioneers,* Sir Isaac Pitman & Sons, Ltd., 1959, pp. 28-38.

[*In the following essay, Urwick and Brech discuss Taylor's life and work.*]

Almost half a century after Charles Babbage, the mathematician and philosopher, observing British industry from without, had propounded the essential principles of the scientific approach to business management, F. W. Taylor, an American engineer, arrived at precisely similar conclusions as the hard-won prize of practical experience. There was no plagiarism in Taylor. He never read Babbage. His ideas were his own, wrung by sheer force of personal effort, energy and originality from the unsympathetic environment of the machine-shops of the United States in the eighteen-eighties. The similarity in the two men's work was born of minds of fundamentally similar training brought by circumstances to a detached examination of identical phenomena.

If Babbage's work produced little subsequent impression, despite his large contemporary circulation, while Taylor's has received world-wide recognition, that was due not so much to any wide difference in the intellectual methods, or the principles which they enunciated, as to the period in which they lived and worked. In Babbage's time, and for some decades after, men were too preoccupied with the sheer technical adventure of developing a new economy based on power-driven machinery to pay much attention to its deeper implications. The excitement of exploitation was more attractive than the pains of exploration, unless this was directed to areas purely technical and material. As Professor Bowie has observed, "business did not turn to operating profits until promotion profits had begun to dwindle."

But by the time Taylor was ready to make public the results of his experiments, a profound unease with the whole rationale of capitalist industry had replaced the earlier complacency, an unease of which his work on management was only one form of expression. The fact that he was at the same time an innovator of genius on the purely technical side of engineering hindered rather than helped popular recognition of his philosophy of organisation, though he himself regarded the latter as infinitely the more important part of his total achievement.

Taylor was born in 1856 of well-to-do parents, and received an excellent general education which included European travel and attendance at French and German schools. He was intended for the law, and had in fact qualified for entry to Harvard. He encountered trouble with his eyes, however, as the result of heavy reading, and though it proved temporary it turned him to an alternative profession.

In 1875 he began his apprenticeship as a machinist and turner. Three years later, having found difficulty in securing an opening in the industrial depression of the late eighteen-seventies, he joined the Midvale Steel Works as a machine-shop labourer. His better education secured him a shop clerkship, which brought him into close contact with the tool room and started him thinking in terms of standardisation. But he did not like clerical work and applied to return to the shop as a machinist.

As long as he remained a member of the rank and file he had no option but to concur with the deliberate "soldiering" (restriction of output) which was endemic in the shop. But shortly after he was promoted gang boss and later foreman. Once he was on the side of the management, he set to work with unflinching loyalty to see that every man under him did a fair day's work—an output which he knew from his own experience at the bench could be secured without undue strain.

It was not a pretty struggle. The machine shop of that date was no kindergarten. And Taylor was challenging what his fellow-workers regarded as the inalienable privilege of setting their own pace. He was fortunate in that family contacts with one of the controlling interests in the company secured him a greater measure of support than would have been accorded in ordinary circumstances. That could not protect him, however, from constant unpopularity, direct sabotage and threats of personal violence. After two years he won through. A humane, friendly and thoughtful man, he was sickened by the forceful methods he had been compelled to employ to achieve a result which he knew to be fair and reasonable, and which ought to have been secured through the spontaneous co-operation of the men. He directed the full force of his trained mind to the development of alternative methods.

He appreciated from the beginning that the root of the whole problem was ignorance—ignorance on the part of the management as to what the men could and should produce, or as how to convince the men that if they did produce what they should, they would receive a fair reward for their efforts; ignorance on the part of the men as to how they could secure a proper output given the assistance they should receive from the management and as to the possibility of securing permanently enhanced earnings as a result.

The methods of both sides were traditional and fortuitous. The craftsman "picked up" his trade from others round him during his apprenticeship. Afterwards he practised it at the conventional speed of the shop. The thousand and one petty delays and interruptions due to faulty supply of materials and tools, uneven running of machines, and the other details which management should have corrected, he accepted without active protest as an inevitable part of his industrial environment. Management left the question of output almost entirely to the men, relying on various forms of wage incentive, or even mere ganging by foremen, to achieve what was reasonable. They set rates crudely and cut them even more crudely if some worker broke loose and started to earn big money. There was not a hint of real fact finding, of precise and accurate knowledge, about the whole business.

Taylor started with an individual worker at a lathe, started, as the trained research worker starts, to find out all about it, to observe what he was doing and leaving undone, to analyse and to measure every factor in his task which could be made susceptible to measurement. In short, he began to build up a "science" of cutting metals on a lathe. Gradually he isolated the various elements and set to work to improve the factors which made for high performance, to eliminate causes of delay and interruption, to reduce the craft of the tradesman to precise and detailed written instructions.

All the features of the practice to which he subsequently gave the title ***Scientific Management*** sprang from that central principle. He approached any form of industrial work, any problem, not as a "mystery," skill in which could be acquired only by years of use and wont, but as a definite logical structure of cause and effect which could and should be mastered along the lines followed by a scientist dealing with a new gas or liquid.

Every development, and they were many, sprang from that root, that attitude towards industrial problems. Thus it became clear that successful lathe work depended on a combination of nine variables including speed of the machine, depth of cut, angle of cut, angle of tool, and so on. In association with Carl Barth, who was a better mathematician, Taylor developed a slide rule on which any foreman could calculate these nine variables for any job. It was apparent that many of the delays and interruptions in work were the consequences of faulty planning. A new job was not ready when the previous job was finished, tools had to be fetched from the other side of the shop, essential materials were not available. Correction of these conditions revealed the fact that few men could be found at a foreman's wage who could be trusted to look after all the factors equally well. Hence his separation of planning from performance and the evolution of the idea of "functional foremanship."

Of course, these developments did not occur simultaneously. Taylor's early career before he left Midvale in 1890 was an impressive combination of material progress and theoretical study. He passed in six years from labourer to chief engineer. At the same time, he completed his technical qualifications by taking a Master's Degree in Engineering at the Stevens Institute solely through evening study.

His method of study in dealing with "management" problems was not in itself original. The originality resided in applying to this field, which had hitherto been regarded as the domain of custom and tradition, of personalities and politics, the detached analysis of the trained engineer. Indeed, many of his followers subsequently described their work in the simple phrase "the engineering approach."

As used by Taylor, this method was reinforced by vigour, great intellectual powers, and, what is not so generally understood, a very vivid human sympathy. Had he not been a great pioneer and originator in the field of management, his technical achievement in itself would have earned him an enduring place in the history of engineering.

One of the factors restricting output on lathe work which had attracted his attention almost from the beginning of his investigations was the inability of existing tool steels to stand up to a really high rate of working owing to overheating. When in 1898 he joined the Bethlehem Steel Company, he found a field for experiment and a support for this aspect of his work which rapidly led to the most dramatic results. At the Paris Exhibition of 1900, British tool steel manufacturers, who had hitherto led the world in machine tool practice, were amazed and alarmed to find on the Bethlehem Steel Company's stand a machine tool running red hot at a quite unprecedented speed without any apparent loss of cutting edge. Here was a revolution in the hardening of tool steel which they could neither neglect nor ignore.

The reaction of the British machine tool trade was twofold. They made a determined effort to recapture their technical supremacy, an effort which deflected their attention from the incipient interest in management issues which had been developing both in U.S.A. and Great Britain for the previous decade. They became involved in proceedings in the United States brought by the Bethlehem Steel Company for infringement of the Taylor-White patents which dragged on from 1903 to 1908. The circumstances were not favourable for the dispassionate consideration of a series of ideas in another field, presented by one of the protagonists in the case. In two directions Taylor, the technical inventor, slammed the door on the work of Taylor, the philosopher of organisation.

His concepts in the management field were first made public in a paper entitled **"A Piece Rate System,"** presented to the American Society of Mechanical Engineers in 1895. This paper focused the growing interest in management questions mentioned in the previous paragraph, which occurred simultaneously in Great Britain and the United States about this time. H. R. Towne had read papers to the same society on *The Engineer as an Economist* in 1886 and on *Gain Sharing* in 1889. F. A. Halsey spoke on *The Premium Plan for Paying Labour* in 1891.

Taylor himself fully recognised that he was one of a group who were developing a revised technique. And it is perhaps one of the clearest signs of his genuine scientific temper that he acknowledged publicly and generously the directions in which he had drawn on the work of others.

"Among the many improvements for which the originators will probably never receive the credit which they deserve may be mentioned"—and he proceeded to list seven innovations. A progressing system (William H. Thorne at the William Sellers Co.); an employment department (at the Chicago Plant of the Western Electric); a messenger system (Mr. Emrie at the Ingersoll Sargent Drill Co.); a mnemonic system of order numbers (Mr.

Oberlin Smith, with amplifications by H. R. Towne); an inspection system (Charles D. Rogers at the American Screw Co.); an apprenticeship system (Mr. Vauclair at the Baldwin Locomotive Works); and "the card system of shop returns introduced as a complete system by Captain Henry Metcalfe at the Frankford Arsenal."

At the time of the publication of his paper, attention was concentrated chiefly, much to Taylor's personal disappointment, on the wage payment aspect of it. There was a lively interest in this particular issue at the time and Taylor's much wider doctrine was treated in the U.S.A. primarily as an alternative to Halsey's plan. With the publication of Mr. James Rowan's *A Premium System of Remunerating Labour* in 1901, exactly the same thing happened in Great Britain. It was not until 1903, when an expanded version of his paper was republished in book form under the title ***Shop Management,*** that the larger implications of Taylor's work began to be recognised in his own country. And it was only in 1912, three years before his death, that the advocacy of Charles D. Brandeis in the Eastern Rates Case called popular attention to its significance.

Only once did Taylor address an audience in England. He was present at the Joint Meeting of the Institution of Mechanical Engineers and the American Society of Mechanical Engineers held at Birmingham in 1910. But the programme reflected the preoccupation with the purely technical aspects of highspeed steel already mentioned. The only opportunity of expressing his ideas was at a session on *High Speed Tools and Machines to Fit Them,* opened by Mr. H. J. Brackenbury. Taylor and F. B. Gilbreth, who was also present, attempted to describe some of their experiments in motion study. But the opener in his reply, while agreeing with the importance of the issues raised, said that "unfortunately the paper had not dealt with that subject."

Taylor left the Bethlehem Steel Company in 1901 and devoted the rest of his life to trying to spread an understanding of his fundamental ideas. While there was never a strike at any factory at which he himself was operating, one of his followers became involved in a very ugly political situation at the Watertown Arsenal. The workers were strongly organised in craft unions, and the Arsenal, being a Government establishment, was rife with the jobbery which inevitably accompanies the "spoils" system, which has proved so great a handicap to public administration in the U.S.A.

As a consequence, the man whose disgust with the slave-driving aspect of conventional methods of industrial management had led him to devote a lifetime to developing a more human alternative, found himself the target of a storm of labour criticism. It was a dirty fight. And in the upshot Taylor, in the witness chair, was "hazed" by a hostile committee of Congress for three days. It was a heart-breaking experience for a generous and honest man, who knew both the value of his own work and the real motives for much of the opposition.

One outburst, however, defined his basic attitude and principles more clearly than any of his more formal writings—"Scientific management is not any efficiency device . . . nor is it any bunch or group of efficiency devices. It is not a new system of figuring costs; it is not a new scheme of paying men; it is not holding a stop watch on a man and writing things down about him; it is not time study; it is not motion study nor an analysis of the movements of men; it is not the printing and ruling and unloading of a ton or two of blanks on a set of men and saying 'Here's your system; go to it.' It is not divided foremanship or functional foremanship; it is not any of the devices which the average man calls to mind when scientific management is spoken of. . . .

"Now, in its essence, scientific management involves a complete mental revolution on the part of the workingman engaged in any particular establishment or industry. . . . And it involves an equally complete mental revolution on the part of those on the management's side—the foreman, the superintendent, the owner of the business, the board of directors. . . . And without this complete mental revolution on both sides, scientific management does not exist.

"The great revolution that takes place in the mental attitude of the two parties under scientific management is that both sides take their eyes off the division of the surplus as the all-important matter, and together turn their attention toward increasing the size of the surplus. . . . There is one more change in viewpoint which is absolutely essential to the existence of scientific management. Both sides must recognise as essential the substitution of exact scientific investigation and knowledge for the old individual judgment or opinion, either of the workman or the boss, in all matters relating to the work done in the establishment."

In Great Britain the preoccupation with technical issues already described prevented any general application of his ideas prior to the war of 1914-1918. One or two progressive firms, such as Hans Renold, made some interesting experiments; there was a little discussion in the press. But that was all. When the needs of war production emphasised the importance of increasing effectiveness in management, the bad odour created by the craft unions in the United States penetrated to this country and was a grave handicap to a clearer understanding of his philosophy and a wider application of his methods. The National Institute of Industrial Psychology felt it necessary to explain on a number of occasions that their work had nothing to do with "Taylorism." This prejudice still persists, but a clearer appreciation of his principles and their value to all ranks in industry is gradually developing. In hundreds of factories which have never heard his name, conceptions of industrial management which he originated are now commonplace practice. His books have been translated into scores of languages. Above all, his basic idea that only through scientific methods of thought can mankind learn to control effectively the tools developed by the physical sciences, is increasingly the inspiration of progressive workers in the sociological sciences throughout the world.

Taylor was sometimes dogmatic. He had need to be to break through the hard shell of habit, prejudice, custom and vested interest which always stands between the originator and a general acceptance of his ideas. Even in the recent war, twenty-five years after his death, millions of pounds were wasted and essential production was held up because administrators and managers were still basically uneducated in the technique of their profession, a technique which he did so much to further.

To see clearly and to express ideas firmly is not to be inhuman, save in the minds of those who regard blinkers as their greatest comfort. Taylor knew very well the limitations of the scientific knowledge which he had to use—

> There is another type of scientific investigation which should receive special attention, namely, the accurate study of the motives which influence men.

But as far as his knowledge went, he was human, generous and large-minded. His ready recognition of his fellow workers in the management field has already been described. He was in favour of high wages. His attitude towards promotion was that it is an employer's duty to see openings elsewhere for any men or women whose abilities cannot be used to the full in his own organisation. While he was a strict disciplinarian, he managed to convince everyone with whom he worked that discipline began with F. W. Taylor. These things are of the stuff of greatness. And it is likely that as our industrial civilisation develops, broadens and deepens, there will be an increasing recognition both of his originality and of the fundamental value of the ideas which he initiated. Already it may justly be said of him in a phrase applied to another great teacher, "Alike in his personality and in his substitution of reason for authority, his work was an enfranchisement of the human mind."

L. Urwick and E. F. L. Brech (essay date 1959)

SOURCE: "The Acceptance of F. W. Taylor by British Industry (1895-1915)," in *The Making of Scientific Management Volume II: Management of the British Industry,* Sir Isaac Pitman & Sons, Ltd., 1959, pp. 88-107.

[*In the following essay, Urwick and Brech discuss the application of scientific management in British industry, noting opposition to the movement that considered its principles "hideous" and "dehumanising."*]

It is remarkable that F. W. Taylor, considered as a pioneer of scientific management, aroused comparatively little practical interest among contemporary British industrial circles, despite the fact that the period was one in which the engineers in this country were becoming increasingly conscious of the significance of sound works management. Searches of a dozen likely periodicals yield no reference to his death or obituary comment on his work. Only *The Engineer* (April, 1915) and *The Efficiency Magazine* (June, 1915) saw fit to make any mention of his passing, and that in but a few lines of biographical comment. Though he had been a participant in joint meetings between the American and British Mechanical Engineers, and had been an outstanding figure in the professional ranks of his own country, the Institution did not include his name among its obituary notices.

During his life-time, when the full concept of scientific management was evolving, the interest displayed by British industrial and engineering circles was limited. Even as late as July, 1917, one finds H. N. Casson, in giving a series of six lectures on *Efficiency* to the staff of Messrs. Mather and Platt, Ltd., Manchester, speaking of "a man called Taylor," who was the first to apply scientific methods to efficiency and to work out efficiency methods. Immediately prior to the war of 1914-1918, there was a brief spell of active interest, but its quality and insight can be judged from the label "Taylorism" which was attached to a great deal of the discussion in the press. But for this interlude British interest remained vague, cool and distant.

The cause of this attitude can only be surmised. But it can probably be traced to the predominantly technical character of those who were responsible for management in this country. This had two consequences—the one, that management itself was not a subject claiming any high degree of time and attention; the other, that interest in Taylor the specialist in high-speed steel overshadowed acquaintance with Taylor the pioneer of management. That "scientific management" itself was not more warmly welcomed on this side of the Atlantic was due to many factors. First among them were the opposition of organised British labour and a sentimental recoil in many quarters on the grounds that this "system" was inhuman in its approach to, and treatment of, workers.

Such views sprang from a complete misunderstanding of Taylor's teachings. He was little read in the original and such versions of his principles from other hands as did become available over here were not well calculated to give readers a true picture of his attitude. None of them recaptured the fervour of his outburst before the Committee of the House of Representatives, or the enthusiastic emphasis with which he there expounded his first basic principle of "a mental revolution" on the part of managers and workers alike.

It is a pity that the teachings of Taylor, Gilbreth and Gantt were not more closely associated in their published form. As was recorded in the early chapters of the first volume the three men were close associates both in their consultancy and in their teaching work. Their published work was unfortunately in strictly separate form. Gilbreth and Gantt, in writing of scientific management, emphasised precisely those aspects of "human interest" which would have won ready response in British political and social circles just before the first Great War. Had readers associated their work with Taylor's principles the idea of scientific management would have been more palatable. But unfortunately, save among a very limited group, Gilbreth was known only as "an academic apostle of motion study" and Gantt as the inventor of a chart.

The key dates in Taylor's development and exposition of scientific management are as follow:

1895 **"A Piece Rate System,"** his first paper to the American Society of Mechanical Engineers.

1903 ***Shop Management,*** a paper to the A.S.M.E. subsequently published in book form.

1906 **"The Art of Cutting Metals,"** a paper to the A.S.M.E.

1910 (July) Joint meeting of the A.S.M.E. and the Institution of Mechanical Engineers at Birmingham. Taylor and Gilbreth took part in the discussion.

1911 ***The Principles of Scientific Management*** published privately after it had been rejected by the Meetings Committee of the A.S.M.E. This was shortly followed by a public edition and by a version in instalment form in *The American Magazine.*

The reaction of British industrialists to each of these events is an interesting story, though it must be told in a setting which indicates the extent and angle of contemporary interest in the problems of factory management generally.

Broadly speaking, the period as a whole was one in which management was at last beginning to get a solid grip on British industry. Primary interest tended to centre on problems of costing and cost control, and among these, especially in the earlier years of the period, the various proposals for premium bonus schemes held pride of place. The landmarks are two or three outstanding publications. The year 1887 had seen the publication of Garcke and Fells' *Factory Accounts,* the first British attempt to use accounting techniques for the systematic control of costs and operations. Less than ten years later (1896), J. Slater Lewis published his comprehensive book on *The Commercial Organisation of Factories.* The end of the period was marked by two further noteworthy books: Dempster-Smith and Pickworth's *Engineers' Costs* (1914) and Elbourne's *Factory Administration and Accounts* (1914). The intervening years witnessed the publication of numerous other more limited and less important works on similar subjects, but greater significance attaches to the many series of articles that appeared in the technical journals.

For instance, *The Engineer* carried a series of eight articles on *Some Aspects of Workshop Management* from July-October, 1902: *The Mechanical World* (Manchester) had a series of five on *The Organisation of a Small Engineering Works* in January-February, 1909, followed by a series of twenty in 1909-1910 on *Economical Workshop Production.* Running concurrently with these it published a series of eighty-two in the years 1908-1912 on *Commercial Engineering* by "A General Manager" (believed to be A. J. Liversedge). Thus the technical press was beginning to build up in its manager and engineer readers a broad general knowledge of more modern methods of management. In the main these articles were little concerned with principles. They were factual and descriptive, expounding their authors' own particular ways of dealing with shop planning, cost assessment, job tickets, drawing office procedures, and the like. Almost every series had several articles devoted to purely technical matters of machine feeds and speeds, tooling and design for certain types of operation—the features which twenty years later led to "production planning" in the engineering sense, as the basis of the task of the production or planning engineer.

Thus, at the turn of the century, the apathy of British industry on questions of management was disappearing. A century of technical concentration on the production side and of "accounting management" on the commercial side was gradually drawing to its close, making way for a new epoch in which the "sides" were to become fused and an integrated functional management to be the new principle. Not that in these years, 1895-1915, there was much in the way of practical advance on a broad front. The reports of the Committee on the Health of Munition Workers illustrated only too clearly the lamentable standard of management that prevailed over much of British industry at the opening of the war of 1914-1918. But certainly ideas on management were much more in the air and were discussed fairly frequently in industrial clubs and technical societies. Taylor's teaching was not coming to a Britain devoid of knowledge or background. It was reception which was at fault. The industrial milieu presented an infertile soil because of scepticism and apathy—an incapacity to understand that anything other than technology was of consequence—rather than because of any active opposition or obstructive ignorance.

In 1895, when Taylor read his first paper, he was an unknown person in this country. American engineering circles already knew him and his work—hence the invitation to read the paper to the Society. But the reception it had in the States did not cast even a pale shadow over here, despite the fact that the subject of "premium bonus" was among the foremost industrial topics of the day. Of the three leading engineering periodicals, *The Engineer* (London), *Engineering* (London) and *The Mechanical World* (Manchester), only one made any reference to Taylor's paper: that was *The Engineer* which reproduced it in full in three instalments, April-May, 1896, nearly a year after it was given. *Cassier's Magazine* (better known now by its later titles *Industrial Management* and *Mechanical Handling*) printed excerpts from the paper in October, 1895, and an abridged version of it in February, 1898, as an article by F. W. Taylor under the title **"A Partial Solution to the Labour Problem."** But except for Rowan's reference to the latter article in the course of his own paper on "The Premium System," given in 1901 to the Institution of Mechanical Engineers, there is no trace of any interest aroused by Taylor's proposals.

The second paper was given to the American Society in June, 1903, on ***Shop Management.*** Broadly speaking, it was a full study of workshop organisation and management, expounding Taylor's particular principles and methods, including such features as the thoroughgoing use of time study and establishment of "functional foremanship." The term "scientific management" was not yet used. In fact, in his opening paragraphs, Taylor himself speaks of "the art of management" defined as "knowing exactly what you want men to do and then seeing that they do it in the best and cheapest way." It is significant of his own thought and of the extent to which he has been misunderstood and misrepresented that he goes on to say . . . "but relations between employers and men form without question the most important part of this art." Neither of the three British technical periodicals—or rather four by this date, including, the new one *Mechanical Engineering* (Manchester) which commenced in 1898—made any reference whatsoever to the paper. Nor even did *Cassier's Magazine* review it or refer to it in any way. In fact, a fairly exhaustive search through the most widely used channels of publication in this country, including the proceedings of the leading institutions, has failed to produce any reference whatsoever to this paper, or to its subsequent publication in book form, save an indirect one in the Manchester paper in 1911. Yet by this time, the general British interest in management methods briefly described above was gaining a substantial momentum of which the technical press carried ample evidence.

With the reading of his paper on **"The Art of Cutting Metals,"** December, 1906, Taylor encountered quite a different reception in this country. Here at last was something that the British engineer could appreciate! *The Engineer* had an editorial on it in January, 1907, calling it "the most remarkable paper ever produced to a learned Society." Then in the following weeks the entire text was reproduced in instalments. *Engineering* for January 11th, 1907, carried a summary article outlining the paper, while both the Manchester periodicals reprinted the text in serial form early in the year: in fact, *Mechanical Engineering* published its first instalment in the issue of 29th December, 1906. Interest elsewhere was equally alive. The attitude of the Engineering Institutions is perhaps best exemplified by a comment in the *Journal of the Iron and Steel Institute* (Vol. I, 1907) referring to the paper as "an address that deserves to become one of the engineers' classics." Indeed one reads with a sense of keen surprise a paper given in 1908 to the Liverpool Engineering Society by Mr. H. H. Hill on *High Speed Steel* in which no reference at all is made to Taylor's experiments or findings.

The next scene forms an interesting close to the "tool steels" act. The place was Birmingham and the occasion a Joint Meeting of the Institution and the American Society of Mechanical Engineers in July, 1910. The subject was *High Speed Tools and Machines,* and there were four papers, two each by British and American members. Among the American delegates were Taylor, Gilbreth and Gantt, though none of them was reading a paper. In the discussion, Dempster-Smith made extensive references to Taylor's technical work, particularly as published in the **"Art of Cutting Metals."**

In due course Taylor rose to speak. "The proceedings of the American Society," he said, "have been burdened to such an extent with what I have said on the subject of high-speed steel and similar topics, that I feel it would be improper for me to make any further remarks on that point. I do, however, welcome the opportunity of speaking upon the far broader subject of which the art of cutting metals and the proper use of machine tools is but one of the small elements, namely, the great opportunity, as well as the duty, which lies before us as engineers of taking such steps as will, during the next few years, result in a very material increase in the output of every man and every machine in their manufacturing establishments. The importance of obtaining this increase of output is that, in my mind, it presents the only opportunity open to us, measurably speaking, of settling the great labour problem which faces both of our countries. I say without hesitation, that in the average establishments in America, not in all the establishments, it is possible to double the output of the men and the machines just as they stand now, and I believe the same is true throughout this country. It gives us the opportunity at the same time to give the men what they want most—higher wages, shorter hours, better working conditions; and, on the other hand, to give the companies what they most need—a lower labour cost, so that they might be able more successfully to compete at home and abroad."

One can imagine the sense of disappointment that greeted this opening. Dr. Taylor, the high-speed tool expert, appeared to be hiding himself behind F. W. Taylor, the father of scientific workshop management. Even more, it was almost as if he was deliberately using this unique opportunity of teaching the British engineers how much they had missed by their neglect of ***Shop Management.*** That the whole of his lengthy contribution—six and a half pages in the printed proceedings—was devoted to management was nothing more than the natural consequence of his conviction of the significance of management as the key to all industrial problems. He sensed acutely that the engineering industry had more serious matters to consider than the technicalities of their machines and materials. He expressed this concern in his remark that the first duty lying upon engineers was that of counteracting and overcoming the blighting fallacy which rested upon every one of their workmen, and which was paralysing their energies, that it was to the best interests of the workmen to go slow instead of going fast, to do as little as possible for the money they were getting instead of as much as possible.

There was hardly a labour union in either of the countries which had not already enacted restrictive regulations upon those principles. Every workman, from the time that he started to serve his apprenticeship, was deliberately taught by the men who were older than himself that it was to his best interests to "soldier," as Americans called it, or to "hang it out," as Englishmen called it, instead of going fast. But what were the engineers doing to meet the problem? With perhaps characteristic modesty, Taylor refrained from enlarging upon his own twenty years of work in the provision of an answer. He pointed instead to the efforts of his colleagues in "increasing output of their working men through a deliberate scientific study of the motions of men, followed by a time-study of their motions." He predicted that "during the next fifty years a very considerable part of the time of engineers would be spent in the minute motion study of every man in the trade." Already he could say that "motion study had been going on in the United States for more than thirty years in increasing volume, and invariably with the same result, namely an enormous increase in the productivity of man if it was properly carried out."

For the rest of his remarks he gave a summary of Gilbreth's four years of work in motion-study in brick laying—"perhaps the oldest of the mechanic arts that are now practised." What Gilbreth had done in this field was typical of what could be accomplished in every trade without exception. He called his hearers' particular attention to the two key principles: the one, that working methods are laid down and workmen trained to use them without deviation; the other, that equipment and tools are analysed and standardised in accordance with the best methods for the job. "Thus," he concluded, "it becomes clear that the new or scientific method calls for deliberate co-operation between the workmen and those over them, as well as for pains-taking thoughtful motion and time study which must be made by those in the management, and which, in fact, is, in most cases, entirely beyond the ability and training of the workman."

As Taylor sat down, the President called on Dr. Gilbreth to speak, but he rose only to remark that he had nothing to add to the discussion. Had he sensed a coolness and lack of interest in the reception given to Taylor's contribution? What the meeting really thought remains unknown because on Gilbreth's reply the President closed the session. Mr. Brackenbury, who had read the opening paper, was called on to wind up as shortly as possible. He "entirely agreed with the remarks Dr. Taylor had made with regard to the importance of the study of the movements of men. Unfortunately," he went on, "the paper did not deal with that subject and he would very much have valued any remarks Dr. Taylor might have made on tools and machines, of which he had had such great experience. In passing, he might remark that machine-builders were studying the movements of men very carefully, and had done so for a long time. Nearly every new machine brought out had some device added to it which made the movements of the operator less, and certainly a great deal of time was saved in that way."

There is no record of Taylor having spoken at any other gathering of engineers or managers in this country.

The next few years were to witness a remarkable change in British interest in "scientific management." The doctrine became as it were popular or fashionable as a topic for the press and publishers. It was, in fact, only just at this time that the term "scientific management" itself had come into use. Drury records that it came into active use only through Brandeis, the lawyer, who used the "scientific management" standpoint in defending the shippers of the Eastern seaboard against the railways in the *Eastern Rates* case, 1910-11. Prior to that date it had been just a technical term used within the very limited circle of Taylor and his immediate associates and its appearance in the earlier reference in ***Shop Management*** must be regarded as an accident. The *Eastern Rates* case was also the source of the sudden wide emergence of interest in the Taylor doctrines, and was probably among the most significant incidents in the story of scientific management, since it gave to the ideas of Taylor and his group the wide popular publicity which they had hitherto lacked.

Briefly, this occurred through the decision of Louis D. Brandeis, a public-spirited Boston lawyer, to use arguments based on scientific management before the Interstate Commerce Commission in opposing the application by the railway companies for an increase in freight rates. Brandeis subsequently rose to the highest rank in his profession, becoming a Justice of the Supreme Court. He maintained that "the practical management of the railroads was completely out of date and inefficient, and that they could save, through efficient management, far more than they could accomplish by an increase of freight rates." He quoted the experience of several companies that were being managed on Taylor principles and was supported by Harrington Emerson who claimed that the railroads had a potential economy of a million dollars a day, which could be secured through the application of scientific management.

Brandeis had apparently been interested by ***Shop Management*** and had made the acquaintance of Taylor himself, Gantt, Dodge, Carl Barth and others of the group supporting the movement. In preparing his brief against the Rates Application he first took advice from these men, and in fact met them in joint session in October, 1910, to decide on a formal title for their methods. *Functional Management* had been one of Taylor's favourites in his earlier years, but the group decided that the name which they had been casually using more recently should be adopted and so came the "official" title of scientific management.

The case went against the railway companies, on the grounds of their liberal earnings in past years. "The subject of scientific management was dismissed (in the decision) with the remark that it was everywhere in an experimental stage . . . but there is reason to believe that the Commission was more influenced by the testimony than it cared to acknowledge." That the proceedings should have had an exceedingly wide and ample press report in America—and even abroad—is only natural. So, too, was the other consequence. Taylor was beseiged by requests for articles and papers, as well as by letters and visitors. But this was not the origin of the paper on the ***Principles of Scientific Management,*** the first draft of which was in preparation a year before the Railway Case opened. It finally appeared as a private publication circulated to members of the American Society in January, 1911, and very shortly afterwards was issued publicly both in instalment form in *The American Magazine* and as a book by Harper's in New York and London.

For British readers the first significant publication was a series of articles in May, June and July, 1911, in *World's Work* (better known by its modern title *The Review of Reviews*). The first of these was by Ray Stannard Baker, under the title *The Gospel of Efficiency—A New Science of Business Management,* and was based primarily on what Baker learned at the Railway Rates hearing. In the following three articles the editor was proud to offer F. W. Taylor's own views: "the first authoritative presentation of the whole subject, the first comprehensive account of the history of the discoveries." The substance was an abridgment of the "principles" and for the first and only time in this period there appeared in a British periodical an emphatic statement of the heart of Taylor's teaching—"but the chief and essential feature of scientific management is the change in the mental attitude of both employers and employees towards their common work."

In its August issue *World's Work* carried a reproduction of some of the criticisms that its articles had aroused. Two of these are of particular interest. *The Engineer* of 19th May, though admitting that there was a lot to be said for "Taylorism," maintained that there was far more to be said against it, and went on to denounce it as inhuman, dehumanising man, depriving him of the use of his intelligence in work and destroying all the best features of a bonus system. Three weeks later *Engineering* took up the theme, commenting that the articles contained little that was new to its own readers, but would arouse strong opposition.

Although such opposition may have been roused it did not appear to be vociferous. On the contrary, for a brief spell immediately prior to the outbreak of war (1914), it seems that there was a sizable group of protagonists. The term "Taylorism" was tending to stick, but the two synonyms "scientific management" and "efficiency" undoubtedly held the field. Some idea of the extent of the interest may be gleaned from mention of a few articles and papers between 1911 and 1913.

Cassier's Magazine printed an article by P. Ballard on "Scientific Management and Science" in 1912. *The Engineer* in the first half of 1911 carried an article and a letter on "Taylorism." These were followed by "Taylorism Again" about a year later and "Scientific Management and Work Efficiency" in 1913. *Engineering* published a "Note on Taylor's Task-Work System" in 1911 and an editorial on "Scientific Management" a year later. The latter, which was primarily concerned with motion study, attracted a letter to the editor, followed by two notes on the same subject. *Mechanical World* and *The Mechanical Engineer,* the two Manchester papers, were more sympathetic in tone. Numerous articles and notes on the subject of management appeared during these three years. Late in 1911 "one of the foremost exponents of scientific management" referred to ***Shop Management*** in an article, "Systematic v. Scientific Management."

The subject figured little in the papers to the technical institutions, although presidential addresses tended often to deal with wider issues of management or industrial relations. Outstanding in these years was the paper given by G. C. Allingham to the Junior Institution of Mechanical Engineers in 1912, entitled "Scientific Shop Management on the Taylor System." Based on ***The Principles,*** the paper was a very full and fair account of Taylor's views, including the comments that "the system demands an understanding of the men" and that "proper personal relations must exist" if it is to succeed. The discussion that followed it was very mixed but on the whole not favourable, many of the adverse comments being along the lines already indicated by *The Engineer.* One member reminded the meeting of the big difficulty that "organised labour here is antagonistic" to scientific management. This paper and discussion were naturally widely reported. About a year later, an equally important address was given by Hans Renold to the Manchester Association of Engineers on "Engineering Workshop Organisation."

Renold had met Taylor and understood the real significance of his thought. Not only had he absorbed it fully, but had been able to mould and re-apply the principles of scientific management along lines that would best suit his own works. He could, in fact, adopt the simple standpoint of defining scientific management as "neither more nor less than commonsense tabulated and applied with tact and reason when facing the everyday problems as they arise." One thus finds in Renold's paper the first signs of assimilation—the process of adapting to British thought and conditions what had hitherto been regarded, frankly and exclusively, as an American "invention."

Two other references of about the same period are also of special interest. The first was an article in *The Nation* (now incorporated with the *New Statesman*) of August, 1912, under the title "An Essay on Scientific Management." This gave a very fair presentation of the case for Taylor's doctrines and analysed a few of the dangers. Particular point was made of the "spirit" in which scientific management is approached and the comment added that "in Taylor's spirit, it can do little but good." Its importance, it was stressed, must not be overlooked, but a warning was given to expect strong opposition from organised labour.

In a following issue Miss Margaret Bondfield replied in a letter to the editor, pointing out that the article underestimated the dangers inherent in the system, and illustrating her argument by a detailed description of the McKee Rock Strike (American Pressed Steel Car Co.) of 1909. A desultory correspondence ensued in which the main issue was soon lost in wider social questions. A vigorous letter was published from H. Gordon Selfridge professing his belief in scientific management which he had used in his shop for years and which ought not to be obstructed by childish sentiment such as "making men like machines." He had given a copy of the original article to each of his managers.

The second source of comment was an article by J. A. Hobson on "Scientific Management" in *The Sociological Review* for July, 1913. In principle he found Taylor's methods of value and importance to industrial efficiency and to economic progress. But they involved sacrifice by the human beings employed in industry—a loss of initiative, of individual freedom, of the use of intelligence and responsibility and a narrowing influence exerted by the subdivision of work. An analysis of the balance of gains and losses led him to the conclusion that society had a lot to gain from scientific management, and that the employee must be compensated by a shorter working day. No discussion appeared to have been provoked by this article. The whole subject was taken up at a meeting of the Sociological Society in November, 1913. Edward Cadbury read the paper on "Some Principles of Industrial Organisation," an analysis of the case for and against scientific management. A good level of discussion followed, among the participants being J. A. Hobson, G. D. H. Cole, Walter Hazell (of Hazell, Watson and Viney Ltd.), and C. G. Renold and W. H. Jackson (both of Hans Renold Ltd.). The proceedings were reproduced in full in the April, 1914, issue of *The Sociological Review.* A few months later the *Review* carried a further article, this time by C. Bertrand Thompson of the Harvard Graduate School of Business Administration, who had had close contacts with Taylor himself. In the same issue Edward Cadbury replied to some of the criticisms that had been made against his paper.

The outbreak of war in August, 1914, as might have been expected, interrupted discussion of the subject from the academic standpoint. But the progress of the war itself and the accompanying demand for production put the substance of scientific management on the map of British industry. That story is not relevant to the present context but its final incident is of interest. Taylor died when the war was but a few months old, and though the British technical press paid so little respect to his departure, a fitting British "memorial" was erected in no less a form than an official publication—*Scientific Business Management,* a pamphlet published and sold by His Majesty's Stationery Office, issued in 1919 on the authority of the Ministry of Reconstruction as one of its series on reconstruction problems. There is, of course, no reference to Taylor or his work in the booklet, but the principles of his teaching are the fundamental thoughts on which the text is based.

"The prosperity of an industry," say the opening words, "and of every man concerned in it is intimately bound up with efficiency of management." And the rest of the paragraph goes on to stress the importance of the "human" aspects of effective management. The whole line of thought expounded rests firmly on Taylor's cardinal principle of a mental revolution in employer and worker alike and of their mutuality of interest. Perhaps the best portrayal of the pamphlet is to say that it represents the completion of the process of anglicising scientific management. The contrast between say, Allingham's paper of 1912, and this pamphlet of only seven years later is extraordinarily marked.

Scientific management remains the same in essence, but it has matured and consolidated, and in the process it has undergone certain shifts of emphasis. "Motion Study" forms one of the sections of the booklet, so do "Labour-Saving Devices" and "Progressive Methods"; bonus schemes are also discussed. But the longest section of all is entitled "Personal Intercourse," starting from the view that employees will look to their employer or chief manager as "a leader, educated to guide and stimulate them towards a higher standard of intellectuality and efficiency in life . . ." And this is a responsibility which he can only discharge by identifying their interests with his and deliberately seeking to build up sound personal relations. "In management itself it is decidedly advantageous to cultivate the personal interest of the workers"; one of the results accruing being that "the overhead employee cost is greatly reduced."

Such thinking is not a new addition to Taylor's presentation of scientific management. Its emphasis is slightly different. And if we take scientific management as represented by the trinity—Taylor, Gilbreth and Gantt—even the emphasis was the same. Taylor failed to recruit his following in British industry largely because he was misrepresented and misunderstood. Admittedly he met in British industrial minds a soil so pre-empted with technical issues that there was little room for the seeds of more effective management. But the greatest opposition to scientific management was rallied round the suggestion that it was "dehumanising"—almost the negation of Taylor's real teaching and absolutely the antithesis of the interpretation of Gilbreth and Gantt.

In the underlying cause of this opposition, there is a warning of great significance for the present time. The Labour movement in the United States was, in Taylor's time, fundamentally on a "craft" basis. The greatest stronghold of these "craft" unions was the metal working industries. One of Taylor's associates was called in as a consultant to the Watertown Arsenal. He found a situation in which craft unionism had joined hands with nepotism and the jobbery which was characteristic at that date of the less reputable political circles in the United States. Not only was "ca' canny" endemic. Every supervisory post was filled by political nominees, relations, and so on. He determined to stand up to this situation, as was his duty to those who had employed him. A strike resulted and its outcome was to align the craft unions in the metal-working industries and their political lobby at Washington against "scientific management."

In the course of the struggle which followed and which led to the House of Representatives Enquiry before which

Taylor gave evidence, the most extreme and violent things were said and written by the Labour side. To give but a single instance; at an Annual Conference of the American Federation of Labour a formal resolution was submitted which referred to:

> the hideous so-called Taylor System of scientific management. No tyrant or slave-driver in the ecstasy of his most delirious dream ever sought to place upon abject slaves a condition more repugnant to commonly accepted notions of freedom of action and liberty of person.

It must not be forgotten that our kinsmen on the other side of the Atlantic speak a language which appears to be the same as our own. But the emphasis given to words and phrases, the whole political tradition which dictates their use in controversial issues and consequently the real meaning to be attached to any given clause, differ profoundly. There is no doubt that the immense prejudice against the idea of scientific management and the profound misunderstanding of the social attitude of the groups who initially formulated its philosophy in the ranks of British Labour was produced not by practical experience, but by the fact that they could read reports and documents formulated by Trade Union colleagues on the other side of the Atlantic. They tended to interpret such documents with a fraternal sympathy which they did not deserve and which their authors would have been the last to expect. In consequence, they formed a picture of the methods implicit in the term which was wholly mistaken and which was founded on the passionate and partial descriptions characteristic of an acute political controversy.

The methods of scientific management can, of course, be abused. They can be applied ruthlessly and for purposes of exploitation, but to describe such abuse as scientific management is no more accurate than to describe the use of poison gas in warfare as chemistry. And indeed, as has been shown, the men who were responsible for designing and developing these methods, the men who really appreciated the philosophy of the scientific approach to management problems, were as a body profoundly concerned with the human element in industry, and with raising the standard of life for the masses of the people. Nor, as the experience of Russia has shown us, can any form of government, whether it is controlled by employers on a capitalist basis, or by the mass of the workers on a communist basis, ignore the technique by which production is made more efficient and effort reduced. "Stakhanovism," of which so much has been heard in the U.S.S.R., is in fact no more than a variation of F. W. Taylor's philosophy.

The fact that so deep-seated a misunderstanding, in its effects so deleterious to the development of British industry, should have arisen because the workers on both sides of the Atlantic speak what is apparently, but not in fact, the same language, is of great importance in the light of the enormous number of problems which will have to be settled by conjoint action between the representatives of the Anglo-Saxon races in the future.

Hugh G. J. Aitken (essay date 1960)

SOURCE: "The Taylor System," in *Taylorism at Watertown Arsenal: Scientific Management in Action 1908-1915,* Harvard University Press, 1960, pp. 13-48.

[*In the following essay, Aitken provides a detailed analysis of Taylor's system.*]

Questioned by Colonel Wheeler about his explanation of the molders' strike, John Frey admitted that workmen sometimes seemed to behave irrationally. "I know," he said, "the fiendish deviltry with which we throw down our things and go out on strike. They deliberately go in in the morning, and say 'Boys, we'll say "No" to this,' and then they take their time, putting away their things or not, and taking their time about things as they go out." But underlying this apparent irrationality, he insisted, was an attitude that made sense. A walkout was not always a rejection of the job; sometimes it was a means of defending it. "The workman believes when he goes on strike that he is defending his job. . . . Because he has quit, he has simply ceased working, and he is not going to let anyone else take it."

When a man goes on strike, according to Frey, he is defending his job. What did this mean? Implicit in the statement was the conviction that a workman had, in a certain sense, a property right to his job; it was not something that could equitably be changed or taken away by management without the consent, passive or active, of the man involved. Implied, too, was a certain view of what was involved in the concept of "the job." The job was something which could be, or had to be, defended. It involved much more than just a contract for the sale of a certain amount of a man's time, energy, and skill for a certain price. It involved an accepted place, in terms of prestige and power, in the organization of the establishment and of the community; an accepted routine for performing certain accepted tasks; and accepted relationships with other individuals and with the physical environment of tools and machines. It involved also a man's feelings: it gave him a point of view from which he could orient himself toward the world in which he worked and provided him with a stable set of expectations as to how he could count on other people's acting toward him. These elements, and others, were involved in the seemingly simple concept of "the job." All of them were subject to change, and a change in any one of them was a change in the job. Some changes—particularly ones that were unpredictable, that made no sense from the point of view of the individual concerned, or that lowered a man's status in his own eyes and the eyes of others—could be regarded as threats, as dangers to a man's image of himself and his world. Against such threats the job had to be defended. One of the possible defenses was withdrawal—the refusal to continue cooperating with the persons from whom the threat emanated.

The idea that the job was something which on occasion might have to be defended against managerial action was not one which would have appealed, or even made sense, to Frederick Winslow Taylor. Already in 1915—the year in which he died—Taylor was generally accepted as the "father" of scientific management. Public repute, in this case, was not an incorrect reflection of the facts. Though modestly stating that he personally had contributed little that was truly new and original, Taylor nevertheless regarded himself as an inventor and creator, on the grounds that he was the first to synthesize and systematize the best that was known about the management of men and to point out the techniques by which this art might be advanced in the future. True, he had not even coined the phrase "scientific management": that had been Louis Brandeis' contribution in the Eastern Rate Case of 1910. Taylor himself had preferred the more accurate but less propagandistic term "task management." But he was the accepted leader of the group of management consultants, engineers, and businessmen who had gathered under the banner of scientific management; his publications on the subject were accepted as the authentic gospel of his sect, at least; the firms which he personally had reorganized according to his principles were regarded as models to be imitated; and in public debate he had taken the position of official spokesman for his cause.

What held the Taylor group together were a vision and a doctrine: a vision of what could be achieved by the application of scientific analysis to the performance of work and a doctrine of approved procedures whereby this vision could be made real. Together, vision and doctrine constituted a cultural innovation of considerable importance—one which has, in little more than half a century, become so much a part of our thinking and activity that today we take it for granted and find it hard to conceive how things could ever have been done differently. Yet Taylor and his colleagues knew that they were innovating. Like all innovators, they tended to overlook their own debt to the past and exaggerate the extent to which they were cutting loose from the pioneers who had preceded them. But in their conviction that they were breaking with tradition, they did not deceive themselves.

Every innovation is a creative synthesis of elements already known. So it was with the concept of scientific management. Essentially it was a late manifestation of the rationalist philosophy, and in this sense it had roots in the eighteenth century and earlier. Prominent too were analogies with Benthamite utilitarianism of the early nineteenth century, in particular the conception of the individual as a social atom, responding to calculations of pleasure and pain that are purely private to himself. What was new in scientific management, or relatively new, was the self-conscious and deliberate extension of rationalism to the analysis of industrial work. It is no coincidence that Taylor and most of his immediate disciples were engineers, for it was by way of engineering that scientific analysis had made its most powerful and continuing impact upon industrial production. They accepted without question the engineering approach that had already proved itself in the design of physical objects, and they extended it to the analysis and control of the activities of people. The essential core of scientific management, regarded as a philosophy, was the idea that human activity could be measured, analyzed, and controlled by techniques analogous to those that had proved successful when applied to physical objects.

So conceived, the idea of scientific management had tremendous implications. Potentially its relevance extended far beyond the organization of industrial work, which was the problem area in which it was first applied. Probably today we have not yet explored the full implications of the concept. Certainly Taylor and his group did not. They were practical men, not philosophers, and their interest was in the immediate problems of industrial production at that time. Thus their conception of scientific management was partial and selective, reflecting the economic and social environment in which they operated. Their preconceptions and their economic interests gave a particular slant to scientific management as they expounded and practiced it. The resistance they encountered stemmed partly from the particular devices and objectives they chose to emphasize; but partly too it was resistance to the basic philosophy of scientific management itself.

Taylor was an aggressive, self-confident individual, seldom at a loss for words and with no small opinion of his own importance. When he expounded the meaning of scientific management, he was capable of making it sound like a turning point in the history of the human race. Yet it is important to distinguish between the idea of scientific management and scientific management as Taylor thought of it and practiced it. In the first place, he was concerned particularly with industry. Some of his colleagues and followers were interested in extending the system to other fields of activity, for instance political and university administration, but Taylor was not. Secondly, within industry he was concerned particularly with metalworking establishments, especially machine shops. In the hands of colleagues and disciples, the system was applied to many other types of business, but it was in machine shops that Taylor did his best and most original work. Thirdly, he was concerned almost exclusively with organization at the shop level—from the superintendent and foreman down. He had nothing to say about finance or pricing or the higher levels of business administration beyond enunciating the so-called "exception principle"—that is, the rule that each level in the administrative hierarchy should concern itself only with matters that are exceptions to the standard procedures of the level immediately below. This is not to say that the principles of scientific management were not thought of as being potentially applicable to a great variety of other problems; on the contrary, Taylor would have insisted that they were universally applicable. The point is that scientific management as Taylor expounded it stemmed from a concern with the organization of work in machine shops. This left an enduring mark on the development of the system.

That Taylor's methods and doctrines were an important innovation can hardly be doubted, but he was far from the first to think seriously about management problems or to try to formulate general principles about the organization of industrial work. In the United States in the period after the Civil War the problem was being attacked from at least three different angles. First, executives and their advisers in large-scale business were concerned with problems of formal organization and control at the administrative level. Leaders in this area were the railroads, notably the Pennsylvania; here we find, for example, discussions of staff and line organization, of executive recruitment and training, and of the formal structure of executive authority. These men were wrestling with the problems of bureaucratic hierarchies and attempting to adapt to the technological imperatives of large businesses the general principles already worked out for other large organizations, such as armies. Secondly, there was the shop management movement. Here the leaders were the mechanical engineers—the men who were responsible for the design and operation of the capital equipment that had come to play such a vital part in American industry. Just as the railroad journals provided the forum for the discussions of the first group, so for the second the publications of the American Society of Mechanical Engineers and other engineering journals were the essential media. Thirdly, there was the reform movement in cost accounting. This was on a slightly different level from the other two, because there is no single group or industry to which we can point as the seedbed of change. The public utilities, operating under the threat or fact of public regulation, naturally showed a special interest in this area; but every man who tried to think or write responsibly about management problems in this period found himself eventually discussing costs and the problems of controlling and measuring costs. Reforms in cost accounting, however, deserve special mention as a source of managerial improvement, for in this area was germinated the seminal idea of costing as a technique not for recording aggregate past performance but for controlling work in process.

Taylor originally made his reputation as a member of the second group: he was part of the shop management movement—an outstanding engineer working along parallel lines with such plant managers as Slater Lewis in Britain and Church, Halsey, and Towne in the United States. He was concerned, as they were, with problems of productivity at the shop level, and he shared their interest in incentive wage payments as a means of increasing productivity. What distinguished Taylor was not that he adopted a radically different approach from his contemporaries and immediate predecessors; rather it was that, accepting many of their assumptions, he carried them to their logical conclusions and embodied the results in an allegedly complete *system* of management that was more inclusive, more self-contained, and more powerful in its practical implications than their proposals and devices. Taylor's system was also much more suitable to serve as the nucleus of a dedicated movement than were the tentative, pragmatic suggestions of other students of the problem. It lent itself excellently, by its drastic oversimplifications and the fact that it could be codified into a relatively small number of rules, to publicity and salesmanship. This is one of the reasons why Taylorism or, as it was later called, scientific management, still evokes recognition and emotional response, while only specialists know the work of men like Halsey and Slater Lewis.

Taylor's interest in managerial reform stemmed from his experiences in industry. While still a young man he was employed as foreman and later as chief engineer at the Midvale Steel Company in Philadelphia, a relatively small engineering and metalworking firm. As foreman his job was to supervise the work of men who were cutting, shaping, or otherwise manipulating metal. Supervision involved seeing to it that certain standards of precision and workmanship were met. At this stage of industrial development this function largely came down to hiring men properly experienced in their craft and firing those who proved incompetent. The foreman's job also involved, however, seeing to it that a certain rate of output was maintained. With given tools and facilities, this implied getting the men to maintain a pace of work that Taylor and his superiors regarded as acceptable.

Taylor quickly became convinced that the men under his charge were soldiering—deliberately restricting output. He took it as his responsibility to break up this practice and increase the pace of work to a rate closer to that of which the physical equipment was capable. He relied at first on the methods normally used by foremen at that time: the threat of discharge, verbal persuasion, and piecework. None of these proved effective. He even recruited some unskilled laborers and taught them the rudiments of the machinist's trade on the understanding that they would back him up in his efforts to increase the work pace. Unfortunately, as soon as they had learned the job, they fell into line with the rest of the machinists and refused to deviate from the norm. Clearly Taylor was being frustrated by the highly effective sanctions operating against any workman who deviated from the normal work pace of his fellows. This frustration, combined with Taylor's compulsion to attain higher labor productivity, led to his initial innovations.

Since this situation was crucial in determining the direction of Taylor's efforts, it deserves analysis. It might be said that Taylor believed that his men were not working hard enough. This, however, would be a misrepresentation of Taylor's views. It was not the expenditure of effort that concerned Taylor. There is no simple one-to-one correlation between expenditure of effort and the rate of work: many other factors influence the relationship—the frequency and duration of waste motions, the number of rest periods, and the degree of nervous tension involved, to mention only the most obvious. Taylor's problem, correctly stated, was to induce his men to increase their pace of work. This was a problem only because of his conviction that their habitual pace of work was inadequate. The crux of the matter was the discrepancy between Taylor's conception of a proper work pace and that of his workmen.

To say that one work pace is proper and another improper is clearly a value judgment. What is possible can on occasion be determined by technological or economic tests; what is proper can be determined only by reference to a given scale of values. When an individual informs us that a certain group of men is working too slowly—that they are slacking or soldiering—he is giving us information about his own values. He is not making a meaningful statement about the group under inspection. The work pace is what it is because the group of persons involved in the work has determined that it shall be so. There is no simple method by which the adequacy, or propriety, or "goodness" of a given work pace can be determined.

Frederick Taylor thought otherwise. He asserted positively that the rate at which work ought to be done could be determined without undue difficulty if the proper procedures were followed, and further, that it could be determined by any person willing to abide by the rules that Taylor stated. This claim was the heart of scientific management as Taylor interpreted it. That such a rate could in fact be determined, and that different individuals observing the same behavior and measuring it by the same techniques would finally determine the same rate as quantitatively correct, was the basic justification for the use of the adjective "scientific."

Taylor's claim was, of course, fallacious. There was, in principle, no difficulty involved in determining the length of time in which a given piece of work *could* be done, assuming that the relevant characteristics of the work, the individual worker, his tools and equipment, and so on were specified. There was even less difficulty involved in determining the length of time in which, on the average, such a job *was in fact done* by a specified workman or group of workmen. But there was no scientific bridge between objective measurements of this kind and the normative judgments that Taylor sought to make. The "can be" and the "ought to be" were not identical. The positive statement was poles apart from the normative judgment.

While at Midvale, Taylor began working out the techniques that were later to become the hallmarks of scientific management. Essentially his method of determining a proper work pace had two elements: job analysis and time study. Job analysis meant that each job was to be divided into particular operations, each of which was taken as a complete unit. The total job was then the sum of these individual operations. In its later developments, particularly at the hands of Lillian and Frank Gilbreth, job analysis was carried to a point at which individual motions of the operator's limbs were taken as the units, and later still the idea began to gain acceptance that the total job was more than the arithmetic sum of its parts. Taylor did not go to these lengths. The primary purpose of job analysis, for him, was to determine the operations that were essential to the performance of the job as distinguished from those that were superfluous or "waste."

This procedure implied a decision, on the part of the individual conducting the analysis, as to what the job really was. Failing this, no isolation of "waste" from "nonwaste" motions was possible. This decision, which to Taylor seemed a simple matter, was in reality a very complex affair. Evaluative criteria entered the picture even at this stage. For example, a machinist assigned the task of turning down a piece of metal to certain dimensions on a lathe might find that his cutting tool required sharpening. To the machinist this might seem a normal part of the job, perhaps a welcome and valued break in routine, certainly a skill that every good machinist prided himself on possessing and exercising. To Taylor, however, or to any of the men he trained, the sharpening of tools was not part of the job. It was *a* job, certainly, but somebody else's job, not the machinist's. To permit the machinist to do it was a waste of his skill and of the money the employer was paying for that skill. Similarly it would not be part of the machinist's job to determine the correct speed of his lathe or the correct angle of cut; even more obviously, it was not part of his job to obtain materials or tools from the storeroom or to move work in progress from place to place in the shop or to do anything but turn the piece of metal on his lathe. Job analysis, as Taylor interpreted it, almost invariably implied a narrowing down of the functions included in the job, an extension of division of labor, a trimming off of all variant, nonrepetitive tasks. This narrowing down was carried out with no consideration for what were traditional parts of a job and with no appreciation of the possible value to the operator of actions which seemed superfluous to the observer. Taylor did not think it necessary to ask the operator what he conceived his job to include, nor would he have considered this to be relevant information.

The second basic element in Taylor's system was time study. After a job had been analyzed into its component operations, these were timed by means of a stop watch. By adding the unit or elementary times for each operation, a total time for the whole job was calculated. In machine-shop work and in similar operations it was found useful to distinguish between machine time and handling time. The former covered the time that elapsed while the piece of work was actually on the machine, with the operative's function confined to supervision and adjustment. Machine times were susceptible to rather precise calculation, as they depended on the physical characteristics of the metal being worked, the cutting instrument, and the machine tool. Frequently machine times could be calculated from data obtained on other jobs. Handling times, in contrast, referred to the time taken by the operative in setting the work up on the machine and removing it after the operation was completed. The sum of all machine times and handling times gave the total time for the job.

This total time, however, was not equated directly with the time in which the job *ought* to be done, which was the measurement it was desired to find. Instead, certain customary percentages were added to the calculated time to obtain what was called the standard or task time for the job. These "allowances" were added both to the machine time and to the handling time—in the former case to allow for unexpected variations in the hardness of the metal or the speed of the machine, in the latter to allow for fatigue and accidental interruptions. The percentages involved were quite large. At Watertown Arsenal, for example, it was standard practice to add from 25 to 75 per cent to the sum of the elementary handling times and similar percentages to the sum of the machine times to obtain the calculated task time.

Carl G. Barth, one of Taylor's leading disciples, once stated in public: "Our method is called scientific because it determines exactly—scientifically—the length of time in which a man can do a piece of work." In several respects, however, the setting of a standard time for a job involved arbitrary, nonscientific decisions. First, there was the decision as to what constituted the job—what operations were in fact to be timed. Secondly, there was the decision as to which particular men were to be timed, how often, and under what circumstances. When questioned on this point Taylor and his followers usually stated that they would select a "good, fast man," or an "average, steady man," or some similar impressionistic phrase. They would time such a man on the job not once but several times, but the exact number of measurements required to give a satisfactory average was not specified. A man with experience in time study, it was said, would know when he had taken enough measurements. As for the circumstances under which a job should be timed, these were in some respects rigorously specified, but in other respects almost completely ignored. Taylor insisted that all the technical conditions of production should be standardized at the highest attainable level of efficiency before any time studies were made. He saw that there could be no stable measurement of a job time if factors affecting the rate of work were allowed to vary haphazardly. The factors that were relevant, however, he saw as almost entirely mechanical: the speed and feed of the machine, the angle of the cutting tool, the supply of parts and material, and so on. He had no corresponding appreciation of the relevance of social and psychological factors—such as an awareness on the operative's part that he was being timed or a fear that the setting of a task time would result in a cut in pay—nor was any attempt made to reduce the variability of such factors. The furthest Taylor would go in this regard was to recommend that the time-study man should see to it that the operative knew and understood the purpose of the stop watch and that the time study should be made, as far as possible, in a spirit of friendly cooperation.

Lastly, the size of the allowances that were added to the calculated time was decided upon in an arbitrary, rule-of-thumb manner. If technical conditions in the shop had been standardized as Taylor stipulated, there should have been no need to add allowances to the machine time. The only exception rests upon the fact that at the time Taylor was developing his system no convenient workshop method was known for determining the hardness of metals, though laboratory methods were available. The hardness of the metal was thus a variable that could not be completely controlled, and this was a case for making allowances. But with this exception, to add allowances to the calculated machine time was to admit that technical conditions had not been completely standardized and that extra time was being allowed to compensate for an error, whose existence was known but whose magnitude could not be calculated, in the rest of the computation. There was no assurance that this procedure made the total time any less inaccurate than it would have been without the allowances. To introduce one unknown error to compensate for another is hardly scientific procedure.

Allowances were added to the handling time to take account of the fact that, because of varying degrees of fatigue on the part of the operative and uncontrollable interruptions in the flow of work, the time taken even by a "good, steady man" might be greater than the calculated time. To the extent that there were uncontrolled interruptions, this was again an admission that the stipulated conditions for the measurement had not been met. Allowances for fatigue were made for basically the same reason: the operative's accuracy and rate of work varied because of factors not under the control of the man making the time study. Precisely how much time to allow for fatigue was not known, as the problem of industrial fatigue had at that time received no serious study. Here again, the time-study man had to rely on experience.

The apparent accuracy and objectivity of stop-watch time study was therefore to a large extent an illusion. When a task time was set for a certain job, one part of the total had been set by reading measurements from a precise instrument—the stop watch. The other part had been set by a whole series of conventional decisions, in which the values and preconceptions of the individual doing the timing were foremost. It is tempting, though it is only part of the truth, to define time study as a ritual whose function it was to validate, by reference to the apparently objective authority of the clock, a subjective estimate of the time a job should take. Critics of stop-watch time study during Taylor's lifetime often attacked the procedure for its alleged inaccuracies. A more fundamental criticism is that it was never clear exactly what was being measured. Was it the minimum time in which a job could be done? If so, why the allowances, and why not select the fastest man for the measurement? Was it the average time—something Taylor would never have admitted? If so, why the attention paid to the elimination of waste motions and the selection of a particular individual to be timed? Was it, perhaps, an ideal time? In a sense it was. But an ideal—however defined—could not conceivably be measured by a stop watch, nor could it be inferred from any evidence a stop watch could provide. No measuring instrument can produce an "ought to be" from an "is." The so-called inaccuracies and the conventional allowances were not regrettable deviations from scientific precision. On the contrary, they were the means for reaching what was hoped would be a viable compromise between two conflicting work norms: that of the worker and his fellows on the one hand and that of the time-study man, his professional colleagues, and his employers on the other.

Taylor insisted that, for stop-watch time study to be carried out correctly, all the conditions of work should be standardized at the highest possible level of efficiency. His conception of what conditions of work were relevant and therefore demanded standardization was a limited one. Nevertheless, his search for methods of standardization produced some of his most solid and remarkable achievements. For example, at the time Taylor was doing his pioneer work the machines in most factories were run by systems of belts, pulleys, and shafts from a central power source; the individual electric motor was not then in general use. The speed of each machine, and therefore the work pace of the operator, depended directly upon the mechanical efficiency of the belt and pulley system. Incorrect tension on the belts caused slippage; inadequate maintenance led to breakdowns and sometimes to serious injury. What was required, as Taylor saw it, was first a method for determining scientifically the correct tension to be put on a belt and the correct methods of maintenance, and second the establishment of belt maintenance and adjustment as a separate job, to be attended to by men trained in the work under special supervision. Here was, in microcosm, Taylor's basic method in action: the analysis of a piece of work, the determination of the best methods of handling it, and the reorganization of the division of labor in the factory so as to insure that these methods were applied. Typically, it involved the divorce of ancillary functions from established jobs—ordinarily no one in particular looked after the belting—and the establishment of new jobs.

To the layman there was nothing very remarkable about this: surely an idea like this could occur to anyone? Indeed it might, and probably some such arrangement had occurred to other shop engineers before Taylor. But to Taylor it was not an incidental detail; it was something that *had* to be done if time study was to be feasible. Like all factors influencing the pace at which work was done, it had to be studied and standardized. His studies of belt maintenance and adjustment were an integral part of his attempt to secure total control over the pace of work.

Precisely the same analysis can be made of Taylor's other contributions to shop management; all were designed to achieve total control of the job and its performance and in particular to enable management to prescribe and enforce a standard work pace. With the advent of the individual electric-motor drive—revolutionizing as it did the whole art of factory layout—Taylor's work on belting lost much of its practical significance, though it remains a classic example of the controlled experiment applied to shop engineering. Other problems to which he turned his attention, however, produced solutions of more enduring significance: the idea of planned routing and scheduling of work in progress, foreshadowing the techniques of the assembly line and continuous-flow production, with the route of each assembly and subassembly scheduled in advance from a central planning room; the introduction of systematic inspection procedures between each operation; the use of printed job and instruction cards, informing the worker in detail what operations were to be performed on each component and informing management precisely how much of each machine's and man's working time was devoted to each product or batch of products; the introduction of refined cost-accounting techniques, based on the routinized collection of elapsed times for each worker and machine on each job; the systematization of stores procedures, purchasing, and inventory control; and the concept of "functional foremanship," with its four or five supervisors with specialized functions in place of the normal multifunctional single foreman. Of all these innovations, only functional foremanship failed to win general acceptance. The remainder quickly became standard workshop practice and, with modifications, have remained so to this day. Because there was nothing spectacular about any one of them, and because they were all organizational changes which could not be patented or branded with the Taylor name, there has been a tendency on the part of historians of industry to play down their importance. In this respect history has done Frederick Taylor less than justice, for these inconspicuous innovations have probably exercised a more far-reaching influence on industrial practice than has the conspicuous innovation of stop-watch time study.

There is one of Taylor's innovations that deserves special comment, not only because of its relevance to what happened at Watertown Arsenal but also because it furnished Taylor with considerable prestige among industrialists and engineers for reasons independent of his strictly managerial reforms. This was the invention, or rather the discovery, of high-speed tool steel. The primary object of Taylor's endeavors was to find a means of determining the rate at which work should be done. Every factor which could influence the pace of work had to be brought under control and standardized at the optimum level of efficiency. In the machine shops where Taylor did most of his early work, a factor of obviously crucial importance was the speed at which the machine tools were run. Taylor was therefore confronted with the problem of determining the proper speed at which any given metal-cutting tool should be operated. This was a problem which, up to that time, no one had tackled systematically.

What Taylor was after was not a new tool steel; he was concerned rather to find out which of the tool steels then available was the best, in order that he might take it as his standard. The crucial series of experiments were run by Taylor and his colleague Maunsel White, a metallurgist, at the Bethlehem Iron Company in 1898. Experimenting with different methods of heat treatment, Taylor and White discovered that cutting tools made of steel containing 7.7 per cent tungsten and 1.8 per cent chromium (high-speed steel, as it was called) attained their optimum cutting efficiency at temperatures just below the melting point of the steel. A cutting tool made of high-speed steel operated at maximum efficiency when run at the highest speed possible without melting the steel.

What had Taylor and White discovered? A new tool steel? Certainly not: the chromium-tungsten steels with which they were working had been purchased commercially from the Midvale Steel Company. A new method of heat treatment? Possibly, for up to that time it had been generally accepted that a tool heated to a temperature above cherry red was permanently ruined. But much more than this was involved. What Taylor and White had done was to show how the new alloy steels could be used to cut metal at rates several hundred per cent faster than had been possible before; they had opened the way to a revolution in machine-shop practice. Incidentally, and this was probably Taylor's contribution rather than White's, they had upset one of the most hallowed precepts of the machinist's craft: the belief that the proper cutting speed was the one that maximized the life of the cutting edge of the tool. Not so, said Taylor: tools can and should be reground regularly and systematically; what we should maximize is the amount of metal removed per unit of time, and cutting speeds should be set accordingly.

The Taylor system of management in later years came to be known by the labor unions as a "speed-up" system. The phrase had strong emotional connotations and did less than justice to what Taylor was trying to do. Taken as referring solely to what Taylor called "the art of cutting metals," however, it is literally correct. Taylor's experiments convinced him that most machine tools used in American industry were being operated too slowly. If a machine tool was being operated at its correct speed, it was purely by chance; not one machinist in a thousand, said Taylor, realized that there existed clearly defined laws governing the speed and duration of cut. Cutting speeds that might have been not too inappropriate at an earlier day, when straight carbon steel was the only tool steel available and when the horsepower applied to each machine was smaller, were still being used in machine shops that had available vastly greater horsepower and improved tool steels. The reason, as Taylor saw it, lay in ignorance of the scientific laws of metal cutting—an ignorance characteristic not only of wage-earning machinists but also of machine builders and mechanical engineers.

Taylor once expressed the relationship between his experiments on tool steels and his system of management as a whole in these terms: "The moment that scientific management was introduced in a machine shop," he said, "that moment it became certain that the art or science of cutting metals was sure to come." This statement certainly expressed one aspect of the relationship. If Taylor was to attain his primary goal of securing complete control over the pace of work, it was essential that he know precisely the maximum rate of output of which his machines were capable. This in turn involved careful analysis of elements in the work situation which previously had been left to tradition and common sense.

There is, however, another way of looking at the relationship between the discovery of high-speed steel and the development of scientific management. This was expressed concisely by James Mapes Dodge, president of the Link-Belt Engineering Company, a warm friend of Taylor's and a close observer of the development of Taylor's ideas. "The whole development of Mr. Taylor's work," wrote Dodge in 1909, "is based on the ability of high-speed steel to remove more metal per minute than any previously used or discovered steel could do." The implication of this statement is that scientific management was essentially a method for exploiting the full productive potentialities of the new cutting tools. The discovery of high-speed steel marked a sharp discontinuity in machine-shop practice. Machines could now be run at from two to four times their former speeds. The organization of the machine shop, and indeed of the whole factory, had to be adjusted to this new level of productivity.

Historically, Dodge's statement is incorrect. Taylor had begun his work with job analysis, time study, and incentive payments before his discovery of high-speed steel. The experiments with tool steels were carried out because time study required the standardization of machine-tool practice. Nevertheless, Dodge's words show considerable insight. Without high-speed steel Taylor's managerial reforms might have been highly desirable; with high-speed steel they became well-nigh indispensable, at least in machine shops. The innovation of high-speed steel spread much more quickly through American industry than did the innovation of scientific management. Its advantages were more obvious, its nature more familiar, and its adoption more easy. Employers and wage-earning machinists alike might well be suspicious of Taylor's managerial reforms, but they would find it much more difficult to resist the introduction of a superior piece of technology. But if high-speed steel was to be effectively utilized, scientific management or something very close to it had to be adopted too.

The discovery of high-speed steel did not solve the problem that Taylor had originally set himself. Indeed, it raised new problems. By reducing machine times by a half or more, it focused attention on the proportionately greater importance of handling times. Efforts to reduce handling time by job analysis and time study therefore were increased. And it now became even more urgent than before to find a method for determining exactly, for any given piece of work, the correct speed and feed of the machine tool.

In tackling this latter problem Taylor had at Bethlehem the help of two men who later became leading exponents and practitioners of his system: Henry L. Gantt and Carl G. Barth. Gantt had earlier worked with Taylor at Midvale and was familiar with what he was trying to do. With his assistance, Taylor succeeded in determining empirically, by a prolonged series of experiments, the optimum relationship between all the variables that influenced the rate at which metal could be cut on a lathe: the depth of cut, feed, speed, and type of tool, the hardness of the metal, the power applied to the machine, and so on. These results were plotted on graph paper, giving a set of geometric curves from which the proper speed of the lathe could be determined when the values of all the other variables were known. This method of solving the problem was, however, too slow and inconvenient for ordinary workshop use. Barth, soon after he came to join Taylor at Bethlehem in June 1899, reduced the relationships discovered by Taylor and Gantt to a mathematical equation and transferred the functional relationships involved to specially made slide rules, which made it possible to determine the correct speed of a machine tool quickly and with all the accuracy required for practical use. Slide rules of this type, usually made by Barth personally, became in time a standard feature of the Taylor system. Like that other hallmark of the Taylor system, the stop watch, Barth slide rules provided management with a quantitatively precise and ostensibly nondebatable method for determining the rate at which work should be done. Whereas in stop-watch time study, however, an element of human motivation was involved—the operator had somehow to be induced to work at the pace prescribed—all the variables included on a Barth slide rule were subject to mechanical control.

The industrial worker, suggests Daniel Bell, lives within a set of constraints imposed on him by three related logics: the logic of size, dictating the concentrating of men at a common place of work; the logic of metric time, which sets his task and determines his pay by reference to the clock; and the logic of hierarchy, which concentrates in management all significant decisions as to the job and how it shall be performed. These three logics are made inescapable by the complex division of labor characteristic of modern industry; they determine the nature of work in the plant and indirectly the nature of life in industrial society. Scientific management, as expounded by Taylor, was in effect an attempt to translate into a set of practical managerial procedures these logics of size, time, and hierarchy.

Taylor's insight into the general logic of industrial work, however, was combined with particular assumptions about human psychology and a particular approach to the problem of incentives. Taylor, like almost all his contemporaries, accepted with little question the view of human nature implied by Benthamite utilitarianism. This acceptance determined Taylor's approach to the problem of incentives in the workshop. It was necessary to create an environment within which the individual, by rational calculation of what was to his own advantage, would do that which management wished him to do. Such an environment, in its mechanical and administrative aspects, could be created by the many detailed reforms in shop practice that made up the Taylor system. There remained the problem of providing a direct and powerful incentive to the individual worker to induce him to put forth his best efforts—to create that spirit of friendly cooperation which Taylor insisted was essential to the success of his methods. The goals of the worker had to be brought into coincidence with the goals of the enterprise. This problem was to be solved by gearing the worker's wage to his production through a system of incentive wages.

Taylor had his own incentive-payments system which he had devised and which he regarded as more powerful than any of the alternatives: the differential piece rate. He realized that no incentive-payments system could by itself bring about important increases in productivity in the absence of the other reforms in shop management that he advocated; nevertheless in his early expositions of his system—specifically in papers presented to the American Society of Mechanical Engineers—the differential piece rate was made the central feature of the presentation, other reforms in shop management being introduced as prior changes that were essential if the differential piece rate were to function effectively. This emphasis on incentive wages was to have important consequences in molding the public image of the Taylor system; but, as an engineer speaking to and writing for other engineers, Taylor had to phrase his presentation in terms that would be familiar and acceptable to his audience. In this case he knew what he was about.

Founded in 1880, the American Society of Mechanical Engineers during the first six years of its existence concerned itself with problems relevant to the duties of mechanical engineers as these had been traditionally conceived—that is, with questions of machine design and operation. The span of discussion did not begin to enlarge until 1886, when for the first time papers on problems that were clearly managerial in nature were presented. Chief among these was a short but brilliant paper by Henry R. Towne, president of the Yale and Towne Manufacturing Company. Bearing the significant title, "The Engineer as Economist," the paper stressed that the engineer employed in industry could no longer with impunity concern himself solely with mechanical efficiency—that is, with doing things in the best way by engineering standards. He had to recognize other criteria of efficiency, and in particular of economic efficiency, expressed in terms of costs and revenues. If engineers employed in industry, argued Towne, are to be called upon to function as executives rather than, or in addition to, their functions as engineers, then they must widen their intellectual horizons and learn to think and act as economists, or in other words be aware that business decisions necessarily involve consideration of money costs.

But how was an engineer to learn to be a manager? Where was the body of accepted theory and practice to which he could refer? Could management be learned and taught and reduced to standard principles as engineering was? No, Towne admitted, it could not—not, that is, if the art or science of management was permitted to remain in its then inchoate and rule-of-thumb condition. What was needed was analysis and systematization: a search for the best practices, an analysis of what worked in management, a beginning with the task of deducing general principles of management analogous to those of sound engineering. A vast amount of accumulated experience in shop management already existed, but it had never been systematically collected and generalized. Each established business went along in its own way, receiving little benefit from the parallel experience of similar enterprises; while each new business gradually developed its own methods of operation, learning little if anything from all that had been done previously. To serve as a clearinghouse for the best available information on managerial practice would be, Towne suggested, a fitting function for the A.S.M.E.

Towne's analysis was penetrating, but his recommendations were general. From the starting point he had provided, progress could have been made in a variety of directions. Actually the men who followed Towne's lead at later meetings of the A.S.M.E. tended to concentrate on one specific problem: the design of incentive-payments schemes. There was nothing in what Towne had said to direct their attention to this managerial device rather than others, beyond the general injunction to pay heed to the cost calculus. The explanation must be sought in the practical problems the members of the A.S.M.E. were encountering in their industrial work and the way in which they interpreted these problems. The last quarter of the nineteenth century was a period when heavy capital equipment was coming into use on an unprecedented scale in American industry. The substitution of capital for labor in production brought tremendous increases in productivity—and a new importance to mechanical engineers. Increases in productivity, however, were limited by the carry-over from an earlier period of crude methods of work training and organization at the shop level. American industry was relying for its skilled labor upon traditional craft training and for its unskilled upon mass immigration. Shop management, now that factories had grown too large to be supervised by a single owner or his agent, was left almost wholly to foremen, recruited from the ranks of wage labor and unassisted by specialized staff except in strictly engineering matters. However sophisticated American industry was becoming in matters of finance and corporate strategy, and however complex in technology, at the level where in the last analysis the work was done and the goods produced, its organization and methods remained primitive. The uneven quality of the work force, reliance upon immigration for new recruits, the relative shortage of supervision, and the growing complexity of division of labor in the workshop—these factors, among others, encouraged an intense interest in incentive-payments systems. Consistent as they were with the American business ethos of competition and the profit motive, piecework and its variants appealed strongly to industrial executives; to industrial engineers such systems seemed to offer the dynamic they needed to translate machine potential into man-hour production.

Concerned professionally to design and operate machines that would run efficiently, and reminded by Towne that efficiency was a matter of dollar costs as well as of minimum energy loss, the engineers of the A.S.M.E.—or those of them whose interest was aroused—interpreted the problem facing them in the same terms they would have applied to a problem in technology. The machine—the lathe, the loom, the rolling mill, or the drill press—could produce so many units of output in twenty-four hours. Ordinarily it produced less than this, and unit costs were higher as a result. The way to reduce costs was to operate the machine at capacity, or as close to it as possible. Some concessions had to be made to human frailty and social custom. It was not ordinarily possible to run a machine twenty-four hours a day, though as far as the machine alone was concerned, assuming repairs and maintenance were adequately provided for, this would represent optimum economy. More realistically, it was not usually possible to operate the machine continuously at its maximum efficiency even during working hours. The reason for this was not a technological one; it involved, in the words commonly used at the time, "the human aspect." Workers apparently did not wish, and could not be induced by any normal methods, to work at the pace of which the machine was capable.

This was a psychological problem, not a technological one. The mechanical engineers who tackled it fell back on the cruder versions of the crude psychological knowledge of their day. The worker, like every other human being, was motivated by rational self-interest. Self-interest, in this case, meant the monetary reward he received for his work. To get him to work harder, all that was necessary was to offer him more pay on condition that he did so. This resolved itself into the problem of designing incentive-payments schemes—systems of buying labor that would make the total daily pay received by the worker depend on his daily output. This was a problem by no means uncongenial to men with engineering training and experience: it was quantitative and mathematical; it was susceptible to refinement in detail; and, by its apparent practical adequacy, it made superfluous any attempt to explore more comprehensively the factors that influence motivation. A problem of considerable psychological complexity was to be disposed of by a mechanical linkage of pay to productivity.

To anyone looking at the problem of incentives from this point of view, ordinary daywork had little to recommend it, since it gave the worker no financial interest in increasing output. Straight piecework was apparently ideal, since it related pay received to volume of output in a direct one-to-one fashion. In practice, however, it had proved disappointing. Employers had consistently found it necessary to cut the rate of pay per piece as their wage costs rose, and employees, expecting such cuts, had acquired the habit of holding back so as not to "spoil the job." The incentive effects were lost, because as soon as a pieceworker began earning more than his employer expected, the rate was cut. Efforts were therefore directed toward designing more complex payment systems, in particular ones that would obviate the necessity for rate cutting. A system of this type had to have two characteristics: the total wage received by the worker had to increase in proportion to increases in output, though not necesarily in direct proportion, and labor costs per unit of product had to fall, or at least not increase, as output rose.

Henry Towne presented such a plan to the A.S.M.E. in 1889. Christened "gain sharing," it involved essentially the drawing up of a contract between employer and employees, to last at least one year. This contract was to be based upon a division of costs of production into those that the worker could influence by his own efforts and those that he could not. Any savings achieved in the former class of costs would be divided up at the end of the year between the management (50 per cent), the foremen (10 to 15 per cent), and the workers (40 to 35 per cent). Towne made two stipulations, however: first, costs should be reckoned, when the contract was first drawn up, not at the true book costs to the company but at a figure from 10 to 30 per cent less than this, so as to enable management to hedge against the possibility of substantial subsequent reductions; and secondly, when one contract expired, management should have the right to cut the rates (*i.e.,* the "costs") in the subsequent contract.

More direct than Towne's scheme was an incentive-payments plan presented to the A.S.M.E. by Frederick A. Halsey in 1891, a significant feature of which was that it was based on job times. The time required for any given job was known from previous experience. For any savings made in job times, the worker was to be paid, in addition to his daily wage, a new premium rate at so much an hour for the time saved. This premium rate was always less than the daily wage rate. One third of the day rate was usual, so that for each hour saved, one third of the gain accrued to the employee. Any increase in the rate of production would certainly increase the worker's total pay; but it would also reduce labor costs per unit, since for a marginal increment to output the worker would be paid at only a fraction of his daily rate. This, Halsey argued, would obviate the need for careful cost keeping (required by Towne's scheme), for the setting of individual rates per piece (a delicate and often acrimonious procedure), and for cutting rates when output rose (since average labor costs per unit would inevitably decline). The historical level of output was taken as the basis for the whole calculation.

Frederick Taylor presented his first formal paper to the A.S.M.E. in 1895. At this time he had been working on the development of his system of management for more than ten years, but it was only by indirection that his work on time study, routing, standardization, and so on appeared in the paper. Entitled **"A Piece-Rate System, Being a Step Toward Partial Solution of the Labor Problem,"** it presented an incentive-payments scheme that appeared on the surface to be essentially an elaboration of Halsey's premium plan, since it was based on job times. There were, however, certain significant differences. Job times were to be determined not from past experience but by stop-watch time study. Standard times were to be set for each job and a standard rate of output thereby determined. This was to mark a sharp discontinuity in the rate of pay. Workers who took a longer time to complete the job were to be paid at a very low piece rate—a rate so low, in fact, that it would be hardly possible to earn a regular day's pay. Workers who completed the job in a shorter time would be paid at a higher rate per piece. Needless to say, if the time study had been carried out correctly, it would be almost impossible for a worker to do better than the allotted task time, so that there was a built-in guarantee that no man could ever earn excessive wages.

Taylor argued that, under his plan, there would never be any need to cut a piece rate. Rate cutting, he said, had been necessary in the past only because employers had had no means of knowing how fast a job ought to be done. The time required for a new job was always overestimated; then, as the workers became more familiar with the job, they began to earn excessive wages and the original rate had to be cut. Determine the time required correctly in the first place, said Taylor, and you will never find it necessary to change the rate, because you can be sure from the start that the rate of work you set as the norm will never be exceeded.

In some respects Taylor's claim appears rather ingenuous. There were at least two ways in which, under his system, management could reduce piece rates. First, Taylor's plan stipulated only that a higher rate should be paid for work done in less than the task time and a lower rate for work done in more. It laid down no rules for what the higher rate should be. Taylor's presentation, however, made it clear that this so-called higher rate was in fact to be smaller than the regular piece rate. Even to maintain his daily wage at the previous level, far less increase it, the worker was compelled to increase his output substantially. On this basis the very installation of Taylor's differential piece rate might seem, from the worker's point of view, equivalent to a cut in the rates. Secondly, management invariably retained the right to change the rate per piece if any changes were made in the way the work was done. If, for example, a worker operating a drill press was provided with a jig to guide his drill, the rate per piece would be reduced; similarly, in machining work, if any changes were made in the speed of the lathe. In general, any reduction in machine times brought with it a reduction in the piece rate. Some such provision was necessary if management were to have any incentive to adopt new methods. But possibilities of abuse lurked in the background. What was to stop a cost-conscious foreman from making some slight change in the job purely in order to cut the rate? What was rate cutting from one point of view was not necessarily rate cutting from another.

It is clear that the mere introduction of a differential factor in the piece rate and the mere setting of a standard work pace by time study did not in themselves determine what the piece rate should be. This was a matter on which Taylor was capable of deceiving himself, for on more than one occasion he publicly stated that his system of management made possible a scientific determination of how much a worker should be paid. This it certainly did not. Taylor's differential piece rate did involve assumptions as to how large an increment in pay was required to call forth a given increment in output. But it shed no light on how the basic rate was to be determined.

Taylor regarded his differential piece rate as the most powerful type of incentive-payments system that could be devised. It gave the worker a strong and immediate incentive to increase his pace of work; it protected the employer from undesirable increases in average labor costs; and, by penalizing men who failed to maintain the standard output, it gradually weeded out from the work force all but "first-class men." These were weighty advantages for any employer. Nevertheless, the differential piece rate was never widely adopted. Some of Taylor's colleagues, such as Gantt, preferred other systems of their own devising, less powerful and punitive than Taylor's; and even Taylor on occasion approved the use of such earlier and milder methods as the Halsey plan. The differential piece rate, to function effectively, required a degree of standardization and systematizing that could not always be achieved, particularly in shops where the product or the methods of production changed frequently. Then too, it was more complex to administer than straight piecework or the Halsey plan, and the advantages to be gained from the added complexity were not always clear. But in addition, the differential piece rate violated the worker's sense of equity and was almost without exception vigorously opposed by the unions.

It is not easy to generalize about the attitude of the unions to incentive-payments schemes in this period. The consensus of those who have examined the problem is that a distinction can be made between straight piecework and more complex systems such as Taylor's. Opposition to piecework was far from universal: it was preferred or willingly accepted by the coal miners, the textile workers, the cigar makers, and a number of others. The molders' union struggled to drive piecework out of the jobbing foundries, but accepted it in the stove and furnace industry. The International Association of Machinists officially prohibited the acceptance of piecework, but many of its members preferred it and negotiated piecework agreements through their own shop representatives. In general, piecework was accepted and indeed preferred where the unit of output could be defined with precision and where conditions of work could be maintained with substantial uniformity over periods of time. Where both these conditions were met, the workers were likely to prefer piecework to straight time work: their earnings varied directly with their effort, and they were protected from the danger of a speed up without additional compensation, which was possible under the day wage system. Where either or both of these conditions were not met, piecework was likely to be opposed both by the workers and by their unions.

Opposition to the differential piece rate and the premium and bonus systems was both more widespread and more determined. In contrast to straight piecework, which rewarded an increase in output with a proportionally equal increase in pay, these variants provided for a reduction in the rate per piece once the standard output was exceeded. As Slichter puts it, "The fast workers [were] compelled automatically to cut their own piece rates." The concept of "a fair day's pay for a fair day's work" ruled out any incentive system under which a given percentage increase in output over a standard amount was not rewarded by at least an equal percentage increase in pay. The base rate was taken as the standard: a "thirty-cent job" should remain a thirty-cent job, no matter what the worker's rate of output might be. Thus the very feature of such plans that commended them to the employer made them unacceptable to the unions, since they ran counter to the whole philosophy of a standard rate for each job. Unions which accepted piecework rejected premium or bonus plans, while unions which found even piecework unacceptable regarded premium or bonus systems as anathema.

The unions' opposition to his particular type of piece rate, as to his other innovations, helped to confirm Taylor in his conviction that he was right. Unions he regarded as essentially pernicious institutions, for they were responsible for the systematic restriction of output which to him was the unforgivable sin. Scientific management, he was convinced, would do far more for the workers—if only they would "cooperate"—than unions ever had done or could do, for scientific management was based on an understanding of the laws of production, not upon the opinion of the ignorant. These laws could not be bargained over. In particular, there was, Taylor believed, no justification whatever for the doctrine of the standard wage. Insistence upon the payment of the same wage to all workers of a given class, regardless of their contribution to the productivity of the plant, meant that the most efficient and energetic were penalized for the benefit of the inefficient and lazy. This was not only undesirable from the point of view of the employer, it was also ethically wrong.

In contrast to the standard wage doctrine, Taylor claimed that his system of management treated the workers as individuals. It was therefore more democratic. If the Taylor system was adopted, the individual worker was provided with all the instruction he could require. His proper job was explained to him; he was shown the best way to do it; he was furnished with tools properly maintained and machines properly adjusted; and he was paid in proportion to his output. What could be fairer than this? What could give a worker more self-respect than the knowledge that, while everything that could be done to help him had been done, beyond this he was on his own? If he produced more, he would be paid more. If he failed to produce more, but was able and eager to learn, he would be shown the way. All that was necessary was for him to approach his job in the right frame of mind and to be willing to cooperate with those who knew how to help him.

Cooperation meant different things to Taylor in different contexts. For the workers (in Taylor's own words) it meant "to do what they are told to do promptly and without asking questions or making suggestions." Whatever changes Taylor or his colleagues might make in the job, the worker was to accept them without question. His role was to be passive—that of an efficient but self-effacing servant of the real producer, the machine. Human ability and motives, not the potentiality of the machine, set the ceiling on the feasible work pace. To raise this ceiling, Taylor relied on the inducement of the dollar. A carefully engineered incentive-payments scheme, operating within a work environment routinized and standardized in every detail, was to overcome the final barrier to increased productivity: the traditional work pace of the worker and his mates.

General William Crozier, Chief of Ordnance, carefully feeling his way toward the adoption of the Taylor system in the government arsenals, once asked Taylor, with disconcerting directness, why he laid such stress on incentive payments. Had not Taylor assured him repeatedly that the men would have to work no harder under the new system, that they would in fact find their work much easier and more pleasant? Why then pay them more? Taylor replied that it was true that a great deal of time could be saved by such things as eliminating waste motions, insisting on the proper sequence of movements, and so on; but that, even after all this preliminary work had been done, it was still necessary to induce the men to exert their skill and energy to full effectiveness, so that each one of them could attain "the quickest time in which a job should be done by a first-class man." As for paying them more, Crozier should have no worry on that account. A worker might on occasion do more than was asked of him (*i.e.*, exceed the norm), but it would be most unusual. "It may happen once in a thousand times . . ."

It was not because Taylor felt that men deserved higher pay for more production that he stressed incentive-payments schemes. Such a system, and preferably one that punished low output as well as rewarded high, was the necessary keystone to the Taylor system of management. Whatever changes were made in the institutional and mechanical framework within which the job was performed—reorganization of stores and supply procedures, planned routing of work, systematic inspection, instruction, maintenance, and even the respeeding of machines—none attacked directly what Taylor had from the start believed to be the principal cause of low output: soldiering. Only an incentive-payments scheme, as Taylor saw the matter, could do that. After all the preparatory work had been done, then was the time for the carefully planned break-through that would shatter the deeply entrenched work habits of the wage earner.

What Taylor called soldiering, however, was by no means as simple a matter as he imagined. Ignorance, malice, stupidity, false doctrine spread by the unions, memories of rate cutting: these were, in his mind, the only possible explanations of why workers deliberately produced less than they knew they could. Nothing in his upbringing, education, or experience, nothing even in the practical or academic knowledge of his time, furnished him with the concepts that might have made possible a different view of the problem. But restriction of output is not restriction unless measured against some relevant standard, and the standards of the engineer and employer have no more claim to absolute validity than the standards of those who are alleged to be doing the restricting. Rates of work are not determined by chance or by the quirks of individual personality. The idea of a norm of output as a universal feature of all organized groups, set and maintained by the group itself and often defended by highly effective sanctions, would, however, have been entirely alien to Taylor, as to most others of his time. Highly sophisticated in its approach to problems of formal organization and technology, in its analysis of motivation and group behavior the Taylor system was crude in the extreme.

Samuel Haber (essay date 1964)

SOURCE: *Efficiency and Uplift: Scientific Management in the Progressive Era 1890-1920,* The University of Chicago Press, 1964, 181 p.

[*In the following excerpt from his book* Efficiency and Uplift, *Haber examines Taylor's early leanings toward scientific management, including early events in his life that may have led to his later obsession with systematizing, and explains the practical application of Taylor's system in factories.*]

YOUNG GENTLEMAN IN THE STEEL WORKS

At the summer meeting of the American Society of Mechanical Engineers in 1895, a small, thin, pernickety engineer named Frederick Winslow Taylor read a paper entitled, **"A Piece-Rate System, Being a Step toward a Partial Solution of the Labor Problem."** Most of those who heard it considered this paper but one more in the series of papers on the question of wage payments that had been presented to the Society over the years. Actually it was much more. It was the first inkling of a new order for the factory which Frederick W. Taylor was rearing at Midvale Steel Company in Nicetown, Pennsylvania.

Ostensibly, Taylor's paper dealt with incentive systems, and thereby fitted in with the growing interest in methods of wage payments which appeared in the last decades of the nineteenth century. America was a country of high labor costs, in which almost any effort to save labor or use it more intensively was worth considering. The spread of cost accounting techniques and the reports of the growing strength of trade unions underscored the high cost of labor and gave the question of incentive wage payment added importance. Taylor's "differential piece rate" was more stringent than most incentive systems. It required that the shortest possible time for each job be computed and fixed. If the worker finished the job in this time he was given a good price per piece. If he failed, he was given a rate so low that the "lazy or inferior" worker could not hold the job. Taylor's piece rate was a carrot-and-stick device to make the laborer work harder and more quickly. The increased work speed rewarded the worker with a higher total wage, and the low cost per piece provided the employer with larger profits. Thus it made "each workman's interest the same as that of his employers."

The differential piece rate, Taylor asserted, would root out the demoralizing effects which attended other wage systems. Other systems allowed or encouraged loafing and led to deceit between workers and employers. Fixing an honest day's work would put an end to all that. Hard work, Taylor believed, built inner strength. From **"A Piece-Rate System,"** the first public statement of his ideas on management, to the last statement of his program, twenty years later, Taylor always opened his lectures with a discussion of "soldiering"—the worker's loafing on the job. The factory, for Taylor, was not only an instrument for the production of goods and profits, it was also a moral gymnasium for the exercise of character.

Yet morality worked hand in hand with science. Taylor proposed that an "honest day's work" be fixed scientifically, by methods free from human bias. This immediately set Taylor's piece rate system apart from all others. At first Taylor tried to calculate a day's heavy labor by "how many foot-pounds of work a man could do in a day." But he discovered that there was no relation between work measured in foot-pounds and its tiring effects on the laborer. He then hit on the idea of breaking the job down into its "elementary operations" and timing each operation by use of a stop watch and a first-rate worker. He hoped to develop a handbook which would list the "elementary operations" from which the correct speed of any job could be reckoned. To get an "honest day's work" did not require the selection of only honest workers or urging the workers to honesty. "If a man won't do what is right," Taylor said, "*make* him." The differential piece rate was an attempt to make the worker do what was right. It meant the transfer of the category of wages from economics to physics—from a realm (as then understood) beyond direct control to one where most things could be manipulated.

"Scientific rate-fixing" had ramifications throughout the factory. The speed at which the laborer worked was inextricably tied to the kind and the quality of his tools, the shop procedures, and even the over-all organization of the factory. If one were really to fix an honest day's work "scientifically," then the entire plant had to be brought under control. In retrospect, Taylor's reorganization of the factory can be seen as logically following from his notion of "scientific rate-fixing." Yet clearly, logic alone was not enough to draw him on. For this logic led through a long series of flops and frustrations that afforded much bitterness and derision. It led to exacting experiments on machine belting which extended over a period of nine years, and to between thirty and fifty thousand experiments on metal cutting over a period of twenty-six years. It led to schemes which often seemed unprofitable or beyond good sense. The logic is clear, but to understand the relentless drive behind that logic, the vehemence which sometimes made even Taylor's friends uncomfortable, we must take a closer look at Taylor the man.

Frederick Winslow Taylor was born into Proper Philadelphia. The Winslows and the Taylors were important families in America as far back as the seventeenth and eighteenth centuries. The Philadelphia branches were Quaker, but even before Frederick was born Quakerism had become a faded and parochial creed to many of its followers. Frederick's mother, Emily Taylor, took up more ardent beliefs. She was interested in transcendentalism and active in the anti-slavery and women's suffrage movements. When she broke her ties to the Society of Friends she chose Unitarianism, the communion of the high-born and high-minded, as her religion.

Franklin Taylor, Frederick's father, was a lawyer who devoted himself to literature, languages, and the good works of charity rather than the practice of law. It is unexpected and yet suggestive that the father of the man who tried to revolutionize the world of work was a leisured gentleman. Emily Taylor was said to have had "the stronger personality." She was blunt and exacting; Franklin was sensitive and delicate. He loved poetry; she did not. Frederick wrote that his father had a "soft, mild manner and a gentleness which was almost that of a woman." And the son often showed concern with his own manliness. Though young Taylor was noted for his full-dress female impersonations in the skits at the Philadelphia Cricket Club, he wished that he were bigger and more brawny. He studiously developed the knack of cussing, and was terribly earnest in sports.

Young Fred was an obedient son, likable but rigid and intense. One of his childhood friends remembered that Fred's quarrels with his playmates often stemmed from his insistence on subjecting their games to strict and elaborate rules. He was disturbed by oppressive dreams and decided that they were related to sleeping on his back. Taylor therefore made a harness of straps and wooden points which he wore to bed at night and which would wake him when he turned. This was but one of his nightmare-fighting machines. Throughout his life he used many devices to force himself to sleep in a sitting position.

Many who knew Taylor commented on what his biographer called his "nervous disposition" and what his doctor decribed as his "extraordinary intense nature." Taylor's youthful pictures seem to show much feminine sweetness. Yet the man who looks out from the later photographs usually adopts an even more brisk and belligerent stance than was customary in the scowling pictures of that day. There is something anxious and obstructed-looking about the man. Taylor gave many signs of deep emotional turmoil. He would turn white at any talk of illness or death. He suffered from recurrent sleeplessness and indigestion, and even in sport found it hard to relax. He worked at play. At one time he appealed to his doctor to help him stop thinking, to get rid of the thoughts that were oppressing him.

Taylor's program for systematizing the factory should be seen in terms of his attempt to systematize most things, including himself. Order can serve to curb impulse and to limit hazards and perhaps pain. The machines and machine-like organizations with which Taylor busied himself resembled human beings in their capabilities, but were more malleable and predictable and were exempt from human feeling and hurt. Taylor's frenzy for order was the counterpart of the disorder within him.

Taylor's very entry into industry was linked to a psychological crisis. The family had planned that he should be a lawyer like his father. He was sent to Phillips Exeter to prepare for college, but toward the end of his studies developed unusual headaches and eye troubles. At this point, young Taylor wanted to give up law and study medicine at Yale or perhaps engineering at Rensselaer Polytechnic Institute. After a long family conference, however, he took the Harvard entrance examination and passed with honors. Yet his eye-sight soon became so poor that he could not even complete the work at Exeter. After a few month's rest at home, Taylor went to work as an apprentice patternmaker, a job which called for the reading of complicated mechanical drawings. He persisted in this apprenticeship though his eye troubles soon disappeared. Clearly, this troublous period of impaired vision hinged as much upon problems of the mind as of the body.

The decision not to become a lawyer might plausibly be linked to the psychological difficulties of following in his father's footsteps. However, the decision to enter industry as a laborer, once the legal career was abandoned, suggests the influence of his mother. Emily Taylor presided over his early education and the shaping of his first precepts and pursuits. His ascetic and use-minded temperament mirrored hers. Like his mother, Taylor identified himself with the Unitarian Church. Though in later years he assumed an agnostic position, he remained a member of that church until his death. Of the many attitudes and beliefs which passed from mother to son, by far the most important was the general tendency to demand much of onself.

Many children of the well-to-do found the work-centered morality of the second half of the nineteenth century menacing. Riches and ease, it was believed, arrested the development of character. The achievements of one generation seemed to threaten destruction of the next. Henry Ward Beecher told his wealthy congregation that their business losses might be their children's gain. "How blessed, then, is the stroke of disaster which sets the children free, and gives them over to the hard but kind bosom of Poverty, who says to them 'Work!' and, working, makes them men." Carnegie's proposal for returning the "surplus" wealth to society seemed too radical an answer. A professional career for the children of the rich was more acceptable. When Taylor's way to the legal profession was blocked, however, he was given over to a mock poverty with the understanding that he would work his way to the top.

Of course, Taylor did just that. He became an apprentice patternmaker at the age of eighteen and promptly raced up the familiar ladder of success. After his apprenticeship he went to work at Midvale Steel Company as a journeyman machinist and in six years was chief engineer. He went on to independent consulting work, the discovery of high-speed steel, and the presidency of the American Society of Mechanical Engineers. After he retired from active engineering, at forty-five, he often described his accomplishment in public lectures on success and education. He extolled "the real monotonous grind which trains character" and directed the young man to go out of his way, if necessary, to find it. He condemned the "kindergarten plan of interesting and amusing children," the lax college discipline, and the university elective system. Every student, whether intending to be a minister or a mechanical engineer, should leave college at the end of the freshman year and spend at least one year "in actual hard work . . . under careful and constant supervision." He preached the strenuous life of the workshop and foundry. The Midvale Steel Company was to Taylor what the Big Horn Mountains were to Theodore Roosevelt.

It must be noted that Taylor's rise did not strictly follow the rules of Ragged Dick. When young Taylor left the shop after a day's work he went home to Germantown, one of the most exclusive sections of Philadelphia. He was probably the only laborer in America with a membership in the local cricket club. Because he could work for little or no money, he moved quickly through his apprenticeships. During the early years of Taylor's rise at Midvale, one of the principal owners was a friend and neighbor. His social connections undoubtedly gave him entry to places otherwise inaccessible.

Taylor brought to the factory the type of sustained and methodical thinking derived from the formal academic world he had left. In his early days at Midvale he felt the need of increasing his scientific education and took home-study courses in mathematics and physics. Through an arrangement with Stevens Institute of Technology, he planned a course of study which brought him a degree in Mechanical Engineering. Taylor became a member of the newly formed American Society of Mechanical Engineers and found his way into a milieu within which he developed his ideas. The impulse toward order came from within; the imperatives of hard work came from his education and upbringing; and the specific content of his work owed much to the profession in which Taylor found himself.

Before the middle years of the nineteenth century, the direct influence of contemporary science on engineering practice was quite uneven. Some of America's most prominent mechanical engineers, even in the last decades of that century, were still men of little or no scientific training who had happened into apprenticeships at various engine works and evinced a knack for machine building. However, the scientific and mathematical achievements of such technologists as William Rankine and Rudolph Clausius soon gave the mechanical engineers with scientific and mathematical training such a decided advantage that they, in effect, blocked entry into the field for most engineers who were not graduates of the engineering colleges. This brought important changes in the social composition of the engineering fellowship. For a college education was often costly and required, even in the state colleges which were nominally free, a sum of leisure which in itself was an expensive luxury. The elevation which science provided and the new sources of recruitment which it demanded converted mechanical engineering from what had been often considered a trade to what was now more often called a profession.

The mechanical engineers of the late nineteenth century strained for the prestige of the traditional "learned professions" and took much of the pre-capitalist professional ethic as their own. In appraising motive, manner, and accomplishment in their new profession, they often looked to standards which stood outside the market place. Within their profession, the engineers frowned on advertising, urged *esprit de corps* rather than competition, insisted that prerogatives and prestige should derive from proven competence, and proclaimed responsibility to the social good as a solemn duty.

This professionalism was invested with an aura of independence. The engineer apparently would not simply do his client's bidding. He saw himself as standing closer to the doctor who gave the patient what he needed than to the merchant who gave the customer what he wanted. Those who enlarged upon the ideals of the engineering profession often designated the engineers as a new industrial intelligentsia, standing between capital and labor, and peculiarly fitted to resolve the nation's social conflicts.

The lofty temperament of the professional ethic seems particularly to have appealed to many of the engineers who came to the field from established old-stock families like Taylor's. Men of this sort provided the American Society of Mechanical Engineers with much of its initial leadership. They demanded that engineering be esteemed and influential. Of course, there were other, less exalted, aspects of the enthusiasm for professionalism. The fixing of minimum fees and the elimination of jurisdictional disputes among the various branches of engineering were also considered important steps toward improving the status of the profession. Economic gain itself was never condemned; only grasp and greed. Acquisition was a just reward of hard work and character. The mechanical engineer of the late nineteenth century often spoke of his own reward as a "competence"—an adequacy of means for living comfortably, but without excess. The engineer's task was not "the piling of gold and silver in treasury vaults, and not the aggregation of fictitious values in Wall Street," wrote the first president of the American Society of Mechanical Engineers, but the production of "durable materials" essential to the comforts of mankind. The engineer was in the market place, but not completely of it. This was true of his day-to-day work as well as his broader social outlook.

Efficiency, the unifying concept of mechanical engineering, lives a double life—having one meaning in mechanics and another in commerce. Mechanical efficiency is an output-input ratio of matter or energy, whereas commercial efficiency is the relation between price and cost. Occasionally, these efficiencies are opposed. Taylor's first paper before the American Society of Mechanical Engineers concerned just such a conflict. Comparing the efficiency of two gases in the steel-making process, he found that the one which yielded the greatest heat per unit did not yield the greatest heat per dollar. The solution was straightforward. In the event of such a divergency, profit obligations prevailed and the mechanically less efficient gas was used. But at times, this decision was made with some suggestion of discomfort.

The intellectual fascination of a scientifically trained mind with the skillful adaptation of material means to ends was quite a distinct and separate thing from the profit to be produced. Costs and prices varied with time and place and were dependent upon apparently accidental circumstances, while matter and energy could be dealt with in accordance with enduring scientific laws. Science had a luster all its own. For a generation in which most people believed that progress was written into the laws of the universe, true and good often seemed to be indistinguishable. Science, which was a more certain form of the true, could also appear as a more rigorous form of the good. The very fruitfulness of science seemed to substantiate this. Furthermore, for the engineers, science was the passkey into their new profession. It is not surprising, therefore, that the problems of mechanical efficiency and the skills employed in their solution afforded considerable prestige. "Economy may be taught even if the material costs nothing," declared a speaker at the same meeting where Taylor delivered his first paper. "We can teach intrinsic values without meddling with market values. The former are permanent, the latter fluctuating. . . . "

Nevertheless, in the day-to-day work of the engineer, more clearly than in the presidential addresses at conventions, the demands of the market place prevailed. If the better mousetrap which the engineer built was unprofitable, hardly a soul would beat a path to his door. The constant awareness of the commercial limitations of engineering was essential to success within the profession. And it was with a certain grimness that the engineers who seemed to believe that engineering could be practiced without regard to money values were condemned. "These men may be ingenious inventors or designers, they may be great mathematicians, they may even be eminent as scientists, but they are not engineers." On at least two issues, this conflict between the scientific and business emphasis broke out into the open. These were the question of the adoption of the metric system and the problem of the engineer's attitude toward conservation.

The metric system had various attractions for the scientist. Its smaller unit was more useful for exact measurement and was well on the way toward being internationally accepted. Equally attractive was the fact that the metric system mirrored in the realm of measurement the unified picture of the world that was presented by the physical sciences. Like science, the metric system presented simple and elegant relations between the different kinds of units and allowed the scientist to interconvert mass, length, and capacity. The unity of science seemed to make intelligible, and the metric system to reflect, the unity of reality itself.

At the very first meeting of the American Society of Mechanical Engineers, a prominent member delivered a paper attacking the metric system. He insisted that it was unwise to tamper with the English standard because of its central position in the system of interchangeable parts so important to American industry. The speaker personified American industry's huge investment in the inch: he was manager and later president of the machine works whose system of screw sizes prevailed in America. The Society endorsed his view.

Metric reform, however, could not be turned aside so easily. It seemed to have a fascination for engineers. The issue was debated back and forth again in 1885, in 1902 and in 1906. The arguments and the results, however, remained much the same. The "scientific enthusiasts . . . captivated by the nicety of the thing," were amply denounced. And the picture which was drawn of catastrophic cost and confusion which would result from conversion to the meter was admonition enough to secure a rejection of metric reform proposals.

Conservation ideas found a more favorable reception at the meetings of the American Society of Mechanical Engineers. Conservation presented a problem quite similar to Taylor's juggling of material and economic efficiencies in his first paper. The process which yielded the maximum coal per mine, for example, often did not yield the greatest amount of coal per dollar. Conservation reformers, nevertheless, urged the elevation of physical values above market values. The particular business ties of the mechanical engineers were not as directly challenged by the conservation programs as they had been by the proposals for conversion to the metric system. Moreover, the social and moral interest which the conservationists aroused in their cause gave it a compelling force which metrics never had. The appeal to the social responsibility of the engineer (of which the advocates of professionalism spoke so much and so often) helped to lift conservation ideas out of the class of dangerous scientific distractions.

Official representatives of the American Society of Mechanical Engineers attended Roosevelt's conservation conference in 1908 and approved its resolutions. The Society devoted a meeting to the subject and listened patiently to exhortations that engineers must direct themselves to "the larger interests of humanity." The engineering societies must fall in with the conservation idea, the Society president declared. Perhaps the doctrine of government "appropriation and beneficial use" was needed as an antidote to "the uncontrolled greed for gain." However, the engineer had to build and operate works so as to compete with others in the same line. The crucial test remained in the cost per unit of output. Therefore "the real work of the engineer, in the field of conservation, will be measured by the ability of the works designed by him to compete in the markets of the world." The engineer supported conservation but with conspicuous qualifications and confusions.

This was the situation of the mechanical engineer of this era—he could not feel completely at ease either as a scientist or as a businessman. Though the values of business prevailed, the values of science, especially in questions of broader scope, occasionally provided a counterforce which left the engineer off-balance.

At first glance it would appear that Taylor made common cause with those who stressed the exigencies of the commercial enterprise of which technical engineering was but a part. This is not at all surprising, for during those very important years at Midvale his close personal ties to its owners surely made him aware of the interests and needs of a business venture. At the time when the metric controversy was provoking tempers at the meetings of the ASME, he dutifully testified against a law which would have required metric units of all contractors for the government. He was particularly interested in the early papers on management problems and presented two management papers of his own. He cautioned young engineering students to "remember that the kind of engineering that is most wanted is that which saves money; that your employer is first of all in business to make money and not to do great and brilliant things."

Yet he did not arrive at this outlook without struggle, and, once attained, it was not easily held. The occasional tug-of-war within engineering between science and business found its counterpart within Taylor. Though he testified against the metric-system bill he admitted that he had earlier favored it, now thought it should be introduced voluntarily, and used metrics himself. He also showed sympathy for conservation principles. When he lectured the engineering students about their employers being in business to make money and not to do great things, he was probably lecturing to himself as well. After he left Midvale, Taylor frequently got into difficulty with his employers because of his habit of "making money fly." In a letter to a friend he confessed that if he had followed his personal inclinations he would have given a greater part of his time to invention and scientific investigation. Taylor loved the quiet of the laboratory and the study and often became worried by the diverse and clashing activities of the shop. His biographer tells us that "he seemed always in danger of reverting to the pure engineer." Yet Taylor is important to us precisely because he did not revert; rather, he thrust the laboratory and the study directly into the realm of the factory. But there was always something ambiguous about this intrusion.

This ambiguity was implicit in Taylor's first presentation of his ideas on management. The discussion which followed his paper, **"A Piece-Rate System,"** was lively and generally sympathetic; yet Taylor was disappointed. The method of "scientific rate-fixing," which he considered its most important feature, was almost completely ignored. This was a portent for the future. What Taylor thought to be the crux of the matter, his ever widening audience often felt to be simply a tendency to carry things to crazy extremes.

The very notion of a completely integrated, scientific system for the factory was a distraction. The truly "scientific" standard for "an honest day's work" (the point of maximum mechanical efficiency of the human machine) could not be established and maintained unless the entire factory was systematized. Yet most business firms, as Taylor himself once noted, need only be more efficient than their competitors. This was one of the reasons that businessmen preferred efficiency stunts, devices, and mechanisms to a complete system of scientific management. The adoption of a complete system was often not the most profitable use of investment capital. Here, unlike the discussion of which gas to use in steelmaking, commercial efficiency did not automatically come first. The system should be adopted, Taylor's most orthodox disciple asserted, even when it might not be a paying investment.

Though Taylor and his followers directed their attention toward business, they seemed to be looking beyond it. Their occupation was management, but their preoccupation often was "science."

The sources and supports of Taylor's program for the factory were manifold. His own personality furnished the initial thrust. The morality of hard work, in which Taylor had been sedulously schooled, played an important role. And of course, the new profession of engineering, with its occasional dissonance between the modes of science and business, provided a persistent influence. This dissonance was responsible, in part, for the limited appeal that Taylor's system had for businessmen, as well as some of its particular attractiveness for many progressive reformers.

TAYLOR'S FACTORY WORLD

In applying "science" to what had been considered strictly business problems, Taylor overstepped the interest of many of his fellow engineers—both those of technical and those of commercial bent. In 1910 the ASME shelved a paper on management by Taylor on the grounds that the membership was not interested in papers of this sort and that there was nothing new in it. This work subsequently became world-famous under the title, ***The Principles of Scientific Management.***

Of course, Taylor was not alone in the study of management. In fact, the placing of Taylor's program against the background of contemporary ideas in this field helps to emphasize his special accomplishment. There were at least two usually distinct groups that devoted themselves to these matters: the "systemizers" and the proponents of "industrial betterment." "Industrial betterment" or "industrial welfare" was an uneven and varying mixture of philanthropy, humanitarianism, and commercial shrewdness. Some of its outstanding exponents were ministers seeking redemptive agencies supplementary to the Word of God. Pullman's model town of the 1880's was an early industrial betterment venture in America, but the "practical religion" of John H. Patterson's National Cash Register Company soon dominated the field and became the archetype of almost all the programs that followed. One of the important aims of these schemes was to prevent "labor troubles" and get better work from the workman. This was to be accomplished by providing lunchrooms, bathhouses, hospital clinics, safety training, recreational facilities, thrift clubs, benefit funds, profit-sharing plans, and Ruskinesque garden cities. Industrial betterment proclaimed that human happiness was a business asset.

The "systemizers" were a diverse group of accountants, engineers, and works managers who rose to some prominence in the last decades of the nineteenth century, along with the growing size of American factories and business enterprises. The systemizers attacked improvisation in business and taught the profitability of orderly arrangements. "The object of modern administrative organization," wrote one of the leaders in the field, "is to readjust the balance of responsibilities disturbed by the expansion of industrial operations, and to enable central control to be restored in its essential features." The literature of system leaned heavily upon analogies to the human body, the machine, and the military. The body and the machine usually illustrated the need for close integration within the factory while military organization exemplified hierarchy and discipline. At times, these illustrations passed beyond analogy and appeared as instances of natural laws of organization which justified the hierarchy and discipline of the factory as well as described it. But for the most part the systemizers had no explicit theory, and system usually took the form of a series of maxims based on recent shop practice and business arrangements.

Like the industrial betterment advocates, Taylor tied productiveness to morality and well-being. But Taylor stressed one side of the equation (hard work yields morality and well-being), while the advocates of industrial betterment insisted upon the other (morality and well-being yield hard work). Taylor concentrated on the worker in the factory and the industrial betterment advocates on the worker after work. This was more than a difference in interest. It stemmed from contrasting views of the human being and differing moral outlooks. The literature of industrial betterment made much of the goodness which would flower if man were nurtured in a benevolent environment. Against this, Taylor emphasized the weakness in man which must be curbed by the "habit of doing what is right." "Too great liberty," Taylor wrote, "results in a large number of people going wrong who would be right if they had been forced into good habits." Out of this difference came arguments, perplexing to both sides, in which the spokesmen of industrial betterment pursued Taylor and his followers with accusations of "ignoring the human element," while the Taylorites declared that they alone actually paid attention to it.

There was less open controversy with the systemizers. In fact, Taylor often described his own work as "systemizing." He fully accepted the imperatives derived from the division of labor and the expansion of industry—co-ordination, hierarchy, and discipline. Like many of the systemizers, Taylor favored the analogy between the organization and the machine. Taylor was not satisfied, however, simply with an orderly arrangement of parts. He wanted to know how well each component performed its task, and he intended to bring each component "to its highest state of excellence." The usual standard for judging an innovation of the systemizers was whether it paid off in dollars and cents. Though profit was important, Taylor decided that the adequacy of a shop's management frequently was not reflected in the dividends it paid. Science, he thought, could supply a more precise and well-founded standard. First, by way of calculations in foot-pounds, and later with the aid of his techniques of time and motion studies, Taylor went in search of scientific laws of work to answer the closely related questions of how a job could best be done and how much could be produced. He derived a "science" of shoveling, pig-iron lifting, lathe work, etc., through a controlled variation of the isolated elements in each task. This usually meant the conversion of the task into its physical quantities. Taylor thus passed from commercial to mechanical efficiency.

Taylor's work was more comprehensive and complex than that of most systemizers and writers on industrial betterment. He posed questions, explicitly and by implication, which were beyond the bounds of their inquiries. He developed a system of factory polity with an image of the worker and a shop hierarchy which referred directly to his science of work.

Taylor's image of the worker had within it a personal as well as a more generalized component. Copley tells us that he deliberately adopted "much of the culture of working people" in protest against the overrefinement and effeminacy of polite society. When Harvard invited him to lecture on scientific management he shocked his audience by sprinkling his talk with a good number of cusswords from the shop. He would bring a steelworker as his dinner guest to Philadelphia's plush Hotel Bellevue-Stratford and also warn college students that there were first-class mechanics who were their mental equals. But if he rattled the genteel by proclaiming the virtues and virility of workers, when he confronted the working man, it was usually as a boss.

The worker was like everyone else but also quite different. His motives were the ordinary motives of men (that is, middle-class motives), but his abilities were usually of a more limited order. When Taylor discussed the incentives which brought special effort from the worker, he drew upon these middle-class motives, such as the desires to excel, to rise, and to increase one's income. Even "Schmidt," Taylor's famous pig-iron handler, whom he calls "a man of the type of the ox," is depicted as buying a plot of land and building a house on it. Incentives were important because man was naturally lazy and the worker had learned under most previous systems of management that it was not in his interest to work hard. In addition, the work of the factory was often tiresome and uninteresting and might become even more so. For one of the aspects of applying "science" to work was elimination of the elements of play that are intermingled with it.

When discussing the place of each worker in the factory, Taylor turned to Platonic metaphors of racehorses and dray horses, songbirds and sparrows. He saw the factory hierarchy as one of abilities. The division of labor did not constrict the worker excessively, because he might rise to that level of competence of which he was capable. Taylor insisted that workers be treated individually and not *en masse*. Each was to be rewarded and punished for his particular deeds. In this way Taylor introduced individualism into the factory, but individualism in a diminished form. It could not measure up to the model of the entrepreneur in the market. The worker was granted an individuality of incentive but not of discretion; the intricate interrelation of parts in the factory did not allow for that. There was no "invisible hand" in the factory to bring order out of complexity. This order was to be discovered and realized by the systemizer. The workers must "do what they are told promptly and without asking questions or making suggestions. . . . it is absolutely necessary for every man in an organization to become one of a train of gear wheels."

The worker's power of free decision was further limited by the necessities of the "science" of work. For one of the most important general principles of Taylor's system was that the man who did the work could not derive or fully understand its science. The result was a radical separation of thinking from doing. Those who understood were to plan the work and set the procedures; the workmen were simply to carry them into effect. This separation might have been reinforced by the need of Taylor's system for exact measurement. The stop watch, an instrument for timing overt action, could gauge only the most routine mental processes. Therefore, to the extent that Taylor's science strained at strict precision, to that degree it had to externalize work and remove the thinking from it.

The Taylor System placed restrictions upon the entrepreneur and the manager in the factory as well as the worker. Taylor attacked the cult of personality in management. Methods were primary, not particular to men. The discovery of a science of work meant a transfer of skill from the worker to management and with it some transfer of power. Yet this power was fixed not directly at the top but in the new center of the factory, the planning department. Taylor asserted:

> The shop (indeed the whole works) should be managed, not by the manager, superintendent, or foreman, but by the planning department. The daily routine of running the entire works should be carried on by the various functional elements of

> this department, so that, in theory at least, the works could run smoothly even if the manager, superintendent, and their assistants outside the planning room were all to be away for a month at a time.

The planning department was to be the repository of the science of production and therefore to possess a new kind of authority which stemmed from the unveiling of scientific law rather than the expression of arbitrary will. Taylor warned that scientific law should not be tampered with by either worker or employer. "Nine-tenths of our troubles," Taylor said, "come in trying to make men on the management side do what they ought to do. . . ."

The "military system" of factory organization, with ranks built of the successive levels of worker, foreman, assistant manager, manager, and a chain of command which allowed for much undirected choice at all levels, was no longer adequate. Under Taylor's program the foreman, for example, could no longer hire and fire or assign tasks. These functions were to be performed in the planning department by the "disciplinarian" and the "instruction card clerk." Much of the traditional hierarchy of the factory was to be maintained for the surveillance of the work, but some of its authority on all levels would be drained into the planning department.

The new demands on management would necessarily raise the proportion of auxiliary employees to those directly involved in production. In this sense Taylorism was in step with the overall trends in American industry. But the popular notion which equates Taylor's system with the outstanding features of modern industrial order, with exaggerated forms of division of labor, mass production, and mechanization and technological innovation, is inaccurate on all three counts. Taylor did not disapprove of these developments, but they were not a significant part of his particular program. Converting each job into a "science" often made possible routinization and the accompanying increase of dexterity in each task without further dividing it among different workmen. Taylor's system had its first complete developments and its typical subsequent applications in small and medium-sized plants which made diverse items. This placed severe limits to the further division of labor. Also, Taylor could not be considered a fervent advocate of technological innovation and mechanization. In fact, he was suspicious of new and radical inventions in machinery and instead laid emphasis upon perfecting the tools at hand to a point of high efficiency. In order to press the broadest application of his stop-watch studies, he did insist upon extensive standardization and synchronization of machines. Yet while he would eliminate any obviously antiquated tools, his inclination was toward getting the most out of existing equipment.

Taylor's system not only applied to the factory but reached out to society as a whole. He tried to broaden the scope of his proposals to an extent unimagined by most systemizers and by a method more definite and internally consistent than that of the industrial betterment advocates. He proposed to make each workman's interest the same as his employer's. The differential piece rate was to give the worker a high daily wage and the employer a low labor cost per piece. For society as a whole, the increased production would lower prices and raise the general standard of living. Especially in Taylor's later writings, increased productivity became a salient point of his social program. He asserted that "the one element more than any other which differentiates civilized countries from uncivilized countries—prosperous from poverty-stricken peoples—is that the average man in one is five or six times as productive as in the other." When critics contended that scientific management might be helpful in the realm of production but ignored the problems of distribution, Taylor replied that this was precisely its great accomplishment. Scientific management brought about a "mental revolution" which set the employer and worker pulling together rather than apart. For "both sides take their eyes off the division of the surplus until this surplus becomes so large that it is unnecessary to quarrel over how it shall be divided."

At first sight, this was a twentieth-century Whiggism. The commonplaces about the harmony of interest among all groups in the American social order were given a current appropriateness and a "scientific" cogency. In the Whiggism of former generations, the tariff had served as the economic bond between employer and worker. In Taylor's program, increased productivity was to play that role. It was from the standpoint of this credo of production that he criticized the profit-sharing schemes which were so dear to advocates of industrial betterment. Profit-sharing, he said, did not lend itself to increased production, and even if all profits were divided among the working people, the addition to wages would be slight. Furthermore, this belief in the primacy of production also led Taylor to condemn the entrepreneur's restriction of output to maintain prices, just as he had disapproved of the worker's "soldiering." On occasion, he contrasted the engineer as hero to the "financier" as villain; the one constantly in the presence of the production process and sensitive to its needs, and the other distant from production but with the power to control it.

Because scientific management allowed for operation at low cost, Taylor thought that it would be thrust upon entrepreneurs through competition. However, it became apparent that in important sectors of the economy, competition was no longer an effective force and, therefore, could not be relied on exclusively. When the Eastern Rate Case splashed scientific management before a large public audience, Taylor came upon a new way to spread his program. He appealed to the "whole people" to repudiate "the type of employer who has his eye on dividends alone," or the laborer who demands more pay and shorter hours but resists efficiency. The "whole people" would be the agents of his system. The role of the consulting scientific management engineer, upholding "science" in the factory against the narrow vision and vested interests of worker and employer, bore some resemblance to that of the middle-class reformer in society upholding the public interest against the pressures of both capital and labor. When Taylor invoked the public interest, scientific management was drawn toward that growing company of progressives who set the tone for the era.

Though Taylor appealed to public opinion for support, he did not look to public opinion for any sort of guidance. All the guidance, so far as scientific management was concerned, would come from experts. The application of science to business, Taylor thought, would have effects much like those which had followed the application of science to engineering a half a century earlier. There would be handbooks of "elementary operations," codifying the laws of work, similar to those engineering handbooks which codified the laws of machines. But, most important, authority would be placed in the hands of those who followed the rules of science rather than the "rule of thumb." The scientific management expert would replace arbitrary command with the dictates of science. And science, Taylor thought, was an oracle free from human bias and selfishness which would point the way to an elevating moral purpose. It would bring a professional attitude. "It is inconceivable," Taylor declared, "that a man should devote his time and life to this sort of thing for the sake of making money for a whole lot of manufacturers."

Many of the shifts in emphasis in Taylor's program over the years were tied to its widening audience. Taylor's first paper, **"A Piece-Rate System,"** was addressed to a small group of engineers and manufacturers and printed in the *Transactions of the American Society of Mechanical Engineers;* his last paper, ***The Principles of Scientific Management,*** was serialized in the *American Magazine,* which spoke the vernacular of reform to a large segment of America. "Early" Taylor cast his proposals primarily in the form of a business service, while "late" Taylor stressed their more widely beneficial aspects. His picture of his own work was changing. Those close to Taylor toward the end of his life tell of "his dreams of the ultimate applicability of Scientific Management principles and ideas, not only to every industrial activity but to every conceivable human activity."

Paradoxically, Taylor's stress on the broader relevance of his system was accompanied by a lessening in his specifically moral tone. This, at first, is even more perplexing, since his new audience was deeply imbued with moral sentiment. Yet Taylor's code differed from theirs. His underscored man's weakness and placed punishment at its center, while theirs usually dealt with man's potential and emphasized precepts of permissiveness. While Taylor, for the most part, did not bring himself to accept the moral outlook which prevailed among most of his new audience, he gradually muffled his own. In the "science" of work, the problem of how work was to be done began to overshadow the determination of the time in which work ought to be done. The differential piece rate, which embodied a dedication to hard work and some fear of its material products (if men have too much they become "shiftless, extravagant and dissipated"), almost disappeared. While in 1895 the Taylor System always meant hard work, by 1911 it sometimes meant easy work.

Taylor could make this transition because scientific management had become almost an end in itself for him. "Indeed, so intense was his will to get there, so grim was his resolution not to let anything stand in his way, that sometimes he resorted to stratagems and subterfuges so far from guileless as rather to puzzle and pain some of his most devoted followers." The toning down of the "old fashioned" moralism of his system gave it the appearance of a neutral device. Because scientific management became almost an end in itself for Taylor, it could become simply a means for others.

Yet the continuity within scientific management must not be overlooked. Taylor's system, from his first public statement of it in 1895 to his last, twenty years later, encompassed three things: it was a method of business therapy; it was a "science"; and it was a social program. During Taylor's lifetime these were three aspects of one outlook. In the generation of his disciples they were separated and each set in its own direction.

Louis W. Fry (essay date 1976)

SOURCE: "The Maligned F. W. Taylor: A Reply to His Many Critics," in *The Academy of Management Review,* Vol. 1, No. 3, July, 1976, pp. 124-129.

[*In the following essay, Fry attempts to answer Taylor's critics, conceding that Taylor's means were not always desirable, but concluding that his goals were indispensible to modern organizational behavior theory.*]

Frederick W. Taylor has been criticized and praised by theorists from various schools of organizational thought. Some say his view of man is too simplistic, as are his theories for solving the interaction of man with organization. Others state that he laid the very foundation for the vastly improved productivity of the modern economic enterprise. This article traces Taylor's thinking and the historical developments which set the stage for his intellect, noting positive and negative comments about his theories.

Although Taylor did not reach his goal of perfecting management into a true science, his impact upon the field—industrial engineering and management—is monumental. Scientific management, as Taylor envisioned it, fell into disfavor shortly after his work was published in 1911. Instead of utilizing his whole system as a philosophy of management, many later followers used time-study as a means to further exploit and speed up work, rather than to determine the best method and the *fair* pace to perform a job. Thus, his scientific means were used for ends other than achieving the greater prosperity he envisioned for not only the employer but the employee and all of society. This abuse was so great that the U. S. Congress passed a law in 1915 forbidding the use of any timing devices to measure work performance within any government facility. The law was not repealed until 1949.

Circumstances such as this slowed but did not stop Taylorism, and perhaps caused a shift in emphasis. Gore and Silander credit the continued probe into decision-making techniques for increasing productivity, to those who seek to develop a management science:

> If it is accidental that the term management science is almost a simple reversal of scientific management, it is not without significance, for there is a sense in which the current scientific rationalistic movement is essentially scientific management with new, vastly more powerful, tools.

THE CRITICS

Taylor's impact upon management thinking, both theoretically and operationally, has been considerable. But he has received scathing criticisms for his concept of man as a total economic being motivated by money alone. Wolin sums up the attitude of many theorists, when he states that the real danger to the organization in an age of industrialism does not lie in stagnation but in the disruptive effects of technological innovation as fostered by Taylor's disciples, the industrial engineers. Drawing upon Mayo's *Human Problems,* Wolin states:

> The modern manager, therefore must in defense of "human values" stand ready to resist the changes proposed by the "logicians" of industrial engineering who are just as eager to subordinate social values to the mathematics of production schedules as the French revolutionaries were ready to lop away regional loyalties and sentiments in order to tidy up the boundary of an arrondissement.

While Wolin's view may be extreme it is not completely unfounded. Even industrial engineers have begun to recognize this fact. But his statement does reflect some theorists' almost outright rejection of Taylor's theories.

Bell accuses Taylor of losing sight of the person as a being, with the smallest unit of motion and time becoming the measure of a worker's worth. Silverman labels the techniques offered by scientific management as combining "spurious scientific" appeal and practical ideas which seemed in harmony with intuition.

Mouzellis states that Taylor neglected the psychological and sociological variables within organizations. Scott and Hart call Taylor's basic assumption of human moral nature Hobbesean, stating that managers and workers were equally culpable in violating Taylor's economic views of rationality.

Even the Russians have noted and criticized Taylor. Gvishiani, in the official Russian communist version of capitalistic management theory, treats Taylor's theories with great respect. This is primarily because Lenin respected Taylor to the point that he proposed making a critical study of Taylorism to determine the feasibility of applying it in communist industry—stripped of its capitalistic exploitationist ideology of course. Gvishiani claims that Taylor advocated that "growth of labor productivity and an increase in production rates be achieved only through coercion, through an enforced standardization of the instruments, conditions, and methods of work."

Finally, some critics attempt to prove that Taylor plagiarized the ideas of others and fraudulently represented data he used to support his theories.

A HISTORICAL PERSPECTIVE

From a historical standpoint, Taylor's enduring importance is derived from his leadership in introducing to work the concept of the scientific method approach, with its corresponding Positivist approach best expressed in Compte's "Know to foresee, foresee to forestall." The forces which compelled Taylor to improvise a more organized means of production are also rooted in his period of history and its particular technological constraints.

Most of Taylor's theories and works were developed during the "Progressive Era", which gave rise to an efficiency craze in which a gospel of efficiency was prescribed without embarrassment by men as disparate as William Jennings Bryan and Walter Lippmann. The words "efficient" and "good" were often used synonymously, to describe such disparate attributes as a personal quality, energy output-input, ratio of dollars, and relationships between people. According to Haber:

> Efficiency meant social harmony and the leadership of the "competent." Progressives often called this social efficiency. And it is this meaning that has particular importance for the understanding of the progressive era.

The underlying force which formed the springboard for this era was the unprecedented expansion of capitalism and the industrialized world. Important technological and economic developments caused the creation and proliferation of large scale organizations, many of which were monopolistic.

The focus of this problem was most acutely felt by individuals, such as Frederick Taylor, who had to deal with daily problems at the workshop level. Taylor rose from an apprentice worker to chief engineer at the Midvale Iron Works, then became a prominent and controversial member of the American Society of Mechanical Engineers. Following Taylor's own view, Mouzelis states:

> Taylor's originality did not consist so much in the invention of any one of his particular techniques to scientific management, but rather in the fact that he succeeded in integrating into a cohesive system various techniques, and ideas about management

> which had existed before his time but never systematized.

Before any attempt at rebuttal, it is appropriate to examine Taylor's main work, ***The Principles of Scientific Management,*** to try to resolve what he really meant when he spoke of scientific management. Taylor abhorred the then current management philosophy of "initiative and incentive" which:

> makes it necessary for each workman to bear almost the entire responsibility for the general plans as well as for each detail of his work, and in many cases for his implements as well. In addition to this he must do all of the actual labor.

This, Taylor felt, was entirely too much of a burden for the worker to bear alone. He thus rejected management by "initiative and incentive" and called for management to assume the burden of planning, controlling and directing workers by taking on additional duties which were grouped under four headings:

1. Development of a science for determining the elements of work, replacing the old rule-of-thumb method;

2. Scientific selection, training and develment of the worker;

3. Management's cooperation with workers to insure implementation of the principles of the science which has been developed;

4. An equal division of work and responsibility between the management and workers.

FREDERICK W. TAYLOR—ORGANIZATIONAL BEHAVIORIST

The third duty of management is perhaps the most surprising. Taylor calls for cooperation, stating: "This close, intimate, personal cooperation between the management and the men is of the essence of modern scientific or task management." He felt that this cooperation must be present for the other areas of scientific management to be implemented. One method through which this cooperation can be gained is by special incentives to the worker, such as:

1. Hope of rapid promotions or advancement;

2. Higher wages, in the form of generous piece-work prices or a premium or bonus;

3. Shorter labor hours;

4. Better surroundings and working conditions.

All this must be accompanied by a genuine interest in the worker's welfare. Taylor attacks those who look upon payment schemes as practically the whole system of management. He states: "Under scientific management, however, the particular pay system which is adopted is merely one of the subordinate elements."

Taylor has been criticized for emphasizing only the economic nature of people. Taylor indeed felt economic incentives to be the primary motivator of the industrial worker; he stated that maximum prosperity can be achieved by "giving the workman what he wants—high wages—and the employer what he wants—a low labor cost—for his manufacturers." In other words, the pie could be enlarged so that all could be satisfied.

But to further explain Taylor's theories, two familiar concepts of organizational behavior can be cited. As is seen from the list of incentives, Taylor recognized other motivators than economic ones. Douglas McGregor's Theory X and Theory Y concepts are contrasts in assumptions concerning inherent human nature. McGregor's position was that under the right conditions, many people (not necessarily all) could find sufficient satisfaction in work to devote more effort to it than they would in response to coercion or coaxing (Taylor's definition of the then current "initiative and incentive" type of management). Taylor recognized this when he stated: "There is a large class of men who require really no discipline in the ordinary acceptance of the term, men who are sensitive, conscientious and desirous of doing just what is right." Theory Y is thus partly what Taylor was advocating when he spoke of the essence of scientific management.

Taylor did not embrace Theory Y totally. He saw people as naturally lazy, identifying two forms of loafing or "soldiering." The first is the natural human instinct to be lazy, and the second, "systematic soldiering," is the result of collusion between workers to restrict productivity. Rather than taking a totally "Theory X" perspective of workers, Taylor was somewhere along the continuum between the Theory X and Y extremes.

Taylor also recognized the existence and dysfunctional aspects of the informal group, while at the same time ignoring its functional properties. Drawing from Perrow, this approach is seen to directly contrast with those of theorists such as Chester Barnard who noted the informal group as functional while ignoring its dysfunctional aspects; Herbert Simon who recognized informal groups and sought to control them through the organization's decision making system (i.e., structure, hierarchy, communications channels, training and indoctrination, etc.); or Phillip Selznick who went one step further in seeing the informal group as "infused" with the values of the organization, thereby institutionalizing the goals of the informal group by making them identical to those of the organization.

"Systematic soldiering"—the result of informal groups as fostered by the then current "initiative and incentive" type of management—was thus seen by Taylor as the greatest barrier to the achievement of maximum efficiency and productivity. Taylor's solution to this problem was the effective implementation of scientific management, the two most important elements of this mechanism being the task and the bonus. Scientific management would remove these barriers to productivity with the correct application of the task through scientific principles, the timely completion of this task, and its ensuing just monetary rewards.

Maslow's concept of a hierarchy of needs, as modified by Lawler and Suttle, offers further explanation of Taylor's choice of motivators. The industrial worker of Taylor's era, being neither well educated nor affluent, emphasized needs different from those of workers today. Education and greater affluence have caused a shift of emphasis in needs from Maslow's primary physiological and security needs to his secondary social, esteem, and self-actualization needs. People were more worried in Taylor's time about where to find their next meal than about self-actualization. Taylor spoke of scientific management as the means of developing each person to a state of maximum efficiency, to enable one to perform "the highest grade of work for which his natural abilities fit him, and it further means giving him, when possible, this class of work to do."

Thus the worker of the progressive era was as complex as the worker of today, but the needs for esteem, recognition and self-actualization were overridden by the most basic needs for shelter and security. Satisfaction of these basic needs was the primary reason for the progressive era workers' greater response to economic incentives. Taylor did not neglect the psychological and sociological variables within organizations; he correctly addressed the means through which people in the early 20th century satisfied basic needs of safety and shelter—money. In fact, money is seen by some sociologists as a primary motivator, years after Taylor's death. Robert and Helen Lynd in *Middletown,* their study of small city American life during the mid 1920's, noted that "for both working and business class no other accompaniment of getting a living approaches in importance the money received for their work."

Taylor was also charged with neglecting the relevant variables of the informal organization, conflict of interest, etc., which concerned the worker within the social context. But it seems clear that Taylor clearly perceived these phenomena instead of neglecting them. He did not ignore the social and ethical aspects of labor. He dealt with them drastically, in the sense that the old management by "initiative and incentive" would be replaced by his then radically new philosophy of scientific management. The worker is not regarded as a work horse (unless he or she is a pig iron handler). Each job has its type of worker, with natural talents to perform the tasks of that job. The job will place the worker in the highest grade of work suitable to his or her natural abilities.

Charges of fraud and plagiarism against Taylor center around the suspicious similarity between much of his work and Morris L. Cooke's unpublished book, *Industrial Management.* But according to Wrege, Cooke obtained most of the material for his book from various Taylor conversations, primarily drawing from his "Boxly talks." It is ludicrous to accuse Taylor of plagiarizing Cooke if in fact Cooke's material was based on Taylor's own talks.

CONCLUSION

Not all criticisms of Taylor are invalid. In many respects he was almost obsessed with his theories, calling their implementation not only a necessity, but a duty. But Taylor cannot be classified as Hobbesean, since he also felt that people could be trained to overcome their inherent deficiencies (à la Locke). His view of human nature is pessimistic, but not without hope for improvement.

Another criticism of Taylor is his failure to recognize the potential functional aspects of informal groups. To him, the only solution was to destroy the very nucleus of these groups, in order to assure worker accountability for actions and to diffuse what he saw as the collusion of the work group to restrict output. Throughout his work, Taylor's philosophies are apparent—reward greatly those who adapt and excel; weed out and reject those who do not—all the while emphasizing the individual divorced from the group.

As for those who have criticized Taylor for what they perceive as a totally economic solution for worker motivation, this article relates other underlying reasons for his choice of such a motivator. Taylor recognized the impact of human behavior in organizations, in terms of both individuals and groups. His solution to what he saw as a dysfunctional phenomenon directly addressed this problem and offered a remedy to help the worker better satisfy the primary need of food and shelter. Kakar directly addresses the many critics of Taylor:

> These arguments with Taylorism have to do with the matter of means; with Taylor's ends there is no quarrel. All who reject Taylor's system for its ignorance or depreciation of the social and psychological dimensions of work gear their arguments and justify their cases with reference to a common goal—increased productivity.

Although Taylor's means may be disputed, his end—to increase organizational productivity through the description, prediction and control of behavior in organizations—is still a major goal of organizational behavior.

Peter F. Drucker (essay date 1976)

SOURCE: "The Coming Rediscovery of Scientific Management," in *Toward the Next Economics and Other Essays,* Harper & Row, Publishers, 1981, pp. 96-106.

[*In the following essay, originally published in* The Conference Board Record *in 1976, Drucker advocates the application of Taylor's principles to what Drucker calls "knowledge work."*]

Everybody "knows" the following "facts" about Frederick Winslow Taylor: His aim was "efficiency," which meant reducing costs and increasing profits. He believed that workers responded primarily to economic incentives. He invented the "speed-up" and the assembly line. He saw only the individual worker, and not the work group. He considered workers to be "machines" and to be used as machines. He wanted to put all power and control into the hands of management, while he had deep contempt for the workingman. And he was the father of "classical organization theory," with its hierarchical pyramids, its concept of the span of control, its functions, and so on.

But even the most cursory reading of Taylor immediately shows that every one of these "well-known facts" is pure myth.

Taylor's central theme, which he repeated again and again, was the need to substitute industrial harmony for industrial warfare and mutual trust for fear in the industrial plant. This required, he maintained, four major changes:

1. It first required high wages. Indeed, Taylor demanded of every management starting to introduce "scientific management"—that is, the systematic study of work and tasks—that it commit itself at the outset, before beginning the study itself, to a wage increase of 30 to 100 percent. And in his first attempt to describe what he then called the "task system" in ***Shop Management,*** he stated almost at the outset: "This book is written mainly with the object of advocating *high wages*—as the foundation of the best management."

He believed that productivity brought about by doing work right would make possible high wages and would, in effect, provide what we today would call "affluence." And Taylor strongly believed that the worker should receive the *full* benefit of higher productivity obtained through "scientific management," whether in the form of higher wages or of shorter hours.

Yet Taylor did not believe that economic incentives by themselves would motivate. He anticipated practically all the later research of the human relations school or of Frederick Herzberg in stating that higher wages by themselves do not provide motivation, but that dissatisfaction with wage incomes is a major deterrent and destroys motivation. (The word "motivation" was, of course, unknown to Taylor—it did not come into general usage until the twenties; Taylor speaks of "initiative.")

2. The second major need, according to Taylor, was to eliminate physical strain and bodily damage caused by doing the work the wrong way. Again and again, he pointed out that "scientific management" lightened the heavy physical toil and maintained energy. Again and again, he pointed out how traditional work creates injuries, fatigue, strain, dulls the faculties, and wears out the body. In a passage in the introduction to ***Principles of Scientific Management,*** which sounds strangely contemporary, Taylor contrasts the then-popular concern with the wanton destruction of such physical resources as forests, coal, or oil with the disregard of the wastage and destruction of the human resource.

3. Thirdly, Taylor believed that "scientific management" would produce industrial harmony through providing the means for the fullest development of the human personality. In his Testimony he said:

> It becomes the duty of those on the management side to deliberately study the character, the nature, and the performance of each workman, with a view to finding out his limitations, on the one hand, but even more important, his possibilities for development on the other hand; and then, as deliberately and as systematically as possible, to train and help and teach this workman, giving him, wherever it is possible, those opportunities for advancement which will finally enable him to do the highest and most interesting and most profitable class of work for which his natural abilities fit him and which are open to him in the particular company in which he is employed. This scientific selection of the workman and his development is not a single act; it goes on from year to year and is the subject of continual study on the part of the management.

Taylor not only preached this, he practiced it. One of his most interesting innovations, and one on which he insisted in every plant in which he introduced "scientific management," was the appointment of people whose main duty it was to identify abilities in the work group and to help workers acquire the training and the skill for advancement to better, more highly skilled, more responsible, and, above all, bigger jobs. He insisted—most successfully in his work at Bethlehem Steel—that no one be fired as a result of "scientific management," but that attrition and normal turnover be used to place the workman in another job in the plant. Again and again, he stressed the need to enrich jobs and work and to make them bigger, rather than confine them to one repeated operation. And he stressed the duty of management of find what a man is suited for—and then to make sure that he gets to do this kind of work. Taylor maintained that except for those few capable of work but unwilling to do it, there are only "first-rate men." It is management's job to make sure that they get the opportunity to excel.

4. Finally, "scientific management" to Taylor meant the elimination of the "boss."

> If there is anything that is characteristic of scientific management, it is the fact that the men who were formerly called bosses under the old type of management, under scientific management become the servants of the workmen. It is their duty to wait on the workmen and help them in all kinds of ways.

Moreover, what Taylor meant by "functional foremanship" is what we now call "matrix organization." He had nothing to do with "classical organization" and its "hierarchy"; it clearly runs contrary to Taylor's basic principles.

THE TRUE TAYLOR

Contrary to everything one reads about Taylor, he was concerned neither with profits nor with costs. His concern was what we today would call "productivity" (a word unknown seventy years ago). Far from being an admirer of management, Taylor was exceedingly critical of it: "Nine-tenths of our trouble has been to bring those on the management side to do their fair share of the work, and only one-tenth of our trouble has come on the workmen's side."

He did not hesitate, in his Testimony, to speak of U.S. Steel's management as "deplorable" and indeed "shameful." He repeatedly, and with great bitterness, attacked the people in top management who refused to pay a worker more than the "going wage" and who opposed "scientific management" because a worker under it will immediately earn $6.50 a day, where the "going wage" at the time was $5 a day. He was forced out as superintendent of Midvale Steel—the company where he had begun as an apprentice journeyman at age eighteen and where he first developed what was later to be known as "scientific management"—because he insisted on giving the workers the full benefit of their increased productivity, rather than keep wages low and raise profits. Altogether, most managements of the time kept him out of their plants as a "dangerous radical" and "troublemaker."

Taylor strongly believed in teamwork. He went to great lengths, in his Testimony, to point to the Mayo Medical Clinic as the finest example of "scientific management" at work, because it had succeeded in enabling a group of ten physicians and surgeons to work together as one team.

Taylor equally did not, as everybody seems to believe, want to give management all the control and to divorce the worker from management. On the contrary, this is what he said—and practiced:

> . . . under this new type of management, there is hardly a single act or piece of work done by anyone in the shop which is not preceded and followed by some act on the part of one of the men in the management. . . . First the workman does something; then the man on the management side does something and then the workman does something; and under this intimate, close, personal cooperation between the two sides, it becomes practically impossible to have a serious problem.

Indeed, Taylor considered "scientific management" a joint task of management and workers.

Finally, Taylor had absolutely nothing to do with the assembly line. There is no shred of evidence that Otto Doering of Sears, Roebuck and Henry Ford, who—between 1903 and 1910—developed the first assembly lines in the mail order house and the automobile plant respectively, had ever heard of Taylor or of "scientific management." Taylor certainly had never heard of the assembly line. In 1911-12, when Taylor last wrote (he was only fifty-six years old by then, but already aging), the assembly line was still below the horizon. It did not become fully visible until after the end of World War I, by which time Taylor was dead. And there is ample reason to believe that Taylor would have been highly critical of the assembly line and would have considered it very poor engineering. It violates his basic principles: the freeing of the initiative of the individual worker; the strengthening of the work group; and, above all, the finding, training, and developing of the individual for the job he is best fitted for.

FLYING IN THE FACE OF IGNORANCE

There are few cases in intellectual history where what a man actually said and did, and what he is generally believed to have said and done, are so totally at variance. The question, therefore, is why Taylor is being so totally misrepresented.

The standard explanation is that he was a "captive of nineteenth-century psychology." But this is nonsense. The trouble with Taylor was that he was so far ahead of his time that no one—or very few people—listened, let alone understood what he was saying and doing. In many ways, indeed in most ways, Taylor was a strong believer in what is now called Theory Y. He stated again and again that management by fear was counter-productive. At times he sounds like McGregor, at others, like Argyris—in his constant criticism of the resistance of organization to accepting the worker as a human being, for instance. At times he sounds very much like Frederick Herzberg. He was concerned with the "quality of life," to use today's terminology. Early in his Testimony he said:

> Scientific management is not an efficiency device, not a device of any kind for securing efficiency. Nor is it any bunch or group of efficiency devices. It is not a new system of figuring costs; it is not a new scheme of paying men; it is not a piecework system; it is not a bonus system; it is not a premium system; it is no scheme for payment; it is not holding a stopwatch on a man and writing things down about him; it is not time study; it is not motion study nor an analysis of the movements of men; it is not divided foremanship or functional foremanship; it is not any of the devices which the average man calls to mind when scientific management is spoken of. *In essence, scientific management involves a complete mental revolution on the part of the working men—and on the part of those on the management side, the foreman, the superintendent, the owner of the business, the Board of Directors—as to their duties towards their fellow workers in the management, towards their workmen and toward all of their problems.* (emphasis added)

But this was so far ahead of 1910 that few even heard what Taylor said. What people heard instead were the very things which Taylor asserted that scientific management is not. And to this day, those are the things which are taught in most engineering schools as "scientific management" and industrial engineering, and are stated in most books to be what Taylor stood for.

But Taylor also committed the unpardonable offense of proving the "isms" to be irrelevant—and for this neither the Right nor the Left will ever forgive him. The "system," Taylor implies, hardly matters. Job, task, and work do. The economy is not made by "capitalism" or "socialism." It is made by productivity. Taylor spoke of the "duty" of owners; he never spoke of their "rights." He spoke of the "responsibility" of workers; he never spoke of their being "exploited." In other words, Taylor did not hold the "system" responsible, nor did he expect any great change to come from a "change in the system." His "revolution" was a "mental" revolution, and not a social one. This flew directly in the face of the most cherished beliefs of 1910—and it still flies in the face of the prevailing beliefs of today.

This would not matter so much if Taylor had not been successful. Wherever his approach has been applied, productivity has increased manyfold, workers' real wages have gone up sharply, hours have gone down, and the physical and mental strain on the workers has been reduced. At the same time, sales and profits have gone up and prices have gone down. The more successful Taylor is, the more hostile to him the prevailing ideologies must become.

Finally, there is the horrible fact that Taylor concerned himself with work. Taylor was the first man in history who actually studied work seriously. This is his historical importance. People had, of course, been talking about work since time immemorial. But no one had thought work worthy of serious study. Indeed, work was clearly beneath the attention of educated people.

Taylor was well aware of this: " . . . the professors of this country . . . resent the use of the word 'science' for anything quite so trivial as the ordinary, everyday affairs of life." But it was not just the use of the word "science," even in Taylor's definition as "classified or organized knowledge of any kind," which "the professors of this country" (we would say "the intellectuals") resent and reject. It is altogether the belief that work—sweaty, dirty, back-breaking labor such as shoveling sand or moving pig iron—offers intellectual challenge and could and should be pleasant, rewarding—both economically and psychologically.

"Professors" believe in "creativity." Taylor believed in systematic, hard, principled work. The "professors" believe in an "elite," no matter how much they preach "equality." Taylor did not believe in "equality." He knew that people differed in their abilities. But he considered everyone a "first-rate man" who did the job and task he was fitted for, and as such entitled to full opportunity, to a good income, and above all, to respect. Management had the duty, he thought, to find what each man was best fitted for, to help him to get there, and to enable him to perform and to achieve by organizing his task, by providing the tools and the information needed, and by giving him adequate managerial support and continuing training. But the "professors" of this world still tend to believe, albeit only unconsciously, that work is something slaves do.

AS THE WORLD LEARNS

Among the "makers of the modern world" Taylor is rarely mentioned. And yet he has had as much impact as Marx or Freud. To be sure, we have gone beyond Taylor and need to go beyond him. But to attack Taylor because he had, for instance, more faith in the power of reason to convince and to convert people than we, living after two world wars, can muster, is foolishness. It is very much like attacking Newton because he did not invent non-Euclidean geometry or discover the theory of relativity.

Taylor has triumphed, despite his detractors. He has triumphed where his main concern was—in manual work. When he predicted, in his Testimony, that "the workman of that day [a hundred years hence] will live as well, or almost, as a high-class businessman lives now, as far as the necessities of life and most of the luxuries of life are concerned," people laughed—yet this is, of course, exactly what has come to pass in the developed countries, and primarily as a result of the application of Taylor's principles. It has come to pass precisely the way Taylor predicted—namely, by "greatly increasing the output of the man without materially increasing his effort." It has come about because we have learned to study tasks, to organize them, to plan them, to provide the right tools and the right information—though no one would claim that we have reached perfection.

But Taylor's greatest impact may still be ahead. In the first place, the underdeveloped and developing countries are now reaching the stage where they need Taylor and "scientific management." They have now reached the stage where their main aim has to be higher wages and yet lower labor costs—that is, increased productivity of manual work. It is now as true of them as it was for the United States eighty years ago that "underproduction" is mainly responsible for the fact that, as Taylor said of America in 1900, "the poorer people have just so much fewer things to live on; that they have poorer food to eat; pay higher prices for their rent; can buy fewer clothes to wear than they ought to have; in other words, that they lack in many cases the necessities and in all cases the luxuries of life that they ought to have."

But the need to study Taylor anew and to apply him may be the greatest in the developed countries, that is, in the countries which have become developed because they have applied Taylor's principles to manual work. These are the countries in which Taylor now has to be applied to knowledge work.

MAKING MENTAL WORK MORE PRODUCTIVE

In his writings and in his Testimony, Taylor emphasized that no plant, no factory, and no railroad had used more than a few elements of "scientific management." The one perfect example of "scientific management" in action, which Taylor cited, was the Mayo Clinic (for which Taylor claimed no credit). Taylor himself, in other words, was fully aware that "scientific management" applies to knowledge work as well as to manual work.

To make knowledge work fully productive requires many things Taylor did not concern himself with. It requires objectives and goals. It requires priorities and measurements. It requires systematic abandonment of the tasks that no longer produce and of the services that are no longer needed. It also requires organization, largely along the lines of the "matrix organization" which Taylor reached for in his "functional foremanship."

But making knowledge work productive also requires "task study" and "task management." It requires the analysis of the work itself. It requires understanding of the steps needed, their sequence and their integration into an organized process. It requires systematic provision of the information needed and of the tool needed. All of these are concepts of "scientific management." It does not require "creativity." It requires the hard, systematic, analytical, and synthesizing work which Taylor developed to deal with shoveling sand, lifting pig iron, running paper machines, or laying brick.

Knowledge work already has the high wages which were Taylor's aim. Now it has to achieve the productivity which alone can justify the high wages. And this requires, above all, changes in "mental attitudes" and Taylor's "complete mental revolution" on the part of both the knowledge worker and his management.

The need today is neither to bury Taylor nor to praise him. It is to learn from him. The need is to do for knowledge work and knowledge worker what Taylor, beginning a century ago, did for manual work and manual worker.

Edwin A. Locke (essay date 1982)

SOURCE: "The Ideas of Frederick W. Taylor: An Evaluation," in *The Academy of Management Review*, Vol. 7, No. 1, January, 1982, pp. 14-24.

[In the following essay, Locke defends Taylor's methods, maintaining that Taylor produced the "most objectively valid" theories in modern thought.]

Few management theorists have been more persistently criticized than has Frederick W. Taylor, the founder of scientific management, despite his being widely recognized as a key figure in the history of management thought (Wren, 1979). Taylor and scientific management frequently were attacked in his own lifetime, prompting, among other responses, Gilbreth's *Primer* (Gilbreth, 1914/1973), and the criticisms have continued to this day.

The present author agrees with Drucker (1976), although not with all of his specific points, that Taylor has never been fully understood or appreciated by his critics. Many criticisms either have been invalid or have involved peripheral issues, and his major ideas and contributions often have gone unacknowledged.

Wren (1979) did a superb job of showing how Taylor's major ideas permeated the field of management both in the United States and abroad. However, Wren was not concerned primarily with evaluating all of Taylor's techniques or the criticisms of his ideas. Boddewyn (1961), Drucker (1976), and Fry (1976) have made spirited defenses of Taylor, but more by way of broad overviews than in systematic detail. The present paper summarizes Taylor's major ideas and techniques and considers both their validity and their degree of acceptance in contemporary management. In addition, the major criticisms made of Taylor are systematically evaluated.

TAYLOR'S PHILOSOPHY OF MANAGEMENT

An essential element of Taylor's philosophy of management, as the name of the movement implies, was a scientific approach to managerial decision making (Taylor, 1912/1970b; Sheldon, 1924/1976). The name was intended to contrast his approach with the unscientific approaches that characterized traditional management practices. By scientific, Taylor meant: based on proven fact (e.g., research and experimentation) rather than on tradition, rule of thumb, guesswork, precedent, personal opinion, or hearsay (Taylor, 1911/1967).

There can be no doubt that this element of Taylor's philosophy is accepted in modern management. This is not to say that all contemporary managers are fully rational decision makers. Clearly this is not the case. However, most would subscribe to the principle of scientific decision making and many actually practice it, at least with respect to some of their decisions. In most business schools there now is a specialized field called management science (which includes operations research), but the scientific approach is reflected in other areas of business as well (e.g., cost accounting). [See Kendall, (1924/1976) for a discussion of Taylor's early influence.] Taylor's goal was to forge a "mental revolution" in management, and in this aim he clearly succeeded. Drucker wrote that "Taylor was the first man in history who actually studied work seriously" (1976).

A second element of Taylor's philosophy of management, and the other key aspect of the mental revolution that he advocated, concerned the relationship between management and labor. At the turn of the century, management-labor strife was widespread, violence was not uncommon, and a number of radical labor groups were advocating the violent overthrow of the capitalist system. Many believed that labor-management conflict was virtually inevitable.

Taylor argued that this view was false, that, at root, the interests of both parties were the same. Both would benefit, he argued, from higher production, lower costs, and higher wages, provided that management approached its job scientifically. Taylor believed that there would be no conflict over how to divide the pie as long as the pie were large enough (Taylor, 1912/1970b).

In logic, one cannot argue with Taylor's fundamental premise of a community of interest between management and labor. There were virtually no strikes in plants in which he applied scientific management (Taylor, 1911/1967; 1912/1970a). Wren (1979) argues that during the 1920s Taylor's hopes for union cooperation in introducing scientific management and in reducing waste were realized to a considerable extent in two industries. Unfortunately this attitude of cooperation ended in the 1930s when unions turned their attention to the passage of prolabor legislation.

In general, management-labor relations now are far more amicable than they were at the turn of the century, but all conflict has not been eliminated. One reason for this is that no matter how big the pie is, there still can be disagreements over how to divide it up. Taylor did not anticipate that as the pie got bigger, aspirations would rise accordingly.

TAYLOR'S TECHNIQUES

Time and Motion Study

Before Taylor, there was no objective method for determining how fast a job should be done. Most managers simply used past experience as a guide. Taylor's solution was to break down the work task into its constituent elements or motions; to eliminate wasted motions so the work would be done in the *"one best way"* (Taylor, 1912/1970a)—a principle even more strongly emphasized by Frank Gilbreth (1923/1970); and to time the remaining motions in order to arrive at an expected rate of production (a proper day's work).

Time study now is used routinely in industrialized countries. However, there has been no final solution to the problem of (partially) subjective elements in time study (e.g., fatigue allowances); nor has worker resistance to time study disappeared, although it should be noted that resistance is most likely when there is a lack of trust in management (Bartlem & Locke, 1981). Such lack of trust often is earned by practices such as rate-cutting—something that Taylor explicitly warned against.

Standardized Tools and Procedures

Before scientific management, every workman had his own private tool box. This resulted in great inefficiencies because the proper tools were not always used or even owned. Taylor pushed strongly for standardization in the design and use of tools. The tools and procedures were standardized in accordance with what designs that experiments had shown to be most effective in a given context (e.g., the best size and shape for coal shovels).

Like time study, the principle of standardization is now well accepted. Combined with the principle of designing tools to fit people, the technique of standardization has evolved into the science of human engineering. Standardization also has been extended beyond the sphere of tool use to include other types of organizational procedures, especially in large firms.

The Task

Taylor advocated that each worker be assigned a specific amount of work, of a certain quality, each day based on the results of time study. This assigned quota he called a "task" (Taylor, 1911/1967). The term task (which was not original to Taylor) is roughly equivalent to the term goal. Thus, the use of tasks was a forerunner of modern day goal-setting. It is worth noting that Wren's (1979) discussion of scientific management at DuPont and General Motors implies that there is an historical connection between it and the technique of management by objectives (MBO). Pierre DuPont adapted Taylor's cost control ideas in order to develop measures of organizational performance (such as "return on investment") for the DuPont Powder Company. One of his employees, Donaldson Brown, further developed the return on investment concept so that it could be used to compare the efficiency of various departments *within* DuPont. When Pierre DuPont became head of General Motors, he hired Brown and Alfred P. Sloan, who institutionalized Brown's ideas at General Motors. Thus, although the technique of MBO may have been an outgrowth of scientific management, it developed more directly from the concepts of feedback, performance measurement, and cost accounting than from the task concept. Taylor had introduced an interlocking cost and accounting system as early as 1893 (Copley, 1923, Vol. 1).

Drucker acknowledges that Sloan was one of the earliest users of the MBO technique, but the term evidently was coined by Drucker (1954) himself, based not just on his studies at GM but on his work at General Electric with Harold Smiddy (Greenwood, 1980). At GE, the technique of MBO came to mean objectives set jointly by the manager and his superior rather than simply assigned objectives and/or work measurement.

Another term used widely today is organizational behavior modification (OB Mod); most OB Mod studies merely involve goal-setting with feedback, described in behavioristic terminology (Locke, 1977). Virtually every contemporary theory of or approach to motivation now acknowledges the importance of goal setting either explicitly or implicitly (Locke, 1978).

The main effect of the post-Taylor research has been to support the validity of his practices. For example, it has been learned that specific challenging goals lead to better performance than do specific, easy goals or vague goals such as "do your best" or "no" goals (Locke, 1968; Locke, Shaw, Saari, & Latham, 1981). Taylor anticipated these results. The tasks his workers were assigned were, in fact, both specific (quantitative) and challenging; they were set by time study to be reachable only by a trained, "first class" workman (Taylor, 1903/1970). Remarkably, Alfred P. Sloan himself said: "The guiding principle was to make our standards difficult to achieve, but possible to attain, which I believe is the most effective way of capitalizing on the initiative, resourcefulness, and capabilities of operating personnel" (Odiorne, 1978).

Further, it now seems clear that feedback (knowledge of one's progress in relation to the task or goal) is essential for goal setting to work (Locke et al., 1981), just as it is essential to have goals if feedback is to work (Locke et al., 1968). Again Taylor anticipated these findings. His workers were given feedback at least daily indicating whether or not they had attained their assigned task (Taylor, 1911/1967). A precursor of evaluative feedback for workers, developed a century before Taylor, was Robert Owen's "silent monitor" technique, described by Wren (1979).

The Money Bonus

Taylor claimed that money was what the worker wanted most, and he argued that the worker should be paid from 30 percent to 100 percent higher wages in return for learning to do his job according to scientific management principles, that is, for *"carrying out orders"* (Boddewyn, 1961), and for regularly attaining the assigned task.

Although money has been attacked frequently by social scientists from the time of the Hawthorne studies to the present, on the grounds that it is an inadequate motivator, Taylor's claim—that money is what the worker wants most—was not entirely misguided. A plethora of new incentive schemes have developed since Taylor's time, and new ones are still being tried (Latham & Dossett, 1978), not only for workers but for managers as well. Most labor-management conflicts still involve the issue of wages or issues related to wages, such as senority, rate setting, layoffs, and fringe benefits. New analyses of the Hawthorne studies indicate that their disparagement of money as a motivator was wrong (Carey, 1967; Franke & Kaul, 1978; Sykes, 1965; Lawler, 1975), and recent books and articles again are advocating the use of money to motivate workers (Lawler, 1971; Locke, 1975; Vough, 1975).

Pay has become a major issue even in the famous Topeka experiment at General Foods, which was intended to stress job enrichment and participation (Walton, 1977), and it is a key element in the still popular Scanlon Plan (Frost, Wakeley & Ruh, 1974), long considered a human relations/organizational development technique. The pendulum now clearly seems to be swinging back toward Taylor's view (Locke, Feren, McCaleb, Shaw, & Denny, 1980). It is notable that one of the most outspoken contemporary advocates of money as a motivator is, like Taylor, an industrial engineer, Mitchell Fein. Fein has developed a new plant-wide incentive system called "Improshare" (Fein, 1977), which is coming into increasingly wide use.

Individualized Work

Taylor was a staunch advocate of individual as opposed to group tasks, as well as individual rewards, because he believed that group work and rewards undermined individual productivity, due to such phenomena as "systematic soldiering." Taylor wrote, "Personal ambition always has been and will remain a more powerful incentive to exertion than a desire for the general welfare" (1912/1976). In this respect, Taylor's views are in clear opposition to the trend of the past four to five decades, which has been toward group tasks.

Nevertheless, Taylor's warnings about the dangers of group work have proven to have some validity. For example, Janis (1972) has demonstrated that groups that become too cohesive are susceptible to groupthink, a cognitive disorder in which rational thinking is sacrificed in the name of unanimity. Latané, Williams and Harkins (1979) have documented a phenomenon called "social loafing," in which people working in a group put out less effort than when working alone even when they claim to be trying their hardest in both cases.

Studies of group decision making indicate that there is no universal superiority of groups over individuals or vice versa. Although a group might outperform the average individual member, the best group member is often superior to the group as a whole (Hall, 1971).

The current view seems to hold that although people may work less hard in groups (as Taylor claimed), the benefits in terms of cooperation, knowledge, and flexibility generally outweigh the costs. Overall, the evidence is not conclusive one way or the other. Most likely the final answer will depend on the nature of the task and other factors.

Management Responsibility for Training

In line with his emphasis on a scientific approach to management, Taylor argued that employees should not learn their skills haphazardly from more experienced workers, who may not be using the "one best way," but from management experts who are thoroughly familiar with the job. There can be no doubt that most contemporary managers fully accept the notion that training new employees is their responsibility. Furthermore, the objective evaluation of training is becoming increasingly common.

Scientific Selection

Taylor advocated selecting only "first class" (i.e., high aptitude) men for a given job because their productivity would be several times greater than that of the average man. Colleague Sanford E. Thompson's use of a measure of reaction time to select bicycle ball bearing inspectors (Taylor, 1911/1967) was one of the earliest efforts at objective selection.

Thompson's selection testing antedated the pioneering work of Hugo Munsterberg (1913) as well as the more systematic attempts at validation of selection tests conducted by American psychologists for the Army during World War I. Since that time, personnel selection has mushroomed enormously and has become a science in its own right. Wren (1979) notes that Taylor's emphasis on scientific selection was an impetus to the development of the fields of industrial psychology and personnel management.

Shorter Working Hours and Rest Pauses

Taylor's experiments with pig iron handlers and ball bearing inspectors determined that fatigue would be reduced and more work would be accomplished if employees were given shorter working hours and/or rest pauses during the day in proportion to the difficulty of the work. The findings with respect to shorter work week were corroborated by the British experiments during World War I (Vernon, 1921) and are now fully accepted. Similarly, the beneficial effects of periodic rest pauses have been documented in numerous experiments. Ryan (1947) summarizes the evidence on both issues.

CRITICISMS OF TAYLOR

View of Work Motivation

A number of criticisms have been made of Taylor and his ideas. Taylor is frequently criticized for having an oversimplified view of human motivation. Although he never claimed to have a complete view (Taylor, 1911/1967), he did claim that what the worker wanted most was money. Taylor believed that men would not work or follow directions unless they attained some permanent, personal benefit from it. This assumption is fully in accord with the tenets of expectancy theory (Vroom, 1964).

What is the evidence for the power of money as motivator? The present author and his students recently analyzed all available field studies that examined the effectiveness of four motivational techniques: money, goal setting, participation in decision making, and job enrichment (Locke et al., 1980). It was found that the median performance improvement resulting from individual incentive systems was 30 percent. This figure was far higher than that for any of the other incentives. The median figure for group or plantwide incentive schemes was 18 percent, still higher than for any nonmonetary technique. These findings (which were based mainly on studies of blue collar workers) coincide with the results of numerous recent studies which indicate that extrinsic incentives such as money are more important for blue collar than for white collar employees (Locke, 1976). This should not be taken to imply that money is unimportant to white collar and professional workers.

Taylor's other major motivational technique was goal setting, that is, assigning specific tasks. A critical incident study by White and Locke (in press) found that goal setting and its equivalents (e.g., deadlines, a heavy work load) were associated with high productivity (and absence of goal setting or goal blockage with low productivity) more frequently than were any other factors. In the Locke et al. (1980) analysis referred to above, goal setting was the second most effective motivational technique. The mean improvement in performance in studies in which workers were assigned specific, challenging goals was 16 percent.

If the effects of Taylor's two main motivators, money and goals—or the task and the bonus, as he called them—are combined, there is an expected or potential performance improvement of 46 percent. The figure is very close to the figure of a 40 percent mean performance improvement obtained in studies of individual task and bonus systems (Locke et al., 1980). A survey of 453 companies (Fein, 1973) found that task and bonus systems combined yielded productivity increases even greater than 40 percent. This figure far exceeds the combined effect of two more recently promulgated motivational techniques, job enrichment and participation (Locke, et al., 1980). Although Taylor offered nothing approaching a complete theory of human motivation, one must be impressed by the effectiveness of his techniques and by the little that has been added, at least by way of effective techniques, since his time.

Social Factors

The Hawthorne studies (Roethlisberger & Dickson, 1939/1956) were supposed to represent a great enlightenment. They allegedly "discovered" the influence of human relations or social factors on worker motivation. It has been noted that most of the conclusions that the Hawthorne researchers drew from their own data were probably wrong (Franke & Kaul, 1978). But, beyond this, much of what they said was not even original. Much has been made of the studies in the Bank Wiring Observation room, which found that workers developed informal norms that led to restriction of output. It has been claimed that this discovery refuted Taylor's alledged assumption that workers respond to incentives as isolated individuals. Actually Taylor made no such assumption. In fact, he had identified exactly the same phenomenon as the Hawthorne researchers several decades earlier. He called it "systematic soldiering." (See also comments by Boddewyn, 1961.) Not only did Taylor recognize restriction of output, but one of the chief goals of scientific management was to eliminate it! He viewed soldiering as wasteful and as contrary to the interests of both management and the worker. The main difference between Taylor and Mayo (director of the Hawthorne studies) was that Taylor viewed soldiering as a problem caused by poor management and one that could and should be eliminated by scientific management; Mayo saw it as a reflection of an ineradicable human need.

Nor was Taylor unaware of the effect of social comparisons on worker morale. Discussing the need for the worker to perceive incentive systems as fair, relative to what other workers were getting, he said, "sentiment plays an important part in all our lives; and sentiment is particularly strong in the workman when he believes a direct injustice is being done him" (Copley, 1923, Vol. 2). Taylor also was aware of social factors at a deeper level. Scientific management itself involved a social revolution in that it advocated replacing management-labor conflict with cooperation.

Authoritarianism

Authoritarianism means the belief in obedience to authority simply because it is authority—that is, obedience for the sake of obedience. Such a doctrine clearly was in total contradiction to everything Taylor stood for. First and foremost he stood for obedience to facts—to reason, to proof, to experimental findings. It was not the rule of authority that he advocated but the rule of knowledge. To quote Taylor biographer F. B. Copley, "there is only one master, one boss; namely, knowledge. This, at all events, was the state of things Taylor strove to bring about in industry. He there spent his strength trying to enthrone knowledge as king" (1923, Vol. 1).

Taylor did not advocate participation in management matters by his uneducated, manual workers because they did not have the requisite knowledge to do their jobs in the one best way. For example, he shortened the working hours of ball bearing inspectors even when they opposed any such reduction (despite the promise of no loss in pay), because the evidence indicated that their work day was too long (Taylor, 1911/1967). The positive results vindicated his judgement. Similarly, most workers, when they first heard about the task and bonus system, wanted no part of it. But when Taylor (1903/1947) showed them how such a system would actually benefit them (sometimes, to be sure, accompanied by pressures) most embraced it enthusiastically and performed far better as a result. Taylor was not averse to suggestions from the workers. He wrote, "Every encouragement . . . should be given to him to suggest improvements in methods and in implements" (1911/1967). (See also Gilbreth, 1914/1973.) Fisher quotes Copley on this issue as follows: "If you could prove that yours was the best way, then he would adopt your way and feel very much obliged to you. Frequently he took humble doses of his own imperious medicine" (1925/1976).

Specialization of Labor

There is little doubt that Taylor emphasized maximum specialization, not only for workers but for foremen (e.g., functional foremanship) and managers as well. His argument was the traditional one, that specialization decreases learning time and increases competence and skill. To evaluate the criticism that Taylor overemphasized specialization one must ask: How much emphasis is overemphasis?

Advocates of job enrichment have argued with some validity that extreme specialization leads to boredom and low morale and lack of work motivation due to underutilized mental capacity. However, it should be noted that Taylor always argued for a matching of men to jobs in accordance with their capacities. People who do jobs that require very little mental capacity should be people who have very little mental capacity (Taylor, 1903/1947). Those with more capacity should have more complex tasks to perform (e.g., by being promoted when they master the simple tasks). See Gilbreth (1914/1973) and Taylor (1912/1970a). In this respect Taylor might very well approve of individualized job enrichment, although, as noted earlier, its effects on performance may be limited. The present author does not agree, however, with Drucker's (1976) claim that Taylor anticipated Herzberg's theory.

There is a potential benefit of job enrichment (e.g., multicrafting and modular working arrangements), however, that Taylor did not foresee. There are fewer and fewer jobs in existence today that stay unchanged for long periods of time. If such jobs exist, they eventually are automated. People are more versatile than machines precisely because of their greater flexibility and adaptability. In times of rapid technological change, such as the present, spending months training a worker for one narrow specialty would not be very cost-efficient. It is more practical to have each worker master several different jobs and to work each day or hour where they are most needed.

With respect to supervision, Taylor's concept of functional foremanship clearly has not been accepted and probably is not very practical.

Men as Machines

The criticism that Taylor's system treated men as machines is related to the previous one. It usually refers to scientific management's requirement of complete uniformity for a given job with respect to the tools and motions used by the workmen (the one best way). As noted earlier, Taylor was not against the workers making suggestions for improvements, provided they first mastered the best known methods. Taylor's well-chosen example of this principle was that of training a surgeon: "he is quickly given the very best knowledge of his predecessors [then] . . . he is able to use his own originality and ingenuity to make *real additions to the world's knowledge, instead of reinventing things which are old*" (1911/1967). The alternative to treating men as machines in the above sense was the prescientific method of management, which allowed men to choose tools and methods based on personal opinions and feelings rather than on knowledge.

It often is forgotten that standardization included the redesign of machines and equipment in order to enable men to become more skilled at the tasks they performed. Taylor applied this principle as much to himself as to others. His unique modifications of the tennis racket and the golf putter for his own use are cases in point. (Both items are on display at the Stevens Institute of Technology.) As noted earlier, he did not force people to fit existing equipment. He, and the Gilbreths, (re-)designed equipment to fit people. It might be more accurate to say that Taylor, rather than treating men as machines, helped to develop the science of integrating men with machines.

Exploitation of the Workers

During Taylor's lifetime, socialist Upton Sinclair and others claimed that Taylor's system was exploitative because, although under scientific management the worker might improve his productivity by around 100 percent, his pay was generally increased by a lesser amount. In fairness, they argued, the pay increase should match the productivity increase.

Taylor easily refuted this argument (Fisher, 1925/1976; Copley, 1923, Vol. 1). He pointed out, for example, that the increase in productivity was not caused by the worker only, but also by management; it was management who discovered the better techniques and designed the new tools, at some cost to themselves. Thus they deserved some of the benefits as well (Taylor, 1911/1967).

Ironically, Lenin, the self-proclaimed enemy of so-called "capitalist exploitation," himself strongly advocated the application of scientific management to Russian industry in order to help build socialism. However, socialist inefficiency, hostility to capitalist ideas, and resistance to change prevented the application of virtually all scientific management techniques in Russia except for the Gantt chart (Wren, 1980). The Soviets, however, may have been influenced by the Polish manager and theorist Karol Adamiecki, who developed his own scientific management theory independently of Taylor (Wesolowski, 1978).

Antiunionism

The criticism that Taylor was antiunion is true in only one sense. Taylor foresaw no need for unions once scientific management was properly established, especially because he saw the interests of management and labor as fundamentally the same (Copley, 1925/1976). It is worth noting in this respect that companies that are known for treating their employees well, such as IBM, do not have unions. The belief that unions were unnecessary under the proper type of management did not indicate lack of concern for employee welfare. The leaders of the scientific management movement, including Taylor, showed great concern about the effects of company policies on employee well-being (Sheldon, 1924/1976). For example, they were constantly preoccupied with eliminating or reducing fatigue. This benevolence, however, did not always characterize the followers of Taylor, who often tried to shortcut the introduction of his methods and engaged in rate-cutting and other deceptive practices.

Dishonesty

The strongest condemnations of Taylor, specifically of Taylor's character, have come in two recent articles (Wrege & Perroni, 1974; Wrege & Stotka, 1978). The first asserts that Taylor lied about the conduct of the famous pig iron handling experiments at Bethlehem Steel, and the second claims that Taylor plagiarized most of his ***Principles of Scientific Management*** from a colleague, Morris L. Cooke.

As for the pig iron experiments, it seems clear from Wrege and Perroni (1974) that Taylor did stress different things in the three reports that appeared in his writings. However, these descriptions were *not* contradictory to one another; they differed only in terms of emphasis and in the amount of detail presented. This in itself does not constitute dishonesty. Taylor apparently was in error as to certain details (e.g., the amount of tonnage of iron involved), but this could have involved errors of memory rather than deliberate deception. Nor do these details change the thread of his arguments.

Wrege and Perroni also claim that Schmidt (actual name: Henry Knolle) was not selected scientifically for the job of pig iron handling as claimed, but was simply the only worker who stuck with the task from the beginning to the end of the introductory period. This claim would appear to be true unless James Gillespie and Hartley Wolle, who conducted most of the research, omitted pertinent information in their report. However, if one accepts the idea that by a "first class" workman Taylor meant one who was not just capable but also highly motivated, then the choice of Schmidt was not inconsistent with Taylor's philosophy.

In addition, Wrege and Perroni could find no evidence that local papers had opposed Taylor's experiments as he had claimed. However, it is possible that Taylor was referring to some other paper or papers. Wrege and Perroni do not indicate whether the papers they looked at were the only ones published in the Bethlehem area or surrounding areas at that time.

Werge and Perroni argue further that Taylor never acknowledged that his "laws of heavy laboring" were based on the work of "two extraordinary workers" (1974). However in ***Principles of Scientific Management,*** Taylor clearly states that "*a first class laborer,* suited to such work as handling pig iron could be under load only 42 percent of the day and must be free from load 58 percent of the day" (1911/1967, italics added). In short, these laws were specifically *for* extraordinary workers.

Wrege and Perroni claim that Taylor lied about giving the workers rest pauses, because all of the rest periods referred to involved only the return walk after loading the pig iron rather than an actual seated or motionless rest period. However, if one reads Taylor's ***Principles*** carefully, one notes that he specifically described his laws of heavy laboring in terms of how much of the time the worker can be "under load" (1911/1967). This implies that the return walk was the part not under load. Furthermore, near the end of footnote 1, Taylor states, "Practically the men were made to take a rest, generally by sitting down, after loading ten to twenty pigs. *This rest* *was in addition to the time which it took them to walk back from the car to the pile*" (1911/1967, italics added). No evidence in Wrege and Perroni's (1974) paper contradicts this assertion; nor do they even mention it.

As to the Wrege and Stotka (1978) claim that Taylor plagiarized most of his ***Principles*** from a manuscript written by a colleague, Morris Cooke, several facts should be noted. First, Cooke's manuscript was based on a talk written and presented by Taylor himself. Apparently Cooke added to it, but the source of the additional material is not actually known; it could have been from other talks by or discussions with Taylor. Cooke himself gave Taylor credit for this allegedly plagiarized material (Wrege & Stotka, 1978). Fry argues, "It is ludicrous to accuse Taylor of plagiarizing Cooke if in fact Cooke's material was based on Taylor's own talks" (1976). Second, Taylor published ***Principles*** with Cooke's full knowledge and apparent consent. Third, Taylor offered Cooke all the royalties lest his book reduce the sales of a similar book Cooke planned to author himself. All of this is hardly consistent with Wrege and Stotka's implication that Taylor was a dishonest exploiter. Actually, the reasons why Cooke agreed to let Taylor be sole author of the manuscript are not known. At most Taylor can be accused of lack of graciousness due to his failure to acknowledge Cooke's editorial work. It also is puzzling why, if Cooke actually wrote most of ***Principles,*** Wrege, Perroni, and Stotka did not accuse Cooke as well as Taylor of dishonesty in reporting the pig iron experiments.

Wrege and Perroni (1974) also accuse Taylor of not giving credit to Gillespie and Wolle for their work on the Bethlehem studies. Although Taylor did not acknowledge in print every assistant who ever worked with him, in ***Principles*** he did acknowledge his indebtedness to many colleagues, including, Barth, Gilbreth, Gantt, and Thompson. He also used the term "we" when describing the Bethlehem experiments. Thus he was clearly not in the habit of taking all credit for himself, as Wrege and Stotka (1978) charge. Again, however, a footnote acknowledging the work of Gillespie and Wolle would have been appropriate.

In the present author's opinion, not only is the evidence that Taylor was dishonest far from conclusive, it is virtually nonexistent. On the grounds of practicality alone, it seems doubtful that Taylor, who worked and performed experiments with so many different people, would deliberately attempt to distort what was done or who did it and thus leave himself open to exposure by any one of them.

CONCLUSION

With respect to the issues of a scientific approach to management and the techniques of time and motion study, standardization, goal setting plus work measurement and feedback, money as a motivator, management's responsibility for training, scientific selection, the shortened work week, and rest pauses, Taylor's views not only were essentially correct but they have been well accepted by management. With respect to the issues of management-labor relations and individualized work, Taylor probably was only partially correct, and he has been only partially accepted. . . .

With respect to criticisms, the accusations regarding the following points are predominantly or wholly false: Taylor's inadequate model of worker motivation, his ignorance of social factors, his authoritarianism, his treatment of men as machines, his exploitation of workers, his antiunionism, and his personal dishonesty. Several of them verge on the preposterous. The accusation of overspecialization seems partly but not totally justified. . . .

Considering that it has been over 65 years since Taylor's death and that a knowledge explosion has taken place during these years, Taylor's track record is remarkable. The point is not, as is often claimed, that he was "right in the context of his time" but is now outdated, but that *most of his insights are still valid today.* The present author agrees with those who consider Taylor a genius (Johnson, 1980). His achievements are all the more admirable because, although Taylor was highly intelligent, his discoveries were not made through sudden, brilliant insights but through sheer hard work. His metal-cutting experiments, for example, spanned a period of 26 years (Taylor, 1912/1970a)!

Drucker (1976) claims that Taylor had as much impact on the modern world as Karl Marx and Sigmund Freud. This may be true in that Taylor's influence was certainly worldwide and has endured long after his death (Wren, 1979). Of the three, however, the present author considers Taylor's ideas to be by far the most objectively valid. But the historical figure that Taylor most reminds one of is Thomas Edison (Runes, 1948)—in his systematic style of research, his dogged persistence, his emphasis on the useful, his thirst for knowledge, and in his dedication to truth.

REFERENCES

Bartlem, C. S., & Locke, E. A. The Coch and French study: A critique and reinterpretation. *Human Relations,* 1981. 34. 555-566.

Boddewyn, J. Frederick Winslow Taylor revisited. *Academy of Management Journal,* 1961, 4, 100-107

Carey, A. The Hawthorne studies: A radical criticism. *American Sociological Review,* 1967, 32, 403-416.

Copley, F. B. *Frederick W. Taylor: Father of scientific management* (2 Vols.). New York: Harper & Row, 1923,

Copley, F. B. Taylor and trade unions. In D. DelMar & R. D. Collins (Eds.), *Classics in scientific management.* University, Ala.: University of Alabama Press, 1976, 52-56. (Originally published, 1925.)

Drucker, P. F. *The practice of management.* New York: Harper, 1954.

Drucker, P. F. The coming rediscovery of scientific management. *Conference Board Record,* 1976, 13 (6), 23-27.

Fein, M. Work measurement and wage incentives, *Industrial Engineering,* 1973, 5, 49-51.

Fein, M. An alternative to traditional managing. Unpublished manuscript, 1977.

Fisher, I. Scientific management made clear. In D. DelMar & R. D. Collins (Eds.), *Classics in scientific management.* University, Ala.: University of Alabama Press, 1976, 154-193. (Originally published, 1925.)

Franke, R. H., & Kaul, J. D. The Hawthorne experiments: First statistical interpretation. *American Sociological Review,* 1978, 43, 623-643.

Frost, C. F., Wakeley, J. H., & Ruh, R. A. *The Scanlon plan for organization development: Identity, participation, and equity,* East Lansing: Michigan State University Press, 1974.

Fry, L. W. The maligned F. W. Taylor: A reply to his many critics. *Academy of Management Review,* 1976, 1 (30), 124-139.

Gilbreth, F. B. Science in management for the one best way to do work. In H. F. Merrill (Ed.), *Classics in management.* New York: American Management Association, 1970, 217-263. (Originally published, 1923.)

Gilbreth, F. B. *Primer of scientific management.* Easton, Pa.: Hive Publishing Co., 1973. (Originally published, 1914.)

Greenwood, R. Management by objectives: As developed by Peter F. Drucker assisted by General Electric's management consultation services. Paper presented at the Academy of Management meetings, 1980, Detroit.

Hall, J. Decisions, decisions, decisions. *Psychology Today,* 1971, 5 (6), 51ff.

Janis, I. *Victims of groupthink.* Boston: Houghton Mifflin, 1972.

Johnson, M. J. Fred Taylor '83: Giant of non-repute. *Stevens Indicator,* 1980, 97 (2), 4-8.

Kendall, H. P. A decade's development in management trends and results of scientific management. In D. DelMar & R. D. Collins (Eds.), *Classics in scientific management.* University, Ala.: University of Alabama Press, 1976, 118-133. (Originally published, 1924.)

Latané, B., Williams, K., & Harkins, S. Social loafing. *Psychology Today,* 1979, 13 (4), 104ff.

Latham, G. P., & Dossett, D. L. Designing incentive plans for unionized employees: A comparison of continuous and variable ratio reinforcement schedules. *Personnel Psychology,* 1978, 31, 47-61.

Lawler, E. E. *Pay and organizational effectiveness: A psychological view.* New York: McGraw-Hill, 1971.

Lawler, E. E. Pay, participation and organization change. In E. L. Cass & F. G. Zimmer (Eds.), *Man and work in society.* New York: Van Nostrand Rienhold, 1975, 137-149.

Locke, E. A. Toward a theory of task motivation and incentives. *Organizational Behavior and Human Performance,* 1968, 3, 157-189.

Locke, E. A. Personnel attitudes and motivation. *Annual Review of Psychology,* 1975, 26, 457-480.

Locke, E. A. The nature and causes of job satisfaction. In M. D. Dunnette (Ed.), *Handbook of industrial and organizational psychology.* Chicago: Rand McNally, 1976, 1297-1349.

Locke, E. A. The myths of behavior mod in organizations. *Academy of Management Review,* 1977, 2, 543-553.

Locke, E. A. The ubiquity of the technique of goal setting in theories of and approaches to employee motivation. *Academy of Management Review,* 1978, 3, 594-601.

Locke, E. A., Cartledge, N., & Koeppel, J. Motivational effects of knowledge of results: A goal-setting phenomenon? *Psychological Bulletin,* 1968, 70, 474-485.

Locke, E. A., Shaw, K. N., Saari, L. M., & Latham, G. P. Goal setting and task performance: 1969-1980. *Psychological Bulletin,* 1981, 90, 125-152.

Locke, E. A., Feren, D. B., McCaleb, V. M., Shaw, K. M., & Denny, A. T. The relative effectiveness of four methods of motivating employee performance. In K. Duncan, M. Gruneberg, & D. Wallis (Eds.), *Changes in working life.* Chichester, England: Wiley, 1980, 363-387.

Munsterberg, H. *Psychology and industrial efficiency.* Boston: Houghton Mifflin, 1913.

Odiorne, G. S. MBO: A backward glance. *Business Horizons,* October 1978, 14-24.

Roethlisberger, F. J., & Dickson, W. J. *Management and the worker.* Cambridge, Mass.: Harvard University Press, 1956. (Originally published, 1939.)

Runes, D. D. (Ed.). *The diary and sundry observations of Thomas Alva Edison.* New York: Philosophical Library, 1948.

Ryan, T. A. *Work and effort.* New York: Ronald, 1947.

Sheldon, O. Taylor the creative leader. In D. DelMar & R. D. Collins (Eds.), *Classics in scientific management.*

University, Ala.: University of Alabama Press, 1976, 35-51. (Originally published, 1924.)

Sykes, A. J. M. Economic interest and the Hawthorne researchers. *Human Relations,* 1965, 18, 253-263.

Taylor, F. W. *Shop management* (published as part of *Scientific management*). New York: Harper, 1947. (Originally published, 1903.)

Taylor, F. W. *The principles of scientific managment.* New York: Norton, 1967. (Originally published, 1911.)

Taylor, F. W. Time study, piece work, and the first-class man. In H. F. Merrill (Ed.), *Classics in management.* New York: American Management Association, 1970, 57-66. (Originally published, 1903.)

Taylor, F. W. The principles of scientific management. In H. F. Merrill (Ed.), *Classics in management.* New York: American Management Association, 1970a. (Originally published, 1912.)

Taylor, F. W. What is scientific management? In H. G. Merrill (Ed.), *Classics in management.* New York: American Management Association, 1970b, 67-71. (Original testimony given, 1912.)

Taylor, F. W. Profit sharing. In D. DelMar & R. D. Collins (Eds.), *Classics in scientific management.* University, Ala.: University of Alabama Press, 1976, 17-20. (Originally written, 1912.)

Vernon, H. N. *Industrial fatigue and efficiency.* New York: Dutton, 1921.

Vough, C. F. *Tapping the human resource.* New York: Wiley, 1964.

Vroom, V. *Work and motivation.* New York: Wiley, 1969.

Walton, R. E. Work innovations at Topeka: After six years. *Journal of Applied Behavioral Science,* 1977, 13 (3), 422-433.

Wesolowski, Z. P. The Polish contribution to the development of scientific management. *Proceedings of the Academy of Management, 1978.*

White, F., & Locke, E. A. Perceived determinants of high and low productivity in three occupational groups: A critical incident study. *Journal of Management Studies,* in press.

Wrege, C. D., & Perroni, A. G. Taylor's pig-tale: A historical analysis of Frederick W. Taylor's pig-iron experiments. *Academy of Management Journal,* 1974, 17, 6-27.

Wrege, C. D., & Stotka, A. M. Cooke creates a classic: The story behind F. W. Taylor's principles of scientific management. *Academy of Management Review,* 1978, 3, 736-749.

Wren, D. A. *The evolution of management thought* (2nd ed.). New York: Wiley, 1979.

Wren, D. A. Scientific management in the U.S.S.R., with particular reference to the contribution of Walter N. Polakov. *Academy of Management Review,* 1980, 5, 1-11.

Stephen Wood and John Kelly (essay date 1982)

SOURCE: "Taylorism, Responsible Autonomy and Management Strategy," in *On Work: Historical, Comparative and Theoretical Approaches,* edited by R. E. Paul, Basil Blackwell, 1988, pp. 173-89.

[*In the following essay, originally published in 1982, Wood and Kelly argue in favor of a conservative reading and application of Taylor's method, keeping in mind that Taylor's principles may not be universally practical or desirable.*]

A curious feature of much previous discussion of Braverman's *Labor and Monopoly Capitalism* (1974) has been a marked tendency to portray capitalist management as virtually omniscient. The implementation of management strategy is therefore taken to be unproblematic. By equating Taylorism with capitalist management in its essence, Braverman is able to depict post-Taylorist developments as either complementary or irrelevant; anti-Taylorist strategies are inconceivable.

By contrast, Friedman (1977a,b) and R. Edwards (1979) have attempted to argue for the existence and importance of such alternatives. Friedman in particular has argued that it is precisely because of resistance to direct control that in certain situations managements have adopted less restrictive systems, involving the concession of 'responsible autonomy'. While Edwards lays equal stress on the need for managements to adapt to worker resistance, his argument rests as much on the reasons for the extensive non-implementation of Taylorism as on the problems created by its utilization. It was resisted by workers but was also not popular with managers and was not adopted in any general fashion. Those managements who adopted it did so in a piecemeal way; in short it was a failed experiment.

Despite this, Edwards concludes that managements did learn from and adopt some of the underlying ideas of Taylorism, such as the need to wrest control of production knowledge from workers or to define jobs in terms of output and to link this with pay, and these features were taken up and have endured. Any conclusion about the implementation and efficacy of Taylorism depends in part on how broadly it is defined at the outset. The broader one's definition of Taylorism, the more one sees it as all pervasive, as Braverman appears to regard it, while a narrower definition suggests a lesser degree of influence (cf. Palmer, 1975). But there is equally the danger that in reacting to Braverman's over-reliance on Taylorism we fall into the trap of minimizing its importance. In this [essay] we shall attempt to show that one way in which these problems may be circumvented is through a recognition of the limits and constraints of Taylorism. This involves more than simply emphasizing worker or managerial resistance to Taylorism: it also requires a reconsideration of the nature of Taylorism in order to clarify its limitations. This [essay] will thus fall into three sections. The first deals with Braverman's treatment of Taylorism; the second outlines certain important but neglected features of Taylorism; and the third concludes by discussing the question of alternatives to Taylorism.

BRAVERMAN: TAYLORISM AS THE QUINTESSENCE OF CAPITALIST MANAGEMENT

According to Braverman, *all* labour processes require some degree of coordination, in so far as they are based on division of labour. In modes of production based on social classes there also arises the necessity for control, a need which is far more thorough and more comprehensive under capitalism because of its dynamic character, evidenced by the constant drive to accumulate. Capitalism is also distinguished, however, by formally free labour—workers may dispose of their own labour power as they wish—and this, according to Braverman, further imparts to capitalist production an unusually antagonistic character.

These features of capitalism resulted, in Braverman's view, in constant attempts throughout the nineteenth century to develop a specifically capitalist mode of management that would exercise control over the labour process. Braverman sees the domestic, sub-contracting and putting-out systems as imperfect approximations to Taylorism, 'the specifically capitalist mode of management'. Detailed control over the labour process at the turn of the century was exercised, in Taylor's (and Braverman's) view, not by management but by skilled workers, who could and did thereby obstruct capitalist innovation and rationalization.

Deskilling originated historically in the management drive against such skilled workers, but the tendency is found throughout all sectors of the economy and continues well beyond the alleged decline of traditional craft work. This is because deskilling allows increased capitalist control over production, since opposed centres of knowledge are destroyed and the labour process is fragmented. It also permits, on the Babbage (1971) principle, a considerable cheapening of labour and an increased rate of exploitation.

For Braverman, Taylorism and its assumptions 'reflect nothing more than the outlook of the capitalist with regard to the conditions of production' (1974), because it articulates the need to control labour, provides means (in the form of time-and-motion study and other techniques) for dispossessing workers of their knowledge of production and thereby provides management with the basis on which to *control* the labour process. Braverman describes Taylorism in the more abstract terms of three principles: the rendering of the labour process independent of craft, tradition or workers' knowledge, and their replacement with experiments (or science); the separation of conception from execution; and the use of the managerial monopoly over knowledge to control the labour process in detail. Post-Taylorist developments in management are seen as complementary to Taylorism ('human relations'), dismissed as inconsequential (for example, job redesign) or ignored (for example, productivity bargaining). Since management under capitalism is taken to have reached its purest expression in Taylorism, no further development of an anti-Taylorism character is possible. Braverman regards the human relations movement simply as a means for adjusting workers to the deleterious consequences of Taylorism.

The key to Braverman's assessment of Taylorism and its significance lies in his structuralist conception of capitalism as a law-governed system whose laws inevitably work themselves out without contradiction (Elger and Schwarz, 1980; Burawoy, 1978). For neither the capitalist mode of production itself nor the practices derived (analytically) from it, are treated as potentially contradictory. There is no notion of capitalist development itself issuing in pre-socialist forms, such as rudimentary planning, the growing interdependence of enterprises and the increasing democratization of work. Braverman's concept of control is also far from adequate, even in his own terms. His inflation of the control or autonomy exercised by pre-Taylorian craftsmen has been commented upon elsewhere but there is another difficulty, which is that he works implicitly with a zero-sum concept of control and its bases, particularly knowledge. Thus if management investigates, and acquires, knowledge of a production process, the workers are supposed either to lose this knowledge or to be incapable of regaining it, however partially. In other words, Braverman conflates acquisition of knowledge with monopoly of knowledge and examines control historically in terms of a simple shift from worker to employer control (see also Burawoy, 1978). He cannot, then recognize different modes of managerial control, post-Taylor, and as we have said must treat Taylorism as the highest form of management under capitalism and as incapable of being transcended.

Against Braverman's conception of a working class dominated by the laws of capitalism and its consequences has been counterposed worker resistance and struggle. This has been seen by many writers as a methodological corrective, but has also been used (Friedman 1977a) as the ground from which to explain the limits of management control as well as major changes in the means and relations of production. Yet the 'class struggle' critique of Braverman also remains within the Taylorist problematic of control. It does so by assigning great theoretical and empirical significance to the potential for working-class organization and struggle to evade full capitalist control of the labour process and thereby to thwart capitalist objectives. This tendency to inflate control to the point at which it becomes the central problem of capitalist management is at variance with most analyses of capitalism, including that of Marx, which emphasize the pursuit of profit as the directing aim of capitalist management.

But this is not all, because even in Marxist terms surplus value has not only to be *produced* but also to be *realized.* Control of the labour process by capital, the maximum rate of extraction of surplus value (consistent with continued accumulation and labour supply) and the realization of surplus value were analysed by Marx as integral but separate moments in capitalist production. This means that it is possible for contradictions to arise between any of these moments. Labour exploitation may be relatively high but control weak, as may be the case with skilled craft workers; or realization of surplus value may be constrained by structural or other limits to its production, such as output regulation.

THE DEVELOPMENT OF TAYLOR'S SCIENTIFIC MANAGEMENT

While Braverman is correct to emphasize the significance of the labour process (Elger, 1979), and of Taylorism within that process, it should also be recognized that management in general does not revolve simply around labour. Taylorism is very much more complex than Braverman suggests, and although it has always centred on labour productivity, there was a growing emphasis throughout Taylor's work on the technical preconditions for raising it, such as adequate materials flow and machine maintenance, and implicitly on the problems of implementing his proposals in the face of worker suspicion or hostility. The initial and central concern was 'task management'—that is, the determination of possible levels of performance (given improved methods and so on) and the search for ways of securing these levels as effectively as possible. Hence Taylor emphasized the importance of financial incentives and the pay-performance link and later came to stress the importance of assigned work quotas for individual workers.

As Braverman notes, Taylor's system arose from his observations of output regulation by workers, a practice that was adopted as a defence against rate cutting and a possible loss of jobs as a result of an increase in productivity. For its part, management was compelled to resort to rate cutting to increase its exploitation of labour, because it lacked the detailed knowledge of production required to raise productivity. It was this knowledge which Taylor set out to acquire through time-and-motion study, though he soon came to realize that if labour productivity was to be raised, then simultaneous improvements had to be effected in machine maintenance, materials and tools supply, work flow and detailed supervision (F. W. Taylor, 1919).

Taylor's conception of control, however, occupies an ambivalent position within his work, a fact obscured by Braverman's abstract and monolithic account of a 'Taylorism' that was free of contradiction and that underwent no development. In **'A Piece-Rate System,'** Taylor's second published work, there was very little emphasis on control. At that stage Taylor still worked within a classical economics conception of the employment relationship as an economic exchange. Time-and-motion study would be accepted because workers would realize that with increased productivity would come increased wages. His own experiences at Midvale and Bethlehem Steel eventually convinced him that economic interest was insufficient to promote change, and that it was necessary to use the knowledge gathered through the 'scientific' investigation of production to control the labour process. Thus in 1906 Taylor could write of the slide rule used to codify and apply knowledge of machining:

> The gain from these slide rules is far greater than that of all the other improvements combined, because it accomplishes the original object, for which in 1880 the experiments were started; i.e. that of taking the control of the machine-shop out of the hands of the many workmen, and placing it completely in the hands of the management, thus superseding 'rule of thumb' by scientific control. (Taylor, 1906).

This much quoted statement is also much misunderstood, by Braverman and others. In short, they argue that if management does in fact acquire such knowledge of production, then workers either lose it or are unable to regain it. Yet knowledge is not a commodity that can be 'lost' in this manner, and Braverman has conflated the acquisition of knowledge with its monopoly (Burawoy, 1978). Even after time-and-motion study craft wrokers continue to possess their knowledge; they 'simply' lose the advantage of management ignorance. On this basis craft workers have continued to resist deskilling and have retained important positions in many branches of production (see Brown, 1977).

It is possible that Taylor himself recognized this problem, even if only dimly, because by 1912, in his Testimony to the House Committee, he was stressing heavily the necessity for a 'mental revolution' among workers and managers. In view of the American Federation of Labour's campaign against Taylorism (which culminated in the House Committee hearing) and the strike in the previous year at the Watertown Arsenal against time-and-motion study (Aitken, 1960; Nadworny, 1955), it is tempting to dismiss the 'mental revolution' as a public relations exercise designed to allay public hostility and suspicion. A more plausible interpretation, in the light of Taylor's experiences and the hostility of both employers and unions, was that Taylor was beginning to articulate the preconditions for the implementation of his techniques. It was the same issue which led his associates, Cooke and Valentine, to the very different conclusion that Taylorism could only be implemented with trade-union co-operation in a framework of 'industrial democracy' (Haber, 1964, ch. 3; Nadworny, 1955, ch. 5).

Implicit in these observations is a distinction between techniques—time-and-motion study, control of work flow, stores inventories—and the strategy required for their implementation. For Taylor the introduction of scientific management did not require union co-operation and would in time render unions superfluous. It was to be introduced by a paternalistic but autocratic management which was itself subject to Taylorist principles. Managers would therefore demonstrate that their decisions were subject to the same discipline as the workers, namely, the authority of science, but in practice Taylor protested in 1912 that 'nine-tenths' of the problems of introducing his system could be laid at management's door. A key component of the strategy was individualism. Workers were to be paid by their individual performance; grievances and suggestions were to be received only from individuals; and the labour process, as far as possible, was to be composed of individualized work roles (Kelly, 1982). As the embodiment of collectivism, unions occupied no place in Taylor's world.

The techniques/strategy distinction is absent from Braverman because he assumes its implementation to be unproblematic. In fact, Taylorist techniques have been implemented within a number of quite different strategic frameworks. In the Japanese context Taylor's emphasis on managerial control of workers and of work processes harmonized well with the paternalistic structures of large industrial organizations and with their drive to modernize Japan and to attack the arbitrary role of owners (Nakase, 1979; Okuda, 1972). Taylor's works were quickly translated into Japanese and sold in enormous quantities, and the Japanese branch of the Taylor Society was one of the first to be formed. It was the larger Japanese organizations, including government bodies and foreign companies inside Japan, that pioneered Taylorism. This strategy coexisted throughout the 1920s both with welfare strategies which constituted the foundation of the life-long employment security system and with collective bargaining and joint consultation with trade unions. Taylorism as such began to decline during the Depression, when workers started to resist it more strongly and it began to be located within nationalist discourse as a foreign ideology alien to Japanese culture.

In Britain, by contrast, the existence of strong union organization in the major branches of production limited the spread of time-and-motion study. Where piece rates were introduced on the basis of such study, as in the car industry, they were often the subject of bargaining and regulated by mutuality clauses (limiting unilateral management changes) rather than by 'science' (Friedman, 1977b; Brown, 1977).

There was also a very intense debate on the nature of Taylorism and its applicability to a socialist mode of production in the early Soviet Union. Lenin's 1914 moral critique of Taylorism's oppression and exploitation of the workers (Lenin, 1965a) and its contrast with the economic anarchy outside the enterprise was replaced with a quite different view in 1918. Writing during the Civil War, at a time of serious economic dislocation, Lenin stressed the importance of using the 'scientific' components of Taylorism, such as time-and-motion study and planned work flow, as opposed to its 'bourgeois' ideological elements, principally intensification of labour. Having said this, Lenin introduced a critical ambiguity into his view by asserting that the overall intensity of labour in Russia was low by international standards and would have to be raised (Lenin, 1965b).

The ensuing debate in the USSR centred on the question of labour intensification, with one group (the Council on Scientific Management) arguing it was unnecessary and counter-productive, while the eventually successful Gastev and his supporters argued for the introduction of piecework and method study and increased labour intensity (Bailes, 1977; Traub, 1978). Taylorism also found favour in Fascist Italy, where it was often introduced in a very authoritarian manner and, instead of raising wages and reducing working hours, was used to achieve precisely the reverse (by contrast with the Soviet Union, where wages did increase in some sectors under piecework) (Carr, 1966; Rollier, 1979). What perhaps unites these otherwise distinct applications of Taylorism is, as Maier (1970) suggests, a radical, technocratic opposition to liberal capitalism. Equally, the insistence in Taylorism on the non-zero-sum basis of conflict, of the possibility of raising wages and profits simultaneously, appealed to the national, anti-class views of Fascism and the unitarist ideology of some American employers in the 1920s.

For many writers evidence of the diffusion of Taylorism emerges from its equation with enhanced division of labour. Braverman, as well as Littler (1978), argues that 'Taylorism' entails a 'dynamic of deskilling' because of its insistence on the division between conception and execution and its implicit acceptance of the Babbage principle. In 1835 Babbage wrote: 'The manufacturer, by dividing the work to be executed into different processes, each requiring different degrees of skill and of force, can purchase exactly that precise quantity of both which is necessary for each process' (Babbage, 1971). While it is undoubtedly the case that Taylorist techniques were used to further the detail division of labour, it is also true that the phenomenon was not peculiar to Taylorism and predated it by a considerable period. Division of labour was subordinated in Taylor's work to his overriding objectives: securing control over the labour process and raising the productivity of labour (Haber, 1964; Kelly, 1982).

DISTINGUISHING MANAGEMENT STRATEGIES

Given the importance of the context in which Taylorism is implemented and of avoiding the conflation of scientific management with specific techniques, it is necessary to develop modes of discussing strategies which are not rooted in Taylorism. The most recent attempt at such discussion is that of Friedman (1977a, 1977b, 1978). His attempt to delineate different managerial strategies is an important corrective to Braverman's view that one can isolate an invariant and essentially capitalist managerial practice, namely, Taylorism. Equally, Friedman implicitly rejects the arguments of a number of French sociologists that contemporary efforts to 'humanize' or reorganize work through the devolution of autonomy and by other methods are merely new forms of Taylorism (see, for example, Montmollin, 1974).

Although as we shall see there is some ambiguity in Friedman's conceptualization, he seems to identify two types of strategy according to their mode of control: direct control and responsible autonomy. In the first (of which Taylorism is the clearest expression) management exercises its control directly, by means of the specification of work methods, close supervision and coercion. The second type entails the concession of elements of control, or 'responsible autonomy', to workers so that they can exercise discretion over the immediate process of production. In another formulation he argues that the direct control strategy seeks to control or suppress the variability inherent in labour power, whereas the responsible autonomy strategy seeks to exploit it and to harness it to capitalist objectives.

These two types of strategy relate to a series of specific determinants, namely, the phase of development of capitalism, the competitive conditions of the industry, the production position of groups of workers (whether central or peripheral) and the central or peripheral position of particular industries. Direct control is thought to be more effective with peripheral workers and peripheral industries and in less developed areas of capitalism.

Despite its intuitive appeal, there are a number of difficulties with this conception. First, the components of both strategies are not clearly identified. Responsible autonomy is variously described as consisting of worker discretion and commitment to capitalist objectives (a job-redesign type of practice); as counselling, improvements in social relations, the stimulation of intergroup competition, suggestion schemes and participation (a classical 'human relations' type of exercise); and as the concession of improved material benefits—high wages and incentives, job security, good fringe benefits and working conditions (Friedman, 1977a; 1977b). These practices may coincide empirically, but there are many cases where they do not, and it is thus important to be clear about the components of the posited strategy and to avoid defining strategies, or even tactics, in terms of techniques.

Equally, direct control is variously described as Taylorism (separation of conception and execution, centralization of conception and close supervision and pay incentives), and as an effort to limit the variable effects of labour power. The critical ambiguity in both conceptions (since they are related by exclusion) centres on the role of pay and pay incentives, described by Friedman as attempts both to control and to harness labour power variability (1977a; 1977b). Friedman's attempt to resolve this issue by distinguishing money piecework (where work methods remain unspecified and payment is by the piece) from time piecework (where methods are specified and payment is by time saved) seems unsatisfactory. For many contemporary pay systems fall between these two extremes, combining method specification and piece payment, and both systems reflect the attempt to control output through the pay system, rather than by the manipulation of other non-financial rewards (1977a).

Secondly, on the narrower conception of responsible autonomy (as argued especially in 1977b) which resembles forms of job redesign, Friedman is empirically incorrect to trace their origins to worker resistance or struggle, unless one wants to extend these latter terms to cover labour turnover and absenteeism. Thirdly, Friedman tends to accept at face value the theories of 'responsible autonomy' as defined in the terms of their originators and disseminators rather than subjecting them to independent and critical analysis. Thus when management theorists describe concessions of autonomy to work groups and posit a dichotomy between their practices and Taylorism (or 'direct control') Friedman accepts their arguments. He therefore fails to consider the possibility that autonomy, or control, may not be a zero-sum concept, and that management control over production may increase simultaneously with worker control over its more immediate aspects (Brighton Labour Process Group, 1977; Pignon and Querzola, 1976).

More seriously, Friedman fails to analyse the connections between responsible autonomy and direct control and to consider that certain forms of the former actually function because of classic Taylorist mechanisms and may conform to Taylorist principles. There is also a strong tendency in Friedman, as in Braverman, to treat management under capitalism principally as a control function, in which the recalcitrance of labour—class struggle—is elevated to paramount status. Yet for Marx the two principal defining features of the capitalist mode of production were that labour existed as a commodity and that the major objective of social production was the production and realization of surplus value. Although formally acknowledging these features, Friedman draws the conventional (but crude) distinction between the co-ordinating (or technical) and the authoritative functions of management: the latter is specific to capitalism while the former is 'part of any complicated economic process' (1977a). What is missing from either of these functions is the production of profit in its various modes, an activity that has been reduced to the ahistorical category of 'co-ordination'. Capitalism therefore ends up being characterized in effect specifically by control over labour and its various modes.

A further consequence of Friedman's argument is that managerial activity tends to be abstracted from tactical or strategic frameworks, incorporating finance, sales, marketing, and to be conceptualized at the level of task management, or control over directly productive activity. He assigns considerable significance to the 'product cycle' under capitalism, in which sales of a new product rise at first only slowly, accelerate and then fall off, and links this with changes in managerial strategy towards 'responsible autonomy'. Yet this useful link is not carried through into an analysis of differences *within* managements.

Finally, one can question the justification for writing of management strategy, rather than say, tactics or practices. The first concept has connotations of comprehensiveness, coherence, long-term perspectives and consciousness. Do we really want to attribute these characteristics uniformly to capitalist management, or would the latter concepts (tactics, practices) be more appropriate?

Taken overall, then, Friedman's work may provide a valuable starting-point, but his central dichotomy as formulated seems unable to support the weight that one could reasonably expect it to bear. A more elaborated conception of managerial practices must recognize shifts in principal managerial objectives. Equally, such a conception must recognize both the connections between practices and the different forms which a single practice—such as Taylorism—may assume under different conditions.

What is important here is Friedman's insistence on the theoretical significance of analysing management practices in relation to class struggle. He argues that worker-initiated schemes of shop-floor control are more likely to reflect workers' own interests than those originating with management, and while this may be true in some cases, for example Fiat as compared with Volvo, there is a further level of analysis which complicates the picture. In their transition from conception to implementation, managerial schemes are invariably modified (to differing degrees) by workers' own counter-initiatives, and it would be necessary to appreciate such modifications in any analysis of managerial practices and their consequences (Goodrich, 1975; Wood and Kelly, 1978). We must also take into account some of the contradictions generated by Taylorism and the detail division of labour under the changing circumstances of the post-war economic boom (cf. Burawoy, 1978; Elger, 1979).

LIMITS AND DEVELOPMENTS OF TAYLORISM AND DETAIL DIVISION OF LABOUR

During the economic boom after the Second World War both Taylorism and detail division of labour encountered problems, stemming in part from worker resistance but much more from structural contradictions (see Pichierri, 1978). To appreciate these contradictions, we must abandon Braverman's implicit treatment of manufacturing industry as a homogeneous sector and distinguish, for example, along the lines of Woodward (1958) mass production, batch production and continuous process industry (see also Heckscher, 1980).

The Ford moving assembly line, pioneered in the Highland Park vehicle works in 1914, was used solely for the mass production of the Model T Ford. Likewise, its extension into other car industries and into the manufacture of consumer goods such as electrical appliances was based on long production runs of a small range of products. Throughout the 1950s manufacturers of domestic appliances and of other mass-produced items expanded their product ranges in line with growing domestic and world markets (Corley, 1966). This process, however, increasingly came into conflict with the structure and limits of the assembly line. Realization of surplus value dictated that an ever-growing range of commodities be produced to meet diverse consumer 'demands'. Production of surplus value dictated that product range should be kept small to ensure long production runs and thereby to minimize production time lost because of product, parts and tools change-over (for examples, see Gowler, 1970; Kelly, 1982).

The major strategy used to resolve this contradiction was product obsolescence: this allowed old lines to be deleted from the product range (see Baran and Sweezy, 1968, ch. 5; Mandel, 1978, ch. 7). Manufacturers also attempted to reorganize distribution, either by stipulating a minimum batch size for wholesalers' orders or by allocating small orders into a 'queue' until there were sufficient orders for a single product to justify a production run. Other manufacturers tried (though unsuccessfully) to reach agreements on production swapping, whereby each of two companies would produce only one type of appliance in a particular factory and obtain other appliances through barter (Corley, 1966).

But a small number of firms reorganized production rather than distribution, either by shortening assembly lines or by abolishing them altogether. Instead of changing a long flowline every day or two in response to market fluctuations, firms could specialize in each of a number of shorter lines or single work situations on the same product, and thus reduce the frequency of product change-over. This trend was represented within management theory as an 'enrichment' of jobs—which, of course, it was, although its origins had less to do with underutilized and bored workers than with overstretched production systems.

This reversal of detail division of labour did not signify the abandonment of Taylorism. On the contrary, such transformations of assembly lines frequently led to an individualization of work roles, to the replacement of group by individual incentives and to greater management control arising out of increased worker visibility (Kelly, 1982; Coriat, 1980). These new work roles were invariably determined by Taylorist techniques—time-and-motion study—within a Taylorist strategy of individualization. At the same time, many of these instances involved simultaneous increases in both worker's control over immediate aspects of production and management control, through the greater ease of accountability of individualized work roles. If we operate with a zero-sum concept of control, as is implicit in Braverman, this feature of mass-production systems cannot be grasped.

The limits to Taylorism are revealed in a different industrial sector, that of continuous process production. Precise specification of individual work roles depends for its efficacy on a relatively predictable input of work. Where there is considerable and unpredictable variability in production, either because of variations in the raw materials (for example, in coal mining, textiles, certain chemicals) or because of variations in the production process itself (for example, in certain branches of metal manufacture and processing), the application of Taylorist techniques generates a series of 'problems' for capital. Workloads are likely to vary significantly between individuals, and with an interdependent production process some individuals or groups are likely to be under-utilized while others are kept very busy. Sudden upsurges of work are likely to strain the production system or will generate higher labour costs if a reserve pool of utility workers is employed for such emergencies (Kelly, 1977).

The significance of sociotechnical systems theory, in this context, is that it articulated this contradiction between detail division of labour and the means of production, that is, between control over the labour process and the production of surplus value, and recommended the creation of autonomous groups. Each group is assigned a series of tasks and is responsible for their distribution within the group. The results of such initiatives have been to iron out work-load inequalities through flexibility of labour and, therefore, to raise the average intensity of labour, under the influence of group pay incentive schemes. Clearly, there are instances where shortened assembly lines and 'autonomous' groups have been inaugurated in response to trade-union initiatives, as Friedman has noted. Though the examples of Fiat and Volvo involve an industrial sector which is generally highly organized throughout the world, the majority of examples of the reorganization of mass-production systems have occurred not in vehicle manufacture but in electrical engineering, a sector characterized (in the UK) by lower union density, weaker union organization and a higher proportion of women employees.

The extent to which reversals of Taylorism or of detail division of labour are responses to structural contradictions and/or class struggle is a purely empirical question and cannot be determined *a priori* on the basis of a desire to upgrade the elements of class struggle or of contradiction, so obviously neglected in Braverman.

CONCLUSIONS

Our discussion of Braverman and Friedman and our analysis of Taylorism and its limitations and contradictions clearly raise a wide range of substantive issues in the analysis of management and organization. Yet a number of key conceptual and methodological distinctions can be identified as necessary components of any analysis that aims to transcend some of the oversimplified views we have discussed.

The first point is that one cannot infer the successful implementation of a management strategy merely from its existence. In other words, the determinants of successful strategy formation are unlikely to coincide exactly with the conditions required for implementation. Taylor himself recognized the problems of implementation, even if he was unable to theorize about them effectively and could produce only the concept of a 'mental revolution' whose social determinants were not articulated.

Several writers have observed carefully the ways in which the implementation of a strategy or practice become the object of class struggle, and the best example here is that of incentive or piecework payment systems. By the more or less systematic modification of work methods and the regulation of output, workers have often been able to thwart the objectives of managerial initiatives (Roy, 1952, 1954; Lupton, 1963; Friedman, 1977a), and it has also been observed that Taylorism was implemented in the 1920s only in a piecemeal fashion (Edwards, 1979; Palmer, 1975). Once implementation is seen as problematic and uncertain, we can avoid the kind of error made by Bosquet (1972) in his assessment of increased worker participation in management decision-making. Bosquet argued that the concession of a degree of autonomy to workers would engender a desire for even greater influence and thereby precipitate an unstable and (to management) threatening process that could even call into question management's control of production. The argument is based on the premise that managerial initiatives are successfully implemented in the forms discussed by management theorists, which overlooks the problems of implementation, not to mention the ideological character of some management theory.

The second conclusion we can draw is that it is dangerous to privilege one particular area of management concern as the overriding problem in need of solution. Braverman's (1974) insistence that the problem of management can be reduced to the problem of control is true in the sense that control can never be complete and predictable. But the significance of control over labour and the labour process has to be understood in the context of management's having a series of objectives (and hence potential problems) linked with the full cycle of capitalist production. Labour supply, job performance and surplus value extraction, product sale and product markets all can and do present problems for managements. The heads of several large British corporations such as British Steel or BL are currently less concerned with control over the labour process and surplus value production than with declining markets because of the world recession (see also Mandel, 1978).

The significance of a 'labour problem' is also likely to vary over time and to be associated with the capital-labour ratio of the company or firm, and we noted that detail division of labour had thrown up different kinds of problems in mass-production, flowline industries as compared with continuous-process production (see also Heckscher, 1980; Woodward, 1958). We cannot therefore assign priority to a single factor in management strategy, whether it be labour, technology or markets, but must determine such problems empirically.

Third, the notion of 'management strategy' is itself open to question on two counts. Management, except in very small firms or at departmental level in larger firms, is unlikely to function as a homogeneous entity, united in the pursuit of a single objective. Specialization of function has also generated specialization or differentiation of interests (Crozier, 1964). Equally, the notion of strategy cannot be taken at face value, with its connotations of conscious and clearsighted formulation of means and ends. In other words, the degree to which management holds and operates a strategy has also to be determined empirically (Thurley and Wood, 1982).

Both the differentiation of management and the variations between firms suggest, as we argued before, that alternative strategies are certainly available. Taylorism, for instance, may have been appropriate under conditions of an abundant labour supply, expanding markets and weak union organization but may reach the limits of its effectiveness in different circumstances.

Overall, the thrust of this [essay] has been to argue for a more careful and more detailed study of management strategy, coupled with a sensitivity to the complexities of employing organizations, which together will enable us to transcend simplistic formulations and generalizations (Wood, 1980).

REFERENCES

Aitken, H. G. J. (1960), *Taylorism at Watertown Arsenal: Scientific Management in Action 1908-1915,* Cambridge, Mass.: Harvard University Press.

Babbage, C. (1971), *On the Economy of Machinery and Manufactures,* Fairfield, NJ: Kelley (first published 1835).

Bailes, K. E. (1977), 'Alexei Gastev and the Soviet controversy over Taylorism, 1918-24', *Soviet Studies,* vol. 29, no. 3, July, pp. 373-94.

Baran, P., and Sweezy, P. (1968), *Monopoly Capital,* Harmondsworth: Penguin.

Bendix, R., ed. (1974), *Work and Authority in Industry,* Berkeley: University of California Press.

Bosquet, M. (1972), 'The prison factory', *New Left Review,* no. 73, May-June, pp. 23-34.

Braverman, H. (1974), *Labor and Monopoly Capital,* New York: Monthly Review Press.

Brighton Labour Process Group (1977), 'The capitalist labour process', *Capital and Class,* no. 1, Spring, pp. 3-26.

Brown, G. (1977), *Sabotage: a Study in Industrial Conflict,* Nottingham: Spokesman Books.

Burawoy, M. (1978), 'Towards a Marxist theory of the labour process', *Politics and Society,* vol. 8, nos 3-4, pp. 247-312.

Carr. E. H. (1966), *The Bolshevik Revolution,* vol. 2, Harmondsworth: Penguin.

Coriat, B. (1980), 'The restructuring of the assembly line: a new economy of time and control', *Capital and Class,* no. 11, Summer, pp. 34-43.

Corley, T. A. (1966), *Domestic Electrical Appliances,* London: Jonathan Cape.

Crozier, M. (1964), *The Bureaucratic Phenomenon,* London: Tavistock.

Drucker, P. (1976), 'The coming rediscovery of scientific management', *Conference Board Record,* vol. 13, no. 6. pp. 23-7.

Edwards, R. (1979), *Contested Terrain,* London: Heinemann.

Elger, A. (1979), 'Valorisation and deskilling—a critique of Braverman', *Capital and Class,* no. 7, Spring, pp. 58-99.

Elger, A., and Schwarz, B. (1980), 'Monopoly capitalism and the impact of Taylorism: notes on Lenin, Gramsci, Braverman and Sohn-Rethel', in T. Nichols (ed.), *Capital and Labour: A Marxist Primer,* London: Fontana, pp. 358-69.

Fridenson, P. (1978), 'Corporate policy, rationalisation and the labour force: French experiences in international comparison; 1900 to 1929', paper given at Nuffield Deskilling Conference, Windsor.

Friedman, A. (1977a), *Industry and Labour,* London: Macmillan.

Friedman, A. (1977b), 'Responsible autonomy versus direct control over the labour process', *Capital and Class,* no. 1, Spring, pp. 43-57.

Friedman, A. (1978), 'Worker resistance and Marxian analysis of the capitalist labour process', paper given at Nuffield Deskilling Conference, Windsor.

Goodrich, C. L. (1975), *The Frontier of Control,* London: Pluto Press (first published 1920).

Gowler, D. (1970), 'Sociocultural influences on the operation of a wage-payment system: an exploratory case study', in D. Robinson (ed.), *Local Labour Markets and Wage Structures,* London: Gower, pp. 100-26.

Haber, S. (1964). *Efficiency and Uplift: Scientific Management in the Progressive Era,* Chicago: University of Chicago Press.

Heckscher, C. (1980), 'Worker participation and management control', *Journal of Social Reconstruction,* vol. 1, no. 1, pp. 77-102.

Kelly, J. E. (1977), 'Scientific management and work "humanisation"', paper read at BSA Industrial Sociology Group Conference, London School of Economics and Political Science.

Kelly, J. E. (1982), *Scientific Management, Job Redesign and Work Performance,* New York: Academic Press.

Lenin, V. I. (1965a), 'Taylorism: man's enslavement to the machine' (first published 1914), in V. I. Lenin, *Collected Works,* vol. 20, London: Lawrence & Wishart, pp. 152-4.

Lenin, V. I. (1965b), 'The immediate tasks of the Soviet government: raising the productivity of labour' (first published 1918), in V. I. Lenin, *Collected Works,* vol. 27, London: Lawrence & Wishart, pp. 235-77.

Littler, C. R. (1978), 'Understanding Taylorism', *British Journal of Sociology,* vol. 29, no. 2, pp. 185-202.

Lupton, T. (1963), *On the Shop Floor,* Oxford: Pergamon Press.

Maier, C. S. (1970), 'Between Taylorism and technocracy: European ideologies and the vision of industrial productivity in the 1920s', *Journal of Contemporary History,* vol. 5, no. 2, pp. 27-61.

Mandel, E. (1978), *Late Capitalism,* London: New Left Books.

Montmollin, M. de (1974), 'Taylorisme et anti-Taylorisme', *Sociologie du Travail,* vol. 16, no. 4, pp. 374-82.

Nadworny, M. (1955), *Scientific Management and the Unions 1900-1932,* Cambridge, Mass: Harvard University Press.

Nakase, T. (1979), 'The introduction of scientific management in Japan and its characteristics', in K. Nakagawa (ed.) *Labor and Management,* Tokyo: University of Tokyo Press, pp. 171-202.

Okuda, K. (1972), 'Managerial evolution in Japan', *Management Japan,* vol. 6. no. 1, pp. 28-37.

Palmer, B. (1975), 'Class, conception and conflict: the thrust for efficiency, managerial views of labor, and the working class rebellion, 1903-1922', *Review of Radical Political Economics,* vol. 7, no. 2, pp. 31-49.

Pichierri, A. (1978), 'Diffusion and crisis of scientific management in European industry', in S. Giner and M. S. Archer (eds), *Contemporary Europe,* London: Routledge & Kegan Paul, pp. 55-73.

Pignon, D., and Querzola, J. (1976), 'Dictatorship and democracy in production', in A. Gorz (ed.), *The Division of Labour,* Brighton: Harvester Press, pp. 63-99.

Roberts, C., and Woods, S. J. (1982), 'Collective bargaining and job redesign' in J. Kelly and C. W. Clegg (eds.), *Autonomy and Control at the Workplace: Contexts for Job Design,* London: Croom Helm.

Rollier, M. (1979), 'Taylorism and the Italian Unions', in C. Cooper and E. Mumford (eds.), *The Quality of Working Life in Western and Eastern Europe,* London: Associated Press, pp. 214-25.

Roy, D. (1952), 'Quota restriction and goldbricking in a machine shop', *American Journal of Sociology,* vol. 57, no. 3, pp. 427-42.

Roy, D. (1954), 'Efficiency and the fix', *American Journal of Sociology,* vol. 60, no. 3, pp. 255-66.

Sohn-Rethel, A. (1978), *Intellectual and Manual Labour,* London: Macmillan.

Taylor, F. W. (1906), *On the Art of Cutting Metals,* New York: American Society of Mechanical Engineers.

Taylor, F. W. (1919), *A Piece-Rate System* (first published 1895), in F. W. Taylor, *Two Papers on Scientific Management: A Piece-Rate System; Notes on Belting,* London: Routledge & Sons, pp. 31-126.

Taylor, P. S. (1979), 'Labour time, work measurement and the commensuration of labour', *Capital and Class,* no. 9. Autumn, pp. 23-38.

Thurley, K., and Wood, S., eds (1982), *Managerial Strategy and Industrial Relations,* Cambridge: Cambridge University Press.

Traub, R. (1978), 'Lenin and Taylor: the fate of "scientific management" in the (early) Soviet Union', *Telos,* no. 37, pp. 82-92.

Wood, S. J. (1980), 'Corporate strategy and organizational studies', in D. Dunkerley and G. Salaman (eds), *Organizational Studies Yearbook 1980,* London: Routledge & Kegan Paul, pp. 52-71.

Wood, S. J. and Kelly, J. E. (1978), 'Towards a critical management science', *Journal of Management Studies,* vol. 15, no. 1, pp. 1-24.

Woodward, J. (1958), *Management and Technology,* London: HMSO.

Hindy Lauer Schachter (essay date 1989)

SOURCE: *Frederick Taylor and the Public Administration Community: A Reevaluation,* State University of New York Press, 1989, 175 p.

[*In the following excerpt from his book* Frederick Taylor and the Public Administration Community, *Schachter addresses the major points of Taylor's method as laid out in* The Principles of Scientific Management *and* Shop Management *and recounts the reaction to Taylor's ideas during his lifetime.*]

SCIENTIFIC MANAGEMENT

Shop Management and ***The Principles of Scientific Management*** are the two works that embody Taylor's mature ideas on organizational improvement and motivation. Although the first originated as a 1903 ASME presentation and the second was originally serialized in the April, May, and June, 1911 *American Magazine* (circulation 340,000), they can be examined as a single entity. Taylor wrote them for the same audience, chiefly industrial managers and engineers; their arguments are similar to the extent that the author quotes chunks of ***Shop Management*** in the later ***Principles.***

A third published source for Taylor's ideas is his January 1912 testimony before a special House of Representatives committee convened to investigate the social impact of shop management systems. This is a particularly valuable source for people who want to understand how Taylor envisioned management principles, since here he replies to criticisms of the earlier presentations. . . .

SHOP MANAGEMENT

For Taylor, management, alternately described as an art and as a science, is essentially a question of the relations between employers and employees. What is wanted is a system that gives satisfaction to both, shows that their best interests are mutual and can"bring about such thorough and hearty cooperation that they can pull together instead of apart."

Historically, Taylor argues, such cooperation has been impossible because employers, ignorant of actual work time and indifferent to individual workers, have equated low wages with the low labor costs they desired, to the point that,

> it is safe to say that the majority of employers have a feeling of satisfaction when their workmen are receiving lower wages than those of their competitors.

This attitude defeats any chance to increase productivity because employees, seeing that hard work brings no monetary reward, adopt a slow pace, marking time or "soldiering." The end result is loss to employers and employees, the former paying higher prices per piece than required and the latter receiving poor wages.

This system, with its "bickering, quarreling, and . . . hard feeling . . . between the two sides," need not continue. A contrasting high-wage/low-labor-cost system can be created if organizations generate the necessary information. This means developing procedures for completing work more quickly and efficiently. A major component of such development is work time study, deconstructing jobs into elementary components and studying the time it takes workers to perform each of these actions under varying conditions. The time-and-motion researcher with the cooperation of the workers gets a sense of the best way of handling each component by first recording how long it takes a first-class employee to complete the motions and then adding a given percentage of this time to cover unavoidable delays and interruptions, and rest periods. Comparative experiments then reveal which changes in layout, equipment, or the order of physical motions would improve the time taken for the job.

Time study is not an end in itself. It is one tactic to improve shop production, which itself is simply a strategy to reach the goal of industrial cooperation, the assumption being that employers will be less relentless in pursuing low wages if profits are greater.

Time study does not determine a precise and unvarying count of seconds it takes to do each motion. Any set of experiments is tentative, yielding advances that themselves become subject to later improvements. Taylor never claims that time study yields perfect knowledge of how to labor; all he avers in its defense is that it gives "a vastly closer approximation as to time than we ever had before."

Among the most-often-quoted passages from Taylor's books are vignettes illustrating what he accomplished with accurate time studies at Bethlehem Steel. This material shows how his work studies are applied to what are generally viewed as simple, repetitive, unskilled manual jobs.

Taylor opens one narrative by asserting that "the average man would question whether there is much of any science in the work of shoveling." Yet

> for a first-class shoveler there is a given shovel load at which he will do his biggest day's work. What is this shovel load? Will a first-class man do more work per day with a shovel load of 5 pounds, 10 pounds, 15 pounds, 20, 25, 30, or 40 pounds? Now this is a question which can be answered only through carefully made experiments.

By varying shovel loads, Taylor found that shovelers were most productive with 21 pounds on their shovel. As a result he rescinded Bethlehem's practice of having each worker use his own implement and issued each man a shovel that would hold 21 pounds of whatever material he was lifting, a small one for iron ore and a large one for ashes.

A more elaborate illustration involved loading pig iron on railroad cars. Taylor's research assistant timed its constituent tasks, such as picking up the pig iron from the ground, walking with it on a level and an incline, throwing the iron down and walking back empty to get another load. Based on over three months of observations, Taylor concluded that workers were most productive if they were under load and allowed to rest at specified periods of the day. He offered a worker whom he calls "Schmidt" (actually Henry Knolle) a chance to earn $1.85 a day, rather than the regulation $1.15, if he would follow the researcher's work/rest regimen so that "When he tells you to pick up a pig and walk, you pick it up and you walk, and when he tells you to sit down and rest, you sit down. You do that right straight through the day." Schmidt agreed, and following Taylor's methods he learned to handle 47.5 tons per day, rather than the 12.5 tons that he and other Bethlehem workers routinely loaded. This meant lower labor costs for Bethlehem and higher wages for an unskilled employee.

The Schmidt episode is often used to castigate Taylor because of the way he describes pig iron loading and the mentality of loaders. Because Taylor wants to emphasize the universality of his methods, he goes to great pains to show that the task is so crude that most people would not associate it with science. He calls it "the most elementary form of labor that is known." To clinch the case he uses two offensive animal analogies.

> This work is so crude and elementary in its nature that the writer firmly believes that it would be possible to train an intelligent gorilla so as to become a more efficient pig-iron handler than any man can be.
>
> Now one of the very first requirements for a man who is fit to handle pig iron as a regular occupation is that he shall be so stupid and so phlegmatic that he more nearly resembles . . . the ox than any other type.

While these remarks are inexcusable, they represent a miniscule fraction of Taylor's writings on work and have to be taken in the context of asserting the importance of studying even such routine labor, rather than a simple assertion that Schmidt himself was a gorilla or an ox. They are a deviation from Taylor's own stricture against being patronizing and condescending, but they cannot be used to assert his contempt for labor; in his letters, he uses equally offensive analogies concerning managers (e.g., financiers as hogs).

The point of the narratives is to leave the skeptical reader "convinced that there is a certain science back of the handling of pig iron," and other menial chores. Taylor could assert that he had never met a single contractor to whom it had even occurred that there was such a thing as a science of labor. Since the books address practitioners, Taylor uses cases to make his points; he embellishes work stories so that they interest an audience of managers and engineers through their particularity as well as their applications. The stylistic problem is to write entertaining narrative while linking each case with the assertion that all work—no matter how repetitive and manual—benefits from study and experimentation. Taylor's awkward, even offensive, handling of the issue should not obscure the purpose of the stories: to show that "there is no class of work which cannot be profitably submitted to time study," whether pig-iron loading, clerical work, or solving problems in mathematics. While the animal analogies can be argued as showing Taylor's distancing himself from labor, the idea behind his narratives is actually to unite skilled and unskilled work by showing that both are capable of study; the thrust of the narratives is to deny the notion that any work is truly unskilled.

Planning

A new approach to studying work leads inexorably to proposing a new organization structure. Developing and maintaining a valid work science or art requires reorganization, particularly creation of a planning department. This is a central record-keeping repository that stores information derived from time and motion studies and serves as a clearing house, sending instructions to and receiving reports from operating personnel. Besides performing all work experiments, the planning department staff analyze all incoming orders for products, for which they perform required design and drafting, and then route those orders from place to place in the plant. The planning department's written archives supplant the foreman's memory as the repository of information on requests and plans for new work, materials in inventory, cost of items manufactured, pay, and discipline. The company regulates and prints the various forms that the new department requires, including shop reports, time cards, instruction sheets on preferred work methodologies, pay sheets, and storeroom records. As in Metcalfe's arsenal system, these are filled out by the workers and directly submitted to the central repository—bypassing the shop foremen.

With so much new information being created, organizations must abandon the military form of command where each worker reports to a single agent. Functional management is needed, with each worker receiving daily orders and help directly from eight different supervisors, each of whom has a different function.

Located in the planning room are those supervisors concerned principally with recordkeeping—the order-of-work, instruction card, and time-and-cost clerks—and those who discipline workers for lateness or absences. On the shop floor, the "gang boss" prepares work. The "speed boss" supervises the use of tools and setting of machine speeds. The "inspector" is in charge of quality control. The "repair boss" supervises the care and maintenance of the machines.

Some of these supervisors relate to each individual worker for such short periods that they can function for the entire shop. Other supervisors have heavy hands-on contact, and consequently must oversee only a small group where they "should be not only able but willing to pitch in . . . and show the men how to set the work in record time."

The shop management has to change worker-supervisor grouping under the new Taylor system. Each entry-level employee belongs to eight different aggregations which shift according to the particular functional supervisor who guides him at a given moment. Since Taylor advocates competence in specific tasks (e.g., setting up work or repairing machines) as the basis for supervisory appointment, this system emphasizes the role of knowledge or skill as legitimators of supervisor's authority. It also stresses the disparate skills necessary to run an organization; opportunities for promotion should be found for those with record-keeping abilities, for those who can repair tools, and for those with the many other discrete skills. This is in line with the philosophy that each workman should be given as far as possible the highest grade of work for which his individual ability and physique fit him. A reorganized factory offers many opportunities for promotion not found in a foreman-do-all establishment.

Chance for Success

While optimism pervades Taylor's work, he did not perceive either managers or workers rushing to embrace so novel a system—the first use of work experiments and a pervasive repudiation of the rule that each worker have only one boss. To use Taylor's ideas, every hierarchical level would have to experience a change in its vertical relations from "suspicious watchfulness and antagonism and frequently open enmity . . . to that of friendship." Employees, duped so many times in the past, might find it hard to cooperate during the experimentation and training phases. They might well regard as "impertinent interference" attempts to teach them new ways of handling their chores, unless they can be made to see that the experimentally derived standards were advantageous to their own interests. Managers will be even harder to convince because "money must be spent, and in many cases a great deal of money, before the changes are completed which result in lowering cost."

Conversion requires initial sacrifices at all levels, none more daunting than the need for a "complete revolution in the mental attitude and the habits of all those engaged in . . . management, as well as . . . the workmen." Because the system relies on cooperation, it cannot be imposed by force. If the owners want to convert, they must stress to managers "a broad and comprehensive view of the general objects to be attained," including the eventual economic usefulness of non-producers such as the trainers and recordkeeping clerks.

A convinced manager receives the task of explaining the system to the workers, giving them every chance to express their views. During a two- to five-year period, volunteers are requested for work training and development, no attempt being made to coerce those who prefer using their own methods.

> The first few changes which affect the workmen should be made exceedingly slowly, and only one workman at a time should be dealt with at the start. Until this single man has been thoroughly convinced that a great gain has come to him from the new method, no further change should be made. Then one man after another should be tactfully changed over. After passing the point at which from one-fourth to one-third of the men in the employ of the company have been changed . . . practically all of the workmen who are working under the old system become desirous to share in the benefits which they see have been received by those working in the new plan.

Object lessons—rather than talk—convince employees that experimentation not only aids the company by increasing productivity but helps the workers personally by extending new material and psychic rewards, including higher wages, improved communication and, most important, advancement opportunities. The presence of peers who enjoy these satisfactions convinces the recalcitrants of the superiority of the new methods.

At no point does Taylor predicate workers' conversion based on higher wages alone. A chance to earn more money is cited as a necessary—rather than a sufficient—prerequisite. Taylor states flatly that of more importance still is "the development of each man . . . so that he may be able to do, generally speaking, the highest grade of work for which his natural abilities fit him." It is difficult to see how modern textbooks can speak of "pure" or "sole" economic motivation when Taylor insists that despite the importance of wages, the "most important object . . . should be the training and development." His motivational approach is clearly tri-dimensional, centering on higher wages, improved communication, and opportunities for advancement.

Higher Wages—After training, an employee who performs a suggested fair day's task receives from 30 to 100 percent more per day than the company's previous average pay for that task. A differential piece work system ensures high pay for a large output and lower wages for poorer or more careless performance, giving those who learn the new methods "a good liberal increase, which must be permanent."

Improved Communication—With its emphasis on information flow and new methods, shop management required more two-way communication than the traditional foreman-do-all setup with its extremes of driving or coercing workers and leaving them to their own unaided devices. Taylor was well aware that anxiety develops when workers lack knowledge about how their efforts are viewed. At a time when employees received almost no written feedback, he recommends giving each a slip of paper identifying daily progress on tasks. He suggests bulletin boards to keep work units posted on the status of orders. He insists that

> Each man should be encouraged to discuss any trouble which he may have. . . . Men would far rather even be blamed by their bosses . . . than be passed by day after day without a word.

Interaction includes supervisors' listening to the worker's point of view and reacting with respect to the information they receive so that workers "feel that substantial justice is being done them."

In particular, training involves "close, intimate, personal cooperation between the management and the men," where each worker gets "the most friendly help from those who are over him." At a bicycle ball factory where Taylor consulted,

> each girl was made to feel that she was the object of especial care and interest on the part of management and that if anything went wrong with her she could always have a helper.

For the workers, training involves learning new methods and then suggesting improvements. Taylor notes that "the first step is for each man to learn to obey the laws as they exist, and next, if the laws are wrong, to have them reformed in the proper way." In a factory, this means that the employees learn the planning department's latest methods before suggesting improvements. All suggestions are tested by the planning staff, and if they increase productivity they are adopted by the entire crew.

As a consultant, at the Link Belt Company, Taylor used esteem as a motivator by telling workers he would test their suggestions and name useful changes after those who proposed them. He justifies this by saying, "It is quite a thing for a man to have the best method about the works called Jones' method." Why should this matter at all if money is the sole motivator?

In ***Principles*** Taylor addresses the charge that training diminishes worker autonomy, that employees lose something if they are not left to their own devices unaided. His reply centers on the anomaly of proscribing training for workers while accepting it for surgeons or dentists, when

> the training of the surgeon has been almost identical in type with the teaching and training which is given to the workman. The surgeon, all through his early years, is under the closest supervision of more experienced men, who show him the minutest way how each element of his work is best done. They provide him with the finest implements, each one of which has been the subject of special study and development, and then insist upon his using each . . . in the very best way.

Only when the student learns the basis of his craft is he invited to "use his originality and ingenuity to make *real additions to the world's knowledge instead of reinventing things which are old.*" The only innovation in worker training is in extending education to the factory, providing the shoveler with an activity normally reserved for his "betters" with high school and college diplomas. A painful discrepancy exists when people praise academic education for a small elite and disparage efforts to teach manual workers better ways to handle their jobs, reinforcing a distinction between work that requires skill and work that needs no particular ability. Taylor sees no such distinction, noting that,

> if it were true that the workman would develop into a larger and finer man without all this teaching . . . then it would follow that the young man who now comes to college to have the help of a teacher in mathematics, physics, chemistry, Latin, Greek, etc., would do better to study these things unaided and by himself.

Yet no one suggests solitary academic labor as a generic alternative to universities. At the academic level, the advantages of teacher-pupil interaction are clear. Why is the person at the bottom of the hierarchy the only one who cannot benefit from education?

A letter from an Australian judge extends this analogy to the arts, a field Taylor relied on as much as the sciences for a model of how careful preparation is prerequisite to real discovery. Taylor was fond of quoting Judge Charles Heydon's assertion that music teachers were longstanding shop management advocates because they knew that the "genius who plays the piano without having been taught the proper, i.e., the most efficient method of fingering, will come short of his very best." Why should imposed technique serve the artist and stifle the pig-iron loader? Why should specialized training not serve as a foundation for helping each do a proper task?

Modern management theory emphasizes the importance of training and feedback. A recent article uses the artistic analogy for a strongly argued proposition that freedom in organizations cannot occur without training. In words that would have engaged Taylor, political scientist Larry Preston notes that creativity is only

> possible for those who have mastered established ideas and practices. . . . The virtuoso pianist, exemplifying creative freedom at the keyboard, builds on years of training and practice. And his or her creativity is primarily an extension of the methods developed and learned by past teachers and masters of the piano. No one sits at a piano and invents a technique. . . . If we want to enhance individuals' freedom, we must be willing to provide an understanding of prevailing practices and the resources needed to decide and act with respect to them.

Taylor does not expect the full-time line worker to have as many new ideas as people performing experiments all day, since the full-time worker lacks the time for and habits of generalizing—which seems obvious and does not raise hackles with regard to professions. Do general practitioners discover as many new drugs as researchers attached to universities? Is it elitist to name this disparity? He does insist that workers who suggest improvements be given encouragement and full credit when their innovations are useful. Through such procedures, "the true initiative of the workman is better attained under scientific management than under the old individual plan."

Training and concomitant two-way communication are important motivators both directly and in permitting the company to offer a career ladder where each person is challenged by the highest grade of work that he can learn to perform well. Education not only facilitates workers' mastering their own jobs but it enables the company to groom the most able for higher-paying tasks or lateral transfers where people who are poor at one job may prove excellent at another. Training accompanied by structural reorganization sets the stage for those advancement opportunities that Taylor sees as the ultimate motivational strategy.

Opportunities for Advancement—Creating a career ladder is a paramount "duty of employers . . . both in their own interest and in that of their employees." Both ***Shop Management*** and ***Principles*** assert the motivational power of having

> the laborer who before was unable to do anything beyond, perhaps shoveling and wheeling dirt from place to place . . . taught to do the more elementary machinist's work, accompanied by the agreeable surroundings and the interesting variety and higher wages which go with the machinist's trade,

while at the same time, the best "machinists become functional foremen and teachers. And so on, right up the line."

Training enables workers to learn more highly skilled work that might well have been closed to them in the past. Functional restructuring demands

> a larger number of men in this class, so that men, who must otherwise have remained machinists all their lives, will have the opportunity of rising to a foremanship.

New opportunities to do "much higher, more interesting, and finally more developing" work are an important motivational strategy.

Some of Taylor's modern critics condemn functional foremanship for creating "a master class of scientific managers ruling over a servant class of workers." This anachronistic criticism is predicated on modern corporate personnel practices, where few, if any, managerial vacancies are filled by blue-collar workers without college degrees. Taylor makes it perfectly clear that he intends to use the most competent workers to fill executive positions without regard to academic credentialing because the most vital managerial attributes are "grit" and "constructive imagination" and "success at college or the technical school does not indicate the presence of these qualities, even though the man may have worked hard." In a letter to Edwin Gay, dean of Harvard University's Graduate Business School, he objects to graduates appearing at factories to inquire if they can commence their careers with shop-management research; he notes that "one trouble with the man who has had a very extensive academic education is that he fails to see any good coming to him from long continued work as a workman," while Taylor, on the contrary, sees such long, continued work as the best way to learn how to plan and manage work experiments. Managers and workers do not constitute autonomous classes; task labor is the advocated route into task management. ***Principles*** contains an oblique warning against managers trying to install scientific management without taking the time and trouble to train employees as functional foremen and teachers so that their very presence serves as an object lesson on the new system's personal benefits. Possibilities for promotion are an essential feature of a system that emphasizes cooperation, one whose technical mechanism of time study should not be

> used more or less as a club to drive the workmen, against their wishes . . . to work much harder, instead of gradually teaching and leading them towards new methods, and convincing them through object-lessons that task management means for them somewhat harder work, but also far greater prosperity.

IMMEDIATE RECEPTION

Taylor wrote to precipitate action—immediate, measurable results. He told an associate, "the people whom I want to reach . . . are principally those men who are doing the manufacturing and construction work of our country, both employers and employees." To interest such a large, variegated audience, he insisted on giving his books a narrative form, including recital of anecdotes with semifictional dialogue. He changed the title of his second book from *Philosophy of Scientific Management* to ***Principles,*** noting, "I am afraid that the word 'philosophy' in the title will tend to make the thing sound rather high-falutin."

The man's language often seems coarse to the modern scholar's ear, particularly the language in the Schmidt anecdotes. While one cause of this may lie in the passage of time (we think we are more honest in our expression than our grandparents, but we have our own circumlocutions), Taylor's insistance on using unvarnished shop-floor language elicited complaints from his own associates. One, Morris Cooke, notes,

> The term "Gang Boss" especially seems to me objectionable and out of harmony with the spirit of scientific management. . . . The word "supervisor" seems to me to be better adapted to our business.

Here, Taylor is cautioned to use a softer word with positive personnel-management connotations, a request he quickly denies, noting, "I . . . do not like 'supervisor.'" "Gang boss" it remained, Taylor's delight in actual shop-floor expressions overwhelming any interest in using more academically respectable nomenclature.

Just as Taylor decried the gulf between skilled and unskilled work, he also tried to break down the conceptual distinction between professional and popular publishing. He takes the stance that his work can have professional insights worthy of discussion at ASME meetings while at the same time being couched in popular prose for publication in *American Magazine* with its mass circulation. Again Cooke remonstrates:

> The principal disadvantage of publishing in this magazine is that you are a technical man and that until quite recently it was not considered good professional practice for technical men to use mediums of this kind for bringing out new scientific doctrine.

Taylor ignored this criticism, his goal being to provide technical information to a mass audience, not a summary of technical data (say, a three-page article based on ***Principles***), but the identical message presented to people who shared his educational pedigree. At his own expense, he printed copies of ***Principles*** for all ASME members while seeing to its *American Magazine* serialization. This ensured simultaneous scholarly and popular discussion.

The decade before America entered World War I saw extensive professional and popular-press debate over Taylor's theories. A 1912 ASME committee described the work as spawning enthusiastic advocates and vigorous opponents. As Taylor foresaw, his ideas also produced a sizable cadre of managers who borrowed discrete techniques (e.g., time study and differential piece rates) while abjuring the underlying principles of cooperation, employee development, and mutual gain. Although Taylor vigorously criticized those who borrowed discrete aspects of his system, many outsiders confused their practice with Taylor's theories. The written legacy produced by adherents, opponents, and those who used only some aspects of Taylorism gives a unique picture of scientific management as it was viewed in its own time. The work of Taylor's supporters is particularly interesting because it stresses facets totally absent from most modern textbooks.

ADHERENTS

From the Midvale years on, Taylor was the center of a small circle of engineer acolytes. Henry Gantt and Carl Barth (his Midvale assistants) were charter members. Others include Horace Hathaway, hired to help Barth improve the Link Belt Company's productivity in 1904, and Morris Cooke, a publishing executive.

Outside this group, scientific management was most attractive to public-sector-oriented Progressive reformers rather than to business leaders. The first quarter of the twentieth century marks the heyday of Progressivism, a pervasive but diffuse political movement based on the belief that (1) a corrupt political system benefited a few rich people at the poor's expense and (2) planned progress towards a better system was possible as well as desirable. Typical Progressives condemned some excesses of the new plutocracy and were in full cry against monopoly, but they were not anti-business. They accepted the large corporate industrial capitalist system as a natural product of social evolution, and associated its evils with particular corrupt financiers and acts of fraud. They were fundamentally conservative to the extent that they offered programs that did not alter business supremacy over the control of wealth, although they sympathized with the workers whom they viewed as underdogs. They displayed a Taylorite optimism in believing that a good society would, should, and could alleviate the lot of poor people.

In the legal sphere, the movement pressed for specific governmental changes to push the country towards reform, some affecting procedures (for example, direct primaries, initiatives, referenda) and others, policy (child labor laws, progressive income taxes, etc.). On the local level, sympathizers opposed electoral "machines," which were generally viewed as corrupt.

Key Progressives perceived shop management as a means for initiating organizational reform on a manageable and practical scale without damaging business. Taylor's views on training were congenial to professionals (lawyers, ministers, college professors) who loomed large in the reform ranks and whose own status depended on training that enabled them to apply a corpus of knowledge and techniques on the job. Taylor's ideas seemed to offer an equivalent way of increasing the satisfaction and esteem of blue-collar factory occupations. The notion that scientific management decreased the conceptual gap between the status-rich professions and the underdog workers led one adherent to label the theory "part of a larger movement, the realization of a sense of social solidarity, of social responsibility of each for all."

The muckraker, Ida Tarbell, stresses this interpretation in a series of *American Magazine* articles asserting that scientific management dignifies factory labor by considering it worthy of study, thus eliminating any skilled-unskilled dichotomy. Tarbell also paints a very positive picture of the human-relations changes wrought by the new management style. Her narrative places Taylor as a New England Butt Company consultant holding open meetings to explain the project's benefits for the workers, describing the information he needs to collect and its usefulness, giving his audience a chance to ask questions and raise objections to participating in work experiments. The new system is described in terms of its psychological advantages to the worker's self-respect and its propensity to minimize arbitrary orders that can now be challenged on the basis of data learned in training or by calling for experimentation. Tarbell echoes Taylor himself in considering higher wages only one motivation for participation in the new mode of worker-manager relations; the opportunity for training and a chance to rise through the ranks and perform more varied and interesting tasks are also motivating.

One suprise Tarbell has for the modern reader is her assumption that scientific management's principal opponents will be selfish employers who resist diminution of arbitrary power, who prefer the role of taskmasters to experimenters and educators. Her title, "The Golden Rule in Business," indicates her missionary zeal to convert old-fashioned employers and her understanding that scientific management enables executives to treat a laborer as they themselves would wish to be treated. Her work emphasizes the centripetal aspect of Taylor's ideas, how their implementation bridges the gap between the treatment of skilled and unskilled employees.

Taylor demonstrated his relation to Tarbell and other Progressives by serializing ***Principles*** in *American Magazine,* a journal known for publishing reform writers. Its editor solicited the manuscript because of his interest in "insurgency," acknowledging that Taylor and his associates represented the insurgents in the factory management sphere.

Cautioned against publishing in a radical journal, Taylor answers in language that gives the lie to his personally favoring factory owners over employees:

> Among a certain class of people the *American Magazine* is looked upon as a muck-raking magazine. I think that any magazine which opposed the "stand-patters" and was not under the control of the moneyed powers of the United States would now be classed among the muck-rakers. This, therefore, has no very great weight with me.

Before World War I, ASME conferences often erupted into imbroglios between Progressives and "stand-patters." The reformist faction found a staunch ally in Taylor, whose stance in these controversies almost always weighed in against the short-term economic interests of factory owners. He unsuccessfully fought to have the society sponsor a section on public matters that would investigate how industrial practices such as polluting affected city life. In April 1909, he signed a petition requesting that the Association hold a conference on air pollution, open to the public and including speakers from the public health field, a request that the society's officers, under pressure from industry, denied. His official biographer quotes him as saying shortly before his death, "Throughout my life I have been very much inclined toward the radical side in all things." This is almost certainly an avowal of Progressive leaning.

Brandeis—Taylor's most useful Progressive adherent was Louis Dembitz Brandeis, known in his day as "the people's lawyer." Brandeis originally approached Taylor for help in a difficult case. In the spring of 1910, the railroads east of the Mississippi gave their employees a pay raise and applied to the Interstate Commerce Commission (ICC) for permission to raise freight rates. Brandeis saw this move as a corporate attempt to recoup operating losses by overcharging consumers. Representing the Trade Association of the Atlantic Seaboard as unpaid counsel, he opposed the increase, arguing that the railroads could support the pay hike through more efficient management.

Hearings in Washington, D.C. began on October 12, 1910. Two weeks later, Brandeis wrote Taylor, asking for data on scientific management (a term he seems to have coined—Taylor previously used "shop management" or "task management"). Readers of post-World-War-II textbooks might surmise that Taylor would reply by explaining how his system motivates worker productivity through higher wages. But those who have read Taylor's own books will be ready for his return letter outlining the system's use of noneconomic motivation. Taylor asserts that shop management democratizes the plant and removes class distinctions by extending training to all. The system provides new advancement opportunities, increasing worker ambition.

Taylor asked Morris Cooke and Henry Gantt to work with Brandeis on his presentation. Gantt was particularly active. He unsuccessfully tried to persuade the ASME council to endorse the anti-increase brief. He testified at the hearing, reiterating Taylor's emphasis on noneconomic motivation, gains the system brings by checking arbitrary supervisors and allowing talented mechanics to rise into the planning department. Scientific management increases worker performance because,

> we get from our men . . . who have worked at routine work . . . the material for more responsible positions. . . . Inefficiency in the workman is not his fault. . . . We have spent a tremendous amount of money in developing machinery and . . . very little money in developing men.

The hearings proved a publicity bonanza. A February 1911 ICC decision against the railroads was one factor that propelled scientific management into people's minds. Taylor thanked Brandeis for bringing his theories to wide public notice.

Had Brandeis simply appropriated scientific management to win a case, he would have relinquished his interest after the victory. In reality, he made it a point to advocate Taylor's approach in a wide array of later speeches. At the 1912 Brown University commencement, he stresses the Taylor system's cooperative basis, noting, "The old idea of a good bargain was a transaction in which one man got the better of another. The new idea . . . is a transaction which is good for both parties to it." At a talk before the Boston Central Labor Union Brandeis stressed how training gives employers a stake in conserving labor. Even unscrupulous owners will not want to arbitrarily fire or overwork people in whom they have invested development money.

Brandeis' forward to Frank Gilbreth's *Primer of Scientific Management* emphasizes the system's equalizing effect through training and promotion opportunities that afford workers a chance for the same self-respect and satisfaction held by professionals. A 1920 address in the Taylor Society's memorial volume notes that scientific management "makes the hire worthy of the laborer," and with Progressive optimism proposes that its impact may be to "make work . . . the greatest of life's joys." Brandeis' understanding of scientific management is very close to Tarbell's. Both had an interest in Taylor's ideas because they believed his system would bring workers material and nonmaterial benefits and bridge the gap between professionals and factory labor. The Taylorism they support foreshadows much of Elton Mayo's advocacy of better human relations in the factory and the work-as-motivator insights currently credited to Douglas McGregor and Abraham Maslow. While neither Brandeis nor Tarbell can be considered radicals in the sense that either wanted to replace the economic dominance of the corporate sector, they were concerned with meliorist changes from noneconomic motivation, particularly the increase in worker self-respect and interest that develops from training and a chance at frequent promotion.

OPPONENTS

Taylor's earliest opponents were old-line plant managers objecting to the fiscal implications of higher wages and company-sponsored training and foremen jealous of their traditional prerogatives. Few modern summaries of Taylor analyze this rebuttal of Taylor's work, but ***Shop Management*** labels "the opposition of the heads of departments and the foremen and the gang bosses . . . the greatest problem in organization." Taylor asserts that he can more readily persuade workers to try the new way than superintendents and foremen.

A second, somewhat later antagonist was the American Federation of Labor (AFL). Representing skilled workers, it argued that scientific management was a ploy to break their members' monopolies on shop expertise. For union leaders, the time-study man was sent into the factory to steal their members' trade secrets, thus enabling employers to fire them and hire unskilled laborers at low wages and train them to perform those craft tasks, heretofore the province of the small elite possessing the requisite skills. Frank Hudson sums up the union view in a thoughtful *American Machinist* article in 1911 expressing a willingness to hear about better methods but rejecting company-wide training. An International Association of Machinists circular of April 1911 denounces the system for enabling companies to hire unskilled manual laborers for machinist positions, which "will mean the wiping out of our trade and organization with the accompanying low wages, life-destroying hard work, long hours and intolerable conditions generally."

Labor opposition may have surprised Taylor more than managerial intransigence because he was not intrinsically anti-union, while his work does attack prevailing managerial practices. He saw a necessary union role in traditional factories without other channels for curbing authority. To a Harvard business school professor, he wrote that he is "heartily in favor of unions" where the employer is a hog or careless of employee rights. ***Shop Management*** states:

> When employers herd their men together in classes, pay all of each class the same wages, and offer none of them any inducements to work harder or do better than the average, the only remedy for the men lies in combination; and frequently the only possible answer to encroachments on the part of their employers is a strike.

However, he did believe that scientific management would supplant the trade union movement as a means of helping the worker, that as scientific management increased productivity, employers would be able to raise wages and shorten work weeks, thus eliminating the need to bargain over these issues. With workers and managers cooperating to develop better methods together, "the close, intimate cooperation, the constant personal contact . . . will tend to diminish friction and discontent," thus eliminating almost all causes for dispute and disagreement.

He agreed with Brandeis—generally considered a union sympathizer—who writes, "There is absolutely nothing in scientific business management opposed to organized labor." He believed that workers and right-thinking managers could cooperate in a manager-initiated system, a view that may have appeared naive to union leaders, who would have asked, "Where is the evidence?"

Modern works dealing with Taylor make few if any references to his old-line manager opposition, with its reactionary complaints that now seem so irrelevant. Much more is written about the AFL critique, spearheaded by the International Association of Machinists, which does seem to bolster scientific management's anti-labor image. It is easy to read the quarrel as Exeter-educated "have" versus blue-collar "have nots." This obscures the fact that union opposition represented labor's own elite fighting to prevent less fortunate or less skilled workers from taking even a few steps up the factory ladder.

Taylor argues that his system benefits all workers:

> It is true, for instance, that the planning room, and functional foremanship, render it possible for an intelligent laborer or helper in time to do much of the work now done by a machinist. Is not this a good thing for the laborer and helper? He is given a higher class of work, which tends to develop him and gives him better wages.
>
> [Concurrently,] the machinist, with the aid of the new system, will rise to a higher class of work which he was unable to do in the past, and in addition, divided or functional foremanship will call for a larger number of men in this class, so that men, who must otherwise have remained machinists all their lives, will have the opportunity of rising to a foremanship.

The International Association of Machinists protested the lumping together of their members who do not become foremen with people who start as common laborers, thus diluting the pool of skilled workers and making it easier to hire machinists at low wages. The association's quarrel with Taylor is partly a matter of vantage point. Quite understandably, the union is concerned with the welfare of its members. While Taylor can assert, "In the sympathy for the machinist the case of the laborer is overlooked," the association is in business to ignore the laborers when their interests conflict with the AFL machinists. (The quarrel might have been totally different if helper/laborer unions had existed in 1911.)

To some extent the controversy can be clarified with empirical evidence. What happens when a factory adopts some scientific management variant? Do machinist wages sink? Are unskilled laborers eventually promoted?

Some empirical support does exist supporting the contention that scientific management in practice brings machinists closer to the status of laborers; but it does so by raising the unskilled workers rather than tangibly lowering the machinists. In 1915, Robert Hoxie, by no means a Taylor supporter, studied factories that had adopted some variant of scientific management. He concludes that the new system tends to realign wages, leveling the skilled/unskilled disparity but that it does so by raising the pay of the unskilled. What the craft workers are protesting is a decline in relative financial superiority. This is an understandable cause for a proud machinists' union but hardly an appropriate one for a battle of "haves" and "have nots."

The second union fear is that planning departments cut the worker's independence and use of his own good judgment. To the extent that planning departments standardize tools and methodologies, this cutback is inherent in the system. The defense is that the best workers move into the planning department, which encourages suggestions from employees working on the shop floor.

Particularly after 1911, Taylor tried to respond to union criticisms. He arranged for the president of the Boot and Shoe Makers Union to talk to workers at plants where he had consulted. Morris Cooke writes

> I think the most important thing to be accomplished by his visit is to convince him beyond any doubt that we really mean it when we say that our relations with the workmen are not only friendly but are of such a nature that it will be impossible for him to find any of them who will criticize what we are doing.

In addition, Taylor fought to break the easy assumption that any company using time and motion studies was actually committed to his ideas. No union chief was ever angrier than Taylor himself at managers adopting his mechanisms as a club to force workers into higher productivity. He realized quite early that his worst enemies were managers who borrowed some of his mechanical devices (notably the stopwatch) without any commitment to his aim at cooperation and increased benefits for all. Specific union complaints were often based on misapplications of his system—even when such misapplications contradicted explicit arguments in his major works.

To the extent that Taylor perceived managers as his worst enemies, he loses points as a prophet. The union critique has been much more damaging, particularly in the political arena. The only salve for his prophetic ego could be his contention that the union critique stemmed from managerial misapplication of his methods, that the AFL distrust arose from managerial antagonism to change in basic reward patterns. Complaints about a planning room divorced from workers cannot stem from ***Shop Management*** or ***Principles,*** both of which make abundantly clear that the workers rise to the planning department. Such complaints can come as a reaction to managers bent on using time study and centralization to extract gain for management alone. With this interpretation, the way to minimize union dissent is to eliminate managerial misapplication. In practical terms, this means condemning half-hearted imitators borrowing specific mechanisms but not the new system's underlying philosophy, those who time employees' work but will not create a planning department staffed by the workers.

IMITATORS

As early as his time at Bethlehem, Taylor was forced to realize that the committed enthusiast and the workaday line manager have radically different perspectives. The theorist can afford to emphasize the long-term benefits of two-way communication and worker training. Most managers are more concerned with short-term profits even if they consider human relations worthwhile.

Taylor's system contains practices that may increase short-term productivity without helping the workers. A company can force its workers to have their motions timed and then enforce new production quotas based on the knowledge obtained. This violates Taylor's explicit stricture against timing without consent, and certainly cannot be considered an aspect of the Taylor system. But why should managers focused on the present bother with consent, when, as Henry Gantt notes, "people value these methods only as new ways of controlling workmen . . . a chance to get something for nothing."

A new occupation soon arose made up of engineering consultants offering to systematize plants by using some of Taylor's methods but with shortcuts, such as testing work time without prior explanations or worker permission. In January 1910, for example, Taylor complained to Cooke that commentators were associating their names with consulting work done at the American Locomotive Company:

> In reality, the facts are that our methods were not all being used there. Harrington Emerson went there with his various shortcuts . . . and Van Alstyne had a whole lot more shortcuts of his own, and then enforced all of this with a club. Now this combination, which uses many of the details of our system and leaves out the essential underlying principles, is the worst thing that can happen to us. Van Alystne has used time study as a club, not as a means of harmonizing the interests of employers and employees.

To separate his ideas from those of such imitators, Taylor refused to join the National Society for Promoting Efficiency nor the New York and Philadelphia Efficiency Societies because Harrington Emerson and other perceived half-way implementers were members. Explaining his conduct, he notes

> All the world, of course, wants Efficiency now, as it has always wanted it. This is not, however, a sufficient basis for a group of men to get together any more than you would get together a society of men, say, to be good. All the world wants to be good.
>
> It is only when you have some particular scheme for promoting goodness that people are able to get together profitably.

Taylor was intent on distinguishing his "scheme" from that of other engineer consultants.

The most destructive conflation of Taylor and his imitators occurs in recrimination over the Watertown arsenal strike. Because management tactics leading to the strike misused scientific management—and were explicitly objected to by Taylor before the labor unrest—it is important to examine and disentangle this particular conflation.

Watertown Arsenal—In January 1909, General William Crozier, head of the Army Ordnance Department, visited Taylor in Germantown, Pennsylvania, to learn how standardizing tools might improve arsenal production. During the next half year, Taylor met personally and corresponded with Crozier about using scientific management in armament manufacture, eventually recommending that Carl Barth reorganize the machine shop at Watertown Arsenal in Massachusetts.

Controversy hung over Crozier's efforts. At its Washington headquarters, the International Association of Machinists issued an anti-Taylor circular urging workers to complain to their congressman. In the plant itself, many workers were afraid that any pay gains Barth brought would be temporary because of subsequent rate cuts, an understandable fear with such cuts common at the turn of the century.

Some of the foremen objected to using incentives to reward workers instead of simply punishing the less productive. One supervisor proclaimed:

> If a man is so lazy—to use no better word—that he will not do a day's work without being put on a premium system, he should be immediately removed from the shop and a better man put in his place.

Barth arrived at the arsenal in June 1909, and did little to dispel the controversy, by, for example, soliciting input from the machinist's union. He did follow Taylor's injunction to involve the workers from the start and show them how the new system benefits them in both material and noneconomic ways. An early step was creating a planning department staffed from men in the machine shop. The arsenal's master mechanic was put in charge, with three long-time foremen serving as assistants. Gang boss promotions went to three workers who now had the responsibility to route information between the planning room and the shop floor.

Dwight Merrick, the time-study person, did not arrive until May 1911, when the machine-shop workers could already see that Barth's presence had brought promotions to some of their own. Following Taylor's advice, Merrick explained why he was bringing a stop watch into the plant. No worker was timed without that person's consent. When one machinist complained that the watch made him nervous, Merrick stopped timing his motions. At least one foreman recalled challenging planning-room methods and having these methods changed after proper experimentation.

This process of consultation and consent looked incredibly drawn out to some of the officers for whom it was an idealistic and unworkable method to increase production. Major Clarence Williams showed his displeasure by telling a machinist who was complaining about a planning department method, "Shut right up."

By June 1911, Barth was encountering pressure from Arsenal officers to either speed up his work or allow them to implement an incentive plan of their own choosing in the foundry. Taylor immediately warned Crozier that such action would bring labor trouble; the necessary change was not a speedier system but more understanding by the officers of the workers' fears through more contact between them. Taylor's advice is clear:

> If you go right straight ahead in introducing our system, one step after another, and do not attempt short cuts and do not try to hurry it too fast . . . you will meet with practically no opposition.

Taylor might have been able to withstand the officers' pressure. But in August 1911, Barth gave in to the complaints of Lieutenant Colonel Charles Wheeler and Major Williams, permitting them to introduce their own incentive plan in the foundry, as long as they understood that their process did not represent an application of Taylor's methods.

On August 10, with Barth absent from the arsenal, Wheeler and Williams introduced time study into the foundry without any prior preparation. No planning department had been created to show that changes might develop and promote workers. No explanations were offered for the presence in the foundry of Merrick and his stop watch; certainly the officers wasted no time soliciting permission for timing their own subordinates' motions. Shifting Merrick to the foundry was, in itself, a violation of Taylor's dictum that a time-study person has to know the task. Merrick had a background in machine shop work and knew very little about foundry molding, a point that became painfully apparent as he tried to time specific motions.

After the first day's timing, the molders met informally and agreed not to cooperate with any of Merrick's attempts to time their labor, and to compose a petition protesting the new shop techniques. The next morning, an unsuspecting Merrick arrived at the foundry brandishing his stop watch. He first tried to time Joseph Cooney who, adhering to the molder's decision, refused to work with Merrick standing nearby. After a heated exchange, Merrick called Major Williams, who ordered Cooney to cooperate (a clear violation of Taylor's written advice and quite the contrary of Barth's practice in the machine shop). Cooney again refused. To Williams this was gross insurbordination. He discharged Cooney, sparking a mass exit from the foundry.

The strike lasted until August 18, when Colonel Wheeler promised Cooney's reinstatement and an Ordnance Department investigation of the new management techniques. For the molders, the job action was brief and inconclusive, for the changes continued while the investigation was in progress. The major consequence of Cooney's dismissal lay in its publicity value for the International Association of Machinists' campaign against Taylorism. Although the job action did not encompass the association's members, it forged an emotional focus for calls to end the timing of work motions. Because the arsenals were public organizations, with public funding, the union lobbied Congress to examine the Taylor system and prohibit further government agency use of stop watches and premium pay. Under the chairmanship of William Wilson (Dem., Pa.), a former United Mine Workers' official, the House Labor Committee heard a request for such examination from James O'Connell, International Association of Machinists' president, and Nick Alifas, a local Machinists' official, but none, interestingly, from any molders or other workers employed at Watertown. On August 21, the Committee appointed a three-person group to investigate the Taylor system—the first of many attempts to link the foundry strike and Taylor's theories, rather than to see the job action as a result of repudiating Taylor's principles.

Those closest to the situation appreciated the difference. Taylor himself saw the strike as validating his concern with worker involvement. To Cooke he wrote, "This ought to be a warning not to try to hurry task work too fast." Crozier receives a harsher message:

> No time study whatever should have been undertaken in the foundry. You will remember that I have told you time and again that without a whole lot of preliminary training no set of workmen should be subjected to the ordeal of time study.

Barth laments that "in the eyes of the world, the Taylor system is responsible for the trouble, while the fact is that the real Taylor system man at the Arsenal has never . . . been inside the foundry." More strikingly, the molder's own lawyer noted "the system in operation is not either the Taylor system or scientific management according to the principles of Frederick W. Taylor." An exhaustive modern study of the strike concludes, "Wheeler and Williams were clear in their own minds that they were not installing the Taylor system." If public administration textbooks want to write about the "Wheeler/Williams management theory," they can use Watertown as an example of these officers' gross insensitivities; the only thing the strike tells us about Taylor's ideas is that they are relatively easy to misapply, a point which does constitute a deficiency in an imperfect world but hardly the deficiency for which he is usually held culpable. Taylor was correct in perceiving that people like Wheeler and Williams were more dangerous to him than committed opponents. No old-line manager, no union chief acting alone could have caused the intense public scrutiny following the foundry strike. Only two partial imitators could have precipitated the House hearings. Antagonism mounted after misapplied attempts to study work without worker involvement in the use of that knowledge to create incentive schemes.

CONGRESSIONAL HEARINGS: ATTACK AND REBUTTAL

The House hearings, which lasted from October 1911 to February 1912, took place before a committee chaired by Representative William Wilson and consisting in addition of William Redfield (Dem., N.Y.) and John Tilson (Rep., Conn.). The committee's composition provided an aura of impartiality, given Wilson's labor background and Redfield's pre-politics business career, an impartiality furnished a further *post hoc* seal of approval when President Woodrow Wilson appointed Redfield Secretary of Commerce and William Wilson Secretary of Labor in 1914.

Taylor's opponents hoped that the hearing would lead to a condemnation of his ideas as oppressive. But by organizing a public forum, they gave their target an unprecedented opportunity to clarify his ideas and distinguish them from imitations. Brandeis, fully aware of the session's publicity value, warned his friend that it was crucial to let the legislature "see scientific management as it is, and not as it is represented."

Taylor, who enjoyed verbal combat, gave twelve hours of testimony spread over four days in January 1912. He challenged the testimony of people who spoke against his system without having read any of his books. His evidence has particular importance because it explicitly rebuts the picture that dominates modern public administration, a portrait that actually seems to describe what he considered misapplications rather than his original theory.

Post-World-War-II public administration literature often argues that Taylorism enthrones efficiency as a public goal. But the January 25, 1912, testimony states: "Scientific management is not any efficiency device, not a device of any kind for securing efficiency; nor is it any bunch or group of efficiency devices." Its goal is a mental change in managers and workers with "the substitution of hearty brotherly cooperation for contention and strife; of both pulling hard in the same direction instead of pulling apart." Efficiency is only important as a means enabling managers and workers to

> take their eyes off of the division of the surplus as the all-important matter, and together turn their attention toward increasing the size of the surplus until this surplus becomes so large that it is unnecessary to quarrel over how it shall be divided.

Since elements associated with increased efficiency (e.g., time studies) can be used "for good and for bad," the intention to cooperate is the only way of differentiating adherents of scientific management. An employer may well increase production by wielding a club, but he is not thus advancing the goals of Taylorism, for "without this complete mental revolution of both sides, scientific management does not exist."

The testimony reiterates Taylor's insistence that time and motion studies require worker agreement, with volunteers recruited through a variety of economic and ego rewards. He suggests the following for recruiting shovelers, for example:

> See here, Pat and Mike, you fellows understand your job all right; both of you fellows are first-class men; you know what we think of you; you are all right now; but we want to pay you fellows doubles wages. We are going to ask you to do a lot of damn fool things, and when you are doing them there is going to be some one out alongside of you all the time, a young chap with a piece of paper and a stop watch and pencil. . . . Now we want to know whether you fellows want to go into that bargain or not? If you want double wages while that is going on all right, we will pay you double; if you don't, all right, you needn't take the job unless you want to; we just called you in to see if you want to work this way or not.

While this sounds patronizing to the modern ear, it is a long way from Major William's insistence on firing workers who would not cooperate; one method should not be confused with the other.

Taylor also reiterates his insistance on urging workers to challenge the planning department's methods. Before any change occurs, a manager should say:

> Try the methods and implements which we give you . . . and then after you have tried our way if you think of an implement or method better than ours, for God's sake come and tell us about it and then we will make an experiment to prove whether your method or ours is the best, and you, as a workman, will be allowed to participate in that experiment.

This give and take is not window dressing but, for Taylor, absolutely crucial as a way of making progress. (General Crozier noted that challenges were allowed by Barth in the Watertown machine shop, where each worker had "the privilege of raising any point he desires and of having it attended to.")

The testimony also records Taylor's emphasis on worker development. One motivation is that "in most cases those who set the daily tasks have come quite recently from doing work at their trades." Union fears about scientific management's eliminating skilled jobs are goundless because what actually should happen is that the best workers are transferred to the management domain as "teachers, guiders, and helpers." This means higher wages and more interesting work, two sources of worker satisfaction. Fewer hands needed at machines is good for workers as long as factories are restructured to need more supervisors and planning personnel.

Concurrent with Taylor's testimony, the ASME subcommittee on administration prepared a report reiterating several of the key points in the House exposition. This nine-member committee, chaired by Progressive businessman James Dodge, stressed the new management system's "appreciation of the human factor" with its potential for educating workers and gaining their cooperation. Taylor, present at the group's discussions, agreed that good relations were essential, a point that Wheeler and Williams seem to have proved beyond possibility of refutation.

The work of the ASME group may have played a role in the House committee's final determination on scientific management. Taylor's own testimony certainly influenced the conclusion that no evidence existed to label his system injurious to workers. The machinists union had lobbied for the hearing to produce a report attacking the new system. The actual outcome was inconclusive; it did not provide the union with the desired victory. The army continued to use its version of the new methods in arsenals; in direct outcome, the hearings protected Taylor as well as his imitators.

DIETRICK AMENDMENT

Despite this setback, the machinists union continued to lobby legislators to end time-and-motion studies in arsenals. One politician who pledged his support was Representative Frederick Dietrick, from the Watertown arsenal district, who succeeded in putting a rider on the 1914 Army and Navy Appropriations Bills to supress such research and payment premiums in government-managed armaments manufacture.

Dietrick made no pretense at being an expert on Taylor's ideas. According to his own testimony, he had not read the two major books in their entirety, and what he had perused he had not always been able to understand (an amazing admission since the volumes were written for the average high school graduate). His amendments to the appropriations bills were, obviously, not directed against scientific management as theory but rather its practical application at the Watertown Arsenal and, to an even greater extent perhaps, its reputation with the International Association of Machinists as a way to eliminate their crafts.

The riders passed the House but not the Senate. This meant that two versions of both bills were sent to the joint Congressional Legislative Conference Committee for reconciliation. By chance, the committee chose to handle the Navy bill first. Since the Navy was not engaged in time-and-motion studies, its officers made no objection to using the House language against such research, and when the Army bill was handled afterwards this precedent was allowed to stand. A recent case study of this reconciliation process concludes, "If the Army Bill had been taken up first, the result might have been different." But the Dietrick amendments did pass. The International Association of Machinists achieved a notable political victory—stop watches and premium pay were henceforth banned from federal armed forces production operations.

The American poet John Greenleaf Whittier notes:

> Of all sad words of tongue or pen
> The saddest are these: "It might have been!"

The passage of the riders overshadowed the benign "wait-and-see" attitude of William Wilson's committee, which had examined scientific management and heard Taylor's human-relations-oriented testimony. It had arrived at no condemnation, while the man responsible for the riders was imperfectly aware of what the system meant. Yet to much of the public, it must have seemed as if congress had studied and condemned the Taylor system.

The political realities of the rider's passage were clear. Taylor's theories and officers Wheeler and William's practice were lumped together as forbidden in defense installations and hence, for at least part of the public, as equally unwise choices. Taylor's pre-eminent fear, that his theories and their misapplications might become indistinguishable, became reality in a law that lumped together voluntary and enforced time-and-motion research. The bill's major impact, then, was not so much its mandate, but rather its implicit assumption that Taylor's ideas and their use in other people's hands should be dealt with in only one way and without investigating the different conditions under which scientific management techniques might be implemented in organizations. The legislative acceptance of this assumption was a severe blow to Taylor's attempts to erect a wall between his proposals and their misapplication, to claim separate intellectual territories for his ideas and for the industrial practices spearheaded by others, particularly industrial practices he had already explicitly condemned in ***Shop Management*** and ***Principles***.

THE PROBLEM OF TAYLOR'S IDEALISM

It is not absurd to call Taylor a scientific management prophet. He was so involved in promoting his ideas that his dedication assumes a religious quality, both in its intensity and in its appearance of proselytizing without financial reward. When the question arose at the Wilson committee hearings if he had money interests in scientific management, he responded:

> I have not a cent. I have not accepted any employment money under scientific management of any kind since 1901, and everything I have done in that cause has been done for nothing. I have spent all of the surplus of my income in trying to further the cause for many years past, and am spending it now.

He did not even accept reimbursement for his lectures or travel expenses in discussing scientific management.

A quasi-religious idealism is also present in the optimistic, millenial predictions that more compassionate human behavior would eventually prevail and lead to a better world. Vintage Taylor is his exchange with Rep. William Wilson:

> The Chairman (Wilson.) Mr. Taylor, do you believe that any system of scientific management . . . would revolutionize the minds of the employers to such an extent that they would immediately, voluntarily, and generally enforce the golden rule?
>
> Mr. Taylor. If they had any sense, they would.

In one sense this idealism is Taylor's least attractive feature, because he takes the attitude that misapplication of his ideas on labor-management cooperation is a unique problem rather than a dilemma that happens to many theorists whose work must be applied by others. The idealistic argument for cooperation would also be strengthened if Taylor had related it to his own experience with situations where cooperation was impossible. He knew the thorny road he had walked at Bethlehem Steel. He saw his own associates having petty quarrels. He must have understood the difficulties in gaining cooperation, and yet he embraced it as a realizable ideal, thus limiting the real-world usefulness of his ideas. The most valuable theories on motivation will explain how to create cooperation in a world where thorny paths and petty quarrels are almost the norm.

Miner Chipman, lawyer for the Watertown molders, grasped that idealizing human nature defeated Taylor in his confrontations with practicing managers who borrowed some of his methods. Chipman argues that Taylor "indulged in Utopian dreams equally as panacean as that of the radical socialist." These dreams were bound to fail because they ignored fallen human nature. Chipman notes, "If we were truly righteous, truly just, truly altruistic, if we really loved our brother man, the socialistic commonwealth would not be a bad sort of thing . . . and . . . scientific management would also be a very good thing."

For the real world, Taylor gives too little thought to situations where the impetus for mutually beneficial cooperation coexists with a potential for conflict over how to cooperate (what the political scientist Thomas Schelling calls "mixed-motive" situations). Taylor envisions a future where managers and workers are so closely allied that the need for collective bargaining disappears. Chipman argues:

> It is not for scientific management to build up Utopian conditions, wherein organized labor would be unnecessary. Organized labor IS. It is our job to take it as it is, not as it ought to be, and work out, slowly, if necessary, the conflicting ideals that separate employer and employee.

Towards the end of Taylor's life, University of Chicago economist Robert Hoxie wrote a study also dismissing Taylor as an "idealist" who failed to distinguish between what might be and what actually was. The critique of scientific management as overidealized is borne out in the actual behavior of business managers and government officers. Many of them like Taylor's discrete methods but reject the moral shift that he postulates should accompany these techniques, being skeptical whether their employees are ripe for such conversions.

At the end of the House testimony, Rep. John Tilson asks Taylor, "How many concerns, to your knowledge, use your system in its entirety?" Taylor replies, "In its entirety—none; not one." . . .

Terry Mulcaire (essay date 1991)

SOURCE: "Progressive Visions of War in 'The Red Badge of Courage' and 'The Principles of Scientific Management'," in *American Quarterly,* Vol. 43, No. 1, March, 1991, pp. 46-72.

[*In the following essay, Mulcaire argues that Stephen Crane's depiction of war in* The Red Badge of Courage *as mechanical and systematic indicates the widespread acceptance at the end of the nineteenth century of Taylor's principles.*]

As Henry Fleming turns his back on war at the end of *The Red Badge of Courage* (1895), Stephen Crane describes Henry's retreat with a biblical allusion that collapses the difference between war and peace. "He came from hot plowshares to prospects of clover tranquility," Crane writes, "and it was as if hot plowshares were not." His text is the famous passage from Isaiah 2:4: "They shall beat their swords into plowshares, and their spears into pruning hooks; nation shall not lift up swords against nation, neither shall they learn war any more." But Crane mangles the logic of Isaiah's text, reversing its association of war with swords and violence and peace with plowshares and agriculture, as if the battle Henry is retreating from—the place of "hot plowshares"—were the scene of a violently heated beating of swords into plowshares, or war itself the peaceful activity which produces plowshares from swords. Readers are left with the sense that the difference between war and peace can be established and maintained only by means of violence itself. Readers of *The Red Badge* have always noticed how detached its violence appears to be from any of the specific ideological or political issues of the Civil War, and the image of the hot plowshare affirms that detachment: violence, in Crane's eyes, seems a general condition of peace as much as it is of war.

In recent years some of Crane's most sophisticated critics have taken this apparent absence of ideological context in *The Red Badge* to indicate its critique of the progressive, reformist ideology of its era. These critics focus in common on Crane's tendency to visualize war as a normative social condition, the same tendency displayed briefly in the image of the hot plowshare. For Donald Pease and Amy Kaplan, for example, Crane's overriding focus on spectacles of war stripped of ideological justifications makes *The Red Badge* into a kind of demystifying camera lens directed at the ideology of American industrial capitalism. Underneath the era's attempt to rewrite the Civil War as the historical origin of a new, peaceful, and progressive union, *The Red Badge,* in this critical view, unmasks new social divisions and sources of conflict which were emerging from the systematic transformation of American society to an industrial base.

Such readings of Crane leave out of the context of the era's ideology, however, the way that progressive industrial reformers embraced the same ideologically critical realism that Crane practiced, as a means of promoting a positive vision of industrialization's potential to transform society. These reformers, worried about the "overcivilizing" and softening effects of peace and prosperity on the national character, proposed that America beat its swords into mass industrial machinery, uniting the nation on a mass industrial war footing and reproducing what they considered to be the social benefits of war—heroic individual effort and democratic cooperation—while eliminating the destructive violence of past wars. Crane's figure of the hot plowshare, far from indicating a literary vision which escapes the era's ideology, captures with remarkable accuracy a widespread progressive vision of a generalized, systematic, and industrial "war on nature," in William James's words, which was to provide the basis for a healthy industrial society.

The most sweeping and influential statement of this ideology appeared in Frederick Winslow Taylor's ***The Principles of Scientific Management*** (1911). Taylor promoted a "new viewpoint" on industry, a vision of industrial inefficiency itself as society's natural enemy. He argued that scientific management's systematic division of labor would end "wars" between labor and management by uniting them in a democratically cooperative battle against inefficiency. Scientific management would systematically produce or "develop first-class men," as he put it, and, at the same time, produce an identity of interests between the laboring and the managerial classes. *The Red Badge*—with its battle scene imagery of machines and mass production and with its account of the development of Henry Fleming into a hero—shares with ***Principles*** an ideologically progressive realism, exemplified by a vision which fuses war and peace, heroic individuals and systematized workers, in an imagination of a progressive and democratic union.

I

Such a vision of industrial reform comes vividly into focus in 1885, the year Edward Bellamy published his hugely popular utopian novel *Looking Backward 2000-1887* (1888). In the year 2000 Bellamy's hero Julian West finds that world society has been transformed through the institution of a democratic "industrial army," designed to organize and amplify the martial drives of each member of society and to direct those drives toward the elimination of humanity's natural needs. This ultimate reformation and rationalization of society, in Bellamy's imagination, would be the result simply of a clarified vision of the potential of such a martial, industrial cooperation to overcome natural needs. Bellamy's novel could have been titled "Hindsight is Better than Foresight"; what is only seen darkly in 1887, Bellamy tells us, will be clearly visible by 2000. Bellamy, however, cannot resist directing some aggression of his own at humanity circa 1887, out of frustration with their very dullness of vision. Julian West returns in a dream to the Boston of 1887 with his vision of a cooperative, socialist, industrial army, only to be rejected by his conservative, upper-class former friends as "an enemy of society." West is relieved to wake up once again in the year 2000, and his relief is an index of Bellamy's sense of the blindness of America in the 1880s to his vision of industrial progress.

Looking Backward shows that progressive industrial reformers saw their task as the reform of their society's vision of industrialization's democratic potential, while it also exhibits the critical paradox which afflicted that visionary reform. If progressives such as Bellamy proposed to unite humanity in a shared vision of a natural enemy of industrial society, they almost always ended by attacking that element of human society which failed to share in the vision, reproducing a new version of the social antagonisms they had set out to reform. For William James, as for Bellamy, this element was made up of the leisured classes, which remained "blind," as James put it in an essay entitled "The Moral Equivalent of War," to the antagonism subsisting between humanity and a hostile natural environment. James's response to this problem of blindness to the reformist potential of industry was itself industrial: as a cure for the blindness of the leisured, James proposed an industrial draft, through which each generation would be sent off in its youth to coal mines and factories in order to have their eyes opened to the necessity of industrial exertions, to pay their "blood tax" in the "moral equivalent of war," the "immemorial human warfare against nature."

The concern showed by Bellamy and James over the blindness of the leisured classes manifested a much broader concern, felt by progressives of all stripes, that the successful winning of wealth and comfort eventually led to indifference, or even antagonism, toward the larger social good. Such a concern rose out of an enduring commitment in the dominant American culture to basic Protestant values of individual labor and social productivity, values which progressives hoped to preserve precisely by systematizing and rationalizing them. The clearest statement of such a rationalization was Thorstein Veblen's *The Theory of the Leisure Class* (1899), where he elevated a Protestant work ethic to the level of a first scientific principle. Veblen argued that an "instinct of workmanship," or an instinctive drive efficiently to exploit nature to human ends, was the very biological basis of human evolutionary progress. Since the exertion of this instinct in modern times was restricted to the engineering and industrial classes, Veblen argued that the leisured classes, because of their lack of contact with physical work, had become detached from a process of biological progressivism. The ideological blindness of the leisured classes to the value of industrial progress, in Veblen's analysis, was due to this detachment, which left them in an epistemological fog, where they seized upon the superficial traits of a prior, essentially feudal level of social evolution—walking sticks, extravagant dress, elaborate social proprieties—and confused these surfaces with the evolution of civilization itself.

In his 1911 address on "The Genteel Tradition in American Philosophy," George Santayana identified as an enduring structural principle of American cultural history an opposition very much like Veblen's distinction between the engineering, industrial classes and the leisured classes. His essay can situate for us the progressive industrial reform movement within a larger tradition of American critical realism in philosophy and literature. Santayana praised an iconoclastic, enterprising, and critical tradition of American culture, rooted in the Calvinism of the Puritans, and attacked a conservative, complacent, and genteel tradition, which had detached itself from the first tradition to embrace a comfortable, materialistic, Victorian status quo. He praised the first tradition and attacked the genteel tradition as little more than a drag on the advance of civilization, insofar as the first preserved the true spirit of what he felt was a deeply valuable Protestant world view. This was the view of a rational and critical natural philosophy humble enough never to presume that the answers it found were more than temporary, contingent ones. It was an essentially evolutionary view of the type Veblen embraced; the great nineteenth-century practitioner of this way of seeing, for Santayana, was Emerson, and he found it embodied, in his day, in the pragmatism of his friend and colleague William James. Along with James, then, Santayana believed that a progressive realism was necessarily at once a practical and a critical pursuit; cast in the tones of Calvinism, it was a constant struggle to make nature reveal itself to human understanding, a struggle which could no more ultimately succeed than it could be abandoned. "Eternal vigilance," Santayana concluded, "is the price of knowledge; perpetual hazard, perpetual experiment keep quick the edge of life."

"Vigilance," "hazard," and "experiment" mark the points of affinity between Santayana's philosophical history and the practical, progressive ideal of a combined martial and scientific industry, an ideal which was to be produced through a strenuous visualization of nature and which opposed itself to the self-satisfied blindness of the genteel leisured classes. What sets Frederick Winslow Taylor apart from the reformers and thinkers surveyed here is the intensity and focus of the vision he shared with them:

Taylor recognized within the practical pursuit of industry itself the uncritical blindness found by the others in the leisured classes who were exempted from industrial practice. Late in his life Taylor described the genesis of this project in the language of the visionary progressive, writing that he had his "eye on the bad industrial conditions which prevailed at the time and gave a good deal of time and thought to some possible remedy for them." These bad conditions within industry, Taylor concluded, were due to the same epistemological mistake Veblen attributed to the leisured classes: management and labor, he believed, had both fixed on a certain stage of industrial development, the stage of violent industrial conflict, as the natural structure of industry itself. "There is no question," he wrote in the opening pages of ***Principles,*** "that, throughout the industrial world, a large part of the organization of employers as well as employees, is for war rather than for peace, and that perhaps the majority on either side do not believe that it is possible so to arrange their mutual relations that their interests become identical." Taylor felt that because labor and management were each so committed to seeing the other as the enemy, they were blind to the inefficiencies in the labor process which were their real, common enemy. He set out to reform this situation by getting labor and management to take their eyes off of each other, in effect, so that they might once again begin scientifically to search out inefficiencies in the industrial process itself. The scientific manager, he wrote, must make "an effort of the imagination" in order to "appreciate," as he put it, "awkward, inefficient, or ill-directed movements of men," phenomena which "leave nothing visible" to the unreformed eye. Along with this appreciation of inefficiency as the real enemy of industry, Taylor claimed further, would come a new appreciation for the potential of cooperative industry to improve the lives of both labor and management. It was the adoption of this "new outlook," Taylor claimed, this "new viewpoint," which was "of the very essence of scientific management."

As a practical system for the rationalization of industrial production, Taylorism is extraordinary for its foundation in a socially critical mode of vision, an aesthetic vision of industry as the arena of human activity where a universal interest might appear and be realized. Before he could efficiently produce pig iron, or gun carriages, or ball bearings, Taylor wanted to produce this new viewpoint in both workers and managers, a production he equated with that of scientific managers. The scientific manager was thus not simply the heroic, reforming agent of the industrial system; he was also the system's original product. "In the past," Taylor proclaimed, "the man has been first; in the future the system must be first"; and Taylor's system was clearly designed to "make this competent man," or to "develop first-class men," from the ranks of both labor and management. Both would achieve first-class status simply by opening their eyes to the new viewpoint of scientific management.

If his reformed management originated in a democratic, aesthetic vision of a universal industrial interest, in practice Taylor called for a systematic division between the tasks of management and labor in industrial shops—where management became the eyes and mind and labor the hands and body of the system. Each job was to be split into distinct supervisory and physical aspects with one man "watching" and one man "working," as Taylor put it. In these terms, Taylor's worker was figuratively blind: his every action, down to the slightest movement of his limbs, was overseen and prescribed for him by his manager. On the other hand, the work of the scientific manager for Taylor involved an intense, even obsessive focus on seeing and making visible the content of every task in a shop and then singling out and eliminating the inefficiency "hidden" in each task. The manager performed first a sort of studious spectatorship at a given worker's task, followed by a series of mathematical calculations aimed at breaking the task down into parts and finding the most efficient way to perform it. Taylor's early disciples would then produce a graphic diagram of the task in order to make visible the difference between its efficient and inefficient components. His protégés Frank and Lillian Gilbreth ultimately pioneered the use of stop-action photography and movies as a means of visualizing each task as a series of distinct, abstract movements which could then be efficiently reorganized by the scientific manager.

Taylor's opponents among labor leaders of the day attacked him above all for this tendency of his system to reduce the ability of workers to supervise themselves, and to put that capacity under the strict control of management. In other words, Taylor's new viewpoint on industry, when put into practice, seemed to its critics to blind laborers effectively and to reserve all intellectual and supervisorial capacity to management. Historians of era have continued to attack Taylor in these terms until he has come to be seen as the embodiment of the worst aspects of a progressive ideology which, under the banner of social progress, cloaked a drive to dominate and control social and individual behavior. In Harry Braverman's *Labor and Monopoly Capital,* the most thorough of these critiques, Taylor appears as the virtual embodiment of the interests of capital and of capital's power to degrade the quality and autonomy of skilled labor. "The perfect expression of the concept of skill in capitalist society is to be found in the bald and forthright dictums of the early Taylorians," Braverman writes, "who had discovered the great truth of capitalism that the workers must become the instrument of labor in the hands of the capitalist, but had not yet learned the wisdom of adorning, obfuscating, and confusing this straightforward necessity." It has been left to "modern managers and sociologists," according to Braverman, to obscure Taylorism's "forthright" promotion of a rational division of labor by appealing to a reactionary, hypostatic realism which dictates that "all that is real [is] necessary, all that exists . . . inevitable," and thus that "the present mode of production [is] eternal."

Braverman's account of the way the techniques of scientific management have transformed industrial working conditions is careful and thorough, but he is less careful in his account of Taylor's ideological interests and practices. To say that Taylor "had not yet learned the wisdom of obfuscating" the division of labor that his system called for is itself an obfuscation, one which makes Taylor into a straw man for Braverman's Marxist model of ideological demystification. By the terms of this model, the more closely tied one's interests are to a capitalist system of production, the more deeply involved one necessarily must be in the ideological mystifications that obscure those processes of accumulation. Taylor, however, was clearly dedicated to displaying and publicizing his plan for scientific management, in a way entirely consistent with his conviction that industrial progress depended on a strenuous visualization of the content of industrial practice. Indeed, Braverman himself admits that Taylor "is still the most useful source" for a critique of scientific management because of the forthright way he explains and illustrates its practices; and in his critique, Braverman relies heavily on citations from Taylor's own writings.

Principles represents Taylor's own attempt to unmask an ideology of reactionary realism that viewed the present mode of production as eternal and to practice a more progressive realism which would "point out, through a series of simple illustrations," the virtues of a new viewpoint of industrial cooperation. In his testimony before a 1912 House Committee considering the status of scientific management in army arsenals, Taylor claimed that the real source of opposition to scientific management lay in such conservative adherence to the status quo, which he believed could be found across the social spectrum, both within and without industry. In any shop, Taylor claimed, scientific management always uncovered a few "incorrigibly lazy" men, or men who "can work and won't work." "There are a few men who remain, you might say, incorrigibly lazy," he wrote, "and when those men are proved to be unchangeable shirkers they have to get out of the establishment in which scientific management is being introduced." Taylor's problem with these men was not that they were *shirkers;* he understood the laziness of workers—"soldiering" in the slang of the day—who felt it was not in their interest to work. His problem was that these men were *unchangeable;* that they refused to adopt his new viewpoint of scientific management, a viewpoint which would make visible to them that it was in their best interests to work efficiently and cooperatively. Taylor went on later in his testimony to claim that the ultimate source of this unchangeably conservative way of seeing was to be found outside of industry, not in the working classes, but in the genteel literary classes. "For the almost universality with which this view is found among workingmen," he testified,

> and still more for the fact that this view is growing instead of diminishing, that the men who are not themselves working in cooperative industry and who belong, we will say, taking a single example, to the literary classes, men who have the leisure time for study and investigation and the opportunity for knowing better, are mainly to blame.

Taylor's animus against the literary classes in this passage does not rise from his sense that they opposed him, that they were working, for example, to convince labor that their interests were opposed to those of management; it arose from his sense that the literary classes were taking no interest at all in the nation's industrial affairs. In other words, Taylor felt that the literary classes were an entire class of people who, like the rare, incorrigibly lazy man found within shops, *could* work to promote the better interests of the nation but would not. Taylor's hostility to the leisured literary classes echoes here the antagonism to the leisured classes shared by the industrial reformers, in particular Santayana's hostility towards a genteel traditionalism which divorces itself from the practice of a progressive, visionary social criticism. These sympathies are further evident in a letter in which Taylor explained his decision not to publish a paper on scientific management in the *Atlantic.* "The readers of the *Atlantic,*" he wrote:

> consist probably very largely of professors and literary men, who would be interested more in the abstract theory than in the actual good which would come from the introduction of scientific management. . . . The people whom I want to reach with the article are principally those men who are doing the manufacturing and construction work of our country, both employers and employed.

That George Santayana was both a professor and, most likely, a reader of the *Atlantic* does not diminish the ideological sympathies evident here between Taylor's opposition to the presumed gentility of the *Atlantic*'s readers and Santayana's opposition to a genteel philosophical tradition. Both defined their progressive way of seeing in terms of its resistance to a stolid and conservative mainstream which appeared even within industry itself, according to Taylor, in the persons of the few "unchangeable shirkers" to be found in any shop. In imaginative and ideological terms Taylor's system did not oppose supervisorial watchers to blind workers so much as it opposed two ways of seeing: a progressive industrial realism against a conservative, literary view which in its blind commitment to the status quo exerted a passive resistance to progress.

For Taylor, the new viewpoint of scientific management transcended and made obsolete the specific interests of both labor and management; he was able to imagine opposition to his system, then, only in terms of a point of view that held no interest at all in industry or social progress. Evidently, in imagining that his own interests represented a universal interest, Taylor simply distorted the particular interests of laborers and labor leaders, managers and factory owners, all of whom had their reasons for opposing the idea that they should surrender control of the conditions of production to a disinterested managerial class. As David Montgomery has shown, Taylor's insistence that there were no particular interests attached to scientific management helped to create a state of affairs where the interests of capital were able to dominate the applications of Taylor's techniques: workers could be compelled to conform to the strict control called for by those techniques, but managers and owners could not be compelled to conform to Taylor's philosophy of cooperation and mutual benefit. The point of taking seriously Taylor's distorted account of the conservative ideological opposition he encountered is not to defend Taylor against critics who attack the role of scientific management in degrading the autonomy of industrial labor, but simply to note that Taylor practiced a system of ideological critique which critics of industrialism such as Braverman continue to practice, a critique which they can direct at Taylor only at the expense of distorting the way in which ideology is produced and criticized.

II

In his study of turn-of-the-century culture, Stephen Kern has linked the stop-action photographic techniques of Taylor's protégés, the Gilbreths, to the modernist aesthetics of Cubism and Futurism which were germinating at the time. In reading *The Red Badge* along with ***Principles,*** one can begin to link Taylor's views on industrial reform to the realist aesthetic Crane adopted. Crane's friend Joseph Conrad, in his preface to *The Nigger of the Narcissus,* professed his desire "by the power of the written word to make you hear, to make you feel . . . before all, to make you see"—a motto which could have served Taylor in his attempts to "point out, through a series of simple illustrations," the virtues of his vision of industry. Crane's critics focus on this power of realism to make *The Red Badge* an ideologically demystifying lens through which readers clearly see the violent social transformations brought about by industrialization in the 1890s. Thus the socially critical force of Crane's battle scenes, according to Donald Pease, comes from their discarding the kind of "adequate ideological underpinnings" which would make social sense out of war, in favor of pure, photographic spectacles of violence. In the same vein, Andrew Delbanco claims that "[r]eading *The Red Badge* relieves us of our ideology and, to the extent that this is ever possible, replaces it with raw experience." *The Red Badge,* however, can be praised for escaping the ideological context of its day, and for criticizing progressive society as a warlike spectacle, only by ignoring its imbrication in the ideologically critical context of progressive martial industrialism, a movement which already had set out to make society see itself in terms of war.

The aesthetics of literary realism that Crane embraced in *Maggie, a Girl of the Streets* (1893) shared the hostility to genteel traditionalism and the commitment to a strenuously critical vision of life which is evident in the ideology of progressive industrial reform. Taylor dropped out of college and turned his "eye to the bad industrial conditions prevailing at the time"; Crane dropped out of college, as he put it, "to study faces on the streets." *Maggie,* the result of this study, shocked genteel readers with its photographically precise visions of slum violence, but it earned extravagant praise from the era's most powerful spokesman for a progressive literary aesthetic, William Dean Howells, who toasted Crane as a writer who had "sprung into life fully armed." A few years before *Maggie,* Howells had praised the *Personal Memoirs* (1885) of a real soldier, Ulysses S. Grant, in terms which can begin to explain why and how Crane chose to follow *Maggie* with a Civil War novel. "He does not cast about for phrases," Howells wrote of Grant, "but takes the word, whatever it is, that will best give his meaning, as if it were a man or a force of men for the accomplishment of a feat of arms. There is not a moment wasted in preening and prettifying, after the fashion of literary men." In Howells's disparagement of "preening and prettifying" literary men, one finds once again, here within the realm of literary culture itself, a by now familiar hostility to a genteel literariness which detaches itself from real life in order to uphold conventional aestheticist notions of beauty. When Howells describes Crane as "fully armed" with literary talent and praises Grant for writing as if literature could be "a man or a force of men" accomplishing "a feat of arms," one sees him importing into literature the valorization of martial effort which Bellamy, James, and Taylor set out to import into industry.

Grant's memoirs were an especially popular example of a huge body of literature produced between 1880 and 1900, which aimed to revise the nation's view of the Civil War from a nearly disastrous shattering of national identity into a violent crucible which had produced a new and vigorous post-war ideology of union. Grant, for example, singled out the valor of both Confederate and Union soldiers at Shiloh as proof of the quality of the post-war American military establishment. This vision of war as a socially cooperative effort dovetailed neatly with visions of martial industrial reform such as *Looking Backward;* indeed, the Civil War memoirs themselves occasionally partook of the language of martial industrialism. A theme of industrial management runs through Warren Lee Goss's *Recollections of a Private* (1890), for example, which Goss sums up by writing: "The whole military machine must be lubricated with general, special, necessary and unnecessary, ornamental and practical orders," while the component soldiers of the machine must learn "the trade of war thoroughly and systematically."

In 1895, Crane gave Howells a signed copy of *The Red Badge* with an inscription thanking Howells for "many things he [Crane] has learned, and above all, for a certain readjustment of his point of view victoriously concluded some time in 1892." His war novel makes clear that, in winning his way to the point of view of Howells's progressive realist aesthetic, Crane also effectively adopted the realism of Taylor's view on industrial reform. *The Red Badge* virtually catalogs the concerns of industrial reformers, picturing the Civil War both as the historical source of the problems those reformers addressed and as the genesis of the martial, industrial solution. As the book opens, Henry Fleming is afflicted by a typically progressive fear of the softening and levelling character of modern life. Where Taylor was extraordinarily acute in finding this softening effect even within industrial shops, Crane uncovers such softening and levelling effects not within the leisured comfort of modern peacetime, but within modern war. War seems to Henry Fleming to have become an overcivilized, overrationalized "blue demonstration," which has made obsolete the kind of traditional heroism Henry admiringly pictures as "Greeklike struggles." He paraphrases the fears of a soft and comfortable industrial peace expressed by advocates of a martial industrialism: "Men were better, or more timid. Secular and religious education had effaced the throat-grappling instinct, or else firm finance held in check the passions." His fear is that his own experience in the army will be merely a blue demonstration, or a systematic and artificial substitute for war in which he is merely "drilled and drilled and reviewed, and drilled and drilled and reviewed," that the army will "make victories as a contrivance turns out buttons," and that he himself, in the heat of battle, will turn out to lack Greeklike qualities.

Thus Henry's actions are motivated not by his opposition to Southern interests or his commitment to the Union, but rather by his consuming desire to see the appearance of a real, Greeklike war within what looks to him like an overly civilized, mechanized blue demonstration, a desire which implies the pre-existence of a certain unity between the antagonists of the war: both sides are committed to seeing violence. Henry wants to see war itself rather than any human enemy, and this vision becomes identified with a pure, antagonistic agency: a visionary war on war. On the way into battle, Henry thinks: "They were going to look at war, the red animal—war, the blood-swollen god." At the same time, Henry is afraid of being seen with his back turned to the war, of failing in his soldierly job of "looking at war." As he skulks behind the lines after fleeing battle, Henry imagines the innocent questions of a comrade in terms a soldiering laborer might have applied to the supervision of a Tayloresque manager: "The simple questions of the tattered man had been knife thrusts to him. They asserted a society that probes pitilessly at secrets until all is apparent. . . . He admitted that he could not defend himself against this agency. It was not within the power of vigilance." After he flees the battle, Henry is not ashamed of himself so much as he is afraid of being seen by the "society" of his regiment in such a shameful position; indeed, this kind of visibility would literally constitute his shame. "He would truly be a worm" he thinks as he makes his way back toward the lines, "if any of his comrades should see him returning thus."

The advice Henry's mother gives him as he leaves home to join the army—"You watch out Henry, an' take good care of yerself in this here fighting business—you watch out"—functions as a kind of ruling principle to Henry's career, as it might for a scientific manager. Henry, as both subject and object of an aggressive form of vision, figures the slippage observed in Taylor's systematic division of men into watchers and workers in terms which virtually mimic the scientific terms of Taylorism. Private Fleming may be constantly drilled and reviewed by his generals, but at the same time he becomes the Tayloresque, scientific general-manager of his own performance. He tries "mathematically to prove to himself that he would not run from a battle" and makes "ceaseless calculations," but this mental supervision is useless without a physical object. Henry finally concludes that he will have to watch the work of his own body, or "figuratively to watch his legs to discover their merits or faults. He reluctantly admitted that he could not sit still and with a mental slate and pencil derive an answer. To gain it, he must have blaze, blood, and danger, even as a chemist requires this, that, and the other."

This identification of the battlefield soldier and the scientist explains Henry's rationalization of his own flight from battle. He attributes it to his commitment to a martial form of rational, industrial efficiency, which he imagines as a democratic enterprise in which the meaning of the military terms "private" and "general"—or the Tayloresque terms "worker" and "manager"—become totally interchangeable.

> He had done a good part in saving himself, who was a little piece of the army. . . . Later the officers could fit the little pieces together again, and make a battle front. . . . It was all plain that he had proceeded according to very correct and commendable rules. His actions had been sagacious things. They had been full of strategy. They were the work of a master's legs.

Henry completely dehumanizes himself by imagining himself as a "little piece" of the army, "fit" in by the officers; but at the same time he claims for himself as a little piece the strategic capacity to supervise the work of his own legs, reducing the officers to the mere mechanical labor of fitting together the independently "sagacious" little pieces of the army.

In the terms of a Tayloresque system, the problem with Henry's masterful management of his own legs in fleeing battle is precisely that no one besides Henry saw it. In the world of *The Red Badge,* courage as well as shame is not integral to the soldier but systematic, defined by its visibility before the eyes of the army. Henry is not courageous until his desire to see violence is itself made visible by the painful "knife thrusts" of his own army's visionary agency. His fear that the tattered man's questions will bring his shame into visibility is accompanied by his approval of, and desire for, a visible courage: "He conceived persons with torn bodies to be peculiarly happy. He wished that he, too, had a wound, a red badge of courage." As he approaches the front, this is exactly what he gets when he meets a panicked member of his own retreating army who "adroitly" crushes his rifle on Henry's head. In this soldier's fusion of panic and adroitness, one sees in microcosm the fusion of irrational Greeklike violence and rational blue demonstrations.

His wound, of course, is interpreted by his regiment as the badge of his courage, and in turn is seen almost universally with some degree of irony by Crane's critics as an empty sign of something which remains absent:

Henry's courage, the possibility of heroism in a modern war. In particular, the superficial, visual character of this red badge has been taken as a prominent example of the book's lack of ideological roots. But the very terms with which Henry rationalizes his flight betray his deep commitment to the system of blue demonstrations where he is drilled and reviewed; and this commitment translates directly into Henry's Greeklike conception that people with torn bodies are peculiarly happy. They are happy, in other words, because they have been torn; their courage—their commitment to the system—has been made visible, available to review. Precisely because Henry's wound is both produced by the army and subject to review by the army's vigilant eye, it signifies his unambiguous commitment to that system of vigilance and to a definition of heroism, not as something internal, or integral, to the individual, but as something mass-produced by a martial system.

This process of systematic, visionary development is completed the next day in battle when Henry momentarily surrenders all of his own rationalizing and supervisorial faculties. "He lost sense of everything but his hate," one reads, and he becomes "so engrossed in his occupation that he was not aware of a lull." In the manner of a worker under Taylorism, Henry does not stop until someone tells him to: "He turned then and . . . looked at the blue line of his comrades. . . . [T]hey all seemed to be engaged in staring at him. They had become spectators. . . . 'By heavens,'" Henry's lieutenant crows in admiration, "'if I had ten thousand wild cats like you I could tear the stomach outa this war in less'n a week!'" Henry realizes that "as he had gone on loading and firing and cursing . . . they had found time to regard him. And they now looked upon him as a war devil."

By figuring Henry as both subject and object of something very much like Taylor's conception of managerial vision, Crane imagines the population of a Civil War battlefield as a progressive, Tayloresque society, united in its commitment to a systematic vision of war. In Crane's imagination, the system no longer exactly directs violence at an enemy; rather, it seems to reproduce enmity itself, and its successful function comes to be defined as a production of violence, a war on war, in which final victory—"tearing the stomach outa this war"—becomes literally inconceivable. Henry does not want to see victory so much as he wants to see violence, and the enemy on which Henry is systematically compelled to gaze is not only the "red animal, the blood-swollen god," but also the industrial system itself. Henry thinks to himself: "The battle was like the grinding of an immense and terrible machine. . . . Its complexities and powers, its grim processes, fascinated him. He must go and see it produce corpses." The battle's grim processes, then, figure the same system which produces Henry Fleming, "first-class" soldier: the "torn bodies" with whom Henry wishes to identify himself "expressed the awful machinery in which the men had been entangled." The "tattered man" captures the function of this violent system in an anecdote he tells Henry.

> I was talkin' cross pickets with a boy from Georgie, onct, an' that boy, he ses, "Your fellers'll all run like hell when they onct hearn a gun," he ses. "Mebbe they will," I ses, "but I don't b'lieve none of it," I ses; "an b'jiminey," I ses back t'um, "mebbe your fellers'll all run like hell when they onct hearn a gun," I ses. He larfed. Well, they didn't run t'day, did they, hey? No, sir! They fit, an' fit, an' fit." His homely face was suffused with a light of love for the army which was to him all things beautiful and powerful.

By the time the tattered man gets to the end of this passage, "they" are both the tattered man's "fellers" and the Georgie boy's "fellers." "The army" has become a blanket term unifying blue and grey in a they who "didn't run," but "fit, an' fit, an' fit": an exceptionally violent, but otherwise faithful version of the cooperative industrial armies imagined by James and Bellamy and a strict example of the unionist revisions of the Civil War in the literature of the 1880s and 1890s. Heroism here is both democratic and systematic: one need only "fit" as a little piece within a system of blaze, blood, and danger; one need only become visible there by being torn, in order to be regarded as a war devil. His love for this "beautiful" vision of the army makes the tattered man's tatters a quality of his vision, as well as his body.

Crane graphically represents as a tear or tattering the division of the individual into visionary and physical components called for by the Taylor system: The system of blaze, blood, and danger in *The Red Badge,* however, does not simply produce men whose tatters display to one another their courage; it also produces corpses, which would seem to represent a scandalous breakdown of the society of the battlefield, that its democratic system of violent vigilance is grounded in the brutal victimization of a certain class. Crane's literary view of the Civil War seems to anticipate Taylor's critics: in order to produce managers systematically, a scientific industry, it appears, must also produce a blind and brutalized work force. Crane's corpses, however, appear to be neither blind nor precisely victimized. He characterizes them, consistently, by both their uncanny capacity to see and their remarkable military potency. Such is the "invulnerable dead man" they encounter on their way into battle, who lies on his back, "staring at the sky." Such, in particular, is the corpse that a terrified Henry Fleming encounters in chapter eight of *The Red Badge.* Here Henry, in his efforts to put distance between himself and the battle, is pushing deeper and deeper into the woods on the edge of the battlefield. Suddenly he stops:

> horror-stricken at the sight of a thing. He was being looked at by a dead man who was seated with his back against a columnlike tree. . . . The youth gave a shriek as he confronted the thing. He was for moments turned to stone before it. He remained staring into the liquid-looking eyes. The dead man and the living man exchanged a long look.

Far from representing a scandalous breakdown of the cooperative social system of the battlefield, or a victimized body, emptied of all capacity to manage or oversee its own fate, this corpse is much closer to being an uncanny scientific manager *par excellence:* a "supervisor" without an effective body, rather than a body effectively blind. The "long look" Henry exchanges with the corpse is the ultimate instance of his being reviewed by the hostile knife thrusts of his society's visionary agency, an agency which corpses continue to possess and to exert on the living. This spectatorial power is implied first by Crane's phrasing—Henry stops at "the sight of a thing"—and then aggressively literalized by Crane—"he was being looked at by a dead man." When he reaches the limits of the battlefield, Henry does not encounter a hidden scandal which refutes the ideology underpinning the battle; he finds a pure form of the same visionary violence which constitutes the battle, and it has the same effect on him that it always has. Leaving the dead man, Henry immediately begins "to run in the direction of the battle" in order to "witness" it, and—but this amounts to the same thing—to fight in it again.

III

In Crane's imagination of a martial industrial system, the system's violence peaks not in the production of blind corpses, but rather in a doubled vision of corpses, in the seeing of corpses who themselves see. These corpses, in turn, evoke Taylor's incorrigibly lazy men who hold what Taylor disparaged as the literary view of industry: they watch the industrial system's functioning but do not actually work at it. The corpse with whom Henry exchanges a long look is a threat to Henry, but not because he represents the interests of a class victimized by Henry's commitment to the systematic machinery of battle. The corpse is terrifying because his view of the war is empty of any perceptible interest in war. Unlike the tattered man, he does not quite fit on the battlefield; he does nothing to make himself visible there; he just looks at it. His spectatorship, if anything, is disinterested, and the fear Henry feels under the eyes of the corpse is clarified by noting that Crane himself felt a similar horror for the idea of a disinterested literary vision. This horror comes out in a letter in which Crane wondered about the aesthetic principles of Henry James. "What," Crane wondered:

> does the man mean by disinterested contemplation? It won't wash. If you care enough about a thing to study it, you are interested and have stopped being disinterested. It clamours in my skull that there is no such thing as disinterested contemplation except that empty as a beerpail look that a babe turns on you and shrivels you to grass with. . . . [T]he horrible thing about a kid is that it makes no excuses, none at all. They are much like the breakers on the beach.

As the look of Crane's "babe" approaches complete aesthetic disinterest, the babe, mysteriously and ominously, is at once objectified and naturalized, appearing to become first a "beerpail" and then a "breaker on the beach." What worries Crane is that, at the same time, the unlucky human subject of the babe's disinterested look—in this scenario, Crane himself—is violently objectified, naturalized, "shriveled to grass," just as Henry Fleming felt himself "turned to stone" by the gaze of the corpse. Crane seems to feel that a truly disinterested vision threatened the definition of human existence itself, which, simply, was to be interested in what one sees. Thus his babe dissolves into the aspect of an ocean wave, and the yellow and green corpse Henry meets in the woods seems a part of the forest it inhabits, except that the babe and corpse turn a terrifyingly disinterested gaze on their human witness.

Crane is not attacking James here—they became friends and mutual admirers—so much as he is expressing his inability to conceive the possibility of a vision both disinterested and fully human. The invulnerably hostile corpses in *The Red Badge,* however, do represent Crane's real hostility to the genteel, moralistic elements of his society which rejected the socially critical visions of his literature—for example, the critic who denounced *Maggie* in *The Nation.* "His types are mainly human beings of the order which makes us regret the power of literature to portray them," wrote this anonymous reviewer. "We resent the sense that we must in certain points resemble them." But Crane did not find this genteel hostility only in the class of fastidious "literary men." Like Taylor, he found it across the social spectrum, for example, in the eyes of the proper old ladies he met in Jacksonville on his way to Cuba, "sitting on hotel porches saying how well the climate suits them and hurling the same lances with their eyes to begin bloodshed." Crane found it in the slums themselves, in very persons whose resemblance to himself the genteel reviewer in *The Nation* wanted to deny. In a letter discussing the Bowery, Crane complained about the "conceit" of its population, about the "person who thinks himself superior to the rest of us because he has no job and no pride and no clean clothes"; and he attributed the misery of the Bowery's residents to a lack of willingness to fight, to "a sort of cowardice . . . a lack of ambition or to willingly be knocked flat and accept the licking." In his sketch entitled "An Experiment in Misery," Crane described his encounter in a flophouse with one such "person," in a scene which he revised and put into the war novel he would soon write:

> Beneath the inky brows could be seen the eyes of the man exposed by the partly opened lids. To the youth it seemed that he and this corpse-like being were exchanging a prolonged stare and that the other threatened with his eyes. . . . The man did not move once through the night, but lay in this stillness as of death.

How close Taylor's antipathy to the "literary view" of industry was to Crane's hostility to a genteel way of seeing is evident in an anecdote in which Taylor's language echoes the kind of language Crane used to describe the vision of his antagonists. Describing one of the "college men" at Midvale whose aloofness from the society of the shop floor infuriated him, Taylor wrote: "He had a rather imperturbably wooden face, and looked at one with an expressionless eye. . . . This man was not only disliked, but cordially hated by all men." Taylor's figuration of his opponent's vision, or better his disfiguration, locates his writing style and diction, if just for a moment, clearly within the borders of the literary realism exemplified in the era by Stephen Crane.

The liminal quality of these antagonists of Crane's—the way they seem to straddle a border between life and death, between human and natural existence—marks Crane's acknowledgement that despite their apparently irremediable hostility, he and they did "resemble" one another. There is no peaceful exterior to the battlefield of *The Red Badge;* in attempting to leave it, Henry Fleming inevitably finds himself at its heart. Crane once referred to his own career as a "beautiful war" between the progressive realists such as himself, Garland, and Howells and the genteel conservatives who promoted a tendentiously moralistic literature. When he tried to paraphrase his conservative opponents, however, he found it impossible. They were "those who say—well, I don't know what they say. They don't, they can't say much, but they fight villainously [*sic*] and keep Garland and I out of the big magazines." Crane imagines his critics here in the same way he imagines the disinterested babe, as persons who mark a kind of mute, passive limit to human existence, where a form of violent vision is detached from any visible or articulate interests which might justify that violence.

IV

The point of the preceding examination of the systems of critical visualization shared by Taylor and Crane has not been, of course, to argue for the accuracy of their visions of American culture around the turn of the century but to show that the literary and industrial visualizations rose directly out of a shared ideology and a shared practice of realism. To the extent that *The Red Badge* is an apology for the progressive ideology of industrial systematization, it is pointless to try to use literary realism to locate a critical perspective outside of that ideology. The affinities between *The Red Badge* and ***Principles*** indicate that there is no such outside perspective any more than there is an outside to the battlefield of Crane's novel. The industrial system of the Progressive Era produced its own internal ideological critique, in the form of literary realism such as Crane's, as well as in the form of Taylor's industrial realism.

The important place of Taylor's vision of industrial reform in the context of Crane's realism has been ignored, perhaps out of an understandable desire on the part of modern-day literary critics to deny any point of resemblance between their own critical practice and the practice of Taylorism. Nonetheless, when a reader of Crane such as Amy Kaplan attributes the critical potency of his book to its capacity to "isolate discontinuous moments of vision"—making visible the inadequacy of the mythological narratives imposed on the Civil War during the 1890s—she adopts the language and techniques of the same critical realism Taylor adopted, using Crane as a kind of camera eye to locate the hidden sources of violence within the era's ideological status quo. These techniques recall the double edge of Crane's hot plowshare: recognizable in the violence of *The Red Badge* is how far the industrial systematization of labor actually was from progressivism; but one sees this only by adopting a systematically and rationally critical perspective shared with Taylorism.

In identifying a critical view of the Progressive Era with Crane's literary view, we identify with a technique which criticizes and, at the same time, reproduces ideology in a capitalist era, a technique embodied, above all, by the ultimate technique of Taylorism: photography. The conflicting ideological consequences of such an identification are the subject of Walter Benjamin's seminal essay on "The Work of Art in an Age of Mechanical Reproduction," in which Benjamin argues that the camera's capacity to reproduce its images destroyed the possibility of authentic art, thereby wrecking the conditions for an authentic selfhood which, for him, were linked closely to the ability to unburden oneself of ideological mystification through the appreciation of true art. Despite these negative effects of photography, Benjamin hailed its advent because, in the process of destroying the traditional conditions for authentic art, it also shattered the traditional distinction between aesthetics and political economy. As W. J. T. Mitchell has put it, on the one hand, the camera embodied for Benjamin the ideology of capitalism in the way that it reduced reality to a reproducible effect of a technological means of production. On the other hand, the camera also embodied in the art form of photography the natural tendency of capitalism to expose the social contradictions it creates and which ideology has always functioned to hide. For Benjamin, in an era of mechanical reproduction the aesthetic question of what was true and beautiful in art could never again be separated from the technical question of how an industrial means of production mediates our perception of truth and beauty: the photograph had bound art and industry together, and it was in this divided form that the ideological battles of industrial society would be fought.

For Benjamin, it was not difficult to distinguish between the liberating and the oppressive functions of the mechanical reproduction of art; he believed it was essential to the nature of history eventually to distinguish between the two, to eliminate the repressive and mystifying function, and to unfetter once and for all the liberatory and clarifying one. One can now see clearly enough the extent to which Benjamin's classically Marxist historical optimism, in which history itself would eventually bring about a kind of progressive super-realism, was a wishful distortion. The tendency of capitalism to expose its contradictions is not a natural effect of history at all. As Taylor shows plainly, it is part of the essential practices of capitalism, part of its constant process of self-criticism and evolutionary reform. Reading *The Red Badge* together with ***Principles,*** as camera eyes trained on one another, may show how difficult it is to separate the capacity of critical realism to relieve people of ideology from its tendency to reproduce ideology and its mystifying and distorting effects, a tendency which goes on behind our backs. One continues to need opposing perspectives to make visible the ideological distortions which have gone into raw historical experience.

The reader of *The Red Badge,* then, seems to be figured within the text—not so much in Henry Fleming as in the more broadly representative figure of the tattered man whose love for the "beauty and power" of his violent society might make readers want to deny any points of resemblance between themselves and him. After witnessing the horrific death of Jim Conklin, the tattered man says to Henry Fleming, "Look-a-here, pardner. He's up an' gone, ain't 'e, an' we might as well begin t' look out fer ol' number one." He and Henry are both always looking out, watching out, which makes the two of them as one: tattered, torn, divided, and thus marked for all to see as fit members of a progressive society. The hot plowshare might be this society's emblem, but its motto could come from Walter Benjamin, from his picture of what would be necessary for authors to become agents of progressive social change in an age of mechanical reproduction. "It is not spiritual renewal," Benjamin wrote, "that is desirable: technical innovations are suggested."

George Will (essay date 1997)

SOURCE: "Faster Mousetrap," in *The New York Times Book Review,* June 15, 1997, p. 10.

[*In the following essay, Will reviews* The One Best Way: Frederick Winslow Taylor and the Enigma of Efficiency.]

In November 1910 some railroads were trying to prove, as it had recently become their burden to do, that they merited Federal permission for rate increases. Representing opponents was Louis Brandeis, the future Justice, who questioned railroad officials about their costs. Were new efficiencies in operations an alternative to rate increases? No, said the railroaders. How did they know? Brandeis asked. Trust us, they said.

But Brandeis was in no mood to trust people who trusted their hunches, intuitions and experiences rather than the rising clerisy of experts. He caused a sensation by asserting that the railroads could save $1 million a day—serious money then—by "scientific management." How did he know? He knew about Frederick Winslow Taylor, who was about to become famous, and frequently unhappy, for the remaining five years of his life.

Taylor is still renowned among historians of American business. Peter Drucker, the well-known student of management, says that Taylor, not Marx, deserves to be ranked with Darwin and Freud in the trinity of makers of the modern world and that Taylorism is perhaps "the most powerful as well as the most lasting contribution America has made to Western thought since the Federalist Papers." Robert Kanigel's judgment is more measured: "The coming of Taylorism made our age what it was going to become anyway—only more so, more quickly, more irrevocably." However, Mr. Kanigel's richly detailed biography, *The One Best Way: Frederick Winslow Taylor and the Enigma of Efficiency,* shows how much drama there was in the mundane when Taylor was making it the stuff of a new "science" of efficiency.

Taylor, whose life (1856-1915) coincided with America's period of pell-mell industrialization, was born into an affluent, landed family in suburban Philadelphia. At the age of 13, during extended travel with his parents in Europe, he watched his impatient father use the power of his purse to get reluctant local laborers to repair a bridge so the family's touring could proceed. This was, for young Fred, an intensely practical epiphany: money can make working men move faster.

He was to become one of those men, briefly, and would use his years on the factory floor to achieve moral ascendancy through downward mobility. For the rest of his life he would invoke his laboring experience to claim the moral high ground in fierce debates about whether he understood, respected and served working people. At Phillips Exeter Academy (where, the saying was, there were "no rules, only absolute freedom, tempered by expulsion") he passed Harvard's admission exam with distinction. However, he chose to work in a factory making iron castings. There he learned that life is real, life is earnest.

He entered what Mr. Kanigel calls a "world of wood, iron, rope, leather, cloth," a world of steam power transmitted through belts and pulleys that amplified human muscle, which was abundant. Abundant and hence, Taylor saw, squandered. As he rose quickly into the ranks of management, he could act on his one seminal idea: the key to productivity is knowledge, not muscle power—although sometimes the most important knowledge is how to organize the use of muscles.

The instruments of organization included stopwatches, with dials marking tenths and hundredths of a minute for easy calculations. Taylor's interest was less in what could be done in 10 hours than in 10 seconds. How much time did it take to perform a properly analyzed task—fill a wheelbarrow, drive a nail, shovel coal? Assembly lines, like Ford's, or even disassembly lines, like those of Chicago's meatpackers, required the disassembly of work. "Amid the blur of activity of human work," Mr. Kanigel writes, "where did one element end and another begin?" Well, time-and-motion studies would tell. "Now, gentlemen, shoveling is a great science compared with pig-iron handling," Taylor said to a Congressional committee in 1912.

The committee was hostile and Taylor was bewildered. Theatrical in temperament, brimful of certitudes and vehement in expressing them, he was not just offended, he was uncomprehending when politicians and other people reacted furiously to his statements like: "In our scheme, we do not ask the initiative of our men. We do not want any initiative. All we want of them is to obey the orders we give them, do what we say, and do it quick." Although he could address workers with appalling brutality ("I have you for your strength and mechanical ability, and we have other men paid for thinking"), he considered himself a progressive, as did Brandeis, Ida Tarbell and other reformers.

This was, after all, a time of self-conscious modernity, defined in part by faith in science. In 1912 the nation would elect a political scientist President. There was a strong paternalistic streak in the progressivism of Walter Lippmann; Herbert Croly, the founder of The New Republic and leader of progressivism; and others who believed that modern life was too complicated for the untutored masses to cope with. A tutoring class, in government and business, would lead the people up from backward practices. However, it now seems that such workplace paternalism often is, well, inefficient. The unending search for enhanced productivity now often leads to something like workplace democracy, empowering the workers to help organize their toils.

In Mr. Kanigel's telling, there is much pathos in Taylor's sense of being ill used by critics. He was sure his system would dissolve tensions between labor and capital by demonstrating that high wages are not a problem but a solution. His mantra was "Men will not do an extraordinary day's work for an ordinary day's pay." So pay better for workers who will pay the price in new techniques for enhanced productivity. However, that price included more than the heightened stress of a more revved-up workplace. It also involved the moral insult of diminished prestige inherent in the transfer of all thinking from labor to the new management class. The result was a world of work that felt and even sounded different. As Mr. Kanigel says, "Everything clacked and whirred faster."

Taylor passionately believed Taylorism would raise what has come to be called the "standard of living." However, the controversy that engulfed him demonstrated that that concept is too complex to be reduced to a few indexes of material betterment. The man who helped ratchet up the level of stress in modern life may have had his life shortened—he died the day after his 59th birthday—by the strain of living with the controversy he caused. This in spite of the fact that in his last years he stopped to smell the roses: one of his final searches was for the one best way to cultivate them.

In 1916, the year after Taylor's death, Lenin passed some of his time in Zurich annotating a German translation of a Taylor book. The year after that, America's entry into World War I secured the nation's embrace of efficiency as a sovereign value and of Taylor as a prophet. In the 1920's a Parisian cleric declared, "The love of God is the Taylor System of our spiritual life." In 1927, at the end of an Italian conference on scientific management, Mussolini gave Taylor's widow a photograph of himself in exchange for one of Taylor. In 1928 the United States elected as President an engineer who had written a report on waste in industry. It has been reported that when Charlie Chaplin's "Modern Times," with its depiction of a man meshed with a machine and reduced to a machine-like jerkiness of movements, was shown to audiences in industrial Pittsburgh, they did not find it funny.

Mr. Kanigel is an award-winning science writer, but his prose could use an infusion of efficiency. (He uses "kid-glove" as a verb.) And he is not as attentive to intellectual history as he should be. His scanting of that allows his narrative to suggest that Taylorism triggered a spanking new anxiety about a Faustian bargain that degrades workers while making them materially better off. Actually, that anxiety is as old as industrialism. Mr. Kanigel does cite Adam Smith's famous hymn to the division of labor in that pin factory where "one man draws out the wire, another straightens it, a third cuts it, a fourth points it, a fifth grinds it at the top for receiving the head," a process "divided into about 18 distinct operations." Smith was sanguine about this because specialization increases a worker's "dexterity," and hence "the quality of the work he can perform." However, Marx thought the division of labor produces alienation but that all would be well under Communism, "where nobody has one exclusive sphere of activity." He was vague about the details.

Mr. Kanigel could have lengthened the pedigree of the controversy that engulfed Taylor had he considered the fact that in the second quarter of the 19th century, when American industrialism was in its infancy, Alexis de Tocqueville anticipated the ambivalence that Taylor catalyzed early in this century: "When a workman is unceasingly and exclusively engaged in the fabrication of one thing, he ultimately does his work with singular dexterity; but, at the same time, he loses the general faculty of applying his mind to the direction of the work. He every day becomes more adroit and less industrious; so that it may be said of him, that, in proportion as the workman improves, the man is degraded."

Taylor's critics worried about both "deskilling" and the creation of an "aristocracy of the capable," and about work becoming scarce because of what is now called "downsizing"—a productive few displacing the less fit. Mr. Kanigel believes, reasonably, that Taylor's legacy—a new kind of seriousness about enhancing workers' productivity—has been, on balance, benign. It certainly came in handy when Hitler was rampant. Mr. Kanigel quotes Mr. Drucker: during the war, "by applying Taylor's Scientific Management, U.S. industry trained totally unskilled workers, many of them former sharecroppers raised in a pre-industrial environment, and converted them in 60 to 90 days into first-rate welders and shipbuilders." One ship, launched in South Portland, Me., in 1942, was the 7,176-ton S.S. Frederick W. Taylor.

FURTHER READING

Biography

Copley, Frank Barkley. *Frederick W. Taylor: Father of Scientific Management* Vol. 2. New York and London: Harper and Brothers, 1923, 472 p.

Comprehensive biography of Taylor.

Kakar, Sudhir. *Frederick Taylor: A Study in Personality and Innovation.* Cambridge, Mass., and London: MIT Press, 1970, 221 p.

Scholarly biography of Taylor and the development of his theories.

Kanigel, Robert. *The One Best Way: Frederick Winslow Taylor and the Enigma of Efficiency.* New York: Viking, 1997, 675 p.

Comprehensive biographical and theoretical study of Taylor.

Wrege, Charles D., and Greenwood, Ronald G. *Frederick W. Taylor, The Father of Scientific Management: Myth and Reality.* Homewood, Ill.: Richard D. Irwin, Inc., 1991, 286 p.

Presents recently uncovered information on Taylor's life and works.

Criticism

Downs, Robert B. "Efficiency Expert: Frederick Winslow Taylor's *Principles of Scientific Management." In Molders of the Modern Mind: 111 Books that Shaped Western Civilization*, pp. 347-350. New York: Barnes and Noble, Inc., 1961.

Surveys Taylor's influence on modern culture.

Frederick Winslow Taylor: A Memorial Volume. New York: Taylor Society, 1920, 108 p.

Contains addresses delivered at Taylor's funeral and at a memorial meeting of the Taylor Society.

Hagen, Robert P. "Frederick Taylor's Challenge to Management: 'Is There a Better Way?'" *SAM Advanced Management Journal* 53, No. 2 (Spring 1988): 45-8.

Provides an overview of Taylor's objectives and argues that Taylorism is still relevant in the workplace.

Hathaway, H. K., ed. "Tributes to Frederick W. Taylor," *Transactions* 37 (1915): 1459-1496.

Contains personal and professional memorials to Taylor and his work.

Layton, Edwin T., Jr. "Measuring the Unmeasurable: Scientific Management and Reform." In *The Revolt of the Engineers. Social Responsibility and the American Engineering Profession*, pp. 134-53. Cleveland and London: The Press of Case Western Reserve University, 1971.

Discusses the social and professional implications of scientific management on engineers.

Gerhard Masur. "The Social Fabric." In *Prophets of Yesterday. Studies in European Culture, 1890-1914*, pp. 353-410. New York: The Macmillan Company, 1961.

Analyzes social and political trends in the early twentieth century, focusing on Taylorism, feminism, the youth movement, and socialism.

Nelson, Daniel. *Frederick W. Taylor and the Rise of Scientific Management.* Madison, Wis.: The University of Wisconsin Press, 1980, 259 p.

Investigates the development and impact of scientific management.

Thompson, C. Bertrand. The Taylor System of Scientific Management. Easton: Hive Publishing Company, 1974, 175 p.

Originally published in 1917, provides a report on the status of scientific management in the workplace.

Wrege, Charles D. "Tayor's Pig-Tale: A Historical Analysis of Frederick W. Taylor's Pig-Iron Experiments." *Academy of Management Journal* 17, No. 1 (March 1974): 6-27.

Provides evidence suggesting that Taylor's study of the loading of pig-iron at the Bethlehem Iron Company was fictionalized.

Wrege, Charles D., and Stotka, Anne Marie. "Cooke Creates a Classic: The Story behind F. W. Taylor's Principles of Scientific Management." *The Academy of Management Review* 3, No. 4 (October 1978): 736-49.

Alleges that Taylor liberally used the ideas first set out in an unpublished manuscript by Morris L. Cooke to write his book *The Principles of Scientific Management.*

Twentieth-Century Literary Criticism

Cumulative Indexes
Volumes 1-76

How to Use This Index

The main references

Calvino, Italo 1923–1985 .... **CLC 5, 8, 11, 22, 33, 39, 73; SSC 3**

list all author entries in the following Gale Literary Criticism series:

BLC = *Black Literature Criticism*
CLC = *Contemporary Literary Criticism*
CLR = *Children's Literature Review*
CMLC = *Classical and Medieval Literature Criticism*
DA = *DISCovering Authors*
DAB = *DISCovering Authors: British*
DAC = *DISCovering Authors: Canadian*
DAM = *DISCovering Authors: Modules*
DRAM: *Dramatists Module;* ***MST***: *Most-Studied Authors Module;*
MULT: *Multicultural Authors Module;* ***NOV***: *Novelists Module;*
POET: *Poets Module;* ***POP***: *Popular Fiction and Genre Authors Module*
DC = *Drama Criticism*
HLC = *Hispanic Literature Criticism*
LC = *Literature Criticism from 1400 to 1800*
NCLC = *Nineteenth-Century Literature Criticism*
PC = *Poetry Criticism*
SSC = *Short Story Criticism*
TCLC = *Twentieth-Century Literary Criticism*
WLC = *World Literature Criticism, 1500 to the Present*

The cross-references

See also CANR 23; CA 85-88; obituary CA116

list all author entries in the following Gale biographical and literary sources:

AAYA = *Authors & Artists for Young Adults*
AITN = *Authors in the News*
BEST = *Bestsellers*
BW = *Black Writers*
CA = *Contemporary Authors*
CAAS = *Contemporary Authors Autobiography Series*
CABS = *Contemporary Authors Bibliographical Series*
CANR = *Contemporary Authors New Revision Series*
CAP = *Contemporary Authors Permanent Series*
CDALB = *Concise Dictionary of American Literary Biography*
CDBLB = *Concise Dictionary of British Literary Biography*
DLB = *Dictionary of Literary Biography*
DLBD = *Dictionary of Literary Biography Documentary Series*
DLBY = *Dictionary of Literary Biography Yearbook*
HW = *Hispanic Writers*
JRDA = *Junior DISCovering Authors*
MAICYA = *Major Authors and Illustrators for Children and Young Adults*
MTCW = *Major 20th-Century Writers*
NNAL = *Native North American Literature*
SAAS = *Something about the Author Autobiography Series*
SATA = *Something about the Author*
YABC = *Yesterday's Authors of Books for Children*

Literary Criticism Series Cumulative Author Index

See also CA 81-84; CANR 19, 54; DLB 130
Appleman, Philip (Dean) 1926- .... **CLC 51**
See also CA 13-16R; CAAS 18; CANR 6, 29, 56
Appleton, Lawrence
See Lovecraft, H(oward) P(hillips)
Apteryx
See Eliot, T(homas) S(tearns)
Apuleius, (Lucius Madaurensis) 125(?)-175(?) **CMLC 1**
Aquin, Hubert 1929-1977 .... **CLC 15**
See also CA 105; DLB 53
Aragon, Louis 1897-1982.. **CLC 3, 22; DAM NOV, POET**
See also CA 69-72; 108; CANR 28; DLB 72; MTCW
Arany, Janos 1817-1882.................. **NCLC 34**
Arbuthnot, John 1667-1735 .... **LC 1**
See also DLB 101
Archer, Herbert Winslow
See Mencken, H(enry) L(ouis)
Archer, Jeffrey (Howard) 1940- ..... **CLC 28; DAM POP**
See also AAYA 16; BEST 89:3; CA 77-80; CANR 22, 52; INT CANR-22
Archer, Jules 1915- .... **CLC 12**
See also CA 9-12R; CANR 6; SAAS 5; SATA 4, 85
Archer, Lee
See Ellison, Harlan (Jay)
Arden, John 1930-**CLC 6, 13, 15; DAM DRAM**
See also CA 13-16R; CAAS 4; CANR 31; DLB 13; MTCW
Arenas, Reinaldo 1943-1990 . **CLC 41; DAM MULT; HLC**
See also CA 124; 128; 133; DLB 145; HW
Arendt, Hannah 1906-1975 .... **CLC 66, 98**
See also CA 17-20R; 61-64; CANR 26, 60; MTCW
Aretino, Pietro 1492-1556..................... **LC 12**
Arghezi, Tudor .... **CLC 80**
See also Theodorescu, Ion N.
Arguedas, Jose Maria 1911-1969 **CLC 10, 18**
See also CA 89-92; DLB 113; HW
Argueta, Manlio 1936- .... **CLC 31**
See also CA 131; DLB 145; HW
Ariosto, Ludovico 1474-1533 .... **LC 6**
Aristides
See Epstein, Joseph
Aristophanes 450B.C.-385B.C.**CMLC 4; DA; DAB; DAC; DAM DRAM, MST; DC 2; WLCS**
See also DLB 176
Arlt, Roberto (Godofredo Christophersen) 1900-1942**TCLC 29; DAM MULT; HLC**
See also CA 123; 131; HW
Armah, Ayi Kwei 1939-**CLC 5, 33; BLC; DAM MULT, POET**
See also BW 1; CA 61-64; CANR 21; DLB 117; MTCW
Armatrading, Joan 1950- .... **CLC 17**
See also CA 114
Arnette, Robert
See Silverberg, Robert
Arnim, Achim von (Ludwig Joachim von Arnim) 1781-1831 ...... **NCLC 5; SSC 29**
See also DLB 90
Arnim, Bettina von 1785-1859 .... **NCLC 38**
See also DLB 90
Arnold, Matthew 1822-1888**NCLC 6, 29; DA; DAB; DAC; DAM MST, POET; PC 5; WLC**
See also CDBLB 1832-1890; DLB 32, 57
Arnold, Thomas 1795-1842 .... **NCLC 18**
See also DLB 55
Arnow, Harriette (Louisa) Simpson 1908-1986 **CLC 2, 7, 18**
See also CA 9-12R; 118; CANR 14; DLB 6; MTCW; SATA 42; SATA-Obit 47
Arp, Hans
See Arp, Jean
Arp, Jean 1887-1966 .... **CLC 5**
See also CA 81-84; 25-28R; CANR 42
Arrabal
See Arrabal, Fernando
Arrabal, Fernando 1932-.... **CLC 2, 9, 18, 58**
See also CA 9-12R; CANR 15
Arrick, Fran .... **CLC 30**
See also Gaberman, Judie Angell
Artaud, Antonin (Marie Joseph) 1896-1948 **TCLC 3, 36; DAM DRAM**
See also CA 104; 149
Arthur, Ruth M(abel) 1905-1979 ...... **CLC 12**
See also CA 9-12R; 85-88; CANR 4; SATA 7, 26
Artsybashev, Mikhail (Petrovich) 1878-1927 **TCLC 31**
Arundel, Honor (Morfydd) 1919-1973**CLC 17**
See also CA 21-22; 41-44R; CAP 2; CLR 35; SATA 4; SATA-Obit 24
Arzner, Dorothy 1897-1979 .... **CLC 98**
Asch, Sholem 1880-1957 .... **TCLC 3**
See also CA 105
Ash, Shalom
See Asch, Sholem
Ashbery, John (Lawrence) 1927-**CLC 2, 3, 4, 6, 9, 13, 15, 25, 41, 77; DAM POET**
See also CA 5-8R; CANR 9, 37; DLB 5, 165; DLBY 81; INT CANR-9; MTCW
Ashdown, Clifford
See Freeman, R(ichard) Austin
Ashe, Gordon
See Creasey, John
Ashton-Warner, Sylvia (Constance) 1908-1984 **CLC 19**
See also CA 69-72; 112; CANR 29; MTCW
Asimov, Isaac 1920-1992 **CLC 1, 3, 9, 19, 26, 76, 92; DAM POP**
See also AAYA 13; BEST 90:2; CA 1-4R; 137; CANR 2, 19, 36, 60; CLR 12; DLB 8; DLBY 92; INT CANR-19; JRDA; MAICYA; MTCW; SATA 1, 26, 74
Assis, Joaquim Maria Machado de
See Machado de Assis, Joaquim Maria
Astley, Thea (Beatrice May) 1925- ... **CLC 41**
See also CA 65-68; CANR 11, 43
Aston, James
See White, T(erence) H(anbury)
Asturias, Miguel Angel 1899-1974 **CLC 3, 8, 13; DAM MULT, NOV; HLC**
See also CA 25-28; 49-52; CANR 32; CAP 2; DLB 113; HW; MTCW
Atares, Carlos Saura
See Saura (Atares), Carlos
Atheling, William
See Pound, Ezra (Weston Loomis)
Atheling, William, Jr.
See Blish, James (Benjamin)
Atherton, Gertrude (Franklin Horn) 1857-1948 **TCLC 2**
See also CA 104; 155; DLB 9, 78
Atherton, Lucius
See Masters, Edgar Lee
Atkins, Jack
See Harris, Mark
Atkinson, Kate .... **CLC 99**
Attaway, William (Alexander) 1911-1986 **CLC 92; BLC; DAM MULT**
See also BW 2; CA 143; DLB 76
Atticus
See Fleming, Ian (Lancaster)
Atwood, Margaret (Eleanor) 1939-**CLC 2, 3, 4, 8, 13, 15, 25, 44, 84; DA; DAB; DAC; DAM MST, NOV, POET; PC 8; SSC 2; WLC**
See also AAYA 12; BEST 89:2; CA 49-52; CANR 3, 24, 33, 59; DLB 53; INT CANR-24; MTCW; SATA 50
Aubigny, Pierre d'
See Mencken, H(enry) L(ouis)
Aubin, Penelope 1685-1731(?) .... **LC 9**
See also DLB 39
Auchincloss, Louis (Stanton) 1917-**CLC 4, 6, 9, 18, 45; DAM NOV; SSC 22**
See also CA 1-4R; CANR 6, 29, 55; DLB 2; DLBY 80; INT CANR-29; MTCW
Auden, W(ystan) H(ugh) 1907-1973**CLC 1, 2, 3, 4, 6, 9, 11, 14, 43; DA; DAB; DAC; DAM DRAM, MST, POET; PC 1; WLC**
See also AAYA 18; CA 9-12R; 45-48; CANR 5, 61; CDBLB 1914-1945; DLB 10, 20; MTCW
Audiberti, Jacques 1900-1965**CLC 38; DAM DRAM**
See also CA 25-28R
Audubon, John James 1785-1851 .. **NCLC 47**
Auel, Jean M(arie) 1936-**CLC 31; DAM POP**
See also AAYA 7; BEST 90:4; CA 103; CANR 21; INT CANR-21; SATA 91
Auerbach, Erich 1892-1957............ **TCLC 43**
See also CA 118; 155
Augier, Emile 1820-1889 .... **NCLC 31**
August, John
See De Voto, Bernard (Augustine)
Augustine, St. 354-430 .... **CMLC 6; DAB**
Aurelius
See Bourne, Randolph S(illiman)
Aurobindo, Sri 1872-1950 .... **TCLC 63**
Austen, Jane 1775-1817 **NCLC 1, 13, 19, 33, 51; DA; DAB; DAC; DAM MST, NOV; WLC**
See also AAYA 19; CDBLB 1789-1832; DLB 116
Auster, Paul 1947- .... **CLC 47**
See also CA 69-72; CANR 23, 52
Austin, Frank
See Faust, Frederick (Schiller)
Austin, Mary (Hunter) 1868-1934 . **TCLC 25**
See also CA 109; DLB 9, 78
Autran Dourado, Waldomiro
See Dourado, (Waldomiro Freitas) Autran
Averroes 1126-1198 .... **CMLC 7**
See also DLB 115
Avicenna 980-1037 .... **CMLC 16**
See also DLB 115
Avison, Margaret 1918- **CLC 2, 4, 97; DAC; DAM POET**
See also CA 17-20R; DLB 53; MTCW
Axton, David
See Koontz, Dean R(ay)
Ayckbourn, Alan 1939- **CLC 5, 8, 18, 33, 74; DAB; DAM DRAM**
See also CA 21-24R; CANR 31, 59; DLB 13; MTCW
Aydy, Catherine
See Tennant, Emma (Christina)
Ayme, Marcel (Andre) 1902-1967 .... **CLC 11**
See also CA 89-92; CLR 25; DLB 72; SATA 91
Ayrton, Michael 1921-1975 .... **CLC 7**
See also CA 5-8R; 61-64; CANR 9, 21
Azorin .... **CLC 11**
See also Martinez Ruiz, Jose
Azuela, Mariano 1873-1952 . **TCLC 3; DAM MULT; HLC**
See also CA 104; 131; HW; MTCW
Baastad, Babbis Friis
See Friis-Baastad, Babbis Ellinor
Bab
See Gilbert, W(illiam) S(chwenck)
Babbis, Eleanor
See Friis-Baastad, Babbis Ellinor

Babel, Isaac
See Babel, Isaak (Emmanuilovich)
Babel, Isaak (Emmanuilovich) 1894-1941(?) **TCLC 2, 13; SSC 16**
See also CA 104; 155
Babits, Mihaly 1883-1941 .... **TCLC 14**
See also CA 114
Babur 1483-1530 .... **LC 18**
Bacchelli, Riccardo 1891-1985 .... **CLC 19**
See also CA 29-32R; 117
Bach, Richard (David) 1936- **CLC 14; DAM NOV, POP**
See also AITN 1; BEST 89:2; CA 9-12R; CANR 18; MTCW; SATA 13
Bachman, Richard
See King, Stephen (Edwin)
Bachmann, Ingeborg 1926-1973 .... **CLC 69**
See also CA 93-96; 45-48; DLB 85
Bacon, Francis 1561-1626 .... **LC 18, 32**
See also CDBLB Before 1660; DLB 151
Bacon, Roger 1214(?)-1292 .... **CMLC 14**
See also DLB 115
Bacovia, George .... **TCLC 24**
See also Vasiliu, Gheorghe
Badanes, Jerome 1937- .... **CLC 59**
Bagehot, Walter 1826-1877 .... **NCLC 10**
See also DLB 55
Bagnold, Enid 1889-1981 .... **CLC 25; DAM DRAM**
See also CA 5-8R; 103; CANR 5, 40; DLB 13, 160; MAICYA; SATA 1, 25
Bagritsky, Eduard 1895-1934 .... **TCLC 60**
Bagrjana, Elisaveta
See Belcheva, Elisaveta
Bagryana, Elisaveta .... **CLC 10**
See also Belcheva, Elisaveta
See also DLB 147
Bailey, Paul 1937- .... **CLC 45**
See also CA 21-24R; CANR 16, 62; DLB 14
Baillie, Joanna 1762-1851 .... **NCLC 2**
See also DLB 93
Bainbridge, Beryl (Margaret) 1933-**CLC 4, 5, 8, 10, 14, 18, 22, 62; DAM NOV**
See also CA 21-24R; CANR 24, 55; DLB 14; MTCW
Baker, Elliott 1922- .... **CLC 8**
See also CA 45-48; CANR 2
Baker, Jean H. .... **TCLC 3, 10**
See also Russell, George William
Baker, Nicholson 1957- **CLC 61; DAM POP**
See also CA 135
Baker, Ray Stannard 1870-1946 .... **TCLC 47**
See also CA 118
Baker, Russell (Wayne) 1925- .... **CLC 31**
See also BEST 89:4; CA 57-60; CANR 11, 41, 59; MTCW
Bakhtin, M.
See Bakhtin, Mikhail Mikhailovich
Bakhtin, M. M.
See Bakhtin, Mikhail Mikhailovich
Bakhtin, Mikhail
See Bakhtin, Mikhail Mikhailovich
Bakhtin, Mikhail Mikhailovich 1895-1975 **CLC 83**
See also CA 128; 113
Bakshi, Ralph 1938(?)- .... **CLC 26**
See also CA 112; 138
Bakunin, Mikhail (Alexandrovich) 1814-1876 **NCLC 25, 58**
Baldwin, James (Arthur) 1924-1987**CLC 1, 2, 3, 4, 5, 8, 13, 15, 17, 42, 50, 67, 90; BLC; DA; DAB; DAC; DAM MST, MULT, NOV, POP; DC 1; SSC 10; WLC**
See also AAYA 4; BW 1; CA 1-4R; 124; CABS 1; CANR 3, 24; CDALB 1941-1968; DLB 2, 7, 33; DLBY 87; MTCW; SATA 9; SATA-Obit 54
Ballard, J(ames) G(raham) 1930-**CLC 3, 6, 14, 36; DAM NOV, POP; SSC 1**
See also AAYA 3; CA 5-8R; CANR 15, 39; DLB 14; MTCW; SATA 93
Balmont, Konstantin (Dmitriyevich) 1867-1943 **TCLC 11**
See also CA 109; 155
Balzac, Honore de 1799-1850**NCLC 5, 35, 53; DA; DAB; DAC; DAM MST, NOV; SSC 5; WLC**
See also DLB 119
Bambara, Toni Cade 1939-1995 **CLC 19, 88; BLC; DA; DAC; DAM MST, MULT; WLCS**
See also AAYA 5; BW 2; CA 29-32R; 150; CANR 24, 49; DLB 38; MTCW
Bamdad, A.
See Shamlu, Ahmad
Banat, D. R.
See Bradbury, Ray (Douglas)
Bancroft, Laura
See Baum, L(yman) Frank
Banim, John 1798-1842 .... **NCLC 13**
See also DLB 116, 158, 159
Banim, Michael 1796-1874 .... **NCLC 13**
See also DLB 158, 159
Banjo, The
See Paterson, A(ndrew) B(arton)
Banks, Iain
See Banks, Iain M(enzies)
Banks, Iain M(enzies) 1954- .... **CLC 34**
See also CA 123; 128; CANR 61; INT 128
Banks, Lynne Reid .... **CLC 23**
See also Reid Banks, Lynne
See also AAYA 6
Banks, Russell 1940- .... **CLC 37, 72**
See also CA 65-68; CAAS 15; CANR 19, 52; DLB 130
Banville, John 1945- .... **CLC 46**
See also CA 117; 128; DLB 14; INT 128
Banville, Theodore (Faullain) de 1832-1891 **NCLC 9**
Baraka, Amiri 1934-**CLC 1, 2, 3, 5, 10, 14, 33; BLC; DA; DAC; DAM MST, MULT, POET, POP; DC 6; PC 4; WLCS**
See also Jones, LeRoi
See also BW 2; CA 21-24R; CABS 3; CANR 27, 38, 61; CDALB 1941-1968; DLB 5, 7, 16, 38; DLBD 8; MTCW
Barbauld, Anna Laetitia 1743-1825**NCLC 50**
See also DLB 107, 109, 142, 158
Barbellion, W. N. P. .... **TCLC 24**
See also Cummings, Bruce F(rederick)
Barbera, Jack (Vincent) 1945- .... **CLC 44**
See also CA 110; CANR 45
Barbey d'Aurevilly, Jules Amedee 1808-1889 **NCLC 1; SSC 17**
See also DLB 119
Barbusse, Henri 1873-1935 .... **TCLC 5**
See also CA 105; 154; DLB 65
Barclay, Bill
See Moorcock, Michael (John)
Barclay, William Ewert
See Moorcock, Michael (John)
Barea, Arturo 1897-1957 .... **TCLC 14**
See also CA 111
Barfoot, Joan 1946- .... **CLC 18**
See also CA 105
Baring, Maurice 1874-1945 .... **TCLC 8**
See also CA 105; DLB 34
Barker, Clive 1952- .... **CLC 52; DAM POP**
See also AAYA 10; BEST 90:3; CA 121; 129; INT 129; MTCW
Barker, George Granville 1913-1991 **CLC 8, 48; DAM POET**
See also CA 9-12R; 135; CANR 7, 38; DLB 20; MTCW
Barker, Harley Granville
See Granville-Barker, Harley
See also DLB 10
Barker, Howard 1946- .... **CLC 37**
See also CA 102; DLB 13
Barker, Pat(ricia) 1943- .... **CLC 32, 94**
See also CA 117; 122; CANR 50; INT 122
Barlow, Joel 1754-1812 .... **NCLC 23**
See also DLB 37
Barnard, Mary (Ethel) 1909- .... **CLC 48**
See also CA 21-22; CAP 2
Barnes, Djuna 1892-1982**CLC 3, 4, 8, 11, 29; SSC 3**
See also CA 9-12R; 107; CANR 16, 55; DLB 4, 9, 45; MTCW
Barnes, Julian (Patrick) 1946-**CLC 42; DAB**
See also CA 102; CANR 19, 54; DLBY 93
Barnes, Peter 1931- .... **CLC 5, 56**
See also CA 65-68; CAAS 12; CANR 33, 34; DLB 13; MTCW
Baroja (y Nessi), Pio 1872-1956**TCLC 8; HLC**
See also CA 104
Baron, David
See Pinter, Harold
Baron Corvo
See Rolfe, Frederick (William Serafino Austin Lewis Mary)
Barondess, Sue K(aufman) 1926-1977**CLC 8**
See also Kaufman, Sue
See also CA 1-4R; 69-72; CANR 1
Baron de Teive
See Pessoa, Fernando (Antonio Nogueira)
Barres, Maurice 1862-1923 .... **TCLC 47**
See also DLB 123
Barreto, Afonso Henrique de Lima
See Lima Barreto, Afonso Henrique de
Barrett, (Roger) Syd 1946- .... **CLC 35**
Barrett, William (Christopher) 1913-1992 **CLC 27**
See also CA 13-16R; 139; CANR 11; INT CANR-11
Barrie, J(ames) M(atthew) 1860-1937 **TCLC 2; DAB; DAM DRAM**
See also CA 104; 136; CDBLB 1890-1914; CLR 16; DLB 10, 141, 156; MAICYA; YABC 1
Barrington, Michael
See Moorcock, Michael (John)
Barrol, Grady
See Bograd, Larry
Barry, Mike
See Malzberg, Barry N(athaniel)
Barry, Philip 1896-1949 .... **TCLC 11**
See also CA 109; DLB 7
Bart, Andre Schwarz
See Schwarz-Bart, Andre
Barth, John (Simmons) 1930-**CLC 1, 2, 3, 5, 7, 9, 10, 14, 27, 51, 89; DAM NOV; SSC 10**
See also AITN 1, 2; CA 1-4R; CABS 1; CANR 5, 23, 49; DLB 2; MTCW
Barthelme, Donald 1931-1989**CLC 1, 2, 3, 5, 6, 8, 13, 23, 46, 59; DAM NOV; SSC 2**
See also CA 21-24R; 129; CANR 20, 58; DLB 2; DLBY 80, 89; MTCW; SATA 7; SATA-Obit 62
Barthelme, Frederick 1943- .... **CLC 36**
See also CA 114; 122; DLBY 85; INT 122
Barthes, Roland (Gerard) 1915-1980**CLC 24, 83**
See also CA 130; 97-100; MTCW
Barzun, Jacques (Martin) 1907- .... **CLC 51**
See also CA 61-64; CANR 22
Bashevis, Isaac
See Singer, Isaac Bashevis
Bashkirtseff, Marie 1859-1884 ...... **NCLC 27**
Basho
See Matsuo Basho

See Bennett, Hal
See also BW 1; CA 97-100
Bennett, Hal .... **CLC 5**
See also Bennett, George Harold
See also DLB 33
Bennett, Jay 1912- .... **CLC 35**
See also AAYA 10; CA 69-72; CANR 11, 42; JRDA; SAAS 4; SATA 41, 87; SATA-Brief 27
Bennett, Louise (Simone) 1919-**CLC 28; BLC; DAM MULT**
See also BW 2; CA 151; DLB 117
Benson, E(dward) F(rederic) 1867-1940 **TCLC 27**
See also CA 114; 157; DLB 135, 153
Benson, Jackson J. 1930- .... **CLC 34**
See also CA 25-28R; DLB 111
Benson, Sally 1900-1972 .... **CLC 17**
See also CA 19-20; 37-40R; CAP 1; SATA 1, 35; SATA-Obit 27
Benson, Stella 1892-1933 .... **TCLC 17**
See also CA 117; 155; DLB 36, 162
Bentham, Jeremy 1748-1832 .... **NCLC 38**
See also DLB 107, 158
Bentley, E(dmund) C(lerihew) 1875-1956 **TCLC 12**
See also CA 108; DLB 70
Bentley, Eric (Russell) 1916- .... **CLC 24**
See also CA 5-8R; CANR 6; INT CANR-6
Beranger, Pierre Jean de 1780-1857**NCLC 34**
Berdyaev, Nicolas
See Berdyaev, Nikolai (Aleksandrovich)
Berdyaev, Nikolai (Aleksandrovich) 1874-1948 **TCLC 67**
See also CA 120; 157
Berdyayev, Nikolai (Aleksandrovich)
See Berdyaev, Nikolai (Aleksandrovich)
Berendt, John (Lawrence) 1939- .... **CLC 86**
See also CA 146
Berger, Colonel
See Malraux, (Georges-)Andre
Berger, John (Peter) 1926- .... **CLC 2, 19**
See also CA 81-84; CANR 51; DLB 14
Berger, Melvin H. 1927- .... **CLC 12**
See also CA 5-8R; CANR 4; CLR 32; SAAS 2; SATA 5, 88
Berger, Thomas (Louis) 1924-**CLC 3, 5, 8, 11, 18, 38; DAM NOV**
See also CA 1-4R; CANR 5, 28, 51; DLB 2; DLBY 80; INT CANR-28; MTCW
Bergman, (Ernst) Ingmar 1918- **CLC 16, 72**
See also CA 81-84; CANR 33
Bergson, Henri 1859-1941 .... **TCLC 32**
Bergstein, Eleanor 1938- .... **CLC 4**
See also CA 53-56; CANR 5
Berkoff, Steven 1937- .... **CLC 56**
See also CA 104
Bermant, Chaim (Icyk) 1929- .... **CLC 40**
See also CA 57-60; CANR 6, 31, 57
Bern, Victoria
See Fisher, M(ary) F(rances) K(ennedy)
Bernanos, (Paul Louis) Georges 1888-1948 **TCLC 3**
See also CA 104; 130; DLB 72
Bernard, April 1956- .... **CLC 59**
See also CA 131
Berne, Victoria
See Fisher, M(ary) F(rances) K(ennedy)
Bernhard, Thomas 1931-1989 **CLC 3, 32, 61**
See also CA 85-88; 127; CANR 32, 57; DLB 85, 124; MTCW
Bernhardt, Sarah (Henriette Rosine) 1844-1923 **TCLC 75**
See also CA 157
Berriault, Gina 1926- .... **CLC 54**
See also CA 116; 129; DLB 130
Berrigan, Daniel 1921- .... **CLC 4**
See also CA 33-36R; CAAS 1; CANR 11, 43; DLB 5
Berrigan, Edmund Joseph Michael, Jr. 1934-1983
See Berrigan, Ted
See also CA 61-64; 110; CANR 14
Berrigan, Ted .... **CLC 37**
See also Berrigan, Edmund Joseph Michael, Jr.
See also DLB 5, 169
Berry, Charles Edward Anderson 1931-
See Berry, Chuck
See also CA 115
Berry, Chuck .... **CLC 17**
See also Berry, Charles Edward Anderson
Berry, Jonas
See Ashbery, John (Lawrence)
Berry, Wendell (Erdman) 1934- **CLC 4, 6, 8, 27, 46; DAM POET**
See also AITN 1; CA 73-76; CANR 50; DLB 5, 6
Berryman, John 1914-1972**CLC 1, 2, 3, 4, 6, 8, 10, 13, 25, 62; DAM POET**
See also CA 13-16; 33-36R; CABS 2; CANR 35; CAP 1; CDALB 1941-1968; DLB 48; MTCW
Bertolucci, Bernardo 1940- .... **CLC 16**
See also CA 106
Berton, Pierre (Francis De Marigny) 1920- **CLC 104**
See also CA 1-4R; CANR 2, 56; DLB 68
Bertrand, Aloysius 1807-1841 .... **NCLC 31**
Bertran de Born c. 1140-1215 .... **CMLC 5**
Besant, Annie (Wood) 1847-1933 .... **TCLC 9**
See also CA 105
Bessie, Alvah 1904-1985 .... **CLC 23**
See also CA 5-8R; 116; CANR 2; DLB 26
Bethlen, T. D.
See Silverberg, Robert
Beti, Mongo ...... **CLC 27; BLC; DAM MULT**
See also Biyidi, Alexandre
Betjeman, John 1906-1984 **CLC 2, 6, 10, 34, 43; DAB; DAM MST, POET**
See also CA 9-12R; 112; CANR 33, 56; CDBLB 1945-1960; DLB 20; DLBY 84; MTCW
Bettelheim, Bruno 1903-1990 .... **CLC 79**
See also CA 81-84; 131; CANR 23, 61; MTCW
Betti, Ugo 1892-1953 .... **TCLC 5**
See also CA 104; 155
Betts, Doris (Waugh) 1932- ...... **CLC 3, 6, 28**
See also CA 13-16R; CANR 9; DLBY 82; INT CANR-9
Bevan, Alistair
See Roberts, Keith (John Kingston)
Bialik, Chaim Nachman 1873-1934**TCLC 25**
Bickerstaff, Isaac
See Swift, Jonathan
Bidart, Frank 1939- .... **CLC 33**
See also CA 140
Bienek, Horst 1930- .... **CLC 7, 11**
See also CA 73-76; DLB 75
Bierce, Ambrose (Gwinett) 1842-1914(?) **TCLC 1, 7, 44; DA; DAC; DAM MST; SSC 9; WLC**
See also CA 104; 139; CDALB 1865-1917; DLB 11, 12, 23, 71, 74
Biggers, Earl Derr 1884-1933 .... **TCLC 65**
See also CA 108; 153
Billings, Josh
See Shaw, Henry Wheeler
Billington, (Lady) Rachel (Mary) 1942- **C L C 43**
See also AITN 2; CA 33-36R; CANR 44
Binyon, T(imothy) J(ohn) 1936- .... **CLC 34**
See also CA 111; CANR 28
Bioy Casares, Adolfo 1914-**CLC 4, 8, 13, 88; DAM MULT; HLC; SSC 17**
See also CA 29-32R; CANR 19, 43; DLB 113; HW; MTCW
Bird, Cordwainer
See Ellison, Harlan (Jay)
Bird, Robert Montgomery 1806-1854**NCLC 1**
Birney, (Alfred) Earle 1904- **CLC 1, 4, 6, 11; DAC; DAM MST, POET**
See also CA 1-4R; CANR 5, 20; DLB 88; MTCW
Bishop, Elizabeth 1911-1979 **CLC 1, 4, 9, 13, 15, 32; DA; DAC; DAM MST, POET; PC 3**
See also CA 5-8R; 89-92; CABS 2; CANR 26, 61; CDALB 1968-1988; DLB 5, 169; MTCW; SATA-Obit 24
Bishop, John 1935- .... **CLC 10**
See also CA 105
Bissett, Bill 1939- .... **CLC 18; PC 14**
See also CA 69-72; CAAS 19; CANR 15; DLB 53; MTCW
Bitov, Andrei (Georgievich) 1937- ... **CLC 57**
See also CA 142
Biyidi, Alexandre 1932-
See Beti, Mongo
See also BW 1; CA 114; 124; MTCW
Bjarme, Brynjolf
See Ibsen, Henrik (Johan)
Bjornson, Bjornstjerne (Martinius) 1832-1910 **TCLC 7, 37**
See also CA 104
Black, Robert
See Holdstock, Robert P.
Blackburn, Paul 1926-1971 .... **CLC 9, 43**
See also CA 81-84; 33-36R; CANR 34; DLB 16; DLBY 81
Black Elk 1863-1950**TCLC 33; DAM MULT**
See also CA 144; NNAL
Black Hobart
See Sanders, (James) Ed(ward)
Blacklin, Malcolm
See Chambers, Aidan
Blackmore, R(ichard) D(oddridge) 1825-1900 **TCLC 27**
See also CA 120; DLB 18
Blackmur, R(ichard) P(almer) 1904-1965 **CLC 2, 24**
See also CA 11-12; 25-28R; CAP 1; DLB 63
Black Tarantula
See Acker, Kathy
Blackwood, Algernon (Henry) 1869-1951 **TCLC 5**
See also CA 105; 150; DLB 153, 156, 178
Blackwood, Caroline 1931-1996**CLC 6, 9, 100**
See also CA 85-88; 151; CANR 32, 61; DLB 14; MTCW
Blade, Alexander
See Hamilton, Edmond; Silverberg, Robert
Blaga, Lucian 1895-1961 .... **CLC 75**
Blair, Eric (Arthur) 1903-1950
See Orwell, George
See also CA 104; 132; DA; DAB; DAC; DAM MST, NOV; MTCW; SATA 29
Blais, Marie-Claire 1939-**CLC 2, 4, 6, 13, 22; DAC; DAM MST**
See also CA 21-24R; CAAS 4; CANR 38; DLB 53; MTCW
Blaise, Clark 1940- .... **CLC 29**
See also AITN 2; CA 53-56; CAAS 3; CANR 5; DLB 53
Blake, Fairley
See De Voto, Bernard (Augustine)
Blake, Nicholas
See Day Lewis, C(ecil)
See also DLB 77
Blake, William 1757-1827 . **NCLC 13, 37, 57; DA; DAB; DAC; DAM MST, POET; PC 12; WLC**
See also CDBLB 1789-1832; DLB 93, 163;

MAICYA; SATA 30
Blake, William J(ames) 1894-1969 ...... **PC 12**
See also CA 5-8R; 25-28R
Blasco Ibanez, Vicente 1867-1928 **TCLC 12; DAM NOV**
See also CA 110; 131; HW; MTCW
Blatty, William Peter 1928-**CLC 2; DAM POP**
See also CA 5-8R; CANR 9
Bleeck, Oliver
See Thomas, Ross (Elmore)
Blessing, Lee 1949- .... **CLC 54**
Blish, James (Benjamin) 1921-1975 . **CLC 14**
See also CA 1-4R; 57-60; CANR 3; DLB 8; MTCW; SATA 66
Bliss, Reginald
See Wells, H(erbert) G(eorge)
Blixen, Karen (Christentze Dinesen) 1885-1962
See Dinesen, Isak
See also CA 25-28; CANR 22, 50; CAP 2; MTCW; SATA 44
Bloch, Robert (Albert) 1917-1994 .... **CLC 33**
See also CA 5-8R; 146; CAAS 20; CANR 5; DLB 44; INT CANR-5; SATA 12; SATA-Obit 82
Blok, Alexander (Alexandrovich) 1880-1921 **TCLC 5**
See also CA 104
Blom, Jan
See Breytenbach, Breyten
Bloom, Harold 1930- .... **CLC 24, 103**
See also CA 13-16R; CANR 39; DLB 67
Bloomfield, Aurelius
See Bourne, Randolph S(illiman)
Blount, Roy (Alton), Jr. 1941- .... **CLC 38**
See also CA 53-56; CANR 10, 28, 61; INT CANR-28; MTCW
Bloy, Leon 1846-1917 .... **TCLC 22**
See also CA 121; DLB 123
Blume, Judy (Sussman) 1938- ... **CLC 12, 30; DAM NOV, POP**
See also AAYA 3; CA 29-32R; CANR 13, 37; CLR 2, 15; DLB 52; JRDA; MAICYA; MTCW; SATA 2, 31, 79
Blunden, Edmund (Charles) 1896-1974 **CLC 2, 56**
See also CA 17-18; 45-48; CANR 54; CAP 2; DLB 20, 100, 155; MTCW
Bly, Robert (Elwood) 1926-**CLC 1, 2, 5, 10, 15, 38; DAM POET**
See also CA 5-8R; CANR 41; DLB 5; MTCW
Boas, Franz 1858-1942 .... **TCLC 56**
See also CA 115
Bobette
See Simenon, Georges (Jacques Christian)
Boccaccio, Giovanni 1313-1375 ... **CMLC 13; SSC 10**
Bochco, Steven 1943- .... **CLC 35**
See also AAYA 11; CA 124; 138
Bodenheim, Maxwell 1892-1954 .... **TCLC 44**
See also CA 110; DLB 9, 45
Bodker, Cecil 1927- .... **CLC 21**
See also CA 73-76; CANR 13, 44; CLR 23; MAICYA; SATA 14
Boell, Heinrich (Theodor) 1917-1985 **CLC 2, 3, 6, 9, 11, 15, 27, 32, 72; DA; DAB; DAC; DAM MST, NOV; SSC 23; WLC**
See also CA 21-24R; 116; CANR 24; DLB 69; DLBY 85; MTCW
Boerne, Alfred
See Doeblin, Alfred
Boethius 480(?)-524(?) .... **CMLC 15**
See also DLB 115
Bogan, Louise 1897-1970 . **CLC 4, 39, 46, 93; DAM POET; PC 12**
See also CA 73-76; 25-28R; CANR 33; DLB 45, 169; MTCW
Bogarde, Dirk .... **CLC 19**
See also Van Den Bogarde, Derek Jules Gaspard Ulric Niven
See also DLB 14
Bogosian, Eric 1953- .... **CLC 45**
See also CA 138
Bograd, Larry 1953- .... **CLC 35**
See also CA 93-96; CANR 57; SAAS 21; SATA 33, 89
Boiardo, Matteo Maria 1441-1494 .... **LC 6**
Boileau-Despreaux, Nicolas 1636-1711 . **LC 3**
Bojer, Johan 1872-1959 .... **TCLC 64**
Boland, Eavan (Aisling) 1944- .. **CLC 40, 67; DAM POET**
See also CA 143; CANR 61; DLB 40
Bolt, Lee
See Faust, Frederick (Schiller)
Bolt, Robert (Oxton) 1924-1995**CLC 14; DAM DRAM**
See also CA 17-20R; 147; CANR 35; DLB 13; MTCW
Bombet, Louis-Alexandre-Cesar
See Stendhal
Bomkauf
See Kaufman, Bob (Garnell)
Bonaventura .... **NCLC 35**
See also DLB 90
Bond, Edward 1934- **CLC 4, 6, 13, 23; DAM DRAM**
See also CA 25-28R; CANR 38; DLB 13; MTCW
Bonham, Frank 1914-1989 .... **CLC 12**
See also AAYA 1; CA 9-12R; CANR 4, 36; JRDA; MAICYA; SAAS 3; SATA 1, 49; SATA-Obit 62
Bonnefoy, Yves 1923- ... **CLC 9, 15, 58; DAM MST, POET**
See also CA 85-88; CANR 33; MTCW
Bontemps, Arna(ud Wendell) 1902-1973**CLC 1, 18; BLC; DAM MULT, NOV, POET**
See also BW 1; CA 1-4R; 41-44R; CANR 4, 35; CLR 6; DLB 48, 51; JRDA; MAICYA; MTCW; SATA 2, 44; SATA-Obit 24
Booth, Martin 1944- .... **CLC 13**
See also CA 93-96; CAAS 2
Booth, Philip 1925- .... **CLC 23**
See also CA 5-8R; CANR 5; DLBY 82
Booth, Wayne C(layson) 1921- .... **CLC 24**
See also CA 1-4R; CAAS 5; CANR 3, 43; DLB 67
Borchert, Wolfgang 1921-1947 .... **TCLC 5**
See also CA 104; DLB 69, 124
Borel, Petrus 1809-1859 .... **NCLC 41**
Borges, Jorge Luis 1899-1986**CLC 1, 2, 3, 4, 6, 8, 9, 10, 13, 19, 44, 48, 83; DA; DAB; DAC; DAM MST, MULT; HLC; SSC 4; WLC**
See also AAYA 19; CA 21-24R; CANR 19, 33; DLB 113; DLBY 86; HW; MTCW
Borowski, Tadeusz 1922-1951 .... **TCLC 9**
See also CA 106; 154
Borrow, George (Henry) 1803-1881 **NCLC 9**
See also DLB 21, 55, 166
Bosman, Herman Charles 1905-1951 **TCLC 49**
See also Malan, Herman
See also CA 160
Bosschere, Jean de 1878(?)-1953 ... **TCLC 19**
See also CA 115
Boswell, James 1740-1795 . **LC 4; DA; DAB; DAC; DAM MST; WLC**
See also CDBLB 1660-1789; DLB 104, 142
Bottoms, David 1949- .... **CLC 53**
See also CA 105; CANR 22; DLB 120; DLBY 83
Boucicault, Dion 1820-1890 .... **NCLC 41**
Boucolon, Maryse 1937(?)-
See Conde, Maryse
See also CA 110; CANR 30, 53
Bourget, Paul (Charles Joseph) 1852-1935 **TCLC 12**
See also CA 107; DLB 123
Bourjaily, Vance (Nye) 1922- .... **CLC 8, 62**
See also CA 1-4R; CAAS 1; CANR 2; DLB 2, 143
Bourne, Randolph S(illiman) 1886-1918 **TCLC 16**
See also CA 117; 155; DLB 63
Bova, Ben(jamin William) 1932- ...... **CLC 45**
See also AAYA 16; CA 5-8R; CAAS 18; CANR 11, 56; CLR 3; DLBY 81; INT CANR-11; MAICYA; MTCW; SATA 6, 68
Bowen, Elizabeth (Dorothea Cole) 1899-1973 **CLC 1, 3, 6, 11, 15, 22; DAM NOV; SSC 3, 28**
See also CA 17-18; 41-44R; CANR 35; CAP 2; CDBLB 1945-1960; DLB 15, 162; MTCW
Bowering, George 1935- .... **CLC 15, 47**
See also CA 21-24R; CAAS 16; CANR 10; DLB 53
Bowering, Marilyn R(uthe) 1949- .... **CLC 32**
See also CA 101; CANR 49
Bowers, Edgar 1924- .... **CLC 9**
See also CA 5-8R; CANR 24; DLB 5
Bowie, David .... **CLC 17**
See also Jones, David Robert
Bowles, Jane (Sydney) 1917-1973 **CLC 3, 68**
See also CA 19-20; 41-44R; CAP 2
Bowles, Paul (Frederick) 1910- **CLC 1, 2, 19, 53; SSC 3**
See also CA 1-4R; CAAS 1; CANR 1, 19, 50; DLB 5, 6; MTCW
Box, Edgar
See Vidal, Gore
Boyd, Nancy
See Millay, Edna St. Vincent
Boyd, William 1952- .... **CLC 28, 53, 70**
See also CA 114; 120; CANR 51
Boyle, Kay 1902-1992**CLC 1, 5, 19, 58; SSC 5**
See also CA 13-16R; 140; CAAS 1; CANR 29, 61; DLB 4, 9, 48, 86; DLBY 93; MTCW
Boyle, Mark
See Kienzle, William X(avier)
Boyle, Patrick 1905-1982 .... **CLC 19**
See also CA 127
Boyle, T. C. 1948-
See Boyle, T(homas) Coraghessan
Boyle, T(homas) Coraghessan 1948-**CLC 36, 55, 90; DAM POP; SSC 16**
See also BEST 90:4; CA 120; CANR 44; DLBY 86
Boz
See Dickens, Charles (John Huffam)
Brackenridge, Hugh Henry 1748-1816**NCLC 7**
See also DLB 11, 37
Bradbury, Edward P.
See Moorcock, Michael (John)
Bradbury, Malcolm (Stanley) 1932- **CLC 32, 61; DAM NOV**
See also CA 1-4R; CANR 1, 33; DLB 14; MTCW
Bradbury, Ray (Douglas) 1920-**CLC 1, 3, 10, 15, 42, 98; DA; DAB; DAC; DAM MST, NOV, POP; SSC 29; WLC**
See also AAYA 15; AITN 1, 2; CA 1-4R; CANR 2, 30; CDALB 1968-1988; DLB 2, 8; MTCW; SATA 11, 64
Bradford, Gamaliel 1863-1932 ...... **TCLC 36**
See also CA 160; DLB 17
Bradley, David (Henry, Jr.) 1950- .. **CLC 23; BLC; DAM MULT**
See also BW 1; CA 104; CANR 26; DLB 33
Bradley, John Ed(mund, Jr.) 1958- .. **CLC 55**
See also CA 139
Bradley, Marion Zimmer 1930-**CLC 30; DAM**

See Aragon, Louis
Derrida, Jacques 1930- .... **CLC 24, 87**
See also CA 124; 127
Derry Down Derry
See Lear, Edward
Dersonnes, Jacques
See Simenon, Georges (Jacques Christian)
Desai, Anita 1937-**CLC 19, 37, 97; DAB; DAM NOV**
See also CA 81-84; CANR 33, 53; MTCW; SATA 63
de Saint-Luc, Jean
See Glassco, John
de Saint Roman, Arnaud
See Aragon, Louis
Descartes, Rene 1596-1650 .... **LC 20, 35**
De Sica, Vittorio 1901(?)-1974 .... **CLC 20**
See also CA 117
Desnos, Robert 1900-1945 .... **TCLC 22**
See also CA 121; 151
Destouches, Louis-Ferdinand 1894-1961**CLC 9, 15**
See also Celine, Louis-Ferdinand
See also CA 85-88; CANR 28; MTCW
de Tolignac, Gaston
See Griffith, D(avid Lewelyn) W(ark)
Deutsch, Babette 1895-1982 .... **CLC 18**
See also CA 1-4R; 108; CANR 4; DLB 45; SATA 1; SATA-Obit 33
Devenant, William 1606-1649 .... **LC 13**
Devkota, Laxmiprasad 1909-1959 . **TCLC 23**
See also CA 123
De Voto, Bernard (Augustine) 1897-1955 **TCLC 29**
See also CA 113; 160; DLB 9
De Vries, Peter 1910-1993 **CLC 1, 2, 3, 7, 10, 28, 46; DAM NOV**
See also CA 17-20R; 142; CANR 41; DLB 6; DLBY 82; MTCW
Dexter, John
See Bradley, Marion Zimmer
Dexter, Martin
See Faust, Frederick (Schiller)
Dexter, Pete 1943- ... **CLC 34, 55; DAM POP**
See also BEST 89:2; CA 127; 131; INT 131; MTCW
Diamano, Silmang
See Senghor, Leopold Sedar
Diamond, Neil 1941- .... **CLC 30**
See also CA 108
Diaz del Castillo, Bernal 1496-1584 .... **LC 31**
di Bassetto, Corno
See Shaw, George Bernard
Dick, Philip K(indred) 1928-1982**CLC 10, 30, 72; DAM NOV, POP**
See also CA 49-52; 106; CANR 2, 16; DLB 8; MTCW
Dickens, Charles (John Huffam) 1812-1870 **NCLC 3, 8, 18, 26, 37, 50; DA; DAB; DAC; DAM MST, NOV; SSC 17; WLC**
See also CDBLB 1832-1890; DLB 21, 55, 70, 159, 166; JRDA; MAICYA; SATA 15
Dickey, James (Lafayette) 1923-1997 **CLC 1, 2, 4, 7, 10, 15, 47; DAM NOV, POET, POP**
See also AITN 1, 2; CA 9-12R; 156; CABS 2; CANR 10, 48, 61; CDALB 1968-1988; DLB 5; DLBD 7; DLBY 82, 93, 96; INT CANR-10; MTCW
Dickey, William 1928-1994 .... **CLC 3, 28**
See also CA 9-12R; 145; CANR 24; DLB 5
Dickinson, Charles 1951- .... **CLC 49**
See also CA 128
Dickinson, Emily (Elizabeth) 1830-1886 **NCLC 21; DA; DAB; DAC; DAM MST, POET; PC 1; WLC**
See also AAYA 22; CDALB 1865-1917; DLB 1; SATA 29
Dickinson, Peter (Malcolm) 1927-**CLC 12, 35**
See also AAYA 9; CA 41-44R; CANR 31, 58; CLR 29; DLB 87, 161; JRDA; MAICYA; SATA 5, 62, 95
Dickson, Carr
See Carr, John Dickson
Dickson, Carter
See Carr, John Dickson
Diderot, Denis 1713-1784 .... **LC 26**
Didion, Joan 1934-**CLC 1, 3, 8, 14, 32; DAM NOV**
See also AITN 1; CA 5-8R; CANR 14, 52; CDALB 1968-1988; DLB 2, 173; DLBY 81, 86; MTCW
Dietrich, Robert
See Hunt, E(verette) Howard, (Jr.)
Dillard, Annie 1945- **CLC 9, 60; DAM NOV**
See also AAYA 6; CA 49-52; CANR 3, 43, 62; DLBY 80; MTCW; SATA 10
Dillard, R(ichard) H(enry) W(ilde) 1937- **CLC 5**
See also CA 21-24R; CAAS 7; CANR 10; DLB 5
Dillon, Eilis 1920-1994 .... **CLC 17**
See also CA 9-12R; 147; CAAS 3; CANR 4, 38; CLR 26; MAICYA; SATA 2, 74; SATA-Obit 83
Dimont, Penelope
See Mortimer, Penelope (Ruth)
Dinesen, Isak .... **CLC 10, 29, 95; SSC 7**
See also Blixen, Karen (Christentze Dinesen)
Ding Ling .... **CLC 68**
See also Chiang Pin-chin
Disch, Thomas M(ichael) 1940- .... **CLC 7, 36**
See also AAYA 17; CA 21-24R; CAAS 4; CANR 17, 36, 54; CLR 18; DLB 8; MAICYA; MTCW; SAAS 15; SATA 92
Disch, Tom
See Disch, Thomas M(ichael)
d'Isly, Georges
See Simenon, Georges (Jacques Christian)
Disraeli, Benjamin 1804-1881 .... **NCLC 2, 39**
See also DLB 21, 55
Ditcum, Steve
See Crumb, R(obert)
Dixon, Paige
See Corcoran, Barbara
Dixon, Stephen 1936- .... **CLC 52; SSC 16**
See also CA 89-92; CANR 17, 40, 54; DLB 130
Doak, Annie
See Dillard, Annie
Dobell, Sydney Thompson 1824-1874 **NCLC 43**
See also DLB 32
Doblin, Alfred .... **TCLC 13**
See also Doeblin, Alfred
Dobrolyubov, Nikolai Alexandrovich 1836-1861 **NCLC 5**
Dobyns, Stephen 1941- .... **CLC 37**
See also CA 45-48; CANR 2, 18
Doctorow, E(dgar) L(aurence) 1931- **CLC 6, 11, 15, 18, 37, 44, 65; DAM NOV, POP**
See also AAYA 22; AITN 2; BEST 89:3; CA 45-48; CANR 2, 33, 51; CDALB 1968-1988; DLB 2, 28, 173; DLBY 80; MTCW
Dodgson, Charles Lutwidge 1832-1898
See Carroll, Lewis
See also CLR 2; DA; DAB; DAC; DAM MST, NOV, POET; MAICYA; YABC 2
Dodson, Owen (Vincent) 1914-1983 **CLC 79; BLC; DAM MULT**
See also BW 1; CA 65-68; 110; CANR 24; DLB 76
Doeblin, Alfred 1878-1957 .... **TCLC 13**
See also Doblin, Alfred
See also CA 110; 141; DLB 66
Doerr, Harriet 1910- .... **CLC 34**
See also CA 117; 122; CANR 47; INT 122
Domecq, H(onorio) Bustos
See Bioy Casares, Adolfo; Borges, Jorge Luis
Domini, Rey
See Lorde, Audre (Geraldine)
Dominique
See Proust, (Valentin-Louis-George-Eugene-) Marcel
Don, A
See Stephen, Leslie
Donaldson, Stephen R. 1947- **CLC 46; DAM POP**
See also CA 89-92; CANR 13, 55; INT CANR-13
Donleavy, J(ames) P(atrick) 1926-**CLC 1, 4, 6, 10, 45**
See also AITN 2; CA 9-12R; CANR 24, 49, 62; DLB 6, 173; INT CANR-24; MTCW
Donne, John 1572-1631**LC 10, 24; DA; DAB; DAC; DAM MST, POET; PC 1**
See also CDBLB Before 1660; DLB 121, 151
Donnell, David 1939(?)- .... **CLC 34**
Donoghue, P. S.
See Hunt, E(verette) Howard, (Jr.)
Donoso (Yanez), Jose 1924-1996**CLC 4, 8, 11, 32, 99; DAM MULT; HLC**
See also CA 81-84; 155; CANR 32; DLB 113; HW; MTCW
Donovan, John 1928-1992 .... **CLC 35**
See also AAYA 20; CA 97-100; 137; CLR 3; MAICYA; SATA 72; SATA-Brief 29
Don Roberto
See Cunninghame Graham, R(obert) B(ontine)
Doolittle, Hilda 1886-1961**CLC 3, 8, 14, 31, 34, 73; DA; DAC; DAM MST, POET; PC 5; WLC**
See also H. D.
See also CA 97-100; CANR 35; DLB 4, 45; MTCW
Dorfman, Ariel 1942- ...... **CLC 48, 77; DAM MULT; HLC**
See also CA 124; 130; HW; INT 130
Dorn, Edward (Merton) 1929- ... **CLC 10, 18**
See also CA 93-96; CANR 42; DLB 5; INT 93-96
Dorsan, Luc
See Simenon, Georges (Jacques Christian)
Dorsange, Jean
See Simenon, Georges (Jacques Christian)
Dos Passos, John (Roderigo) 1896-1970 **CLC 1, 4, 8, 11, 15, 25, 34, 82; DA; DAB; DAC; DAM MST, NOV; WLC**
See also CA 1-4R; 29-32R; CANR 3; CDALB 1929-1941; DLB 4, 9; DLBD 1, 15; DLBY 96; MTCW
Dossage, Jean
See Simenon, Georges (Jacques Christian)
Dostoevsky, Fedor Mikhailovich 1821-1881 **NCLC 2, 7, 21, 33, 43; DA; DAB; DAC; DAM MST, NOV; SSC 2; WLC**
Doughty, Charles M(ontagu) 1843-1926 **TCLC 27**
See also CA 115; DLB 19, 57, 174
Douglas, Ellen .... **CLC 73**
See also Haxton, Josephine Ayres; Williamson, Ellen Douglas
Douglas, Gavin 1475(?)-1522 .... **LC 20**
Douglas, Keith (Castellain) 1920-1944**TCLC 40**
See also CA 160; DLB 27
Douglas, Leonard
See Bradbury, Ray (Douglas)
Douglas, Michael
See Crichton, (John) Michael
Douglas, Norman 1868-1952 .... **TCLC 68**
Douglass, Frederick 1817(?)-1895**NCLC 7, 55; BLC; DA; DAC; DAM MST, MULT; WLC**

See also CDALB 1640-1865; DLB 1, 43, 50, 79; SATA 29

Dourado, (Waldomiro Freitas) Autran 1926- **CLC 23, 60**
See also CA 25-28R; CANR 34

Dourado, Waldomiro Autran
See Dourado, (Waldomiro Freitas) Autran

Dove, Rita (Frances) 1952-**CLC 50, 81; DAM MULT, POET; PC 6**
See also BW 2; CA 109; CAAS 19; CANR 27, 42; DLB 120

Dowell, Coleman 1925-1985 .... **CLC 60**
See also CA 25-28R; 117; CANR 10; DLB 130

Dowson, Ernest (Christopher) 1867-1900 **TCLC 4**
See also CA 105; 150; DLB 19, 135

Doyle, A. Conan
See Doyle, Arthur Conan

Doyle, Arthur Conan 1859-1930**TCLC 7; DA; DAB; DAC; DAM MST, NOV; SSC 12; WLC**
See also AAYA 14; CA 104; 122; CDBLB 1890-1914; DLB 18, 70, 156, 178; MTCW; SATA 24

Doyle, Conan
See Doyle, Arthur Conan

Doyle, John
See Graves, Robert (von Ranke)

Doyle, Roddy 1958(?)- .... **CLC 81**
See also AAYA 14; CA 143

Doyle, Sir A. Conan
See Doyle, Arthur Conan

Doyle, Sir Arthur Conan
See Doyle, Arthur Conan

Dr. A
See Asimov, Isaac; Silverstein, Alvin

Drabble, Margaret 1939-**CLC 2, 3, 5, 8, 10, 22, 53; DAB; DAC; DAM MST, NOV, POP**
See also CA 13-16R; CANR 18, 35; CDBLB 1960 to Present; DLB 14, 155; MTCW; SATA 48

Drapier, M. B.
See Swift, Jonathan

Drayham, James
See Mencken, H(enry) L(ouis)

Drayton, Michael 1563-1631 .... **LC 8**

Dreadstone, Carl
See Campbell, (John) Ramsey

Dreiser, Theodore (Herman Albert) 1871-1945 **TCLC 10, 18, 35; DA; DAC; DAM MST, NOV; WLC**
See also CA 106; 132; CDALB 1865-1917; DLB 9, 12, 102, 137; DLBD 1; MTCW

Drexler, Rosalyn 1926- .... **CLC 2, 6**
See also CA 81-84

Dreyer, Carl Theodor 1889-1968 ...... **CLC 16**
See also CA 116

Drieu la Rochelle, Pierre(-Eugene) 1893-1945 **TCLC 21**
See also CA 117; DLB 72

Drinkwater, John 1882-1937 .... **TCLC 57**
See also CA 109; 149; DLB 10, 19, 149

Drop Shot
See Cable, George Washington

Droste-Hulshoff, Annette Freiin von 1797-1848 **NCLC 3**
See also DLB 133

Drummond, Walter
See Silverberg, Robert

Drummond, William Henry 1854-1907**TCLC 25**
See also CA 160; DLB 92

Drummond de Andrade, Carlos 1902-1987 **CLC 18**
See also Andrade, Carlos Drummond de
See also CA 132; 123

Drury, Allen (Stuart) 1918- .... **CLC 37**
See also CA 57-60; CANR 18, 52; INT CANR-18

Dryden, John 1631-1700**LC 3, 21; DA; DAB; DAC; DAM DRAM, MST, POET; DC 3; WLC**
See also CDBLB 1660-1789; DLB 80, 101, 131

Duberman, Martin 1930- .... **CLC 8**
See also CA 1-4R; CANR 2

Dubie, Norman (Evans) 1945- .... **CLC 36**
See also CA 69-72; CANR 12; DLB 120

Du Bois, W(illiam) E(dward) B(urghardt) 1868-1963**CLC 1, 2, 13, 64, 96; BLC; DA; DAC; DAM MST, MULT, NOV; WLC**
See also BW 1; CA 85-88; CANR 34; CDALB 1865-1917; DLB 47, 50, 91; MTCW; SATA 42

Dubus, Andre 1936- **CLC 13, 36, 97; SSC 15**
See also CA 21-24R; CANR 17; DLB 130; INT CANR-17

Duca Minimo
See D'Annunzio, Gabriele

Ducharme, Rejean 1941- .... **CLC 74**
See also DLB 60

Duclos, Charles Pinot 1704-1772 .... **LC 1**

Dudek, Louis 1918- .... **CLC 11, 19**
See also CA 45-48; CAAS 14; CANR 1; DLB 88

Duerrenmatt, Friedrich 1921-1990**CLC 1, 4, 8, 11, 15, 43, 102; DAM DRAM**
See also CA 17-20R; CANR 33; DLB 69, 124; MTCW

Duffy, Bruce (?)- .... **CLC 50**

Duffy, Maureen 1933- .... **CLC 37**
See also CA 25-28R; CANR 33; DLB 14; MTCW

Dugan, Alan 1923- .... **CLC 2, 6**
See also CA 81-84; DLB 5

du Gard, Roger Martin
See Martin du Gard, Roger

Duhamel, Georges 1884-1966 .... **CLC 8**
See also CA 81-84; 25-28R; CANR 35; DLB 65; MTCW

Dujardin, Edouard (Emile Louis) 1861-1949 **TCLC 13**
See also CA 109; DLB 123

Dulles, John Foster 1888-1959 .... **TCLC 72**
See also CA 115; 149

Dumas, Alexandre (Davy de la Pailleterie) 1802-1870 .. **NCLC 11; DA; DAB; DAC; DAM MST, NOV; WLC**
See also DLB 119; SATA 18

Dumas, Alexandre 1824-1895 **NCLC 9; DC 1**
See also AAYA 22

Dumas, Claudine
See Malzberg, Barry N(athaniel)

Dumas, Henry L. 1934-1968 .... **CLC 6, 62**
See also BW 1; CA 85-88; DLB 41

du Maurier, Daphne 1907-1989**CLC 6, 11, 59; DAB; DAC; DAM MST, POP; SSC 18**
See also CA 5-8R; 128; CANR 6, 55; MTCW; SATA 27; SATA-Obit 60

Dunbar, Paul Laurence 1872-1906. **TCLC 2, 12; BLC; DA; DAC; DAM MST, MULT, POET; PC 5; SSC 8; WLC**
See also BW 1; CA 104; 124; CDALB 1865-1917; DLB 50, 54, 78; SATA 34

Dunbar, William 1460(?)-1530(?) .... **LC 20**
See also DLB 132, 146

Duncan, Dora Angela
See Duncan, Isadora

Duncan, Isadora 1877(?)-1927 .... **TCLC 68**
See also CA 118; 149

Duncan, Lois 1934- .... **CLC 26**
See also AAYA 4; CA 1-4R; CANR 2, 23, 36; CLR 29; JRDA; MAICYA; SAAS 2; SATA 1, 36, 75

Duncan, Robert (Edward) 1919-1988**CLC 1, 2, 4, 7, 15, 41, 55; DAM POET; PC 2**
See also CA 9-12R; 124; CANR 28, 62; DLB 5, 16; MTCW

Duncan, Sara Jeannette 1861-1922 **TCLC 60**
See also CA 157; DLB 92

Dunlap, William 1766-1839 .... **NCLC 2**
See also DLB 30, 37, 59

Dunn, Douglas (Eaglesham) 1942- **CLC 6, 40**
See also CA 45-48; CANR 2, 33; DLB 40; MTCW

Dunn, Katherine (Karen) 1945- .... **CLC 71**
See also CA 33-36R

Dunn, Stephen 1939- .... **CLC 36**
See also CA 33-36R; CANR 12, 48, 53; DLB 105

Dunne, Finley Peter 1867-1936 ...... **TCLC 28**
See also CA 108; DLB 11, 23

Dunne, John Gregory 1932- .... **CLC 28**
See also CA 25-28R; CANR 14, 50; DLBY 80

Dunsany, Edward John Moreton Drax Plunkett 1878-1957
See Dunsany, Lord
See also CA 104; 148; DLB 10

Dunsany, Lord .... **TCLC 2, 59**
See also Dunsany, Edward John Moreton Drax Plunkett
See also DLB 77, 153, 156

du Perry, Jean
See Simenon, Georges (Jacques Christian)

Durang, Christopher (Ferdinand) 1949-**CLC 27, 38**
See also CA 105; CANR 50

Duras, Marguerite 1914-1996**CLC 3, 6, 11, 20, 34, 40, 68, 100**
See also CA 25-28R; 151; CANR 50; DLB 83; MTCW

Durban, (Rosa) Pam 1947- .... **CLC 39**
See also CA 123

Durcan, Paul 1944-**CLC 43, 70; DAM POET**
See also CA 134

Durkheim, Emile 1858-1917 .... **TCLC 55**

Durrell, Lawrence (George) 1912-1990 **CLC 1, 4, 6, 8, 13, 27, 41; DAM NOV**
See also CA 9-12R; 132; CANR 40; CDBLB 1945-1960; DLB 15, 27; DLBY 90; MTCW

Durrenmatt, Friedrich
See Duerrenmatt, Friedrich

Dutt, Toru 1856-1877 .... **NCLC 29**

Dwight, Timothy 1752-1817 .... **NCLC 13**
See also DLB 37

Dworkin, Andrea 1946- .... **CLC 43**
See also CA 77-80; CAAS 21; CANR 16, 39; INT CANR-16; MTCW

Dwyer, Deanna
See Koontz, Dean R(ay)

Dwyer, K. R.
See Koontz, Dean R(ay)

Dye, Richard
See De Voto, Bernard (Augustine)

Dylan, Bob 1941- .... **CLC 3, 4, 6, 12, 77**
See also CA 41-44R; DLB 16

Eagleton, Terence (Francis) 1943-
See Eagleton, Terry
See also CA 57-60; CANR 7, 23; MTCW

Eagleton, Terry .... **CLC 63**
See also Eagleton, Terence (Francis)

Early, Jack
See Scoppettone, Sandra

East, Michael
See West, Morris L(anglo)

Eastaway, Edward
See Thomas, (Philip) Edward

Eastlake, William (Derry) 1917-1997 **CLC 8**
See also CA 5-8R; 158; CAAS 1; CANR 5; DLB 6; INT CANR-5

Eastman, Charles A(lexander) 1858-1939 **TCLC 55; DAM MULT**

See also Clutha, Janet Paterson Frame
France, Anatole .... **TCLC 9**
See also Thibault, Jacques Anatole Francois
See also DLB 123
Francis, Claude 19(?)- .... **CLC 50**
Francis, Dick 1920-**CLC 2, 22, 42, 102; DAM POP**
See also AAYA 5, 21; BEST 89:3; CA 5-8R; CANR 9, 42; CDBLB 1960 to Present; DLB 87; INT CANR-9; MTCW
Francis, Robert (Churchill) 1901-1987 **CLC 15**
See also CA 1-4R; 123; CANR 1
Frank, Anne(lies Marie) 1929-1945**TCLC 17; DA; DAB; DAC; DAM MST; WLC**
See also AAYA 12; CA 113; 133; MTCW; SATA 87; SATA-Brief 42
Frank, Elizabeth 1945- .... **CLC 39**
See also CA 121; 126; INT 126
Frankl, Viktor E(mil) 1905- .... **CLC 93**
See also CA 65-68
Franklin, Benjamin
See Hasek, Jaroslav (Matej Frantisek)
Franklin, Benjamin 1706-1790 .. **LC 25; DA; DAB; DAC; DAM MST; WLCS**
See also CDALB 1640-1865; DLB 24, 43, 73
Franklin, (Stella Maraia Sarah) Miles 1879-1954 .... **TCLC 7**
See also CA 104
Fraser, (Lady) Antonia (Pakenham) 1932- **CLC 32**
See also CA 85-88; CANR 44; MTCW; SATA-Brief 32
Fraser, George MacDonald 1925- ...... **CLC 7**
See also CA 45-48; CANR 2, 48
Fraser, Sylvia 1935- .... **CLC 64**
See also CA 45-48; CANR 1, 16, 60
Frayn, Michael 1933-**CLC 3, 7, 31, 47; DAM DRAM, NOV**
See also CA 5-8R; CANR 30; DLB 13, 14; MTCW
Fraze, Candida (Merrill) 1945- .... **CLC 50**
See also CA 126
Frazer, J(ames) G(eorge) 1854-1941**TCLC 32**
See also CA 118
Frazer, Robert Caine
See Creasey, John
Frazer, Sir James George
See Frazer, J(ames) G(eorge)
Frazier, Ian 1951- .... **CLC 46**
See also CA 130; CANR 54
Frederic, Harold 1856-1898 .... **NCLC 10**
See also DLB 12, 23; DLBD 13
Frederick, John
See Faust, Frederick (Schiller)
Frederick the Great 1712-1786 .... **LC 14**
Fredro, Aleksander 1793-1876 .... **NCLC 8**
Freeling, Nicolas 1927- .... **CLC 38**
See also CA 49-52; CAAS 12; CANR 1, 17, 50; DLB 87
Freeman, Douglas Southall 1886-1953**TCLC 11**
See also CA 109; DLB 17
Freeman, Judith 1946- .... **CLC 55**
See also CA 148
Freeman, Mary Eleanor Wilkins 1852-1930 **TCLC 9; SSC 1**
See also CA 106; DLB 12, 78
Freeman, R(ichard) Austin 1862-1943**TCLC 21**
See also CA 113; DLB 70
French, Albert 1943- .... **CLC 86**
French, Marilyn 1929-**CLC 10, 18, 60; DAM DRAM, NOV, POP**
See also CA 69-72; CANR 3, 31; INT CANR-31; MTCW
French, Paul
See Asimov, Isaac
Freneau, Philip Morin 1752-1832 ... **NCLC 1**
See also DLB 37, 43
Freud, Sigmund 1856-1939 .... **TCLC 52**
See also CA 115; 133; MTCW
Friedan, Betty (Naomi) 1921- .... **CLC 74**
See also CA 65-68; CANR 18, 45; MTCW
Friedlander, Saul 1932- .... **CLC 90**
See also CA 117; 130
Friedman, B(ernard) H(arper) 1926- **CLC 7**
See also CA 1-4R; CANR 3, 48
Friedman, Bruce Jay 1930- ...... **CLC 3, 5, 56**
See also CA 9-12R; CANR 25, 52; DLB 2, 28; INT CANR-25
Friel, Brian 1929- .... **CLC 5, 42, 59**
See also CA 21-24R; CANR 33; DLB 13; MTCW
Friis-Baastad, Babbis Ellinor 1921-1970**CLC 12**
See also CA 17-20R; 134; SATA 7
Frisch, Max (Rudolf) 1911-1991**CLC 3, 9, 14, 18, 32, 44; DAM DRAM, NOV**
See also CA 85-88; 134; CANR 32; DLB 69, 124; MTCW
Fromentin, Eugene (Samuel Auguste) 1820-1876 .... **NCLC 10**
See also DLB 123
Frost, Frederick
See Faust, Frederick (Schiller)
Frost, Robert (Lee) 1874-1963**CLC 1, 3, 4, 9, 10, 13, 15, 26, 34, 44; DA; DAB; DAC; DAM MST, POET; PC 1; WLC**
See also AAYA 21; CA 89-92; CANR 33; CDALB 1917-1929; DLB 54; DLBD 7; MTCW; SATA 14
Froude, James Anthony 1818-1894**NCLC 43**
See also DLB 18, 57, 144
Froy, Herald
See Waterhouse, Keith (Spencer)
Fry, Christopher 1907- **CLC 2, 10, 14; DAM DRAM**
See also CA 17-20R; CAAS 23; CANR 9, 30; DLB 13; MTCW; SATA 66
Frye, (Herman) Northrop 1912-1991**CLC 24, 70**
See also CA 5-8R; 133; CANR 8, 37; DLB 67, 68; MTCW
Fuchs, Daniel 1909-1993 .... **CLC 8, 22**
See also CA 81-84; 142; CAAS 5; CANR 40; DLB 9, 26, 28; DLBY 93
Fuchs, Daniel 1934- .... **CLC 34**
See also CA 37-40R; CANR 14, 48
Fuentes, Carlos 1928-**CLC 3, 8, 10, 13, 22, 41, 60; DA; DAB; DAC; DAM MST, MULT, NOV; HLC; SSC 24; WLC**
See also AAYA 4; AITN 2; CA 69-72; CANR 10, 32; DLB 113; HW; MTCW
Fuentes, Gregorio Lopez y
See Lopez y Fuentes, Gregorio
Fugard, (Harold) Athol 1932-**CLC 5, 9, 14, 25, 40, 80; DAM DRAM; DC 3**
See also AAYA 17; CA 85-88; CANR 32, 54; MTCW
Fugard, Sheila 1932- .... **CLC 48**
See also CA 125
Fuller, Charles (H., Jr.) 1939- **CLC 25; BLC; DAM DRAM, MULT; DC 1**
See also BW 2; CA 108; 112; DLB 38; INT 112; MTCW
Fuller, John (Leopold) 1937- .... **CLC 62**
See also CA 21-24R; CANR 9, 44; DLB 40
Fuller, Margaret .... **NCLC 5, 50**
See also Ossoli, Sarah Margaret (Fuller marchesa d')
Fuller, Roy (Broadbent) 1912-1991**CLC 4, 28**
See also CA 5-8R; 135; CAAS 10; CANR 53; DLB 15, 20; SATA 87
Fulton, Alice 1952- .... **CLC 52**
See also CA 116; CANR 57
Furphy, Joseph 1843-1912 .... **TCLC 25**
Fussell, Paul 1924- .... **CLC 74**
See also BEST 90:1; CA 17-20R; CANR 8, 21, 35; INT CANR-21; MTCW
Futabatei, Shimei 1864-1909 .... **TCLC 44**
See also DLB 180
Futrelle, Jacques 1875-1912 .... **TCLC 19**
See also CA 113; 155
Gaboriau, Emile 1835-1873 .... **NCLC 14**
Gadda, Carlo Emilio 1893-1973 .... **CLC 11**
See also CA 89-92; DLB 177
Gaddis, William 1922- **CLC 1, 3, 6, 8, 10, 19, 43, 86**
See also CA 17-20R; CANR 21, 48; DLB 2; MTCW
Gage, Walter
See Inge, William (Motter)
Gaines, Ernest J(ames) 1933- **CLC 3, 11, 18, 86; BLC; DAM MULT**
See also AAYA 18; AITN 1; BW 2; CA 9-12R; CANR 6, 24, 42; CDALB 1968-1988; DLB 2, 33, 152; DLBY 80; MTCW; SATA 86
Gaitskill, Mary 1954- .... **CLC 69**
See also CA 128; CANR 61
Galdos, Benito Perez
See Perez Galdos, Benito
Gale, Zona 1874-1938**TCLC 7; DAM DRAM**
See also CA 105; 153; DLB 9, 78
Galeano, Eduardo (Hughes) 1940- ... **CLC 72**
See also CA 29-32R; CANR 13, 32; HW
Galiano, Juan Valera y Alcala
See Valera y Alcala-Galiano, Juan
Gallagher, Tess 1943- ...... **CLC 18, 63; DAM POET; PC 9**
See also CA 106; DLB 120
Gallant, Mavis 1922- ... **CLC 7, 18, 38; DAC; DAM MST; SSC 5**
See also CA 69-72; CANR 29; DLB 53; MTCW
Gallant, Roy A(rthur) 1924- .... **CLC 17**
See also CA 5-8R; CANR 4, 29, 54; CLR 30; MAICYA; SATA 4, 68
Gallico, Paul (William) 1897-1976 ..... **CLC 2**
See also AITN 1; CA 5-8R; 69-72; CANR 23; DLB 9, 171; MAICYA; SATA 13
Gallo, Max Louis 1932- .... **CLC 95**
See also CA 85-88
Gallois, Lucien
See Desnos, Robert
Gallup, Ralph
See Whitemore, Hugh (John)
Galsworthy, John 1867-1933**TCLC 1, 45; DA; DAB; DAC; DAM DRAM, MST, NOV; SSC 22; WLC 2**
See also CA 104; 141; CDBLB 1890-1914; DLB 10, 34, 98, 162; DLBD 16
Galt, John 1779-1839 .... **NCLC 1**
See also DLB 99, 116, 159
Galvin, James 1951- .... **CLC 38**
See also CA 108; CANR 26
Gamboa, Federico 1864-1939 .... **TCLC 36**
Gandhi, M. K.
See Gandhi, Mohandas Karamchand
Gandhi, Mahatma
See Gandhi, Mohandas Karamchand
Gandhi, Mohandas Karamchand 1869-1948 **TCLC 59; DAM MULT**
See also CA 121; 132; MTCW
Gann, Ernest Kellogg 1910-1991 ...... **CLC 23**
See also AITN 1; CA 1-4R; 136; CANR 1
Garcia, Cristina 1958- .... **CLC 76**
See also CA 141
Garcia Lorca, Federico 1898-1936**TCLC 1, 7, 49; DA; DAB; DAC; DAM DRAM, MST, MULT, POET; DC 2; HLC; PC 3; WLC**
See also CA 104; 131; DLB 108; HW; MTCW

Author Index

See also CA 85-88
Gippius, Zinaida (Nikolayevna) 1869-1945
See Hippius, Zinaida
See also CA 106
Giraudoux, (Hippolyte) Jean 1882-1944 **TCLC 2, 7; DAM DRAM**
See also CA 104; DLB 65
Gironella, Jose Maria 1917- .... **CLC 11**
See also CA 101
Gissing, George (Robert) 1857-1903**TCLC 3, 24, 47**
See also CA 105; DLB 18, 135, 184
Giurlani, Aldo
See Palazzeschi, Aldo
Gladkov, Fyodor (Vasilyevich) 1883-1958 **TCLC 27**
Glanville, Brian (Lester) 1931- .... **CLC 6**
See also CA 5-8R; CAAS 9; CANR 3; DLB 15, 139; SATA 42
Glasgow, Ellen (Anderson Gholson) 1873(?)-1945 .... **TCLC 2, 7**
See also CA 104; DLB 9, 12
Glaspell, Susan 1882(?)-1948 .... **TCLC 55**
See also CA 110; 154; DLB 7, 9, 78; YABC 2
Glassco, John 1909-1981 .... **CLC 9**
See also CA 13-16R; 102; CANR 15; DLB 68
Glasscock, Amnesia
See Steinbeck, John (Ernst)
Glasser, Ronald J. 1940(?)- .... **CLC 37**
Glassman, Joyce
See Johnson, Joyce
Glendinning, Victoria 1937- .... **CLC 50**
See also CA 120; 127; CANR 59; DLB 155
Glissant, Edouard 1928- . **CLC 10, 68; DAM MULT**
See also CA 153
Gloag, Julian 1930- .... **CLC 40**
See also AITN 1; CA 65-68; CANR 10
Glowacki, Aleksander
See Prus, Boleslaw
Gluck, Louise (Elisabeth) 1943-**CLC 7, 22, 44, 81; DAM POET; PC 16**
See also CA 33-36R; CANR 40; DLB 5
Glyn, Elinor 1864-1943 .... **TCLC 72**
See also DLB 153
Gobineau, Joseph Arthur (Comte) de 1816-1882 .... **NCLC 17**
See also DLB 123
Godard, Jean-Luc 1930- .... **CLC 20**
See also CA 93-96
Godden, (Margaret) Rumer 1907- ... **CLC 53**
See also AAYA 6; CA 5-8R; CANR 4, 27, 36, 55; CLR 20; DLB 161; MAICYA; SAAS 12; SATA 3, 36
Godoy Alcayaga, Lucila 1889-1957
See Mistral, Gabriela
See also BW 2; CA 104; 131; DAM MULT; HW; MTCW
Godwin, Gail (Kathleen) 1937- **CLC 5, 8, 22, 31, 69; DAM POP**
See also CA 29-32R; CANR 15, 43; DLB 6; INT CANR-15; MTCW
Godwin, William 1756-1836 .... **NCLC 14**
See also CDBLB 1789-1832; DLB 39, 104, 142, 158, 163
Goebbels, Josef
See Goebbels, (Paul) Joseph
Goebbels, (Paul) Joseph 1897-1945**TCLC 68**
See also CA 115; 148
Goebbels, Joseph Paul
See Goebbels, (Paul) Joseph
Goethe, Johann Wolfgang von 1749-1832 **NCLC 4, 22, 34; DA; DAB; DAC; DAM DRAM, MST, POET; PC 5; WLC 3**
See also DLB 94
Gogarty, Oliver St. John 1878-1957**TCLC 15**
See also CA 109; 150; DLB 15, 19
Gogol, Nikolai (Vasilyevich) 1809-1852**NCLC 5, 15, 31; DA; DAB; DAC; DAM DRAM, MST; DC 1; SSC 4, 29; WLC**
Goines, Donald 1937(?)-1974 **CLC 80; BLC; DAM MULT, POP**
See also AITN 1; BW 1; CA 124; 114; DLB 33
Gold, Herbert 1924- .... **CLC 4, 7, 14, 42**
See also CA 9-12R; CANR 17, 45; DLB 2; DLBY 81
Goldbarth, Albert 1948- .... **CLC 5, 38**
See also CA 53-56; CANR 6, 40; DLB 120
Goldberg, Anatol 1910-1982 .... **CLC 34**
See also CA 131; 117
Goldemberg, Isaac 1945- .... **CLC 52**
See also CA 69-72; CAAS 12; CANR 11, 32; HW
Golding, William (Gerald) 1911-1993**CLC 1, 2, 3, 8, 10, 17, 27, 58, 81; DA; DAB; DAC; DAM MST, NOV; WLC**
See also AAYA 5; CA 5-8R; 141; CANR 13, 33, 54; CDBLB 1945-1960; DLB 15, 100; MTCW
Goldman, Emma 1869-1940 .... **TCLC 13**
See also CA 110; 150
Goldman, Francisco 1955- .... **CLC 76**
Goldman, William (W.) 1931- .... **CLC 1, 48**
See also CA 9-12R; CANR 29; DLB 44
Goldmann, Lucien 1913-1970 .... **CLC 24**
See also CA 25-28; CAP 2
Goldoni, Carlo 1707-1793**LC 4; DAM DRAM**
Goldsberry, Steven 1949- .... **CLC 34**
See also CA 131
Goldsmith, Oliver 1728-1774**LC 2; DA; DAB; DAC; DAM DRAM, MST, NOV, POET; WLC**
See also CDBLB 1660-1789; DLB 39, 89, 104, 109, 142; SATA 26
Goldsmith, Peter
See Priestley, J(ohn) B(oynton)
Gombrowicz, Witold 1904-1969**CLC 4, 7, 11, 49; DAM DRAM**
See also CA 19-20; 25-28R; CAP 2
Gomez de la Serna, Ramon 1888-1963**CLC 9**
See also CA 153; 116; HW
Goncharov, Ivan Alexandrovich 1812-1891 **NCLC 1, 63**
Goncourt, Edmond (Louis Antoine Huot) de 1822-1896 .... **NCLC 7**
See also DLB 123
Goncourt, Jules (Alfred Huot) de 1830-1870 **NCLC 7**
See also DLB 123
Gontier, Fernande 19(?)- .... **CLC 50**
Gonzalez Martinez, Enrique 1871-1952 **TCLC 72**
See also HW
Goodman, Paul 1911-1972...... **CLC 1, 2, 4, 7**
See also CA 19-20; 37-40R; CANR 34; CAP 2; DLB 130; MTCW
Gordimer, Nadine 1923-**CLC 3, 5, 7, 10, 18, 33, 51, 70; DA; DAB; DAC; DAM MST, NOV; SSC 17; WLCS**
See also CA 5-8R; CANR 3, 28, 56; INT CANR-28; MTCW
Gordon, Adam Lindsay 1833-1870 **NCLC 21**
Gordon, Caroline 1895-1981**CLC 6, 13, 29, 83; SSC 15**
See also CA 11-12; 103; CANR 36; CAP 1; DLB 4, 9, 102; DLBY 81; MTCW
Gordon, Charles William 1860-1937
See Connor, Ralph
See also CA 109
Gordon, Mary (Catherine) 1949- **CLC 13, 22**
See also CA 102; CANR 44; DLB 6; DLBY 81; INT 102; MTCW
Gordon, N. J.
See Bosman, Herman Charles
Gordon, Sol 1923- .... **CLC 26**
See also CA 53-56; CANR 4; SATA 11
Gordone, Charles 1925-1995**CLC 1, 4; DAM DRAM**
See also BW 1; CA 93-96; 150; CANR 55; DLB 7; INT 93-96; MTCW
Gore, Catherine 1800-1861 .... **NCLC 65**
See also DLB 116
Gorenko, Anna Andreevna
See Akhmatova, Anna
Gorky, Maxim **TCLC 8; DAB; SSC 28; WLC**
See also Peshkov, Alexei Maximovich
Goryan, Sirak
See Saroyan, William
Gosse, Edmund (William) 1849-1928**TCLC 28**
See also CA 117; DLB 57, 144, 184
Gotlieb, Phyllis Fay (Bloom) 1926- .. **CLC 18**
See also CA 13-16R; CANR 7; DLB 88
Gottesman, S. D.
See Kornbluth, C(yril) M.; Pohl, Frederik
Gottfried von Strassburg fl. c. 1210- **CMLC 10**
See also DLB 138
Gould, Lois .... **CLC 4, 10**
See also CA 77-80; CANR 29; MTCW
Gourmont, Remy (-Marie-Charles) de 1858-1915 .... **TCLC 17**
See also CA 109; 150
Govier, Katherine 1948- .... **CLC 51**
See also CA 101; CANR 18, 40
Goyen, (Charles) William 1915-1983**CLC 5, 8, 14, 40**
See also AITN 2; CA 5-8R; 110; CANR 6; DLB 2; DLBY 83; INT CANR-6
Goytisolo, Juan 1931- . **CLC 5, 10, 23; DAM MULT; HLC**
See also CA 85-88; CANR 32, 61; HW; MTCW
Gozzano, Guido 1883-1916 .... **PC 10**
See also CA 154; DLB 114
Gozzi, (Conte) Carlo 1720-1806 .... **NCLC 23**
Grabbe, Christian Dietrich 1801-1836**NCLC 2**
See also DLB 133
Grace, Patricia 1937- .... **CLC 56**
Gracian y Morales, Baltasar 1601-1658**LC 15**
Gracq, Julien .... **CLC 11, 48**
See also Poirier, Louis
See also DLB 83
Grade, Chaim 1910-1982 .... **CLC 10**
See also CA 93-96; 107
Graduate of Oxford, A
See Ruskin, John
Grafton, Garth
See Duncan, Sara Jeannette
Graham, John
See Phillips, David Graham
Graham, Jorie 1951- .... **CLC 48**
See also CA 111; DLB 120
Graham, R(obert) B(ontine) Cunninghame
See Cunninghame Graham, R(obert) B(ontine)
See also DLB 98, 135, 174
Graham, Robert
See Haldeman, Joe (William)
Graham, Tom
See Lewis, (Harry) Sinclair
Graham, W(illiam) S(ydney) 1918-1986**CLC 29**
See also CA 73-76; 118; DLB 20
Graham, Winston (Mawdsley) 1910- **CLC 23**
See also CA 49-52; CANR 2, 22, 45; DLB 77
Grahame, Kenneth 1859-1932**TCLC 64; DAB**
See also CA 108; 136; CLR 5; DLB 34, 141, 178; MAICYA; YABC 1
Grant, Skeeter
See Spiegelman, Art
Granville-Barker, Harley 1877-1946**TCLC 2; DAM DRAM**

See also DLB 38
Gunn, Thom(son William) 1929-**CLC 3, 6, 18, 32, 81; DAM POET**
See also CA 17-20R; CANR 9, 33; CDBLB 1960 to Present; DLB 27; INT CANR-33; MTCW
Gunn, William Harrison 1934(?)-1989
See Gunn, Bill
See also AITN 1; BW 1; CA 13-16R; 128; CANR 12, 25
Gunnars, Kristjana 1948-.................. **CLC 69**
See also CA 113; DLB 60
Gurdjieff, G(eorgei) I(vanovich) 1877(?)-1949 **TCLC 71**
See also CA 157
Gurganus, Allan 1947-. **CLC 70; DAM POP**
See also BEST 90:1; CA 135
Gurney, A(lbert) R(amsdell), Jr. 1930-. **C L C 32, 50, 54; DAM DRAM**
See also CA 77-80; CANR 32
Gurney, Ivor (Bertie) 1890-1937 ... **TCLC 33**
Gurney, Peter
See Gurney, A(lbert) R(amsdell), Jr.
Guro, Elena 1877-1913 .... **TCLC 56**
Gustafson, James M(oody) 1925- ... **CLC 100**
See also CA 25-28R; CANR 37
Gustafson, Ralph (Barker) 1909- ..... **CLC 36**
See also CA 21-24R; CANR 8, 45; DLB 88
Gut, Gom
See Simenon, Georges (Jacques Christian)
Guterson, David 1956- .... **CLC 91**
See also CA 132
Guthrie, A(lfred) B(ertram), Jr. 1901-1991 **CLC 23**
See also CA 57-60; 134; CANR 24; DLB 6; SATA 62; SATA-Obit 67
Guthrie, Isobel
See Grieve, C(hristopher) M(urray)
Guthrie, Woodrow Wilson 1912-1967
See Guthrie, Woody
See also CA 113; 93-96
Guthrie, Woody .... **CLC 35**
See also Guthrie, Woodrow Wilson
Guy, Rosa (Cuthbert) 1928- .... **CLC 26**
See also AAYA 4; BW 2; CA 17-20R; CANR 14, 34; CLR 13; DLB 33; JRDA; MAICYA; SATA 14, 62
Gwendolyn
See Bennett, (Enoch) Arnold
H. D. .... **CLC 3, 8, 14, 31, 34, 73; PC 5**
See also Doolittle, Hilda
H. de V.
See Buchan, John
Haavikko, Paavo Juhani 1931- .. **CLC 18, 34**
See also CA 106
Habbema, Koos
See Heijermans, Herman
Habermas, Juergen 1929- .... **CLC 104**
See also CA 109
Habermas, Jurgen
See Habermas, Juergen
Hacker, Marilyn 1942- **CLC 5, 9, 23, 72, 91; DAM POET**
See also CA 77-80; DLB 120
Haggard, H(enry) Rider 1856-1925**TCLC 11**
See also CA 108; 148; DLB 70, 156, 174, 178; SATA 16
Hagiosy, L.
See Larbaud, Valery (Nicolas)
Hagiwara Sakutaro 1886-1942**TCLC 60; PC 18**
Haig, Fenil
See Ford, Ford Madox
Haig-Brown, Roderick (Langmere) 1908-1976 **CLC 21**
See also CA 5-8R; 69-72; CANR 4, 38; CLR 31; DLB 88; MAICYA; SATA 12
Hailey, Arthur 1920-**CLC 5; DAM NOV, POP**
See also AITN 2; BEST 90:3; CA 1-4R; CANR 2, 36; DLB 88; DLBY 82; MTCW
Hailey, Elizabeth Forsythe 1938- ..... **CLC 40**
See also CA 93-96; CAAS 1; CANR 15, 48; INT CANR-15
Haines, John (Meade) 1924- .... **CLC 58**
See also CA 17-20R; CANR 13, 34; DLB 5
Hakluyt, Richard 1552-1616 .... **LC 31**
Haldeman, Joe (William) 1943- .... **CLC 61**
See also CA 53-56; CAAS 25; CANR 6; DLB 8; INT CANR-6
Haley, Alex(ander Murray Palmer) 1921-1992 **CLC 8, 12, 76; BLC; DA; DAB; DAC; DAM MST, MULT, POP**
See also BW 2; CA 77-80; 136; CANR 61; DLB 38; MTCW
Haliburton, Thomas Chandler 1796-1865 **NCLC 15**
See also DLB 11, 99
Hall, Donald (Andrew, Jr.) 1928- **CLC 1, 13, 37, 59; DAM POET**
See also CA 5-8R; CAAS 7; CANR 2, 44; DLB 5; SATA 23
Hall, Frederic Sauser
See Sauser-Hall, Frederic
Hall, James
See Kuttner, Henry
Hall, James Norman 1887-1951 ..... **TCLC 23**
See also CA 123; SATA 21
Hall, (Marguerite) Radclyffe 1886-1943 **TCLC 12**
See also CA 110; 150
Hall, Rodney 1935- .... **CLC 51**
See also CA 109
Halleck, Fitz-Greene 1790-1867 .... **NCLC 47**
See also DLB 3
Halliday, Michael
See Creasey, John
Halpern, Daniel 1945- .... **CLC 14**
See also CA 33-36R
Hamburger, Michael (Peter Leopold) 1924- **CLC 5, 14**
See also CA 5-8R; CAAS 4; CANR 2, 47; DLB 27
Hamill, Pete 1935- .... **CLC 10**
See also CA 25-28R; CANR 18
Hamilton, Alexander 1755(?)-1804 **NCLC 49**
See also DLB 37
Hamilton, Clive
See Lewis, C(live) S(taples)
Hamilton, Edmond 1904-1977 .... **CLC 1**
See also CA 1-4R; CANR 3; DLB 8
Hamilton, Eugene (Jacob) Lee
See Lee-Hamilton, Eugene (Jacob)
Hamilton, Franklin
See Silverberg, Robert
Hamilton, Gail
See Corcoran, Barbara
Hamilton, Mollie
See Kaye, M(ary) M(argaret)
Hamilton, (Anthony Walter) Patrick 1904-1962 **CLC 51**
See also CA 113; DLB 10
Hamilton, Virginia 1936- .... **CLC 26; DAM MULT**
See also AAYA 2, 21; BW 2; CA 25-28R; CANR 20, 37; CLR 1, 11, 40; DLB 33, 52; INT CANR-20; JRDA; MAICYA; MTCW; SATA 4, 56, 79
Hammett, (Samuel) Dashiell 1894-1961 **C L C 3, 5, 10, 19, 47; SSC 17**
See also AITN 1; CA 81-84; CANR 42; CDALB 1929-1941; DLBD 6; DLBY 96; MTCW
Hammon, Jupiter 1711(?)-1800(?) .. **NCLC 5; BLC; DAM MULT, POET; PC 16**
See also DLB 31, 50
Hammond, Keith
See Kuttner, Henry
Hamner, Earl (Henry), Jr. 1923- ...... **CLC 12**
See also AITN 2; CA 73-76; DLB 6
Hampton, Christopher (James) 1946- **CLC 4**
See also CA 25-28R; DLB 13; MTCW
Hamsun, Knut .... **TCLC 2, 14, 49**
See also Pedersen, Knut
Handke, Peter 1942-**CLC 5, 8, 10, 15, 38; DAM DRAM, NOV**
See also CA 77-80; CANR 33; DLB 85, 124; MTCW
Hanley, James 1901-1985 ..... **CLC 3, 5, 8, 13**
See also CA 73-76; 117; CANR 36; MTCW
Hannah, Barry 1942- .... **CLC 23, 38, 90**
See also CA 108; 110; CANR 43; DLB 6; INT 110; MTCW
Hannon, Ezra
See Hunter, Evan
Hansberry, Lorraine (Vivian) 1930-1965**CLC 17, 62; BLC; DA; DAB; DAC; DAM DRAM, MST, MULT; DC 2**
See also BW 1; CA 109; 25-28R; CABS 3; CANR 58; CDALB 1941-1968; DLB 7, 38; MTCW
Hansen, Joseph 1923- .... **CLC 38**
See also CA 29-32R; CAAS 17; CANR 16, 44; INT CANR-16
Hansen, Martin A. 1909-1955 .... **TCLC 32**
Hanson, Kenneth O(stlin) 1922- .... **CLC 13**
See also CA 53-56; CANR 7
Hardwick, Elizabeth 1916- .... **CLC 13; DAM NOV**
See also CA 5-8R; CANR 3, 32; DLB 6; MTCW
Hardy, Thomas 1840-1928**TCLC 4, 10, 18, 32, 48, 53, 72; DA; DAB; DAC; DAM MST, NOV, POET; PC 8; SSC 2; WLC**
See also CA 104; 123; CDBLB 1890-1914; DLB 18, 19, 135; MTCW
Hare, David 1947- .... **CLC 29, 58**
See also CA 97-100; CANR 39; DLB 13; MTCW
Harford, Henry
See Hudson, W(illiam) H(enry)
Hargrave, Leonie
See Disch, Thomas M(ichael)
Harjo, Joy 1951- .... **CLC 83; DAM MULT**
See also CA 114; CANR 35; DLB 120, 175; NNAL
Harlan, Louis R(udolph) 1922- .... **CLC 34**
See also CA 21-24R; CANR 25, 55
Harling, Robert 1951(?)- .... **CLC 53**
See also CA 147
Harmon, William (Ruth) 1938- .... **CLC 38**
See also CA 33-36R; CANR 14, 32, 35; SATA 65
Harper, F. E. W.
See Harper, Frances Ellen Watkins
Harper, Frances E. W.
See Harper, Frances Ellen Watkins
Harper, Frances E. Watkins
See Harper, Frances Ellen Watkins
Harper, Frances Ellen
See Harper, Frances Ellen Watkins
Harper, Frances Ellen Watkins 1825-1911 **TCLC 14; BLC; DAM MULT, POET**
See also BW 1; CA 111; 125; DLB 50
Harper, Michael S(teven) 1938- .... **CLC 7, 22**
See also BW 1; CA 33-36R; CANR 24; DLB 41
Harper, Mrs. F. E. W.
See Harper, Frances Ellen Watkins
Harris, Christie (Lucy) Irwin 1907- **CLC 12**
See also CA 5-8R; CANR 6; CLR 47; DLB 88; JRDA; MAICYA; SAAS 10; SATA 6, 74
Harris, Frank 1856-1931 .... **TCLC 24**
See also CA 109; 150; DLB 156

Author Index

Henley, Beth .... **CLC 23; DC 6**
See also Henley, Elizabeth Becker
See also CABS 3; DLBY 86
Henley, Elizabeth Becker 1952-
See Henley, Beth
See also CA 107; CANR 32; DAM DRAM, MST; MTCW
Henley, William Ernest 1849-1903 .. **TCLC 8**
See also CA 105; DLB 19
Hennissart, Martha
See Lathen, Emma
See also CA 85-88
Henry, O. .... **TCLC 1, 19; SSC 5; WLC**
See also Porter, William Sydney
Henry, Patrick 1736-1799 .... **LC 25**
Henryson, Robert 1430(?)-1506(?) ...... **LC 20**
See also DLB 146
Henry VIII 1491-1547 .... **LC 10**
Henschke, Alfred
See Klabund
Hentoff, Nat(han Irving) 1925- .... **CLC 26**
See also AAYA 4; CA 1-4R; CAAS 6; CANR 5, 25; CLR 1; INT CANR-25; JRDA; MAICYA; SATA 42, 69; SATA-Brief 27
Heppenstall, (John) Rayner 1911-1981 **CLC 10**
See also CA 1-4R; 103; CANR 29
Heraclitus c. 540B.C.-c. 450B.C. .. **CMLC 22**
See also DLB 176
Herbert, Frank (Patrick) 1920-1986**CLC 12, 23, 35, 44, 85; DAM POP**
See also AAYA 21; CA 53-56; 118; CANR 5, 43; DLB 8; INT CANR-5; MTCW; SATA 9, 37; SATA-Obit 47
Herbert, George 1593-1633..... **LC 24; DAB; DAM POET; PC 4**
See also CDBLB Before 1660; DLB 126
Herbert, Zbigniew 1924- .. **CLC 9, 43; DAM POET**
See also CA 89-92; CANR 36; MTCW
Herbst, Josephine (Frey) 1897-1969 **CLC 34**
See also CA 5-8R; 25-28R; DLB 9
Hergesheimer, Joseph 1880-1954 .. **TCLC 11**
See also CA 109; DLB 102, 9
Herlihy, James Leo 1927-1993 .... **CLC 6**
See also CA 1-4R; 143; CANR 2
Hermogenes fl. c. 175- .... **CMLC 6**
Hernandez, Jose 1834-1886 .... **NCLC 17**
Herodotus c. 484B.C.-429B.C. ...... **CMLC 17**
See also DLB 176
Herrick, Robert 1591-1674**LC 13; DA; DAB; DAC; DAM MST, POP; PC 9**
See also DLB 126
Herring, Guilles
See Somerville, Edith
Herriot, James 1916-1995**CLC 12; DAM POP**
See also Wight, James Alfred
See also AAYA 1; CA 148; CANR 40; SATA 86
Herrmann, Dorothy 1941- .... **CLC 44**
See also CA 107
Herrmann, Taffy
See Herrmann, Dorothy
Hersey, John (Richard) 1914-1993**CLC 1, 2, 7, 9, 40, 81, 97; DAM POP**
See also CA 17-20R; 140; CANR 33; DLB 6; MTCW; SATA 25; SATA-Obit 76
Herzen, Aleksandr Ivanovich 1812-1870 **NCLC 10, 61**
Herzl, Theodor 1860-1904 .... **TCLC 36**
Herzog, Werner 1942- .... **CLC 16**
See also CA 89-92
Hesiod c. 8th cent. B.C.- .... **CMLC 5**
See also DLB 176
Hesse, Hermann 1877-1962**CLC 1, 2, 3, 6, 11, 17, 25, 69; DA; DAB; DAC; DAM MST, NOV; SSC 9; WLC**
See also CA 17-18; CAP 2; DLB 66; MTCW; SATA 50
Hewes, Cady
See De Voto, Bernard (Augustine)
Heyen, William 1940- .... **CLC 13, 18**
See also CA 33-36R; CAAS 9; DLB 5
Heyerdahl, Thor 1914- .... **CLC 26**
See also CA 5-8R; CANR 5, 22; MTCW; SATA 2, 52
Heym, Georg (Theodor Franz Arthur) 1887-1912 .... **TCLC 9**
See also CA 106
Heym, Stefan 1913- .... **CLC 41**
See also CA 9-12R; CANR 4; DLB 69
Heyse, Paul (Johann Ludwig von) 1830-1914 **TCLC 8**
See also CA 104; DLB 129
Heyward, (Edwin) DuBose 1885-1940 **TCLC 59**
See also CA 108; 157; DLB 7, 9, 45; SATA 21
Hibbert, Eleanor Alice Burford 1906-1993 **CLC 7; DAM POP**
See also BEST 90:4; CA 17-20R; 140; CANR 9, 28, 59; SATA 2; SATA-Obit 74
Hichens, Robert S. 1864-1950........ **TCLC 64**
See also DLB 153
Higgins, George V(incent) 1939-**CLC 4, 7, 10, 18**
See also CA 77-80; CAAS 5; CANR 17, 51; DLB 2; DLBY 81; INT CANR-17; MTCW
Higginson, Thomas Wentworth 1823-1911 **TCLC 36**
See also DLB 1, 64
Highet, Helen
See MacInnes, Helen (Clark)
Highsmith, (Mary) Patricia 1921-1995**CLC 2, 4, 14, 42, 102; DAM NOV, POP**
See also CA 1-4R; 147; CANR 1, 20, 48, 62; MTCW
Highwater, Jamake (Mamake) 1942(?)- **CLC 12**
See also AAYA 7; CA 65-68; CAAS 7; CANR 10, 34; CLR 17; DLB 52; DLBY 85; JRDA; MAICYA; SATA 32, 69; SATA-Brief 30
Highway, Tomson 1951-**CLC 92; DAC; DAM MULT**
See also CA 151; NNAL
Higuchi, Ichiyo 1872-1896 .... **NCLC 49**
Hijuelos, Oscar 1951- **CLC 65; DAM MULT, POP; HLC**
See also BEST 90:1; CA 123; CANR 50; DLB 145; HW
Hikmet, Nazim 1902(?)-1963 .... **CLC 40**
See also CA 141; 93-96
Hildegard von Bingen 1098-1179 . **CMLC 20**
See also DLB 148
Hildesheimer, Wolfgang 1916-1991 .. **CLC 49**
See also CA 101; 135; DLB 69, 124
Hill, Geoffrey (William) 1932- **CLC 5, 8, 18, 45; DAM POET**
See also CA 81-84; CANR 21; CDBLB 1960 to Present; DLB 40; MTCW
Hill, George Roy 1921- .... **CLC 26**
See also CA 110; 122
Hill, John
See Koontz, Dean R(ay)
Hill, Susan (Elizabeth) 1942- . **CLC 4; DAB; DAM MST, NOV**
See also CA 33-36R; CANR 29; DLB 14, 139; MTCW
Hillerman, Tony 1925- . **CLC 62; DAM POP**
See also AAYA 6; BEST 89:1; CA 29-32R; CANR 21, 42; SATA 6
Hillesum, Etty 1914-1943 .... **TCLC 49**
See also CA 137
Hilliard, Noel (Harvey) 1929- .... **CLC 15**
See also CA 9-12R; CANR 7
Hillis, Rick 1956- .... **CLC 66**
See also CA 134
Hilton, James 1900-1954 .... **TCLC 21**
See also CA 108; DLB 34, 77; SATA 34
Himes, Chester (Bomar) 1909-1984**CLC 2, 4, 7, 18, 58; BLC; DAM MULT**
See also BW 2; CA 25-28R; 114; CANR 22; DLB 2, 76, 143; MTCW
Hinde, Thomas .... **CLC 6, 11**
See also Chitty, Thomas Willes
Hindin, Nathan
See Bloch, Robert (Albert)
Hine, (William) Daryl 1936- .... **CLC 15**
See also CA 1-4R; CAAS 15; CANR 1, 20; DLB 60
Hinkson, Katharine Tynan
See Tynan, Katharine
Hinton, S(usan) E(loise) 1950- **CLC 30; DA; DAB; DAC; DAM MST, NOV**
See also AAYA 2; CA 81-84; CANR 32, 62; CLR 3, 23; JRDA; MAICYA; MTCW; SATA 19, 58
Hippius, Zinaida .... **TCLC 9**
See also Gippius, Zinaida (Nikolayevna)
Hiraoka, Kimitake 1925-1970
See Mishima, Yukio
See also CA 97-100; 29-32R; DAM DRAM; MTCW
Hirsch, E(ric) D(onald), Jr. 1928- .... **CLC 79**
See also CA 25-28R; CANR 27, 51; DLB 67; INT CANR-27; MTCW
Hirsch, Edward 1950- .... **CLC 31, 50**
See also CA 104; CANR 20, 42; DLB 120
Hitchcock, Alfred (Joseph) 1899-1980**CLC 16**
See also AAYA 22; CA 159; 97-100; SATA 27; SATA-Obit 24
Hitler, Adolf 1889-1945 .... **TCLC 53**
See also CA 117; 147
Hoagland, Edward 1932- .... **CLC 28**
See also CA 1-4R; CANR 2, 31, 57; DLB 6; SATA 51
Hoban, Russell (Conwell) 1925- . **CLC 7, 25; DAM NOV**
See also CA 5-8R; CANR 23, 37; CLR 3; DLB 52; MAICYA; MTCW; SATA 1, 40, 78
Hobbes, Thomas 1588-1679 .... **LC 36**
See also DLB 151
Hobbs, Perry
See Blackmur, R(ichard) P(almer)
Hobson, Laura Z(ametkin) 1900-1986**CLC 7, 25**
See also CA 17-20R; 118; CANR 55; DLB 28; SATA 52
Hochhuth, Rolf 1931- .. **CLC 4, 11, 18; DAM DRAM**
See also CA 5-8R; CANR 33; DLB 124; MTCW
Hochman, Sandra 1936- .... **CLC 3, 8**
See also CA 5-8R; DLB 5
Hochwaelder, Fritz 1911-1986**CLC 36; DAM DRAM**
See also CA 29-32R; 120; CANR 42; MTCW
Hochwalder, Fritz
See Hochwaelder, Fritz
Hocking, Mary (Eunice) 1921- .... **CLC 13**
See also CA 101; CANR 18, 40
Hodgins, Jack 1938- .... **CLC 23**
See also CA 93-96; DLB 60
Hodgson, William Hope 1877(?)-1918 **TCLC 13**
See also CA 111; DLB 70, 153, 156, 178
Hoeg, Peter 1957- .... **CLC 95**
See also CA 151
Hoffman, Alice 1952- ... **CLC 51; DAM NOV**
See also CA 77-80; CANR 34; MTCW
Hoffman, Daniel (Gerard) 1923-**CLC 6, 13, 23**
See also CA 1-4R; CANR 4; DLB 5
Hoffman, Stanley 1944- .... **CLC 5**

Brief 27
Hugo, Richard F(ranklin) 1923-1982 **CLC 6, 18, 32; DAM POET**
See also CA 49-52; 108; CANR 3; DLB 5
Hugo, Victor (Marie) 1802-1885**NCLC 3, 10, 21; DA; DAB; DAC; DAM DRAM, MST, NOV, POET; PC 17; WLC**
See also DLB 119; SATA 47
Huidobro, Vicente
See Huidobro Fernandez, Vicente Garcia
Huidobro Fernandez, Vicente Garcia 1893-1948 .... **TCLC 31**
See also CA 131; HW
Hulme, Keri 1947- .... **CLC 39**
See also CA 125; INT 125
Hulme, T(homas) E(rnest) 1883-1917 **TCLC 21**
See also CA 117; DLB 19
Hume, David 1711-1776 .... **LC 7**
See also DLB 104
Humphrey, William 1924-1997 .... **CLC 45**
See also CA 77-80; 160; DLB 6
Humphreys, Emyr Owen 1919- .... **CLC 47**
See also CA 5-8R; CANR 3, 24; DLB 15
Humphreys, Josephine 1945- .... **CLC 34, 57**
See also CA 121; 127; INT 127
Huneker, James Gibbons 1857-1921**TCLC 65**
See also DLB 71
Hungerford, Pixie
See Brinsmead, H(esba) F(ay)
Hunt, E(verette) Howard, (Jr.) 1918-. **CLC 3**
See also AITN 1; CA 45-48; CANR 2, 47
Hunt, Kyle
See Creasey, John
Hunt, (James Henry) Leigh 1784-1859**NCLC 1; DAM POET**
Hunt, Marsha 1946- .... **CLC 70**
See also BW 2; CA 143
Hunt, Violet 1866-1942 .... **TCLC 53**
See also DLB 162
Hunter, E. Waldo
See Sturgeon, Theodore (Hamilton)
Hunter, Evan 1926-. **CLC 11, 31; DAM POP**
See also CA 5-8R; CANR 5, 38, 62; DLBY 82; INT CANR-5; MTCW; SATA 25
Hunter, Kristin (Eggleston) 1931- .... **CLC 35**
See also AITN 1; BW 1; CA 13-16R; CANR 13; CLR 3; DLB 33; INT CANR-13; MAICYA; SAAS 10; SATA 12
Hunter, Mollie 1922- .... **CLC 21**
See also McIlwraith, Maureen Mollie Hunter
See also AAYA 13; CANR 37; CLR 25; DLB 161; JRDA; MAICYA; SAAS 7; SATA 54
Hunter, Robert (?)-1734 .... **LC 7**
Hurston, Zora Neale 1903-1960**CLC 7, 30, 61; BLC; DA; DAC; DAM MST, MULT, NOV; SSC 4; WLCS**
See also AAYA 15; BW 1; CA 85-88; CANR 61; DLB 51, 86; MTCW
Huston, John (Marcellus) 1906-1987 **CLC 20**
See also CA 73-76; 123; CANR 34; DLB 26
Hustvedt, Siri 1955- .... **CLC 76**
See also CA 137
Hutten, Ulrich von 1488-1523 .... **LC 16**
See also DLB 179
Huxley, Aldous (Leonard) 1894-1963 **CLC 1, 3, 4, 5, 8, 11, 18, 35, 79; DA; DAB; DAC; DAM MST, NOV; WLC**
See also AAYA 11; CA 85-88; CANR 44; CDBLB 1914-1945; DLB 36, 100, 162; MTCW; SATA 63
Huysmans, Charles Marie Georges 1848-1907
See Huysmans, Joris-Karl
See also CA 104
Huysmans, Joris-Karl .... **TCLC 7, 69**
See also Huysmans, Charles Marie Georges
See also DLB 123
Hwang, David Henry 1957- ... **CLC 55; DAM DRAM; DC 4**
See also CA 127; 132; INT 132
Hyde, Anthony 1946- .... **CLC 42**
See also CA 136
Hyde, Margaret O(ldroyd) 1917- ..... **CLC 21**
See also CA 1-4R; CANR 1, 36; CLR 23; JRDA; MAICYA; SAAS 8; SATA 1, 42, 76
Hynes, James 1956(?)- .... **CLC 65**
Ian, Janis 1951- .... **CLC 21**
See also CA 105
Ibanez, Vicente Blasco
See Blasco Ibanez, Vicente
Ibarguengoitia, Jorge 1928-1983 ..... **CLC 37**
See also CA 124; 113; HW
Ibsen, Henrik (Johan) 1828-1906 **TCLC 2, 8, 16, 37, 52; DA; DAB; DAC; DAM DRAM, MST; DC 2; WLC**
See also CA 104; 141
Ibuse Masuji 1898-1993 .... **CLC 22**
See also CA 127; 141; DLB 180
Ichikawa, Kon 1915- .... **CLC 20**
See also CA 121
Idle, Eric 1943- .... **CLC 21**
See also Monty Python
See also CA 116; CANR 35
Ignatow, David 1914- .... **CLC 4, 7, 14, 40**
See also CA 9-12R; CAAS 3; CANR 31, 57; DLB 5
Ihimaera, Witi 1944- .... **CLC 46**
See also CA 77-80
Ilf, Ilya .... **TCLC 21**
See also Fainzilberg, Ilya Arnoldovich
Illyes, Gyula 1902-1983 .... **PC 16**
See also CA 114; 109
Immermann, Karl (Lebrecht) 1796-1840 **NCLC 4, 49**
See also DLB 133
Inchbald, Elizabeth 1753-1821 ...... **NCLC 62**
See also DLB 39, 89
Inclan, Ramon (Maria) del Valle
See Valle-Inclan, Ramon (Maria) del
Infante, G(uillermo) Cabrera
See Cabrera Infante, G(uillermo)
Ingalls, Rachel (Holmes) 1940- .... **CLC 42**
See also CA 123; 127
Ingamells, Rex 1913-1955 .... **TCLC 35**
Inge, William (Motter) 1913-1973 . **CLC 1, 8, 19; DAM DRAM**
See also CA 9-12R; CDALB 1941-1968; DLB 7; MTCW
Ingelow, Jean 1820-1897 .... **NCLC 39**
See also DLB 35, 163; SATA 33
Ingram, Willis J.
See Harris, Mark
Innaurato, Albert (F.) 1948(?)- .. **CLC 21, 60**
See also CA 115; 122; INT 122
Innes, Michael
See Stewart, J(ohn) I(nnes) M(ackintosh)
Ionesco, Eugene 1909-1994**CLC 1, 4, 6, 9, 11, 15, 41, 86; DA; DAB; DAC; DAM DRAM, MST; WLC**
See also CA 9-12R; 144; CANR 55; MTCW; SATA 7; SATA-Obit 79
Iqbal, Muhammad 1873-1938 .... **TCLC 28**
Ireland, Patrick
See O'Doherty, Brian
Iron, Ralph
See Schreiner, Olive (Emilie Albertina)
Irving, John (Winslow) 1942-**CLC 13, 23, 38; DAM NOV, POP**
See also AAYA 8; BEST 89:3; CA 25-28R; CANR 28; DLB 6; DLBY 82; MTCW
Irving, Washington 1783-1859 . **NCLC 2, 19; DA; DAB; DAM MST; SSC 2; WLC**
See also CDALB 1640-1865; DLB 3, 11, 30, 59, 73, 74; YABC 2
Irwin, P. K.
See Page, P(atricia) K(athleen)
Isaacs, Susan 1943- .... **CLC 32; DAM POP**
See also BEST 89:1; CA 89-92; CANR 20, 41; INT CANR-20; MTCW
Isherwood, Christopher (William Bradshaw) 1904-1986 .... **CLC 1, 9, 11, 14, 44; DAM DRAM, NOV**
See also CA 13-16R; 117; CANR 35; DLB 15; DLBY 86; MTCW
Ishiguro, Kazuo 1954- **CLC 27, 56, 59; DAM NOV**
See also BEST 90:2; CA 120; CANR 49; MTCW
Ishikawa, Hakuhin
See Ishikawa, Takuboku
Ishikawa, Takuboku 1886(?)-1912 **TCLC 15; DAM POET; PC 10**
See also CA 113; 153
Iskander, Fazil 1929- .... **CLC 47**
See also CA 102
Isler, Alan (David) 1934- .... **CLC 91**
See also CA 156
Ivan IV 1530-1584 .... **LC 17**
Ivanov, Vyacheslav Ivanovich 1866-1949 **TCLC 33**
See also CA 122
Ivask, Ivar Vidrik 1927-1992 .... **CLC 14**
See also CA 37-40R; 139; CANR 24
Ives, Morgan
See Bradley, Marion Zimmer
J. R. S.
See Gogarty, Oliver St. John
Jabran, Kahlil
See Gibran, Kahlil
Jabran, Khalil
See Gibran, Kahlil
Jackson, Daniel
See Wingrove, David (John)
Jackson, Jesse 1908-1983 .... **CLC 12**
See also BW 1; CA 25-28R; 109; CANR 27; CLR 28; MAICYA; SATA 2, 29; SATA-Obit 48
Jackson, Laura (Riding) 1901-1991
See Riding, Laura
See also CA 65-68; 135; CANR 28; DLB 48
Jackson, Sam
See Trumbo, Dalton
Jackson, Sara
See Wingrove, David (John)
Jackson, Shirley 1919-1965 . **CLC 11, 60, 87; DA; DAC; DAM MST; SSC 9; WLC**
See also AAYA 9; CA 1-4R; 25-28R; CANR 4, 52; CDALB 1941-1968; DLB 6; SATA 2
Jacob, (Cyprien-)Max 1876-1944 .... **TCLC 6**
See also CA 104
Jacobs, Jim 1942- .... **CLC 12**
See also CA 97-100; INT 97-100
Jacobs, W(illiam) W(ymark) 1863-1943 **TCLC 22**
See also CA 121; DLB 135
Jacobsen, Jens Peter 1847-1885 .... **NCLC 34**
Jacobsen, Josephine 1908- .... **CLC 48, 102**
See also CA 33-36R; CAAS 18; CANR 23, 48
Jacobson, Dan 1929- .... **CLC 4, 14**
See also CA 1-4R; CANR 2, 25; DLB 14; MTCW
Jacqueline
See Carpentier (y Valmont), Alejo
Jagger, Mick 1944- .... **CLC 17**
Jakes, John (William) 1932- .. **CLC 29; DAM NOV, POP**
See also BEST 89:4; CA 57-60; CANR 10, 43; DLBY 83; INT CANR-10; MTCW; SATA 62
James, Andrew
See Kirkup, James
James, C(yril) L(ionel) R(obert) 1901-1989

CLC 33
See also BW 2; CA 117; 125; 128; CANR 62; DLB 125; MTCW
James, Daniel (Lewis) 1911-1988
See Santiago, Danny
See also CA 125
James, Dynely
See Mayne, William (James Carter)
James, Henry Sr. 1811-1882 .... **NCLC 53**
James, Henry 1843-1916 **TCLC 2, 11, 24, 40, 47, 64; DA; DAB; DAC; DAM MST, NOV; SSC 8; WLC**
See also CA 104; 132; CDALB 1865-1917; DLB 12, 71, 74; DLBD 13; MTCW
James, M. R.
See James, Montague (Rhodes)
See also DLB 156
James, Montague (Rhodes) 1862-1936 **TCLC 6; SSC 16**
See also CA 104
James, P. D. .... **CLC 18, 46**
See also White, Phyllis Dorothy James
See also BEST 90:2; CDBLB 1960 to Present; DLB 87
James, Philip
See Moorcock, Michael (John)
James, William 1842-1910 .... **TCLC 15, 32**
See also CA 109
James I 1394-1437 .... **LC 20**
Jameson, Anna 1794-1860 .... **NCLC 43**
See also DLB 99, 166
Jami, Nur al-Din 'Abd al-Rahman 1414-1492 **LC 9**
Jammes, Francis 1868-1938 .... **TCLC 75**
Jandl, Ernst 1925- .... **CLC 34**
Janowitz, Tama 1957- .. **CLC 43; DAM POP**
See also CA 106; CANR 52
Japrisot, Sebastien 1931- .... **CLC 90**
Jarrell, Randall 1914-1965 **CLC 1, 2, 6, 9, 13, 49; DAM POET**
See also CA 5-8R; 25-28R; CABS 2; CANR 6, 34; CDALB 1941-1968; CLR 6; DLB 48, 52; MAICYA; MTCW; SATA 7
Jarry, Alfred 1873-1907 .. **TCLC 2, 14; DAM DRAM; SSC 20**
See also CA 104; 153
Jarvis, E. K.
See Bloch, Robert (Albert); Ellison, Harlan (Jay); Silverberg, Robert
Jeake, Samuel, Jr.
See Aiken, Conrad (Potter)
Jean Paul 1763-1825 .... **NCLC 7**
Jefferies, (John) Richard 1848-1887 **NCLC 47**
See also DLB 98, 141; SATA 16
Jeffers, (John) Robinson 1887-1962 **CLC 2, 3, 11, 15, 54; DA; DAC; DAM MST, POET; PC 17; WLC**
See also CA 85-88; CANR 35; CDALB 1917-1929; DLB 45; MTCW
Jefferson, Janet
See Mencken, H(enry) L(ouis)
Jefferson, Thomas 1743-1826 .... **NCLC 11**
See also CDALB 1640-1865; DLB 31
Jeffrey, Francis 1773-1850 .... **NCLC 33**
See also DLB 107
Jelakowitch, Ivan
See Heijermans, Herman
Jellicoe, (Patricia) Ann 1927- .... **CLC 27**
See also CA 85-88; DLB 13
Jen, Gish .... **CLC 70**
See also Jen, Lillian
Jen, Lillian 1956(?)-
See Jen, Gish
See also CA 135
Jenkins, (John) Robin 1912- .... **CLC 52**
See also CA 1-4R; CANR 1; DLB 14
Jennings, Elizabeth (Joan) 1926- . **CLC 5, 14**
See also CA 61-64; CAAS 5; CANR 8, 39; DLB 27; MTCW; SATA 66
Jennings, Waylon 1937- .... **CLC 21**
Jensen, Johannes V. 1873-1950 ...... **TCLC 41**
Jensen, Laura (Linnea) 1948- .... **CLC 37**
See also CA 103
Jerome, Jerome K(lapka) 1859-1927 **TCLC 23**
See also CA 119; DLB 10, 34, 135
Jerrold, Douglas William 1803-1857 **NCLC 2**
See also DLB 158, 159
Jewett, (Theodora) Sarah Orne 1849-1909 **TCLC 1, 22; SSC 6**
See also CA 108; 127; DLB 12, 74; SATA 15
Jewsbury, Geraldine (Endsor) 1812-1880 **NCLC 22**
See also DLB 21
Jhabvala, Ruth Prawer 1927- **CLC 4, 8, 29, 94; DAB; DAM NOV**
See also CA 1-4R; CANR 2, 29, 51; DLB 139; INT CANR-29; MTCW
Jibran, Kahlil
See Gibran, Kahlil
Jibran, Khalil
See Gibran, Kahlil
Jiles, Paulette 1943- .... **CLC 13, 58**
See also CA 101
Jimenez (Mantecon), Juan Ramon 1881-1958 **TCLC 4; DAM MULT, POET; HLC; PC 7**
See also CA 104; 131; DLB 134; HW; MTCW
Jimenez, Ramon
See Jimenez (Mantecon), Juan Ramon
Jimenez Mantecon, Juan
See Jimenez (Mantecon), Juan Ramon
Joel, Billy .... **CLC 26**
See also Joel, William Martin
Joel, William Martin 1949-
See Joel, Billy
See also CA 108
John of the Cross, St. 1542-1591 .... **LC 18**
Johnson, B(ryan) S(tanley William) 1933-1973 **CLC 6, 9**
See also CA 9-12R; 53-56; CANR 9; DLB 14, 40
Johnson, Benj. F. of Boo
See Riley, James Whitcomb
Johnson, Benjamin F. of Boo
See Riley, James Whitcomb
Johnson, Charles (Richard) 1948- **CLC 7, 51, 65; BLC; DAM MULT**
See also BW 2; CA 116; CAAS 18; CANR 42; DLB 33
Johnson, Denis 1949- .... **CLC 52**
See also CA 117; 121; DLB 120
Johnson, Diane 1934- .... **CLC 5, 13, 48**
See also CA 41-44R; CANR 17, 40, 62; DLBY 80; INT CANR-17; MTCW
Johnson, Eyvind (Olof Verner) 1900-1976 **CLC 14**
See also CA 73-76; 69-72; CANR 34
Johnson, J. R.
See James, C(yril) L(ionel) R(obert)
Johnson, James Weldon 1871-1938 **TCLC 3, 19; BLC; DAM MULT, POET**
See also BW 1; CA 104; 125; CDALB 1917-1929; CLR 32; DLB 51; MTCW; SATA 31
Johnson, Joyce 1935- .... **CLC 58**
See also CA 125; 129
Johnson, Lionel (Pigot) 1867-1902 **TCLC 19**
See also CA 117; DLB 19
Johnson, Mel
See Malzberg, Barry N(athaniel)
Johnson, Pamela Hansford 1912-1981 **CLC 1, 7, 27**
See also CA 1-4R; 104; CANR 2, 28; DLB 15; MTCW
Johnson, Robert 1911(?)-1938 .... **TCLC 69**
Johnson, Samuel 1709-1784 **LC 15; DA; DAB; DAC; DAM MST; WLC**
See also CDBLB 1660-1789; DLB 39, 95, 104, 142
Johnson, Uwe 1934-1984 .. **CLC 5, 10, 15, 40**
See also CA 1-4R; 112; CANR 1, 39; DLB 75; MTCW
Johnston, George (Benson) 1913- ..... **CLC 51**
See also CA 1-4R; CANR 5, 20; DLB 88
Johnston, Jennifer 1930- .... **CLC 7**
See also CA 85-88; DLB 14
Jolley, (Monica) Elizabeth 1923- **CLC 46; SSC 19**
See also CA 127; CAAS 13; CANR 59
Jones, Arthur Llewellyn 1863-1947
See Machen, Arthur
See also CA 104
Jones, D(ouglas) G(ordon) 1929- ...... **CLC 10**
See also CA 29-32R; CANR 13; DLB 53
Jones, David (Michael) 1895-1974 **CLC 2, 4, 7, 13, 42**
See also CA 9-12R; 53-56; CANR 28; CDBLB 1945-1960; DLB 20, 100; MTCW
Jones, David Robert 1947-
See Bowie, David
See also CA 103
Jones, Diana Wynne 1934- .... **CLC 26**
See also AAYA 12; CA 49-52; CANR 4, 26, 56; CLR 23; DLB 161; JRDA; MAICYA; SAAS 7; SATA 9, 70
Jones, Edward P. 1950- .... **CLC 76**
See also BW 2; CA 142
Jones, Gayl 1949- .... **CLC 6, 9; BLC; DAM MULT**
See also BW 2; CA 77-80; CANR 27; DLB 33; MTCW
Jones, James 1921-1977 ...... **CLC 1, 3, 10, 39**
See also AITN 1, 2; CA 1-4R; 69-72; CANR 6; DLB 2, 143; MTCW
Jones, John J.
See Lovecraft, H(oward) P(hillips)
Jones, LeRoi .... **CLC 1, 2, 3, 5, 10, 14**
See also Baraka, Amiri
Jones, Louis B. .... **CLC 65**
See also CA 141
Jones, Madison (Percy, Jr.) 1925- .... **CLC 4**
See also CA 13-16R; CAAS 11; CANR 7, 54; DLB 152
Jones, Mervyn 1922- .... **CLC 10, 52**
See also CA 45-48; CAAS 5; CANR 1; MTCW
Jones, Mick 1956(?)- .... **CLC 30**
Jones, Nettie (Pearl) 1941- .... **CLC 34**
See also BW 2; CA 137; CAAS 20
Jones, Preston 1936-1979 .... **CLC 10**
See also CA 73-76; 89-92; DLB 7
Jones, Robert F(rancis) 1934- .... **CLC 7**
See also CA 49-52; CANR 2, 61
Jones, Rod 1953- .... **CLC 50**
See also CA 128
Jones, Terence Graham Parry 1942- **CLC 21**
See also Jones, Terry; Monty Python
See also CA 112; 116; CANR 35; INT 116
Jones, Terry
See Jones, Terence Graham Parry
See also SATA 67; SATA-Brief 51
Jones, Thom 1945(?)- .... **CLC 81**
See also CA 157
Jong, Erica 1942- . **CLC 4, 6, 8, 18, 83; DAM NOV, POP**
See also AITN 1; BEST 90:2; CA 73-76; CANR 26, 52; DLB 2, 5, 28, 152; INT CANR-26; MTCW
Jonson, Ben(jamin) 1572(?)-1637 .. **LC 6, 33; DA; DAB; DAC; DAM DRAM, MST, POET; DC 4; PC 17; WLC**
See also CDBLB Before 1660; DLB 62, 121
Jordan, June 1936- ...... **CLC 5, 11, 23; DAM**

See also CA 101; CAAS 9; CANR 39, 59; MTCW
Koontz, Dean R(ay) 1945- ..... **CLC 78; DAM NOV, POP**
See also AAYA 9; BEST 89:3, 90:2; CA 108; CANR 19, 36, 52; MTCW; SATA 92
Kopit, Arthur (Lee) 1937-**CLC 1, 18, 33; DAM DRAM**
See also AITN 1; CA 81-84; CABS 3; DLB 7; MTCW
Kops, Bernard 1926- .... **CLC 4**
See also CA 5-8R; DLB 13
Kornbluth, C(yril) M. 1923-1958 .... **TCLC 8**
See also CA 105; 160; DLB 8
Korolenko, V. G.
See Korolenko, Vladimir Galaktionovich
Korolenko, Vladimir
See Korolenko, Vladimir Galaktionovich
Korolenko, Vladimir G.
See Korolenko, Vladimir Galaktionovich
Korolenko, Vladimir Galaktionovich 1853-1921 .... **TCLC 22**
See also CA 121
Korzybski, Alfred (Habdank Skarbek) 1879-1950 .... **TCLC 61**
See also CA 123; 160
Kosinski, Jerzy (Nikodem) 1933-1991**CLC 1, 2, 3, 6, 10, 15, 53, 70; DAM NOV**
See also CA 17-20R; 134; CANR 9, 46; DLB 2; DLBY 82; MTCW
Kostelanetz, Richard (Cory) 1940- .. **CLC 28**
See also CA 13-16R; CAAS 8; CANR 38
Kostrowitzki, Wilhelm Apollinaris de 1880-1918
See Apollinaire, Guillaume
See also CA 104
Kotlowitz, Robert 1924- .... **CLC 4**
See also CA 33-36R; CANR 36
Kotzebue, August (Friedrich Ferdinand) von 1761-1819 .... **NCLC 25**
See also DLB 94
Kotzwinkle, William 1938- ..... **CLC 5, 14, 35**
See also CA 45-48; CANR 3, 44; CLR 6; DLB 173; MAICYA; SATA 24, 70
Kowna, Stancy
See Szymborska, Wislawa
Kozol, Jonathan 1936- .... **CLC 17**
See also CA 61-64; CANR 16, 45
Kozoll, Michael 1940(?)- .... **CLC 35**
Kramer, Kathryn 19(?)- .... **CLC 34**
Kramer, Larry 1935- .... **CLC 42; DAM POP**
See also CA 124; 126; CANR 60
Krasicki, Ignacy 1735-1801 .... **NCLC 8**
Krasinski, Zygmunt 1812-1859 .... **NCLC 4**
Kraus, Karl 1874-1936 .... **TCLC 5**
See also CA 104; DLB 118
Kreve (Mickevicius), Vincas 1882-1954**TCLC 27**
Kristeva, Julia 1941- .... **CLC 77**
See also CA 154
Kristofferson, Kris 1936- .... **CLC 26**
See also CA 104
Krizanc, John 1956- .... **CLC 57**
Krleza, Miroslav 1893-1981 .... **CLC 8**
See also CA 97-100; 105; CANR 50; DLB 147
Kroetsch, Robert 1927-**CLC 5, 23, 57; DAC; DAM POET**
See also CA 17-20R; CANR 8, 38; DLB 53; MTCW
Kroetz, Franz
See Kroetz, Franz Xaver
Kroetz, Franz Xaver 1946- .... **CLC 41**
See also CA 130
Kroker, Arthur 1945- .... **CLC 77**
Kropotkin, Peter (Aleksieevich) 1842-1921 **TCLC 36**
See also CA 119
Krotkov, Yuri 1917- .... **CLC 19**
See also CA 102
Krumb
See Crumb, R(obert)
Krumgold, Joseph (Quincy) 1908-1980 **CLC 12**
See also CA 9-12R; 101; CANR 7; MAICYA; SATA 1, 48; SATA-Obit 23
Krumwitz
See Crumb, R(obert)
Krutch, Joseph Wood 1893-1970 ...... **CLC 24**
See also CA 1-4R; 25-28R; CANR 4; DLB 63
Krutzch, Gus
See Eliot, T(homas) S(tearns)
Krylov, Ivan Andreevich 1768(?)-1844**NCLC 1**
See also DLB 150
Kubin, Alfred (Leopold Isidor) 1877-1959 **TCLC 23**
See also CA 112; 149; DLB 81
Kubrick, Stanley 1928- .... **CLC 16**
See also CA 81-84; CANR 33; DLB 26
Kumin, Maxine (Winokur) 1925- **CLC 5, 13, 28; DAM POET; PC 15**
See also AITN 2; CA 1-4R; CAAS 8; CANR 1, 21; DLB 5; MTCW; SATA 12
Kundera, Milan 1929- . **CLC 4, 9, 19, 32, 68; DAM NOV; SSC 24**
See also AAYA 2; CA 85-88; CANR 19, 52; MTCW
Kunene, Mazisi (Raymond) 1930- .... **CLC 85**
See also BW 1; CA 125; DLB 117
Kunitz, Stanley (Jasspon) 1905-**CLC 6, 11, 14; PC 19**
See also CA 41-44R; CANR 26, 57; DLB 48; INT CANR-26; MTCW
Kunze, Reiner 1933- .... **CLC 10**
See also CA 93-96; DLB 75
Kuprin, Aleksandr Ivanovich 1870-1938 **TCLC 5**
See also CA 104
Kureishi, Hanif 1954(?)- .... **CLC 64**
See also CA 139
Kurosawa, Akira 1910-**CLC 16; DAM MULT**
See also AAYA 11; CA 101; CANR 46
Kushner, Tony 1957(?)-**CLC 81; DAM DRAM**
See also CA 144
Kuttner, Henry 1915-1958 .... **TCLC 10**
See also Vance, Jack
See also CA 107; 157; DLB 8
Kuzma, Greg 1944- .... **CLC 7**
See also CA 33-36R
Kuzmin, Mikhail 1872(?)-1936 ...... **TCLC 40**
Kyd, Thomas 1558-1594**LC 22; DAM DRAM; DC 3**
See also DLB 62
Kyprianos, Iossif
See Samarakis, Antonis
La Bruyere, Jean de 1645-1696 .... **LC 17**
Lacan, Jacques (Marie Emile) 1901-1981 **CLC 75**
See also CA 121; 104
Laclos, Pierre Ambroise Francois Choderlos de 1741-1803 .... **NCLC 4**
La Colere, Francois
See Aragon, Louis
Lacolere, Francois
See Aragon, Louis
La Deshabilleuse
See Simenon, Georges (Jacques Christian)
Lady Gregory
See Gregory, Isabella Augusta (Persse)
Lady of Quality, A
See Bagnold, Enid
La Fayette, Marie (Madelaine Pioche de la Vergne Comtes 1634-1693 .... **LC 2**
Lafayette, Rene
See Hubbard, L(afayette) Ron(ald)
Laforgue, Jules 1860-1887**NCLC 5, 53; PC 14; SSC 20**
Lagerkvist, Paer (Fabian) 1891-1974 **CLC 7, 10, 13, 54; DAM DRAM, NOV**
See also Lagerkvist, Par
See also CA 85-88; 49-52; MTCW
Lagerkvist, Par .... **SSC 12**
See also Lagerkvist, Paer (Fabian)
Lagerloef, Selma (Ottiliana Lovisa) 1858-1940 **TCLC 4, 36**
See also Lagerlof, Selma (Ottiliana Lovisa)
See also CA 108; SATA 15
Lagerlof, Selma (Ottiliana Lovisa)
See Lagerloef, Selma (Ottiliana Lovisa)
See also CLR 7; SATA 15
La Guma, (Justin) Alex(ander) 1925-1985 **CLC 19; DAM NOV**
See also BW 1; CA 49-52; 118; CANR 25; DLB 117; MTCW
Laidlaw, A. K.
See Grieve, C(hristopher) M(urray)
Lainez, Manuel Mujica
See Mujica Lainez, Manuel
See also HW
Laing, R(onald) D(avid) 1927-1989 .. **CLC 95**
See also CA 107; 129; CANR 34; MTCW
Lamartine, Alphonse (Marie Louis Prat) de 1790-1869**NCLC 11; DAM POET; PC 16**
Lamb, Charles 1775-1834 ..... **NCLC 10; DA; DAB; DAC; DAM MST; WLC**
See also CDBLB 1789-1832; DLB 93, 107, 163; SATA 17
Lamb, Lady Caroline 1785-1828 ... **NCLC 38**
See also DLB 116
Lamming, George (William) 1927- **CLC 2, 4, 66; BLC; DAM MULT**
See also BW 2; CA 85-88; CANR 26; DLB 125; MTCW
L'Amour, Louis (Dearborn) 1908-1988 **CLC 25, 55; DAM NOV, POP**
See also AAYA 16; AITN 2; BEST 89:2; CA 1-4R; 125; CANR 3, 25, 40; DLBY 80; MTCW
Lampedusa, Giuseppe (Tomasi) di 1896-1957 **TCLC 13**
See also Tomasi di Lampedusa, Giuseppe
See also DLB 177
Lampman, Archibald 1861-1899 ... **NCLC 25**
See also DLB 92
Lancaster, Bruce 1896-1963 .... **CLC 36**
See also CA 9-10; CAP 1; SATA 9
Lanchester, John .... **CLC 99**
Landau, Mark Alexandrovich
See Aldanov, Mark (Alexandrovich)
Landau-Aldanov, Mark Alexandrovich
See Aldanov, Mark (Alexandrovich)
Landis, Jerry
See Simon, Paul (Frederick)
Landis, John 1950- .... **CLC 26**
See also CA 112; 122
Landolfi, Tommaso 1908-1979 .... **CLC 11, 49**
See also CA 127; 117; DLB 177
Landon, Letitia Elizabeth 1802-1838 **NCLC 15**
See also DLB 96
Landor, Walter Savage 1775-1864 **NCLC 14**
See also DLB 93, 107
Landwirth, Heinz 1927-
See Lind, Jakov
See also CA 9-12R; CANR 7
Lane, Patrick 1939- ... **CLC 25; DAM POET**
See also CA 97-100; CANR 54; DLB 53; INT 97-100
Lang, Andrew 1844-1912 .... **TCLC 16**
See also CA 114; 137; DLB 98, 141, 184; MAICYA; SATA 16
Lang, Fritz 1890-1976 .... **CLC 20, 103**

See also Ngugi wa Thiong'o
Ngugi wa Thiong'o 1938-**CLC 36; BLC; DAM MULT, NOV**
See also Ngugi, James T(hiong'o)
See also BW 2; CA 81-84; CANR 27, 58; DLB 125; MTCW
Nichol, B(arrie) P(hillip) 1944-1988 **CLC 18**
See also CA 53-56; DLB 53; SATA 66
Nichols, John (Treadwell) 1940- .... **CLC 38**
See also CA 9-12R; CAAS 2; CANR 6; DLBY 82
Nichols, Leigh
See Koontz, Dean R(ay)
Nichols, Peter (Richard) 1927- **CLC 5, 36, 65**
See also CA 104; CANR 33; DLB 13; MTCW
Nicolas, F. R. E.
See Freeling, Nicolas
Niedecker, Lorine 1903-1970 .... **CLC 10, 42; DAM POET**
See also CA 25-28; CAP 2; DLB 48
Nietzsche, Friedrich (Wilhelm) 1844-1900 **TCLC 10, 18, 55**
See also CA 107; 121; DLB 129
Nievo, Ippolito 1831-1861 .... **NCLC 22**
Nightingale, Anne Redmon 1943-
See Redmon, Anne
See also CA 103
Nik. T. O.
See Annensky, Innokenty (Fyodorovich)
Nin, Anais 1903-1977 **CLC 1, 4, 8, 11, 14, 60; DAM NOV, POP; SSC 10**
See also AITN 2; CA 13-16R; 69-72; CANR 22, 53; DLB 2, 4, 152; MTCW
Nishiwaki, Junzaburo 1894-1982 .... **PC 15**
See also CA 107
Nissenson, Hugh 1933- .... **CLC 4, 9**
See also CA 17-20R; CANR 27; DLB 28
Niven, Larry .... **CLC 8**
See also Niven, Laurence Van Cott
See also DLB 8
Niven, Laurence Van Cott 1938-
See Niven, Larry
See also CA 21-24R; CAAS 12; CANR 14, 44; DAM POP; MTCW; SATA 95
Nixon, Agnes Eckhardt 1927- .... **CLC 21**
See also CA 110
Nizan, Paul 1905-1940 .... **TCLC 40**
See also DLB 72
Nkosi, Lewis 1936- .... **CLC 45; BLC; DAM MULT**
See also BW 1; CA 65-68; CANR 27; DLB 157
Nodier, (Jean) Charles (Emmanuel) 1780-1844 **NCLC 19**
See also DLB 119
Nolan, Christopher 1965- .... **CLC 58**
See also CA 111
Noon, Jeff 1957- .... **CLC 91**
See also CA 148
Norden, Charles
See Durrell, Lawrence (George)
Nordhoff, Charles (Bernard) 1887-1947 **TCLC 23**
See also CA 108; DLB 9; SATA 23
Norfolk, Lawrence 1963- .... **CLC 76**
See also CA 144
Norman, Marsha 1947-**CLC 28; DAM DRAM**
See also CA 105; CABS 3; CANR 41; DLBY 84
Norris, Frank 1870-1902 .... **SSC 28**
See also Norris, (Benjamin) Frank(lin, Jr.)
See also CDALB 1865-1917; DLB 12, 71
Norris, (Benjamin) Frank(lin, Jr.) 1870-1902 **TCLC 24**
See also Norris, Frank
See also CA 110; 160
Norris, Leslie 1921- .... **CLC 14**
See also CA 11-12; CANR 14; CAP 1; DLB 27
North, Andrew
See Norton, Andre
North, Anthony
See Koontz, Dean R(ay)
North, Captain George
See Stevenson, Robert Louis (Balfour)
North, Milou
See Erdrich, Louise
Northrup, B. A.
See Hubbard, L(afayette) Ron(ald)
North Staffs
See Hulme, T(homas) E(rnest)
Norton, Alice Mary
See Norton, Andre
See also MAICYA; SATA 1, 43
Norton, Andre 1912- .... **CLC 12**
See also Norton, Alice Mary
See also AAYA 14; CA 1-4R; CANR 2, 31; DLB 8, 52; JRDA; MTCW; SATA 91
Norton, Caroline 1808-1877 .... **NCLC 47**
See also DLB 21, 159
Norway, Nevil Shute 1899-1960
See Shute, Nevil
See also CA 102; 93-96
Norwid, Cyprian Kamil 1821-1883 **NCLC 17**
Nosille, Nabrah
See Ellison, Harlan (Jay)
Nossack, Hans Erich 1901-1978 .... **CLC 6**
See also CA 93-96; 85-88; DLB 69
Nostradamus 1503-1566 .... **LC 27**
Nosu, Chuji
See Ozu, Yasujiro
Notenburg, Eleanora (Genrikhovna) von
See Guro, Elena
Nova, Craig 1945- .... **CLC 7, 31**
See also CA 45-48; CANR 2, 53
Novak, Joseph
See Kosinski, Jerzy (Nikodem)
Novalis 1772-1801 .... **NCLC 13**
See also DLB 90
Novis, Emile
See Weil, Simone (Adolphine)
Nowlan, Alden (Albert) 1933-1983 **CLC 15; DAC; DAM MST**
See also CA 9-12R; CANR 5; DLB 53
Noyes, Alfred 1880-1958 .... **TCLC 7**
See also CA 104; DLB 20
Nunn, Kem .... **CLC 34**
See also CA 159
Nye, Robert 1939- .. **CLC 13, 42; DAM NOV**
See also CA 33-36R; CANR 29; DLB 14; MTCW; SATA 6
Nyro, Laura 1947- .... **CLC 17**
Oates, Joyce Carol 1938-**CLC 1, 2, 3, 6, 9, 11, 15, 19, 33, 52; DA; DAB; DAC; DAM MST, NOV, POP; SSC 6; WLC**
See also AAYA 15; AITN 1; BEST 89:2; CA 5-8R; CANR 25, 45; CDALB 1968-1988; DLB 2, 5, 130; DLBY 81; INT CANR-25; MTCW
O'Brien, Darcy 1939- .... **CLC 11**
See also CA 21-24R; CANR 8, 59
O'Brien, E. G.
See Clarke, Arthur C(harles)
O'Brien, Edna 1936- **CLC 3, 5, 8, 13, 36, 65; DAM NOV; SSC 10**
See also CA 1-4R; CANR 6, 41; CDBLB 1960 to Present; DLB 14; MTCW
O'Brien, Fitz-James 1828-1862 ..... **NCLC 21**
See also DLB 74
O'Brien, Flann .... **CLC 1, 4, 5, 7, 10, 47**
See also O Nuallain, Brian
O'Brien, Richard 1942- .... **CLC 17**
See also CA 124
O'Brien, (William) Tim(othy) 1946- . **CLC 7, 19, 40, 103; DAM POP**
See also AAYA 16; CA 85-88; CANR 40, 58; DLB 152; DLBD 9; DLBY 80
Obstfelder, Sigbjoern 1866-1900 ... **TCLC 23**
See also CA 123
O'Casey, Sean 1880-1964 **CLC 1, 5, 9, 11, 15, 88; DAB; DAC; DAM DRAM, MST; WLCS**
See also CA 89-92; CANR 62; CDBLB 1914-1945; DLB 10; MTCW
O'Cathasaigh, Sean
See O'Casey, Sean
Ochs, Phil 1940-1976 .... **CLC 17**
See also CA 65-68
O'Connor, Edwin (Greene) 1918-1968 **CLC 14**
See also CA 93-96; 25-28R
O'Connor, (Mary) Flannery 1925-1964 **CLC 1, 2, 3, 6, 10, 13, 15, 21, 66, 104; DA; DAB; DAC; DAM MST, NOV; SSC 1, 23; WLC**
See also AAYA 7; CA 1-4R; CANR 3, 41; CDALB 1941-1968; DLB 2, 152; DLBD 12; DLBY 80; MTCW
O'Connor, Frank .... **CLC 23; SSC 5**
See also O'Donovan, Michael John
See also DLB 162
O'Dell, Scott 1898-1989 .... **CLC 30**
See also AAYA 3; CA 61-64; 129; CANR 12, 30; CLR 1, 16; DLB 52; JRDA; MAICYA; SATA 12, 60
Odets, Clifford 1906-1963 **CLC 2, 28, 98; DAM DRAM; DC 6**
See also CA 85-88; CANR 62; DLB 7, 26; MTCW
O'Doherty, Brian 1934- .... **CLC 76**
See also CA 105
O'Donnell, K. M.
See Malzberg, Barry N(athaniel)
O'Donnell, Lawrence
See Kuttner, Henry
O'Donovan, Michael John 1903-1966 **CLC 14**
See also O'Connor, Frank
See also CA 93-96
Oe, Kenzaburo 1935- **CLC 10, 36, 86; DAM NOV; SSC 20**
See also CA 97-100; CANR 36, 50; DLB 182; DLBY 94; MTCW
O'Faolain, Julia 1932- .... **CLC 6, 19, 47**
See also CA 81-84; CAAS 2; CANR 12, 61; DLB 14; MTCW
O'Faolain, Sean 1900-1991 **CLC 1, 7, 14, 32, 70; SSC 13**
See also CA 61-64; 134; CANR 12; DLB 15, 162; MTCW
O'Flaherty, Liam 1896-1984 **CLC 5, 34; SSC 6**
See also CA 101; 113; CANR 35; DLB 36, 162; DLBY 84; MTCW
Ogilvy, Gavin
See Barrie, J(ames) M(atthew)
O'Grady, Standish (James) 1846-1928 **TCLC 5**
See also CA 104; 157
O'Grady, Timothy 1951- .... **CLC 59**
See also CA 138
O'Hara, Frank 1926-1966 . **CLC 2, 5, 13, 78; DAM POET**
See also CA 9-12R; 25-28R; CANR 33; DLB 5, 16; MTCW
O'Hara, John (Henry) 1905-1970 **CLC 1, 2, 3, 6, 11, 42; DAM NOV; SSC 15**
See also CA 5-8R; 25-28R; CANR 31, 60; CDALB 1929-1941; DLB 9, 86; DLBD 2; MTCW
O Hehir, Diana 1922- .... **CLC 41**
See also CA 93-96
Okigbo, Christopher (Ifenayichukwu) 1932-1967 .... **CLC 25, 84; BLC; DAM MULT, POET; PC 7**
See also BW 1; CA 77-80; DLB 125; MTCW
Okri, Ben 1959- .... **CLC 87**
See also BW 2; CA 130; 138; DLB 157; INT

Author Index

Pilnyak, Boris .... **TCLC 23**
See also Vogau, Boris Andreyevich
Pincherle, Alberto 1907-1990 ... **CLC 11, 18; DAM NOV**
See also Moravia, Alberto
See also CA 25-28R; 132; CANR 33; MTCW
Pinckney, Darryl 1953- .... **CLC 76**
See also BW 2; CA 143
Pindar 518B.C.-446B.C. .... **CMLC 12; PC 19**
See also DLB 176
Pineda, Cecile 1942- .... **CLC 39**
See also CA 118
Pinero, Arthur Wing 1855-1934 ... **TCLC 32; DAM DRAM**
See also CA 110; 153; DLB 10
Pinero, Miguel (Antonio Gomez) 1946-1988 **CLC 4, 55**
See also CA 61-64; 125; CANR 29; HW
Pinget, Robert 1919-1997 .... **CLC 7, 13, 37**
See also CA 85-88; 160; DLB 83
Pink Floyd
See Barrett, (Roger) Syd; Gilmour, David; Mason, Nick; Waters, Roger; Wright, Rick
Pinkney, Edward 1802-1828 .... **NCLC 31**
Pinkwater, Daniel Manus 1941- .... **CLC 35**
See also Pinkwater, Manus
See also AAYA 1; CA 29-32R; CANR 12, 38; CLR 4; JRDA; MAICYA; SAAS 3; SATA 46, 76
Pinkwater, Manus
See Pinkwater, Daniel Manus
See also SATA 8
Pinsky, Robert 1940-**CLC 9, 19, 38, 94; DAM POET**
See also CA 29-32R; CAAS 4; CANR 58; DLBY 82
Pinta, Harold
See Pinter, Harold
Pinter, Harold 1930-**CLC 1, 3, 6, 9, 11, 15, 27, 58, 73; DA; DAB; DAC; DAM DRAM, MST; WLC**
See also CA 5-8R; CANR 33; CDBLB 1960 to Present; DLB 13; MTCW
Piozzi, Hester Lynch (Thrale) 1741-1821 **NCLC 57**
See also DLB 104, 142
Pirandello, Luigi 1867-1936**TCLC 4, 29; DA; DAB; DAC; DAM DRAM, MST; DC 5; SSC 22; WLC**
See also CA 104; 153
Pirsig, Robert M(aynard) 1928-**CLC 4, 6, 73; DAM POP**
See also CA 53-56; CANR 42; MTCW; SATA 39
Pisarev, Dmitry Ivanovich 1840-1868 **NCLC 25**
Pix, Mary (Griffith) 1666-1709 .... **LC 8**
See also DLB 80
Pixerecourt, Guilbert de 1773-1844**NCLC 39**
Plaatje, Sol(omon) T(shekisho) 1876-1932 **TCLC 73**
See also BW 2; CA 141
Plaidy, Jean
See Hibbert, Eleanor Alice Burford
Planche, James Robinson 1796-1880**NCLC 42**
Plant, Robert 1948- .... **CLC 12**
Plante, David (Robert) 1940- **CLC 7, 23, 38; DAM NOV**
See also CA 37-40R; CANR 12, 36, 58; DLBY 83; INT CANR-12; MTCW
Plath, Sylvia 1932-1963 **CLC 1, 2, 3, 5, 9, 11, 14, 17, 50, 51, 62; DA; DAB; DAC; DAM MST, POET; PC 1; WLC**
See also AAYA 13; CA 19-20; CANR 34; CAP 2; CDALB 1941-1968; DLB 5, 6, 152; MTCW
Plato 428(?)B.C.-348(?)B.C. ... **CMLC 8; DA; DAB; DAC; DAM MST; WLCS**
See also DLB 176
Platonov, Andrei .... **TCLC 14**
See also Klimentov, Andrei Platonovich
Platt, Kin 1911- .... **CLC 26**
See also AAYA 11; CA 17-20R; CANR 11; JRDA; SAAS 17; SATA 21, 86
Plautus c. 251B.C.-184B.C. .... **DC 6**
Plick et Plock
See Simenon, Georges (Jacques Christian)
Plimpton, George (Ames) 1927- .... **CLC 36**
See also AITN 1; CA 21-24R; CANR 32; MTCW; SATA 10
Pliny the Elder c. 23-79 .... **CMLC 23**
Plomer, William Charles Franklin 1903-1973 **CLC 4, 8**
See also CA 21-22; CANR 34; CAP 2; DLB 20, 162; MTCW; SATA 24
Plowman, Piers
See Kavanagh, Patrick (Joseph)
Plum, J.
See Wodehouse, P(elham) G(renville)
Plumly, Stanley (Ross) 1939- .... **CLC 33**
See also CA 108; 110; DLB 5; INT 110
Plumpe, Friedrich Wilhelm 1888-1931**TCLC 53**
See also CA 112
Po Chu-i 772-846 .... **CMLC 24**
Poe, Edgar Allan 1809-1849**NCLC 1, 16, 55; DA; DAB; DAC; DAM MST, POET; PC 1; SSC 1, 22; WLC**
See also AAYA 14; CDALB 1640-1865; DLB 3, 59, 73, 74; SATA 23
Poet of Titchfield Street, The
See Pound, Ezra (Weston Loomis)
Pohl, Frederik 1919- .... **CLC 18; SSC 25**
See also CA 61-64; CAAS 1; CANR 11, 37; DLB 8; INT CANR-11; MTCW; SATA 24
Poirier, Louis 1910-
See Gracq, Julien
See also CA 122; 126
Poitier, Sidney 1927- .... **CLC 26**
See also BW 1; CA 117
Polanski, Roman 1933- .... **CLC 16**
See also CA 77-80
Poliakoff, Stephen 1952- .... **CLC 38**
See also CA 106; DLB 13
Police, The
See Copeland, Stewart (Armstrong); Summers, Andrew James; Sumner, Gordon Matthew
Polidori, John William 1795-1821 . **NCLC 51**
See also DLB 116
Pollitt, Katha 1949- .... **CLC 28**
See also CA 120; 122; MTCW
Pollock, (Mary) Sharon 1936-**CLC 50; DAC; DAM DRAM, MST**
See also CA 141; DLB 60
Polo, Marco 1254-1324 .... **CMLC 15**
Polonsky, Abraham (Lincoln) 1910- **CLC 92**
See also CA 104; DLB 26; INT 104
Polybius c. 200B.C.-c. 118B.C. ...... **CMLC 17**
See also DLB 176
Pomerance, Bernard 1940- .... **CLC 13; DAM DRAM**
See also CA 101; CANR 49
Ponge, Francis (Jean Gaston Alfred) 1899-1988 **CLC 6, 18; DAM POET**
See also CA 85-88; 126; CANR 40
Pontoppidan, Henrik 1857-1943 .... **TCLC 29**
Poole, Josephine .... **CLC 17**
See also Helyar, Jane Penelope Josephine
See also SAAS 2; SATA 5
Popa, Vasko 1922-1991 .... **CLC 19**
See also CA 112; 148; DLB 181
Pope, Alexander 1688-1744 **LC 3; DA; DAB; DAC; DAM MST, POET; WLC**
See also CDBLB 1660-1789; DLB 95, 101
Porter, Connie (Rose) 1959(?)- .... **CLC 70**
See also BW 2; CA 142; SATA 81
Porter, Gene(va Grace) Stratton 1863(?)-1924 **TCLC 21**
See also CA 112
Porter, Katherine Anne 1890-1980**CLC 1, 3, 7, 10, 13, 15, 27, 101; DA; DAB; DAC; DAM MST, NOV; SSC 4**
See also AITN 2; CA 1-4R; 101; CANR 1; DLB 4, 9, 102; DLBD 12; DLBY 80; MTCW; SATA 39; SATA-Obit 23
Porter, Peter (Neville Frederick) 1929-**CLC 5, 13, 33**
See also CA 85-88; DLB 40
Porter, William Sydney 1862-1910
See Henry, O.
See also CA 104; 131; CDALB 1865-1917; DA; DAB; DAC; DAM MST; DLB 12, 78, 79; MTCW; YABC 2
Portillo (y Pacheco), Jose Lopez
See Lopez Portillo (y Pacheco), Jose
Post, Melville Davisson 1869-1930 **TCLC 39**
See also CA 110
Potok, Chaim 1929- . **CLC 2, 7, 14, 26; DAM NOV**
See also AAYA 15; AITN 1, 2; CA 17-20R; CANR 19, 35; DLB 28, 152; INT CANR-19; MTCW; SATA 33
Potter, (Helen) Beatrix 1866-1943
See Webb, (Martha) Beatrice (Potter)
See also MAICYA
Potter, Dennis (Christopher George) 1935-1994 **CLC 58, 86**
See also CA 107; 145; CANR 33, 61; MTCW
Pound, Ezra (Weston Loomis) 1885-1972 **CLC 1, 2, 3, 4, 5, 7, 10, 13, 18, 34, 48, 50; DA; DAB; DAC; DAM MST, POET; PC 4; WLC**
See also CA 5-8R; 37-40R; CANR 40; CDALB 1917-1929; DLB 4, 45, 63; DLBD 15; MTCW
Povod, Reinaldo 1959-1994 .... **CLC 44**
See also CA 136; 146
Powell, Adam Clayton, Jr. 1908-1972**CLC 89; BLC; DAM MULT**
See also BW 1; CA 102; 33-36R
Powell, Anthony (Dymoke) 1905-**CLC 1, 3, 7, 9, 10, 31**
See also CA 1-4R; CANR 1, 32, 62; CDBLB 1945-1960; DLB 15; MTCW
Powell, Dawn 1897-1965 .... **CLC 66**
See also CA 5-8R
Powell, Padgett 1952- .... **CLC 34**
See also CA 126
Power, Susan 1961- .... **CLC 91**
Powers, J(ames) F(arl) 1917-**CLC 1, 4, 8, 57; SSC 4**
See also CA 1-4R; CANR 2, 61; DLB 130; MTCW
Powers, John J(ames) 1945-
See Powers, John R.
See also CA 69-72
Powers, John R. .... **CLC 66**
See also Powers, John J(ames)
Powers, Richard (S.) 1957- .... **CLC 93**
See also CA 148
Pownall, David 1938- .... **CLC 10**
See also CA 89-92; CAAS 18; CANR 49; DLB 14
Powys, John Cowper 1872-1963**CLC 7, 9, 15, 46**
See also CA 85-88; DLB 15; MTCW
Powys, T(heodore) F(rancis) 1875-1953 **TCLC 9**
See also CA 106; DLB 36, 162
Prado (Calvo), Pedro 1886-1952 ... **TCLC 75**
See also CA 131; HW

Prager, Emily 1952- .... **CLC 56**
Pratt, E(dwin) J(ohn) 1883(?)-1964 **CLC 19; DAC; DAM POET**
See also CA 141; 93-96; DLB 92
Premchand .... **TCLC 21**
See also Srivastava, Dhanpat Rai
Preussler, Otfried 1923- .... **CLC 17**
See also CA 77-80; SATA 24
Prevert, Jacques (Henri Marie) 1900-1977 **CLC 15**
See also CA 77-80; 69-72; CANR 29, 61; MTCW; SATA-Obit 30
Prevost, Abbe (Antoine Francois) 1697-1763 **LC 1**
Price, (Edward) Reynolds 1933-**CLC 3, 6, 13, 43, 50, 63; DAM NOV; SSC 22**
See also CA 1-4R; CANR 1, 37, 57; DLB 2; INT CANR-37
Price, Richard 1949- .... **CLC 6, 12**
See also CA 49-52; CANR 3; DLBY 81
Prichard, Katharine Susannah 1883-1969 **CLC 46**
See also CA 11-12; CANR 33; CAP 1; MTCW; SATA 66
Priestley, J(ohn) B(oynton) 1894-1984**CLC 2, 5, 9, 34; DAM DRAM, NOV**
See also CA 9-12R; 113; CANR 33; CDBLB 1914-1945; DLB 10, 34, 77, 100, 139; DLBY 84; MTCW
Prince 1958(?)- .... **CLC 35**
Prince, F(rank) T(empleton) 1912- .. **CLC 22**
See also CA 101; CANR 43; DLB 20
Prince Kropotkin
See Kropotkin, Peter (Aleksieevich)
Prior, Matthew 1664-1721 .... **LC 4**
See also DLB 95
Prishvin, Mikhail 1873-1954 .... **TCLC 75**
Pritchard, William H(arrison) 1932- **CLC 34**
See also CA 65-68; CANR 23; DLB 111
Pritchett, V(ictor) S(awdon) 1900-1997 **C L C 5, 13, 15, 41; DAM NOV; SSC 14**
See also CA 61-64; 157; CANR 31; DLB 15, 139; MTCW
Private 19022
See Manning, Frederic
Probst, Mark 1925- .... **CLC 59**
See also CA 130
Prokosch, Frederic 1908-1989 ...... **CLC 4, 48**
See also CA 73-76; 128; DLB 48
Prophet, The
See Dreiser, Theodore (Herman Albert)
Prose, Francine 1947- .... **CLC 45**
See also CA 109; 112; CANR 46
Proudhon
See Cunha, Euclides (Rodrigues Pimenta) da
Proulx, E. Annie 1935- .... **CLC 81**
Proust, (Valentin-Louis-George-Eugene-) Marcel 1871-1922 **TCLC 7, 13, 33; DA; DAB; DAC; DAM MST, NOV; WLC**
See also CA 104; 120; DLB 65; MTCW
Prowler, Harley
See Masters, Edgar Lee
Prus, Boleslaw 1845-1912 .... **TCLC 48**
Pryor, Richard (Franklin Lenox Thomas) 1940- **CLC 26**
See also CA 122
Przybyszewski, Stanislaw 1868-1927**TCLC 36**
See also CA 160; DLB 66
Pteleon
See Grieve, C(hristopher) M(urray)
See also DAM POET
Puckett, Lute
See Masters, Edgar Lee
Puig, Manuel 1932-1990**CLC 3, 5, 10, 28, 65; DAM MULT; HLC**
See also CA 45-48; CANR 2, 32; DLB 113; HW; MTCW
Pulitzer, Joseph 1847-1911 .... **TCLC 76**
See also CA 114; DLB 23
Purdy, Al(fred Wellington) 1918-**CLC 3, 6, 14, 50; DAC; DAM MST, POET**
See also CA 81-84; CAAS 17; CANR 42; DLB 88
Purdy, James (Amos) 1923- **CLC 2, 4, 10, 28, 52**
See also CA 33-36R; CAAS 1; CANR 19, 51; DLB 2; INT CANR-19; MTCW
Pure, Simon
See Swinnerton, Frank Arthur
Pushkin, Alexander (Sergeyevich) 1799-1837 **NCLC 3, 27; DA; DAB; DAC; DAM DRAM, MST, POET; PC 10; SSC 27; WLC**
See also SATA 61
P'u Sung-ling 1640-1715 .... **LC 3**
Putnam, Arthur Lee
See Alger, Horatio, Jr.
Puzo, Mario 1920-**CLC 1, 2, 6, 36; DAM NOV, POP**
See also CA 65-68; CANR 4, 42; DLB 6; MTCW
Pygge, Edward
See Barnes, Julian (Patrick)
Pyle, Ernest Taylor 1900-1945
See Pyle, Ernie
See also CA 115; 160
Pyle, Ernie 1900-1945 .... **TCLC 75**
See also Pyle, Ernest Taylor
See also DLB 29
Pym, Barbara (Mary Crampton) 1913-1980 **CLC 13, 19, 37**
See also CA 13-14; 97-100; CANR 13, 34; CAP 1; DLB 14; DLBY 87; MTCW
Pynchon, Thomas (Ruggles, Jr.) 1937-**CLC 2, 3, 6, 9, 11, 18, 33, 62, 72; DA; DAB; DAC; DAM MST, NOV, POP; SSC 14; WLC**
See also BEST 90:2; CA 17-20R; CANR 22, 46; DLB 2, 173; MTCW
Pythagoras c. 570B.C.-c. 500B.C. . **CMLC 22**
See also DLB 176
Qian Zhongshu
See Ch'ien Chung-shu
Qroll
See Dagerman, Stig (Halvard)
Quarrington, Paul (Lewis) 1953- ..... **CLC 65**
See also CA 129; CANR 62
Quasimodo, Salvatore 1901-1968 ..... **CLC 10**
See also CA 13-16; 25-28R; CAP 1; DLB 114; MTCW
Quay, Stephen 1947- .... **CLC 95**
Quay, The Brothers
See Quay, Stephen; Quay, Timothy
Quay, Timothy 1947- .... **CLC 95**
Queen, Ellery .... **CLC 3, 11**
See also Dannay, Frederic; Davidson, Avram; Lee, Manfred B(ennington); Marlowe, Stephen; Sturgeon, Theodore (Hamilton); Vance, John Holbrook
Queen, Ellery, Jr.
See Dannay, Frederic; Lee, Manfred B(ennington)
Queneau, Raymond 1903-1976 **CLC 2, 5, 10, 42**
See also CA 77-80; 69-72; CANR 32; DLB 72; MTCW
Quevedo, Francisco de 1580-1645 .... **LC 23**
Quiller-Couch, Arthur Thomas 1863-1944 **TCLC 53**
See also CA 118; DLB 135, 153
Quin, Ann (Marie) 1936-1973 .... **CLC 6**
See also CA 9-12R; 45-48; DLB 14
Quinn, Martin
See Smith, Martin Cruz
Quinn, Peter 1947- .... **CLC 91**
Quinn, Simon
See Smith, Martin Cruz
Quiroga, Horacio (Sylvestre) 1878-1937 **TCLC 20; DAM MULT; HLC**
See also CA 117; 131; HW; MTCW
Quoirez, Francoise 1935- .... **CLC 9**
See also Sagan, Francoise
See also CA 49-52; CANR 6, 39; MTCW
Raabe, Wilhelm 1831-1910 .... **TCLC 45**
See also DLB 129
Rabe, David (William) 1940- ... **CLC 4, 8, 33; DAM DRAM**
See also CA 85-88; CABS 3; CANR 59; DLB 7
Rabelais, Francois 1483-1553**LC 5; DA; DAB; DAC; DAM MST; WLC**
Rabinovitch, Sholem 1859-1916
See Aleichem, Sholom
See also CA 104
Rachilde 1860-1953 .... **TCLC 67**
See also DLB 123
Racine, Jean 1639-1699 . **LC 28; DAB; DAM MST**
Radcliffe, Ann (Ward) 1764-1823**NCLC 6, 55**
See also DLB 39, 178
Radiguet, Raymond 1903-1923 ...... **TCLC 29**
See also DLB 65
Radnoti, Miklos 1909-1944 .... **TCLC 16**
See also CA 118
Rado, James 1939- .... **CLC 17**
See also CA 105
Radvanyi, Netty 1900-1983
See Seghers, Anna
See also CA 85-88; 110
Rae, Ben
See Griffiths, Trevor
Raeburn, John (Hay) 1941- .... **CLC 34**
See also CA 57-60
Ragni, Gerome 1942-1991 .... **CLC 17**
See also CA 105; 134
Rahv, Philip 1908-1973 .... **CLC 24**
See also Greenberg, Ivan
See also DLB 137
Raine, Craig 1944- .... **CLC 32, 103**
See also CA 108; CANR 29, 51; DLB 40
Raine, Kathleen (Jessie) 1908- ...... **CLC 7, 45**
See also CA 85-88; CANR 46; DLB 20; MTCW
Rainis, Janis 1865-1929 .... **TCLC 29**
Rakosi, Carl .... **CLC 47**
See also Rawley, Callman
See also CAAS 5
Raleigh, Richard
See Lovecraft, H(oward) P(hillips)
Raleigh, Sir Walter 1554(?)-1618 . **LC 31, 39**
See also CDBLB Before 1660; DLB 172
Rallentando, H. P.
See Sayers, Dorothy L(eigh)
Ramal, Walter
See de la Mare, Walter (John)
Ramon, Juan
See Jimenez (Mantecon), Juan Ramon
Ramos, Graciliano 1892-1953 .... **TCLC 32**
Rampersad, Arnold 1941- .... **CLC 44**
See also BW 2; CA 127; 133; DLB 111; INT 133
Rampling, Anne
See Rice, Anne
Ramsay, Allan 1684(?)-1758 .... **LC 29**
See also DLB 95
Ramuz, Charles-Ferdinand 1878-1947**T C L C 33**
Rand, Ayn 1905-1982**CLC 3, 30, 44, 79; DA; DAC; DAM MST, NOV, POP; WLC**
See also AAYA 10; CA 13-16R; 105; CANR 27; MTCW
Randall, Dudley (Felker) 1914-**CLC 1; BLC; DAM MULT**
See also BW 1; CA 25-28R; CANR 23; DLB

MTCW
Rimbaud, (Jean Nicolas) Arthur 1854-1891 **NCLC 4, 35; DA; DAB; DAC; DAM MST, POET; PC 3; WLC**
Rinehart, Mary Roberts 1876-1958**TCLC 52**
See also CA 108
Ringmaster, The
See Mencken, H(enry) L(ouis)
Ringwood, Gwen(dolyn Margaret) Pharis 1910-1984 .... **CLC 48**
See also CA 148; 112; DLB 88
Rio, Michel 19(?)- .... **CLC 43**
Ritsos, Giannes
See Ritsos, Yannis
Ritsos, Yannis 1909-1990 .... **CLC 6, 13, 31**
See also CA 77-80; 133; CANR 39, 61; MTCW
Ritter, Erika 1948(?)- .... **CLC 52**
Rivera, Jose Eustasio 1889-1928 ... **TCLC 35**
See also HW
Rivers, Conrad Kent 1933-1968 .... **CLC 1**
See also BW 1; CA 85-88; DLB 41
Rivers, Elfrida
See Bradley, Marion Zimmer
Riverside, John
See Heinlein, Robert A(nson)
Rizal, Jose 1861-1896 .... **NCLC 27**
Roa Bastos, Augusto (Antonio) 1917-**CLC 45; DAM MULT; HLC**
See also CA 131; DLB 113; HW
Robbe-Grillet, Alain 1922- **CLC 1, 2, 4, 6, 8, 10, 14, 43**
See also CA 9-12R; CANR 33; DLB 83; MTCW
Robbins, Harold 1916- ... **CLC 5; DAM NOV**
See also CA 73-76; CANR 26, 54; MTCW
Robbins, Thomas Eugene 1936-
See Robbins, Tom
See also CA 81-84; CANR 29, 59; DAM NOV, POP; MTCW
Robbins, Tom .... **CLC 9, 32, 64**
See also Robbins, Thomas Eugene
See also BEST 90:3; DLBY 80
Robbins, Trina 1938- .... **CLC 21**
See also CA 128
Roberts, Charles G(eorge) D(ouglas) 1860-1943 **TCLC 8**
See also CA 105; CLR 33; DLB 92; SATA 88; SATA-Brief 29
Roberts, Elizabeth Madox 1886-1941 **TCLC 68**
See also CA 111; DLB 9, 54, 102; SATA 33; SATA-Brief 27
Roberts, Kate 1891-1985 .... **CLC 15**
See also CA 107; 116
Roberts, Keith (John Kingston) 1935-**CLC 14**
See also CA 25-28R; CANR 46
Roberts, Kenneth (Lewis) 1885-1957**TCLC 23**
See also CA 109; DLB 9
Roberts, Michele (B.) 1949- .... **CLC 48**
See also CA 115; CANR 58
Robertson, Ellis
See Ellison, Harlan (Jay); Silverberg, Robert
Robertson, Thomas William 1829-1871**NCLC 35; DAM DRAM**
Robeson, Kenneth
See Dent, Lester
Robinson, Edwin Arlington 1869-1935**TCLC 5; DA; DAC; DAM MST, POET; PC 1**
See also CA 104; 133; CDALB 1865-1917; DLB 54; MTCW
Robinson, Henry Crabb 1775-1867**NCLC 15**
See also DLB 107
Robinson, Jill 1936- .... **CLC 10**
See also CA 102; INT 102
Robinson, Kim Stanley 1952- .... **CLC 34**
See also CA 126
Robinson, Lloyd
See Silverberg, Robert
Robinson, Marilynne 1944- .... **CLC 25**
See also CA 116
Robinson, Smokey .... **CLC 21**
See also Robinson, William, Jr.
Robinson, William, Jr. 1940-
See Robinson, Smokey
See also CA 116
Robison, Mary 1949- .... **CLC 42, 98**
See also CA 113; 116; DLB 130; INT 116
Rod, Edouard 1857-1910 .... **TCLC 52**
Roddenberry, Eugene Wesley 1921-1991
See Roddenberry, Gene
See also CA 110; 135; CANR 37; SATA 45; SATA-Obit 69
Roddenberry, Gene .... **CLC 17**
See also Roddenberry, Eugene Wesley
See also AAYA 5; SATA-Obit 69
Rodgers, Mary 1931- .... **CLC 12**
See also CA 49-52; CANR 8, 55; CLR 20; INT CANR-8; JRDA; MAICYA; SATA 8
Rodgers, W(illiam) R(obert) 1909-1969**CLC 7**
See also CA 85-88; DLB 20
Rodman, Eric
See Silverberg, Robert
Rodman, Howard 1920(?)-1985 .... **CLC 65**
See also CA 118
Rodman, Maia
See Wojciechowska, Maia (Teresa)
Rodriguez, Claudio 1934- .... **CLC 10**
See also DLB 134
Roelvaag, O(le) E(dvart) 1876-1931**TCLC 17**
See also CA 117; DLB 9
Roethke, Theodore (Huebner) 1908-1963**CLC 1, 3, 8, 11, 19, 46, 101; DAM POET; PC 15**
See also CA 81-84; CABS 2; CDALB 1941-1968; DLB 5; MTCW
Rogers, Thomas Hunton 1927- .... **CLC 57**
See also CA 89-92; INT 89-92
Rogers, Will(iam Penn Adair) 1879-1935 **TCLC 8, 71; DAM MULT**
See also CA 105; 144; DLB 11; NNAL
Rogin, Gilbert 1929- .... **CLC 18**
See also CA 65-68; CANR 15
Rohan, Koda .... **TCLC 22**
See also Koda Shigeyuki
Rohlfs, Anna Katharine Green
See Green, Anna Katharine
Rohmer, Eric .... **CLC 16**
See also Scherer, Jean-Marie Maurice
Rohmer, Sax .... **TCLC 28**
See also Ward, Arthur Henry Sarsfield
See also DLB 70
Roiphe, Anne (Richardson) 1935- .. **CLC 3, 9**
See also CA 89-92; CANR 45; DLBY 80; INT 89-92
Rojas, Fernando de 1465-1541 .... **LC 23**
Rolfe, Frederick (William Serafino Austin Lewis Mary) 1860-1913 .... **TCLC 12**
See also CA 107; DLB 34, 156
Rolland, Romain 1866-1944 .... **TCLC 23**
See also CA 118; DLB 65
Rolle, Richard c. 1300-c. 1349 ...... **CMLC 21**
See also DLB 146
Rolvaag, O(le) E(dvart)
See Roelvaag, O(le) E(dvart)
Romain Arnaud, Saint
See Aragon, Louis
Romains, Jules 1885-1972 .... **CLC 7**
See also CA 85-88; CANR 34; DLB 65; MTCW
Romero, Jose Ruben 1890-1952 .... **TCLC 14**
See also CA 114; 131; HW
Ronsard, Pierre de 1524-1585 ... **LC 6; PC 11**
Rooke, Leon 1934- .. **CLC 25, 34; DAM POP**
See also CA 25-28R; CANR 23, 53
Roosevelt, Theodore 1858-1919 ..... **TCLC 69**
See also CA 115; DLB 47
Roper, William 1498-1578 .... **LC 10**
Roquelaure, A. N.
See Rice, Anne
Rosa, Joao Guimaraes 1908-1967 .... **CLC 23**
See also CA 89-92; DLB 113
Rose, Wendy 1948-**CLC 85; DAM MULT; PC 13**
See also CA 53-56; CANR 5, 51; DLB 175; NNAL; SATA 12
Rosen, R. D.
See Rosen, Richard (Dean)
Rosen, Richard (Dean) 1949- .... **CLC 39**
See also CA 77-80; CANR 62; INT CANR-30
Rosenberg, Isaac 1890-1918 .... **TCLC 12**
See also CA 107; DLB 20
Rosenblatt, Joe .... **CLC 15**
See also Rosenblatt, Joseph
Rosenblatt, Joseph 1933-
See Rosenblatt, Joe
See also CA 89-92; INT 89-92
Rosenfeld, Samuel 1896-1963
See Tzara, Tristan
See also CA 89-92
Rosenstock, Sami
See Tzara, Tristan
Rosenstock, Samuel
See Tzara, Tristan
Rosenthal, M(acha) L(ouis) 1917-1996. **CLC 28**
See also CA 1-4R; 152; CAAS 6; CANR 4, 51; DLB 5; SATA 59
Ross, Barnaby
See Dannay, Frederic
Ross, Bernard L.
See Follett, Ken(neth Martin)
Ross, J. H.
See Lawrence, T(homas) E(dward)
Ross, Martin
See Martin, Violet Florence
See also DLB 135
Ross, (James) Sinclair 1908- **CLC 13; DAC; DAM MST; SSC 24**
See also CA 73-76; DLB 88
Rossetti, Christina (Georgina) 1830-1894 **NCLC 2, 50; DA; DAB; DAC; DAM MST, POET; PC 7; WLC**
See also DLB 35, 163; MAICYA; SATA 20
Rossetti, Dante Gabriel 1828-1882. **NCLC 4; DA; DAB; DAC; DAM MST, POET; WLC**
See also CDBLB 1832-1890; DLB 35
Rossner, Judith (Perelman) 1935-**CLC 6, 9, 29**
See also AITN 2; BEST 90:3; CA 17-20R; CANR 18, 51; DLB 6; INT CANR-18; MTCW
Rostand, Edmond (Eugene Alexis) 1868-1918 **TCLC 6, 37; DA; DAB; DAC; DAM DRAM, MST**
See also CA 104; 126; MTCW
Roth, Henry 1906-1995 ..... **CLC 2, 6, 11, 104**
See also CA 11-12; 149; CANR 38; CAP 1; DLB 28; MTCW
Roth, Philip (Milton) 1933-**CLC 1, 2, 3, 4, 6, 9, 15, 22, 31, 47, 66, 86; DA; DAB; DAC; DAM MST, NOV, POP; SSC 26; WLC**
See also BEST 90:3; CA 1-4R; CANR 1, 22, 36, 55; CDALB 1968-1988; DLB 2, 28, 173; DLBY 82; MTCW
Rothenberg, Jerome 1931- .... **CLC 6, 57**
See also CA 45-48; CANR 1; DLB 5
Roumain, Jacques (Jean Baptiste) 1907-1944 **TCLC 19; BLC; DAM MULT**
See also BW 1; CA 117; 125
Rourke, Constance (Mayfield) 1885-1941 **TCLC 12**
See also CA 107; YABC 1
Rousseau, Jean-Baptiste 1671-1741 ...... **LC 9**
Rousseau, Jean-Jacques 1712-1778**LC 14, 36; DA; DAB; DAC; DAM MST; WLC**

Roussel, Raymond 1877-1933 .... **TCLC 20**
See also CA 117
Rovit, Earl (Herbert) 1927- .... **CLC 7**
See also CA 5-8R; CANR 12
Rowe, Nicholas 1674-1718 .... **LC 8**
See also DLB 84
Rowley, Ames Dorrance
See Lovecraft, H(oward) P(hillips)
Rowson, Susanna Haswell 1762(?)-1824 **NCLC 5**
See also DLB 37
Roy, Gabrielle 1909-1983 **CLC 10, 14; DAB; DAC; DAM MST**
See also CA 53-56; 110; CANR 5, 61; DLB 68; MTCW
Rozewicz, Tadeusz 1921- .. **CLC 9, 23; DAM POET**
See also CA 108; CANR 36; MTCW
Ruark, Gibbons 1941- .... **CLC 3**
See also CA 33-36R; CAAS 23; CANR 14, 31, 57; DLB 120
Rubens, Bernice (Ruth) 1923- .... **CLC 19, 31**
See also CA 25-28R; CANR 33; DLB 14; MTCW
Rubin, Harold
See Robbins, Harold
Rudkin, (James) David 1936- .... **CLC 14**
See also CA 89-92; DLB 13
Rudnik, Raphael 1933- .... **CLC 7**
See also CA 29-32R
Ruffian, M.
See Hasek, Jaroslav (Matej Frantisek)
Ruiz, Jose Martinez .... **CLC 11**
See also Martinez Ruiz, Jose
Rukeyser, Muriel 1913-1980**CLC 6, 10, 15, 27; DAM POET; PC 12**
See also CA 5-8R; 93-96; CANR 26, 60; DLB 48; MTCW; SATA-Obit 22
Rule, Jane (Vance) 1931- .... **CLC 27**
See also CA 25-28R; CAAS 18; CANR 12; DLB 60
Rulfo, Juan 1918-1986 ...... **CLC 8, 80; DAM MULT; HLC; SSC 25**
See also CA 85-88; 118; CANR 26; DLB 113; HW; MTCW
Rumi, Jalal al-Din 1297-1373 .... **CMLC 20**
Runeberg, Johan 1804-1877 .... **NCLC 41**
Runyon, (Alfred) Damon 1884(?)-1946**TCLC 10**
See also CA 107; DLB 11, 86, 171
Rush, Norman 1933- .... **CLC 44**
See also CA 121; 126; INT 126
Rushdie, (Ahmed) Salman 1947- **CLC 23, 31, 55, 100; DAB; DAC; DAM MST, NOV, POP; WLCS**
See also BEST 89:3; CA 108; 111; CANR 33, 56; INT 111; MTCW
Rushforth, Peter (Scott) 1945- .... **CLC 19**
See also CA 101
Ruskin, John 1819-1900 .... **TCLC 63**
See also CA 114; 129; CDBLB 1832-1890; DLB 55, 163; SATA 24
Russ, Joanna 1937- .... **CLC 15**
See also CA 25-28R; CANR 11, 31; DLB 8; MTCW
Russell, George William 1867-1935
See Baker, Jean H.
See also CA 104; 153; CDBLB 1890-1914; DAM POET
Russell, (Henry) Ken(neth Alfred) 1927-**CLC 16**
See also CA 105
Russell, Willy 1947- .... **CLC 60**
Rutherford, Mark .... **TCLC 25**
See also White, William Hale
See also DLB 18
Ruyslinck, Ward 1929- .... **CLC 14**
See also Belser, Reimond Karel Maria de
Ryan, Cornelius (John) 1920-1974 ..... **CLC 7**
See also CA 69-72; 53-56; CANR 38
Ryan, Michael 1946- .... **CLC 65**
See also CA 49-52; DLBY 82
Ryan, Tim
See Dent, Lester
Rybakov, Anatoli (Naumovich) 1911-**CLC 23, 53**
See also CA 126; 135; SATA 79
Ryder, Jonathan
See Ludlum, Robert
Ryga, George 1932-1987**CLC 14; DAC; DAM MST**
See also CA 101; 124; CANR 43; DLB 60
S. H.
See Hartmann, Sadakichi
S. S.
See Sassoon, Siegfried (Lorraine)
Saba, Umberto 1883-1957 .... **TCLC 33**
See also CA 144; DLB 114
Sabatini, Rafael 1875-1950 .... **TCLC 47**
Sabato, Ernesto (R.) 1911-**CLC 10, 23; DAM MULT; HLC**
See also CA 97-100; CANR 32; DLB 145; HW; MTCW
Sacastru, Martin
See Bioy Casares, Adolfo
Sacher-Masoch, Leopold von 1836(?)-1895 **NCLC 31**
Sachs, Marilyn (Stickle) 1927- .... **CLC 35**
See also AAYA 2; CA 17-20R; CANR 13, 47; CLR 2; JRDA; MAICYA; SAAS 2; SATA 3, 68
Sachs, Nelly 1891-1970 .... **CLC 14, 98**
See also CA 17-18; 25-28R; CAP 2
Sackler, Howard (Oliver) 1929-1982 **CLC 14**
See also CA 61-64; 108; CANR 30; DLB 7
Sacks, Oliver (Wolf) 1933- .... **CLC 67**
See also CA 53-56; CANR 28, 50; INT CANR-28; MTCW
Sadakichi
See Hartmann, Sadakichi
Sade, Donatien Alphonse Francois Comte 1740-1814 .... **NCLC 47**
Sadoff, Ira 1945- .... **CLC 9**
See also CA 53-56; CANR 5, 21; DLB 120
Saetone
See Camus, Albert
Safire, William 1929- .... **CLC 10**
See also CA 17-20R; CANR 31, 54
Sagan, Carl (Edward) 1934-1996 ..... **CLC 30**
See also AAYA 2; CA 25-28R; 155; CANR 11, 36; MTCW; SATA 58; SATA-Obit 94
Sagan, Francoise .... **CLC 3, 6, 9, 17, 36**
See also Quoirez, Francoise
See also DLB 83
Sahgal, Nayantara (Pandit) 1927- .... **CLC 41**
See also CA 9-12R; CANR 11
Saint, H(arry) F. 1941- .... **CLC 50**
See also CA 127
St. Aubin de Teran, Lisa 1953-
See Teran, Lisa St. Aubin de
See also CA 118; 126; INT 126
Saint Birgitta of Sweden c. 1303-1373**CMLC 24**
Sainte-Beuve, Charles Augustin 1804-1869 **NCLC 5**
Saint-Exupery, Antoine (Jean Baptiste Marie Roger) de 1900-1944**TCLC 2, 56; DAM NOV; WLC**
See also CA 108; 132; CLR 10; DLB 72; MAICYA; MTCW; SATA 20
St. John, David
See Hunt, E(verette) Howard, (Jr.)
Saint-John Perse
See Leger, (Marie-Rene Auguste) Alexis Saint-Leger
Saintsbury, George (Edward Bateman) 1845-1933 .... **TCLC 31**
See also CA 160; DLB 57, 149
Sait Faik .... **TCLC 23**
See also Abasiyanik, Sait Faik
Saki .... **TCLC 3; SSC 12**
See also Munro, H(ector) H(ugh)
Sala, George Augustus .... **NCLC 46**
Salama, Hannu 1936- .... **CLC 18**
Salamanca, J(ack) R(ichard) 1922-**CLC 4, 15**
See also CA 25-28R
Sale, J. Kirkpatrick
See Sale, Kirkpatrick
Sale, Kirkpatrick 1937- .... **CLC 68**
See also CA 13-16R; CANR 10
Salinas, Luis Omar 1937- ...... **CLC 90; DAM MULT; HLC**
See also CA 131; DLB 82; HW
Salinas (y Serrano), Pedro 1891(?)-1951 **TCLC 17**
See also CA 117; DLB 134
Salinger, J(erome) D(avid) 1919-**CLC 1, 3, 8, 12, 55, 56; DA; DAB; DAC; DAM MST, NOV, POP; SSC 2, 28; WLC**
See also AAYA 2; CA 5-8R; CANR 39; CDALB 1941-1968; CLR 18; DLB 2, 102, 173; MAICYA; MTCW; SATA 67
Salisbury, John
See Caute, David
Salter, James 1925- .... **CLC 7, 52, 59**
See also CA 73-76; DLB 130
Saltus, Edgar (Everton) 1855-1921 . **TCLC 8**
See also CA 105
Saltykov, Mikhail Evgrafovich 1826-1889 **NCLC 16**
Samarakis, Antonis 1919- .... **CLC 5**
See also CA 25-28R; CAAS 16; CANR 36
Sanchez, Florencio 1875-1910 .... **TCLC 37**
See also CA 153; HW
Sanchez, Luis Rafael 1936- .... **CLC 23**
See also CA 128; DLB 145; HW
Sanchez, Sonia 1934- ..... **CLC 5; BLC; DAM MULT; PC 9**
See also BW 2; CA 33-36R; CANR 24, 49; CLR 18; DLB 41; DLBD 8; MAICYA; MTCW; SATA 22
Sand, George 1804-1876**NCLC 2, 42, 57; DA; DAB; DAC; DAM MST, NOV; WLC**
See also DLB 119
Sandburg, Carl (August) 1878-1967**CLC 1, 4, 10, 15, 35; DA; DAB; DAC; DAM MST, POET; PC 2; WLC**
See also CA 5-8R; 25-28R; CANR 35; CDALB 1865-1917; DLB 17, 54; MAICYA; MTCW; SATA 8
Sandburg, Charles
See Sandburg, Carl (August)
Sandburg, Charles A.
See Sandburg, Carl (August)
Sanders, (James) Ed(ward) 1939- .... **CLC 53**
See also CA 13-16R; CAAS 21; CANR 13, 44; DLB 16
Sanders, Lawrence 1920-**CLC 41; DAM POP**
See also BEST 89:4; CA 81-84; CANR 33, 62; MTCW
Sanders, Noah
See Blount, Roy (Alton), Jr.
Sanders, Winston P.
See Anderson, Poul (William)
Sandoz, Mari(e Susette) 1896-1966 .. **CLC 28**
See also CA 1-4R; 25-28R; CANR 17; DLB 9; MTCW; SATA 5
Saner, Reg(inald Anthony) 1931- .... **CLC 9**
See also CA 65-68
Sannazaro, Jacopo 1456(?)-1530 .... **LC 8**
Sansom, William 1912-1976 **CLC 2, 6; DAM**

NOV; SSC 21
See also CA 5-8R; 65-68; CANR 42; DLB 139; MTCW
Santayana, George 1863-1952 .... **TCLC 40**
See also CA 115; DLB 54, 71; DLBD 13
Santiago, Danny .... **CLC 33**
See also James, Daniel (Lewis)
See also DLB 122
Santmyer, Helen Hoover 1895-1986. **CLC 33**
See also CA 1-4R; 118; CANR 15, 33; DLBY 84; MTCW
Santoka, Taneda 1882-1940 .... **TCLC 72**
Santos, Bienvenido N(uqui) 1911-1996. **CLC 22; DAM MULT**
See also CA 101; 151; CANR 19, 46
Sapper .... **TCLC 44**
See also McNeile, Herman Cyril
Sapphire 1950- .... **CLC 99**
Sappho fl. 6th cent. B.C.- ...... **CMLC 3; DAM POET; PC 5**
See also DLB 176
Sarduy, Severo 1937-1993 .... **CLC 6, 97**
See also CA 89-92; 142; CANR 58; DLB 113; HW
Sargeson, Frank 1903-1982 .... **CLC 31**
See also CA 25-28R; 106; CANR 38
Sarmiento, Felix Ruben Garcia
See Dario, Ruben
Saroyan, William 1908-1981**CLC 1, 8, 10, 29, 34, 56; DA; DAB; DAC; DAM DRAM, MST, NOV; SSC 21; WLC**
See also CA 5-8R; 103; CANR 30; DLB 7, 9, 86; DLBY 81; MTCW; SATA 23; SATA-Obit 24
Sarraute, Nathalie 1900-**CLC 1, 2, 4, 8, 10, 31, 80**
See also CA 9-12R; CANR 23; DLB 83; MTCW
Sarton, (Eleanor) May 1912-1995**CLC 4, 14, 49, 91; DAM POET**
See also CA 1-4R; 149; CANR 1, 34, 55; DLB 48; DLBY 81; INT CANR-34; MTCW; SATA 36; SATA-Obit 86
Sartre, Jean-Paul 1905-1980**CLC 1, 4, 7, 9, 13, 18, 24, 44, 50, 52; DA; DAB; DAC; DAM DRAM, MST, NOV; DC 3; WLC**
See also CA 9-12R; 97-100; CANR 21; DLB 72; MTCW
Sassoon, Siegfried (Lorraine) 1886-1967**CLC 36; DAB; DAM MST, NOV, POET; PC 12**
See also CA 104; 25-28R; CANR 36; DLB 20; MTCW
Satterfield, Charles
See Pohl, Frederik
Saul, John (W. III) 1942-**CLC 46; DAM NOV, POP**
See also AAYA 10; BEST 90:4; CA 81-84; CANR 16, 40
Saunders, Caleb
See Heinlein, Robert A(nson)
Saura (Atares), Carlos 1932- .... **CLC 20**
See also CA 114; 131; HW
Sauser-Hall, Frederic 1887-1961 ...... **CLC 18**
See also Cendrars, Blaise
See also CA 102; 93-96; CANR 36, 62; MTCW
Saussure, Ferdinand de 1857-1913 **TCLC 49**
Savage, Catharine
See Brosman, Catharine Savage
Savage, Thomas 1915- .... **CLC 40**
See also CA 126; 132; CAAS 15; INT 132
Savan, Glenn 19(?)- .... **CLC 50**
Sayers, Dorothy L(eigh) 1893-1957 **TCLC 2, 15; DAM POP**
See also CA 104; 119; CANR 60; CDBLB 1914-1945; DLB 10, 36, 77, 100; MTCW
Sayers, Valerie 1952- .... **CLC 50**
See also CA 134; CANR 61
Sayles, John (Thomas) 1950- . **CLC 7, 10, 14**
See also CA 57-60; CANR 41; DLB 44
Scammell, Michael 1935- .... **CLC 34**
See also CA 156
Scannell, Vernon 1922- .... **CLC 49**
See also CA 5-8R; CANR 8, 24, 57; DLB 27; SATA 59
Scarlett, Susan
See Streatfeild, (Mary) Noel
Schaeffer, Susan Fromberg 1941- **CLC 6, 11, 22**
See also CA 49-52; CANR 18; DLB 28; MTCW; SATA 22
Schary, Jill
See Robinson, Jill
Schell, Jonathan 1943- .... **CLC 35**
See also CA 73-76; CANR 12
Schelling, Friedrich Wilhelm Joseph von 1775-1854 .... **NCLC 30**
See also DLB 90
Schendel, Arthur van 1874-1946 ... **TCLC 56**
Scherer, Jean-Marie Maurice 1920-
See Rohmer, Eric
See also CA 110
Schevill, James (Erwin) 1920- .... **CLC 7**
See also CA 5-8R; CAAS 12
Schiller, Friedrich 1759-1805**NCLC 39; DAM DRAM**
See also DLB 94
Schisgal, Murray (Joseph) 1926- .... **CLC 6**
See also CA 21-24R; CANR 48
Schlee, Ann 1934- .... **CLC 35**
See also CA 101; CANR 29; SATA 44; SATA-Brief 36
Schlegel, August Wilhelm von 1767-1845 **NCLC 15**
See also DLB 94
Schlegel, Friedrich 1772-1829 .... **NCLC 45**
See also DLB 90
Schlegel, Johann Elias (von) 1719(?)-1749**L C 5**
Schlesinger, Arthur M(eier), Jr. 1917-**CLC 84**
See also AITN 1; CA 1-4R; CANR 1, 28, 58; DLB 17; INT CANR-28; MTCW; SATA 61
Schmidt, Arno (Otto) 1914-1979 ...... **CLC 56**
See also CA 128; 109; DLB 69
Schmitz, Aron Hector 1861-1928
See Svevo, Italo
See also CA 104; 122; MTCW
Schnackenberg, Gjertrud 1953- .... **CLC 40**
See also CA 116; DLB 120
Schneider, Leonard Alfred 1925-1966
See Bruce, Lenny
See also CA 89-92
Schnitzler, Arthur 1862-1931**TCLC 4; SSC 15**
See also CA 104; DLB 81, 118
Schoenberg, Arnold 1874-1951 ...... **TCLC 75**
See also CA 109
Schonberg, Arnold
See Schoenberg, Arnold
Schopenhauer, Arthur 1788-1860 . **NCLC 51**
See also DLB 90
Schor, Sandra (M.) 1932(?)-1990 ...... **CLC 65**
See also CA 132
Schorer, Mark 1908-1977 .... **CLC 9**
See also CA 5-8R; 73-76; CANR 7; DLB 103
Schrader, Paul (Joseph) 1946- .... **CLC 26**
See also CA 37-40R; CANR 41; DLB 44
Schreiner, Olive (Emilie Albertina) 1855-1920 **TCLC 9**
See also CA 105; DLB 18, 156
Schulberg, Budd (Wilson) 1914- ... **CLC 7, 48**
See also CA 25-28R; CANR 19; DLB 6, 26, 28; DLBY 81
Schulz, Bruno 1892-1942**TCLC 5, 51; SSC 13**
See also CA 115; 123
Schulz, Charles M(onroe) 1922- .... **CLC 12**
See also CA 9-12R; CANR 6; INT CANR-6; SATA 10
Schumacher, E(rnst) F(riedrich) 1911-1977 **CLC 80**
See also CA 81-84; 73-76; CANR 34
Schuyler, James Marcus 1923-1991**CLC 5, 23; DAM POET**
See also CA 101; 134; DLB 5, 169; INT 101
Schwartz, Delmore (David) 1913-1966**CLC 2, 4, 10, 45, 87; PC 8**
See also CA 17-18; 25-28R; CANR 35; CAP 2; DLB 28, 48; MTCW
Schwartz, Ernst
See Ozu, Yasujiro
Schwartz, John Burnham 1965- .... **CLC 59**
See also CA 132
Schwartz, Lynne Sharon 1939- .... **CLC 31**
See also CA 103; CANR 44
Schwartz, Muriel A.
See Eliot, T(homas) S(tearns)
Schwarz-Bart, Andre 1928- .... **CLC 2, 4**
See also CA 89-92
Schwarz-Bart, Simone 1938- .... **CLC 7**
See also BW 2; CA 97-100
Schwob, (Mayer Andre) Marcel 1867-1905 **TCLC 20**
See also CA 117; DLB 123
Sciascia, Leonardo 1921-1989 . **CLC 8, 9, 41**
See also CA 85-88; 130; CANR 35; DLB 177; MTCW
Scoppettone, Sandra 1936- .... **CLC 26**
See also AAYA 11; CA 5-8R; CANR 41; SATA 9, 92
Scorsese, Martin 1942- .... **CLC 20, 89**
See also CA 110; 114; CANR 46
Scotland, Jay
See Jakes, John (William)
Scott, Duncan Campbell 1862-1947 **TCLC 6; DAC**
See also CA 104; 153; DLB 92
Scott, Evelyn 1893-1963 .... **CLC 43**
See also CA 104; 112; DLB 9, 48
Scott, F(rancis) R(eginald) 1899-1985**CLC 22**
See also CA 101; 114; DLB 88; INT 101
Scott, Frank
See Scott, F(rancis) R(eginald)
Scott, Joanna 1960- .... **CLC 50**
See also CA 126; CANR 53
Scott, Paul (Mark) 1920-1978 .... **CLC 9, 60**
See also CA 81-84; 77-80; CANR 33; DLB 14; MTCW
Scott, Walter 1771-1832**NCLC 15; DA; DAB; DAC; DAM MST, NOV, POET; PC 13; WLC**
See also AAYA 22; CDBLB 1789-1832; DLB 93, 107, 116, 144, 159; YABC 2
Scribe, (Augustin) Eugene 1791-1861 **NCLC 16; DAM DRAM; DC 5**
Scrum, R.
See Crumb, R(obert)
Scudery, Madeleine de 1607-1701 .... **LC 2**
Scum
See Crumb, R(obert)
Scumbag, Little Bobby
See Crumb, R(obert)
Seabrook, John
See Hubbard, L(afayette) Ron(ald)
Sealy, I. Allan 1951- .... **CLC 55**
Search, Alexander
See Pessoa, Fernando (Antonio Nogueira)
Sebastian, Lee
See Silverberg, Robert
Sebastian Owl
See Thompson, Hunter S(tockton)
Sebestyen, Ouida 1924- .... **CLC 30**
See also AAYA 8; CA 107; CANR 40; CLR 17; JRDA; MAICYA; SAAS 10; SATA 39
Secundus, H. Scriblerus

See also CA 49-52; CANR 1, 59; DAM POET
Smith, Florence Margaret 1902-1971
See Smith, Stevie
See also CA 17-18; 29-32R; CANR 35; CAP 2; DAM POET; MTCW
Smith, Iain Crichton 1928- .... **CLC 64**
See also CA 21-24R; DLB 40, 139
Smith, John 1580(?)-1631 .... **LC 9**
Smith, Johnston
See Crane, Stephen (Townley)
Smith, Joseph, Jr. 1805-1844 .... **NCLC 53**
Smith, Lee 1944- .... **CLC 25, 73**
See also CA 114; 119; CANR 46; DLB 143; DLBY 83; INT 119
Smith, Martin
See Smith, Martin Cruz
Smith, Martin Cruz 1942- ..... **CLC 25; DAM MULT, POP**
See also BEST 89:4; CA 85-88; CANR 6, 23, 43; INT CANR-23; NNAL
Smith, Mary-Ann Tirone 1944- .... **CLC 39**
See also CA 118; 136
Smith, Patti 1946- .... **CLC 12**
See also CA 93-96
Smith, Pauline (Urmson) 1882-1959**TCLC 25**
Smith, Rosamond
See Oates, Joyce Carol
Smith, Sheila Kaye
See Kaye-Smith, Sheila
Smith, Stevie .... CLC 3, 8, 25, 44; PC 12
See also Smith, Florence Margaret
See also DLB 20
Smith, Wilbur (Addison) 1933- .... **CLC 33**
See also CA 13-16R; CANR 7, 46; MTCW
Smith, William Jay 1918- .... **CLC 6**
See also CA 5-8R; CANR 44; DLB 5; MAICYA; SAAS 22; SATA 2, 68
Smith, Woodrow Wilson
See Kuttner, Henry
Smolenskin, Peretz 1842-1885 .... **NCLC 30**
Smollett, Tobias (George) 1721-1771 .... **LC 2**
See also CDBLB 1660-1789; DLB 39, 104
Snodgrass, W(illiam) D(e Witt) 1926-**CLC 2, 6, 10, 18, 68; DAM POET**
See also CA 1-4R; CANR 6, 36; DLB 5; MTCW
Snow, C(harles) P(ercy) 1905-1980**CLC 1, 4, 6, 9, 13, 19; DAM NOV**
See also CA 5-8R; 101; CANR 28; CDBLB 1945-1960; DLB 15, 77; MTCW
Snow, Frances Compton
See Adams, Henry (Brooks)
Snyder, Gary (Sherman) 1930-**CLC 1, 2, 5, 9, 32; DAM POET**
See also CA 17-20R; CANR 30, 60; DLB 5, 16, 165
Snyder, Zilpha Keatley 1927- .... **CLC 17**
See also AAYA 15; CA 9-12R; CANR 38; CLR 31; JRDA; MAICYA; SAAS 2; SATA 1, 28, 75
Soares, Bernardo
See Pessoa, Fernando (Antonio Nogueira)
Sobh, A.
See Shamlu, Ahmad
Sobol, Joshua .... CLC 60
Soderberg, Hjalmar 1869-1941 ..... **TCLC 39**
Sodergran, Edith (Irene)
See Soedergran, Edith (Irene)
Soedergran, Edith (Irene) 1892-1923 **TCLC 31**
Softly, Edgar
See Lovecraft, H(oward) P(hillips)
Softly, Edward
See Lovecraft, H(oward) P(hillips)
Sokolov, Raymond 1941- .... **CLC 7**
See also CA 85-88
Solo, Jay
See Ellison, Harlan (Jay)
Sologub, Fyodor .... TCLC 9
See also Teternikov, Fyodor Kuzmich
Solomons, Ikey Esquir
See Thackeray, William Makepeace
Solomos, Dionysios 1798-1857 .... **NCLC 15**
Solwoska, Mara
See French, Marilyn
Solzhenitsyn, Aleksandr I(sayevich) 1918- **CLC 1, 2, 4, 7, 9, 10, 18, 26, 34, 78; DA; DAB; DAC; DAM MST, NOV; WLC**
See also AITN 1; CA 69-72; CANR 40; MTCW
Somers, Jane
See Lessing, Doris (May)
Somerville, Edith 1858-1949 .... **TCLC 51**
See also DLB 135
Somerville & Ross
See Martin, Violet Florence; Somerville, Edith
Sommer, Scott 1951- .... **CLC 25**
See also CA 106
Sondheim, Stephen (Joshua) 1930- . **CLC 30, 39; DAM DRAM**
See also AAYA 11; CA 103; CANR 47
Sontag, Susan 1933-**CLC 1, 2, 10, 13, 31; DAM POP**
See also CA 17-20R; CANR 25, 51; DLB 2, 67; MTCW
Sophocles 496(?)B.C.-406(?)B.C. ... **CMLC 2; DA; DAB; DAC; DAM DRAM, MST; DC 1; WLCS**
See also DLB 176
Sordello 1189-1269 .... **CMLC 15**
Sorel, Julia
See Drexler, Rosalyn
Sorrentino, Gilbert 1929-**CLC 3, 7, 14, 22, 40**
See also CA 77-80; CANR 14, 33; DLB 5, 173; DLBY 80; INT CANR-14
Soto, Gary 1952- **CLC 32, 80; DAM MULT; HLC**
See also AAYA 10; CA 119; 125; CANR 50; CLR 38; DLB 82; HW; INT 125; JRDA; SATA 80
Soupault, Philippe 1897-1990 .... **CLC 68**
See also CA 116; 147; 131
Souster, (Holmes) Raymond 1921-**CLC 5, 14; DAC; DAM POET**
See also CA 13-16R; CAAS 14; CANR 13, 29, 53; DLB 88; SATA 63
Southern, Terry 1924(?)-1995 .... **CLC 7**
See also CA 1-4R; 150; CANR 1, 55; DLB 2
Southey, Robert 1774-1843 .... **NCLC 8**
See also DLB 93, 107, 142; SATA 54
Southworth, Emma Dorothy Eliza Nevitte 1819-1899 .... **NCLC 26**
Souza, Ernest
See Scott, Evelyn
Soyinka, Wole 1934-**CLC 3, 5, 14, 36, 44; BLC; DA; DAB; DAC; DAM DRAM, MST, MULT; DC 2; WLC**
See also BW 2; CA 13-16R; CANR 27, 39; DLB 125; MTCW
Spackman, W(illiam) M(ode) 1905-1990**C L C 46**
See also CA 81-84; 132
Spacks, Barry (Bernard) 1931- .... **CLC 14**
See also CA 154; CANR 33; DLB 105
Spanidou, Irini 1946- .... **CLC 44**
Spark, Muriel (Sarah) 1918-**CLC 2, 3, 5, 8, 13, 18, 40, 94; DAB; DAC; DAM MST, NOV; SSC 10**
See also CA 5-8R; CANR 12, 36; CDBLB 1945-1960; DLB 15, 139; INT CANR-12; MTCW
Spaulding, Douglas
See Bradbury, Ray (Douglas)
Spaulding, Leonard
See Bradbury, Ray (Douglas)
Spence, J. A. D.
See Eliot, T(homas) S(tearns)
Spencer, Elizabeth 1921- .... **CLC 22**
See also CA 13-16R; CANR 32; DLB 6; MTCW; SATA 14
Spencer, Leonard G.
See Silverberg, Robert
Spencer, Scott 1945- .... **CLC 30**
See also CA 113; CANR 51; DLBY 86
Spender, Stephen (Harold) 1909-1995**CLC 1, 2, 5, 10, 41, 91; DAM POET**
See also CA 9-12R; 149; CANR 31, 54; CDBLB 1945-1960; DLB 20; MTCW
Spengler, Oswald (Arnold Gottfried) 1880-1936 **TCLC 25**
See also CA 118
Spenser, Edmund 1552(?)-1599**LC 5, 39; DA; DAB; DAC; DAM MST, POET; PC 8; WLC**
See also CDBLB Before 1660; DLB 167
Spicer, Jack 1925-1965 **CLC 8, 18, 72; DAM POET**
See also CA 85-88; DLB 5, 16
Spiegelman, Art 1948- .... **CLC 76**
See also AAYA 10; CA 125; CANR 41, 55
Spielberg, Peter 1929- .... **CLC 6**
See also CA 5-8R; CANR 4, 48; DLBY 81
Spielberg, Steven 1947- .... **CLC 20**
See also AAYA 8; CA 77-80; CANR 32; SATA 32
Spillane, Frank Morrison 1918-
See Spillane, Mickey
See also CA 25-28R; CANR 28; MTCW; SATA 66
Spillane, Mickey .... CLC 3, 13
See also Spillane, Frank Morrison
Spinoza, Benedictus de 1632-1677 .... **LC 9**
Spinrad, Norman (Richard) 1940- ... **CLC 46**
See also CA 37-40R; CAAS 19; CANR 20; DLB 8; INT CANR-20
Spitteler, Carl (Friedrich Georg) 1845-1924 **TCLC 12**
See also CA 109; DLB 129
Spivack, Kathleen (Romola Drucker) 1938- **CLC 6**
See also CA 49-52
Spoto, Donald 1941- .... **CLC 39**
See also CA 65-68; CANR 11, 57
Springsteen, Bruce (F.) 1949- .... **CLC 17**
See also CA 111
Spurling, Hilary 1940- .... **CLC 34**
See also CA 104; CANR 25, 52
Spyker, John Howland
See Elman, Richard
Squires, (James) Radcliffe 1917-1993**CLC 51**
See also CA 1-4R; 140; CANR 6, 21
Srivastava, Dhanpat Rai 1880(?)-1936
See Premchand
See also CA 118
Stacy, Donald
See Pohl, Frederik
Stael, Germaine de
See Stael-Holstein, Anne Louise Germaine Necker Baronn
See also DLB 119
Stael-Holstein, Anne Louise Germaine Necker Baronn 1766-1817 .... **NCLC 3**
See also Stael, Germaine de
Stafford, Jean 1915-1979**CLC 4, 7, 19, 68; SSC 26**
See also CA 1-4R; 85-88; CANR 3; DLB 2, 173; MTCW; SATA-Obit 22
Stafford, William (Edgar) 1914-1993 **CLC 4, 7, 29; DAM POET**
See also CA 5-8R; 142; CAAS 3; CANR 5, 22; DLB 5; INT CANR-22
Stagnelius, Eric Johan 1793-1823 . **NCLC 61**
Staines, Trevor
See Brunner, John (Kilian Houston)

Stairs, Gordon
See Austin, Mary (Hunter)
Stannard, Martin 1947- .... **CLC 44**
See also CA 142; DLB 155
Stanton, Elizabeth Cady 1815-1902**TCLC 73**
See also DLB 79
Stanton, Maura 1946- .... **CLC 9**
See also CA 89-92; CANR 15; DLB 120
Stanton, Schuyler
See Baum, L(yman) Frank
Stapledon, (William) Olaf 1886-1950 **TCLC 22**
See also CA 111; DLB 15
Starbuck, George (Edwin) 1931-1996**CLC 53; DAM POET**
See also CA 21-24R; 153; CANR 23
Stark, Richard
See Westlake, Donald E(dwin)
Staunton, Schuyler
See Baum, L(yman) Frank
Stead, Christina (Ellen) 1902-1983 **CLC 2, 5, 8, 32, 80**
See also CA 13-16R; 109; CANR 33, 40; MTCW
Stead, William Thomas 1849-1912 **TCLC 48**
Steele, Richard 1672-1729 .... **LC 18**
See also CDBLB 1660-1789; DLB 84, 101
Steele, Timothy (Reid) 1948- .... **CLC 45**
See also CA 93-96; CANR 16, 50; DLB 120
Steffens, (Joseph) Lincoln 1866-1936 **TCLC 20**
See also CA 117
Stegner, Wallace (Earle) 1909-1993**CLC 9, 49, 81; DAM NOV; SSC 27**
See also AITN 1; BEST 90:3; CA 1-4R; 141; CAAS 9; CANR 1, 21, 46; DLB 9; DLBY 93; MTCW
Stein, Gertrude 1874-1946**TCLC 1, 6, 28, 48; DA; DAB; DAC; DAM MST, NOV, POET; PC 18; WLC**
See also CA 104; 132; CDALB 1917-1929; DLB 4, 54, 86; DLBD 15; MTCW
Steinbeck, John (Ernst) 1902-1968 **CLC 1, 5, 9, 13, 21, 34, 45, 75; DA; DAB; DAC; DAM DRAM, MST, NOV; SSC 11; WLC**
See also AAYA 12; CA 1-4R; 25-28R; CANR 1, 35; CDALB 1929-1941; DLB 7, 9; DLBD 2; MTCW; SATA 9
Steinem, Gloria 1934- .... **CLC 63**
See also CA 53-56; CANR 28, 51; MTCW
Steiner, George 1929- ... **CLC 24; DAM NOV**
See also CA 73-76; CANR 31; DLB 67; MTCW; SATA 62
Steiner, K. Leslie
See Delany, Samuel R(ay, Jr.)
Steiner, Rudolf 1861-1925 .... **TCLC 13**
See also CA 107
Stendhal 1783-1842**NCLC 23, 46; DA; DAB; DAC; DAM MST, NOV; SSC 27; WLC**
See also DLB 119
Stephen, Leslie 1832-1904 .... **TCLC 23**
See also CA 123; DLB 57, 144
Stephen, Sir Leslie
See Stephen, Leslie
Stephen, Virginia
See Woolf, (Adeline) Virginia
Stephens, James 1882(?)-1950 .... **TCLC 4**
See also CA 104; DLB 19, 153, 162
Stephens, Reed
See Donaldson, Stephen R.
Steptoe, Lydia
See Barnes, Djuna
Sterchi, Beat 1949- .... **CLC 65**
Sterling, Brett
See Bradbury, Ray (Douglas); Hamilton, Edmond
Sterling, Bruce 1954- .... **CLC 72**
See also CA 119; CANR 44
Sterling, George 1869-1926 .... **TCLC 20**
See also CA 117; DLB 54
Stern, Gerald 1925- .... **CLC 40, 100**
See also CA 81-84; CANR 28; DLB 105
Stern, Richard (Gustave) 1928- .... **CLC 4, 39**
See also CA 1-4R; CANR 1, 25, 52; DLBY 87; INT CANR-25
Sternberg, Josef von 1894-1969 .... **CLC 20**
See also CA 81-84
Sterne, Laurence 1713-1768**LC 2; DA; DAB; DAC; DAM MST, NOV; WLC**
See also CDBLB 1660-1789; DLB 39
Sternheim, (William Adolf) Carl 1878-1942 **TCLC 8**
See also CA 105; DLB 56, 118
Stevens, Mark 1951- .... **CLC 34**
See also CA 122
Stevens, Wallace 1879-1955 **TCLC 3, 12, 45; DA; DAB; DAC; DAM MST, POET; PC 6; WLC**
See also CA 104; 124; CDALB 1929-1941; DLB 54; MTCW
Stevenson, Anne (Katharine) 1933-**CLC 7, 33**
See also CA 17-20R; CAAS 9; CANR 9, 33; DLB 40; MTCW
Stevenson, Robert Louis (Balfour) 1850-1894 **NCLC 5, 14, 63; DA; DAB; DAC; DAM MST, NOV; SSC 11; WLC**
See also CDBLB 1890-1914; CLR 10, 11; DLB 18, 57, 141, 156, 174; DLBD 13; JRDA; MAICYA; YABC 2
Stewart, J(ohn) I(nnes) M(ackintosh) 1906-1994 .... **CLC 7, 14, 32**
See also CA 85-88; 147; CAAS 3; CANR 47; MTCW
Stewart, Mary (Florence Elinor) 1916-**CLC 7, 35; DAB**
See also CA 1-4R; CANR 1, 59; SATA 12
Stewart, Mary Rainbow
See Stewart, Mary (Florence Elinor)
Stifle, June
See Campbell, Maria
Stifter, Adalbert 1805-1868**NCLC 41; SSC 28**
See also DLB 133
Still, James 1906- .... **CLC 49**
See also CA 65-68; CAAS 17; CANR 10, 26; DLB 9; SATA 29
Sting
See Sumner, Gordon Matthew
Stirling, Arthur
See Sinclair, Upton (Beall)
Stitt, Milan 1941- .... **CLC 29**
See also CA 69-72
Stockton, Francis Richard 1834-1902
See Stockton, Frank R.
See also CA 108; 137; MAICYA; SATA 44
Stockton, Frank R. .... **TCLC 47**
See also Stockton, Francis Richard
See also DLB 42, 74; DLBD 13; SATA-Brief 32
Stoddard, Charles
See Kuttner, Henry
Stoker, Abraham 1847-1912
See Stoker, Bram
See also CA 105; DA; DAC; DAM MST, NOV; SATA 29
Stoker, Bram 1847-1912**TCLC 8; DAB; WLC**
See also Stoker, Abraham
See also CA 150; CDBLB 1890-1914; DLB 36, 70, 178
Stolz, Mary (Slattery) 1920- .... **CLC 12**
See also AAYA 8; AITN 1; CA 5-8R; CANR 13, 41; JRDA; MAICYA; SAAS 3; SATA 10, 71
Stone, Irving 1903-1989 .. **CLC 7; DAM POP**
See also AITN 1; CA 1-4R; 129; CAAS 3; CANR 1, 23; INT CANR-23; MTCW; SATA 3; SATA-Obit 64
Stone, Oliver (William) 1946- .... **CLC 73**
See also AAYA 15; CA 110; CANR 55
Stone, Robert (Anthony) 1937-**CLC 5, 23, 42**
See also CA 85-88; CANR 23; DLB 152; INT CANR-23; MTCW
Stone, Zachary
See Follett, Ken(neth Martin)
Stoppard, Tom 1937-**CLC 1, 3, 4, 5, 8, 15, 29, 34, 63, 91; DA; DAB; DAC; DAM DRAM, MST; DC 6; WLC**
See also CA 81-84; CANR 39; CDBLB 1960 to Present; DLB 13; DLBY 85; MTCW
Storey, David (Malcolm) 1933-**CLC 2, 4, 5, 8; DAM DRAM**
See also CA 81-84; CANR 36; DLB 13, 14; MTCW
Storm, Hyemeyohsts 1935- ...... **CLC 3; DAM MULT**
See also CA 81-84; CANR 45; NNAL
Storm, (Hans) Theodor (Woldsen) 1817-1888 **NCLC 1; SSC 27**
Storni, Alfonsina 1892-1938 . **TCLC 5; DAM MULT; HLC**
See also CA 104; 131; HW
Stoughton, William 1631-1701 .... **LC 38**
See also DLB 24
Stout, Rex (Todhunter) 1886-1975 ..... **CLC 3**
See also AITN 2; CA 61-64
Stow, (Julian) Randolph 1935- .. **CLC 23, 48**
See also CA 13-16R; CANR 33; MTCW
Stowe, Harriet (Elizabeth) Beecher 1811-1896 **NCLC 3, 50; DA; DAB; DAC; DAM MST, NOV; WLC**
See also CDALB 1865-1917; DLB 1, 12, 42, 74; JRDA; MAICYA; YABC 1
Strachey, (Giles) Lytton 1880-1932 **TCLC 12**
See also CA 110; DLB 149; DLBD 10
Strand, Mark 1934- **CLC 6, 18, 41, 71; DAM POET**
See also CA 21-24R; CANR 40; DLB 5; SATA 41
Straub, Peter (Francis) 1943- **CLC 28; DAM POP**
See also BEST 89:1; CA 85-88; CANR 28; DLBY 84; MTCW
Strauss, Botho 1944- .... **CLC 22**
See also CA 157; DLB 124
Streatfeild, (Mary) Noel 1895(?)-1986**CLC 21**
See also CA 81-84; 120; CANR 31; CLR 17; DLB 160; MAICYA; SATA 20; SATA-Obit 48
Stribling, T(homas) S(igismund) 1881-1965 **CLC 23**
See also CA 107; DLB 9
Strindberg, (Johan) August 1849-1912**TCLC 1, 8, 21, 47; DA; DAB; DAC; DAM DRAM, MST; WLC**
See also CA 104; 135
Stringer, Arthur 1874-1950 .... **TCLC 37**
See also DLB 92
Stringer, David
See Roberts, Keith (John Kingston)
Stroheim, Erich von 1885-1957 ..... **TCLC 71**
Strugatskii, Arkadii (Natanovich) 1925-1991 **CLC 27**
See also CA 106; 135
Strugatskii, Boris (Natanovich) 1933-**CLC 27**
See also CA 106
Strummer, Joe 1953(?)- .... **CLC 30**
Stuart, Don A.
See Campbell, John W(ood, Jr.)
Stuart, Ian
See MacLean, Alistair (Stuart)
Stuart, Jesse (Hilton) 1906-1984**CLC 1, 8, 11, 14, 34**

Wakoski, Diane 1937- **CLC 2, 4, 7, 9, 11, 40; DAM POET; PC 15**
See also CA 13-16R; CAAS 1; CANR 9, 60; DLB 5; INT CANR-9
Wakoski-Sherbell, Diane
See Wakoski, Diane
Walcott, Derek (Alton) 1930-**CLC 2, 4, 9, 14, 25, 42, 67, 76; BLC; DAB; DAC; DAM MST, MULT, POET; DC 7**
See also BW 2; CA 89-92; CANR 26, 47; DLB 117; DLBY 81; MTCW
Waldman, Anne 1945- .... **CLC 7**
See also CA 37-40R; CAAS 17; CANR 34; DLB 16
Waldo, E. Hunter
See Sturgeon, Theodore (Hamilton)
Waldo, Edward Hamilton
See Sturgeon, Theodore (Hamilton)
Walker, Alice (Malsenior) 1944- **CLC 5, 6, 9, 19, 27, 46, 58, 103; BLC; DA; DAB; DAC; DAM MST, MULT, NOV, POET, POP; SSC 5; WLCS**
See also AAYA 3; BEST 89:4; BW 2; CA 37-40R; CANR 9, 27, 49; CDALB 1968-1988; DLB 6, 33, 143; INT CANR-27; MTCW; SATA 31
Walker, David Harry 1911-1992 .... **CLC 14**
See also CA 1-4R; 137; CANR 1; SATA 8; SATA-Obit 71
Walker, Edward Joseph 1934-
See Walker, Ted
See also CA 21-24R; CANR 12, 28, 53
Walker, George F. 1947- . **CLC 44, 61; DAB; DAC; DAM MST**
See also CA 103; CANR 21, 43, 59; DLB 60
Walker, Joseph A. 1935- .... **CLC 19; DAM DRAM, MST**
See also BW 1; CA 89-92; CANR 26; DLB 38
Walker, Margaret (Abigail) 1915- **CLC 1, 6; BLC; DAM MULT**
See also BW 2; CA 73-76; CANR 26, 54; DLB 76, 152; MTCW
Walker, Ted .... **CLC 13**
See also Walker, Edward Joseph
See also DLB 40
Wallace, David Foster 1962- .... **CLC 50**
See also CA 132; CANR 59
Wallace, Dexter
See Masters, Edgar Lee
Wallace, (Richard Horatio) Edgar 1875-1932 **TCLC 57**
See also CA 115; DLB 70
Wallace, Irving 1916-1990 **CLC 7, 13; DAM NOV, POP**
See also AITN 1; CA 1-4R; 132; CAAS 1; CANR 1, 27; INT CANR-27; MTCW
Wallant, Edward Lewis 1926-1962**CLC 5, 10**
See also CA 1-4R; CANR 22; DLB 2, 28, 143; MTCW
Walley, Byron
See Card, Orson Scott
Walpole, Horace 1717-1797 .... **LC 2**
See also DLB 39, 104
Walpole, Hugh (Seymour) 1884-1941**TCLC 5**
See also CA 104; DLB 34
Walser, Martin 1927- .... **CLC 27**
See also CA 57-60; CANR 8, 46; DLB 75, 124
Walser, Robert 1878-1956 **TCLC 18; SSC 20**
See also CA 118; DLB 66
Walsh, Jill Paton .... **CLC 35**
See also Paton Walsh, Gillian
See also AAYA 11; CLR 2; DLB 161; SAAS 3
Walter, Villiam Christian
See Andersen, Hans Christian
Wambaugh, Joseph (Aloysius, Jr.) 1937-**CLC 3, 18; DAM NOV, POP**
See also AITN 1; BEST 89:3; CA 33-36R; CANR 42; DLB 6; DLBY 83; MTCW
Wang Wei 699(?)-761(?) .... **PC 18**
Ward, Arthur Henry Sarsfield 1883-1959
See Rohmer, Sax
See also CA 108
Ward, Douglas Turner 1930- .... **CLC 19**
See also BW 1; CA 81-84; CANR 27; DLB 7, 38
Ward, Mary Augusta
See Ward, Mrs. Humphry
Ward, Mrs. Humphry 1851-1920 .. **TCLC 55**
See also DLB 18
Ward, Peter
See Faust, Frederick (Schiller)
Warhol, Andy 1928(?)-1987 .... **CLC 20**
See also AAYA 12; BEST 89:4; CA 89-92; 121; CANR 34
Warner, Francis (Robert le Plastrier) 1937- **CLC 14**
See also CA 53-56; CANR 11
Warner, Marina 1946- .... **CLC 59**
See also CA 65-68; CANR 21, 55
Warner, Rex (Ernest) 1905-1986 ...... **CLC 45**
See also CA 89-92; 119; DLB 15
Warner, Susan (Bogert) 1819-1885 **NCLC 31**
See also DLB 3, 42
Warner, Sylvia (Constance) Ashton
See Ashton-Warner, Sylvia (Constance)
Warner, Sylvia Townsend 1893-1978 **CLC 7, 19; SSC 23**
See also CA 61-64; 77-80; CANR 16, 60; DLB 34, 139; MTCW
Warren, Mercy Otis 1728-1814 ..... **NCLC 13**
See also DLB 31
Warren, Robert Penn 1905-1989**CLC 1, 4, 6, 8, 10, 13, 18, 39, 53, 59; DA; DAB; DAC; DAM MST, NOV, POET; SSC 4; WLC**
See also AITN 1; CA 13-16R; 129; CANR 10, 47; CDALB 1968-1988; DLB 2, 48, 152; DLBY 80, 89; INT CANR-10; MTCW; SATA 46; SATA-Obit 63
Warshofsky, Isaac
See Singer, Isaac Bashevis
Warton, Thomas 1728-1790 ..... **LC 15; DAM POET**
See also DLB 104, 109
Waruk, Kona
See Harris, (Theodore) Wilson
Warung, Price 1855-1911 .... **TCLC 45**
Warwick, Jarvis
See Garner, Hugh
Washington, Alex
See Harris, Mark
Washington, Booker T(aliaferro) 1856-1915 **TCLC 10; BLC; DAM MULT**
See also BW 1; CA 114; 125; SATA 28
Washington, George 1732-1799 .... **LC 25**
See also DLB 31
Wassermann, (Karl) Jakob 1873-1934**TCLC 6**
See also CA 104; DLB 66
Wasserstein, Wendy 1950- ... **CLC 32, 59, 90; DAM DRAM; DC 4**
See also CA 121; 129; CABS 3; CANR 53; INT 129; SATA 94
Waterhouse, Keith (Spencer) 1929- . **CLC 47**
See also CA 5-8R; CANR 38; DLB 13, 15; MTCW
Waters, Frank (Joseph) 1902-1995 .. **CLC 88**
See also CA 5-8R; 149; CAAS 13; CANR 3, 18; DLBY 86
Waters, Roger 1944- .... **CLC 35**
Watkins, Frances Ellen
See Harper, Frances Ellen Watkins
Watkins, Gerrold
See Malzberg, Barry N(athaniel)
Watkins, Gloria 1955(?)-
See hooks, bell
See also BW 2; CA 143
Watkins, Paul 1964- .... **CLC 55**
See also CA 132; CANR 62
Watkins, Vernon Phillips 1906-1967 **CLC 43**
See also CA 9-10; 25-28R; CAP 1; DLB 20
Watson, Irving S.
See Mencken, H(enry) L(ouis)
Watson, John H.
See Farmer, Philip Jose
Watson, Richard F.
See Silverberg, Robert
Waugh, Auberon (Alexander) 1939- .. **CLC 7**
See also CA 45-48; CANR 6, 22; DLB 14
Waugh, Evelyn (Arthur St. John) 1903-1966 **CLC 1, 3, 8, 13, 19, 27, 44; DA; DAB; DAC; DAM MST, NOV, POP; WLC**
See also CA 85-88; 25-28R; CANR 22; CDBLB 1914-1945; DLB 15, 162; MTCW
Waugh, Harriet 1944- .... **CLC 6**
See also CA 85-88; CANR 22
Ways, C. R.
See Blount, Roy (Alton), Jr.
Waystaff, Simon
See Swift, Jonathan
Webb, (Martha) Beatrice (Potter) 1858-1943 **TCLC 22**
See also Potter, (Helen) Beatrix
See also CA 117
Webb, Charles (Richard) 1939- .... **CLC 7**
See also CA 25-28R
Webb, James H(enry), Jr. 1946- .... **CLC 22**
See also CA 81-84
Webb, Mary (Gladys Meredith) 1881-1927 **TCLC 24**
See also CA 123; DLB 34
Webb, Mrs. Sidney
See Webb, (Martha) Beatrice (Potter)
Webb, Phyllis 1927- .... **CLC 18**
See also CA 104; CANR 23; DLB 53
Webb, Sidney (James) 1859-1947 .. **TCLC 22**
See also CA 117
Webber, Andrew Lloyd .... **CLC 21**
See also Lloyd Webber, Andrew
Weber, Lenora Mattingly 1895-1971 **CLC 12**
See also CA 19-20; 29-32R; CAP 1; SATA 2; SATA-Obit 26
Weber, Max 1864-1920 .... **TCLC 69**
See also CA 109
Webster, John 1579(?)-1634(?) ... **LC 33; DA; DAB; DAC; DAM DRAM, MST; DC 2; WLC**
See also CDBLB Before 1660; DLB 58
Webster, Noah 1758-1843 .... **NCLC 30**
Wedekind, (Benjamin) Frank(lin) 1864-1918 **TCLC 7; DAM DRAM**
See also CA 104; 153; DLB 118
Weidman, Jerome 1913- .... **CLC 7**
See also AITN 2; CA 1-4R; CANR 1; DLB 28
Weil, Simone (Adolphine) 1909-1943**TCLC 23**
See also CA 117; 159
Weinstein, Nathan
See West, Nathanael
Weinstein, Nathan von Wallenstein
See West, Nathanael
Weir, Peter (Lindsay) 1944- .... **CLC 20**
See also CA 113; 123
Weiss, Peter (Ulrich) 1916-1982**CLC 3, 15, 51; DAM DRAM**
See also CA 45-48; 106; CANR 3; DLB 69, 124
Weiss, Theodore (Russell) 1916-**CLC 3, 8, 14**
See also CA 9-12R; CAAS 2; CANR 46; DLB 5
Welch, (Maurice) Denton 1915-1948**TCLC 22**
See also CA 121; 148
Welch, James 1940- ..... **CLC 6, 14, 52; DAM MULT, POP**

See also CA 85-88; CANR 42; DLB 175; NNAL
Weldon, Fay 1933- . **CLC 6, 9, 11, 19, 36, 59; DAM POP**
See also CA 21-24R; CANR 16, 46; CDBLB 1960 to Present; DLB 14; INT CANR-16; MTCW
Wellek, Rene 1903-1995 .... **CLC 28**
See also CA 5-8R; 150; CAAS 7; CANR 8; DLB 63; INT CANR-8
Weller, Michael 1942- .... **CLC 10, 53**
See also CA 85-88
Weller, Paul 1958- .... **CLC 26**
Wellershoff, Dieter 1925- .... **CLC 46**
See also CA 89-92; CANR 16, 37
Welles, (George) Orson 1915-1985**CLC 20, 80**
See also CA 93-96; 117
Wellman, Mac 1945- .... **CLC 65**
Wellman, Manly Wade 1903-1986 .... **CLC 49**
See also CA 1-4R; 118; CANR 6, 16, 44; SATA 6; SATA-Obit 47
Wells, Carolyn 1869(?)-1942 .... **TCLC 35**
See also CA 113; DLB 11
Wells, H(erbert) G(eorge) 1866-1946**TCLC 6, 12, 19; DA; DAB; DAC; DAM MST, NOV; SSC 6; WLC**
See also AAYA 18; CA 110; 121; CDBLB 1914-1945; DLB 34, 70, 156, 178; MTCW; SATA 20
Wells, Rosemary 1943- .... **CLC 12**
See also AAYA 13; CA 85-88; CANR 48; CLR 16; MAICYA; SAAS 1; SATA 18, 69
Welty, Eudora 1909- **CLC 1, 2, 5, 14, 22, 33; DA; DAB; DAC; DAM MST, NOV; SSC 1, 27; WLC**
See also CA 9-12R; CABS 1; CANR 32; CDALB 1941-1968; DLB 2, 102, 143; DLBD 12; DLBY 87; MTCW
Wen I-to 1899-1946 .... **TCLC 28**
Wentworth, Robert
See Hamilton, Edmond
Werfel, Franz (V.) 1890-1945 .... **TCLC 8**
See also CA 104; DLB 81, 124
Wergeland, Henrik Arnold 1808-1845**NCLC 5**
Wersba, Barbara 1932- .... **CLC 30**
See also AAYA 2; CA 29-32R; CANR 16, 38; CLR 3; DLB 52; JRDA; MAICYA; SAAS 2; SATA 1, 58
Wertmueller, Lina 1928- .... **CLC 16**
See also CA 97-100; CANR 39
Wescott, Glenway 1901-1987 .... **CLC 13**
See also CA 13-16R; 121; CANR 23; DLB 4, 9, 102
Wesker, Arnold 1932- .... **CLC 3, 5, 42; DAB; DAM DRAM**
See also CA 1-4R; CAAS 7; CANR 1, 33; CDBLB 1960 to Present; DLB 13; MTCW
Wesley, Richard (Errol) 1945- .... **CLC 7**
See also BW 1; CA 57-60; CANR 27; DLB 38
Wessel, Johan Herman 1742-1785 .... **LC 7**
West, Anthony (Panther) 1914-1987 **CLC 50**
See also CA 45-48; 124; CANR 3, 19; DLB 15
West, C. P.
See Wodehouse, P(elham) G(renville)
West, (Mary) Jessamyn 1902-1984**CLC 7, 17**
See also CA 9-12R; 112; CANR 27; DLB 6; DLBY 84; MTCW; SATA-Obit 37
West, Morris L(anglo) 1916- .... **CLC 6, 33**
See also CA 5-8R; CANR 24, 49; MTCW
West, Nathanael 1903-1940 **TCLC 1, 14, 44; SSC 16**
See also CA 104; 125; CDALB 1929-1941; DLB 4, 9, 28; MTCW
West, Owen
See Koontz, Dean R(ay)
West, Paul 1930- .... **CLC 7, 14, 96**
See also CA 13-16R; CAAS 7; CANR 22, 53; DLB 14; INT CANR-22
West, Rebecca 1892-1983 .... **CLC 7, 9, 31, 50**
See also CA 5-8R; 109; CANR 19; DLB 36; DLBY 83; MTCW
Westall, Robert (Atkinson) 1929-1993**CLC 17**
See also AAYA 12; CA 69-72; 141; CANR 18; CLR 13; JRDA; MAICYA; SAAS 2; SATA 23, 69; SATA-Obit 75
Westlake, Donald E(dwin) 1933- **CLC 7, 33; DAM POP**
See also CA 17-20R; CAAS 13; CANR 16, 44; INT CANR-16
Westmacott, Mary
See Christie, Agatha (Mary Clarissa)
Weston, Allen
See Norton, Andre
Wetcheek, J. L.
See Feuchtwanger, Lion
Wetering, Janwillem van de
See van de Wetering, Janwillem
Wetherell, Elizabeth
See Warner, Susan (Bogert)
Whale, James 1889-1957 .... **TCLC 63**
Whalen, Philip 1923- .... **CLC 6, 29**
See also CA 9-12R; CANR 5, 39; DLB 16
Wharton, Edith (Newbold Jones) 1862-1937 **TCLC 3, 9, 27, 53; DA; DAB; DAC; DAM MST, NOV; SSC 6; WLC**
See also CA 104; 132; CDALB 1865-1917; DLB 4, 9, 12, 78; DLBD 13; MTCW
Wharton, James
See Mencken, H(enry) L(ouis)
Wharton, William (a pseudonym)CLC 18, 37
See also CA 93-96; DLBY 80; INT 93-96
Wheatley (Peters), Phillis 1754(?)-1784**LC 3; BLC; DA; DAC; DAM MST, MULT, POET; PC 3; WLC**
See also CDALB 1640-1865; DLB 31, 50
Wheelock, John Hall 1886-1978 .... **CLC 14**
See also CA 13-16R; 77-80; CANR 14; DLB 45
White, E(lwyn) B(rooks) 1899-1985 **CLC 10, 34, 39; DAM POP**
See also AITN 2; CA 13-16R; 116; CANR 16, 37; CLR 1, 21; DLB 11, 22; MAICYA; MTCW; SATA 2, 29; SATA-Obit 44
White, Edmund (Valentine III) 1940-**CLC 27; DAM POP**
See also AAYA 7; CA 45-48; CANR 3, 19, 36, 62; MTCW
White, Patrick (Victor Martindale) 1912-1990 **CLC 3, 4, 5, 7, 9, 18, 65, 69**
See also CA 81-84; 132; CANR 43; MTCW
White, Phyllis Dorothy James 1920-
See James, P. D.
See also CA 21-24R; CANR 17, 43; DAM POP; MTCW
White, T(erence) H(anbury) 1906-1964 **CLC 30**
See also AAYA 22; CA 73-76; CANR 37; DLB 160; JRDA; MAICYA; SATA 12
White, Terence de Vere 1912-1994 ... **CLC 49**
See also CA 49-52; 145; CANR 3
White, Walter F(rancis) 1893-1955 **TCLC 15**
See also White, Walter
See also BW 1; CA 115; 124; DLB 51
White, William Hale 1831-1913
See Rutherford, Mark
See also CA 121
Whitehead, E(dward) A(nthony) 1933-**CLC 5**
See also CA 65-68; CANR 58
Whitemore, Hugh (John) 1936- .... **CLC 37**
See also CA 132; INT 132
Whitman, Sarah Helen (Power) 1803-1878 **NCLC 19**
See also DLB 1
Whitman, Walt(er) 1819-1892 . **NCLC 4, 31; DA; DAB; DAC; DAM MST, POET; PC 3; WLC**
See also CDALB 1640-1865; DLB 3, 64; SATA 20
Whitney, Phyllis A(yame) 1903- ..... **CLC 42; DAM POP**
See also AITN 2; BEST 90:3; CA 1-4R; CANR 3, 25, 38, 60; JRDA; MAICYA; SATA 1, 30
Whittemore, (Edward) Reed (Jr.) 1919-**CLC 4**
See also CA 9-12R; CAAS 8; CANR 4; DLB 5
Whittier, John Greenleaf 1807-1892**NCLC 8, 59**
See also DLB 1
Whittlebot, Hernia
See Coward, Noel (Peirce)
Wicker, Thomas Grey 1926-
See Wicker, Tom
See also CA 65-68; CANR 21, 46
Wicker, Tom .... **CLC 7**
See also Wicker, Thomas Grey
Wideman, John Edgar 1941- **CLC 5, 34, 36, 67; BLC; DAM MULT**
See also BW 2; CA 85-88; CANR 14, 42; DLB 33, 143
Wiebe, Rudy (Henry) 1934- .. **CLC 6, 11, 14; DAC; DAM MST**
See also CA 37-40R; CANR 42; DLB 60
Wieland, Christoph Martin 1733-1813**NCLC 17**
See also DLB 97
Wiene, Robert 1881-1938 .... **TCLC 56**
Wieners, John 1934- .... **CLC 7**
See also CA 13-16R; DLB 16
Wiesel, Elie(zer) 1928- **CLC 3, 5, 11, 37; DA; DAB; DAC; DAM MST, NOV; WLCS 2**
See also AAYA 7; AITN 1; CA 5-8R; CAAS 4; CANR 8, 40; DLB 83; DLBY 87; INT CANR-8; MTCW; SATA 56
Wiggins, Marianne 1947- .... **CLC 57**
See also BEST 89:3; CA 130; CANR 60
Wight, James Alfred 1916-
See Herriot, James
See also CA 77-80; SATA 55; SATA-Brief 44
Wilbur, Richard (Purdy) 1921-**CLC 3, 6, 9, 14, 53; DA; DAB; DAC; DAM MST, POET**
See also CA 1-4R; CABS 2; CANR 2, 29; DLB 5, 169; INT CANR-29; MTCW; SATA 9
Wild, Peter 1940- .... **CLC 14**
See also CA 37-40R; DLB 5
Wilde, Oscar (Fingal O'Flahertie Wills) 1854(?)-1900**TCLC 1, 8, 23, 41; DA; DAB; DAC; DAM DRAM, MST, NOV; SSC 11; WLC**
See also CA 104; 119; CDBLB 1890-1914; DLB 10, 19, 34, 57, 141, 156; SATA 24
Wilder, Billy .... **CLC 20**
See also Wilder, Samuel
See also DLB 26
Wilder, Samuel 1906-
See Wilder, Billy
See also CA 89-92
Wilder, Thornton (Niven) 1897-1975**CLC 1, 5, 6, 10, 15, 35, 82; DA; DAB; DAC; DAM DRAM, MST, NOV; DC 1; WLC**
See also AITN 2; CA 13-16R; 61-64; CANR 40; DLB 4, 7, 9; MTCW
Wilding, Michael 1942- .... **CLC 73**
See also CA 104; CANR 24, 49
Wiley, Richard 1944- .... **CLC 44**
See also CA 121; 129
Wilhelm, Kate .... **CLC 7**
See also Wilhelm, Katie Gertrude
See also AAYA 20; CAAS 5; DLB 8; INT CANR-17
Wilhelm, Katie Gertrude 1928-
See Wilhelm, Kate
See also CA 37-40R; CANR 17, 36, 60; MTCW

Wordsworth, Dorothy 1771-1855 .. **NCLC 25**
See also DLB 107
Wordsworth, William 1770-1850 .. **NCLC 12, 38; DA; DAB; DAC; DAM MST, POET; PC 4; WLC**
See also CDBLB 1789-1832; DLB 93, 107
Wouk, Herman 1915- **CLC 1, 9, 38; DAM NOV, POP**
See also CA 5-8R; CANR 6, 33; DLBY 82; INT CANR-6; MTCW
Wright, Charles (Penzel, Jr.) 1935- **CLC 6, 13, 28**
See also CA 29-32R; CAAS 7; CANR 23, 36, 62; DLB 165; DLBY 82; MTCW
Wright, Charles Stevenson 1932- ... **CLC 49; BLC 3; DAM MULT, POET**
See also BW 1; CA 9-12R; CANR 26; DLB 33
Wright, Jack R.
See Harris, Mark
Wright, James (Arlington) 1927-1980 **CLC 3, 5, 10, 28; DAM POET**
See also AITN 2; CA 49-52; 97-100; CANR 4, 34; DLB 5, 169; MTCW
Wright, Judith (Arandell) 1915- **CLC 11, 53; PC 14**
See also CA 13-16R; CANR 31; MTCW; SATA 14
Wright, L(aurali) R. 1939- .... **CLC 44**
See also CA 138
Wright, Richard (Nathaniel) 1908-1960 **C L C 1, 3, 4, 9, 14, 21, 48, 74; BLC; DA; DAB; DAC; DAM MST, MULT, NOV; SSC 2; WLC**
See also AAYA 5; BW 1; CA 108; CDALB 1929-1941; DLB 76, 102; DLBD 2; MTCW
Wright, Richard B(ruce) 1937- .... **CLC 6**
See also CA 85-88; DLB 53
Wright, Rick 1945- .... **CLC 35**
Wright, Rowland
See Wells, Carolyn
Wright, Stephen Caldwell 1946- .... **CLC 33**
See also BW 2
Wright, Willard Huntington 1888-1939
See Van Dine, S. S.
See also CA 115; DLBD 16
Wright, William 1930- .... **CLC 44**
See also CA 53-56; CANR 7, 23
Wroth, LadyMary 1587-1653(?) .... **LC 30**
See also DLB 121
Wu Ch'eng-en 1500(?)-1582(?) .... **LC 7**
Wu Ching-tzu 1701-1754 .... **LC 2**
Wurlitzer, Rudolph 1938(?)- .... **CLC 2, 4, 15**
See also CA 85-88; DLB 173
Wycherley, William 1641-1715 **LC 8, 21; DAM DRAM**
See also CDBLB 1660-1789; DLB 80
Wylie, Elinor (Morton Hoyt) 1885-1928 **TCLC 8**
See also CA 105; DLB 9, 45
Wylie, Philip (Gordon) 1902-1971 ... **CLC 43**
See also CA 21-22; 33-36R; CAP 2; DLB 9
Wyndham, John .... **CLC 19**
See also Harris, John (Wyndham Parkes Lucas) Beynon
Wyss, Johann David Von 1743-1818 **NCLC 10**
See also JRDA; MAICYA; SATA 29; SATA-Brief 27
Xenophon c. 430B.C.-c. 354B.C. ... **CMLC 17**
See also DLB 176
Yakumo Koizumi
See Hearn, (Patricio) Lafcadio (Tessima Carlos)
Yanez, Jose Donoso
See Donoso (Yanez), Jose
Yanovsky, Basile S.
See Yanovsky, V(assily) S(emenovich)
Yanovsky, V(assily) S(emenovich) 1906-1989 **CLC 2, 18**
See also CA 97-100; 129
Yates, Richard 1926-1992 .... **CLC 7, 8, 23**
See also CA 5-8R; 139; CANR 10, 43; DLB 2; DLBY 81, 92; INT CANR-10
Yeats, W. B.
See Yeats, William Butler
Yeats, William Butler 1865-1939 **TCLC 1, 11, 18, 31; DA; DAB; DAC; DAM DRAM, MST, POET; WLC**
See also CA 104; 127; CANR 45; CDBLB 1890-1914; DLB 10, 19, 98, 156; MTCW
Yehoshua, A(braham) B. 1936- .. **CLC 13, 31**
See also CA 33-36R; CANR 43
Yep, Laurence Michael 1948- .... **CLC 35**
See also AAYA 5; CA 49-52; CANR 1, 46; CLR 3, 17; DLB 52; JRDA; MAICYA; SATA 7, 69
Yerby, Frank G(arvin) 1916-1991 . **CLC 1, 7, 22; BLC; DAM MULT**
See also BW 1; CA 9-12R; 136; CANR 16, 52; DLB 76; INT CANR-16; MTCW
Yesenin, Sergei Alexandrovich
See Esenin, Sergei (Alexandrovich)
Yevtushenko, Yevgeny (Alexandrovich) 1933- **CLC 1, 3, 13, 26, 51; DAM POET**
See also CA 81-84; CANR 33, 54; MTCW
Yezierska, Anzia 1885(?)-1970 .... **CLC 46**
See also CA 126; 89-92; DLB 28; MTCW
Yglesias, Helen 1915- .... **CLC 7, 22**
See also CA 37-40R; CAAS 20; CANR 15; INT CANR-15; MTCW
Yokomitsu Riichi 1898-1947 .... **TCLC 47**
Yonge, Charlotte (Mary) 1823-1901 **TCLC 48**
See also CA 109; DLB 18, 163; SATA 17
York, Jeremy
See Creasey, John
York, Simon
See Heinlein, Robert A(nson)
Yorke, Henry Vincent 1905-1974 ...... **CLC 13**
See also Green, Henry
See also CA 85-88; 49-52
Yosano Akiko 1878-1942 .... **TCLC 59; PC 11**
Yoshimoto, Banana .... **CLC 84**
See also Yoshimoto, Mahoko
Yoshimoto, Mahoko 1964-
See Yoshimoto, Banana
See also CA 144
Young, Al(bert James) 1939- . **CLC 19; BLC; DAM MULT**
See also BW 2; CA 29-32R; CANR 26; DLB 33
Young, Andrew (John) 1885-1971 ...... **CLC 5**
See also CA 5-8R; CANR 7, 29
Young, Collier
See Bloch, Robert (Albert)
Young, Edward 1683-1765 .... **LC 3, 40**
See also DLB 95
Young, Marguerite (Vivian) 1909-1995 **C L C 82**
See also CA 13-16; 150; CAP 1
Young, Neil 1945- .... **CLC 17**
See also CA 110
Young Bear, Ray A. 1950- ...... **CLC 94; DAM MULT**
See also CA 146; DLB 175; NNAL
Yourcenar, Marguerite 1903-1987 **CLC 19, 38, 50, 87; DAM NOV**
See also CA 69-72; CANR 23, 60; DLB 72; DLBY 88; MTCW
Yurick, Sol 1925- .... **CLC 6**
See also CA 13-16R; CANR 25
Zabolotskii, Nikolai Alekseevich 1903-1958 **TCLC 52**
See also CA 116
Zamiatin, Yevgenii
See Zamyatin, Evgeny Ivanovich
Zamora, Bernice (B. Ortiz) 1938- .. **CLC 89; DAM MULT; HLC**
See also CA 151; DLB 82; HW
Zamyatin, Evgeny Ivanovich 1884-1937 **TCLC 8, 37**
See also CA 105
Zangwill, Israel 1864-1926 .... **TCLC 16**
See also CA 109; DLB 10, 135
Zappa, Francis Vincent, Jr. 1940-1993
See Zappa, Frank
See also CA 108; 143; CANR 57
Zappa, Frank .... **CLC 17**
See also Zappa, Francis Vincent, Jr.
Zaturenska, Marya 1902-1982 ...... **CLC 6, 11**
See also CA 13-16R; 105; CANR 22
Zeami 1363-1443 .... **DC 7**
Zelazny, Roger (Joseph) 1937-1995 . **CLC 21**
See also AAYA 7; CA 21-24R; 148; CANR 26, 60; DLB 8; MTCW; SATA 57; SATA-Brief 39
Zhdanov, Andrei A(lexandrovich) 1896-1948 **TCLC 18**
See also CA 117
Zhukovsky, Vasily 1783-1852 .... **NCLC 35**
Ziegenhagen, Eric .... **CLC 55**
Zimmer, Jill Schary
See Robinson, Jill
Zimmerman, Robert
See Dylan, Bob
Zindel, Paul 1936- **CLC 6, 26; DA; DAB; DAC; DAM DRAM, MST, NOV; DC 5**
See also AAYA 2; CA 73-76; CANR 31; CLR 3, 45; DLB 7, 52; JRDA; MAICYA; MTCW; SATA 16, 58
Zinov'Ev, A. A.
See Zinoviev, Alexander (Aleksandrovich)
Zinoviev, Alexander (Aleksandrovich) 1922- **CLC 19**
See also CA 116; 133; CAAS 10
Zoilus
See Lovecraft, H(oward) P(hillips)
Zola, Emile (Edouard Charles Antoine) 1840-1902 **TCLC 1, 6, 21, 41; DA; DAB; DAC; DAM MST, NOV; WLC**
See also CA 104; 138; DLB 123
Zoline, Pamela 1941- .... **CLC 62**
Zorrilla y Moral, Jose 1817-1893 .... **NCLC 6**
Zoshchenko, Mikhail (Mikhailovich) 1895-1958 **TCLC 15; SSC 15**
See also CA 115; 160
Zuckmayer, Carl 1896-1977 .... **CLC 18**
See also CA 69-72; DLB 56, 124
Zuk, Georges
See Skelton, Robin
Zukofsky, Louis 1904-1978 **CLC 1, 2, 4, 7, 11, 18; DAM POET; PC 11**
See also CA 9-12R; 77-80; CANR 39; DLB 5, 165; MTCW
Zweig, Paul 1935-1984 .... **CLC 34, 42**
See also CA 85-88; 113
Zweig, Stefan 1881-1942 .... **TCLC 17**
See also CA 112; DLB 81, 118
Zwingli, Huldreich 1484-1531 .... **LC 37**
See also DLB 179

Literary Criticism Series Cumulative Topic Index

This index lists all topic entries in Gale's *Classical and Medieval Literature Criticism, Contemporary Literary Criticism, Literature Criticism from 1400 to 1800, Nineteenth-Century Literature Criticism,* and *Twentieth-Century Literary Criticism.*

Twentieth-Century Literary Criticism
Cumulative Nationality Index